Proceedings of the Thirty-sixth

SIGCSE

TECHNICAL SYMPOSIUM ON COMPUTER SCIENCE EDUCATION

St. Louis, Missouri USA • February 23-27, 2005

SIGCSE 2005

Symposium Chairs: **Wanda Dann**, *Ithaca College*
Tom Naps, *University of Wisconsin – Oshkosh*

Program Chairs: **Doug Baldwin**, *SUNY Geneseo*
Paul Tymann, *Rochester Institute of Technology*

Publications Chair: **John Dougherty**, *Haverford College*

Sponsored by:
The Association for Computing Machinery
Special Interest Group on Computer Science Education

The Association for Computing Machinery
1515 Broadway
New York, New York 10036

ISBN: 1-58113-997-7

Additional copies may be ordered prepaid from:

ACM Order Department
PO Box 11405
New York, NY 10286-1405

Phone: 1-800-342-6626
(US and Canada)
+1-212-626-0500
(all other countries)
Fax: +1-212-944-1318
E-mail: acmhelp@acm.org

ACM Order Number 457050
Printed in the USA

Message from the SIGCSE Chair

Welcome to SIGCSE 2005! This annual Symposium draws together a wonderful group of people who are interested in computing education. In that distinguished tradition, this year's Symposium contains an impressive listing of workshops, paper presentations, special sessions, panels, birds-of-a-feather events, faculty posters, and meetings. Also in the spirit of experimentation that is so important within computing, this Symposium incorporates some new ideas.

- The Symposium Luncheon is moved from Friday to Saturday, so it can serve as a concluding high point for the conference.
- The Symposium has a plenary session with an exciting address each day:
  - Kim Bruce, the winner of SIGCSE's Award for Contributions to Computer Science Education, will present a keynote address on Thursday.
  - Mordechai Ben-Ari, last year's winner of SIGCSE's Award for Contributions to Computer Science Education, will present a keynote address on Friday.
  - Maria Klawe, immediate past ACM President, will present a talk at the SIGCSE Symposium Luncheon on Saturday.
- Times for faculty posters have been greatly expanded.
- Morning sessions on Saturday extend somewhat later than in the past, expanding the technical program.

Also, as in past years, coordinating activities at the Symposium enrich opportunities for recognition, dialog, and professional growth. The following list highlights some events, following long tradition.

- Andrew McGettrick, winner of SIGCSE's Award for Lifetime Service, will be recognized at the SIGCSE Symposium Luncheon.
- Exhibitors organize Vendors Sessions that are scheduled through coordination with other Symposium Technical Sessions.
- The SIGCSE Doctoral Consortium meets on Wednesday and reaches out to those working on their doctoral degrees.
- ACM organizes several Student Research Competitions, including one held in coordination with this Symposium.
- The Consortium for Computing Sciences in Colleges holds meetings in cooperation with this Symposium.

The organization, coordination, and implementation of all of these wonderful activities require tremendous energy, effort, and insight. Many, many thanks the SIGCSE 2005 Committee for their outstanding work. Particular thanks to Wanda Dann and Tom Naps, Symposium Co-Chairs, and to Douglas Baldwin and Paul Tymann, Program Co-Chairs, for your outstanding leadership, resourcefulness, hard work, creativity, and collaborative skills.

These Proceedings provide an outstanding reference for the many stimulating sessions for this conference. In addition, I encourage participants to use this time for dialog -- catching up with old friends and getting to know new colleagues.

Finally, I encourage Symposium attendees and Proceedings readers to participate in upcoming events. SIGCSE is an exciting and expanding organization, and it owes its strengths to the contributions and insights of its members. Please consider participating in these events:

- Each summer, SIGCSE sponsors a European conference. This year, please join us June 27–29, 2005, at ITiCSE 2005, to be held in Monte de Caparica, Portugal, and hosted by the Faculdade de Ciências e Tecnologia of Universidade Nova de Lisboa. For more details, please see http://www.iticse05.unl.pt/
- Beginning this fall, SIGCSE will be sponsoring a new conference that will focus on computing education research. The first meeting of this conference, the International Computing Education Research Workshop 2005 (ICER'05), is scheduled for October 1-2, 2005 in Seattle, Washington, USA. For more details, please see the links at http://www.sigcse.org.

I hope you enjoy these Proceedings and hope all attendees will enjoy the conference!

Henry Walker, *SIGCSE Chair*

Message from the Symposium Chairs

Welcome to St. Louis for the 36th year of the SIGCSE Technical Symposium on Computer Science Education. We are excited about SIGCSE 2005 and we hope you have as much fun as we have had in planning this event. There is much to see and do with a record number of paper presentations, panels, special sessions, and workshops. We also suggest you take the time to relax and stroll along the Mississippi to visit the famous Gateway to the West arch. Or enjoy a reunion with old friends, find an experienced colleague and discuss topics of common interest over dinner, make plans for collaboration, or meet new friends in the inviting renaissance environment of the conference setting.

We are pleased to announce the winners of the two annual SIGCSE awards: Kim Bruce for Outstanding Contributions to Computer Science Education and Andrew McGettrick for Lifetime Service. Kim will give the opening keynote talk on Thursday morning. Other invited speakers for the Symposium are Mordechai (Moti) Ben-Ari and Maria Klawe. You may recall that Moti was the SIGCSE 2004 outstanding contributions award winner but was unable to make his presentation at the symposium in 2004. We are delighted that Moti will be joining us to present his keynote talk on Friday morning. We are also honored that Maria Klawe will present the final keynote address at the luncheon on Saturday.

This year we experienced a 4% increase in submitted papers (following on the heels of a 37% increase last year). In all, 330 papers were submitted! Approximately 1650 blind reviews were completed, with each paper receiving at least 4 reviews and most receiving 5 or 6 reviews. An all time high of 104 papers will be presented. All submissions of Panels, Special Sessions, Workshops, Birds of a Feather, and Posters were reviewed carefully and selections were made based on considerations of quality, diversity of topics, and available space. In addition to the technical sessions, and invited talks, we again provide a Thursday first-timer's lunch and the Thursday evening reception. This year, the luncheon will be held Saturday as a culminating event, where the final keynote address will be given. A large exhibit hall is the location of vendor presentations where you can view and experiment with the latest in instructional software, hardware, and publications. Events co-located with the symposium include the SIGCSE Doctoral Consortium, the ACM SIGCSE Student Research Competition, and a CRA-W workshop for women CS educators.

We are most grateful to the many volunteers who make this conference possible. First, we'd like to thank our committee – Myles, Susan, Cary, Larry, Frank, Bonnie, Don, Todd, Mark, Scott, Dennis, Guido, Henry, John, Pam, Constance, Cathy, and Rich – you've been a terrific team. We are grateful to all the authors, reviewers, and session chairs. Thank you to Ann Sobel for continuing the ACM research competition at SIGCSE and to Todd Stevens and Mark Guzdial for leading the Doctoral Consortium. Thanks to the people at ACM headquarters for their assistance, especially Erin Dolan. It's been a pleasure working with our exhibit managers, Matthew Campagni and Tom D'Auria, of Information Methods Incorporated, and with our conference manager Tracy Pendleton and his staff, and the folks at the Renaissance hotel in St. Louis. We are most grateful for the editorial contributions provided by Lisa Tolles at Sheridan Printing. Thanks to St. Louis University for providing lab facilities and to our home institutions for their support: Ithaca College, University of Wisconsin – Oshkosh, Rochester Institute of Technology, SUNY Geneseo, and Haverford College.

If you are viewing the proceedings on-line, or are holding a printed copy in your office or at home, enjoy the wealth of material within. We hasten to add that although we offer much of the conference within the pages of these proceedings; it is not possible to capture the experience of a SIGCSE symposium on paper. You really do have to be there. So, please plan to attend an upcoming symposium soon.

Wanda Dann, *Symposium Chair*
Tom Naps, *Symposium Chair*
Paul Tymann, *Program Chair*
Doug Baldwin, *Program Chair*
John (J.D.) Dougherty, *Publications Chair*

Table of Contents

Special Session (Thursday, February 24, 2005, 10:30 AM)

Paper Session: Databases (Thursday, February 24, 2005, 10:30 AM)

Session Chair: Mohammad Neilforosham *(Stockton College)*

Panel Session (Thursday, February 24, 2005, 10:30 AM)

Special Session (Thursday, February 24, 2005, 10:30 AM)

Paper Session: Networks (Thursday, February 24, 2005, 2:00 PM)

Session Chair: Bina Ramamurthy *(SUNY at Buffalo)*

Paper Session: Capstone Projects (Thursday, February 24, 2005, 2:00 PM)

Session Chair: Chang Liu *(Ohio University)*

Paper Session: Computer Organization (Thursday, February 24, 2005, 2:00 PM)

Session Chair: Timothy Stanley *(Brigham Young University – Hawaii)*

Panel Session (Friday, February 25, 2005, 10:30 AM)

Paper Session: Courseware (Friday, February 25, 2005, 2:00 PM)

Session Chair: Lynda Thomas *(University of Wales)*

Paper Session: Programming with Images (Friday, February 25, 2005, 2:00 PM)

Session Chair: Larry Griffith *(Westfield State College)*

Paper Session: Active and Lab-Based Learning (Friday, February 25, 2005, 2:00 PM)

Session Chair: Graciela Gonzalez *(Sam Houston State University)*

Paper Session: The First Year: Breadth First Approaches (Friday, February 25, 2005, 2:00 PM)

Session Chair: Rhys Price-Jones *(Rochester Institute of Technology)*

Panel Session (Friday, February 25, 2005, 2:00 PM)

Special Session (Friday, February 25, 2005, 2:00 PM)

Panel Session (Friday, February 25, 2005, 2:00 PM)

Paper Session: Issues in Secondary Education & Introductory Programming (Friday, February 25, 2005, 4:00 PM)

Session Chair: Troy Vasiga *(University of Waterloo)*

Paper Session: Ethics and Computing (Friday, February 25, 2005, 4:00 PM)

Session Chair: James Huggins *(Kettering University)*

Paper Session: Non-Majors Courses (Friday, February 25, 2005, 4:00 PM)

Session Chair: Mark Jones *(Kutztown University)*

Special Session (Friday, February 25, 2005, 4:00 PM)

Paper Session: Evaluating Student Work (Friday, February 25, 2005, 4:00 PM)
Session Chair: Holly Patterson-McNeill *(Lewis-Clark State College)*

Special Session (Friday, February 25, 2005, 4:00 PM)

Special Session (Friday, February 25, 2005, 4:00 PM)

Paper Session: Gender Issues (Saturday, February 26, 2005, 8:30 AM)
Session Chair: Hilary Holz *(California State University, Hayward)*

Paper Session: The First Year: Studies of Student Performance (Saturday, February 26, 2005, 8:30 AM)
Session Chair: Tzu-Yi Chen *(Pomona College)*

Panel Session (Saturday, February 26, 2005, 11:00 AM)

Special Session (Saturday, February 26, 2005, 11:00 AM)

Keynote (Saturday, February 26, 2005, 1:00 PM)

SIGCSE 2005 Symposium Committee

Wanda Dann, Symposium Co-Chair
Ithaca College

Tom Naps, Symposium Co-Chair
University of Wisconsin - Oshkosh

Paul Tymann, Program Co-Chair
Rochester Institute of Technology

Doug Baldwin, Program Co-Chair
SUNY Geneseo

John P. Dougherty, Publications
Haverford College

Susan Rodger, Special Sessions and Panels
Duke University

Myles McNally, Workshops
Alma College

Don Goelman, Birds-of-a-Feather
Villanova University

Ann Sobel, ACM Student Research Competition
Miami University, OH

Bonnie McVey, Faculty Posters
St. Norbert College

K. Todd Stevens, Doctoral Consortium
Radford University

Mark Guzdial, Doctoral Consortium
Georgia Institute of Technology

Cary Laxer, Registration
Rose-Hulman Institute of Technology

Larry Merkle, Registration
Rose-Hulman Institute of Technology

Frank Young, Registration
Rose-Hulman Institute of Technology

Scott Grissom, Treasurer
Grand Valley State University

Pam Lawhead, Student Volunteers
University of Mississippi

Constance Bland, Student Volunteers
Mississippi Valley State University

Henry Walker, Database Administrator
Grinnell College

John Dooley, Database Administrator
Knox College

Cathy Bareiss, Evaluations
Olivet Nazarene University

Rich Kick, High School Liason
Hinsdale Central High School, Illinois

Dennis Bouvier, Local Arrangements
St. Louis University

Guido Rößling, International Liason
Darmstadt University of Technology, Germany

SIGCSE 2006

Houston, Texas, USA
March 1 – 5, 2006

`http://www.cs.rit.edu/~sigcse06/`

Symposium Co-Chairs for SIGCSE 2006

Paul Tymann
Rochester Institute of Technology
ptt@cs.rit.edu

Doug Baldwin
SUNY Geneseo
baldwin@geneseo.edu

SIGCSE 2005 Doctoral Consortium

Coordinators

Todd Stevens, *Radford University*

Mark Guzdial, *Georgia Tech*

Description

The SIGCSE Doctoral Consortium is held on Wednesday, February 23, 2005, the day before the regular sessions of the SIGCSE Technical Symposium begin. The aims of the Doctoral Consortium are:

- To offer a friendly forum for students to discuss their work and receive constructive feedback
- To offer relevant information on issues important to doctoral candidates
- To nurture a community of researchers

The Consortium is designed primarily for students currently enrolled in a Ph.D. program at any stage of study. Students in any area of computing are welcome to apply. The Consortium allows participants to interact with established researchers and with other students. It is a forum to discuss the process of research and life in academia. Each participant will give a short, critiqued research presentation.

Discussants

J. Philip East, *University of Northern Iowa*

Marian Petre, *The Open University, UK*

Orit Hazzan, *Technion – Israel Institute of Technology*

Ann Fleury, *Aurora University*

Mike Clancy, *UC Berkeley*

Zachary Kurmas, *Grand Valley State University*

Participants

Rebecca Grasser, *Lakeland Community College*

Kate Deibel, *University of Washington*

Titus Winters, *University of California, Riverside*

Adrienne Decker, *University at Buffalo, SUNY*

Marjahan Begum, *The University of Nottingham*

Anna Eckerdal, *Uppsala University, Sweden*

Haitham S. Hamza, *University of Nebraska-Lincoln*

Matt Bower, *Macquarie University, Sydney*

Becky Blackshaw, *Unitec Institute of Technology, New Zealand*

Ken Yasuhara, *University of Washington*

Jaime Spacco, *University of Maryland*

I-Ju Liao, *University of Illinois at Urbana-Champaign*

Tony Clear, *Auckland University of Technology, New Zealand*

Recipients of the SIGCSE Award for Outstanding Contributions to Computer Science Education

1981 **William F. Atchison**, *University of Maryland*
1982 **Alan Perlis**, *Yale University*
1983 **Karl V. Karlstrom**, *Prentice-Hall*
1985 **Elliot I. Organick**, *University of Utah*
1986 **Donald Knuth**, *Stanford University*
1987 **Niklaus Wirth**, *ETH, Zurich*
1988 **Grace Murray Hopper**, *Rear Admiral, USN, Digital Equipment Corp.*
1989 **Edsger W. Dijkstra**, *The University of Texas at Austin*
1990 **Curriculum '68 Committee**:

William F. Atchison	Samuel D. Conte	John Hamblen
Thomas E. Hull	Thomas A. Keenan	William B. Kehl
Edward J. McClusey	Silvio O. Navarro	Werner Rheinboldt
Earl J. Schweppe	William Viavant	David M. Young, Jr.

1991 **David Gries**, *Cornell University*
1992 **Daniel D. McCracken**, *City College, City University of New York*
1993 **Alan C. Kay**, *Apple Computer*
1994 **Norman E. Gibbs**, *Software Engineering Institute*
1995 **Robert M. Aiken**, *Temple University*
1996 **Nell B. Dale**, *The University of Texas at Austin*
1997 **Andrew Tannenbaum**, *Vrije University*
1998 **William A. Wulf**, *University of Virginia and National Academy of Engineering*
1999 **Peter J. Denning**, *George Mason University*
2000 **Andries Van Dam**, *Brown University*
2001 **Allen B. Tucker**, *Bowdoin College*
2002 **Elliot Soloway**, *University of Michigan*
2003 **Eric Roberts**, *Stanford University*
2004 **Mordechai Ben-Ari**, *Weizmann Institute of Science*
2005 **Kim Bruce**, *Williams College*

Recipients of the SIGCSE Lifetime Service Award

1997 **Richard Austing**, *University of Maryland*
1998 **Della Bonnette**, *University of Southwestern Louisiana*
1999 **Robert Aiken**, *Temple University*
2000 **James E. Miller**, *University of Southern Mississippi*
2001 **Lillian N. (Boots) Cassel**, *Villanova University*
2002 **Joe Turner**, *Clemson University and Zayed University*
2003 **Harriet Taylor**, *National Science Foundation and Louisiana State University*
2004 **Bruce Klein**, *Grand Valley State University*
2005 **Andrew McGettrick**, *University of Strathclyde*

SIGCSE'05 Reviewers

Adel Abunawass
State University of West Georgia

Evans Adams
Fort Lewis College

Adeolu Afolabi
Ladoke Akintola University of Technology

Kirsti Ala-Mutka
Tampere University of Technology

Mir Farooq Ali
Virginia Tech

Vicki Almstrum
University of Texas at Austin

Carl Alphonce
University at Buffalo, The State University of New York

Jamal Alsabbagh
Grand Valley State University

Juan Alvarez
Universidad de Chile

Alaaeldin Aly
College of Information Technology, UAE Uinversity

Jay Anderson
Franklin Marshall College

Ruth Anderson
University of Virginia

Steven K. Andrianoff
St. Bonaventure University

Karen Anewalt
Mary Washington College

Florence Appel
Saint Xavier University

Clark B. Archer
Mount Union College

Charles Ashbacher
Charles Ashbacher Technologies

Owen Astrachan
Duke University

Moshe Augenstein
Brooklyn College

John Avitabile
College of Saint Rose

John Aycock
University of Calgary

Pavel Azalov
Penn State University

Donald Bagert
Rose-Hulman Institute of Technology

Mark Bailey
Hamilton College

Bettina Bair
Ohio State University

Laura Baker
St. Edward's University

Doug Baldwin
SUNY Geneseo

Catherine Bareiss
Olivet Nazarene University

David Barnes
University of Kent

Lewis Barnett
University of Richmond

John Barr
Ithaca College

Martin Barrett
East Tennessee State University

Joao Barros
Instituto Politecnico de Beja

Jose L. Barros Justo
University of Vigo

Robert Beck
Villanova University

Byron Weber Becker
University of Waterloo

John Beidler
University of Scranton

Mordechai Ben-Ari
Weizmann Institute of Science

Jens Bennedsen
IT-West

Joseph Bergin
Pace University

Seth Bergmann
Rowan University

Mikael Berndtsson
School of Humanities and Informatics, University of Skovde

Dave Berque
DePauw University

Gian Mario Besana
CTI DePaul University

Bhagyavati
Columbus State University

Robert Biddle
Carleton University

Judith M. Bishop
University of Pretoria

Cathy Bishop-Clark
Miami University

Joyce Blair-Crowell
Belmont University

M. Brian Blake
Georgetown University

Michael Blumenstein
Griffith University

Rosa Maria Bottino
Consiglio Nazionale Ricerche

Marie-Michele Boulet
Universite Laval

Dennis Bouvier
Saint Louis University

Ilona Box
University of Western Sydney

Roger Boyle
School of Computing, University of Leeds

Ed Boyno
Montclair State University

Alyce Brady
Kalamazoo College

Stefan Brandle
Taylor University

Josef Breutzmann
Wartburg College

Robert Bryant
Gonzaga University

Barry Burd
Drew University

Kevin Burger
Rockhurst University

Debra Burhans
Canisius College

Helmar Burkhart
University of Basel

Vicky Bush
University of Gloucestershire

Greg Butler
Regis University

Anne Cable
Eastern New Mexico University

Mary Elaine Califf
Illinois State University

Andre Paul Calitz
University of Port Elizabeth

Johan Calu
KHBO

Greg Cameron
Brigham Young University - Idaho

Mario Camilleri
University of Malta

James Caristi
Valparaiso University

Martin Carlisle
US Air Force Academy

Janet Carter
University of Kent at Canterbury

Lori Carter
Point Loma Nazarene University

Lillian N. Cassel
Villanova University

Tim Chamillard
University of Colorado at Colorado Springs

Maiga Chang
Chung-Yuan Christian University

Ranjan Chaudhuri
Eastern Michigan University

Tom Cheatham
Middle Tennessee State University

James Chegwidden
Tarrant County College

Tzu-Yi Chen
Pomona College

Li-hsiang Cheo
William Paterson University of New Jersey

Carlos Ivan Chesnevar
Universitat de Lleida

Chia-Chu Chiang
University of Arkansas at Little Rock

Sei-Jong Chung
Northern Illinois University

John Cigas
Rockhurst University

Charmain Cilliers
University of Port Elizabeth

Dawn Cizmar
University of Texas at Austin

Michael Clancy
University of California, Berkeley

Martyn Clark
University of Leeds, School of Continuing Education

Tony Clear
Auckland University of Technology

Joe Clifton
University of Wisconsin, Platteville

Avi Cohen
Ministry of Education, State of Israel

Maxine Cohen
Nova Southeastern University

Constantinos Constantinides
Concordia University

Curtis Cook
Oregon State University

Stephen Cooper
Saint Joseph's University

David Cordes
University of Alabama

Jose L. Cordova
University of Louisiana at Monroe

Lee Cornell
Minnesota State University, Mankato

Jill Courte
Miami University Hamilton Campus

Al Cripps
Middle Tennessee State University

James Cross
Auburn University

Jose Cunha
New University of Lisbon

Sally Jo Cunningham
University of Waikato

Edwin P. Curran
University of Ulster

Robert Cutler
The Harker School

Pamela Cutter
Kalamazoo College

Mohammad Dadfar
Bowling Green State University

Roy Daigle
University of South Alabama

Nell Dale
University of Texas at Austin

Mats Daniels
Uppsala University

Douglas Dankel
University of Florida

Nasir Darwish
King Fahd University of Petroleum and Minerals

Sergiu Dascalu
University of Nevada, Reno

Gordon Davies
UK eUniversities Worldwide

Renzo Davoli
University of Bologna

Paul De Palma
Gonzaga University

Susan Dean
UMUC - Maryland in Europe

Joan DeBello
St. John's University

Adrienne Decker
University at Buffalo, The State University of New York

Akim Demaille
LRDE/EPITA

William Denny
McNeese State University

Peter DePasquale
The College of New Jersey

Molisa Derk
Oklahoma City University

Herbert L. Dershem
Hope College

Richard Detmer
Middle Tennessee State University

Kamyar Dezhgosha
University of Illinois at Springfield

Paloma Diaz
Universidad Carlos III de Madrid

Martin Dickey
University of Washington

Suzanne W. Dietrich
Arizona State University

Adair Dingle
Seattle University

Zachary Dodds
Harvey Mudd College

John Dooley
Knox College

David L. Doss
Illinois State University

John P. Dougherty
Haverford College

Peter Drexel
Plymouth State University

Anthony Duben
Southeast Missouri State University

Rick Duley
School of Engineering Science, Murdoch University

J. Philip East
University of Northern Iowa

Nick Efford
University of Leeds

Mary Anne Egan
Siena College

Christopher Egert
University at Buffalo, The State University of New York

Roger Eggen
University of North Florida

Joseph Ekstrom
Brigham Young University

Richard Enbody
Michigan State University

Gerald Engel
University of Connecticut, Stamford

Eileen B. Entin
Aptima, Inc.

Ed C. Epp
Intel Corporation

John Estell
Ohio Northern University

Henry Etlinger
Rochester Institute of Technology

Deidre Evans
Florida A&M University

Soundararajan Ezekiel
Indiana University of Pennsylvania

Barry Fagin
US Air Force Academy

Alan Fekete
University of Sydney

John Fendrich
Bradley University

Ernest Ferguson
Northwest Missouri State University

Francesc J. Ferri
Universitat de Valencia

Leslie Fife
Brigham Young University - Hawaii

Sue Fitzgerald
Metropolitan State University

Ann Fleury
Aurora University

Adeolua Folabi
Ladoke Akintola University of Technology

William Fone
Staffordshire University

Jeffrey Forbes
Duke University

Timothy Fossum
University of Wisconsin - Parkside

Kent Foster
Winthrop University

Charles Frank
Northern Kentucky University

Robert Franks
Central College

Frank Friedman
Temple University

Vashti Galpin
School of Computer Science, University of the Witwatersrand

Dick Gayler
Kennesaw State University

Edward M. Gellenbeck
Central Washington University

Carlisle E. George
Middlesex University, London

Jill Gerhardt
Richard Stockton College of New Jersey

Judith Gersting
University of Hawaii at Hilo

Ahmad Ghafarian
North Georgia College & State University

Marguerite Giguette
Xavier University of Louisiana

David Ginat
Tel-Aviv University

Don Goelman
Villanova University

Michael Goldwasser
Saint Louis University

Evan Golub
University of Maryland

Annegret Goold
Deakin University

Leila Goosen
University of Pretoria

Aaron Gordon
Fort Lewis College

Cary Gray
Wheaton College

Jean Greyling
University of Port Elizabeth

Scott Grissom
Grand Valley State University

Mario Guimaraes
Kennesaw State University

Jiang Guo
California State University, Los Angeles

Mark Guzdial
Georgia Institute of Technology

Tibor Bela Gyires
Illinois State University

Hisham Haddad
Kennesaw State University

Berqia Hafssa
University of Geneva

Max Hailperin
Gustavus Adolphus College

Susan Haller
University of Wisconsin - Parkside

Farid Hallouche
Saginaw Valley State University

Ranette Halverson
Midwestern State University

Mohamed Hamada
The University of Aizu

Denis Hamelin
Ryerson University

John Hamer
University of Auckland

Haitham Hamza
University of Nebraska-Lincoln

Judy Hankins
Middle Tennessee State University

Brian Hanks
University of California, Santa Cruz

Stuart Hansen
University of Wisconsin - Parkside

Ed Harcourt
St. Lawrence University

Ronald Harkins
Miami University

Douglas Harms
DePauw University

Stephen J. Hartley
Rowan University

Jessen Havill
Denison University

Christopher Haynes
Indiana University

Carol Hazlewood
Texas State University

Orit Hazzan
Technion -- Israel Institute of Technology

Jerrolyn Hebert
University of South Alabama

James Heliotis
Rochester Institute of Technology

Rachelle Heller
George Washington University

Tyson Henry
California State University, Chico

Thomas B. Hilburn
Embry-Riddle Aeronautical University

Lewis Hitchner
California Polytechnic State University

Jesper Holck
Copenhagen Business School

Mark A. Holliday
Western Carolina University

Joe Hollingsworth
Indiana University

Geoffrey Holmes
University of Waikato

Hilary Holz
California State University, Hayward

Joan E. Hoopes
Marist College

Charles Hoot
Oklahoma City University

Dwight House
Fayetteville State University

Brian Howard
DePauw University

James Howatt
Luther College

Trudy Howles
Rochester Institute of Technology

Michelle Hribar
Pacific University

Wen-Jung Hsin
Park University

Chenglie Hu
Carroll College

James Huggins
Kettering University

Richard Hull
Lenoir-Rhyne College

Dalton R. Hunkins
St. Bonaventure University

Frances Hunt
Educational Testing Service

Deborah Hwang
University of Evansville

Rahat Iqbal
Coventry University

Lubomir Ivanov
Iona College

Eric Jacopin
Ecoles de Coetquidan/Centre de Recherches Saint-Cyr

Richard James
Rollins College

Ricardo Jimenez-Peris
Technical University of Madrid

Mike Jipping
Hope College

David John
Wake Forest University

Bruce W. Johnston
University of Wisconsin-Stout

Edward Jones
Florida A&M University

Paul Jorgensen
Grand Valley State University

Anthony Joseph
Pace University

Daniel Joyce
Villanova University

Lisa Kaczmarczyk
University of Texas at Austin

Debbie Kaneko
Hampton University

Elizabeth Katz
Millersville University

David G. Kay
University of California, Irvine

Jennifer Kay
Rowan University

Thomas Kelliher
Goucher College

Mark Kerstetter
Western Michigan University

Sami Khuri
San Jose State University

K. N. King
Georgia State University

Nancy Kinnersley
University of Kansas

David Klappholz
Stevens Institute of Technology

Myungsook Klassen
California Lutheran University

Frank Klassner
Villanova University

Bruce J. Klein
Grand Valley State University

Joe Klerlein
Western Carolina University

Peter J. Knoke
University of Alaska Fairbanks

Deborah Knox
The College of New Jersey

Jane Kochanov
Pennsylvania State University - Capital College

Elliot Koffman
Temple University

Michael Kolling
University of Southern Denmark

Ari Korhonen
Helsinki University of Technology

Yana Kortsarts
Widener University

Larry Kotman
Grand Valley State University

Janet Kourik
Webster University

Joan Krone
Denison University

Amruth Kumar
Ramapo College of New Jersey

Stan Kurkovsky
Columbus State University

Jose Emilio Labra Gayo
University of Oviedo

Thomas Lancaster
University of Central England

H. Chad Lane
University of Southern California

Mary Last
University of Mary Hardin-Baylor

Patterson Laurie
University of North Carolina at Wilmington

Cary Laxer
Rose-Hulman Institute of Technology

Alina Lazar
Youngstown State University

Cathie LeBlanc
Plymouth State College

Jae Young Lee
Colorado School of MInes

Chuck Leska
Randolph-Macon College

Anany Levitin
Villanova University

Gary Lewandowski
Xavier University

John A. Lewis
Villanova University

Billy Lim
Illinois State University

Ivan Liss
Radford University

Raymond Lister
University of Technology, Sydney

Jigang Liu
Metropolitan State University

Tim Long
Ohio State University

Andy Lopez
University of Minnesota at Morris

Dian Lopez
University of Minnesota at Morris

Antonio M. Lopez, Jr.
Xavier University of Louisiana

Stephanie Ludi
Rochester Institute of Technology

Geoffrey Lund
University of Abertay Dundee

William Lyle
Murray State University

Ian Macdonald
Curtin University

Peter Macpherson
Rogers State University

David E. Maharry
Wabash College

John S. Mallozzi
Iona College

Bill Manaris
College of Charleston

Yannis Manolopoulos
Aristotle University of Thessaloniki, Greece

Bill Marion
Valparaiso University

Kenneth Martin
University of North Florida

Joseph Mast
Eastern Mennonite University

Bruce R. Maxim
University of Michigan- Dearborn

Johannes Mayer
University of Ulm

Lester McCann
The University of Arizona

Renee A. McCauley
College of Charleston

Robert McCloskey
University of Scranton

O. William McClung
Nebraska Wesleyan University

Charlie McDowell
University of California, Santa Cruz

Scott McElfresh
Carnegie Mellon University

Ryan McFall
Hope College

James McGuffee
St. Edward's University

John A. McTaggart
Drake University

Bonita McVey
St. Norbert College

Dee Medley
Augusta State University

Veijo Meisalo
University of Helsinki

Sigurd Meldal
San Jose State University

Cindy Meyer
Oklahoma Baptist University

Gail Miles
Lenoir-Rhyne College

James Miller
Bradley University

Ted Mims
University of Illinois at Springfield

William Mitchell
University of Arkansas at Little Rock

Alvaro Monge
California State University, Long Beach

Ralph Morelli
Trinity College

Ted Morris
RMIT University

Briana Morrison
Southern Polytechnic State University

Mary-Alice Muraski
University of Wisconsin – River Falls

Laurie Murphy
Pacific Lutheran University

Michael Murphy
Southern Polytechnic State University

Keitha Murray
Iona College

Nachiappan Nagappan
North Carolina State University

Lasse Natvig
Norwegian University of Technology and Science

Rance Necaise
Washington and Lee University

Robert Neufeld
McPherson College

Jaime Niño
University of New Orleans

Daniel Nohl
Benedictine University

Robert Noonan
College of William and Mary

Cindy Norris
Appalachian State University

Linda Null
Penn State Harrisburg

William Oblitey
Indiana University of Pennsylvania

Rainer Oechsle
Trier

Chris Okasaki
United States Military Academy at West Point

Amos Olagunju
St. Cloud State University

Joseph Oldham
Centre College

Lynn J. Olson
Wartburg College

Lawrence Osborne
Lamar University

Michael Oudshoorn
Montana State University

Youwen Ouyang
California State University at San Marcos

Cherry Owen
The University of Texas of the Permian Basin

Barbara Boucher Owens
Southwestern University

Claus Pahl
Dublin City University

Victor Pankratius
AIFB Institute, University of Karlsruhe

Abelardo Pardo
Carlos III University of Madrid

Crist'obal Pareja-Flores
Universidad Complutense de Madrid

Young Park
Bradley University

Brenda C. Parker
Middle Tennessee State University

David Parker
Salisbury University

Dee Parks
Appalachian State University

Allen Parrish
The University of Alabama

Marta Patino
Technical University of Madrid

Holly Patterson-McNeill
Lewis-Clark State College

Richard E. Pattis
Carnegie Mellon University

John Paxton
Montana State University - Bozeman

Teresa Peterman
Grand Valley State University

Chrisila C. Pettey
Middle Tennessee State University

Phil Pfeiffer
East Tennessee State University

Jennifer Polack-Wahl
University of Mary Washington

Wayne Pollock
Hillsborough Community College

Lori Postner
Nassau Community College

Kris Powers
Berry College

Jon Preston
Clayton College and State University

John-Paul Pretti
University of Waterloo

Rhys Price-Jones
Rochester Institute of Technology

Ann Quade
Minnesota State University

John Rager
Amherst College

Rajendra Raj
Rochester Institute of Technology

Muthu Ramachandran
Leeds Metropolitan University

Sub Ramakrishnan
Bowling Green State University

M.R.K. Krishna Rao
King Fahd University of Petroleum and Minerals

A. Joseph Turner
Clemson University

Elise Turner
University of Maine

William Turner
Wabash College

Sharon Tuttle
Humboldt State University

Paul Tymann
Rochester Institute of Technology

Susan D. Urban
Arizona State University

Ian Utting
University of Kent at Canterbury

David Valentine
Slippery Rock University

Robert Van Camp
West Virginia University at Parkersburg

Patricia Van Verth
Canisius College

Tammy VanDeGrift
University of Washington

Troy Vasiga
University of Waterloo

Steven Vegdahl
University of Portland

J. Angel Velazquez-Iturbide
Universidad Rey Juan Carlos

Phil Ventura
State University of West Georgia

Gabriela Vilanova
Universidad Nacional de la Patagonia Austral

Tamar Vilner
The Open University of Israel

Ken Vollmar
Southwest Missouri State University

Paul Wagner
University of Wisconsin - Eau Claire

Ellen Walker
Hiram College

Henry Walker
Grinnell College

Stan Warford
Pepperdine University

Richard Wasniowski
California State University Dominguez Hills

Michael Way
Florida Southern College

Thomas Way
Villanova University

Stephen Weiss
University of North Carolina at Chapel Hill

Linda Werner
University of California, Santa Cruz

Suzanne Westbrook
University of Arizona

Curt White
DePaul University

Laurie White
Mercer University

Richard Wicentowski
Swarthmore College

Michael Wick
University of Wisconsin - Eau Claire

Sheila Wiggins
Morgan State University

Samuel Wiley
La Salle University

Linda Wilkens
Providence College

James Wilkes
Appalachian State University

Dawn Wilkins
University of Mississippi

Craig Wills
Worcester Polytechnic Institute

Charles Winton
University of North Florida

Michael Wirth
University of Guelph

Lee Wittenberg
Kean University

Denise Woit
Ryerson University

Marty Wolf
Bemidji State University

Walter Wolf
Rochester Institute of Technology

Rosalee Wolfe
DePaul University

David Wolff
Pacific Lutheran University

Greg Wolffe
Grand Valley State University

Karl Wurst
Worcester State College

Arthur Yanushka
Christian Brothers University

Ken Yasuhara
University of Washington

Sung Yoo
Middle Tennessee State University

Frank H. Young
Rose-Hulman Institute of Technology

Qing Yuan
East Tennessee State University

Carol Zander
University of Washington, Bothell

Alan Zaring
Ohio Wesleyan University

Larry Zettel
Loras College

Guy Zimmerman
Bowling Green State University

Jill Zimmerman
Goucher College

Teresa Zollo
SUNY College at Geneseo

Keynote Talk

Using Abstractions to Make Concepts Concrete

Kim B. Bruce
Williams College
Williamstown, MA, USA
kim@cs.williams.edu

Abstract

As instructors we work hard at teaching our students why and how to create appropriate abstractions in order to simplify program design and implementation. Interestingly, we sometimes neglect to take advantage of the fact that we can also use abstractions to benefit teaching and learning. In this talk I'll present some examples of useful abstractions that can make computer science concepts more concrete for novices. I'll also discuss the importance of understanding and using languages that provide support for creating abstractions in developing software.

Bio

Kim Bruce is Frederick Latimer Wells Professor of Computer Science at Williams College. He received his B.A. from Pomona College and his Ph.D. from the University of Wisconsin at Madison, both in Mathematics. He was an instructor in Mathematics at Princeton University for two years before going to Williams in 1977. He has been a visiting Professor or researcher at M.I.T., Princeton University, Stanford University, the University of Pisa, Cambridge University, the Ecole Normale Superieure in Paris, and is currently on leave at the University of California at Santa Cruz. Bruce's primary research interest is in the design and semantics of programming languages, particularly the design of static type systems for object-oriented languages. He is the author of "Foundations of Object-Oriented Languages: Types and Semantics", published by MIT Press.

His interests in Computer Science education include the design of introductory courses, the role of mathematical thinking in computer science, and general mechanisms for making abstract ideas more concrete for students. He is co-author with Andrea Danyluk and Tom Murtagh of the introductory text, "Java: An eventful approach", which will be published this spring by Prentice Hall. Together with Danluk and Murtagh, he designed the objectdraw library for teaching Java to novices. He is one of the founding members of the Liberal Arts Computer Science Consortium, and has been deeply involved in the design of all three of their curricula for Computer Science at liberal arts colleges. He also served on the ACM / IEEE CS Curricula 1991 task force, and chaired the Programming Languages Knowledge Area Focus Group for Curricula 2001. He is currently serving on the ACM Java Task Force. His website is http://www.cs.williams.edu/~kim/.

SIGCSE'05, February 23-27, 2005, St. Louis, Missouri, USA.
ACM 1-58113-997-7/05/0002.

Building an XQuery Interpreter in a Compiler Construction Course

Sara Miner More   Tim Pevzner   Alin Deutsch
Scott Baden   Paul Kube

{more, tpevzner, deutsch, baden, kube}@cs.ucsd.edu
Department of Computer Science & Engineering
University of California, San Diego
La Jolla, CA 92093-0114

ABSTRACT

For two years, we have been teaching a quarter-long compiler construction course where students implement an interpreter for a variant of the XML query language XQuery. Our goal is to motivate students' interest in the course by exposing them to an interesting and powerful new language which they see as relevant to potential future experiences.

In this paper, we first explain the workings of the course itself, and then describe some pedagogically interesting variants of the XQuery language. We close with a discussion of challenges faced and conclusions.

Categories and Subject Descriptors

K.3 [**Computers & Education**]: Computer & Information Science Education—*Computer Science Education*

General Terms

Languages, Theory, Design

Keywords

Compiler construction, XQuery, XML, Capstone courses

1. INTRODUCTION

For years, our department taught a typical two-quarter sequence of courses on compiler construction. This sequence represented an integrated, capstone experience which spanned the two quarters. The assigned projects afforded students experience following a detailed specification, writing modular software and testing code. However, faculty described several problems with the existing situation. First, it was difficult to motivate students to learn about compilers. Most students were aware that it was unlikely that they would write a compiler or interpreter for a source language in their later careers, and seemed to devote less time and energy to the compiler sequence than to subjects which they perceived as more "relevant". Secondly, projects were completed in teams, and the second quarter project relied on work completed in the first quarter. This situation led to difficulties for students whose teammates did not remain enrolled in the course for the second quarter (either changed major, or took the second course during a later quarter). Furthermore, at the beginning of the second quarter, students were not starting off on even footing - those who had performed very well in the first quarter had a stronger base of code from which to begin the second half of the project.

Therefore, two years ago, with support from the department and university, we undertook a major change in our compiler sequence. First, we separated the courses so that the project in the second quarter did not depend on work completed in the first quarter. Then, we changed the focus language in the first quarter of the sequence in an attempt to improve student motivation for the course. Additionally, we tried to retain the integrative, capstone nature of the student experience, albeit only over a single quarter. To accomplish these goals, we selected the the World Wide Web Consortium's (W3C [6]) XML query language XQuery [9] as our new focus language, and asked students to build an interpreter for a subset of XQuery. In this paper, we describe our experiences using XQuery as the focus language in the first quarter of our compiler construction sequence.

2. WHY XQUERY?

As mentioned above, the selection of XQuery as a new focus language for this course was, in part, a response to faculty perception that the existing sequence of compiler construction courses was difficult to motivate. As Debray [11] noted, most computer science majors do not write a source language compiler or interpreter after graduation, so students often feel that the sequence of compiler courses is less relevant to contemporary practice. To mitigate this problem, we sought to relate the study of translators to emerging technologies that would be relevant to students' likely postgraduate experiences. Many of our undergraduates are interested in databases, and have expressed a desire to learn about XML. Since understanding the syntax and semantics of XQuery would require first obtaining a basic understanding of XML, we reasoned that students might become more enthusiastic about the subject matter from the start.

Secondly, we wanted students to come away from the compiler sequence with the sense that, with minimal effort, they would be capable of writing a compiler for a fairly complex language. Requiring them to work with XQuery, a rich language currently undergoing standardization, would

SIGCSE'05, February 23–27, 2005, St. Louis, Missouri, USA.

leave them with confidence about their ability to apply their knowledge to different languages. Admittedly, there is not enough time in a ten-week quarter to expect students to implement an interpreter for the entire language, so we ended up restricting the language somewhat.[1] However, we use a language subset that retains the flavor of the full language.

Furthermore, an XQuery interpreter lends itself nicely to a modular XML-centric design, as we will describe below. This design helps to reinforce students' newly gained knowledge about XML, allows for automated grading, and gives the instructor flexibility in terms of requirements.

3. DESCRIPTION OF THE COURSE

3.1 Concepts Covered

The course in question traditionally focused on lexical analysis, syntactic analysis, error analysis, type-checking and, to some degree, syntax-directed translation. (The second course in the sequence covers code generation and optimization, which are not included in the first quarter.) With the change to XQuery as our focus language, we did not want to sacrifice any of this conceptual core. However, we did now need to devote some time to teaching students about XML and the Document Object Model [2], as well as about XQuery itself. As a result, we reduced the amount of time spent on the theory of lexing and parsing. However, we do provide students with useful exposure to real-world language specifications and the process of dealing with an evolving standard. Furthermore, we introduce students to tools for automating the lexer and parser generation process, which they may encounter again after graduation.

In addition, in order to foster interest in the language and to help students relate it to potential real-world experiences, we invite an XQuery expert to give a guest lecture about how XQuery is used in practice and where it is headed.

3.2 Student Teams

We have a large number of CS majors in our department, and, as a result, even upper-level major courses have large enrollments. In the past two years, we have taught this class with sizes ranging from 75 to 250 students. Students are permitted to work in teams of two on the task of constructing the interpreter. (Teams typically remain together for the entire quarter, though this is not strictly required, and some students elect to work individually for some or all of the quarter.) Working in pairs ameliorates the problem of large enrollments by reducing the amount of time spent grading, and it carries with it the added benefits of encouraging student interaction, and allowing us to assign a more complex project. In fact, for most students, the project completed in this course is by far the largest programming project they have undertaken. They are also given much more flexibility and independence during the quarter than they have encountered in previous courses. Unfortunately, this freedom causes some students to struggle; we will discuss this problem further in Section 5.1.

[1]An alternative would be to create a simpler language such as MinimL [10], which was built to contain just enough features to be interesting, but not so many that students are overwhelmed. We opt for the subset approach because we feel that students are more excited about a language which they might imagine using in future employment. We discuss various subsets of the language in Section 4.

3.3 Phases of Interpreter Construction

The task of building an interpreter is often broken into three phases. We follow this traditional sequence of phases as follows. First, the lexer translates source code into a stream of tokens. Secondly, while enforcing syntax rules, the parser translates this stream of tokens into an abstract syntax tree (AST) or some other intermediate representation. Finally, the semantic engine evaluates the AST, performing type checking, and executes the code it represents.

In our XML-centric project design, XML output is used during intermediate phases. Specifically, in the first phase, students write driver programs for their lexers which, when given XQuery input, output the stream of tokens as an XML document. In the second phase, their driver programs output an XML representation of the abstract syntax tree, a natural fit with the tree-based structure of XML documents.

3.3.1 Lexer

At the beginning of the lexer portion of the course, students are introduced to the Java-centric JFlex [3] scanner-generator tool. They are then provided with a Lexical Specification documenting the requirements of their lexer. The goal of the lexer itself is to generate a stream of tokens found in the given input, including line and column information from the input file. A lexer driver extracts this token stream and outputs it in XML format. If any errors are found, they are reported in XML as well.

An interesting issue in the lexer phase (which also arises in Pascal compilers) is that XQuery comments are delimited by matching `(:` and `:)`. That is, comments may be nested. In the traditional division of labor within an interpreter, the lexer identifies comments and strips them from the input rather than tokenizing them, so that the parser is not burdened with them. However, a lexer which is a finite automaton is not sufficient for recognizing nested comments. Without the power of a stack, an XQuery lexer cannot reliably determine how to tokenize the text occurring after `:)`. This feature of XQuery breaks the traditional clean modular structure of an interpreter, but exposes students to real-world language issues. In addition, some XQuery language constructs require the use of lexical states, so we provide students with a Lexical State Specification.

3.3.2 Parser

We begin the parser portion of the course with an introduction to the Java-centric CUP [1] parser-generator. Students are given a Syntax Specification which contains the grammar rules for the language. (As mentioned above, the language is a subset of the full XQuery language, with minor modifications.) Their task is to generate an abstract syntax tree (AST) representing any given source input which conforms to the grammar. We also provide a specification for the representation of the AST, which we call the XQueryX Specification. (It is loosely based on an early version of the W3C's XQueryX specification document [8], which specifies a standard XML representation of an XQuery program.) In the case that the program contains syntax errors, the parser generates an XML file describing the location of the error.

There is one practical issue to mention here. When CUP is used to generate a parser, it creates a file called *sym.java* which contains list of token names and integers representing those tokens. The symbolic constants contained in this file are actually necessary for the scanner produced by running JFlex. Since the lexer phase of the project occurs prior to the parser phase, students have not created their own *sym.java* file yet. To rectify this problem, we provide students with the *sym.java* file generated from our reference parser to use during the lexer phase. Furthermore, parsers generated from different CUP files will generate different mappings in the resulting *sym.java* file. Providing a single file from which all teams can work avoids the problem of grading lexers which output different integers corresponding to a particular token. In the parser phase, however, students abandon the provided *sym.java* file from the earlier phase and run CUP to create their own. Since the output of the parser does not include tokens, the internal integer representation for a particular token does not affect the output.

3.3.3 *Semantic Engine*

In the final phase of the interpreter construction, the goal is evaluation of ASTs generated by the parser. Students are given a full Semantic Specification detailing the meaning of language constructs and its type system.

Evaluation of some XQuery constructs is quite straightforward for students, e.g., literals or the *if-then-else* statement. A central construct in an XQuery program, however, is a *FLWOR expression*, which supports iteration and binding of variables to values. Students are unfamiliar with the semantics of this expression, so implementing its evaluation takes some time. In particular, the *order-by* clause of a FLWOR is most troublesome for students. Furthermore, *constructors* and *path expressions* are constructs which allow for the creation and traversal, respectively, of nodes within XML document trees, and seem to be the most troubling for students to implement. In addition, the preexisting XML and XPath[7] schema on which XQuery was based introduce some unusual constructs into the language, adding to the complexity of the assignment. Luckily, the Java standard packages org.w3c.dom, org.xml.sax, and javax.xml.parsers provide much functionality for manipulating XML documents and Document Object Model interfaces. To assist students further, we supply them with our own utility package for manipulating XML in Java that provides much of the components of path expression functionality. Students are left with the task of combining these different given components of a path expression in the appropriate way.

Type checking is also performed in this phase. XQuery has a detailed hierarchical structure of predefined datatypes. We include a subset of these, consisting of what we believe is a manageable number of types (approximately 15, about half of which are the various XML node types). In addition, we simplify the language further by disallowing user-defined types. It turns out that implementing an XQuery interpreter in Java is convenient, as there is a nice mapping of most XQuery types to Java types. Furthermore, we encourage students to make use of Java inheritance when implementing the hierarchical type system of XQuery.

Because some students begin the course without prior knowledge of XML and nearly all students begin without prior knowledge of XQuery, we spend some time introducing these languages during lecture. In addition, we have found it useful to include an initial programming assignment that forces students to use these languages. Students write several fairly short XQuery programs which are intended to acquaint them with unfamiliar language constructions such as FLWOR expressions, constructors, path expressions and predicates. Although it delays the beginning of the lexer assignment, we find that familiarity with XQuery is very helpful for students during the semantic analysis phase.

3.4 The Grading Process

The XML-centric nature of the interpreter project allows fairly clean automation of the grading process. By running all test inputs through our reference implementation, we generate reference XML output files. Students use a script to turn in their source code electronically, and we use our own script to collect the turn-in files, compile them, and run them. We then use *xmldiff* [4], a freely available *diff*-like tool for comparing XML files, to compare student output to our reference output. We take an all-or-nothing approach to assigning points. For a 100-point assignment, we test each team's code on 100 different input files designed to cover all language features. The team earns one point for each output file which matches the corresponding reference output according to xmldiff. Generally, we do not award partial credit for partial matches, as this would require too much time for such a large class. This means that even minor spacing errors can cost a team significant points. To make this process more fair, we do provide a small set of public test inputs and outputs to the students while they work on a particular phase, and they have access to the xmldiff tool. This gives them the opportunity to check their output against the posted output, to help eliminate these types of errors. Grades are returned to students via email, along with the xmldiff output from the test runs and some individual comments on their progress, so that they can determine which types of tests they did not pass. Because the next phase of the interpreter builds on the current phase, timely feedback about mistakes is important for student progress.

In addition to the programming projects, we give midterm and final examinations to test the students' knowledge of course concepts. Students take these exams individually. Inevitably, there are some project teams in which one student performs a disproportionate amount of the work, and these individual assessments help us to assign appropriate grades. To this end, it is important to test understanding of the XQuery language in addition to compiler theory on the exams. This allows us to identify students who did not learn XQuery well because they did not put in their share of effort on the projects.

4. OUR VARIANTS OF XQUERY

In this section, we describe a language based on XQuery which we believe is interesting from a pedagogical standpoint. First, however, we begin with a very elementary overview of some of the features of full XQuery.

4.1 Some Basic Features of XQuery

XQuery is a functional language. The basic building blocks in XQuery are expressions, whose values consist of sequences of items. Designed as a query language for the widely-used markup language XML, XQuery allows concise yet powerful queries over XML documents. As such, built-in types in XQuery are based on the XML type system. A large number of standard functions are specified in XQuery, for tasks such as arithmetic, logical and set operations. Both user-defined types and functions are also allowed.

A central construct in the language is the FLWOR expression, where the letters in the acronym stand for the clauses available in the expression, namely, *for*, *let*, *where*, *order by* and *return*. This type of expression allows iteration over and binding of values to variables, along with selection of particular values. Specifically, *for* clauses permit iteration, *let* clauses permit binding, and an optional *where* clause "gates" the execution of the *return* clause. That is, for a particular iteration, the boolean expression associated with the *where* clause is evaluated. If the expression is true, the *return* clause is executed for that iteration. The value of a FLWOR expression is the concatenation of all values returned by each execution of the *return* clause of the FLWOR into a single sequence. The optional *order by* clause may be used to sort the items in the returned sequence.

FLWOR expressions are useful for computing joins between two or more documents and for restructuring data.

Data in a well-formed XML document is logically arranged in a tree specified by the Document Object Model (DOM), and different nodes in the tree are of different types (e.g., *element*, *attribute*, *text*, *comment*, etc.). XQuery's path expression construct allows the selection of nodes in an XML document based on their position in the document's DOM tree, their types, and the names given to the nodes. For example, using a path expression within a FLWOR, one can iterate over a sequence of nodes in a particular document, such that, at every node n in the sequence, all logical children of n which are *element* type nodes that have name foo are selected. The full syntax of such an expression is as follows, where we assume that the variable `$sequence` is already bound to a sequence of XML nodes:

```
for $n in $sequence return $n/child::element(foo)
```

Because the path expression appearing in the above return clause is a common type of query, XQuery permits a shorthand version of it. Thus, the following expression is equivalent to the one above:

```
for $n in $sequence return $n/foo
```

That is, expressions of the form a/b indicate that all *element* children of node a with name b are to be returned.

A related path expression allows queries for all element nodes which are descendants (on any level in the tree) of a node. There are many other sorts of path expressions, allowing queries based on different position specifiers within the DOM tree and different node types. Some of these path expressions can be expressed using full path expression syntax as well as specialized shorthand notation.

XML documents on which path expressions queries are made can be read in from external files, or, alternatively, XML nodes may be constructed within the XQuery program themselves. *Direct constructors* allow literal XML to be written verbatim within an XQuery program. *Computed constructors* allow XML nodes to be specified using keywords to identify the type of node to be created.

4.2 Our Variations on XQuery

Because XQuery has many additional features (which we lack sufficient space to mention here), students in a quarter-long course can implement only a subset of the actual XQuery standard language. Here we discuss several variants of XQuery that include language features which we found to be interesting in our compiler construction course. In some cases, our variants are not strictly subsets of the official XQuery language; we do deviate from the official specification somewhat. However, we believe that the flavor of the official language is retained.

First, we restrict the type system of the language, so that only approximately 15 types are included. (Note that nine of these are XML node types or groups of of XML nodes, and much of the functionality required to implement them is available in standard Java classes.) We do not allow user-defined types. We also restrict the number of built-in functions, the different types of path expressions and the types of constructors allowed. We give detailed instructions about implicit type conversions used in function calls.

We are experimenting with the idea of treating path expressions as built-in functions, rather than using their official syntax. We also intend to eliminate the shorthand versions of path expressions, which students found confusing and which do not provide significant pedagogical interest.

We also found it useful to rework the XQuery grammar so that, for example, literals are derived in a small number of steps. This allows testing of parser code to be performed incrementally, instead of requiring that students have a large section of the grammar in place before testing can begin.

To combat plagiarism, we modify our project requirements from quarter to quarter in an attempt to avoid the "code migration" problem, where students in the course during a previous quarter share their code with students currently enrolled in the course. Of course, these change in requirements necessitate the preparation of a new reference implementation each quarter, but we feel the gains are worth the additional instructor effort.[2]

Changing the AST specification from quarter to quarter is one way to drastically change the code required for the project. For example, we changed the AST representation of a FLWOR expression dramatically one quarter. This not only helped combat plagiarism, it was also a representation that simplified the interpretation of the expression. In other quarters, we removed the *order by* clause from the language completely, allowing only FLWR expressions instead.

More simple changes include using different subsets of official XQuery's many built-in functions, or specifying new built-in functions which allow any number of parameters. Modifications to the error handling requirements are another option. Furthermore, we have incorporated different language features from the official XQuery specification at different times, such as the explicit specification of parameter and return types in user-defined functions and quantified expressions.

5. DISCUSSION

In the past two years, we have offered this course five different times. We now mention some general challenges that we faced along with the XQuery-specific issues we mentioned earlier. We close with some summary remarks.

5.1 Challenges

One of the goals of our compilers course is to expose students to large-scale programming projects. Since this is a new experience for a majority of the enrolled students, they have initial difficulties in grasping the big picture of the assignment and budgeting their time.[3] (These problems are typical of capstone courses, regardless of topic.) We address

[2]Because we use a different language each quarter, students sometimes find bugs in the project specifications. For some, this may be a good learning experience, but other students understandably find this frustrating.

[3]As last-minute desperation engenders plagiarism, we also

these challenges as follows. In order to encourage students to begin working on the phases of the project as soon as they are assigned, we have instituted voluntary checkpoints midway through the longer phases. In the future, these may include students turning in part of the assignment for feedback. This checkpoint would not be counted in their grade for the course, but might help them determine what areas need attention before the final project is handed in. Although it increases our administrative burden, we hope that this potential boost to their final score will motivate students to work steadily on the project from the beginning, increasing their chances for success. Adding software engineering topics [12] to the course may also be helpful, though there is not much time to spare during a ten-week quarter. On a departmental level, we would like to increase the effectiveness of prerequisite courses at preparing students to handle assignments of this size, so the long-term nature of the interpreter project does not come as a shock.

Because students work in pairs on the projects, we face the usual team-related issues. For example, is each partner is pulling his or her own weight? As mentioned above, we try to address this problem by including project-related material on the individual exams. When assigning final letter grades, students who have high project scores but low exam grades raise a red flag. Another minor problem arises when one student from a team withdraws during the quarter. We try to assist the remaining partner by finding another individual in the same situation, and in our large classes, we are usually successful. Another team-related challenge is that students become accustomed to asking a peer for assistance. We wonder if working in teams increases the likelihood of different pairs working together, which is not allowed.

Finally, we find that some topics covered in lectures and exams seem disconnected from the interpreter project. For example, the textbook and lectures include descriptions of top-down and bottom-up parsing algorithms, but students do not feel this knowledge is helpful, since CUP automates the parser generation process. Throughout the quarter, student interest level during lecture seems fairly low except when we are discussing project details. Students have repeatedly expressed their feelings that the book is "useless until it is time to study for the exams".

5.2 Conclusions

We conclude with some observations about using XQuery as the focus language in our compiler construction course. First, we note that none of the major challenges we faced were introduced when we began using XQuery. These challenges could arise during any team-based large project.

Compared with prior offerings of the course, we now spend more time discussing the base language and XML, as well as interpreter design. These come at the expense of some parsing theory, and add to the list of new ideas that students must juggle. An argument can be made that reducing the time spent on parsing theory is warranted, and we feel that the exposure to languages and tools which are more "real-world relevant" is useful for the students.

Looking toward the future, we can imagine several other versions of this course which use XQuery as a focus language. The XML-based modular design of the system allows students to concentrate on any particular part of the compiler. For example, we could provide students who write a lexer and parser with a web interface to an existing semantic engine, so that they could more easily verify the correctness of the AST output by their parser. (A similar approach where a parser is provided would allow students to verify the correctness of the token stream output by their lexer.) Alternatively, we may want to design a course emphasizing software design that would concentrate more on database issues, and less on lexing and parsing. To acheive this, we could provide a web interface to a parser that would generate an appropriate AST. Interpreters written by students would then take the generated AST as input, freeing them from the burden of writing the lexer and parser. Furthermore, the Java DOM implementation could be used as the AST representation, providing a simple interface. The convenience of the XML-based architecture of an XQuery interpreter makes other variations possible as well.

---

run student submissions through MOSS[5, 13], a tool which checks software similarity. MOSS is most useful on the semantic engine portion of the assignment, because it does not work on the JFlex and CUP files which constitute the majority of the earlier assigments.

6. REFERENCES

[1] CUP Parser Generator For Java. `http://www.cs.princeton.edu/appel/modern/java/CUP/`, August 2004.

[2] Document Object Model (DOM). `http://www.w3.org/DOM/`, August 2004.

[3] JFlex - The Fast Scanner Generator For Java. `http://jflex.de/`, August 2004.

[4] Logilab's xmldiff. `http://www.logilab.org/projects/xmldiff/`, August 2004.

[5] MOSS: A System for Detecting Software Plagiarism. `http://www.cs.berkeley.edu/aiken/moss.html`, August 2004.

[6] W3C World Wide Web Consortium. `http://www.w3.org/`, August 2004.

[7] XML Path Language (XPath) Version 1.0. `http://www.w3.org/TR/xpath`, August 2004.

[8] XML Syntax for XQuery 1.0 (XQueryX). `http://www.w3.org/TR/2001/WD-xqueryx-20010607`, August 2004.

[9] XQuery 1.0: An XML Query Language. `http://www.w3.org/TR/xquery/`, August 2004.

[10] D. Baldwin. A compiler for teaching about compilers. In *Proceedings of the 34th SIGCSE Technical Symposium on Computer Science Education*, pages 220–223. ACM SIGCSE, February 2003.

[11] S. Debray. Making compiler design relevant for students who will (most likely) never design a compiler. In *Proceedings of the 33rd SIGCSE Technical Symposium on Computer Science Education*, pages 341–345. ACM SIGCSE, February 2002.

[12] W. G. Griswold. Teaching software engineering in a compiler project course. *ACM Journal of Educational Resources in Computing*, 2(4):1–18, December 2002.

[13] S. Schleimer, D. S. Wilkerson, and A. Aiken. Winnowing: Local algorithms for document fingerprinting. In *Proceedings of the ACM SIGMOD International Conference on Management of Data*, pages 76–85. ACM SIGMOD, June 2003.

Teaching Compiler Construction Using a Domain Specific Language

Tyson R. Henry
Department of Computer Science
California State University, Chico
Chico, CA 95929-0410
tyson@ecst.csuchico.edu

ABSTRACT

Building a compiler for a domain specific language (a language designed for a specific problem domain) can engage students more than traditional compiler course projects. Most students feel that compiler courses are irrelevant because they are not likely to get a job writing compilers[2]. However, the technologies used to construct a compiler are widely applicable [2,5]. Using a domain specific language demonstrates to students the wide applicability of compiler construction techniques. This paper presents the results of using a domain specific language in an upper division compiler course.

Categories and Subject Descriptors

K.3 [Computers and Information Science Education]: *Computer Science Education*.

General Terms

Design, Languages

Keywords

Compiler Construction, Domain Specific Languages, Educational Projects

1. INTRODUCTION

After working several years in industry, I taught a compiler course for the first time. On the first day I told the students that compiler construction technologies could be used for many applications other than traditional compilers. I told them about the several times in my career that flex/bison (GNU compiler construction tools) provided a very efficient way to solve complex input problems. I explained that in some situations a language-based user interface was more elegant and more powerful than a graphical user interface. Ironically, I then assigned a typical compiler class project – I had the students write a compiler for a subset of C.

SIGCSE'05, February 23–27, 2005, St. Louis, Missouri, USA.

The students were not very excited by the project. While the compiler construction tools are not overly complicated, learning them seemed entirely pointless to many of them. Not a single student in my class thought he or she would get a job writing a C compiler. It did not matter to them that I had insisted these technologies were useful for applications other than writing a compiler for a high level programming language. Soon after the semester was underway, I realized that if I wanted students to learn compiler construction technologies and recognize that compiler construction technologies are widely useful, I should give them a project that demonstrated their usefulness.

Of all the course projects that I have assigned, the projects that have included graphics have engaged students more than any others; of all the graphics projects the games were the most popular. Thus I set about developing a compiler course project that included both graphics and games.

I developed the Game Programming Language (GPL), a specialized language for programming graphical computer games. GPL is a simple but expressive language that can be learned in a couple hours. It is well suited for simple video games such as Pong, Space Invaders, Centipede, etc. A simple one-player Pong game can be written in about 75 lines of code, and Space Invaders in about 120 lines. I then developed a course project to implement a compiler/interpreter for GPL. The resulting project is reasonable in scope and does not require students to perform any graphics programming. It is well suited for upper division computer science majors at a typical state teaching university such as Chico State.

I have used this project for two semesters with great results. This paper describes the GPL project and students' reactions to it. My intention of this paper is not to sell this particular language or project, but to demonstrate that it is possible and valuable to stray from the traditional compiler course project of writing a compiler for a subset of a language such as C or Pascal.

2. THE GAME PROGRAMMING LANGUAGE (GPL)

The Game Programming Language (GPL) provides a good example of a domain specific language appropriate for an upper division compiler course. It is expressive enough that it can be used to describe an interesting set of games, but simple enough that it is very easy to learn. It is particularly well suited for implementing early video games (*circa* 1970's). Students have used it to write simplified versions of dozens of games including: Pong, Space Invaders, Centipede, Break-Out, Frogger, and Pac Man. The compiler/interpreter is small enough that most students at Chico State can write it in a single semester. The development goals of GPL were:

- Interesting enough to engage students
- Expressive enough so students can create interesting games
- Simple enough for students at a state teaching university to implement in a single semester
- Powerful enough to demonstrate the usefulness of creating a domain specific language
- Would not require any graphics programming experience

The language is based around animated graphical objects called *game objects*[3]. Each game object has a geometry (e.g. a rectangle) that is parameterized by a set of attributes (e.g. color, size, location), and a code block, called an animation block, that changes its attributes. The language provides definitions for triangle, rectangle, circle, and text-box game objects. Game object attributes can be initialized at instantiation time and modified at run time. For example, a rectangle can be instantiated as follows:

```
new rectangle ball(
    x = 100, y = 100, w = 10, h = 10,
    animation = ball_animation);
```

The above will create a rectangle named `ball` with the specified size, location, and animation block.

```
int window_width = 500;
int window_height = 500;
int paddle_increment = 30;

int ball_x_increment = 3;
int ball_y_increment = 2;
int ball_size = 10;

int computer_score = 0;
int player_score = 0;

// declare ball's animation handler
animation ball_animate(rectangle cur_ball);

// create paddle rectangle
rectangle paddle(x = .75 * window_width,
                 y = .5 * window_height,
                 w = 5, h = 40);

// create ball rectangle
rectangle ball(x = window_width/2,
               y = window_height/2,
               w =  ball_size,
               h = ball_size,
               animation = ball_animate);

textbox c_score_tbox(x = 0, y = 0,text= "0");

textbox p_score_tbox(x = window_width - 20,
                     y = 0, text = "0");

// when user presses up arrow, move paddle up
on uparrow
{
    if (paddle.y < window_height - 40)
        paddle.y += paddle_increment;
}

// when user presses down arrow, move paddle down
on downarrow
{
    if (paddle.y > paddle_increment)
        paddle.y -= paddle_increment;
}
```

```
// animation handler for the ball
animation ball_animate
{
    // if ball has reached top or bottom
    // reverse its direction
    if (cur_ball.y < 0
        || cur_ball.y > window_width – ball_size)
    {
        ball_y_increment = -ball_y_increment;
    }

    // if ball has reached left wall
    // increment score & reverse its direction
    if (cur_ball.x < 0 )
    {
        ball_x_increment = -ball_x_increment;
        player_score += 1;
        p_score_tbox.text = player_score;
    }

    // if ball has reached right wall
    // increment score & reverse its direction
    if (cur_ball.x > window_width - ball_size)
    {
        ball_x_increment = -ball_x_increment;
        computer_score += 1;
        c_score_tbox.text = computer_score;
    }

    // if ball touches the paddle, reverse
    if (cur_ball touches paddle)
    {
        ball_x_increment = -ball_x_increment;
    }

    // on each step of the animation, move ball
    cur_ball.x += ball_x_increment;
    cur_ball.y += ball_y_increment;
}
```

Figure 1: Simple Pong Game Implemented Using GPL

Animation blocks are named blocks of code that are executed at regular intervals (specifically, the run-time system executes all animation blocks at regular intervals). An object can be animated by placing code that alters the object's attributes in its animation block. For example, the following animation block[1] will cause the ball to move to the right until it disappears off the window:

```
animation ball_animation
{
    ball.x += 10;
}
```

In addition to graphical objects and animation blocks, the language contains event handlers. Event handlers are blocks of code for handling user actions. Each event handler is tied to a specific user event, e.g. up-arrow, down-arrow, space-bar. It is specified using the keyword `on` followed by the keyword for the type of event (e.g. `uparrow`, `downarrow`, `space`). The following event handler moves the rectangle `ball` up when the user pressed the up-arrow:

```
on uparrow
{
    ball.y += 5;
}
```

There are four types of statements that can be used in animation blocks and event handler blocks:

1. assignment
2. if
3. for-loop
4. print (used primarily for debugging)

In addition to graphical object declarations, animation blocks, and event handlers, the language contains global numeric variables (float and int), and system variables. System variables are predefined variables that are used for setting window attributes such as the size and title of the window. In order to simplify the parsing of the language, all declarations (ints, floats, games objects) must come before the animation blocks and event handlers. Figure 1 shows a simple Pong game written using GPL.

3. PROJECT OVERVIEW

The project is part compiler and part interpreter. It has the front-end of a compiler (lexical, syntactic, and semantic analysis) and the back-end of an interpreter (program execution). In order to limit the size of the project, it does not perform any code generation like traditional compiler course projects. Students were given the choice of working independently or with one other student. The project was broken up into eight phases as shown in Figure 2; the remainder of this section describes each phase. A complete description of the project is described in [4].

1. Extend a simple expression parser
2. Write a game using GPL
3. Write a lexical analyzer and parser for the GPL grammer
4. Implement a symbol table and insert numeric variable declarations
5. Add expressions to the initialization of numeric variable declarations
6. Add code to parse the declaration of game objects (graphics objects)
7. Implement statements and event handlers
8. Implement animation blocks

Figure 2: Project Phases

In phase one, students are given a simple integer expression parser written using flex and bison. They must then extend it to include more operators and doubles. The project is simple, but forces students to learn the syntax of flex and bison.

The second phase is to write a game using GPL. I provide a working GPL interpreter, and students must develop a game with a level of complexity similar to Pong. The vast majority of students write games much more complex than required. This is a great example of how graphical computer games engage and motivate students to do more work than required. The goal of this phase is to introduce students to GPL. Afterwards students understand all the components of the language and how it works.

The next phase is to write a lexical analyzer and a parser for the GPL grammar. This phase is largely mechanical – the students must convert the grammar into the format accepted by bison and extend the flex script used in Phase 1 so that it recognizes all the tokens in GPL. Since all students understand the syntax of flex and bison from the first phase, no one has difficulty with this phase. The length of the project could be reduced by giving the students the lexical analyzer and parser, but many students have commented that they enjoyed starting from scratch; it gives them a strong sense of accomplishment.

The fourth phase is to implement a symbol table and parse numeric variable declarations. The symbol table is very straight forward and can be written in isolation from the parser. Thus, few students have any problem completing this phase. The parsing of numeric variable declarations is the first task that requires students to insert actions into the parser. This task is difficult for some students.

For many students the fifth phase is the most difficult. In this phase, expressions are implemented to handle the initialization of numeric variables. In order to complete this phase, students must develop an understanding of the recursive nature of the parser and must understand more details of bison. Since expressions are used throughout the language, students implement an expression tree that can be used for both the initialization of variables and evaluating expressions at run-time.

1 This is a slight simplification, animation blocks are parameterized and can be used for multiple objects.

In the sixth phase, students implement the declarations of game objects (graphical objects). This phase requires students to use a set of classes that I provide. These classes encapsulate all the graphics and windowing aspects of the interpreter, thus students don't have to learn how to program using OpenGL. Graphical objects (square, circle, etc.) are created by instantiating the provided classes. The only graphics programming that has to be done is to specify the x and y coordinates of the graphical objects. Students without any graphics programming experience have no trouble using these classes.

By this point in the project, students have a good working knowledge of bison. Once this phase is implemented, graphics appear on the screen. Students like seeing the graphics; it gives them a sense of accomplishment. At this point most students feel they they are over the hump and appear to gain momentum.

Phase seven is the implementation of statements and event handlers. Students write a C++ class for each type of statement. When a statement is parsed, their parser instantiates an instance of the corresponding class. Once the first statement is implemented, implementing the rest of the statements is trivial. Event handlers are the blocks of statements that are executed when the user presses a key. Once the statement classes are implemented, the event handler is easy.

The final phase is to implement the animation blocks. The animation blocks are mostly a specialization of event handlers. However, since an animation block can be associated with many different game objects, a parameter passing mechanism must be implemented. This mechanism is hard for students to grasp, but once they understand it, they don't have any problem implementing it.

At this point students can use their compiler/interpreter to run the game they wrote for phase two. They usually have a big grin on their face when they demonstrate their game using their interpreter.

3.1 Programming Environment

The project was written in C++ using the GNU C++ compiler. The scanner was generated using the GNU compiler construction tool flex (a lexical analyzer generator similar to lex), and the parser was generated by GNU's bison (a parser generator similar to yacc). The graphics were implemented using OpenGL and GLUT (the GL Utility Toolkit). All of these are available free of charge on a wide range of UNIX and Linux platforms. They are also available for the Macintosh and for Cygwin (Cygwin is a public domain UNIX emulator for Microsoft operating systems). Students developed on Linux, Mac, and Windows operating systems. There were very few problems porting the code between the three.

4. STUDENT REACTION

Most students like the project. Many report learning more from it then they have in any other course project. Several students remarked on the usefulness of the interpreter; they felt they had built something meaningful that they could use. On average, students felt the project was more fun, more exciting, and more engaging than previous course projects. The survey in Figure 3 was given to students in four different compiler courses. Two courses used the GPL project (21 and 17 students). In one course students wrote a compiler for a subset of C (12 students), and in the fourth, students augmented a working C compiler (12 students). Averages of the student answers are shown in Figure 4.

The GPL project is difficult for students at Chico State. Sixty percent of all students rate it as the hardest of all their computer science class projects. Another 32% rate it as one of the hardest. Fifty-nine percent of the students finish the entire project. The majority of the other 41% were close to finishing; all of the students who did not finish reported starting the assignment too late. In order to prevent students from giving up when they realized they would not finish, I gave significant partial credit and allowed students to turn components in late. Most students who got behind never caught up.

5. FUTURE DIRECTIONS

Many games include a large number of objects, thus GPL would be much more expressive if it contained arrays. However, arrays make the implementation more complex. I have offered the implementation of arrays as extra credit, but no one has been able to get them fully working. I plan to to reduce the complexity of the project by providing part of the solution so that students will have time to implement arrays. The addition of arrays will allow the students to write more complex games and potentially better engage them.

Not all students can finish this project and thus I provide a liberal late policy so that students can get credit for the work they accomplish and so they don't give up. However, when students start to fall behind, they tend to start putting off the phases until the last few weeks of the semester. Next time I teach this class I will provide a set of milestones students must meet to receive an A, one for a B, and one for a C. I will provide some leeway for students to catch up and move back to a higher grade track, but students who fall significantly far behind will not be allowed to catch up. This should prevent students from thinking they can catch up during the last few weeks of the semester. If this approach does not improve completion rate, an alternative approach would be to give students a completed component if they failed to meet a deadline [1].

The project does not touch on the compiler construction topics of code generation and optimization. These are important topics and it would be good to include them. One way to include them would be to change the project into an actual compiler that generates a specialized byte code. The students could be provided with a byte code interpreter to run the programs. This approach would probably make the project less complicated for the students, but would require significant effort to develop the byte code and its interpreter. The disadvantage of this approach is that the project would be less representative of how compiler construction technologies are used to build front-ends for applications.

For each question, students circled a number (0,1,2,3,4).

1. How confident are you that you can recognize a problem that could be efficiently solved using flex and bison? *Not Confident(0) — Very Confident(4)*
2. How confident are you that you could solve a problem using flex and bison on your own? *Not Confident(0)—Very Confident(4)*
3. How confident are you that you could create a new special purpose language for describing complex input (for example, a language for describing the input to a project scheduling program)? *Not Confident(0)—Very Confident(4)*
4. Compared to all your other class programming assignments, how would you rate your compiler course project?
   a: *Learned less(0)—Learned more than other projects(4)*
   b: *Not applicable to my career(0)—Applicable(4)*
   c: *Easy(0)—Hardest of all class projects(4)*
5. How do you feel about the project? The project was:
   a: *Not engaging(0)—Very engaging(4)*
   b: *Not fun(0)—Fun(4)*
   c: *Boring(0)—Exciting(4)*
   d: *Hard to motivate self(0)—Wanted to work on it(4)*
   e: *Busywork(0)—Made me think a lot(4)*

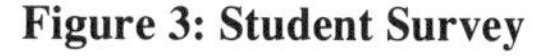

Figure 3: Student Survey

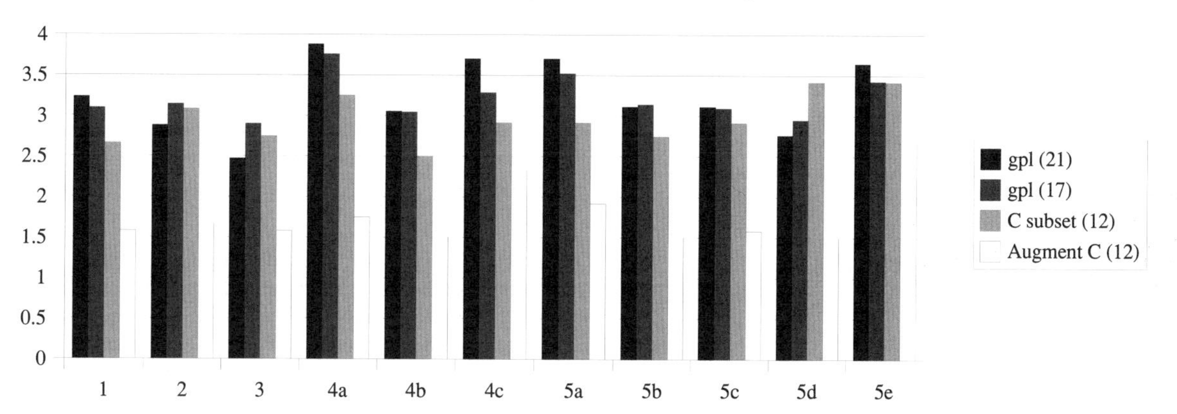

Figure 4: Student Survey Results by Question

6. CONCLUSION

Traditional compiler courses have students implement a compiler for a subset of a high level programming language. Many students do not find such projects engaging or pertinent to their career. Most students do not believe they will get a job writing a compiler and thus will never use compiler construction technologies again. However, the technologies used to construct compilers are widely applicable. For example, domain specific languages are sometimes better for user input than a graphical user interface.

As an alternative, I have developed a compiler course project around a domain specific language for the specification of graphical computer games. I have used the project in two courses with good success. Students report being more engaged and having more fun than students that complete a traditional compiler project. Students also have more confidence that they can solve problems using compiler construction technology and many students report learning more from this project than from any other project they have completed. The project clearly demonstrates the wide applicability of compiler construction technology.

7. REFERENCES

[1] D. Baldwin, "A Compiler for Teaching about Compilers," in *Proceedings of the 34th SIGCSE Technical Symposium on Computer Science Education*, pages 220-223, February 2003.

[2] S. Debray, "Making Compiler Design Relevant for Students who will (Most Likely) Never Design Compiler," in *Proceedings of the 33h SIGCSE Technical Symposium on Computer Science Education*, pages 220-223, February 2002.

[3] T. Henry, "The Game Programming Language (GPL)", on-line document, http://www.ecst.csuchico.edu/~tyson/gpl/gpl_manual.html.

[4] T. Henry, "The GPL project description," on-line document, http://www.ecst.csuchico.edu/~tyson/gpl/project.html.

[5] M. Werner, "A Parser Project in a Programming Languages Course", in *The Journal of Computing Sciences in Colleges*, Volume 18, Issue 5, May 2003.

Hide and Show – Using Real Compiler Code for Teaching

Elizabeth White
Computer Science Department
George Mason University
Fairfax, VA
(703) 993-1586
white@cs.gmu.edu

Ranjan Sen
Microsoft Corporation
Washington, DC
(425) 443-5621
ranjans@microsoft.com

Nina Stewart
Computer Science Department
George Mason University
Fairfax, VA
(703) 993-1530
nstewart@gmu.edu

ABSTRACT

In this paper, we present a novel approach that enables students in graduate compiler courses to examine and experiment with a real compiler without becoming overwhelmed by complexity. The key to the idea is the use of a debugger directly on a compiler during the compilation process. By providing instructions on breakpoints and variables of interest, the student is only shown the relevant portions of the compiler; the rest is hidden. We describe our strategy of using exercise sessions targeted toward illustration of core compiler concepts such as lexical analysis, parsing and code generation.

Categories and Subject Descriptors

D.3.4 [**Programming Languages**]: Processors – *compilers, debuggers, parsing, code generation*

General Terms

Languages, Experimentation

Keywords

Compilers, parsing, SSCLI

1. INTRODUCTION

The study of programming language environments and language processing tools is a core subject in the field of computer science [1]. Traditionally, these topics are taught by combining language and compiling theory with programming assignments designed to illustrate the concepts. Often these assignments require the use of compiler generation tools such as Lex and YACC[7] to write a rudimentary compiler for a small language [3,4,10]. While this approach provides students with much of the background knowledge necessary to understand underlying basic concepts such as lexical analysis, parsing, symbol tables, runtime environments, it typically does not provide an accurate picture of how these concepts are addressed in a real, industrial strength compiler.

SIGCSE'05, February 23-27, 2005, St. Louis, Missouri, USA.

One approach to addressing this issue is to use a complete compiler for a very small language, as described in [5]. We want to take this approach a step further and demonstrate the inner workings of a real compiler to students. Demonstrations that use real software to illustrate basic concepts and theory can be educationally very significant [9]. A concrete example compiler can help in the examination and understanding of the formal models, engineering, data structures and algorithms that help in solving the language processing problem. However, in order to do this, we needed to find a way to highlight the parts of the compiler that relate to the concept being studied while hiding the unneeded details.

This paper describes our work developing and using exercises that allow students to examine the source code of a real compiler as an illustration of basic compiler concepts. We are using the described approach in the Fall 2004 graduate compiler classes in the Computer Science Department at George Mason University. We also present how hide and show exercises are developed for curriculum use and give initial impressions of the feasibility and utility of this approach as part of the compiler curriculum. Finally in Section 5, we briefly describe the technologies that we are using in this work.

2. HIDE AND SHOW LESSONS

As described in the introduction, our goal was to develop a way to use a real, industrial strength compiler as a teaching tool for compiler theory. In order to do this, we needed to be able to show only the relevant parts of the compiler and hide the rest. Our approach (Figure 1) to achieving this goal is to use a debugging tool directly *on the compiler* in a manner tailored directly to the relevant basic concepts. The tailoring is achieved by providing students with basic debugger configurations (for example, breakpoints in given compiler modules, and important variables and data structures) and input programs to be compiled, along with a lab manual and questions. The lab manual provides any needed background documentation on the part of the compiler relevant to the concept under study, as well as a step-by-step list of activities. The activities include examination of source code as well as the contents of different variables and data structures to understand the state of a compilation. Using this information, the student can see the real inner workings with respect to the concept under study.

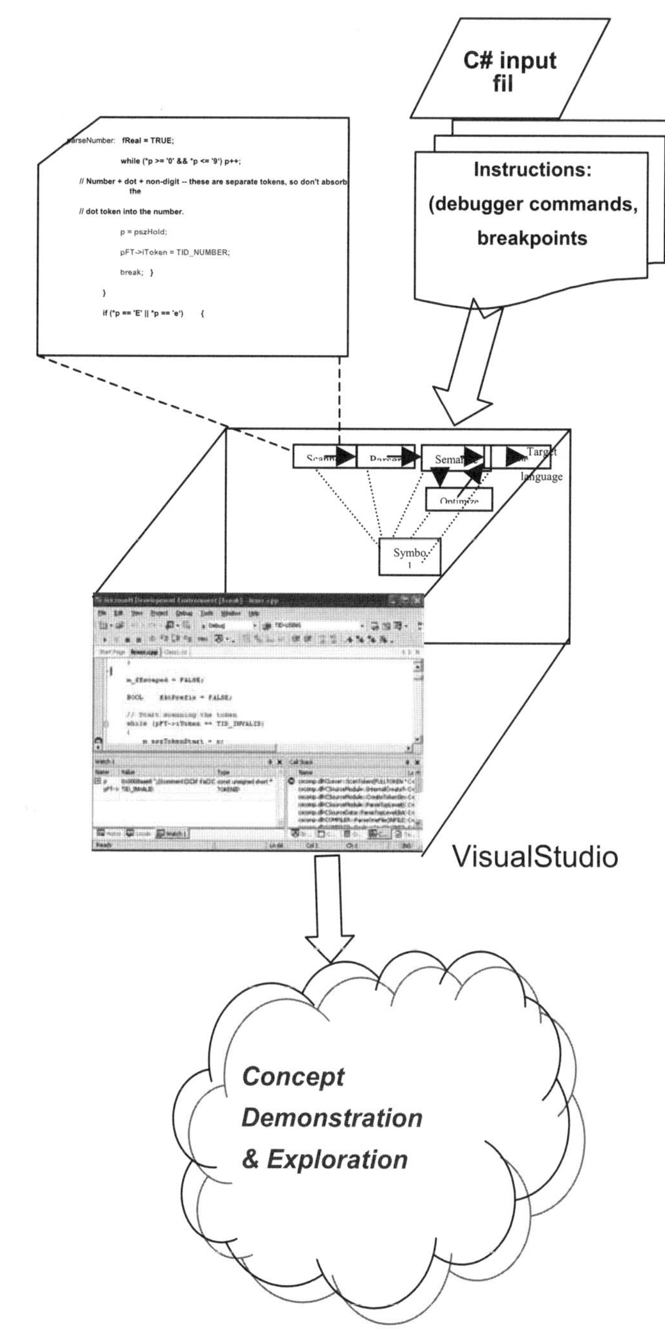

Figure 1. Hide and Show.

For example, to illustrate symbol table maintenance, a carefully chosen input program along with pre-chosen breakpoints inside source code of a real compiler component could be combined into a set of instructions to be used in a debugger. If done properly, the student would step through the processing of an input program and watch how the input program triggers changes to the compiler symbol table without having to look at the rest of the work being done. We believe that a carefully planned exercise of this type may provide insights that would be difficult to provide to the students using other techniques.

```
anIdentifier = b
//comment
if iff
<  << <= <<=
7       8876    3.2     5.2     9
```

Figure 2. Input Code for Lexical Analysis

We currently have four different exercises planned for use in the Fall 2004 class. Two of these, lexical analysis and parsing basics are described in the rest of this section. The third exercise covers additional parsing issues, such as error handling and name binding; the fourth exercise covers symbol table management.

2.1 Lexical Analysis

As an example of using the hide and show approach for concept illustration, consider lexical analysis. The primary tasks of the lexical analysis phase are to break the input string of characters into the tokens associated with the input language and to discard white space [2]. Although we could give the students the lexical analysis code to examine directly, the associated module is more than 800 lines long, making this a daunting task for some students.

In the hide and show approach, we use the debugger to selectively display the lexer module of the C# compiler as it processes the input program. Before beginning the code walkthrough, the student is given a list of break points in the source file `lexer.cpp` and the names of the relevant variables and data structures for the watch window. In the case of lexical analysis, there are six different break points to set, each illustrating some aspect of lexical analysis. There are also two variables of interest, one that captures the current input stream and another that holds the value of any token that is found.

Once setup is complete, the student starts the compiler running in the debugger to parse a given input file. Different exercises will use different input files for illustration. For example, we use the input file in Figure 2 for the lexical analysis exercise. Although this code is not a legal C# program, it has several different types of lexical elements. It is evident that various types of input programs may be used to show how the lexical analyzer handles different types of tokens.

Once it starts running, the debugger stops at the given breakpoints and the student examines the code and variables in order to understand the state of the processing. The student may also have to answer questions at these points. A snapshot of what the exercise looks like to the student is given in Figure 5 (included at the end). The breakpoint in the Visual Studio .net window corresponds to the code just before the lexer decides that it has found an identifier (`TID_IDENTIFIER`) token. The watch window (bottom left) shows the remaining input (`pzsName`). The call stack is also shown at the bottom right of the figure.

2.2 Parsing Basics

The C# parser itself works in two phases. In the first phase, only the top-level of the code is analyzed; the function bodies are only analyzed in the second phase. This behavior provided a natural way to divide the study of parsing into two exercises.

The first parser exercise focuses on two concepts related to parsing: the lexer/parser interface and type analysis. To run the exercise, the student is again given a list of breakpoints and variables to watch, this time for file `parser.cpp`. This information, in conjunction with a provided input file (Figure 3), provides the starting point for the exercise.

While stepping through the compiler execution for the given input file, students can see how tokens received from the lexer interface drive the progress through the compilation. The exercise also shows how both predefined and user defined types are recorded and used.

```
using System;
namespace SphereMathSpace
{
class SphereMath
{
public static int Main(string[] args)
   {
     const double Pi = 3.14;
     double radius = 3.957;
     Console.WriteLine(Pi + " " + radius);
      return 0;
     }
}
}
```

Figure 3. Input Code for Parsing Basics

2.3 Advanced use

We envision these exercises as starting points in the learning process. Interested students can develop additional test programs to further expose the working of the lexical analyzer. With sufficient knowledge of the process the student could also add new types of tokens and code to process them. Alternately, students can modify existing code in the lexical analyzer, then rebuild, and test compilation in the same manner. Finally, if after working through the exercise an advanced student wanted to know more about the implementation associated with the illustration, it would be straightforward for him or her to expand and examine the parts of the compiler that were of interest.

3. CREATING HIDE AND SHOW EXERCISES

Creating hide and show exercises is not a trivial activity. It is not enough to just give a tour of the running code; this tour must be tied back into the basic concepts. During exercise development, we saw that not all concepts are easy to demonstrate in this manner. For example, the actual LR parsing algorithm is difficult to show.

Once we were clear on the concepts that we wanted to demonstrate, it was necessary to locate the actual code (line numbers in the source) and data structures that illustrate these concepts. Unfortunately, complicated data structures are not easy to show in a debugger. Currently, students need to use some imagination to see their shapes change. We hope to eventually interface to visualization tools to solve this problem.

Finally, it is not enough to find all of the interesting points in the compiler source code. There must be input files that cause the relevant paths to be taken in the compiler. For example, in lexical analysis we wanted to illustrate different tokens and to show the students what happens to white space. The input file is a legal C# program but did not perform any interesting computation; rather it used different types of white space and interesting tokens.

Once the interesting parts of the source code have been identified, there should be instructional materials that both walk the student through the code and pose questions that will help the student understand what he/she is seeing.

4. INITIAL ASSESSMENT

When considering a new approach for use in a class, there are several issues that need to be considered.

- What the role of the approach is in the curriculum,
- How to deliver the material, and
- Whether there will be valued added by the integration.

The current graduate compilers course at George Mason University is fairly traditional, providing theoretical concepts that are tied into programming assignments that have the students build small compilers using standard development tools. We are using the hide and show exercises as supplemental material once the base concepts have been discussed.

In terms of delivery, we are combining small in-class demonstrations with out of classroom assignments. The role of the in-class demonstrations is to give the students an idea of what they will be seeing; however, we believe that the real learning will take place when they must take an active role in running the exercises themselves.

The question of value added is perhaps the important of the three issues raised. We have no plans to formally evaluate this question in the current semester. Our Fall 2004 goal is to evaluate feasibility and overall mechanics, as well as to informally see how the students feel about the utility of the exercises. We will use this feedback to refine our techniques and plan to put more formal evaluation techniques in place during the Spring 2005 semester use.

5. TECHNOLOGIES

We constructed the exercises described in this paper using two different technologies: SSCLI (Shared Source Common Language Infrastructure) and Visual Studio .Net. We briefly describe these technologies in this section with a particular emphasis on SSCLI because we believe that SSCLI has broader uses in Computer Science instruction.

5.1 SSCLI

SSCLI [11,12], also known as Rotor, is freely available source code for an actual implementation of the Common Language Infrastructure (CLI). CLI is an industry standard architecture for component inter-operability [6]. The CLI specification consists of a Common Type System (CTS), Common Intermediate Language (CIL) and a Common Language Runtime (CLR). The specification of the C# language is a companion to the CLI specification. SSCLI is drawn out from an earlier version of the production code of the .NET framework. The SSCLI contains C#, Jscript, Clisp compilers, ILASM assembler, disassembler, class libraries, debugging utility, cache for sharing assemblies, code access security service. It is made available to OEMs and researchers for understanding of the CLI. The SSCLI package can be downloaded from the web and its contents extracted. The doc directory contains the documentation of the software distribution [11].

The part of the SSCLI package of interest to us in this work is the included source of the C# compiler. This compiler has a modular architecture that includes many separate components, including components for compilation staging, lexical analysis, parsing, intermediate code generation, symbol table and name management, memory allocation, and code generation. The size of C# source is 29.5 MB(200,000 lines). The C# compiler is written in C++.

Figure 4 gives an overview of compilation of high level CLI compliant code (e.g. C# source) and its subsequent load and execution in the CLR. The CLR provides a runtime where types are checked, modules are loaded and compiled on demand (just-in-time compilation), code access security enforced, versions verified etc. It also supports platform independence through a platform adaptation layer (PAL). Details can be found in [12]

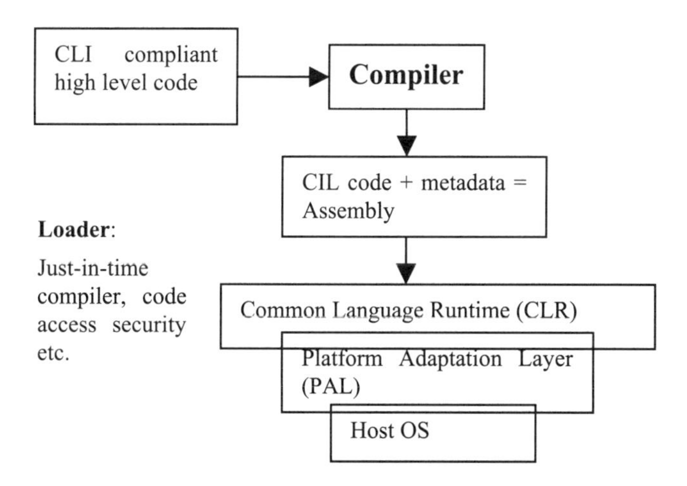

Figure 4. Compilation and execution in SSCLI

5.2 Visual Studio .Net

Visual Studio .Net was used as the debugger interface for the students in this class. One reason for this choice was that the interface provided a simple way for students to look at the source code and any relevant variables, as well as a view of the runtime stack. Visual Studio is easily available via the Microsoft MSDN Academic Alliance program [8].

6. CONCLUSION

The use of source code and a debugger can implement the hide and show strategy that can help deal with the complexity of a real compiler. Although some preliminary study shows hopeful results, it is not yet clear how effective this approach would be in a large scale classroom situation. How can courses using standard texts such as [2] be complemented with experiments about real compilers? Can a carefully planned set of debugger driven actions, performed by a student, successfully illustrate implementation of these basic concepts in a large compiler?

There are a number of further issues related to the use of a real infrastructure that we intend to explore in future work. First, past experience [13] has shown that visualization can be valuable to the learning process in a course such as this; we believe that tools built on top of this infrastructure can provide similar value. Second, we are interested in whether this infrastructure could be used as part of a more advanced course in compilers. Given the appropriate foundation and experience, students could extend/modify the existing code generation and optimization components in order to experiment with different back-end strategies.

7. REFERENCES

[1] ACM Computing Curricula 2001 - Appendix A: CS Body of Knowledge http://www.computer.org/education/cc2001/final/pl.htm

[2] Aho. A.V et al. *Compilers – Principles, Techniques and Tools*, Addison-Wesley. 1988.

[3] Aiken, A. Cool: a portable project for teaching compiler construction. ACM SIGPLAN Notices, Volume 31 Issue 7 (July 1996).

[4] Appelbe, B. Teaching Compiler Development. Proceedings of the 10th SIGCSE technical symposium on Computer Science Education (January 1979)

[5] Baldwin, D. A Compiler for Teaching about Compilers. Proceedings of the 34th SIGCSE technical symposium on Computer Science Education (March 2003).

[6] ECMA C# and Common Language Infrastructure. Standards. http://www.dotnetexperts.com/ecma

[7] Levine, J., T. Mason and D. Brown, *lex & yacc*, O'Reilly & Associates, Inc., 1995.

[8] Microsoft Developer Network Academic Alliance. www.msdnaa.net

[9] Prey, J.C. Cooperative learning and closed laboratories in an undergraduate Computer Science curriculum. Integrating Technology into Computer Science Education. ACM SIGCSE, SIGCSE Bulletin, Volume 28, Special Issue, 1996.

[10] Sathi, H.L. A project-based course in compiler construction. Proceedings of the 17th SIGCSE technical symposium on Computer Science Education (February 1986).

[11] Shared Source Common Language Infrastructure (SSCLI). www.microsoft.com/sharedsource, http://msdn.microsoft.com/net/sscli

[12] Stutz, D. et al. *Shared Source CLI*, O'Reilly, 2003.

[13] White, E., L. Deddens, J. Ruby. Software Visualization of LR parsing and Syntax Directed Translation, Software: Practice and Experience, 29,1, January 1999.

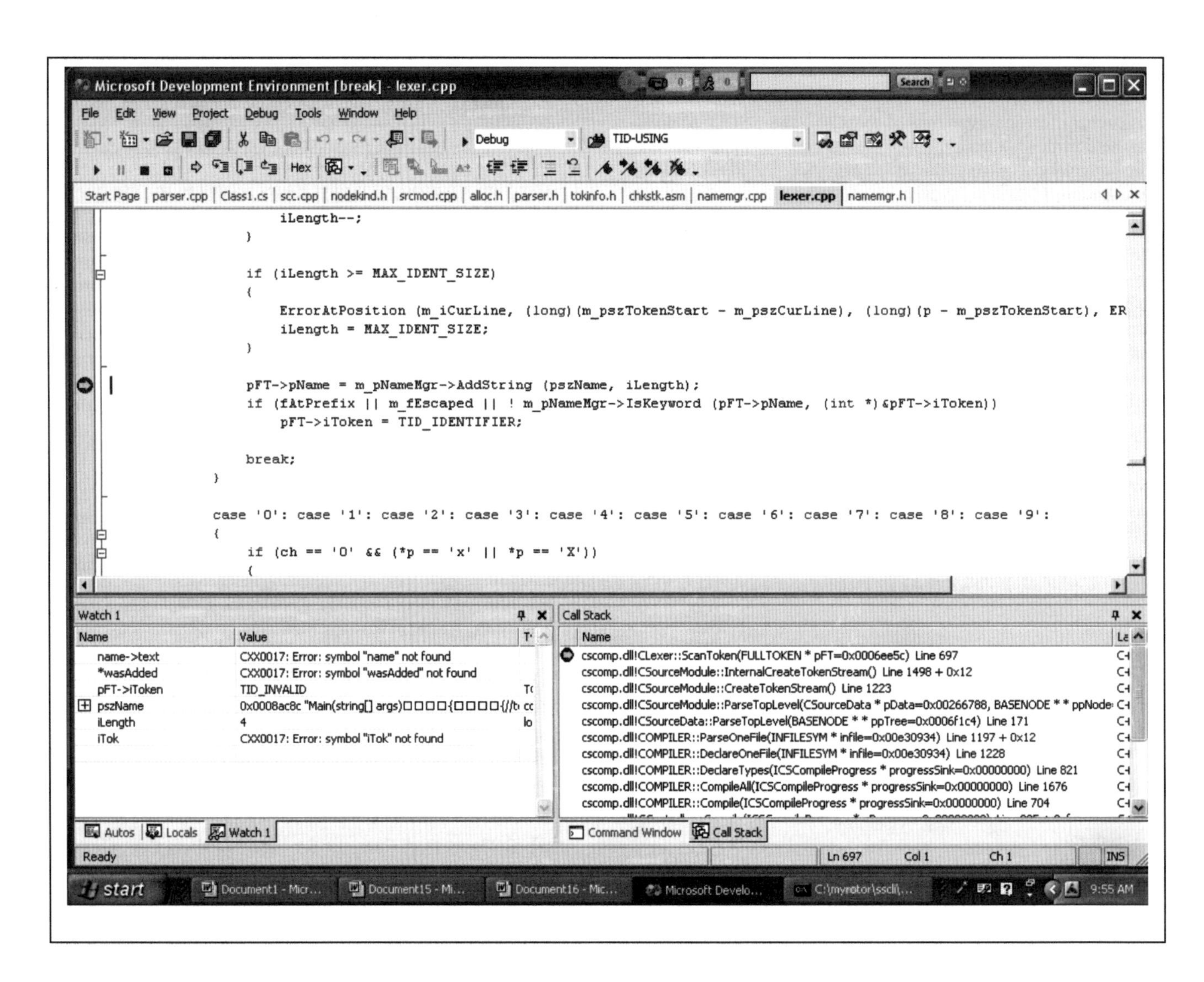

Figure 5. Screen shot of Lexical Analysis exercise

Accessibility in Introductory Computer Science

Robert F. Cohen
rfc@cs.umb.edu

Alexander V. Fairley
vegas@cs.umb.edu

David Gerry
gerrydk@cs.umb.edu

Gustavo R. Lima
glima@cs.umb.edu

+1 617 287 6452

Department of Computer Science
University of Massachusetts Boston
Boston, Ma 02125

ABSTRACT

This paper describes our efforts to integrate software accessibility into the CS1 curriculum. Accessibility is an important aspect of modern software systems for both legal and ethical reasons. The acceptance of Java as language for CS1 gives us the opportunity to teach accessibility from the beginning, since Java Accessibility is simple and integrated into Swing components. We present simple guidelines on how to incorporate Accessibility into a Java based CS1, and describe programming projects that incorporate accessibility.

Categories and Subject Descriptors

K.3.2 [Computer and Information Science Education]: Computer Science Education

General Terms

Human Factors

Keywords

Accessibility, Java Programming Language

1. INTRODUCTION

Software accessibility has been legally mandated by recent laws, e.g. section 508 of the Rehabilitation Act, amended in 1998 and enacted in June of 2001 [13]. Beyond legal requirements, ensuring that software is accessible to all users is a concern shared by all socially responsible developers. However, we have found very few computer science programs that address the issue. Curricula 2001[3] includes no direct mention of accessibility or where it should be covered in the undergraduate curriculum. The wide spread use of Java as a programming language provides us with the opportunity to teach this important topic in computer science programs. Because of the simplicity of specifying accessibility factors to Swing components, accessibility can be included in the CS1 curriculum without taking much additional time or resources.

This paper describes our efforts to integrate software accessibility into the CS1 curriculum. In particular, we focus on accessibility for visually impaired, because of our recent experience teaching a blind programmer. Section 2 reviews accessible computing and accessibility for the visually impaired. Section 3 explains our motivation for including accessibility in the CS1 curriculum. Section 5 outlines our guidelines for accessibility appropriate for CS1. Section 5 describes some programming projects that fit our guidelines. Section 6 offers some conclusions.

SIGCSE'05, February 23–27, 2005, St. Louis, Missouri, USA.

2. ACCESSIBLE COMPUTING

2.1 Definition

A computer system is accessible if it can be used by any person, including those who have some type of disability. To achieve that purpose, computer applications and assistive technologies, such as a screen magnifier or a screen reader, must be compatible with one another, so that a person with disabilities is able to fully use the computer and its applications.

2.2 The Need for Accessibility in CS1

The demand for accessible software has increased continuously over the past years. In the U.S., section 508 of the Rehabilitation Act, amended in 1998 and enacted in June of 2001, requires that all Federal agencies give the disabled equal access to information that is available to others. It requires that all electronic government technology and IT to be accessible [13].

Computer Science has increasingly become a popular undergraduate major for disabled students over the past years. The American Disabilities Act (ADA) of 1990 [1] states that students with disabilities can not waive course requirements in High School. Disabled students take the same math and science preparation as other students. Therefore, many finish High School with the math and science background and interests required for Computer Science programs at the post-secondary level [4]. Additionally, many disabled students see how current computer based tools improve their lives and are motivated to enter the field in order to further advance the technology [4].

Educational institutions nationwide must adapt themselves to best address the needs of disabled students and to educate the general student population of these needs. In Computer Science, efforts must be made to ensure that students with disabilities have full access to computer applications and programming tools. The current trend towards teaching Graphical User Interfaces (GUI) at the introductory level presents a hurdle to visually impaired students, since they are not able to see the output of their programs.

In addition to providing accommodations to the handicapped, Computer Science programs need to encourage their students to start thinking about these problems from the beginning of their academic careers. Our project focuses on how to teach students in an introductory Computer Science course (CS1) how to build accessible software. We focus on the needs of blind students, because of our recent experience educating a blind programming student.

2.3 Assistive Technologies

Assistive technology is a general term used to describe devices or software that helps an individual provide input or receive output from the system. Many assistive technology products are available on the market, such as special keyboards, intelligent mice, typing aids, text-to-speech software, speech recognition software, easy-touch screens, etc.

Assistive technologies also play an important role in providing alternative modalities of input and output to ordinary systems. For example, speech recognition plays a role in assisting both physically handicapped and mobile users. Consequently, the need for assistive software will continue to grow.

The main technology that visually impaired users use to access a computer is a *screen reader*. A screen reader is a device that reads text rendered on the computer screen and "speaks" the information out loud to the user. Not all applications are screen reader friendly. In Java, some essential and simple programming techniques must be applied in order to make GUI components (such as buttons and text fields) work well with screen readers. These techniques are discussed later in section 5.

3. ACCESSIBLE CS1

The primary goal of CS1 is to teach good programming and problem solving skills. In recent years, there has been movement to include in CS1 topics and themes relating to best practices in software development, including design [11], teamwork [12],[16], testing [4][5] and these topics need to be balanced so not to interfere with the primary objectives of CS1. Many Java-based CS1 courses now include some aspect of user interfaces using Java Swing, and this is supported by popular textbooks (e.g. [10]). A course that teaches Swing basics can easily include accessibility (see subsection 5.1). A CS1 course that teaches accessibility needs to first be accessible itself. In particular, programming projects need to be designed to engage all students, even those with disabilities. The course then needs to present and exercise programming techniques that produce an end product usable by anyone.

3.1 Why introduce accessibility?

All courses need to be inclusive. Computer science courses need additionally to teach programmers to be aware of inclusion issues. We see two motivations:

1. *It is a good habit.* Accessibility is required by law, and therefore is an employability skill. Programmers need to be taught to consider accessibility issues from project inception, since the process of retrofitting accessibility can be costly and time consuming.
2. *It is lightweight to introduce.* Accessibility is easy to include using Java Swing. We have simple guidelines (Section 5) that can be implemented with only a few lines of code. Accessibility can be explained in a few pages in a textbook and a few minutes in a lecture. Accessibility can be seamlessly embedded into any existing curriculum with little overhead.

4. PROJECTS

4.1 Qualities of Accessible Projects

The 1997 Trace Center [2] report on Java Accessibility divides applications into three types based on their support for Accessibility. *Type I* applications are those which are designed with accessible features built in; *Type II* applications are those compatible with current assistive technology, either incidentally or by design; and *Type III* applications are those which are neither directly accessible, nor readily compatible with existing assistive technology. Accessibility oriented project based learning should involve students creating Type I or Type II projects, and help students learn the difference.

There are several ways of teaching accessibility in CS1. GUI projects involving the appropriate use of the Java accessibility package are Type II applications. Console applications are Type II, because blind users can access them with the simplest of screen reader technology. Projects can use the Java sound API to produce applications which have both audio and visual outputs. However, because of the complexity of Java Sound, we believe adaptor classes are required, much in the way many introductory texts include classes to hide the complexity of console input (prior to J2SE version 5) (e.g. [10]). If done properly, these audio/visual assignments are accessible to several kinds of users, while being intriguing to beginning programmers.

The Java accessibility package is a set of classes and interfaces which are used in the design of accessible GUIs. It defines a contract between the program and assistive technologies where the program provides information needed by screen readers and screen magnifiers [17]. Its main components are a set of interfaces implemented by accessible objects, and a set of classes which are the return types for the methods required to implement these interfaces. These classes encapsulate the information needed by a screen reader to provide access to the application. Java Swing has a great deal of built-in support for these interfaces. Creating Type II applications using Swing becomes largely a method of setting parameters appropriately. It is simple enough to be done by students who have a basic understanding of object orientation and the Java Event Model. If custom components are designed which do not extend swing classes, the use of javax.accessibilty is somewhat complicated, but can be simplified through the use of instructor provided components.

Console based applications, long a mainstay of computer science projects, are generally accessible without requiring any extra work on the part of students or instructors.

Sound output is not frequently addressed within the context of CS1. The Java Sound API is not extraordinarily complicated to use, but it does present more language specific material than may be appropriate at the introductory level. However, instructors can provide adaptor classes which have public methods for accepting student calls for generating sound and private methods for dealing with the Java Sound API. These classes allow students to design applications which simultaneously present output audibly and visually. Such applications, if appropriately designed, are accessible to both blind and deaf users. Furthermore, the novelty of such an assignment may help to capture the interest of beginning programmers, and give them a better feel for the full capabilities of modern programming languages.

4.2 Sample Accessible Projects

We have designed a number of projects that include accessibility. The projects range from quite simple to moderately large and exercise many concepts typically taught in CS1. We summarize a few here:

Number Format Converter

This assignment consists of designing an accessible GUI for an application which converts numbers from one radix format to another. It is a very simple interface from an accessibility standpoint, and serves as an excellent first accessible programming assignment.

Accessible Calculator

This assignment involves the use of a customized component that we have written. Using the component (a *KeyPad*) as a utility class, the student builds a calculator using mainly control statements and the Java Event Model. In addition to implementing the calculator controls, students are required to provide accessibility settings for the KeyPad component.

Audio Visualizer

The Audio Visualizer application illustrates the use of both graphical and aural elements to display its output. The project is designed to allow the student to concentrate on learning the course concepts while offering a means for any student to interact and test their work.

5. GUIDELINES

What follows are simple accessibility guidelines appropriate for a CS1 course. Professional guidelines are also available (e.g. from IBM [7].

Assistive technologies, such as screen readers, get information from GUI components via the Java Accessibility API. Most of the support needed to make a Java application accessible (for visually impaired students) is already built into the swing components. However, some steps need to be taken to make an application work well with a screen reader:

1) *Provide Accessible Names for all Components.*

The accessible name of a component is the main source information to be spoken by a screen reader. Most Swing components have their default accessible name be the same as their textual display name (the String displayed on the component). For example, a `JLabel` displaying the text "social security number" would automatically have its accessible name set to be "social security number". Therefore, for most components nothing needs to be done to achieve name accessibility. Components that do not display a string as a default name can get an accessible name using the `setAccessibleName` method of the component's `AccessibleContext` class. The accessible name only needs to be set if the component's name needs to be spoken by the screen reader. If the component is not intended to receive the keyboard focus, there is no need to set its accessible name. For example, suppose we have a panel containing radio buttons that are associated with grades for a course evaluation. Since a blind student needs to know what the buttons are referring to, we need to set the panel's accessible name:

```
JPanel evalPanel = new JPanel();
AccessibleContext ctext = evalPanel.getAccessibleContext();
ctext.setAccessibleName("Course Evaluation Panel");
```

2) *Provide Accessible Descriptions for components that need to have one.*

Screen Readers can speak extra information when requested to do so. This information is usually accessed through a component's accessible description. One way to set this property is by calling the `setToolTipText` method on the component. This method sets information both for sighted and sightless students. If this is not possible – as in the case of objects that do not inherit from `JComponent` (e.g. `JFrame`, `JApplet`) - the `setAccessibleDescription` method should be used. Examples:

```
JButton btn = new JButton("Access");
btn.setToolTipText(
   "This text is also the button's " +
   "accessible description");
```

```
AccessibleContext context =
   btn.getAccessibleContext();
context.setAccessibleDescription (
   "This is the accessible description," +
   "but not the tool tip");
```

3) *Provide keyboard navigation and focus for all components that a sighted person would want to see or interact with.*

Focus should be given only to those components that users interact with or to textual components that need to be spoken by the screen reader. The default focus traversal policy (which defines the components that will get focus and the order in which they will be traversed) already meets these needs. The programmer needs to modify the traversal policy only if the application requires a tailored focus traversal characteristics. In the Windows operation system, the default traversal keys are "TAB" for forward traversal and "SHIFT + TAB" for backward traversal.

Keyboard alternatives should be provided for navigation besides the tab key. Java supplies some features for that purpose:

4) *Provide Mnemonics for keyboard control.*

Mnemonics are underlined characters that appear on menu items and some buttons. They provide instant access to components. Examples:

```
JButton b = new JButton ("Submit");
b.setMnemonic(KeyEvent.VK_S);
```

In this example, when the user presses alt+s, keyboard focus is given to the button.

```
JLabel  label  =  new  JLabel("First  Name");
JTextField firstNameText = new JTextField();
label.setLabelfor(firstNameText);
label.setDisplayedMnemonic('KeyEvent.VK_F');
```

On the previous example, we have two components: a text field and a label. Unlike labels and buttons, text fields do not carry a textual display name. Therefore we cannot directly assign a hotkey to them. First, we need to create a label and link it to the text field using the `setLabelFor` method. Then, we assign a mnemonic to this label through the `setDisplayedMnemonic` method. This way, when the user activates the hotkey (by pressing alt+f in this case), keyboard focus is given to the associated text field.

Menus also support accelerators: combination of keys that provide a shortcut for the program's most important actions. For example, "save" can be associated with (Ctrl + s). Other components also can associate user typing with actions. For example, in operating system environments, pressing the space bar is equivalent to clicking on a button or checking off a check box.

5) Customized components should support accessibility.

Every component in a java application should implement the `Accessible` interface and provide an implementation for its only method, `getAccessibleContext()`. Fortunately, most Swing components meet this need. Any custom component should implement this interface in order to be accessible.

6) Other issues:

- Always use a layout manager for Containers. Different individual settings and systems may require a different font (a larger font for a low vision user, for instance) or may have the application's frame resized. If no layout manager is used (by setting the container's layout to null), the application does not adjust well to these changes.
- Provide textual descriptions for all `ImageIcon` objects, so that the visually impaired has a text alternative to the graphic. That can be done either by setting one of the Strings in the ImageIcon constructor or by the setDescription method.
- If a set of components form a logical group, try placing them in a single container. For example, a set of check boxes related to the same purpose could be grouped together in a JPanel. Then, a description could be set to the panel (by setting AccessibleName or AccessibleDescription), such as the purpose of the boxes. This way, the application is better organized and its navigation is facilitated. Consequently, a person with visual disabilities using a screen reader finds his way on the screen more easily.

5.1 Including Accessibility in Textbook Code Examples

We analyzed the popular CS1 textbook by Lewis and Loftus [8] in order to determine how much would have to change to include accessibility. Accessibility would need to be covered in the text, most likely as a subsection of chapter 5 which includes an introduction to the Java event model.

Additionally, small modifications need to be made to the code examples. For example, chapter 5 includes a simple GUI for converting temperatures from Fahrenheit to Celsius.

The current code in the text includes the following constructor:

```
public FahrenheitGUI() {
  frame = new JFrame (
      "Temperature Conversion");
  frame.setDefaultCloseOperation(
      JFrame.EXIT_ON_CLOSE);
  inputLabel = new JLabel (
      "Enter Fahrenheit temperature:");
  outputLabel = new JLabel (
      "Temperature in Celcius: ");
  resultLabel = new JLabel ("---");
  fahrenheit = new JTextField (5);
  fahrenheit.addActionListener (
      new TempListener());
  // Code that builds a panel of components
  // …
  frame.getContentPane().add (panel);
}
```

The following is an accessible version of the GUI that would work well with a screen reader. Only six additional lines of code are required:

```
public AccessibleFahrenheitGUI() {
  // as above
  // additional code follows
  AccessibleContext ctx =
      frame.getAccessibleContext();
  ctx.setAccessibleDescription(
      "Press alt+e to enter input in " +
      "Fahrenheit and alt+t to read the " +
      "converted temperature in Celsius");
  inputLabel.setLabelFor(fahrenheit);
  inputLabel.setDisplayedMnemonic (
      KeyEvent.VK_E);
  outputLabel.setLabelFor(resultLabel);
  outputLabel.setDisplayedMnemonic (
      KeyEvent.VK_T);

  }
```

6. ACKNOWLEDGMENTS

We wish to thank EAST Alliance (http://www.eastalliance.org/) and BATEC (http://www.batec.org/) who provided student scholarships. We also thank Nancy Lightbody and Virginia Stern for their valuable comments.

7. REFERENCES

[1] ADA: Americans With Disabilities Act. http://www.usdoj.gov/crt/ada/adahom1.htm.

[2] Chisholm, W., Illingworth, C., Novak, M., Vanderheiden, G. Java Accessibility Preliminary Examination. March 14, 1997. http://trace.wisc.edu/docs/java_access_rpt/report.htm.

[3] Computing Curricula. Final Draft. December 15, 2001. http://www.computer.org/education/cc2001/final/.

[4] Edwards, S. Using Software Testing to Move Students from Trial-and-Error to Reflection-in-Action. In *Proceedings of the 35th SIGCSE technical symposium on Computer science*

education (SIGCSE '04) (Norfolk, VA, USA, March 3-7 2004). ACM Press, New York, NY, 2004, 26-30.

[5] Etheredge, J. CMeRun: Program Logic Debugging Courseware for CS1/CS2 Students. In *Proceedings of the 35th SIGCSE technical symposium on Computer science education (SIGCSE '04)* (Norfolk, VA, USA, March 3-7 2004). ACM Press, New York, NY, 2004, 22-25.

[6] Francioni, J.M. and Smith, A.C. Computer Science Accessibility for Students with Visual Disabilities. in *Proceedings of the 33rd SIGCSE Technical Symposium on Computer Science Education*, Northern Kentucky, February 2002, pages 91-95.

[7] Grissom,S. *A pedagogical framework for Java I/O.* Volume 32, Issue 4, December 2000, pages 57 – 59.

[8] IBM Accessibility Center. Accessibility in an on Demand Era. http://www-306.ibm.com/able/access_ibm/AC_Accessibility_QA_031104.pdf.

[9] IBM Accessibility Center. Developer Guidelines. http://www-306.ibm.com/able/guidelines/java/snsjavag.html

[10] Lewis,J., and Loftus,W. *Java Software Solutions, Foundations of Program Design.* 3rd edition. Addison Wesley. 2003.

[11] Lewis, T., W., Rosson, M.B., and Pérez-Quiñones, M. What Do The Experts Say? Teaching Introductory Design from an Expert's Perspective. In *Proceedings of the 35th SIGCSE technical symposium on Computer science education (SIGCSE '04)* (Norfolk, VA, USA, March 3-7 2004). ACM Press, New York, NY, 2004, 296-300.

[12] Nagappan, N. et al., Improving the CS1 experience with pair programming. In *Proceedings of the 34th SIGCSE technical symposium on Computer science education (SIGCSE '03)* (Reno, Nevada, USA, 2003). ACM Press, New York, NY, 2003, 359-362.

[13] Section 508: The Road to Accessibility, http://www.section508.gov.

[14] Smith, A.C., Francioni, J. M. , and Matzek, S.D. A Java Programming Tool for Students with Visual Disabilities. in *Proceedings of Assets 2000*, Washington D.C., November 2000.

[15] The Java Tutorial. How to Support Assistive Technologies. http://java.sun.com/docs/books/tutorial/uiswing/misc/access.html.

[16] Waite, W., Jackson, M., Diwan, A., and Leonardi, P. Student Culture vs Group Work in Computer Science. In *Proceedings of the 35th SIGCSE technical symposium on Computer science education (SIGCSE '04)* (Norfolk, VA, USA, March 3-7 2004). ACM Press, New York, NY, 2004, 12-16.

[17] Walker, W. Overview of the Java Accessibility Features. *Sun Microsystems Java Accessibility Team.* http://java.sun.com/products/jfc/jaccess-1.3/doc/guide.html.

Opening the Eyes of Those Who Can See to the World of Those Who Can't: A Case Study

Susan M. Harrison
Computer Science Department
University of Wisconsin-Eau Claire
Eau Claire, WI 54701
1-715-836-5381
harrison@uwec.edu

ABSTRACT

While some web page or user interface design courses include a lecture or two highlighting issues related to users with visual impairments, it is rare that such courses make this a recurring theme. This paper describes how a web page design course weaves the idea of designing for screen reader users throughout the entire course with minor changes to the standard curriculum of the course. Included are examples of how the eyes of the students are opened to the world of blind users, to the requirements of the law, to the code to make pages accessible, and to ways to test accessibility.

Categories and Subject Descriptors

K.4.2 [**Computers and Society**]: Social Issues – *assistive technologies for persons with disabilities, handicapped persons/special needs;* H.5.4 [**Information Interfaces and Presentation**]: Hypertext/Hypermedia – *navigation, user issues.* H.5.2 [**Information Interfaces and Presentation**]: User interfaces – *screen design.*

General Terms

Design, Human Factors, Standardization.

Keywords

Web accessibility, Blindness, Screen readers, Visually impaired, Web page design, Web page development.

1. INTRODUCTION

The main goal of any web design course is to help the students design pages that are visually pleasing and usable by a wide audience. For a web site to be usable, it must be accessible.

However, "the most serious accessibility problems, given the current state of the Web, relate to blind users and users with other visual disabilities because most web pages are highly visual" [10]. With less than one third of all websites being accessible to visually impaired people [3], a real need exists for educating future designers and developers on how to create accessible web pages.

Curtis Chong, Director of Technology, National Federation of the Blind, recommends eight principles for the web developer to follow [4].

- Provide screen access software with the ASCII text it needs to produce speech or Braille.
- Make it possible for blind web surfers who explore your web page by tabbing from link to link to determine the meaning and purpose of all hypertext links on the page.
- Enable screen access software to provide information to the blind web surfer about purely graphical objects on the page.
- Ensure that the use of tables and multi-column text on your web site does not preclude the ability of screen access software to render your pages in an intelligible and useful manner.
- Make it possible for the blind web surfer to fill out web-based forms in an efficient manner.
- Provide an alternative way to access your site which does not compel the blind web surfer to use a Java applet or plug-in that is inaccessible to screen access software.
- Provide a means for blind web surfers to avoid redundant links on a web page.
- Provide a means for blind web surfers to avoid splash screens or other displays that are updated on a timed basis.

These principles provided a base for the type of accessibility issues discussed and the coding examples included in this three-credit, 15-week course in web page design.

2. OPENING THE EYES

The majority of undergraduate students interested in web page design are often unaware of the challenges faced by the blind. To help open the eyes of the students to these challenges, two lecture periods and one lab session were used to establish the need for accessible pages and to provide opportunities for students to personally experience some of the challenges encountered when using the Web.

2.1 Need Explained

More than one million Americans, age 40 and older, are affected by blindness [5]. Each one, attempting to acquire information in the cyber-world, must overcome multiple barriers. The challenge of overcoming these barriers is "frightening" [6] as these barriers cannot be overcome through training the blind, but only through the intentional development of accessible pages.

The Workforce Rehabilitation Act of 1973 was amended by Congress in 1998 to require all Federal agencies to make electronic and information technology accessible to people with disabilities. This amendment, known as Section 508, helps ensure that agencies give disabled employees and members of the public access to information that is comparable to the access available to others [1]. In addition, Section 508 required the U. S. Architectural and Transportation Barriers Compliance (ACCESS) Board to publish standards including functional performance criteria necessary for electronic and information technology to comply with section 508 [2]. Web Content Accessibility Guidelines 1.0 was released in May 1999 by the World Wide Web Consortium [17].

New York Attorney General Eliot Spitzer spent over two years investigating whether web sites complied with the federal act and state law that required all "places of public accommodation" and all "goods, services, facilities, privileges, advantages, or accommodations" to be accessible to the disabled. On August 19, 2004, the Associated Press reported that Priceline.com and Ramada.com reached a settlement with Spitzer by agreeing to make changes that would allow users of screen reader software to navigate and listen to the text throughout their web sites [7].

It was stressed to students that thinking about how to make web pages accessible and creating accessible pages were good habits to form since the audience is growing, the law requires it, and the industry trend is toward it. As Spitzer said, "accessible web sites are the wave of the future and the right thing to do" [7].

2.2 Challenges Experienced

To experience how screen readers work and to gain an appreciation of the challenges facing the blind, students were asked to use screen reader software, Window-Eyes [8], to locate a particular reference book on the local library's web site and to select a greeting card from a commercial greeting card web site. Students worked in teams with the blind-folded member using the keyboard and screen reader software and the other sighted member serving as a guide. After a few minutes, students switched roles. In addition, students were asked to check existing web pages for compliance with WCA Guidelines 1.0 for accessibility.

During the following class period, a blind member of the university community who daily uses a screen reader spoke to the class. By demonstrating how she navigates web sites, she showed students how a screen reader user does not listen to every word on the page, but listens to just enough to determine where to go next. Students witnessed how she rapidly scanned the web page with her ears; much like sighted users scan a web page with their eyes.

From these experiences, students were able to learn about the challenges faced and the differences that exist between the sighted user and the blind user [9]. Table 1 summarizes these differences.

Table 1. Difference between sighted and blind users

Sighted	Blind
Assimilate page structure and visual cues within first few seconds on the web page	Hear about 20 spoken words, from top left to bottom right, within first few seconds on the web page
Whole screen of information, through visual cues, available for refreshing memory	Small portion of screen, through words heard at beginning of links or line, available for refreshing memory
Consistency of visual layout easy to determine	Layout difficult to determine; every page seems different

3. PROVIDING THE BASICS

The "challenge to web publishers and designers is to create sites which are not only visually attractive and informative, but comply with the Disability Discrimination Act by being accessible to visually impaired people," stated Helen Brazier of the National Library for the Blind [3]. After students gained a sense of the barriers, some basic ways to design accessible web pages without sacrificing visual attractiveness were provided.

3.1 Images

Guideline 1.1 of the Web Content Accessibility (WCA) Guidelines 2.0 [19] reads: "Provide text alternatives for all non-text content." Since screen readers read the URL of the image if nothing is placed in the ALT attribute, students were expected to use the ALT attribute for every IMG element in the HTML code of every page developed for the course. Students were also reminded that the alternative text should be descriptive, meaningful, and useful [14], conveying the same information that is communicated by the image. Alternative text should be brief and to the point, typically no more than eight to ten words [10]. Embedded spaces and separators to aid the screen reader should be included [12]. For example, consider images used in on-line catalogs. ALT= "skirt" and ALT= "blue skirt" are less informative, less meaningful, and less useful than ALT= "36 inch long blue cotton skirt back zipper".

One exception to the "ALT for every image" rule is allowed when an image is used purely for decoration. Blind users working through a series of web sites stated their objection to listening to descriptions of bullets that added no meaning to the page and delayed the user from reaching the real information behind the bullet [15]. Rather than using a meaningless ALT= "yellow bullet", an empty ALT, ALT="", should be used. (Remember without the ALT, the URL will be read.)

3.2 Headers and Links

Guideline 2.4: "Facilitate the ability of users to orient themselves and move within the content" [19]. For web pages to be accessible, navigation mechanisms must be clear and consistent. Targets of each link should be clearly identified and "skip links" should be used to allow the screen reader user the option of skipping over repetitive navigation links and access the main content [11].

Students were asked to think of how the content of the page could be written in outline form and then add headings accordingly using <H1> for the highest level, <H2> for the main parts of information within the <H1>, and <H3> for finer divisions. Using standard HTML heading tags, <H1> through <H6>, rather than creating user-defined styles for headers, facilitates scanning, emphasizes the page structure, and allows users with assistive technologies that support this markup to quickly jump between headers and gain an overview of the structure of the content [10, 16].

Just like the ALT of an image, "active" words composing a link within text should be informative, meaningful, and useful. Common, but poor, links often found on web pages include:

```
<a href="resources.htm">Click here.</a>
<a href="resources.htm">Link to resources.</a>
```

Since users are notified by the screen reader that a link has been encountered, the use of the word 'link' in the link text is redundant. Using 'Click here' provides no meaningful information to the user as he quickly skips from link to link with the screen reader. Students are asked to provide the most meaningful information within the first few words of the link such as:

```
<a href="resouces.htm">Accessibility
        Resources</a> are available.
```

When images are used as links, the ALT within the IMG tag becomes the means for conveying the linking information to the user. Therefore, one should never use an empty ALT on an image within a link as the user will be informed that a link has been encountered, but receive no meaningful information about the link.

When asked to provide an appropriate ALT for the image in Figure 1, students may be tempted to include the fact that a girl is in the picture. Since this fact provides no meaningful information to the user, ALT= "Come visit campus!" is adequate (see Figure 1).

```
<a href="visit.htm"><img src="comevisitgirl.jpg"
        alt="Come visit campus!"></a>
```

Figure 1. Come visit image and HTML code for link

When creating client-side image maps in the course, students are again reminded of the need to use ALT tags for every area of the map that is a link. Since the ALT information is not accessible to screen readers for server-side image maps [10], client-side image maps are emphasized in the course.

To aid screen reader users, hidden skip links are also emphasized. As the name implies, skip links allow the user to jump directly to another area of the page such as the main content. Skip links are usually found at the top of the page near the search engine option on a well-designed accessible page and may be invisible to the sighted user or contained within a decorative image. A common way to include a skip link is to use a 1x1 pixel transparent GIF and use the image's ALT text as the means for notifying the user of the skip link's destination [13]. The following lines of code, using named internal targets, help accomplish this:

```
<a href ="#MainContent">
<img alt ="Skip to main content"
     src="1.gif" width=1> </a>
<a name=MainContent>
</a>… main content begins here…
```

Another method is to include a text-based link of the same color as the background. However, this 'hidden' text may become visible if a user chooses to alter the font or background color.

3.3 Tables

When a screen reader encounters a table, it linearizes or spreads out the table lining up the contents of each cell one after another working from left to right across each row. Tables embedded within a cell are completely linearized prior to continuing on to the next cell [14]. To help students properly construct tables used for page layout purposes that are screen-reader friendly, students are asked to 'think like a screen reader' by reading the content of the cells in the order encountered in the HTML code. If this method is applied to Table 2, the student would say: Title, Nav Link 1, Nav Link 2, Nav Link 3, Banner, Ad Link 1, Ad Link 2, Ad Link 3, Main content area filled by a story consisting of a lot of text.

Table 2. Sample table to help illustrate linearization

	Title	
Nav Link 1 Nav Link 2 Nav Link 3	Banner Main content area filled by a story consisting of a lot of text.	Ad Link 1 Ad Link 2 Ad Link 3

Since the information found in the 'Main content' cell relates to the 'Banner', a screen reader user would have difficulty understanding the structure of this table. One way to make the 'Main content' be heard immediately after the 'Title' and 'Banner', but before any list of links, is to include empty cells as the first and last part of row 2 and rearrange the items slightly as shown in Figure 2 [14].

Banner *followed by* Title		
(empty cell) Nav Link 1 Nav Link 2 Nav Link 3	Main content area filled by a story consisting of a lot of text.	*(empty cell)* Ad Link 1 Ad Link 2 Ad Link 3

Figure 2. Table with empty cells to aid linearization

To help make data tables more understandable to screen reader users, the caption element, usually located at the top of the table, and the summary attribute containing a description of the contents, as shown in the following lines, are commonly used.

```
<table width="200" border="1"
summary="Descriptive summary">
<caption align="top">Caption here</caption>
```

After working with these basic ways to improve tables, students are directed to the on-line reference of the web page editor used in the course to learn about other helpful features, such as <TH> to indicate table headers.

3.4 Forms

During the section of the web page design course which deals with forms, the importance of keeping the label physically close to, but not below, the associated form object is stressed. Even though a screen reader states the default value, the use of a default value associated with the input type "text" requires the removal of the text before new information can be entered (see Figure 3).

```
<input type="text" name="dorm name"
   value="type dorm name here">
```

is rendered as:

type dorm name here

Figure 3. Form object using default value

The preferred method of directing the user is to include either a LABEL element to specifically connect the text of the label with the INPUT element or the title attribute, specifying the element's purpose [14].

A common error found on web forms is the use of color to indicate required fields. An asterisk can be used to indicate required fields, but users of screen readers often turn off punctuation. Figure 4 shows how the use of a simple (R) can be used to indicate which fields are required.

Fields with (R) are required.

First name (R)

Last name (R)

Figure 4. Required fields designated

4. REINFORCING THE CONCEPTS

Students were asked to demonstrate their understanding of the concepts of the course by creating an accessible web site. Although more rigorous accessibility testing software may be available, a free service, Bobby, provided by Watchfire [18], was used. Student web sites were required to be free of Priority 1 and 2 Accessibility problems as identified by Bobby testing the site against WCA Guidelines 1.0. (Bobby also includes the option of checking submitted pages again Section 508 guidelines and was periodically used in previous labs to test accessibility.) Even though students expressed frustration that an 'error free' report was never generated even after correcting all the reported errors, students found that Bobby was able to help highlight problem areas and accessibility issues to consider.

For students wanting to dig deeper into issues of accessibility or consider adding advanced accessibility features to their web site, a list of resources relating to accessibility was provided.

- *Accessibility & Disability Information & Resources.* Ten areas of links to articles and other resources on such topics as accessibility issues in psychology training and practice, the civil rights of people with disabilities, assistive technology, accessibility standards for web sites, disability-related legal issues in higher education and professional licensing, and the American Psychological Association's mentoring program. http://kpope.com/index.php
- *DRM WebWatcher: Web Page Design.* Includes 19 links to resources for making web pages more accessible. http://www.disabilityresources.org/WEB.html
- *HiSoftware Solutions.* Software to aid users in creating and managing corporate standards for accessibility, privacy and content quality. http://hisoftware.com
- *IBM Home Page Reader.* A talking browser. http://www.ibm.com/able/hpr.html
- *JAWS.* Screen reader from Freedom Scientific. http://www.freedomscientific.com/
- *JimThatcher.com.* A short course written by James W. Thatcher, a web accessibility consultant, on designing for web accessibility as it relates to Section 508 written for the Information Technology Technical Assistance and Training Center. Screen shots and HTML code provided along with a list of 66 resources. http://jimthatcher.com/index.htm
- *Lynx.* A text-only browser replacing images with the alternate text. http://lynx.browser.org
- *National Federation of the Blind.* http://www.nfb.org/emptrn/tech.htm
- *Section 508 of the Rehabilitation Act: Electronic and Information Technology Accessibility Standards with Technical Assistance.* http://www.access-board.gov/508.htm
- *WAVE.* A free on-line service, sponsored by Temple University Institute on Disabilities that helps one judge if a web page is accessible to people with disabilities. http://www.wave.webaim.org/index.jsp
- *Web Accessibility Initiate (WAI).* News and resources about accessibility in five primary areas of work: technology, guidelines, tools, education and outreach, and research and development. http://www.w3.org/WAI/
- *Web Accessibility Survey Site* created by Axel Schmetzke. A form of clearing house for research in the area of web accessibility. Includes numerous studies, developments, evaluations of web accessibility checkers, and on-line library resources. http://library.uwsp.edu/aschmetz/Accessible/websurveys_p.htm
- *Web Content Accessibility Guidelines 2.0.* W3C Working Draft dated July 30, 2004. http://www.w3.org/TR/WCAG20/
- *WebABLE.* Web site for disability-related internet resources with various 'how to' links. http://www.webable.com

5. SUMMARY

With minimal curricular change to a web page or user interface design course, one can emphasize accessibility for screen reader users. If students are given the challenge of designing an accessible site, they will rise to meet that challenge. During presentations, made at the end of the semester in this course, students highlighted the various features that made their site as accessible as possible to the blind. Web pages created were visually attractive as well as accessible, indicating to the instructor that the course had met one of its major goals: *opening the eyes of those who can see to the world of those who can't.*

6. REFERENCES

[1] *508 Law. Section 508.* http://www.section508.gov/index.cfm?FuseAction=Content&ID=3.

[2] *Architectural and transportation barriers compliance board Electronic and information technology accessibility standards.* 36 CFR Part 1194. [Docket No. 2000-01]. Federal Register, 2000. http://www.access-board.gov/sec508/508standards.htm

[3] BBC News. *Awards for websites with 'vision'.* (Dec. 3, 2003). http://news.bbc.co.uk/2/hi/ technology/3256346.stm

[4] Chong, C. *Making your web site accessible to the blind.* Online. http://www.nfb.org/tech/webacc.htm.

[5] Friedman, D. S. *Vision problems in the U. S. prevalence of adult vision impairment and age-related eye disease in America.* Prevent Blindness America. (2002) http://www.nei.nih.gov/eyedata/pdf/VPUS.pdf

[6] Gashel, J. The state of the law on technology and the blind: what it is and what it ought to be. *Information Technology and Disabilities*, 9, 1 (Oct. 2003). http://www.rit.edu/%7Eeasi/itd/itdv09n1/gashel.htm.

[7] Gormley, M. Web sites agree to be accessible to blind. On Washingtonpost.com. *The Associated Press*, (August 19, 2004). http://www.washingtonpost.com/ac2/wp-dyn/A15979-2004Aug19?language=printer.

[8] GW Micro. *Window-Eyes.* http://www.gwmicro.com/

[9] Harper, S., Goble, C. and Stevens, R. A pilot study to examine the mobility problems of visually impaired users traveling the web. *ACM SIGCAPH Computers and the Physically Handicapped*, 68 (Sept. 2000), 10-19.

[10] Nielsen, J. *Designing Web Usability: The Practice of Simplicity.* New Riders Publishing, Indianapolis, IN, 2000.

[11] Sierkowski, B. Achieving web accessibility. In *Proceedings of the 30th annual ACM SIGUCCS conference on User services* (SIGUCCS'02) (Providence, Rhode Island, USA, November 20-23, 2002). ACM Press, New York, NY, 2002, 288-291.

[12] Sullivan, T. The Art of ALT. *All things web.* 1998. http://www.pantos.org/atw/35534.html.

[13] Sullivan, T. and Manning, K. Could Helen Keller read your page. *All things web.* 1998. http://www.pantos.org/atw/35412.html

[14] Thatcher, J. *508 Web Tutorial.* Online. (2000-2002). http://jimthatcher.com/webcourse1.htm.

[15] Theofanos, M. F., Redish, J. Bridging the gap between accessibility and usability. *Interactions, 10,* 6 (Nov.-Dec. 2003), 36-51.

[16] Thompson, T., Burgstahler, S. and Comden, D. Research on web accessibility in higher education. *Information Technology and Disabilities*, 9, 2 (Dec. 2003). http://www.rit.edu/%7Eeasi/itd/itdv09n2/thompson.htm.

[17] Waddell, C. The growing digital divide in access for people with disabilities: overcoming barriers to participation in the digital economy. *Understanding the Digital Economy: Data, Tools and Research.* US Department of Commerce, Washington, DC. (May 25-26, 1999). http://www.icdri.org/Cynthia W/the_digital_divide.htm.

[18] Watchfire Corporation. *Bobby.* (2002-2004). http://bobby.watchfire.com/bobby/html/en/index.jsp

[19] World Wide Web Consortium. Web Content Accessibility Guidelines 2.0. *W3C Working Draft* (July, 2004). http://www.w3.org/TR/WCAG20/

Students with Asperger's Syndrome in the CS Classroom

Mary Anne L. Egan
Siena College
515 Loudon Rd.
Loudonville, NY 12211
(518)782-6546
maegan@siena.edu

ABSTRACT

More students with Asperger's Syndrome are entering higher education and a majority of these students are choosing a computer science curriculum. With an increasing number of students with disabilities in the classroom, it is important to understand the particular aspects of a disability that will affect classroom situations. This paper presents common characteristics of students with Asperger's Syndrome and offers techniques that will maximize the student's educational experience and minimize disturbance to other students.

Categories and Subject Descriptors

K.3.2 [**Computers and Education**]: Computer and Information Science Education – *computer science education.*

General Terms

Management, Human Factors

Keywords

Computer Science Education, Asperger's Syndrome, Classroom Management, Non-traditional Students

1. INTRODUCTION

Very few Ph.D. students in computer science take classes aimed at educating students with disabilities. Since students with Asperger's Syndrome tend to do well in computer and math related disciplines, it seems that their professors should have some knowledge of classroom management issues that are helpful when dealing with students with Asperger's Syndrome. Before each semester starts, the campus disabilities office notifies professors of any student with a disability in their classroom (assuming the student has given permission for this information to be shared). When I received a notice for my fourth student with Asperger's Syndrome in six years, I realized that certain classroom management issues benefit both the student with Asperger's Syndrome and the remainder of the class. Through first hand knowledge, extensive use of the local disabilities office and review of current literature, several recurring techniques were very effective in dealing with Asperger's Syndrome students both in and out of the classroom.

SIGCSE'05, February 23–27, 2005, St. Louis, Missouri, USA.

Classroom management is an important issue not only to the students with Asperger's Syndrome, but for other students in the classroom as students with Asperger's Syndrome can be disruptive. Therefore, it is in everyone's interest that the professor learn how to discourage problem behavior and encourage cooperation in the classroom. As Hans Asperger, the Austrian pediatrician who originally described this disorder, wrote in 1944, "These children often show a surprising sensitivity to the personality of the teacher... They can be taught, but only by those who give them true understanding and affection, people who show kindness towards them and, yes, humour... The teacher's underlying emotional attitude influences, involuntarily and unconsciously, the mood and behaviour of the child." [1]

The structure of this paper is to first outline some of the characteristics that typify students with Asperger's Syndrome and how it could affect a classroom or lab situation. It also discusses several techniques that are effective in managing problems that these characteristics present in the classroom. Finally, a list of resources that are helpful when dealing with students with Asperger's Syndrome is given. The hope of the author is to give other faculty an advantage when they find that they have one or more students with Asperger's Syndrome in their classroom.

2. WHAT IS ASPERGER'S SYNDROME?

Asperger's Syndrome (AS) is a developmental disorder characterized by major difficulties in social interaction, and restricted or unusual patterns of interest and behavior. AS is the term applied to the mildest and highest functioning end of the spectrum of pervasive developmental disorders (or the autism spectrum) and occurs in approximately 25 per 10,000 people. Like all conditions along the autism spectrum it is felt to represent a neurologically-based disorder of development, most often of unknown cause, in which there are deviations of abnormalities in three broad aspects of development: social skills, language skills and certain behavioral characteristics. People with the syndrome are of normal or above average intelligence, some are even considered gifted. Because AS is more commonly found in boys than in girls, this paper will refer to the student with AS as "he".

Why are students with AS drawn to computer science? A recurring theme in case histories of AS is an attraction to highly organized systems and complex machines. Clumsy and easily overwhelmed in the physical world, AS minds excel in the virtual realms of mathematics, symbols and code. The culture of the computer world has subtly evolved to meet the social needs of adults in high-functioning regions of the autism spectrum which include AS. In the geek warrens of engineering and R&D, social graces are beside the point. You can be as off-the-wall as you want to be, but if your code is bulletproof, no one's going to point out that you've been wearing the same shirt for two weeks. People with AS have a hard time multi-tasking – particularly when one of the channels is face-to-face communication. Replacing the commotion of the traditional office with a screen and an email address inserts a controllable interface between a programmer and the chaos of everyday life. A world where respect and rewards are based strictly on merit is an Asperger's dream. [6]

Students with AS present a special challenge in the classroom in several ways. They are typically viewed as eccentric and peculiar by classmates because of their lack of social skills, clumsiness and obsessive interest in obscure objects. Other students often view these students as "odd" because they tend to misread social situations and interact with others based on these misinterpretations. They also lack an understanding of human relationships, rules of social convention and have difficulty sustaining the "give and take" of conversations. While most students with AS express a desire to fit in socially and have friends, they are often deeply frustrated and disappointed by their social difficulties. This is not due to a lack of interaction so much as lack of effectiveness in interactions.

Additionally, there are usually some observable differences in how students with AS use language. Their aspects of spoken language such as volume of speech, intonation, inflection, and rate are frequently unusual, making the language sound overly formal. In many cases, idioms and slang are often not used or are misused, and language is often taken too literally. Compounding the language issues, these students are usually naïve and lacking in common sense. These are important concepts in a classroom setting, as the professor needs to understand why these students may have a difficult time following an example or a particular lecture.

Another characteristic that many students with AS share is that they are easily overwhelmed when dealing with changes or frustrating situations. Suggestions for handling this in the classroom will be given in the next section, but one major difficulty to keep in mind is that many students, with or without AS, find computer programming inherently frustrating. Students without AS deal with the frustrating aspects of CS by focusing on the reward of creating a working program. It is difficult for students with AS to realize the eventual reward and handle the frustration without causing a major disruption to those around them.

3. CHARACTERISTICS AND STRATEGIES

This section presents several common characteristics of students with AS and their manifestations in a classroom and/or office setting. It also provides guidelines to teachers of these students. The purpose of this section is to raise awareness of the pervasive nature of differences associated with AS. In other words, there is no universal description of ideal provision. Not only will needs vary enormously between individuals, but there may also be fluctuations in sensory and attentional circumstances that make performance by the same student somewhat erratic over time. However, an attempt needs to be made to give concrete solutions to recurring problem behaviors.

3.1 Difficulty with Change

Students with AS are easily overwhelmed by minimal change. They worry obsessively when they do not know what to expect. This can manifest itself in the classroom by insisting that the syllabus be followed exactly, sitting in the same seat each class period, insisting on a particular writing utensil or asking many questions about the content of an upcoming test or project.

One of the first things that must be done if there is a student with AS in the classroom is to create a detailed syllabus informing the students about the topics to be covered each week and listing the dates of major exams and projects. If a change is necessitated, announce it at least a week in advance and mention it on several occasions. The student may be upset at first, but by the time the change occurs, he will be ready for it.

Other behavioral issues that a professor will more than likely encounter in the classroom include the insistence to sit in the same seat each class and write with a particular utensil. If the student needs to sit in the same seat, try to ensure that the arrangement of the seating does not vary too much between classes. If the student is missing his preferred writing utensil, see how he will work with an alternate. If his agitation level is increasing, suggest that he take his belongings to the hall to more thoroughly search for the one he wants. Allowing him to remain in an agitated state in the classroom doesn't benefit anyone. The student with AS will not be attentive to the lecture and will also disrupt those around him.

When assigning a project, be as explicit as possible to minimize possible confusion and hence the number of visits to office hours. Be sure to explicitly state the desired input and output, include a detailed grading scheme, the date assigned, the due date and submission procedures (even if it doesn't change from project to project). A sample run of the program is also necessary to ensure clarity. While the detail on the project description may seem obvious, it is especially critical when dealing with students with AS. Additionally, the description and discussion of the project should be as concise as possible because these students have a difficult time gleaning necessary information from the extraneous.

Before an exam it is helpful for the student with AS to receive a detailed list of topics that will be covered to minimize office visits. In order for this list to be helpful to the student, it must contain a list of topics, not just sections of the book. Additionally, be sure to indicate the date, time, duration, location and proctors for the exam. Preparing students with AS for an unknown situation, such as an exam, decreases their agitation levels both preceding and during the event.

3.2 Social Interaction Issues

This is an area that can affect a larger classroom, but will mainly affect smaller discussion type classes, lab classes and office hours where working with other people is required. Students with AS have an inability to understand complex rules of social interaction and therefore, may use inappropriate body language, have difficulty initiating and sustaining conversations, and may be insensitive and lack tact. When using office hours, these students may be in the office every five minutes, may cut to the beginning of the line, may enter the office even if the professor is working with another student and will more than likely pace outside the office door while waiting for their turn.

The primary method of managing these behavioral issues is to remind the student of appropriate behavior. When a student with AS has been unintentionally insulting or insensitive, it must be explained to them why the response was inappropriate and what response would have been correct. Be prepared to correct the student kindly, but firmly. For example in each of the office hour situations mentioned above, appropriate responses may be found in Table 1.

Table 1. Sample Issues with Appropriate Responses

Issue	Response
Visit office every 5 minutes	"Could you please wait at least 15 minutes before coming back and asking another question?"
Cut to the beginning of line	"Are there any other students in line waiting to see me?"
Enter the office even when professor is working with another student	"When I am working with other students, you must wait out in the hallway."
Pacing outside the office door while waiting their turn	"I should be done with this student in ten minutes, why don't you come back then?"

Notice the use of concrete periods of time in the above examples. Students with AS have a difficult time with vague phrases such as "come back later". Does "later" mean five minutes from now? An hour? Next week? Consequently, if ambiguous times are given, their frustration level increases, their pacing increases and they become more disruptive to those around them.

As far as physical contact is concerned, students with AS may be at one end of the spectrum or another. Some students may avoid any form of physical contact as they find physical contact literally painful. Accommodations may need to be made if group work around a single computer is required, as accidental contact needs to be avoided. On the other end of the spectrum are those students who cannot judge "social distance" and invade another person's space while talking or working with them. The invading space problem is handled by reminding the student about appropriate behavior. The students with AS who find contact painful are a little more difficult to accommodate. One option may be to set them up at a computer next to the group so they can participate, but still maintain physical distance.

People with AS have difficulty understanding jokes, irony or metaphors. This may cause several problems in the classroom if the teacher incorporates any of these techniques in their teaching. While jokes or metaphors may be a good way to reinforce difficult concepts, it is good to keep in mind that this technique may be confusing to some students. While it is not necessary to remove the use of jokes or metaphors from your classroom, it may be necessary to explain the concepts separately after class.

3.3 Poor Motor Skills

Students with AS are physically clumsy and awkward. While this may not seem to affect a classroom setting, it does include fine motor skills. Deficits in this area cause handwriting problems and reduce note-taking speed. Some solutions to this problem include distributing class notes or making them available online so that the students need only to add details or fill in missing information. The less the students need to write, the more they can focus on the topic being taught and keep up with everyone else. Also, the slowness in handwriting should warrant extra time on exams.

3.4 Emotional Issues

The main characteristics that must be managed when working with students with AS are rage reactions and temper outbursts. These are common responses to stress and frustration. Unfortunately, both stress and frustration are common when working with computers. The best way to handle these situations is to work at avoiding them. Easier said than done, but if the professor notices that a student is getting increasingly agitated, he/she may suggest that the student take a walk or get a drink. Sometimes the change of locale is enough to diffuse the situation. Other students in the classroom notice the cues and may also make suggestions to the student with AS while working in the lab. But, there may be times when the student is so frustrated that they become violent. This may reveal itself in shouting and throwing or slamming objects interspersed with manic pacing around the room. These are situations where the local security officers should be called. They are trained to deal with outbursts like these and for students with AS, it reinforces the idea that there are consequences to their actions.

Sometimes a student with AS will become confrontational with another student or the professor. The avoidance of an escalating power struggle is the best solution. They often do not understand anger and will become more stubborn if forcefully confronted. It is best to avoid the confrontation through calmness, negotiation, presentation of choices or diversion of attention elsewhere.

In addition to all the other issues that a student with AS must face, they are especially prone to depression, have low self-esteem, are self-critical and unable to tolerate making mistakes. It is important to compliment these students when they do a task well. More importantly, the professor must be unafraid to suggest a visit to the local counseling center if they notice signs of depression. Signs of depression may include greater levels of disorganization, inattentiveness, decreased stress threshold, tiredness, crying, or suicidal remarks.

It would be helpful to create a support network for the student if they feel isolated. Study groups may be useful, as can paired or group assignments.

3.5 Limited Field of Interest

Students with AS will often focus on a particular interest. They may refuse to learn about anything outside their limited field of interest causing them to "zone out" during certain topics. Typically, they will be interested in computer science, but have another outside interest that keeps surfacing in the classroom. Their desire to talk about this area of interest is exacerbated by the fact that they typically do not have a group of friends with whom to discuss these interests. One technique for managing this issue is to give the student an allotted amount of time to discuss his interest. For example, giving the student a 15-minute appointment every three weeks to discuss whatever he wants, will often satisfy his need to share information and/or ask questions about his area of interest.

3.6 Poor Concentration

A student with AS who is enrolled in higher education should have learned compensation techniques for difficulties associated with distractions, but the professor needs to be aware that the student may sometimes be off-task and distracted by internal stimuli. Typically these students have learned that sitting in the front of the classroom is more conducive to remaining on-task. Additionally, the professor should direct questions to the student to help him attend to the lecture.

Another difficulty that arises from poor concentration is disorganization. Many students with AS have learned methods for remembering to submit assignments. But, many other papers will be lost, including lecture notes, project descriptions, and returned projects and exams. To minimize the headaches, be sure to make at least three extra copies of everything for every student with AS. If this is done, when they come to the office looking for a particular note packet that they lost, there is one readily available.

Difficulty determining what is relevant in a conversation is often a problem many students with AS share. This often occurs when trying to explain a concept to a student with AS. With students without AS, if the professor notices that the students are having trouble understanding the method used to explain a topic, he/she will typically try another method. This technique does not work well with students with AS. Unfortunately, they will confuse and mingle the two methods that were used to clarify a concept and will typically end up more confused than when they started. Just stay with the original method for explaining a concept and be patient, they will eventually understand it.

3.7 Academic Difficulties

Students with AS tend to be very literal thinkers. In general, try to keep teaching fairly concrete. Avoid language that may be misunderstood by the student with AS, such as sarcasm, confusing figurative speech, idioms, etc. Work to break down and simplify more abstract language and concepts. Try to use visual methods to teach abstract concepts.

Explain metaphors and words with double meanings as students with AS may find abstract language, metaphors and irony difficult to understand. Try to use clear and literal language and be explicit about what is being taught. Pause occasionally to check understanding. It may be helpful, especially at the beginning of the course, to provide extra time immediately after group sessions to check that sessions have been understood; short-term auditory memory is often poor and learning is visual, often through reading.

Finally, be clear when a new topic or concept is introduced. There should be a definite end to one topic and a beginning to the next. This can be accomplished by something as simple as erasing the whole board, starting a new heading and stating that this is a different topic. If handouts are given to the students, paper color is very helpful to indicate separate topics. For example, all notes related to decision structures are on yellow paper, all notes on iterative structures are printed on green, etc. This gives the students several cues that they are now studying a different topic.

4. RESOURCES

In addition to the books and articles listed under the reference section of this paper, the following links were helpful when working with students with AS in the classroom.

General autism links include the University Students with Autism and Asperger's Syndrome (www.users.dircon.co.uk/~cns), the Autism Society of America (www.autism-society.org) and the Center for the Study of Autism (www.autism.org).

While AS is a form of autism, there is also a useful site dedicated just to AS: Online Asperger Syndrome Information and Support (www.udel.edu/bkirby/asperger).

For the student with AS, there is a booklet of advice available from The University of Melbourne and the Australian Catholic University entitled "Towards Success in Tertiary Study with Asperger's Syndrome and other Autistic Spectrum Disorders". (www.services.unimelb.edu.au/ellp/publications/towards.html)

5. CONCLUSION

This paper has given a brief introduction to Asperger's Syndrome, together with a general outline of some of the ways in which access to higher education might be restricted for students with related special needs. In offering general guiding principles aimed at increasing accessibility for students on the spectrum, the need for explicit instructions, firm reminders in social situations, diffusing frustrating situations, patience, and consistency were highlighted.

6. REFERENCES

[1] Asperger, H. Autistic Psychopathy in Childhood. In Frith, U. ed. *Autism and Asperger's Syndrome*. Cambridge University Press, UK, 1991.

[2] Committee on Educational Interventions for Children with Autism, Division of Behavioral and Social Sciences and Education, National Research Council. *Educating Children with Autism.* National Academy Press, Washington, DC, 2001.

[3] Harpur, J., Lawlor, M. and Fitzgerald, M. *Succeeding in College with Asperger Syndrome*. Jessica Kingsley Publishers, London, UK, 2004.

[4] Klin, A. and Volkmar, F. *Asperger's Syndrome Guidelines for Treatment and Intervention.* Learning Disabilities Association of America, 1995.

[5] Luckett, T. and Powell, S. Students with Autism and Asperger's Syndrome. *Special Teaching in Higher Education*. Kogan Page, London and Sterling, VA, 2003.

[6] Silberman, S. The Geek Syndrome, *Wired Magazine, 9, 12* (December 2001).

[7] Williams, K Understanding the Student with Asperger Syndrome: Guidelines for Teachers. *Focus on Autistic Behavior, 10,* 2 (June 1995).

Integrating Science and Research in a HCI Design Course

Robert Pastel
Department of Computer Science
Michigan Technological University
Houghton, MI 49931, USA
1-906-487-2209
rpastel@mtu.edu

ABSTRACT

Undergraduate computer science students have few opportunities to experience scientific investigation and computer science research. A human-computer interaction (HCI) course can offer many opportunities for research that are accessible to undergraduate students, and because of the similarity between the design and research processes, a design project based HCI course is particularly suited to introducing undergraduate computer science students to the research process. In this paper, we describe and discuss the challenges of integrating research projects into a design HCI course. We also present example research projects and discuss the feedback form students attending the course.

Categories and Subject Descriptors

K.3.2 [**Computer and Information Science Education**]: Computer science education

H.5.2 [**User Interfaces**]: Theory and methods

General Terms

Measurement, Design, Experimentation, Human Factors

Keywords

Undergraduate research, human-computer interaction research, group projects.

1. INTRODUCTION

The term group design project based human-computer interface (HCI) course is extensively discussed in the computer science educational literature [3,4,9] and is becoming a standard model for teaching HCI. The group design project is generally favored by students because they can "learn by doing," and they can implement a substantial project of their own design. But McCrickard, et al. [6] have argued for teaching the full spectrum of HCI by including design, science, and engineering topics in a case-study pedagogical model. This paper outlines a technique for including science in a project based HCI course by guiding a few groups through the scientific investigation process as a substitute for their design projects. This alternative project track, *research project*, is possible because of the striking similarities between the software design and scientific research processes.

The research projects are beneficial to the students directly involved in the projects because they experience and receive training in a scientific process. The research projects are also beneficial to students engaged in the traditional design projects because they observe the scientific process in progress. All students become aware of scientific issues in HCI, and the research projects can help motivate the more theoretical lectures. Because many of the research projects attempt to measure usability directly, the concepts of measurement and usability are demonstrated in the course. Also because research projects can employ unique HCI devices or implementations and all students participate in the tests, the students experience using alternative user interfaces. For students considering continuing their education through graduate school, the research project experience provides a glimpse at life in graduate school. Often the research projects can serve as the bases for publication in the general literature [8].

2. DESIGN PROJECT BASED COURSE

Our HCI course is an elective junior level course for computer science majors and required for software engineering majors. Generally students take the course their junior or senior year after they have had a year of introductory Java programming, one semester of data structures, advanced C++ programming with object oriented design, and team software courses. Thus, the students are proficient programmers familiar with more than one GUI toolkit and managing their own groups. Consequently, the course lectures can concentrate on design and theory. Also because our students are very proficient programmers and have already implemented several GUIs, they are eager to implement their interface design; in fact, the major challenge for the instructor is insuring that students cycle through several low-fidelity prototypes before implementation.

Course lectures progress through vaguely segmented sections: introductory, design, theory, and HCI examples. The design lectures emphasize usability and user-centered design. The theory lectures includes topics such as Norman's interaction, GOMS CMN and KLM models, information theory, and Fitts's and Hick's laws. Besides generalizing the applicability of design principles, the theory lectures provide context for many of the

Table 1. Correspondences between design and research course assignments

Design Process	Corresponding Research Process
1. Proposal	Research Proposal • Research goals and hypothesis • Literature study, articles provided by instructor
2. User/task Analysis	Participant/test Analysis • Test-participants, administrators, analysts, and other users specifications • Test description and scenarios • Data and data-format specifications
3. Initial Design	Initial Test Development • Spike implementations and evaluations • Initial test platform implementation and debugging • Test platform presentation and feedback from experts
4. Second Design	Initial Testing and Evaluation • Initial participant testing, observations and participant feedback • Evaluation using observations, collected data and feedback from participants • Test Redesign
5. Final Design	Reimplementation and Retesting • Test platform modifications • Participant retest
6. Implementation	Data Analysis • Preliminary data analysis • Evaluation of results • Graphs and presentation

research projects. The HCI example lectures are synchronized with the students implementing their projects. Initial HCI example lectures discuss toolkits and the capstone lectures demonstrate alternative interfaces, for example interfaces and devices using gesturing.

Students work in groups of three to five on projects that they specify. The design assignments stress user-centered design and by necessity encourage iterative rapid prototyping. After the project proposal presentation, the design assignments progress through user/task analysis, initial design, final design and implementation. Paper documents are produced at each phase, and the groups present their initial design near mid semester and final designs before the end of the semester to the class. The format of the presentations mimics brief cognitive walkthroughs [7], where the rest of the class participates as experts. In addition the class formally evaluates the designs using a heuristic evaluation survey [7]. At the end of the semester the instructor evaluates the implementations generally in an interview conducted with the group.

3. INTEGRATING RESEARCH PROJECTS

The crux of guiding undergraduate students through a research project is the delicate balance between specific supervision and free exploration that the instructor must constantly maintain. Although the computer science undergraduate students are extensively trained at problem solving, they receive little training in making progress in vaguely defined, large projects. If the instructor solely assigns a sequence of tasks, then the experience lacks the essential characteristic of research, the discovery of new principles in science. Guiding undergraduate students through research in a semester course has greater time constraints than advising graduate students; at the conclusion of the course an undergraduate student expects to have completed the research and receive a grade. Completing a significant portion of the research in a single semester is also important to all students so that they can observe the complete research process.

Many of the challenges of guiding undergraduate research can be surmounted by the structure of the HCI design course and the parallels between the design and research processes. Table 1 compares the design assignments and corresponding research tasks. The essential *scientific hypotheses* correspond with the design's project proposal. The design process's user/task analysis corresponds to the test-participants/task analysis in the research process. The iterative quality of the design process is reflected by the cyclic process of testing and evaluating results in research. The design implementation is the final assignment for the design students while data analysis is the final assignment for the research students. Students conducting research are required to make corresponding documents and presentations. Besides informing the students not involved in the research project of the research, the presentations insure that the research students equally participate in the course. Typically the initial research presentations demonstrate the tests and administer the tests to the class, and the final research presentations discuss the experimental results.

Success of a delicately balanced process is critically sensitive to detail and agility. The research project is not appropriate for every student. The course syllabus explains that students may ask to work on a research project under the instructor's guidance only after an agreement between the instructor and students. Although students meet a general academic threshold before they are permitted to work on a research project, our criteria for selecting students is primarily dependent on the students' maturity and motivation. A critical provision for success of the research project is the students' investment in the project; students must feel that the project is their own. But the project must also be important to the instructor, otherwise the student will feel that the project is not important. So in the initial interview the students are given a choice among a variety of projects of interest to the instructor and involve different skills and interests.

Weekly meetings between individual research groups and the instructor are required to maintain progress. Besides assuring the students of the instructor interest, research problems frequently have subtle solutions and students are often shy to admit failure. But the instructor must not offer too much assistance or the students will become disinvested. Generally the instructor provides the scientific background but rarely technical support. During the meetings the instructor naturally helps the students interpret the assignments. The participant/test analysis emphasizes the people involved in the test including participants, programmers, administrator and analyst. Also at this time data collection is discussed. Because the primary goal of the research project is to give the students experience in the full spectrum of research, from hypotheses formulation to data analysis and reporting results, implementation of the testing programs must start early. Typically testing programs require an unusual programming technique, so the students are encouraged to write spikes [2], small programs illustrating the unusual technique.

4. EXAMPLE RESEARCH PROJECTS

A possible classification of HCI research appropriate for undergraduate students is:

- Studying user-interfaces or interface-tools
- Developing new user-interfaces and interface tools
- Testing interfaces or human-computer interactions

Although all three categories of HCI research have been pursued in the HCI design course, the latter and specifically testing human-computer interactions have been the most successful. The study of user interfaces and tools is too vague for all but the most mature student to make progress in the project. Although developing a new interface tool has clear goals, the programming involved is generally too extensive and abstract for most undergraduate students. The paradigm for introducing research into an HCI design course described in this article is based on testing human-computer interactions, and the following examples best illustrate the technique.

Figure 1. Maze image with cursor track

4.1 Maze Project

The goal of the maze project is to verify the steering law [1] and eventually extend the steering law to more complex tasks. The participants are sequentially presented with images, called mazes, one of which is shown in Figure 1. The participant is asked to click in the green disc, darker grey in Figure 1, and move the cursor to the red disc, lighter grey in the figure, while remaining in the black area. After the cursor reaches the red disc, a new maze is presented to the participant. The light grey dots in Figure 1 indicate a cursor's motion for a typical participant. The raw data collected is the time and cursor screen coordinates at approximately 16-msec intervals. Figure 2 is a graph of cursor's maze-center line speed against the width of the maze at that location. Because the participants move the cursor from a wide section of the maze to a narrow section, the passage of time on the graph is from right to left. The graph displays a typical participant's behavior of acceleration, slow down and speed up and slowing down again towards the goal.

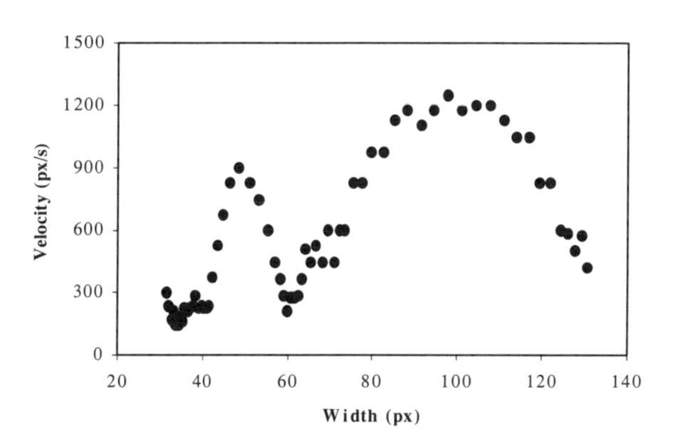

Figure 2. Cursor velocity verses width

Implementing and administrating this test was a lesson in user/participant feedback. The original test platform gave only the standard user feedback, a cursor image. While debugging, the researchers found it difficult to determine if the cursor was inside or outside the maze near the maze boundary. So the student researchers modified the test platform so that the cursor changed its image when it moved outside the maze. From the participant feedback after the initial participant testing, we learned that the participants wanted more feedback; in particular they wanted to know how well they had done on the mazes. So the researchers added a feedback window that appears after the completion of each maze informing the participant of the total time and accuracy completing the maze. In addition the participants wanted feedback when they click on the green disc, so the researchers added a third cursor image, while the cursor is moved to the green disc and before it is clicked. After the final testing the researchers were not happy with the general accuracy of the participants, so the researches modified the test platform such that when a participant performs below an accuracy threshold the participant is required to repeat the maze. The student researchers hope that in future testing the participant will quickly learn to maintain accuracy. All students in the class and especially the researchers learned techniques and roles of user-interface feedback.

4.2 Gravity Mouse Project

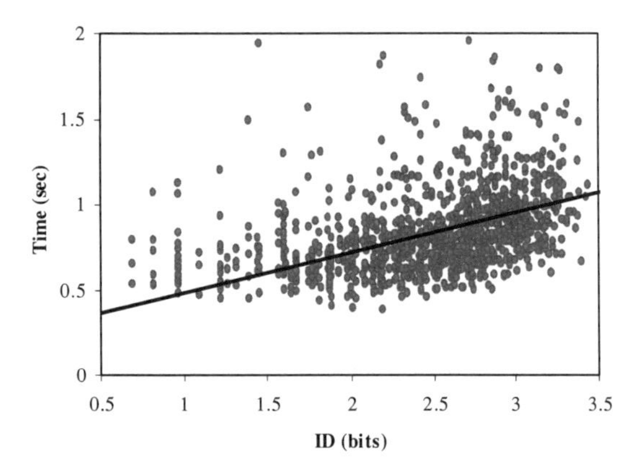

Figure 3. Time to click verses index of difficulty

The goal of the gravity mouse project is to test the usability of a mouse that is "accelerated" toward buttons. The project's name and initial design of gravity mouse is based on an analogy in physics. The cursor is *accelerated*, moved an additional amount, in the direction of the mouse motion. Gravity mouse accelerates the cursor inversely proportional to the square of the separation of the button and cursor locations. In general the acceleration is maximum closes to a button and minimal far from a button. Buttons are given mass, so the acceleration is also proportional to the button's mass. The usability test is similar to a Fitts's Law verification, in this case the participants are sequentially presented with randomly located buttons and asked to move the cursor to the button and click. After clicking, new buttons are immediately displayed and randomly located. Figure 3 graphs the time to click as a function of the index of difficult (ID) [5], proportional to the initial cursor and button separation, for a moderate button mass. Figure 4 graphs the throughput (TP) [5], reciprocal slope of the ID vs. time regression, for four button masses. Note that locating the zero mass, the test without acceleration, along the veridical axes is arbitrary.

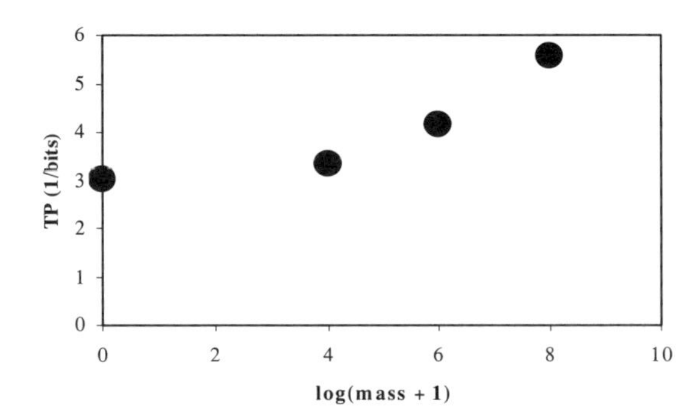

Figure 4. Throughput verses logarithm of button mass

Gravity mouse testing was a lesson in the pros and cons of assisting or controlling the user. Figure 4 clearly illustrates the advantages to assisting the user on controlling the cursor. The TP increases with mass or additional assistance. But subsequent administrators' tests found that distracter-buttons, non target buttons with mass, can inhibit the cursor from reaching the target button. The amount of inhibition increases with the button mass and the number of distracters. Subsequent research students can study the inhibition and improve the computer control of the cursor.

5. FEEDBACK FROM STUDENTS

A class survey given near the end of the semester was used to learn students' feelings about the research projects and the course as a whole, 15 students participated in the survey. Figure 5 presents the survey result when asked, "How interested are you in the research projects?" Although the responses appear split, clearly the students are not bored by the research projects. Two students surveyed, approximately 13%, were directly involved in the research project as researchers; removing their responses from the "very interested" category makes the responses more uniform, and implying that the average design student was "interested" in the research project. Confidence in the survey results can be increased by asking students how definite they feel about their response. This confidence was

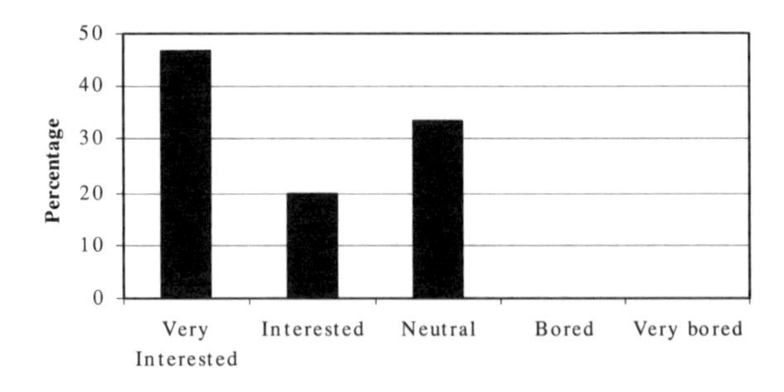

Figure 5. Student interest in research projects

elicited by the follow up question, "Please rate your feeling or commitment to your choice in the above question on a scale of A to E, where A is 'I feel very strongly' and E is 'I have no feeling, I just picked one.'" A *mushiness percentage* [10] can be calculated where 0% implies very definite and 100% implies the choice is arbitrary, very *mushy*. The mushy percentage for the students' interest in the research projects is 17%, which is definite. In addition a validity index or *appropriateness percentage* can be determined by asking a factual question to determine if it is appropriate for the respondents to be answering the question. In this case 93% of the students answered yes to the question; "Did you participate as a subject in the research tests?"

The survey was also used to gain insight into the course as a whole; students were asked, "what is your favorite and least favorite lecture/discussion category: introductory, design, theory, and example-HCI?" The favorite lecture category was split between design and example-HCI lectures, 47% and 40% respectively, with mushiness 37%. We believe the higher mushy percentage represents the choice most students had to make between design or example lectures. The least favorite lecture category is more unanimous; 60% of the students respond that the theory lectures are their least favorite with mushiness 32%. Even after the research experience students are still not interested in theory; the survey does not determine if the students have a better perspective about research then before taking the course. Further insight into the personality of the students can be gained by their response to the question; "The course has 3 components: lectures, design homework, and user interface implementation, which component did you enjoy the most?" 67% of the students with mushiness 28% choose the user-interface implementation as their favorite course component. Probably not surprising, our students are application orientated and prefer learning "hands on." Even the students involved in the research unanimously favored implementation over lecture and design homework, research documentation in this case. We believe their response is indicative of their enjoyment in doing the research or design projects.

6. CONCLUSION

Although undergraduate research integrates smoothly into an HCI design course, the process requires continuous monitoring and mentoring the student researchers. They need guidance through a vaguely defined project, and examples of how to agilely solve subtle problems and respond to unexpected results. Although the students are frequently very technically competent, for example programming skills, they are very inexperienced in scientific skills, such as data analysis. For the project to conclude successfully the instructor must provide varying degrees of scaffolding.

Student researchers benefit by gaining research experience and some research skills. We believe that undergraduate students with this experience will transition quickly to graduate research. Students not directly involved in the research are engaged in the research by participating in the testing, evaluating the test platform, and learning about the experimental results.

We plan to continue including research projects in our HCI design course.

7. ACKNOWLEDGMENTS

The author wishes to acknowledge the contribution made by the undergraduate students that have participated in HCI research projects: Joseph Vaillancourt, Greg Murphy, Ryan Antkowiak, Robert Moore, Chris Blazek, Scott Gross, Jacob Champlin, and Chris Fuller. The author also wishes to thank the reviewers for their thoughtful suggestions.

8. REFERENCES

[1] Accot, J., Zhai, S. Beyond Fitts' Law: Models for Trajectory-Based HCI Tasks. In *Proceedings of theACM CHI97 Conference on Human in Computer Systems (SIGCHI97)* (Atlanta, GA, USA, March 22-27, 1997) ACM Press, 1997, 295-302.

[2] Beck, K. *Extreme Programming Explained*. Addison-Wesley, Reading, MA, 1999.

[3] Hartfield, B., Winograd, T., and Bennett, J. Learning HCI Design: Mentoring Project Groups in a Course on Human-Computer Interaction. In *Proceedings of the Twenty-third SIGCSE Technical Symposium on Computer science Education (SIGCSE92)* (Kansas City, Missouri, USA, 1992) ACM Press, 1992, 246-251.

[4] Leventhal, L. M., Barnes, J., and Chao, J. Term Project User Interface Specifications in a Usability Engineering Course: Challenges and Suggestions. In *Proceedings of the 35th SIGCSE Technical Symposium on Computer science Education (SIGCSE'04)* (Norfolk, Virginia, USA, March 3-7, 2004) ACM Press, New York, NY, 2004, 41-45.

[5] MacKenzie, I. S., Kauppinen, T., and Silfverberg, M. Accuracy Measures for Evaluating Computer Pointing Devices. In *Proceedings of the ACM CHI'01 Conference on Human in Computer Systems (SIGCHI'01)* (Seattle, WA, USA, March 31-April 4, 2001) ACM Press, 2001, 9-16.

[6] McCrickard, D. S., Chewar, C. M., and Somervell, J. Design, Science, and Engineering Topics?: Teaching HCI with a Unified Method. In *Proceedings of the 35th SIGCSE Technical Symposium on Computer Science Education (SIGCSE'04)* (Norfolk, Virginia, USA, March 3-7, 2004) ACM Press, New York, NY, 2004, 31-35.

[7] Nielsen, J. and Mack, R. L. *Usability Inspection Methods*. John Wiley and Sons, 1994.

[8] Pastel, R., and Skalsky, N. Demonstrating Information in Simple Gestures. In *Proceedings of the Conference for Intelligent User Interface (IUI'04)* (Maderia, Portugal, January 13-16, 2004) ACM Press, 2004, 360-361.

[9] Willshire, M. J. A Usability Focus for an HCI Project. *J. Comput. Small Coll. 17, 2* (2001) 50-58.

[10] Yankelovich, D. A New Direction for Survey Research. Intl. J. for Public Opinion Research, 1, (March 1996). Available at http://www.danyankelovich.com/anew.htm

Interpreting Java Program Runtimes

Stuart Hansen
Department of Computer Science
University of Wisconsin - Parkside
Kenosha, WI 53144
(262) 595 - 3395
hansen@cs.uwp.edu

ABSTRACT
Many instructors use program runtimes to illustrate and reinforce algorithm complexity concepts. Hardware, operating systems and compilers all influence the runtimes, but generally not to the extent of making the data difficult to interpret. The Java virtual machine adds an additional layer of software, making it much harder to see the relationship between the runtimes and the underlying algorithm. This paper presents some of the basic issues the author and his students have encountered when analyzing Java program runtimes and briefly discusses strategies to address them.

Categories and Subject Descriptors
C.4 [**Performance of Systems**]: Measurement Techniques, Performance

General Terms
Algorithms, Performance, Experimentation.

Keywords
Java virtual machine, Program runtime, Garbage Collection,

1. INTRODUCTION
The author recently taught Data Structures and Algorithms for the first time since his department's curriculum was converted from C++ to Java. Like many instructors, he wished to demonstrate how the complexity of an algorithm directly impacts its implementation's runtime. The importance of this type of activity is well recognized by computer science educators [2, 7]. During the semester, the author and his students collected runtime data from a variety of programs, but found themselves repeatedly confused by the data because of influences from the virtual machine. Figures 1 through 3 show runtimes for sample programs. The data presented in these figures were obtained using Sun's SDK 1.4.1 running under Debian Linux, Version 3.0 on a 2.4 Gigahertz machine with 512 Megabytes of memory. Times were measured using the method `System.currentTimeMillis()`. Similar results may be obtained using other hardware and software configurations.

SIGCSE'05, February 23-27, 2005, St. Louis, Missouri, USA.

Figure 1 shows the runtimes for repeated calls to `Arrays.sort()` with random `int` arrays of size 20,000. `Arrays.sort` uses a version of Quicksort, which is an unstable algorithm. In the long run we expect to see some fluctuation in runtimes. This is not the cause of the problem here, however, as repeated runs of our program with different random arrays produce very similar results. The virtual machine is causing the method to run more slowly on the first call than on subsequent calls.

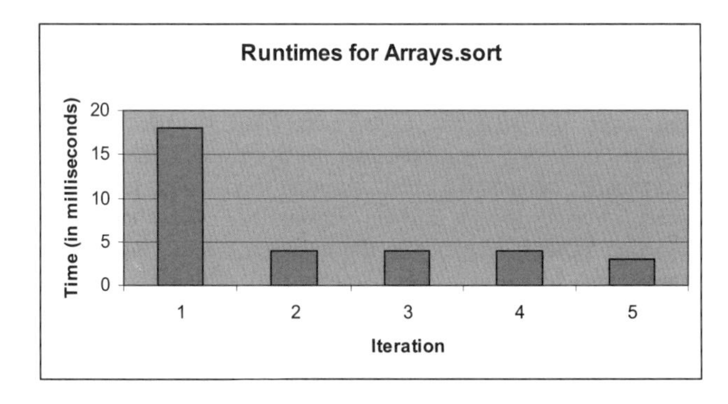

Figure 1. Runtimes of `Arrays.sort` called five times in succession on random `int` arrays of size 20,000. The first run took significantly longer than any of the others.

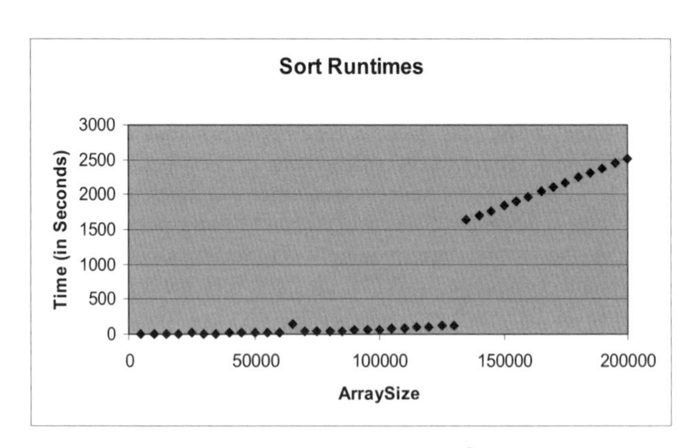

Figure 2. Runtimes obtained for a $O(n^2)$ sort program.

Figure 2 shows the runtimes for a Java program implementing a $O(n^2)$ sort algorithm. The sort is not one of the standard $O(n^2)$ sorts, however. The author had recently introduced his students to the fact that instantiating a Java array is a O(n) operation, since all cells in the array are initialized. To reinforce this idea, he modified the merge() method from a MergeSort program to use a temporary array the size of the entire array being sorted. This one line change makes the MergeSort program $O(n^2)$. The author was expecting the graph to be roughly parabolic. Instead, it appears to have near linear behavior, with a major discontinuity occurring between 130,000 and 135,000.

Figure 3 shows runtimes for rehashing a Java Hashtable. This experiment was suggested by Michael Clancy during a panel discussion at SIGCSE 2002 [7]. A Hashtable of size 1,000,000 was created and a varying number of Integers was added to it. Since the size of the Hashtable is fixed, rehashing is linear in the number of elements added. The author was expecting the graph in Figure 3 to be roughly a single straight line. Instead, the graph consists of two line segments, with the runtimes for larger data sets being significantly faster than runtimes for smaller data sets. Somehow between 120,000 and 130,000 the program speeds up by over a factor of five.

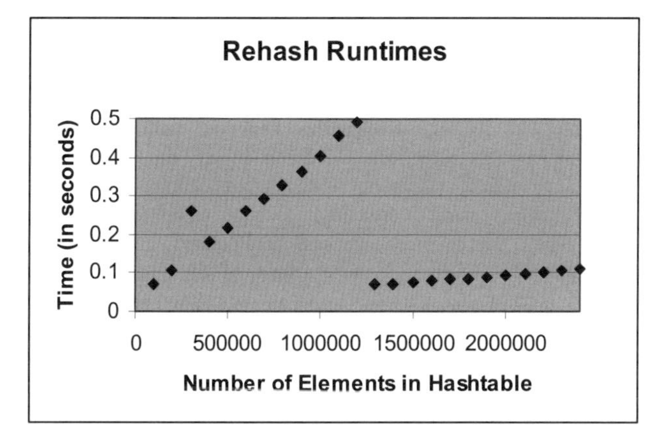

Figure 3. Runtimes obtained when rehashing a hashtable of size 1,000,000.

These examples illustrate that interpreting Java program runtimes is difficult. The goal of this paper is to explain the features of the Java virtual machine that are major influences on program runtimes and show how they may be explained and at least partially controlled to obtain runtimes that reflect the complexity of the underlying algorithm. What we want is to be able to time a $O(n^2)$ algorithm and plot the results, obtaining something akin to a parabola.

This goal is very different than performance tuning. Performance tuning looks at the virtual machine's features with the goal of making a program run faster. There are many texts and papers that address Java performance tuning [1, 6, 8, 9, 10]. Sun's Hotspot virtual machine even tries to tune performance of the program dynamically. This paper does not discuss how to make Java programs run faster. In fact, we will sometimes accept a hit in overall performance if we can thereby obtain runtimes more consistent with the underlying algorithm.

2. JAVA VIRTUAL MACHINES

Most CS instructors are aware of how a computer's hardware and system software influence the runtime of a program. The CPU speed, the amount of main memory, the amount of cache, the operating system and the compiler all play significant roles. We take these into account when designing experiments to illustrate algorithm complexity. For example, if we are working with data structures, we limit their size so that they will fit into physical memory, because we know that as soon as the program starts swapping pages to virtual memory it will slow down significantly. In general, however, it is not difficult to obtain runtimes that are consistent with the underlying algorithm.

Java virtual machines impose another level of software between the program and the operating system. There are many different Java virtual machines available. This paper only discusses Sun's Hotspot virtual machine (JVM). As Java and the JVM have matured, a number of issues have arisen that make designing experiments and interpreting empirical data more difficult. Among the issues are:

1) Starting a Java application incurs a sizable cost. Processes and threads must be created and the JVM must be initialized. Library files must be opened and a fairly large set of classes must be loaded. Only then is programmer code invoked.
2) The JVM automates heap management. The heap is the area of memory where all objects are allocated. Heap management consists of controlling the size of the heap and removing objects from the heap that are no longer in use. All Java instructors know that programmers no longer need to explicitly free memory resources, as the garbage collector takes care of it for us. We also realize that garbage collection takes time. It is important that we understand how garbage collection works and the effect it can have on a program's runtime.
3) The JVM interprets byte code but also compiles byte code into native code for better performance. There are tradeoffs as compiling takes time, but the resulting native code may run significantly faster.
4) The JVM dynamically optimizes running programs. The Hotspot virtual machine takes its name from its ability to analyze a running program, find the bottlenecks, or hotspots, in the program and apply optimizations on the fly.

3. PROGRAM STARTUP

The JVM is resource intensive at program startup. As an example, consider the data presented in Figure 1. It shows the runtimes obtained when invoking `Arrays.sort()` five times in succession on random `int` arrays of size 20,000. The first invocation takes 18 milliseconds, which is more than the next four invocations combined.

Figure 1 only presents part of the picture, however. There are startup costs that are not captured by `System.currentTimeMillis()`. The operating system creates one or more processes for the virtual machine. The JVM is loaded and initialized. Standard libraries must be located and opened. Since these actions occur before the first call to `System.currentTimeMillis()`, they affect the measured elapsed time for running a Java program, but do not influence our recorded runtime and are not discussed further here.

Once the JVM is started, running an application requires loading and initializing a collection of classes. The simplest possible Java application, one with a completely empty main method, loads 280 classes during execution. Loading classes into the JVM is generally a disk-bound activity which is slow compared to CPU activities.

The high cost of the first call to `Arrays.sort()` in Figure 1 is due to loading the `Arrays` class. On the system where the data was collected, the Java libraries are installed on a file server, which slowed the class loader even further.

Frequently, when we are measuring program runtimes, we are interested in taking a series of measurements. It is best to warm up the virtual machine before we start taking collecting data. As a rule of thumb, call each method to be timed at least twice before beginning to record times.

4. HEAP MANAGEMENT

All objects in a Java program live in the JVM's heap. When an object is instantiated, memory is allocated for it in the heap. Sometime after the program finishes using an object, the memory is returned to the free portion of the heap for reallocation. Because Java is object-oriented, many objects are created during the run of even a simple Java program, making heap management important. The two most important issues related to heap management are garbage collection and heap size.

4.1 The JVM's Garbage Collector

When an object is no longer referenced by a program it becomes garbage. Unlike older programming languages, e.g. Pascal, C and C++, it is no longer the programmer's responsibility to return garbage to the heap for reuse. Instead, the JVM's garbage collector takes care of it automatically. The garbage collector finalizes each object and then returns its memory to the heap [3, 4, 5]. There are many different garbage collection algorithms, each with various strengths and weaknesses [5]. The Java Virtual Machine Specification does not indicate which algorithm(s) should be used. It is left to the virtual machine implementer to choose [6]. Sun's JVM can use different algorithms than IBM's Jikes, but both still implement correct Java virtual machines.

4.1.1 Generational Garbage Collection

Sun made its decisions about garbage collecting algorithms based on program observation. Programs allocate many objects that have very short lifetimes. These objects are instantiated, used and discarded in rapid succession. For example, the extent of an object that is local to a method is just the single invocation of that method. If the method is called again, a new object is created for the next invocation. Java programs also have many objects with much longer lifetimes. In fact, if an object survives for more than a short time, it has a high probability of having a very long lifetime. Sun organized the JVM's heap around these different categories of objects, using different garbage collection algorithms for each of them.

The JVM uses a hierarchical garbage collector. It separates the heap into Young and Tenured generations. New objects are allocated in the Young generation. Since there are many objects with very short lifetimes, the Young generation fills up quickly. Many of the objects also become garbage quickly. Minor garbage collections clean up the Young generation using an algorithm that is very fast when most of the space is garbage. If an object survives several minor garbage collections, it is moved to the Tenured generation.

The Tenured generation is garbage collected only when most of its space is used. These full garbage collections use a mark and compact algorithm that runs efficiently when there are still many objects in use. A full garbage collection still takes significantly longer to run than a minor garbage collection. It may be slowed down even further by sometimes doing extra work, like allocating more memory for the heap, if it is still too full after completing the collection.

Garbage collections take place frequently. They are generally transparent to the user, however. If an application is started with the `-verbose:gc` option information about each garbage collection is printed as it occurs. The garbage collector runs in a separate thread from the application program. It does influence the time reported by `System.currentTimeMillis()`, however, because `System.currentTimeMillis()` records elapsed time, not just time dedicated to the application.

4.1.2 Incremental Garbage Collection

The JVM contains an alternative garbage collection algorithm named incremental garbage collection. Incremental garbage collection is specified on the Java command using the `-Xincgc` option. Incremental garbage collection replaces the full garbage collection with a series of smaller steps run more frequently. Since full garbage collection, which can be very time consuming, never takes place, program runtimes are often much more consistent when using incremental garbage collection. On the other hand, incremental garbage collection can cause a performance hit to the overall runtime of the program. Sun included incremental garbage collction primarily for programs with hard deadlines. These programs cannot afford to wait for a full garbage collection to complete, but can wait for the more frequent, but faster incremental garbage collections.

4.2 Heap Size

The amount of memory dedicated to the heap is not fixed. If the heap is still relatively full after a garbage collection, more memory will be allocated to it, up to a specified maximum. The heap's initial size may be set explicitly using the `-Xms` option. The default maximum heap size is usually set so that the entire heap will still reside in main memory. The heap's maximum size may be set using the `-Xmx` option. There are no hard and fast rules for specifying the heap parameters. Specifying a large enough initial heap size can prevent the need for garbage collections in programs with small memory footprints and can delay the need for major garbage collections in others. On the other hand, large heaps take more time for garbage collection when it does occur.

4.3 The Modified MergeSort Explained

The modified MergeSort example shown in Figure 2 illustrates anomalies associated with the heap.

4.3.1 The MergeSort Data

As you recall, Figure 2 charts the runtimes for a modified MergeSort that is a $O(n^2)$ sort algorithm when implemented in Java. There are three anomalies that need explanation:

1) Why isn't the graph parabolic?
2) What is the blip at 65,000?
3) Finally, what is the discontinuity between 130,000 and 135,000?

In fact, the left portion of the data is close to parabolic. It is just that the scale of the y-axis is so perturbed that the parabola is hard to see. Figure 4 re-graphs the data from Figure 2, up to an array of size 130,000. The graph appears roughly parabolic.

There are two outlying blips in Figure 4, one at 25,000 and one at 65,000. These blips are caused by full garbage collections running very frequently. After the heap expands, full garbage collections again run less frequently and the runtimes go back down.

The discontinuity between 130,000 and 135,000 is also a garbage collection problem. Using the `-verbose:gc` option shows that there is a full garbage collection following each minor garbage collection at 135,000. The Tenured generation contains enough objects that full garbage collections take place very frequently and the entire program becomes garbage collection bound. The linux `ps` command shows the system is spending 97% of its time doing garbage collection and very little time actually sorting data.

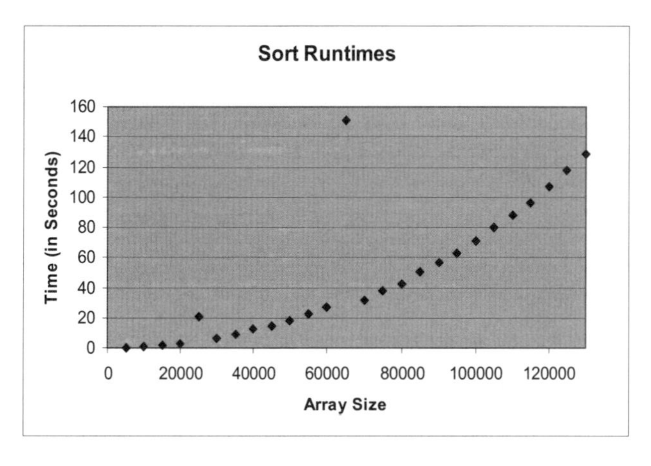

Figure 4. The initial portion of the sort data is close to a parabola.

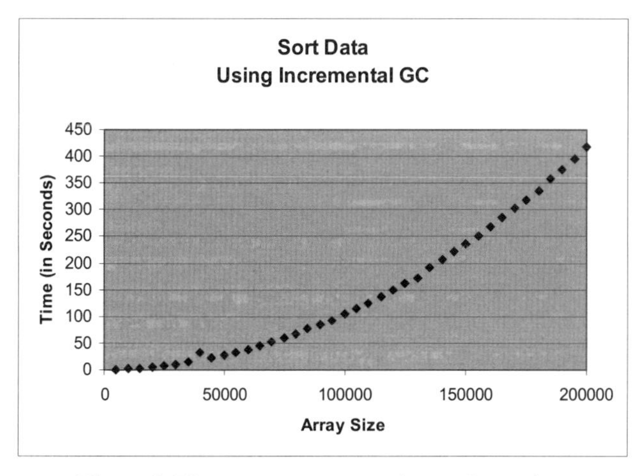

Figure 5. The sort program runtimes when using incremental garbage collection.

Figure 5 shows runtimes from the MergeSort program running with the incremental garbage collector. Recall that the incremental garbage collector is used in place of full garbage collections. Full garbage collections never take place, so the blips disappear and the full garbage collection bottleneck is gone.

5. DYNAMIC OPTIMIZATION

Sun's Hotspot JVM introduced several improvements that can also impact runtime performance.

5.1 Dynamic Compilation

The Hotspot JVM executes both byte code and native code. It takes responsibility for compiling byte code to native code when it feels the performance to be gained is worth the time spent compiling. Most methods are not compiled the first time they are called. This is because many methods are only called once, and compiling such methods would slow down the runtime considerably. While there are several different rules that govern when a method is compiled, the default behavior is to compile a method when it has been called 1500 times.

5.2 Dynamic Optimizations

The Hotspot JVM also applies dynamic optimizations to code that appears to be a bottleneck, or hotspot. Sun claims that this approach shows major advantages over static code optimizers of the type that come with languages like C++. The idea is that the virtual machine will find hotspots in the program and apply optimizations only to those areas. For example, a primary optimization is method inlining, where a method invocation is replaced by the body of the method. Polymorphism makes this very difficult to do at compile time, as any of a number of methods might be called at each invocation. At runtime, however, the JVM has additional information that may let it know which method will be invoked.

Dynamic compilation and dynamic optimizations can play important roles in improving the performance of programs with long runtimes. We have encountered them infrequently in student programs. Most of the time, programmer supplied code is compiled early enough that the runtimes collected reflect executing native code. Occasionally there will be an unexplained blip in runtimes that can be attributed to dynamic optimizations, but the JVM does not give us an easy way to capture when this is occurring.

5.3 Rehashing Explained

The rehashing experiment created and populated a `Hashtable` with `Integers` and timed how long it took to rehash. The runtimes for various numbers of `Integers` were shown in Figure 3. There is one major anomaly in the data. When the number of elements in the `Hashtable` grows large enough, the program actually speeds up. Both segments of the graph illustrate close to linear behavior, but the program runs faster and the slope of the line is much less steep for the larger data sets. This is completely due to dynamic optimizations. The JVM inlined method calls and applied other optimizations when approximately 90% of its time was taken up by rehashing. The improvement in performance is dramatic.

Rehashing is a memory intensive process. While the rehashing is taking place there are two hash tables in existence, the old one from which data is being removed and the new one to which data is being inserted. In this example, full garbage collections were frequently taking place when the heap was small, because more space was needed. As the program runs, the heap grows larger, making garbage collection less frequent and increasing the time spent on rehashing. We can obtain improved performance more quickly by starting with a larger heap. Figure 6 shows runtimes for the same program as Figure 3, but with the initial heap size set to 500 Megabytes. Incremental garbage collection was not used. The graph displays the linear behavior consistent with the right hand segment in Figure 3.

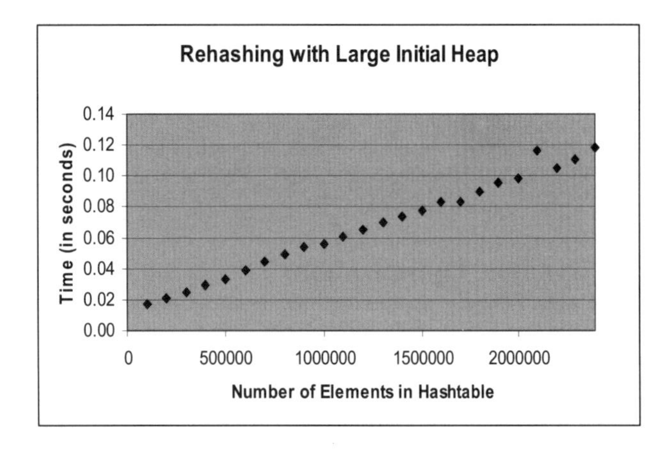

Figure 6. Runtimes obtained by rehashing program when using a large initial heap.

6. CONCLUSIONS

In this paper we have explained three major causes of runtime anomalies in Java programs: program startup consideration, heap management and dynamic optimizations. Our approach is still ad hoc, however. Each time we encounter runtimes in a student program that don't reflect the underlying algorithm, we start from scratch looking for possible causes. Our long term goal is to develop a clear, simple set of instructions for our students so that they can perform runtime experiments on their own and obtain meaningful results.

Source code for all examples presented in this paper is available from the author.

7. REFERENCES

[1] Armstrong, E., *HotSpot: A New Breed of Virtual Machine*, Java World, March 1998. Available on-line at http://www.javaworld.com/javaworld/jw-03-1998/jw-03-hotspot_p.html.

[2] Braught, G., Miller, C., and Reed, D., *Core Empirical Concepts and Skills for Computer Science,* Proceedings of the Thirty-Fifth SIGCSE Technical Symposim on Computer Science Education, Norfolk, VA, March 3-7, 2004.

[3] Goetz, B., *Java Theory and Practice: A Brief History of Garbage Collection*, DeveloperWorks, IBM, October 2003. Available on-line at http://www-106.ibm.com/developerworks/java/library/j-jtp10283.

[4] Goetz, B., *Java Theory and Practice: Garbage Collection in the 1.4.1 JVM*, DeveloperWorks, IBM, November 2003, Available on-line at http://www-106.ibm.com/devloperworks/java/library/j-jtp11253.

[5] Jones, R., Lins, R., *Garbage Collection: Algorithms for Automatic dynamic Memory Management,* John Wiley and Sons, New York, NY, 1996.

[6] Lindholm, T. and Yellin, F., *The Java Virtual Machine Specification, Second Edition,* Addison-Wesley, Boston, MA, 2003.

[7] Reed, D., moderator, *Integrating Empirical Methods into Computer Science,* Proceedings of the Thirty-Third SIGCSE Technical Symposium on Computer Science Education, Covington, KY, February 27-March 3, 2002.

[8] Shirazi, J., *Java Performance Tuning,* O'Reilly and Associates, Sebastopol, CA, 2000.

[9] Venners, B., *The Hotspot Virtual Machine: How Hotspot Can Improve Java Program Performance and Designs*, Developer.com, May 1998. Available on-line at http://www.artima.com/desingtechniques/hotspotP.html.

[10] Wilson, S. and Kesselman, J., *Java Platform Performance: Strategies and Tactics,* Addison-Wesley, Boston, MA, 2000.

Teaching Empirical Skills and Concepts in Computer Science using Random Walks

Grant Braught
Dickinson College
Department of Mathematics and Computer Science
Carlisle, PA 17013
717-245-1401
braught@Dickinson.edu

ABSTRACT
An argument is made for integrating the study of empirical skills and concepts into the computer science curriculum. With reference to past work an incremental approach is advocated for the study of these skills and concepts. A unique assignment that exemplifies the advocated approach is presented. This assignment, based on the study of random walks, is intended to introduce empirical investigation as early as is possible, during the first week of the first course. Two extensions to this assignment, one for the first course and one for a programming languages course, are discussed and used to illustrate the advocated incremental approach.

Categories and Subject Descriptors
K.3.2 [**Computers and Education**]: Computer and Information Science Education — *computer science education, curriculum.* G.3 [**Probability and Statistics**].

General Terms
Experimentation, Languages.

Keywords
Empirical concepts, empirical skills, random walk, turtle graphics.

1. INTRODUCTION
From software engineering [1] to the design of human-computer interfaces [5] to the validation of new hardware designs [11] the problems faced by computer scientists are becoming increasingly empirical in nature. This fact combined with a traditionally poor track record for experimentation [20, 18] has led to calls for better and more extensive experimentation by computer scientists [17]. The Computing Curricula 2001 [7], recognizing this need and the role of educators in addressing it, advocates that students receive a "solid exposure" to the scientific method. Indeed, individual computer science educators have also recognized this need and many have incorporated empirical studies into course projects. In particular, the literature contains reports of projects involving experimentation at the introductory level [8, 12, 13], in operating systems [6, 15], architecture and organization [2], human-computer interaction [5, 10], software engineering [1] and scientific programming [19].

Despite these efforts the words of Paul Schneck, founding director of the Super Computing Research Center, still ring true:

> *Many (most?) students of computer science are not educated as scientists. They are trained as programmers. This results in a situation, reflected in our literature, where many practitioners form unstructured phenomenological inferences instead of creating models, forming hypotheses, and performing experiments to validate (or invalidate) the hypotheses and models. [11]*

In an effort to address this situation David Reed, Craig Miller and I recently advocated a more systematic approach. We argued that all computer science students should be exposed to a core set of empirical skills and concepts [3]. In addition, we have argued that, like important computer science concepts, empirical skills and concepts should be introduced early and revisited often to facilitate students' mastery of them [14, 15]. Further, we have advocated a progressively rigorous introduction of empirical skills and concepts. This approach encourages students to develop intuition about concepts during introductory courses before encountering more formal or mathematical definitions in their intermediate and advanced courses.

In earlier papers [3, 4, 11, 12, 14] we have described sample assignments that illustrate the above approach. The assignments described in those papers highlight the progressively rigorous introduction of empirical skills and concepts. Those assignments also demonstrate how this content can be added to an already full curriculum with only a small marginal cost. As part of an NSF funded project to develop and disseminate materials supporting this approach, we have created an on-line repository of classroom-tested assignments with empirical content (See: http://empirical.cs.creighton.edu). Cover sheets for each assignment in the repository indicates not only the core empirical skills and concepts that each assignment addresses but also where it fits within a traditional computing curriculum.

This paper presents an in depth discussion of the "Exploring Random Walks" assignment that can be found in our repository. This assignment is based on earlier assignments created by David Reed [13] that also have students conduct experiments modeling random walks by using turtle graphics. The "Exploring Random

SIGCSE '05, February 23–27, 2005, St. Louis, Missouri, USA.

Walks" assignment discussed here builds on the ideas from these earlier assignments, introducing more formal treatments of the empirical concepts of accuracy and consistency. In addition, the new assignment addresses the relationships between consistency, accuracy, data distributions and hypothesis testing through the use of a new piece of pedagogical software.

The "Exploring Random Walks" assignment, like other assignments described in our earlier papers, clearly illustrates the incremental approach that we are advocating. Beyond this illustration, there are also several other unique aspects of this assignment that justify its extended discussion here. First, this assignment introduces empirical inquiry as early as is possible – during the first week of the first course in computer science. By introducing empirical inquiry early, the groundwork is laid for future assignments with empirical content. Further, early introduction helps to firmly establish in the minds of the students the central role of empirical investigation in the computing disciplines. Second, because lab periods during the first week of school are often underutilized, this assignment provides a way to introduce empirical skills and concepts while minimizing the impact on the coverage of traditional CS topics. Third, the supporting software for the "Exploring Random Walks" assignment has been structured to allow for several carefully planned extensions; one later in the first course and another in a subsequent programming languages course. These extensions provide natural opportunities for students to revisit and expand upon the empirical skills and concepts introduced earlier. In addition, because they address CS topics that most likely already to appear in class projects, they again demonstrate how empirical studies can be integrated into existing courses with a minimum of effort.

The remainder of this paper has the following organization. Section 2 describes the "Exploring Random Walks" assignment along with the Java applet that supports it. Section 3 discusses how extensions of this assignment can be used later in an objects first CS course and also in a programming languages course. Finally, Section 4 provides some brief concluding remarks.

2. EXPLORING RANDOM WALKS

The primary objective of the "Exploring Random Walks" assignment is to expose students to the empirical skills and concepts most critical to performing experiments with simulations. In particular, consistency, accuracy, the effects that averaging multiple trials has on them, and a rudimentary form of hypothesis testing are explored. The primary vehicle for exploring these concepts is the Random Walks Application (RWapp) shown in figure 1. Students use this Java applet to write small turtle graphics programs that simulate random walks (Section 2.1). They then explore the effect of averaging multiple walks on the accuracy of experimental results (Section 2.2). Students then examine distributions of experimental results, highlighting the relationship between accuracy, consistency and the effect of averaging multiple walks (Section 2.3). Finally, they form hypotheses about two different types of random walk and perform an experiment to test their hypotheses (Section 2.4).

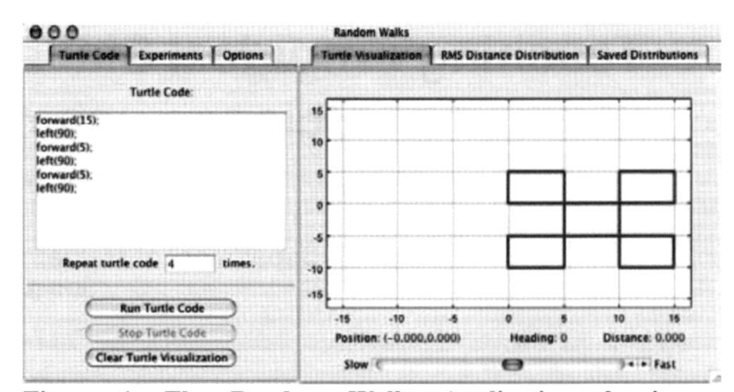

Figure 1: The Random Walks Application showing a geometric figure that students use to learn about the turtle graphics language.

2.1 Turtle Graphics

The RWapp supports the subset of the turtle graphics language shown in Table 1. To familiarize students with this language they begin by writing several short programs that create line drawings and simple geometric figures (see Figure 1 for an example). These programs are written by entering instructions into the text area on the "Turtle Code" tab as shown in Figure 1. The "Turtle Code" tab also contains a text field for specifying the number of times the turtle code is to be repeated. As the turtle code is executed the graph on the "Turtle Visualization" tab shows a live visualization of the turtle's path.

Once students are familiar with the turtle graphics language, they are asked to write a program that simulates a random walk. They are instructed that each step in the walk should cause the turtle to turn randomly to one of 360 possible directions and then take one step forward. They are also instructed that the random walk should consist of 100 steps. They then use this program to investigate the ideas of consistency and accuracy as described in the following sections.

Table 1: Subset of the turtle graphics language supported by the Random Walks Application.

Command
`forward(<steps>)` Move the turtle forward by `<steps>` steps.
`left(<deg>)` Rotate the turtle heading left by `<deg>` degrees.
`right(<deg>)` Rotate the turtle heading right by `<deg>` degrees.
`randomInt(<low>,<high>)` Return a random integer in [`<low>`,`<high>`).
`randomOneOf([<i1>,<i2>,…,<in>])` Return one of the listed integers selected at random.

2.2 Accuracy

One property of random walks that can be studied is the distance between the starting and ending points of the walk (i.e. its net distance). For the random walk programmed by the students, it is known that the expected value of the root mean square (RMS) distance is the square root of the number of steps in the walk [9]. Thus, because there is a known theoretical value for the RMS distance it is a natural quantity to use in an investigation of the effects of averaging multiple trials on the accuracy of the results.

Figure 2 shows the RWapp setup to perform an experiment that computes the RMS distance of a set of five walks. The Runs/Experiment text field controls the number of random walks in the experiment. The Experiments field allows for multiple experiments to be run in succession and its usefulness will be discussed in the next section. When an experiment is run, the turtle visualization is cleared prior to each walk and the turtle starts each walk at the origin. After the experiment is complete the RMS distance for the set of walks is reported.

Students are asked to use the familiar percent error calculation to compare the accuracy of results obtained from experiments consisting of 1, 5 and 20 walks. This exercise confirms the students' expectations that using more runs tends to produce more accurate results. Though, the students are also pushed to recognize that more runs does not universally yield more accurate results. While this recognition seems to trouble many of them, the activities described in Section 2.3 help them in gaining insights into why this is the case.

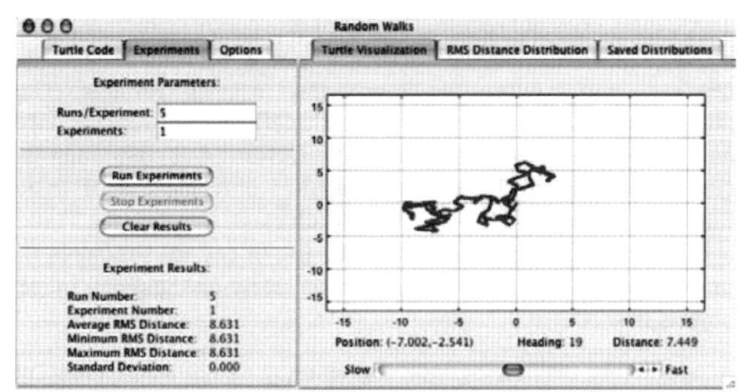

Figure 2: The Random Walks Application configured to measure the RMS distance of a set of 5 walks.

2.3 Consistency

While most students entering the first CS course can tell you that averaging more trials will generate more accurate results, few can articulate why they believe this to be true. Further, many students believe that when increasing the number of trials fails to yield a more accurate result they have done something wrong. This belief is exemplified by the fact that after performing the experiments described in the previous section, students have frequently asked if they should perform them again until they get the "right" result! The activities in this section are designed to combat this belief by examining the effect of averaging multiple runs on the consistency of experimental results and the relationship between consistency and accuracy.

Students begin by examining the distribution of results from 50 experiments each consisting of 1 walk. The RWapp, as shown in Figure 3, simplifies this process by displaying a histogram of the results on the "RMS Distance Distribution" tab. Students compare this distribution with ones they obtain from 50 experiments consisting of 5 walks and 50 experiments consisting of 20 walks. The RWapp facilitates this comparison by allowing distributions to be saved for later review, as shown in Figure 4.

Comparing the distributions shown in Figures 3 and 4 illustrates the striking difference in distributions observed by the students. The students are asked to state which distribution represents more consistent data and to describe why. They then formalize this intuitive visual sense of consistency in two ways. First they examine the range of the data as a percentage of the mean, finding that this measure agrees with their visual intuition. Second, they are introduced to standard deviation and observe that the standard deviations reported by the RWapp agree both with their visual sense of consistency and their calculations of the range as a percentage of the mean.

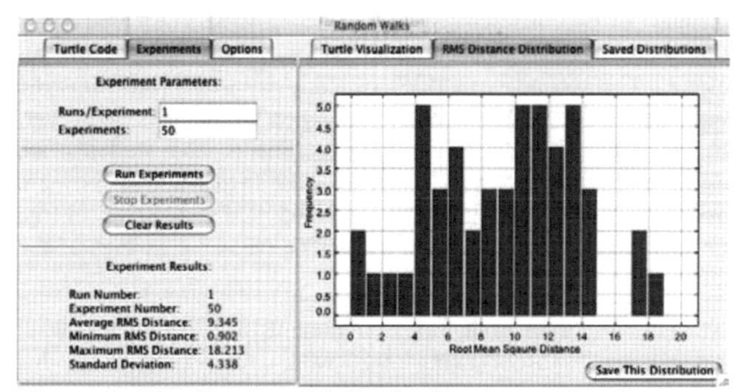

Figure 3: The Random Walks Application makes it easy to conduct a set of experiments and observe the distribution of results.

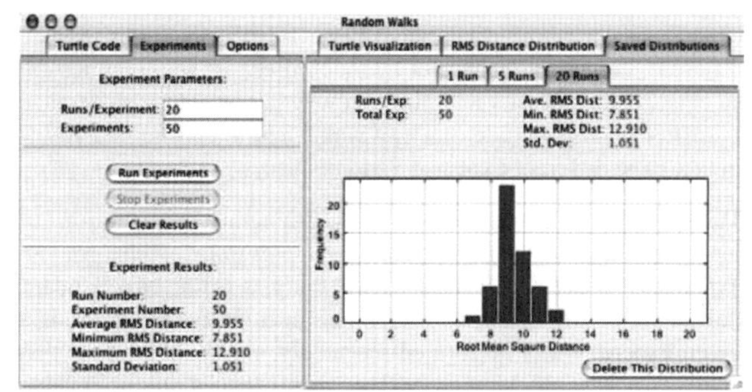

Figure 4: The Random Walks Application allows distributions to be saved making it easy to perform comparisons.

It is important to note that at this point students are not asked to compute the standard deviation, or even to understand how it is computed. Rather, they are only asked to understand that it is a measure of consistency and that *most* of the results lie within plus or minus one standard deviation. Consistent with the approach we have advocated, this early informal treatment is intended to plant the seeds for a later more formal presentation of standard deviation.

After exploring the effects of the number of runs on consistency, students are presented with several exercises to help them relate the concepts of consistency and accuracy. First they are asked to count the number of experiments that give results within 10% of the expected value for each number of runs (1, 5, 20). Based on this data they are asked to draw a conclusion about the relationship between the number of runs performed in an experiment, the consistency of the results and the likelihood of producing accurate results (i.e. within 10% of the expected value). At this point most students have begun to realize that increasing the number of runs that are averaged does not guarantee anything, but that it simply increases the likelihood of obtaining an accurate result (or conversely that it decreases the likelihood of obtaining an outlier result). Of course this relationship can be dramatically affected by the presence of systematic error. This issue is addressed by a discussion of the effect of systematic errors and program bugs as a primary source of such errors in simulation experiments.

2.4 Hypothesis Testing

The final portion of the "Exploring Random Walks" assignment asks students to experimentally compare the expected RMS distance of two different types of random walk. The first type is the *unconstrained random walk* that they have been using all along. The second type, often called a *city walk*, constrains the turn between each step to be 0, 90, 180 or 270 degrees. However, before actually conducting any experiments, the students are asked to form a hypothesis to be tested. In particular, they are asked to predict whether the expected RMS distance of the unconstrained walk is longer, shorter or the same as that of the city walk.

After making their prediction, the students perform 50 city walk experiments each consisting of 20 walks. Of course, to do this they must first write turtle graphics code that simulates a city walk. After this code is written and the experiments performed, they are asked to compare the average RMS distance of the 50 unconstrained walk experiments to that of their city walk experiments. In all likelihood these two RMS distances are different, though probably not by much. Because these values are so close, most students will question whether or not the difference is sufficient to conclude that city walks and unconstrained walks in fact have different expected RMS distances.

To help the students resolve this ambiguity, the notion of plausible values is introduced. A *plausible value* for an experiment is defined to be any value that lies within two standard deviations of the mean for that experiment. In other words, if a given experiment is performed repeatedly, we should expect that nearly every result obtained (95% of them) to be a plausible value for the experiment. Or conversely, we should expect it to be rare for an experiment to yield a result that is not a plausible value for the experiment.

This notion of plausible values forms the basis for a rudimentary hypothesis test. The students are asked to determine the range of plausible values for their two experiments. They are then asked to determine if the RMS distance for the city walk is a plausible value for an unconstrained walk and vice versa. If the RMS distance for the city walks experiment is a plausible value for the unconstrained walks experiment and vice versa, the students are lead to reject any hypothesis stating that the two types of walks have different expected RMS distances. Conversely, if either RMS distance is not a plausible value for the other experiment, then the students are lead to reject any hypothesis stating that the walks have the same expected RMS distance.

Clearly, this form of hypothesis testing is rudimentary. Its purpose is only to bring the students to the realization that considering the distributions of data can help to provide more convincing arguments than simply comparing mean values. As with the earlier informal introduction of standard deviation, this introduction serves not as an end point but rather as a way to set the stage for a more formal treatment later in the curriculum (see Sections 3.2 for one possibility).

3. ASSIGNMENT EXTENSIONS

The Random Walks Application has been designed in such a way that two classes contained within it can be used as independent assignments. A class representing the turtle can be used as an early assignment in an objects first CS1 course. A class encapsulating the interpreter for the turtle graphics language makes an ideal assignment for a programming languages course. The following sub-sections provide a brief description of each of these assignments and how they can be used to revisit or formalize previously introduced empirical skills and concepts, or to introduce new ones.

3.1 A First Objects First Assignment

Within the RWapp there is a class named Turtle that represents the turtle by maintaining its current position and heading. This Turtle class also provides accessor methods for accesing the turtle's x and y coordinates, its heading and its distance from the origin. In addition, there are mutator methods for moving the turtle forward, rotating it left or right and resetting it to the origin.

Careful consideration reveals that the implementation of the Turtle class does not require the use of any control structures. The accessor methods for the turtle's x and y coordinates and its heading simply return the appropriate instance variable. The mutator methods for rotating the turtle left or right require only modular arithmetic. Moving the turtle forward and computing its current distance from the origin requires only the use of basic functions available in the java.lang.Math class. Because the Turtle class can be implemented without the use of control structures its implementation is well suited for an early assignment in an objects first course.

In addition to making a good programming assignment, revisiting the RWapp later in the first course has some benefits for teaching empirical skills and concepts. For example, having introduced the idea of standard deviation earlier in the semester, this assignment might provide an opportunity to introduce its formal mathematical definition. Alternatively, the earlier experience gained with consistency could be used to gain insight into how to answer the question of how many trials are enough when performing an experiment? Another option would be to divide the empirical content of the "Exploring Random Walks" assignment into two, doing the first half at the beginning of the semester and the second half in conjunction with implementing the Turtle class.

3.2 A Parser/Interpreter Assignment

The RWapp delegates the validation and execution of the turtle graphics code to a class named TurtleInterpreter. This class, as its name suggests, encapsulates an interpreter for the turtle graphics language. Each time the turtle graphics code is executed the program statements in the Turtle Code text area (see Figure 1) are passed to a method in the TurtleInterpreter. This method checks the syntax of the statements and if all of the statements are syntactically correct they are executed, otherwise an error message is displayed.

The implementation of the syntax checker and interpreter make an ideal assignment for a programming languages course. The students could be given a grammar for the turtle graphics language, or they could develop the grammar from a description of the language. It is also possible to create an entirely new language, as the functionality of the RWapp does not depend on the specifics of the language. Rather it depends only on the fact that the TurtleInterpreter class properly interprets and executes the language that is used. This opens the door to including things such as variables, assignments, arithmetic expressions, conditional execution, iteration and function calls.

As with the assignment discussed in Section 3.1, this assignment also provides an excellent opportunity for revisiting and formalizing empirical skills and concepts introduced earlier. Here the most likely candidate is to formalize the informal approach to hypothesis testing described in Section 2.4 by introducing z-scores and t-tests. A nice twist at this point is to have the students form and test a hypothesis regarding the relative RMS distances of the unconstrained random walk and a one-dimensional random walk. Quite surprisingly these two types of walk also have the same expected RMS distance (but different standard deviations)!

4. CONCLUSION

A brief argument, with reference to prior work, was presented for integrating the study of empirical skills and concepts into the computer science curriculum. The "Exploring Random Walks" assignment and the associated Random Walks applet were presented as a way to introduce several empirical skills and concepts critical to experimenting with simulations. Particular attention was paid to the ideas of consistency, accuracy, the effects of averaging multiple trials and hypothesis testing. In addition, several extensions to the assignment were discussed that provide opportunity to expand upon and formalize some of these ideas later in the curriculum.

As mentioned earlier the assignment presented here was developed as part of an ongoing project (See: http://empirical.cs.creighton.edu). Continuing work on this project includes the creation of additional new assignments and materials. These new assignments and materials will address different empirical skills and concepts and will be targeted at use at a variety of points in the computer science curriculum. In addition, the existing assignments are being continually revised based on classroom testing. Finally, an effort is beginning that will conduct an assessment of the effectiveness of these assignments in terms of how well they address the targeted empirical skills and concepts as well as the ease with which they are integrated into existing computer science courses.

5. ACKNOWLEDGMENTS

Partial support for this work was provided by the National Science Foundation's Course, Curriculum, and Laboratory Improvement Program under grant DUE-0230950.

6. REFERENCES

[1] Basili, V. R. (1996). "The role of experimentation in software engineering: past, current, and future." *IEEE Proceedings of ICSE 18.*

[2] Bem, E. Z. (2002). "Experiment-based project in undergraduate computer architecture." *SIGCSE Bulletin* **34**(1): 171-175.

[3] Braught, G., Miller, C. S. and Reed, D. (2004). "Core Empirical Concepts and Skills for Computer Science." *SIGCSE Bulletin* **36**(1): 245-249.

[4] Braught, G. and Reed, D. (2002). "Disequilibration for Teaching the Scientific Method in Computer Science." *SIGCSE Bulletin* **34**(1): 106-110.

[5] Clarke, M. C. (1998). "Teaching the empirical approach to designing human-computer interaction via and experimental design group project." *SIGCSE Bulletin* **30**(1): 316-320.

[6] Downey, A. (1999). "Teaching Experimental Design in an Operating Systems Class." *SIGCSE Bulletin* **31**(1): 316-320.

[7] Joint IEEE Computer Society/ACM Task Force for CC2001 (2001). "Computing Curricula 2001." Online at http://www.sigcse.org/cc2001/.

[8] Laxer, C. (2001). "Treating Computer Science as Science: An Experiment with Sorting." *Proceedings of ITICE '01*, 189.

[9] McCrea, W. and Whipple, F. (1940). "Random Paths in Two and Three Dimensions." *Proceedings of the Royal Society of Edinburgh* **60**: 281-298.

[10] Miller, C. S. (2003). "Relating Theory to Actual Results in Computer Science and Human-Computer Interaction." *Computer Science Education* **13**(3): 227-240.

[11] Mudge, T. (1996). "Report on the panel: How can computer architecture researchers avoid becoming a society for irreproducible results" *Computer Architecture News* **24**(1): 1-5.

[12] Reed, D. (2001). "Developing Empirical Skills in an Introductory Computer Science Course." Proceeding of the 34th Midwest Instruction and Computing Symposium. Online at http://www.creighton.edu/~davereed/Papers/Developing.pdf

[13] Reed, D. (2002). "The Use of Ill-Defined Problems for Developing Problem-Solving and Empirical Skills in CS1." *Journal of Computing Sciences in Colleges* **18**(1): 121-133.

[14] Reed, D., Miller, C. S. and Braught, G. (2000). "Empirical Investigation throughout the CS Curriculum." *SIGCSE Bulletin* **32**(1): 202-206.

[15] Reed, D., Baldwin, D., Clancy, M., Hansen, S. and Downey, A. (2002). "Panel: Integrating Empirical Methods into CS." *SIGCSE Bulletin* **34**(1): 48-49.

[16] Robbins, S., and Robbins, K. (1999). "Empirical exploration in undergraduate operating systems." *SIGCSE Bulletin* **31**(1): 311-315.

[17] Tichy, W. (1998). "Should computer scientists experiment more?" *Computer* **31**(5): 32-40.

[18] Tichy, W., Lukowicz, P., Prechel, L. and Heinz, E. (1995). "Experimentation and Evaluatoin in Computer Science: A quantitative study." *Journal of Systems and Software* **28**: 1-18.

[19] Zachary, J. (1997). "The Gestalt of Scientific Programming: Problem, Model, Method, Implementation, Assessment." *SIGCSE Bulletin* **29**(1): 238-242.

[20] Zelkowitz, M. V., and Wallace, D. R. (1998). "Experimental models for validating technology." *Computer* **31**(5): 23-31.

Special Session Proposal
The ACM Java Task Force: Status Report

Eric Roberts (chair)
Stanford University
eroberts@cs.stanford.edu

Kim Bruce
Williams College
kim@cs.williams.edu

Rob Cutler
The Harker School
robbc@harker.org

James H. Cross II
Auburn University
cross@eng.auburn.edu

Scott Grissom
Grand Valley State University
grissom@gvsu.edu

Karl Klee
Alfred State College
kleekj@alfredstate.edu

Susan Rodger
Duke University
rodger@cs.duke.edu

Fran Trees
Drew University
fran@ftrees.com

Ian Utting
University of Kent
i.a.utting@kent.ac.uk

Frank Yellin
Sun Microsystems
frank.yellin@sun.com

SUMMARY
SIGCSE 2004 marked the official announcement of the ACM Java Task Force, which is working to develop a stable collection of pedagogical resources that will make it easier to teach Java to first-year computing students. The Java Task Force has received funding from the ACM Education Board, the SIGCSE Special Projects Fund, and the National Science Foundation (NSF Award DUE-0411905). This session offers an update on the work of the Java Task Force over the past year and provides an opportunity for community feedback prior to the publication of the final report in June 2005.

Categories and Subject Descriptors
K.3.2 [**Computer and Information Science Education**]: computer science education, curriculum.

General Terms
design

Keywords
Computer science education, CS1, teaching libraries, Java.

1. SPECIAL SESSION DESCRIPTION
Since its introduction in 1995, the use of Java as an instructional language has shown a steady increase. At the same time, those who have tried to teach Java have identified a number of problems in the language in terms of its suitability for students, particularly at the introductory level [1]. Concern about these problems prompted the ACM Education Board to create the ACM Java Task Force with the following charter:

> To review the Java language, APIs, and tools from the perspective of introductory computing education and to develop a stable collection of pedagogical resources that will make it easier to teach Java to first-year computing students without having those students overwhelmed by its complexity.

The Java Task Force was announced at SIGCSE 2004 and has been meeting throughout the past year. A paper outlining the rationale behind the task force [2] and a summary of the goals and timetable [3] appeared in the SIGCSE 2004 proceedings.

At this year's special session, we will give a brief presentation covering of the highlights of the preliminary Java Task Force report. The presentation will be followed by an extensive feedback session in which we will listen to comments from the SIGCSE community. The preliminary report will be out at the end of December 2004, which means that the audience at the special session will have had two months to read and reflect on the proposed design. The feedback that we get at the meeting will provide useful guidance for the task force as we prepare to publish our final report in June 2005.

The Java Task Force reports and associated materials are available from the following URL:

http://www.acm.org/education/jtf/

2. EXPECTATIONS
The intended audience for the special session consists of computer science teachers who use—or are planning to use—Java in first-year computer science courses. Although most SIGCSE attendees teach at colleges and universities, we believe that this special session will have particular relevance to high-school teachers.

The feedback that we get at SIGCSE is essential to producing a report that has the support of the community. In part, we expect the comments, questions, and concerns that come up at the

SIGCSE'05, February 23–27, 2005, St. Louis, Missouri, USA.
ACM 1-58113-997-7/05/0002

meeting will help us refine our proposals so that they better serve the needs of people who are, if you will, in the trenches teaching Java to novices. At the same time, having an open process and providing opportunities for feedback are essential to developing the community support that is essential to the success of the project.

REFERENCES

1. ACM Java Task Force. Taxonomy of problems in teaching Java, February 2004.
2. Eric Roberts. The dream of a common language: The search for simplicity and stability in computer science education. Proceedings of the 35th SIGCSE Technical Symposium on Computer Science Education, Norfolk, VA, March 2004.
3. Eric Roberts. Resources to support the use of Java in introductory computer science. Proceedings of the 35th SIGCSE Technical Symposium on Computer Science Education, Norfolk, VA, March 2004.

Design Patterns for Database Pedagogy – A Proposal

Thomas J. Marlowe
Seton Hall University
Dept. of Math and Computer Science
South Orange, NJ 07079, USA
973-761-9784
marlowto@shu.edu

Cyril S. Ku
William Paterson University
Department of Computer Science
Wayne, NJ 07470, USA
973-720-3719
kuc@wpunj.edu

James W. Benham
Montclair State University
Department of Computer Science
Montclair, NJ 07043, USA
973-655-7249
benham@pegasus.montclair.edu

ABSTRACT
Courses in Relational Databases largely use a domain-specific design approach different from that used in the rest of the curriculum. Use of the Unified Process, UML, and Design Patterns as a pedagogical approach for Databases can leverage previous student experience with design, make knowledge from Database courses more immediately relevant elsewhere, and create greater continuity across the curriculum. This approach allows issues in logical design and in implementation to be more easily connected with similar concerns in other courses (for example, Software Engineering), and supports greater and easier transfer of design between Relational and Object-Oriented Databases, and between databases and embedding applications.

Categories and Subject Descriptors
D.2.2 [Design Tools and Techniques]: Object-oriented design methods. **D.2.11 [Software Architectures]:** Patterns. **H.2.1** [**Database Management**]: Logical Design – *Data models.*

General Terms: Design.

Keywords: Database, Database Design, Design Pattern, UML, Unified Process.

1. INTRODUCTION
The growing importance of design considerations for large applications, driven by both technical and economic considerations, make design a major issue in all practically-oriented courses in computer science and information technology. A common and standardized approach to design will aid students' acquisition of both knowledge and concepts. The UML specification language [3, 15] is now the standard design syntax, and the Unified Process [7] the standard approach in software engineering. Most students will have seen UML, sometimes even in 1st- or 2nd-year computer science courses. UML is also migrating to other courses; in particular, recent database texts and technical works (for example, [4, 10]) now include UML as an alternative for, or in preference to, ER and EER notation. *Design Patterns* [5,8], which capture common idioms, patterns, and guidelines in the software design and development process, are a more recent development [at least in their current formulation], and not yet universal in software engineering texts, but are certain to become so in the next few years. Design patterns are useful in software engineering courses not only for structuring large projects, but also to suggest complex concerns, or to make connections between topics in a few strokes. Examples in [5] also show applicability to other areas, including networking, graphics, and systems programming.

Design patterns can also be of great use in database courses, particularly if they have been used throughout the curriculum. The cost of their introduction is recovered when a pattern simplifies or clarifies an explanation, facilitates communication, or applies to a design challenge, and in addition is amortized across the curriculum. This repeated use also assures that most students come out of the computer science major with a good feel for design and for this suite of tools.

There are several direct benefits for database courses. First, their use results in a more structured and standard project implementation; used together with UML and the Unified Process, the result is a greater design emphasis and better group project interaction, without requiring a simpler project. Second, a wide range of database issues and concepts are readily illustrated and understood using patterns and UML, allowing students to make connections with similar concepts in other courses. Third, use of UML and patterns provides a common vocabulary and notation, allowing exams and problem sets to ask more complex, more precisely-defined, and more open-ended questions, while allowing students resources and guidelines in conceptualizing, formulating, and expressing their answers. Finally, recent work [17] suggests that working with design patterns, even for relative novices, results in better and faster design. Since many of the design improvements will translate naturally to the relational database world, this should result in better database design.

Two caveats: First, we are proposing a *pedagogical* approach; we are not suggesting that industrial database design immediately switch to a UML/Design Pattern approach (although the translation back to more conventional database notation is relatively straightforward), nor that database implementation be changed to follow an object-oriented paradigm. Second, while this paper examines the use of generic design patterns, these should be complemented by use of database-specific and other domain-specific (for example, transaction management) patterns.
The rest of this paper is organized as follows. In Section 2, we briefly overview design patterns, and in Section 3 show how they

occur naturally (and sometimes surprisingly) in database design and system implementation, and suggest how patterns might be used in teaching and testing. (A more comprehensive list will be available in an extended version at http://cs.wpunj.edu/~kuc/dp.html.) Section 4 introduces a sample project and discusses three possible subprojects emphasizing design, table and query realization, and system implementation, respectively, indicating the advantages of using design patterns in the course. Finally, Section 5 briefly discusses related work, and Section 6 gives our conclusions.

2. AN OVERVIEW OF DESIGN PATTERNS

Design patterns provide a standardized approach for specifying the toolbox of recurrent guidelines and patterns that are a major part of a software architecture methodology [18] for object-oriented design. Larman's GRASP patterns [8] provide general guidelines for assigning responsibilities to classes. In contrast, the "Gang-of-Four" Design Patterns in [5] are building-block patterns that provide design and code scaffolding. We are dealing with building-block patterns.

In their seminal book [5], Gamma, *et al.*, describe a design pattern as the general outline of a solution to a commonly occurring problem that can be reused over and over. A design pattern has four essential elements:

(1) a *pattern name* that allows efficient communication about the pattern—in fact, we will be referring to patterns by name in the balance of this paper,
(2) a problem statement that describes in general terms when to apply the pattern,
(3) a solution that "describes the elements that make up the design, their relationships, responsibilities, and collaborations," and
(4) consequences of applying the pattern, including trade-offs.

Using design patterns often incurs costs in terms of space and time, but increases the flexibility, extensibility, and maintainability of the system. There are three varieties of patterns in [5]: Creational, Structural, and Behavioral.

Creational patterns separate the creation of objects or classes from their use in the system. For example, *Builder* separates the construction of a complex object from the creation of the simpler components that comprise it. In particular, one creates an interface *Builder* with a method to build each type of component. Concrete subclasses build components for the specific system. A *Director* calls the *Builder* to create the components needed for a complex object.

Structural patterns provide ways to combine classes or objects into larger structures. Many of these patterns provide a uniform interface between a complex object or class structure and the rest of the system. For example, the *Adapter* pattern converts the interface of a server class to the interface that its clients expect. This allows the developer to easily adapt the system to different server classes. Another structural pattern, *Proxy,* represents a surrogate that controls access to another object. Proxies have multiple uses, including: allowing requests to a real object in a different address space (remote proxies), caching information about the real object to postpone accessing it (virtual proxies), or checking that the caller has permission to execute a request (protection proxies).

Behavioral patterns deal with the collaboration and communication among objects to achieve some desired behavior of the system. For example, the *Observer* pattern supports dependent objects: when a principal object changes state (and an appropriate trigger condition is met), its dependent objects are notified and updated automatically. Another behavioral pattern, *Iterator,* decouples access to an aggregate object's contents from its internal structure. This allows one to vary the structure of the aggregate without having to rewrite code for objects that access its contents, improving maintainability and extensibility.

3. DESIGN PATTERNS IN DATABASES

3.1 Database Design

Design patterns show up in database design in both obvious and surprising ways. Among the more evident examples:

- *Command*, which supports the *undo* of operations, can be used together with *Proxy* to enforce domain and key constraints (including referential integrity) by rejecting or modifying illegal updates. *Proxy* can also be used for access control.
- *Memento*, which allows access to old state, can be used (possibly together with *Proxy*) to model transactions.

Somewhat less evident, but more useful:

- Maintained views are really *Observers* of the tables referenced in their defining queries. Data warehouses and data marts can likewise be viewed as Observers of sets of databases and or a data warehouse, respectively, using *Mediator* to handle the more complex deferred triggers.
- Unions and subclasses in relational databases admit of a number of different table and query realizations, with various tradeoffs. Use of *State* or *Strategy* allows a uniform approach to be used in high-level design, deferring the decision or allowing off-line or even on-line changes in structure. Specific realizations of unions may be instances of various patterns, such as *Decorator* (shared attributes in base relation, differing attributes decorating the various sets) or *Observer* again (the union stored in a common table, and the subsets isolated from it).

3.2 Database Implementation

Design patterns can also be used to express concerns in database implementation; this is helpful even if (or especially if) course projects do not touch the implementation layer.

- *Proxy* and *Memento* can also be used to model distributed queries and the needed locking.
- *Adapter* is a natural model for translating user interfaces (whether an interface language such as JDBC [13], forms and reports, or a graphical interface) to the underlying query language. *Adapter* or *Bridge* can be used to model the interface between the table-oriented DBMS layer and varying file decompositions and structures in the file system layer. *State* and/or *Strategy* can be used in cases where dynamic conversion between file structures is desirable.

- *Iterator* expresses table traversal for simple queries; complex queries are probably better modeled by using *Visitor* (which allows interrupted and repeated traversals) together with *Composite* (which models recursive structures) on the structure of the query (or at another level, on the access plan).
- *State* and *Strategy* can again be used in optimization to support selection among multiple implementations for join and for temporary files, particularly in stored queries and views.

3.3 Relational and Object-Oriented Databases

An important side benefit of this approach is increased portability of design between a relational approach and an object-oriented or a hybrid approach. If EER diagrams and notations are used, transition to an OO approach requires far more work than if UML and design patterns have been employed, where the transition is immediate.

4. DATABASE PROJECTS USING DESIGN PATTERNS

A typical class project in a relational database management course usually involves the following four major steps (sub-projects)—together with review and testing at each stage, and limited phase iteration if required.

- Analyze the database problem and capture the requirements specification in a conceptual model such as Entity-Relationship Model;
- Map the conceptual schema to a logical database model (e.g., relational schema) and make use of various database design concepts (e.g., normalization);
- Create and populate relational tables;
- Create views, stored queries, and ad hoc queries to solve various database problems.

In transferring knowledge between databases and software engineering, the first knowledge to transfer is the design and implementation processes. An appropriate of subset of UML and the Unified Process [3, 7, 15] is used to express design and implementation concepts in building the database system from requirements, following the software engineering life cycle. As the steps are followed, design pattern concepts and other software engineering concepts are introduced by the instructor and used by student groups.

Consider for example a project to design a database for a regional repertory theater, a small subset of which will be implemented. (A fuller description is available at http://cs.wpunj.edu /~kuc/dp.html.) Entities include repertory personnel (actors, musicians, directors, technical staff, house staff, and others) and guest personnel, plays, technical assets (costumes, sets, props and lighting), current and pending productions (with directors, casts, and technical assets) and timelines (casting, rehearsal, preview, performance), customers of various types, subscription plans and special events, funding sources, and so on. In addition to the standard key and domain constraints, many others, including scheduling, casting (both temporal and personal), and ticket sales, must be enforced. Ticket purchases, cancellations, and exchanges are handled differently depending on the class of customer and other factors. The target system includes a computer on premises, and a small network hosted at a state university, shared with other regional arts organizations.

There are multiple classes of user, with different permissions, query sets, and user interfaces. Access is through forms and reports, although house and technical staff also use programmed parametric queries. Ad hoc queries may occur, for example in searching for technical assets. Seating status must be available per production and performance as graphics derived from maintained views. There is a special need for undo-able "what-if" updates as production, schedule, subscription and casting alternatives are considered.

In summary, we have the following complications: subsets and unions (disjoint, overlapping, and—in Customer—non-categorical (non-class-based)); maintained views; undo-able operations (from both requirements and constraints, as well as transactions); file interfaces and distribution; security, visibility, and access control; and multiple kinds of (simple and complex) queries and user interfaces, including embedded queries.

From experience, students find it quite difficult to capture many of these distinctions and features in the first two stages of the project, even given substantial interaction with the instructor. Identification of database design idioms and their correspondence with design patterns brings these issues to the forefront, facilitates their solution, and in some cases assists in design-level consideration of alternatives. Particular benefits of design patterns in this example, and possible ideas for milestones in the project, include:

- Design. After determining the basic entities, identify and classify instances of subsets and unions. Use UML and design patterns to express different realizations, and evaluate tradeoffs.
- Table and query realization. Model table access and query planning using *Iterator, Visitor,* and *Composite*. Use OCL [19] together with *Proxy, Memento,* and *Command* to model constraint enforcement, or to model support for "what-if" updates. Implement "what-if" updates using subqueries with named results, relation assignment, and conditional flow. Use *State* and/or *Strategy* to provide both a "committed" and a "what-if" mode for queries.
- Implementation. Use a protection *Proxy* plus *Adapter* to model security, visibility, and access control. Assume that other software identifies and validates the current user, and that his/her ID is provided to the DBMS, and further that it can be found among the repertory personnel (but is not super-user). Also assume that rules for visibility and access control are available as meta-information. Implement messages that deny access for invalid queries (via *Command*), and views (via *Observer*) that provide filtered information if the query is allowed.

We illustrate our approach using a simplified model of personnel. Performers have a *name* (first, last, MI, title), a *salary*, and a *status* (Available, Unavailable, NotWithCompany) where Unavailable is used for situations such as injury or outside commitments. Performers comprise Actors (with *age, sex,* and *vocalRange*) and Musicians (with, for simplicity, a single *instrument*).

There are three different standard approaches for implementing this disjoint union in database design—common attributes and differences, unified table with discriminator, and table of references to separate tables—with various tradeoffs. Figure 1 shows the first approach implemented with a non-recursive version of *Decorator*, while Figure 2 shows the second approach implemented with *Observer*. Method *getName( )* recovers a printable name from the *name* record. (There is a simplification in Figure 2, since in reality we need both Actor to be an *Observer* of Performer, and ActorTable [not shown] to be an *Observer* of PerformerTable, and likewise for Musician.)

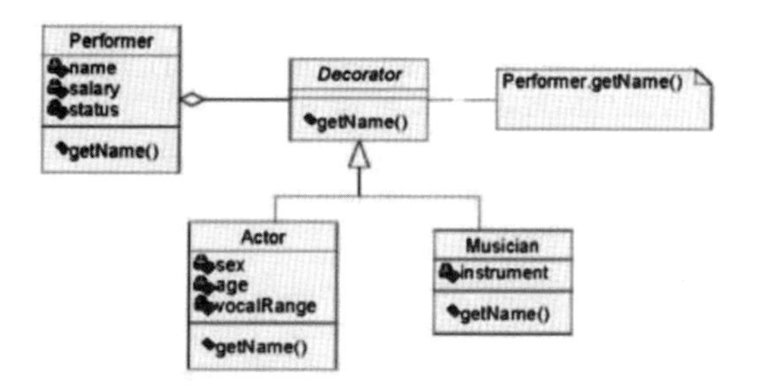

Figure 1. Performer Specified Using the Decorator Pattern

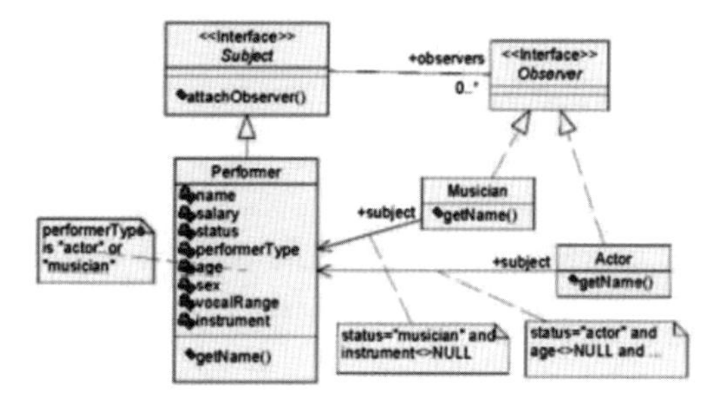

Figure 2. Performer Specified Using the Observer Pattern

An access permissions example, omitted for lack of space, considers the CastableActor view of Performer and Actor provided to the casting director—only Available actors are visible (so *status* need not be shown), and *salary* cannot be seen. This view is implemented via Proxy (to redirect the query from Performer and Actor to CastableActor) and Observer (to filter appropriate, up-to-date entries and fields from the base tables).

5. RELATED WORK

Related work falls into two categories: discussion of design patterns in course pedagogy, and use of design patterns in database design. There are large numbers of articles in the first group, many in SIGCSE conferences, or the newsletter. These apply design patterns of course to Software Engineering (as in [8]), but also to the introductory CS sequence (up to proposals to completely restructure the sequence as in [1, 9]) and to courses in data structures and algorithms (see for example [13]), as well as courses devoted to specific applications or devices.

A number of papers suggest use of design patterns for developing or teaching object-oriented databases, but few if any for relational databases. An approach motivated by the Unified Process, software architectures, and design patterns is presented in [2]. Use of a Factory (called a Database Factory) to support differing transaction and query implementations is proposed in [16]. Finally, database-specific and other domain-specific patterns have been developed, following the practice in software architectures. Nock [11] discusses five categories of database-specific patterns (Decoupling, Resource, Input/Output, Cache, and Concurrency), addressing both logical and implementation design; Grand [6] includes patterns relevant to concurrency, transactions, and databases within a broad catalog of (largely pre-existing) patterns.

6. CONCLUSIONS

Design is an intrinsic and critical concern for all application-oriented courses in computing, but most particularly in areas in which application structure is driven by modeling of fuzzy, complex real-world phenomena, such as artificial intelligence, software engineering, and databases. Use of a uniform approach, with a uniform set of tools and idioms, supports better concept acquisition and a more challenging course structure.

It is interesting to view applications courses and design issues in light of software engineering standards. The CMM (Capability Maturity Models) of the SEI [12] classifies software engineering approaches at five levels of maturity/capability: initial, repeatable, defined, managed, and optimized. Shaw and Garlan [18] define the steps in the evolution of an engineering discipline as *production* and *craft,* which combine to give *commercial*, which together with *science (theory)* gives *professional engineering*. With the Unified Process, aided by design patterns and other developments, software engineering, we would claim, supports managed commercial development—the tool base is there, but there is as yet no body of theory. Relational databases have a solid mathematical theory and a good theory of optimization, but, without a well-recognized set of standard tools and idioms, design remains more a craft than a commercial profession [18]. Adding a richer set of design structures, including design patterns, increases replicability, and, in one view, allows a transition through *commercial development* to *engineering*. Use of the Design Patterns with UML and the Unified Process throughout the computer science major has equally significant benefits for both the nature and level of (non-theory) courses. More complex problems can be modeled and implemented, and design issues and tradeoffs confronted more directly. Students, working with a common approach that is becoming standard in industry, will develop better abstraction and conceptualization skills, benefiting their future education, professional development, and career opportunities. A database course, with its strong emphasis on modeling of complex problems, offers a natural and effective stage for further presentation and use of these techniques.

7. REFERENCES

[1] Alphonce, Carl. Curricular Patterns. *ACM SIGPLAN Notices, 39, 5* (May 2004) 7-14.

[2] Ambler, Scott W. *Agile Database Techniques: Effective Strategies for the Agile Software Developer*, Wiley & Sons, 2003.

[3] Booch, Grady, Rumbaugh, James and Jacobson, Ivar. *The Unified Modeling Language User Guide*, Addison Wesley, 1998.

[4] Elmasri, Rame and Navathe, Shamkant B. *Fundamentals of Database Systems,* 4th edition, Addison Wesley, 2003.

[5] Erich Gamma, Richard Helm, Ralph Johnson, John Vlissides, *Design Patterns: Elements of Reusable Object-Oriented Software*, Addison Wesley, 1995.

[6] Grand, M. *Patterns in Java,* 3 volumes, J. Wiley & Sons, 2002.

[7] Jacobson, Ivar, Booch, Grady, Rumbaugh, James, *The Unified Software Development Process*, Addison Wesley, 1999.

[8] Larman, Craig. *Applying UML and Patterns: An Introduction to Object-Oriented Analysis and Design and the Unified Process*, 2nd edition, Prentice-Hall, 2001.

[9] Lewis, Tracy L., Rosson, Mary Beth, and Pérez-Quiñones, Manuel. What do the Experts Say? Teaching Introductory Design from an Expert's Perspective. *Proceedings of the 35th SIGCSE Technical Symposium on Computer Science Education*, 2004, 296—300.

[10] Naiburg, Eric J. and Maksimchuk, Robert A.*UML for Database Design*, Addison Wesley, Reading, MA, 2001.

[11] Nock, Clifton. *Data Access Patterns: Database Interactions in Object-Oriented Applications,* Addison Wesley, 2004.

[12] Paulk, M. C., Weber, C. V., Curtis, B. and Chrissis, M. B. *The Capability Maturity Model: Guidelines for Improving the Software Process*, Addison Wesley, 1995.

[13] Preiss, Bruno R. Design Patterns for the data structures and algorithms course. *Proceedings of the 30th Annual SIGCSE Technical Symposium on Computer Science Education, 1999,* 95—99.

[14] Reese, George. *Database Programming with JDBC and Java*, 2nd edition, O'Reilly, 2000.

[15] Rumbaugh, James, Jacobson, Ivar, Booch, Grady, *The Unified Modeling Language Reference Manual*, 2nd edition, Addison Wesley, 2004.

[16] Selvaraj, A. and Ghosh, D. Implementation of a Database Factory. *ACM SIGPLAN Notices, 32 6*, (June, 1997) 14—16.

[17] Shalloway, Alan and Trott, James R. *Design Patterns explained: a new perspective on object-oriented design,* Addison-Wesley, 2005.

[18] Shaw, Mary and Garlan, David. *Software Architecture: Perspectives on an Emerging Discipline*, Prentice Hall, 1996.

[19] Warmer, Jos and Kleppe, Anneke. *The Object Constraint Language: Getting Your Models Ready for MDA*, Addison Wesley, Reading, MA, 2003.

Exploring XML for Data Exchange in the Context of an Undergraduate Database Curriculum

Suzanne W. Dietrich Susan D. Urban Hua Ma Yang Xiao Shama Patel
Department of Computer Science and Engineering
Arizona State University
Tempe, AZ 85287-8809
dietrich@asu.edu s.urban@asu.edu

ABSTRACT

The relationship between XML and database management systems has become an important topic for coverage at the undergraduate level. This paper presents an approach to teaching the use of XML through the study of data exchange. After a brief review of XML, the paper provides a tutorial on the different features that are provided in major relational database products for the import and export of XML, providing a discussion of how these features can be used as implementation exercises for students. In addition to addressing the use of XML for data exchange in relational systems, the paper also provides an overview of several teaching tools that are also used in the study of XML for object-oriented data and also for the exchange of object-oriented and object-relational data.

Categories and Subject Descriptors

H.2.4 [**Database Management**]: Systems – *relational databases, object-oriented databases, textual databases.*

General Terms

Languages

Keywords

XML, data exchange, undergraduate database curriculum, relational databases, object-oriented databases, object-relational databases.

1. INTRODUCTION

The Extensible Markup Language (XML) [13] is an important topic to address when teaching database concepts to undergraduates. The SQL:2003 standard [8] includes a new part on XML-related specifications, called SQL/XML [6]. Further advancements to SQL/XML can be found in [7]. However, there is varying support in database products for features described in the standard. Database educators are now faced with the challenge of upgrading course content based on the evolving SQL/XML standards and understanding how to use XML-enabled database products as a teaching tool in the classroom.

SIGCSE'05, February 23–27, 2005, St. Louis, Missouri, USA.

At Arizona State University, we have developed an advanced database concepts course (http://www.eas.asu.edu/~cse494db) for undergraduates that assumes a prerequisite course on relational database systems (e.g., http://www.eas.asu.edu/~cse412). A recent textbook [5] provides detailed coverage of the advanced database topics addressed in this course. A companion Web site (http://www.eas.asu.edu/~advdb) gives curriculum examples that support the concepts covered in the book. One module of the course includes coverage of XML and its relationship to data management. The standard for XML is introduced, including Document Type Definitions (DTDs) and XML Schema for representing the valid content of an XML document. The use of XML is addressed in the context of both object-oriented and relational data, with a specific focus on how XML can be used to support data exchange between different applications and database systems. Related work on the use of XML in the classroom has been reported in [12], describing the use of XML for exercises involving data modeling, converting an XML schema to a relational schema, using XPath to query an Oracle XMLType, and parsing XML documents.

This paper provides an overview of our approach to using XML for data exchange as a means for teaching students the relationship between XML and databases. The paper is presented in a tutorial style, outlining the XML features of several different relational database products that we have explored for use in the classroom, including Microsoft Access, Oracle, SQL Server 2000, and the new SQL Server 2005 Express [9]. In addition to discussing how these features can be used for exercises involving relational data exchange, we also provide an overview of several teaching tools that are also used in the study of XML for object-oriented data (using Objectivity/DB) and for the exchange of object-oriented and object-relational data between Objectivity/DB and Oracle implementations of the same conceptual design. Students therefore experience the use of XML with several different database paradigms.

The remainder of this paper is structured as follows. Section 2 provides a brief overview of XML. Section 3 then describes the data exchange support for XML in the four relational systems mentioned above, providing a discussion of how these features can be used as a teaching tool. Section 4 addresses our experience with the use of XML in an object-oriented database, whereas Section 5 focuses on a tool that we have developed for using XML for data exchange between object-relational and object-oriented databases. Section 6 concludes the paper with a discussion of our exploration.

2. A BRIEF INTRODUCTION TO XML

XML is widely used for representing textual knowledge. The markup language allows for user-defined tags to provide the semantics of the data contained in the document. Consider the schema of a simple employee table [3]:

employee(eID, eLast, eFirst, eTitle, eSalary)

Figure 1 shows a sample XML document representing a canonical table-based mapping of the employee relational table in XML based on the format discussed in [6]. A *tag* is a label that is contained within a < and >. A label is case sensitive in XML and cannot contain white space. Each opening tag must be matched with a closing tag that has the same label except that the label is preceded by a / character. The term *element* refers to an opening tag, the enclosed text, and the corresponding ending tag. A well-formed XML document must contain a distinguished root element, which is employee in the example shown in Figure 1. Additionally, a well-formed XML document must contain a proper nesting of all elements. As shown in Figure 1, each tuple of the table is enclosed within a row element, which has elements corresponding to each column in the employee table.

```
<employee>
  <row>
      <eID>456</eID>
      <eLast>Last456</eLast>
      <eFirst>First456</eFirst>
      <eTitle>Software Engineer</eTitle>
      <eSalary>45456</eSalary>
  </row>
<!-- This is an XML comment: other rows are not shown -->
  <row>
      <eID>999</eID>
      <eLast>Last999</eLast>
      <eFirst>First999</eFirst>
      <eTitle>Manager</eTitle>
      <eSalary>100999</eSalary>
  </row>
</employee>
```

Figure 1. XML Data for an employee Table

Figure 1 illustrates an element-based representation of the XML data. The opening tags of elements may contain attributes, which have a name and a value that is enclosed in quotes. The following is an alternative attribute-based representation of a table row in XML:

```
<row eID="456" eLast="Last456" eFirst="First456"
      eTitle="Software Engineer" eSalary="45456" />
```

3. RELATIONAL SYSTEMS

This section provides an overview of the support for XML in the four relational systems that we have explored: Access, SQL Server 2000, Oracle and the recently announced SQL Server 2005 Express. Initial support for representing XML in relational database products used CLOBs (Character Large OBjects) or varying length character strings (varchar), while more recent releases have introduced an explicit type for XML.

3.1 Access

Access has the capability to export and import XML data. To export the XML representation of data in a relational table, select the table in Access and then select the Export item from the File menu. (Another alternative is to use the shortcut of a right-mouse click on the table to open a pop-up window that shows the Export option.) Choose the "Save as Type XML Documents" option. Access generates several files on the export of a table:

- *xml*: The xml data corresponding to the table, where the XML distinguished root element is dataroot and each tuple of the table is enclosed by an element given by the table name.
- *xsd*: The XML Schema Definition for the generated XML data.
- *xsl*: An Extensible Stylesheet Language file that provides a transformation of the XML to HTML for viewing in a browser.

There are several options for importing XML data into Access. From the File menu, select Get External Data and then Import. There is an Options button that allows one of the following choices:

- *structure and data*: The structure of the XML document and its corresponding data is imported into a table, given by the name of the element enclosing each row. By default, the fields corresponding to imported XML data are defined in Access as text with maximum length of 255.
- *structure only*: Only the structure of the XML document is used to define a table.
- *append to an existing table*: By defining a table with the appropriate field types first, the import of XML data can be appended into the table and the textual data will be imported as the predefined type.

3.2 SQL Server 2000

SQL Server 2000 uses strings (varchar) for representing XML data. The FOR XML clause of the SELECT statement provides the capability to return XML data. The Transact-SQL (T-SQL) programming language provides programmatic support with the OPENXML function for importing XML data into a relational table.

The SELECT statement allows a FOR XML clause to return the result of a query in XML format:

SELECT ... FROM ... FOR XML *mode* [,ELEMENTS]

The *mode* specification indicates the structure of the resulting XML. By default, an attribute-based XML representation for the data is provided, where the columns of the table are represented as attributes in XML. The use of the ELEMENTS option changes the XML representation to be element-based, where each column of the table is represented as an XML element. The choices for the *mode* specification are: RAW, AUTO and EXPLICIT. The following query will be used to illustrate the XML result based on the *mode*:

```
SELECT * FROM employee WHERE eID='456' FOR XML
```

The RAW mode returns each tuple of the resulting query in a generic row element:

```
<row eID="456" eLast="Last456" eFirst="First456"
      eTitle="Software Engineer" eSalary="45456" />
```

The AUTO mode returns each tuple in an element named by the table name:

```
<employee  eID="456" eLast="Last456" eFirst="First456"
           eTitle="Software Engineer" eSalary="45456" />
```

```
CREATE PROCEDURE insertEmployeeXML
  @myxml varchar(2000)
AS
DECLARE
  @iTree int
  EXEC sp_xml_preparedocument @iTree OUTPUT, @myxml
  INSERT employee(eID, eLast, eFirst, eTitle, eSalary)
    SELECT * FROM OPENXML(@iTree,'/dataroot/employee',2)
      WITH (eID          varchar(5)   'eID',
            eLast        varchar(20)  'eLast',
            eFirst       varchar(20)  'eLast',
            eTitle       varchar(50)  'eTitle',
            eSalary      float        'eSalary')
  EXEC sp_xml_removedocument @iTree
```

Figure 2. Inserting XML Data in SQL Server 2000

The EXPLICIT mode provides the capability to specify the structure of the resulting XML. Due to space limitations, the full details of the EXPLICIT specification are beyond the scope of this paper. The ELEMENTS option returns an element-based XML representation:

```
<employee>
    <eID>456</eID>
    <eLast>Last456</eLast>
    <eFirst>First456</eFirst>
    <eTitle>Software Engineer</eTitle>
    <eSalary>45456</eSalary>
</employee>
```

Figure 2 illustrates the population of the employee table in SQL Server 2000. The OPENXML function parses and queries an XML document to return values in the form of rows and columns. The sp_xml_preparedocument and sp_xml_removedocument are two system procedures that are associated with the OPENXML function. The sp_xml_preparedocument procedure takes an XML string as a parameter and parses it to build an XML internal tree representation (pointed to by @iTree). Once the document is prepared, OPENXML can be used to query the document and return a result set. The sp_xml_removedocument procedure should be executed after XML processing to release the allocated memory.

3.3 Oracle

Oracle (Version 9) introduced a data type for XML, called XMLType. The attributes of a table can be defined to be of type XMLType, allowing the storage of XML within a table. Oracle provides two packages for supporting XML: DBMS_XMLGEN and DBMS_XMLSave.

DBMS_XMLGEN is a PL/SQL package that supports the creation of XML from an SQL query. To generate an XML document, first create a context handle by passing the query to the parameter of the newContext method, where employeeCtx is declared to be of type DBMS_XMLGEN.ctxhandle:

```
employeeCtx :=
  DBMS_XMLGEN.newContext('SELECT * FROM employee');
```

By default, Oracle uses an element-based representation of the table having the element ROWSET as the distinguished root and each tuple of the table is enclosed in a ROW element. The setRowSetTag and setRowTag methods allow for changing the defaults to the second parameter, where the first parameter is the XML context handle:

```
DBMS_XMLGEN.setRowSetTag(employeeCtx, 'employees');
DBMS_XMLGEN.setRowTag(employeeCtx, 'employee');
```

The XML results can be stored in either a CLOB or an XMLTYPE, using the getXML or getXMLType methods, respectively:

```
empXMLclob := DBMS_XMLGEN.getXML(employeeCtx);
```

or

```
empXMLtype := DBMS_XMLGEN.getXMLType(employeeCtx);
```

where empXMLclob is defined to be of type CLOB and empXMLtype is defined to be of type XMLType. A procedure can then be written to store the result in a file.

The import of XML data to be stored as a relational table requires calling the methods provided by the DBMS_XMLSave package in Oracle. Assuming that the table employee is already defined (but not populated), a context named empCtx is defined as type DBMS_XMLSave.ctxType and assigned as the context for the save of the XML data to the employee table:

```
empCtx := DBMS_XMLSave.newContext(employee);
```

The setRowTag method allows for the specification of the row tag that encloses each tuple. In this example, it is assumed to be called employeeRow:

```
DBMS_XMLSave.setRowTag(empCtx, 'employeeRow');
```

The following call to the setIgnoreCase method tells Oracle to ignore any case differences in matching XML element names to database attribute names, since the database convention is to ignore case sensitivity in attribute names:

```
DBMS_XMLSave.setIgnoreCase(empCtx, 1);
```

A call to the insertXML method inserts the employee data represented in XML as a CLOB into the employee table, returning the number of rows inserted into the table:

```
numberOfRows :=
    DBMS_XMLSave.insertXML(empCtx, empXMLclob);
```

The closeContext method releases the resources associated with the context:

```
DBMS_XMLSave.closeContext(empCtx);
```

The new XMLType in Oracle allows for storing XML directly in the database. Consider the following table definition:

```
CREATE TABLE sampleXMLtable
    (xmlColumn XMLType);
```

Assume that the variable myXMLclob contains a CLOB representation of XML data, the following code snippet shows how to create an instance myXMLdata of an XMLType from a CLOB and insert the XML into the table:

```
myXMLdata := XMLType.createXML(myXMLclob);
INSERT INTO sampleXMLtable VALUES (myXMLdata);
```

3.4 SQL Server 2005 Express

The recently announced SQL Server 2005 Express [9] also supports a new type called XML, extending the features discussed for SQL Server 2000 with inherent support for XML. The stored procedure sp_xml_preparedocument has been extended to support a parameter of type XML rather than a string (varchar) and the FOR XML clause has been extended with several new features.

The FOR XML clause of the select statement allows a TYPE option, returning an instance of type XML, which is assigned to the myxml variable:

```
DECLARE @myxml XML
SET @myxml =
        (SELECT * FROM employee WHERE eID='456'
         FOR XML, ELEMENTS, TYPE)
```

The FOR XML clause of the select statement has also been extended to allow a PATH mode and ROOT directive for specifying a more complex XML structure. Consider as a motivational example, the creation of an XML representation of the employee data that

- returns the eID as an id attribute in XML,
- encloses the eLast and eFirst attributes within a name element,
- encloses each tuple within an element named employeeTuple, and
- names the distinguished root of the XML document as employeeDataRoot.

The following select statement illustrates the query specification:

```
SELECT     eID AS '@id',
           eLast AS 'name/eLast',
           eFirst AS 'name/eFirst',
           eTitle,
           eSalary
FROM       employee
FOR XML    PATH('employeeTuple'),
           ROOT('employeeDataRoot')
```

The following indicates the resulting XML (with only one employee tuple shown for brevity of presentation):

```
<employeeDataRoot>
   <employeeTuple id="456">
     <name>
       <eLast>Last456</eLast>
       <eFirst>First456</eFirst>
     </name>
     <eTitle>Software Engineer</eTitle>
     <eSalary>45456</eSalary>
   </employeeTuple>
 ...
</ employeeDataRoot >
```

SQL Server 2005 Express also has the capability to store XML data as an attribute value. Consider the following table definition:

```
CREATE TABLE sampleXMLtable
      (xmlColumn XML);
```

The INSERT statement can be used to populate a column of type XML:

```
INSERT INTO sampleXMLtable VALUES (@xmlColumnValue);
```

where the variable @xmlColumnValue can be declared either as type XML or varchar, and is assumed to have the value of an XML document. The system automatically converts a varchar argument to type XML for inserting the values.

3.5 Relational Data Exchange

The features described in the previous subsections provide useful tools that can be used in exercises to explore XML through data exchange between different database products. Exercises can be designed to use the export/generation feature of one product and then use the import/loading feature of the other product. Depending on the products available, exercises can either focus on the transfer of data between a relational table and XML format or the storage of an XML file as an XML type in a relational table. For example, the use of the FOR XML, ELEMENTS option of the SELECT statement in SQL Server (2000 or 2005 Express) results in an element-based representation of the table, with the table name as the element enclosing each tuple. The Oracle DBMS_XMLSave package can then be used to load the XML data into a table, specifying the table name as the row tag in the setRowTag method.

4. AN OBJECT-ORIENTED EXPLORATION

Our exploration of XML in the classroom includes the use of XML with object-oriented and object-relational database systems so that students also have an understanding of how to use XML to represent object-oriented data. The study of XML with the use of object-oriented databases makes use of the Object Manager tool developed at ASU and presented in [4]. The Object Manager is a graphical user interface tool for interacting with object-oriented databases such as Objectivity/DB. An XML file is used to communicate the schema of an object-oriented database to the Object Manager, allowing students to define the classes in the database, the attributes and keys of each class, inverse relationships between classes, and method names for getting and setting attributes and relationships. The Object Manager uses this schema information in the XML file to generate a generic user interface that allows students to create objects, delete objects, and manage relationships between objects. The Object Manager also supports importing of XML data into an object-oriented database as well as exporting of data to an XML file. Specific XML examples of schema and data files used with the Object Manager can be found in [4].

Our most current use of the Object Manager is integrated with a tool that we have developed known as the Object Database Generator [10]. The Object Database Generator, outlined in the following section on object-relational exploration, allows students to use XML to study similarities and differences between object-oriented and object-relational representations of data.

5. AN OBJECT-RELATIONAL EXPLORATION

XML for the representation of object-relational data is explored through the use of the Object Database Generator (ODG) [10]. The ODG was developed to support the portability of data between an Oracle object-relational database system and the Objectivity/DB object-oriented database system. Figure 3 shows the architecture of the ODG. Beginning with a database schema described using the Object Definition Language (ODL) of the Object Data Management Group (ODMG) standard [1], the ODG supports the creation of Objectivity and Oracle database implementations from the same ODL schema. For Objectivity, the ODG compiles an ODL schema to generate an XML file that conforms to the schema description required by the Object Manager tool. Students then implement the Java classes for the object-oriented database implementation. For Oracle, the ODG gives students a choice of bidirectional or unidirectional relationships for all inverse relationships in the ODL schema based on an object-relational mapping approach described in [5]. Furthermore, for the many side of a 1:N or a M:N relationship, the user must specify the implementation to be either a varray or a nested table, which are the choices for representing collections in Oracle. The ODG then generates the appropriate object type, object table, varray, and nested table definitions for the creation of an object-relational database. Students complete the implementation with the creation of the appropriate stored procedures and functions.

A subcomponent of the ODG is the Oracle-to-Objectivity Converter (OOC), originally developed in [11] and modified in [10] for use as part of the ODG. The OOC transforms data in the object-relational implementation of the ODL schema into an XML data file that conforms to the data format used by the Object Manager. As part of the transformation, the OOC generates the inverse data for unidirectional relationships. Students then experiment with exporting data from the Oracle object-relational implementation into the corresponding Objectivity database through the XML data import feature of the Object Manager. The ODG together with the OOC allows students to study the similarities and differences between the object-oriented and object-relational implementations, using XML to transfer data from one implementation to the other.

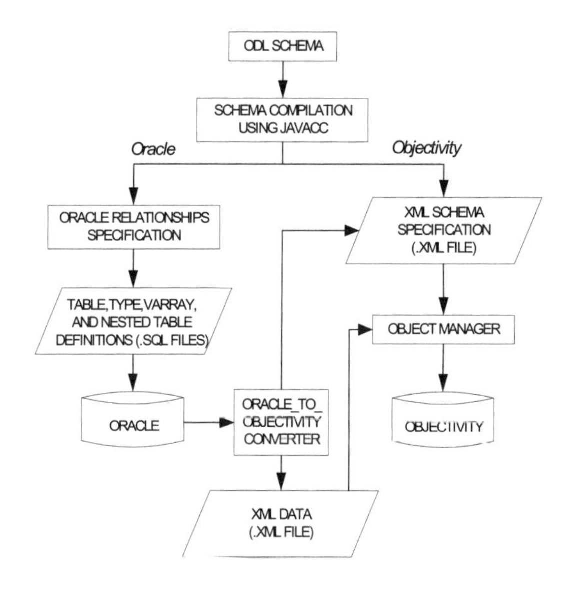

Figure 3. Architecture of the Object Database Generator

6. DISCUSSION

This paper has explored the use of XML for data exchange between relational systems as well as data exchange between object-oriented and object-relational database systems. It is important to note that many existing relational database systems also provide the capability to export a database in a format compatible for another product. For example, SQL Server 2000 has a tool, known as the Data Transformation Service, which transforms data from SQL Server to Oracle without the use of XML. Also, some products may also provide separate tools for mapping tables and views to XML documents, such as Oracle's XML SQL Utility. We have found, however, that an XML-based approach to data exchange is a useful learning tool, where students are exposed to the universal nature of XML as a means for representing data and its corresponding description, together with relevant database tools that support the import and export of XML data.

As the support for XML in commercial database products continues to grow, so will our approach to the incorporation of XML into the database curriculum. For example, some of the products discussed in this paper already have some form of support for querying XML [2]. We anticipate the expression of queries over XML data as the next module in our approach to teaching XML within an advanced database curriculum for undergraduates.

7. ACKNOWLEDGMENTS

We would like to thank Ingrid Biswas and Alexey Ushakov who supported earlier versions of this exploration. This research was supported by NSF Grant No. DUE-9980417 and the Microsoft Research Content and Curriculum Program.

8. REFERENCES

[1] Cattell, R. G. G. et al. (eds.) *The Object Database Standard: ODMG 3.0*. Morgan Kaufmann, San Franciso, 2000.

[2] Chaudhri, A. B., Rashid, A., and Zicari, R. (eds.) *XML Data Management: Native XML and XML-Enabled Database Systems*. Addison-Wesley, Boston, 2003.

[3] Dietrich, S. W. *Understanding Relational Database Query Languages*. Prentice Hall, Upper Saddle River, NJ, 2001.

[4] Dietrich, S. W., Suceava, D., Cherekuri, C., and Urban, S. D. A Reusable Graphical Interface for Manipulating Object-Oriented Databases Using Java and XML. In *Proceedings of the ACM Technical Symposium on Computer Science Education* (*SIGCSE '01*) (North Carolina, Feb. 2001). ACM Press, New York, NY, 2001, 362-366.

[5] Dietrich, S. W. and Urban, S. D. *An Advanced Course in Database Systems: Beyond Relational Databases*. Prentice Hall, Upper Saddle River, NJ, 2005.

[6] Eisenberg, A. and Melton, J. SQL/XML is making good progress. *ACM SIGMOD Record*, 31, 2 (Jun. 2002), 101-108.

[7] Eisenberg, A. and Melton, J. Advancements in SQL/XML. *ACM SIGMOD Record*, 33, 3 (Sep. 2004), 79-86.

[8] Eisenberg, A., Melton, J., Kulkarni, K., Michels, J., and Zemke, F. SQL:2003 has been published. *ACM SIGMOD Record*, 33, 1 (Mar. 2004), 119-126.

[9] Microsoft Corporation. SQL Server 2005 Express Edition, 2004. http://lab.msdn.microsoft.com/express/sql/

[10] Patel, S. *The Object Database Generator*. M.C.S. Project, Department of Computer Science and Engineering, Arizona State University, 2003.

[11] Ushakov, A. *Oracle_to_Objectivity Converter*. Undergraduate Independent Study Report, Department of Computer Science and Engineering, Arizona State University, Fall 2002.

[12] Wagner, P. and Moore, T. Integrating XML into a Database Systems Course. In *Proceedings of the ACM Technical Symposium on Computer Science Education (SIGCSE '03)*, (Nevada, Feb. 2003). ACM Press, New York, NY, 2001, 26-60.

[13] World Web Wide Consortium. XML. http://www.w3.org/XML/

Automated Tutoring for a Database Skills Training Environment

Claire Kenny
School of Computing
Dublin City University
Dublin, Ireland
++353 1 7005616
ckenny@computing.dcu.ie

Claus Pahl
School of Computing
Dublin City University
Dublin, Ireland
++353 1 7005620
cpahl@computing.dcu.ie

ABSTRACT

Universities are increasingly offering courses online. Feedback, assessment, and guidance are important features of this online courseware. Together, in the absence of a human tutor, they aid the student in the learning process. We present a programming training environment for a database course. It aims to offer a substitute for classroom based learning by providing synchronous automated feedback to the student, along with guidance based on a personalized assessment. The automated tutoring system should promote procedural knowledge acquisition and skills training. An automated tutoring feature is an integral part of this tutoring system.

Categories and Subject Descriptors

K.3.1 [**Computers and Education**]: Computer Uses in Education – *Computer-assisted instruction (CAI).*

General Terms

Management, Design, Human Factors, Languages.

Keywords

Structured Query Language, tool-mediated independent learning, skills training.

1. INTRODUCTION

The School of Computing at Dublin City University offers a second year undergraduate module, an introduction to databases, which is presented online. Courseware is comprised of lectures in textual, pictorial, and audio format, along with animated tutorials. Also included are interactive lab sessions, one of which tutors students in SQL (structured query language), a database definition and manipulation language.

SQL is a declarative database programming language, comprised of approximately thirty English commands, such as select, insert, and update. It is the most widely used language for relational database data definition and data manipulation. For this reason, it is commonly included in introductory database courses.

SIGCSE'05, February 23–27, 2005, St. Louis, Missouri, USA.

Our automated tutoring system is concerned with the SQL select statement, for a variety of reasons. This statement is used to retrieve information from a database, and can be viewed as being the most fundamental of the SQL statements. It can be simple, but also has the capacity to become quite complex, thus lending itself to being taught to students with a wide range of ability.

Learning is a complex domain. With classroom-based modules a human lecturer or tutor is generally available to personally correct answers and offer specific advice to students. This type of support is not immediately available with an online course. Disadvantages can result, such as being unable to offer personalized guidance.

Accordingly, to facilitate independent and self-reliant learning with an online environment, there needs to be a certain level of advice and guidance. Our tutoring system aims to provide this by using feedback, assessment, and personalized guidance, all of which are available at all times, to support the learner due to the absence of synchronous human tutoring. This is available at all times. The tutoring system focuses on training and development of skills rather than on knowledge and learning. It is similar in aspects to intelligent tutoring systems [10], and so interaction is primarily learner-content, rather than learner-learner.

Similar database tutoring systems exist. One such system is SQL-Tutor [7]. Like our system, it is intended as a practise environment and supposes that students have previously been exposed to the concepts of database management in lectures. SQL-Tutor uses constraint-based modelling to create a model of and deliver feedback to the student. Another system, Acharya [1], uses truth table processing to correct SQL select statements. It too offers feedback to the student.

While SQL tutoring systems exist [1] [7], it has been noted that many do not use an assessment of the student's previous progress throughout the tutorial in order to offer an optional personalized and adaptive guidance element. We aim to rectify this issue in our system. Additionally, students will submit statements to an actual Oracle database that can be used for coursework and projects, a feature often absent in other online SQL tutors.

This paper will outline the pedagogical issues we address in our project. We will then describe the conceptual structure of the system, including examples of student-system interaction. We will conclude with an evaluation and discussion.

2. PEDAGOGICAL ISSUES

Educational technology combines trusted and new information technologies with established and emerging pedagogical methods. We discuss a number of these to address the quality of automated tutoring systems.

2.1 Cognitive and Virtual Apprenticeship

Traditional apprenticeship is a process by which the student learns through observing and actively aiding the master as he completes a certain task. Through time, the apprentice will complete the task with the master looking on, and offering help when necessary.

Collins et al. [4] propose a form of apprenticeship called cognitive apprenticeship. This form of apprenticeship is suitable for tasks that are more knowledge based than those dealt with by traditional apprenticeship. Here, a given task is divided into parts. Students may then complete sub-parts suited to their level of ability and hence the complexity of the task is slowly increased. This process is carried out in an authentic setting in which the student is actively involved, thus having real-world relevance.

The virtual apprenticeship model [8] adapts the cognitive apprenticeship theory, by using scaffolding and activity theory, to make it suitable for the Web context. When developing our tutoring system we aimed to replicate components of the virtual apprenticeship model. The online tutor assumes the role of the master.

2.2 Learning Structure

Learning is often a broad and general term. It may refer to theory and knowledge acquisition. Alternatively, training and obtaining practical skills may be in question. Online learning is often focused on knowledge acquisition. Occasionally, the online environment acts simply as a replacement for a book – knowledge is presented, but skills training is not accommodated.

The automated tutoring system described in this paper is concerned with training and the development of skills rather than factual and theoretical knowledge. Students submit SQL statements to an actual database; hence they are actively involved in a realistic database programming environment.

An additional aim is to encourage guided discovery [2]. With this the primary emphasis is placed on the student and his ability to seek information, rather than the system overwhelming him with data. It is often a productive method of learning in one-to-one situations.

2.3 Learning Supports

In the traditional classroom-based learning environment, a student is usually supported while partaking in some form of learning activity. As he gains confidence and ability this support is removed, and thus the student can complete the activity independently. This support is called scaffolding [6], and its removal is referred to as fading.

In keeping with the virtual apprenticeship model, scaffolding and fading should be offered in the online classroom. In fact, scaffolding can be seen as crucial to an online tutoring system, as the teacher-student relationship is often absent.

Our system uses feedback as a means of learning support. This is described in more detail later in this paper.

3. SYSTEM DESCRIPTION

Important features of the automated tutoring system presented here include it's architecture, the error classification scheme being used, the interface, and the feedback and guidance elements present. This section describes each of these features in detail.

3.1 Tutoring architecture

The system consists of four main components – interface, correction model, pedagogical model, and student model, as illustrated below (Figure 1) in the dataflow model. These are further outlined in the following subsections.

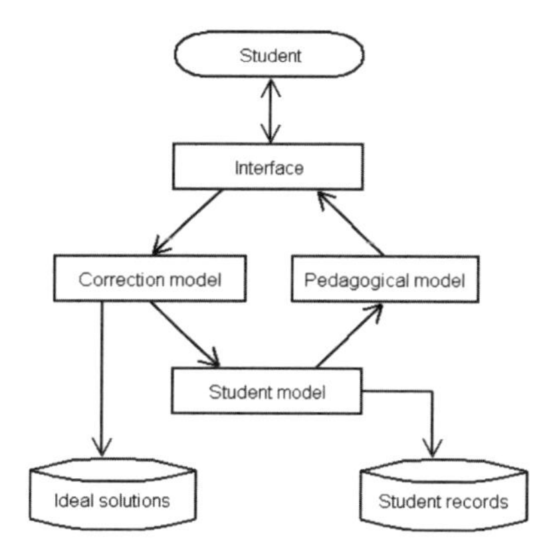

Figure 1. System architecture

3.2 Error classification

SQL is a formal language and, as with any formal language, properties of it may be *syntactical*, *semantic*, or *pragmatic*. As such, errors can also be grouped into the above three properties.

- Syntax errors are those caused by problems with the actual syntax of the language, such as misspelling a keyword.
- Semantic errors occur when the student creates a syntactically correct statement that does not reflect his intentions correctly.
- Pragmatic errors are considerably more generic and are concerned with rules and conventions within the language.

Incorrect expressions are central to the training and feedback context in question here. It is important to base error categories on the difficulties the student may encounter. These may include the correct use of basic syntax, using operations in the manner intended, or dealing with combinations of operations.

A basic implementation of the automated tutoring system analyses syntax and semantic errors. These are further grouped into separate categories we devised based on the elements commonly found in the SQL select statement – tables names, attributes, prefixes, symbols, aggregate functions, and a miscellaneous category for specific instances, such as when a proper noun needs to be referred to in the solution. While error groupings are based on the various elements of an SQL statement, the notion can be extended to most other formal languages.

SQL statements are generally made up of three clauses - *select – from – where*. Errors can occur in any of these clauses. The basic aspects of the language consist of input elements *(from)*, a computation (usually based on a condition - *where*), and an output element (*select*). While various errors can be made at each part of the formal language sentence the nature of the sentence makes it relatively easy to partition and analyse.

The tutoring system is currently being extended to include a multi-level error categorization scheme. Errors types will be further grouped according to the six fundamental SQL select statement clauses, i.e. select, from, where, group by, having, order by. Thus, errors will be classed as being syntactical or semantic, of a certain type (such as being concerned with table names), and occurring in a particular clause. Errors will also be assigned a severity level – some mistakes indicate more fundamental student difficulties than other errors made. By using a multi-level scheme, the system will be able to pinpoint mistakes and accompanying misconceptions (which may suggest pragmatic errors) in a more precise manner.

3.3 Interface

All interaction with the student is via the interface. There are a number of primary tasks (or questions), based on a particular SQL concept, for the learner to attempt (Figure 2). Central to each task is the testing of the student on a combination of error types; this is in a guided tutorial format.

Index of Queries

1) SIMPLE QUERY - ONE TABLE
This question is based on one table. Tasks included are prefixes, attributes, tables, symbols, and miscellaneous tasks

Go!

2) QUERY - JOINS (MULTIPLE TABLES)
This question is based on multiple tables. Tasks included are prefixes, attributes, tables, and symbols

Go!

3) NESTED QUERY
This question is based on multiple tables and nested queries. Tasks included are prefixes, attributes, tables, symbols, syntax, and miscellaneous tasks

Go!

Figure 2. Question index

Having selected a task to attempt, the student is shown an initial input screen (as shown in Figure 3). The selected task is described in English. The student must submit his SQL answer to the given task, by typing into a dedicated text area, in order for his proposed solution to be executed. Initially the statement is used to query an actual database of relevant tables. The submitted solution is then evaluated by the correction model through a series of steps whereby patterns in the student's solution are matched with patterns in the stored idea solution. A graphical representation of the student's submission is displayed at this stage to aid clarity, and continues to be displayed until the user moves on to the next task.

Various items of data are produced by the correction model. The most fundamental piece of information notes if the proposed solution is deemed to be correct or incorrect. Other important data relates to errors that may have been made, such as type and location.

All such correction information, along with the student's preferences, is stored and arranged by the student model. This model is updated for each student every time they submit an answer, regardless if submissions are made during one session or over a range of sessions.

The pedagogical model analyses the information stored by the student model, and so it plays an important role in the overall system. It is concerned with three main functions – *feedback*, *assessment*, and *guidance*.

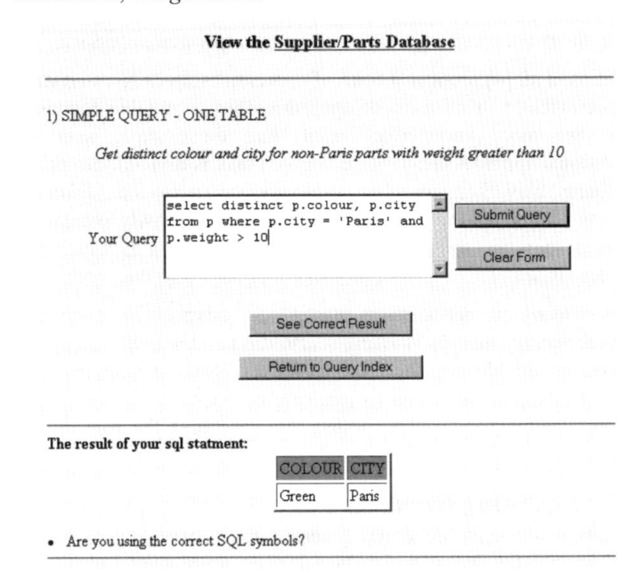

Figure 3. Input screen with hint displayed

3.4 Feedback

The Oxford English dictionary defines feedback as information on some activity or system return on input. In the educational context in question here, feedback is immediate advice given to a student based on solutions previously submitted by the student. Its objectives are self-reliant learning and the achievement of competency in a domain. It may be synchronous or asynchronous i.e. it may be returned immediately or returned after a period of time.

Our system provides increasing degrees of feedback support by offering a three-tiered synchronous feedback strategy, comprised of error flagging, hints, and partial solutions.

- *Error flagging*, which the system automatically displays, is a form of integrated feedback. It shows the user if their submission is deemed to be correct or incorrect. A syntax error results in a system error message being created by the actual Oracle database in use. This error message is amended for the learner or novice user, so that the student can more easily comprehend it. It is then printed on screen, integrating Oracle into the learning environment, in keeping with a realistic setting. Should the submission be semantically incorrect the student may choose to view hints, partial solutions, or both.
- *Hints* indicate the part of the query that is causing an error. This aims to guide the student towards the solution, without explicitly telling him the correct answer. He is encouraged to rethink and restructure his proposed solution in the

context of the given hint. In the example shown in Figure 1 the student has used the "equals" symbol instead of the "is-not-equal-to" symbol. The corresponding hint displayed is "*Are you using the correct SQL symbols?*"

- *Partial solutions* give the student precise advice. However, while this advice is directly related to the incorrect input sentence, it is not so specific as to tell the student the complete answer. He must judge how to use the partial solution in his answer. Regarding the example in Figure 1, the partial solution displayed would be "*The question specifies non-Paris parts. Therefore, you need to use the <> symbol.*"

Each type of feedback is displayed when the user selects a particular option. In keeping with guided discovery, it is not compulsory to view hints or partial solutions. Additionally, allowing the student to choose the level of feedback may result in fewer negative motivational consequences [5]. Should the student find he is unable to successfully complete the given task, with or without the aid of feedback, he may choose to view the correct answer.

3.5 Assessment and Guidance

Other SQL tutors provide a feedback feature of varying degrees [1][7]. As far as we are aware, however, there is no optional personalized guidance element available to the student.

The term guidance is defined by the Oxford English dictionary as help or advice. We extend this definition to describe guidance as offering the student advice and recommendations for areas to concentrate on, based on data collected in a previous determination. This may be a single determination (i.e. a single session), or data collected over a period of time (over a number of sessions). When teaching a classroom-based module, a lecturer's advice is commonly based on the results of continuous assessment or coursework. Ideally an online tutoring system should also assume this role.

- You are having a small number of problems with selecting correct attributes
- You are having a lot of of problems with aggregate functions
- You are having a moderate amount of problems using SQL symbols

These results have been analysed, and a set of practise queries have been selected for you

1) SIMPLE QUERY - ONE TABLE
This question is based on one table. Tasks included are
prefixes, attributes, tables, symbols, and
miscellaneous tasks

2) QUERY WITH AGGREGATE FUNCTIONS
Supplier-Parts Database
This question is based on aggregate functions and a single table.
Tasks included are attributes, tables,
and aggregate functions

3) QUERY WITH AGGREGATE FUNCTIONS
Supplier-Parts Database
This question is based on aggregate functions and a single table.
Tasks included are prefixes, attributes, tables, symbols,
aggregate functions, and miscellaneous tasks

Figure 4. Portion of guidance feature

Information about the student is recorded as he works through the various tasks available on the tutoring system. This information consists primarily of the number of attempts made for each task along with the amount and category of any errors made for those attempted tasks.

The system uses the data obtained by the assessment element in order to formulate personalized guidance for the student (Figure 4). This data is divided into various categories based on the types of error the student has made. Also, the number of errors and attempts the student has made for each error type weights it. Guidance includes explicitly telling the student the level of difficulty they are having with each error group, be it low, moderate, or high. The system makes this evaluation by studying the weighted information available for each student. They are then presented with a list of tasks to practise, from which they may choose to complete any number or combination. Guidance is weighted according to the amount of errors made. Making a large number of mistakes within a certain error group results in more tasks based on that group being suggested for practise.

It is not compulsory for the student to attempt the extra set of tasks. Each task is described in full to allow the student to decide which they wish to attempt.

A further improvement to the guidance element of the tutoring system can be achieved through the use of data mining or, more specifically, web usage mining. Chang et al. [3] define data mining as being the process of extracting information or knowledge from a data set for the purposes of decision making. We wish to achieve this using the information stored in the access logs created by the web server. In order to analyse this raw data in order to discover learning and training patterns, we will adopt a three-tier architecture [11], which consists of data gathering and pre-processing, pattern discovery, and pattern analysis. By dynamically assessing the previous actions of the student, for example the SQL topics he has recently browsed, personalization of feedback and guidance can be enhanced, and fading of scaffolding can be further supported.

4. EVALUATION

An evaluation was conducted to assess student acceptance and usage of the system. This was carried out over a period of time by surveying students, studying web logs created by the server, and analyzing student results.

4.1 Usage

It was noted that high usage occurred during the week, particularly in the late afternoons and evenings. However, a significant amount, 20%, of usage was observed on weekends. In a traditional classroom setting, a tutor would not typically be available on weekends. With an online tutoring system, however, the student may continue with coursework when they wish.

Students expressed the opinion that feedback is the most important feature of an online system; we have found that 84% of students surveyed have used the scaffolding provided. Feedback and guidance are integral parts of this scaffolding, and should be faded over time.

4.2 Student opinion

Students taking the Introduction to Databases module were surveyed to determine their attitude towards online learning as opposed to traditional classroom based learning [9]. In excess of 85% appreciate online teaching and skills training as part of an on-campus degree programme. Students indicated that key advantages to the system include its constant availability and the self-paced learning opportunities.

When asked for their opinion regarding traditional labs versus online labs, the students surveyed did not greatly prefer one over the other. This indicates that both types of lab delivery are accepted.

4.3 Student results

Student performance is a substantial part of a degree programme.. Over the course of the last four years there has been a 2% increase per annum in the marks obtained by students in SQL exams [9]. During this time the system has been improved; other factors have remained constant.

5. CONCLUSION

The popularity of online tutorials is increasing as university class numbers expand and the availability of the Internet grows. Online tutoring however can be a complex task. Often learning through technology results in the computer simply acting as a substitute for a textbook. In order to maximise the potential offered by technology, online tutoring systems should reflect the role of the teacher rather than the textbook. For example, it would be beneficial to offer feedback to the student when they are having difficulty. A further benefit would be to note the areas the student is excelling in or having problems with and offer advice based on this.

Formal languages are particularly suited to automated tutoring. Their structure makes the expressions in these languages relatively easy to analyse and are often easy to define. Therefore, the comprehensive automated tutoring of a formal language becomes a realistic goal.

The system we presented here is an automated tutor for a database skills training environment. It aims to help students develop their SQL skills and is focused on training rather than knowledge acquisition. SQL is a formal language and so it is suited to automated tutoring. As with most formal languages errors can be easily classified as syntactical, semantic, or pragmatic, and thus can be analysed.

Our strategy for the automated tutoring of a formal language, SQL, is based on the virtual apprenticeship model. As with a traditional apprenticeship the student is engaged in a learning-by-doing process. The master observes and offers assistance when necessary. The automated tutoring system presented uses attempts to emulate this using scaffolding in the form of feedback and guidance. In keeping with guided discovery the student may view increasing levels of feedback, namely error flags, hints, and partial solutions.

Typically the student will attempt a number of tasks over one or more sessions. Information about each attempt and any errors made are stored. This is retrieved and used if the student wishes to obtain dynamically created personalized guidance.

Analysis of student activities and surveying of students have shown this automated tutoring system to positively influence exam results, and students have accepted it equally with classroom based lectures. The tutoring system presented here attempts to move beyond teaching the basic constructs of SQL alone. By encouraging the student to repeatedly practise the use of certain concepts he will gradually learn the pragmatics of the language, such as rules and conventions.

6. ACKNOWLEDGEMENTS

Our work was supported by the Dublin City University Teaching and Learning Fund.

7. REFERENCES

[1] Bhagat, S., Bhagat, L., Kavalan, J., Sasikumar, M., Acharya: An Intelligent Tutoring Environment for Learning SQL. In *Proceedings of the Vidyakash 2002 International Conference on Online Learning,* Mumbai, India, 2002.

[2] Boyle, T., *Design for Multimedia Learning*, Prentice Hall, Europe, 1997.

[3] Chang, G, *Mining The World Wide Web*, Kluwer Academic Publishers, 2001.

[4] Collins, A., Brown, J. S., & Newman, S. E. Cognitive apprenticeship: Teaching the crafts of reading, writing, and mathematics. In L. B. Resnick (Ed.), *Knowing, learning, and instruction: Essays in honor of Robert Glaser* (pp. 453-494). Hillsdale, NJ: Lawrence Erlbaum Associates.

[5] Corbett, A., Anderson, J., *Locus of Feedback Control in Computer-Based Tutoring: Impact on Learning Rate, Achievement and Attitudes*. In *Proceedings of the SIGCHI conference on Human factors in computing systems (CHI'01),* New York, USA, 2001.

[6] McLoughlin, C., Winnips, J. C., and Oliver R., Supporting Constructivist Learning through Learner Support On-line. In *Proceedings of the World Conference on Educational Multimedia, Hypermedia and Telecommunications EDMEDIA 2000*, Montreal, Canada. 2000, pp 674-680.

[7] Mitrovic, A., A Knowledge-Based Teaching System for SQL. In *Proceedings of the World Conference on Educational Multimedia, Hypermedia and Telecommunications ED-MEDIA/ED-TELECOM'98*, AACE, Freiburg, 1998, pp. 1027-1032.

[8] Murray, S., Ryan, J., and Pahl, C., A tool-mediated cognitive apprenticeship approach for a computer engineering course. In *Proceedings of the IEEE International Conference on Advanced Learning Technologies ICALT'03*, 2003.

[9] Pahl, C., Barrett, R., and Kenny, C., Supporting Active Database Learning and Training through Interactive Multimedia. In *Proceedings of the Annual conference on Innovation and Technology in Computer Science Education ITiCSE'04*, Leeds, UK, ACM, 2004.

[10] Wenger, E., *Artificial intelligence and tutoring systems : computational and cognitive*, Morgan Kaufmann Publishers, 1987

[11] Zaïane, O., Luo, J., Towards Evaluating Learner's Behaviour in a Web-Based Distance Learning Environment. In *Proceedings of the IEEE International Conference on Advanced Learning Technologies ICALT01*, pp 357-360, Madison, WI, USA, 2001.

Contrasting Women's Experiences in Computer Science at Different Institutions

Ela Zur
Computer Science Department
The Open University of Israel
108 Ravutski Street, Raanana, Israel 43107
tami,ela@cs.openu.ac.il

Lecia Barker
ATLAS Evaluation and Research, U. Colorado
Stadium 262E; 320 UCB
Boulder, Coloardo 80309-0320
lecia.J.Barker@colorado.edu

Lilly Irani
Computer Science Department
Stanford University
353 Serra Mall, 1B
Stanford, CA 94305
lirani@cs.stanford.edu

Mark Guzdial (Moderator)
College of Computing/GVU
Georgia Tech
Atlanta, GA 30332-0280
guzdial@cc.gatech.edu

SUMMARY

The SIGCSE community has produced much analysis of the dynamics causing women to choose Computer Science in disproportionately low numbers. In truth, we have learned that the factors are complex and contextual. This panel presents dynamics affecting women in four different institutions and explores the possibilities for common solutions to unique contextual problems.

In the last five years, there has been extensive attention paid to the gender-gap in computer science courses (e.g., [1, 5]). Women are not succeeding in our introductory computer science courses, nor are they continuing in the curriculum, at the same rate as men. The reasons why have much to do with the context of individual courses, which can differ markedly between institutions. This panel explores how markedly different institutions can have similar outcomes, and how there may be some cross-institutional contextual issues that we might address.

We will begin presenting an analysis of the results found in one university regarding the success of women in CS. Then we will present how classroom climate and the way CS is sometimes taught can lead to negative experience of studying CS at a different institution. We will suggest that interventions are necessary while students are building images of CS. We will end by presenting such an intervention that changes the classic CS1 course, and leads to changing the focus of what we're teaching.

Categories and Subject Descriptors

K.3 [**Computers and Education**]: Computer and Information Sciences Education

General Terms: Design

Keywords: Gender issues, CS1, success rates

SIGCSE'05, February 23-27, 2005, St. Louis, Missouri, USA.
ACM 1-58113-997-7/05/0002.

POSITION STATEMENTS

Ela Zur: The Open University of Israel (OUI) is a distance-learning university with an open admissions policy. Nonetheless, our courses are on an uncompromisingly high academic level. We noticed that over the years the percentage of women among students completing an undergraduate degree in Computer Science (CS) is very low: only 16% of the graduates are women.

We decided to investigate this phenomenon beginning with the first courses that students take in CS. The program of studies in CS begins with the introductory CS course, CS1, and with one of two Math courses. We found that women comprise about 20% of the students enrolled in all CS courses; about 17% of the students in the first Math courses; and 22% of the students in CS1.

When we measured success in CS1 by gender, we found significant differences. While 43% of the men passed the course, only 30% of the women did. In the math courses, the differences were a bit smaller: but still, while 30% of the men passed, only 24% of the women did. The low overall percentages are a reflection of the combination of open admissions and high academic standards mentioned above.

It is interesting that in advanced CS courses, the differences, if any, are much smaller. This is true for both theoretical courses (e.g., Algorithms, Automata) and programming courses (e.g., Advanced Programming with Java, Introduction to System Programming with C). The data suggests that there is no difference in success between men and women after the first courses. This means that when women make the initial effort and pass the first courses, they are as capable of succeeding, as are the men. Therefore, it is worthwhile investing efforts to increase the percentage of women enrolled in the CS program.

Lecia Barker: One long-standing explanation for the low participation of women in the sciences is the social and pedagogical climate of the classroom. In our research at the University of Colorado, however, we found few of the overtly anti-woman characteristics of the "chilly climate" first described in 1982 by Hall and Sandler. Nevertheless, we found that classroom climate in introductory classes was difficult and inhospitable for both men and women. Unfortunately, however, the characteristics leading to the "defensive climate" more acutely affect women than they do men, chipping away at their confidence and motivation because women enter computer science with less experience and coursework than men, must overcome a general societal belief that computing is in the male domain (thus making their presence a violation of an unspoken norm), and because they are so few in number, feel both isolated and conspicuous.

Our observations showed infrequent interpersonal interaction among students and professors, inexperienced students left behind by the fast pace, an unusually low frequency of questions or help-seeking, an environment where making mistakes was not allowed, and unchecked bids for attention and status among a few outspoken students. In interviews with 51 students, students said they often wanted to compare their performance with that of others, yet the individual nature of assignments made it impossible to know whether one was performing well or poorly. Students also perceived that one needed prior knowledge to succeed, so that in reality, the introductory course was not for beginners. Less experienced students interviewed felt intimidated by the outspoken students, and feared asking questions because they would slow down the class or expose their lack of knowledge. In combination with other changes (e.g., making assignments more concrete and palatable), changing the classroom climate to remove several of these characteristics could go a long way toward increasing the participation of women in computing.

Lilly Irani: A study of students in a CS course at Stanford during 2001-2003 surveyed a cohort of students who began in CS1 and continued through the core. Surveys at the beginning and end of the quarter, coupled with ethnographic interviews of a subset of the cohort, shed light on students' reasons for their choices to continue their CS educations. The researcher was not associated with the course.

Interviews and survey responses reveal that women's choices cannot simply be attributed to disproportionate lack of interest. Students found the course to be well-taught and assignments to be enjoyable. In CS1 at Stanford, socialization proved more important a gender-related factor than "chilly climates," inexperience with computers, or interpersonal gender issues.

Students, both male and female, who did not continue past CS1 typically told one of three stories about their choice, all beginning "It was fun but…": "I'm not really a computer person" and "I don't want to be a programmer all my life." Only one of 22 students interviewed did not enjoy her experience in the course.

However, research found that only students who knew adults involved in computing had a notion of options for computer science graduates that extended beyond the images of a solitary, "Office Space" coder developing lines of script. Work in sociology of gender found that even where women have interest and current competence in a field, the perceived utility, or value, of a field is critical to justifying its pursuit [2]. If choices that are atypical for one's gender are sociologically risky, then the potential risk-takers' rewards must be more valuable or more certain.

Our findings suggest the necessity of interventions that enrich students' awareness of rich possibilities in CS at the times when students are building images of various disciplines. [3] and [4] are case studies of such pedagogical efforts.

Mark Guzdial: Computer science departments have failed to attract the numbers or kinds of students for which there is currently demand. Despite the concerns about "off-shoring," information technology jobs in the U.S. economy go unfilled. What factors dampen interest in CS-related fields?

Typically in our courses, we over-emphasize *computer science* at the expense of teaching *computing*. Computer science is about the abstractions of how computational processes and devices work. Computing is about using these abstractions in concrete ways that provide service. We tend to teach the abstractions, but students learn best starting from the concrete.

Students want to learn for careers that are *useful*. Why is biology one of the most popular majors on most campuses, especially among women? Cells are not inherently more motivating than processes. I propose that it's clear to students that the *applications* of biology serve the needs of people. Is it obvious to a first year student that linked lists and recursion help people?

At Georgia Tech, we created a new introductory course *Introduction to Media Computation* that teaches introductory computer science in the context of manipulating media—a useful application of computers that students recognize. We developed the course because our campus required computing of all students, but we were only offering one form of CS1. The result was the same that we see around the world in CS1: High drop-out and failure rates, and very few transfers into the major. With the new course, we have some 90% of the students succeeding at the class, including women and minorities—and asking for *more* computing courses! The content of the new courses that we are creating for these students is computer science, but by explicitly starting from the *computing*, we create a sequence that attracts a different and wider range of students.

REFERENCES

[1] AAUW—America Association of University Women. (2000.) *Tech-Savvy: Educating Girls in the New Computer Age.* New York: AAUW Education Foundation.

[2] Eccles, J. S., Barber, B. L., & Jozefowicz, D. (1998). Linking gender to educational, occupational, and recreational choices: Applying the Eccles et al. model of achievement related choices. W. B. Swann, J. H. Langlois, & L. C. Gilbert (Eds.). *Sexism and stereotypes in modern society: The gender science of Janet Taylor Spence* Washington DC: American Psychological Association. 153-192.

[3] Margolis, J. and Fisher, A. (2002). *Unlocking the Clubhouse: Women in Computing*. Cambridge, MA: MIT Press.

[4] Rich, L., Perry, H., and Guzdial, M.. (2004). A CS1 Course Designed to Address Interests of Women. *Proceedings of the ACM SIGCSE Conference*. 190-194.

[5] Roberts, S. E., Kassianidou M. and Irani L., (2002), Encouraging women in computer science, *ACM SIGCSE Bulletin, v.34(2).*

A Synthesis and Ontology of All of Computing

Lillian (Boots) Cassel
Dept. of Computing Sciences
Villanova University
cassel@acm.org

Russell Shackelford
Chair, ACM Education Board
shackelford@acm.org

Robert H. Sloan
Dept. of Computer Science
University of Illinois at Chicago
sloan@uic.edu

Categories and Subject Descriptors

K.3.2 [**Computing Milieux**]: Computers and Education—*Computer and Information Science Education*

General Terms

Documentation, Standardization

Keywords

education, ontology, curricula

1. SUMMARY

In recent years, the discipline of computing has matured to the point of having distinct sub elements, each of which is developing curriculum recommendations, accreditation criteria, conferences, professional societies and publications. In particular, five distinct curriculum projects range in status from completed some time ago (*Computing Curricula 2001: Computer Science (CS-2001) [4]* and *IS 2002 Model Curriculum and Guidelines for Undergraduate Degree Programs in Information Systems (IS-2002)* [1]), through almost completed as of the writing of this special session proposal, and very likely to be published by the time of SIGCSE 2005 (*Computing Curricula 2004: Software Engineering* [2] and *Computing Curricula: Computer Engineering* [5]) to one that will likely be finished in late 2005 or early 2006 (*Computing Curricula: Information Technology*). More broadly, recent work in the UK to identify the variety of computing related programs currently offered in British universities identified 2,400 distinct program names [3]!

We are making an interim report on, and seeking input into, a project to keep the family of computing related disciplines together. This project is partially funded by the National Science Foundation (NSF grant 0338546, *Special Project: All in the Family: A unified representation of the computing and information related disciplines*), and is being run by a joint task force from several professional societies, with ACM taking the lead.

Very roughly, the goals of the project are to provide a synthesis of all that is computing, and various ways of organizing and visualizing that synthesis. This project began in late 2003, and got started in earnest in early 2004. We anticipate completing the work late in 2005 or early in 2006. Thus SIGCSE 2005 is the perfect time for us both to report on our work to date, and to get valuable feedback from the community.

2. OUTLINE

1. History and goals of this "ontology project." In Section 4 of this proposal for a special session, we discuss what those goals are.
2. Summary of progress so far.
3. Questions that the task force has about how best to proceed.
4. Discussion with those present about how we should go forward.

We expect that the "presentation" parts may occupy 20-35 minutes altogether, and that the remainder of the session will run as a group discussion.

3. EXPECTATIONS FOR SESSION

We expect that this session will be of broad interest to many members of the SIGCSE community. We do not think that this will be controversial in the way that *Computing Curricula: Computer Science* occasionally was. Nevertheless, we think that most computer science educators are very interested in the totality of computing and in particular the place of computer science within this totality. Of course the session will also be of great interest to those SIGCSE attendees who have strong interests in one of the other computing disciplines. In particular, the session will be of interest to those whose departments or colleges offer more than one type of computing degree or are planning to add an option for their computing students.

This session is important because, as we discuss at more length in Section 4, the overall project is important. Now that the breadth of computing has grown to include five distinct possible undergraduate programs, it is really important that we keep some sense of the computing disciplines as a related family of disciplines. We need to work *today* to ensure that in a future school where there are roughly equal sized

SIGCSE'05, February 23–27, 2005, St. Louis, Missouri, USA.
ACM 1-58113-997-7/05/0002.

departments of, say, computer science, information technology, and software engineering (which, incidentally, is approximately how Rochester Institute of Technology is now), that those three programs are seen as close neighbors, in the manner of, say, mechanical engineering, industrial engineering, and civil engineering, and not as three unrelated entities that have no common ties.

We expect to elicit feedback both by discussion during the session, and by calling for written and web feedback.

4. GOALS OF OVERALL PROJECT

This project seeks to produce an interactive representation of all of the computing and information related disciplines. This representation will include all of the topic areas that comprise the various sub disciplines and will show the relationships between them and between the topic areas and various outcomes that are associated with proficiency in the topic areas. The structure will be web accessible and will allow exploration for a variety of purposes. Some of these are sketched here to give a flavor for the goals of this project.

- Support of program development. Innovative and creative programs will be able to identify where they are in the spectrum of computing related topics and will be able to describe their offerings clearly.
- Support updates of curriculum recommendations. Because this mechanism will be extensible and easily updateable, massive curriculum recommendation efforts will not be required. Instead, the contents of a computing related program can be derived from the dynamic list of topics and activities, and associated with the desired objectives.
- Development of interdisciplinary programs. The integration of computing and various other disciplines is leading to a number of exciting new areas of study and research. This representation of the union of all the computing disciplines will give a clear view of the areas that they bring to the table in these new areas. For example, a program in bioinformatics can clearly see the topics that computing has to offer and can select the ones that are best suited to the goals of the interdisciplinary program. A similar structure for biology would be a very useful partner in this effort but is outside the scope of this proposal.
- Relationships with related disciplines. The computing disciplines rely on related areas and need to remain connected with relevant advances in such areas as electronics, physics, mathematics, psychology, management, biosciences, neurosciences, linguistics, and more. These connections will be easy to add to this structure.
- Visualization of the union of the bodies of knowledge of the computing disciplines. We are working to find a way to visualize, along many different dimensions, the union of the information in the five curriculum reports. (To date concept mapping seems the most promising approach, but nothing we have tried so far is perfect.)
- Possible updating of the ACM Computing Classification scheme. The ACM classification scheme (used, for instance, to classify articles in both ACM's and IEEE Computer Society's scholarly journals) is somewhat dated. The output of this project may be useful in helping to bring this scheme into the twenty-first century.

5. ACKNOWLEDGMENTS

This project has been supported by National Science Foundation (CISE Directorate) grant number 0338546. Additional funding has come from ACM; participation of the IEEE Computer Society members of the task force has been funded by IEEE Computer Society.

6. ADDITIONAL AUTHORS

Additional author: Andrew McGettrick (University of Strathclyde, email: andrew@cis.strath.ac.uk).

7. REFERENCES

[1] J. T. Gorgone, G. B. Davis, J. S. Valacich, H. Topi, D. L. Feinstein, and J. Herbert E. Longenecker. *IS 2002 Model Curriculum and Guidelines for Undergraduate Degree Programs in Information Systems.* Association for Information Systems, 2002. Also available on-line from http://www.computer.org/education/cc2001/.

[2] R. LeBlanc and A. Sobel. *Computing Curricula 2004: Software Engineering.* IEEE Computer Society Press, 2004. To appear.

[3] UK Quality Assurance Agency. Subject benchmark statements:computing. Technical report, Qulity Assurance Agency for Higher Education, 2000. Available from http://www.qaa.ac.uk/crntwork/benchmark/computing.html.

[4] E. Roberts, G. Engel, J. H. Cross, R. Shackelford, R. Sloan, R. Austing, D. Carver, C. K. Chang, G. Davies, P. J. Denning, R. Eckhouse, W. King, F. Lau, A. McGettrick, S. Mengel, G. M. Schneider, P. Srimani, and U. Wolz. *Computing Curricula 2001: Computer Science.* IEEE Computer Society Press, 2001. Also available on-line from http://www.computer.org/education/cc2001/.

[5] D. Soldan, M. Theys, J. Hughes, P. Srimani, A. McGettrick, V. P. Nelson, M. Varanasi, A. Clements, R. H. Sloan, D. J. Neebel, E. A. Hughes, B. Klenke, R. Hoelzeman, J. Aylor, G. Engel, J. Impagliazzo, D. Lyon, and G. Peterson. *Computing Curricula 2004: Computer Engineering.* IEEE Computer Society Press, 2004. In press. Final draft available on-line from http://www.eng.auburn.edu/ece/CCCE/.

Using SeSFJava in Teaching Introductory Network Courses

Tamer Elsharnouby
Department of Computer Science,
University of Maryland,
College Park, MD 20742
sharno@cs.umd.edu

A. Udaya Shankar
Department of Computer Science,
University of Maryland,
College Park, MD 20742
shankar@cs.umd.edu

ABSTRACT

Networking course projects are usually described by an informal specification and a collection of test cases. Students often misunderstand the specification or oversimplify it to fit just the test cases. Using formal methods eliminates these misunderstandings and allows the students to test their projects thoroughly, but at the expense of learning a new language. SeSF (Services and Systems Framework) is one way to overcome this obstacle. In SeSF, both implementations and services are defined by programs in conventional languages, thereby, eliminating the need to teach the students a new language. SeSF is a markup language that can be integrated with any conventional language. The integration of SeSF and Java is called SeSFJava. SeSFJava provides a technique to mechanically test whether student projects conform to their corresponding specifications, thereby, providing the instructors with a technique for semi-automated grading.

We present a four-phase transport protocol project, and describe how SeSFJava is used in specifying, testing and grading the different phases of this project. The use of SeSF significantly (1) increased the percentage of students who completed the projects, (2) reduced their email queries about the specification, and (3) reduced the grading time.

Categories and Subject Descriptors

C.2.2 [**Computer-Communication Networks**]: Network Protocols; D.2.5 [**Software Engineering**]: Testing And Debugging—*distributed debugging, testing tools*; F.4 [**Theory Of Computation**]: Mathematical Logic And Formal Languages

General Terms: Design, Verification.

1. INTRODUCTION

The goal of the programming assignments of the introductory networking senior-level course at University of Maryland is to teach the students the following:

- The role of network protocols.
- The different roles of the layers of the network and how they stack above each other.
- How to enhance the performance of the network in the face of changing network conditions.
- How to implement a distributed multi-threading applications, for example, client-server or peer-to-peer applications.

In fall 1999, we introduced a three-phase project that takes the above goals into account. The project was to implement client and server TCP sockets. Phase I implements a data transfer protocol. Phase II implements congestion control in order to enhance the performance of the data transfer protocol. Phase III implements the connection management and the two-way data transfer protocols of TCP/IP. All project specifications were described informally, and test cases were provided.

During the course, a number of problems emerged. Some students misunderstood the specification or oversimplified it to just fit the test cases provided with the project assignment. Other students did not test their projects thoroughly with various inputs. Others did not finish the project because they did not budget enough time, especially in phase III which involved much more work than the other two phases.

The teaching assistants (TAs) spent excessive time in testing and grading the student projects.

These problems prompted us to integrate formal methods into the networks course. Formal methods, in theory, removes all misunderstandings about the project specifications. It provides techniques to test the projects extensively, which helps the students to discover more bugs. It permits division of the project into more phases, for example, the third phase can be divided into two phases: one that implements connection management, and another that puts everything together. Formal methods also provides a testing harness on the actual platform.

But on the other hand, formal methods is not without drawbacks. One drawback is that students have to learn a new formal language, which paves the way to more misunderstandings by the students, because of their lack of expertise. Another drawback is that they have to learn new techniques to test their implementation against the project specifications. All these have to be learned under the tight time constraints of the semester.

SIGCSE'05, February 23–27, 2005, St. Louis, Missouri, USA.

To overcome these drawbacks, we used a framework that we have developed, called SeSF (**Se**rvices and **S**ystems **F**ramework), that (1) allows definitions in conventional languages of implementations and services of distributed systems, (2) formalizes the notion of an implementation satisfying its services, and (3) provides a means for mechanical testing [9]. SeSF is an imperative, or procedural, version of the formalism in [4]. The main difference between SeSF and most other formalisms [4–7], is that SeSF stays close to the programming world.

The remainder of the paper is organized as follows. Section 2 describes an overview of SeSF. Section 3 describes an overview of SeSFJava and SeSFJava Harness. Section 4 introduces the network project. Section 5 describes our experience with the students. Section 6 concludes.

2. SESF OVERVIEW

Like most formalisms, SeSF provides a **compositional methodology** for the design and implementation of concurrent systems. Compositionality means that the design and implementation of a concurrent system can be broken up into the design and implementation of component concurrent systems. We refer to implementations as **systems** and external behavior specifications as **services**. In SeSF, both systems and services are specified by programs in conventional programming languages.

A system specification is intended for execution. Hence, its programs must satisfy the computational, synchronization, and other constraints of the underlying platform – for example, accounting for whether the platform has a single processor, a multi-processor with shared memory, or a set of loosely-coupled message-passing processors.

The service specification states all (and only) the desired properties of the system's execution, unencumbered by internal structure and computational, implementation and synchronization issues. In most formalisms, the service defines the permissible interactions between the system and its environment. However, our interest is in **layered compositionality**. Here, a composite system consists of layers of component systems, and services define the allowed sequences of interactions between layers.

Roughly speaking, a system **satisfies** its services above and below if the interactions it initiates are allowed by the services, *assuming* the interactions initiated by the system's environment are allowed by the services. Our **compositionality property** is that, given a composite system consisting of layers of component systems with services in between, if every component system in isolation satisfies its services, then the composite system as a whole satisfies its services.

Because services are defined by conventional programming languages, they are **executable**. The adoption of executable services, in general and in SeSF in particular, has the following consequences. First, the notion of a system satisfying a service is equivalent to the composite program of the system and service satisfying certain correctness properties. Second, developers can *test* a concurrent system against its service simply by executing the composite program of the system and the service, and checking whether those properties are satisfied.

Using conventional languages for specifying services, instead of a high-level specification language, has certain advantages and disadvantages. One advantage is that the service specification language is familiar to programmers, perhaps even the same language as that of implementation. This reduces the possibility of the service specification being misunderstood by implementors. Another advantage is that it allows actual implementations to be tested, rather than an abstract model. The main disadvantage is that most programming languages suffer from inconsistencies and ambiguities, and one has to avoid such constructs in service specifications. For example, Java has an ambiguous memory model, and different Java implementations have different memory models.

3. SESFJAVA OVERVIEW

SeSF is a markup language that can be integrated with any programming language. **SeSFJava** [3] is the integration of SeSF with Java. Java is chosen because of its relatively precise semantics, popularity, and built-in concurrency constructs. A SeSFJava program is a Java program with SeSF tags inserted as Java comments. Hence, a SeSFJava program can be compiled and executed as a Java program. But because of the SeSF tags, it can also be tested. We have developed a testing harness, called **SeSFJava Harness**, that can execute a distributed system of SeSFJava programs and check whether the resulting execution satisfies the relevant services and any other desired correctness assertions (also specified in SeSFJava).

SeSFJava Harness is able to handle general Java programs (e.g., parameterized unbounded-state programs) and general safety and progress assertions (e.g., parameterized invariant and leads-to assertions). It tests the implementation on the actual final platform, without altering the program to run on a simplified platform (e.g., over TCP/IP network sockets rather than a thread-based emulation). It helps the programmer check systems during the development phase; we are not concerned with black-box testing.

To test a system against its service, we execute the services and the systems together with a harness process. The harness process runs on an arbitrary machine and ensures that only one thread in the distributed system is proceeding at any time. This approach is rather conservative (because it prevents parallel execution of processes). However, it is simple and provides the global snapshots needed to check the assertions.

To participate in the testing, the system and service programs need to be instrumented, and there is a SeSFJava Preprocessor for this purpose [2, 3]. But in the case of the networking projects, we gave the students preprocessed code to manually insert in their system programs, thereby relieving them of the preprocessing hassle.

4. PROJECT OVERVIEW

The goal of the project is to build a full-fledged transport protocol between a client entity and a server entity over unreliable channels that (exactly like IP) can lose, reorder and duplicate messages in transit subject to a maximum message lifetime. The transport service [8] consists of connection management between the client and server entities augmented with reliable two-way flow-controlled data transfer. A reliable data transfer from a source to a sink ensures that data is delivered in the same sequence it was sent and without loss.

The project is divided into four phases. Each phase is independently tested for correctness.

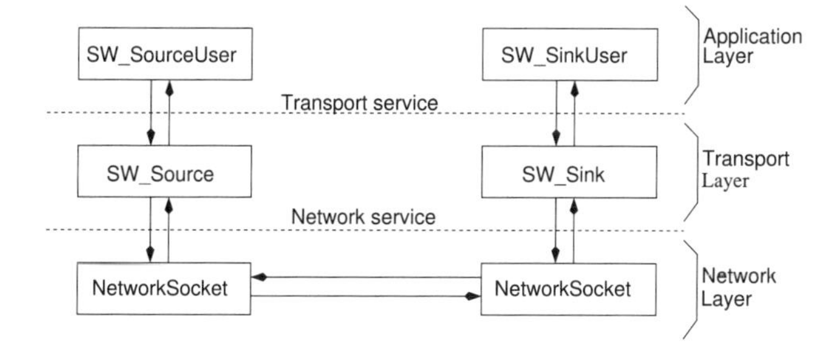

Figure 1: Phase I Overview

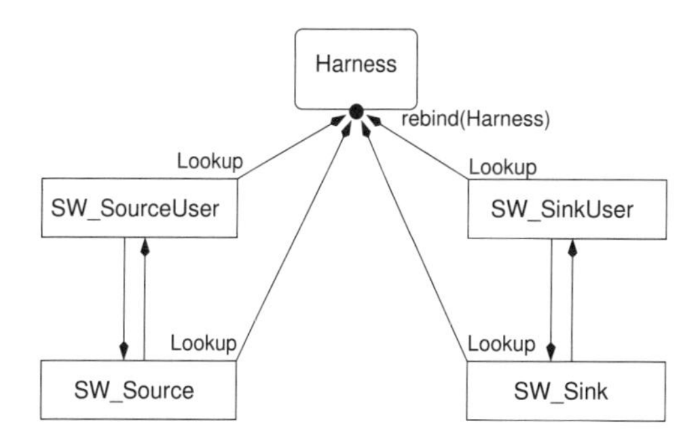

Figure 2: Phase I Harness Outline

4.1 Phase I: Data Transfer Protocol (Correctness)

In this phase, the student implements a protocol that achieves reliable data transfer over unreliable network channels. Specifically, the project consists of two interacting programs, a Source and a Sink, as shown in fig. 1. The Source consists of three components: SW_SourceUser, SW_Source and NetworkSocket. The Sink consists of three components: SW_SinkUser, SW_Sink and NetworkSocket. SW_SourceUser passes data to SW_Source. SW_Source buffers the data (in a send window) and transfers it to SW_Sink, resending until it is acknowledged by SW_Sink. SW_Sink buffers data received out of sequence (in a receive window) and delivers data in sequence to SW_SinkUser.

The students are provided with:

- The applications, SW_SourceUser and SW_SinkUser, which transfer a file from the source to the sink.
- The NetworkSocket entity which provides the unreliable channels to be used by the transport entities. NetworkSocket entity is a wrapper to the standard sockets. It is used instead of the usual UDP sockets, because in a LAN environment, the standard sockets display hardly any loss, reordering or duplication. The students can change the probabilities of loss, reordering and duplication on the fly, which is important for testing.
- The SeSFJava Harness module and the data transfer service specification, which defines the signature of the interactions between the layers, as well as the permissible sequences of these interactions (e.g., the data sequence delivered to SW_Sink must be a prefix of the data sequence accepted from SW_Source).

The students are to implement SW_Source and SW_Sink so that they conform to the provided data transfer service. The students are free to choose the particulars of the design, including message types and formats, sequence number space, data block size, retransmission policy, acknowledgment (cumulative and/or selective) policy, round-trip time estimator, etc.

4.1.1 *Testing Phase I*

The data transfer service and the SeSFJava Harness are illustrated in file Harness.java (fig. 3). For full version of the harness, see the class homepage [1]. This file consists of the following parts:

- The main method which binds an instance of the Harness to Remote Method Invocation (RMI) port "Harness".
- Lock and unlock methods for the Harness main lock, for synchronizing the programs and threads of the project. When a thread acquires the main lock, no other thread in the network system can proceed, until the lock is released. This allows a global snapshot of the network system to be collected at the Harness and evaluated against the service. (This is a simplified version of the general SeSFJava Harness.)
- Methods that represent the interactions between the transport layer and the application layer. There are three of them: sendData and ackData on the source side, and deliverData on the sink side.
- Invariants of the data transfer protocol, for example, the number of bytes delivered to Sink's user cannot exceed the number of bytes sent by Source's user.

After developing the source and sink entities, the student connects the distributed system (SW_SourceUser, SW_Source, SW_SinkUser and SW_Sink) to the Harness, as shown in fig. 2. Initially, the student inserts, in the constructor of each network entity, an RMI "lookup" call for the Harness RMI port. For each of the interactions mentioned above, the student inserts code to obtain the Harness lock and issue an RMI call in the corresponding method in class Harness.

For example, SW_Source.sendData method after the student insertion is as follows:

```
// Inside SW_Source.java
void sendData (byte []data) throws Exception {
    harness.lock();              // obtain Harness main lock
    harness.sendData(data);      // RMI call of Harness method
                                 // with same parameters
    ...                          // sendData method body
    harness.unlock();            // release Harness main lock
}
```

Consequently, a student can determine the correctness of both source and sink sides by checking that no errors were thrown during the execution of Harness. (To detect deadlocks, we add an extra condition: a file sent by the source has to be received.)

The program is executed as follows: (1) Execute the Harness module, so it can bind to port "Harness", (2) Execute the sink side so it can hook to the Harness class, (3) Execute the source side to start sending the file. A log file is recorded for every execution.

4.1.2 *Grading Phase I*

The TAs grade the data in a semi-mechanical way. They run scripts to execute the projects with different input files and different network conditions. Each execution is stored in a different log file, which is checked for thrown errors. If there is an error, the TA checks the log file to print out the trace that has generated this error, and determines the grade accordingly. The student can resort to a very simple solution, say a send window size of 1, but they will then suffer in Phase II.

4.2 Phase II: Data Transfer Protocol (Performance)

This phase emphasizes the protocol's performance; that is, the grade is primarily based on the throughput achieved under varying network conditions, which in turn depends on how well the protocol adapts to congestion, the overhead of the congestion control mechanism, etc.

The students strip the RMI calls inserted in Phase I, and enhance their code to perform better. Enhancements are of two kinds: (1) network optimizations, for example, adding Tahoe congestion control, and (2) code optimizations, for example, reducing the thread-switching in their code. In this phase, the NetworkSocket has the ability to play scenarios that emulate real-life network traffic. Thus, the students can view how their code performs under various conditions.

The TAs grade this project by running scripts that execute the students projects a number of times for every test scenario, and record the throughput for each run. The average throughput is computed and the students are classified according to the performance into four groups, from fast to slow, and the grade is determined accordingly.

4.3 Phase III: Connection Protocol

In this phase, the students build a connection management protocol over unreliable network channels. The grade in this phase is primarily based on the protocol's correctness. Specifically, the project consists of two interacting programs, a Client and a Server, as shown in fig. 4. Client consists of three components: ClientUser, CM_Client and NetworkSocket. Server consists of three components: ServerUser, CM_Server and NetworkSocket.

The students are to implement CM_Client and CM_Server which are the transport entities at the two ends. They are provided with the other entities. ClientUser and ServerUser are the users of the transport entities. These applications open and close hundreds of connections under different circumstances. The pair of NetworkSockets are as in phases I and II. The specifications formally describe the three-way handshaking connection establishment, and the two-way handshaking of the disconnection procedure. Similar to that of phase I, the service specifications and the Harness are provided in Harness file, and the network system is constructed as in fig. 5, The testing and grading are carried out similarly to that of phase I. Because of limited space, we will not describe the methods in detail.

4.4 Phase IV: Putting It All Together

In this phase, the students build a full-fledged transport service over unreliable network channels, specifically, com-

```
import . . .;
class Harness  extends UnicastRemoteObject implements HarnessInterace{
  // HarnessInterface contains the headers of all the methods defined
  // in this file except methods correctData and checkAssertions.
  . . .
  Harness() throws RemoteException {super();}
  public static void main(String args[]) throws Exception {
    . . .
    Naming.rebind("Harness", new Harness());
  }

  public void lock () throws RemoteException  { . . . }
  public void unlock () throws RemoteException { . . . }

  // Source entity variables.
  ByteArrayOutputStream srcHist = new ByteArrayOutputStream ();
  long srcBufSize = 32*1024;
  int srcBufUsed;
  long srcNumSent, srcNumAcked;
  long sinkNumDelivered;   // Sink entity variable

  // Sends data from source user to source entity to deliver it to
  // remote user.
  // Called by SW_Source.sendData
  public void sendData(byte []data) throws RemoteException {
    synchronized (lock){
      checkAssertions();
      if (srcBufUsed + data.length <= srcBufSize && data.length > 0){
        srcHist.write (data, 0, data.length);
        srcNumSent + = data.length ;
        srcBufUsed + = data.length ;
      } else System.out.println("usr sendDataSource failed ");
    }
  }

  // Notifies user that n bytes have been acked.
  // Called by SW_SourceUser.ackData
  public void ackData(int n) throws RemoteException {
    synchronized(lock){
      checkAssertions();
      if (srcNumAcked + n  <=srcNumSent ){
        srcBufUsed = srcBufUsed - n ;
        srcNumAcked = srcNumAcked + n ;
      } else System.out.println("usr ackedData failed ");
    }
  }

  // Delivers "data" received to entity user.
  // Called by SW_SinkUser.deliverData
  public void deliverData(byte []data) throws RemoteException {
    synchronized(lock){
      checkAssertions();
      if (sinkNumDelivered + data.length <= srcNumSent &&
          data.length > 0 && correctData(data))
        sinkNumDelivered = sinkNumDelivered + data.length ;
      else System.out.println("usr deliverData failed ");
    }
  }

  boolean correctData (byte []data) {
    byte srcData[] = srcHist.toByteArray();
    for (int i = 0; i < data.length; i++)
      if (srcData [((int) sinkNumDelivered) + i] != data[i])
        return false ;
    return true ;
  }

  // ASSERTIONS section
  void checkAssertions() throws RemoteException{
      if (!((srcBufUsed >= 0) && (srcBufUsed <= srcBufSize)))
        System.out.println(":bufCondition(false)");
  }
}
```

Figure 3: Harness program (file Harness.java)

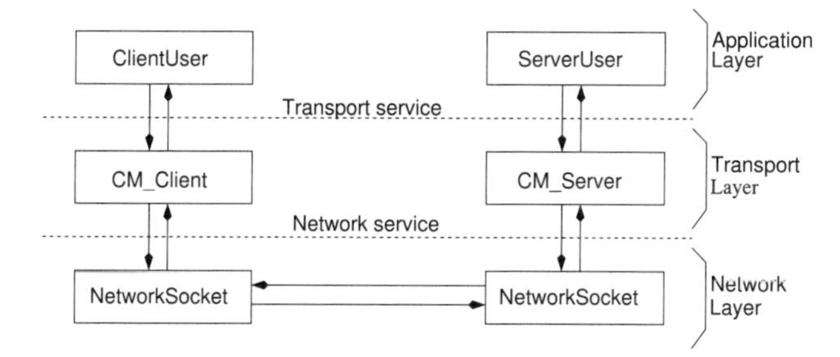

Figure 4: Phase III Overview

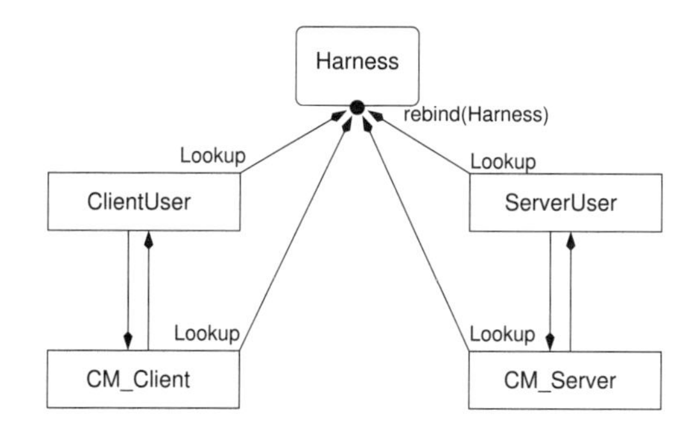

Figure 5: Phase III Harness Outline

bining phases II and III (after stripping the RMI calls). The grade of this project is based on the correctness and the performance of the students' implementations.

5. EXPERIENCE WITH THE STUDENTS

We have been using SeSFJava in the senior-level undergraduate computer networks course for the past three years. The projects are mandatory: no student can pass the course without passing the projects. The average number of students per class is 50. Most students have not been exposed to formal methods before taking this course.

Using SeSFJava significantly improves the performance of the students. Table 1 compares the use of detailed informal description of the projects (without SeSF) against the use of SeSF in specifying these projects. The number of students who completed all the phases of their projects almost doubled. Their questions about the specifications decreased by 40%. The student drop rate decreased by almost half.

	Without SeSF	With SeSF	Improv.
% of students who completed their projects	45%	88%	95%
# of email queries per students	16	10	60%
% of students dropping the class	27%	14%	93%

Table 1: Improvement using SeSFJava

From the TA perspective, using SeSF reduces the grading time per student, because considerable amount of the grading is carried mechanically. The number of regrading requests fell by 60%. We think this is because a student can test his/her implementation against the project specification, and because the TA provides the student with the trace demonstrating any errors (and thus grade penalties).

6. CONCLUSION

This work presented a design for an incremental transport protocol project. We integrated formal methods, SeSFJava in particular, into this project to achieve several goals. First, misunderstandings of the project specifications are almost entirely eliminated, because the specifications are presented formally in a language that is familiar to the students. Second, we are able to test and grade each phase thoroughly and independently, which results in better management of time for the students and the TAs. Third, the students and the TAs are able to mechanically test whether the project implementations conform to the specifications.

SeSFJava and the Harness have been used in computer network courses [1, 10]. It is not limited to networking projects, and can be used in introductory concurrent programming courses.

Acknowledgment

This work was supported in part by the Maryland Information and Network Dynamics (MIND) Laboratory, Fujitsu Laboratories of America, and by the Department of Defense through a University of Maryland Institute for Advanced Computer Studies (UMIACS) contract.

7. REFERENCES

[1] T. Elsharnouby. Class homepage on computer networks (CMSC417) at University of Maryland, 2003. http://www.cs.umd.edu/class/spring2003/cmsc417/.

[2] T. Elsharnouby and A. U. Shankar. SeSFJava: A framework for design and testing of concurrent systems. Technical Report CS-TR 4619, UMIACS-TR 2004-61, University of Maryland, 2004.

[3] T. Elsharnouby and A. U. Shankar. SeSFJava harness: Service and assertion checking for protocol implementations. *IEEE Journal on Selected Areas in Communucations*, 2004.

[4] S. S. Lam and A. Shankar. A theory of interfaces and modules I – composition theorem. *IEEE Transactions on Software Engineering*, 20(1):55–71, January 1994.

[5] N. Lynch and M. Tuttle. Hierarchical correctness proofs for distributed algorithms. In *Proceedings of the ACM Symposium on Principles of Distributed Computing*, Vancouver, B.C., August 1987.

[6] J. Misra. *A Discipline of Multiprogramming.* Springer-Verlag, 2001.

[7] A. Roscoe. *The Theory and Practice of Concurrency.* Prentice Hall Series in Computer Science, 1998.

[8] A. U. Shankar. Transport layer principles. published in The Communication Handbook, CRC Press, 1996.

[9] A. U. Shankar. *Concurrent Systems and Services: Design, Verification and Testing.* in preparation, 2005.

[10] Y. Yang. Class homepage on computer networks (CS433) at Yale University, 2003. http://zoo.cs.yale.edu/classes/cs433/assignments/prog1.

A Pattern-based Development Tool for Mobile Agents

Vishal D. Modak
School of Computer & Info. Sc.
University of South Alabama
Mobile, AL 36688
251-343-1263
vdm303@jaguar1.usouthal.edu

David D. Langan
School of Computer & Info. Sc.
University of South Alabama
Mobile, AL 36688
251-460-6390
dlangan@usouthal.edu

Thomas F. Hain
School of Computer & Info. Sc.
University of South Alabama
Mobile, AL 36688
251-460-6390
thain@usouthal.edu

ABSTRACT

Mobile agents are a technology that is applicable in several courses. However, the development of applications using mobile agents can be difficult and time-consuming for students. To address this problem, a tool called Mobile Agent Development Environment (MADE) is presented. MADE facilitates the rapid creation of mobile agent based applications through a pattern-based code generating wizard. MADE organizes and offers the creation of mobile agents based on their characteristics and behavior. MADE is based on the IBM Aglets API. MADE also offers easy-to-use plug-ins for course specific domains such as database and networking. Initial testing has shown that 55% of the code needed for simple applications can be generated quickly and automatically using the described tool.

Categories and Subject Descriptors

D.2.2 [**Software**]: Design tools and techniques. Programmer workbench.

General Terms

Design, Experimentation.

Keywords

Mobile agents, development tool, design patterns, distributed systems.

1. INTRODUCTION

The widespread use of communication and computing technologies on the Internet in areas such as E-commerce, information retrieval, mobile devices, and monitoring systems has increased the need for customizability, configurability, and flexibility in distributed applications. In this context, distributed applications have been developed using standard client-server technologies such as RPC, RMI and CORBA. However, these technologies have limitations such as voluminous traffic, high network latency, and inflexibility.

SIGCSE'05, February 23–27, 2005, St. Louis, Missouri, USA.

Mobile agents are a powerful, uniform paradigm for distributed computing. Mobile agents are autonomous entities that move in the network, executing themselves and performing tasks on an arbitrary or pre-defined set of machines.

In the mobile agent paradigm, the service-related code (provided exclusively by the server in the client-server model) is encapsulated in the mobile agent. The execution of the code is not limited to the machine on which the mobile agent was created, but is available throughout the network. In this manner, mobile agents allow a network host maximum flexibility in accessing logic, resources and processors. The advantages of mobile agents have been extensively discussed by Lange [7].

There are numerous application areas where mobile agents can make a significant contribution, including distributed information retrieval [4], distributed network management [3,6], distributed databases, workflow applications, load balancing [2,9] and parallel processing [8].

A mobile agent can monitor the network traffic load on a router and switch to a more expensive (higher bandwidth) connection when there is congestion. An information retrieval agent can search for information residing on remote nodes and report back to the source machine. A computation agent can identify lightly loaded network hosts to perform CPU-intensive processing functions. A communication agent can send messages back and forth between clients residing on various network nodes. A mobile agent can encapsulate a service that dynamically configures itself to the changing network conditions. A mobile agent can also be used to trace an intruder's path through a network by reading host logs, determining the intruder's source, and moving to that host for further tracking.

Design patterns have proven to be highly useful in the object-oriented community helping programmers to develop well-designed applications through approved reusable components. The objective of design patterns is to provide general solution models for common problems. Similarly, a mobile agent design pattern describes the characteristic behavior of a genre of mobile agents to solve a particular problem type. For example, consider the problem of gathering information from a list of sites. Once the search criterion is known, an exhaustive search can be performed on each site, either locally or by remote invocation. If none of the sites yield the desired data, it can be concluded that the data does not exist in that list. The Itinerary mobile agent design pattern is a generic solution to problems of this nature. The list of sites to be searched is the itinerary, and searching the data on each site is the repetitive task that is to be performed by the mobile agent. Patterns are flexible, understandable and reusable, and have become an essential element for intelligent software engineering. Mobile agent design patterns have been proposed to solve various kinds of problems [1,5,10]. Some of these patterns have fairly intuitive names like Boomerang, Itinerary, Master-Slave, Messenger and Finder.

The rest of the paper is structured as follows: in Section 2 we present the motivation for using mobile agents in some advanced computer science courses; in Section 3 we list some of the problems faced by students in developing mobile agents; Section 4 highlights the features of our visual pattern-based mobile agent development environment, MADE; in Section 5 we present results of the preliminary evaluation of MADE; finally summarizing conclusions in Section 6.

2. MOBILE AGENTS IN ACADEMICS

Mobile agents can be seen as a useful paradigm that could be integrated into several advanced courses in a computer science curriculum. For example, in a networking class, a variety of concepts are presented that involve gathering the status of a system of computers, and, based on that status, making centralized decisions. Mobile agents provide a suitable abstraction, and a mobile agent design pattern provides a solution template. In most operating systems classes the concept of distributed algorithms is presented. It is often covered only at a conceptual level because of implementation overhead. Again, mobile agents may provide a suitable abstraction, and one or more patterns can be composed into a solution. In a database course scenario, data needed by an application may be distributed over databases found at multiple sites. The solutions to these problems can again be easily addressed in terms of mobile agents based on a collection of design patterns.

These three examples provide possible course candidates for the use of mobile agent technology. Mobile agents may be thought of as a special case of threads or as processes that travel as well as communicate, and as such, the implementation of mobile agents could be covered in an advanced programming class. However, in advanced networking, operating systems, or database courses, the focus is on the domain problems being addressed, and little room is available for coding overhead. Thus the use of mobile agents in such academic settings may be dependent on how easily one can deal with the programming problems associated with them.

3. OBSTACLES TO DEVELOPING MOBILE AGENTS

While most of the available mobile agent toolkits provide an API, they lack a visual development environment with automatic code generation. Thus, the majority of the mobile agent code is generated by hand and can be a very complex and error-prone task.

Based on our experience in developing mobile agents, we present some common programming problems faced by students, that are tedious, complex, and error-prone:

1. Implementing the various mobile agent design patterns such as Itinerary, Master-Slave, Star-shaped, Branching, Meeting and others.
2. Programming mobile agents to perform various tasks such as database querying and retrieving network statistics using SNMP protocol.
3. Handling mobile-agent intercommunication.
4. Centrally monitoring the execution of the aglets in the network. Since the Aglets framework does not provide any centralized monitoring of an aglet's execution, monitoring the aglet's execution and determining the location of error/exception is very difficult.
5. Step-by-step debugging a mobile agent's execution in a network to determine the exact cause of error/exception.

4. A SOLUTION

An analysis of various existing mobile agent applications developed so far suggests the importance of mobile agent design patterns. Most of these applications used multiple mobile agent design patterns, and multiple agents in their design.

To simplify the creation of mobile agents, we have developed a visual pattern-based Mobile Agent Development Environment (MADE). MADE is based on the IBM Aglets API [11]—a commonly used, and easy to understand mobile agent toolkit. This was a natural choice since several mobile agent applications have been developed using the Aglets API. This approach does require that each participating machine on the network be running the Tahiti aglet server. MADE will help a student create mobile agents, and using a selected design pattern, create an application framework. Some domain specific reusable components (plug-ins for SNMP and JDBC) provide additional domain specific capabilities.

With the help of a step-by-step wizard, the student first selects a mobile agent design pattern (see Figure 1) and in a corresponding number of additional steps adapts it to the requirements of target application. On the basis of the pattern selected, the wizard provides various choices for selecting events to be handled, execution order, protections, type of remote messaging, itinerary destinations, task allocation policy, timeout, logging choices, and others (see Figures 2 and 3). These choices give the developer the flexibility to adapt the pattern to the specific target requirements. Finally, the code generator—an integral part of MADE—generates the skeleton source code for the selected pattern. The mobile agent is now programmed to follow the selected pattern.

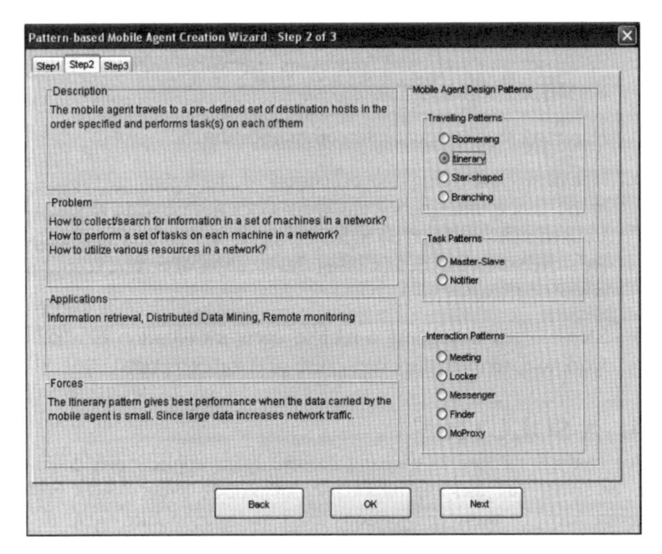

Figure 1 Selecting a design pattern.

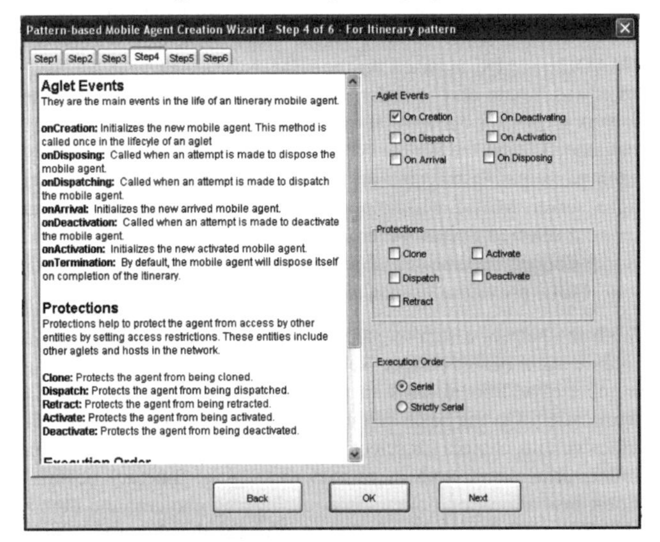

Figure 2 Specifying event handlers and execution order.

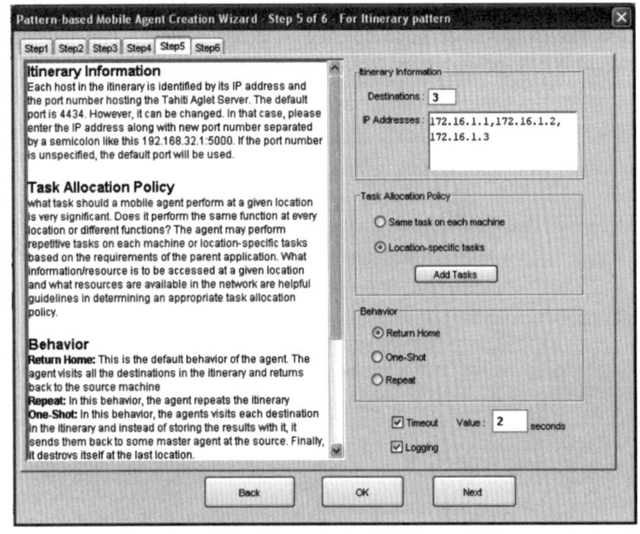

Figure 3 Specifying a specific itinerary.

To further simplify the task of developing mobile agents for various domains, MADE provides a collection of plug-ins. MADE currently provides three such plug-ins: JDBCConnection for making JDBC connections, JDBCResultSet for making queries, and one for SNMP.

The JDBCConnection plug-in provides support for four drivers—JDBC-ODBC, Oracle, Ms SQLServer and PostgresSQL. The JDBCResultSet allows the developer to configure the SQL query and set the characteristics for the Resultset object. These two components greatly simplify the task of querying and reporting data from various databases.

The SNMP plug-in called SNMPManager provides support for four RFCs—RFC 1213, RFC 1514, RFC 1643 and RFC 1755. These RFCs enable the collection of information about hosts in a network, such as attached interfaces, available resources, and running processes. In addition, various network traffic parameters can be monitored, such as bandwidth consumption, link utilization, packet error rate, SNMP statistics, and various protocol statistics.

These toolbox components facilitate the creation of mobile agents having the ability to perform database-related and SNMP-related tasks. The student drags and drops the necessary components into the agent's design area and configures them to add the necessary functionality to the mobile agent (see Figure 4). Component-specific source code is automatically generated and added into the agent's source code.

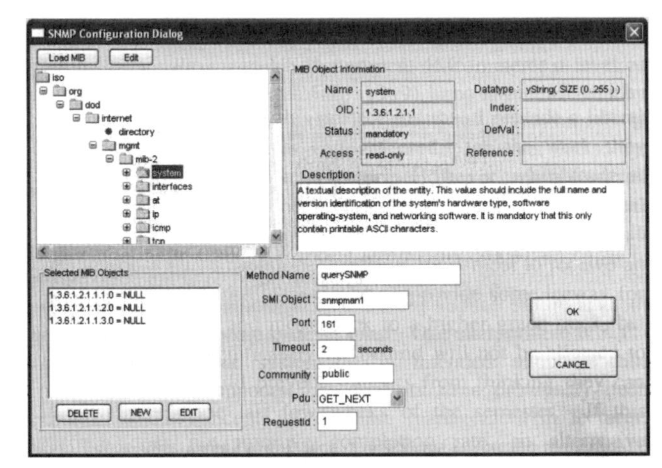

Figure 4 The SNMP configuration plug-in.

As mentioned, remote debugging a mobile agent's execution in a network is very daunting task. So far, none of the existing mobile agent systems have been able to provide an acceptable solution to this problem. One way of minimizing the initial occurrence of errors, is to auto-generate validated error free code for the commonly known programming errors and exceptions. The automatic generation of pattern-specific and component-specific code in MADE has been shown to considerably reduce occurrence of common programming errors.

MADE currently provides support for implementing three patterns—Itinerary, Master-Slave and Notifier with full pattern source-code generation. MADE also provides support for integrating mobile agents based on multiple design patterns.

5. EVALUATION

The evaluation of MADE consisted of two phases. The test group consisted of students familiar with the basic concepts underlying mobile agents and their various design patterns. In the first phase, the students were given two programming assignments involving mobile agents, without using MADE. The two assignments were based on two mobile agent design patterns, namely *Itinerary* and *Master-Slave*. A survey was conducted to collect information about their experiences and the difficulties faced. The test group was also asked for their suggestions, and features they would like in a proposed tool. The survey provided valuable information for formulating the requirements and features incorporated into MADE.

In the second phase, the same test group of students was asked to carry out the same assignments using MADE. A survey was conducted to determine the experience of the test group. The survey questions were designed to evaluate the intuitiveness, real world match, usability, accessibility, and error handling.

The time taken to perform the assignments, and the total length of the source code, were also collected in both the phases.

The comparative survey responses indicate that MADE is very intuitive and easy to use. In phase one, the average time taken to complete the assignments was 10-12 hours. In phase two, the average time taken to complete the same assignments was reduced to a "1–3 hours" category. This is a huge reduction in the development time. While some of the reduction may be explained by the experience gained in phase one, it is unlikely that this would be anywhere near the 80% observed time savings, particularly since there was a ten-month interval between the two phases. Also, one of the test subjects who had not participated in phase one, experienced a development time in the "1–3 hours" category. We feel that a substantial amount of the development time reduction is due to the elimination of the complex low-level code. We found that 55% of the total code was autogenerated. Programming errors, such as those relating to the migration of the agents, serialization, JDBC exceptions, and other runtime exceptions, were reduced.

6. CONCLUSION

The described features of MADE[1] make the mobile agent design process easy and accessible. Abstracting the implementation details allows the user to concentrate on the overall semantics of the target application, thus helping to reduce the tedium and complexity involved in its implementation. The visual development tool and code generator synergistically aid in the rapid development of mobile agents.

With a reduction of about 80% of the development time using MADE, and the elimination of the complex low-level code, the concept of the mobile agent paradigm becomes a viable implementation mechanism. A number of computer science courses can now make profitable and practical use of this technology.

[1] Available at www.cis.usouthal.edu/~vmodak/made.htm

7. REFERENCES

[1] Aridor, Y., and Lange D., Agent Design Patterns: Elements of Agent Application Design, In *Proceedings of 2nd International Conference on Autonomous Agents*, ACM Press, 1998

[2] Cao, J, Sun, Y., Wang, X., and Das, S.K., Scalable Load Balancing on Distributed Web Servers Using Mobile Agents, *Journal of Parallel and Distributed Computing*, 63(10), 2003, pp 996–1005.

[3] Du, T.C., Li, E.Y., and Chang, A-P., Mobile agents in distributed network management, *CACM*, 46(7), 2003, pp. 127–142.

[4] Gray, R., Kotz, D., Cybenko, G., and Rus, D., Mobile Agents: *Motivations and state-of-the-art systems*, Thayer School of Engineering, Dept. Of Computer Science, Dartmouth College, April 2000.

[5] Hung, E., and Pasquale, J., Agent Usage Patterns: Bridging the conceptual gap between Agent-Based Applications and Middleware, *Technical Report*, Univ. Of California, San Diego, 2000.

[6] Kona, M.K., and Xu, C-Z, A framework For Network Management using Mobile agents, *IEEE International Parallel and Distributed Processing Symposium*, Fort Lauderdale, FL, 2002, pp. 225–233.

[7] Lange, D., and Oshima, M., *Programming and Deploying Java Mobile Agents with Aglets*, Addison and Wesley Publications, August 1998 Edition.

[8] Noy, P.,and Schroeder, M., Mobile Agents for Distributed Processing. *Agents Workshop on Infrastructure for Multi-Agent Systems*, Barcelona, Spain, 2000, pp. 263-265,

[9] Sawano, T., Zhang, Y., and Takagi, H., Load Balancing Facility Using Aglets, a Java mobile agent system, *Institute of Policy and Planning Sciences*, Discussion Paper Series No. 894, February 2001.

[10] Tahara, Y., Ohsuga, A., and Honiden, S., Agent System Development Method based on Agent Patterns, *Proceedings of the 21st International Conference on Software Engineering.* IEEE Computer Society Press, pp. 356–367, 1999

[11] The IBM Aglets Software Development Kit Version 2.0.2, www.trl.ibm.com/aglets/

The Virtual Network System

Martin Casado
Department of Computer Science
Stanford University
Stanford, CA 94305-9030
casado@cs.stanford.edu

Nick McKeown
Department of Electrical Engineering
Stanford University
Stanford, CA 94305-9030
nickm@stanford.edu

ABSTRACT

The goal of our work is to give students a hands-on experience designing, deploying and debugging parts of the Internet infrastructure, such as an Internet router that routes real network traffic, or a security firewall. To do so normally requires that the students have access to snoop and generate raw network traffic, which is a risk to privacy and security. And it normally requires each student to have a dedicated computer, and to modify the kernel. The Virtual Network System (VNS) is a teaching tool designed for undergraduate and graduate networking courses. With VNS, each student can build a router (or any packet-processing device) in user-space, in their own private, protected topology, and process real Internet traffic. VNS has been used by over 500 students at Stanford and remotely from other universities. This paper describes the VNS tool, and our experiences using it in the classroom.

Categories and Subject Descriptors

K.3.2 [**Computers and Education**]: Computer and Information Science Education

General Terms

Measurement, Design, Experimentation

Keywords

Network Simulation, TCP, Internet Infrastructure, Router Design, VNS

1. BACKGROUND

The typical undergraduate introductory networking class includes programming assignments. A canonical first assignment gives students experience with API-level sockets programming by implementing a simple web-client or ftp-client. Further assignments typically build on the sockets layer, and the students implement remote procedure calls, network games, distributed file systems and other applications. Yet the sockets layer is quite a high level abstraction of the underlying network, and sits on top of TCP, IP and the link-layer. Projects at this level don't provide students with experience in packet re-transmission, congestion control, routing nor other concepts key to an introductory class.

To provide hands-on access with lower-level networking concepts, the computer science education community has developed a number of project environments to supplement introductory networking courses [6, 7, 15, 8, 11, 16, 18, 10]. These reflect an oft-cited need for active learning environments in networking courses. Active learning in networks gives students experience in the subtleties of the design of a complex system, as well as prepare them for the networking industry.

These environments are typically variants of the following:

- Infrastructure for implementation of transport level protocols over a connection-less protocol such as UDP [15, 8].
- Virtual, simulation or emulation environments for developing simplified link layer or network layer protocols [11, 9, 6, 2, 3].
- Administration and/or kernel level development of network topologies of dedicated hardware or networked virtual machines [14, 16, 18, 12, 17].
- Simplified access to link-layer network traffic for analysis [10]

.

At the introductory level however there is a lack of teaching tools that allow students to develop and deploy Internet infrastructure components such as routers that interact with actual hardware on the Internet. Projects at the network level and below are typically taught theoretically or using special-purpose simulation environments. Simulation environments often require the students to learn and use non-standard scripting interfaces and libraries [9, 2] and are not designed to provide real time access to the Internet. Larger computer science programs may have labs with dedicated hardware in which students can develop network functionality at the kernel level [14, 17]. However, such environments require extensive resources to setup and and manage and are not suitable for introductory courses where the students may not have sufficient systems development expertise.

Giving students experience below the sockets layer with live traffic is quite difficult[5]. At the machine level, this

SIGCSE'05, February 23–27, 2005, St. Louis, Missouri, USA.

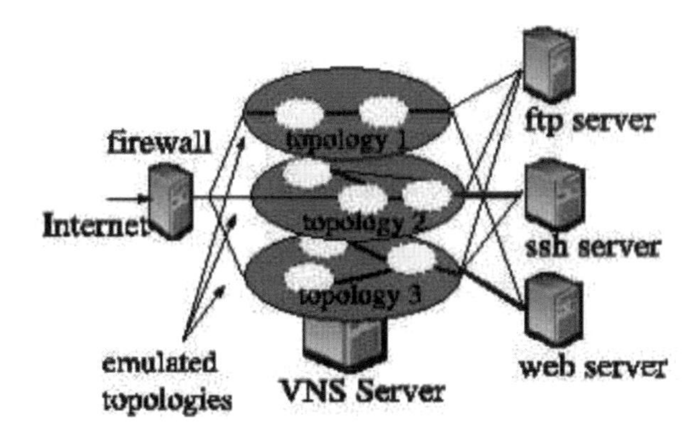

Figure 1: A simple VNS server setup with three virtual topologies and three application servers

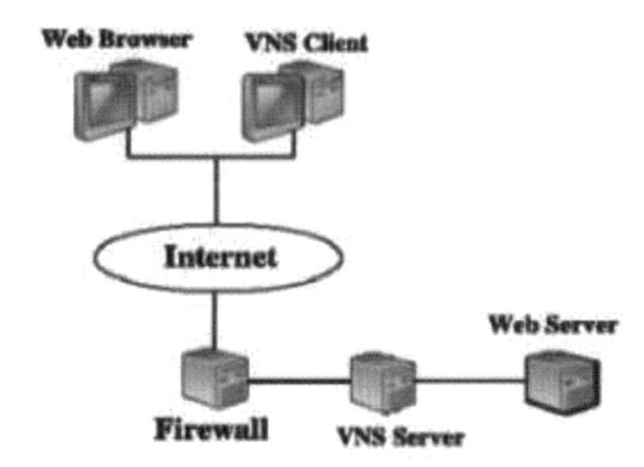

Figure 2: Web browser accessing a web server connected to VNS

usually requires modifying the kernel, which requires a computer per student, and a highly unstable development environment. It also requires great care in the security of the network. Most universities don't allow students to snoop or generate arbitrary raw IP packets on the campus network. And even if it was possible for a student to implement a router, it would be cumbersome to build a realistic topology to test one or more instances.

In this paper we present an educational tool we developed to support projects below the socket layer safely and using few resources. The Virtual Network System (VNS) was designed to allow hundreds of students working remotely (anywhere on the Internet) to develop user space programs that function as network infrastructure components, which operate on the actual Internet handling live, real-time traffic. We have developed a number of programming assignments using VNS that are suitable for undergraduate and graduate level courses. All course materials are publicly available. Fundamental to the design of VNS is the ability to support multiple remote classes working on different projects simultaneously. VNS is a production system currently being used in a number of courses locally and remotely. It has been used in undergraduate and graduate networking courses here at Stanford and at Johns Hopkins to teach the implementation of routers and to support the development of functional TCP compatible stacks that interact with other hosts on the Internet.

2. THE VIRTUAL NETWORK SYSTEM

The core of VNS is a server daemon written in standard C++ that can simulate multiple, virtual network topologies from a single host as shown in figure 1. Each virtual topology is reachable from the Internet and can integrate with actual hardware devices such as commodity PCs running common Internet services. The VNS server daemon can support hundreds of users and topologies from a single machine.

The VNS server accepts connections from VNS clients which are user space programs that will operate as hosts on the virtual topologies. Clients upon connecting can request that the server forward them traffic as seen by a particular host on a given topology. The client may then inspect, discard, modify or inject new traffic into the network, giving it the full capabilities of an actual host on the network.

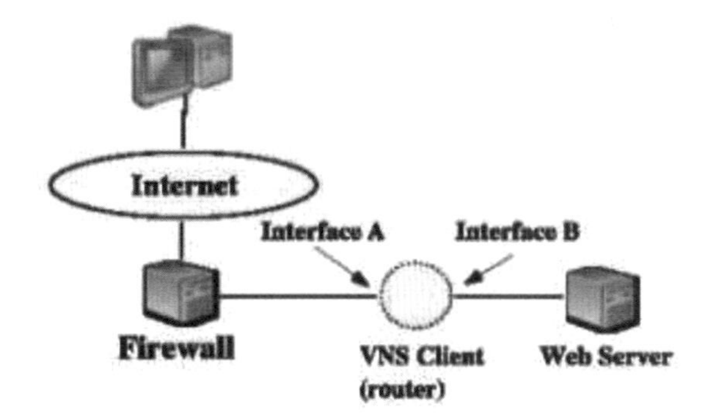

Figure 3: View of virtual topology as seen by web browser

We describe the operation of VNS using a simple example. Figure 2 shows a physical network topology in which a web browser application is trying to access a web server. The VNS server provides a virtual topology such that the web browser sees the network topology shown in figure 3.

In effect, the VNS server inserts the VNS client (the student's code) into the topology, even though the VNS client is physically located somewhere else on the internet (Figure 2). The VNS server achieves this by receiving all packets destined for interfaces A and B and passing them via a separate socket to the VNS client. The VNS client receives each packet exactly as the router would have received it (as raw Ethernet packets) and then determines what action, if any, to take. For example, when the VNS client receives an http (web) request packet on interface A, it will send the packet back to the VNS server with instructions for the VNS server to forward the packet out of interface B to the web server.

Security considerations regarding student access to low-level network functionality are addressed in VNS by placing a firewall with a stringent set of rules between the server and the Internet. The firewall rules only pass valid TCP and UDP packets without forged source addresses (egress filtering). Gateway based rate limiting makes it hard to implement client-initiated DOS style traffic patterns (e.g. SYN floods; although we've yet to experience this type of behaviour).

Projects using VNS typically involve writing a client to perform a specific function on the network. We've developed simple libraries in C, C++ and Java to serve as the base for clients. These libraries provide low level primitives for interaction with the server such as reserving a host, reading interface information about a particular host, reading a packet from the network and injecting a packet back into the network. All communications between the server and clients are done via a proprietary protocol over a TCP connection. Using a simple, user-level library to handle low level packet access has the advantages of simplicity, portability and simplified debugging. The libraries have the ability to create *pcap* [4] compatible packet trace files of all packets sent to or received by the client for analysis standard tools such as *tcpdump* [4] or *ethereal* [1].

3. REPRESENTATIVE PROJECTS

VNS is a good candidate environment for any project requiring low-level network access. While initially designed to aid students in developing network infrastructure components it is equally useful for demonstrating network concepts such as TCP characteristics using real Internet traffic. In this section we describe two assignments designed around VNS and our current effort to create a visual demonstration tool for use in class lectures and student lab environments.

3.1 Building an Internet Router with VNS

Here at Stanford VNS is used in the introductory networking course to teach the implementation of Internet routers. The assignment is structured around a simple topology consisting of a router with three interfaces connected to two application servers running standard Internet services such as http and ftp. Each student is assigned their own private topology and an IP range to allocate to the router's interfaces. Using the VNS client library as a base, the students develop fully functional routers. The routers must support the following basic functionality:

- ARP query/response capability
- ARP cache with timeout
- IP header checksum calculation
- TTL decrement on forwarded packets
- generate ICMP TTL exceeded when necessary
- NEXT hop lookup in forwarding table
- response to ICMP echo request
- generate ICMP Port Unreach for TCP/UDP packets destined to a local interface

A completed router will be able to route traffic from anywhere on the Internet to the connected Internet servers and will respond correctly to ping and traceroute. During development a student can test his or her router by using a standard web or ftp client directed at one of the application servers connected to their topology. Ambitious students may wish to add support for advanced functionality on their routers. Students have extended their routers to support NAT, web servers and IP filtering.

3.2 Implementing a Full TCP/IP Network Stack

VNS is used by students in our introductory networking course to develop a TCP compliant transport layer called STCP. While STCP can inter-operate with any standard TCP implementation it consists of a subset of TCP functionality leaving out more complex features such as congestion control. Students begin the project by implementing STCP over UDP, using UDP for the network layer. They manage both sides of the TCP connection. When they believe they have working implementations, they migrate their transport code to IP using VNS and test their implementations against standard TCP stacks anywhere on the Internet. The VNS portion of the assignment is done using a simple one host, one interface topology. Testing is done using an ftp client they develop in their direct programming assignment. Armed with an application and a transport layer, they can transfer files from any ftp-server in the Internet.

There are a number of advantages to using an IP based, TCP compatible transport layer. Students get to experience the subtleties of inter-operating with commodity TCP stacks. Exposure to the IP layer is representative of real world transport layer implementations which for example may have to handle checksumming over the IP pseudo-header. Students can extend their code to support standard TCP features such as slow-start, dynamic window-resizing, and the Karn-Partridge algorithm.

3.3 Clack : A GUI Router Builder

We also use VNS in the classroom to graphically demonstrate network concepts. To this end, we developed Clack, a Click-inspired, GUI VNS client written in Java [13]. Clack is a graphical, component-based router builder that can be used to demonstrate various router aspects using live Internet traffic. It currently contains a working subset of Click's basic ipv4 router components and supports ARP handling, IP header checks, IP forwarding, IP TTL decrement and basic ICMP handling and generation. Clack connects to the VNS server just like any other VNS client and can route real network traffic.

Clack is designed to visually illustrate network infrastructure concepts. For example, we show students in real-time how the buffer in a router evolves with network congestion; how performance changes if packets are dropped randomly instead of from the tail of a queue; and what happens if the router mis-sequences the packets. The client contains many user-configurable components, such as a FIFO queue component with configurable size and drop policy that displays its occupancy in real time. The queue also has a graphing feature which plots the absolute and average queue occupancy over a period of time. This can be used to show the TCP slow-start algorithm, or the saw-tooth of a TCP flow in congestion avoidance.

Development on Clack is ongoing. We plan to develop a set of loadable router configurations that can be used for demonstrations during lectures and by students in a lab environment.

4. EXPERIENCES WITH VNS IN THE CLASSROOM

VNS has become an integral part of two annual courses at Stanford and is used remotely by an upper level IP protocols course at Johns Hopkins University. The current con-

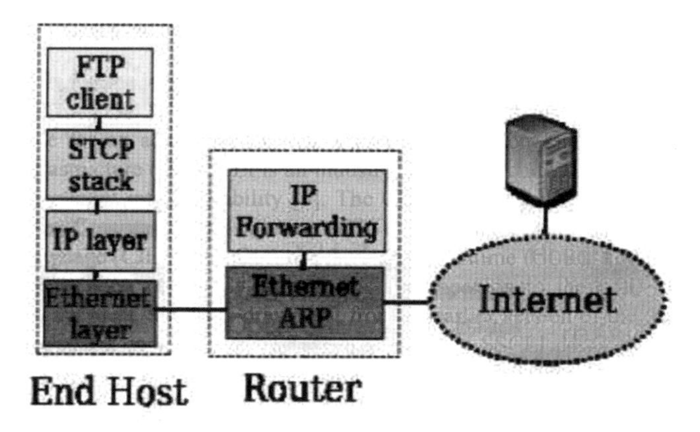

Figure 4: Full network stack and router developed by students in our introductory network course using VNS

figuration has handled tens of students simultaneously and hundreds of students in a quarter.

With VNS we have been able to organize the projects in our introductory networking course so that by the end of the quarter the students have developed a full networking stack that can inter-operate with live hosts on the Internet. The final project for the course requires the students to piece together all of their previously completed programming projects: Their ftp client application operates over their TCP transport layer, from which packets are forwarded through their own routers to connect to the Internet. The VNS topology and components of the final project are shown in figure 4.

Feedback from the students has been very positive. While most admit that the projects are a lot of work, implementations typically range from 1,000 - 2,000 lines of code per project, many find tremendous value in working directly with real Internet traffic using standard protocols. In the words of one student responding to a question on an anonymous, formal evaluation

> "Yes, it greatly helped my understanding. I feel that I could go work commercially on routers now."

We've had numerous requests from students after the quarter is over to allow them to use VNS to experiment with ideas of their own.

We have found that students' experiences are greatly affected by the transparency of the system. That is, a student must have access to all possible paths that traffic might take in order to debug their implementations. Providing *pcap*-compatible dump files is very useful to the students and we are continuing to explore other methods for providing debug access to VNS at runtime.

5. CONCLUSIONS AND FUTURE WORK

VNS gives students the opportunity to process real Internet traffic in user-space from anywhere in the Internet. Our implementation of the VNS server is robust, and can support hundreds or thousands of students from remote schools, with each student having their own private topology.

With support from the National Science Foundation, we are prototyping a national center for internet infrastructure teaching. Our lab setup has the necessary infrastructure, including global IP space, network and server capacity to support thousands of students simultaneously. The idea is to offer full support, curriculum and supplemental source code to institutions interested in using VNS. Technical details and complete assignment materials are posted on the project website at http://yuba.stanford.edu/vns. We are seeking to expand the number of courses that use VNS in remote colleges and universities. We encourage any faculty considering using the project to contact us directly by e-mail.

6. ACKNOWLEDGMENTS

This work was funded by the NSF, grant 02-082. We would like to thank Andreas Terzis of Johns Hopkins for providing very helpful feedback and suggestions, Greg Watson for general guru-ness and Guido Apenzeller and Vikram Vijayaraghavan for help in designing, developing and debugging the next generation virtual router system.

7. REFERENCES

[1] The ethereal network analyzer. http://www.ethereal.com.

[2] The network simulator - ns-2. http://www.isi.edu/nsnam/ns/.

[3] Opnet network simulator. http://www.opnet.com.

[4] tcpdump network sniffer. http://www.tcpdump.org.

[5] S. Akhtar, N. Al-Holou, M. Fienup, G. T. Finley, R. S. Roos, and S. Tannouri. The networks course: Old problems, new solutions. *The proceedings of the thirtieth SIGCSE technical symposium on Computer science education*, pages 360 – 361, 1999.

[6] I. B. Lewis Barnett. An ethernet performance simulator for undergraduate networking. *Proceedings of the twenty-fourth SIGCSE technical symposium on Computer science education*, pages 145–150, 1993.

[7] N. W. Brad Richards. Illustrating networking concepts with wireless handheld devices. *Proceedings of the 7th annual conference on Innovation and technology in computer science educatio*, pages 29–33, 2002.

[8] P. Dinda. The minet tcp/ip stack. *Northwestern University Department of Computer Science Technical Report NWU-CS-02-08*, January 2002.

[9] R. D. Enrico Carniani. The netwire emulator : a tool for teaching and understanding networks. *ACM SIGCSE Bulletin*, 33(3):153–156, 2001.

[10] M. J. Jipping, A. Bugaj, L. Mihalkova, and D. E. Porter. Using java to teach networking concepts with a programmable network sniffer. *Proceedings of the 34th SIGCSE technical symposium on Computer science education*, pages 120 – 124, 2003.

[11] L. E. Joseph D. Touch, Yu-Shun Wang. Virtual internets for lab and class experiments. *ISI-TR-563*, August 2002.

[12] B. Kneale and L. Box. A virtual learning environment for real-world networking. *Information Science*, page 71, June 2003.

[13] E. Kohler, R. Morris, B. Chen, J. Jannotti, and M. F. Kaashoek. The click modular router. *ACM*

Transactions on Computer Systems, 18(3):263 – 297, August 2000.

[14] J. M. Mayo and P. Kearns. A secure unrestricted advanced systems laboratory. *The proceedings of the thirtieth SIGCSE technical symposium on Computer science education*, pages 165–169, 1999.

[15] B. Richards. Rtp: A transport layer implementation project. *Proceedings of the sixth annual CCSC northeastern conference on The journal of computing in small colleges*, pages 134 – 141, 2001.

[16] J. Rickman, M. McDonald, G. McDonald, and P. Heeler. Enhancing the computer networking curriculim. *Proceedings of the 6th annual conference on Innovation and technology in computer science education*, pages 157–160, 2001.

[17] P. Steenkiste. A network project course based on network processors. *Proceedings of the 34th SIGCSE technical symposium on Computer science education*, pages 262 – 266, 2003.

[18] S. Yoo and S. Hovis. Remote access internetworking laboratory. *Proceedings of the 35th SIGCSE technical symposium on Computer science education*, pages 311–314, 2004.

The Course Scheduling Problem as a Source of Student Projects

William Combs
combsw@dickinson.edu

Robert Hawkins
hawkinsr@dickinson.edu

Thomas Pore
poret@dickinson.edu

Arik Schechet
schechet@dickinson.edu

Tim Wahls
wahlst@dickinson.edu

Louis Ziantz
ziantzl@dickinson.edu

Dickinson College, P.O. Box 1773, Carlisle, PA 17013, USA

ABSTRACT

The course scheduling problem is simple to understand, yet complex enough to admit a wide range of solutions at varying levels of difficulty in implementation. In this work, we outline four types of student projects based on this problem, discuss how these projects can be approached and how they might integrate into a computer science curriculum, and describe two example projects that we have used.

Categories and Subject Descriptors: K.3.2 [**Computers and Education**]: Computer and Information Science Education – computer science education, curriculum; F.2.2 [**Analysis of Algorithms and Problem Complexity**]: Nonnumerical Algorithms and Problems – sequencing and scheduling; D.3.2 [**Programming Languages**]: Language Classifications – constraint and logic languages

General Terms: Algorithms, Languages

Keywords: curriculum development, student projects, scheduling, constraint programming, user interface design, search

1. INTRODUCTION

The course scheduling problem is familiar and easily stated. Each course to be taught in a given academic term must be assigned an instructor, an appropriate classroom and a time period (start time, duration, and a set of days on which the course meets). This assignment must obey certain constraints. For example, the same instructor usually can not teach two courses with overlapping time periods, and two courses with overlapping time periods can not meet in the same classroom. Although this problem seems simple at first glance, it is actually quite complex. Even this version of the problem is NP complete [3]. Adding additional constraints (balancing faculty loads, specifying that particular courses should or should not be taught at the same time, giving preference to the wishes of senior faculty, ...) does not change the time complexity, but it does make implementing a solution even more interesting. The problem can be approached in many different ways covering a wide range of the computer science curriculum. Simplified versions of the problem are approachable by sophomore level students, while more complex versions can be used as senior projects. Hence, the course scheduling problem is an ideal source of student projects. Additionally, solutions (or even partial solutions) are obviously very useful for academic institutions, so a successful project is likely to actually be used and to become the basis for additional projects in following terms, rather than simply being discarded at the end of the term.

In this work, we first describe some project types based on this problem, and the difficulty of these projects. Next, we outline some possible approaches to solving the problem. Finally, we describe two example projects that students at our institution have completed.

SIGCSE'05, February 23–27, 2005, St. Louis, Missouri, USA.

2. PROJECT TYPES

We have identified four types of projects based on the course scheduling problem. In order from least to most difficult, they are:

1. implementing a graphical user interface
2. checking schedules for conflicts
3. generating feasible schedules
4. optimizing schedules by minimizing the number of unsatisfied preferences

Note that this ordering also gives an incremental approach to the problem as a whole, as each level is useful in implementing the next. We briefly describe each project type in the following subsections.

2.1 The User Interface

An academic course schedule should ideally be displayed as a grid (usually with days of the week on one axis and time periods on the other), as this format is familiar and facilitates visual checking for scheduling conflicts. This format is also very useful for inputting and modifying schedules, as those who are constructing the schedule can try various options and make changes until the schedule is satisfactory. The ability to modify schedules is also useful when the schedule to be constructed is based on the schedule from a previous term. For maximum usability, the user should be able to drag and drop courses from one scheduling period to another with the mouse. This kind of graphical interface is very different from a standard menu or dialog box based one, and requires considerably more creativity in implementation.

2.2 Conflict Checking

Even if a course schedule is constructed by hand, it is useful to check it for conflicts or other problems in an automated way. Typical aspects that could be checked include:

- courses taught by the same instructor or in the same classroom should not have overlapping time periods,
- the number of courses being taught by each instructor should be correct,
- courses that many students would wish to take simultaneously should not have overlapping time periods,
- courses that students would frequently switch between (at the beginning of the term) should be offered at exactly the same time.

Other aspects can be checked depending upon the policies and needs of the school or department in question.

2.3 Generating Schedules

The problem of generating course schedules is a classic example of a Constraint Satisfaction Problem (CSP) [6]. A *CSP* consists of a set of variables, a finite and predetermined set of possible values for each variable (referred to as the domain of the variable), and a set of constraints. A solution is an assignment to each variable of a value from its domain that satisfies all of the constraints. The variables are often referred to as *finite domain variables.* For the course scheduling problem, each of the attributes of a course that are of interest (the instructor, classroom and meeting time, for example) can be modeled as a finite domain variable, with appropriate sets of values specified for each. The constraints are exactly the kinds of conflicts or properties listed in the previous section. Such constraints are sometimes referred to as *hard constraints*, as any feasible schedule must satisfy all of them. CSPs can be solved in a number of ways, including search or constraint programming techniques as described in Section 3.

2.4 Optimization Using Preferences

Certain properties of a schedule may be desirable, but not absolutely required. For example, an instructor may prefer not to teach early in the morning, or not to teach two courses back to back, but would be willing to do so if it were necessary in order to find a feasible schedule. These sorts of properties are referred to as *soft constraints* or *preferences.* In the presence of such preferences, schedule generation can be optimized so as to find schedules that violate the minimal number of preferences. In optimization problems, the relative "goodness" of a solution is measured by an *objective function*, and optimization refers to finding solutions that minimize the objective function. In this paper, we use the number of unsatisfied preferences for a schedule as the objective function directly, although many other objective functions could be defined. For example, it is relatively straightforward to weight preferences, so that violating one preference has a larger impact on the value of the objective function than violating another would.

3. POSSIBLE APPROACHES

3.1 Approaches to the First Level Project

The course scheduling problem can be solved in many ways. For the first level project (user interface design), any programming language that has appropriate graphical user interface components can be used. Examples include Java, Tcl/Tk, and the Microsoft Visual languages. These languages can also be used to implement persistent storage of schedules (i.e. to hard disk), which is critical for usability. If all courses must be scheduled in standard time slots, this project is relatively straightforward. It becomes considerably more complex otherwise, especially for cleanly displaying courses with overlapping time periods.

3.2 Approaches to the Second Level Project

For the conflict checking version of the problem, the primary concern is a data structure for storing schedules that allows conflicts to be checked simply and efficiently. The simplest approach is a one dimensional list of courses (including the assigned instructor, room and time period) that is scanned repeatedly during conflict checking. A useful refinement (especially for large problem instances) is to use indices on each attribute of interest to speed up the search for potential conflicts. A related option is to store course information in a table in a standard relational database, and then check for conflicts using SQL queries. In this way, appropriate indices could be created and managed through the database system. The use of a database system for conflict checking is further explored in Section 4.1. All of these options can also be used to implement checking the number of preferences that are unsatisfied. Although we have not explored this option, it would likely also be useful to model a schedule as a graph for conflict checking purposes.

3.3 Approaches to the Remaining Projects

3.3.1 *Brute Force Enumeration*

The simplest approach to the remaining project types (generating and optimizing schedules) is brute force enumeration. If the problem is formulated as a CSP (so that each course has an associated set of possible instructors, possible rooms and possible meeting times), then all possible schedules can be generated using nested loops that step through all values in the domain of each attribute. If only a feasible schedule is required, then this process can stop as soon as the first schedule that satisfies all of the specified constraints is found. For optimization purposes, all schedules must be checked under this approach. The number of unsatisfied preferences for each feasible schedule is computed, and the best candidate schedule encountered so far is saved.

Although this approach is simple to implement, it is only usable for very small inputs. For example, suppose that 10 courses are to be scheduled, and for each course there are 3 possible instructors, 4 possible classrooms and 5 possible meeting times. Using the brute force approach, each of approximately 6×10^{17} possible schedules ($3^{10} \times 4^{10} \times 5^{10}$) must be checked in the worst case. The most direct implementation for this example would be to write 30 nested loops, although of course this should be modularized for maintainability and so that varying numbers of courses can be scheduled.

3.3.2 Search

A somewhat more efficient approach is to use backtracking to search for feasible schedules. The space of all possible schedules can be organized as a search tree, with each node representing a *choice point* (a point where a domain value is assigned to an attribute of a schedule), and each child of that node representing a choice of one of the domain values. Each child node in turn becomes a choice point for the next attribute to be assigned, and each leaf node represents a complete course schedule. Simply searching the entire tree is equivalent to brute force enumeration. However, a partial schedule can become unfeasible at a relatively high level in the tree. For example, the first two courses scheduled could be assigned the same classroom and overlapping meeting times on one branch of the search tree. Clearly, all of the schedules represented by the subtree rooted at the point where the second choice was made are not feasible – no assignment to the attributes of the remaining courses can cause such a schedule to become feasible. Hence, if this kind of situation is detected as soon as it occurs, the entire subtree can be skipped during search. Although this approach has the same time complexity as brute force enumeration in the worst case, it is often considerably better in practice.

If an optimal schedule (the fourth level project) is desired, then the objective function can be used to implement *branch and bound* search under certain conditions. In particular, the preferences to be checked must have the following properties:

- it is possible to calculate the number of unsatisfied preferences (so far) for a partial schedule (i.e. without scheduling all courses first)
- scheduling additional courses can never cause a previously unsatisfied preference to become satisfied

For example, if an instructor has a preference of teaching at least four courses, then branch and bound can only be applied if this preference is not considered unsatisfied until all courses are scheduled (or at least all courses for which this hypothetical instructor is a possible instructor). Under these conditions, if the number of unsatisfied preferences (so far) for a partial schedule is larger than the number of unsatisfied preferences for the best known candidate schedule, then an optimal schedule can not exist in the subtree rooted at that partial schedule. Hence, the subtree need not be searched.

This approach is most easily implemented in a declarative language such as Prolog. In these languages, partial schedules can easily be represented by using logic variables to represent attributes that have not yet been assigned values. Additionally, depth first exploration of search trees is the fundamental evaluation mechanism of these languages. Branch and bound can be implemented on top of depth first search by evaluating the objective function on a partial schedule and explicitly failing if its value is too high. Depth first search can also be implemented in more standard programming languages such as Java, although this requires using a stack (or recursion) to keep track of the next search tree node to visit during search, and most likely some explicit data structure for representing partial schedules as well.

3.3.3 Constraint Programming

An even more sophisticated approach is to use a *constraint programming language* such as Oz [7, 8] or clp(FD) [4] that has a built-in solver for finite domain constraints. The basic idea is to eliminate values from the domains of the variables that can not be included in any feasible schedule both before any search is done, and again each time a variable is assigned a value during search. For example, suppose that course A and course B are constrained to meet at the same time, that the possible meeting times for course A are Monday, Wednesday, Friday (MWF) at 11:00 a.m., 1:00 p.m. and 2:00 p.m. with a 50 minute duration, and that the possible meeting times for course B are MWF at 1:00 p.m. and 2:00 p.m. with a 50 minute duration, and also Tuesday, Thursday (TTh) at 1:30 p.m. or 3:00 p.m. with a 75 minute duration. The domains of the variables representing the meeting times for each course can immediately be reduced to MWF at 1:00 p.m. and 2:00 p.m. with no search, because none of the other values in the domains of these variables can appear in a schedule satisfying the given constraint. Additionally, if a meeting time of MWF at 1:00 p.m. is chosen for one of the courses during the search, then that same meeting time can immediately be assigned to the other course. As a final example, suppose that the possible classrooms for both courses A and B are Rooms 1, 2, and 3. Given the constraints that the courses must meet at the same time and that two different courses can not meet at the same room at the same time, then as soon course A is assigned Room 1 (during the search), Room 1 can be removed from the domain of the variable representing the classroom assignment for course B.

The effect of this domain pruning is exactly to avoid exploring large subtrees of the search tree, and so is much the same as the backtracking approach previously described. In fact, the worst case time complexity is still the same as for brute force enumeration. However, the average case running time is greatly improved, as the constraint programming approach is even more effective at avoiding search. For example, the scheduler described in Section 4.2, which is implemented in Oz, can generate schedules consisting of 25 or 30 courses without noticeable delays. Additionally, as the finite domain constraint solver is built in to the language, the kinds of domain reductions described above require very little effort on the part of the programmer. Many constraint programming languages also include features to support optimization. For example, branch and bound search as previously described is built in to Oz. The programmer need only implement the objective function appropriately, and then pass it as a parameter to the search mechanism.

The practical difficulty of the constraint programming approach, of course, is that the students and faculty involved must learn a constraint programming language. As these languages are quite different from "standard" programming languages, this is a significant challenge. We have offered a topics course in constraint programming at our institution, and so had students that were prepared to implement a system in Oz in a single semester. Otherwise, this project would have required two semesters – one to study constraint programming, and the second for the project. An alternative is to use a constraint solver that interfaces with a more standard programming language. For example, the Java Constraint Kit (JCK) [1, 2] is a tool for implementing constraint solvers in Java. Using such a tool would allow work on the project to begin more quickly, although the project itself would be more difficult as compared to doing the implementation in a constraint programming language.

3.4 Integration into the Curriculum

These projects incorporate concepts from a wide range of the computer science curriculum. A graphical interface for entering and/or presenting schedules is complex enough to require substantial design work, and is also excellent for reinforcing event-driven and perhaps even object-oriented programming techniques. Different stakeholders (faculty members, staff, the registrar, ...) are likely to have very different requirements for the user interface, the kinds of constraints and preferences that can be expressed on schedules, the relative weight of various preferences, and so on. Resolving these kinds of differences is a great lesson in real-world software engineering. Several of the approaches require significant data structure and algorithm design. Even the problem of representing possible class meeting times can require an interesting data structure. For example, the possibilities may include different combinations of days for the class meeting (MWF vs. TTh), and a class with a lab could meet at two different times on the same day. The data structure used must allow efficient detection of overlaps in meeting times, as this operation will be heavily used in both checking and search. Analyzing the worst and average case time complexity of the various approaches is also an interesting problem. Implementing a conflict checker using a relational database is obviously an appropriate project for a database course, and would integrate naturally into a larger project such as implementing a database for the registrar's office. Finally, implementing a schedule generating system in Prolog would exemplify many of the declarative programming concepts and techniques that are often taught in a programming languages or artificial intelligence course.

4. EXAMPLE PROJECTS

4.1 Checking Conflicts

The first student project involved writing a tool to check for conflicts in existing schedules. The system is implemented in Java, with Java Swing components used to create the user interface. The JDBC API is employed to communicate with IBM Cloudscape [5], which is a object-relational database management system that supports SQL queries. Given that all system components are Java-based, the schedule conflict checker can be used on a variety of systems.

The final user-interface implemented is quite simple and includes options to add rules for conflicts, to add courses, and to force a conflict check. Options can be initiated via pull-down menus or buttons on the interface. Choosing to add a course or a conflict opens a dialog box for the user to enter appropriate information. Information required for adding a course includes course subject (a string indicating both the department and course number), instructor name, time, and room. Defining a new conflict requires entering two different course subjects representing courses that should not be allowed to meet at the same time. Note that this is the only type of conflict that can be set by the user since checks for two courses meeting in the same room at the same time or having the same instructor at the same time are built in to the system. A check for one instructor teaching more than a set number of courses was not part of this implementation. Due to time constraints, a visual display of the current schedule (much like the first level project) was not implemented. Instead, when the user initiates a conflict check, a dialog box is displayed with the full schedule if there are no conflicts, or with a list of conflicts if any exist. The underlying implementation assumes predefined time slots. For example, a course in timeslot "A" would meet on Mondays, Wednesdays, and Fridays (MWF) from 8:30-9:20 AM, and a course in time slot "B" would meet MWF from 9:30-10:20 AM. This is based upon recommendations from the registrar's office on when courses should be scheduled. However, during the development of the project it became clear that laboratory sections of courses were not always scheduled within recommended time slots. In the interest of completing a working prototype of a conflict checker, the students decided to keep their simplifying assumptions and leave handling lab sections as a possible extension that future students could undertake. Having an enumerated set of time slots simplifies some of the processing since the software does not have to check for overlaps in time ranges. As implemented, course information is placed in a separate table based on time slot, and SQL queries are done to check for conflicts. Any conflicts are then recorded in a list data structure for later display.

The students involved in this project had extensive experience in Java and some background in SQL. They had significantly less experience with Swing components and had never used the JDBC API, so they had to invest time becoming accustomed to both. Additionally, they spent some time installing and configuring Cloudscape. While these were useful learning experiences, the students would have been able to accomplish even more if they had a more extensive background. Their final product has been tested on schedules for the Mathematics and Computer Science program, but has not been used on schedules beyond 25 courses.

Initial plans for this project included a web interface with many of the same properties as the first level project. The intent was to allow collaboration while building schedules so that individuals from the same department could contribute to the schedule independently, and then the final schedule could be checked for conflicts. Several departmental schedules could then be easily merged to check for conflicts across related disciplines. For example, the Physics and Astronomy department at our institution recommends Linear Algebra for students planning to attend graduate school in Physics, so they might wish to check for conflicts between that class and their upper-level Physics courses. Thus, a future extension to the conflict checker could involve making the interface web accessible.

4.2 Generating Schedules

The second student project consisted of writing a system to generate feasible schedules. This system is implemented in the Oz programming language, which supports constraint, declarative, object-oriented and graphical user interface programming (as well as several additional programming paradigms). Using Oz allowed the data structures representing schedules and courses to be implemented as classes, constraint programming techniques to be used for finding feasible schedules, and a graphical interface to be implemented for the system. Oz is free software and is available for Windows, Unix and Macintosh platforms.

This project includes two graphical interfaces – one for

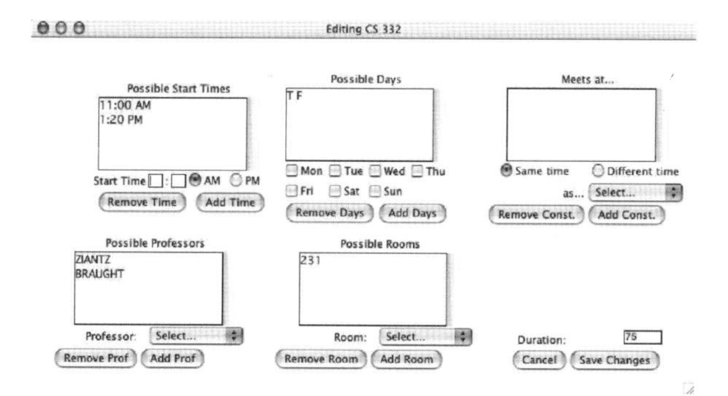

Figure 1: The Add/Edit Window

specifying the constraints on schedules, and a second for stepping through feasible schedules one at a time. The first interface (referred to as the Add/Edit window) allows the user to specify the sets of possible instructors, classrooms and meeting times for each course, and to specify that the meeting times for one course either must be exactly the same as for another course (so that students could easily switch between the courses), or must not overlap (so that students could take both courses simultaneously). These constraints can be saved in a file and later reloaded for generating more schedules or for modification. A screen shot of this interface is displayed in Figure 1.

The second interface allows the user to choose a set of courses to schedule, and then to step through all feasible schedules one at a time. A screen shot of this interface is displayed in Figure 2. Again, the students had planned to implement a graphical display of the schedule itself, but ran out of time and so a simple textual display was used. The Add/Edit window can be used to adjust the constraints on the schedule while possible schedules are being displayed. For example, if the schedule currently being displayed is satisfactory except that two courses taught by the same instructor are scheduled back to back, the sets of possible meeting times for these courses can be edited, and then the schedule can immediately be redisplayed. This approach allows preferences to be applied incrementally and interactively until either the schedule is satisfactory to all concerned, or the set of constraints on the schedule becomes unsatisfiable. During testing, this approach seemed to be at least as effective in finding good schedules as optimization using preferences would have been, and was considerably easier to implement.

Because the students had previously taken a course in constraint programming, they were able to use some reasonably sophisticated constraint programming techniques (reification, 0/1 propagators, ...) to control the amount of search done by their system. The system can easily schedule upwards of 30 courses, as long as the number of possibilities for each attribute of a course remains relatively small and the constraints are not so tight as to permit only a few feasible schedules. For smaller scheduling problems, the system can detect and report that no feasible schedules exist.

5. CONCLUSION

We have found the course scheduling problem to be intuitive and interesting for students, and to be a useful source of projects of various sizes and complexities. Because the problem can be approached in so many ways, these projects can

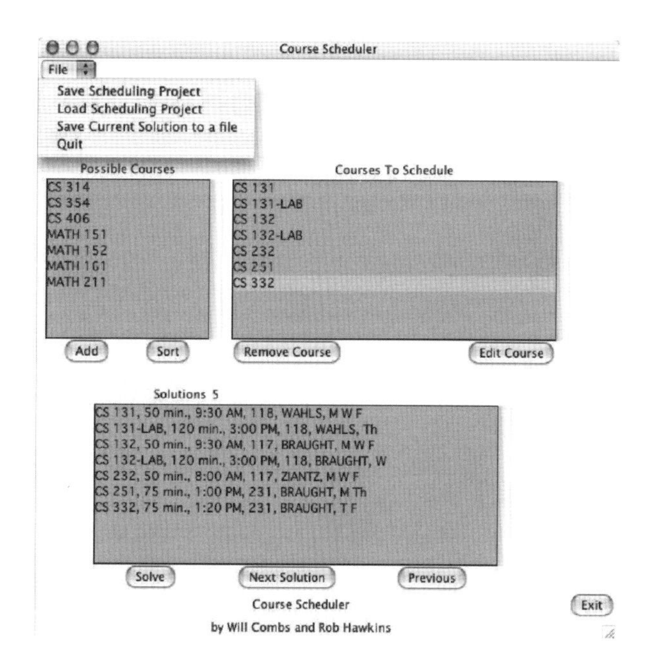

Figure 2: The Course Scheduler

be integrated into many different courses in the computer science curriculum, including data structures, algorithms, database, software engineering and programming languages courses. Larger projects based on this problem are ideal candidates for independent study or senior projects. Because solutions to the problem are immediately useful for academic institutions, projects are likely to be used and to be extended in future semesters. Of course, students are much more inspired to work on a project when the result will actually be used. We hope that we have inspired you to try some of these projects with your students.

6. REFERENCES

[1] S. Abdennadher, T. Frühwirth, E. Krämer, M. Saft, and M. Schmauss. Java Constraint Kit website, 2004. http://www.pms.ifi.lmu.de/software/jack/index.html.

[2] S. Abdennadher, E. Krämer, M. Saft, and M. Schmauss. JACK: A Java constraint kit. In M. Hanus, editor, *Electronic Notes in Theoretical Computer Science*, volume 64. Elsevier, 2002.

[3] T. B. Cooper and J. H. Kingston. The complexity of timetable construction problems. In E. Burke and P. Ross, editors, *Proceedings of the First International Conference on the Practice and Theory of Automated Timetabling*, volume 1153 of *Lecture Notes in Computer Science*, pages 283 – 295. Springer-Verlag, 1995.

[4] D. Diaz. *clp(FD) 2.21 User's Manual.* INRIA-Rocquencourt, Domaine de Voluceau, 78153 Le Chesnay, France, July 1994.

[5] IBM Corporation. Cloudscape website, 2004. http://www-306.ibm.com/software/data/cloudscape/.

[6] K. Marriott and P. J. Stuckey. *Programming with Constraints: An Introduction.* The MIT Press, Cambridge, Massachusetts, 1998.

[7] Mozart Consortium. Mozart Programming System website, 2004. http://www.mozart-oz.org.

[8] P. Van Roy and S. Haridi. *Concepts, Techniques and Models of Computer Programming.* The MIT Press, Cambridge, Massachusetts, 2004.

A Real-Time Information Warfare Exercise On A Virtual Network

James Walden
University of Toledo
1005 Abbe Rd N
Elyria, OH 44035
jwalden@eecs.utoledo.edu

ABSTRACT

Information warfare exercises, such as "Capture the Flag," serve as a capstone experience for a computer security class, giving students the opportunity to apply and integrate the security skills they learned during the class. However, many information security classes don't offer such exercises, because they can be difficult, expensive, time-consuming, and risky to organize and implement. This paper describes a real-time "Capture the Flag" exercise, implemented using a virtual network with free, open-source software to reduce the risk and effort of conducting such an exercise.

Categories and Subject Descriptors

K.3 [**Computers & Education**]: Computer & Information Science Education—*Computer Science Education*

General Terms

Experimentation, Security, Virtual Machine

Keywords

Information Warfare, Capture the Flag, Computer Security, Network Security, Laboratory, Exercise, Virtual Machine, User-mode Linux

1. INTRODUCTION

An overview course in computer security covers a wide range of theoretical and practical topics. While exercises on individual topics aid student understanding of particular aspects of security, effectively securing information systems requires consideration of multiple areas of security theory and technology simultaneously. An exercise where students secure and defend systems against live attack serves as a capstone experience, integrating student understanding of theoretical and practical aspects of security. To provide such a capstone experience for our first offering of a computer security class at the University of Toledo in the Spring 2004 semester, we developed a live information warfare exercise.

Information warfare is the defensive and offensive use of information and information systems to exploit an opponent's information resources. "Capture the Flag" is a symmetric information warfare exercise, where students work in teams to defend their own computer system while also attempting to exploit systems controlled by other teams by planting their team's flag on the other systems. Due to the unusual nature of this exercise, where students design and execute attacks on live systems, it is essential to educate students beforehand about the ethical and legal implications of attacking computer systems outside of the exercise.

We implemented our exercise using a network of virtual machines. A virtual machine (VM) is software that emulates the hardware of a computer. The virtual machine software is started on the host computer, then users run an operating system and their applications on the virtual machine as they would on a physical computer. A virtual network is constructed using network emulation software to connect the virtual machines' emulated network interfaces to each other. Virtual machines reduce the hardware and maintenance requirements of an information warfare exercise.

"Capture the Flag" exercises have been run since 1996 at the Defcon conference[1, 4, 7] and recent papers describe their use as teaching tools in computer security courses[15, 16, 18]. The exercise described in this paper differs from those in prior educational papers in its real-time nature, scoring system, and in its use of a virtual network.

2. INFORMATION WARFARE EXERCISE

2.1 Goals

The purpose of the exercise was to integrate theoretical and practical student understanding of security concepts and technologies presented in the course. The exercise was designed to achieve this purpose through three specific goals:

1. Students would gain experience securing a host as a team, preparing it for live attacks during the exercise.
2. Students would gain experience reacting to an attack in real time, learning to adapt their defenses in a crisis situation.
3. Students would gain experience with attacker strategies and tactics, as they researched, designed, and constructed attacks against other teams.

We emphasized to students that attack strategies and tactics were taught because of their importance in understanding how to effectively construct and test defenses against such attacks. Students were warned that use of attack tools or tactics outside of an authorized context such as the "Capture the Flag" exercise or a pre-approved penetration test was unethical and likely to result in legal consequences.

2.2 Rules

Students chose teams of 3-4 people to participate in the exercise. They had a one week preparation period before the exercise to research the operating system and software that they would use in the exercise, ask questions of the instructor, download defensive and offensive tools, prepare configuration files, and write their own tools.

Teams met in the computer lab on a Saturday for the actual 8 hour exercise, which was divided into two 4 hour segments with a short break between them. Having the teams sitting adjacent to each other in the lab facilitated interaction between teams during the exercise, including offering the opportunity for social engineering attacks.

When the exercise began, each team was given the root password and IP address of their assigned virtual machine. They had access to their machines via ssh. During the first half of the exercise, student teams installed and configured software to secure their respective virtual machines. Teams also installed offensive software for use during the second half of the exercise. All virtual machines had limited access to the campus network and Internet during this period to facilitate downloading software and applying security patches. A firewall on the machine hosting the virtual machines blocked outgoing packets destined for ports other than ssh, ftp, http, and https. The firewall also prevented the virtual machines from contacting each other during the defensive phase. All packets on the network were captured and examined to ensure that no team attempted to begin the attack phase early.

After the initial defensive segment ended, students were given a break to eat while the virtual network was reconfigured to isolate it from the campus network for the offensive phase of the exercise. It is important to isolate the exercise network in order to avoid stray packets from causing damage to production networks. The virtual network was also reconfigured to allow the participating teams' virtual machines full access to each other. Teams were permitted to react to attacks and enhance their defenses during the offensive period, as well as to research and launch attacks. The attack segment of the exercise was conducted in real time in order to simulate the crisis situation of an actual attack.

Teams were scored according to the number of times their team's flag was read on the scored network services by the scoring system. Teams received points for maintaining their flag on their own machines, as well as for placing their flag on other team's machines. Flags were simple text strings created by appending the team's numerical identifier to the constant string "team."

One point was awarded to a team for each of the three scanned network services that displayed that team's flag during a scan by the scoring system, for a maximum of three points per machine on the virtual network. The scoring system scanned the network once every 10 minutes during the offensive segment of the exercise. The three network services chosen for scoring the exercise were telnet, SMTP, and HTTP.

Teams were permitted to patch or even remove the scored services, but no points were assigned unless the service was available and displayed the team's flag to the scoring server. Blocking IP addresses on those ports so that only the scoring system could access a team's services was forbidden, as was sending spoofed data to the scoring server. The network was scanned from different IP addresses to check for any illegal firewalling of the flagged services. Scores were announced on a regular basis, but several teams independently checked their host's integrity by writing their own software to scan its flags.

Several types of attacks were forbidden, including attacks on the host machine or outside network, denial-of-service attacks except as a short term part of another attack such as IP spoofing, and destructive attacks designed to disable a hacked host. Network traffic during the exercise was recorded and examined to check for forbidden attacks, including attempts to spoof to the scoring system.

Afterward, teams were required to write a report on the exercise, detailing defensive preparations made before and during the exercise, successful and unsuccessful attacks that they attempted, and defensive and offensive reactions to attacks against their own machine.

3. IMPLEMENTATION

3.1 Virtual Networks

An information warfare exercise requires an isolated network, that is, a network which is separated by a physical or software barrier from other networks in order to protect their integrity. A "Capture the Flag" exercise generates a wide array of dangerous network traffic, some of which may damage networks that are not participating in the exercise unless the exercise network is isolated. Students also need to have administrative access to their machines, so that they can harden systems and use attacker tools that require root access. Machines are extensively reconfigured during the exercise by defenders and possibly also by attackers who penetrate the machine's defenses.

The common solution to these issues is to construct a lab with an isolated network of physical machines[9, 12, 13, 14, 19]. However, such laboratories require time, money, and space to set up. Computers need to have operating systems and software installed and reconfigured before, after, and possibly during the exercise, and networks need to be specially configured, requiring extensive maintenance skill and effort.

Virtual networks offer instructors the ability to set up an information warfare exercise at a lower cost in resources. A network of virtual machines doesn't require a dedicated space or dedicated machines. The virtual network can be instantiated when needed and shut down when not used, allowing ordinary lab machines to be used temporarily to create an isolated network for computer security exercises without a great deal of effort. The virtual network provides the necessary isolation for a security exercise by default, but can be connected to the Internet if so desired. Restoring a virtual machine to its initially configured state simply requires deleting a single file and restarting the virtual machine software.

A variety of free, open source virtual network and virtual machine software exists today. We chose User Mode Linux (UML)[6] for our virtual machine software because it is free, open source, and has good performance. UML is limited to emulating a computer running the Linux operating system, but that was not a problem for the exercise as each team was assigned only one virtual machine and we wanted all teams to be using the same operating system.

If we had wanted to use an operating system other than Linux or to assign multiple machines, each running a different OS, to each team, we could have used a program like the commercial product VMware[17], which is a virtual machine that can run a variety of operating systems, including FreeBSD, Microsoft Windows, and Solaris x86. Open source virtual machine programs that support multiple operating systems exist, such as Bochs[3] and Xen[2], but are either slower or not as stable as VMware.

We used the open source TUN/TAP virtual Ethernet interface[11] and bridge-utils[8] for Linux to construct our virtual network[5]. To instantiate the virtual network on the host computer, a script ran bridge-utils to create a virtual network switch with one network port for each virtual machine. The script also created one virtual Ethernet interface per virtual machine and connected it to a virtual port on the switch, so that traffic sent through that interface would be forwarded by the switch to its destination. When each UML virtual machine was started, it was given one of the virtual Ethernet interfaces so that it could communicate on the network.

At this point in the process, the virtual network switch only connects the virtual machines to each other. The network is completely isolated. In order to connect the virtual machines to the campus network, bridge-utils is used to connect the Linux host machine's physical network interface to the virtual switch. Network packets from the virtual machines destined for the campus network are then forwarded by the virtual switch to the host machine's physical network interface which is connected to the campus network.

Maintenance is simple, as User Mode Linux virtual machines store changes to the filesystem in a copy-on-write (COW) file containing the user's modifications to the VM filesystem. Restoring the virtual machine to its original state is simply a matter of deleting the COW file and restarting the UML software. Multiple virtual machines can share a filesystem image, using their own COW files to store their different modifications. Virtual networks are also portable, easily moved to another host machine by copying the UML software and filesystem image. After the exercise, the virtual machines and network are shut down, making the host machine immediately available for normal use.

There are some disadvantages to virtual machines. They cannot be used for exercises involving physical security. Virtualization also imposes some overhead costs, so that a virtual machine is not quite as fast as the physical machine on which it is running. However, the virtual network can be faster than the host machine's physical network since it is not limited to Ethernet speeds.

3.2 Specifics

We created a Redhat Linux 9.0 image for each virtual machine to run. No security patches were installed on the image, and, in fact, the system's security was reduced by introducing user and guest accounts with weak passwords and by turning on unnecessary network services. The filesystem image was stored as a sparse file on the host machine.

Each virtual machine used the same filesystem image file but had its own COW file. The only differences between machines at the start of the exercise were their hostnames, IP addresses, and their root passwords. All files, including both startup scripts and the filesystem image are available from the exercise web site[10].

Three network services were set up and modified for the scoring system. The services chosen were telnet, SMTP, and HTTP, in order to require teams to maintain and defend a commonly used set of network services. Since these services were necessary to gain points, there was no need to impose additional rules requiring that students run specific services on their machines. The modifications were small changes to the service's configuration or source code so that the service would produce the team's flag on request. Teams were permitted to modify the configuration of these services, or even run different programs to provide the same services, but would not receive any points if they broke the flag functionality.

The telnet service displayed the team's flag on its login banner; the flag was simply included in the `/etc/issue` file. The `sendmail` program provided SMTP service and was patched to add a new SMTP protocol command `FLAG`, which would output the team's flag when issued. The Apache web server provided HTTP service, and the flag for this service was retrieved by sending a request with the appropriate form parameters to an intentionally insecure CGI script.

The Linux `iptables` firewall on the host machine was set up to allow Internet access for the initial defensive half of the exercise, and was reconfigured after the break to prevent Internet access during the offensive portion of the exercise. The host machine monitored all packets on the virtual network.

3.3 Issues

We originally planned to give teams access to their virtual machines using ssh to contact the host machine, where they could access the virtual serial consoles of their machine. This method would have permitted the virtual network to be completely isolated from the campus network during the offensive phase of the exercise. However, due to problems we experienced with virtual serial consoles, we gave teams direct ssh access to their machines and provided isolation by blocking all outbound connections initiated from the virtual machines during the attack phase using the firewall on the host machine.

While our host machine, a 2.8GHz Pentium 4 temporarily upgraded with 1.5GB of RAM borrowed from other lab machines, was able to run over a dozen UML network servers without any performance issues, we discovered that 5 virtual machines on which 3-4 interactive users each were compiling tools and cracking passwords required much more processing power. The virtual machines slowed to a crawl, with keystrokes taking minutes to be echoed back to students' terminals until we paused the exercise to reconfigure the virtual network. We moved two virtual machines from the original host machine to another host machine and reconfigured the firewall and virtual switch to forward packets between the two hosts.

The reconfigured network solved our performance problems for the remainder of the exercise. We plan to benchmark an identical system using Linux 2.6 kernel-based UML virtual machines to determine if the interactive scheduler enhancements in the 2.6 kernel will provide a sufficient performance improvement to run the exercise on a single host machine next year.

4. LEARNING EXPERIENCES

Students discovered that designing and carrying out an attack on a live system was much more difficult than they expected. While most teams were able to gain user level access to at least one other team's machine, they were unprepared to elevate their privileges to gain root access. One team gained root access by obtaining another team's root password without their knowledge through a simple social engineering attack. No other team was able to gain root access. We used the success of the social engineering attack in the post-mortem analysis of the exercise as an example to illustrate that security is a process involving people, not purely a technical exercise.

We suspect that part of the difficulty was the students' focus on downloaded remote root exploits, especially as no such tool worked successfully for any team. One such tool crashed the attacking team's machine, losing them points for not having their flag displayed on their own machine during one scoring scan. After the exercise, several teams wrote in their reports that they should have focused on multiple part exploits, where initial user-level access was gained then later elevated to root access. Students developed only one unique offensive a tool, a program to set all flags on the current machine to their own, but that team did not gain the root access required to successfully run their program.

Most teams focused more of their efforts on defense than attack. Network security was generally good, but host security was weaker. Besides one team that accidentally left an ftp server running that they thought they had disabled, all unnecessary network services were shut down as part of the initial defensive stage. Teams also deployed a variety of defensive network software, including firewalls and intrusion detection systems.

However, most teams missed some elementary host security problems, such as the existence of insecure user and guest accounts. Only one team disabled those accounts before experiencing an attack using them. Some teams enhanced host security by backing up system binaries in case of their replacement with trojan horse versions through a rootkit, while others deployed tripwire.

Several teams wrote and deployed their own defensive software. Multiple teams deployed software to scan their flags at regular intervals, and one deployed a program that restored the flags to their initial state every minute, requiring a successful attacker to either synchronize their attack carefully with the scoring scans or to find and disable this unique defensive software as part of their attack. Another team wrote a shell wrapper, which required a password to be entered before a shell would be launched. This wrapper saved their insecure user and guest accounts from being exploited, but the wrapper also caused a delay when their machine crashed and the wrapper had to be disabled before it would restart in multiple user mode.

Student response to the exercise was enthusiastic, despite having to come into the lab on a Saturday. Students comments rated the exercise highly, both in terms of fun and in terms of its educational value, with one student writing "Capture the Flag was fun, in a mentally exhausting way that I really wasn't expecting. While our defense made progress the entire time, offense was frustrating for the first 5 or 6 hours; but when things started to make sense and we began to get into other machines, it was a rush. It takes weeks of lectures and applies them all at once, which is a great experience." Another student suggested running the exercise again as part of the final exam.

5. LESSONS LEARNED

5.1 Issues

While one team requested more time for defense in their report, the extent of the defensive measures deployed and the difficulty all teams had in carrying out successful attacks suggests that the exercise needs to be biased more toward offense, not defense. We plan to emphasize the importance of multiple part exploits involving privilege escalation during lecture and laboratory sessions next year. We also plan to modify the flags used for scoring and to insert additional security flaws into the system image in order to increase the difficult of securing systems.

Several teams stated in their reports that they felt underprepared for the UNIX system administration aspects of the exercise. While most students could use common UNIX utilities and programming tools, they had little experience building and installing software packages, administering user accounts, or configuring servers. We intend to address this lack next year by creating additional exercises using UML virtual machines to give students hands-on experience with these tasks before the "Capture the Flag" exercise.

5.2 Future Directions

In order to improve the chances of attackers next year, we intend to add new flags to the scoring system, including ones that will require logging into student machines to check them and others that will require the ability to transfer files to and from the machine to be checked. We also intend to create flags that do not require root access to modify. These requirements should increase the effort require to harden and defend a team's host machine, while decreasing the effort required for a successful attack, which should result in more teams gaining experience with intrusion detection and incident response.

If we can obtain sufficient resources, we would like to provide an entire virtual network for each team to defend, including multiple virtual machines running different operating systems. Such an environment would offer a better simulation of a network, allowing us to create additional flagged services for students to defend, such as authentication and database servers.

We would also like to improve the simulation by adding virtual hosts to the environment that are not administered by student teams. Such hosts would have trust relationships with machines administered by student teams, offering more complex configurations to defend and opportunities for students to attempt more complex attacks. In addition, we plan to insert decoy traffic into the virtual network to better simulate a production network environment. Students will have to sift through network traffic to discover which packets were sent by attackers and which were normal parts of the environment, instead of being able to assume that any packets destined for their machine from IP addresses other than that of the scoring system were hostile.

6. CONCLUSIONS

We found that a "Capture the Flag" information warfare exercise provided an excellent capstone experience for an overview of computer security class. Students were highly enthusiastic about the exercise and expressed their appreciation of how it helped them integrate and apply much of what they learned in the course.

The use of open source User-Mode Linux virtual machines and Linux virtual networking software allowed us to construct the isolated network we needed for the exercise without the requirement of a dedicated space or machines. The two machines used in the exercise were removed from normal use for only the 8 hours of the actual exercise plus an hour of setup and tear down time. The virtual machines were run one at a time after the exercise for grading purposes, while leaving the machine in normal use.

Tying the scoring system's flags to the network services we wanted students to defend eliminated the need to create a separate scanning system for those services. The scoring system also offered minimal opportunities for attackers to gain points by requiring that the servers be present and be configured to provide the flag when requested. We plan to continue using a "Capture the Flag" exercise as a capstone experience for our security class and to improve the rules, scoring system, and virtual network in future iterations.

7. REFERENCES

[1] Defcon IV announcement. http://www.defcon.org/html/defcon-4/, 1996.

[2] P. Barham, B. Dragovic, K. Fraser, S. Hand, T. Harris, A. Ho, R. Neugebauer, I. Pratt, and A. Warfield. Xen and the art of virtualization. In *Proceedings of the nineteenth ACM symposium on Operating systems principles*, pages 164–177. ACM Press, 2003.

[3] Bochs. http://bochs.sourceforge.net/.

[4] C. Cowan, S. Arnold, S. Beattie, C. Wright, and J. Viega. Defcon capture the flag: Defending vulnerable code from intense attack. In *Proceedings of the DARPA DISCEX III Conference*, pages 120–129. IEEE CS Press, 2003.

[5] D.Cannings. Networking UML using bridging. http://edeca.net/articles/bridging/index.html, 2004.

[6] J. Dike. A user-mode port of the Linux kernel. In *Proceedings of the 4th Annual Linux Showcase and Conference (Usenix 2000)*, 2000.

[7] Ghetto-Hackers. Root-fu. http://www.ghettohackers.net/rootfu/, 2004.

[8] S. Hemminger. Bridge-utils. http://bridge.sourceforge.net/.

[9] J. M. D. Hill, C. A. Carver, Jr., J. W. Humphries, and U. W. Pooch. Using an isolated network laboratory to teach advanced networks and security. In *Proceedings of the thirty-second SIGCSE technical symposium on Computer Science Education*, pages 36–40. ACM Press, 2001.

[10] J.Walden. Capture the flag. http://www.eecs.utoledo.edu/~jwalden/ctf.html, 2004.

[11] M. Krasnyansky and M. Yevmenkin. Universal TUN/TAP driver. http://vtun.sourceforge.net/tun/, 2001.

[12] P. Mateti. A laboratory-based course on internet security. In *Proceedings of the 34th SIGCSE technical symposium on Computer science education*, pages 252–256. ACM Press, 2003.

[13] M. Micco and H. Rossman. Building a cyberwar lab: lessons learned: teaching cybersecurity principles to undergraduates. In *Proceedings of the 33rd SIGCSE technical symposium on Computer science education*, pages 23–27. ACM Press, 2002.

[14] J. Schafer, D. J. Ragsdale, J. R. Surdu, and C. A. Carver. The iwar range: a laboratory for undergraduate information assurance education. In *Proceedings of the sixth annual CCSC northeastern conference on The journal of computing in small colleges*, pages 223–232. The Consortium for Computing in Small Colleges, 2001.

[15] G. Vigna. Teaching Hands-On Network Security: Testbeds and Live Exercises. *Journal of Information Warfare*, 3(2):8–25, 2003.

[16] G. Vigna. Teaching Network Security Through Live Exercises. In C. Irvine and H. Armstrong, editors, *Proceedings of the 3rd Annual World Conference on Information Security Education (WISE 3)*, pages 3–18, Monterey, CA, June 2003. Kluwer Academic Publishers.

[17] VMware. http://www.vmware.com/.

[18] P. J. Wagner and J. M. Wudi. Designing and implementing a cyberwar laboratory exercise for a computer security course. In *Proceedings of the 35th SIGCSE technical symposium on Computer science education*, pages 402–406. ACM Press, 2004.

[19] T. Wulf. Implementing a minimal lab for an undergraduate network security course. *J. Comput. Small Coll.*, 19(1):94–98, 2003.

Experience with an Industry-Driven Capstone Course on Game Programming

[Extended Abstract]

Ian Parberry
Department of Computer Science & Engineering
University of North Texas
Denton, TX, USA
ian@unt.edu

Timothy Roden
Department of Computer Science & Engineering
University of North Texas
Denton, TX, USA
roden@cs.unt.edu

Max B. Kazemzadeh
School of Visual Arts
University of North Texas
Denton, TX, USA
maxk@unt.edu

ABSTRACT

Game programming classes have been offered at the University of North Texas continuously since 1993. The classes are project based, and feature collaborative coursework with art majors in UNT's School of Visual Arts. We discuss the design that enables them to simultaneously provide both training for students intending employment in the game industry, and a capstone experience for general computer science undergraduates.

Categories and Subject Descriptors

K.3.2 [**Computing Mileux**]: Computers and Education-Computer and Information Science Education[Computer science Education]

General Terms

Design, Experimentation, Measurement

Keywords

Game programming, capstone, undergraduate education

1. INTRODUCTION

In 1993 we introduced a game programming course to the undergraduate computer science program at the University of North Texas. At the time, this was a controversial, much-challenged, and difficult move. There were no course materials, books, or web pages available. Interestingly, the only objections were from faculty — both the students and the administration were in favor of the class. During the first few years the class was offered, objections were raised about the industry-driven focus of the class and the perceived trivial nature of entertainment computing. Since 1993 the initial game programming class has evolved with the fast-moving game industry, and spawned a second, advanced game programming class. After more than a decade of operation, our game programming classes have positioned our alumni for employment in companies including Acclaim Entertainment, Ensemble Studios, Gathering of Developers, Glass Eye, iMagic Online, Ion Storm, Klear Games, NStorm, Origin, Paradigm Entertainment, Ritual, Sony Entertainment, Terminal Reality, and Timegate Studios.

Game programming classes are now gaining acceptance in academia (see, for example, Feldman [6], Moser [10], Adams [1], Faltin [5], Jones [8], Becker [3], Alphonce and Ventura [2], and Sindre, Line, and Valvåg [13]), resulting in a proliferation of new classes and programs nationwide, and a move towards a professionally recommended curriculum in game studies [7]. In contrast to institutions such as Digipen, Full Sail, and SMU's Guildhall that offer specialized degrees or diplomas in game programming, we offer game programming as an option within a traditional computer science curriculum. Keeping in mind that many institutions are starting game programs, and many of them are designing their curricula in an *ad hoc* manner, the purpose of this paper is to share some of what we have learned from experience over the last decade by describing our game programming classes, the design philosophy behind them, and some of the potential pitfalls.

We begin by discussing game industry needs in Section 2, and some important issues in the design of a game programming class in Section 3. We will discuss the introductory class in more detail in Section 4. Finally, in Section 5 we examine the impact of game programming on the computer science program at UNT.

2. WHAT GAME COMPANIES WANT

Game companies want C and C++ programmers with general competence in technical subjects typically found in an undergraduate computer science program such as programming, computer architecture, algorithms, data structures, graphics, networking, artificial intelligence, software engineering, and the prerequisite math and physics classes. In addition, they usually demand evidence of the following skills and experience:

1. Work on a large project, that is, larger than the typical "write a program for a linked list" kind of programs that are typically used as homeworks in programming courses.

SIGCSE'05, February 23–27, 2005, St. Louis, Missouri, USA.

2. Creation of a game demo or two, something nontrivial that plays well and showcases the programmer's ability. This shows that the applicant is devoted enough to have spent their own time to create something, and the perseverance to see it through to completion.
3. That the applicant is a "team player", somebody who can work with other programmers, and just as importantly work with artists and other nontechnical people.
4. That the applicant can learn independently, because the game industry continues to push the boundaries of what can be done using new computer technology.
5. That the applicant is well-versed in game technology, who the important development houses are, and what they are currently reputed to be doing.

While our undergraduates can technically learn enough about the game industry in general and game programming in particular from books to satisfy most of these requirements, our game programming classes are designed to help students achieve them more effectively than they could alone, and encourage them to higher levels of achievement. The requirements listed above are similar to the "Ideal Programmer Qualities" listed by Marc Mencher [9]: self-starters, who possess a team attitude, will follow-through on tasks, can communicate with nonprogrammers, and take responsibility for what they have done.

In addition to satisfying the needs of aspiring game programmers, we quickly found that the game programming classes are attractive to general students as a capstone experience, paralleling the experience of Jones [8]. Indeed, our class projects meet most of the requirements of the capstone project CS390 in [4]. Other employers are also attracted to students who have experience with a group software project with nontechnical partners. Feedback has suggested that game demos created with artists tend to show better in interviews than the typical project created by programming students.

3. DESIGNING A GAME PROGRAMMING CLASS

There are a number of key decisions in the design of a game programming class that affect the outcome in a fundamental way:

1. Should the classes be theory based, or project based?
2. What software tools should be used?
3. Where do programming students find art assets?
4. Should students be free to design any game in any genre, or should their choices be limited?
5. Should students write their own game engine, or work with a pre-existing engine?

On the first question, the options were either a theory class with homeworks and exams, perhaps augmented with small programming projects, versus a project class in which the grade is primarily for a large project programmed in groups. We chose the project option, understanding that students would come out of the classes with two substantial game demos that will play a major role in their first job interview in the game industry.

On the second question, the Computer Science department at UNT was until recently almost exclusively Unix based, with g++ being the compiler of choice and graphics programming taught using OpenGL. We chose to use Windows, Visual C++, and Microsoft DirectX instead, for two reasons: for those students bound for the game industry it makes sense to expose them to tools actually in use in a significant segment of the industry, and for the rest, it is advantageous to expose them to a different set of software tools before graduation (both of which are encouraged in Section 10.2.2 of [4]).

On the third question, that of art assets, the obvious choice is to have students take advantage of the free art on the web. Our experience is that students benefit substantially from working with art students. We will describe more of our collaboration with the School of Visual Arts at the University of North Texas in Section 4.

On the fourth question, on whether students should be allowed to design and implement a game in any genre, our experience is similar to that of Sindre, Line, and Valvåg [13]. Constraints on the type of game being created (as in [1, 2, 3, 5, 6, 8]) may seem attractive from a managerial point of view because, for example:

- It allows for a more shared experience, enabling students to learn and collaborate across group lines.
- It gives the flexibility to reassign group membership in response to late drops and overheated group dynamics.
- It allows the art class to streamline their process by using a pipeline art production line where necessary.

However, we have found that the element of creativity, student morale, the quality of the resulting games, and the outcomes all suffer when any kind of constraint is placed on the game being developed.

On the fifth and final question, whether to teach with a pre-existing game engine and tools or to have the students create their own custom game engines, the pre-existing game engine option may seem the most attractive at first for several reasons:

- It allows the students to "stand on the shoulders of giants", that is, to achieve more than they can on their own by leveraging existing code.
- It prepares them for the game industry, where they will likely find themselves working on an existing engine, or at least with an existing code base.
- It is easier for faculty to teach from an existing game engine than to teach students to create their own game engines.

However, we have found that the arguments for not using a pre-existing game engine are more compelling in practice:

- Teaching students to use a single game engine simply trains them in its use. The learning curve in a single 15-week class is typically so steep that they run the risk of spending their time wrestling with code rather than developing general skills.
- Existing game engines for educational use tend to be poorly documented, low in features, and unstable. Students find that they spend most of their time trying to force a recalcitrant engine to do what they want it to do, or coding around obscure bugs. They are often resentful of the fact that their grade depends on somebody else's ability to write code, particularly when it is obvious that "somebody else" writes bad code.

- The code for existing game engines is generally *production code*, code that is designed to run fast and be maintainable, rather than *teaching code*, which is further designed to teach basic concepts.
- Students who write their own game engines get first-hand experience with their internal workings, and are thus able to more quickly pick up the details of the proprietary game engine at their first job.
- Students entering the game industry will most likely spend the majority of their professional lives modifying and making additions to somebody else's code. This is the last opportunity that they will have to devote major slices of their time on their own game engine.

For these reasons, we opted to teach game engine programming with the class project being to create a game engine using some standard utilities, rather than modifying a free or proprietary game engine.

4. THE INTRODUCTORY GAME PROGRAMMING CLASS

The introductory game programming class was introduced in 1993 as a special topics class. Despite some initial resistance from faculty, it received its own course code CSCI 4050 and catalog entry in 1997, effective in Fall 1998. It is offered once a year in Fall semesters.

CSCI 4050 started out in 1993 as a 2D game programming class for DOS, changed to DirectX 3, and has been updated annually to keep pace with each new release of DirectX, from DirectX 5–9. Recently, elementary 3D techniques for a simple billboard game has been introduced to the curriculum. CSCI 4050 is a project class. Students must attend lectures, but the final grade is for a game programmed in teams. To make this as real-world as possible, the students are given an ill-defined objective, as recommended in Sections 10.3.2 and 10.4 of [4]. In the first class meeting, the students are shown a slide that describes the grading system as follows:

A: it really knocks my socks off
B: it's a pretty cool game
C: it's an OK game
D: it's not there, but at least you tried
F: you really blew it off, didn't you?

Two kinds of points are awarded: completeness points and techno points. Completeness points are awarded for things such as:

- Does it run without crashing?
- Are there few (preferably no) bugs?
- Does it have an intro, a title screen, a credits screen, a menu screen, help screens?
- Does it play with the keyboard, mouse, and/or joystick?
- Does it have sound support?
- How is the game play? Is it fun?

Techno points are awarded for implementing technology not covered in class. Examples include, but are not limited to:

- MP3 instead of WAV format sounds
- Showing video clips using DirectShow
- Lighting effects (eg. directional light, sunset, shadows, lense flare)
- Pixel and vertex shaders
- Network play using TCP/UDP/DirectPlay

The students in CSCI 4050 are usually seniors in the computer science program, who are technologically savvy and experienced programmers. They are usually quite capable of reading the DirectX documentation themselves. For them, the biggest road-block is picking the small subset of techniques that they actually need from the wealth of options available. The lectures in CSCI 4050 focus on getting started, and leave exploration of options in the more than capable hands of the students.

The first author has developed a novel teaching technique called *incremental development*. Rather than going through the DirectX documentation in detail, we teach using a basic game called *Ned's Turkey Farm*, a simple side-scroller in which the player pilots a biplane and shoots crows. The aim is not to teach this game *per se*, but rather to teach the development of games in general using this engine as an example. It is designed to have many of the features of a full game in prototype form so that students can, if they wish, use code fragments from it as a foundation on which to build their own enhancements. Earlier versions of the code and lecture notes have been published in book form (Parberry [11, 12]).

During lectures we have a laptop with 3D acceleration and an overhead projector available in the classroom. The laptop is set up as a game development platform, with Visual C++ and the DirectX SDK. It is important to be able to show and manipulate the code in class, rather than just show a pre-prepared slideshow. This hands-on attitude to the code in class helps us avoid a disconnect between the code and the lectures: in many classes the code and the lecture material seem to have very little intersection.

The code is currently organized into a sequence of 11 demos. Each demo is built on top of its predecessor. A file difference application, such as `windiff` is used in class to highlight the changes in code that must be made to add the new features. An average of one demo is presented per week. A typical class begins by running the demo and pointing out the new features, followed by a powerpoint slideshow describing the new demo, its new features, the theory or principles behind them, and any implementation details, but at a high level without getting bogged down in the code. This is followed by running `windiff` and going through the code changes in more or less detail depending on the complexity and difficulty of the code. Often, we run Visual C++ to show students in real time the effects of minor code tweaks.

CSCI 4050 is taught in parallel with a game art class taught to art students in the School of Visual Arts at UNT. Part of the art students' grade is to produce the art work for a game programmed by the students in CSCI 4050. To encourage group synergy we teach both the art and programming classes at the same time in different rooms in the same building. Classes run for 3 hours in the evening, and the final hour is reserved for group meetings between the artists and programmers. We have experimented with running the classes at different times, and at the same time in different buildings, resulting in both cases in a massive drop-off in meeting attendance, and a corresponding decrease in the quality and number of completed games at the end of the semester.

Allowing students to form their own groups based on common interests has proved to be the best way of maintaining interest and excitement about the projects. At the end of the first class we take the students in both classes — typically 30–35 programmers and 15–20 artists — into a large classroom and have them stand up sequentially and introduce themselves to the class, asking them specifically to talk about what kind of games they like to play, what kind of game they would like to create, and any prior experience. We then allow them to wander around at random, and come to the front of the room when they have formed a group of two programmers with one artist. We have found that the amount of artwork required by a simple sprite game is within the ability of a single art student to create in a single class. However, we always have one or two groups of odd sizes, which are handled in a case-by-case manner.

The final projects in CSCI 4050 are presented to the instructor in a series of 30-minute slots over two days during Finals week. They are graded on the final executable only, the instructor does not look at source code. After demonstrating the game and allowing the instructor to play, the students are quizzed on their individual contributions to the game, to ensure that they actually did what they claimed to have done. Grading on the executable only is a radical departure from other classes that the students have taken in the computer science curriculum, but is an important real-world constraint.

Starting in the Fall 2002, we instituted a game contest for students in CSCI 4050 and the associated game art class. Entry is strictly optional, and does not contribute to grades. The contest is judged by a panel of 4 or 5 local representatives from the game industry. Prizes are donated by Texas game and publishing industries, ranging from the more expensive books and games to less expensive T-shirts and posters. The contest lasts 2–3 hours, and is open to the general public.

Holding the contest in the final week of classes, approximately one week before the deadline for turn-in of the final projects, encourages students to start coding early. Previous attempts at getting students to get started early were focussed on checkpoints and documentation. Preliminary progress reports and play testing dates proved to be positive up to a certain point, after which insistence on more checkpoints and documentation took up valuable time that could more profitably be spent creating the actual game. The game contest is a much more positive way of reinforcing the final deadline.

Our proximity to the DFW metroplex with its high density of game development companies makes it easy to attract guest lecturers. We encourage visits by teams from development houses including artists, programmers, and designers, and have them speak to the combined class of artists and programmers. Rather than technical presentations, we have guest lecturers speak about what it is like to work in the game industry, what it takes to get their first job, and what educational paths the students should pursue. Typically, we have two or three presentations per semester.

5. ENROLMENT TRENDS

We believe that the game programming classes at UNT have had a significant effect on student enrolment and retention. Student numbers are currently dropping in computer science and engineering programs nationwide, which is mirrored at UNT (see Figure 1). Figure 2 shows enrollment figures for the introductory and advanced game programming classes from Fall 1997 to Spring 2004 compared to the total number of Bachelor's degrees awarded by the Department of Computer Science and Engineering. The introductory class was capped at 35 students in 2002. We see that a substantial fraction — between one-third and one-half – of departmental graduates have taken the introductory game programming class.

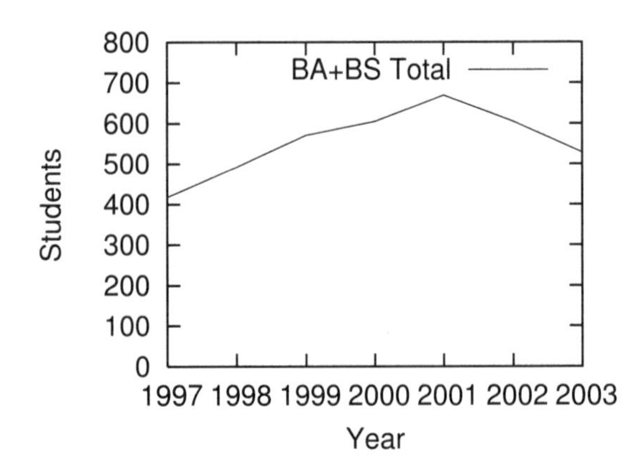

Figure 1: Total enrollments in BA and BS degrees in CSE, 1997-2003.

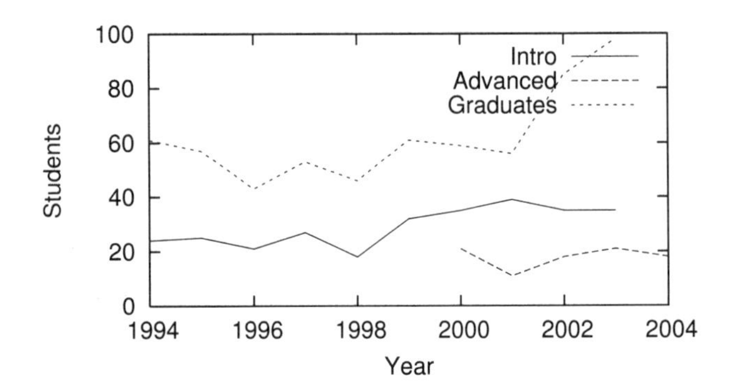

Figure 2: Game class enrollment versus number of CSE Bachelor's degrees awarded. Degrees are listed by academic year, for example, the 2003 figure lists graduation in Fall 2002, Spring 2003, and Summer 2003.

Table 1 shows the results of a survey of students in the undergraduate computer science and engineering programs at UNT in Fall 2003. A total of 197 students were polled in three classes, the two-course freshman-year C++ programming sequence CSCI 1110, CSCI 1120, and the junior-year Data Structures prerequisite to the intro game programming course, CSCI 3400. Despite the total absence of an advertising budget, 79% of students had heard of the game programming classes, and about half of those had heard of them before coming to UNT. We can see future demand for game programming classes, e.g. that 49% of students polled intend to take the intro game programming class, and a further 32% say that they may take it. We can also see the effect on the makeup of the undergraduate population, e.g. it was a factor in choosing UNT for 37% of them.

Response	1110	1120	3400	Total
When did you hear about the game programming classes?				
Before coming to UNT	47%	40%	27%	41%
While at UNT	33%	33%	55%	38%
Only during survey	20%	26%	16%	21%
Do you plan to take the intro game programming class?				
Yes	50%	40%	59%	49%
Maybe	32%	35%	27%	32%
No	18%	25%	14%	19%
Did they influence your decision to come to UNT?				
The only reason for choosing UNT	6%	4%	5%	5%
Major reason for choosing UNT	19%	12%	5%	14%
Minor reason for choosing UNT	13%	21%	27%	18%
No influence on choice of UNT	63%	63%	64%	63%
Number of respondents	96	57	44	197

Table 1: Responses to Fall 2003 survey. Columns list percentages for the two-course introductory C++ programming sequence CSCI 1110, CSCI 1120, and the Data Structures prerequisite to the intro game programming course, CSCI 3400.

6. CONCLUSIONS

We have had great success over the last decade with a two-course sequence in game programming in a traditional computer science undergraduate curriculum. The classes are project based, and feature collaborative work with art students in the School of Visual Arts. In addition to training aspiring students for the game industry, the classes also provide a capstone style project experience for all computer science students.

Our experience with game industry involvement is that while companies are, with a few notable exceptions, reluctant to provide any sort of concrete support for game development programs in academia, individuals are much more positive. Requests for guest lecturers from industry almost always results in great presentations from motivated, knowledgable, and experienced game programmers and artists.

7. REFERENCES

[1] J. C. Adams. Chance-It: An object-oriented capstone project for CS-1. In *Proceedings of the 29th SIGCSE Technical Symposium on Computer Science Education*, pages 10–14. ACM Press, 1998.

[2] C. Alphonce and P. Ventura. Object orientation in CS1-CS2 by design. In *Proceedings of the 7th Annual Conference on Innovation and Technology in Computer Science Education*, pages 70–74. ACM Press, 2002.

[3] K. Becker. Teaching with games: The minesweeper and asteroids experience. *The Journal of Computing in Small Colleges*, 17(2):23–33, 2001.

[4] Computing Curricula 2001: Computer Science. Steelman draft, The Joint Task Force on Computing Curricula, IEEE Computer Society, ACM, 2001.

[5] N. Faltin. Designing courseware on algorithms for active learning with virtual board games. In *Proceedings of the 4th Annual Conference on Innovation and Technology in Computer Science Education*, pages 135–138. ACM Press, 1999.

[6] T. J. Feldman and J. D. Zelenski. The quest for excellence in designing CS1/CS2 assignments. In *Proceedings of the 27th SIGCSE Technical Symposium on Computer Science Education*, pages 319–323. ACM Press, 1996.

[7] IGDA Curriculum Framework. Report Version 2.3 Beta, International Game Developer's Association, 2003.

[8] R. M. Jones. Design and implementation of computer games: A capstone course for undergraduate computer science education. In *Proceedings of the 31st SIGCSE Technical Symposium on Computer Science Education*, pages 260–264. ACM Press, 2000.

[9] M. Mencher. *Get in the Game!* New Riders Publishing, 2003.

[10] R. Moser. A fantasy adventure game as a learning environment: Why learning to program is so difficult and what can be done about it. In *Proceedings of the 2nd Conference on Integrating Technology into Computer Science Education*, pages 114–116. ACM Press, 1997.

[11] I. Parberry. *Learn Computer Game Programming with DirectX 7.0.* Wordware Publishing, 2000.

[12] I. Parberry. *Introduction to Computer Game Programming with DirectX 8.0.* Wordware Publishing, 2001.

[13] G. Sindre, S. Line, and O. V. Valvåg. Positive experiences with an open project assignment in an introductory programming course. In *Proceedings of the 25th International Conference on Software Engineering*, pages 608–613. ACM Press, 2003.

CAMERA: Introducing Memory Concepts via Visualization

Linda Null
The Pennsylvania State University, Harrisburg
777 West Harrisburg Pike
Middletown, PA 17057
+01 717 948-6089
LNull@psu.edu

Karishma Rao
The Pennsylvania State University, Harrisburg
307 First Montgomery Blvd
Thorndale, PA 19372
+01 610 219-6477
Karishma.Rao@siemens.com

ABSTRACT
CAMERA, *Cache and Memory Resource Allocation*, is a collection of workbenches for cache mapping schemes (including direct, fully associative, and set associative) and virtual memory (including paging and TLBs). Its goals are to provide users with interactive tutorials and simulations to help them better understand the fundamental concepts of memory management. Implemented in Java Swing, these workbenches allow users to observe the processes of memory to cache mapping, and virtual memory using paging. The workbenches have proven useful in both introductory architecture classes and operating system classes. Students find CAMERA easy to use, even without the supplied user's guide. In the paper, we compare CAMERA to various existing systems and explore the software's features in detail in addition to discussing future enhancements.

Categories and Subject Descriptors
C.0 [**Computer Systems Organization**]: General – *modeling of computer architecture*; I.6.5 [**Simulation and Modeling**]: Model Development – *modeling methodologies*; K.3.1 [**Computers and Education**]: Computer Uses in Education – *CAI*

General Terms
Design

Key words
Computer memory workbenches, Tutorial, Education

1. INTRODUCTION
CAMERA (Cache and Memory Resource Allocation), is a collection of concise, intuitive, and visually inspiring workbenches for cache mapping schemes and virtual memory. The best way to learn any new concept is hands-on experience, and CAMERA's primary goal is to provide users with the means to step along while it simulates and demonstrates various concepts of cache mapping and virtual memory. Workbenches, by their very nature, lend themselves to exploration, and with CAMERA, students can modify some basic features of the components and follow their changes through the cycle of the application.

SIGCSE'05, February 23–27, 2005, St. Louis, Missouri, USA.

There are other applications similar to CAMERA. The ones most comparable to CAMERA include the following:

1. **Acme Cache Simulator** [4]. This simulator, written in C++, supports multiple configurations and runs faster than many other full-featured cache simulators (such as Dinero, discussed below). It must be compiled before being run, and the interface is not particularly user friendly. It is a cache simulator only (no paging or TLBs), but is quite complete. It was less usable for our introductory class, as the concepts it covers (and their related complexities) are beyond the scope of a first year architecture class.
2. **Dinero IV** [3]. This trace-driven uniprocessor cache simulator simulates the hierarchy of cache as one or more trees, with the processors as leaves and a memory at each root, and requires a somewhat complex initial configuration in addition to setting parameters. Although powerful, it was difficult for our beginning students to use and understand. In addition, it has not been tested on Windows machines. It provides no paging or virtual memory simulation.
3. **HASE Dinero Cache Simulator** [2]. This simulator has two components: Hierarchical computer Architecture design and Simulation Environment (HASE) and Dinero, a cache simulator. It provides good user instructions, but is available for limited platforms only (it has not been tested under Linux, for example). It is basically an implementation of Dinero in HASE created to address the difficulty of using the original Dinero and to provide a method for teaching the fundamentals of cache operation and architecture via an animation of the HASE display window. It is a command-line driven simulator written in C++ and has many parameters that must be set (simulation mode and level, various counters, and trace input file). It was too sophisticated for our beginning courses.
4. **Java Cache Simulator** [9]. This tool addresses the concepts of the three cache mapping schemes and is considerably flexible in that it allows for modifications to cache size, block size and, in the set associative cache, the number of ways. It is not, however, a true simulation as it does not demonstrate the flow of data, nor does it supply any details on how it advances from one point to another.
5. **Virtual Memory Workbench** [7]. This applet demonstrates the flow of information and displays vital statistics (page faults, TLB hit ratio, etc.) in the operation of a virtual memory system. In addition, the workbench can be executed in step-by-step or continuous modes. It is an independent workbench for virtual memory so other concepts of memory

management such as cache mapping schemes are not addressed.

6. **PAGE** [5]. This is a stand-alone application written in Java 1.2. It is intended for use in an operating systems course, and it simulates five page replacement algorithms. It does not address the use of TLBs or cache mapping.

7. **MOSS Memory Management Simulator** [8]. Modern Operating Systems Simulators (MOSS) is a collection of Java-based simulation programs that illustrates key concepts presented in [10]. The memory management simulator focuses on page fault behavior in a paged virtual memory system, and does not address caching or the TLB.

Although each of the tools mentioned above has its significant features, it has been our experience that CAMERA is more useful for beginning architecture and operating systems classes, and for more than one reason. First, CAMERA provides for both cache mapping as well as virtual memory concepts. Not only does it afford all the attributes of each in one single package that is usable on any platform, but it also has some of its own unique characteristics. It describes each step using graphical as well as textual aids, and it permits user interaction and adapts accordingly to provide a clear understanding of the principles of direct mapped cache, fully associative cache, set associative cache, and virtual memory and paging. Each application comprising CAMERA is a tutorial, a workbench, and a simulator, all brought together to produce a comprehensive learning tool.

2 CACHE MAPPING AND VIRTUAL MEMORY DESIRED FEATURES

The goal of CAMERA is to provide a comprehensive tool for the memory concepts presented in both computer organization and architecture classes as well as operating system classes. Therefore, we include the features that follow.

2.1 Cache Mapping Schemes

CAMERA supports three cache mapping schemes: direct mapped, fully associative, and set associative. In direct mapping, each block of memory is mapped to exactly one cache block. Memory addresses are partitioned into three fields: *tag*, *block* and *word*. Main memory blocks are mapped in a modular fashion to cache locations. Since there are more blocks in memory than in cache, it is obvious that there is contention for the cache blocks. The tag field is stored with each memory block when it is placed in cache so the block can be uniquely identified. When cache is searched for a specific memory block, the CPU knows exactly where to find the block just by looking at the main memory address bits. CAMERA currently uses a fixed number of blocks in cache (16) and a fixed block size of 8 words, although plans are underway to allow users a choice of block size.

With fully associative cache, instead of specifying a unique location for each main memory block, we allow a block of memory to be placed anywhere in cache. Memory addresses are partitioned into two fields: *tag* and *word*. When cache is searched for a specific memory block, the tag field of the main memory block is compared to all the valid tags in cache and, if a match is found, the block is found. While there are empty blocks in cache, the memory blocks are placed in the nearest available free cache block. Once cache is full, a replacement algorithm is used to evict an existing memory block from cache and place the new memory block in its place. In CAMERA, the replacement algorithm used is the *least recently used (LRU)* algorithm. Future enhancements include adding additional replacement algorithms.

The third cache mapping scheme is N-way set associative cache mapping. It is similar to direct mapped cache because the memory address is used to map to a cache location. The difference is that an address maps to a set of cache blocks instead of a single cache block. Memory addresses are partitioned into three fields: *tag*, *set* and *word*. When cache is searched for a specific memory block, the CPU uses the set field to go to the appropriate set. The tag bits then identify the desired memory block. CAMERA currently allows the user a choice of either 2-way or 4-way set associative cache. CAMERA uses the LRU replacement algorithm to determine the victim block that will be removed from a given cache set to make available free space for a new memory block.

2.2 Virtual Memory and Paging

Some computer organization and architecture classes introduce the notion of virtual memory and paging; but the concepts are generally covered in depth in an operating systems class. The most common method of implementing virtual memory is paging, in which memory is divided up into page frames, and the process memory space is divided into virtual pages.

Each process has its own page table, which keeps track of the physical location of the virtual pages of the process and usually resides in main memory. CAMERA's page tables consist of N rows, where N is the number of virtual pages in a process. Each row has two fields: the *valid bit* and the *frame number*. The valid bit indicates whether or not that particular virtual page resides in main memory, and the frame number indicates the location in main memory where the page exists. (Future plans include the addition of a modify bit and multi-level page tables.)

As a process executes, it generates virtual addresses, resulting in an *address reference string*. CAMERA can generate random reference strings, but also allows the user to specify an address reference string. Each virtual address is partitioned into two fields: *page* and *offset*. To access data at a given virtual address, the page number and offset are extracted from the address and translated into a physical page frame number using the page table, if the page actually exists in main memory. If not, a page fault occurs and the page needs to be brought into memory from the disk. CAMERA currently uses the LRU replacement algorithm to select a victim page if memory is full.

The page table lookup can be done more efficiently using a *translation look-aside buffer (TLB)*, a page table cache that stores the most recently accessed pages. Each TLB entry consists of a virtual page number and its corresponding frame number as they exist in the page table. To use a TLB, the page number and offset are extracted from the virtual address, the TLB is searched using the virtual page number and, if it is found, the corresponding frame number is added to the offset, resulting in the physical address. If the virtual page number is not found in the TLB, the page table is used to retrieve the frame number and, if found, the page is accessed from main memory. At this time the TLB is updated. If a page fault occurs, the page is brought from disk into memory, the page table and TLB are updated, and then the page can be accessed.

3 CAMERA

On more than one occasion, students have expressed dissatisfaction in their inability to grasp concepts of memory management — cache mapping schemes in particular. Although a well-written book with diagrams and illustrations can be very educational, a simulation that models the actual process and also allows user input and manipulation can provide an entirely new perspective to learning [1]. CAMERA was developed to give students graphical representations of the memory system, provide them with step-by-step descriptions of the current activity, and furnish them with appropriately flexible interfaces to observe and experiment with the system.

3.1 Description

The CAMERA package consists of four independent Java Swing applications illustrating three cache mapping schemes, including direct mapped cache, fully associative cache, and set associative cache, and virtual memory and paging, including the use of TLBs.

Each interface representing the cache mapping schemes contains a 16-block cache, a 32-block memory, an address reference string, and the binary representation of the main memory address represented currently being processed. CAMERA also maintains the statistics on the cache hits and misses occurring during one run-through of the simulation, provides a detailed explanation of each step, and supports forward and backward navigation through the simulation with buttons.

The basic idea governing each cache mapping simulation is to highlight each architectural element involved, such as main memory, cache, or memory address, as the CPU attempts to retrieve a required main memory block from cache. The simulation demonstrates how the CPU obtains an address reference for the required main memory block, converts this hexadecimal address to binary, extracts information about the cache location to be searched for the required memory block, searches cache for the block and, either accesses the memory block if it finds it in cache, or brings the memory block into the appropriate cache location and then accesses it from there.

The interface representing the virtual memory and paging concepts is governed by the same principles as those illustrating the cache mapping schemes. The architectural elements involved are the address reference string, the virtual and physical address bits, the TLB, the page table, and the physical and virtual memory space for each process. Statistics on TLB hits and misses and page hits and faults are also maintained. The simulation describes how the CPU obtains a virtual address string from the address reference string, converts this hexadecimal value into its binary equivalent, extracts the virtual page number and then uses it to find a matching entry in the TLB or the page table. If a match is found in either, the virtual address is translated into a physical address, the physical page frame is accessed, and the data is retrieved. If a match is not found, the page frame into which the faulting page will be placed is determined, the page table and TLB are updated, and the data is accessed from physical memory.

3.2 Design Decisions

Java Swing was selected as the implementation language due to its consistency across platforms and clean look and feel. The key goals of the interface design were to capture the user's attention and offer ease of usability. Therefore, another consideration was the placement and size of the components on the screen, since each screen represents a snapshot of the memory architecture. We avoid scrolling controls and use a fixed-size screen. The 256-word memory size is a starting point; future enhancements will include a choice of memory size. The 16-block cache size was decided upon as the best intermediate choice. This value can be made suitably variable in the future as well.

We were also careful in choosing colors for the interface. Approximately 1 in 12 people have weaknesses relating to perception of color. Research shows that shades of yellow and blue are safe choices, as are bright colors as they are the easiest to tell apart [6]. CAMERA uses a basic and bright color scheme, striving for strong color contrasts.

Another design issue was the choice of the step-by-step traversal mode of the simulation and the lack of a continuous mode. This was governed by two factors: the need to urge the user to study the occurring events in detail at each stage, and the existence of the progress text field. At each step, the actions taken by the CPU are displayed graphically and explained in the progress field. This information could be challenging to follow in a continuous mode simulation. As a future enhancement, the user could be allowed to choose a continuous mode simulation at a specified speed and disregard the textual information if so desired.

The decision to allow backward traversal of the simulations was a challenging one. The implementation demanded some amount of memory space but, after some consideration, memory was sacrificed for functionality, as this feature has proven to be one of the most useful features of the CAMERA workbenches.

3.3 Functionality

We now describe how to use CAMERA. We begin with cache mapping. Since our three cache mapping simulators have a very similar look and feel, only one of them will be addressed in detail. A screen shot of a complete cache access for memory address 19 is shown in Figure 1. On the start of the simulation, the cache is cleared and the user is prompted to generate an address reference string. There are two options for creation of the string: (1) the user can request that the application generate an address reference string of a predefined length; or, (2) the user can enter single valid addresses one at a time up to a predefined maximum.

Once the address reference string is created, the simulation can begin. As the user steps forward using the `Next` button, the application retrieves an address from the string, converts it into its binary equivalent, and displays the bits, which are partitioned into the tag, block, set, and word fields (as appropriate to that particular cache mapping scheme). The progress/update window not only tells the user to click `Next` to continue, but it also describes what is happening at each step. Once the cache location is determined, the CPU looks in the appropriate cache location for the memory block. The cache block that is accessed as well as the tag used are both highlighted. In this example, there was a cache miss because the required cache block was originally empty. The number of cache misses is incremented.

The required memory block is brought into cache, but each step of the retrieval is highlighted for users to watch. The cache now contains the memory block and the CPU can access the main memory block from here. The required cache block is highlighted as is the work within that block. The tag field is also updated and highlighted.

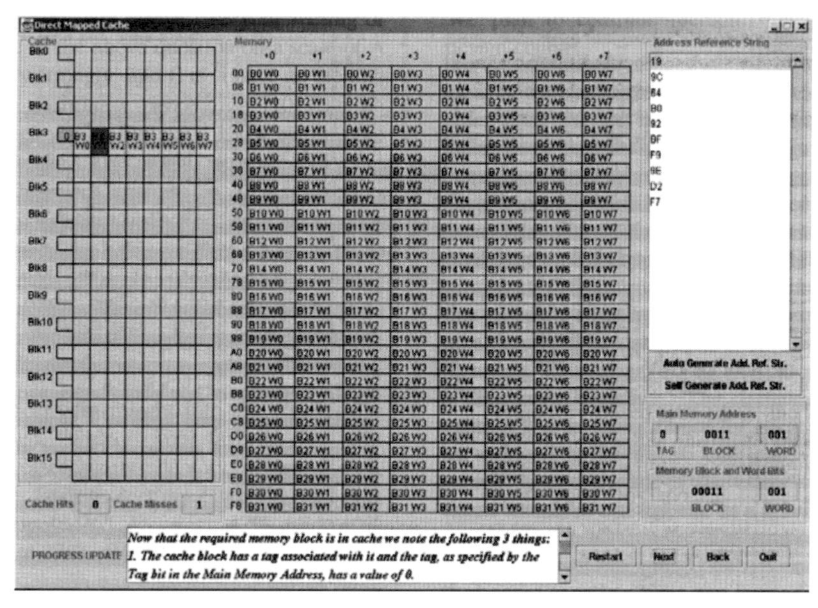

Figure 1: Direct Mapped Cache Access in CAMERA

Fully associative cache and set associative cache have much of the same functionality as direct mapped cache in the way that they illustrate the process starting from the generation of the memory address to the mapping of memory to cache and the retrieval of the memory block. The only differences in the interfaces lie in the partitioning of the bits in main memory address and the cache design.

Figure 2 illustrates the simulator layout at the start of a virtual memory simulation. The physical memory is empty and the user is prompted to generate an address reference string. As the user steps forward using the `Next` button, the application retrieves a virtual address from the string, converts it into its binary equivalent and displays the bits, which are partitioned into the page and offset fields. Once the virtual page number is determined, the CPU looks in the TLB for a matching entry. Since the TLB contains pairs of virtual page numbers and physical page numbers, a match on the virtual page number can provide the corresponding physical page frame. CAMERA uses a fixed-size TLB of 4 entries. If there is a TLB miss, the CPU goes to the page table to retrieve the information. Either the entry is highlighted, or a page fault occurs. If a page fault occurs, it is illustrated in detail, highlighting, as necessary, an available memory frame, a "victim" page (using LRU), and corresponding address bits used to determine these items. In addition, the page table and TLB are updated to reflect any changes.

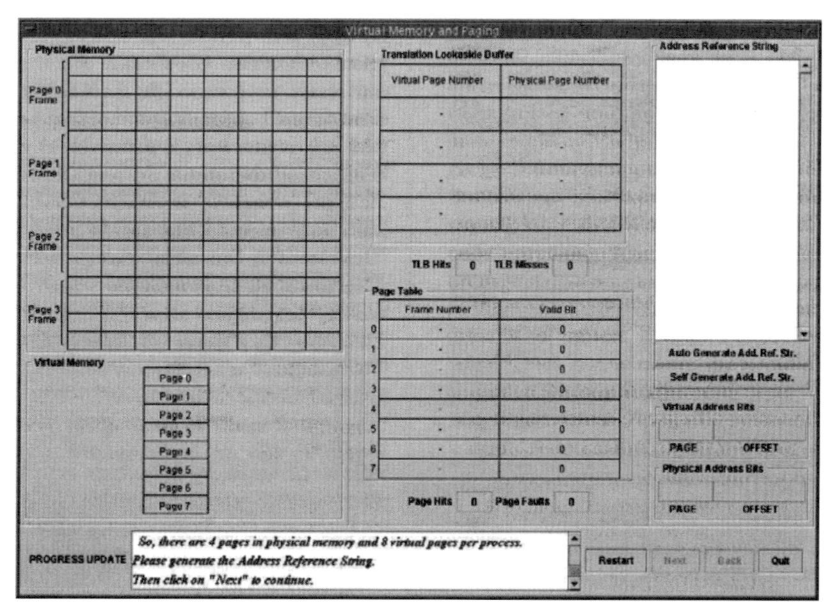

Figure 2: CAMERA's Virtual Memory Layout

The CAMERA software has many distinctive features:

- Progression through each simulation is illustrated with visual effects and reinforced by the current updates offered by the progress status field.
- Along with the detailed explanation the progress field presents, it also provides guidance to the user on how to proceed to the next step.
- The main memory address retrieved from the address reference string is converted to its binary equivalent at each step to clearly show the user the mapping between the memory address and its corresponding cache location.
- The navigation buttons provide easy maneuverability back and forth so the user doesn't overlook any important information during a simulation cycle.
- The user is offered several choices in the generation of the address reference string.
- The color scheme used to represent the process flow is attention grabbing.
- Each workbench represents a snapshot of the memory architecture so the user can perceive it in its entirety in one glance. There are no scrolling controls and no multiple windows that clutter the interface.
- CAMERA, with its workbenches for cache mapping as well as virtual memory, is a comprehensive package of applications for memory management concepts that has proven to be a great teaching aid. It can assist instructors in explaining memory management concepts and in providing students with interesting tools to further their knowledge of the same.

4. CONCLUSION

CAMERA is a complete collection of workbenches for cache mapping schemes and virtual memory. It acts as a visual and textual learning aid and provides students with interactive tutorials to help them better understand the fundamental concepts of memory management. The CAMERA workbenches are available at http://computerscience.jbpub.com/ecoa (on the student resources page).

Although CAMERA was built to be an effective standalone set of applications useful for learning memory management, there are a few enhancements that could be made to this toolset to improve its scope, functionality, and flexibility. These future enhancements include: (1) giving users a choice of cache, block, and memory sizes; (2) supporting continuous mode simulation; (3) providing the user with a selection of other common replacement algorithms; (4) addressing other performance issues such as CPU cycles, read versus write operations, and write-thru versus write-back caching; (5) adding segmentation; (6) adding multi-level page tables; and, (7) adding more information on context switching and clean versus dirty pages.

At our university, there has been a statistically significant improvement of student scores for those students using CAMERA. Pre-CAMERA scores for quizzes covering memory concepts (gathered over 5 semesters) averaged 78 out of 100 in our computer organization class, and 81 out of 100 in our operating systems class. Similar quizzes given to students who had access to CAMERA yielded average quiz scores of 85/100 and 91/100 respectively (over a 3 semester period). Students appear to have a better understanding of how memory works as indicated by not only these quiz scores but also class discussions. In addition, student response to CAMERA has been very positive, as evidenced by the encouraging comments in student evaluations. Although these results are strictly anecdotal, future research plans include a more formal study to verify the impact of CAMERA applications in both introductory computer architecture and operating systems classes.

REFERENCES

[1] BOWERMAN, C., ERIKSSON, A., HUCKVALE, M., ROSNER, M., TATHAM, M. AND WOLTERS, M. Tutorial Design for Web-based Teaching and Learning. *ECSA/Socrates MATISSE Workshop*. London, April 1999.

[2] EDINBURG UNIVERSITY. HASE Dinero Cache Simulator, 1999. Available at: *http://www.dcs.ED.ac.uk/home/hase/ projects/dinero/ index.html* or *http://www.dcs.ed.ac.uk/ home/hase/projects/dinero /html/guide.html.*

[3] EDLER, J. AND HUNT, M. Dinero IV, 1999. Available at: *http://www.cs.wisc.edu/~markhill/DineroIV/.*

[4] HUNT, B. R. Acme Cache Simulator, 1997. Developed at Parallel Architecture Research Laboratory, Department of Electrical & Computer Engineering, New Mexico State University, Las Cruces, NM. Available at: *ftp://tracebase.nmsu.edu/pub/tracebase4/src/acs/.*

[5] KHURI, S. AND HSU, H. Visualizing the CPU Scheduler and Page Replacement Algorithms. *Proceedings of the 30th SIGCSE Technical Symposium.* March 1999, pp. 277-231. Software available at: *http://www.mathcs.sjsu.edu/faculty /khuri/animation.html.*

[6] NEWMAN, C. Considering the Color Blind, 2000. Available at: *http://webtechniques.com/archives/ 2000/08/newman/.*

[7] NGON, T. Virtual Memory Workbench. Available at: *http://cne.gmu.edu/workbenches/vmsim/vm.html.*

[8] REEDER, A. AND ONTKO, R. MOSS Memory Management Simulator. Available at *http://www.ontko.com/moss/ memory/user_guide.html.*

[9] RICH, K., PANG, H., WEATHERS, E. AND ZHONG, G. Java Cache Simulator. Available at: *http://huron.cs.ucdavis.edu students/ weathers/public_html/index.html.*

[10] TANENBAUM. A. *Modern Operating Systems, 2/e*. Prentice-Hall, Englewood Cliffs, NJ, 2001.

Computer Architecture and Mental Models

CecileYehezkel
Department of Science Teaching,
Weizmann Institute
of Science,
Rehovot 76100 Israel
ntcecile@wisemail.weizmann.ac.il

Mordechai Ben-Ari
Department of Science Teaching,
Weizmann Institute
of Science,
Rehovot 76100 Israel
moti.ben-ari@weizmann.ac.il

Tommy Dreyfus
Department of Science Education,
School of Education,
Tel Aviv University
Tel Aviv 69978 Israel
tommyd@post.tau.ac.il

ABSTRACT

The EasyCPU visualization environment was developed for teaching computer architecture to novice students of computer science. During the development, the process of choosing the appropriate conceptual model of the computer for the visualization motivated research on the *mental models* that arise in the students as they learn. These mental models come from attempts by the students to make sense of the *conceptual models* presented to them by the software tool and their learning materials (textbook and exercises). The research findings support the view that the visualization was critical in enabling the construction of a viable mental model, a process that did not occur from textbook learning alone, because for the majority of students, their mental models were based upon their end-user experience rather than on the theoretical learning.

Categories and Subject Descriptors

K3.2. Computer and Information Science Education., C.0 [**Computer architecture and organization**]: General.

General Terms

Measurement, Design, Human Factors.

Keywords

Computer architecture education, mental models, visualization.

1. Introduction

The EasyCPU environment was developed for teaching computer architecture to high school students of computer science. As a result of experience during the development, it was decided to perform research on the *mental models* that arise in the students as they learn. These mental models come from attempts by the students to make sense of the *conceptual models* presented to them by the software tool and their learning materials (textbook and exercises). These conceptual models concern the various components of the computer and their interconnections.

The development of a visualization environment requires that the developers engage in analysis and decision-making concerning the conceptualization of the model that will be presented to students [6]. The model may be of an actual computer, a simplified model or a hypothetical model, and each model may be presented at different levels of abstraction, such as transistors or logic gates. The model and abstraction level have to be appropriate for the target population and syllabus [10]. Additional decisions required during the development concern the selection of methods to facilitate interaction between the student and the environment.

We wished to investigate the relationship between the conceptual models that were presented and the mental models of the students.

2. Theoretical background

The first researcher to use the concept of mental models was Craik [1], but the development of the theory of mental models was advanced by the later birth of cognitive science. The renewal of interest in mental models dates from the publication of [7] and [2].

Johnson-Laird [7] saw mental models as a way of describing the thought processes of people as they solved deductive problems. Gentner and Stevens [2] collected the work of several researchers on this topic, and claimed that mental models supply people with a means of understanding the functioning of physical systems. Norman's paper [4] defines a mental model M(T) as a conceptualization of a target system T by a user. According to him, this conceptualization defines the manner in which the user will carry out an operation on T. The mental model M(T) develops over time as a result of the interaction of the user with the target system T. M(T) is distinct from C(T), the conceptual model, which is the conceptualization of T by the developer. The conceptual model should be based on the user's task requirements and capabilities, taking in consideration the user's background, experience, and the cognitive limits on the user's information processing mechanism [4]-[5].

The mappings of models involved in the user-system interaction research are complex. Sasse [8] clarified these mappings in a taxonomy of mental models. Norman [4] claimed that mental models do not have to be accurate, but they must be functional. The factors which affect the development of a mental model include: the technical background of the user, previous experience with similar systems and the structure of the user's own thought patterns. The user has a tendency to make up general rules that seem to fit all target systems. The mental model serves to guide decisions: the user can "run" the model to predict the outcome of an operation on the system. In effect, the model enables the user to mentally exercise the system. Nielsen [3] recommends that user interfaces should "speak the user's language" which includes having good mappings between the user's mental model of the system and the computer's interface for it.

When studying computer architecture, a student may not interact directly with a target system T, but rather with a *learning model* of the system L(T) that is presented by the visualization system on a computer platform. Therefore, it is possible that the resultant mental model M(T) may be different than it would have been had the student worked directly with T (Figure 1). In this paper we deal with a conceptual model aimed at learning: a *learning model* L(T) of a target system T and the investigation of student's mental model M(L(T)) resulting from the learning process.

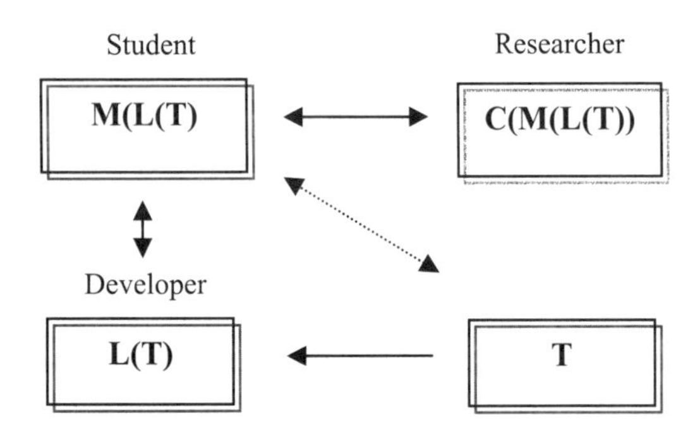

Figure 1: Hierarchy of models

3. The EasyCPU environment

The EasyCPU environment is based on a simplified model of an 8-bit version of the Intel 80X86 microprocessor family [9]. EasyCPU has two modes of operation: a basic mode and an advanced mode. The basic-mode enables the novice student to learn the syntax and semantics of individual assembly language instructions (Figure 2). The visualization shows the main units of the computer: CPU, memory segments, and elementary I/O. The units are connected by control, address, and data busses, which are animated during the execution of an instruction. The student can simulate a single instruction's execution and follow the data transfer between the CPU's registers and the data flow between the units. This way the student can observe the dynamic processes involved in instruction execution.

4. The computer model L(T)

By the means of a visualization environment, the developer is able to present to the student both static and dynamic elements that form a conceptual model of the computer in the learning system L(T). The *static* viewpoint is the description of the different units and a map of their interconnections, and the *dynamic* viewpoint is the description of the interaction and data transfer between the units. The conceptual model is based on four units (CPU, memory, input and output), and is composed of:

- The layout of the units and their interconnections.
- The method of transferring data along the connections.
- Standard interaction scenarios based on bus cycles.

The first two form the static viewpoint and the third describes the dynamic viewpoint. From the specific instruction being executed and its operands, you can predict what operations will be performed and describe them in a scenario.

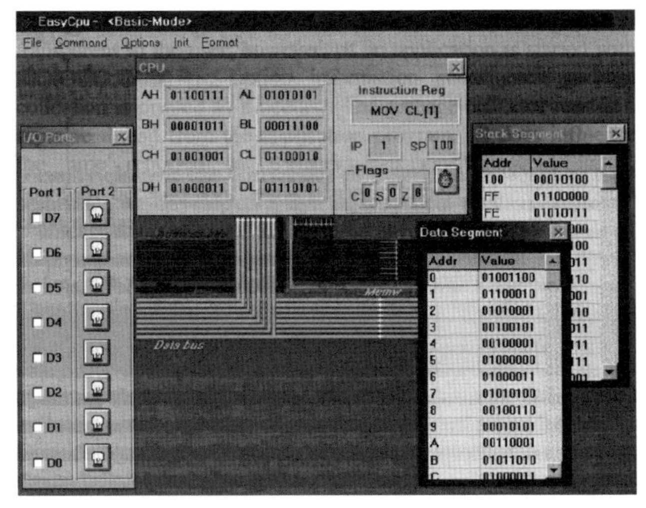

Figure 2: A screenshot of the EasyCPU Basic Mode during the execution of MOV CL, [1]

5. Methodology

The research was carried out on a class of eleven tenth-grade students. They studied a one-year 90-hour course in computer architecture and assembly language programming. The students were evaluated on the basis of a project that they developed.

The first learning phase was based only on theoretical learning. The theoretical topics included: data representation, computer organization, basic instruction set (symbolic representation) and the program execution process. A conceptual model of the computer C(T) was described through various static representations of the computer layout of the various units and graphical descriptions of dynamic information transactions between units during instruction execution.

The second learning phase included hands-on experimentation, carrying out tasks using the EasyCPU visualization environment which formed the L(T). The main subjects treated were instruction syntax and addressing modes.

The mental models of the students were investigated at two points of time. Once, after the first learning phase, where they studied the material theoretically from the textbook, but before they were exposed to the EasyCPU environment, and once after the second phase where they carried out tasks using the environment. We will refer to the former mental model as M(C(T)) and the later mental model as M(L(T)).

The research tools were two questionnaires, a pretest and a posttest and interviews. The students were asked to describe both the static viewpoint (the topology of the interconnections between the units), and the dynamic viewpoint (six scenarios describing data transfer as a result of executing specific instructions).

In the pretest, the instructions were presented in symbolic form, for instance, AL←[10h], which means *copy the content of the memory cell addressed by 10h to register AL*. This was the instruction form learned during the first theoretical learning phase. In the posttest, the instructions were written in assembly language learned during the second learning phase, for instance, *MOV AL, [10h]* (see Table 1). The six scenarios included the main basic types of instructions involving all the types of interaction between the CPU, Memory and Input and Output Units.

Table 1: Six basic scenarios presented in pretest and posttest

Type of scenario	Pretest	Posttest
Internal to CPU	AL ← BL	MOV CH, BL
Internal to CPU with data	AL ← 03h	MOV BH, 02h
Reading memory	AL ←[02h]	MOV BL, [03h] MOV AL, [BX]
Writing to memory	[01h] ←CL	MOV [01h], BH MOV [BX], CL
Reading Input Port	AL←Input	IN AL, 02h
Writing to Ouput Port	Output ←AL	OUT 03h, AL

The students were asked to describe the static and dynamic system model. They were provided with seven schemas representing the four units but the connections between them were omitted. We provided the basic layout of the four units to determine the level of refinement required in the graphical description and to make the visual analysis of all the graphical schemas easier. The first one was dedicated to the static model and the other six to the description of the scenarios of the dynamic model. For each one they had to complete the schemas with arrows, to describe graphically the dynamic transactions between the units using arrows and they add a description in written text alongside the schemas. Afterwards, four students were interviewed and asked to comment verbally on their graphical and textual descriptions both on the pretest and on the posttest.

6. Results

The results were summarized in a table, with a row for each student, showing the six dynamic models that the student drew. Table 2 shows the row for one student, both for the pretest and the posttest. This enabled us to identify the characteristic topologies of the drawings and to assign to each one a category defining the mental model associated with the topology. This gave us a mental model for each student at the pretest and then again at the posttest.

In order to validate the results, the written text was also analyzed. The written text included the textual description provided by the student during the test and the verbal explanations provided when interviewed. The text was analyzed, searching for textual evidence that would support or contradict the categorization of the graph that was drawn.

Then we grouped the results of the graphical and textual categorization for each student for the static and dynamic model, and conducted an evaluation of the predominant model that emerged from each description The whole process is too complex to be described in this paper; see [11] for details.

We found that the students developed mental models that can be categorized into the four different topologies shown in Figure 3.

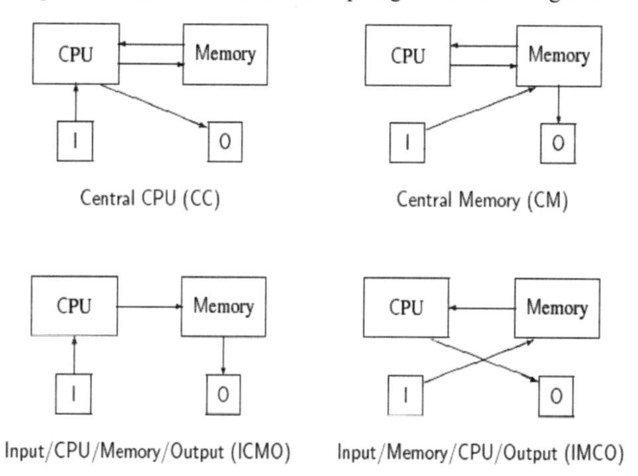

Figure 3: The four topologies

For this target system, the CC model is the correct one, since all memory accesses and input-output are performed via the CPU. The CM model incorrectly assumes that I/O is done directly to memory, while the ICO model stresses input and output operations, downplaying the role of the main memory. There were two variations of the ICO model: one with the memory inserted before the CPU (IMCO) and one with the memory inserted after the CPU (ICMO).

On the pretest, five of the eleven students chose to draw systems consistent with the ICO model, two more drew CM models, and only four drew the correct CC model. We interpret this as occurring because the students are used to interacting with the computer as end-users, which would tend to encourage the construction of a mental model M(T) consistent with the ICO model. The end-user interacts with the computer T through I/O and experiences the computer as a processor of information, streaming from input to the CPU for processing and then to the output. As one student said:

> *The data and instructions are entered through the input to the CPU, during this process the data is translated to the binary base and the instructions are translated to machine code. Then the CPU executes the operation. The result is transferred to the memory and then displayed onto the output.*

On the posttest, after the students had interacted with the L(T) model presented by the visualization, all the students drew models consistent with the correct CC model. This supports the view that the visualization was critical in enabling the construction of a viable mental model, a process that did not occur from textbook learning alone, when for the majority of students, mental models were based upon their end-user experience M(T) rather than on theoretical learning M(C(T)). For example, in the posttest, one student, identified in the pretest as holding an ICO mental model, correctly described the instruction execution "MOV CH, BL":

The content of the register BL is transferred to CH. There is no need to use the memory and the Input/Output devices because the registers are in the CPU.

7. Discussion

Norman [4] has shown how mental models develop naturally as a result of the interaction between the user and the system. The students, during the first phase of the experiment, were not exposed to any computerized visualization of the processes involved during instruction execution inside the computer. Their source of information was frontal teaching with theoretical materials and books. Our hypothesis is that their mental model developed as a result of a superposition of the assimilation of the theoretical materials, and their daily experience as end–users and novice programmers who had experience with a high level language.

Programming development can also be characterized by a similar pattern of interaction with the computer in each stage of the development: program editing, compilation and execution. It seems that this pattern of interaction is the cause of a typical mental model ICO (Input–Central processing–Output) identified in the pretest. This model of the computer processing is compatible at both the software and hardware levels of abstraction. At the software level of abstraction, the program processes the input data and generates the output. At the hardware levels of abstraction, the input unit supplies the information to the central processing unit, which transfers the processed information to the output. The similarity of the models at the two levels of abstraction is a source of confusion for the students.

Students who described CM models were influenced by what they learned about the stored-program architecture. A typical explanation by these students is:

The instructions are entered through the input to the memory...The memory executes the instruction and controls the information flow.

8. Conclusions

After studying theoretical materials, the majority of the students still held mental models that had been influenced by their experience as end-users. The visualization of the EasyCPU environment enabled the students to develop a viable model of the computer architecture by visualizing dynamic interaction between the units during scenarios of instruction execution. The conceptual models presented in a visualization environment have to be designed through an evaluation procedure to ensure that the model is correctly interpreted by the students. The experiment presented in this paper was carried out within the context of a larger evaluation research, which enabled us to validate the findings described here. This kind of experiment may be applicable to other domains, because it can shed some light on students' mental models and can be helpful in the visualization development process.

9. ACKNOWLEDGMENTS

We thank the teacher and the students who participated in this research.

10. REFERENCES

[1] Craik, K. *The Nature of Explanation*. Cambridge University Press, Cambridge, 1943.

[2] Gentner, D., & Stevens, A. L. (Eds.), *Mental models*. Hillsdale, NJ: Lawrence Erlbaum Associates, 1983.

[3] Nielsen, Jakob. *Usability Engineering*. Morgan Kaufmann Publishers Inc. San Francisco, CA, USA, 1995.

[4] Norman, D. A. User-centered system design: New perspectives in human-computer interaction. In D. Gentner & A. L. Stevens (Eds.), *Mental Models* (pp. 7-14). Hillsdale, NJ: Lawrence Erlbaum Associates, 1983.

[5] Norman, D. A. Cognitive engineering. In D. A. Norman & S. W. Draper (Eds.), *User-Centered System Design: New Perspectives in Human-Computer Interaction* (pp. 32-65). Hillsdale, NJ: Lawrence Erlbaum Associates, 1986.

[6] Petre, M., Blackwell, A., & Green, T. Cognitive questions in software visualization. In J. Stasko, J. Domingue, M. Brown, & B. Price (Eds.), *Software Visualization* (pp. 453-480). Cambridge, MA: MIT Press, 1998.

[7] Johnson-Laird, P. N., *Mental Models: Towards a Cognitive Science of Language, Inference and Consciousness.* Cambridge, MA: Harvard University Press, 1983.

[8] Sasse, M. A., *Eliciting and Describing Users' Models of Computer Systems*. Unpublished PhD Thesis, School of Computer Science, University of Birmingham, 1997.

[9] Yehezkel, C., Yurcik, W., Pearson, M., & Armstrong, D., Three simulator tools for teaching computer architecture: EasyCPU, Little Man Computer, and RTLSim. *Journal on Educational Resources in Computing, 1*(4), 60-80, 2001.

[10] Yehezkel, C., A taxonomy of computer architecture visualizations. *ACM SIGCSE Bulletin*, *34*(3), 101-105, 2002.

[11] Yehezkel, C., *A Visualization Environment for Computer Architecture*. Unpublished PhD Thesis, Weizmann Institute of Science, 2004.

Table 2. The six schemas representing the dynamic model that one of the students drew in pretest (a) and in posttest (b)

Table 2.a Dynamic Models drawn in pretest

AL ← BL	AL ← 03h	AL ←[02h]	[01h] ←CL	AL←Input	Output ←AL
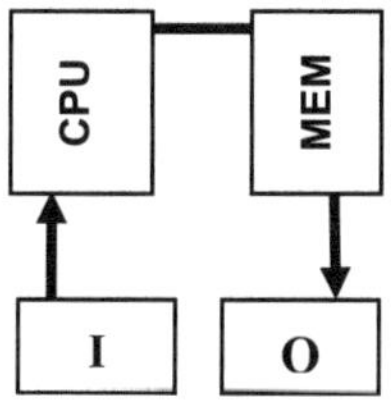 CPU MEM I O	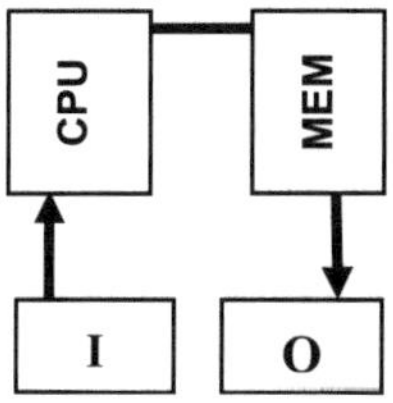 CPU MEM I O	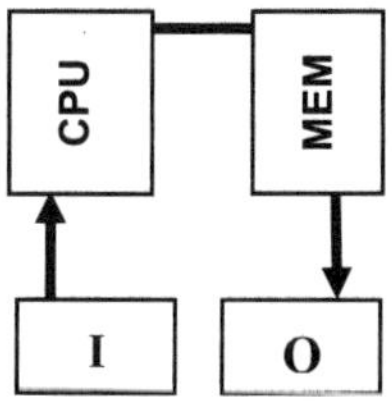 CPU MEM I O	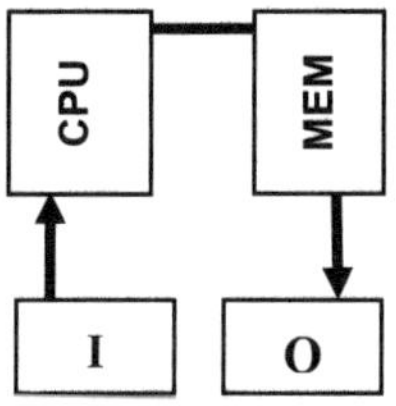 CPU MEM I O	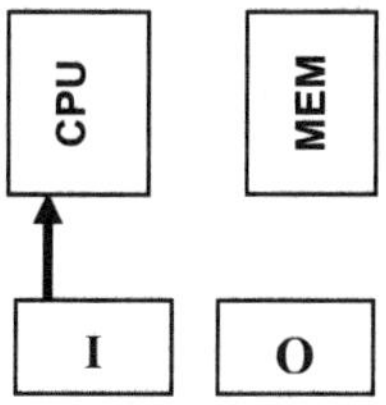 CPU MEM I O	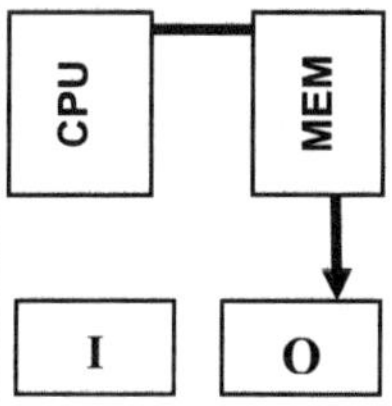 CPU MEM I O
The BL moves through the memory to AL in the CPU then to the output.	The number 3 moves from the intput to the memory to AL in CPU, then to the output	The number 2 is tranlated to binary base, then it is transferred to AL.	The input gives the value to CL, from CL to the memory cell which addressed is 01h, then to the output.	The input is transferred to AL.	AL is transferred through memory to output.
ICMO	ICMO	ICMO	ICMO	CC	ICMO

Table 2.b. Dynamic Models drawn in posttest

MOV CH, BL	MOV BH, 02h	MOV BL, [03h]	MOV [BX], CL	IN AL, 02h	OUT 03h, AL
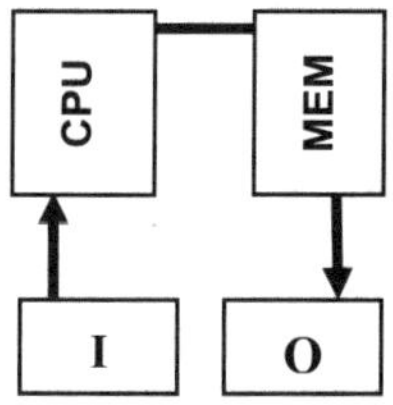 CPU MEM I O	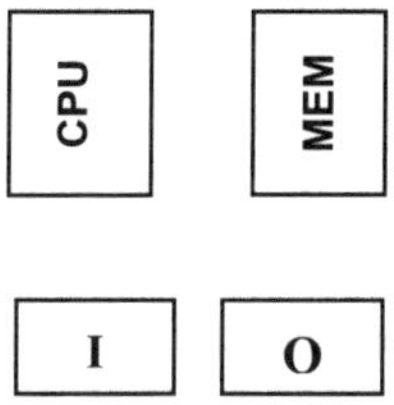 CPU MEM I O	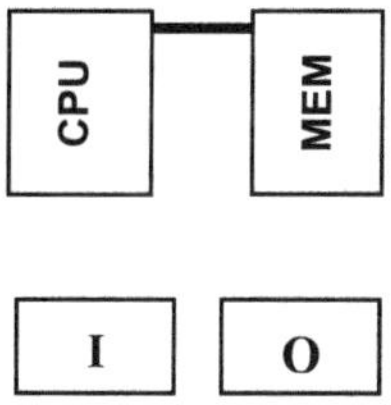 CPU MEM I O	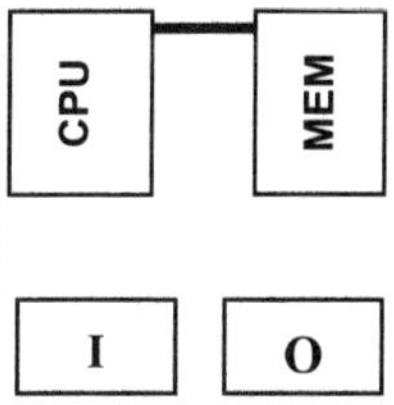 CPU MEM I O	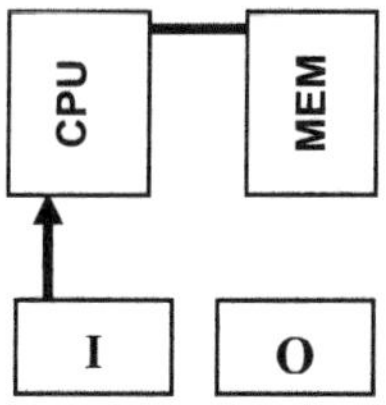 CPU MEM I O	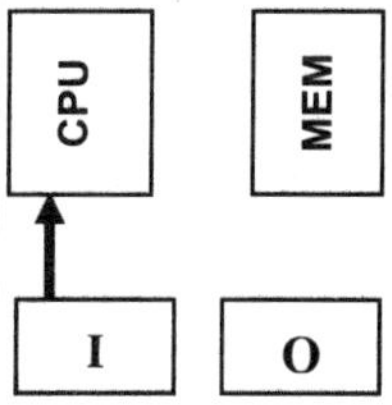 CPU MEM I O
The content of the register BL is transferred to CH. There is no need to use the memory and I/O because the register are in CPU.	There is an input operation to input 02 to the CPU. Then 02 is transferred to CH. Then it is output.	The instruction for the transfer is transferred to memory. We go to memory to the cell 03h . Then we transfer the content of the cell to the register BL through the data bus.	We enter data to BL, BH through input (initialization of BX) Then the memory is activated without interaction of the CPU. CL content is tranfered to BX address.	First she said that the binary value of 3 port address is entered to AL – then she said that the content of the input is entered to AL.	We are able to see in the output : the content of AL.
CC according to textual description	CC	CC according to textual description	CC	CC	CC

SPIMbot: An Engaging, Problem-based Approach to Teaching Assembly Language Programming

Craig Zilles
Department of Computer Science
University of Illinois at Urbana-Champaign
zilles@cs.uiuc.edu

ABSTRACT

This paper describes SPIMbot, an extension to James Larus's widely-used MIPS simulator SPIM, that allows virtual robots to be controlled by writing programs in the MIPS assembly language. SPIMbot was written to provide an engaging environment to motivate students to learn assembly language concepts. The SPIMbot tool allows the development of scenarios—in which students must program the robot to perform certain tasks—and provides the means to compete two robots against each other.

In our sophomore/junior-level class, we structure the programming component as a collection of structured assignments that produce sub-components for the robot; these sub-components are then used in a final open-ended programming assignment to produce an entry for a SPIMbot tournament. In our experience, this has been an effective means of engaging students, with many students investing time to aggressively optimize their implementations. SPIMbot has been effectively used in large classes and its source code is freely available [7].

Categories and Subject Descriptors

D.3.2 [**Programming Languages**]: Language Classifications—*Macro and assembly languages*; K.3 [**Computers & Education**]: Computer & Information Science Education—*Computer Science Education*

General Terms

Human Factors, Languages

Keywords

Education, Assembly language programming, MIPS

1. INTRODUCTION

As one of their "Seven Principles for Good Practice in Undergraduate Education", Chickering and Gamson [1] list **emphasizing time on task** as number 5. They state:

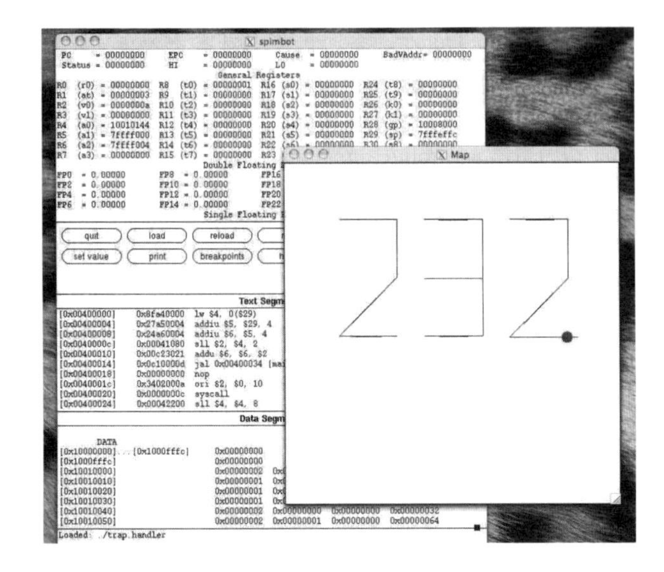

Figure 1: Example SPIMbot screen shot. ***The map window shows the robot's current location, orientation, and virtual environment; in this scenario, SPIMbot can turn on/off a paint trail allowing him to write out messages. Behind the map window is the main window (unmodified from xspim) that shows the MIPS processor's machine state.***

> Time plus energy equals learning. There is no substitute for time on task.

Thus one of our chief tasks as undergraduate educators is to develop activities that encourage our students to spend time on the course concepts and approach them with desire to master them. This paper describes one such set of activities, focused on teaching concepts related to assembly language programming.

In the remainder of this section, we describe the motivation for this work (Section 1.1) and abstractly how we use SPIMbot to achieve our pedagogical goals. After discussing the capabilities of the software (Section 2), we discuss, in detail, how it was used in the Spring 2004 semester (Section 3). We conclude, in Section 4, with a discussion of student feedback that supports our assertion that SPIMbot is an engaging way for students to learn assembly language programming concepts.

1.1 Motivation

In teaching assembly programming in our Computer Science curriculum[1], we have two primary goals: 1) to provide students a mental model of how a computer executes their high-level language (HLL) programs, and 2) to provide the background knowledge necessary for later courses on compilers and operating systems. To this end, we teach the students about instruction sets, stacks and their management (including recursion), calling conventions, floating point arithmetic, instruction encoding, I/O interfacing, and interrupt handling.

If one is not careful, these topics can come across as dry. The students' limited programming experience (this class is early in the curriculum) coupled with the inherent inefficiency of assembly programming can limit the scope of programming assignments. Furthermore, the demands of grading, especially in large enrollment classes where some form of automation is necessary, require most assignments to be rather structured. Examples of common assembly programming assignments found at many universities include: producing the Fibonacci sequence, string manipulation (reversing a string, `toupper()`, etc.), and sorting arrays. In many cases, HLL source is provided, reducing such assignments to somewhat mechanical translation.

The goal of SPIMbot was to produce an environment for teaching assembly programming that was fun and interesting, to motivate students to want to learn the material. While there is a long history of using robots for instruction (*e.g.*, [5]), the author's inspiration came from Patricia Teller's presentation [6] at the 2003 Workshop for Computer Architecture Education. In their semester-long course on assembly programming concepts, students program 68HC11-based robots to escape from mazes and chase other robots. Pedagogically, programming robots has three appealing features: 1) it is visceral: students like seeing their code control motions and actions of objects in the physical world, 2) it is cognitively challenging: debugging requires mapping robot behavior back to the behavior specified in the code, and 3) it provides a non-contrived way to expose students to I/O programming.

The problem with (physical) robots is one of logistics; in a high enrollment class—we have 100-150 students per semester—acquiring, maintaining, and scheduling sufficient resources is prohibitive. In contrast, virtual robots are cheap, plentiful, take-up no space, require no maintenance, yet (for students accustomed to interpreting computer-rendered virtual realities) still provide the fundamental qualities of physical robots.

[1] Assembly programming is taught in the context of the second semester-long class in a required two-class sequence in computer architecture. The first class in the sequence teaches digital fundamentals: the digital abstraction, combinational logic, finite-state machines, and basic architecture concepts (*e.g.*, a single-cycle implementation). The second class covers three main topics: assembly programming, machine organization, and memory and I/O systems; each topic receiving roughly a third of a semester. As our undergraduates predominantly pursue software-oriented (rather than hardware-oriented) careers, the goal of this second class is to provide the practical understanding of computer hardware necessary to be an effective programmer. Most students continue their architecture sequence, taking a third course in either high-performance architecture or embedded systems.

1.2 How we use SPIMbot

The central part of our implementation is the SPIMbot tournament, a friendly competition between the programs that the students write. The contest presents a challenging, multi-part task for the robots to perform. We use this concrete task to motivate the presentation of the desired assembly language concepts and the problem solving/design process.

As most of our students have not been exposed to assembly language previously, the SPIMbot tournament is the last activity in our assembly language segment. We work up to the contest by solving isolated sub-problems as programming assignments. We start with small structured assignments and then move onto larger structured assignments before attempting the contest (a large open-ended assignment). This structure lets us provide the students with early, motivating successes.

Although it is the last assignment, we present the contest first, because it allows us to model a problem solving process: a top-down design, followed by a bottom-up implementation. In class, we brainstorm approaches to the contest task, making it clear that there are multiple approaches. Then, we identify sub-tasks necessary for accomplishing the contest goal; these sub-tasks make up the structured programming assignments leading up to the contest. The contest itself challenges students to figure out what they need to implement and requires them to integrate the components they've completed in previous assignments.

When it comes to covering the desired course material, the fact that SPIMbot exists only in a virtual reality can be an advantage, as we can structure that reality to include those concepts that we want to teach. For example, two concepts that we cover in the course are recursion and the implementation of linked-data structures. To incorporate these concepts into our programming assignments, our Spring 2004 contest (see Section 3) involved an I/O device that returned its output as a tree, requiring students to write a recursive procedure to traverse the nodes of the tree.

After the students have submitted their contest entries, we use one class period to hold a tournament. With each competition lasting about 15 seconds, a double-elimination tournament for 32 teams can easily be held in a 50-minute class period. While this class time could be used for other purposes, we believe that it successfully motivates students to be actively engaged with course material *outside of class* achieving our objectives.

A Note on Competition: As competition can be demotivating if not handled properly [2, 3], we take a number of steps to alleviate the potential downsides of competition: 1) performance in the competition is responsible for a minimal fraction (about 1 percent) of student's final grade, 2) students compete as teams, reducing the pressure on individuals, and 3) teams select team names allowing students to compete anonymously.

2. SPIMBOT SOFTWARE

SPIMbot is an extension of James Larus's widely-used MIPS simulator SPIM [4]. SPIMbot involves three major enhancements: 1) a framework for simulating robots and their interactions with a virtual world, 2) a 2-D graphical display to visualize the robots and their environments, and 3) support for concurrently simulating multiple programs—

each on their own virtual processor—allowing multiple robots to be simultaneously active in a single virtual world.

Simulating the virtual world requires tracking and updating the state of the robots and other objects in the simulated world. In addition to location, orientation, and velocity, we have to keep track of the state of any I/O devices. Updating the world involves computing new locations for objects based on their current velocities. Collision detection is performed to update an object's velocity/orientation (*e.g.*, when a robot runs into a wall) and to allow interaction between robots and simulated objects (*e.g.*, when a robot picks up an object or pushes a button). Events in the virtual world can also trigger events in the MIPS processor, either updating the state of an I/O device and/or triggering an interrupt.

To interact with the virtual world, SPIMbot provides the robot programmer an (extensible) array of input/output devices. These virtual I/O devices, like real I/O devices, have their I/O registers mapped to memory addresses and, thus, are accessed using normal loads and stores. Simple examples include "sensors" that tell SPIMbot its or the opponent's (X,Y) coordinates and "actuators" to control its orientation. The SPIMbot code is structured so that the collection of I/O devices can easily be extended for a particular scenario. Furthermore, SPIMbot includes a programmable interrupt controller (PIC) that allows individual device interrupts to be enabled/disabled. Standard interrupts include the "bonk" interrupt (raised when SPIMbot runs into something) and timer interrupts (SPIMbot includes a programmable timer). The collection of interrupts can also be extended.

To achieve a tight coupling between the virtual world and the simulated MIPS code, we interleave the simulation of the virtual world with that of the MIPS code. Every *cycle* we execute a single instruction for each robot and update the physical world based on the actions of the robots. Simulating multiple concurrent robots required eliminating the use of global variables in SPIM's parsing and simulation of MIPS code; while currently we only simulate two robots, this could easily be extended to any number. As there can be interactions between the robots, we alternate each cycle which robot is simulated first in an attempt to be fair.

The graphics are currently decidedly low tech—XWindows drawing primitives are used to draw geometric shapes (lines, boxes, circles, etc.)—but this appears to actually have two advantages: 1) it is very simple; a minimal amount of development time is required to add the rendering code for a new scenario, and 2) it is not distracting; students can focus on what the graphics represent instead of the graphics themselves. Because the graphics are not demanding, smooth animation can be achieved without state-of-the-art hardware. In part this is because the graphical display need not be rendered every cycle. Currently, we re-draw every 1024 cycles and can achieve a refresh rate over 60 Hz on a 1GHz laptop.

3. AN EXAMPLE SCENARIO

In the Spring 2004 semester, the competition revolved around collecting "tokens": 15 tokens were randomly placed on a square map, tokens could be collected by driving over them, and the location of tokens can be divined by using an I/O device called the "scanner." The winning robot was the one that collected the most tokens by the end of competition.

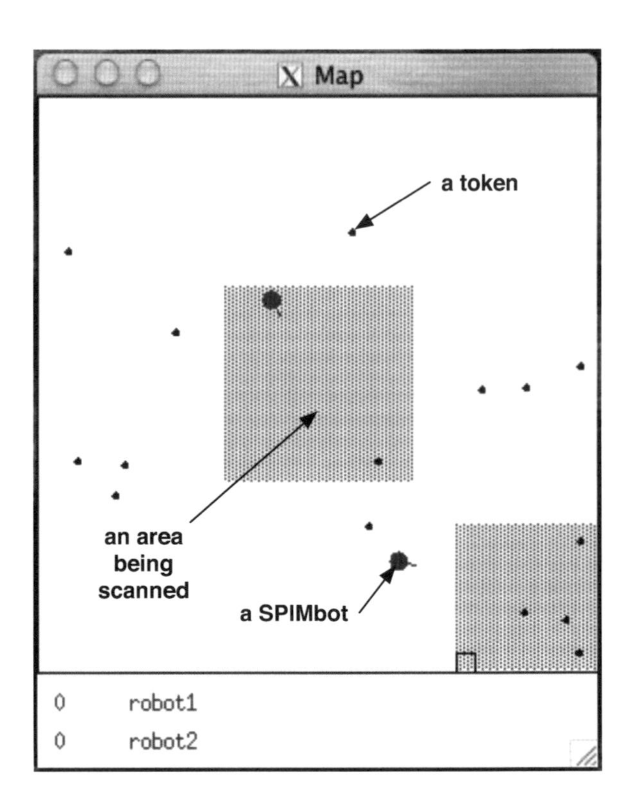

Figure 2: SPIMbot token collection competition.

Writing a program to compete in the contest involved: 1) allocating memory for the results of a scan, 2) communicating with the scanner to initiate a scan, 3) handling the scanner's interrupt, 4) searching the tree-like data structure returned by the scanner for the location of tokens, and 5) repeatedly orienting SPIMbot toward a token and recognizing when it has arrived, until all tokens have been collected. As this represents a relatively difficult programming assignment for students at this point in the curriculum, we broke out major components of the program as individual programming assignments. Below is a list of the structured assignments that led up to the contest:

1. A SPIMbot introduction: write a simple interpreter that reads a string of commands (*e.g.*, turn, wait, paint on/off) and invokes provided functions that perform these actions. *Introduces students to SPIM/SPIMbot and exposes students to loops, arrays, calling functions, control flow and I/O interfacing.*

2. Arctangent Approximation: given the (x,y) location of 2 points, compute the angle to drive from one to the other using a Maclaurin series expansion. *Exposes students to computing in floating point.*

3. Tree Traversal: SPIMbot's scanner returns the location of the tokens embedded as leaves of a tree-like data structure. Students write a recursive function that traverses the tree. *Exposes students to linked data structures and recursive functions in assembly.*

4. Interrupt Handler: write an interrupt handler for the timer interrupt that commands SPIMbot to turn 90

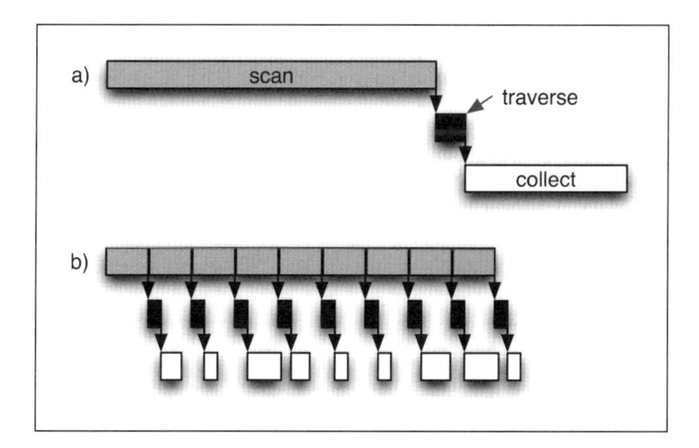

Figure 3: Pipelining the three sub-tasks reduces the latency of the task. ***By scanning one-ninth of the map at a time, the pipelined version (b) overlaps the collection of tokens with the scanner latency, completing the task significantly before the non-pipelined version (a).***

degrees and resets the timer, resulting in SPIMbot driving in a square. *Introduces students to writing interrupt handlers.*

While the solutions to these assignments can be integrated into a working contest entry, designing a competitive entry requires a little more effort. Three activities dominate the execution time of most of the robots: scanner latency, tree traversal, and collecting tokens. In a straight-forward implementation, which scans the whole map at once, these activities are performed completely sequentially (Figure 3a).

A higher performance implementation can be developed which pipelines the scan/traversal/collection process. The scanner can be programmed to scan only a portion of the map at a time, and its latency is largely a function of the area scanned. Once a small portion of the map has been scanned, the robot can begin collecting tokens from that portion while it requests the scan of the next region. In this way, much of the scan latency can be overlapped with the latency of tree traversals and token collection. Students found that breaking the map into 9-36 pieces and pipelining the processing of those pieces resulted in good performance. Another enhancement that students developed was driving to the center of the region currently being scanned after all known tokens had been collected.

Developing such a pipelined solution requires managing concurrent activities and demonstrates the importance of interrupts. The students learn first hand that their interrupt handler must avoid clobbering the applications registers, because it could be called at any time. It also demonstrates that pipelining—a concept we introduce in the machine organization portion of the class—is not a concept that is restricted to hardware.

Scenario Implementation Time: After the Spring 2004 semester, we re-factored SPIMbot's implementation to decouple the scenario-specific aspects from the core of SPIMbot's implementation. With these changes in place, it is rather straight-forward to implement new scenarios, by implementing a collection of functions for supporting scenario-specific initialization, physics, drawing, and I/O devices.

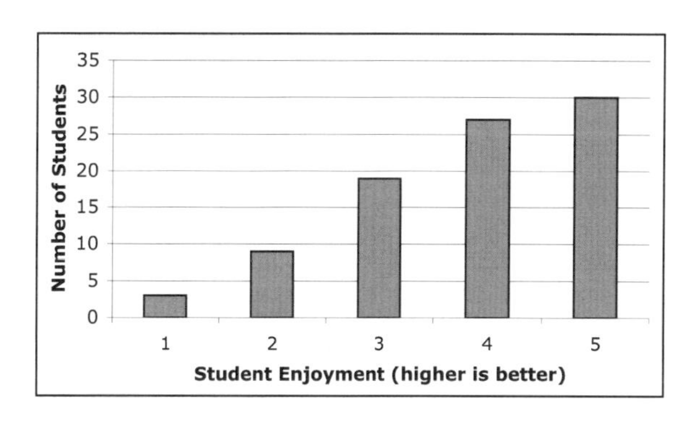

Figure 4: SPIMbot achieved high-level of student enjoyment. ***Data shown for the 88 (out of 99) responding students for the Spring 2004 semester.***

The Fall 2004 scenario required about a day to prepare; this accounts for the time to implement both the SPIMbot code, as well as the MIPS code to test the scenario (which includes solutions to most of the structured assignments).

4. STUDENT REACTION

The Spring 2004 students had a quite positive opinion of the SPIMbot assignments and student anecdotes suggest that they found it engaging. Students were asked in an anonymous electronic survey to rate their enjoyment of the SPIMbot assignments on a 5-point scale (5: "very much so" to 1: "not at all"). Of the 88 out of 99 students that responded, the mode was a 5 and the mean was just under 4 (see Figure 4).

In the course evaluations, six students commented specifically about SPIMbot when asked "What do you like about this course?", including the following quotes:

> "I really liked the SpimBot Tournament. That was the coolest thing I have done in a class. It makes it a lot more fun".
>
> "I liked the MP's, especially the SPIMbot Tournament and how the MP was designed to make us think of optimizations for ourselves."
>
> "... I also really liked the SPIMbot tournament"

The feedback was not uniformly positive, suggesting that there remain opportunities for improvement. One student mentioned SPIMbot in response to the question "What do you NOT like about this course?", giving the following response:

> "Spimbot. Pointless, difficult, and closed source, so hard to see exactly what was happening, so it's not entirely useful".

Another measure of student engagement is the effort they expended. Along with their source code, students handed in a short write-up describing any noteworthy aspects (generally optimizations) of their program. Of the 30 teams, over 3/4's of the teams attempted optimizations with half completing significant optimizations:

- 15 teams (50%) described aggressive optimizations like segmenting the scan and the aforementioned pipelining,

- 5 teams (17%) described modest optimizations like greedily picking up the closest known token at any time,
- 7 teams (23%) reported attempting no optimization, and
- 3 teams (10%) reported attempting aggressive optimizations, but failed to get them working, requiring them to submit unoptimized versions.

Some of the teams that aggressively optimized their code reported trying a variety of techniques or parameterizing their code and tuning those parameters. Here are two student comments:

> "We tried many different strategies, including sorting the nodes in order of increasing distance from the spimbot, using an algorithm which heads toward the closest node to spimbot each time spimbot moves toward a new token, rescanning token locations to determine if they have been picked up, and breaking up the scans into different sizes. After trying all of these, we found that the only one which sped up the collection of tokens was breaking down the scan."

> "Our program does scans of size 25 thus giving 36 scans. We found this to be optimal because we started out with scans of size 5 doing 900 scans and found it to speed up as we approached 36. We even went down to 16 and found it slowed down as the scan sizes got bigger. Thus we have an optimal scan size."

A final metric of effort that students expended on their contest entry is the number of lines of code. While lines of code is a metric of little practical utility, it outlines the of the work and the amount of effort the students put into it. The assignments that the students handed in ranged from 186 to over 608 lines of code and data segments (not counting blank lines and those containing only comments), with most in the 200-400 lines of code range. For comparison, there were about 130 lines of code provided in solutions that most students incorporated into their designs.

5. ACKNOWLEDGMENTS

This work was supported by NSF CAREER award 434 CCF 03-47260.

6. REFERENCES

[1] A. W. Chickering and Z. F. Gamson. Seven principles for good practive in undergraduate education. *American Association for Higher Education Bulletin*, 39:3–7, 1987.

[2] B. G. Davis. *Tools for Teaching.* Jossey-Bass, San Francisco, CA, 2001.

[3] E. M. F. III and L. Silvestri. Effects of Rewards, Competition and Outcome on Intrinsic Motivation. *Journal of Instructional Psychology*, 19:3–8, 1992.

[4] J. Larus. SPIM: A MIPS R2000/R3000 Simulator. http://www.cs.wisc.edu/~larus/spim.html.

[5] S. Papert. *Mindstorms: Children, Computers, and Powerful Ideas.* Basic Books, New York, 1980.

[6] P. Teller, M. Nieto, and S. Roach. Combining Learning Strategies and Tools in a First Course in Computer Architecture. In *Workshop on Computer Architecture Education, held in conjunction with the 30th Annual International Symposium on Computer Architecture*, June 2003.

[7] C. Zilles. SPIMbot. http://www-faculty.cs.uiuc.edu/~zilles/spimbot.

Using Asynchronous Discussions to Enhance Student Participation in CS Courses

Bhagyavati
Columbus State University
4225 University Avenue
Columbus, GA 31907
1-706-565-3519
bhagyavati@colstate.edu

Stan Kurkovsky
Columbus State University
4225 University Avenue
Columbus, GA 31907
1-706-565-3520
kurkovsky_stan@colstate.edu

Christopher C. Whitehead
Columbus State University
4225 University Avenue
Columbus, GA 31907
1-706-565-3527
whitehead_christopher@colstate.edu

ABSTRACT
As Computer Science (CS) educators, we are involved in teaching a variety of undergraduate and graduate courses such as database management systems, networking, software development and web development courses. In addition to the traditional classroom environment, we use online and blended teaching methods to enhance student participation and improve the achievement of learning objectives. Typical online supplements to classroom instruction include posting homework, links to external resources, lecture notes and exams online. Asynchronous discussions and synchronous chat sessions provide additional forums outside the classroom for strengthening interaction and enriching the learning experience for students. This paper focuses on how asynchronous discussions can be used to enhance student participation in CS courses; increased participation leads to learning effectiveness, rich involvement with the course content, and student satisfaction.

Categories and Subject Descriptors
K.3.1 [**Computer Uses in Education**]: Computer-assisted instruction (CAI), Computer-managed instruction (CMI), Distance learning.

General Terms
Management, Experimentation, Human Factors, Measurement.

Keywords
Curriculum, Computer Science, Asynchronous Discussions, Student Participation, Course Related, Split Deadlines, Classroom Management, Learning Communities, Student Engagement.

1. INTRODUCTION
The number of higher education institutions that offer at least one fully online or blended course has grown significantly in recent years [1]. Computer Science educators are experimenting with online modules and courses, just as their counterparts in other disciplines. While academic leadership believes that the quality of online education matches that of the traditional, face-to-face instruction, faculty has been more conservative in their enthusiasm [1], [10]. The majority of CS educators supplement classroom instruction with web-based enhancements such as posting a syllabus on a website, maintaining a repository of external links and resources and so on.

SIGCSE'05, February 23–27, 2005, St. Louis, Missouri, USA.

In the context of modern CS education, the question of online instruction being "as good as" face-to-face instruction has been substituted by the question of how an online environment can provide benefits unavailable in traditional classroom environments. An online component that assists in providing additional benefits to students is the asynchronous discussion implemented as threaded discussion topics. If the full potential of this tool is realized by CS educators, student participation in their courses will be enhanced, thereby maximizing learner effectiveness, student satisfaction and achievement of learning objectives. By offering a richer environment for interaction than the traditional classroom, asynchronous discussions help address several problems inherent in the traditional approach to student-student and student-instructor interaction, which manifest themselves very prominently in most CS courses.

Asynchronous discussion assignments typically comprise a significant component of online and blended environments, and may provide meaningful complements to classroom instruction and student interaction. In this paper, we address the specific issues of topic selection and scheduling of asynchronous discussions so that student participation is maximized for an optimal learning experience within the CS curriculum. Asynchronous discussion topics, if chosen carefully, facilitate the formation of communities that can lead to success in the course [12]. We present our experiences in using asynchronous discussion topics that have proven to be effective in enhancing student participation in our courses. We also describe the issues involved in scheduling discussions that affect successful achievement of learning outcomes. These learning outcomes are specifically focused on CS students and courses which require direct application of the course material.

2. BACKGROUND
The potential of asynchronous discussions to enhance student participation and effective learning has long been recognized [2]. We believe that asynchronous discussions are necessary components of CS courses because of the richness of student

interaction obtainable by them [13], [15]. Online asynchronous discussions also address several problems inherent in classroom discussions: presence of silent and passive students; lack of time; lack of prepared and thoughtful responses; propensity to venture off-topic; lack of focus; and lack of student involvement [11]. Graded asynchronous discussions trivialize the concerns of passivity in students, lack of involvement, lack of focus and preparation. In addition, if responses to these discussions are part of the overall grade of the course, moving them online overcomes the pressure of time typically present in a classroom discussion.

Carefully chosen topics enhance student involvement and keep students engaged in the learning process. Discussions that challenge traditional thinking motivate students to seek external sources to defend their opinions in discussion responses [4]. Peer support and encouragement have a tendency to form strong learning communities, which are instrumental in enhancing student participation and interaction between peers and with the instructor [3]. A learning community of peers motivates students to seek more sources of information than the recommended sources by the instructor; peers continually challenge and support each other in a community. Timely and open-ended questions are more effective in provoking stimulating debate than questions to which answers can be easily found in the textbook [9].

For example, a discussion on the Patriot Act in Computer Security and Information Assurance courses provides more responses than those motivated by grade and course credit. In a recent discussion on opinions about the sharing of airline passenger data with the government, pro-privacy and pro-security students were quite passionate about voicing their divergent opinions. When questioned by peers or by the instructor, students successfully found independent sources to corroborate their viewpoints. Thus, asynchronous discussion topics can be selected to maximize participation and optimize learning outside the classroom. The authors have been successful in incorporating such interesting and even provocative topics into the context of many CS areas such as database management, web development, software development and network security courses, thus enlarging upon the classroom experiences of the students.

Many topics requiring student involvement in independent research fit perfectly into the framework of asynchronous discussions as well. As an example, consider the research involved in obtaining relevant sources of information on security features of the .NET Framework. Ordinarily, this research requires many hours of work for an individual. However, if assigned as a project to a team of students, such a task may lead to a deeper and more informed discussion among team members. In the process of sharing thoughts and debating over important issues within their team, students often come up with thorough and detailed answers to discussion questions. Such interaction is most effective in online asynchronous mode because each participant needs preparation time to provide insightful and relevant summaries independent of other team members. At the same time, contributions of individual members are clearly visible to the instructor and peers, who can critique and assist in development of a deeper understanding of the material than possible in a face-to-face environment.

During the process of researching material, summarizing it independently of team members and posting responses to discussion topics, students often synthesize a collective point of view to the ongoing discussion. For example, a team leader may distill the individual responses of the team members into a cohesive team summary. Therefore, asynchronous discussions add another important feature to the learning process – cultivating the culture of teamwork among students. In today's office environment, teamwork is prevalent in almost all areas of computer science; this added feature of the asynchronous discussion can have a significant impact on students' success in the workplace.

However, without active instructor involvement, students can lose interest and become repetitive in their responses, thereby defeating the purpose of asynchronous discussions. Instructors have to be vigilant in choosing current, relevant and open-ended topics [6]; if the topic lends itself to an easy answer, students quickly become disillusioned after the first few responses because they will not perceive the purpose in rephrasing the same responses. Instructor involvement is also necessary to keep the discussion focused, on track and professional. It is typical to become heavily involved in the beginning, posting a response to almost every student; such in-depth involvement is not required after students become comfortable with the format and expectations of the discussions. Later topics generate more discussion than initial topics, which, along with the formation of learning communities necessitates reduced instructor involvement as the course progresses through the term [5].

3. SIGNIFICANT ISSUES

Several issues impact the effect of asynchronous discussions on student participation and interaction in CS courses. The number of students, nature of the course, primary delivery mode of course content, duration of the course, level of preparedness of the students, the number of topics in a discussion, relevance and type of topics, time assigned for completion of the discussion, percentage of grade allocation and scheduling of due dates are some of the issues we managed effectively through our combined teaching experience. We present two important issues in greater detail below. The nature and type of topics, and scheduling of discussion due dates are significant issues affecting student participation. While effective practices in topic selection can be measured by qualitative means, best practices in scheduling have been supported by quantitative means.

3.1 Topic Selection

As CS instructors, we each differ in our approach to asynchronous discussion in our courses. While there are some similarities, such as weekly discussions and grade-mandated responses, the selection and number of topics we present to our students varies. The number of topics changes according to the primary delivery mode of course content: in a course taught exclusively online, the discussion comprises a major component of the course grade, ranging from 35 to 50% of the overall grade; in a course taught mostly through traditional lectures, the discussion moves online from the classroom due to lack of time; in a blended course taught in the traditional classroom and supplemented heavily via online means, asynchronous discussion occupies the middle ground between the other two modes.

The number of asynchronous discussions in a course also varies based on the duration of the term – summer courses typically generate less number of topics than fall or spring term courses. Nevertheless, irrespective of the primary delivery mode of the class, each of the authors typically engages in weekly discussions online; in other words, a new discussion is opened for students every week. In a weekly discussion, the number of topics is likely to vary between 1 and 4, depending on the number of students, nature of the subject matter, duration of the course, and the interest of the instructor and students.

One of the authors initially started with presenting one topic per weekly discussion. If the number of students in the course ranged between 20 and 30, student-to-student interaction was sufficiently motivated to gain and maintain the momentum required for effective participation in the learning experience. However, if the number of students in the course was less than 15, the presence of a lone topic did not pose an adequate challenge to students, and responses became stilted and repetitive. This problem was remedied by presenting a choice of 2 topics per weekly discussion to sustain the interest level of students in the smaller classes. The topics were related and each student had the choice of responding to one or the other topic. Each student also had to comment on a peer's response to the topic they had not originally chosen. This format enabled variety in responses, thus stimulating greater debate and interaction among students.

Another author requires students to respond to two or three discussion questions concerning the course content, and to respond to a question that requires students to summarize either Internet sources or peer-reviewed/refereed journal articles relevant to the course topic every week. This allows students to independently research computer science areas of interest to them and to acquire knowledge not presented in the course textbook. For software or web development courses, students are also required to post their completed assignments, to describe those assignments, and to describe their "trials and tribulations" in completing them. This technique allows students to see and comment on each other's developmental techniques and to share their experiences with other students. In courses requiring projects, students are also required to post their project deliverables and to comment on other students' deliverables. This technique of varying the required types of responses aids in addressing the different learning styles of the students [7]. Requiring students to comment substantively on classmates' responses encourages them to consistently review other student responses, independently compare these posts to their own and think critically about their own and others' responses.

In the CS curriculum, several courses are enriched by careful selection of topics in asynchronous discussions. Courses involving software development, network and information security, web design and development, and database management systems compel independent, external research among students, which are borne out in discussion responses to thought-provoking topics. Project-based and current topics courses also require experiences involving students beyond the classroom. Because CS students can be motivated by timely hot-button issues such as the privacy and security of biometric identification schemes, the selection of relevant topics for engaging students in asynchronous discussions becomes especially important for CS educators.

3.2 Scheduling Due Dates

We have been engaged in using asynchronous discussions in each of the 3 courses we teach every term, including the summer term. For the last 3 years, each of us has followed different models for topic selection and scheduling due dates for discussions. We typically compare notes on teaching methods, "sit" in on virtual and classroom sessions, exchange ideas on effective practices, and actively participate in professional meetings in the field. Although each author uses the week as a standard format for a discussion, due dates for student responses have been differently scheduled. While one of the authors mandates at least 2 posts per week for grade purposes, another author expects as many as 5 posts per week per student. In addition, in some courses, students are required to post at least one comment to another student's response. This may result in a minimum of 10 posts per week.

Initially, the authors struggled with a single due date for student responses in a week. In some courses, responses were due on Sunday; in others, on Saturday; and in others, on Friday. Since a majority of the students posted their original responses a day before the deadline or on the day of the deadline, regardless of the day of the week of that deadline, there was little time for reading and commenting upon peer responses. Initial discussion topics were laced with one-line comments such as "Great response" or "Good job!" The overhead on instructor time spent on grading also occurred in bursts with periods of little or no grading activity interspersed with periods of intense grading activity.

After a week or two of unsatisfactory responses and marathon grading sessions, one of the authors decided to split the discussion deadline in half – students now needed to post an original response to one of two weekly topics by mid-week; they had until the end of the week to read, understand and comment on peer responses to the other topic. This model immediately improved student participation: students' comments were meaningful, and they sought clarification or added to the substance of the original response. Some students expressed disagreement with their peers' responses, which stimulated lively defenses from the original respondents. Distributed deadlines for weekly topics are now the norm in asynchronous discussions of all the courses that all of the authors teach every term.

From our experiences and survey of literature, we present two additional techniques for improving student interaction:

- clearly state the requirements of discussion responses, such as length required, due date, stylistic requirements (if any) and percentage of grade, up front either in the syllabus or in a "welcome" message to students [14]; and
- provide timely feedback to the students, particularly in the beginning of the term before learning communities have been formed [8].

By clearly stating the requirements for effective interaction up front and quickly pointing out to students when they are failing to meet expectations, comments such as "Great response!" or "Good job!" have been nearly eliminated. This has resulted in significantly more interactivity throughout the discussions.

Initial ad-hoc experimentation with one discussion topic per week did not provide enough of a challenge to students in CS courses. From personal experience in taking online courses, the authors know that one topic to discuss per week is too light a load to maintain interactive momentum among students. Sporadic posts also undermine the teamwork aspect of the courses. Providing two or more topics per weekly discussion presented an adequately challenging assignment to most CS students. Plurality of topics also sustained daily and meaningful interaction among students and between students and instructor. The final adjustment in asynchronous discussions to exploit their full potential occurred as a result of splitting the response and comment deadlines among students. Such a distribution of deadlines, coupled with multiple, related, relevant and timely topics per weekly discussion, furnished optimal interactivity and produced optimum engagement of CS students with the course material otherwise presented in traditional lectures and online supplements.

4. METHODOLOGY AND RESULTS

We believe that scheduling weekly asynchronous discussions with distributed due dates is more effective in enhancing student participation than scheduling weekly discussions with a single due date at the end of the week. Increasing student participation in discussions has a direct impact on achieving better academic results and learning outcomes by students. This is particularly true in CS courses wherein students are expected to understand the underlying theoretical concepts sufficiently thoroughly in order to apply them in different practical contexts. To substantiate our belief, we quantitatively compare student participation in discussions with single due dates, with participation in discussions with split deadlines. Our basic premise is that split deadlines work better than unified deadlines in eliciting higher student involvement and enriching the learning experience of students in CS courses.

Out of a total of 7-8 undergraduate and graduate courses taught by each of the authors over an academic year, we selected 3 to 4 courses per instructor that best represented teaching style and requirements for online asynchronous discussions. The period of teaching ranged from summer 2003 to summer 2004. Messages in discussion topics were grouped by week and compiled together to get a composite listing of all messages in that discussion. Knowledge of the number of students enrolled in the course enabled us to obtain the number of messages per student. This number was normalized to obtain the number of posted messages per day per student per discussion (Table 1). We refer to this measure as the *student participation metric*. The final results were compared graphically as shown in Figure 1 a) through d).

Table 1. Sample numeric data for student participation metric

Day	Course 1	Course 2	Course 3	Course 4
Sun	0.89	1.30	0.23	0.18
Mon	0.24	0.29	0.34	0.33
Tue	0.28	0.20	0.36	0.33
Wed	0.32	0.24	0.32	0.37
Thu	0.42	0.20	0.43	0.53
Fri	0.32	0.28	1.00	1.01
Sat	0.47	0.39	0.22	0.20
# students	17	17	25	15
# discussions	7	13	13	13
Deadlines	Sun	Sun	Fri	Fri

Figure 1 a) and b) show the student participation metric for courses with unified, non-distributed discussion deadlines. Figure 1 a) shows the data for two courses in which discussion messages were due on Sundays while Figure 1 b) shows the data for two courses in which discussion messages were due on Fridays. It is obvious from these two figures that student activity remained relatively low throughout the week, but peaked dramatically on the deadline. Such an approach may encourage students to procrastinate until the last moment. Non-distributed deadlines may lead to the accumulation of work that students need to complete in a short period of time. Our experience indicates that courses with a significant software development component are those that suffer the most when offered in this mode: student performance in coding assignments and software development projects tends to decline. On the other hand, distributed deadlines help keep the students engaged in the course, as explained below.

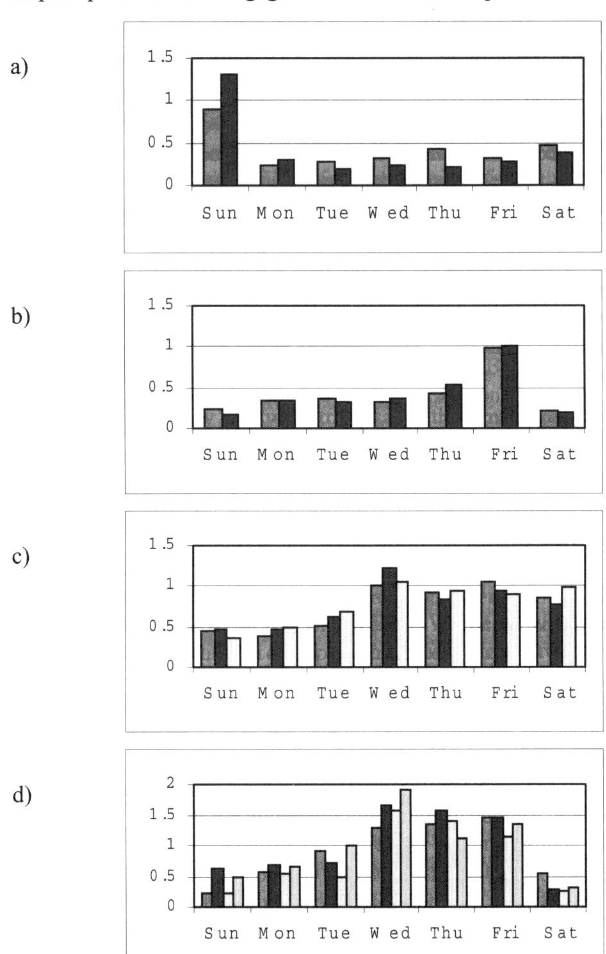

Figure 1. Student participation metric: a) two classes offered by Instructor 1 with a single Sunday deadline; b) two classes offered by Instructor 1 with a single Friday deadline; c) three classes offered by Instructor 2 with a split Wednesday/Saturday deadline; and d) four classes offered by Instructor 3 with a split Wednesday/Friday deadline

Figure 1 c) and d) show the student participation metric for several courses offered by Instructor 2 and Instructor 3 respectively. As can be clearly seen in these figures, student participation is more uniformly spread throughout the entire workweek. This type of deadline structuring encourages students to plan ahead, which yields significantly positive results in CS courses requiring many hands-on activities, such as software development assignments and projects. In network security and forensics courses, lively debate was engendered by distributing the deadlines. There was a marked improvement in student engagement with the subject matter when they were given time to read other students' discussion messages and respond to them appropriately and adequately. Research-oriented courses that require a lot of reading benefit from this structure as well, since students generally have more time to analyze their reading materials and discuss them with other students and the instructor.

As observed by the illustrations, the experimental results clearly demonstrate the higher degree of student participation in asynchronous discussions with distributed deadlines for the mandated posts. Our hypothesis that scheduling weekly asynchronous discussions with distributed due dates is more effective in enhancing student participation than scheduling weekly discussions with a single due date at the end of the week has been borne out by the data. Student survey responses, to be presented at the conference, strongly support this result. An increase in student participation in discussions related to the course has a direct impact on increasing student engagement and involvement with the material. This is especially true in CS courses because of the practical content delivered and the need for students to grasp applications of the concepts studied in lectures.

5. CONCLUSION

This paper focused on effective teaching practices that can be used to enhance student participation and involvement in CS courses. Asynchronous discussion can lead to successful learning outcomes and enhanced student satisfaction. In our collective experience, student participation and achievement of learning outcomes can best be increased by following good practices. These practices relate to online asynchronous discussions in tandem with online or traditional instruction in CS courses:

- posting discussion topics that are timely and relevant to the course material,
- providing a multiplicity of carefully chosen weekly topics, and
- distributing response deadlines on topics such that sufficient time is granted for understanding others' messages so students can post constructive criticism and supplemental information.

Lively and involved discussions conducted asynchronously in an online forum also accelerated the generation of learning communities, thus enhancing the learning experience. Qualitative data, anecdotal evidence and a survey of research literature supported our theories of topic selection and the need for multiple topics per weekly discussion. Quantitative data were collected to evaluate the theory of distribution of response deadlines. The results of the evaluation confirmed our belief that split deadlines worked better than unified deadlines in fostering higher and frequent interaction among students. The beneficial implications of our work can be realized by all CS educators in improving student participation and satisfaction, and stimulating students to seek current knowledge via external and independent research into topics pertaining to course content and learning objectives.

6. REFERENCES

[1] Allen, I. E., Seaman, J. *Sizing the Opportunity: The Quality and Extent of Online Education in the United States, 2002 and 2003.* The Sloan Consortium, September 2003. http://www.sloan-c.org/resources/sizing_opportunity.pdf

[2] Anderson, T., and Elloumi, F., editors. Theory and Practice of Online Learning. Ngwenya, J., Annand, D., and Wang, E., authors: Chapter 13 – *Supporting Asynchronous Discussions among Online Learners.* Athabasca University, 2004. http://cde.athabascau.ca/online_book/pdf/TPOL_book.pdf

[3] Bhagyavati and Whitehead, C. Facilitating Learning Communities. In *Proceedings of the Society for Information Technology and Teacher Education* (Atlanta, GA, March 1-6, 2004).

[4] Cereijo, M. V. P., Young, J., and Wilhelm, R. W. Factors Facilitating Student Participation in Asynchronous Web-Based Courses. *Journal of Computing in Teacher Education,* 18, 1 (Fall 2001), 32-39. http://www.iste.org/jcte/pdfs/te18132cer.pdf

[5] Dudding, C., Gauthier, A., Naderi, N., and Scot, T. *Learning Communities, Asynchronous Discussions: Asynchronous Discussion Guide.* University of Virginia, May 11, 2002. http://onlinelearn.edschool.virginia.edu/discuss/design/async h_disc_guide_blank.pdf

[6] Frey, B. A., and Wojnar, L. C. *Successful Synchronous and Asynchronous Discussions: Plan, Implement and Evaluate.* Educause Information Resources Library, 2004. http://www.educause.edu/ir/library/pdf/MAC0426.pdf

[7] Hardless, C., Lundin, J., and Nulden, U. Mandatory Participation in Asynchronous Learning Networks. In *Proceedings of the 34th Hawaii International Conference on System Sciences* (2001). http://www.alnresearch.org/ Data_Files/articles/full_text/hardless.pdf

[8] Kelly, J. On-line Discussions: Making them work for you. *JISC InfoNet Key Issues.* Northumbria University, 2003. http://www.jiscinfonet.ac.uk/InfoKits/infokit-related-files/on-line-discussions

[9] Kurkovsky, S., Bhagyavati, Summers, W., and Whitehead, C. Online Discussions in Computer Science Courses: How to Make Them an Effective Learning Tool. In *Proceedings of the Information Technology in Research and Education* (London, United Kingdom, June-July 2004).

[10] McDonald, J. Is "As Good as Face-to-Face" As Good As It Gets? *Journal of Asynchronous Learning Networks,* 6, 2 (August 2002).

[11] Murray, B. Reinventing Class Discussion Online. *Monitor on Psychology,* 31 (April 2000). 54-56.

[12] Pelz, B. (My) Three Principles of Effective Online Pedagogy. *Journal of Asynchronous Learning Networks,* 8, 3 (June 2004). Sloan Consortium. http://aln.org/publications/jaln/v8n3/v8n3_pelz.asp

[13] Raleigh, D. Keys to Facilitating Successful Online Discussions. *Teaching with Technology Today,* 7, 3 (November 15, 2000). http://www.uwsa.edu/ttt/raleigh.htm

[14] SUNY. *Enhancing Online Discussion. Teaching, Learning and Technology at State University of New York,* June 28, 2004. http://tlt.suny.edu/discussion.htm

[15] Wu, D., and Hiltz, S. Online Discussions and Perceived Learning. In *Proceedings of the 9th Americas Conference on Information Systems* (Tampa, FL, August 2003). pp. 687-696

Ubiquitous Presenter: Increasing Student Access and Control in a Digital Lecturing Environment

Michelle Wilkerson
Math and Computer Science Dept.
University of San Diego
mw4@sandiego.edu

William G. Griswold
Computer Science and Engineering Dept.
University of California, San Diego
wgg@cs.ucsd.edu

Beth Simon
Math and Computer Science Dept.
University of San Diego
bsimon@sandiego.edu

ABSTRACT

The University of Washington's Classroom Presenter lecturing system enables an active lecturing environment by combining a standard electronic slide presentation format with the capability for extemporaneous ink annotations by instructors and students using Tablet PCs. Thus, it can promote more interactive, student-centered learning. While many students may own laptops, few are yet Tablet devices. Also, Presenter uses multicast networking, which has availability and reliability issues. Ubiquitous Presenter (UP) expands Presenter via common web technologies to support non-Tablet audiences and enhance student control. UP enables students, using internet web browsers, to (a) synchronously or asynchronously view the slides and ink that are broadcast by the instructor, as well as (b) provide contextual submissions via text overlaid on the instructor's slides. The only compromises are that non-Tablet students cannot produce ink, and that professor ink is provided after a small time delay.

Categories and Subject Descriptors

K.3.1 [Computers and Education]: Computers Uses in Education – collaborative learning, computer-assisted instruction, distance learning.

General Terms: Human Factors.

Keywords

Educational technology, active learning, collaborative learning, classroom assessment, Presentation tools, Tablet PC.

1. INTRODUCTION

Emerging classroom technologies, while allowing for innovative pedagogical practice, can experience cost barriers to access and adoption. UW Classroom Presenter (or just Presenter) provides instructors the ability to quickly and intuitively annotate digital slide presentations using the Tablet PC, as well as receive student-annotated slide submissions from audience Tablet PCs. In this work we describe the motivation and design of Ubiquitous Presenter (UP), a system which enables users with a variety of non-Tablet, internet-enabled computer devices to access live lecture materials generated by the instructor with Presenter, including ink annotations. In future work we will evaluate UP's use in CS courses. UP additionally enables (text-based) student submissions without the need for student-accessible Tablet PCs, instead allowing submissions via internet browsers. UP enables widespread deployment of Classroom Presenter without the need for several Tablet PC devices or a multicast network setup, and simplifies the use of Classroom Presenter for student submissions – a powerful pedagogical feature that was previously costly and difficult to utilize.

Ubiquitous Presenter, like Classroom Presenter, enables a more active, student-centered lecture environment without a dramatic shift in established teaching methods. Although instructors still use prepared slides as a guide, the ability for students to have questions addressed quickly and easily during a lecture allows students more control over the learning experience. Additionally, the ability to review archives of annotated slides after a lecture provides students with a lasting resource. Student submissions enable instructors to further address the varying needs of students by allowing anonymous understanding checks and feedback sessions. At its limit, the two-way annotation of the instructor's slides enables a conversation between the instructor and students.

An additional, beneficial side-effect of UP's move from multicast to a client-server architecture is that students can now more readily browse forward and back through slides in a lecture, supporting a wider variety of learning styles. Though technically possible in Presenter, the broadcast communication structure of the system meant this ability was rarely utilized by students. Providing students with such active control over the lecture environment both within and outside of the classroom can promote student involvement in learning [1], and allows student difficulties and concerns to be addressed quickly and effectively.

For these benefits, students using non-Tablet devices sacrifice the ability to submit ink – instead overlaying typed text on slides. Also, slides and ink are provided to non-Tablet students through a polling mechanism, resulting in slight delays. Significantly, Tablet-using instructors and students experience no compromises.

In the following, we begin with some background on UW Classroom Presenter. We then describe UP's design and implementation (based on a download of source code from the Presenter web site), followed by a discussion of its use both inside and outside the classroom. We close with a discussion of related work and closing remarks.

SIGCSE'05, February 23–27, 2005, St. Louis, Missouri, USA.

2. CLASSROOM PRESENTER

UW Classroom Presenter (Presenter), first deployed in 2002, allows an instructor to teach in a dynamic, responsive manner using Tablet PCs. The obvious benefits of pen computing – the ability to freely annotate and move about while lecturing – are combined with Presenter's unique features, enabling a spontaneous, student-centered, yet organized lecture. Slide minimization allows the instructor to produce blank space along the margins of a slide for inking examples in real time, answering questions, or making corrections to slides; while the whiteboard feature allows instructors to create entire slides on-the-fly. Presenter enables students to leave personal (private) notes to themselves on slides. The student submission feature enables instructors to conduct structured (or unstructured) spontaneous understanding checks of students who also have a Tablet PC. UW Classroom Presenter has been used in over 75 Computer Science classes, from introductory courses to Masters level and distance learning programs [2,3].

2.1 Limitations of Presenter

As Presenter has grown in popularity, users have voiced the need for a more reliable, accessible form of it. The features and benefits of Presenter are attractive to many, but there are barriers to use. Students wishing to view slides and ink up-close, or wishing to save lectures for later review, must have access to a Tablet PC with Presenter installed.

Presenter uses a broadcast model of communication. At the start of the class session, the instructor broadcasts slides to all of the student devices. During the lecture ink strokes and slide transitions are broadcast. This creates a problem for late joiners, since they will not have access to the slides or the ink that was broadcast before they joined. Requiring the instructor to rebroadcast materials each time a student joined the session could severely impact performance. The broadcast networking is implemented in Presenter using multicast networking [10]. This introduces two further problems. First of all, multicast networking does not guarantee delivery of packets, leading to reliability problems. This is a particular issue for sending slides in a wireless environment. Second, not all networks support multicast. Routers are often configured to block multicast packets, so in many university environments it may not be possible to use multicast across different subnets.

Student submissions, a powerful feature of Presenter, are not fully utilized due to the need for multiple, student-accessible devices. In order to allow student submissions, instructors must obtain a number of Tablet PCs (one per collaborating group, for example), install Presenter on the device, establish a multicast-enabled network for the class to use, and distribute the Tablets to students. This is costly and interruptive – in one instance; an instructor would bring Tablets to class, distribute them for a submission activity, and then collect the devices after the activity was complete.

3. UBIQUITOUS PRESENTER

In response to these limitations, we undertook the development of Ubiquitous Presenter, a web-based extension to Classroom Presenter that allows Presenter materials to be accessed and annotated by a web browser on any internet-enabled computing device. Our desire was to widen the accessibility of such Presenter features as the ability to review slides with ink and enable student submissions, while taking advantage of the availability and reliability of the internet for broadcast.

3.1 Project Goals

These goals were outlined at the beginning of the project:

1) Availability of full-featured Presenter slides (automatically hiding instructor notes) on the web in a browser-neutral representation such as PNG or JPEG.

2) Synchronization of slides and instructor ink between the instructor machine running Presenter and the web-based repository of UP.

3) Enabling of student submissions via the web interface (without disrupting traditional Presenter multicast submissions).

4) Support for Tablet PC users to continue to use traditional Presenter with no degradation of features.

All four of these goals have been met and the system will be available download (free for academic use) in mid 2005 after a period of in-class testing.

3.2 System Design

UP is a client-server application programmed in PHP, a server-side language that generates simple HTML and limited JavaScript that is passed to student browsers. This reduces cross-browser compatibility issues and client-side processing requirements. Devices capable of running current versions of Internet Explorer, Netscape Navigator, and Mozilla can run UP. JavaScript must be enabled on the browser for some features to work.

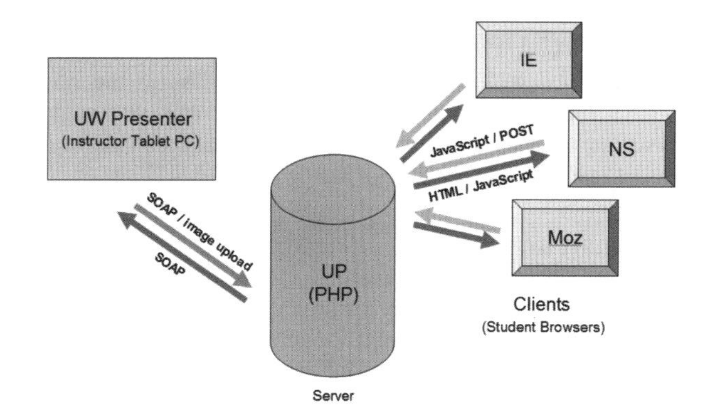

Figure 1. Setup of Ubiquitous Presenter system. A centralized server running UP enables compatibility with a number of browsers.

By isolating most of UP's processing on the server, any failures do not compromise the instructor's Presenter session. Instructors are notified of server errors, but presentations are not interrupted. If students encounter an error or incompatibility in their computers, they are still able to simply unsynchronize from the presentation and manually follow along (synchronization is described in Section 4.1).

Student browsers remain synchronized through a hidden HTML frame that polls a single image file, referred to as the current display file. This current display file is modified whenever an action (such as a slide change, ink overlay, or minimization) occurs. The hidden frame then sends a message to the visible frame to update the image by reloading. Students may experience a short delay – no more than 3 seconds – before the image displayed is the current one.

A majority of the synchronization between Classroom Presenter and UP occurs through short file transfers and SOAP (Simple Object Access Protocol) remote procedure calls. When the instructor changes slides, a SOAP call is made to the PHP server containing the position of the new slide, and PHP executes the call, switching its current slide. When ink is exported to UP, a small snapshot image of the ink overlay in Presenter is sent to the server via an ink-overlay SOAP call. PHP composites the ink with the slide, using PHP GD image library commands, and the resulting image is displayed to students and copied for archiving. Other Presenter features, such as slide minimization or slide clearing, are also executed via simple SOAP calls from Presenter to the UP server.

Student submissions are similarly handled through HTTP POST commands and processed via the central PHP server. Upon beginning a submission, students are provided a copy of the slide being broadcast. Students may annotate the slide with text, and the server composites the text's images with PHP GD library function calls as new blocks of text are added. Once the slide is satisfactory, students choose to 'submit' the slide, and a permanent image copy is created and made available in the presentation's submission directory. The Presenter session running on the instructor's Tablet periodically checks for new images in the submission directory, and downloads the submissions as they become available and converts them into native Presenter slides.

4. USING UBIQUITOUS PRESENTER

In accordance with our goal to increase access to the novel learning modalities enabled by Presenter, attention was paid to preserving as many of its features and uses as possible. Attention was also paid to not changing the instructor's use of Presenter.

4.1 Instructor Use

The instructor creates a presentation in Microsoft PowerPoint and saves it to Presenter's native file format (CSD, or Conferencing Slide Deck). Both a PowerPoint add-in (available when Presenter is installed) and a related standalone application, Deckbuilder, can be used to accomplish this – users without Powerpoint can create CSD files, and those who are already familiar with PowerPoint may export directly from the PPT interface[1]. Deckbuilder and the PowerPoint add-in have been modified to allow the presentation to be uploaded by the instructor to a UP web server. Upon upload, the slides are available for review in the UP interface. Students may peruse the slides independently, with synchronization turned off (since there is no active lecture), as soon as slides have been uploaded. Instructors also have the option to password protect their presentation, preventing others from editing preferences or synchronizing to the presentation, as well as providing a student password, preventing public access to UP slide presentations.

To begin a UP lecture, the instructor selects "Synchronize to Web" from the Presenter menu, and a list of available uploaded presentations are shown. Upon selection of the appropriate presentation (and password, if necessary), it becomes "live" and students using UP with slide synchronization enabled will see the first slide of the instructor's presentation appear in their browsers. The instructor now may change slides, ink on slides, and use whiteboard and slide minimization features, with the results automatically displayed on students' browsers within a few seconds. Ink is automatically exported when a natural pause occurs in inking patterns, indicating the instructor is discussing an annotation, or is encouraging students to pause and consider it.

If desired, instructors may conduct understanding checks or request feedback from students using UP's student submission feature. From the Classroom Presenter menu, instructors select "Enable Web Submissions". Students are then allowed to, via their browsers, position text over the active slide, and save the annotated slide for instructors to load back into the Presenter interface for review. As students submit their annotated slides, they appear automatically as another "Web Submissions" slide deck in the instructor's Presenter interface for review.

4.2 Student Use

Students using UP are not required to install anything – all that is needed is a web browser (recent versions of Internet Explorer, Netscape Navigator or Mozilla) and a URL exported by UP.

A key feature is that students may use UP to view live presentations in class as broadcast by an instructor either synchronously or asynchronously as they choose – likely, a combination of the two in the course of a lecture. In general, we expect students to stay synchronized with the instructor's active slide and ink. However, students may still be reviewing a slide when the instructor moves to the next [4, 5, 11]. In UP a student can temporarily switch to asynchronous mode to review (or preview) slides at their own rate, choosing to resynchronize at any time. Since all ink is captured on the web-server, students who unsynchronize do not lose the ability to access inked slides that occurred while they were unsynchronized. Figure 2 shows a student browser view of a live lecture. Student control over synchronization is set at the top right of the page with a radio button. While synchronized, navigation buttons (top left) are disabled.

---

[1] While importing of lecture materials from non-PPT images is supported, Presenter's instructor objects are only supported in PPT.

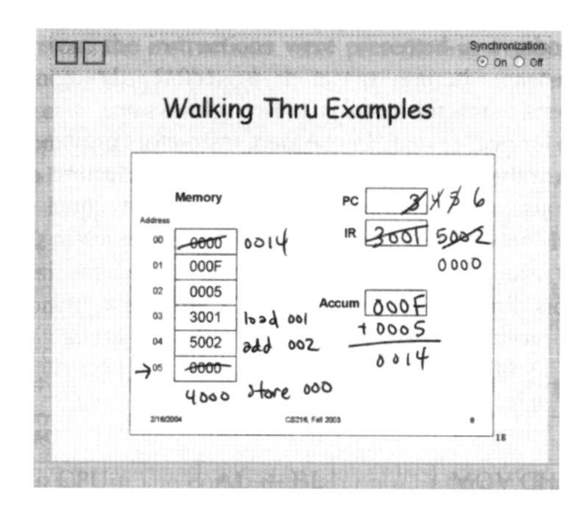

Figure 2. Student view of synchronized presentation. Slides update automatically to include ink or slide transitions.

Outside of class, students may preview slides as soon as they are uploaded and review slides plus ink annotations once a presentation is complete. As an instructor gives a presentation and ink is displayed in UP, archives of the ink are saved chronologically. In Figure 3, the various versions of inked slides occur as [1] [2] etc. at the bottom of each slide as it is displayed. Note that the original un-inked slides are always available for student viewing. This allows students to replay a lecture, viewing any annotations, examples, or corrections as added during a lecture.

4.3 Active Learning with Student Submissions

A powerful feature of Classroom Presenter, extended and made more accessible in UP, is the ability to accept student submissions contextualized in the presentation. These submissions are often comprised of annotations on top of a slide the instructor has designed for the purpose, though an instructor can also create a student activity extemporaneously using the Presenter whiteboard. Currently, UP supports text submissions on top of pre-loaded presentation slides, though plans exist to extend this feature to include 'ink' submissions from student browsers using a Java applet to allow "drawing" using a mouse or other pointer device. Such ink capability is considered an important component of student submissions; both in expanding the types of activities allowed and allowing students greater freedom of expression. Thus activities involving or requiring graphical responses may be limited by the current UP student submission feature.

Once student submissions are enabled by an instructor, students view a "Create a Submission" button below the slide display area. Students may click this button to open a new window, displaying the slide. Students may fill a textbox, then click on the slide to place the text onto the slide. Students may add several blocks of text, and edit previous annotations as shown in Figure 4. Once satisfied, the students click 'submit', at which point the slide plus annotations is sent to the instructor's Presenter interface. Note that students retain complete control over their submissions. Any text box can be edited multiple times before submission. Anecdotal use of Presenter student submissions with Tablets has shown that students frequently rework their answers and do not want initial results transmitted to the instructor.

4.4 Use Outside the Live Lecture

Just as slides and ink may be reviewed after a presentation is complete, instructors may opt to leave the "allow student submissions" feature on after a presentation. This enables students to complete an assignment based on a slide or leave feedback and questions about a presentation. To access these submissions, the instructor need only resynchronize to the presentation, and all submitted slides will reload into the Presenter interface. Additionally, the instructor has the option of making student submissions available for review within the UP interface, allowing both students and the instructor to access submissions without the need for Presenter. These student submission slides appear as an [SSx] link underneath the slide to which the submission text was added, as shown in Figure 3.

When submissions are displayed online, slides remain anonymous, but students are able to compare their results with others, or review their own work. This feature may also be employed within the class, enabling an instructor to have students

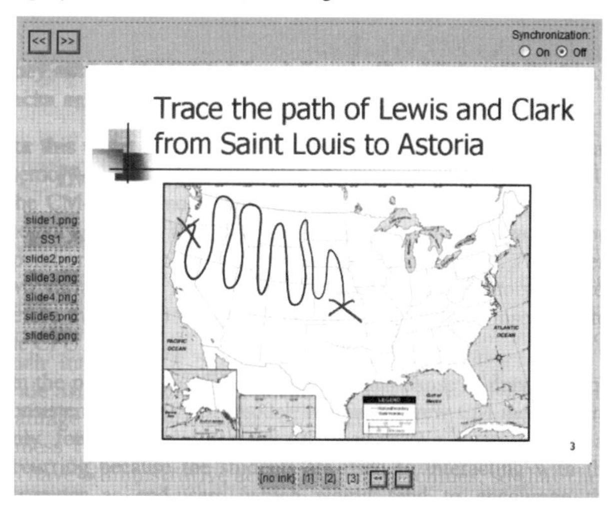

Figure 3. Student view of unsynchronized presentation. Students may peruse original slides, inked slides and student submissions that occurred during the live presentation.

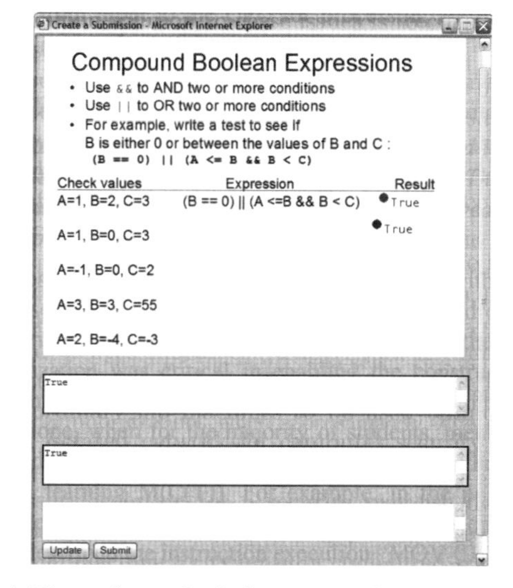

Figure 4. The student submission screen allows students to add an unlimited number of text blocks to the slide.

review their peers' submissions anonymously, or have the class collectively review a specific, particularly interesting submission.

5. OTHER USES OF UBIQUITOUS PRESENTER

5.1 Distance Learning

Perhaps the most flexibility is afforded by Ubiquitous Presenter in distance learning. In order to utilize traditional Presenter in such instances, a multicast network must be established between the instructor and the remote location. Students using UP, however, need only to log onto the URL representing the presentation they know will occur at class time. Thus students unable to attend class, distance classes conducted at remote locations, etc. may all attend a Presenter lecture without any special setup, and may utilize all of the features of Presenter – including student submissions, which like submissions done on-site, are immediately available for review by the instructor.

6. RELATED WORK

A number of projects have addressed the issue of using technology to support lecturing and learning environments.

Early work focused on integrating slides and writing includes Lecturer's Assistant [6] and ZenPad [7], the presentation component of the Classroom 2000 system. Golub [8] has independently developed a system for presenting material from a Tablet PC known as Tablet Mylar Slides.

The DyKnow system [5] has goals similar to our own. In DyKnow, students sit at PCs, optionally equipped with pen enabled technology, while the instructor lectures from an electronic whiteboard, video tablet or PC. DyKnow encourages students to annotate instructor material synchronously, with the option to review class work asynchronously. DyKnow Vision utilizes progressive disclosure to help keep students on task. Students can go back at any point within a class session to review material, but they are not able to get ahead of the instructor. DyKnow is focused on an effective classroom experience that fosters collaboration as well as the development of a good set of notes. UP differs in that we target a minimal classroom infrastructure where only the instructor must have a Tablet PC and students may interact using any internet-enabled device.

In the Virtual MultiBoard System [4], they address the lack of context enabled by a single digitally projected slide in comparison to multiple sliding blackboards. They develop software to support the use of multiple video-projector based presentations in order to address students' need to see more than the current slide – though the entire class will be shown this same view.

Engaging the class is a major goal of Active Class [1] which has currently targeted the PDA-platform to bring interaction to the classroom. Also, commercial systems exist allowing students to respond to multiple choice polls using remote controllers [9].

7. CONCLUSIONS

Ubiquitous Presenter not only expands accessibility of the popular Tablet PC Presenter system, but helps to address a wide variety of learning styles. Students are able to review slides and instructor ink annotations at their own pace either during or after a presentation. Instructors may choose to review student comprehension during or after a lecture through student submissions, and may make these submissions anonymously available for peer review. In one step, instructors provide students with reviewable lecture materials, an interactive lecture including spontaneous annotations addressing student questions or additional information, and a means for assessing student comprehension or extracting student concerns. Through Ubiquitous Presenter, student access comes not only through expanded access to the live lecture itself, but through extended accessibility of lecture slides, instructor ink, and peer submissions even after a lecture has concluded.

8. ACKNOWLEDGEMENTS

This work is based on the Classroom Presenter project available for download from http://www.cs.washington.edu/education/dl/presenter. This work was funded, in part, by an NSF REU from the National Partnership for Advanced Computing Infrastructure's Education, Outreach and Training program, gifts from Microsoft Research, and a gift from Hewlett Packard.

9. REFERENCES

[1] Griswold, W., Shanahan, P., Brown, S., Boyer, J., Ratto, M., Shapiro, R., and Truong, T., ActiveCampus - Experiments in Community-Oriented Ubiquitous Computing. *IEEE Computer*, To Appear.

[2] Simon, B., Anderson, R., Hoyer, C., and Su, J. Preliminary Experiences with a Tablet PC Based System to Support Active Learning in Computer Science Courses. *9th ITICSE,* June 2004.

[3] Anderson, R., Anderson, R., Simon, B., Wolfman, S. A., VanDeGrift, T., and Yasuhara, Ken. Experiences with a Tablet PC Based Lecture Presentation System in Computer Science Courses. 35th *SIGCSE*, March 2004.

[4] Rößling, G., Trompler, C., Muehlhäuser, M., Köler, S., Wolf, S. Enhancing Classroom Lectures with Digital Sliding Blackboards. *9th ITICSE*, June 2004.

[5] Berque D., Bonebright T., and Whitesell M. Using Pen-based Computers Across the Computer Science Curriculum. 35th *SIGCSE,* 2004.

[6] Buckalew, C., Porter, A., The Lecturer's Assistant. *25th SIGCSE*, pp 193-197. 1994.

[7] Brotherton, J. A. *College of Computer*. Ph.D. Thesis, Georgia Tech, Atlanta, GA, 2001.

[8] Golub, E. Handwritten Slides on a TabletPC in a Discrete Mathematics Course. *35th SIGCSE*, 2004.

[9] eInstruction http://www.einstruction.com

[10] Schulzrinne, H., Casner, S., Frederick., R., Jacobson., V., RTP: A Transport Protocol for Real-Time Applications. IETF RFC 3550, July 2003. http://www.ietf.org/rfc/rfc3550.txt

[11] Anderson R., Anderson R., VanDeGrift, T., Wolfman, S., Yasuhara, K., Promoting Interaction in Large Classes with Computer-Mediated Feedback. In *Computer Support for Collaborative Learning,*2003.

Research to Classroom: Experiences from a Multi-institutional Course in Smart Home Technologies

Charles Hannon
Texas Christian University
Box 298860
Fort Worth, TX 76129
817.257.7166
C.Hannon@tcu.edu

Manfred Huber
Univ. of Texas
Box 19015
Arlington, TX 76019
817.272.2345
Huber@cse.uta.edu

Lisa Burnell
Texas Christian University
Box 298850
Fort Worth, TX 76129
817.257.6378
L.Burnell@tcu.edu

ABSTRACT
Bringing the excitement and challenges of active research into the classroom offers unique learning experiences. This is particularly true for undergraduate students not otherwise exposed to the processes, methods, and results of research. Designing and delivering such a course, however, presents many challenges. In this article, we describe our recent experience co-teaching a multi-institutional course in smart home technologies. From our experience and analysis of student evaluations, we offer a number of lessons learned and recommendations.

Categories and Subject Descriptors
K.3.2 [Computer and Information Science Education]

General Terms
Measurement, Experimentation.

Keywords
Pedagogy, CS education research, using emerging instructional technology, research in the classroom,

1. INTRODUCTION
The exposure of students to emerging technologies in an active learning environment is important to prepare them for today's work place or for the pursuit of an advanced academic degree. Recently, two universities offered a course intended to provide such opportunities through the integration of advances in on-going, multi-disciplinary and cross-institutional research in Smart Home technologies. This course, held in the spring semester of 2004, was introduced into the upper-level undergraduate and beginning graduate curricula at two universities. The first, which we will refer to as U1, is a large public university with undergraduate and graduate programs in Computer Science Engineering. The second, U2, is a small private university with undergraduate programs in Computer Science and Computer Information Technology. Cross-disciplinary, cross-institutional course activities are open to students from different engineering disciplines and co-taught by faculty from both universities. Emulating the future industry experience many students will experience, the course is designed to expose students to multi-disciplinary teams working together, and the challenges inherent in such teams. A central goal is the enhancement of the educational experience and preparation of students through the use of state-of-the-art tools and curriculum components that integrate research and educational experiences.

Some of the most current technology was used for delivering the course to both local and remote students. Communication was over Internet 2, with an ISDN backup. At U2, the course was held in a dedicated studio/classroom managed by the Instructional Services Department (Figure 1). A technician was always available to assist the instructors. A large screen plasma monitor displayed transmitted lecture notes, while a second TV displayed images of either the instructor or students at the remote site. At U1, a standard classroom with portable communication equipment was used. An interactive whiteboard was acquired, but proved too slow to be effectively used.

In this article, we describe the course and its development, the course experience, evaluation, and the results of the evaluation. A number of recommendations and lessons learned conclude the discussion.

Figure 1. Studio/classroom for the course. The local projector screen and a monitor at the back of the room are not shown.

2. THE SMART HOME COURSE

A key objective of the course was to use the smart home application as a unifying theme through which a broad range of issues, technologies, and methods could be introduced to the student. One advantage of using a complex application domain area is that it helps illustrate systems integration issues, the design trade-offs necessary, and the fact that real problems often do not have a "right" answer. An advantage of using smart homes is that it brings active research into the classroom. The topics covered in the course are shown below. Except for the last two, topics were covered in two to three lectures.

1)	Smart home overview	2)	Sensors and actuators
3)	Networking	4)	Distributed computing
5)	Data storage & retrieval	6)	Adaptive behavior
7)	Decision making	8)	Robotic assistants
9)	Privacy, security	10)	System design issues

The prerequisites for the course were 1) ability to program in one high-level programming language such as Java, C, or C++ at least equivalent to the completion of a first programming course, and 2) upper division or graduate status in Engineering or Computer Science. We kept the course prerequisites minimal to allow students from multiple engineering disciplines to take the course, but insisted they had some demonstrated level of maturity through the upper division requirement.

Three instructors, each involved in smart home research, shared teaching responsibilities. Their overlapping areas of expertise allowed coverage of the broad range of topics in the course. Because this was the first time the course was offered, all instructors attended each lecture. This allowed each of our perspectives to contribute to the course evaluation. Furthermore, it helped ensure a smooth transition between topics.

No textbooks were used for the course. We examined a number of books and paper collections, ranging from specific areas such as sensors or decision making to general books on intelligent or multi-agent systems. None of these seemed to cover what we needed at the appropriate depth or level. Instead, we opted for presentation slides. For some of the topics, lecture notes and at most two published articles were also provided. Topic lectures included discussion of the current state of research and open issues. All materials were posted on the course website.

Students toured the smart home research lab spaces at one of the schools and were able to interact with researchers. They were able to see sophisticated versions of the solutions they were developing in their labs. This gave them a greater appreciation of how the various technologies must work together to achieve real functionality.

Lab 1: Gain practical knowledge about sensors, actuators and micro-controllers.

Things you need: Lab power supply (5V), Protoboard with Javelin, Digital Multimeter, Javelin IDE and cable, Photoresistor, 6V lamp, LM34DZ, LED, Various resistors, capacitors and jumpers

Part A:

1) Using the lecture notes, build the light and temperature sensor circuit and the three actuator circuits (lamp, speaker and LED)
2) Test these using the sample program
3) Look up the data sheet for the LM34DZ. Using your multimeter and a heat source, measure the relationship between the output voltage and temperature at several points. Plot these values. Explain how your results compare to what you expected from reading the data sheet. Based on your data, propose a voltage range that you would expect the LM34DZ to produce over a temperature range of 32 - 120(F).
4) Explain how the ADC process being used in the lab should work. Using your multimeter, plot the relationship between the actual voltage input to the ADC circuit and the output value reported of the ADC.
5) Submit as part of the overall lab report a write-up covering what you learned from doing steps 1 and 2, and the results of your research on steps 3 and 4.

Part B:

6) Write a program that senses when an object moves between the lamp and the photoresistor.
7) Modify the program (from step 6) to try to use the LED instead of the lamp. Explain what happens.
8) Submit as part of the overall lab report a write-up including your code from step 6 and 7 and test results from step 7.

Part C:

9) Write a program that fuses the light and temperature data of your sensors to generate the following set of alerts:
   a) A/C failure (high temp.), b) Heating failure (low temp.), c) Loss of lighting (low light), d) Too much afternoon sun (high light, medium temp), e) Fire (medium light, high temp), f) Teenager in the house (low light, high temp), g) Ghost in the house (high light, low temp.)

   The program should set a unique audio and visual alarm for each alert condition. It should also allow you to turn off either or both types of alert notification (alarm) both before and during an alert.
10) Demo this program to an instructor or TA.
11) Submit as part of the overall lab report a write-up including your code from step 9, your results, and what you learned.

Figure 2. One of the most popular lab assignments given in the course.

2.1 Assignments and Exams

Assignments were primarily lab-based and covered 6 of the technology topic areas. An initial assignment asked student to review and critique a selection of articles that discusses the goals and challenges of smart home systems. One of the students' favorite labs is shown in Figure 2. There are three possible reasons for this: 1) students enjoyed working with something physical that provided immediate feedback of success or failure, 2) more time was spent in lecture about doing this lab than on most other labs, and 3) it required less student time to prepare and conduct the lab than most others. Some of the labs used software under active development in the instructors' research labs.

Based on student feedback and observation of performance, the last few labs were simplified for the U2 students. For example, the machine learning lab allowed students to select one of two exercises on learning techniques, rather than complete both. The students were not always notified of these differences. In hindsight, perhaps the students should have been informed of the reductions made to their workload, since a number of students commented on the course survey that they believed the work load was geared primarily to graduate level work.

Quizzes were given in the first twenty minutes of class approximately every two weeks and were not comprehensive. We tried to schedule quizzes so they were given in a week in which a lab assignment was not due. This did not always work out, as we had to extend the lab due dates in a few cases because of either technical difficulties with provided software or students needing more time. Instructors shared responsibility for quiz construction, with the instructor at U1 adding or modifying a few questions on each quiz for the graduate students. Otherwise, students at both campuses took the same quizzes. Local instructors graded their respective students' quizzes.

3. EVALUATION AND FINDINGS

Twenty-eight students, majoring in Computer Science Engineering, Computer Science, or Computer Information Technology, enrolled in the course. The ten students from U1 were primarily graduate students, while the eighteen at U2 were all undergraduates. The grade distributions for the course were comparable to those in other courses at the same level.

At the semester end, all students completed a course evaluation developed specifically for this course. The questions are grouped into three categories. The first measures the students' experiences regarding the course content and its impact on their learning experience. The second group assesses students' perceived preparation for the course and the courses' impact on motivating them to continue in research. Finally, the third group regards the instructional format. The questions are listed in Table 1.

3.1 Student Learning Experience

Concerning the breadth of topics (question 1), some students would have preferred fewer topics covered at greater depth. They felt they had insufficient background knowledge to quickly grasp the broad range of topics. Reflecting this group of students, one reported "It is very difficult to understand a topic when there is no time spent on it.". This did not match our initial belief that the students' prior background in databases, hardware, networking, etc. would allow a fast-paced survey of many techniques.

For more students, covering a breadth of topics was satisfactory, but concerns were raised that the labs required more in-depth knowledge that was not covered in the lectures. The undergraduates had difficulty extending the lecture concepts on their own to enable them to complete the labs, and understand what they were doing in them.

Table 1. Questions from the student evaluations. Some questions have been abridged for space.

Category	Question
Learning	1) It was a good idea to cover a broad range of topics, rather than covering fewer topics in more detail
	4) The labs helped me understand the lecture topics
	5) Visualization tools would have helped me understand the labs better (for example, a tool that visually showed simulator actions—when a light was turned on, a person entered a room, etc.).
	10) My favorite topic from the course was (the most interesting to you, not the easiest!). Choices were: Sensors/Actuators; Networks; Active Databases; Learning/Prediction; Decision Making
	11) My least favorite topic from the course was: (same choices as 10)
	12) The lab I learned the most from was: (same choices as 10)
Student	2) I had enough background knowledge to understand most of the course topics
	8) This course has increased my interest in research
	9) I plan to go to graduate school to study science, mathematics or technology
Instruction	3) I understood which instructor I should contact when I had a question
	6) I was distracted from the lecture because of the technical difficulties of delivering the lectures between the 2 schools (disconnects, choppy audio, etc.).
	7) It was easier to understand the lecture when the instructor was lecturing from my location.

One option for a future course is to cover the same top level topics, but cover just one or two sub-topics within each. A second option is to limit the number of topic areas, for example databases and prediction. With either option, depth should be emphasized over breadth.

Student experiences in the labs (questions 4, 5, and 12) sharply differed between the two schools. Every student at U1 strongly agreed that the labs aided understanding of the lecture topics, whereas those at U2 were generally neutral. Both schools agreed that better visualization tools would have aided understanding. This suggests that it may be worth the effort developing such tools, however, there is a big difference evaluating direct vs. imagined experiences, so it is suggested that any development effort happen incrementally and reevaluated. The sensors and networks labs were by far the labs students reported learning the most from, with the database lab being a distant third. For most students, the sensors lab was the easiest lab while the networks lab was by far the most challenging, indicating that something else besides difficulty is affecting learning (or perception of learning). The most likely hypothesis is that these two labs had the most instructor involvement, giving the students more support completing their tasks. This is suggested by the student comment: "The labs took a small piece of the topics and went extremely in depth on it. We basically had to teach ourselves to do the labs. I think the lectures should have focused a bit more on the labs". Students' preferences for topics (questions 10 and 11) correlated with the lab experiences and, for the U2 students, with the amount of lecture time spent preparing students for the labs.

3.2 Student Preparation and Motivation

Students were mixed in feeling they had adequate background for covering the course material (question 2). While students at both schools had backgrounds in programming, databases, and hardware, students at U1 have more background studying algorithms. This difference became apparent when covering the learning and decision making topics, both of which presented a survey of common algorithms. Regarding incentive for continuing their studies (questions 8 and 9), students at U2 covered the full range of answers. Since most of the students at U1 were graduate students, the responses were predictably skewed towards the higher end.

3.3 Distributed, Multi-institutional Format

The last category of questions (3, 6, and 7) evaluated students' experience regarding instructor contact and the method of delivery. Students generally felt instructor contact was good. We made a consistent effort to communicate which instructor to contact for a given topic or task, and each instructor was conscientious in communicating with students at both campuses. The students overwhelmingly prefer the instructor to be local, reporting that it enhanced motivation, attention, and willingness to ask questions. Receiving a slide lecture over a monitor is akin to watching television and caused some students difficulties in focusing their attention. Technical difficulties did not overly distract from the class experience for most students, most likely because we adequately prepared the students to expect such difficulties. When difficulties of more than a minute did occur, local instructors engaged the students in dialog to keep them focused.

4. LESSONS LEARNED

In addition to the analysis of student surveys, our experience resulted in other lessons that we believe must be considered when developing a course of this nature. University culture and student expectations, instructor ability, and support services are all important to successful execution of a research-oriented course.

The culture of each participating university should be considered. In addition to the student mix of graduates and undergraduates at U1 versus the undergraduate only population at U2, the cultures of the programs at the two universities is quite dissimilar. We were aware of this difference, and attempted to find a balance, but we underestimated the effect on students of changes to their standard course experience. At U2, most of the courses offer significant structure to support student learning. Course time is spent working through numerous examples and demonstrating how to use tools. Self-learning of concepts and tools is limited in most courses. Detailed, pre-tested assignments that sometimes include code frameworks are the norm. The U2 instructors involved believe this culture needs to change in order to better prepare students, but it must be done more gradually than was attempted in this course. While there were students that rose to the challenge and thrived in the environment, other students became aggravated, and others apathetic. Within this culture is the expectation that everything works and that the instructor has all the answers. Rather than avoid teaching research, the student's attitudes and perceptions need to change, a challenge best approached gradually over a number of courses.

The instructor's technical expertise, teaching styles and personalities melded well, an important consideration for supporting students. An instructor at the site receiving the day's lecture could interject comments or questions when they perceived the need for clarification. While the instructor received live images of the remote students, subtle cues of body language and inattention cannot easily be perceived. Moreover, students sought the help of a particular instructor with whom they felt most comfortable. We made clear who the contact for each topic and assignment was, but some students (especially weaker ones) expressed a strong preference to work with one instructor.

Support services are needed. The U2 instructional services department fully cooperated in preparing for and delivering the course, freeing the instructors to teach rather than operate the delivery technology. U1 did not have this same level of support and relied on the instructor and the teaching assistant to set-up and manage the equipment. This has obvious repercussions to the flow of the lectures. The instructors agreed in advance how to handle equipment trouble and this proved to be needed a few times. Another support service we would have benefited from is experienced programming staff that could help with installing and testing software tools, creating test fixtures, and preparing primers for the lab software. This need is echoed in [2]: "From an instructional viewpoint, a vital ingredient of the course is having an experienced [...] programmer on the staff".

5. RECOMMENDATIONS

In this section, we make a number of recommendations for improving the course or one like it. We plan to institute some of these changes in the next offering, planned for the spring semester of 2005.

The most straightforward enhancement of the course is to apply the key lessons to address student concerns and improve pedagogy. We keep the breadth of topics, but within each topic select an area to cover at some depth. Use abstraction so that, for example, students do not need to understand computer networking fundamentals. Instead they can focus on an architectural model, its benefits and limitations, and how it might be configured in a home environment.

There may be an alternative to a breadth-based course that retains the objective of exposing students to large, complex systems research. Select a topic, for example decision making in smart homes, for in-depth study. Expose the students to the other subsystems of the smart home through lab tours and video demonstrations. A simulator or the ability to plug into an existing smart home research prototype would be necessary so that students can develop code that must work in a given environment, exposing them to issues such as systems integration, and dealing with noisy and incomplete data.

Labs should be integrated with one another. Each lab should build on a stable result of the previous labs. Thus rather than have students continue to build on their past lab results, each lab should begin with the same instructor-supplied inputs. Any questions or problems need to be addressed rapidly to keep students motivated. We did this to some extent, but not enough to support undergraduates with limited research experience.

One or a few textbooks should be used, particularly for undergraduates. Lecture slides, instructor notes, and technical articles offer insufficient examples and background information. The ideal solution would be a text on pervasive intelligent environments that contained a running smart home case study. Exercises, additional case studies, sample projects, reviews of basic prerequisite knowledge, and references to both research and fielded systems, would aid student learning.

Avoid the straight lecture format in favor of learning activities that keep students at both campuses engaged and participated. For some topics, like sensors and robots, this can readily be achieved if sufficient equipment is available for small groups of students to interact with the hardware in the class. The instructor then leads the students through exercises while explaining concepts. How to do this for, say data warehousing, is more challenging.

It would be useful to have factory tours or speakers from industry discuss how their successful products have moved from the lab to the market. At least some of the undergraduates had difficulty envisioning the practical uses of the research and how they might ever have employment that resembled the activities we asked of them or that they saw in the research labs.

The research process is one topic we should have covered early in the semester, at least for the undergraduates, who are accustomed to most problems having reasonably good, and well-defined, solutions. In addition, subsequent topics should all have included discussion of the current maturity of research in the area and its application to smart homes.

Lest one perceives the course experiences were all negative, we did do a number of things right. We list some of these below:

- Have good tools for the labs. The most significant achievement was the development of a distributed simulator for a smart-home sensor-actuator network. This was introduced in the second lab assignment and used in the information processing lab interacting with an active database system. The simulator is continuing to be developed and used for both research and teaching.
- Make clear which instructor is to be contacted for help with topics, assignments, and administrative issues, and the proper method of contact.
- Do significant up-front planning and preparation. Recognize that you generally cannot just simplify graduate-level material.
- Coordinate frequently with the other instructors and be willing to adapt assignments and due dates.
- Exchange instructors. The two campuses were close to one another. Instructors delivered lectures occasionally from the other campus, giving them some face time with the other students. Students appeared to be more comfortable asking questions of the remote instructor after such visits occurred.

6. CONCLUSIONS

Even with many years of teaching experience, designing a course like the one described here presents many challenges. Teaching in a distributed, collaborative, instructional environment requires some special skills [3]. As many others have reported, extra time is required as well, especially when the course is new. Given that the course covers emerging technologies, it may well be that extra time will continue to be required to update the frequently evolved material. It is crucial that the lecturers are dynamic speakers; it's even worse to listen to a monotone, dull lecture over a TV screen. We agree that "there is no doubt that people prefer face-to-face communication over electronic" [1], at least for establishing a student-instructor relationship. How well technology can overcome this seemingly fundamental characteristic of human nature remains to be seen.

7. ACKNOWLEDGMENTS

This work was sponsored in part by the National Science Foundation under grant EIA-0203499. Thanks also to the anonymous reviewers.

8. REFERENCES

[1] George, B., Mansour, M.,and Williams, L.. A Multidisciplinary Virtual Student Team. In *Proceedings of the 14th Conference on College Teaching and Learning*, 2002. http://collaboration.csc.ncsu/laurie/.

[2] Hemmingway, B., Brunette, W., Anderl, T., and Borriello, G.. The Flock: Mote Sensors Sing in Undergraduate Curriculum, *Computer* 37(8), August 2004, 72-78

[3] McAlpine, I. "Collaborative Learning Online", Distance Education 21(1), Jan. 2000, 66-80.

Using History of Computing to Address Problems and Opportunities in Computer Science Education

Orit Hazzan (moderator)
Department of Education in Technology & Science
Technion – Israel Institute of Technology
Haifa, Israel 32000
oritha@tx.technion.ac.il

John Impagliazzo
Department of Computer Science
Hofstra University
Hempstead, New York 11549-1030 USA
cscjzi@Hofstra.edu

Raymond Lister
Faculty of Information Technology
University of Technology, Sydney
Broadway NSW 2007, Australia
raymond@it.uts.edu.au

Shimon Schocken
Efi Arazi School of Computer Science
The Interdisciplinary Center Herzliya (IDC)
Herzliya, Israel 46150
schocken@idc.ac.il

Categories and Subject Descriptions: K.2 [**History of Computing**]: *hardware, people, software, systems, theory.*

General Terms: Human Factors

Keywords: history of computing, computer science education, computer science, software engineering, CS education research.

Summary

Like nations and peoples, professions have histories too. Similar reasons for teaching history of nations and peoples may explain the importance of teaching prospective professionals the history of their profession. Indeed, much of K-16 education evolves around the teaching of history. Computing is not different with this respect. However, in the computing field, that often lacks attention to the societal impact of its products or an appreciation of the human side of the field, the inclusion of history of computing courses (or incorporating historical perspectives in computer science courses) is rare. In addition, the lack of formal education in computing history and the lack of relevant effective resources does not encourage faculty to incorporate history in their courses.

Traditional historians often classify the history of computing as "recent or contemporary history". Indeed, the majority of undergraduate students currently in university and college programs were born after the personal computer and their teachers educated after the advent of email. Thus, though computers have strongly influenced their lives, they are generally unaware of the antecedents of the machines and tools they use every day. Hence, they usually do not build on the foundations of the field to explain a subject. Equally, myths and fallacies fill the field, including textbooks.

The panel illustrates how teachers can integrate history of computing into traditional computer science education. Open discussion with the audience will follow the panelists' short presentations.

SIGCSE'05, February 23-27, 2005, St. Louis, Missouri, USA.
ACM 1-58113-997-7/05/0002.

Panelists' Statements

Orit Hazzan

In his July column in the CACM, Peter Denning tells a story that describes how the history of CS has influenced its public image ([2]). In that story, Denning mentions both events (like the NATO conference held in 1968) and people (e.g., Fredrick Brooks).

In my presentation, I follow a similar style and illustrate, with respect to three topics, how the history of computing (people and events) can be integrated in CS education. Specifically, in a Programming Paradigms course, history is used to inspire students with the vivid and dynamic nature of our discipline. In a Methods of Teaching Computer Science course, history is used to enhance teacher construction of their professional perception. In a project that aims at promoting female high school students to learn computer science, the history of the field is used to highlight personal stories of female role models. Table 1 summarizes my perspective by outlining the messages of each case.

Beyond discussing the above issues, I would argue that history is, in fact, a narrative. As the ITiCSE 2003 keynote speaker Christos Papadimitriou argued, narratives become increasingly more accepted ways to convey ideas. This provides yet another great vehicle for integrating the history of computer science in computer science education.

Table 1: Messages conveyed by the history of computer science

	Messages of the history of computer science
Traditional computer science courses	▫ The field is young and dynamic. ▫ Its development and nature have been influenced and shaped by people like you and me.
Teacher preparation courses	▫ Increasing pupils' awareness to the fact that computer science goes beyond programming. ▫ Contribution to the professional perception of prospective computer science teachers: Why we teach what we teach.
Gender issues	▫ Female role models in the history of computer science.

John Impagliazzo

In 1996, the United States National Science Foundation, Division of Undergraduate Education recommended that faculty members build into every course inquiry, the processes of science (or mathematics or engineering), a knowledge of what practitioners do, and the excitement of cutting-edge research. An excellent way to do this is through the introduction of historical perspectives into the computer science curriculum. To accomplish this, the various fields of computing need to develop greater exposure to its own history and the historical resources surrounding it. Indeed, computing education has lost myriad opportunities by not taking advantage of this recent history to better present up-to-date concepts. A brief examination of computing education would lead one to believe that professionals are likely repeat past mistakes. Therefore, make your profession more meaningful. Make your courses more interesting. *Use history!*

Raymond Lister

We cannot credibly argue that an historical perspective is an important part of the education of a computer scientist unless we also embrace an historical perspective on our teaching. Brookfield [1] gave five reasons why we should all read education theory (p. 186-188). Those reasons also apply to reading education history: (1) It lets us name our practice, (2) it breaks the circle of familiarity, (3) it can substitute for absent colleagues, (4) it prevents groupthink and improves conversation with colleagues, and (5) it locates our practice in a social context.

Many who advocate teaching history of computing to students argue (like my co-panelists) that it brings a human edge to computing – computer science is primarily about people, and how they think and communicate, not machines. However, computer science educators have had a long love affair with trying to replace teachers with machines. If computer science educators were more aware of the history of education, then they would be more skeptical that salvation is to be found in the latest technological toy. The lesson of education history is that teaching–and–learning is a very human, social process.

Shimon Schocken

As computer science educators, we blissfully think that computer science – in and by itself – is a fascinating field of inquiry and practice. This naïve assumption can make us complacent and ineffective in the classroom. For many students, computer science can be dreadfully boring and technically intimidating – just like math, with the added trauma of programming. Therefore, if we want computer science students to love the field as much as we do, and if we want to draw more non-majors and minority groups into computer science programs, we must find ways to spice up computer science education without compromising rigor. The history of ideas underlying the computer science discipline provides a rich plethora of stories, personalities, and insights that can help achieve this goal.

I have learned this lesson first hand, in the process of developing a new capstone course in computing systems (www.idc.ac.il/tecs). This course guides students in the construction of a modern computer system, from the ground up. In particular, the students build a complete hardware platform (in HDL) and a modern software hierarchy, culminating in the design of a simple Java-like language and a mini operating system. The course is rather challenging, involving many technical details and a series of programming projects. Therefore, students can easily lose the forest for the trees, or simply be intimated by the sheer volume of specifications, APIs and design documents.

To help bring the course and the projects closer to the student's hearts, I start and end each lecture in this course with historical anecdotes that cut across the history of the field. For example, when we talk about building the computer's chip-set, I describe how hardware design evolved from the binary algebra of George Boole to the circuit logic of Cluade Shannon to the contemporary design and fabrication of a modern chip-set. When I talk about assemblers, I tell the students about how symbolic programming was invented by Ada Lovelace, before computers were actually born. When I present virtual machines, I follow their roots to P-code and further on to the universal Turing machine. And so on.

References

[1] Brookfield, S. (1995) "Becoming a Critically Reflective Teacher", San Francisco: Jossey-Bass.

[2] Denning, P. J. (2004). The field of programmers Myth, *Communication of the ACM* **47**(7), pp. 15-20.

The Voice of Experience: National Science Foundation Funded Projects

Steve Cunningham
National Science Foundation
4201 Wilson Blvd
Arlington, VA 22230 USA
1.703.292.4729
scunning@nsf.gov

ABSTRACT

The National Science Foundation wants STEM faculty to be able to develop projects that will succeed in attracting funding from NSF programs. For the SIGCSE Symposium audience, this probably means being successful in being funded from the CCLI program. This special session gives attendees the opportunity to learn from those who have built successful CCLI-funded projects.

Categories & Subject Descriptors

K.3.2 Computer and Information Science Education

Keywords: Grants, awards, proposals, National Science Foundation, education.

1. TOPICS

This session differs from the special session on NSF education-related programs because the presenters come from within the ranks of computer science faculty who have been successful in developing projects that have attracted NSF funding. This will create a very special opportunity for those who have not yet had a funded project to how successful projects are developed and presented.

Four PIs of successful projects will give a short presentation on how their projects were developed, made into proposals, and managed after they were funded. These will be some 15 minutes each, followed by a final 15 minutes of general questions and discussions. The session contact person will moderate the session. The PIs and the award abstracts for their projects are listed below.

Leland Beck, San Diego State

This project is developing a more effective way of teaching the introductory computer programming course (CS1) by creating a set of cooperative learning materials for use in the course, building on a previous CCLI proof-of-concept project. The effectiveness of the materials in improving student learning is being evaluated at a variety of types of institutions, serving students with diverse backgrounds and career goals. The project is also adding to the educational research base by studying ways of using cooperative learning in Computer Science courses.

Scott Grissom, Grand Valley State

This project brings together experienced developers from three institutions to develop a suite of materials for teaching data structures and algorithms using the algorithm visualization tool JHAVÉ. These materials and the tool support student work in active, engaged learning outside the classroom. The project is developing new materials and refining existing materials, based on formative evaluation by outside reviewers and experiences in the classroom. It also provides workshops that train faculty on how to use the developed materials and how to create their own materials. Workshop participants will use project materials in their teaching and contribute to additional evaluation. Project outcomes will include a published student laboratory manual, a digital library of high quality Web-based visualizations, and an instructor's guide describing best practices in using these materials.

Zachary Dodds, Harvey Mudd College

Computational interaction with the physical world—intelligent sensing, actuation, and embodied reasoning—has historically required expensive equipment with steep learning curves. Recently, resources for undergraduate intelligent systems courses have grown rapidly at prices, and capabilities, an order of magnitude lower. What is striking is the lack of options between the extremes of high cost and capability and low cost and capability. By combining and extending current trends in curricula, software, and hardware, this project uses off-the-shelf PCs and the adapts the NSF-supported Python Robotics (Pyro) software system to create a low-cost integration of research-caliber physical agents with common computing resources, refocusing undergraduate intelligent systems courses away from toy problems and platforms toward opportunities for open inquiry. This curriculum weaves units from the PIs' research subfields into courses serving a variety of students across the Claremont Colleges and beyond, to the women of Chatham College and the students of the Community College of Allegheny County. The software and curricular resources developed will be mainstreamed into their existing efforts for widespread distribution. An evaluation team of AI/robotics researchers from Bryn Mawr College, the University of Delaware, and Southern Illinois University will help adapt existing assessment instruments and will provide an external

SIGCSE'05, February 23–27, 2005, St. Louis, Missouri, USA.
ACM 1-58113-997-7/05/0002

perspective on the results. Their feedback will both serve and measure progress toward the project's fundamental goal: raising the expectations of the power, flexibility, and cost-effectiveness possible in an undergraduate robotics laboratory.

John Carroll, Pennsylvania State University

A prior proof of concept project has developed a prototype set of usability engineering case studies, a case browsing tool, and several classroom activities based on the case studies. This work was coordinated with the development and publication of a new HCI undergraduate textbook (Morgan Kaufmann, 2002). The textbook differs dramatically from current offerings, interleaving the presentation of HCI content with a comprehensive scenario-based framework for the development of interactive systems. A key innovation of the new textbook is its use of a case study to introduce and exemplify the analysis, design, and evaluation framework. The proof of concept project enhanced the case study material presented in the book, by developing richer and more flexible online materials, and by building cases from three additional problem domains. This project, submitted to the CCLI-EMD track, further develops and validates the learning effectiveness of case studies as an element of teaching HCI. Using the marketing channels of Morgan Kaufmann, we recruit professors and students from 8-10 other universities interested in using the book, and participating in the evaluation of the case study materials. We work with these instructors and students to develop new activities, as well as packaging the prototype activities for convenient use. We also refine the browsing tool, responding to formative evaluation received during the prototype project, and add new functionality to support traceability of concerns throughout the life cycle, more flexible views and case study reporting schemes, and authoring by both experts and students. This project leverages our ongoing research on scenario-based development methods, incorporating the methodology concepts into undergraduate education. It also highlights the use of information technology in undergraduate education, for both content access and student project support. The graduate students who develop the case studies are becoming experts in presenting and illustrating the scenario-based framework, helping to prepare them for careers in HCI education.

Agile Development in Computer Science Education: Practices and Prognosis

Joseph Bergin
Computer Science
Pace University
New York, NY
845-225-4369
berginf@pace.edu

Clifton Kussmaul
(Moderator)
Mathematical Sciences
Muhlenberg College
Allentown, PA 18104-5586
484-664-3352
kussmaul@muhlenberg.edu

Thomas Reichlmayr
Software Engineering
Rochester Institute of Technology
Rochester, NY 14623-5608
585-475-2852
tjrese@rit.edu

James Caristi
Mathematics & Computer Science
Valparaiso University
Valparaiso, IN 46383
219-464-5342
James.Caristi@valpo.edu

Gary Pollice
Computer Science
Worcester Polytechnic Institute
Worcester, MA, 01609-2280
508-831-6793
gpollice@cs.wpi.edu

Categories and Subject Descriptors
D.2.9 [**Software Engineering**]: Management – *productivity, programming teams, software process models.* K.3.2 [**Computers and Education**]: Computer and Information Science Education – *computer science education, curriculum, information systems education.* K.6.3 [**Management of Computing and Information Systems**]: Software Management – *software development, software process.*

General Terms
Design, Documentation, Management, Standardization

Keywords
agility, curriculum, development, methodology, process, software, XP

1. SUMMARY
Agile approaches to software development share a particular set of values [2,4]:

- Individuals and interactions over processes and tools.
- Working software over comprehensive documentation.
- Customer collaboration over contract negotiation.
- Responding to change over following a plan.

SIGCSE'05, February 23–27, 2005, St. Louis, Missouri, USA.
ACM 1-58113-997-7/05/0002.

Many agile methodologies were developed in response to so-called disciplined methodologies that emphasize detailed documentation and formal processes, and that are often associated with ISO compliance or the CMM. However, there is growing recognition that both agile and disciplined approaches have advantages, and that often a combination can be very effective [1].

Many faculty are exploring and experimenting with ways to integrate agile concepts and practices into academic programs in areas such as computer science, software engineering, and information systems. This special session will help us work together in agile ways to better understand the importance and role(s) of agile concepts and practices, successful ways to incorporate them in academic settings, potential pitfalls, and key questions that should be explored further. We want to gather input from a wide range of people in different sub-disciplines and programs.

We will begin with a very brief overview of agile concepts and practices, followed by brief statements from each of the five speakers, to give other participants a sense of the range of possibilities (25 min). Next, we will poll participants to identify a set of topics within agility that they want to discuss further (5 min). Participants will then gather into subgroups for each topic, and each subgroup will identify best practices, interesting ideas, and open questions for that topic (30-35 min). Each subgroup will then give a brief report to the entire group, and we will conclude with a few minutes of general discussion (10-15 min).

2. JOSEPH BERGIN
Many of the techniques of agile methods are beneficial to novices as well as to professionals. In fact the practices of XP are just good practices that can be taught early. It is also true that some of the tools and techniques of XP can be used to enhance the teaching process itself. One such tool is the GeneralFixture of Fitnesse [3], which permits an instructor to present a Java exercise to a student as an executable

specification. This specification can be easily interleaved with natural language requirements. The tool then provides an executable test of the correctness of implementation of an individual requirement. Moreover, the students can easily add additional tests to help them get the program correct. The executable specification is equivalent to a test in JUnit, but it doesn't involve programming so is accessible to students earlier in their education.

GeneralFixture is an optional component of Fitnesse, which is itself a convenient wiki server that also permits asynchronous communication within a course. The tests in Fitnesse are executed directly within a web page by pushing a button on the page and are developed online by filling in a web form. Tables use a simpler syntax than HTML and can even be pasted from Excel spreadsheets.

3. JAMES CARISTI

A number of students resist using some of the agile practices that we try to teach them. In particular, strong students occasionally have difficulty accepting test first and pair programming. Research in pair programming has indicated a few promising strategies. And the experience of several instructors with test first has uncovered a few ideas that seem to work and some that definitely do not.

4. CLIFTON KUSSMAUL

I have used agile practices successfully in consulting projects, and I am experimenting with agile practices in a variety of educational contexts. I encourage, but don't yet require, pair programming in CS I. I find that Iterative development of software projects and written proposals is very effective in both non-majors courses and capstone courses. The emphasis on individuals and interactions, and the lack of detailed formal processes, give students an incentive to reflect on and adjust the process, rather than blindly following it. Multiple iterations and the emphasis on responding to change give students more opportunities to see the interactions between activities, and encourage students to react to and recover from errors early in the project. For me, these advantages are just as important as helping students become more effective developers. I am also trying to show students that many of these ideas are more broadly applicable; for example, agile concepts and techniques can be used to improve student writing.

5. GARY POLLICE

Should we develop agility or analytical skills? Are they distinct?

The Agile Software Development movement has matured and become an effective approach to software development for many industrial environments. However, it is but one approach of several that might be selected. The key skill is to understand what the benefits and disadvantages of each approach are and how and when to apply them.

Agility has a lot to offer when teaching CS courses, especially those that are designed to give students basic programming and problem-solving skills. Pair-programming and test-first practices are useful skills to know. As we progress to software engineering courses, we are faced with the need to broaden the student's skills to more than just agile methods. The question I am continually faced with is whether to just present an agile method like XP, for the students to apply to their, necessarily small, term project, or to give them the knowledge that will allow them to select the right set of practices for their context. I choose the latter and find that this almost always works better in the long run.

As educators we need to find the right ways to introduce students to agile practices while preparing them for all kinds of projects they might encounter in their professional careers. Just teaching agile methods is not sufficient for software engineering courses.

6. THOMAS REICHLMAYR

Can an agile software development process be successfully integrated into an undergraduate software engineering curriculum? The introductory software engineering class at RIT has successfully been using an agile process for the past two years in its term long project. As this course represents the first opportunity for students to participate in a team project, the collaborative nature of agile processes has facilitated the challenges of students transitioning from individually focused developers to contributing team players.

The agile process attributes that have been most beneficial to student teams has been the development of project requirements and a raised quality awareness using test driven design.

Time to delivery is always a major challenge of any software project, but even more so in an academic environment. Student teams have a short period in which to deliver their final release of the project. User stories provide a process in which requirements can be elicited and incremental release strategies developed to evolve the product over the term. Exposure to user story prioritization, scheduling and release planning are perhaps the most valuable skills our students leave the course with.

Testing is identified as a skill that students are least prepared for upon graduation and entry into the industrial workplace. Academic project scheduling pressures often short change the testing process by the students' perception that testing is an end of the waterfall activity that is often consumed by the need for additional implementation (coding) effort. Test driven design in concert with a well conceived project release plan puts the focus on continuous working software through out the project life cycle.

7. REFERENCES

[1] Boehm, B. and Turner, R. Balancing Agility and Discipline: A Guide for the Perplexed. Addison Wesley, 2003

[2] Cockburn, A. Agile Software Development. Addison Wesley (2003)

[3] Fitnesse. http://www.fitnesse.org

Highsmith, J. Agile Software Development Ecosystems. Addison Wesley (2002)

A Company-based Framework for a Software Engineering Course

Thomas P. Way
Department of Computing Sciences
Villanova University
800 Lancaster Avenue
Villanova, Pennsylvania 19085
(610) 519-5033
thomas.way@villanova.edu

ABSTRACT

The subject matter of a typical undergraduate software engineering course, while providing necessary background, can be quite dry. Team-based programming projects often complement the more theoretical textbook and lecture content by giving students valuable hands-on practice, albeit on a small scale and within a traditional classroom setting. This paper describes a company-based framework used in two semesters of a software engineering course. This approach incorporates a novel, collaborative framework to simulate the real-world experience of working for a medium-sized software design company or research laboratory, while giving students a vested interest in the overall outcome.

Categories and Subject Descriptors

D.2.9 [**Software Engineering**]: MANAGEMENT – *programming teams*. K.3.2 [**Computers and Education**]: COMPUTER AND INFORMATION SCIENCE EDUCATION – *Computer science education*.

General Terms

Management, Design, Human Factors.

Keywords

Software engineering education, distributed group working, collaborative learning, team-based projects, pedagogy, capstone.

1. INTRODUCTION

Providing a grounding in theoretical concepts while reinforcing their importance in a real-world context is a major challenge in designing and implementing an undergraduate software engineering course [1]. Team-based programming projects frequently are used to engage students by affording them the opportunity to participate in the type of teamwork found in a software industry setting [2,6,8]. The use of such a team- or group-based approach, with small groups of three to five members each, has gained significant acceptance and support as a means to simulate the industry experience for software engineering students while reinforcing other course material [5].

The use of a larger project team format which more closely resembles the reality of the industry workplace is perceived as being more difficult to implement, and is infrequently reported in the literature [8,10]. When such an immersive model is used, however, students can learn more about "real" software engineering than with less ambitious frameworks [3,7,8]. Additional benefit is gained when students experience a distributed group working environment, where members of teams are physically, or virtually, separated while participating in cooperative tasks [4]. As the business structure of the software industry continues to become more distributed geographically, providing students with exposure to this way of working is a desirable part of their formal software engineering education and a valuable asset to their future employers.

This paper describes the design and use of two variations of such an industry-focused large group project as part of an upper-level undergraduate course in software engineering. Based on the author's extensive prior research laboratory and industry experience, novel attributes not normally found in a software engineering course were incorporated including class-wide product brainstorming sessions, overlapping subgroups of students, distributed group working, weekly engineering meetings, and business and marketing strategic planning aimed at releasing the finished product to the outside world. Observations, feedback from industry contacts, and the results of a follow-up survey with students are presented and discussed.

2. THE COMPANY-BASED FRAMEWORK

Two approaches to a company-based framework have been developed and used in the design of an undergraduate software engineering course. The company-based framework involves organizing students into a simulated software development company, with each student being delegated specific individual and group tasks plus a shared responsibility to the company for the design, development and ultimate distribution of a new software product.

The first variation models a university-based research laboratory and was used in a single section of the course. Based on experience with the first model, adjustments were made the following year to produce a second variation that models a medium-sized bicoastal software development firm combining two sections of the course into a single entity. This framework attempts to simulate as realistically as possible the experience of programming-in-the-large as part of a large software development team developing a new product under deadline pressure.

2.1 Motivation and General Framework

"Give a man a fish and you feed him for a day. Teach him how to fish and you feed him for a lifetime." Lao Tzu

The principal motivation behind the use of a large group project framework was the belief that providing students with practical experience in working in a real software lab or company setting would reinforce the lecture and reading content of the course while demystifying the process of developing software in the real world. The initial vision was that of a newly hired computer science graduate sitting in a first engineering meeting and feeling completely at home, on familiar turf, ready to immediately contribute. To realize this vision required gaining complete buy-in by the students involved.

Engaging students in the process was accomplished by providing each a direct and personal stake in the outcome, beyond mere grades which were downplayed to the extent that was possible. A variety of justifications were presented, including experiencing exactly what a first job will be like, being a part of a project that will be released to the public at the end of the semester, having access to a permanent web product site to serve as concrete proof to potential employers of just what the student is capable, the chance to have a lot of fun and learn new technology, and the potential that the initial version of the product could lead to bigger things. Gaining the students' enthusiastic commitment amounted to being equal parts motivation speaker, experienced industry pro, and, occasionally, a red-pen-wielding professor.

The general framework for the course included a grounding in fundamental software engineering theory, including software processes, requirements engineering, system modeling and architecture, prototyping, user-interface design, verification and validation, project management and planning, software re-engineering and configuration management, all part and parcel of an undergraduate software engineering course [1,8]. Assigned readings and lectures were used to formally present this theoretical side, with lecture and discussion filling approximately 1.5 to 2.0 of the 2.5 hours of weekly class meeting time. Lectures were based on a required text [8], but were amply counterpointed with appropriate software industry anecdotes from the instructor's past. The flow of lecture topics was matched to corresponding stages of the hands-on product development cycle whenever possible. Midterm and final exams provided more traditional, and expected, assessments of the theoretical material covered.

As a result of a variety of individually produced student writing assignments throughout the semester, the course fulfilled a university requirement as a "writing intensive" course. All students crafted a rough design outline and prototype design, which led to an initial software requirements specification (SRS). Students were free to be creative and incorporate any new, unique and innovative features into their SRS that they could devise. A very complete final SRS served as a culmination of each student's individual design experience.

The remaining 30 to 60 minutes of class time was allocated to a weekly "engineering meeting." This meeting was run from an agenda provided to students in advance, with each student expected to be prepared to field questions that may arise within their area of responsibility at any time. Minutes of each meeting were recorded and posted on a continuously updated course web site, along with all lecture notes, assignments, deadlines and handouts. During initial weekly engineering meetings, the company was organized into smaller, overlapping teams, which formed the core of the two variations of the company-based framework. Later meetings addressed ongoing product design and development concerns, including product naming, feature identification, specification, problem solving, student demonstrations of web site and application versions, and other technological, business and aesthetic issues.

2.2 Novasoft Research Laboratories

In the Spring 2003 semester, one section of the software engineering course was organized into a simulated university-style research lab called "Novasoft Research Laboratories," or "NRL." On the first day of class, students were "hired" by NRL, and were presented with the main company goal: the production of an experimental image processing tool for release to the academic research community, and the world at large, by the end of the semester. The tool had to be designed for ease of use and extensibility, written in Java for wide compatibility, distributed as open source, and suited to legitimate research tasks. Thus, the "employees" were provided with a worthwhile, realizable and significant goal and a personal stake in the outcome.

The company structure is illustrated in Figure 1. The instructor served as Project Manager, and students were placed on the five teams based on interest or need. A very high degree of collaboration among teams was necessary and expected.

The **GUI Team** was responsible for development of the application user-interface, or front-end, which included an initial prototype, and for collaboration with the Module, Specification and Testing/Docs Teams. The GUI Team took the lead on integration of all modules into the finished product, known as the Villanova Image Processing Research (VIPeR) Tool (Figure 2).

The **Module Team** designed the software interface between the front-end and a generic image processing module, working very closely with the GUI Team. Later, this module interface was used company-wide to develop a range of plugable modules, resulting in information that was then provided to the Specification and Testing/Docs Teams.

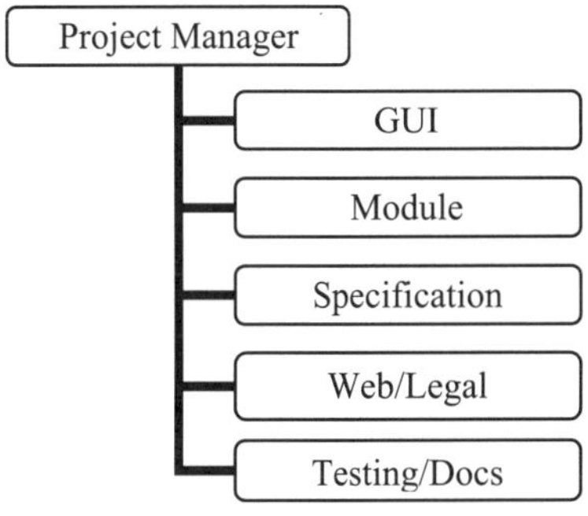

Figure 1. Organization of NRL Teams

Figure 2. VIPeR Tool, edge detection filter.

The **Specification Team** had the job of gathering the best of individual ideas and features, and incorporating those ideas in a shared final product specification. Design information and product screen shots were gathered from the GUI and Module Teams for use in the specification document, and also passed on the Testing/Docs Team.

The **Web/Legal Team** was charged with developing a company web site [11], including general product description, user support, a legal licensing agreement (a variation of the Gnu Public License), and product download capability. The Specification and Testing/Docs Teams provided content to the Web/Legal Team for inclusion on the site, while hands-on experience with early versions of the product in collaboration with the GUI and Module Teams was needed to generate user support information.

The **Testing/Docs Team** was responsible for devising a testing plan and working with the GUI and Module Teams to test and debug the product. It also collaborated with the Specification Team to write user and developer documentation, and created a product installer that was given to the Web/Legal Team to enable easy distribution of the product online.

Because of the relative autonomy of teams, twice during the semester team members evaluated each other and themselves by assigning a "contribution factor" of 0 to 100 to each member of the team along with a brief justification of the score. These evaluations were used primarily to identify and rectify "weak links" in teams, assuring that members fully contributed to the team effort. The unavoidability of weekly public-accountability during the engineering meeting seemed to serve as additional motivation for participants to get things done. It was the rare student who failed to contribute sufficiently to the effort.

2.3 Novasoft Game Laboratories

Based on the experience with NRL, the course for the Spring 2004 semester was modified to incorporate multiple, overlapping subgroups and a project with more student appeal. Students from two sections of the course were organized into the "Novasoft Game Laboratories," or "NGL," and given the mission of designing a game-playing software product with three goals in mind. First, it must be a fun-to-play game system that allows a user to enjoy a variety of games, suited to their taste. Second, it must be an extensible platform that allows other programmers or students to create and integrate their own game modules into the product. Third, it becomes a calling card for each team member to use in the future to illustrate their talents, providing experience in an actual software development group.

Organization of the company was more complex. First, members of each section were assigned to one of two geographic office locations: section 1 was at "HQ" located in Palo Alto, California, while section 2 was the "East" office located in Nashua, New Hampshire. The virtual geography of these locations were to be respected, with collaboration between members of different sections of the course to be done either electronically or, with permission of the Project Manager, face-to-face having been approved for such "travel" to the other location.

Students were each assigned to two distinct teams: a **game module development team** and a corporate-level **product development team**. Game module teams consisted of three to five members from the same "office" (section), and were responsible for the complete development from design through implementation of a computer game that integrates seamlessly into the overall product. It was left to the discretion of each team what specific game was developed, although implementation as either a Java application or applet was mandatory.

Product development teams were organized in a similar fashion to those in NRL (Figure 3). Some of the responsibilities of the earlier incarnation of this company-based approach were redistributed to achieve a better balance among workloads for teams. Significant interaction between teams again took place.

The **Front End & Integration Team** was responsible for designing an initial prototype, and for creating the framework to make game module integration work. The resulting application was **JavaGP**, a Java Game Playing application (Figure 4). For the integration phase, company-wide collaboration with all individual game module teams was performed.

The **Web & Legal Team** created a company web site which included product description, product and individual game module download capability, and a password-protected member contact database to facilitate the high communication rate among students at the game module team, corporate development team and company-wide level [11].

The **Specification & Documentation Team** again elicited the best ideas from all students, merging them into a complete product software requirements specification and associated developer and user documentation.

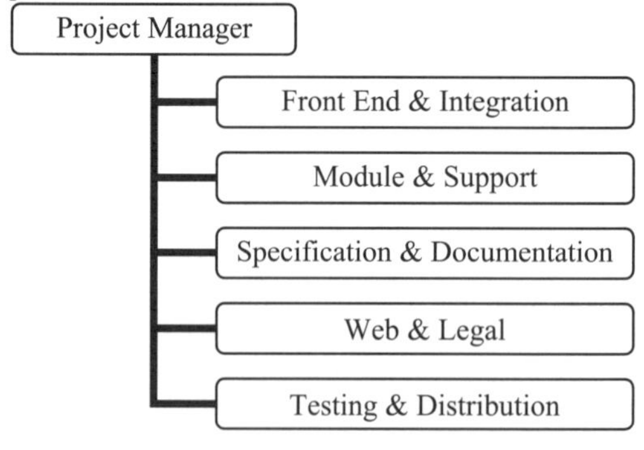

Figure 3. Organization of NGL Teams

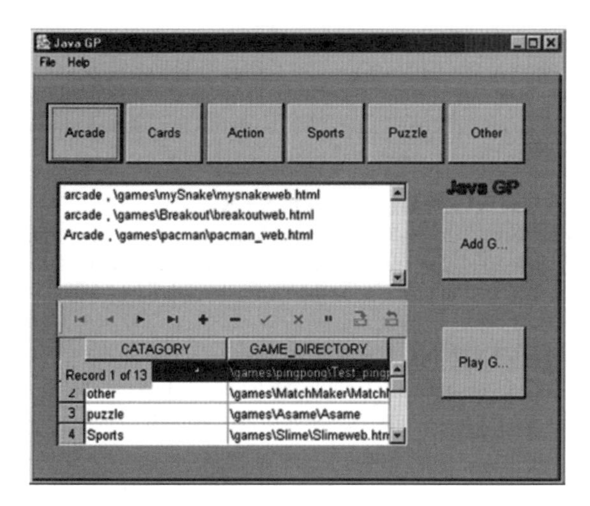

Figure 4. JavaGP main user interface screen.

The **Module & Support Team** collaborated with the Front End & Integration Team to design a flexible interface for adding and playing Java application and applet games via the user interface. This approach was disseminated to all game module development teams to guide their design efforts. A text-based configuration file provided a robust module information database, enabling the addition, deletion and modification of game-related display and execution information to be manipulated via a parser within the user interface or directly using a text editor.

The **Testing & Distribution Team** joined forces with the Front End & Integration Team early to develop and test the product as it evolved from an initial prototype to the completed product. Significant effort was expended creating and testing the executable installer version of the product, since the final version included the Java runtime environment, a myriad of application and applet class files, and various data and image files.

Team member evaluations were again successfully used to assess individual contributions, identify problem areas, and to correct lapses in participation, which were rare.

2.4 Evaluation of Product Outcomes

A single semester is a very short time for a complete software product development cycle, and as a result the software produced is not in a polished state. The evolutionary Unified Process Model used was a good fit given the time constraints, enabling ongoing integration of incremental improvements to the product. The image processing tool still has many bugs related to the user-interface (mostly issues with event-related painting and Java), and fewer interesting image processing modules than a DSP investigator would require, but the framework for adding more modules is well designed and the tool potentially could be a good starting point for a researcher.

The game software is further developed, thanks to a small group of students who took the initiative to work many late nights, solving problems and integrating individual game modules produced by their fellow students. The flexibility with which new modules can be added is solid, and the design decision to use a text file to use the initialization information makes the possibility of downloading and installing upgrades a very simple matter. The use of Java provides very good cross-platform compatibility, and the program seamlessly allows running of games implemented both as applications and applets.

The finished products were solid efforts, especially for unseasoned upper-level undergraduate students. The results were far from professional quality, but that is to be expected given the limited time available and the backgrounds of those involved. The more important result is that the collective group of 25 to 45 students collaborated to accomplish a significant outcome under a strict deadline and with little prior experience. The instructor served as the overseeing Project Manager, but it was the students who poured their creative energy, programming skills, and many long hours into development of the products.

3. OBSERVATIONS AND ANALYSIS

In general, the company-based framework of the courses was successful in exposing students to the theories and practical aspects of software engineering. Students clearly felt engaged in the process, and their enthusiasm fed off of each other. When weekly meetings would, as engineering meetings tend to, digress into the minutia of web site logos or fonts used on user interface buttons, a fair amount of latitude was allowed by the instructor, since recognizing the tendency to digress is a valuable survival skill for a software engineer. The company frequently contracted a nasty case of "creeping featuritis," the tendency to continuously brainstorm new product feature ideas to the exclusion of getting any real work done. This discussion was included in the design process, and students were encouraged to learn to recognize and address these very natural inclinations.

3.1 Survey and Observations

Students were surveyed and asked to provide their assessment of the value of the course as it was structured to both their academic and professional career. An overwhelming majority of students stated that the course was very or extremely valuable on both fronts. Many students have positively drawn on their experience in the software engineering course while undertaking another significant and more-autonomous project as part of the capstone Senior Projects course.

Many students have graduated or held summer jobs in a variety of positions involving computer game development, aerospace, financial, insurance and software industries. All have expressed enthusiastic appreciation for the company-based approach. A sample of the typical remarks from former students includes:

- "I probably had the greatest job ever this summer, making the Madden 2005 video game. I was shocked and most pleased I got to use what I was actually learning in school."
- "I worked for Raytheon this summer and applied all of the software engineering principles we learned. It has been the most valuable class that I have taken at Villanova."
- "I specifically remember being able to use my experience from the course as a response to an interview question with Vanguard. It must have worked, because I got the job and I'm with the company!."
- "This summer I worked at Siemens Medical writing test scripts for their new software. It was great that I could go into the job knowing terms, procedures, and methods of testing software. Everything fell into place when I experienced it with a large software project."

- "I worked in several groups over the summer in my internship and I really used the skills I learned because we had people who did work, people who did not, and people that tried to take over."

Some students were concerned that the self-supervised nature of team tasks was detrimental, due to the natural tendency of students to put off those items which do not have a fixed deadline. A few remarked that the sheer volume of theoretical material covered was excessive, while others noted that imbalance was unavoidable in assigning and carrying out various project tasks.

Recommendations included using more industry-standard tools for modeling and version control, requiring all students to participate in more hands-on programming, and tying company activities more completely to all lecture topics. One student noted that smaller group projects would guarantee that students could not "hide within their comfort zone" since they would be responsible for all phases of product development. Many recognized the value of the company-based framework as being directly applicable to their current or future positions in industry and academia. Additional feedback from students is expected with each iteration of a planned longitudinal study.

Because each company served as its own client, experience in client-interaction, such as requirements elicitation, presentations, and executive buy-in, was lacking. The skills gained in dealing with the instructor-as-client, however, offset some of this shortfall. In prior, small-group versions of this course, student teams sought out "clients" in various university offices to gain client contact experience.

3.2 Industry Feedback

A number of current and former colleagues now working as software engineers and project managers were informally surveyed for feedback on this company-based framework. Comments such as "I wish we had something like that when I was in school" and "Let me know when your students are graduating" were common. No reservations about lack of individual level of participation were expressed. Rather, the consensus was that having new hires already intimately familiar with the business model and normal functioning of a large project team were far more valuable than a more specific background in programming or testing, for example. Most said that they would expect a learning curve as far as the technology was concerned regardless of the level of experience of a new employee, so having that new employee feel comfortable within the team environment, ready to contribute to the process right away would be very desirable to them as a team leader or project manager.

4. CONCLUSIONS

The company-based framework reported in this paper attempted to provide students with a simulated real-world software engineering experience to reinforce the theoretical aspects of the subject. A strong case can be made for the effectiveness of this approach, with positive reviews from the instructor, students and interested industry representatives. A needed improvement is routinely achieving work-load parity among team members.

While there is clearly a place for smaller group projects in a computer science curriculum due to the necessity of hands-on experience with software design and implementation, software engineering as it is practiced in industry is frequently a large group activity. The software engineering course perhaps is the only opportunity within a general computer science curriculum to engage students in the experience of programming-in-the-large, with a company-based approach such as that reported in this paper presenting a viable and valuable option.

5. ACKNOWLEDGMENTS

Thanks to my CSC 4700 students from the Spring semesters of 2003 and 2004 for coming along for the ride, and to Dr. Dan Joyce and Dr. John Lewis for their valuable advice and feedback.

6. REFERENCES

[1] ACM Computing Curricula, October 2001. Available: http://www.acm.org/sigcse/cc2001/steelman/, 2001.

[2] Adams, E. J. *A Project-Intensive Software Design Course*. In *Proceedings of the 25th ACM SIGCSE Technical Symposium on Computer Science Education*, Indianapolis, Indiana, 112-116, March 1993.

[3] Boehm, B. W., Egyed, A., Port, D., Shah, A., Kwan, J., and Madachy, R. J. *A Stakeholder Win-Win Approach to Software Engineering Education*. Ann. Software Eng. 6, 1295-321, 1998

[4] Brereton, P., Lees, S., Gumbley, M., Boldyreff, C., Drummond, S., Layzell, P., Macaulay, L., and Young, R. *Distributed Group Working in Software Engineering Education*. Journal of Information and Software Technology (IST), special issue on Software Engineering Education, 40, 221-227, May 1998

[5] Gotterbarn, D. and Riser, R. *Real-world Software Engineering: A Spiral Approach to a Project-Oriented Course*. In *Proceedings of the 7th IEEE Conference on Software Engineering Education and Training*, 119-150, 1994

[6] Habra, N. and Dubois, E. *Putting into Practice Advanced Software Engineering Techniques through Students Project*. In J.L. Diaz-Herrera (ed.), *Proceedings of the Seventh Conference on Software Engineering Education,* volume 750 of LNCS. Springer-Verlag, San Antonio - Texas, January 303-316, 1994

[7] McCauley, R. A., Adams, E. J., Gotterbarn, D. J., Northrop, L. M., Saiedian, H. and Zweben, S.. *Organizational issues in teaching project-oriented software engineering courses*. ACM SIGCSE Bulletin , Proceedings of the Twenty-Fifth SIGCSE Symposium on Computer Science Education, Volume 26, Issue 1, 392-393, 1994.

[8] Northrop, Linda M. Success with the Project-Intensive Model for an Undergraduate Software Engineering Course. SIGCSE Bulletin 21, 1, 151-155, February 1989.

[9] Somerville, I. *Software Engineering*. Addison-Wesley, 6th Edition, 1996.

[10] Tomayko, J. E. and Shaw, M. *Models for Undergraduate Project Courses in Software Engineering*. In J. Tomayko (ed.) Software Engineering Education (*Proceedings of the 5th Conference on Software Engineering Education)*. Springer-Verlag, pp. 33-71, 1991.

[11] Way, T. P. Software Engineering course web sites, Villanova University, http://www.csc.villanova.edu/~tway/, 2004.

Large Team Projects in Software Engineering Courses

David Coppit
The College of William and Mary
Department of Computer Science
Williamsburg, VA
david@coppit.org

Jennifer M. Haddox-Schatz
Daniel H. Wagner Associates, Inc.
Hampton, VA
jennifer@va.wagner.com

ABSTRACT

A key goal of educators teaching software engineering is to provide students with useful experience that will benefit them after graduation. A key component of this experience is usually a class project that is meant to expose students to the issues associated with real software development efforts. Unfortunately, educators rarely have the time required to manage software projects in addition to their normal pedagogical duties. As a result, many software engineering courses compromise the project experience by reducing the team sizes, project scope, and risk. In this paper, we present an approach to teaching a one-semester software engineering course in which approximately 30 students work together to construct a moderately sized (22 KLOC) software system. This approach provides a more realistic project experience for the students, without incurring significant managerial overhead for the instructor. We present our experiences using the approach for the spring 2004 software engineering course at The College of William and Mary.

Categories and Subject Descriptors: K.3.1 [Computers and Education]: Computer and Information Science Education—Computer science education

General Terms: Design

Keywords: software engineering education, large team projects

1. INTRODUCTION

Software continues to play an increasingly vital role in the functioning of society, and because of this, the demand for skilled software engineers persists. Unfortunately, those who do enter industry as software developers are often ill-prepared for the work that they will be expected to perform [3, 4]. A primary cause of this problem is that the institutions responsible for producing tomorrow's software professionals are still in the process of determining the proper way to teach the concepts and skills students need when they enter the workforce.

A primary component of most software engineering courses is the software development project. For many computer science programs, this is the first opportunity that students have to work together to build a software system of significant size. The course project reinforces the lecture material, making concrete for students the necessity and utility of the tools, processes, and techniques for large software system development.

Of the various models for course projects, the "large project" model often teaches students the most about software engineering [6]. Unfortunately, the overhead of managing a large group of students can make this model a difficult one to implement, even when the professor makes a conscious effort to delegate the work. As a result, many educators opt for an alternative model, such as the "small project" model, where small groups of 4-6 students develop smaller software systems, or perhaps even the same small system.

We believe that smaller projects and teams lack essential elements of realism. Students fail to see the need for key software engineering activities such as up-front design, documentation, version control, etc. They fail to understand the importance and difficulties of communication. Most importantly, the students do not experience the issues that arise when no one person can fully understand the system. Instructors are therefore placed in a difficult situation, balancing the desire to provide a realistic project experience with the practical limitations of a classroom setting.

In this paper we describe our approach for integrating a large-scale development project into a one-semester software engineering course. Our approach results in a course that exposes students to some of the issues they will face on real-world projects, and yet requires only modest amount of additional management overhead on the part of the instructor. We describe our project management structure, the development process we used, and its interaction with the associated lectures. We follow the advice given in [7] that recommends against projects that are "known quantities," choosing large projects that have not been tried before.

We evaluated our approach in a software engineering course at The College of William and Mary during the spring of 2004. During this course, a class of twenty-one undergraduates and three graduate students developed a billiards simulator in Java with 2D and 3D views of the table, and support or multiple games. In addition to our own self-evaluation, we also provide an evaluation of the approach from the students' perspectives, based on survey results collected at the conclusion of the course. Overall, the course was a success in that students learned key software engineering concepts, reinforced by a project in which they dealt with issues such as communication within a large group, working within a management hierarchy, and using new technologies and tools.

The next section characterizes the difficulties associated with large projects in more detail. In Section 3 we describe our approach and how it addresses some of the issues enumerated in the previous section. The last two sections contain an evaluation of our approach and conclusion.

SIGCSE'05, February 23–27, 2005, St. Louis, Missouri, USA

2. LARGE PROJECT CHALLENGES

Unfortunately, most computer science programs emphasize software development skills ("programming"), devoting only a semester or two to *software engineering*. As a result, students only experience software development as a low-risk activity in which small systems are developed by one or a few people, during all-night coding sessions the day before a deadline. Because the systems are small, planning activities such as developing the requirements, specifications, and design are not necessary. Indeed, a single person can easily understand the whole system, and possibly implement it as well. In the end, students know that their software has no long-term use, so the focus is on providing enough quality to pass a professor-supplied test suite.

The professor of a software engineering class must work hard to change these expectations, usually in the student's final year. One good way to do this is to scale up the size of the software project so that students can not possibly use the same techniques that they used in other computer science courses. At the same time, professors must accommodate the realities of a pedagogical setting.

One issue that immediately emerges as the size of the project increases is the additional management overhead. The professor is likely tempted to assume the role of manager because he or she wants to help the students succeed. However taking on all of the responsibilities of a manager (and perhaps the customer as well) is an additional burden on top of the usual responsibilities of teaching.

Unlike true software development projects, professors lack a number of key capabilities of most managers. Managers have the power to interview, hire, and fire project members. In contrast, professors can not hand-pick the students who will take their courses, nor can they "fire" students who are not doing their share of the work. Managers also have the responsibility of performing employee reviews, which can be subjective. Conversely, a professor should ideally have an objective approach for evaluating individual student performance in a group project.

A key difference between professional software developers and students is that professional developers are likely to be far more motivated than students simply because they are being compensated with a salary, benefits, bonuses, etc. Students are not being compensated in a tangible way; they are simply trying to earn an acceptable grade and hopefully trying to learn new topics and concepts. Thus, students do not have the same incentives to perform well as professionals, particularly if the course is one in which the student does not have a high interest. Further compounding this problem is the fact that at many institutions, such a course is not offered until a student's last semester when "senioritis" kicks in.

Another issue is that most professional software engineers are full time employees who can devote each and every hour to the project(s) at hand. In fact, sometimes more than a standard forty hour work week is given to the project by the developer when overtime is required. In contrast, students have multiple courses and varying schedules. As a result, they can not be expected to treat a course project as a full-time job, and can have a difficult time scheduling meetings. This can have a significant detrimental impact on team communication and collaboration, which is an essential component of large software system development.

Finally, where the ultimate goal in industry is the successful completion of the project, the key goal in the classroom must be the education of the students, even when trying to model a real life setting. In industry, a true division of labor is likely to exist: one group works on requirements, one on design, and one on testing. However, limiting students to working on just one of these tasks prevents them from experiencing other activities.

In terms of the project itself, professional developers are often maintainers of software, spending a large amount of time learning the domain and the existing system. Although such an experience would be beneficial to students, the time constraints of a single semester course leave little opportunity for students to acquire detailed domain-specific knowledge, or to become intimately familiar with a large legacy system. Students may also view maintenance as uncreative and uninteresting compared to new development, which could adversely affect student motivation.

These factors combine to present an interesting set of requirements for software engineering instructors who wish to provide a realistic large-systems development experience, while accommodating the realities of an academic setting. Students should work on a system that is large and complex enough that they must specialize their skills and knowledge, and work together in its development. On the other hand, all students should participate in key development activities to ensure that they acquire important practical experience. The project should not require a large amount of domain-specific knowledge, and should be interesting to students. It must be possible to evaluate students individually, despite their group effort. Because of the risk of such a project, the development process and customer must be flexible enough to change requirements as necessary. The course should expose students to state-of-the-art tools supporting fundamental software engineering concepts.

3. APPROACH

In this section we present our approach, which attempts to address the difficulties and requirements described in the previous section. Overall, the course is taught in a single semester, meeting three times a week for 50 minutes, for a total of about 40 meetings. Mondays and Wednesdays the instructor presents lecture material, and Friday is devoted to the project. In addition, small groups of students meet in team meetings for two hours a week.

3.1 Scheduling

The lectures are planned to integrate with the project. The lectures in the first half of the semester provide an overview of the phases of the software development lifecycle, with an emphasis on object-oriented analysis and design. The second half of the semester is devoted to more in-depth lectures on special topics such as formal methods, software architecture, and project management.

Our rationale for this approach is that students must quickly acquire a working knowledge of software engineering in order to become productive in the course project. For example, students must develop the initial requirements, specification, and design for the software early in the course. Without some classroom exposure to these concepts, students will have difficulty performing these tasks well. At the same time, these project activities can not be delayed due to the limited amount of course time.

Overall students work on different aspects of the project. However, we must also ensure that every student learns the fundamental material. For key activities such as requirements definition and system design, we duplicate the project work class-wide in the form of homework assignments. We then either choose the best product to use for the project, or synthesize the project standard from a few of the best submissions. Similarly, we use the first few homework assignments to ensure that every student learns the required development tools. We believe this approach allows students to exploit parallel development on different parts of the project, while still ensuring that every student experiences the most essential elements of software engineering.

The only exception to the use of class-wide homework is the development of the initial high-level design. This work is done by the managers and team leaders during the first few weeks. We believe that a small team of designers can function more efficiently, rapidly creating the framework for the rest of the development effort. This approach also helps to ensure that the managers and team leaders have a shared vision for the product.

At the same time, the rest of the class is learning about the tools that will be used during project development, and brushing up their programming skills. Example tools include the integrated development environment, and software for documentation, testing, and version control. We seek to update the toolset every time the course is offered, so that students are exposed to state-of-the-art tools. However, as other authors have suggested [2, 8], our emphasis is on teaching the fundamental concepts of software engineering, rather than simply learning various tools and technologies.

3.2 Project Management

Project management is performed by students. The professor only makes "command decisions" when intervention is absolutely required. The professor may also serve as the customer, validating the requirements document, test plan, etc., negotiating features and schedule, and evaluating the quality of the resulting software. Of course, the professor is also responsible for resolving course-related administrative issues.

For a class of approximately 30 students, we use three to five managers. The managers are responsible for tasks such as client communication, reallocation of students to teams, setting milestone goals and deadlines, and running the Friday project meetings. Importantly, the managers identify work tasks, assign them importance and timeliness values, and certify their satisfactory completion. As we will soon discuss, this process is essential for reducing most of the management overhead, providing a student evaluation mechanism, and tracking the progress of the project. Managers do little if any software development.

Students self-organize into teams that generally correspond to the major modules of the system, or activities in its development. Each team has a technical lead, chosen either by the team or the managers. The technical lead runs team meetings, performs detailed scheduling of work, communicates with the managers, ensures the quality of the team work, and helps to resolve technical difficulties. Technical leads are hands-on leaders who perform some software development in addition to their other duties. A team may consist of one person, as is the case with the single "buildmaster," who manages the build process for the software.

Developers do most of the software development. They attend all team meetings, and communicate issues weekly to the team lead. Developers are encouraged but not required to work in pairs, especially if a particular developer needs help becoming familiar with the part of the system they are working on. Of course, any student in the class can skip the management hierarchy in order to bring issues to the instructor's attention.

We believe that this approach works well for students, who can choose teams and activities that they want. For example, some students may wish to become adept at documentation, or perhaps a particular module of the system. At the same time, students can freely move from one team to another as their interest in a particular team's work wanes, or as the remaining work is completed. At the same time, student team self-selection, along with the evaluation technique described later, ensure that managers are largely relieved of the difficulties of allocating students to teams.

We have the undergraduates complete short surveys to determine their technical strengths, interests, and prior development experience. Based on survey responses we select several students to serve as managers or technical leads for sub-modules of the system. Team building exercises can also be used early in the semester to help identify the best candidates for management or technical leadership. During the semester, the professor and managers can adjust the management hierarchy as necessary. However, unlike real software development organizations, the professor can not easily hire or fire developers.

3.3 Improving Communication

The team meeting period provides a predefined meeting time for the students. This is crucial in that it provides a guaranteed time for the students to work together in person. Students are free to move from one team meeting to another as their interests change, or if they must resolve cross-team issues. The meetings are therefore scheduled to accommodate the differing schedules of the evolving team members. Managers also meet each week with the professor to discuss the project and resolve any issues that have arisen. Managers also use this time to plan the Friday meetings.

We also advocate several additional mechanisms to improve project communication. A web-based discussion forum provides fast communication, and is easily archived and searched. Students should also configure the version control system so that it notifies them of changes made by others to the modules they are developing. Students should attempt to schedule similar work times outside of the team meetings so that they can communicate via instant messaging when they can not be physically together. We believe that these mechanisms help to ease communication difficulties that students face.

Finally, the Friday classes are devoted to cross-team project communication. In the first few Friday meetings, some students research the project development tools, and present an overview to the rest of the group. Later class meetings are used to elevate important issues from teams to the entire class, and to update the rest of the class on developments within teams.

3.4 Development Process and Grading

We use an agile software process model based on Extreme Programming (XP) [1]. Our primary departures from XP are a more significant emphasis on documentation and up-front design. We believe that this approach is flexible, allowing unexpected risks to be quickly resolved and functionality to be modified as necessary to meet the hard deadlines of an academic course. At the same time, students are exposed to the more traditional notions such as requirements analysis and documentation. (The documentation is evolved along with the code, "faking" the up-front design process as described by Parnas and Clements [5].)

A key component of managing the development process, evaluating the contributions of individual students, and assessing project progress is the *issue tracker*. The issue tracker is a common database of all work that must be completed for the project. Accessed via the web, anyone in the class can view the list of work to be done, create new tasks for the list, and assign themselves to a task. Managers assign each task a 1-10 value for the priority and timeliness, as well as a modifier value. The overall point value of a task is the priority times the timeliness plus the modifier. Managers establish their own guidelines for proper values for these variables, and periodically evaluate each other to ensure consistency.

As developers complete work, they change the status to "Waiting for Technical Lead." At this time, the team leader checks the work to make sure that it has been done satisfactorily, and then promotes the task status to "Waiting for Manager." The manager then reviews the task, potentially modifies the point total, and then closes it. At this time, the points for the task are divided evenly among the people assigned to the task.

The task management system is based on the open-source Issue Tracker software [9]. We heavily modified the software in order to support a number of features we needed, including custom reports that automatically compute the project grade for each student in the class. We compute a student's grade as the average of (1) the percentage of completed points of the total points for all tasks in the system, and (2) the percentage of points that the student has earned for their share of the work. There are a number of additional details that space does not permit us to discuss; they will be presented in a forthcoming paper. For example, one must compensate for "overachievers" who do more than their share of the work, thereby "stealing" earnable points from other students.

We believe that this system provides managers with significant leverage in order to motivate the students. Instead of motivating developers with money, managers can give bonus points for exceptional work, or penalize poor work by subtracting points. The system is also extremely flexible, allowing managers (and the professor) to add all manner of work to the system that needs to be done. For example, tasks can be created for cleaning up the code, writing documentation, fixing a broken build process, etc. From the student's perspective, they can be sure that they will be rewarded for hard work that they do, and that their classmates who work less hard will be rewarded as appropriate.

4. EVALUATION

4.1 Use of the Approach: Spring 2004

We applied the approach presented in the previous section during the spring of 2004 at The College of William and Mary. The class is cross-listed as a graduate course, and consisted of 22 undergraduates and 3 graduate students. The graduate students were part time students, who had all developed software at some time during their employment. The undergraduates consisted mostly of junior-level students.

The project chosen by the instructor was a billiards game. (The professor served as the customer in this case.) The project involved a degree of difficulty for the students as it would require them to deal with graphical user interface issues, both 2D and 3D graphics, and physics to simulate the movement of the pool balls. Early on the requirements included a networked version of the game, but this was dropped fairly quickly as it became clear that achieving that functionality would greatly sacrifice the quality of the software.

The development schedule for the course was divided into three milestones. The first milestone required completion of the 2D 8-ball billiards game. The second milestone required the students to produce a 3D prototype and have the 2D view completed. The last milestone called for the completion of the 3D view and the addition of multiple games. We assigned homework early on to familiarize the students with the tools of the project: CVS for version control, jUnit for testing, Apache Ant for build management, and Issue Tracker for task tracking. As the project went on, students also adopted additional tools, such as Jalopy for automatically reformatting code, and Eclipse as the IDE. Later homework had the students rigorously document the requirements of the system, develop a set of use cases, finish the initial design in UML, develop a test plan, and write a formal specification of the billiard balls and the table, along with key operations on them.

In the issue tracker, the students completed approximately 400 tasks consisting of 2800 points total. Students completed approximately 84% of milestone one by its due date, about 96% of milestone two, and about 90% of milestone three. The key difficulty for the first milestone was a slow start for the project work. We believe that these grades were reflective of the quality of the software.

In the end, the students were able to complete a playable billiards game having both 2D and 3D views, good user documentation, a fairly good software architecture. Implementing proper physics turned out to be too challenging: the results were incorrect in circumstances involving a ball moving at high speed and many collisions (e.g. during the break). Some game rules were not implemented correctly, and there were also cross-platform speed and CPU consumption issues.

4.2 Self-Evaluation

4.2.1 Successes

Overall, we believe our approach was successful in that the project provided all of the students with practical experience with key software development activities, while forcing them to work together as a class to develop approximately 22,000 lines of code (6,000 non-comment, non-whitespace lines). They experienced the difficulties of a large project in which no one person fully understood the entire system. The students were exposed to the technical challenges of defining requirements and creating a design for a large system, and integrating independently developed modules. They also gained experience working with unfamiliar code, both in terms of each other's code and that of the Java3D platform. They learned to use a number of essential software tools, and gained experience working within a management hierarchy and communicating effectively within a large group.

At the same time, the cost of delivering a more realistic project experience was minimal on the part of the professor, whose project-related duties were largely confined to grading the homework assignments (i.e. reviewing requirements, designs, etc.), and grading the milestones by determining whether the milestone requirements were met. Managers performed the day-to-day project management, and the professor only intervened when absolutely necessary.

While our graduate student managers were more experienced in software development than the undergraduates, they were not necessarily more skilled at management. While we have not yet evaluated the hypothesis, we believe that it may be possible to identify suitable managers from the undergraduate class. For example, we found that undergraduate team leaders were quite effective, allowing the managers to delegate many of their decisions regarding the completion of tasks. (On the other hand, managers liked managing the completion of tasks because it allowed them to maintain intimate knowledge of the progress of the project.)

In our subjective judgment, the point system we devised was very effective at both tracking project activities and evaluating the contributions of individuals. The system was sufficiently flexible. We were able, for example, to give bonuses following each milestone to those people who performed exceptionally well. We also feel that the system accurately measured the contributions of each individual, and the group as a whole.

4.2.2 Challenges

However, the system and our use of it can still be improved. For example, the current system does not handle sub-tasks or dependencies between tasks. We also found that it was best to assign intermediate deadlines to tasks to ensure that they would be finished in a timely manner. Items with short deadlines were worth more, encouraging students to complete them sooner. This helped to overcome the procrastination we observed, where the students would try to complete most of the work a few days prior to the deadline. We also found that we needed to improve the traceability of tasks to requirements, to help ensure that all the requirements would be met in the final system.

Our choice of project for the course was not optimal. Initially, we thought the physics component of the game would provide an interesting bit of technical difficulty. Instead, we found that accurately modeling physical interactions was overly difficult, consuming more time than necessary. Otherwise, the choice of a game was good at capturing the interest of the students.

For the spring 2004 course, we did not use scheduled team meetings. We added this component to our approach in response to the most significant difficulty students faced: scheduling conflicts that made it difficult to meet and work on the project together. We had believed that the Friday meetings would provide some communication time, and that students would self-organize outside of class. We now believe that forcing the team members to adhere to a weekly meeting time is essential.

One surprise we encountered was the strong impact of individual personalities on the overall success of the project. For example, people who were content with lower grades frustrated those who wanted the project to be fully complete. We also found that timid people tended to remain disengaged, never becoming active participants. Further, skilled developers may have been best left as developers instead of team leaders because the additional management duties adversely affected their productivity

4.3 Student Feedback on the Project

At the end of the course, we surveyed the students to get their evaluation of the approach. The graduate students who served as managers had a generally positive experience. They felt that the lessons they learned were useful and interesting. One of the graduate students, who also works full-time as a software developer, commented that she has been able to directly apply lessons she learned from this course to her job.

We asked the students to rate various aspects of the course in terms of their usefulness. The ranked averages, starting with the most useful, are as follows: version control, weekly meetings, intermediate deadlines, issue tracker, discussion forums, the management hierarchy, pair programming, coding standards, unit testing, project documentation, software ownership, prototyping.

The students reported in the surveys that the course helped them in a number of ways. It helped them learn a number of tools, and forced them to become involved in software development. They also learned the importance of planning and communication in a real-world project. However, the students reported that the combination of homework and project was too much work, and that more up-front design should be done in order to allow independent work to begin sooner. The managers suggested the use of weekly team meetings sections to help alleviate scheduling problems. The top four challenges the undergraduates reported were communication, scheduling, differing visions for the project, and differing levels of commitment to the project. In fact, one student said that the professor's warning about communication problems was the "understatement of the year."

The students also felt that the lack of a domain expert negatively affected the realism of the physics modeled in the project. They felt that working in a large team is too difficult, and as a result, the workload among students was uneven, scheduling conflicts among students made person-to-person interaction and communication difficult, and that management overhead prevented meaningful feedback on the quality of the design prior to implementation. The undergraduates suggested that we use the system as a starting point for the next class, extending it in some way or even evolving it into a different game that uses similar constructs. This would allow the next class to experience software maintenance issues.

5. CONCLUSION

Providing students with meaningful development experiences in software engineering courses is essential if we are to produce graduates who can enter the workforce and be productive. While the model we have presented has its problems and will continue to be refined, we believe that it is a good first step toward this goal. We believe that it provides students with a software development experience that most had never encountered, at a reasonable cost to the instructor's time.

We have adopted the suggestion of team meetings to improve teamwork. We also plan to make individual schedules a more significant factor in the allocation of people to teams. The students also suggested that we use smaller teams and projects, intuitively understanding that this would ease management overhead. However, this misses the point of what we are trying to accomplish. For many software development efforts, a smaller team is not a luxury one can afford.

We do agree that maintenance was an important component of software engineering that was absent from this course. However, it may be hard to motivate students to perform maintenance on a system with which they have no emotional investment, especially if that system will be discarded part way through the semester to start a new project. A feasible alternative would be to begin the next offering of the course with part or all of the system that was developed by the previous class, and have the next class modify or extend it in some way. For example, the next class could use the physics module to build a bowling game.

6. ACKNOWLEDGMENTS

The authors thank Meghan Revelle for her insightful comments on a previous version of this paper. We also thank the anonymous reviewers for their valuable comments, some of which could not be addressed due to space limitations.

7. REFERENCES

[1] Kent Beck. Embracing change with Extreme Programming. *IEEE Computer*, 32(10):70–77, October 1999.

[2] Bertrand meyer. Software engineering in the academy. URL: http://archive.eiffel.com/doc/manuals/technology/bmarticles/computer/teaching.pdf.

[3] David Lorge Parnas. Software engineering: An unconsummated marriage. *SIGSOFT Software Engineering Notes*, 22(6):40–50, November 1997.

[4] David Lorge Parnas. Software engineering programmes are not computer science programmes. *Annals of Software Engineering*, 6(1–4):19–37, April 1999.

[5] David Lorge Parnas and Paul C. Clements. A rational design process: How and why to fake it. *IEEE Transactions on Software Engineering*, SE-12(2):251–7, 1986.

[6] M. Shaw and J. Tomayko. Models for undergraduate project courses in software engineering. Technical Report CMU/SEI-91-TR-010, Software Engineering Institute, 1991.

[7] Mary Shaw. We can teach software better. *Computing Research News*, 4(4):2–4, 12, September 1992.

[8] Mary Shaw. Software engineering education: A roadmap. In *Proceedings of the 22nd International Conference on Software Engineering—The Future of Software Engineering*, pages 371–80, Limerick, Ireland, 4–11 June 2000. IEEE.

[9] TuxMonkey.com. The issue tracker homepage. URL: http://www.issue-tracker.com/.

AlgorithmA Project: The Ten-Week Mock Software Company

Marc Bernstein
marc@marcanderica.org

Kelly M. FitzGerald
Kelly_fitzgerald@symantec.com

James P. Macdonell
jmacdone@csusb.edu

Arturo I Concepcion
concep@csci.csusb.edu

California State University, San Bernardino
Department of Computer Science
San Bernardino, CA 92407, U.S.A.
(909) 880-5326

ABSTRACT

It is difficult to teach students proper software engineering methodology in a classroom setting. Without hands-on experience, students may not understand why the software engineering process exists. By teaching students via a mock company experience, teaching software engineering can become a rewarding experience while showing the students how simple it is to follow the correct process. Here we show how in the microcosm of a mock software company it is possible to teach very real lessons about software engineering, unfamiliar technologies, teamwork and the realization that when a project ends, the code does not disappear.

Categories and Subject Descriptors

D.2.9 [**Software Engineering**]: Management – software development, software maintenance, software process.

General Terms

Management, Human Factors, Documentation.

Keywords

Software engineering, Software process, Management.

1. INTRODUCTION

Imagine a mock software company that exists only for 10-weeks a year. Each time this company reopens, it hires a completely new set of programmers with different skills and experiences. The resulting maintenance nightmare creates a unique, challenging, yet innovative environment for software engineering. In order to have a realistic maintenance, there were attempts to make the software engineering course as realistic as possible in [1,5].

The AlgorithmA (Algorithm Animation) Project started 13-years ago in the Department of Computer Science, California State University, San Bernardino, as the sole product of a mock software company managed and operated by the undergraduate software engineering class.

Divided into teams, the students are transformed into software engineers of a pseudo-company and then set forth augmenting and maintaining the AlgorithmA Project. All software and design artifacts, namely the software requirements specifications, software project management plan, software quality assurance plan, architecture design, detailed design, unit test plan, integration test plan, system test plan, and source code are inherited from previous software engineering classes, allowing AlgorithmA to develop into a maintainable, feature-rich product.

This paper reports on the interactions within and between teams, highlights the difficulties of the project and offers suggestions for circumventing them. Section 2 gives a brief history of the AlgorithmA Project. Sections 3 and 4 discuss the experiences, organization and activities of the management and programming teams, respectively. Section 5 summarizes lessons learned, section 6 is a conclusion as well as a projection for the future direction of the AlgorithmA Project.

2. HISTORY OF ALGORITHMA PROJECT

The details of the AlgorithmA software project and of its functionality are available in SIGCSE publications [3,4]. In general, AlgorithmA displays and animates the execution of algorithms through three main interfaces: animation, walkthrough, and authoring. The animation interface animates an algorithm giving the user the ability to obtain an overall perspective of an algorithm's functionality. The walkthrough interface allows the user the interactively step through an algorithm animation. The authoring interface allows the user to visualize arbitrary algorithms coded in a custom Pascal-like pseudocode named AL.

At the end of the 10-week course, the class culminates with a presentation, attended by all levels of Computer Science students. During this presentation, the students show off their hard work and the knowledge that they have gained from the class. Frequently, members from years past return from the workforce to see how AlgorithmA has progressed since their year on the project.

SIGCSE'05, February 23-27, 2005, St. Louis, Missouri, USA.

In AlgorithmA's 13-year history, it has undergone many iterations and three core language migrations, detailed below.

Table 1: AlgorithmA History

Year	Project Progress Highlights
1991	Software Design, no implementation.
1992	1st prototype, DOS/UNIX, C and cursor graphics.
1993	1st implementation of authoring system.
1994	C code generator added to authoring system.
1995	Researched migration to OO paradigm via C++.
1996	1st C++ prototype built, improved multimedia.
1997	Code base migration to Java, 1st Web accessible prototype.
1998	Code base stabilized, project focus changed to algorithm animations.
1999	Improved pseudo-code interpreter.
2000	Applets overhauled to use the Java Swing Library.
2001	Organized source tree, 1st top-level makefile.
2002	Authoring system re-engineered and project focus changed to authoring system.
2003	Additions to Authoring system.

3. MANAGEMENT TEAM

Management in our mock company begins with the CEO, who is also the instructor of the class. Like any real corporation, the duty of the CEO is to manage vision, direction and keep the big picture in focus. In AlgorithmA, the CEO/Instructor gives this mock corporation its goals, specifications and objectives. In AlgorithmA 2002, the goal was to re-engineer the authoring system (software capable of compiling and animating pseudo-code) for greater expandability and functionality. In AlgorithmA 2003, the focus was on extending the authoring system functionality and to create more canned applets.

During the first week of the course, the class is separated into two types of teams, management and programmers. For the duration of the class, those who are in the Management Team will direct those in the Programming Teams. Those students interested in joining the Management Team submit a one-page resume and a short questionnaire to the CEO/Instructor. The questionnaire covers the topics of managerial experience, technical competence and why the student is interested in becoming an AlgorithmA Project Leader.

Qualifying management hopefuls enter an interviewing process with the CEO/Instructor to gauge the applicants' interpersonal skills, knowledge, leadership and motivation in the hope of composing a Management Team that maintains the appropriate balance of temperament, finesse and expertise. After the Management Team is chosen, the CEO/Instructor selects one Management Team member to act as Project Leader. The Project Leader acts as the intermediary between the customer (another position employed by the CEO/Instructor) and the programming team. As such, it is important that the Project Leader possesses the best/most balanced leadership experience out of all the applicants.

After the selection of the Project Leader comes the delegation of managerial duties. At this point, each member of the Management Team becomes the manager for one of the Programming Teams (applets, interface, maintenance and authoring). The job of these Team Managers is to ensure that all the directives of proper software engineering process are followed.

There are natural tendencies for projects to have those that are best/fastest at a particular task complete the entire task. This is perhaps the most efficient technique on small, relatively uncomplicated projects. Yet, after twelve years of design and coding, the project is over 100,000 lines of executable Java Code. This excludes the thousands of lines of HTML, Java Script, Flash and CGI. This project is simply too big, unwieldy and complex for a few students to complete in ten weeks. This means that in order to have a successful project, it is vital to delegate the workload, communicate frequently and, by experiencing it first hand, learn the benefits of good software engineering.

3.1 Organizational Duties

In order to construct a realistic simulation of a well-maintained software firm, the RMT (Recursive Multi-Threaded) [2] object-oriented software lifecycle model was used to organize and integrate the components and artifacts used in previous iterations. The student employees are also organized using RMT methodology by the Management Team. In the RMT process, software is developed incrementally and iteratively through threads, where each thread represents a complete software lifecycle. Each year of the AlgorithmA Project completes two iterations or main RMT threads. For every main RMT thread there exists one sub-thread for each team in the project. Each team sub-thread is capable of further recursion (i.e. the applets team can create an additional RMT sub-thread for each applet in the iteration) to provide greater artifact storage and management of more minute details. The end of a thread is indicative of the completion of an iteration.

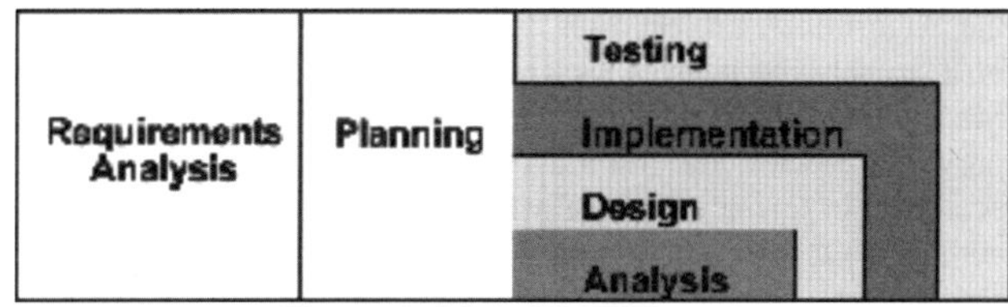

Figure 1: Main RMT Thread

Students of the software engineering course are introduced to the AlgorithmA Project and RMT methodology by collaborating in teams of two and constructing an industry standard Software Requirement Specification (SRS) [IEEE 830-1998]. This step provides every student the experience of creating a well-defined, pertinent, professional document. Of the submitted papers, one is selected by the CEO/Instructor as the official contract for a particular iteration of the project. The creation of the SRS signifies the initiation of the main thread into the RMT lifecycle from which the Management Team can begin creating sub-threads.

In addition to team organization, the Management Team also constructs a Software Project Management Plan (SPMP) [IEEE Std 1058-1987] to define the necessary components and resources needed to bring the thread to completion. The Management Team

also creates the Software Quality Assurance Plan (SQAP) [IEEE Std 730-1998]. The SQAP takes place of the Software Quality Assurance team that might exist in a bigger corporation. In the case of the AlgorithmA SQAP, it is used to ensure that the product described in the SRS is the product delivered. This is accomplished by outlining responsibilities, creating code checklists and testing methods (i.e. white box and black box testing).
Once the organizational foundation of the SRS, SQAP and SPMP has been constructed, the main RMT thread moves to the Design Phase. This phase was hallmarked with an overall architectural design created using a Unified Modeling Language Class Diagram describing the AlgorithmA System in terms of each module. The AlgorithmA Modules were linked together in relation to the means by which they were attached to the initial interface screen. This made the diagram more logical and easier to understand.

In parallel with the development of the architecture, the project moved to the analysis phase. It is here that the Programming Teams write the pseudo-code for the modules that they are building. After the pseudo-code has been composed, it undergoes the scrutiny of the design reviews. Guided by checklists from the SQAP the Management Team and project designers work together to review the pseudo-code to search for any potential faults, weaknesses or watch points.

4. PROGRAMMING TEAMS

Once the Management Team was in place and the Project Leader has been selected, the project focus moved to populating the interface, authoring system, applets and maintenance teams with the remaining students. To aid in this placement, each student software engineer filled out a questionnaire outlining his/her skills, team preferences and pertinent previous experience.

In 2003, Computer Science courses were taught using C++ a majority of the time. To provide for cross-platform compatibility, the AlgorithmA project uses Java as its primary language. In order to help compensate for a potential experience pitfall, a smart Management Team arranges for seasoned Java programmers to provide lectures and tutorials in order to help the students acclimate to this new, generally foreign language. The applet and authoring teams were both generally populated with those students who had had some Java experience.

The interface team needs productive artists to create the interface and hard workers with a practical knowledge base to link all of the applets, HTML, planning and design documents to the central interface. This made for an interface team that was motivated, talented and excited about creating a slick, user-friendly interface. The task of the maintenance team was a collaboration of odds and ends (fixing broken applets, organizing artifacts, updating documentation, etc) and so the team was constructed with self-motivators and students with a desire to obtain some fundamental system administration knowledge.

After the students were placed in programming teams, the Team Managers sought Team Leaders to fill the niche between managers and programmers. Because it would be the duty of the leaders to handle day-to-day motivation and project minutia, finding team leaders who balanced their respective team managers was vital. To help compensate for a potential problem in authority or maturity, the Management Team took care to find personable Team Leaders with excellent management skills. Team Leaders managed to keep things smooth by motivating the programmers and acting as an intermediary if the tasks became too demanding. This created a good cop/bad cop dynamic that produced success.
Once the Team Leaders have been selected and the overall architecture has been constructed the programmers move to module-level design. This involves building sequence diagrams, which help to create test cases that cover both typical and abnormal situations. By teaching the Student Software Engineers to find faults at the design level, they save themselves and their future companies man-hours of debugging and bottom line savings. After the sequence diagram is completed, team members begin writing the pseudo-code for their particular portion of the code. By using industry design standards, these Student Software Engineers received hands-on learning to both the tools and the practices of their trade.

4.1 Peer Evaluation

In order for the Management Team to gain authoritative leverage over the programmers there had to be some mechanism of motivation. In corporate America, this power is derived from the ability to hire, fire and compensate the employee. In AlgorithmA, this control is gained via the ability to influence grades. This grade control was implemented via the use of written evaluations that counted towards a portion of the students' grade. Because these evaluations were completed at the end of each iteration, team members and managers had a chance to receive input in order to improve and refine themselves before the quarter was over.

At the completion of each iteration, every team leader filled out an employee evaluation that outlined the employees' attitude, abilities and work ethic for a particular phase in the project. The team leaders received similar evaluations from the manager of the particular group to which they belonged. The project leader in turn evaluated managers. The members of the Management Team evaluated the Project Leader. Each member of every programming team (Managers, Leads and System Administrators) evaluated

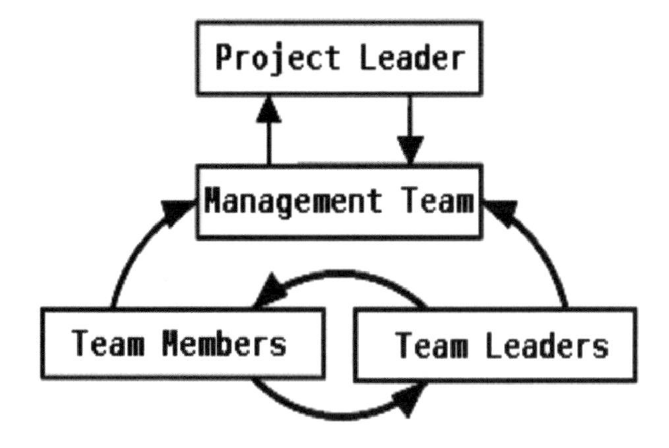

Figure 2: Peer Evaluation

4.2 Two Iterations

In order to provide a more realistic business environment for the students, the project was completed in two iterations. This granted the student the ability to see how software is created in the real world. This also allowed the students a second chance to hone their abilities and learn what does and does not work in software engineering.

As an example of what can be completed in a typical first iteration, AlgorithmA 2003 completed a walkthrough and animation of the heap data structure and radix sort and m-way tree algorithms. In addition to this, both the breadth first search and binary search tree algorithms were added to the authoring system. At this time, the user interface needed to be designed and implemented. The maintenance team concentrated on fixing 50% of the outstanding bugs.

The deliverables for AlgorithmA 2003 iteration 2 were the walkthrough and animation of a priority queue and recursive binary search tree. At the end of this iteration, the Authoring Team was responsible for the release of an Authoring System capable of generating C code from pseudocode, and added a binary search tree and depth first search algorithm to the stored procedures. The interface team worked on fixing up the look and feel of the project. The maintenance team concentrated on fixing the final 50% of the outstanding bugs.

5. LESSONS LEARNED

Taught improperly, Software Engineering can seem impractical in the minds of inexperienced computer science students, simply a class where memorization of the text reins supreme. AlgorithmA provides an environment that allows students to learn the benefits of sound Software Engineering in a programming setting that demands it.

Being a Project Manager for the AlgorithmA project was a rich, rewarding, and sometimes stressful experience. Structuring the project like a software company allowed all involved to experience what life might be like after graduation. For most parts, the class was able to settle within their hierarchical roles. However, the unique problem of having your peers be elevated to an authoritative position for each class session was difficult for some to deal with on both sides of the meeting room table. Some of the managers had problems directing their employees on what to do and when to have it done due to either friendships or confidence problems. Some of the employees also had problems accepting assignments when given by peers. Accordingly, the management team came up with different ways to deal with these problems.

Dealing with a manager's confidence issues was handled by clearly delineating the managerial responsibilities of each management team member. Once the manager knew what they were going to be responsible for having done, they felt more confident in the delegation of assignments. This worked because the managers knew they could not handle everything on their own and thusly were better able to expect assignments to be done knowing the amount of open assignments. The Project manager for 2003 also had a policy of backing up his managers in everything they did. This worked because the Project manager had authority second only to the CEO/Instructor, and the managers felt confident in that higher level of authority.

Dealing with the programmer's issues was slightly trickier for 2003. To their credit, most of the programmers had no problem understanding the hierarchy of the company. Since there was an open interview for the leadership positions at the beginning of the course, most who wanted greater responsibility and authority were able to attempt to gain it. Of 12 interviewees for management positions, five were selected to be on the management team. Most of those who interviewed but were not selected were then offered the team leader position of their respective teams. After this selection process, there were only a few who harbored some kind of unease with the structure of authority. The management team had an established line of command that started with the team leader, then the team manager, and finally the project manager. If things could not be reconciled by that point, issues were forwarded on to the CEO/Instructor of the class. This "ladder" of authority ensured that the person who had a problem had plenty of opportunities to explain their problem and escalate to a higher authority if the situation warranted.

A unique problem also came up during the 2003 project. During the 2003 project, the Applet team experienced a serious setback on one of their goals. The team was responsible for, among other goals listed in section 4.2, creating an applet that demonstrated an m-way tree search algorithm. The UML model and appropriate pseudo-code were approved during the Analysis Phase, and the team had a deadline in which to complete the goal so it could be included into the first iteration of the project (see section 4.2). As the deadline approached, the team's manager assured the management team and the CEO/Instructor during our weekly status meetings that everything was on schedule. At this point, there was no independent review (i.e. Maintenance team's manager checking on the Applet team) to ensure that goals were being met. Once the deadline was a week away, reports began trickling in that the applet was not going to be ready. The team manager had tried to cover for his team, hoping that they would somehow finish in time. The correct software engineering process was not followed in this case, and the failure affected the whole project. The team had deviated from their original pseudocode and decided to program the applet their own way. If the process had been followed as laid down in the Software Project Management Plan, the applet would have been seen to be faulty at an earlier stage and more resources could have been allocated to the team. This failure was a blow to the morale of the entire project, and the entire management team was chastised by the CEO/Instructor for what in the real world would have warranted firings. The team was given another chance to complete the applet for the second iteration of the project. Although this led to resources being stretched thin for the applet team on the seond iteration, the team felt as if they had something to prove and actually ended up boosting morale while getting the goal done correctly.

One of the more poignant lessons learned through the years was that the most critical, yet unpredictable link in the project has more to do with human nature than technical prowess. Human interaction, life circumstances and personal idiosyncrasies are far more complex and robust than even the most sophisticated supercomputer. For example, during the course of the AlgorithmA 2002, a team member became a father, another walked down the aisle of blessed matrimony and a third saw the sudden termination of his relationship by his longtime girlfriend. The class learned that it is possible to write amazing code under the sleep deprived influence of a new baby and losing a girlfriend can bring a massive boost to Java productivity.

Another key lesson learned by Management Teams over the years is that the best way to succeed at leadership is not to emulate others, but to lead with the way that is most inherent to a particular personality. One offbeat tactic utilized by the AlgorithmA 2002 Project Leader was making baked goods for better communication. That year's Project Leader would frequently bake cookies and brownies in order to create a more hospitable environment; students were comfortable and more open to share thoughts and ideas in a non-judgmental way. This communal breaking of the brownies worked well as a conduit to better communication. Though perhaps not a technique taught in Software Engineering books, the method fit the project leader's attitude and personality well and garnered excellent results.

Students in AlgorithmA also have discovered that much can gained by looking at the lessons learned by previous years. The students created their own oral history of the project. By connecting with team members of years past, new students receive advice and learn about elements of the project that might not have been placed in the standard documentation. Because the CEO/Instructor is keen on the importance of past performance, he initiates each class meeting with reading pleasures, e-mails from previous AlgorithmA team members, discussing what they had learned from their experience with the project and how that experience benefited their lives after graduation.

6. CONCLUSION

The AlgorithmA Project is more than programming, more than design and more than social engineering. The AlgorithmA Project is an intense relay race that teaches the finer points of software engineering in a realistic environment. The best way to learn software engineering cannot be taught by book alone; to truly learn this discipline, one must practice it. The 10-week AlgorithmA project allows just that; it allows the student to become the practitioner.

The future direction for the project is to remove the need for canned algorithms via the use of a strong Authoring System. The goal is to have a system where first year students can input any algorithm straight from a textbook and watch it animate right before their eyes. AlgorithmA 2002 took a major step to that goal by creating a framework for the more powerful, expandable, and robust Authoring System. AlgorithmA 2003 took further steps to expand the number of data structures in the system and to promote easier usage of the authoring system.

The first author of this paper was the Project Leader of AlgorithmA 2003, the second author was the Project Leader of AlgorithmA 2002, and the third author was Team Manager of the Authoring System for AlgorithmA 2001. The fourth author was the instructor of the course.

7. ACKNOWLEDGEMENT

The support of the National Science Foundation under the award 9810708 is gratefully acknowledged.

8. REFERENCES

[1] A. Chamillard and K. Braun, the Software Engineering Capstone: Structure and Trade Offs, In Proc. Of the 33rd SIGSCE Symposium, 2002.

[2] A.I. Concepcion, C-P. Lin, and S.J. Simon, The RMT (Recursive Multi-Threaded) Tool: A Computer Aided Software Engineering Tool for Monitoring and Practicing Software Development Progress, In Proc. of the 21st International Conference on Software Engineering, Los Angeles, CA, May 1999.

[3] A.I. Concepcion, L. Cummins, E. Moran, and M. Do, AlgorithmA 98: An Algorithm Animation Project, in Proc. of the 30 SIGSCE Symposium. New Orleans, LA, March 1999.

[4] A.I. Concepcion, N. Leach, and A. Knight, AlgorithmA 1999: An Experiment in Reusability and Component-Based Software Engineering, In Proc. Of the 31st SIGSCE Symposium, Austin, Texas, Mar 2000.

[5] A. Diwan, W. Waite, and M. Jackson, An Infrastructure for Teaching Skills for Group Decision Making and Problem Solving in Programming Projects, In Proc. of the 33rd SIGCSE Symposium, 2002.

Computer Forensics Programs in Higher Education: A Preliminary Study

Larry Gottschalk, Jigang Liu,
Brahma Dathan, Sue Fitzgerald and Michael Stein
Metropolitan State University
St. Paul, MN 55106 USA
+1-651-793-1471
{larry.gottschalk, jigang.liu, brahma.dathan, sue.fitzgerald, michael.stein} @metrostate.edu

ABSTRACT
This paper presents a preliminary survey of computer forensics programs in North America. It summarizes existing requirements for associate, bachelor's, and master's degree programs as well as certificate programs. It briefly discusses factors which must be considered when introducing a new program (curriculum design, faculty, students, facilities, and budget).

Categories and Subject Descriptors
K.3.2 [**Computer and Information Science Education**]: Curriculum – *computer forensics*

General Terms
Security

Keywords
Computer Forensics

1. INTRODUCTION
Computer Forensics deals with identifying, preserving, recovering, analyzing, and documenting computer data allegedly used in crimes committed using computers. This field has arisen since the microcomputer revolution of the 1980s. Criminals using computers may leave some evidence of their activities on their computers. Seizing and analyzing such digital evidence has become an important aspect of criminal prosecution [1, 17].

Computer forensics is a subfield of forensic science, which has its roots in forensic medicine [2]. Well-known criminal forensics techniques include matching fingerprints, ballistic testing, and DNA matching. Computer forensics differs from computer security, the issue of securing computers against malicious attacks. It is also not the same as using computers to solve crimes.

SIGCSE'05, February 23-27, 2005, St. Louis, Missouri, USA.

Network/Internet forensics is a subfield of computer forensics focusing on criminal activity on a computer network [14]. Berghel [2] argues that Internet forensics should be treated as a more independent field. A criminal using a computer may not be technically competent and may not always know how to bypass normal security mechanisms or to hide digital evidence, but a network hacker is likely to be as technically sophisticated as investigators of network crime; this can be a serious challenge to solving this class of crimes.

The need for trained computer forensic experts will grow in the future. Crimes using computers are increasing, threats to computer networks are very real, and the associated financial losses can be substantial. Isner [14] refers to a Carnegie Melon University study that reports that business-to-business e-commerce was expected to be $1.5 trillion dollars this year.

In this paper, we investigate the efforts of colleges and universities across the United States provide computer forensics instruction. To our knowledge, there has been no such study, and our work attempts to fill this gap. We look at two-year, four-year, certificate, and graduate programs. Section 2 surveys articles on computer forensics education. Section 3 reports on existing programs of study. Section 4 discusses sample curricula. Section 5 draws some conclusions.

2. RELATED WORK
Clearly, the field is multidisciplinary by nature, founded on the disciplines of criminology and information technology. Coursework must address social, legal, and ethical considerations for practitioners. Possible topics for a curriculum include the following (with varying emphases): criminal justice, law, and court procedures; criminal investigation; ethics; computer hardware; computer programming; system software; networking; computer security; and computer forensics

An orthogonal approach to the development of a computer forensics curriculum would be to look at careers available to students. The paper by Yasinsac et al. [35] considers four distinct roles and identifies the proper education for these positions:

- *Technicians* with skills to retrieve digital evidence may have an associate's degree or a four-year degree.
- *Enterprise policy makers* responsible for making policies require knowledge of computing and forensic sciences.

- *Forensics professionals* translate the policies established by the policy makers to actual procedures carried out by technicians. Their education should impart technical skills and an understanding of the legal procedures.
- *Researchers* will have masters or doctoral degrees.

Yasinsac et al. [35] also discuss issues related to the establishing a computer forensics program. These include changes in available tools and platforms, finding a suitable home (criminal justice, computer science) for the program, and forensic examinations. Laboratory work is an integral component of the curriculum. Hardware equipment for a forensics lab is expensive and new tools are developed at a rapid rate. Yasinsac et al. report that many of the software tools are freeware.

Troell et al [28] describe the development of an undergraduate and a graduate course in computer forensics. The undergraduate course introduces the student to the basic tools and procedures of the field. The graduate course has the above undergraduate course as a prerequisite and discusses advanced issues related to analysis and presentation of evidence and the tailoring of available tools.

Lang [19] presents a study of issues related to the establishment of a distance learning program in computer forensics. The paper argues that many training programs have limited class size, which justifies an investigation of the viability of online programs. The paper then traces the developments of several training programs and outlines the contents of some of these. Lang also describes the proposals made by the High Tech Crime Consortium (HTCC) for a certificate program, which demonstrates the perspective required of a graduate of a computer forensics program. This proposal recommends two programming courses, security concepts, system administration, web publishing, and two courses in computer forensics. The author points out that much can be learned through self-study.

3. EXISTING PROGRAMS OF STUDY

Our investigation located 32 computer forensics-related programs including two-year associate degrees [7, 9, 13, 18, 20, 23, 26, 27], four-year baccalaureate programs [5, 9, 10, 32], master's degree programs of study [13, 17, 31, 32], graduate certificate programs [12, 29, 30] and non-graduate-level certificate programs [3, 4, 6, 8, 11, 16, 21, 22, 24, 25, 31, 33, 34].

3.1 Associate Degree Programs

There is a great deal of convergence in the core curricula among associate degree programs in Computer Forensics. A successful model seems to have emerged in this arena. We included seven Associate of Science (AS) and Associate of Applied Science (AAS) programs and one Associate in Specialized Business (ASB) degree in the study. Total credits for two-year Computer Forensics programs range from 60 to 71 credits. Generally, one-third of the program credits are in the combined areas of law enforcement, criminal justice and computer forensics with several institutions having a strong focus in computer forensics. Computer technology courses form approximately one-third of the program of study with the remaining third applying toward general education requirements.

Of the eight programs studied, six programs were found on the East Coast, one in the Midwest, and one on the West Coast.

Most programs require one to two courses on law enforcement, in which students explore investigative procedures and police operations. In addition, typically one to four courses in criminal justice explore the requirements for evidence presentation and cover laws used in prosecuting computer-based crime.

Most associate degree programs require two to five courses in computer forensics. Three institutions have 19 to 20 credits in computer forensics, which seems to be the heart of the programs as opposed to the stronger emphasis on general education and elective choices demonstrated by other schools.

Almost all the programs have solid grounding in operating systems, networking, and computer security with one or more courses on how to effectively secure data; how to checkpoint data for safekeeping until used in court; how to find useful traces of criminal activity in the data; and relevant law regarding forensics. Programming courses are required by only one program. There are no database or data structures courses at any of the programs examined. Since database attack is a prevalent form of computer crime, this is surprising.

Among the programs studied, there is a range from zero to two courses in operating systems. These skills-based courses focus on the operational use of common systems. There is a range from one to five largely skills-based courses in networking. Some of the networking courses deal with network security as a sub-topic. There is a range of zero to fifteen credits in computer security, with the typical amount being one to two courses. Typical security coursework is PC-based with an emphasis on web, information and Internet security.

One AAS program [26] is unique. It has no courses in criminal justice and only one course in computer forensics. Its program is heavily oriented toward computer-technology courses. This is the only college which requires programming in its degree program.

All of the programs train their students to secure multiple copies of data for investigation so as to satisfy judicial requirements against tampering with original data. Students are trained to use a set of well established procedures for analyzing hard disk data. Commercially available forensic software packages are often used, making the investigation a standard, repeatable process. Thus computer forensics is being presented as a stepwise laboratory procedure, depending on the procedure, rather than innovation being applied to each case.

Table 1a. Credits for Associate Degree Programs (N=8)

	Avg	Median	Max	Min
LE/CJ[1]	9	9	15	0
Computer Forensics	12	9	20	3
CS/IT	22	19	45	13
Ethics	1	0	3	0
General Education	21	23	25	15
Electives	1	0	5	0
Total Credits	**67**	**67**	**71**	**60**

[1] LE/CJ = Law Enforcement/Criminal Justice

Only two schools require a dedicated ethics course. This topic seems to be covered as a module in other courses. Typical of most AS and AAS programs, there are few elective credits.

Some programs, such as [9], have valuable links to local police and to child protection agencies.

Table 1b. CS/IT Credits in Associate Degree Programs

	Avg	Median	Max	Min
Programming	2	0	9	0
Operating Systems	9	9	21	3
CSec/IA[2]	5	3	15	0
Other	7	6	16	0
Total	**22**	**19**	**45**	**13**

3.2 Certificate Programs

We located 13 programs offering a certificate in Computer Forensics or a closely-related field. Approximately half of the institutions offering these programs are two-year colleges, three are research institutions, and some of the rest have one or more graduate programs. Ten schools are in states abutting the two coasts, one is in West Virginia, one in Idaho, and one in Illinois.

Admission requirements and program length vary greatly among programs. At least three programs are housed in Criminal Justice, five are offered through Continuing Education/Extension programs, and the rest are in Computer Science, Business, and other centers. We found two non-graduate programs in Florida that are identical in almost all respects. Course duration varies from five days in one case to three quarters or two semesters. One institution offers all of its classes online, exclusively.

Table 2a. Credits in Certificate[3] Programs (N=3[4])

	Avg	Median	Max	Min
LE/CJ[1]	2	0	6	0
Computer Forensics	9	9	11	8
CS/IT	8	7	11	6
Ethics	1	0	2	0
Total	**20**	**21**	**24**	**15**

Table 2b. CS/IT Credits in Certificate[1] Programs

	Avg	Median	Max	Min
Operating Systems	1	0	2	0
CSec/IA[2]	7	7	9	6
Total	**8**	**7**	**11**	**6**

Only three programs state course requirements in traditional college credits; requirements vary from 15 to 24 semester credits, with the Computer Forensics portion of the curriculum ranging from 9 to 12 credits. Others specify their program length in terms of a list of courses (7 programs), Continuing Education Credits (2 programs), or daily activities (1 program).

Regarding admission requirements, one university has identical admission requirements for its master's program in computer science and the certificate program. Other programs expect their students to be at least computer literate, two also requiring that applicants undergo a criminal background check..

Given the above variations in admission criteria and program length, we were not surprised to find significant differences in curriculum. Programs requiring two or more quarters/semesters seemed to impart more perspective on the field. Surprisingly, only one program had a course specifically in ethics. Four programs supplied little information about course requirements.

3.3 Baccalaureate Programs

The bachelor's degree programs studied are conspicuously dissimilar. Programs are housed in academic units as diverse as a school of computing, an economic crime institute, a division of accounting and computer systems, and a criminal justice program. Computer forensics is often offered as a concentration or option within a related degree program. The programs vary widely in content, size, and degree of flexibility.

Of the four baccalaureate programs studied, three offer the Bachelor of Science degree and one offers the Bachelor of Technology degree. Two programs are degree-completion programs in the sense that students must complete an associate degree in computer forensics or a closely related field before beginning the bachelor's program. One of these two schools, [9] offers both the associate and bachelor's degrees; the other [5] offers only the last two years of the bachelor's degree. None of these schools offer a graduate program in Computer Forensics.

Table 3a. Credits in Bachelor's Programs (N=4)

	Avg	Median	Max	Min
LE/CJ[1]	26	20	52	14
Forensics[5]	14	12	28	3
CS/IT	11	13	20	0
Ethics	2	2	3	0
Major Electives	1	0	3	0
Other Major	9	10	15	0
Tot. Major Credits[6]	**62**	**60**	**78**	**51**

Table 3b. CS/IT Credits in Bachelor Programs

	Avg	Median	Max	Min
Programming	3	3	6	0
Operating Systems	3.8	3	9	0
CSec/IA[2]	1.8	1.5	4	0
Other	3.5	3.5	7	0
Total Credits	**12**	**14**	**20**	**0**

The bachelor's programs place a strong emphasis on criminal justice and law enforcement coursework. There appears to be a relatively light focus on computer-related coursework. However, some curricula integrate coursework in forensics with IT skills.

[2] CSec/IA = Computer Security/Information Assurance

[3] Does not include graduate certificates.

[4] Only institutions whose requirements are spelled out in terms of traditional college credits have been included.

[5] Includes all forensics courses.

[6] Does not include general education requirements.

In addition, the very nature of a degree-completion program presumes the students have already become adept at computer forensic investigation during their associate degree programs. The majority of the programs require or offer internships. Internships or apprentice experiences are seen as an essential to professional success. Only two programs require an ethics course.

Unlike the associate degree programs, the bachelor's programs explore forensics more generally, placing less specific emphasis on computer forensics per se. Forensics studies are the second most significant component of the degree programs after law enforcement and criminal justice courses. No program requires course work in database management systems or data structures, and only two of the programs require the study of programming.

3.4 Graduate Programs

We located four graduate programs in computer forensics. Three programs offer both certificates and MS degrees; the other only offers an MS degree.

The certificate programs require 12-18 semester credits. Each program requires at least nine credits in computer forensics and security. Other courses are taken in "traditional" forensic science, criminal justice, or computer science, depending on the program. The choices of electives appear meant to allow people with different backgrounds to take electives to shore up the areas in which they are weak. For instance, one university [12] lists electives in criminal justice and in advanced topics in forensics, but notes that people with a law degree may choose to take lower-level computer science courses for electives.

Table 4a. Credits for Graduate Certificates (N=3)

	Avg	Median	Max	Min
LE/CJ[1]	3	3	6	0
Computer Forensics	3	0	9	0
CS/IT	5	6	9	0
General Education	1	0	3	0
Other	4	6	6	0
Total Credits	**15**	**15**	**18**	**12**

Table 4b. CS/IT Credits for Graduate Certificates

	Avg	Median	Max	Min
Operating Systems	1	0	3	0
CSec/IA[2]	1	0	3	0
Other	3	0	9	0
Total Credits	**5**	**6**	**9**	**0**

Each university that offers both a certificate and a degree in computer forensics uses the courses for the computer forensics certificate as the core of the Master's program. All programs require from 33-40 semester credits for a Master's degree.

But the four degree programs differ in a number of ways. In addition to offering graduate certificates in Computer Forensics, two universities also offer a master's degree through the department of Forensic Science [12, 30]. These programs require that most of the work beyond the certificate come from "traditional" Forensic Science courses on the handling of evidence at a crime scene, being a courtroom witness, or dealing with physical evidence.

One university [29] permits students who take the necessary courses for the Computer Forensics certificate to complete a Master of Liberal Studies degree with a concentration in Computer Forensics by filling out their program with approved General Education courses, many not directly related to forensics.

One university [15] offers a Master's degree with no certificate option, through its college of Criminal Justice. Its program has a heavy concentration of graduate courses in Computer Science, Computer Security, and Computer Forensics. No traditional Forensic Science coursework is required.

While graduate certificate programs in Computer Forensics appeared to be fairly similar, degree programs differ greatly in their coursework beyond the core certificate courses.

Table 5a. Credits in Master's Programs (N=4)

	Avg	Median	Max	Min
LE/CJ[1]	5	0	18	0
Computer Forensics	13	9	33	0
CS/IT	7	5	18	0
General Education	5	2	18	0
Other	8	5	22	0
Total Credits	**33**	**38**	**40**	**15**

Table 5b. CS/IT Credits in Master's Programs

	Avg	Median	Max	Min
Operating Systems	1.5	0	6	0
CSec/IA[2]	3	0	12	0
Other	2.25	0	9	0
Total Credits	**6.75**	**4.5**	**18**	**0**

4. ANALYSIS AND RECOMMENDATIONS

It is clear from the overview of existing programs that computer forensics is a multi-disciplinary field with elements taken from criminal justice, law enforcement, ethics, political science, computer science, and information technology. Many factors must be considered before starting a program in computer forensics. These factors include curriculum design, existing programs, faculty, students, facilities, and budget.

We identified four different approaches to computer forensics programs: associate degree programs, baccalaureate degrees, graduate programs and certificate programs. The best approach to starting a program in computer forensics depends on local circumstances. Certificate programs provide a relatively low-cost starting point for institutions with limited resources. For those schools whose existing programs provide multi-disciplinary support, a two or four year program is possible. Ideally, a solid four year program in either computer science or criminal justice is needed before a master's program is offered.

No matter which approach is taken, faculty who are capable of teaching the core computer forensics courses are essential to the success of the program. Industry experts are highly desirable adjunct faculty for these programs. However, in a long run, full-time faculty must be trained.

The choice of department to host a program in computer forensics varied. Our survey found programs hosted by criminal justice departments, computer science departments, and interdisciplinary centers. To avoid unnecessary competition among departments, an interdisciplinary center is recommended, budget permitting.

Student interest in computer forensics is strong. However, some caution must be exercised with regard to admitting students due to the sensitive nature of the field. Although the most common solution is checking the background of students applying for admission, no unified rule emerged from our study. Some schools only check students' backgrounds when they take computer forensics courses. Other schools allow only law enforcement personnel to be admitted to their programs. At other institutions, no mention is made of background checks.

Dedicated computer labs are essential for the study of computer forensics. Because investigations may involved unbroken systems, corrupted systems, or physically damaged systems, computer labs must provide access to multiple computers as well as expensive equipment for recovering data from physically damaged or otherwise corrupted systems.

Budget remains a key issue. Currently available sources of funding include the office of homeland security and other defense and security related government agencies.

5. CONCLUSION

We found that computer forensics is a growing multi-disciplinary field with increasing industry demand. Although there are no publicly recognized program standards to follow at this time, there are a number of good examples of two and four year programs [9]. At the master's level, [15, 30] serve as good examples.

However, few programs exist at this time. The preponderance of the programs is located in the eastern U.S. with about 20% of the programs on the west coast. It seems clear that there is plenty of room for growth.

To promote computer forensics education, coordination and cooperation from criminal justice, law enforcement, ethics, political science, computer science, and information technology will be needed. Further discussion and study are necessary for establishing standardized curricula in this emerging field.

6. ACKNOWLEDGMENTS

We thank those schools and faculty which share their curricula and course descriptions so we may learn from one another.

7. REFERENCES

[1] *Computer Forensics & Electronic Discovery: The Corporate Security Guide for Recovering Electronic Digital Evidence*, Pinkerton Consulting & Investigations, 2001.

[2] Berghel, H. The Discipline of Internet Forensics, *Communications of the ACM*, 46, 8 (August 2003), 15-20.

[3] http://www.blueridge.edu/ContinuingEducation/Programs/CyberCrimeInvest.htm.

[4] http://cte.bridgew.edu/certifications/cdfe.cfm

[5] http://programs.bcit.ca/845CBTECH.

[6] http://web.bryant.edu/~edc/forensics.htm

[7] http://www.bc3.edu/academics/technology/compforensics.htm.

[8] http://www.canyoncollege.edu/lawenforce.htm.

[9] http://digitalforensics.champlain.edu.

[10] http://a-s.clayton.edu/cj/curriculum%20-%20overview.htm.

[11] http://www.curry.edu/Academics/Continuing+Education/Certificate+Programs/Computer+Crime+Investigations+and+Computer+Forensics.htm.

[12] http://www.gwu.edu/~mastergw/programs/com_fraud/.)

[13] http://www.icmschool.com/business-medical-careers-criminal-justice-cybercrime.html.

[14] Isner, J. *Computer Forensics: An Emerging Practice in the Battle Against Cyber Crime*, SANS Institute, Bethesda, Maryland. 2003.

[15] http://www.jjay.cuny.edu/programsGraduate/progGraduateForensicComputing.asp.

[16] http://www.kennesaw.edu/coned/sci/index.htm

[17] Kruse, W. and Heiser, J. What Exactly is Computer Forensics? *Security Bulletin*, July 2004. Hong Kong CERT/CC, 1-7.

[18] http://www.lwtc.ctc.edu/future/programs/list/cfor.htm.

[19] Lang, D. *Design and Development of a Distance Education Paradigm for Training Computer Forensics Examiners: A Limited Review of Literature*, Dec. 6, 1999, http://www.computerteacher.org/CFLR.htm.

[20] http://www.lccc.edu/academics/credit/computer-forensics-aas.asp.

[21] http://www.bus.oregonstate.edu/services/nti.htm.

[22] http://www.polk.edu/INSTRUCT/wfd/ips/programscoursedescriptions.htm.

[23] http://www.southwest.cc.nc.us/acadprog/cct.htm.

[24] http://tech.spokanefalls.edu/InfoSys/default.asp?menu=2&page=CertForensics.

[25] St. Petersburg College, Florida, http://www.spcollege.edu/webcentral/acad/compcrime.htm.

[26] http://www.starkstate.edu/ACADEMICS/it_tech/compnetadmin_secur.htm.

[27] http://www.sunytccc.edu/academic/forensic/main.asp.

[28] Troell, L., Pan, Y. and Stackpole, B. Forensic Course Development, *Proc. Conference on Information Technology Curriculum 4 (CITC4 '03)* (Lafayette, IN, October 16-18, 2003). ACM Press, New York NY, 2003, 265-269.

[29] http://www.graduate.ucf.edu/currentGradCatalog/content/degrees/ACAD_PROG_71.cfm

[30] http://www.newhaven.edu/psps/gradforensicscience.html.

[31] http://www.extension.washington.edu/ext/certificates/cpf/cpf_gen.asp.

[32] http://www.ecii.edu/edu_eci.html

[33] http://www.lcsee.cemr.wvu.edu/forensics/.

[34] http://wright.ccc.edu/department/forensics/index.asp.

[35] Yasinsac, A., Erbacher, R., Marks, D., Pollitt, M., and Sommer, P. Computer Forensics Education. *IEEE Security & Privacy*, July/August 2003, 15-23.

Viruses 101

J. Aycock and K. Barker
Department of Computer Science
University of Calgary
2500 University Drive N.W.
Calgary, Alberta, Canada T2N 1N4
{aycock,barker}@cpsc.ucalgary.ca

ABSTRACT

The University of Calgary introduced a controversial course in the fall of 2003 on computer viruses and malware. The primary objection about this course from the anti-virus community was that students were being taught how to create viruses in addition to defending against them. Unfortunately, the reaction to our course was based on a dearth of information, which we remedy in this paper by describing key pedagogical elements of the course.

Specifically, we present four aspects of our course: how students are vetted for entry, operation of the course, course content, and the instructional materials used. In addition, we pay particular attention to the controversial course assignments, discussing the assignments and the need for balance, objectivity, security, and learning in a university environment. Our experiences with the course and future plans may be helpful for other institutions considering such course offerings. It should also provide opponents of the course with valuable information about the true nature of the course, the pedagogy used, and the value provided to the computer community as computer science graduates with this kind of expertise take their place as the next generation computer security experts.

Categories and Subject Descriptors

D.4.6 [**Operating Systems**]: Security and Protection—*Invasive Software*; C.2.0 [**Computer-Communication Networks**]: General—*Security and Protection*; K.6.5 [**Management of Computing and Information Systems**]: Security and Protection—*Invasive Software*

General Terms

Security

Keywords

Computer viruses, Anti-virus software, Malware, University course

1. INTRODUCTION

It is hard to think of any truly controversial topics in computer science. It is even harder to think of any that are far-ranging beyond computer science: not "religious wars" about a favorite editor or programming language, but topics which incite passion and opinion in the general public.

We stumbled across just such a topic when the University of Calgary introduced a course in computer viruses and malware in the fall of 2003. One distinguishing feature of our course is that students learn about malware by creating their own under strictly controlled conditions. Prior to our announcement of the course, we were aware of only one other institution that did this [6]; since that time, we have found out about a few others. To the best of our knowledge, we are currently the only institution in Canada that offers such a course, and only one of a handful worldwide. Typically, any discussion of computer viruses seems to occur in the abstract, as a small part of some other "legitimate" course offering like operating systems or networking.

The reaction to our virus course announcement astounded us. We were inundated with email, swamped with media attention from all over the world (e.g., [5, 15, 19, 20]), and castigated by the anti-virus community (e.g., [4, 13]).

Much of this reaction took place in the absence of any concrete details about what we would be teaching. In the remainder of this paper, we present these details. Starting with high-level course design issues in Section 2, we move on to course admission and operation in Section 3. Section 4 talks about the course syllabus and material, followed by the assignments in Section 5 and our secure laboratory environment in Section 6. We conclude with our future plans for the course.

2. THREE BIG QUESTIONS

Generally speaking, there are three questions that need to be asked when teaching a course:

1. How do we teach this subject?
2. Can we teach this subject safely?
3. Would teaching the subject make the world worse or better?

Normally, course content is so clearly benign that we do not even consider Questions 2 and 3, but the questions are implicitly present and must be considered as part of an ethical instructional design.

We addressed Question 2, safety, by designing a secure environment for students to work in (see Section 5). Question 3 is somewhat trickier; the full argument is outside the scope of this paper, but it can be summarized as follows. First, malware is a valid area of study, and such computer security research is becoming vital to our increasingly computer-dependent society. Second, it is very easy to learn how to create malware, even for people with no programming expertise. It is not easy, however, to learn this in a safe environment, nor to get an objective view of the entire field, both malware and anti-malware.

Surprisingly, our answer to Question 1 was the thing that caused us the most grief. We took a pedagogical approach to the virus course not unlike that we would use for other courses, trying to ensure that students would learn in the most effective way possible. To this end, many educators would recognize the quote:

> I hear, and I forget.
> I see, and I remember.
> I do, and I understand.
>
> – Anonymous

We wanted to produce high-quality students who possess a deep understanding of this aspect of computer security. We therefore wanted students to "do," which in the context of malware, means that students must write both virus and anti-virus software. However, writing viruses, even if they are not new types of viruses, earned us instant, stiff opposition from the anti-virus community. If we had omitted the virus-writing aspect of the course, we were told that the anti-virus community would have supported our initiative. But we did not back away from this pedagogical principle, because doing so would have compromised our ability to teach students objectively and effectively. Our students, informally polled at the end of the course, confirmed that they thought they learned the material better through doing.

3. COURSE ADMISSION AND OPERATION

Enrollment in the virus course is limited to 16 students – both graduate and undergraduate – due to lab space limitations. The 16 spots are assigned competitively; students must meet the following criteria:

- A grade point average of 3.0 or better.
- Computer Science students only. This restriction allows us to properly enforce penalties for lab protocol violations, should it become necessary to do so.
- Fourth-year (senior) standing or better, which includes graduate students.
- A passing grade in operating systems and computability theory courses. Operating systems background is obviously essential, and this prerequisite also transitively ensures that students have taken assembly language courses. The key elements from the computability theory course are finite automata and undecidability results. Depending on the content covered in the virus class, a computer networking course would also be useful.
- A one-page essay, on why the students wants to take the course, and what learning expectations they have from it.[1] The essays are ranked by committee, and students who meet the other criteria are offered positions in the class using this ordering.

Noteworthy in its absence is the lack of any criminal background checks or other security checks. It was decided at higher levels of administration that such a requirement would run contrary to the mission of a university.

Students are notified in advance that they will have to sign a legal agreement to take the course and abide by strict laboratory protocols. In the interest of full disclosure, applicants are also notified that some companies have made public statements that they will not hire people who have taken the virus course [18]. A discussion of this ban is beyond the scope of this paper, but we have noticed that it has unfortunately dissuaded some students from taking the course.

No auditing or "sitting in" the lectures is allowed by students not admitted to the course, and this policy is enforced by the instructor checking students' identification.

4. SYLLABUS AND COURSE MATERIAL

As a "capstone" course, studying malware combines ideas from across computer science as well as other disciplines: low-level concepts, operating systems, programming language implementation, networking, security, automata theory, law, ethics, psychology, and human-computer interfaces.

Our current syllabus is below. Law and ethics are covered first, deliberately, before any programming assignments are done; this is part of establishing a secure environment. The material on "weaknesses exploited" is actually more closely related to worms, but was moved up to accommodate a guest lecture on the topic.

- Introduction
  - Lab protocol
  - Legal agreement
  - Basic definitions
- Law and malware
  - United States law
  - Canadian law
  - Council of Europe Convention on Cybercrime
  - Extradition
- Ethics and malware
  - General ethical theories
  - Moral development
  - Ethical decision-making processes
  - Codes of ethics
    - Computing profession
    - Anti-virus profession
- Weaknesses exploited

[1]The admission process for graduate students involves a personal interview instead of the essay.

- Software
- Humans
  - Social engineering
  - Hoaxes

- Viruses
- Anti-virus techniques
- Anti-anti-virus techniques
- Worms and deworming
- People and communities
  - Malware creators
  - AV community
- "Applications"
  - Benevolent Malware
  - Information Warfare
  - Cyberterrorism

We are careful to maintain objectivity when presenting material about virus writers. It is not unusual, at anti-virus conferences, to hear virus writers referred to in less-than-flattering terms, but such rhetoric has no place in an objective university environment. We also rely on established research when studying virus writers [8, 9], and not stereotypes [16].

Objectivity plays a strong role when teaching ethics, too. Clearly, we do not want students who think it ethically sound to deliberately unleash malware into the world, yet it is not the job of a university instructor to indoctrinate students with a certain set of ethics. That would neither be objective, nor would it allow students to be inquisitive. We must instead give students an appropriate framework with which to make choices: teaching ethical theories, working through case studies, and emphasizing the effect of actions on others.

Where possible, the material in the syllabus is complemented by guest lectures from domain experts. In our first offering of the virus course, we had three guests, who spoke about criminal law, ethics, and buffer overflow defenses in the OpenBSD operating system.

Finding course material is an ongoing problem. We do not use a textbook at present, because no text exists that covers the correct topics at the appropriate level of detail for a senior/graduate course. Some material is quite easy to find, like computer-related ethics [2]; computer law is similarly easy, although many available resources are U.S.-centric. There are an increasing number of recent books on exploiting software weaknesses [7, 12] and worms [14], too.

Virus material is prolific, but surprisingly, the single hardest area to find detailed information about is anti-virus software. Current books [10, 17] only gloss over some anti-virus techniques, and anti-virus companies treat this information as proprietary. Obviously, anti-virus companies do not want to give anyone a competitive advantage, but neither do they want to leak information to virus writers.[2] For anti-virus material, traditional sources of information are insufficient.

[2]Deciding whether or not security through obscurity is effective is left as an exercise for the interested reader.

As researchers, we have been taught to regard non-peer-reviewed, non-academic publications with extreme suspicion. Virus writers do not tend to publish in *Nature*, however. To dismiss non-academic publications is to disregard a wealth of potential information about both virus and anti-virus software. Preparing course material for our virus course thus took months of painstaking research work, using methods not unlike historians might use: taking bits and pieces from a wide selection of non-academic sources and piecing them together to arrive at some semblance of the truth. Some material unearthed this way, particularly technical detail, is directly verifiable; other material must be qualified appropriately when presented in lectures:

> "Several writers have said that..."

> "One author has said that..."

In lectures, this is a good opportunity to teach analyzing the veracity of source material, and to encourage a healthy level of skepticism.

Sometimes non-academic sources are the simplest ways to get certain information. In one case, the instructor was looking for a specific macro virus' source code to use in a lecture. "Legitimate" sources presented the source code in pseudocode form, if at all. In less than five minutes with a web search engine, the source code was acquired from a non-academic source.

5. ASSIGNMENTS

The virus course has five assignments: one written, four involving programming. The first, written, assignment is a malware-related ethical case study in which students must consider their response to a presented scenario. The programming assignments are grouped, reflecting the balanced nature of the course, with one "offensive" and one "defensive" assignment per group:

- Software weaknesses and defense

  Assignment 2. Basic stack-smashing attack.

  Assignment 3. Defense against stack-smashing attacks.

- Virus and anti-virus

  Assignment 4. Virus creation.

  Assignment 5. Anti-virus software to detect and disinfect.

After each offensive assignment of a group (i.e., Assignments 2 and 4), students share their code with one another. This gives them a larger set of samples to work with for their defensive assignment. For example, students had to write one virus for Assignment 4, then for Assignment 5 had to detect *all* viruses from Assignment 4 and disinfect at least one Assignment 4 virus.

The degree of difficulty for programming assignments is somewhat problematic. Obviously, we do not want to set trivial assignments. On the other hand, if assignments are too hard, an argument could be made – rightly or wrongly – that we had forced students to work outside the secure environment to complete the assignments. We have thus scaled back the assignments somewhat from what we would normally use in a course. For example, allowing students to exploit code of their own for Assignment 2, instead of finding holes in existing code, simplifies their task.

Another constraint with assignment difficulty is bureaucratic. At the University of Calgary, new courses such as the virus course aren't permitted any lab time, just lecture time. Any time spent by the instructor in the lab for instruction or assignment demonstrations detracts from lecture time. This is also a consideration when choosing the operating system used for assignments. Our students use mostly non-Windows operating systems, and so to have students doing assignments under Windows (for instance) would first require labs to instruct them on the finer points of Windows programming – not an effective use of lecture time. This is a temporary problem, however, and the virus course should have real lab time within the year.

6. THE VIRUS LABORATORY

Programming assignments are performed in a secure virus laboratory. This laboratory is one aspect of the secure environment which we have established [1]. We recognize that, by themselves, technical safeguards are insufficient; it only takes one student to work on malware outside a "secure" laboratory to render technical precautions moot.

Instead, we create a secure *environment* by employing five broad categories of safeguards:

Legal. Our legal safeguards are twofold. First, we teach the legal repercussions of writing and releasing malware through course material and a guest lecture.

Second, we impose contractual legal obligations on the students by having them sign a legal agreement prior to taking the course. The legal agreement includes adherence to the laboratory protocol, usage and handling of the course material, and liability and indemnity.

Ethical. As we mentioned in Section 4, teaching ethics with respect to malware is tricky. Again, we use a combination of course material and a guest lecture. We "test" ethics by working through case studies in lectures, and using a written ethics assignment.

Social. Peer pressure is exploited for safety conformance. Programming assignments *must* be done by students in pairs – in fact, students cannot log in to the virus lab machines unless the passwords of all group members are entered. We stress to the students that they are jointly responsible for everything that happens during their login session, and this is reinforced through the laboratory protocol.

Advocates of pair programming [3] might argue that this technique improves safety by improving software quality. It certainly adds an extra layer of security to the virus laboratory, because any illegal or unethical activity would require collusion between students.

Behavioral. Behavioral safeguards refer to conduct in the virus laboratory, which we regulate with a formal laboratory protocol. Recognizing that other sciences have a lot of experience handling dangerous substances, we initially based our protocol on biohazard protocols [11], adapting and extending the protocol to cover computer-specific risks.

Our protocol covers issues like laboratory entry, authorized personnel in the laboratory, prohibited devices and media, and safety mechanisms that must be included in software. The complete protocol may be found in [1, Appendix]. Violating the lab protocol results in an "F" grade in the course.

It is critical to note that the laboratory protocol applies to *everyone*, not just the students: the course instructor and technical staff are not exempt, for instance. This helps to underscore the importance of proper laboratory behavior.

Technical. Our technical safeguards can be divided into two parts: physical and electronic security.

Physical security. Physically, the laboratory is located within two card-key access areas. It has one entrance, with a door closer and an alarm which rings if the door is held open for too long. Two unmonitored cameras are present in the room, sending images to an external machine for recording. The machines in the laboratory are physically locked down, and the laboratory server and network switch are located in a locked cabinet. Network connectors in the room have been both physically and electronically disabled.

Electronic security. The laboratory computers have all unnecessary I/O ports disabled and the BIOS settings locked down. Ports on the network switch are locked to the MAC addresses of these computers.

Once logged in, students only have the option of running VMware, a virtual x86 machine – all work is done inside this virtual machine. The hardware architecture used for the laboratory server is different than that of the students' computers, and different operating systems are used for the server, to run VMware on, and to run inside VMware. The lack of hardware and software monocultures is deliberate, and is intended to limit the spread of any malware that should somehow escape its virtual x86 machine.

It is the combination of these five categories of safeguards, taking both human and computer elements into account, that makes the environment secure.

The safeguards are mutually reinforcing. Consider malware leaving the laboratory on a USB flash RAM drive, for example. This scenario is guarded against by technical, behavioral, legal, and social means. First, the USB ports have been disabled as part of electronic security. Second, the USB port settings cannot be altered without breaching further electronic security – a BIOS password – or the physical security of the locked-down computer case. Third, the laboratory protocol precludes such a USB device from being brought into the lab in the first place. Fourth, the legal agreement enforces adherence to the laboratory protocol. Fifth, even if the USB port were enabled somehow, collusion would be required to log in to the computer to transfer files. Sixth, any unauthorized personnel would have to compromise physical security (and be captured on camera) to get in to the laboratory. It is far easier to find malicious code using a web search engine than to take such elaborate measures!

7. FUTURE PLANS

We will be enhancing the course material in upcoming offerings of the virus course. In particular, we will be expanding coverage of worms, adding a section on virus cryptanalysis, and incorporating new information from both academic and non-academic sources.

There are a number of laboratory enhancements to consider too. The computing environment needs tuning to permit environment customization and multiple operating systems. There is also the question of whether or not to actively jam wireless electronics, but as the current safeguards prevent the use of wireless devices, this may be overkill. As for the human element, we are interested in finding ways to evaluate the efficacy of our non-technical safeguards.

Needless to say, we are committed to continuing to offer the virus course, despite the controversy. The students taking our course receive an in-depth understanding of malware and anti-malware, taught in a balanced, objective, and secure fashion.

8. ACKNOWLEDGMENTS

Many thanks to our technical staff, especially Tim Bliek, Darcy Grant, Shaun Laing, Brian Scowcroft, Jennifer Walker, and Erik Williamson. A number of people reviewed our lab specification and lab protocol to help ensure safety; Randy Abrams, Brad Arlt, Fred Cohen, Sarah Gordon, and Darcy Grant all provided valuable feedback. Thanks also to Gerry Bliss and Sid Tolchinsky from SPIE for their independent review and risk assessment. Stephen Jenuth, Ken Chapman, and Theo de Raadt gave the guest lectures on law, ethics, and OpenBSD, respectively.

9. REFERENCES

[1] J. Aycock and K. Barker. Creating a secure virus laboratory. In *13th Annual EICAR Conference*, 2004. 13pp.

[2] S. Baase. *A Gift of Fire*. Prentice Hall, 2nd edition, 2003.

[3] K. Beck. *Extreme Programming Explained*. Addison-Wesley, 2000.

[4] V. Bontchev. Should we teach virus writing? In *6th Association of anti Virus Asia Researchers Conference (AVAR 2003)*, 2003. 15pp.

[5] CNN Headline News: Hot Wired. News broadcast, 28 May 2004.

[6] F. Cohen. CJ 528/628 – Computer viruses and malicious code. http://unhca.com/CJ628/CJ628.html. Course syllabus, University of New Haven.

[7] J. Erickson. *Hacking: The Art of Exploitation*. No Starch Press, 2003.

[8] S. Gordon. The generic virus writer. In *4th International Virus Bulletin Conference*, 1994.

[9] S. Gordon. The generic virus writer II. In *6th International Virus Bulletin Conference*, 1996.

[10] D. Harley, R. Slade, and U. E. Gattiker. *Viruses Revealed*. Osbourne, 2001.

[11] Health Canada. *The Laboratory Biosafety Guidelines*. M. Best and M. Heisz, eds., 3rd (draft) edition, 2001. http://www.hc-sc.gc.ca/pphb-dgspsp/ols-bsl/lbg-ldmbl/index.html.

[12] J. Koziol, D. Litchfield, D. Aitel, C. Anley, S. Eren, N. Mehta, and R. Hassell. *The Shellcoder's Handbook*. Wiley, 2004.

[13] J. Kuo. Alberta strikes again. *Virus Bulletin*, page 2, July 2003.

[14] J. Nazario. *Defense and Detection Strategies against Internet Worms*. Artech House, 2004.

[15] B. Read. How to write a computer virus, for college credit (cover story). *Chronicle of Higher Education*, 50(19):A33, 2pp., Jan. 2004.

[16] Reuters. Looking into the mind of a virus writer. CNN.com, 19 March 2003.

[17] E. Skoudis. *Malware: Fighting Malicious Code*. Prentice Hall, 2004.

[18] Sophos. Sophos CEO says: "I won't hire virus writing students". http://www.sophos.com/virusinfo/articles/calgary2.html, 28 May 2003.

[19] P. Svensson. Antivirus industry steamed over virus article, college class. Associated Press (New York), 11 June 2003.

[20] E. Wilson. Anger at 'virus' lessons. Sydney Morning Herald (Sydney, Australia), 6 October 2003.

Teaching Students to Hack: Curriculum Issues in Information Security

Patricia Y. Logan Ph.D.
Associate Professor
Marshall University Graduate College
Charleston, West Virginia 25303-1600
(304) 746-1951
Loganp@marshall.edu

Allen Clarkson, M.S., MCSE
Independent Consultant
San Antonio, Texas
(210) 863-0610
allen@espressodonkey.com

ABSTRACT
Teaching "hacking" as a legitimate means of training students in how to protect a future employer's data assets has been introduced into courses with increasing frequency. The introduction of "red teaming" and attack-based exercises into information security courses presents a potential ethical problem. This paper explores the issues involved in designing an information security course with lab components that involve destructive actions.

Categories and Subject Descriptors
Security

General Terms
Security

Keywords
Information security, education, computer security, computer science education, hacking, information assurance, ethics and computers

1. INTRODUCTION
With the introduction of information security courses into the computer science curriculum has come content that includes labs and exercises that emphasize a form of internal security auditing known as "ethical hacking." Instructors have begun to construct labs and develop exercises that teach students how to employ the tactics and exploits of hackers.[1] The practice first emerged within the U.S. intelligence community and military where "tiger teams" would simulate attacks against government IT assets to determine vulnerabilities. The teams would employ the same tools and techniques as malevolent intruders but would cause no harm. [2] The term "ethical hacker" has become popularized by corporations hiring security professionals to test their systems for vulnerabilities and describing these individuals as "ethical hackers". C.C. Palmer in the IBM Systems Journal says, "ethical hackers...employ the same tools and techniques as the intruders, but they...neither damage the target systems nor steal information. Instead, they ...evaluate the target systems' security and report back to owners with the vulnerabilities they found and instructions for how to remedy them." [3] Farmer and Venema advocated an approach to improving security that included breaking into one's own system using the argument that they were "trying to help systems administrators to make informed decisions on how to secure their site." [4]

At its simplest, hacking is accessing a system without authority or beyond one's authority. It includes the application of computer skills to find vulnerable systems, penetrate systems, and to remove evidence of access to a system. These skills most often are acquired from diligent practice, or through directed assistance from experienced hackers (possibly via chat rooms, web resources, black hat groups). With the introduction of information security courses, both proprietary and academic, these skills can now be acquired with less effort. Additionally, vendors have introduced the idea of ethical hacking certification such as the CEH (Certified Ethical Hacker) offered by the EC-Council. [5] Arguments in favor of "ethical hacking" as an important security practice are: 1) that hacking skills are equivalent to audit skills as both are designed to discover flaws in the protection of data and secure operation of a system. Just as auditors test systems for security or operational flaws, hackers "test" systems through attack; 2) knowledge of hacking skills and practice in attacking secured systems improves security by informing network administrators of how an exploit can be executed; and 3) to provide the best security defense, a systems administrator must possess the same skills as the attacker. These arguments in favor of "ethical hacking" have been lifted up as justification for including these skills in information security courses at both the undergraduate and graduate levels. Courses have been designed to teach students to hack, with the implication that it is a necessary security practice and that it will improve employability as a network administrator charged with protecting valuable corporate assets.

This paper deals with the implementation of courses in information security with a lab component that includes exercises in hacking. The authors examine some curriculum issues that should be considered when designing information security curriculum. The paper discusses four issues for universities and CS departments that arise from students learning to hack, write malicious code, or use forensic tool sets. These areas are:

SIGCSE'05, February 23-27, 2005, St. Louis, Missouri, USA.

1. Appropriate hands-on course content for security and forensics classes
2. The design and use of security labs
3. Student awareness of ethical behavior in computing
4. University response to student attacks

2. Appropriate Hands-On Course Content for Security and Forensics Classes

It can be argued that hacking tools, methods, and other types of security course content are readily available on the Internet; a Google™ search reveals hacker web sites and tool sets with instructions and chat rooms for personal assistance. Within CS departments, however, there has been a quiet inclusion of this same content within the context of a course of study in information security without much discussion of the potential for misuse or abuse by students. Courses that include hacking often state that they are providing practical knowledge in identifying, detecting, and responding to intrusions. Students are theoretically being equipped to interpret the output of intrusion sensors, identify whether a system has been compromised, learn to contain the intrusion and perform necessary actions to eliminate the source of the intrusion and return affected systems to secure operation. The problem is that anyone can hack a network and describe the results of a scan but network administrators will need to put the results into a business context in order to manage an intrusion. They must describe to management the nature of the security risk as well as the remedies that will mitigate the risk. Any hack performed on a network should be part of a larger security audit process designed to reveal vulnerabilities and improve security policies and procedures. Professionals in security assessment believe that hacking a network will only give a snapshot in time [6] but an organized security audit is designed to provide an on-going assessment of vulnerability. Students that perform a single exercise perform the actions of hacking and not of defense. Students should learn to protect their networks from common intruder methods of attack but should also be able to perform vulnerability assessments on the entire spectrum of data assets: applications, policies, procedures, and physical infrastructure.

Universities that include undergraduate or graduate majors in information security and offer courses in network or computer forensics often have been designated by the National Security Administration as Centers of Academic Excellence in Information Assurance (CAE). Using the published list (2004) of NSA Centers of Academic Excellence in Information Assurance (CAE) there are 59 U.S. universities that have these courses and offer a major or emphasis in information security at the undergraduate or graduate level. Implementing these courses often means approval by university curriculum committees. At that level, questions are seldom raised about the content of hands-on exercises or the security of the lab facilities. Course developers may offer reassurances that the content would not be dangerous or that the risk is necessary in pursuit of guiding students to be effective network administrators.

Many universities offer information security courses with labs only at the graduate level. Allowing these courses only at the graduate level possibly ensures that students are more mature, gainfully employed, and therefore, less likely to use course content for malicious experimentation. These assumptions are not supported by the history of on-campus hacking cases which involve both undergraduate and graduate students. Some universities avoid the issue altogether by not teaching hands-on content or having separate labs away from general student access to practice their skills. Book and lecture-based instruction is not always as effective in demonstrating concepts as hands-on experience. Separate labs help reduce malicious activity initiated from within their confines, but that solution alone does nothing to protect the wider network from experimentation on other nodes. A question remains about the legitimacy of teaching students to hack in order to improve their intrusion detection skills. The same question was asked last year when the University of Calgary announced plans to offer a virus writing course with the stated goal of improving the understanding of virus mechanisms. Opponents argue that formal instruction in writing viruses only encourages more illegal activity. Dr. Ken Barker, chair of the Department of Computer Sciences at the university, contends that "most computer-science graduates today already have the technical knowledge to create a virus" and that the focus of the course is understanding and prevention. [7]

The authors reviewed the web sites for the CAE schools and where available examined the on-line syllabi for evidence that a course included lab instruction or activities in hacking. Most of the schools had received funding for a specialized computer lab that enabled testing of security precautions. These labs were described as set-up to facilitate the testing of systems through attempts at penetration. The syllabi for information security courses that contained a lab component revealed the following types of activities required of their students: writing port scanners, writing a propagating virus, writing an exploit program, creating a shell to gain root privilege, packet sniffing, injecting a packet, war games competitions, and attack teams hacking a "secure network". The course content in any of these courses did not appear to include recovery activities, intensive vulnerability assessments of a simulated corporate network, network forensic investigations. As systems administrators will reveal, their job is seldom fighting hackers in computer-to-computer combat. Most systems attacked have security applied, including some high-profile systems with better than average security (Microsoft). The most devastating hacks are often exploits that do not include strong technical knowledge (i.e., password guessing, social engineering, using Google). A recent report from the financial industry the *Insider Threat Study: Illicit Cyber Activity in the Banking and Finance Sector* [8] compiled by the U.S. Secret Service and the CERT/CC at Carnegie Mellon showed that 87 percent of the attacks were from insiders who exploited non-technical vulnerabilities (business rules, organization processes, procedures) and were carried out by those with little technical skill. A number of questions should be asked about the appropriate content for courses in information security: How should students be taught to implement network and desktop security? Is hacking and virus-writing a pre-requisite for developing strong technical skills in detecting malicious activity? What course content (if any) should be off-limits? Should courses follow the content for CISSP certification or SANs technical seminars for GIAC certification? Does it necessarily follow that hacking skills for future network administrators will improve security and their employability?

A starting point for designing information security courses is to establish what skills will add the most value to the security of the enterprise. Faculty should examine the value of exercises that attack a system, and assignments that encourage the creation of malicious programs. No research has yet shown a direct positive benefit between the special knowledge of hacking and the subsequent improved security of a network. Red team exercises and attack competitions carried out as events isolated from the over-all responsibilities for security will focus student-attention and their knowledge retention on the "thrill" of the hunt (or attack) rather than on a security message.

In advance of developing assignments and exercises that include the creation of malicious code, attacks on secure networks or the use of tools to find network vulnerabilities, faculty should determine if these activities can be justified within the context of the learning goals of the course. These courses should include assignments that mimic the job responsibilities of security administrators. Students need to be taught methods of detecting attacks from inside that do not use traditional hacker's methods. Recent study shows that 28% of attacks were from existing employees and 21% from former employees. Hacker tools sets and skills do nothing to protect a company from this threat. An over-emphasis on attack scenarios may do a disservice to students as they will believe they possess the total skill set to protect a company from attack focusing on the perimeter and not what is inside the network. [9]

Courses in information security with a lab component should include activities that present the greatest challenges to information security in the enterprise. These include: restoration of a hacked system to full operation, creation of an enterprise security plan, collecting evidence of a network attack for law enforcement, and the skills to perform a proper security audit (meaning people, policies, and technology). Assignments that are weighted heavily toward red team exercises and attack-defense labs present an unrealistic view of the skill sets needed to be an effective information security professional. Students should not assume that technology or policies will insure success: as good security planning includes the plan for an inevitable failure.

Summary: CS departments need to be practicing, considering, and justifying the methods used to train students in information security. Course developers should consider that systems administrators seldom spend their days waiting to respond to an intrusion. The reality of administering a secure network is that it is often practicing to fail. Systems administrators will need to have a variety of skill sets to effectively implement security, not just the skill to hack a system. These skills include the ability to perform security audits, maintaining a secure network, recovering from intrusion, and planning for disaster recovery and business continuity. Course content needs to cover the entire spectrum of security management and not just the exercise in attack and defense or the creation of malicious code.

3. The Design and Use of Security Labs

Universities have received funding for "cyber battlefield" labs that simulate a corporate network and enable students to attack a system in a controlled environment. The lab can simulate a broad range of real-world cyber-threats and enable students to perform vulnerability assessments, test defenses, and implement tool sets. These specialized labs can give instructors an opportunity to provide "hands-on" exercises that provide an "in the trenches perspective and understanding of how the various technologies work." [10]

The configuration of these specialized security labs and their connection to the university network should be carefully considered. University CS departments often depend on university computing services to maintain labs and install software. What happens when security and forensics courses require installation of tools that if connected to a university network would potentially do damage and violate computer law? Where computer science departments use a general purpose university lab for computer science students, who protects against the improper use of the tools? Should departments assume the risk and configure and manage labs for high security to prevent potential rogue activity? What happens when universities, such as Marshall University, West Virginia house the state's digital evidence lab for the state police, as well as student computer forensic training labs? If computing services require additional tools to effectively manage these unique labs, who will pay for them if they are not part of an existing effort to manage security? In at least one course reviewed by the authors, it was obvious that the instructor was using a lab that was not disconnected from the wider university network as the instructions explicitly said, "Do not attack beyond xxx.xxx.xxx.xxx." The list of universities that have been attacked by students (most recently UC Berkeley) would indicate that university resources are not always well-protected. Improperly configured security labs that allow access to the wider university network (whether by mishap or design) may place the university assets in a vulnerable position as well as expose the university to legal liability. Unmonitored penetration testing of a class network that is connected to other networks and systems may be a potential breach of law and licensing restrictions of software. [11] Instructors typically allow students to attack without approving the specific actions that will be used. One instructor stated in such an exercise that any student able to secure the root password, by any means automatically earned an A in the course. In several syllabi, students had assignments that simply requested that a student find a hacking tool, test it, and demonstrate it to the class.

A university and campus computing services has a legitimate interest in knowing about these exercises and making sure that students are properly guided in their actions. Computing services departments have a better understanding of the technical relationships among student labs, administrative databases, university data services, email, and the systems and controls that link them all together. In part, computing services can offer expertise in isolating CS students in these courses, but also they can help identify potential flaws in a lab's design that can lead to security breaches.

Summary: The design of information security labs should involve careful planning and include consultation with computing services. Including computing services in the design of security labs and curriculum can prevent complicating security further by stemming one potential source of intrusion.

4. Student Awareness of Ethical Behavior in Computing

CS students do not often take courses in ethics and law, which are more usually offered in the social science or the business curriculum. Students are not often taught the law with respect to computing and electronic transmission. A survey of a graduate computer security class at Marshall University found that no students had read the university's Acceptable Use Policies (AUP). Most students are surprised to find that there are laws against copying MP3 files and unapproved wireless access to networks on campus. Each year at least one instructor can give an example of students that have managed to find their way into the instructor's network drive, WebCT or other network services that compromise grading or tests. Given the ethical lapses of Enron and Anderson, it appears that business schools were doing an inadequate job of describing to MBA students ethics and the law that resulted in flagrant violations. Universities should never assume that students learn ethical behavior, the laws on illegal network/computer access, outside (or before) their time at the university.

In order to determine whether universities were requiring their CS students to take a course in ethics and computer law, we reviewed computer science major requirements from the websites of the institutions listed on the NSA website as CAEs. These schools were chosen as a representative sample of those that place a high priority on information security curriculum. The statistics represented in Figure 1 ***do not*** reflect an opinion on CAE programs or course offerings, but instead they represent CS programs at these same institutions. No inference should be drawn from this study regarding the individual CAEs. The integration of the CAE varies widely – some integrate directly into student CS curricula, while others are purely research centers, and still others offer their own academic programs entirely separate from the CS tracks.

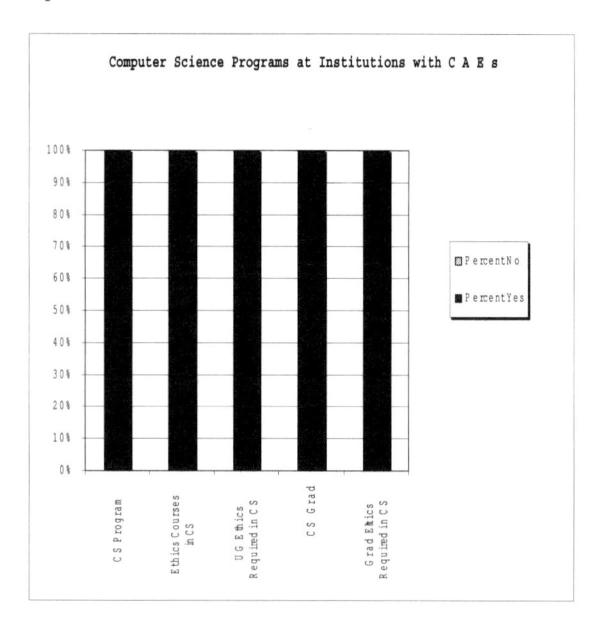

Figure 1.

The statistics show that while a solid majority (62%) have ethics courses in their CS program, an even larger percentage (66%) do not *require* undergraduate students to study ethical and/or legal issues as part of a degree program (includes both those institutions that do and do not *offer* ethics or legal issues courses). Further, 95% of all such institutions with graduate studies programs do not require ethics courses. These same universities often have international students that may be unfamiliar with the legal restrictions on computing activities in the United States. It is evident from these percentages that formal instruction in ethical and/or legal issues of computing is not a universal priority in CS curricula even in those institutions with a focus on security. The authors found in examining the syllabi for a variety of courses in security at CAEs that ethics about the use of computer facilities was not generally covered but unethical behavior with respect to cheating was fully explained in every syllabus. When a CS curriculum does not require a course in ethics and the law, a course in information security should emphasize the ethical responsibility of the security professional who is entrusted to protect data assets.

Could it be that we are training both the "good guys" – security professionals – and the "bad guys" – those with knowledge of techniques and tools but without exposure to ethical and legal issues – at the university level? The statistics from this study show that there may be a disconnect between the study of security and the translation of lessons learned to the rest of the computer-oriented curriculum. Reviewing the CAE schools, the pattern for offering these courses becomes clear: strong technical content and the absence of an ethics and computer law course. Many offer a single course in ethics and law as an elective. What student in this area would by-pass a technical course in order to take a course in ethics? It is apparent that instructors believe that a casual warning about legal/university consequences in a syllabus or brief comment about ethics in an introductory course will be sufficient warning against rogue activity.

Training students to attack systems without the ethical or legal constructs to understand their actions carries the risk of training future security professional and hackers side-by-side. The intent of information security training is to improve information security and to educate future security professionals. The idea of testing the security of a system by breaking it is not new. Is breaking into a system really the best way to teach students how to protect a company's data assets? Training students to be ethical professionals should begin with an instructor that models the behavior of an ethical security professional. Any exercises should include not only the technology but the soft attacks like social engineering, and malware from email attachments. Students should be steered toward the development of tools to assist in detection and strengthen systems to focus attention on their contribution to security. "Ethics do not replace good policies. Promoting ethical principles can instill positive behavior …but policies …provide clear and mandatory guidelines for acceptable conduct. Simply trusting the student to behave in an ethical manner is not enough". Class policies should exist to dissuade students with weak ethics. These policies should clearly present improper forms of hacking as illegal and unethical. All activities should be represented as right or wrong and not neutral or described as "ethical hacking …" [12] Each course should emphasize the role of the systems administrator in applying countermeasures. Proper security training should instill in students a strong ethical sense of what they should and should not do as security professionals.

Summary: As the role of information technology continues to increase in importance to business and critical infrastructures, additional consideration needs to be given to ethics awareness. Other professions, such as medicine, pharmacology and civil engineering, require that students be exposed to ethical and legal issues in their respective fields. Computer-oriented curricula need to include the same focus for those who will be operating modern infrastructure.

What should we teach in a course on ethics and law? Possible topics include: Cases from the CCIPS web site on FBI investigations and convictions of cyber-criminals, which includes some virus writers and improper access; a review of investigative processes and the specifics of the laws on monitoring, search and seizure, and illegal access of protected data; ethical duties owed to employers and for those who are in the field of computing, the ACM code of ethics.

5. University reaction to student attacks

Universities have crafted Acceptable Use Policies (AUPs) to respond to the necessity of maintaining and securing computing facilities. Universities enforce AUPs with banners at logon that students quickly bypass reading. Students involved in security courses with hacking exercises do not usually provide a separate and trackable ID that allows network administrators to monitor their activities. In the absence of strong network security and an awareness of the need for creating monitored accounts, should a university worry about downstream liability? Can a university be held responsible for a student's malicious efforts aimed at a corporation or business? A principle tool in protecting the university is the AUP, but it can be most effective only when introduced to students *before* a violation occurs, as a preventative measure, rather than after the fact as a justification for prosecution. Students need to be made aware of AUPs as a regular practice in CS courses. It seems contradictory to give students tools and knowledge that may damage the university system, not explaining the necessary restrictions on their use, and then punishing students for violations.

Universities have seldom prosecuted students involved in malicious or unethical use of campus networks. Given the knowledge that many students possess from their own education in hacking, and exposure to information about campus network configuration from their security course lab, it is reasonable to assume that some students may cross the line at a moment of temptation or revenge. Students should understand the legal consequences for moving across the legal line and that their university is prepared to prosecute them for their actions. In the authors experience, computer science students that have performed their own network vulnerability scans on university networks and collected data from unauthorized sniffing have been caught and warned rather than prosecuted. This lenient treatment for a criminal act does not reinforce the seriousness of the offense and may reinforce the view that hacking is a trivial activity.

Summary: Most students are unaware of the university acceptable use policies and any restrictions they might impose. Students in security courses may need accounts that work only under monitoring, signed statements of an understanding of their responsibilities in learning security material, and actual dismissal if involved in misuse. CS departments should consider creating course-level AUPs to augment the university's general use policies that clearly delineate what is being explored for instructional purposes and what is expected of students in their extra-curricular application of the knowledge.

6. CONCLUSION

University CS departments are moving quickly into information assurance courses at both graduate and undergraduate levels with the current popularity of the major magnified by the large number of job opportunities available in security, access to large amounts of federal funding (NSF scholarship for service or instructional enhancement), and increased focus on the issues by society at large. Students are being trained to use tools and investigative procedures that provide knowledge of hacking and avoidance of detection. Instructors should carefully consider the design of all "red team" exercises that use tools and techniques that mimic criminal intrusion methods. The ethics of computing activities and the legal issues need to be included in the study of security techniques and tools.

REFERENCES

[1] http://thewhir.com/king/ethical-hacking.cfm, last accessed November 30, 2004.

[2] Greene, Tim, Training Ethical Hackers: Training the Enemy?, www.ebcvg.com/articles.php?id=241, last accessed October 14, 2004.

[3] C.C. Palmer,Ethical Hacking, IBM Systems Journal, www.research.ibm.com/journal/sj/403/palmer.html, last accessed November 30, 2004.

[4] D. Farmer and W. Venema, "Improving the Security of Your Site by Hacking Into It," www.deter.com/unix/papers/improve_by_breakin.html, last accessed November 28, 2004.

[5] http://www.eccouncil.org/CEH.htm, last accessed November 29, 2004.

[6] Bernard, Allen, The Pros and Cons of Ethical Hacking, www.cioupdate.com/trends/article.php/3303001, last accessed September 14, 2004.

[7] http://www.pcworld.com/resource/printable/ar ticle/0,aid,110938,00.asp last accessed February 25, 2004.

[8] *Insider Threat Study: Illicit Cyber Activity in the Banking and Finance Sector* http://www.cert.org/archive/pdf/bankfin040820.pdf

[9] The State of Information Security, 2004, L.C. Ware, CSO Research Reports, http://www.csoonline.com/csoresearch/report75.html, last accessed November 30, 2004.

[10] http://news.com.com/2102-1001_3-898084.html? tag=st_util_print last accessed February 25, 2004.

[11] Appreciating the Art of the Hack, D. Phillips, Legal Times, 02-06-2002

[12] http://news.com.com/2102-1001_3-898084.html? tag=st_util_print last accessed February 25, 2004

Alternatives to Two Classic Data Structures

Chris Okasaki*
United States Military Academy
West Point, NY
Christopher.Okasaki@usma.edu

ABSTRACT

Red-black trees and leftist heaps are classic data structures that are commonly taught in Data Structures (CS2) and/or Algorithms (CS7) courses. This paper describes alternatives to these two data structures that may offer pedagogical advantages for typical students.

Categories and Subject Descriptors

E.1 [**Data Structures**]: Trees

General Terms

Algorithms

Keywords

Red-black trees, maxiphobic heaps, leftist heaps

1. INTRODUCTION

The field of computer science changes so rapidly that few of the topics we teach deserve the appellation "classic". Two common data structures that fall into that category are *red-black trees* [5] and *leftist heaps* [6], both developed in the 1970's. Classic data structures provide a welcome sense of history to the computer science classroom, but, because such data structures were rarely devised with an eye toward pedagogy, we should continue to look for alternatives that may be pedagogically superior. This paper describes two such alternatives.

The first alternative is not a new data structure per se, but rather an alternative approach to inserting an element into a red-black tree. Our algorithm is simpler to understand and dramatically simpler to code than the usual algorithm found in textbooks [3, 9]. The second alternative is a new data structure similar to leftist heaps. This new data structure, called *maxiphobic heaps*, is simpler to design than leftist heaps and hopefully offers greater insight into the process of designing a non-trivial data structure. Both alternatives are suitable for use in either Data Structures (CS2) or Algorithms (CS7).

Our insertion algorithm for red-black trees has previously been descibed in [7]. Maxiphobic heaps have previously been described in [8]. However, both data structures were devised and described in the context of functional programming languages. Unfortunately, few Data Structures or Algorithms courses are taught in functional programming languages. This paper adapts these data structures to an imperative pseudocode that is compatible with all the major imperative and object-oriented languages commonly used in the classroom today, and explicitly considers their potential pedagogical benefits.

*This work was supported, in part, by the National Science Foundation under grant CCR-0098288. The views expressed in this paper are those of the author and do not reflect the official policy or position of the United States Military Academy, the Department of the Army, the Department of Defense, or the U.S. Government.

SIGCSE'05, February 23–27, 2005, St. Louis, Missouri, USA.
ACM 1-58113-997-7/05/0002.

2. RED-BLACK TREES

Red-black trees and AVL trees [1] are probably the two most widely taught forms of balanced binary search trees. The algorithms and presentation of both are similar, involving left single rotations, left double rotations, right single rotations, and right double rotations. Although easy to understand at a superficial level, both kinds of trees are extremely difficult for a beginner to implement. We describe an alternative approach to insertion in a red-black tree that replaces the four kinds of rotations with a single balancing transformation, dramatically reducing the amount of code needed to implement the insertion function.

Besides the usual search-tree ordering, red-black trees obey several invariants related to the color of the nodes. Every node is colored either red or black in such a way that

1. every red node has a black parent, and
2. every path from the root to a node with one or two empty children contains the same number of black nodes.

The trick is to maintain these color invariants when modifying the tree.

To insert an element into a red-black tree, we create a new node containing the element and attach it to the bottom of the tree in the appropriate location to maintain the search-tree ordering, exactly as if we were inserting into an unbalanced binary search tree.

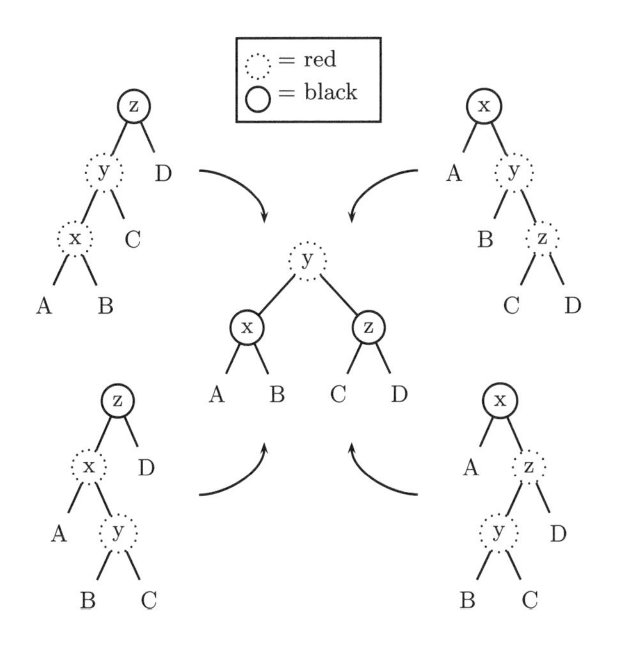

Figure 1: The four cases for balancing a red-black tree.

Next we color the new node. If we color it red, we risk violating the first color invariant. If we color it black, we risk violating the second color invariant. However, note that the first invariant is a local property and the second invariant is a global property. In the hope that a local property will be easier to fix than a global property, we color the new node red.

If the parent of the new node is also red, then we have violated the first color invariant and need to rearrange and recolor the tree to restore the invariant. This is where rotations are used in ordinary red-black trees. Instead of rotations we use the following balancing transformation:

> Take the red child, the red parent, and the (black) grandparent and locally balance these three nodes by making the smallest and largest nodes children of the middle node. Then color the middle node red and the other two nodes black. The middle node is linked back into the tree in place of the former black grandparent.

This balancing transformation is illustrated in Figure 1. Students find this picture satisfying because all four cases *look* like they are making the tree more balanced, whereas the usual pictures of left and right single rotations do not look like they are making any progress.

After the balancing transformation, we might still have a violation of the first color invariant, because the middle node, which is now red, might again have a red parent. However, note that the red-red violation is now closer to the root. By repeating the balancing transformation, we will eventually eliminate the red-red violation or reach the root. (It is worth exploring with students the consequences of trying the opposite color scheme in the balancing transformation, making the middle node black and the other two nodes red. What happens in that scheme is that the algorithm sometimes falls into an infinite loop, repeatedly rotating the same few nodes back and forth.)

```
-- a Tree node contains four fields:
--    Key, Color, Left, and Right

function Insert(K : Key, T : Tree) returns Tree is
   T := Ins(K, T)
   T.Color := BLACK  -- always recolor root black
   return T

function Ins(K : Key, T : Tree) returns Tree is
   if T = null then
      T := allocate a new Tree node
      T.Key := K
      T.Color := RED
      T.Left := null
      T.Right := null
   elseif K < T.Key then
      T.Left := ins(Key, T.Left)
   elseif K > T.Key then
      T.Right := ins(Key, T.Right)
   else return T  -- K is already in T

   -- check for red child and red grandchild
   if IsRed(T.Left) and IsRed(T.Left.Left) then
      T := Balance(T.Left.Left, T.Left, T,
                   T.Left.Left.Right, T.Left.Right)
   elseif IsRed(T.Left) and IsRed(T.Left.Right) then
      T := Balance(T.Left,T.Left.Right,T,
                   T.Left.Right.Left,T.Left.Right.Right)
   elseif IsRed(T.Right) and IsRed(T.Right.Left) then
      T := Balance(T, T.Right.Left, T.Right,
                   T.Right.Left.Left, T.Right.Left.Right)
   elseif IsRed(T.Right) and IsRed(T.Right.Right) then
      T := Balance(T, T.Right, T.Right.Right,
                   T.Right.Left, T.Right.Right.Left)
   return T

function Balance(X : Tree, Y : Tree, Z : Tree,
                 B : Tree, C : Tree) returns Tree is
   X.Right := B
   Y.Left  := X
   Y.Right := Z
   Z.Left  := C
   X.Color := BLACK
   Y.Color := RED
   Z.Color := BLACK
   return Y

function IsRed(T : Tree) returns Boolean is
   return T != null and T.Color = RED
```

Figure 2: Pseudocode for insertion into a red-black tree.

Notice that the first color invariant implies that the root must be black because it has no parent. If the root becomes red as a result of the balancing transformation, we simply color it black. In practice, it is easier to always color the root black than to check whether the root has become red. Pseudocode for the complete insertion algorithm is shown in Figure 2.

If you compare this code to a typical textbook presentation of red-black trees, such as [3], you will immediately be struck by how short this code is compared to an ordinary implementation. Most of this savings is from replacing the four separate kinds of rotations with a single transformation. In addition, ordinary implementations of red-black trees check whether the sibling of the red parent is also red. In such cases, these implementations recolor several of the nodes without rearranging them. Our implementation completely ignores the color of the sibling node, further reducing the amount of code required.

Although the resulting code is quite compact compared to other implementations, the density of the balancing code in the second half of the `Ins` function can be rather daunting at first glance. However, comparing the code side-by-side with the picture in Figure 1 makes it easy to sort out the `.Left`'s and `.Right`'s. Two more comments on this code are in order. First, the reason that we only check for red nodes in `Ins`, instead of also verifying that `T` is black, is that we are guaranteed that `T` is black if its child and grandchild are both red, because there will be at most one red node with a red parent at a time. Second, the reason we do not need to pass the A and D subtrees from Figure 1 into the `balance` function is that they are guaranteed to already be in the right places (to the left of X and the right of Z, respectively).

We omit the analysis showing that insertion into a red-black tree takes $O(\log N)$ time, because it is identical to the analysis for ordinary red-black trees, found in many textbooks [3, 9].

3. MAXIPHOBIC HEAPS

A common failing in the way we teach data structures and algorithms is presenting finished products rather than guiding students through the algorithmic design steps necessary to reach that product. For example, presentations of red-black trees (including our own!) commonly conjure the red-black invariants out of thin air. As a second example, consider leftist heaps [6]. Leftist heaps are simple to understand, simple to code, and simple to analyze, but students typically regard the leftist height invariant as "magic". They see how to proceed once they are given the height invariant, but do not see how they could have come up with the height invariant on their own. *Maxiphobic heaps* are an alternative to leftist heaps that retain the good qualities of leftist heap, but without the "magic".

Maxiphobic heaps, like leftist heaps, are a form of priority queue. Elements can be inserted into a heap, and the minimum element in a heap can be inspected or removed. In addition, two heaps can be merged into a single heap. Like leftist heaps, a maxiphobic heap is represented as a binary tree in *heap order*, meaning that the value at each node is never bigger than the values at any of its descendants. In addition, each node is annotated with the size of the subtree rooted at that node. Unlike leftist heaps, maxiphobic heaps place no restrictions on the shape of the binary tree—a maxiphobic heap can be arbitrarily unbalanced in any direction.

Except for merge, the operations on maxiphobic heaps are trivial. The minimum element in a heap-ordered tree is always the root, so to find the minimum element in a maxiphobic heap, we simply return the value at the root. To delete the minimum element, we simply delete the root and merge its two subtrees. To insert an element, we create a singleton tree containing the new element and merge it with the existing tree. Given the idea of heap-ordered trees and the existence of a merge function, students can readily come up with these algorithms on their own, although they may need a little coaxing to think of implementing insertion using merge.

Only the merge operation remains. To merge two maxiphobic heaps, we first compare their roots. The smaller root becomes the root of the combined tree. Now we reach the crucial step. Having decided on the new root, we next need to determine the two subtrees of the new root. However, we currently have three candidate subtrees vying for those two spots: the tree that lost the comparison of the roots and the two existing subtrees of the winning root. We must somehow reduce these three subtrees into two by (recursively) merging two of them together. But which two should we merge?

```
-- a Heap node contains four fields:
--   Value, Size, Left, and Right

function FindMin(H : Heap) returns Value is
   if H = null then error
   else return H.Value

function DeleteMin(H : Heap) returns Heap is
   if H = null then error
   else return Merge(H.Left, H.Right)

function Insert(V : Value, H : Heap) returns Heap is
   NewH := allocate a new Heap node
   NewH.Value := V
   NewH.Size  := 1
   NewH.Left  := null
   NewH.Right := null
   return Merge(H, NewH)

function Merge(H1 : Heap, H2 : Heap) returns Heap is
   if H1 = null then return H2
   if H2 = null then return H1

   -- force H1 to have smaller root
   if H2.Value < H1.Value then Swap(H1, H2)

   -- calculate size of merged tree
   H1.Size := Size(H1) + Size(H2)

   -- get the three subtrees
   A := H1.Left
   B := H1.Right
   C := H2

   -- force A to be biggest of the three subtrees
   if Size(B) > Size(A) then Swap(A,B)
   if Size(C) > Size(A) then Swap(A,C)

   -- rebuild tree
   H1.Left := A
   H1.Right := Merge(B, C)
   return H1

function Size(H : Heap) returns Integer is
   if H = null then return 0
   else return H.Size
```

Figure 3: Pseudocode for maxiphobic heaps.

Working through a few examples with trees of different sizes and shapes leads students to the following insight: we should always merge the two smallest of the three trees, leaving the largest of the three untouched (hence the name *maxiphobic*, meaning "biggest avoiding", although this name should probably not be introduced until after the students have had a chance to wrestle with the merge algorithm). A pseudocode implementation of maxiphobic heaps appears in Figure 3.

The key point here is that students can come up with this all-important design decision with only the gentlest of prodding from the instructor. They are left with a sense of empowerment, a feeling that they too are capable of *designing* data structures, rather than merely implementing somebody else's design. In comparison, the height invariant of leftist heaps is usually handed down by the instructor or textbook author without any insight into how or why Knuth came up with that invariant.[1] Students are passive spectators in the design process, rather than active participants.

After designing the merge algorithm with students, an easy analysis verifies that `merge` runs in $O(\log N)$ time, and therefore so do `insert` and `deleteMin`. For `merge`, N is the combined number of values in the two heaps being merged. Because the biggest of the three subtrees is avoided at each step, and that tree contains at least $(N-1)/3$ values, it is easy to see that

$$T(N) \leq T(2N/3) + O(1)$$

The solution to this recurrence relation is $O(\log_{3/2} N) = O(\log N)$.

Finally, note that "size" in maxiphobic heaps can be interpreted as either number of nodes or height of the tree. Either interpretation leads to a successful solution, so go with whichever one students come up with. The pseudocode in Figure 3 assumes a number-of-nodes interpretation, but changing to a height interpretation requires changing a single line of code (the size calculation of the merged tree in `merge`). Taking a number-of-nodes interpretation makes maxiphobic heaps similar to *weighted* leftist heaps [2], whereas a height interpretation makes them more similar to ordinary leftist heaps.

4. DISCUSSION

The data structures described in this paper offer several pedagogical advantages over their classical brethren. Our algorithm for insertion into red-black trees is significantly simpler than the usual insertion algorithms, so much so that implementing the insertion algorithm from scratch becomes a feasible task for a typical student. Our second data structure, maxiphobic heaps, offers greater insight into the design process than leftist heaps, without sacrificing simplicity in other areas. We believe that these alternatives could be seamlessly added to many instances of Data Structures (CS2) or Algorithms (CS7) courses, particularly those aimed at students of average or below average ability.

On the other hand, there may be some pedagogical disadvantages for courses aimed at highly talented students. Such a course might want to present deletion from red-black trees in addition to insertion. Our balancing transformation does not extend to deletion, so traditional rotation-based deletion algorithms would need to be used. If both insertion and deletion are to be presented, then it may be preferable to use traditional rotations for both.

For maxiphobic heaps, the elimination of the leftist height invariant may diminish the opportunity to impress upon top students the vital role of such invariants in the design of advanced data structures. If the design and use of such complex invariants is considered a significant objective, then leftist heaps may indeed be preferable, provided substantial attention is paid to the motivation and development of the height invariant.

5. SOURCE CODE

Source code for red-black trees and maxiphobic heaps in a variety of languages is available on the World Wide Web at the author's web site:
`http://www.eecs.usma.edu/personnel/okasaki/sigcse05/`

6. ACKNOWLEDGEMENTS

Thanks to Jean Blair and John Hill for their feedback on an earlier draft of this paper.

7. REFERENCES

[1] G. M. Adel'son-Vel'skiĭ and E. M. Landis. An algorithm for the organization of information. *Soviet Mathematics–Doklady*, 3(5):1259–1263, Sept. 1962. English translation of Russian orginal appearing in *Doklady Akademia Nauk SSSR*, 146:263-266.

[2] S. Cho and S. Sahni. Weight-biased leftist trees and modified skip lists. *ACM Journal of Experimental Algorithmics*, 1998. Article 2.

[3] T. H. Cormen, C. E. Leiserson, R. L. Rivest, and C. Stein. *Introduction to algorithms*. MIT Press, 2001.

[4] C. A. Crane. *Linear lists and priority queues as balanced binary trees*. PhD thesis, Computer Science Department, Stanford University, Feb. 1972. Available as STAN-CS-72-259.

[5] L. J. Guibas and R. Sedgewick. A dichromatic framework for balanced trees. In *IEEE Symposium on Foundations of Computer Science*, pages 8–21, Oct. 1978.

[6] D. E. Knuth. *Searching and Sorting*, volume 3 of *The Art of Computer Programming*. Addison-Wesley, 1973.

[7] C. Okasaki. Red-black trees in a functional setting. *Journal of Functional Programming*, 9(4):471–477, July 1999.

[8] C. Okasaki. *Fun with binary heap trees*, pages 1–16. Palgrave MacMillan, 2003.

[9] M. A. Weiss. *Data Structures & Algorithm Analysis in Java*. Addison-Wesley, 1998.

[1]Ironically, the original data structure by Crane [4] upon which Knuth based leftist heaps, was more similar to maxiphobic heaps, except that it avoided the bigger of the two subtrees of the winning root, even if the losing tree was bigger still.

Experiments with Balanced-Sample Binary Trees

G. Michael Barnes
Computer Science, CSUN
18111 Nordhoff St.
Northridge, CA. 91330-8281
(818) 677-2299
renzo@csun.edu

John Noga
Computer Science, CSUN
18111 Nordhoff St.
Northridge, CA. 91330-8281
(818) 677-6480
jnoga@csun.edu

Peter D. Smith
Computer Science, CSUCI
One University Drive
Camarillo, CA 93012
(805) 437-8882
peter.smith@csuci.edu

Jeff Wiegley
Computer Science, CSUN
18111 Nordhoff St.
Northridge, CA. 91330-8281
(818) 677-2038
jeffw@csun.edu

ABSTRACT

In this paper we propose using experiments with Balanced-Sample Binary Trees (BSBTrees) as assignments and lecture material in intermediate data structures courses (CS2/3). BSBTrees are composite data structures that have a temporarily constructed form that precedes their normal construction. We present them in the context of binary search trees. To do this we first investigate the retrieval properties of randomly generated binary search trees and show how temporary construction can improve both worst case and average case behavior. We provide a brief analysis of BSBTree performance and description of the classes that can be used for BSBTree implementation. Last we discuss the use of BSBTrees in CS2 and CS3 courses and a survey of student opinions about BSBTrees.

Categories and Subject Descriptors

E.1 [**Data Structures**]: Arrays, Trees; E.2 [**Data Storage Representation**]: Composite structures, Object representation

General Terms

Algorithms, Experimentation

Keywords

Binary tree, random binary tree, temporary construction, hybrid data structures, random sample, pedagogy, polymorphism

SIGCSE'05, February 23–27, 2005, St. Louis, Missouri, USA.

1. INTRODUCTION

Niklaus Wirth [11] aptly described approaches to solving problems in the title of his book, "Algorithms + Data Structures = Programs". In computing the solution to a problem there is a spectrum of possibilities ranging from a sequence of executable instructions (at the primarily computational end) to a retrieval from stored values (at the primarily data structures end). Generally, a more computational solution to a problem is preferred over a data structures approach. Computational solutions tend to be quicker and require less maintenance. Between the extreme approaches, we have hybrids such as Michie's memo functions [7] and hash tables with overflow lists. We propose an approach to retrieved value for which we use the term *temporarily constructed* (pre-processed) data structures. In a temporarily constructed approach, an initial small data structure is built first as a "working buffer" for the resultant data structure. The temporary data structure can be considered a sample, or an ideal (heuristic) precursor of the actual data structure.

In the next sections we describe our experiments, analysis, and implementation of temporarily constructed random binary search trees. We call this data structure balanced-sample binary trees (BSBTrees). We believe it to be more of an educational concept and exercise for students than a practical technique for professionals. Last we discuss how one might use BSBTrees in an intermediate data structures course (CS2/3). BSBTrees facilitate educational goals such as experimentation, time complexity trade-offs, Application Programming Interface (API) and non-web available solutions to assignments.

2. RANDOM BINARY SEARCH TREES

Consider a random binary search tree [2, 6], where we mean that the tree results from inserting a random (uniform) permutation of the elements. Note that because of the way that the trees are generated it is not the case that every possible shape of tree is equally likely.

We are interested in the worst case and average case behavior for retrievals represented by the number of key-key comparisons. Worst case is represented by the height of the tree. Gonnet and Baeza-Yates [3] report that the expected number of comparisons to retrieve an item from a random binary tree containing N nodes is approximately

$$1.3863 \log_2 N - 1.8456$$

We ran experiments using a reliable source of random bits [4] that we grouped into 32-bit integers. Using C++ we created random binary trees (700 for each value of N) and computed the average depth of a node (the average retrieval case) and the height of the tree. Table 2 shows results for relatively small values of N, which generally match the expected results quite well.

N	**Random Binary Tree**			**Balanced Binary Tree**	
	Worst Case	Average Case	Formula	Worst Case	Average Case
1	1.000	1.000	−1.846	1	1.000
3	2.672	1.891	0.352	2	1.667
7	4.679	2.930	2.046	3	2.429
15	6.820	4.069	3.571	4	3.267
31	9.148	5.303	5.022	5	4.161
63	11.626	6.613	6.441	6	5.095
127	14.195	7.950	7.843	7	6.055
255	16.757	9.292	9.237	8	7.031
511	19.448	10.663	10.627	9	8.018
1,023	22.118	12.031	12.015	10	9.010

Table 1: Retrieval Parameters of Random Trees

3. BALANCED-SAMPLE BINARY TREES

Sorting algorithms can be used to optimize binary trees [5]. We know that if we have all the data available in a buffer we can sort the buffer and build a balanced tree by adapting a binary search algorithm to select data for insertion. For large values of N, as in the case of records in a database, it is not practical to have a large temporary buffer to sort the keys. Suppose our buffer can hold only M items, (where $M < N$). In the case of a random binary tree, the first M items collected represents a sample from the population of the final tree's set of keys. By storing and sorting the first M items in a temporary buffer (*temporary construction*) we can construct an initially balanced tree from the sorted sample and discard the space used for the buffer. Subsequent insertions proceed straight to the tree in the usual way. It is this hybrid, temporarily constructed, data structure that we term a balanced-sample binary tree (BSBTree). Next we explore its behavior both experimentally and formally.

4. IMPLEMENTATION EXAMPLE

In an object-oriented environment we seek to hide implementation details from the user. The BSBTree would need to remember if it is in the temporary construction or normal construction phase. Figure 1 shows a UML-like representation for BSBTree simulation experiments. Table 2 briefly describes the 6 classes used in the implementation.

Class BSBTree contains methods for binary tree construction and manipulation. These methods are performed on an abstract BSBStore class. BSBPreTree and BSBPostTree extend BSBStore and define the actual binary tree methods invoked. The construction of a BSBTree actually constructs a BSBPreTree. Nodes are initially inserted into the temporarily constructed sample until the sort buffer is full. When the sort buffer is full, it is sorted, a BSBPostTree is constructed using the temporarily constructed tree's sort buffer, and the resulting balanced binary tree is returned. Thereafter BSBTree operations are performed on the post construction tree. Thus, from the driver program's (BSBTreeDemo) perspective the morphing of the temporarily constructed tree (a sort buffer) into the binary tree is transparent. All behaviors are requested via the BSBTree wrapper class for BSBStore and are handled polymorphically via the actual BSBStore subclass object. The Java source listing and HTML Java Documentation for this program is available on the WWW [1].

Node	attributes and methods for a binary tree node
BSBTree	wrapper class with attributes and methods for a BSBTree, actual tree is an instance of a BSBStore
BSBStore	abstract class with attributes and methods for BSBTree
BSBPreTree	temporarily constructed sample, representation of the BSBTree, a subclass of BSBStore
BSBPostTree	resulting binary tree built from the temporarily constructed sorted sample, a subclass of BSBStore
BSBTreeDemo	a "driver" class to build a random binary tree using a BSBTree

Table 2: BSBTree Class Description

5. EXPECTED BSBTREE PERFORMANCE

Consider the two parts of a BSBTree: (1) its initial balanced sample tree of M nodes, and (2) its random binary sub-trees built from the $M + 1$ to N insertions. Each of the $M + 1$ random binary sub-trees are expected to have $(N - M)/(M + 1)$ nodes. We are now going to attempt a more analytical expression of the performance of BSBTrees by comparing them with random binary search trees. Given a sequence of items we could create both a BSBTree and a random binary search tree. Picture both trees with the initial sample of M items colored blue and the remaining nodes green. Both trees will consist of 1 blue sub-tree and $M + 1$ sub-trees with green nodes. The ith green sub-tree

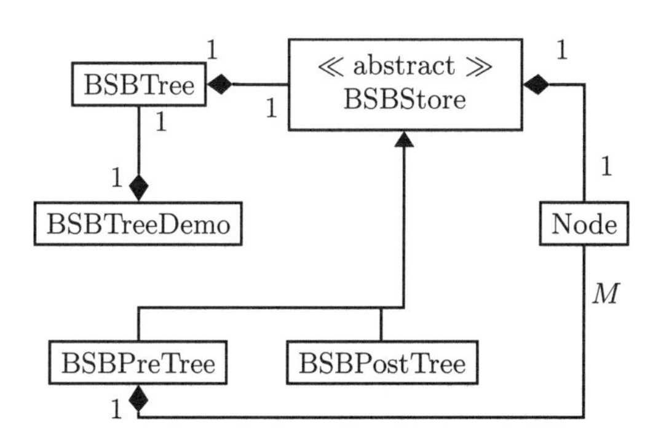

Figure 1: BSBTree Classes

in the BSBTree and the random binary search tree will be identical (both items contained and shape) because the ith sub-tree consists of items that are larger than i items in the sample, but not larger than $i+1$ items in the sample and these items will be inserted in the same order in both trees. In both trees the number of comparisons necessary to access an item can be decomposed into the comparisons with blue nodes and green nodes. The number of comparisons with green nodes will be the same for both trees. Therefore the difference will only be in the number of comparisons with blue nodes. The number of blue comparisons necessary to insert into the BSBTree is $\log_2(M+1)$ The expected number of blue comparisons necessary to insert the kth item into a randomly generated binary search tree satisfies the recurrence

$$C_k = 1 + \frac{1}{k(k-1)} \sum_{i=1}^{k-1} \left[iC_i + (k-i)C_{k-i} \right].$$

After solving the recurrence, it can be seen that the difference in the number of blue comparisons is

$$2 \sum_{i=1}^{M+1} \frac{1}{i} - 2 - \log_2(M+1) \approx 0.3863 \log_2(M+1) - 0.8456.$$

Therefore the expected number of comparisons needed to access an item is approximately:

$$1.3863 \log_2 N - 0.3863 \log_2(M+1) - 1.$$

Notice that the benefit of a BSBTree over a binary search tree is due entirely to the initial perfectly balanced insertion of the buffer. A similar argument can show that the expected depth of a BSBTree differs from a random binary search tree by a constant multiple of $\log_2(M+1)$. See [8] for details.

6. EXPERIMENTAL INVESTIGATION

Using Java we experimentally generated 30 trees without the initial sort (or, $M=1$) and then with the initial sort for various values of M and N. We used $N = 2^k - 1$, where k ranged from 5 to 23 in steps of 2. The key values in our trees ranged from 0 to $2^k - 1$. (N key values were placed in an array in sequential order and the array was randomly shuffled before iterating across the array to insert the N random keys.) We also used the first four values of N for M. Table 6 shows the percent reductions in the worst case and average case. For example, for $M = N = 2,047$ we create a completely balanced tree for the 2047 random keys and gain a 55.58% decrease in the height of a BSBTree relative to a random tree. The more interesting cases are where the ratio of M/N is small. For example BSBTrees built with 8,388,607 keys and a very small sample of 2,047 ($M = 0.000247N$) have a 11.12% improvement for average retrieval.

7. COURSE ASSIGNMENT

The application domain for BSBTrees in practical software development is not obvious. This in no way precludes the educational merit of BSBTrees, or other temporarily constructed data structures, in intermediate data structures courses (CS2/3). A series of related assignments to design, implement, and analyze BSBTrees allow students to focus on the use of abstract classes and polymorphism to hide

	M			
N	**31**	**127**	**511**	**2,047**
31	45.34 21.53			
127	16.58 14.31	50.69 23.83		
511	11.04 10.56	22.25 17.61	53.72 24.81	
2,047	8.08 8.35	15.71 13.97	26.45 19.67	55.58 25.41
8,191	6.30 6.79	12.37 11.52	20.06 16.27	30.21 21.06
32,767	7.03 6.75	10.58 10.77	16.68 14.54	23.52 18.57
131,071	6.04 5.13	8.52 8.08	12.72 11.59	19.09 15.24
524,287	3.18 3.74	7.35 7.02	11.86 10.14	16.31 13.26
2,097,151	3.90 3.62	6.78 6.24	10.06 8.86	14.64 11.81
8,388,607	3.59 3.43	6.11 6.08	9.08 8.50	12.67 11.12

Table 3: Percent Improvement (Worst/Average Case)

implementation of a hybrid data structure. In the first assignment an experimental framework could be developed to collect average and worst case retrieval statistics for random binary search trees (comparisons, execution time). This requires the use of random number sources and experimental design considerations (number of runs for each tree size). Lecture could discuss traditional alternative trees that improve performance like AVL and Red-Black trees. Lecture could then present BSBTrees as an experimental alternative. The second assignment would extend the first's experimental framework to run BSBTree experiments. The hypothesis that large samples would improve average retrieval could be tested in the third assignment. Lecture should discuss what constitutes a meaningful improvement and review time versus improvement tradeoffs. After each assignment is completed the analysis of expected results can be done in lecture or as homework and compared to the experimentally gathered values. Students can be challenged to consider application domains for BSBTrees or propose additional sample-assisted data structures that incorporate temporary construction. Last, the use of such assignments exposes students early to the discovery aspects of Computer Science: the search for new algorithms and problem domains.

8. ACTUAL CLASSROOM EXPERIENCE

During the 2003/2004 academic year BSBTrees were presented to two sections of CS2 and one section of CS3. The data structure itself was presented and explained in lecture and programming projects were assigned. In both cases, the programming project included both implementing the structure as well as testing performance. In the CS2 courses the BSBTrees were presented only as a modification of binary search trees because other tree balancing techniques are not generally covered in the course. The CS3 course covered BSBTrees in the context of a variety of tree balancing techniques. The actual programming projects assigned during the spring semester can be viewed at [9, 10].

8.1 CS2 OBSERVATIONS

Approximately four hours of class time was dedicated to covering binary search trees including approximately one hour on BSBTrees. An additional hour of laboratory time was spent describing implementation details of BSBTrees and the teaching assistant was available for questions and assistance for six more hours.

From the perspective of the professor, including BSBTrees in these sessions of CS2 had both positive features as well as some drawbacks.

The fact that the new data structure had significant similarities to simpler structures, already understood by the students, helped the students to cope with new or more complicated concepts by building on the foundation of knowledge they already possess. BSBTrees are effective in this manner, since they simply augment the already understood binary search tree data structure. This allows students to concentrate on project goals other than implementation complexities that would arise from a more complicated data structure such as Red Black or 2-3-4 Trees. Instead of implementation or theory complexities, the students are free to tackle concepts relating to investigation, analysis and comparison to expected results. These concepts might fail to be realized by students working on more complicated data structures where the majority of their effort was required and consumed by trying to cope with complex implementation theory and debugging.

For the vast majority of students, the topic of BSBTrees was at an appropriate level of difficulty. Nearly all students were eventually capable of understanding and performing the basic operations by hand. Although many students had some difficulty in implementing the data structure for the programming project, it was completed at roughly the same rate and level as the earlier projects. One aspect in particular that did cause difficulty was the recursive method to move the items from the initial buffer into a perfectly balanced binary search tree. The teaching assistant and professor needed to guide many students through designing this method multiple times. The difficulty seemed to be caused by the recursive nature of the method rather than any failure to understand the idea of moving from a buffer to the binary tree structure.

Once a student completed the programming portion of the project, he was to perform testing of performance of the data structure on a variety of data sets and values of M. Most students did not complete adequate performance testing of the structure. While this was not uncommon for some earlier projects, it seemed that the concept that the choice of buffer size presented a tradeoff was not clearly understood.

A problem which arises in teaching CS2 is that marginal students in the course often attempt to complete programming projects by finding code from the web or getting code from students who have completed the course in previous semesters. Obviously, this is ineffective when such code does not exist. Further, even though binary search tree code would greatly assist in completing the project, camouflaging the structure did lead to more code actually being written by students.

Another advantage of teaching BSBTrees was that students saw that analyzing the time complexity of various operations is neither a fixed procedure nor something that can only be done by appealing to a reference.

The main drawback of presenting a non-standard data structure was that some students, particularly those who are already not passing, make a variety of complaints. These complaints included statements that it is unfair to require this additional material ("my friend in the other section doesn't need to learn this"), that it forces attendance at class and labs ("I couldn't make it to class/lab that week, let me do something else"), and that the structure is unreasonably hard. While these concerns are fairly simple to address, they can provide classroom distractions and give a convenient excuse for some to avoid making an attempt.

Overall, the experience of teaching a non-standard data structure such as an BSBTree was a positive one.

8.2 CS3 OBSERVATIONS

When presenting this topic at the CS3 level more advanced concepts can be introduced and discussed. For example, the project specifications spoke of implementing an abstract, opaque associative map data structure. The project had the students implement a standard binary search tree, a red-black tree, and a BSBTree with the API for all implementations required to be the same. Similar to, but more advanced than the CS2 course, once the three implementations were completed the students were responsible for producing a methodical benchmark and graphical comparison of the performance of the implementations.

For these students several advanced concepts existed in this project that were important yet not concerned with the details of the theories of the trees. This project afforded the students the opportunity to learn the benefits of reusing and extending code. Students also found a project that could exhibit the benefits of designing and maintaining a common public API while being free to implement the desired API in a variety of methods ranging from simple, yet inefficient, to complex and efficient. The most significant concept was that the three different implementations allowed the students to benchmark and compare the performances of the three solutions and then to engage in investigation and draw conclusions about their results. This was far more successful than in the CS2 course.

For third semester programming students who have grown beyond the early difficulties of simply mastering syntax requirements and basic data structures, but have yet to master troubleshooting, problem solving and software architecture design issues, BSBTrees provided a good opportunity to exercise these skills.

Typical student projects suffer from being rather "artificial" in nature. They lack practical application or fail to reflect certain difficulties and requirements that students will face on real problems. For well understood textbook-type problems it is easy for students to obtain a full understanding of the problem and they can then predict expected results with accuracy. This artificiality and predictable nature of such projects can result in a lack of student motivation. Why should the task be attempted if it is never going to be useful and they already know what the answer is going to be? BSBTrees provided the students with a a problem were the answers were not easily predictable and students could engage in a more practical experimentation with the products they produced.

More complicated and efficient data structures exist that

do achieve significant performance increases compared to BSBTrees. The significant increase in complexity can equate to a significant obstacle to the students acceptance and understanding of the efficient data structure. Although BSBTrees are not as efficient, they are simpler and can be used effectively to provide students with a data point that encourages adoption of the more advanced and efficient solution. The BSBTree structure's simplicity and performance limitations can be used as a foundation on which to justify the need to develop an understanding of much more unintuitive and complicated structures such as Red Black Trees, AVL trees or B-Trees.

It should be noted that the open nature of the project specifications resulted in some unforeseen difficulties during the course of the project. Loose, poorly defined specifications resulted in several impasses for students. Although these difficulties often set the students back until the issue could be resolved in lecture it provided some benefits as well. These unexpected points allowed students to identify and deduce needs themselves and became material to instruct students on the importance of needs and requirements analysis. The downside to these unexpected events was that they impacted negatively on time and also interfered with students pursuit of the intended investigation as described earlier.

Lack of rigid, narrow project specification scope allowed for deviation in implementations. The differences between any two submissions was generally more diverse than for previous projects based on well understood and defined problems. This helped enrich the set of experimental results obtained by the class. The comparison of results amongst students allowed for a more free form investigation as to the cause of differences. Students were also able to share ideas and concepts without having to share source code.

Although the implementation details of the project were relatively simple it allowed students time to cope with unexpected behaviors and to investigate causes. Theoretical analysis of what the performance of BSBTrees should be when compared to binary search trees and red-black trees was discussed during lecture and provided a foundation for predicting expected results. The variety of implementations and design decisions however led to a wide variety of differences in the measured performances of these trees. Resulting graphs did not always match predicted expectations and comparison of graphs amongst different students revealed wide differences.

These results were excellent at allowing students the opportunity to learn about many external influences that they may not have understood otherwise. Influences such as garbage collection, virtual machine performance, memory issues, code optimization and benchmarking procedures were discussed and investigated as possible causes. In several cases the analysis of the resulting measured data led students to conclude that the outcome was a result of programming error and what the nature of that error might be based on the behavior witnessed. Analysis of measured data also provided students with ideas as to how their solutions could be improved or how external influences could be removed from the problem.

8.3 STUDENT OBSERVATIONS

Student feedback was directly solicited with a fourteen question survey of both courses. See [9] for complete results. For both courses, many of the questions resulted in very mixed results. Points that seemed to stand out were: experimentation can be a useful tool for understanding data structures, experimentation will be a recurring technique in computer science, and code for BSBTrees could not be found on the web. Surprisingly, despite the fact that CS2 students had more difficulty experimenting with the structure than CS3 students, they felt more strongly that experimentation was useful and would be required in future courses.

9. CONCLUSIONS

Even a modest buffer size (in comparison with the number of tree entries) can have a significant reduction in worst case and average case behavior for BSBTrees. In addition, temporarily constructed data structures are memory efficient. They can dispose of their temporarily constructed buffer once the initial sample has been obtained. Thereafter their memory requirements are equivalent to traditional data structures. They could be thought of as using "just-in-time" constructors. We have also demonstrated the use of simulation experiments to investigate the criteria of novel data structures in CS2/3 courses. Last we hope that readers will contribute additional ideas for temporary constructed data structures, investigate their application to problem domains and share their results.

10. REFERENCES

[1] Barnes, G. M. BSBTree source listing and JAVA™ documentation. http://www.csun.edu/~renzo/pub/BSBTree.html, September 2003.

[2] Devroye, L. A note on the height of binary search trees. *Journal of the ACM 33*, 3 (1986), 489–498.

[3] Gonnet, G. H., and Baeza-Yates, R. *Handbook of Data Structures and Algorithms in Pascal and C*, second ed. Addison-Wesley, 1991.

[4] Marsaglia, G. The marsaglia random number cd-rom with the diehard battery of tests of randomness. http://www.stat.fsu.edu/pub/diehard, 1995.

[5] Martin, W.A., and Ness, D.N. Optimizing binary trees grown with a sorting algorithm. *Communications of the ACM 15*, 2 (1972), 88–93.

[6] Martinez, C., and Roura, S. Randomized binary search trees. *Journal of the ACM 45*, 2 (1988), 288–323.

[7] Michie, D. 'Memo' functions and machine learning. *Nature 218* (1968), 19–22.

[8] Noga, J. Sbtree analysis. http://www.csun.edu/~jnoga/pub/BSBTrees.html, September 2003.

[9] Noga, J. Additional BSBTree content. http://www.csun.edu/~jnoga/pub/BSBTrees.html, May 2004.

[10] Wiegley, J. CS3 BSBTree project. http://www.csun.edu/~jnoga/pub/BSBTrees.html, May 2004.

[11] Wirth, N. *Algorithms + Data Structures = Programs*. Prentice-Hall, 1985.

Analyze *That*: Puzzles and Analysis of Algorithms

Anany Levitin
Department of Computing Sciences
Villanova University
Villanova, PA 19085
(610) 519-7349
anany.levitin@villanova.edu

ABSTRACT
The paper advocates a wider use of puzzles and puzzle-like games in teaching the analysis of algorithms. It discusses many specific examples—from classic puzzles of recreational mathematics to newly popular job interview brainteasers—which illustrate all major aspects of algorithm analysis.

Categories and Subject Descriptors
F.2.2 [**Analysis of Algorithms and Problem Complexity**]: Nonnumerical Algorithms and Problems

General Terms
Algorithms

Keywords
Puzzles, algorithm analysis, pedagogy

1. INTRODUCTION
The idea of using puzzles and puzzle-like games has a long tradition in mathematical undergraduate education (e.g., [1]). Computer science educators seem to have been less successful in this regard, even though a few puzzles such as the Tower of Hanoi have become a standard feature of programming textbooks. Recent years have witnessed a welcome change. Thus, Curzon [4] and Mitchell [19] have advocated using puzzles and games in introductory computing courses; many specific examples for doing this can be found in the *Colorful Challenges* column of the SIGCSE Bulletin and other papers by Ginat [10]. Hill et al. [12] and Huang [13] have described their experiences of using games in a variety of teaching situations; Ross [26] has shared his experience of using three well-known puzzles in a junior-level Java course. Levitin and Papalaskari [18] have found puzzles illustrating every major algorithm design technique of a new taxonomy [16]; many of these puzzles have been used in a recently published textbook on the design and analysis of algorithms [17].

SIGCSE'05, February 23-27, 2005, St. Louis, Missouri.

This paper advocates a wider use of puzzles and puzzle-like games in teaching the *analysis* of algorithms. It discusses many specific examples for all the major aspects of algorithm analysis, including efficiency determination techniques, invariants, and NP-hardness.

There are several advantages in using puzzles in teaching analysis of algorithms:

- Puzzles force students to think about algorithms on a more abstract level, divorced from programming and computer language minutiae.
- Puzzles show that algorithm design strategies can be looked upon as general problem-solving tools that might be useful in areas far removed from computer science.
- Solving puzzles helps in developing creativity and problem solving skills—the qualities any future CS professional should strive to acquire.
- Puzzles usually attract more interest on the part of students, making them work harder on the problems assigned to them.

In addition to these advantages of using puzzles in teaching algorithms, there are two other pertinent points that need to be made. First, following Microsoft's lead, more and more employers are making puzzles a standard component of their job interviews. This trend has been documented and discussed in two recent books [20], [23]. Whatever one thinks of the appropriateness of this interviewing practice, it is a fact of today's job-searching reality. Although training for interviews should arguably be the last goal of a college-level education, mentioning this practice might serve as an extra incentive for "practically oriented" students. Computer science educators should also welcome a by-product of this interviewing practice in the form of new sets of puzzles that are potentially much more useful for computer science education than many traditional puzzles of recreational mathematics. We will use one of these "new generation" puzzles in the next section and contrast it with a puzzle from one of the recreational mathematics classics.

Second, puzzles and puzzle-like games constitute a significant part of problems given in different programming contests. (For examples of such problems, see the book by Skiena and Revilla [28] who selected a sample from over 1,000 items at the Universitdad de Valladolid online judge, available at http://online-judge.uva.es.) Hence, using puzzles in algorithms courses can stimulate students' interest in participating in such competitions and serve as training material to prepare for them.

2. TWO EXAMPLES

Slightly different versions of the following problem are mentioned among examples of interview questions in both books [20] and [23] (see also [11]); it provides an excellent example of a puzzle that can be used for demonstrating several facets of an algorithm analysis:

You are at one end of a hallway lined with n *closed lockers. You will make n passes along the lockers returning to the starting point after each pass. On the first pass, you will open all the lockers. On the second pass, you will close every second locker. In general, on the* i*-th pass, you will toggle every* i*-th locker, i.e., open it if it was closed and close it if it was open. How many lockers will be open after pass* n*?*

What is so good about this puzzle? To begin with, it is neither trivial nor too difficult. Almost any student should be able to see, after tracing the algorithm on an instance of a small-to-moderate size, that the doors open after the last pass are in all the positions that are perfect squares between 1 and n. Nevertheless, many students, if our own experience can serve as a guide, may have trouble proving the correctness of this assertion. The proof, based on the observation that a positive integer has an odd number of divisors if and only if it is a perfect square, is actually not difficult, especially if the instructor chooses to provide an appropriate hint. Getting the closed-form answer, which is $\lfloor n \rfloor$, to the puzzle's question is elementary, although a few students may find it not immediately obvious.

Further, there are other instructive questions one can pose about this puzzle in an algorithms course. For example, find the asymptotic order of growth (or an approximate formula) for the number of open lockers if the pass directions alternate instead of always go from the first locker to the last one. Or find the asymptotic order of growth (or an approximate formula) for the total number of times all the locker doors are toggled. The last two questions make an important point that one should not always expect an exact answer in a nice closed form but rather should be prepared to use approximation formulas and empirical analysis.

Finally, the puzzle can be used as an excellent assignment for algorithm visualization. (To our surprise, we were unable to find its visualization on the Web.)

Unfortunately, examples of such ready-to-use puzzles appropriate for teaching algorithmics are relatively rare. Thousands of puzzles collected literally over centuries in books on recreational mathematics are often either hopelessly inapplicable or require a rework. For an example of the latter, consider the "Chickens in the Corn" puzzle by Sam Loyd [8]:

The game is played on an 8-by-8 checkerboard representing a cornfield, with two checkers of one color representing a farmer and his wife and two checkers of another color representing a rooster and a hen. On each move, a person and a chicken can move to a neighboring square, directly up and down or right and left but not diagonally. Starting with the positions indicated in Figure 1, *the man* (`M`) *and woman* (`W`) *each move one square, then each the rooster* (`r`) and the hen (h) *make a move. The play continues by turns until both chickens are captured. A capture occurs when the farmer or his wife can pounce on a square occupied by the chicken. The goal is to accomplish this task in a minimum number of moves.*

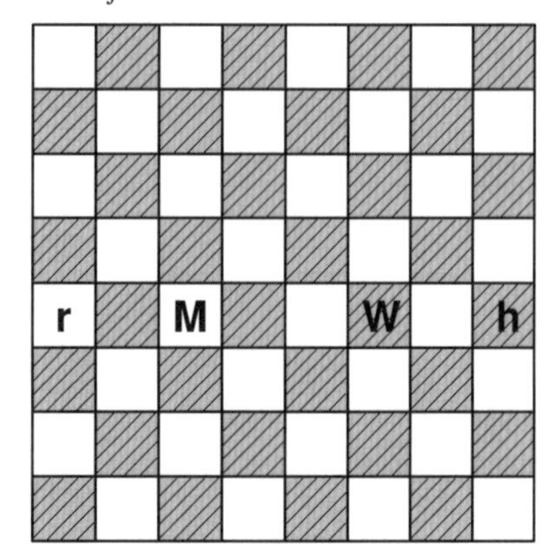

Figure 1. Board of the "Chickens in the Corn" puzzle

It does not take much effort to realize that the man (woman) cannot capture the rooster (hen) by himself (herself): A capture can only occur when they occupy two adjacent squares, which are always of the opposite colors. But they start from the same-color squares (see Figure 1), and this property remains valid after both make one and hence any finite number of moves. Of course, we could make both people go successfully for one of the chickens first, and then send one of them to capture the other chicken. If the birds do not cooperate in a fast capture, this algorithm would require the total of 27 moves of the people and the chickens, which is far from optimal. The optimal algorithm turns out to be making the man go for the hen and the woman go for the rooster; this will require a total of 17 one-piece moves. The solution is arguably ingenious and fun—Sam Loyd did not achieved world fame and posthumous appreciation for nothing—but it hardly makes an important algorithmic point in the clearest way possible.

In our view, it is more instructive to pose a similar problem with just one person and one chicken starting at two arbitrary non-adjacent squares. As mentioned above, for an instance of this problem to have a solution, with the person moving first, the person and the chicken must start at opposite–color squares. This condition is not only necessary but sufficient: A simple greedy algorithm that moves the person vertically (horizontally) towards the chicken if the row distance between them is larger (smaller) than the column distance pushes the non-cooperating chicken into a corner in a minimum number of moves.

In this form, the puzzle clearly illustrates several general points: the importance of identifying an appropriate invariant; the greedy strategy and worst-case analysis (in a non-traditional setting); the usefulness of the Manhattan distance for problems of this kind. And even after the critical insights have been reached, writing a general program implementing the algorithm makes a good assignment in its own right. The original version of the problem with two people and two birds can be added to the basic assignment as an enhancement.

3. PUZZLES AND ANALYSIS OF ALGORITHM EFFICIENCY

In the narrow sense, the analysis of an algorithm is usually understood as establishing the algorithm's efficiency, principally, its asymptotic efficiency class. The difference between the worst-, best-, and average-case efficiencies can be illustrated by the problem of selecting a matching pair of socks from a drawer containing $2n$ socks of two colors, say, n black and n brown. Another question of this type is identifying a fake among n given coins by the brute-force weighing of pairs of coins on a balance scale until the fake coin is found.

For nonrecursive algorithms, the principal tool of investigation is setting up a sum for the number of times the algorithm's basic operation is executed and then simplifying the sum by using standard summation formulas and rules. To train students' counting skills with a puzzle-like example, one can ask about the total number of distinct squares on an n-by-n chessboard. (Note that counting the number of rectangles is, in fact, a simpler problem with the immediate answer $C(n+1,2)^2$, which is the number of different ways to choose two horizontal and two vertical lines forming a rectangle; hence, it is inappropriate for our purposes.)

Here is another example from a recreational mathematics collection [7]: *How many one-by-one squares will be generated by the algorithm that starts with a single square and, on each iteration, adds new squares all around the outside*? (In the parlance of cellular automata theory, the answer is the number of cells in the von Neumann neighborhood of range n.) The results for n = 0, 1, 2, and 3 are illustrated in Figure 2.

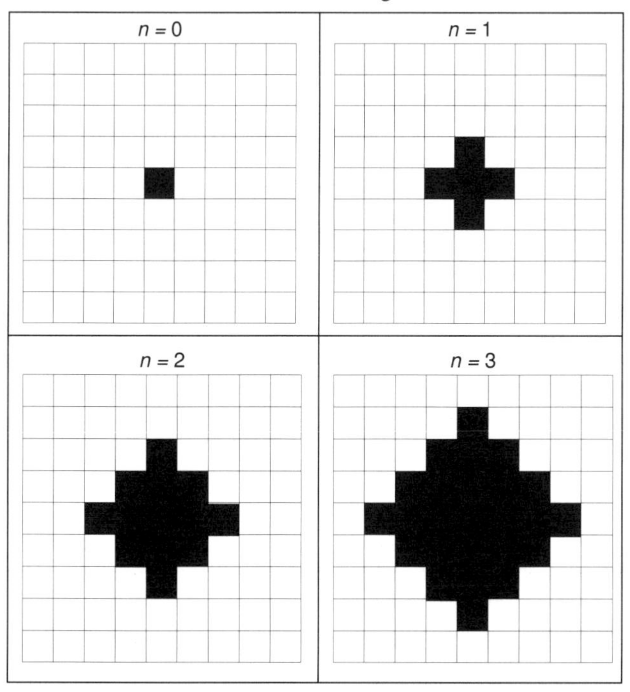

Figure 2. Von Neumann's neighborhood of range n = 0, 1, 2, 3

The answer $2n^2+2n+1$ can be obtained either by a straightforward evaluation of the sum

$$2\sum_{i=1}^{n}(2i-1)+(2n+1)$$

or by solving the recurrence relation

$$S(n) = S(n\text{-}1) + 4n \text{ for } n>0,\ S(0) = 1.$$

(One can also get the closed-form answer by noting that the cells on the alternating diagonals of the von Neumann neighborhood of range n compose two squares of sizes n+1 and n, respectively.)

Here is another example from the same collection [7], generalized for an input of an arbitrary size. It has an obvious similarity with efficiency investigation of insertion sort:

You have a row of 2n *discs of two colors, dark and light. They alternate: dark, light, dark, light, and so on. You want to get all the dark discs to the right-hand end, and all the light discs to the left end* (see Figure 3). *The only moves you are allowed to make are those which interchange the positions of two neighboring discs. How many moves does it take?*

Figure 3. Alternating discs puzzle

The principal tool for investigating recursive algorithms—recurrence relations—can be illustrated by several puzzles. The standard workhorse here is arguably the Tower of Hanoi. Its main advantages are familiarity to students after a typical introductory course and the lack of ceiling and floor roundoffs in the recurrence. On the downside, its recurrence is not the easiest for a novice to solve. The simplest alternative is, probably, the following classic ferrying puzzle:

A detachment of n *soldiers must cross a wide and deep river with no bridge in sight. They notice two boys playing in a rowboat by the shore. The boat is so tiny, however, that it can only hold two boys or one soldier. How can the soldiers get across the river and leave the boys in joint possession of the boat? How many times does the boat need to pass from shore to shore?*

The following interesting puzzle from one of Martin Gardner's collections [9], which seems to be not widely known, leads to a recurrence of a rather rare decrease-by-two type.

There are n *pairs of glasses standing next to each other in a row, the first* n *of them are filled with wine, while the remaining* n *of them are empty* (see Figure 4) . *Make them alternate in the filled-empty-filled-empty and so on pattern with the minimum number of glass moves.*

Figure 4. Alternating glasses puzzle

(Note that the puzzle has a "gotcha" element: we can solve the instance of size n = 3 in one pouring, which can be considered being just one "move." As an excuse, this also provides an opportunity to stress the importance of deciding exactly what constitutes the basic operation of the algorithm in question.)

The binary-search like recurrences can be introduced or reinforced by 20 questions, the classic game of "guessing" a number selected from the first n positive integers. Alternatively, one can use the problem of identifying a lighter counterfeit coin with a balance scale. The latter problem has a pedagogical advantage in leading naturally to two algorithms based on dividing the coins into two and three groups, respectively.

After excluding binary-search like algorithms as examples of the decrease-by-a-constant-factor paradigm rather than degenerative cases of divide-and-conquer [16, 17], we are left with surprisingly few examples of puzzles to illustrate a divide-and-conquer recurrence. One such example is the nuts-and-bolts problem [25]. The perfect divide-and-conquer example of tiling with trominoes a 2^n-by-2^n chessboard with one missing square [21] can also be used for the efficiency analysis demonstration, with the caveat that the number of the algorithm's steps can be obtained directly by counting the number of tiles required, which is obviously equal to $(4^n - 1)/3$.

As to Fibonacci-type recurrences, there are about two dozen puzzle-like questions leading to them in a nice collection on Ron Knott's website [15]. A majority of them are questions about the number of solutions in a problem such as the following one:

Find the number of different ways to climb an n-*stage staircase when each step is either one or two stages.*

The other type of problem with an algorithm analysis flavor mimics the seminal one by Fibonacci about the size of a rabbit population.

Finally, puzzles and puzzle-like games can be used as projects involving an algorithm timing and empirical investigation of relative efficiency of several algorithms for the same problem. A very good example of such a project is to compare empirically the exhaustive search algorithm for finding a magic square of order n with more efficient algorithms for the task (see, e.g., [22]). Puzzles can also be used to demonstrate the usefulness of algorithm visualization. As we already pointed out in Section 2, the locker doors puzzle provides an excellent vehicle for making this point.

All the previous examples dealt with the so-called upper-bound analysis of algorithm efficiency. Typically, a much more difficult task is lower-bound analysis, which seeks to establish a meaningful lower bound on the amount of work any algorithm solving the problem must perform. There are two major methods for establishing nontrivial lower bounds: information-theoretic arguments (usually implemented via decision trees) and adversary arguments. Several textbooks (e.g., [3], [17]) have used different versions of the fake-coin problem to illustrate the usefulness of decision trees for finding both a lower bound and an optimal weighing algorithm. Shasha [27] has an interesting but difficult variation of the fake-coin problem that uses a scale rather than a balance for identifying possible fake coins. As to the adversary argument method, the game of 20 questions has provided textbook writers with an ideal vehicle to introduce this method in a simple setting.

A closely related issue is that of algorithm optimality: when an algorithm performs the minimal amount of work needed to solve the problem in question, the algorithm is obviously optimal in terms of its efficiency. The classic recursive algorithm for the Tower-of-Hanoi puzzle and the insertion sort like algorithm for the alternating discs puzzle (Figure 3) can be used as good illustrations. The chocolate bar puzzle, asking to break an n-by-m chocolate bar into 1-by-1 squares with the minimum number of breaks, makes the same point but in a rather exotic fashion: any algorithm requires nm-1 breaks.

4. INSOLVABILITY AND INTRACTABILITY

Most problems encountered by students in courses on data structures and algorithms have a solution. Two prominent exceptions are the notions of Eulerian and Hamiltonian cycles and paths, which, of course, were introduced as puzzles by their discoverers. We believe it is important to stress the point that there are discrete problems that do not have a solution for all or some of their instances. Puzzles provide natural examples of both kinds. Probably, the most well-known of them are Sam Loyd's Fifteen and covering with dominoes a chessboard missing two opposite-end squares of its main diagonal. Several other examples exploiting invariance and parity can be found on Alexander Bogomolny's website [2]; these examples are supported by attractive applets and detailed discussions. The modification of the "Chickens in the Corn" puzzle, which we suggested in Section 2, provides yet another example of this kind.

If a problem has an algorithmic solution, we are usually interested whether it can be obtained in polynomial time. It should be noted that many classic examples of NP-hard problems such as the traveling salesman, knapsack, and bin packing have a definite puzzle flavor. Computational complexity of puzzles has been studied as a special subarea of algorithmic combinatorial game theory. Demaine [5] and Eppstein [6] provide good surveys of the field. Its recent achievements include establishing NP-completeness of several popular puzzle-like games such as tetris (in its offline version) and minesweeper. Richard Kaye's informal talk [14] about his proof of the latter result is highly recommended as a resource for teaching the difficult topic of NP-completeness.

5. CONCLUSION

Puzzles and puzzle-like games can be very helpful for teaching different aspects of algorithmics. In this paper, we pointed out and discussed about two dozen examples that can be used for illustrating general techniques of algorithm analysis. We hope that the paper will encourage more people to search for other examples of puzzles suitable for teaching algorithmics. Among other benefits, such a search could provide a natural way to involve undergraduate students in research-related activities in computer science. (For a successful example of such an effort see the paper about two classic puzzles by David Singmaster and one of his students, Ian Pressman [24].)

6. REFERENCES

[1] Averbach, B. and Chein, O. Mathematics: Problem Solving Through Recreational Mathematics. W.H.Freeman, San Francisco CA, 1980.

[2] Bogomolny, A. Mathematical Miscellany and Puzzles. http://www.cut-the-knot.org.

[3] Brassard, G. and Bratley, P. Fundamental of Algorithmics. Prentice-Hall, Englewood Cliffs NJ, 1996.

[4] Curzon, P. Computing Without Computers, draft of a book, 2001.

[5] Demaine, E. Playing games with algorithms: Algorithmic combinatorial game theory. in Proceedings of MFCS '01 (Marianske Lazne, Czech Republic, August 2001), Lecture Notes in Computer Science, vol. 2136, Springer, 18-32.

[6] Eppstein, D. Computational Complexity of Games and Puzzles. http://www.ics.uci.edu/~eppstein/cgt/hard.html#sok

[7] Gardiner, A. Mathematical Puzzling. Dover, Mineola NY, 1999.

[8] Gardner, M., ed. Mathematical Puzzles of Sam Loyd. Dover, New York NY, 1959.

[9] Gardner, M. aha! Insight. Scientific American/ W.H.Freeman and Co., New York NY, 1978.

[10] Ginat, D. http://www.tau.ac.il/education/homepg/ginat.html

[11] Ginat, D. Efficiency of algorithms for programming beginners. in Proceedings of SIGCSE '96 (Philadelphia PA, February 1996), ACM Press, 256-260.

[12] Hill, J.M.D. et al. Puzzles and games: addressing different learning styles in teaching operating systems concepts. in Proceedings of SIGCSE '03 (Reno NV, February 2003), ACM Press, 182-186.

[13] Huang, T. Strategy game programming projects. JCSC, vol. 16, no. 4, 2001, 205-213.

[14] Kaye, R. W. How complicated is minesweeper? http://web.mat.bham.ac.uk/R.W.Kaye/minesw/ASE2003.pdf

[15] Knott, R. Fibonacci Numbers and the Golden Section. http://www.mcs.surrey.ac.uk/Personal/R.Knott/Fibonacci.

[16] Levitin, A. Do we teach the right algorithm design techniques? in Proceedings of SIGCSE '99 (New Orleans LA, March 1999), ACM Press, 179-183.

[17] Levitin, A. Introduction to the Design and Analysis of Algorithms. Addison-Wesley, Boston MA, 2002.

[18] Levitin, A. and Papalaskari, M-A. Using puzzles in teaching algorithms. in Proceedings of SIGCSE '02 (Northern Kentucky, March 2002), ACM Press, 292-296.

[19] Mitchell, W. Another look at CS0. JCSC, vol. 17, no. 1, 2001, 194-205.

[20] Mongan, J. and Suojanen, N. Programming Interviews Exposed, Wiley, New York NY, 2000.

[21] Parberry, I. Problems on Algorithms. Prentice-Hall, Englewood Cliffs NJ, 1995.

[22] Pickover, C.A. The Zen of Magic Squares, Circles, and Stars: An Exhibition of Surprising Structures Across Dimensions. Princeton University Press, Princeton NJ, 2002.

[23] Poundstone, W. How Would You Move Mount Fuji? Little, Brown and Company, Boston MA, 2003.

[24] Pressman, I., and Singmaster, D. The jealous husbands and the missionaries and cannibals. Math. Gazette, vol. 73, no. 464 (June 1989), 73-81.

[25] Rawlins, G.J.E. Compared to What? An Introduction to the Analysis of Algorithms. Computer Science Press, New York NY, 1991.

[26] Ross, J. M. Guiding students through programming puzzles: value and examples of Java game assignments. SIGCSE Bulletin, vol. 34, no. 4, 2002, 94-98.

[27] Shasha, D. Codes, Puzzles, and Conspiracy. W.H.Freeman, New York NY, 1992.

[28] Skiena, S.S., and Revilla, M.A. Programming Challenges: the Programming Contest Training Manual. Springer, 2003.

RAPTOR: A Visual Programming Environment for Teaching Algorithmic Problem Solving

Martin C. Carlisle, Terry A. Wilson[1], Jeffrey W. Humphries, Steven M. Hadfield
United States Air Force Academy
Department of Computer Science
2354 Fairchild Dr, Suite 6G149
USAFA, CO 80840-6234
{Martin.Carlisle,Jeffrey.Humphries,Steven.Hadfield}@usafa.af.mil

ABSTRACT

When students are learning to develop algorithms, they very often spend more time dealing with issues of syntax rather than solving the problem. Additionally, the textual nature of most programming environments works against the learning style of the majority of students. RAPTOR is a visual programming environment, designed specifically to help students envision their algorithms and avoid syntactic baggage. RAPTOR programs are created visually and can be executed visually by tracing the execution through the program. Required syntax is kept to a minimum. Students preferred expressing their algorithms visually, and were more successful creating algorithms using RAPTOR than using a traditional language or writing flowcharts.

Categories and Subject Descriptors

D.1.7 [**Visual Programming**]

General Terms

Languages, Algorithms.

Keywords

Visual Programming, Programming Environments, Problem Solving, Flowcharts.

1. INTRODUCTION

Shackelford and LeBlanc [8] previously observed that the use of a particular programming language in an introduction to computing course tends to "annoy and distract attention from the core issue of algorithmic problem solving." In our experience, it also distracts attention from the teaching of algorithmic problem solving. Instructors spend class time where they expect students to have the most difficulty. Consequently, they often focus on syntactic difficulties that they expect students will encounter (e.g. the inappropriate use of "=" instead of "==" in C-based languages, or the improper placement of a semicolon).

[1]Work performed while this author was a member of the faculty at the US Air Force Academy. Current address: ATR Technology Division AFRL/SNAR; Wright Patterson Air Force Base, Ohio; Terry.Wilson@wpafb.af.mil.

SIGCSE'05, February 23–27, 2005, St. Louis, Missouri, USA.
ACM 1-58113-997-7/05/0002.

Furthermore, Felder [2] notes that most students are visual learners and that instructors tend to present information verbally. Studies [6,10] estimate that between 75% and 83% of our students are visual learners. Because of their highly textual rather than visual nature, the use of either traditional programming languages or pseudo-code provides a counter-intuitive framework for expressing algorithms to the majority of our students.

We designed RAPTOR, the Rapid Algorithmic Prototyping Tool for Ordered Reasoning, specifically to address the shortcomings of syntactic difficulties and non-visual environments. RAPTOR allows students to create algorithms by combining basic graphical symbols. Students can then run their algorithms in the environment, either step-by-step or in continuous play mode. The environment visually displays the location of the currently executing symbol, as well as the contents of all variables. Also, RAPTOR provides a simple graphics library, based on AdaGraph [11]. Not only can the students create algorithms visually, but also the problems they solve can be visual.

We teach an "Introduction to Computing" course that is required for all students. Previously, the twelve hour algorithms block of this course was taught in Ada 95 or MATLAB. Beginning in the summer of 2003, we taught the same course using RAPTOR. On the final exam, we tracked three questions that required the students to develop algorithms. The students were allowed to use any method to express their algorithm (Ada, MATLAB, flowcharts, etc.) Given this choice, students preferred a visual representation, and those taught using RAPTOR performed better in general.

2. RELATED WORK

Within the context of End User Development, Fischer, Giaccardi, Ye, Sutcliffe, and Mehandjiev [5] implore the benefits of graphical languages over textual ones by stating:

> "Text-based languages tend to be more complex because the syntax and lexicon (terminology) must be learned from scratch, as with any human language. Consequently, languages designed specifically for end users represent the programmable world as graphical metaphors containing agents that can be instructed to behave by condition-action rules. The aim is to reduce the cognitive burden of learning by shrinking the conceptual distance between actions in the real world and programming." [5]

Indeed, IBM has endorsed the importance of visual programming environments for end users by their use of a flowchart-based development environment within their WebSphere product [7].

Tia Watts [12] developed SFC, a structured flowchart editor. SFC allows the user to develop a flowchart, and always displays a textual representation of the flowchart in either a C or Pascal-like syntax. The user is then required to copy and paste the textual representation into a text editor and make changes to get a complete program.

Calloni and Bagert [1] developed an iconic programming language, BACCII++, which they used as a supplement to C++ in their CS1/CS2 sequence. Their experiments showed that students using both BACCII++ and C++ performed better than those using only C++. Once the program is developed, the user can generate code for any one of five text-based languages (including Pascal and C++).

The FLINT program [3,13] eliminates the shortcoming of having to debug the textual code. Using FLINT, students create a top-down decomposition of their program, and then design flowcharts for each subgoal. These flowcharts are executed within FLINT. This forces the students into a waterfall model [9] of software engineering, whereas students may have more success with a more incremental or spiral approach.

Visual Logic [14] is a follow-on project to FLINT designed for CS 1 before transitioning to Visual Basic. It abandons the waterfall model of programming, and adds support for one-dimensional arrays and turtle graphics.

The combination of RAPTOR features makes it a superior teaching tool compared to these predecessors. RAPTOR enables students to execute their algorithms within the environment, rather than having to separately compile and execute their programs. This means that debugging can be done on the visual representation of the algorithm, rather than the textual one and prevents having to use multiple tools. RAPTOR does not force top-down decomposition, on the student, instead allowing the student to develop his or her code incrementally. Furthermore, RAPTOR adds one and two-dimensional arrays, files, strings and a more sophisticated graphics library allowing user interaction. Students are therefore able to create more interesting programs than with the previous tools.

3. DESCRIPTION OF RAPTOR

RAPTOR is written in a combination of Ada, C# and C++, and runs in the .NET Framework. RAPTOR begins by opening a blank workspace with a start and end symbol. The user can then add symbols corresponding to loops, selections, procedure calls, assignments, inputs and outputs by selecting from the palette in the upper left corner and then inserting at an appropriate point in the program (see Figure 1).

RAPTOR programs are forced to be structured. Selections and loops must be properly nested, and each loop has a single exit point. Loops, however, allow the exit condition to be tested at any point inside the loop body. The student may select to use a pre-test, mid-test, or post-test loop simply by adding symbols before and/or after the loop test. Additionally, the loop structure more closely follows the loop/exit-when structure of Ada, rather than the while loop, as beginning students more naturally express positive logic (when the loop should exit) rather than negative logic (when the loop should keep going) [4].

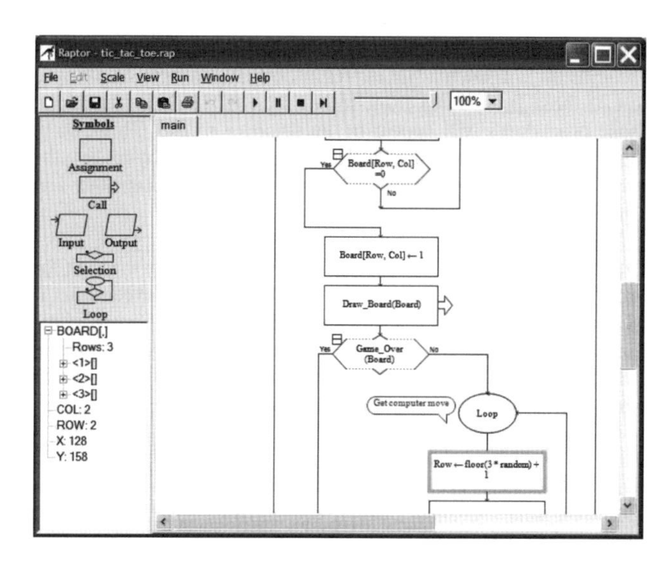

Figure 1: RAPTOR in action.

The syntax used within a symbol is designed to be flexible. Elements have been borrowed from both C and Pascal-style languages. For example, either "**" or "^" may be used as an exponentiation operation, and "&&" or "and" may be used as a Boolean "and" operator. RAPTOR enforces syntax checking on each symbol as it is edited. Therefore, it is impossible to create a syntactically invalid program. If the user enters "x+" as the right hand side of an assignment, they will get an error message and be required to fix the arithmetic expression before leaving the assignment box.

Commenting is done by right-clicking on a symbol and selecting "comment". The comment appears as a "talking bubble" next to the symbol. The comments can be clicked and dragged to improve the aesthetic of the program.

RAPTOR has over 40 built-in functions and procedures which allow the student to generate random numbers, perform trigonometric computations, draw graphics (including circles, boxes, lines, etc.), and interface with pointing devices. As seen in Figure 2, RAPTOR will automatically suggest completions to procedure names.

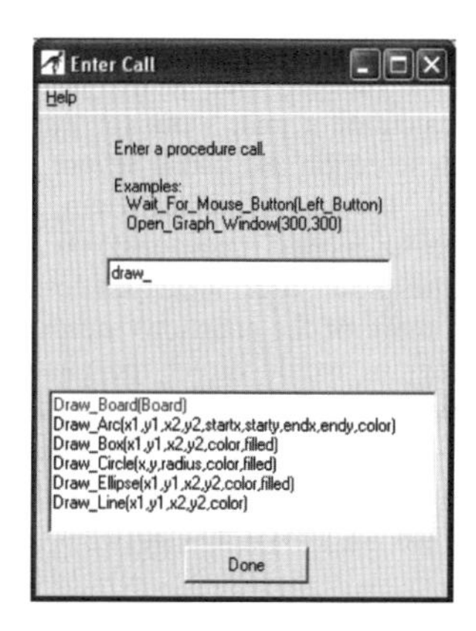

Figure 2: Entering a procedure call.

In addition, RAPTOR will automatically search the current folder for an instructor provided dynamically linked library named "plugins.dll". If such a file is present, the student will be allowed to call those procedures from within the RAPTOR program, and those procedures will appear in the suggestion list. This allows the instructor to create more interesting assignments by raising the level of abstraction. In Figure 2, "Draw_Board" is from the Tic-Tac-Toe sample plug-in.

During execution, the student can select to single step through the program, or run continuously. The speed of execution is adjustable by moving the slider shown at the top of Figure 1. At each step, the currently executing symbol is shown in green. Additionally, the state of all of the variables is shown in a watch window at the bottom left corner of the screen.

4. EXPERIMENTAL RESULTS

The two primary goals of developing and using RAPTOR were to improve student problem solving skills while reducing the syntactical burden inherent in most programming languages. In order to initially assess the achievement of the goal of improving student problem solving skills, we compared the results of three algorithmic design questions on the final exam across the Spring 2003, Fall 2003, and Spring 2004 offerings of our "Introduction to Computing" course, which is required of all students. Final exams are never returned to the students, which helps avoid any effects related to question reuse. The Spring 2003 offering consisted of 365 students with 15 classes using Ada and 4 classes using MATLAB. For the Fall 2003 offering, there were 530 students and RAPTOR was used as the programming language. The Spring 2004 offering consisted of 429 students.

The three final exam questions used for the comparison involved a brief problem statement tasking the students to write an algorithm to solve the problem. The first question asked the students to write an algorithm that would get three numbers from the user and print the numbers starting with the first number through the second number but excluding the third number. Examples of special cases were provided for clarification. For the Spring offering, students could express their algorithms in either a flowchart, Ada, or MATLAB with about 95% choosing to use flowcharts. RAPTOR was the only option provided for the Fall 2003 and Spring 2004 offerings. The second question had a bowling theme testing loops and accumulators. The user would enter the scores for a team of four bowlers playing three games. The program would validate each score, re-prompt on invalid scores, and then calculate a total score for the team. The third question dealt with selection and had a Severe Acute Respiratory Syndrome (SARS) theme. The program asked an airline passenger four health-related questions; one was their body temperature and the other three were yes/no questions. If the answers to two or more of the questions indicated the possibility of SARS, the program would direct the passenger for further examination otherwise it would release the passenger to board the aircraft. For both the bowling and SARS questions, the Spring 2003 offering allowed the solution to be expressed in either Ada or MATLAB and the Fall 2003 and Spring 2004 offerings used RAPTOR.

The results of the final exam questions comparison is shown in Figure 3. In all but one case, the students taught with RAPTOR performed better than the students taught using Ada or MATLAB.

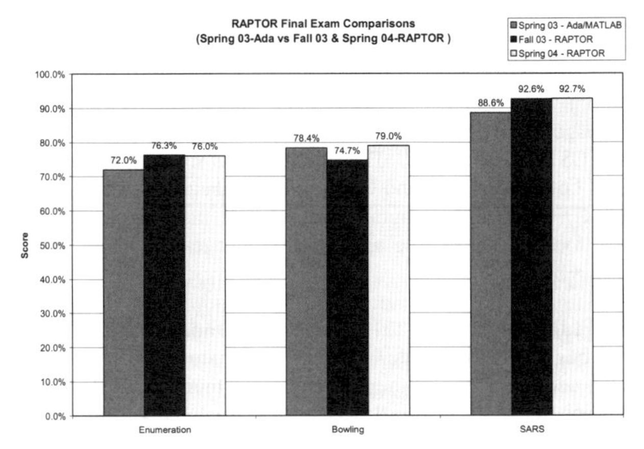

Figure 3: RAPTOR Final Exam Comparison Results

Both one-sided and two-sided, two-sample T-tests were conducted on the results. The null hypothesis for the one sided tests was that the mean for students using RAPTOR was less than or equal to the mean of the students using Ada or MATLAB. For the two-sided tests, the null hypothesis was that the means would be equal. The results of these tests are shown in Table 1. The results indicate statistically significant increases in performance on both the Enumeration and SARS questions when using RAPTOR. The Bowling questions results were less clear cut. For Spring 2003 versus Fall 2003, there was actually a statistically significant decrease when using RAPTOR. The Spring 2003 versus Spring 2004 results showed a slight increased performance when using RAPTOR but it was far from statistically significant. We attribute this lack of increased performance with RAPTOR on the bowling questions to be due to the fact that arrays in RAPTOR are implicitly declared and hence less obvious to the students. In addition, the programming assignment for arrays during the Fall 2003 was far more challenging than the other semesters. We consider it likely that the students in the Fall 2003 semester were confused about arrays due to the complexity of the assignment and hence performed poorly on the array algorithm during the final exam.

Table 1: RAPTOR Final Exam Comparison Statistics

	Spr 03 Average	Fall 03 Average	1-Tailed Significance	2-Tailed Significance
Enumera.	72.0%	76.3%	99.79%	99.57%
Bowling	78.4%	74.7%	97.44%	94.88%
SARS	88.6%	92.6%	99.96%	99.92%
GPA	2.84	2.93		
	Spr 03 Average	Spr 04 Average	1-Tailed Significance	2-Tailed Significance
Enumera.	72.0%	76.0%	98.61%	97.23%
Bowling	78.4%	79.0%	63.74%	27.48%
SARS	88.6%	92.7%	99.97%	99.95%
GPA	2.84	2.87		

Also of note was an observation by the graders of the final exams that student's algorithms from the Fall 2003 and Spring 2004 offerings tended to be much more structured and hence were much easier to read and evaluate. This was attributed to the structured manner in which RAPTOR programs must be constructed using the six primitives provided in the programming environment.

In order to assess the ease-of-use goal, we made use of a survey administered to the Fall 2003 and Spring 2004 students. The survey consisted of nine questions each with a seven-point Likert scale (1-Strongly Disagree..4-Neutral..7-Strongly Agree). Table 2 shows the questions and the average scores.

The survey questions and the Fall 2003 and Spring 2004 results are reported on Table 2 below. The results are also shown graphically in Figure 4. All of the questions except for #7 on their enjoyment of using RAPTOR resulted in average responses that were above the neutral rating of 4.0. Students have traditionally rated the programming section as their least favorite portion of the course.

Unfortunately, we did not have a baseline survey from the Spring 2003 offering using Ada and MATLAB for comparison. However, we were encouraged by these results and have since implemented a number of additional ease-of-use features including most of the suggestions provided by students on the narrative portion of the surveys.

Table 2: RAPTOR Survey Results

Survey Question	Fall 2003 Avg	Spring 2004 Avg
1) I had few problems learning how to use RAPTOR to create my programs.	4.68	4.33
2) I had few problems getting my programs to run once I had created them.	4.56	4.27
3) I found the Help System in RAPTOR to be useful.	4.56	4.51
4) I used the Help System in RAPTOR frequently.	4.37	4.57
5) RAPTOR helped me to develop and improve my problem solving skills.	4.96	4.39
6) RAPTOR helped me to better understand how computer programs operate.	5.13	4.50
7) I enjoyed programming in RAPTOR.	3.77	3.40
8) Being able to view the contents of variables helped me to test and debug my programs.	5.42	4.90
9) My teacher gave me enough instruction on using RAPTOR so that I could use it effectively to create programs.	5.01	4.55

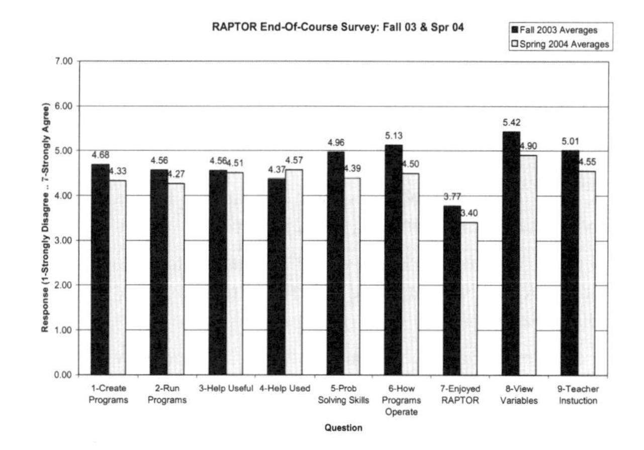

Figure 4: RAPTOR End-Of-Course Survey Results

5. FUTURE WORK

In the upcoming semesters, we plan to further experiment with using RAPTOR to teach algorithmic programming by refining and expanding the programming assignments that we give to our students as well as enhancing the manners in which we teach our students to use RAPTOR. Of particular attention will be the issue of teaching and using arrays in RAPTOR as the final exam results indicated this to be an area for improvement. In addition, we will continue to modify and improve the RAPTOR environment with richer sets of available functions and procedures, enhanced Help facilities, and other ideas to be gleaned from user feedback.

6. CONCLUSIONS

RAPTOR provides a simple environment for students to experiment with developing algorithms. Instructors can customize the environment and facilitate more interesting exercises by adding to the built-in procedures.

Students, when given a choice, overwhelming prefer to express their algorithms visually. Even when primarily taught a third generation programming language, 95% of students chose instead to use a flowchart on the final exam. The visual nature of RAPTOR makes it easier for students to follow the control flow in their programs, and to solve problems more easily.

Experimental results indicate that teaching programming in RAPTOR develops problem solving skills better than teaching programming in a more traditional, non-visual language. Of note here is the observation that this conclusion did not extend to the use of arrays in problem solving. In fact, the first semester with RAPTOR students performed statistically significantly worse on the array question. This would suggest that array handling in RAPTOR might be an area for future improvements.

We have provided a web site where other universities can download RAPTOR. It is located at http://www.usafa.af.mil/dfcs/bios/mcc_html/raptor.html.

7. REFERENCES

[1] Calloni, B. Iconic Programming Proves Effective for Teaching the First Year Programming Sequence. Proceedings of the 28th SIGCSE Symposium (1997), 262-266.

[2] Cardellini, L. An Interview with Richard M. Felder. Journal of Science Education 3(2), (2002), 62-65.

[3] Crews, T., and Ziegler, U. The Flowchart Interpreter for Introductory Programming Courses. Proceedings of FIE '98, 307-312.

[4] Feldman, M., and Koffman E. Ada 95 Problem Solving and Program Design, 3rd edition. Addison-Wesley Publishing Company, 1999.

[5] Fischer, G., Giaccardi, E., Ye, Y., Sutcliffe, A.G., and Mehandjiev, (2004) N. Meta-Design: A Manifesto for End-User Development. *Communications of the ACM*, September 2004, 33-37.

[6] Fowler, L., Allen, M., Armarego, J., and Mackenzie, J. Learning styles and CASE tools in Software Engineering. In A. Herrmann and M.M. Kulski (eds), Flexible Futures in Tertiary Teaching. Proceedings of the 9th Annual Teaching Learning Forum, February 2000. http://ccea.curtin.edu.au/tlf/tlf2000/fowler.html

[7] IBM (2004). WebSphere Studio: Application Developer Integration Edition. Available at http://www-306.ibm.com/software/integration/wsadie/.

[8] Shackelford, R., and LeBlanc, R. Introducing Computer Science Fundamentals Before Programming. Proceedings of FIE '97, 285-289.

[9] Sorensen, R. A Comparison of Software Development Methodologies. Crosstalk (January 1995).

[10] Thomas, L., Ratcliffe, M., Woodbury, J. and Jarman, E. Learning Styles and Performance in the Introductory Programming Sequence. Proceedings of the 33rd SIGCSE Symposium (March 2002), 33-42.

[11] vanDijk, J. AdaGraph. Online. Internet. Available: http://users.ncrvnet.nl/gmvdijk/adagraph.html.

[12] Watts, T. SFC – A Structured Flow Chart Editor Version 3. Faculty Poster SIGCSE 2003. Available at: http://www.cs.sonoma.edu/~tiawatts/SFC/.

[13] Ziegler, U., and Crews, T. An Integrated Program Development Tool for Teaching and Learning How to Program. Proceedings of the 30th SIGCSE Symposium (March 1999), 276-280.

[14] Crews, T., and Murphy, C. Programming Right From the Start with Visual Basic .NET. Pearson Prentice Hall, 2004.

IRONCODE: Think-Twice, Code-Once Programming

Mark W. Bailey
Computer Science Department
Hamilton College
mbailey@hamilton.edu

ABSTRACT

To become proficient programmers, novices must develop the skills of writing, reading, debugging, and testing code. We believe that learning to write short pieces of code correctly the first time helps strengthen all of these skills. In this paper, we describe a type of exercise, called IRONCODE, that helps develop the code-once skill. We describe the exercise, the programming environment, its implementation, and our experiences using IRONCODE in a second semester programming class.

Categories and Subject Descriptors

K.3.2 [**Computers and Education**]: Computer and Information Science Education—Computer science education; D.2.3 [**Software Engineering**]: Coding Tools and Techniques; D.2.5 [**Software Engineering**]: Testing and Debugging—*testing tools*;

General Terms

Design, Reliability, Experimentation.

Keywords

Correct Code, Program Reading, Program Writing

1 INTRODUCTION

An important skill that beginning programmers must develop and master is the skill of writing correct code *the first time*. Unfortunately, the tremendous increases in processor speeds has shortened the edit-compile-run cycle to the point that students often rely too heavily on testing. Frequently, students choose to "try" a code snippet — or hack — over careful craftsmanship of a piece of code. In this paper, we present an exercise we use in a second semester programming course to develop this skill that we call "think-twice, code-once programming."

The ability to construct carefully a few lines of code is critical in software development. In teaching programming, we often focus on clean and elegant solutions at the expense of emphasizing the importance of "correct" solutions. This skill is used in not only writing code, but also reading and modifying code. How often do we have to "debug" a piece of code by examination? Such examination requires the same skills that writing "bullet-proof" code does: the ability to understand the interactions of two or more lines of code. The exercise we use to develop "bullet-proof" coding skills we call IRONCODE (in retrospect, we should have called it KEVLARCODE!).

SIGCSE'05, February 23–27, 2005, St. Louis, Missouri, USA.

2 RELATED WORK

For many years, instructors have used online environments for programming labs. Bowles used drills and programming quizzes to test programming skills [4]. More recently though, online examinations have been used in both closed and open environments [5, 7, 8, 12]. We often evaluate student progress in courses using tests or drills [2, 1, 3, 9, 10]. In addition, online quizzes have been used in introductory programming courses [11]. Main and Savitch provide software with their text that will automatically test methods for correctness [6]. However, to our knowledge, there has never been any experience with online code correctness exercises reported in the literature.

3 SOLUTIONS IN TEN LINES OR FEWER

In order to develop strong code-once programming skills, we hone a student's skill using small programming problems. Each IRONCODE problem asks the student to write a subprogram. Each problem is one that might have been encountered in an introductory programming course. An important characteristic of IRONCODE problems is that a common solution can be written in ten or fewer lines.

We take many of the early IRONCODE problems from the standard **C** library. These include: string copy (strcpy), string comparison (strcmp), string length (strlen), and character search (similar to strtok). These are good starters because students have used these functions (or a variant) in their programming and may already be familiar with their implementation. Additional problems are taken from classic introductory problems: sum the integers from M to N, determine if a number is prime, sum of squares, *etc*. Finally, as the semester progresses and student skills improve, we introduce problems relevant to current data structures course material: find the minimum in a stack, determine the depth of a tree, *etc*. Often, these are problems whose solutions have already been presented in class and have been coded recently by the students. These advanced problems not only further develop a student's IRONCODE skills but help reinforce current concepts in the course.

4 IRONCODE LAB ENVIRONMENT

We introduce IRONCODE in data structures, our second semester programming course. Our course introduces students to C++ after a semester of programming in Java. Our course has a dedicated three-hour weekly lab, though we've used IRONCODE during lecture-only formats as well. Since we lecture in the lab, our enrollments are limited to the lab capacity of 26 students.

Students gather in a closed laboratory to solve the weekly IRONCODE problem. Students work individually on online problems. Each IRONCODE problem asks the student to implement a C++ function. In a space provided on a web page, the student types their solution to the problem. When the student is satisfied with their solution, he submits it for evaluation. Figure 1 shows a snapshot of the IRONCODE programming environment.

During evaluation, the student's solution is compiled and linked with a test harness. If the solution fails to produce an executable program, the student is notified and asked to make appropriate modifications. However, if the solution produces an executable program, the solution undergoes a series of tests to evaluate its correctness. The solution either passes (the test harness failed to identify a problem with the solution) or fails. At this point, the student completes the exercise by receiving the results. Most importantly, if the student's solution fails, the student may not modify the program to receive credit.

The preceding description will undoubtedly seem unreasonably harsh to many readers. However, it doesn't tell the whole story. Students receive instructor support throughout the exercise. At any time, a student may ask the instructor questions. In particular, questions similar to the following are both allowed and encouraged:

- What result should the function return if it is given an empty string?
- What is the question asking?
- I don't know where to begin. Could I solve the problem by searching through the array?
- When is the increment expression of a `for` loop executed?
- What does this compilation error mean? How do I fix it?

These questions help the students understand the nature of the problem they are trying to solve and deal with the simple technology aspects of the exercise. We encourage significant interaction throughout the exercise. There are, however, questions that we deem inappropriate for the instructor to answer. These include:

- Why doesn't my program work?
- What does my solution return if the parameter is an empty string?

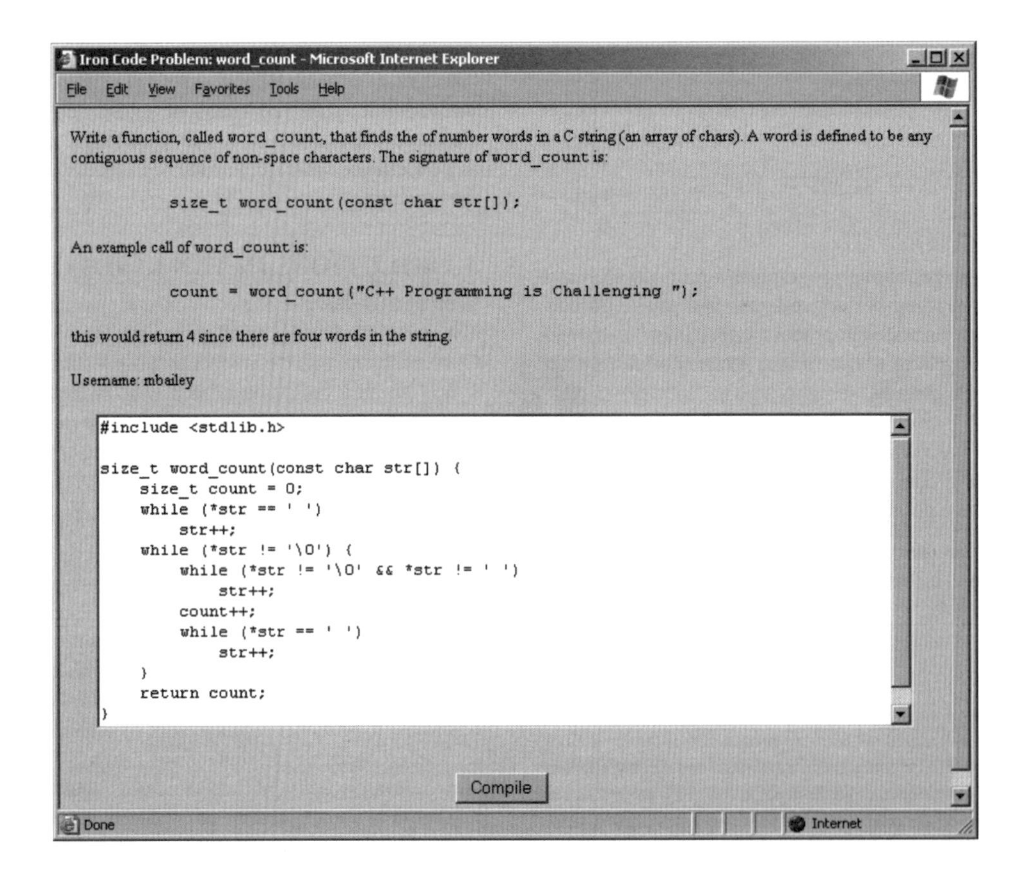

Figure 1. The IRONCODE programming environment.

- Should I place this if statement inside or outside the loop?
- What's the value of variable x at this location?

Each of these questions focuses on the interaction of a sequence of two or more lines of code. Since the purpose of the exercise is to develop exactly these skills, we gently encourage them to answer the question themselves. Often, however, it is possible to guide the student to a different, more appropriate, question that will help them with their solution.

5 IMPLEMENTATION

In order to implement IRONCODE, we needed an environment that allows students to edit and compile programs, but does not allow them to run or test them. Since we were aware of no such system, we constructed a custom-built system for the purpose.

The IRONCODE environment is built using CGI (common gateway interface), a C++ compiler, custom CGI scripts, and testing and support code for the IRONCODE problems. The IRONCODE front page presents the "open" problems. The student selects the appropriate problem and is presented with an IRONCODE coding page. This page always contains an English description of the problem, a function signature (or C++ prototype if you prefer), and an HTML text area for entering code.

The student progresses through the system by entering a proposed solution to the problem. When complete, the student presses the "submit" button (this action is verified before proceeding). Upon submission, the content of the text area is uploaded to the web server.

5.1 Results of Submitting a Solution

When a solution is submitted, it is compiled, run, and tested to evaluate its conformance to the problem's specification. The mechanics for this process will be discussed in the next section. During the evaluation process, any of the following outcomes may occur:

- The program doesn't compile—this is the simplest and most common outcome. The student's source has a compilation error. The errors need to be displayed to the student so he can fix the problem.
- The program doesn't link—a linking error will occur if the student failed to provide the requested function, or if the student failed to provide an auxiliary function that he calls. Again, the errors need to be displayed for the student.
- The program runs correctly—in this case, the run of the program is displayed to the student. This always involves displaying the different instances of calls to the function.
- The program runs, incorrectly—in this case, the student has failed to correctly solve the problem. The run of the program is displayed. Each call to their subprogram is displayed, with a correct result and the student's result shown. Incorrect results are clearly marked for examination. In addition to the run, the version of the function that the student was tested against is shown. We do this for two purposes. Usually, the student wants to see a working version so he can learn from his mistakes. Frequently, this demonstrates a far easier solution than the student proposed. We feel it is important for student to be exposed to superb solutions to problems. Finally, in the event that the solution is not "superb" (the solution has an error), this gives the student "appeal" material. Fortunately, this hasn't happened (yet).
- The program runs, but terminates prematurely. This can occur for many reasons. Any number of exceptions—most notably dereferencing a null pointer—can cause a program to terminate. Again, the program has not executed correctly, so the student doesn't receive credit (or another chance) for a correct solution. This outcome is equivalent to the program running incorrectly.
- The program runs, but doesn't terminate (in a timely manner)—one problem with small, execute-once solutions is that infinite loops are common. To overcome this problem, solutions are required to execute in a timely manner (a couple of seconds). After a predetermined length of time (set on a per-problem basis), the program is terminated. This outcome is equivalent to the program running incorrectly.
- Any of the above, but the program has already been graded—after a program has been graded (the program has executed at least once), the student can continue to work on the problem. However, he will not get credit. This option was added after many students indicated that they wanted to polish their solutions (for no credit!).

5.2 Mechanics of Building a Test Program

In order to evaluate a student's solution, it must be tested. Since IRONCODE solutions always consist of one or more C++ functions, we can repeatedly call the student's function to determine correctness. Operationally determining correctness requires that for each call to the student's function, the correct result must be known. This can be accomplished in at least two ways:

- For each set of parameters, the correct result(s) may be recorded. This can be handled using an array of records that contains the parameters and the corresponding results.
- For each set of parameters, the correct result(s) may be computed. This requires a correct solution be available in the test harness.

It seems that either approach would work, but we felt that providing a correct solution would be less error-prone than providing correct results, so we opted for the correct solution approach.

Such a test harness will have a solution similar in structure to the code in Figure 2. This approach will work, in theory, but fails for even the simplest problems. For example, this approach limits problems to those that return a single result as a return value. Functions that return results through parameters cannot be included in this test harness. In addition, functions such as C's string copy (strcpy) destructively modify one of the parameters causing subsequent use of the same parameters to produce different return results (consider strcat for example). Further, incorrect execution of one function can impact the subsequent execution of other functions if the stack is corrupted. All of these issues therefore require a more general solution than presented previously.

In our first implementation, we simply skirted the problems of developing a "general" test harness by writing custom test harnesses for each problem. At first this sounds tedious, but often test harnesses can be adopted or adapted from previous IronCode problems. For example, the kernel of the test harness for reversing an array of characters is shown in Figure 3.

```
<for each student solution>
    if (student_soln(<parms>) !=
        correct_soln(<parms>))
        <signal incorrect solution>;
<signal correct solution>;
```

Figure 2. A possible structure of a test harness.

```
for (i = 0; tests[i]; i++) {
    strcpy(solution, tests[i]);
    strcpy(theirs, tests[i]);
    solution_reverse(solution);
    start_alarm(2);
    reverse(theirs);
    stop_alarm();
    if (strcmp(solution, theirs)) {
        errors++;
    }
}
```

Figure 3. Test harness for reversing a string.

This illustrates the kinds of contortions that one must go through to test such a simple problem. First, notice that the correct solution is called prior to calling the student's solution. This prevents the student solution from corrupting the stack of the correct solution (for the current iteration of the loop at least!). Second, in the case of string reversal, the single parameter is destructively modified. Thus, a copy of the parameter must be made (strcpy) before calling the first solution. A copy of the result must also be made, or at least it must be placed in a different location. Finally, a type-specific comparison operation (strcmp) must be performed to determine if the result is correct. This technique proves to be acceptable for small numbers of simple IronCode problems, but mounting a more ambitious program requires a more robust system.

A second-generation IronCode test harness system is in development. This system uses a complex collection of templated C++ classes to provide a general solution to this problem. In this system, a separate class is required for each set of problems with differing arity (that is, functions taking four parameters use a different templated class than functions that take three). In addition to these classes, we have constructed a set of operators for copying and comparison of common types. The system can model in, out, and in/out parameters and provides a mechanism for registering instances of tests to be run. Figure 4 shows the complete test harness for the reverse example.

6 CONCLUSIONS

We began the IronCode initiative because we found that students were exiting our first programming course with a firm understanding of programming through experimentation, but with deficiencies in their understanding of fundamental programming language semantics. For example, it was common for students to misunderstand the intricacies of the for loop. We have found that since beginning the IronCode project, students have responded to the close instructor interaction that IronCode promotes. We have also found the environment helps the students quickly identify and strengthen their weaknesses.

We have been experimenting with IronCode for several semesters. For the most part, the experiment seems to be a great success. Since our courses generally have fewer than 20 students each semester, student performance metrics are not statistically significant enough to evaluate IronCode as a pedagogical tool. Instead, we conclude with our observations of how IronCode is working in our course.

When students first experience IronCode, they often feel quite intimidated and anxious (we have tried to find ways to alleviate this but to date have been unsuccessful). They feel this way even though IronCode is not used to determine student grades. However, after a few exercises, most students rise to the challenge of

```
int main() {
    VoidOneParm<char *> TestRun(reverse_solution, reverse, "reverse");

    char *tests[] = {
        "bob",
        "bo",
        "a couple of words",
        "a couple",
        "BOB",
        "Next one is empty!",
        "",
    };

    for (size_t i = 0; i < sizeof(tests) / sizeof(char *); i++) {
        TestRun.addTest(tests[i]);
    }

    return TestRun.performTests();
}
```

Figure 4. A templated test harness for reverse.

IRONCODE. The success rate for IRONCODE typically hovers around 50%. This seems to be sufficiently high to encourage students but sufficiently low to challenge them to improve their IRONCODE skills. By the end of the course, students are more confident about their programming-in-the-small skills and look forward to future IRONCODE challenges.

REFERENCES

1. J. M. Adams and B. L. Kurtz. A state-of-the-art CS undergraduate lab. In *Proceedings of the SEI Conference on Software Engineering Education*, pages 85–94. Springer-Verlag, 1990.
2. H. P. B. Kurtz. Developing programming quizzes to support instruction in abstract data types. *SIGCSE Bulletin*, 21(1):66–70, February 1989.
3. R. Bennett and J. Wadkins. Interactive performance assessment in computer science: the advanced placement computer science (APCS) practice system. *Journal of Education Computing Research*, 12(4):636–678, 1995.
4. K. Bowles. A CS1 course based on stand-alone microcomputers. *SIGCSE Bulletin*, 9(1):125–127, February 1978.
5. M. Joy and M. Luck. Effective electronic marking for on-line assessment. In *Proceedings of the 6th Annual Conference on the Teaching of Computing and the 3rd Annual Conference on Integrating Technology into Computer Science Education*, pages 134–138. ACM Press, 1998.
6. M. Main and W. Savitch. *Data Structures and Other Objects using C++*. Addison-Wesley, 2nd edition, 2001.
7. D. V. Mason and D. M. Woit. Integrating technology into computer science examinations. In *Proceedings of the 29th SIGCSE Technical Symposium on Computer Science Education*, pages 140–144. ACM Press, 1998.
8. M. D. Medley. On-line finals for CS1 and CS2. In *Proceedings of the 6th Annual Conference on the Teaching of Computing and the 3rd Annual Conference on Integrating Technology into Computer Science Education*, pages 178–180. ACM Press, 1998.
9. R. Sanford and P. Nagsue. Selftest, a versatile menu-driven PC tutorial simulates test-taking. *Computers in Education Journal*, pages 58–69, 1992 1992.
10. A. Walworth and R. Herrick. The use of computers for educational and testing purposes. In *Proceedings of Frontiers in Education. 21st Annual Conference. Engineering Education in a New World Order*, pages 510–514, 1991.
11. D. Woit and D. Mason. Enhancing student learning through on-line quizzes. In *Proceedings of the 31st SIGCSE Technical Symposium on Computer Science Education*, pages 367–371. ACM Press, 2000.
12. D. M. Woit and D. V. Mason. Lessons from on-line programming examinations. In *Proceedings of the 6th Annual Conference on the Teaching of Computing and the 3rd Annual Conference on Integrating Technology into Computer Science Education*, pages 257–259. ACM Press, 1998.

Revealing the Programming Process

Jens Bennedsen
IT University West
Fuglesangs Allé 20
DK-8210 Aarhus V
Denmark
jbb@it-vest.dk

Michael E. Caspersen
Department of Computer Science
University of Aarhus
Aabogade 34, DK-8200 Aarhus N
Denmark
mec@daimi.au.dk

ABSTRACT
One of the most important goals of an introductory programming course is that the students learn a systematic approach to the development of computer programs. Revealing the programming *process* is an important part of this; however, textbooks do not address the issue – probably because the textbook medium is static and therefore ill-suited to expose the process of programming. We have found that process recordings in the form of captured narrated programming sessions are a simple, cheap, and efficient way of providing the revelation.

We identify seven different elements of the programming process for which process recordings are a valuable communication media in order to enhance the learning process. Student feedback indicates both high learning outcome and superior learning potential compared to traditional classroom teaching.

Categories and Subject Descriptors
K3.1 [**Computers & Education**]: Computer Uses in Education – *computer-assisted instruction, distance learning.*

K3.2 [**Computers & Education**]: Computer and Information Science Education – *computer science education, information systems education.*

General Terms
Design, Documentation, Experimentation, Human Factors, Languages.

Keywords
CS1, Programming Process, Process Recording, Model-Based Programming, Objects-First, Design, Incremental Development, Testing, Refactoring, Programming Education, UML, Conceptual Modelling, Systematic Programming, Pedagogy.

SIGCSE'05, February 23–27, 2005, St. Louis, Missouri, USA.

1. INTRODUCTION
We believe that one of the most important goals of an introductory programming course is that the students learn a systematic approach to the development of computer programs.. Revealing the programming process is an important part of this, and we have found that process recordings in the form of screen captured narrated programming sessions is a simple, cheap, and efficient way to provide the revelation. We hereby expand the applied apprenticeship approach as advocated in [2, 15].

Revealing the programming process to beginning students is important, but traditional *static* teaching materials such as textbooks, lecture notes, blackboards, slide presentations, etc. are insufficient for that purpose. They are useful for the presentation of a product – a finished program– but not for the presentation of the *dynamic* process used to create that product. Besides being insufficient for the presentation of a development process, the use of traditional materials has another drawback: typically they are used for the presentation of an *ideal* solution which is the result of a non-linear development process. Like others [20, 21, 22], we consider this to be problematic; the presentation of the product independently of the development process will inevitably leave the students with the false impression that there *is* a linear and direct "royal road" from problem to solution. This is very far from the truth, but the problem for novices is when they see their teacher present clean and simple solutions, they think they themselves should be able in a straightforward fashion to develop solutions in a similar way. When they realize they cannot, they blame themselves and feel incompetent. Consequently they will lose self-confidence and in the worst case their motivation for learning to program.

Besides teaching the students about tools and techniques for the development of programs, i.e. a programming language, an integrated development enviroment (IDE), programming techniques, etc., we must also teach them about the development process, i.e. the task of using these tools and techniques to develop, in a systematic, incremental and typically non-linear way, a "good" solution for the problem at hand. An important part of this is to expound and demonstrate that many small steps are better than few large ones, that the result of every little step should be tested, that prior decisions may need to be undone and code refactored, that making errors is common also for experienced programmers, that compiler errors can be misleading/erroneous, that online documentation for class libraries provide valuable information, and that there is a systematic, however non-linear, way of developing a solution for the problem at hand. We cannot rely on the students to learn all of this by themselves, but using an apprenticeship approach we can show them how to do it; for this purpose we use process recordings.

The paper is structured as follows: Section 2 is a brief introduction to the notion of process recordings. In section 3 we discuss the need for exposition of the programming process (e.g. through process recordings) and why textbooks are ill-suited for this purpose. Section 4 is a more detailed description of process recordings and we identify seven different categories. In section 5 we discuss the use of process recordings in a course context. Section 6 is a brief discussion of related work. The conclusions are drawn in section 7, which also points to future work.

2. PROCESS RECORDINGS, A BRIEF INTRODUCTION

Written material in general and textbooks in particular are not a suitable medium through which to convey processes. We have used process recordings, captured and narrated programming sessions, to do that. The creation of a process recording is easy, fast, and cheap, and does not require special equipment besides a standard computer.

The term *process recording* refers to a screen capture of an expert programmer (e.g. the teacher) solving a concrete programming problem, thinking aloud as he moves along. A process recording can be produced using a standard computer; there is no need for a special studio or other expensive equipment. The software for capturing is free, and depending on how advanced post production one needs, that software is either free or very cheap. We have used Windows Media Encoder and Windows Media File Editor, both freeware programs.

We have found that 15-20 minutes is an appropriate duration of a process recording; for some problems the duration can be longer. For convenience, we offer an index (a topic→time mapping) to help retrieve sections of special interest. The index of each recording is stored in a database allowing the students to search for specific material at a later stage. Figure 1 shows a snapshot of a playback of a process recording.

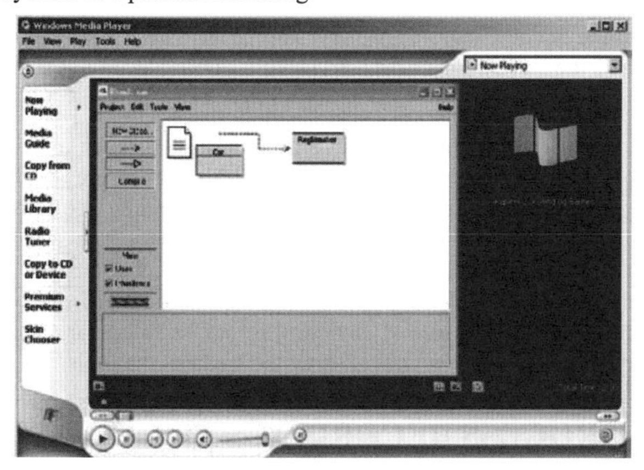

Figure 1: Playback of a process recording

3. TEACHING THE PROCESS OF PROGRAMMING

The concern for teaching process and problem solving is not new; in [10] David Gries wrote:

> *Let me make an analogy to make my point clear. Suppose you attend a course in cabinet making. The instructor briefly shows you a saw, a plane, a hammer, and a few other tools, letting you use each one for a few minutes. He next shows you a beautifully-finished cabinet. Finally, he tells you to design and build your own cabinet and bring him the finished product in a few weeks. You would think he was crazy!*

Clearly, cabinet making cannot be taught simply by teaching the tools of the trade and demonstrating finished products; but neither can programming. Nevertheless, this seems to be what was being attempted thirty years ago when Gries wrote the above analogy, and to a large extent it seems to be the case today.

du Boulay [6] identifies *Pragmatics* – the skills of planning, developing, testing, debugging and so on – as an important domain to master. The latter is concerned with skills related to the programming process; however, only few of these are addressed in traditional textbooks on introductory programming.

3.1 Textbooks Neglect the Issue

At a recent workshop [14], a survey of 39 major selling textbooks on introductory programming was presented. The overall conclusion of the survey was that all books are structured according to the language constructs of the programming language, not by the programming techniques that we (should) teach our students. This is consistent with the findings in [18]: *Typical introductory programming textbooks devote most of their content to presenting knowledge about a particular language* (p. 141). The prevailing textbook approach will help the students to understand the programming language and the structure of programs, but it does not show the student how to program – it does not reveal the programming process.

We know what is needed, so why has the topic not found its way into textbooks on introductory programming? The best answer is that the static textbook medium is unsuitable for this kind of dynamic descriptions.

3.2 New Technology Allows for Changes

Earlier it has been difficult to present actual programming to students. When programs, in the form of finished solutions, were presented to students it was in the form of writings on the blackboard or copies of finished programs (or program fragments) on transparencies for projection.

Programming on a blackboard has the advantage that it is possible to create programs in dialog with the students at a pace the students can follow; also, the teacher and the students can interact during the development of the program. The obvious drawback is that only small programs can be presented, and neither are we able to run and modify the programs nor to demonstrate professional use of the development tool(s) and programming techniques.

Finished programs on transparencies provide a way of presenting larger and more complex programs to the students, programs that we would never consider writing on a blackboard. This approach has the drawback that teachers tend to progress too fast and exclude the students from taking part in the development.

The emergence of new technology has made it possible in a simple and straightforward manner to present live programming to students. Live programming can be presented in two different ways: live programming using computer and projector, and process recordings showing how the expert at work.

Live programming in the lecture theatre using computer and projector is like a combination of using blackboard and slides, but with the important additional ability to run and test the program and to use the programming tools (IDE, online documentation, diagramming tools). This is much closer to the actual programming process than the first two approaches. However, there are still drawbacks: time in the class room is limited and this restricts the complexity of the examples that are presented; also, the presentation vanishes as it takes place; nothing is saved afterwards.

Process recordings showing the programming process of an expert are similar to live programming but without its limitations. In process recordings you can take the time needed to present as complex an example as you wish, and the presentation can be reviewed over and over as many times as a student needs to.

The first three approaches have in common that they are synchronous, one shot events. There is no possibility for the student to go back and review (a step in) the development process if there were something he did not understand. This opportunity is exactly what is added by using process recordings.

4. A CATEGORIZATION OF PROCESS ELEMENTS

In this section we present a more detailed description of the process elements we expose through process recordings, and we identify seven different categories that we have found useful in CS1.

4.1 Elements of Structures and Pragmatics

A typical programming process encompasses the following process elements: use of an IDE, incremental development, testing, refactoring, error handling, use of online documentation, and systematic construction of code from a model/specification. All are unsuitable for textual descriptions, but important for the student to master. For each process element we will discuss how to address it in an introductory programming course and how process recordings can be used to reveal its core aspects.

Use of the IDE: We use a simple IDE [13]. However, a short recording demonstrating the use of special facilities in the IDE makes it still easier for the students to start using it.

Incremental development: Students often try to create a complete solution to a problem before testing it. This is not the behaviour we want the students to exhibit; instead we want them to create the solution in an incremental way taking very small steps alternating between implementing and testing. Following this advice makes it much easier to find and correct errors and it simplifies the whole activity. This is a topic that is very difficult to communicate in a book. With a process recording it is simple and straightforward to demonstrate how to behave.

Testing: We promote two simple techniques for testing: interactive testing through the IDE (BlueJ) or the creation of a special class with test methods. The process aspect of the former technique is covered under "Use of the IDE" above (see also [12]). A textbook is useful for describing principles and techniques for testing but how to integrate testing in the development process is best demonstrated showing a live programming/testing process.

Refactoring: When the students read a textbook they easily get the impression that programmers never make mistakes, that programmers always create perfect, working solutions in take one, and that programmers therefore never have to correct and improve their programs. In [8] it is stated that an experienced programmer should expect to use approximately 50% of his time refactoring his code. If this is the case for an experienced programmer, a novice programmer should expect to use significantly more time refactoring/correcting; clearly, students cannot expect to create perfect solutions in take one. But the students get the impression that they ought to be capable of this.

We have found it difficult to motivate the need for refactoring to students. The goal of refactoring is to create better programs in the sense of exhibiting lower coupling and higher cohesion. The students do not know when it is advantageous to refactor a program; they consider the job done when the program can compile and run. But showing them the refactoring techniques "live" gives them a much better understanding of the techniques and an appreciation of the necessity for refactoring. In order to optimise motivation we often start out with a student's program, showing how refactoring can make that program more readable, and how lower coupling and higher cohesion can be obtained through successive applications of simple standard techniques.

Error handling: In order to make the students feel more comfortable it is important to show them that every programmer makes errors and that error handling is a part of the process. It is important to show the students how errors are handled. In particular it is important to demonstrate to the students that the output from the compiler does not always indicate the real error and that there are different types of errors. The process recordings help by being explicit and by dealing systematically with each kind of error.

Online documentation: Modern programming languages are accompanied by large class libraries which the students need to use. The documentation for Java is available online, and the students have to be acquainted with the documentation and how to use it in order to write programs. When the students write code, we force them to write javadoc too. In order to teach how to write and generate the documentation, we show how to do this as an integrated part of the development process using live programming/process recordings.

Model-based programming: We teach a model-driven, objects-first approach as described in [3]. In order to do so the students need to use more than the traditional programming tools; they need to use a tool for describing the class models. The students also need to understand the interaction between the IDE and the modeling tool as well as the relation between model and code. To reinforce the importance of modeling as an integrated part of program development it is vital to show the students the tools.

5. PROCESS RECORDINGS IN A COURSE CONTEXT

In this section we will describe how the process recording materials are used in an introductory object-oriented programming course.

5.1 Categories of Process Recordings

We have created five different types of process recordings: introduction to assignments, solutions to the assignments, documentation of synchronous activities (lectures and online meetings), alternative teaching materials, and tool support.

Introduction to assignments: Many students struggle with getting started with an assignment: what is the problem, how shall I start, what exactly is it that I have to do? Many such questions can efficiently be addressed in a process recording where also fragments/structure of a solution can be presented.

Solutions to assignments: Presentation of a solution to a programming assignment; besides presenting the solution, we also present aspects of the development process.

Documentation of synchronous activities: By capturing live programming as it takes place, the students get the opportunity to review (parts of) the process at a later stage.

Alternative teaching materials: For the core topics in the text, we create small programming problems to illustrate the use and applicability of the topic. This provides diversity in the course material supporting different styles of learning.

Tool support: We have created different kinds of process recordings for tool support. Like [1] we have found that, instead of creating written descriptions and manuals for these tasks, it is much easier for us as well as the students if we create a process recording showing how to *do* things: just tell what you are doing on the screen while capturing it.

5.2 Production Details

Most process recordings can be captured without too much preparation. It is our experience that a detailed manuscript is superfluous; too detailed a manuscript tend to make the process recording less authentic and in the worst case plain boring. We have created approximately 60 process recordings; it is our experience that we use one hour to prepare a 30-minute recording and another 20 minutes for post-production.

To increase usability we make it possible for students to navigate in the process recording. The addition of the topic→time index has added a new usage of the material: the students can search the material afterwards and use it as yet another part of their learning material repository. In this way the value of the lectures has expanded from something that is only useful if you are present, to a material that can be used repeatedly over time.

5.3 Student Feedback

Recently we taught two introductory programming courses based on distance education with respectively 35 and 20 students (a detailed description of the design of this course can be found in [4]). For these courses we made extensive use of process recordings. All of these materials are stored on a web-server and the students can access them whenever they want and from where they want.

We have evaluated the use of process recordings in our introductory programming course. The evaluation was done quantitatively using a questionnaire as well as qualitatively by interviewing a number of students about their attitude towards the material. From the questionnaire we can see that more than 2/3 of the students have seen more than 50% of the process recordings.

The distribution of hits for the different types of process recordings is as follows: introduction to assignments 28%, solutions to assignments 19%, documentation of synchronous activities 9% alternative teaching materials 21%, and tool support 23%. The interesting thing is that the possibility of reviewing the synchronous activities has by far the smallest hitrate; this indicates that web casting of lectures, which is a widespread use of process recordings [5, 17], is the least useful of the five categories.

The students have self-evaluated the learning outcome of the process recordings; the result of the evaluation is;: None 21%, Small 0%, Ordinary: 21%, High: 14%, Very high: 44%. 58% has indicated a high or very high learning outcome which is very encouraging. In post-course interviews, the students generally confirmed this. One student characterized the use of process recordings as follows: *I claim that the learning potential is better with this teaching form than for traditional class room teaching; in the virtual class room I can eliminate all kind of noise and interruptions. Combined with the opportunity to review (parts of) the session, the return on investment becomes optimal.*

6. RELATED WORK

Streaming video has become more and more popular and common [16, 19]. Compression techniques have been standardized and improved; bandwidth is increasing (also in private homes) making it realistic to use videos in an educational setting.

Web casts of lectures is used by many universities including prominent ones like Berkeley and MIT [5, 17]. While such videos may be valuable to students who are not able to attend the lecture or would like to have (parts of) it repeated, they do not significantly add new value to the teaching material.

The use of process recordings in teaching is not new [19]. Process recordings are used extensively in [11], but the use is somewhat different from ours: all process recordings are very short and focused on explaining a single aspect of the programming language or programming; the process recordings are "perfect", they do not show that it is common to make errors (and how to correct them); and the process recordings do not show the integrated use of the different tools like IDE, online documentation, etc. The process recordings in [11] can be characterized as alternative teaching materials according to our categorization in section 5.1.

Others use a much richer form of multimedia than plain video. One example is the learning objects discussed in [7]. The same differences as described above apply, and on top of that the production cost for creating these learning objects is extremely high.

7. CONCLUSIONS

The idea of revealing the programming process is not new:

> *Anyone with a reasonable intelligence and some grasp of basic logical and mathematical concepts can learn to program; what is required is a way to demystify the programming process and help students to understand it, analyse their work, and most importantly gain the confidence in themselves that will allow them to learn the skills they need to become proficient.*

This quotation is fifteen years old [9]; nevertheless, the issue still has not found its way into programming textbooks.

Revealing the programming process is an important part of an introductory programming course which is not covered by traditional teaching materials such as textbooks, lecture notes, blackboards, slide presentations, etc. This is just as good since these materials are insufficient and ill-suited for the purpose.

We suggest that process recordings in the form of screen captured narrated programming sessions is a simple, cheap, and efficient way of providing a revelation of the programming process. Furthermore we have identified seven elements included in the programming process. For each of these we have discussed how to address it in an introductory programming course and how process recordings can be used to reveal its core aspects.

From our evaluation of the approach we know that the students use and appreciate the process recordings; some students even find the material superior to traditional face-to-face teaching. The creation of video-mediated materials has proven to be easy and cheap as opposed to other approaches to create learning objects.

The advance of new technology in the form of digital media has made it possible to easily create learning material to reveal process elements that in the past only has been addressed implicitly. The students welcome the new material which has great impact on the students' understanding of the programming process and their performance in practical programming. With new technology, in this case computers and video capturing tools, it becomes possible to store information that represent dynamic behaviour, something which is virtually impossible to describe and represent using traditional tools and materials such as blackboards and books. We are looking forward to further pursue this new opportunity.

8. ACKNOWLEDGEMENT

It is a pleasure to thank Carl Alphonce, David Barnes and Michael Kölling for valuable comments and suggestions.

The production of process recordings was initiated in the Flexnet project under IT University West; we will like to thank IT University West for financial support for the project.

9. REFERENCES

[1] Alford, K., "Video FAQs – Instruction-On-Demand", *Proceedings of Frontiers in Education*, Boulder Colorado, 2003.

[2] Astrachan, O. & Reed, D., "AAA and CS1: The Applied Apprenticeship Approach to CS1", *Proceedings of the twenty-sixth SIGCSE Technical Symposium on Computer Science Education*, Nashville, Tennessee, 1995, pp. 1-5.

[3] Bennedsen, J. & Caspersen, M. E., "Programming in Context – A Model-First Approach to CS1", *Proceedings of the thirty-fifth SIGCSE Technical Symposium on Computer Science Education*, Norfolk, Virginia, 2004, pp. .

[4] Bennedsen, J. & Caspersen, M. E., "Rationale for the Design of a Web-based Programming Course for Adults", Proceedings of ICOOL 2003, *International Conference on Open and Online Learning*, Mauritius, 2003.

[5] Berkeley, http://webcast.berkeley.edu/courses/

[6] du Boulay, J.B.H., "Some difficulties of learning to program", in Spohrer, J.C. and Soloway, E. (Eds.), *Studying the Novice Programmer*, Hilldale, NJ, Lawrence Erlbaum Associates, Hillsdale, 1989., pp. 283-299.

[7] Boyle, T., "Design principles for authoring dynamic, reusable learning objects", *Australian Journal of Educational Technology*, 19 (1), 2003, pp. 46-58.

[8] Fowler, M., *Refactoring – Improving the Design of Existing Code*, Addison-Wesley, 1999. ISBN 0-201-48567-2

[9] Gantenbein, R. E., "Programming as Process: A 'Novell' Approach to Teaching Programming", *Proceedings of the twentieth SIGCSE Technical Symposium on Computer Science Education*, Louisville, Kentucky, 1989, pp. 22-26.

[10] Gries, D., "What Should We Teach in an Introductory Programming Course", *Proceedings of the fourth SIGCSE Technical Symposium on Computer Science Education*, 1974, pp. 81-89.

[11] Gries, D. & Gries, P., *ProgramLive*, John Wiley & Sons, 2001.

[12] Kölling, M. & Rosenberg, J., "Testing Object-Oriented Programs: Making it Simple", *Proceedings of the twenty-eighth SIGCSE Technical Symposium on Computer Science Education*, San José, California, 1997, pp. 77-81.

[13] Kölling, M., "Teaching Object Orientation with the Blue Environment", Journal of Object-Oriented Programming, Vol. 12 (2), 1999, pp. 14-23.

[14] Kölling. M, "The Curse of Hello World", *Invited lecture at Workshop on Learning and Teaching Object-orientation – Scandinavian Perspectives*, Oslo, October 2003.

[15] Linn, M. C. & Clancy, M. J., "The Case for Case Studies of Programming Problems", *Communications of the ACM*, 35 (3), 1992, pp. 121-132.

[16] Ma, W., Lee, Y., Du, D.H.C. & McCahill, M. P., "Video-based Hypermedia for Education-On-Demand", *Proceedings of the fourth ACM International Conference on Multimedia*, 1996, pp. 449-450.

[17] MIT, www.swiss.ai.mit.edu/classes/6.001/abelson-sussman-lectures/

[18] Ronins, A., Rountree, J. & Rountree, N., "Learning and Teaching Programming: A Review and Discussion" *Journal of Computer Science Education*, Vol. 13 (2), 2003, pp. 137-172.

[19] Smidth, T, Ruocco, A & Jansen, B., "Digital Video in Education", *Proceedings of the thirtieth SIGCSE Technical Symposium on Computer Science Education*, New Orleans, Louisiana, 1999, pp. 122-126.

[20] Soloway, E., "Learning to Program = Learning to Construct Mechanisms and Explanations", *Communications of the ACM*, 29 (9), 1986, pp. 850-858.

[21] Spohrer, J. & Soloway, E., "Novice Mistakes: Are the Folk Wisdoms Correct?", *Communications of the ACM*, 29 (7), 1986, pp. 624-632.

[22] Spohrer, J. & Soloway, E., "Analyzing the High-Frequenzy Bugs in Novice Programs", In Iyengar, S. & Soloway, E. (Eds.), *Empirical Studies of Programmers*, Ablex, New York, 1986.

Challenges to Computer Science Education Research

Vicki L. Almstrum
Department of Computer Sciences
The University of Texas at Austin
almstrum@cs.utexas.edu

Orit Hazzan (moderator)
Department of Education in Technology & Science
Technion – Israel Institute of Technology
oritha@tx.technion.ac.il

Mark Guzdial
College of Computing
Georgia Institute of Technology
guzdial@cc.gatech.edu

Marian Petre
Faculty of Mathematics and Computing
The Open University
M.Petre@open.ac.uk

Categories and Subject Descriptions: K.3.0 [Computers and Education] - *general.*

General Terms: Human Factors.

Keywords: research in computer science education, research methods, qualitative methods, quantitative methods.

SUMMARY

In recent years, the theme of research in computer science education (CSE) has received a relatively large share of attention in the CSE community [1, 2, 3, 4, 5]. Some specific activities conducted in this direction include:

- 12/02: Nell Dale's summary of her SIGCSE proceedings review: "Beginning in 1998, there is a definite increase in CS Ed research related papers." [2]
- 06/03: Launch of the *Scaffolding Research in CS Education* hands-on workshop, aimed at introducing higher-education faculty to research in CSE (depts.washington.edu/srcse/).
- 03/04: Publication of Sally Fincher and Marian Petre's edited book *Computer Science Education Research* [3].
- 12/04: Publication of the special issue of *Computer Science Education* about import/export relationships to CSE research [1], focusing on mutual relationships of CSE research with research in other educational fields.

Based on our experience with research in CSE, we suggest that the community of CSE researchers should consider future challenges. The panelists will present four challenges, illustrating each with specific cases and research studies. Open discussion with the audience will follow the panelists' short presentations.

PANELISTS' STATEMENTS

Vicki L. Almstrum

A key challenge that prevents many computing educators from attempting CSE research is *isolation*. Isolation can result from existing in an atmosphere where colleagues regularly convey the attitude that educational research is not *real* research. Isolation can come from uncertainty about where to begin digging into the literature from computer science education as well as from a wide variety of related and supporting fields. Isolation can be like a void into which ideas for research questions, designs, and analyses simply disappear without the benefit of collegial discussion and brainstorming. A sense of isolation can emerge from frustrating struggles while dealing with special situations, such as small sample sizes, the need for specialized methods, or difficulty in locating or creating appropriate instruments.

Combating this sense of isolation requires patience, persistence, and creativity. Creating a receptive support network outside of one's own department can help. For example, partnering with an academic from a different department at one's own institution (such as communication, psychology, or mathematics education) can provide inspiration and productive intermixing of specialties — if an appropriate partner can be found. Setting up collaborations with computing educators (or folks in other areas) at other institutions can result in anything from a one-on-one interaction to a multi-institutional cooperative endeavor. On-line forums can also help pull an isolated researcher into richer interactions. With some imagination, practitioners in isolated situations can find research approaches leading to doable studies that add to the collection of knowledge about what works in computing education.

Mark Guzdial

The real challenge to computing education is to avoid the temptation to re-invent the wheel. Computers are a revolutionary human invention, so we might think that teaching and learning about computers requires a new kind of education. That's completely false: The basic mechanisms of human learning haven't changed in the last 50 years.

Too much of the research in computing education ignores the hundreds of years of education, cognitive science, and learning sciences research that have gone before us. We *know* that student opinions are an unreliable measure of learning or teaching quality. We *know* that meta-analyses are very hard to do with any sort of rigor, so there are careful, formal procedures for doing them right. We *know* that the educational value of algorithm animations is subtle, and we're not going to be able to measure the potential benefit from whole-class, quantitative studies.

If we want our research to have any value to the researchers that come after us, if we want to grow a longstanding field that contributes to the improvement of computing education, then we have to "stand on the shoulders of giants," as Newton put it, and stop erecting ant hills that provide too little insight.

Orit Hazzan

While the theme of research in CS education has recently received a lot of attention, most of the research conducted in CSE uses quantitative research tools. My presentation addresses the challenge of diversifying the research methods we employ. Specifically, I illustrate how qualitative research, which has been used extensively in other educational research fields, may be applied in CSE research. I address the nature of qualitative research, its fitness for use in the research in CSE, and its research tools.

Qualitative research can be used to investigate environments, situations, and processes for which quantitative data cannot adequately describe their complexity. For example, how can numerical data describe mental processes involved in learners' comprehension of object-oriented concepts, or student interaction in software development processes? I claim that though quantitative data can shed light on several aspects of such processes, they cannot provide a full picture of what goes on in such situations. I do *not* argue that qualitative data analysis can describe such complex processes entirely; I do argue, however, that qualitative data analysis highlights additional important aspects of these processes.

Qualitative research has different objectives than those of quantitative research. Accordingly, its data-gathering tools are different. Specifically, since the products of qualitative research are descriptive, the data gathering tools, such as interviews and observations, are verbal as well; because qualitative research aims at describing a given situation, rather than at generalizing a theory, in qualitative research it is sufficient to focus on a small number of individuals who participate in the research field.

My presentation will be accompanied with examples of research works that illustrate the use of different qualitative research tools.

Marian Petre

In the absence of a driving theory and an established methodology, we borrow research methods from other disciplines. I take a 'horses for courses' view of research design for CS education. *What* we borrow should be shaped by the questions we wish to address and by an understanding of the nature of evidence. *How* we borrow it should be shaped by vigilant striving for the greatest possible rigour.

There are some key requirements in borrowing and employing methods, among them:

understanding the method in its context: It is essential, in borrowing methods, that we understand the epistemology, focus, and assumptions that underpin them. It's not enough to borrow a method without understanding how it is applied – and constrained – in its discipline of origin, and how that tradition shapes the method and the evidence it can yield.

seeking rigour: Weak or sloppy evidence does no one any good. And so we must concern ourselves with repeatability of studies. We must be vigilant against bias. We must address issues of representativeness and generalisation explicitly. We must consider alternative accounts and potentially contradictory evidence. Whatever the method, it requires full and honest reporting, with articulation of the reasoning that connects question to data to interpretation to conclusions, so that the whole 'audit trail' is exposed to scrutiny and potentially to repetition.

accumulating evidence: It's crucial to remember that no one study stands on its own; one must also understand how the study fits into the body of existing work. How might the results of one study accumulate with those of other studies, how might findings be compared to other evidence, and how might findings be validated?

REFERENCES

[1] Almstrum, V., Hazzan, O. and Ginat, D. (in press, December 2004). Special Issue on Import/Export Relationships to Computer Science Education Research, *Computer Science Education* **15**(3).

[2] Dale, N. (2002). Increasing interest in CS ED research, *SIGCSE Bulletin inroads* **34**(4), pp. 16-17.

[3] Fincher, S. and Petre, M. (2004). *Computer Science Education Research*, Routledge Falmer.

[4] Goldweber, M., Clark, M. and Fincher, S. (2004). The relationships between CS education research and the SIGCSE community. *SIGCSE Bulletin inroads* **36**(1), pp. 147-148.

[5] Valentine, D. W. (2004) CS Educational Research: A meta-analysis of SIGCSE Technical Symposium proceedings. *SIGCSE Bulletin inroads* **35**(1), pp. 255-259.

Taking Advantage of National Science Foundation Funding Opportunities

Steve Cunningham
National Science Foundation
4201 Wilson Blvd
Arlington, VA 22230 USA
1.703.292.4729
scunning@nsf.gov

Diana Gant
National Science Foundation
4201 Wilson Blvd.
Arlington, VA 22230
703.292.4642
dgant@nsf.gov

Harriet Taylor
National Science Foundation
4201 Wilson Blvd
Arlington, VA 22230 USA
1.703.292.7973
htaylor@nsf.gov

ABSTRACT
This session will highlight programs in the National Science Foundation EHR Division of Undergraduate Education and CISE Division of Computer and Network Systems that are of interest to college faculty, discussing the requirements and guidelines for programs in these areas. It will also include a presentation of the characteristics of a competitive proposal and the proposal and review processes, and participants will be encouraged to explore their ideas with the presenters.

Categories & Subject Descriptors
K.3.2 Computer and Information Science Education

Keywords: Grants, awards, proposals, National Science Foundation, education.

1. TOPICS
This year there are some significant changes in the way NSF supports education projects in computer science. The CISE Directorate has been reorganized and there is an increased emphasis on REU sites and on all research programs supporting focused educational activities. At the same time the CCLI program is being changed and there will be some changes in the details of the way CCLI proposals will be presented. We will cover these changes in general terms but will be as concrete as we can in the changing circumstances.

One aspect of our programs is still the same: we are still actively seeking to increase both the number and competitiveness of proposals to all education activities in the National Science Foundation, most particularly to the DUE CCLI (Course, Curriculum, and Laboratory Improvement) program. Funding for many computer science education programs at NSF responds directly to the total proposal pressure, so increasing both the number of proposals and the competitiveness of those proposals will actually increase the amount of funding NSF will target towards computer science education. Most CCLI proposals come from faculty who attend or have attended the SIGCSE Symposium, and we want to help these faculty be more successful. We particularly want to concentrate on helping participants develop their ideas into successful proposals.

Note that this session will precede a planned birds-of-a-feather session in which we will discuss the proposal writing and review process in considerably more detail. The intent of the BOF is two-fold: participants will see what goes into a successful proposal and participants will be able to submit higher quality proposals once they understand the review process for these proposals.

SIGCSE'05, February 23–27, 2005, St. Louis, Missouri, USA.
ACM 1-58113-997-7/05/0002

Status Report on the SIGCSE Committee on the Implementation of a Discrete Mathematics Course

Bill Marion
Dept. of Math and Computer Science
Valparaiso University
Valparaiso, IN 46383
219.464.5422
Bill.Marion@valpo.edu

SUMMARY

This session is a progress report from the first committee created under the SIGCSE Committee Initiative. The Committee on Implementation of a Discrete Mathematics Course is charged with developing implementation models and materials for the one-semester discrete math course proposed in Computing Curriculum 2001. At the time of the session, the Committee will have completed about three-fourths of its task. In this session the committee will present a number of course models which, for each, will include a syllabus/course outline and a list of possible applications which connect the mathematics to fundamental ideas in computer science. Comments and additional input from the SIGCSE community will be solicited. Presentation will by Bill Marion, one of the two committee co-facilitators and two other committee members.

Categories and Subject Descriptors

K.3.2 [Computing Milieux]: Computer and Information Science Education – curriculum, computer science education.

General Terms

Algorithms, Theory.

Keywords

Discrete mathematics, computing curriculum, CC2001, SIGCSE committee initiative, course models, syllabi

1. BACKGROUND

In June 2003, the SIGCSE Committee on the Implementation of a Discrete Mathematics Course was chartered, the first committee operating under the new SIGCSE Committee Initiative. The Committee's charge is to "work toward providing a few ... practical models for a one-semester [discrete math] course that will meet the basic needs of undergraduates in a computer science program."

The need for this committee arises from the discrete math (discrete structures) requirements of Computing Curriculum 2001 [1]. In particular, Computing Curriculum 2001 requires computer science programs to cover six core knowledge areas:

- DS1: Functions, Relations, and Sets
- DS2: Basic Logic
- DS3: Proof Techniques
- DS4: Basic Counting
- DS5: Graphs and Trees
- DS6: Discrete Probability

Computing Curriculum 2001 recommends 43 class hours devoted to topics within these six areas. Two approaches are provided for covering these topics, a single course (CS 115) and a two-course sequence (CS 105 and CS 106). Some guidance is available for departments implementing the two-course sequence [3], but there is little to help departments interested in the one-course approach.

Despite the lack of guidance, the one-course approach is exactly what local constraints lead many departments to favor. However, the material itself does not imply an obvious, coherent, course structure, nor does it lead obviously to lab exercises or group projects. Faculty trying to implement this approach are largely working in isolation, producing ad hoc courses.

The basic goal for the Committee on the Implementation of a Discrete Mathematics Course is to assist those trying to implement a one-semester CC2001-compliant discrete math course, by identifying successful implementations

SIGCSE '05, February 23-27, 2005, St. Louis, Missouri, USA.
ACM 1-58113-997-7/05/0002.

and making them available as models for others to build on. The Committee is hoping to find a small number of models (no more than six), each of which can be characterized by a typical syllabus/course outline, possible laboratory exercises and homework assignments, and a list of possible applications that the course can cover.

At last year's SIGCSE Symposium the committee reported on its preliminary work which included the analysis of a survey which was sent to computer science and mathematics faculty who teach a discrete mathematics course which meets the needs of computer science majors. One hundred and eight surveys were returned, eighty percent of which were from faculty at universities and colleges where there is only a one-semester discrete math course. In addition, over fifty of the faculty who returned the survey included a course syllabus, either as an attachment or a url where it could be obtained.

A random sample of the syllabi received was examined over the summer and certain models began to emerge. From these models the course outlines to be presented were developed.

2. SESSION OUTLINE

We propose the following outline for the special session:

5 minutes: Introduction and overview of the session (Bill Marion).

10 minutes: Update on committee activities, including a review of the survey results, observations about course syllabi received, and a description of what distinguishes one course model from another (Bill Marion).

35 minutes: A description of candidate course models, to include syllabi/course outlines and possible applications (one or two committee members).

35 minutes: Audience discussion, guided by such questions as

1. What other models should be considered?
2. What kinds of lab assignments and homework assignments would be most helpful
3. What products, beyond the Committee's report, would be useful, and how should they be distributed?

(Bill Marion and other committee members).

3. EXPECTATIONS

This session is aimed primarily at people interested in discrete math as an important part of the computer science curriculum. The session should appeal both to people interested in discrete math's role in the abstract, and those with a concrete interest in implementing a course. Judging from the response to the call for Committee members (66 people are currently subscribed to the Committee's mailing list) and interest in recent years in a broader mathematical reasoning interest group [2] (89 e-mail subscribers, 40 to 50 attendees at each SIGCSE birds-of-a-feather session organized by the group in the last two years), there are a large number of such people.

We foresee two specific outcomes from the session:

1. The Committee's ideas concerning models for a one-semester discrete mathematics course will be shared with the audience. While the Committee's work will not be complete by SIGCSE 2005, these concrete ideas should be sound enough to help others implement one-semester discrete math courses.
2. The Committee itself will receive input from its intended constituents, at a time when that input can still influence the Committee's final product.

ACKNOWLEDGEMENTS

Thanks to all the members of the SIGCSE Committee on the Implementation of a Discrete Mathematics Course for their comments on this proposal, and the illuminating discussions leading to it.

REFERENCES

[1]. ACM/IEEE Joint Task Force on Computing Curricula, Computing Curriculum 2001: Computer Science. http://www.computer.org/education/cc2001/final/index.html

[2]. D. Baldwin and P. Henderson, Integrating Mathematical Reasoning into Computer Science Curricula. http://www.math-in-cs.org/

[3]. Pedagogy Focus Group 2 on Supporting Courses of the ACM/IEEE Joint Task Force on Computing Curricula, Draft Report, Version 5.2. http://www.cs.grinnell.edu/~walker/curriculum/pedagogy-5.2.html

Keynote Address

The Concorde Doesn't Fly Anymore

Mordechai (Moti) Ben-Ari
Department of Science Teaching
Weizmann Institute of Science
Rehovot 76100 Israel
moti.ben-ari@weizmann.ac.il

Abstract

While computing technology has undoubtedly changed the world in which we live, the changes have been exaggerated. Talk of a hi-tech internet-driven revolution during the last decade is inaccurate from a historical perspective: (a) It belittles previous technological achievements; for example, the landings on the moon between 1969 and 1972 were achieved with less computing capability than a PDA has today. (b) So much of the "new" technology dates back thirty years or more; for example, how many of our students know when the first email was sent? This loss of historical perspective has led to demands for an artifact-driven curriculum that I believe is inadequate for the education of future computer scientists and computational engineers. (The latter is a new term I wish to propose for people engaged in the scientifically-based design and construction of systems that perform computations. It is linguistically modeled on the terms mechanical and electrical engineer, and is intended to take the place of the term software engineer.) A comparison of the CC2001 curriculum with the curriculum of a traditional, "non-revolutionary" engineering discipline points to what I believe the future of CS education should be.

Bio

Mordechai (Moti) Ben-Ari holds a BSc from MIT and a PhD from the Tel Aviv University. He worked as a programmer and software manager from 1970 until 1995, when he joined the Department of Science Teaching of the Weizmann Institute of Science. His group develops CS courses for high-school students (Foundations of Computer Science, Concurrent and Distributed Computation, Object-Oriented Programming), and runs a CS Teachers' Center in collaboration with the Technion. Prof. Ben-Ari has published six textbooks: *Principles of Concurrent Programming* (1982); *Principles of Concurrent and Distributed Programming* (1990); *Mathematical Logic for Computer Science* (1992; second edition, 2001); *Understanding Programming Languages* (1995); *Ada for Software Engineers* (1998). His next book, *Just a Theory: Exploring the Nature of Science* is forthcoming from Prometheus Books. One of his primary interests is in tools for teaching CS. His recent projects include the jBACI concurrency simulator, the DAJ tool for teaching distributed algorithms, and the Jeliot program visualization system (developed at the University of Joensuu, Finland). Other research interests include the application of cognitive and social theories of education to CSE, and the application of the history and philosophy of science to science teaching. Prof. Ben-Ari held visiting positions at Brandeis University in 1989 and at the University of Joensuu in 2002. He is on the editorial board of the journal Computer Science Education.

SIGCSE'05, February 23-27, 2005, St. Louis, Missouri, USA.
ACM 1-58113-997-7/05/0002.

An Introductory VR Course for Undergraduates Incorporating Foundation, Experience and Capstone.

Sharon Stansfield
Ithaca College
Ithaca, NY 14850
(607) 274-3630
sstansfield@ithaca.edu

ABSTRACT

This paper presents the structure, pedagogy and motivation for an introductory undergraduate course in Virtual Reality. The course is offered as an elective at the 400-level, hence students taking the course are juniors and seniors who have completed a substantial portion of their Computer Science curriculum. The course incorporates multiple components of VR theory and practice, including hardware and software survey and analysis, human perception, and applications. It also contains a semester-long, hands-on development component utilizing a specific virtual reality environment. In addition, because VR is a broad, multidisciplinary field of study, the course provides an ideal environment for incorporating capstone elements that allow undergraduate students to tie together many of the computing principles learned during their undergraduate academic careers.

Categories and Subject Descriptors

I.3.7 [Computer Graphics]: Three-Dimensional Graphics and Realism; K.3.2 [Computer and Information Science Education]: computer science education, curriculum.

General Terms

None.

Keywords

Course design, virtual reality, capstone.

1. INTRODUCTION

In undergraduate education, it is important to take every opportunity to assist students in tying together the threads of their academic computer science experience. This is usually done in a one or two semester capstone course designed specifically for that purpose. But the incorporation of capstone elements into other upper-level computer science courses can serve to both reinforce and broaden this experience. Because Virtual Reality (VR) is such a diverse and multidisciplinary area, an introductory course in VR lends itself naturally to the incorporation of capstone elements. In addition to the more traditional aims of a VR course, such as creating the next generation of VR researchers and end-users [4], such a course could seek to create a capstone experience that encompasses not only aspects of core CS knowledge, but also more general issues of importance to the computing professional, such as communication skills, teamwork, and application (as specified in Computing Curricula 2001 [2].) With this in mind, we have designed an introductory, undergraduate course in VR with the following goals:

1. That the student will gain an understanding of the breadth of the VR discipline, including hardware, software, human perception, and a range of applications.
2. That the student will gain an understanding of the underlying principals and design issues involved in constructing a virtual reality system/application.
3. That the student will gain hands-on experience by developing VR software utilizing an existing VR platform.
4. That the student will utilize a range of knowledge gained throughout his/her undergraduate curriculum in pursuing the above goals.
5. That the student will enhance his/her communication skills by writing and presenting a research paper.

2. OBJECTIVES AND ORGANIZATION

As indicated above, the course is structured around two synergistic aims: to introduce students, who may have a variety of interests, to the field of VR and to provide an opportunity for additional capstone experiences. Toward this end, the course has both a "traditional" lecture-based component and a hands-on experiential component. We have implemented this hands-on component as an on-going, semester-long team project. In our experience this works better than a "big bang" final project coming sometime after the bulk of the course material has been presented. Students develop each software component as the topic is presented in class. For example, the module on navigation in VR consists of a survey of hardware and software methodologies, a analysis of the trade-offs between these various devices and methods, and the incorporation of a navigation component into their VR programming project. The students choose and program the appropriate methodology for their application.

SIGCSE'05, February 23–27, 2005, St. Louis, Missouri, USA.

The prerequisite for the course is our 300-level course in computer graphics. The primary reason for this prerequisite is the need for students to have a reasonable facility with the mathematics of computer graphics, such as coordinate frames, transformations and geometric object representation. While low-level graphics programming is not a component of the VR course, more advanced techniques, such as scenegraphs and stereo viewing, are presented. If desired, in depth coverage of these advanced graphics topics may be skipped – tools exist that permit one to develop virtual worlds without an in depth knowledge of the underlying mathematics and algorithms. In this case, the Computer Graphics requirement may be eliminated and additional introductory mathematics covering topics such as homogeneous transforms, coordinate systems, and geometric transformations, may be presented instead.

2.1 Objectives

After completing the course, students should be able to:

1. Explain the computational models used in VR systems (e.g. scenegraph representations, stereo viewing and collision detection.)
2. Describe the various hardware devices used in VR systems and compare and contrast the features of these devices used for similar purposes (e.g. magnetic tracking vs. optical tracking.)
3. Analyze a particular application specification and determine the best VR system configuration to meet the application's requirements.
4. Do the research and write a paper on a chosen VR topic.
5. Organize and do a presentation on this topic.
6. Program a VR environment utilizing a specific VR platform.
7. Demonstrate an ability to work as part of a programming team.

Student learning outcomes are measured through a midterm and final exam, written paper, presentation, and project demonstration.

2.2 Topics Covered

The course covers the basic hardware, software, methodologies, human factors, and applications relevant to the field and addresses the topics and learning objectives specified for the Virtual Reality elective in Computing Curricula 2001 [2].

VR topics may be organized so that they are somewhat independent of one another -- they are often organized around the various aspects of a VR system and this is the format used in our course. A survey of visual displays, for example, is preceded by a discussion of the human visual system and is followed by a discussion of the technical and human factors trade-offs involved in choosing a device. The module on interaction in VR includes a survey of tracking devices, along with their technical benefits and drawbacks and a presentation of the various models and algorithms for interaction within a VR (e.g. collision detection and voice recognition.) The course also includes assigned readings on and an open discussion of ethical issues, which often provokes the most spirited student participation of the semester.

The following is a complete list of the topics covered:

- Intro and overview of VR
- Human vision
- Visual displays
- 3D stereo viewing
- The scenegraph
- Introduction to the VR software used in class (in our case, VR_Station)
- Networked VR
- VR_station support for shared virtual environments
- Position and posture tracking
- VR_station support for tracking
- Human touch
- Haptic displays
- Interaction in virtual environments
- Navigation in virtual environments
- Human hearing
- Virtual sound
- Equilibrium and simulator sickness
- Autonomous and reactive worlds
- Ethical issues in virtual reality research and application
- Applications of virtual reality: student presentations

Presented materials may be reinforced by assigned readings from a textbook and of survey and/or research papers on the various topics. Two up-to-date and well-organized textbooks that may be used for an undergraduate course are Burdea and Coiffet [1] and Sherman and Craig [8].

In addition to the course materials, each student is expected to write a research paper on a chosen application of VR to a field outside of computer science. Topics chosen by students in the past have included such diverse applications as psychology, education, and archeology, and often reflect the student's interests in other disciplines. The assigned paper is not simply a literature review; in addition to a discussion of relevant work in the chosen area, students must compare and contrast the various methods used by individual researchers and provide an analysis of the approach and its potential. Pedagogically, the aim is to have the students research a topic as though they were preparing to do work in that same area. The last few weeks of the course are then dedicated to a "mini-conference" wherein each student prepares and presents a twenty-five minute presentation based on his/her paper. The goal in this case, of course, is to enhance technical communication skills.

3. Experiential Component

The on-going programming project is central to our VR course. Students utilize our VR laboratory to program a virtual reality environment. As topics are explored, this environment is extended to incorporate several of the major components of a VR system. Obviously, the available resources will influence what is possible – not all institutions will have the same equipment, and even a well-equipped VR research facility will likely not be available at all times to undergraduates enrolled in a VR course. Our own current model is to give the students access to the research facility, with the understanding that the research projects will get highest priority for using the equipment. However, as the popularity of the course (and hence the number of students enrolled) has increased, we have begun to reconsider this issue. Below we describe the VR platform we currently utilize for the programming project. We also consider the minimal requirements to support the underlying pedagogy, for those who have limited access to VR facilities or who might prefer to establish a separate lab dedicated to the VR coursework

3.1 VR platform

VR Software: A reasonably fast PC with a good graphics card and a VR software platform might be considered the minimum requirements for programming Virtual Reality. We are currently using a set of software tools developed at Sandia National Laboratories for both our VR research and instructional environments. The software, which consists of a viewing component (VR_Station) and a network-based communication component (VR_Multicast), was obtained under a research licensing agreement and is fully described in [9]. This software provides support for shared virtual environments and multiple viewing methods (flat screen, head-coupled displays, etc.) It is an open platform that uses networking to support incorporation of independent modules to support such components as tracking and simulation. The course (and research) also utilizes the VR_Sim simulation engine. VR_Sim is an on-going software project to which a number of undergraduates at our institution have contributed as their senior, or capstone, project.

While we have chosen to utilize the above software in our coursework and research, a number of other VR software platforms are also available from both commercial and research organizations that could serve as the basis for the laboratory component of a VR course. Some freely available VR software systems are DIVE, developed at the Swedish Institute of Computer Science [3], Java 3D, developed at Sun Microsystems [5], NPSNET, developed at the Naval Postgraduate School [6] and VR Juggler, developed at Iowa State University [10].

Modeling Software: While a modeling package is not strictly a requirement -- one can download models, or build them before hand and make them available to the class -- it can be a valuable experience for students to build their own VE models. Geometric models form the underpinning of most VR applications and can be one of the bottlenecks in developing a VR system. Some experience with model building is invaluable to any student of VR.

Hardware: Although the popular image of VR is of someone wearing a head-mounted display (HMD), many VR researchers no longer use these devices, due to their cost, lack of resolution and field-of-view, and general discomfort. Since our research is currently utilizing HMD devices, they are available to the students in the course. After an initial demo, however, we have found that the students develop and debug their VR programs primarily using the PC monitor display -- and this is probably adequate for an introductory course. If possible, a visit to the research lab or a near-by facility for a demo of some of the more traditional viewing devices is valuable -- experiencing an HMD, CAVE, or other immersive display provides a better example of the power of immersion. A dedicated device, however, does not appear to be a requirement. The same is true for other types of displays, such as tactile and force feedback. Sound, of course, is a freebie. Arguably, the one indispensable piece of VR hardware is some type of real-time position tracker. Again, these can be expensive, although simple devices with limited range are now available which could support a VR course. The ability to track the user's position is at the heart of both presence and interaction – two of the three required dimensions in Zeltzer's definition of VR [11]. We are currently using MotionStar® electro-magnetic trackers from Ascension Corporation. For the VR course, we use two of these six degree-of-freedom (DOF) trackers: a tracker worn on the head (or HMD) supports updating the user's view as they move and one worn on the hand permits integration of interaction techniques (touching and pointing.) Students are given the option of using more trackers if they would like to create more complex avatars and navigation. If the PC monitor is used for display, then a single six- or even three-DOF tracker would be adequate.

3.2 Programming project

The main focus of the project is to develop a virtual world that is immersive and interactive. In institutions with VR research programs, students in a VR course are often assigned to work on some aspect of a research project. We do not follow this model, since research projects tend to be large, complex, and on-going. Students are often limited to working on some small piece of the larger project. While this is no doubt a beneficial experience, it does not provide as broad an experiential activity as does having the teams build a full-up (albeit small) VR system. The components of the on-going project are discussed below:

Modeling and model hierarchies: Working in teams, students are given the task of building a simple virtual world (e.g. modeling a room and several different associated objects.) The concepts of object complexity, texture mapping, and scenegraphs are introduced. VR_Station is scenegraph-based, and builds its internal representation from a hierarchical data file. Students create this hierarchical representation of their world using the object geometries that they previously created. Using VR_Station, they are then able to view their room in the HMD. Completing this module gives students hands-on experience with modeling and with hierarchical scene representation.

Shared virtual worlds and object behaviors: Our VR software (VR_Station / VR_Multicast / VR_Sim) supports shared VR via network communication of joint values for objects whose state may change. Each viewer loads the same world hierarchy. Simulations programmed using the VR_Sim library then create object behaviors by changing and communicating joint values to all participating viewers, which update the states of these objects. Students utilize this method to add articulated objects to their worlds: each member of the team creates an articulated object and its associated "driver" or simulation. These objects are added to the team's world model hierarchy and world engine. Team members may now independently view a shared world consisting of multiple objects with autonomous behaviors. Completing this module gives students hands-on experience with networked VR and with creating animated virtual objects using joint sets.

Interaction: In the third extension of their virtual reality projects, student teams add interaction to their worlds: The behaviors developed for the second project are modified so that they are only invoked when a user interacts with the object. The project is divided into two components: teams create tracker-driven "avatars" that will represent users within the VR. They then develop the code to determine when an avatar has selected an object. Avatars may be driven using any number of trackers worn on the user's body. A single tracker on the hand or on a wand would represent the minimum configuration. Students may make their avatars as simple or complex as they like in terms of geometry, but each of the avatar parts must move correctly in relationship to both the data input from the trackers and the representation (e.g. head and hands must move with the body as well as independently.) Interaction may consist of pointing or touching. For either method, students must program a simple collision detection method for determining when an object has been selected.

Navigation: The final component of the project is to add a navigation technique to the virtual reality. Teams choose and implement a navigation method using either a position sensor or mouse as input. For simplicity, navigation is implemented by manipulating the model, rather than view (which is controlled by the VR viewing software.)

By the end of the course, students will have built a shared, inhabited VR with behavior and interaction – the foundation of any VR application.

4. CAPSTONE ELEMENTS

The definition of a capstone course varies from institution to institution, however, all definitions have the same fundamental elements. The following definition is taken from [7]:

"Capstone courses generally target undergraduate students who are nearing completion of their studies. They are designed to build on skills acquired in earlier courses and emphasize situations and challenges that exist in the "real world." Specific learning goals and course objectives vary across disciplines and institutions but most capstone courses provide an opportunity for students to demonstrate a range of professional competencies and communication skills." (p. 1)

In general, capstone courses are not advanced courses on a particular topic, such as VR. Most programs, including ours, have a specific one or two semester course dedicated to the capstone experience. However, the incorporation of capstone elements into other upper-level computer science courses serves to both reinforce and broaden this experience. A VR course, such as the one presented here, provides many opportunities for students to utilize and build on previously acquired skills. The on-going, team project requires design and implementation, as well as the very "real-world" task of understanding and using code developed by others. (This is a good argument for using one of the VR platforms described above. None is a commercial product: they are the result of on-going research efforts, with all of the "real world" connotations that implies.) Specific methods and technologies from earlier courses must be applied to the design and implementation of the project, as well -- object-orientation, systems analysis and design, networked communication, and real-time data acquisition, among them. For students who may not have been previously exposed to some of these topics, the platform and project provide an opportunity to gain some experience with them in the context of an actual application. The paper and presentation not only reinforce communication skills, but also require students to understand, analyze, and critique the work of others. (A reason why we have chosen to have students write and present a topic paper, rather than their own project work.) Project demonstrations are also scheduled throughout the semester – another all too familiar real-world task.

Of course, VR is not the only topic which lends itself to the incorporation of capstone elements: robotics and artificial intelligence are examples of others for which such a structure should work.

5. ACKNOWLEDGEMENTS

The author would like to acknowledge the support of Ithaca College and of the Mathematics and Computer Sciences Department, with special thanks to Pat Woodworth, without whose support and effort neither the course nor the lab would have been possible. We would also like to acknowledge the National Science Foundation, which supported the purchase of the VR equipment used for this course under NSF grant EIA0116295.

6. REFERENCES

[1] Burdea, G. and Coiffet, P. *Virtual Reality Technology*. John Wiley and Sons, Inc. 2003.

[2] Computing Curricula 2001 Final Report. IEEE Computer Society Press. 2002

[3] The DIVE Homepage. Retrieved from http://www.sics.se/dive on September 1, 2004

[4] IEEE VR Panel on Teaching VR. R. Darken, moderator, IEEE Virtual Reality Conference. March 29-31, 2004. Chicago, IL.

[5] Java 3D API. Retrieved from http://java.sun.com/products/java-media/3D/ on September 1, 2004

[6] NPSNET-V. Retrieved from http://www.npsnet.org/~npsnet/v/ on September 1, 2004.

[7] Rhodus, T. and Hoskins, J. Toward a Philosophy for Capstone Courses in Horticulture. *Horticulture Technology*. Vol 5, No. 2, (April-June 1995) p. 175-178

[8] Sherman, W. and Craig, A. *Understanding Virtual Reality: Interface, Application, and Design*. Morgan Kaufman Publishers. 2003.

[9] Stansfield , S., Shawver, D., Sobel, A., Prasad, M., and Tapia, L. Design and Implementation of a Virtual Reality System and Its Application to Training Medical First Responders. *Presence: Teleoperators and Virtual Environments*. MIT Press Journals, Vol. 9, No. 6. (Dec. 2000) p. 524-556.

[10] VR Juggler - Open Source Virtual Reality Tools. Retrieved from http://www.vrjuggler.org on September 1, 2004

[11] Zeltzer, D. Autonomy, Interaction and Presence. *Presence: Teleoperators and Virtual Environments,* Vol. 1, No. 1. (1992) p. 127-132.

Photon Mapping Made Easy *

Tin-Tin Yu, John Lowther and Ching-Kuang Shene
Department of Computer Science
Michigan Technological University
Houghton, MI 49931
{tiyu,john,shene}@mtu.edu

ABSTRACT

This paper presents the authors' introduction of photon mapping in an undergraduate computer graphics course, Software was designed as a pedagogical and demonstration tool which permitted students to practice and learn photon mapping. Classroom experience and examples that illustrate soft shadows, color bleeding, indirect illumination and caustic are also discussed.

Categories and Subject Descriptors

I.3.7 [**Three-Dimensional Graphics and Realism**]: Ray-tracing; K.3.2 [**Computers and Education**]: Computer science education

General Terms

Photon Mapping, Ray Tracing

Keywords

Photon Mapping, Ray Tracing

1. MOTIVATION

The *programming approach* is the most popular approach in teaching introductory computer graphics courses. However, it does have some serious drawbacks [4]. **First**, students usually do not know if the created image is correct. C. A. R. Hoare once said: "You can't teach beginning programmers top-down design because they don't know which way is up." Likewise, it is difficult to teach graphics programming to beginners because they do not know what the anticipated effect should be. As a result, we need an easy way for students to recognize the effect of each graphics parameter before they start to program. GraphicsMentor is a tool designed for this purpose [5, 7]. **Second**, the programming approach depends on local illumination-based graphics APIs which, in general, do not support shadow generation, reflection and refraction. **Third**, the design and modeling component is unlikely to be touched upon because students may dedicate too much time on programming and because a typical graphics API has a limited modeling capability.

To overcome this "local illumination" bias and maintain a well-balanced graphics syllabus, we teach students ray tracing. Our experience, as reported in [6], shows that students like ray tracing and learn global illumination models effectively and efficiently from exercises designed to explore the advantages of global illumination models and disadvantages of local illumination models. With this knowledge in hand, in our **Advanced Computer Graphics** course, we present ray tracing implementation details and discuss major shortcomings of ray tracing. We do cover radiosity in our course. However, radiosity theory is complex and, reflection and refraction are not available unless more theory is discussed. This is a very frustrating fact, and leads us to find a simple, easy to understand, and powerful enough global illumination based rendering method between ray tracing and radiosity. The answer is photon mapping.

In the following, Section 2 elaborates why photon mapping is a natural and reasonable choice, Section 3 briefly discusses the theory of photon mapping, Section 4 presents the details of our software tool designed to help students explore photon mapping and generate images, Section 5 demonstrates the quality of our system with a number of examples, Section 6 summarizes our classroom experience, and, finally, Section 7 has our conclusions.

2. WHY PHOTON MAPPING?

Traditional ray tracing systems trace rays from an eye (or a camera) rather than from light sources, and one light ray from a hit point to each light source is used to determine the shadow color of that point. As a result, traditional ray tracing techniques are not able to correctly generate shadows (and hence caustic) of refractive objects, produce indirect illumination from reflective objects, and implement diffuse reflection (*e.g.*, no color bleeding). Although soft shadows are possible, one must use area lights that can significantly increase processing time. On the other hand, radiosity provides soft shadows, color bleeding and indirect illumination for free; however, it does not handle specular reflection, has difficulty in processing transparency (*i.e.*, reflection and refraction), requires the scene to be subdivided into polygons, and is very time consuming. A second pass (*e.g.*, ray tracing) is needed to produce reflection and refraction.

Instead of complicating the radiosity implementation by

*This work is partially supported by the National Science Foundation under grant DUE-0127401. The third author is also supported by an IBM Eclipse Innovation Award 2003.

SIGCSE'05, February 23–27, 2005, St. Louis, Missouri, USA.

post ray tracing, an easier way would collect illumination information of the scene by a pre-trace from light sources. This is the basic idea of photon mapping. Since students have learned ray tracing, converting the process of tracing from the camera to tracing from each light source with some data structure manipulations is not very difficult. Furthermore, since photo mapping can easily generate area light sources, color bleeding, soft shadows, indirect illumination and caustic, we believe it would be easier for students to learn and program these effects via photon mapping rather than with radiosity. The major advantages of photon mapping are (1) using photons to simulate the transport of individual photon energy, (2) being able to calculate global illumination effects, (3) capable of handling arbitrary geometry rather than polygonal scenes, (4) low memory consumption, and (5) producing correct rendering results, even though *noise* could be introduced. Consequently, after the discussion of ray tracing and radiosity, our course adds a 5-hour presentation on photon mapping to its global illumination module.

3. WHAT IS PHOTON MAPPING?

The basic idea of photon mapping is very simple [3]. It tries to decouple the representation of a scene from its geometry and stores illumination information in a global data structure, the *photon map*. Photon mapping is a two-pass method. The first pass builds the photon map by tracing photons from each light source (Section 3.1), and the second pass renders the scene using the information stored in the photon map (Section 3.2).

3.1 Pass 1: Light Emission and Photon Scattering

The first pass of photon mapping consists of two steps: *light emission* and *photon scattering*. In the first step, photons are generated and shot into the scene. A light source with higher intensity will produce more photons, and the direction of each photon is randomly selected based on the type of the light source (*e.g.*, spherical, rectangle, or directional). The processing of these photons is similar to ray tracing with one difference: photons propagate flux while rays gather radiance. When a photon hits an object, it can be reflected, transmitted, or absorbed. If a photon hits a specular object (*e.g.*, a mirror), it is reflected with its intensity scaled by the reflection index of that object. On the other hand, if a photon hits a diffuse surface, it is stored in the photon map and reflected. The direction of this "diffusely" reflected photon is a randomly chosen vector that is above the intersection point with a probability proportional to the cosine of the angle with the normal. This can be implemented by playing "Russian roulette."

The "Russian roulette" technique removes unimportant photons and ensures the same power. In the specular case, a random number $q \in [0,1]$ is generated, and if $q \in [0,f)$, where f is the reflection index, the photo is reflected. Otherwise, it is absorbed. In the diffuse case, a random number $q \in [0,1]$ is generated, and the photon is diffused (*resp.*, reflected) if $q \in [0,d]$ (*resp.*, $q \in (d, d+s]$), where d and s are the diffuse reflection and specular reflection indices, respectively. Otherwise, it is absorbed.

The photon hit information is stored in a photon map, which is usually a balanced *kd*-tree [1]. Each node of the *kd*-tree stores the information of a photon hit, which include the coordinates of the hit point (x, y, z) (used as the key for building the tree), color intensity (r, g, b), incident direction of the photon, and other important information. Since the number of photons and their hit points may be very large, some form of compression may be needed; however, in an undergraduate course, we skip compression concerns. While the concept of *kd*-tree is simple, the implementation of a balanced *kd*-tree is a non-trivial task. Fortunately, good balanced *kd*-tree code is available [3]. After all photons are shot and the *kd*-tree is built, the first pass completes.

3.2 Pass 2: Radiance Estimate and Rendering

The second pass renders the scene with the help of the photon map built in the first pass. A traditional ray tracing procedure is performed by shooting rays from the camera. When a ray hits a point $\mathbf{P}$ on a surface, the illumination information (*i.e.*, flux) of the neighboring photons collected from the first pass and stored in the photon map will be added to the radiance information collected from ray tracing at $\mathbf{P}$. Let the normal vector at $\mathbf{P}$ be $\mathbf{N}$ and $r > 0$ be a predefined small value. Consider all photons in the sphere $\mathcal{S}(\mathbf{P}, r)$ of center $\mathbf{P}$ and radius r (Figure 1).

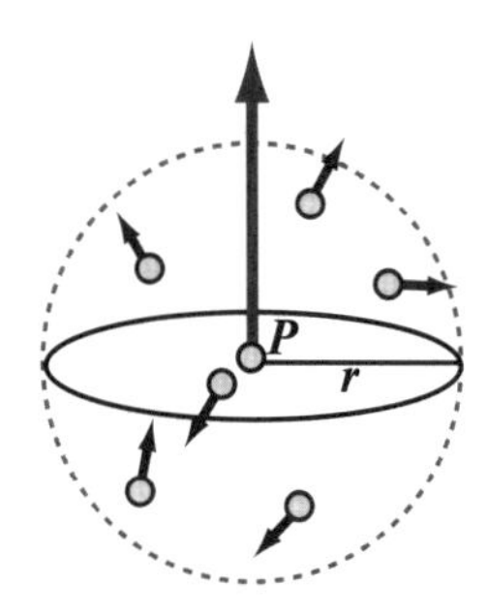

Figure 1: Radiance Estimate

Not every photon in $\mathcal{S}(\mathbf{P}, r)$ would contribute to the radiance at $\mathbf{P}$. In fact, a photon with incident direction $\mathbf{d}$ can contribute only if $\mathbf{d}\cdot\mathbf{N} > 0$, because if $\mathbf{d}\cdot\mathbf{N} \leq 0$, its direction goes inside of the surface. If a photon does not contribute, it is ignored in this radiance estimate for point $\mathbf{P}$. From the illumination equation, the radiance contribution of a photon with incidence direction is:

$$\text{intensity} \times (\mathbf{d} \cdot \mathbf{N}) \times \text{diffuse-factor}$$

Let the sum of all radiance contribution be s. The radiance estimate at $\mathbf{P}$ is $s/(\pi r^2)$, where πr^2 is the area of a great circle of sphere $\mathcal{S}$. Therefore, the color at $\mathbf{P}$ is the sum of this radiance contribution and the radiance calculated from ray tracing. This method is theoretically sound; however, due to its required mathematics, we do not offer any proof. The sum of the radiance estimate and the radiance collected from ray tracing may be larger than one, and normalization is needed. Additionally, if the number of photons that can contribute to radiance estimate is too small, they are all ignored because the computed radiance estimate from very few photons may produce blurred images.

4. SOFTWARE DESIGN

This software that supports ray tracing and photon mapping is the cumulative work of many undergraduate students. It grew out from various undergraduate student research projects on ray tracing and photon mapping. The current design consists of an API written in C++ classes with a structure as shown in Figure 2. Under `GICore`, `GIType` defines various data types, `GIObjIntersection` provides the ray-object intersection mechanism, and `GILightSrc` handles light sources. `GIType` defines object types and light source types via `GIObjType` and `GILightSrcType`. A user may inherit these classes to extend their functionality.

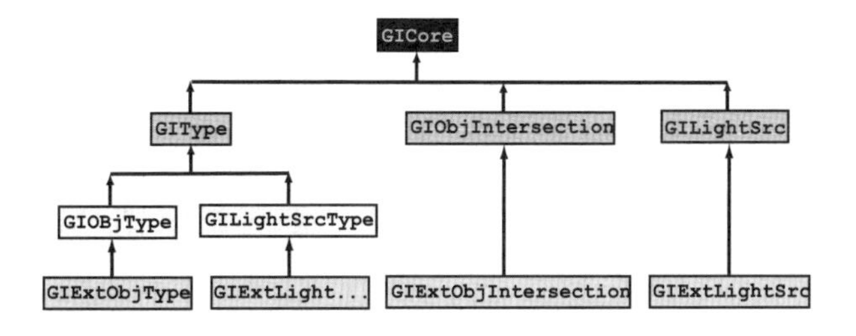

Figure 2: System Programming API

To write a program that performs photon mapping, a user must include the header file `GICore.h`, define a scene class derived from the base class `GIScene`, and provide a constructor. Figure 3 shows that the scene `MyScene` has a rectangular area light, a red sphere and a white floor, Figure 4 has the main program that actually renders the scene, and Figure 5(a) is the result of running this program. Therefore, it is very easy for a user to render a scene using photon mapping. If the call to method `EnablePhotonMapping()` is removed, the system will only ray trace the scene. Figure 5(b) is a ray traced example.

```
class MyScene : public GIScene
{
   public:
      void ConstructScene();
};

void MyScene::ConstructScene()
{
  GI_FLOAT l=-1.0, r=1.0, t=5.5, b=7.5, h=5.25;

  this->backgroundColor = GI_RGB(0.0,0.0,0.0);
  AddRectAreaLight(
    Vector3(0,-1,0),      // normal
    Vector3(l,h,t), Vector3(r,h,t), // vertices:
    Vector3(r,h,b), Vector3(l,h,b),
    1.00,                 // brightness,
    GI_RGB(0.95, 0.85, 0.90) ); // light color

  AddSphere(              // red sphere
    Vector3(1.65,1.000,5.5), 1.995, // center & radius
    red_plastic);         // material (pre-defined)

  AddPlane(               // white floor
    Vector3(0,1,0), Vector3(0,-1.0,0), // normal & vertex
    white_plastic_dull);// material (pre-defined)
}
```

Figure 3: Scene Constructor

```
int main(int argc, char **argv)
{
  MyScene *scene = new MyScene(); // create MyScene
  GIImage img;                    // image area
  int width = 400, height = 400*3.0/4.0;

  GICamera cam = CreateCamera(
     Vector3( 0,  3.20, -24),       // position
     Vector3( 0, -0.05,   1),       // look-at direction
     Vector3( 0,     1,   0),       // up-vector
     45.0,                          // view angle
     width/height);                 // aspect ratio
  scene->EnablePhotonMapping();    // use photon mapping
  img = CreateImage(width, height); // create image

  scene->MaxRayPerLightSrc = 10 * 1000;
  scene->MaxRayTraceDepth     = 3;
  scene->MaxPhotonTraceDepth  = 6;
  scene->photonMap.MaxPhotonSearchRadius = 2.0;
  scene->ConstructScene();          // scene construction
  scene->Render(cam, img);          // render the scene
  SaveImgPPM("test.ppm", img);      // Save to file
  free(img.data);                   // free image memory
  return 0;
}
```

Figure 4: The Main Program

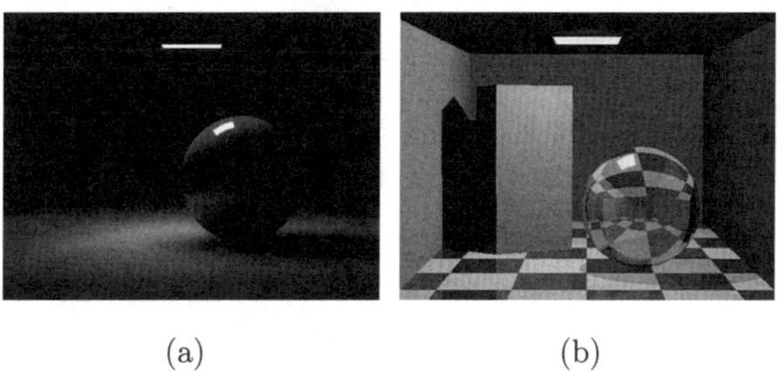

(a) (b)

Figure 5: Sample Photon Mapping and Ray Tracing Images

5. EXAMPLES

Figure 6 demonstrates the quality of our photon mapping API. The scene consists of a box and a glass sphere, with a rectangular light source (*i.e.*, area light) on the ceiling (Figure 5(b)). Thus, we expect to have soft shadows, color bleeding from the green wall to the left side of the box, and some form of caustic produced by the glass ball. In Figure 6, the first image shows the photon hit positions and the second has the rendered result. We choose to use 1,000 photons with $r = 4.0$, 10,000 photons with $r = 2.0$, 100,000 photons with $r = 1.0$ and 200,000 photons with $r = 0.4$. Note that the radius for radiance estimate is inversely proportional to the number of photons shot. The color bleeding effect is weak when the number of photons is small; however, as the number of photons increases, the effect of color bleeding is more evident as shown by the color on the left side of the box. The ceiling above the box also shows a touch of white. Caustic of the glass ball also becomes clearer as the number of photons shot increases. In fact, in the case of 200,000 photons, the glass sphere generates a very pleasant and soft caustic. The effect of soft shadows also becomes more realistic as the number of photons shot increases. Figure 5(b) is the same scene generated by ray tracing. Compared this result with Figure 6(d), it shows a huge difference.

Figure 7 is an example that illustrates the effect of indirect illumination. This scene has an object between the light source and the left wall, and a reflective floor. If this scene is ray traced, the left portion of the ceiling would become dark. With photon mapping, some photons will be bounced to the ceiling, left wall, and even the back side of the blocking object (Figure 7(a)). As a result, these areas are illuminated indirectly by the light reflected from the floor (Figure 7(b)).

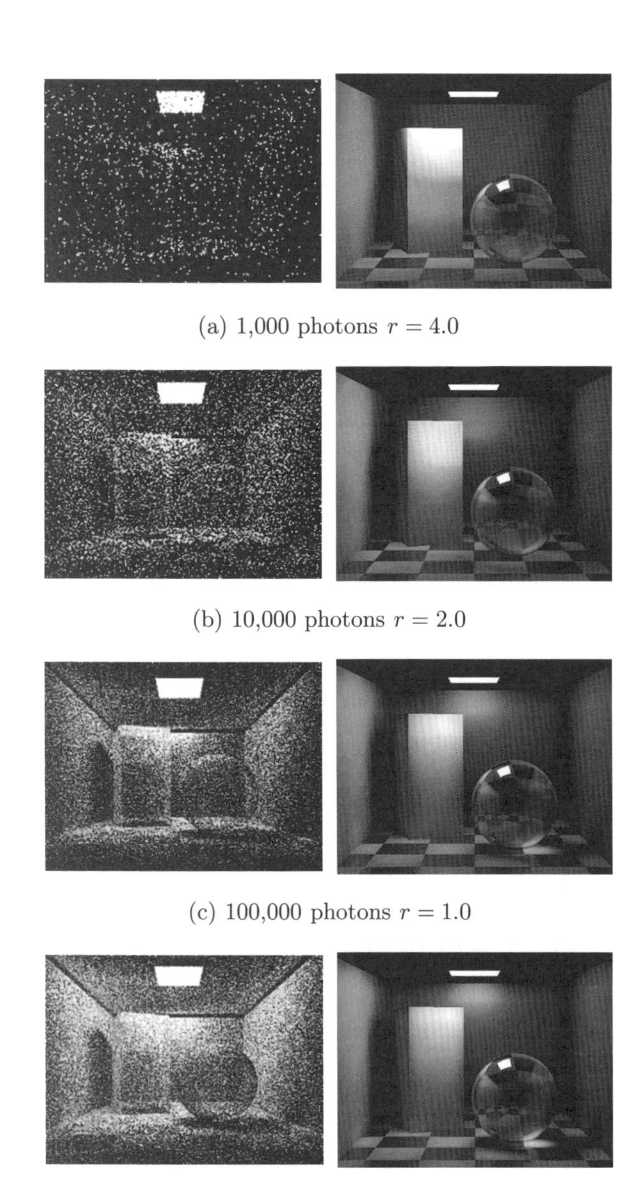

(a) 1,000 photons $r = 4.0$

(b) 10,000 photons $r = 2.0$

(c) 100,000 photons $r = 1.0$

(d) 200,000 photons $r = 0.4$

Figure 6: A Few Photon Mapping Examples

If a glass sphere is bombarded with concentrated photons from a spot light, we will be able to generate very realistic caustic effects. In this case, two photon maps may be needed, one for general rendering while the other for caustic generation. Figure 8, created by undergraduate Josh Anderson with his own caustic code, shows a beautiful and realistic caustic. However, if we use only one photon map to record all photon hits without concentrated photons, caustic may be soft as shown in Figure 9, which is actually Figure 6(d) enlarged to reveal the effect.

6. CLASSROOM EXPERIENCE

Photon mapping was taught twice in our **Advanced Computer Graphics** course, a course designed for those who have completed an introductory course and are interested in more advanced topics beyond graphics programming. Class size was small with around 10 students, most of them were

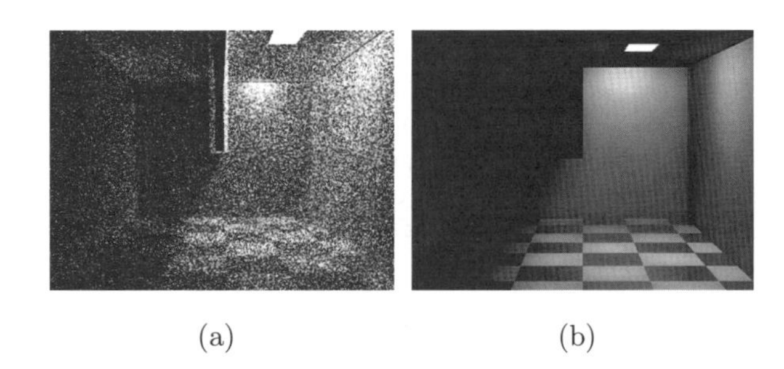

(a) (b)

Figure 7: Indirect Illumination

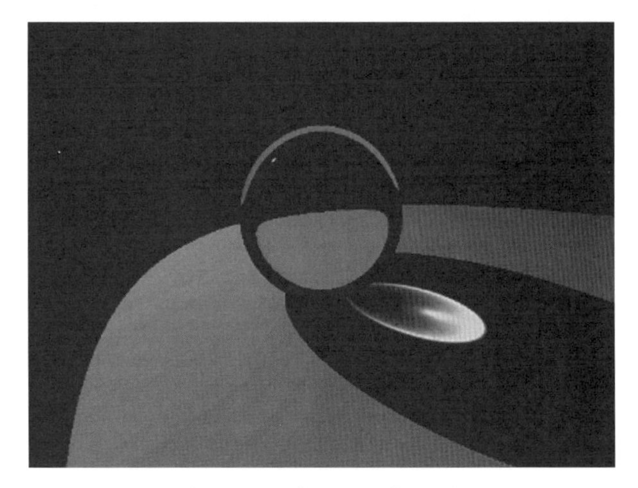

Figure 8: Strong Caustic

undergraduates with a few graduate students. The organization of this course is topic-oriented and project-based. We present about ten topics and each student is required to perform a term project, which includes a report, an implementation, and a presentation with demonstration. In the past, students did ray tracing, photon mapping, radiosity, advanced texture mapping, mesh simplification, geometry compression, multiresolution modeling, morphing and non-photorealistic rendering. We have a long history in ray tracing and photon mapping development by undergraduate students in directed study and other courses. As a result, students who are interested in photon mapping have sample source code to use. Interestingly enough, every student preferred to write their own version of ray tracer and photon mapping system with a difference emphasis (*e.g.*, real-time photon mapping and caustic).

Most students in our class are very competent in ray tracing. Figure 10 shows two student ray traced images using POV-Ray [9]. Hence, we only present the way of building a recursive ray tracer and refer those who are interested to two standard references [2, 8], followed by the discussion of several problems of recursive ray tracing. This usually takes three lecture hours. Then, we spend about six hours on radiosity to address the shortcomings of ray tracing. Topics include the basic heat transfer theory, the radiosity equation, gathering and shooting, progressive refinement, form factor computation, substructuring and adaptive subdivision. After the radiosity discussion, students have a thorough understanding of the basics as well as pros and cons of both global illumination based methods. Photon mapping is introduced as a compromise between ray tracing and

Figure 9: Soft Caustic

radiosity. Since it is easy to understand, students have no difficulty in following the lectures and greatly enjoy photon mapping. This is demonstrated by the success of students' work on photon mapping. For example, Figure 8 is the first successful implementation of caustic using photon mapping. An early version of the software presented here was implemented by the first author of this paper when he was an undergraduate student.

Figure 10: Two Student Ray Tracing Images

Since the size of the class was small and since students follow different research/study paths for the second half of this course with many one-on-one discussions, we believe course evaluation would not help draw any significant conclusion in such a non-traditional course setting.

7. CONCLUSIONS

We have presented our approach of discussing photon mapping in our **Advanced Computer Graphics** course. The major contribution of our work is evidence showing that it is possible to teach global illumination rendering with ray tracing and photon mapping to undergraduate students with very good and convincing results. Our ultimate goal is to provide a good and easy-to-use software tool for students in an introduction computer graphics course to explore, practice and perform photon mapping rendering. Although our software is an API, we plan to add a command processor for users to specify the scene without programming. A long-term goal would be integrating GraphicsMentor and our ray tracing and photon mapping system into a single unit so that students can design a scene using GraphicsMentor and render it with local illumination, ray tracing and photon mapping. In this way, instructors may use this new system to discuss and demonstrate both local and global illumination rendering methods, and students will have a system to practice ray tracing and photon mapping. A radiosity component is also planned. We do hope our effort to making global illumination rendering method available in an introductory course can soon be realized.

8. REFERENCES

[1] J. L. Bentley, Multidimensional Binary Search Trees in Database Applications, *IEEE Transactions on Software Engineering*, Vol. 5 (1979), No. 4 (July), pp. 333–340.

[2] Andrew S, Glassner (editor), *An Introduction to Ray Tracing*, Academic Press, 1989.

[3] Henrik Wann Jensen, *Realistic Image Synthesis Using Photon Mapping*, A K Peters, 2001.

[4] John L. Lowther and Ching-Kuang Shene, Rendering + Modeling + Animation + Postprocessing = Computer Graphics, *The Journal of Computing in Small Colleges*, Vol. 16 (2000), No. 1 (November), pp. 20–28. (reprinted in *Computer Graphics*, Vol. 34 (2000), No. 4 (November), pp. 15–18.

[5] Dejan Nikolic and Ching-Kuang Shene, GraphicsMentor: A Tool for Learning Graphics Fundamentals, *ACM 33rd Annual SIGCSE Technical Symposium*, 2002, pp. 242-246.

[6] Ching-Kuang Shene, Raytracing as a Tool for Learning Computer Graphics, *ASEE/IEEE 32nd Frontiers in Education*, 2002, Volume III, pp. (S4G-7)-(S4G-13).

[7] Ching-Kuang Shene, Teaching and Learning Computer Graphics Made Easy with GraphicsMentor, *Interactive Multimedia Electronic Journal of Computer-Enhanced Learning*, October, 2002 (online journal).

[8] Peter Shirley, *Realistic Ray Tracing*, A K Peters, 2000.

[9] Chris Young and Drew Wells, *Ray Tracing Creations*, Second Edition, Waite Group Press, 1994.

Acknowledgments

The third author appreciates the hospitality of Dr. Horng-jinh Chang, the former President of Tamkang University, Taipei, Taiwan, and Dr. Chuan-Jen Chyan, Chair of Department of Mathematics, for a short-term visit in the summer of 2004 during which the writing of this paper and other research activities were carried out.

A Geographically-Distributed, Assignment-Structured Undergraduate Grid Computing Course

Mark A. Holliday, Barry Wilkinson, Jeffrey House, and Samir Daoud
Department of Mathematics and Computer Science
Western Carolina University
Cullowhee, NC 28723
+1 (828) 227-3951
{holliday, abw, jhouse, sdaoud}@cs.wcu.edu

Clayton Ferner
Department of Computer Science
University of North Carolina at Wilmington
601 South College Road
Wilmington, NC 28403
+1 (910) 962-7129
cferner@uncw.edu

ABSTRACT

Grid computing is now mature enough and important enough to be studied as a full course at the undergraduate level for upper-level computer science majors. We have developed such a course, including a set of lecture slides, assignments, and assignment handouts specifically targeted for this audience. The sequence of assignments is a key part of the course. Some of the assignments are modifications of pre-existing work and others are completely new. We describe the key decisions we made about the course organization and content and describe the assignments. An important feature of the course is that it was geographically distributed with copies of the grid software installed at three campuses. Those campuses plus three others were receiving sites and included students and faculty associated with nine universities.

Categories and Subject Descriptors

C.2.4 [**Computer-Communication Networks**]: Distributed Systems – *client/server, distributed applications, distributed databases, network operating systems.*

General Terms

Design, Experimentation, Security, Standardization.

Keywords

Grid Computing, Assignments, Globus, Web Services, Grid Services.

1. INTRODUCTION

Grid computing is an approach to distributed computing over the Internet that uses open standards [2]. The goal is to virtualize the resources at geographically distributed and often heterogeneous sites. Such resources can include computational devices, data storage, and instrumentation and sensors. Grid computing should lead to more efficient use of these resources by allowing remote and transparent access. Increasing Internet bandwidth and the recent development of key open standards are making the development of production grids increasingly feasible.

SIGCSE'05, February 23-27, St. Louis, Missouri, USA.

We believe that the field of grid computing has matured to the point where a course aimed at the undergraduate, upper-level computer science major is both feasible and desirable. Graduate level courses on grid computing which consist of a seminar reading and presenting a series of papers in the area have been ongoing at a number of universities. However, a true undergraduate course should be different. Such a course should provide a coherent set of lectures that describe the organization of the software that implements grid computing. Just as importantly, such a course should provide a series of hands-on programming assignments so that the students can directly use the key components of the grid infrastructure and develop their own grid-enabled applications.

We have been working over the last year to develop such a course. We received funding from the University of North Carolina Office of the President [9, 10] and the National Science Foundation [11] to support this effort. The first offering of the course is ending at the time of this writing. Undergraduate, grid computing courses for computer science majors are still quite novel. In fact, we chose to offer the course to other universities in North Carolina over the state-supported tele-conferencing network. The response was larger than we expected.

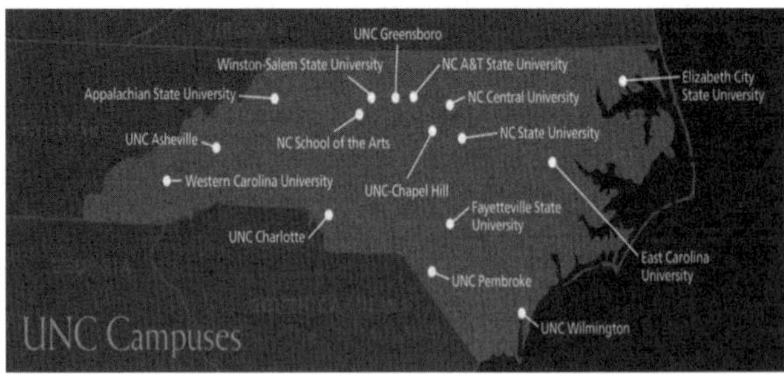

Figure 1: A map of all the University of North Carolina (UNC) campuses. The course originated at the Western Carolina University campus of UNC and was received at Appalachian State University, NC State University, UNC Asheville, UNC Greensboro, UNC Wilmington. In addition, NC Central University, Cape Fear Community College and the private institution Elon University had students or faculty participating.

Over forty students and faculty participated in the course. In addition to the students from our own university, students and faculty at eight other universities participated in the course remotely via the video network. Figure 1, which is a map of the University of North Carolina system, includes the locations of most of the universities involved. The enthusiastic response to our course clearly indicates the need and interest for such a course.

It is our premise that students best learn with hands-on experiences that include working software that they use and modify. In fact, because of the importance of the programming assignments in such a course we structured the course around the assignments. The course involves a series of six assignments including detailed assignment handouts and extensive lecture slides. This paper describes these assignments and thus also explains the course organization.

This paper is organized with the next section addressing some preliminary decisions we had to make about course coverage and expectations of student backgrounds. The third section has a subsection for each of the six assignments. In the fourth section we discuss our experiences. In the last section we review related work and conclude.

2. PRELIMINARY DECISIONS

Deciding on what *not* to have as the first assignment was an early key decision. What we chose not to cover in the lectures or the assignments are the details of installing the grid software. Installation is complex and understanding the details would not be appropriate for an undergraduate course, especially at the start of such a course. Nevertheless, we did develop a detailed installation guide handout that we posted on the website for students to read if they wish.

The posted installation guide served another important purpose which is to ensure consistency across the installations at all the sites. Some of the remote sites had just a few students so we gave those students accounts on our local machines that they could logon to remotely. However, two of the remote sites (NC State University and UNC Wilmington) had about thirteen students each in the course. At those remote sites, the faculty or system administrator performed their own installations or had preexisting installations. Our installation guide provided a point of reference to help ensure consistent installation procedures and resulting grid environments across the sites.

Another issue concerning the installation guide involved what to describe installing. The Globus Toolkit of the Globus Alliance [7] has become the most widely-used basic, open source grid software. However, an installation guide for only the current version of the Globus Toolkit is insufficient. A working grid requires many other pieces of software. Fortunately, the National Science Foundation Middleware Initiative (NMI) [8] has developed a distribution containing many open source grid software contributions. We developed our installation guide based on downloading the NMI distribution and installing selected key parts of it.

Though there is some proprietary grid software, the grid environment is one in which open source software based on open standards is the predominant case. Furthermore, much of the software includes several other features: it is written in the Java programming language, Linux is the operating system, and standard open source software from other application areas (especially software developed as part of the Apache web server project) is used. There are certainly significant efforts with respect to other languages and operating systems, but a representative introduction to current grid software should involve Linux and Java. Consequently we decided that because the course audience consists of upper-level computer science majors we did not think it unreasonable to expect the students to have had some experience with both of these.

Though grid environments are often used to access high-performance computing resources and large capacity storage resources, the hardware requirements needed to install an open source grid environment are not exceptional. At our university we used four 1.3 GHz Pentium IV machines each with 512 megabytes of main memory and a 30 gigabyte disk.

Another key decision we had to make was how the students would use the software. We would characterize a grid as having at least the following key parts:

1. a graphical portal that requires authentication and displays available resources
2. a graphical means to create a workflow (in other words, a) to create job instances out of selected resources, b) to place those job instances at specified sites, and c) to identify execution ordering dependencies between the job instances)
3. the actual procedure of submission and distribution of the jobs that form the workflow
4. monitoring and visualization of the progression of the execution of the workflow and visualization of the results upon completion of the workflow

Because computer science majors make up the audience for this course, we decided to focus on the implementation issues rather than on the user's perspective. Consequently, we chose to use a bottom-up approach. The assignments and lectures start with the lowest level concepts (i.e. web services) and build up to higher levels of software. Thus, the way to use the software is command-level for most of the course. Only after we reach the top level do the students see and start using graphical interfaces for accessing the grid.

3. THE ASSIGNMENTS

Each of the assignments includes a detailed handout available on the course website. Here we merely identify the key points. The lectures for the course cover the material needed for each assignment. The lectures also include introductory material motivating the use of grids and providing a historical context. The last several lectures were by guest speakers on specialized topics.

3.1 Assignment One: Web Services

The standards which grid software implement have been changing rapidly. However, those standards and software appear to be converging to a stable state. A key feature of that state is that the grid is implemented by grid services and that grid services are an extension of web services. Web services, in turn, are based on a set of well-defined standards [12]. Thus, we decided that the series of assignments should start with an assignment where the students learn how to implement and execute a web service.

A web service is often implemented using a Java servlet which in turn requires the presence of a servlet container. Our assignment one uses the widely used Apache Tomcat servlet container. One instance of Tomcat is running on the machine before the student starts the assignment.

All of the assignments have two halves. In the first half the student is guided through the steps of running a version of the software being demonstrated. In the second half the student modifies or extends the provided client and server software and then repeats the steps. Assignment one involves creating all the needed server source files, creating the server executable files, creating the client source file, and compiling and running the client.

The server source files are partially provided. The example service is a MyMath class that includes a method returning the square of the number which is passed to it as an argument. A source file with only that class is provided. The student then uses the Apache Axis software to generate all the other needed server source files. These source files include the WSDL (Web Services Description Language) describing the service, Java interfaces used by the client, a Java stub class to be called by the client, and a Java class to use in locating the service.

The student then compiles the service source files using the Java compiler. We provide and explain the source file for an example client that accesses the server. The student then compiles the client source file and runs the client. The output can be examined to see that the server worked.

The student then extends the MyMath class by adding another method that checks whether the number passed as an argument is even or odd. This assignment and its handout were motivated by one developed by Amy Apon [1].

3.2 Assignment Two: Grid Services

Assignment one does not require the use of any grid software since it involves only a web service. Assignment two adds the complexity of requiring some grid software. However, it only uses the most basic layer of grid software which is implemented by the Globus Toolkit (we are using version 3.2 which is the most recent version).

The assignment two grid service is another mathematics-related class that has methods for changing the value of a state variable by addition or subtraction as well as a method for returning the current value of the state variable. In contrast to the web service, this grid service maintains some state between method calls.

Being a grid service makes the assignment more complex in several ways. One is that Tomcat is not used directly as the servlet container. Instead the servlet container is started through Globus by the student as part of the assignment and terminated by the student as part of the assignment. Since multiple students are using the same machine there will be multiple containers running and the students must ensure that each container is listening on a different TCP port. The students need to learn how to determine which TCP ports are free.

A second way that a grid service is more complex is that deployment of the service is more explicit than it was in assignment one. As in assignment one, the base server source file is provided. However, the WSDL file (actually Grid WSDL) is also provided and described instead of merely generated and used. The student then builds all the other required source files, compiles them, and deploys the resulting service using the Apache Ant build system. Ant is similar to the UNIX make program but based on XML.

At this point the student turns his or her focus to the client software. The source code for an example client is provided and described. The student compiles this code to create the client executable, starts the container on a free port and runs the client. The student then learns to end the session including terminating the container. As in assignment one, the student then extends the server and redoes all the steps. This assignment is a modification of the one in Bojo Sotomayor's tutorial [5] though our handout is significantly more detailed.

3.3 Assignment Three: Job Submission

At this point the student has the basic understanding of how to define, create, deploy, and use a generic grid service. In assignment three we focus on how to use a particular, very important, grid service: the grid service that is used to submit a job. That grid service is called the Globus Resource Allocation Manager (GRAM).

The student first is introduced to the Resource Specification Language-2 (RSL-2). RSL-2 is the language that GRAM uses starting with version 3.2 of the Globus Toolkit. It is an XML schema (RSL-1 was not) with some standard attributes such as the file path to the executable for the job that is being submitted and the file paths for standard input, standard output, and standard error. The RSL-2 file used to submit the executable file /bin/echo is examined.

At this point the student is ready to start the sequence for submitting a job to the grid. As discussed for assignment two, the student must first identify a free port and then start a container on one of those free ports. It would be convenient for the next step to be for the student to submit the job. However, an intermediate step is needed that involves security.

An important part of Globus is its implementation of the Grid Security Infrastructure (GSI). In a grid when a user requests a service that service is often not on the same machine as the user. In fact the service is often on a machine at a different site and that other site may belong to a different organization. Thus, mutual authentication of both the user and the service is essential. Mutual authentication is done by GSI via certificates and the Secure Socket Layer (SSL) protocol. In particular, each user and service in the grid is identified via a certificate in the X.509 certificate format. Each certificate has been signed by a Certificate Authority (CA) through the use of digital signatures and public key cryptography. The mutual authentication is initiated by the user entering a passphrase.

The presence of these certificates and the mutual authentication process have so far not been visible to the user. However, at this point in the use of GRAM, the presence of GSI in the background becomes apparent. In particular, GSI includes a delegation capability which is an extension to the SSL protocol. The service requested by the user often needs to, in turn, make a request of other services in order to complete the user's request. Each of these secondary requests requires mutual authentication and thus an entering of a passphrase by the user. Delegation avoids the need to reenter the passphrase through the creation of a proxy certificate.

Thus, before the student can perform the actual job submission, a proxy certificate must be created to be used by GSI when the job submission takes place. The proxy certificate creation is done by the student executing the grid-proxy-init command. After that command the student can submit the job. GRAM is invoked using the managed-job-globusrun command. That command takes as its argument the RSL-2 file that identifies the job to be run and other information (such as the file to be used for standard output).

The job runs and the student can see that it ran by looking at the output of /bin/echo in the file designated for standard output. The student then repeats this sequence but with a new executable job that she has written and compiled The new job is a Java program that implements the functionality of /bin/echo. In addition to creating the new executable job the student must edit the RSL-2 file appropriately.

Just before assigning assignment three we decided to add another major step. In the additional step the student combines assignment two and assignment three. First, the student writes a grid service called Item, which provides inventory information about the items being sold in a store. Second, the student deploys an instance of the Item grid service. Next the student writes a client called Shopper that accesses that instance of the Item grid service. All of these steps are like parts of assignment two, but are non-trivial since many grid-related files have to be changed as well as the writing of the source code for the grid service and the client.

The next phase of this step involves GRAM job submission and the previous steps of assignment three. First, the student creates a RSL-2 file to submit via GRAM one instance of the Shopper client. That client, once submitted, interacts with the deployed Item grid service as before. Then, the student modifies the RSL-2 file to submit via GRAM four instances of the Shopper client. All four instances of the client then concurrently access the one instance of the deployed Item grid service.

3.4 Assignment Four: Job Distribution

The Globus Toolkit only provides part of the software needed for a grid environment. Assignment four is the first assignment that goes beyond the Globus Toolkit. In particular, GRAM provides only basic job submission. More sophisticated job submission and distribution is done by software such as Condor-G (Grid-enabled Condor) [7]. Fortunately, the National Science Foundation Middleware Initiative (NMI) grid distribution includes many programs including Condor-G (Grid-enabled Condor).

In assignment four the student uses Condor-G to submit a job. The student first learns the format of the submit description text file that Condor-G requires. An example of such a file is provided. The student then creates a proxy certificate, learns how to check the status of the condor pool of machines, and uses the submit description text file and the condor-submit command to submit the job. The student then monitors and manages the progress of the job and the status of the condor pool and verifies the output of the job when the job completes. As in assignment three the student then repeats this sequence but with a job that he or she writes and compiles.

3.5 Assignment Five: Parallel Programming

The previous assignments illustrate how grids can be used to solve important classes of problems. These classes include cases where jobs are single executions but they are embedded within a larger problem such as the parameter sweep of a design space or a step within a workflow. However, grids can also be used for parallel programming. Message Passing Interface (MPI) is widely used to support parallel programming [3]. A version of MPI, called MPICH-G2, works with Globus. Assignment five involves the students writing some parallel programs using MPICH-G2 and running them on our grid.

3.6 Assignment Six: A Workflow Editor

By the end of assignment five the student has an understanding of how the internals of a significant part of a grid environment work. It is now time for the student to turn to the view seen by a user. As mentioned earlier, the user is authenticated via a grid portal and then uses the portal to specify which resources to execute within a workflow. The workflow is then submitted and the user can monitor the progression of the workflow and use visualization to examine the results when the workflow completes.

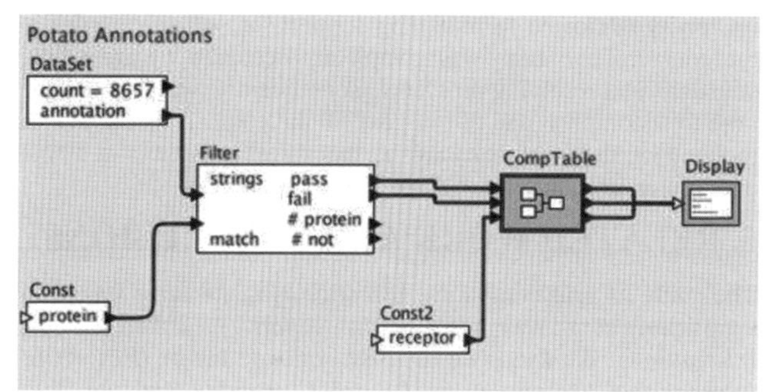

Figure 2: Creation of a workflow [9] using the workflow editor developed at the Department of Computer Science of UNC-Wilmington.

We show the user viewpoint to the student by examining the workflow editor developed at the Department of Computer Science of UNC-Wilmington [9]. An example use of this workflow editor is shown in Figure 2. This example illustrates the flexibility of the UNC-W software. The module selected by the user and placed in the workflow need not be a regular job. Instead it can be the data set resulting from a database query (as in the top left rectangle of the figure), a particular constant value (as in the bottom left rectangle of the figure), or useful general modules such as a filter (left middle rectangle) or a statistical analyzer (right middle rectangle). Assignment six involves the students using this workflow editor in an example grid problem.

4. EXPERIENCES

The course that is structured around the above assignments is now finished except for the final exam. Before the semester started we had carefully tested the first four assignments. We tested them ourselves on our own machines. We also conducted a trial run of using them in a workshop attended by UNC computer science faculty. We were fairly confident at that point that they would work as expected. The one surprise from the pre-course workshop was how memory intensive the servlet container is. If more than a few containers are started on a single machine with 512 megabytes of main memory, thrashing occurs.

During the course those four assignments worked as we expected. Our one mistake was the last minute addition of the last step to assignment three (the store grid service and the shopper client). Completing this step is quite complex and turned out to be beyond the skills of most of the students. We extended the deadline for assignment three in an attempt to give the students sufficient time to complete it. As a result we did not have enough time for all of the remaining assignments. Our solution was to post assignment five (MPI programming) but not to require the students to complete it.

Our experience with assignment three highlights an issue that we debated about the nature of the assignment handouts. If we want the assignment handout to be as useful as possible as a resource for the students then it should contain a great deal of detail. On the other hand, too much detail can make the assignment too straightforward and not require sufficient independent thinking on the part of the student.

The grid software was installed at two of the remote sites as well as at our site. Even though the three sites had different hardware configurations, students were able to complete the assignments at all three sites. We found that supporting the student use of the software was very labor-intensive. We had two students at our university dedicated to providing support for software issues in the course. Their time was completely occupied by answering questions and resolving problems. Consequently, we did not have time to accomplish one of our goals in the course. That goal was to connect the grid software at the three sites into a single operational grid, instead of three independent grids.

5. RELATED WORK AND CONCLUSIONS

The study of grid computing education is in its early stages. A significant step was the set of papers presented at the *International Workshop on Grid Education* at the *4th IEEE/ACM International Symposium on Cluster Computing and the Grid (CCGrid04)* in April of 2004.

The paper [4] by Bini Ramamurthy on the GridForce project is especially noteworthy. The GridForce project involves developing a two course sequence on grid computing at the senior undergraduate/first year graduate student level. The laboratories in the first course involve web services and grid services. However, their approach to grid services is different than ours and aimed at more advanced students. The first grid service laboratory does not use Globus (or Apache Axis); instead it uses a "minimal grid framework". The students build the framework themselves. The second grid service laboratory requires the students to install Globus themselves. The GridForce approach is a useful complement to our approach. It would be attractive to students who complete our course and want to investigate grid computing further.

Bojo Sotomayor has written *The Globus Tookit 3 Programmer's Tutorial* [5]. An early section of the tutorial shows how to write "your first grid service in five easy steps." Our assignment two is an adaptation of this section to our environment with our handout expanding on what we feel are the key points.

The work [1] by Amy Apon at the University of Arkansas is also related. Like us, she recommends starting with a web services assignment and then a grid services assignment. Our web services assignment was motivated by hers. Her grid service assignment, like ours, is a modification of the Bojo Sotomayor example.

In conclusion, we believe that the course we have developed is a significant contribution to the study of grid computing education. The sequence of assignments builds upon earlier work. The overall sequence of assignments is new. Some assignments are completely new. Other assignments are based on earlier work but for all the assignments we have developed unusually detailed handouts to help explain the concepts and to ensure that the student will avoid common pitfalls. The lecture slides are completely new. Materials appropriate for the undergraduate computer science major are significantly different from those appropriate for graduate students or professionals. We believe (and are supported by our experiences) that we have found the right level of assignments and materials for the undergraduate audience.

All of the course materials including lecture slides, assignment slides, the grid software installation handout, and the assignment handouts are available on the web at http://cs.wcu.edu/~abw/CS492F04/index.html.

6. ACKNOWLEDGEMENTS

Our thanks to the National Science Foundation (DUE 0410667) and the Office of the President of the University of North Carolina System for their financial support of this project. Our thanks also to Mark Baker and the Distributed Systems Group at the University of Portsmouth in England for the time Mark Holliday spent there while working on this paper.

7. REFERENCES

[1] Apon, A., Mache, J., Yara, Y., and Landrus, L., *Classroom Exercises for Grid Services*, Proc. of the Linux Cluster Institute Int. Conf. on High Performance Computing, Austin, TX, USA, May 2004.

[2] Foster, I. and Kesselman, C. *The Grid 2: Blueprint for a New Computing Infrastructure, Second Edition*, Morgan Kaufmann, 2004.

[3] Gropp, W., Lusk, E., and Skjellum A., *Using MPI Portable Parallel Programming with the Message-Passing Interface, Second Edition*, MIT Press, 1999.

[4] Ramamurthy, B., *GridForce: A Comprehensive Model for Improving the Technical Preparedness of our Workforce for the Grid*, Int. Workshop on Grid Education (CCGrid04), April 2004, Chicago, IL. USA.

[5] Sotomayor, B., "The Globus Toolkit 3 Programmer's Tutorial," http://www.casa-sotomayor.net/gt3-tutorial/multiplehtml/index.html.

[6] The Condor Project Homepage, http://www.cs.wisc.edu/condor/.

[7] The Globus Alliance: The Globus Toolkit, http://www-unix.globus.org/toolkit/.

[8] The National Science Foundation Middleware Initiative, http://www.nsf-middleware.org/.

[9] Wilkinson, B., et. al. (UNC-Wilmington, lead), *Fostering Undergraduate Research Partnerships through a Graphical User Environment for the North Carolina Computing Grid*, University of North Carolina Office of the President, 2004-2006.

[10] Wilkinson, B., Holliday, M., et. al. (Appalachian State Univ. lead), *A Consortium to Promote Computational Science and High Performance Computing*, University of North Carolina Office of the President, 2004-2006.

[11] Wilkinson, B., Holliday, M., and Luginbuhl, D., *Introducing Grid Computing into the Undergraduate Curriculum*, National Science Foundation, DUE 0410667, 2004-2006.

[12] World Wide Web (W3C) Consortium, Web Services Activity, http://www.w3.org/2002/ws/.

The Grader in ProgrammingLand

Curt Hill
Department of Mathematics
Valley City State University
Valley City, ND
701 845-7103
Curt.Hill@vcsu.edu

Brian M. Slator
Department of Computer Science
North Dakota State University
Fargo, ND
701 231-6124
slator@cs.ndsu.edu

Lisa M. Daniels
Department of Teacher Education
North Dakota State University
Fargo, ND
701 231-8748
Lisa.Daniels@ndsu.edu

ABSTRACT

In this paper, we describe a customized instructional content delivery system named ProgrammingLand with special emphasis on a program evaluation module named TorqueMOODa. The system is fully online and is used as a component of several classroom courses, as well the foundation of comparable distance education classes. The context of these systems is the early programming classes often taken by introductory Computer Science students, among others.

Categories and Subject Descriptors

1.1 K.3.2 [Computers and Education]: Computer and Information Science Education – *computer science education*

General Terms

Design, Experimentation.

Keywords

CS educational research, online instruction, blended education, distance education.

2. INTRODUCTION

The ProgrammingLand MOOseum [3] is an online virtual environment designed to instruct lower level students in the fundamentals of programming and computer science. This system has been in use and development for several years in the CS 1 classroom. The metaphor is that of a museum, where the students move from one exhibit to another choosing what they will view and with what they will interact. The museum is a learner centered experience, where the students control their own path and pace. Several classes have used the system as an online textbook substituting for a regular textbook. In addition the system has been used as the basis for distance education.

The system is based on a MOO [1], a text based virtual environment. Although it has been updated to have a web interface [4] it is organized differently than most web based systems, continuing a room and exit based metaphor that is likened to a Exploratorium style museum.

SIGCSE'05, February 23–27, 2005, St. Louis, Missouri, USA.

The student enters ProgrammingLand by starting a Java enabled web browser and connecting to the class web page. After a login process the student sees a screen similar to that of Figure 1. The student navigates the system by clicking links shown in the right hand pane of the interface. On occasion, interaction may involve typing in the lower left hand pane of the interface. Messages, other than room descriptions are shown in the left middle pane.

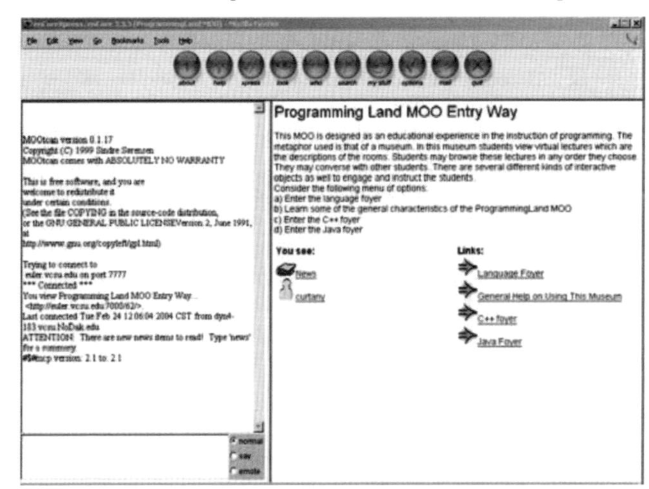

Figure 1. The student view.

The system records where the student has gone, and what interactive objects have been used. This information is used to determine which lessons the student has completed.

3. LESSONS AND ASSIGNMENTS

A lesson in ProgrammingLand contains similar components to lessons in the classroom. Certain prerequisite material must be accomplished; some motivation as to why this material is important is needed; the basic content material is presented with optional material for the interested student; exercises pertinent to the material are given; and a mastery test or application project is assigned. Not every lesson has all of these components since lessons vary in size from small, such as what can be accomplished in five minutes, to large, such as a significant unit in a course, taking more than a week. A course is a set of lessons that contain other lessons, which may contain yet other lessons recursively.

A lesson in ProgrammingLand is a special form of room that has certain properties, most important of which is a set of requirements, that must be accomplished in order to receive credit for completing the lesson. A lesson is also a gateway to the rooms that deliver the content pertaining to that lesson. A lesson may require that a previous lesson be completed, that some subset of the lessons rooms be visited, that contained lessons be completed, and that some interactive objects are used. The first time a student arrives in a lesson room, the requirements are displayed. At any subsequent visit the student may see the requirements again, which also shows those that are completed. A partial display of typical set of requirements is shown in Figure 2.

```
There were 3 different requirements. You
only need to satisfy one of these.
Requirement 1
 Trace of code machine Hello(#7826)
 Room: Executable and non-executable
statements(#694)
 Lesson: Comments in Programs(#691)
 Lesson: Statements(#902)

Requirement 2
 Trace of code machine Hello2(#7827)
```

Figure 2. Portion of the requirements of a lesson.

The student who leaves the lesson space without completing it may be offered the option of satisfying the lesson by taking a quiz. This option is only available in certain instances, such as when the only unsatisfied requirements are unvisited rooms and that there are sufficient questions to produce a five question multiple choice test. Each room may be constructed with one or more quiz questions attached. These are not available to the student until the quiz is generated. In addition the lesson room may have a store of general quiz questions. At the presentation of the quiz, the questions are randomly selected and their right and wrong answers randomly ordered. If the student misses one or fewer questions, he or she receives full credit for the lesson.

It is more common for a student to satisfy a lesson by completing the requirements than passing a quiz. The first time the student enters the lesson room after having completed the requirements, a message noting the completion is sent. Since, the lesson room is the gateway to the lesson's rooms and any subordinate lessons this notification is rather routine and often a student may not notice it. Yet, there are situations where it cannot be ignored, such as when completion of a lesson triggers an assignment.

Each lesson that is completed sends a message to the student but also to another object. This object determines if this lesson has a corresponding assignment. If this is a lesson with an assignment, an agent is dispatched to deliver the assignment. To the student this appears like a person entered the room, gives the assignment, and then leaves. Of course it is just an agent object of the MOO. This assignment is stored such that the student may review it at any later time. The assignment may be of any type, but it is usually a programming assignment that the student is to complete outside of ProgrammingLand.

The assignment given to the student is chosen from a set of equivalent assignments belonging to this agent. This is done to discourage plagiarism in the programming projects. Some of these assignments may be scored by the program grader.

4. THE PROGRAM GRADER

TorqueMOODa, the program grader was introduced as a component of ProgrammingLand in the Fall semester of 2003. During that term it was an optional item that a student could use to check a program before turning it in. In the Fall semester of 2004 it became a required last check of the program before handing in the program. It is both a MOO client and a scripted program grader. The student downloads the install file from the class web page and then runs TorqueMOODa on any program to be handed in.

Briefly, the execution of TorqueMOODa performs the following seven tasks: 1) TorqueMOODa connects to ProgrammingLand to determine which assignments are waiting, 2) the student chooses which assignment is to be scored 3) TorqueMOODa downloads the proper grading script 4) the student selects the executable to be graded 4) TorqueMOODa runs the program through its paces, 5) the student chooses the source files, if there is a source file requirement 6) TorqueMOODa scans the source files looking for various characteristics, and 7) TorqueMOODa save the results in the student's record within ProgrammingLand.

Program graders are not new [2], however one of the things that distinguishes TorqueMOODa, is its integration into an existing learning system. A predecessor system [5] had a lesser scope and completely different implementation. Currently, TorqueMOODA only runs on Microsoft Windows executables, although a Java version is under development.

4.1 TorqueMOODa execution

TorqueMOODa obtains assignment information, including scripts from ProgrammingLand. Therefore it must connect to the MOO and must do so with the student's user name and password. Therefore, the initial execution of the program requires four pieces of information from the student: user name, password, MOO location and port number. The four are stored in an encrypted initialization file after the initial execution for the student's ease of use.

A student's progress in ProgrammingLand is often not completely orderly. It is not uncommon for a student to have acquired a subsequent assignment before completing the previous one. ProgrammingLand allows a student to have at most two pending TorqueMOODa gradable assignments. Students having more than that are not allowed to enter a previously unvisited lesson. They may always return to lessons they have already entered or completed.

TorqueMOODa's first action upon connection is to find the currently pending assignments. Figure 3 shows such a choice. On the left side of Figure 3 are two different program descriptions identified by the agents that delivered them. These agents are named Donald and Fernanda and these names also label radio buttons on the right hand side. The student selects the correct program and clicks the Grade Program button on the bottom.

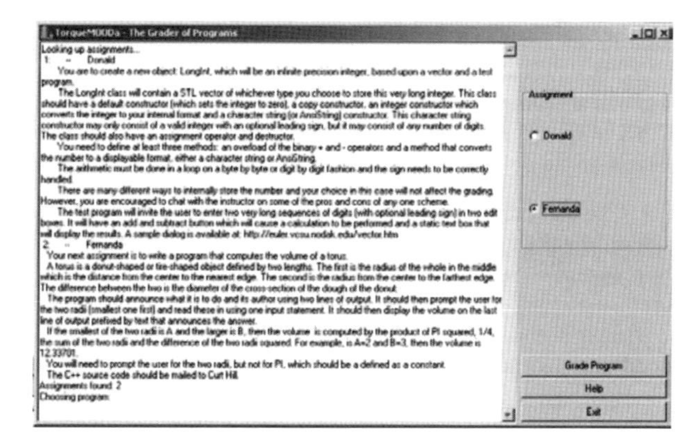

Figure 3. TorqueMOODa offering assignment choice.

What the student does not see at this point is that the program is downloading the correct script from the MOO. Instead the student sees a dialog box asking for an executable file to be chosen. In the initial grading the source language is irrelevant, only the executable is run. The course for which ProgrammingLand and TorqueMOODa have been most heavily used introduces both the console and graphical user interface paradigms, therefore TorqueMOODa must handle either form. However, the script that TorqueMOODa uses must be for one paradigm or the other. Perhaps surprising is that the Graphical User Interface program is generally easier to grade with TorqueMOODa.

The selected program is then run under TorqueMOODa's control and the student just watches the process. In a console program, the standard input and output files of the program are piped to TorqueMOODA, which simulates a user. In a graphical user interface program the components, such as buttons and edit fields are changed and monitored by TorqueMOODa to simulate the user. The typical console program has only these two files as a mechanism to interface with the user, while a graphical user interface complicates this considerably. TorqueMOODa has several mechanisms to make sure that it is reading the correct controls within a window.

Each window component that is to be used in a script is identified by an approximate location. This only includes components such as buttons, edit fields and areas that must be read or written by TorqueMOODa. Labels, graphics, and other items to make the window more attractive or readable will be ignored. A typical assignment specification often refers to a web page containing an image of the desired window. Once the program to be graded is started TorqueMOODa attempts to connect the expected controls with the actual ones within the window, based on location and type. This process is problematic, since students often consider the specifications a suggestion rather than a command. Moreover, they are encouraged to enhance programs beyond the specification for their own edification. Hence, TorqueMOODA needs an additional mechanism to finalize the connection. This is supplied by the mockup window.

The mockup window is another window of shape and size approximating the original window. Those components expected by the script are listed in this window for confirmation. If TorqueMOODa guessed well, the student only has to click the OK button, otherwise corrections may be made to the window. Three figures should illustrate this process. Figure 4 shows a particular program as it is running. Figure 5 shows the expectations of the script displayed by TorqueMOODa. Figure 6 shows the mockup window. All three windows are visible to the student at the same time.

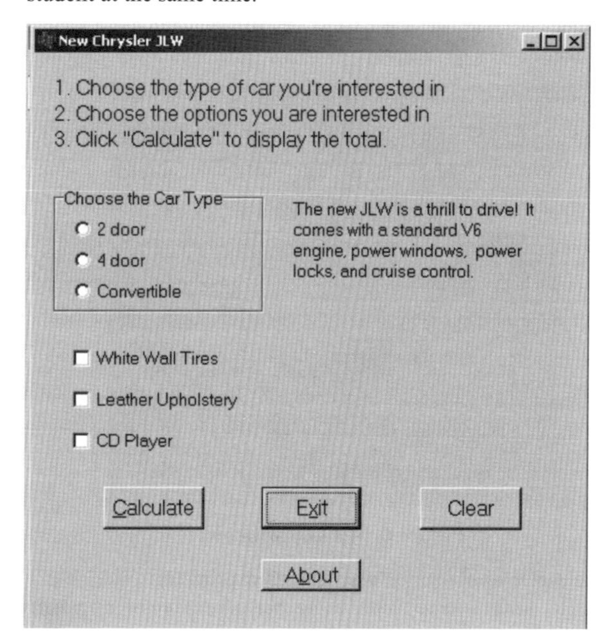

Figure 4. A running program.

```
[1] Regular      << Radio Button >>
[2] Four door    << Radio Button >>
[3] Convertible    << Radio Button >>
[4] Whitewall    << Check Box >>
[5] Leather    << Check Box >>
[6] CD Player    << Check Box >>
[7] Answer    << Static Text >>
[8] Calculate    << Button >>
[9] About    << Button >>
[10] Exit    << Button >>
```

Figure 5. TorqueMOODa display.

Figures 4, 5 and 6 show the grading of a good program which causes TorqueMOODa to not guess correctly. The Clear button in Figure 4 was not in the original requirements, yet the student should not be penalized for using it. Moreover the small box identified by the 7 in Figure 6 will actually only contain a dollar sign, while the box next to it identified by -1, will actually contain the answer, which is the price of an automobile. When these two items are corrected and the OK button clicked, then the program will be graded. There is a similar mechanism for verifying menu entries for windows programs.

At the next step TorqueMOODa proceeds in its script to emulate a user, by entering values and examining results. Each scoring step is typically a sequence of two steps. The first is a preparation step where the input data is given to the graded program. This may be the production of an input line for a console program or in the case of a graphical window the manipulation of one or more controls, followed by a button click or menu selection. The second step pauses for a short delay to allow the program to process its inputs, then the output file or output window components are examined. A series of rules in the script then determines the number of points to be awarded, which are shown in the TorqueMOODa display.

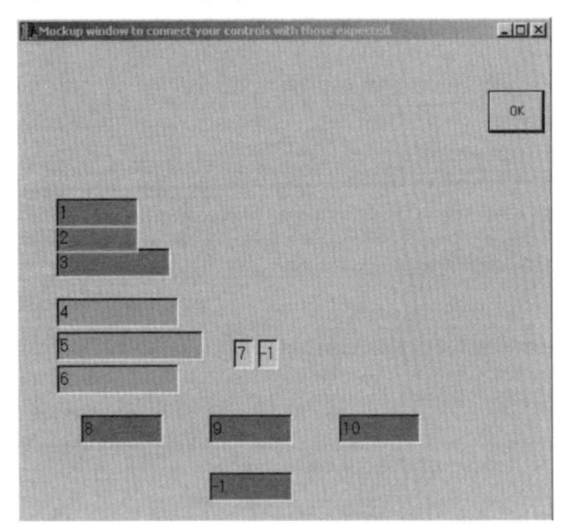

Figure 6. Mockup window.

TorqueMOODa is mainly a script-based program tester, but it may also scan source code using regular expression pattern matching. If the script contains any statements that require source code scanning the program will ask for selection of the source code, which may include several files. The source code scanner recognizes comments and counts the number of words within comments, which may be used in scoring. Those characters not in comments are scanned for regular expressions. For example, the program shown in figure 4 had the requirement to use a C++ *switch* statement. Thus, the scoring script looked for the C++ *switch* keyword and a minimal number of comment words.

At the conclusion of all grading steps, TorqueMOODa sends the results to ProgrammingLand for storage in the student's records. This clears the assignment from the list of pending assignments.

4.2 TorqueMOODa scripts

TorqueMOODa is designed to handle programs in a similar way to a human grader. The typical grader will work out a set of data that will exercise a program in reasonable ways, based on expected types of errors. This data is then run on all programs and the results tabulated. Representing this in a script should be a straightforward process. This is a black box testing scheme.

TorqueMOODA has two forms of script. The first is designed to be easy to create and modify. This script syntax has a superficial resemblance to a C-like language. The first script form is compiled into the second form of script. The second form is equivalent and designed to be compact for easy storage in the MOO, easy to download from the MOO, as well as easy to interpret by TorqueMOODA.

The script is written free form, has C++ style one-line comments, a restricted form of variable that must be declared before it is used, a C style assignment statement, a simple *if* statement with an else and compound statement, and a variety of predefined functions. Unlike C it is not case-sensitive.

Variables in TorqueMOODa scripts are not so much variables in the normal sense, but program inputs or outputs. Console programs and graphical user interface programs are quite different in this way so TorqueMOODa may merely examine variable declarations to determine the paradigm of the graded program.

In a console program a TorqueMOODA variable is a value produced by the graded program that TorqueMOODa must find in the program's output. This is done using regular expression pattern matching specified in the script. Thus the output of the program is scanned and when variable values are found they are placed in the variable. They are then accessed with *if* statements. A console script usually does not use the assignment statement. The input to the graded program is merely a string of characters that is placed into the graded programs console input file.

In a windows program every point of interaction is a variable. These points of interaction are window controls or components. So a TorqueMOODa variable for a GUI program must specify the type of control in question, the location and the purpose. The control may be a button, check box, radio button, text, or an edit field. The location is used for TorqueMOODa's guessing process. The purpose of the variable is a text string used in the mockup window. The TorqueMOODA variable is used in the script to modify or access the current value of the corresponding window component. Reading a control is usually seen inside an *if* condition, while modification is usually performed with an assignment.

An assignment statement changes a variable and its corresponding window control. Of course, not all assignments are legal. A check box may be assigned a *true* or *false* to set it to its desired value, but may not receive a text string. An edit field may receive a constant string. A button may not be the target of an assignment, it is clicked by the use of the function *execute* with the button as a parameter. The *execute* function also delays TorqueMOODa so that the program has time to respond.

The main checking is done by the *if* statement. This is similar to a C style *if* except that there is a mandatory *endif* to remove the common language ambiguity. The comparison of the *if* must compare a variable for equality with a constant or function result. The statement to be executed either when the comparison is true or false must be a single statement, but C style braces may be used to wrap several statements into a single statement. The *if* statement may be nested.

The typical *if* has a single call to the function named score as its alternative if the condition is true and a nested *if* when the condition is false. The score function takes three parameters: the integer value earned, the integer value possible, and a text message. All three are displayed on the TorqueMOODa window when the function is called. If the earned score is less than the available points the message is also saved to be later sent to the MOO.

A few examples are now discussed to illustrate the process of scoring. Setting the values of a control are different for console and windows programs so these will be discussed first.

Figure 7 shows a fragment of a console script, declaring a variable and setting its value. A console script will require just a small number of variables, often just one. The output function processes an output of the program with a regular expression, while the input function sends a string of characters to the graded program's input file.

```
control(variable, product);
output("");  // Prompt
input(" 3 4 ");
output(".* {product,3}");
```

Figure 7. Establishing console variables.

In figure 7, the control is declared first. It has the name of product. The reserved word variable is the type of the control and indicates that this control is not tied to any component in a window. The output statement that follows merely flushes the first output line of the program to be graded. The input function then sends the constant string to the program. The second output function is to find the value to be assigned to product. The initial ".*" is a regular expression that matches any number and type of characters. The braces enclose a pair indicating a value to be found. The first item of the pair indicates the variable, while the 3 indicates that an integer value is desired.

```
Control(radio,regular,(30,90),"Regular");
Control(check,white,(20,200),"Whitewall");
Control(text,answer,(250,200),"Answer");
Control(button,calc,(150,300),"Calculate");
regular = true;
white = false;
execute(calc);
```

Figure 8. A portion of window script.

A similar piece of a script for the windows program is shown in figure 8. This is a fragment of the script that was used on the program shown in figure 4. The controls indicate a position and a purpose, unlike the console version. The last line indicates that the *execute* function is to click the Calculate button.

Once the values of variables are established the process to grade is similar between console and GUI programs. Figure 9 shows the use of *if* and *score.*

```
if(answer == currency(20000.00))
  Score(2,2,"Correct");

else
  Score(0,2,"Incorrect price");
endif;
```

Figure 9. A script rule using score.

The currency function merely strips the excess characters from a text string such as a dollar sign or commas.

5. CONCLUSIONS AND FUTURE WORK

TorqueMOODa adds an important new capability to ProgrammingLand, but not without problems. The program contains no AI, so its scanning of source code is necessarily crude. It cannot read and understand displayed instructions so the student must follow the specifications in ways that seem quite arbitrary. For example, a console program that displays two values on the same line must put them in the specified order, for TorqueMOODa lacks the sophistication of a human tester. Its handling of GUI programs is somewhat better but also with limitations. It may recognize a multi-line edit box, but there is as yet no syntax for accessing individual lines within it and processing data in a multi-line edit box has all the same problems as processing console output. There is still the unanswered question as to how far in the curriculum the grader may be used. First semester programs tend to be simple, thus using simple inputs and outputs. In contrast a grader for a data structures course would be much more concerned with how the source code accomplishes its purpose, the very place where TorqueMOODa is the weakest.

In the first instance of use, TorqueMOODA was optional. At the conclusion of the semester one assignment was analyzed. All the programs for this assignment were graded by four advanced students and also by TorqueMOODa. The correlation for the scores between the graders and TorqueMOODa was a respectable 0.70. Of course, the human graders had a higher correlation with each other. The next attempt will be a more elaborate study where using the grader is mandatory as the last test of an assigned program, but not counted in the student's grade.

TorqueMOODa has successfully graded programs written in Borland's CBuilder, Microsoft's Visual Basic and Microsoft's Visual C compilers. A Java version is under development.

6. ACKNOWLEDGMENTS

The authors wish to acknowledge the work that numerous students have contributed to this project. These include Justin Bearinger, Martina Miteva, and Jacqueline Wolfe, among many others.

The ProgrammingLand MOOseum project has been supported by ND-EPSCoR through the FLARE program under EPS-9874802 and is currently supported by National Science Foundation Grant EIA-0313154.

7. REFERENCES

[1] Curtis, Pavel (1992). Mudding: Social Phenomena in Text-Based Virtual Realities. Proceedings of the conference on Directions and Implications of Advanced Computing (sponsored by Computer Professionals for Social Responsibility)

[2] Foubister, S. P., Michaelson, G.J. and Tomes, N. Automatic assessment of elementary standard ML programs using Ceilidh. *Journal of Computer Assisted Learning.* 13(2), June, 99-108.

[3] Hill, C., Slator, B., and Daniels, L. An Online Resource for the Introductory Programming Class. In *Proceedings of the 2nd International Conference Information Technology Research and Education (ITRE '04)* (London Metropolitan University, London, UK, June 28 -July 1, 2004). IEEE, Piscataway, NJ 08855-1331.

[4] Holmevik, J. R., and Haynes, C. enCore, Open Source MOO project. http://lingua.utdallas.edu/encore/index.html

[5] Peng, Ge (2003). TorqueMOODa: automatic grading in the ProgrammingLand MOOseum. M.S. Thesis, North Dakota State University, Fargo ND.

Results from the Evaluation of the Effectiveness of an Online Tutor on Expression Evaluation

Amruth N Kumar
Ramapo College of New Jersey
505 Ramapo Valley Road
Mahwah, NJ 07430, USA

amruth AT ramapo.edu

ABSTRACT

Researchers have been developing online tutors for various disciplines, including Computer Science. Educators are increasingly using online tutors to supplement their courses. Are online tutors effective? Can they help students learn? If so, what features contribute to their effectiveness? We will examine these questions in the context of an online tutor that we developed for introductory Computer Science. The tutor is designed to help students learn expression evaluation in C++/Java.

We evaluated the tutor over several years, in multiple sections of Computer Science I each year. We used controlled tests with differential treatments, and used pre and post-tests to evaluate the effectiveness of the tutor. Our results show that online tutors indeed help students learn. Students who use the tutor for practice learn better than those who use a printed workbook. Students who receive both graphic visualization and text explanation learn better than those who receive only graphic visualization. Students who use graphic visualization learn better than those who receive no explanation. These results will be of interest to both developers and users of online tutors.

Categories and Subject Descriptors

K.3.1 [**Computing Milieux**]: Computer-Assisted Instruction

General Terms

Experimentation, Languages.

Keywords

Tutor, Programming, Expression, Evaluation, Feedback, Visualization, Computer Science I.

1. INTRODUCTION

The prevalent view of science education is constructivism, which maintains that information cannot simply be transferred from the teacher to the student. Instead the student must construct his or her own meaning [4]. The most productive way to help a student construct his/her own meaning is through scaffolding, where the teacher guides the student during problem-solving [23]. Online tutors are an attractive option for providing such one-on-one guidance.

Therefore, researchers have been developing online tutors for various disciplines, including Computer Science. Examples of tutors developed for Computer Science include JFLAP [21] for Automata Theory, Gateway Labs for discrete mathematics [3], and PILOT [6] for graph algorithms. These tutors engage the user in problem-solving activities, which are known to promote learning. Online tutors for introductory Computer Science courses include:

- Tutors wherein students fill out missing statements in a programming problem, and the tutor points out syntax errors and selected semantic and run-time errors. Examples include WebToTeach [2] (now TuringsCraft), InStep [20] and [24].
- Tutors that preprocess/annotate the student's program so that when the program is executed, either the state of the program is clarified or errors in the program are highlighted. Examples include CMeRun [10] and Expresso [12].
- Tutors that provide detailed feedback about the evaluation/execution of programs, so that they can be used as supplements to classroom instruction [7]. In this category, we have developed several tutors on introductory programming concepts (e.g., expressions [15], loops [9]), advanced concepts (e.g., pointers [16,17], classes [13]) and programming language design (e.g., scope [11, 18], parameter passing mechanisms [22]).

Are such online tutors effective? Do they help students learn? What features contribute to the effectiveness of tutors for Computer Science? To date, one study has shown that students who used the tutor spent less time asking teaching assistants for additional help [20]. Intelligent Tutoring Systems researchers have documented an improvement of one standard deviation through the use of problem-solving tutors in algebra, geometry and LISP [1]. We investigated these questions in the context of a tutor that we developed for expression evaluation in C++/Java.

We chose a tutor on expression evaluation for this study for two reasons: 1) All introductory Computer Science students must learn expression evaluation. Therefore, the sample sizes for experiments would be large. 2) It is easier to evaluate a students' knowledge of expression evaluation, and therefore, the

SIGCSE '05, February 23-27, 2005, St. Louis, MO, USA.

effectiveness of a tutor on expression evaluation. In Section 2, we will present our tutor on expression evaluation and its features. In Section 3, we will discuss the evaluation of the tutor, including the protocol and the results.

2. A TUTOR ON EXPRESSION EVALUATION

We developed an online tutor on expression evaluation to help students learn by solving problems. The tutor generates and presents problems to the student, obtains the student's answer, grades it, and provides detailed feedback about the correct answer. The tutor can be used in one of two modes: in tutoring mode, it generates a problem and demonstrates the step-by-step solution to the problem. In testing mode, it generates a problem, lets the user solve it and grades the user's solution. First developed in 1996, the tutor is currently in its fourth version. The work reported in this paper was carried out using version 3 (2001-02).

The tutor presents problems compiled by the instructor. It can also generate problem expressions randomly. So, it is capable of generating an infinite number of problems with which to practice - a student will never see the same problem twice. Therefore, the same tutor can be used for both tutoring and testing in a course. When used for assignments and tests, random generation of problems helps prevent plagiarism and cheating.

The student is expected to solve each expression one operator at a time. For each sub-expression, the student draws an underbrace across the sub-expression by clicking and dragging the mouse. In response, the tutor pops up a dialog box to enter the intermediate result. The student has the option to undo one or all the previous steps. Please see the left panel in Figure 1 for the problem and the incorrect answer entered by the student.

After the student enters the answer and submits it, the tutor grades the student's answer and provides detailed feedback about the correct answer. It provides two types of feedback:

- Graphic visualization, in which the answer is displayed using underbraces. Underbraces illustrate the order in which the operators in an expression are evaluated. This is intuitive and natural - similar to how a student might evaluate an expression on paper.
- Text explanation, in which each step in the evaluation of the expression is described in prose. The explanation of each step includes a description of the precedence and associativity of the operator, errors, if any in the evaluation of the operator, and finer points in the evaluation of the operator, such as integer division or the inadvisability of comparing real numbers.

Please see the right panel in Figure 1 for the graphic and text feedback provided by the tutor. The tutor provides animation controls for the student to step through the feedback. After reading the feedback, the student clicks on the 'Next Problem' button to go to the next problem and start all over again.

The tutor can be configured to provide feedback at several levels:

- No feedback – the user is just instructed to go to the next problem;
- Minimal feedback – the user is told whether his/her answer is correct.
- Detailed feedback – the user is not only told whether his/her answer is correct, but also shown graphic visualization and/or text explanation for the correct answer.

3. EVALUATION OF THE TUTOR

We evaluated the tutor (arithmetic and relational operators only) in multiple sections of our Computer Science I course from spring 2001 through fall 2002. We tested a different hypothesis each semester. We will describe the evaluation protocol in Section 3.1 and discuss the results in Section 3.2.

3.1 The Protocol

We used controlled tests to evaluate our tutors. We used a between-subjects design, randomly but evenly dividing each class into control and test groups. Further, we used the traditional pre-test, practice, post-test protocol. Both the control and test groups first answered the same pretest, then were exposed to differing treatments for practice learning, and finally came back together to answer the same post-test:

- During the pre-test, students answered a set of questions on the topic. Their score on the test reflected their level of preparation in the topic. The students were neither told whether their answers were correct/wrong, nor were they given any feedback during the test. Typically, the test lasted 6-10 minutes.
- During the practice, the test and control groups practiced with different treatments. Typically, the practice session lasted 10-12 minutes. Students did not have access to any other resource (such as text books, notes, consultation with the instructor or classmates) during the practice session.
- During the post-test, the students answered a new set of questions that were carefully matched with those on the pretest for the concepts they tested and the order in which they appeared. The change in the score from pretest to post-test reflected the effect of the tutor on the student's learning.

The whole procedure took 30-40 minutes. When analyzing the results, we calculated the average points per question rather than the total points in order to eliminate practice effect.

3.2 The Results

In spring 2001, we compared the tutor against textbooks – we tested the hypothesis that practicing with the tutor would be at least as effective as practicing with a printed workbook that included answers to problems as an appendix. The improvement in the score per attempted problem from pretest to post-test was 20.1% for workbook users (N=31) and 29.6% for tutor users (N=33), both the improvements being statistically significant (t-test 2-tailed $p < 0.05$). The effect size, calculated as (post-test average – pretest average) / standard deviation on the pretest was 1.27 for the tutor users versus 0.71 for the workbook users. Table 1 lists these figures.

Table 1: Printed Workbook Vs Tutor

Spring 2001	Pre-Test Score/Problem	Post-Test Score/Problem	% Change	Effect Size
Workbook Users (N=31)				
Average	4.35	5.23	20.10%	0.71
Std-Dev	1.23	1.03		
Tutor Users (N=33)				
Average	3.90	5.06	29.62%	1.27
Std-Dev	0.91	1.10		

In fall 2001, we compared two versions of the tutor – one that provided both graphic visualization and text explanation against one that provided only graphic visualization and no text explanation. Both the control and test groups used the tutor for practice, and both the groups viewed the visualization of the evaluation of the expression. But, only the test group received additional text explanation of the evaluation of the expression. We tested the hypothesis that students who received the text explanation would learn better than those who did not. The improvement in the score per attempted problem from pretest to post-test was 51.2% for the test group (N=33) and 39.8% for the control group (N=33), both improvements being statistically significant ($p < 0.05$). The effect size was 1.30 for those who received both graphic visualization and text explanation versus 1.00 for those who received only graphic visualization. Table 2 lists these figures.

In fall 2002, we compared two different versions of the tutor – one that provided graphic visualization (but no text explanation), versus one that did not provide any explanation except for the correct final answer. Our hypothesis was that those who received graphic visualization only would still learn better than those who received no explanation. The improvement in the score per attempted problem from pretest to post-test was 53.1% for the test group that received graphic visualization (N=24) and 33.4% for the control group that received no explanation (N=24), both improvements being statistically significant ($p < 0.05$). The effect size was 1.35 for those who received graphic visualization versus 0.84 for those who received no explanation. Table 3 lists these figures.

Table 2: Graphic Visualization with and without Text Explanation

Fall 2001	Pre-Test Score/Problem	Post-Test Score/Problem	% Change	Effect Size
Graphic Visualization (N=33)				
Average	3.44	4.80	39.80%	1.00
Std-Dev	1.36	1.05		
Graphic Visualization + Text Explanation (N=33)				
Average	3.12	4.72	51.22%	1.30
Std-Dev	1.23	1.26		

Table 3: No Explanation Vs Graphic Visualization

Fall 2002	Pre-Test Score/Problem	Post-Test Score/Problem	% Change	Effect Size
No Explanation (N=24)				
Average	3.06	4.08	33.43%	0.84
Std-Dev	1.22	1.51		
Graphic Visualization (N=24)				
Average	3.02	4.63	53.13%	1.35
Std-Dev	1.19	0.98		

3.3 Discussion

Students who used the tutor for practice learned better than those who used a printed workbook. We have replicated this result in several other studies [9,13,14]. Clearly, online tutors are at least as effective as textbooks, the traditional source of exercise problems. Online tutors have several advantages over textbooks:

1. Unlike textbooks, online tutors can generate an unlimited supply of problems, thereby providing for as much practice as desired by the learner.
2. Unlike textbooks, online tutors can instantaneously grade the learner's answer.
3. Unlike textbooks, online tutors can provide detailed feedback.

Therefore, online tutors such as ours may be used for learning, reinforcement, assessment, and self-assessment, both in and after class.

Students who received graphic visualization and text explanation learned better than those who received only graphic visualization. This confirms the earlier result in literature that in order to be effective, visualization must be extended with explanation [8,19].

Students who received only graphic visualization still learned better than those who received no explanation. This highlights the importance of providing explanation in online tutors. Other studies that we have conducted also support this conclusion [11,14,16].

The improvement in learning that we observed with our online tutor was in the range of 30-60% after accounting for practice effect. The effect size was over 1.25. This compares favorably with the result that one-on-one human tutoring can improve student learning by two effect sizes over normal classroom instruction [5].

4. ONGOING AND FUTURE WORK

Since testing our tutor, we have made several changes in keeping with the feedback we received from students and teachers who used the earlier versions of the tutor:

- Problem generation in the tutor is now adaptive – the tutor keeps track of the topics that the student has not yet mastered, and generates problems on only those topics.
- The tutor does not generate expressions randomly any more, since it is harder to control the learning outcomes of such expressions. Instead, the tutor now generates problems based on parameterized templates. Since a large number of problem instances can be generated from each template, the tutor is still capable of generating an endless supply of problems. Since the templates are indexed by learning outcomes, the generated problems are better matched to the needs of the learner.

We are currently extending the tutor to cover logical, assignment and bitwise operators. We plan to continue to evaluate the tutor. The tutor is available for general use. Access to the tutor can be obtained by contacting the author.

5. ACKNOWLEDGMENTS

Partial support for this work was provided by the National Science Foundation's Course, Curriculum and Laboratory Improvement Program under grant DUE-0088864 and the Combined Research and Curriculum Development and Educational Innovation Program under grant CNS-0426021.

6. REFERENCES

[1] Anderson J.R., Corbett A.T., Koedinger K.R. and Pelletier R., "Cognitive Tutors: Lessons Learned", The Journal of the Learning Sciences, Vol No 4(2), 1995, Lawrence Erlbaum Associates, Inc., pp 167-207.

[2] Arnow D. and Barshay, O., WebToTeach: An Interactive Focused Programming Exercise System, In proceedings of FIE 1999, San Juan, Puerto Rico (November 1999), Session 12a9.

[3] Baldwin, D. Three years experience with Gateway Labs. In Proceedings of ITiCSE '96 (Barcelona, Spain, June 1996), ACM Press, 6-7.

[4] M. Ben-Ari, Constructivism in Computer Science, Proceedings of 29th SIGCSE Technical Symposium, March 1998, 257-261.

[5] Bloom, B.S.: The 2 Sigma Problem: The Search for Methods of Group Instruction as Effective as One-to-One Tutoring. Educational Researcher, Vol 13 (1984) 3-16.

[6] Bridgeman, S., Goodrich, M.T., Kobourov, S.G., and Tamassia, R. PILOT: An Interactive Tool for Learning and Grading. in Proceedings of SIGCSE '00 (Austin, TX, March 2000), ACM Press, 139-143.

[7] Brusilovsky, P. and Su, H.: Adaptive Visualization Component of a Distributed Web-Based Adaptive Educational System, Proceedings of the 6th international conference on Intelligent Tutoring Systems, June 2002, LNCS 2363, Springer Verlag, 229-238.

[8] Brusilovsky, P., Explanatory Visualization in an educational programming environment: connecting examples with general knowledge. In: B. Blumenthal, J. Gornostaev and C. Unger (eds.) Human Computer Interaction. LNCS 876. Berlin: Springer-Verlag, 202-212.

[9] Dancik, G. and Kumar, A.N., A Tutor for Counter-Controlled Loop Concepts and Its Evaluation, Proceedings of Frontiers in Education Conference (FIE 2003), Boulder, CO, 11/5-8/2003, Session T3C.

[10] Etheredge, J. CMeRun: Program Logic Debugging Courseware for CSi/2 Students. Proceedings of 35th SIGCSE Technical Symposium on Computer Science Education, March 2004, 22-25.

[11] Fernandes, E. and Kumar, A.: A Tutor on Scope for the Programming Languages Course, Proceedings of 35th SIGCSE Technical Symposium, Norfolk, VA, (March 2004), 90-95.

[12] Hristova, M., Misra, A., Rutter, M, and Mercuri, R. Identifying and Correcting Java Programming Errors for Introductory Computer Science Students. Proceedings of 34th SIGCSE Technical Symposium on Computer Science Education, February 2003, 153-156

[13] Kostadinov, R. and Kumar, A.N. A Tutor for Learning Encapsulation in C++ Classes, Proceedings of ED-MEDIA 2003 World Conference on Educational Multimedia, Hypermedia and Telecommunications}, Honolulu, HI, 6/23-28/2003, 1311-1314.

[14] Kumar, A.N., Learning Programming by Solving Problems, in Informatics Curricula and Teaching Methods, L. Cassel and R.A. Reis ed., Kluwer Academic Publishers, Norwell, MA, 2003, 29-39.

[15] Krishna, A., and Kumar A.: A Problem Generator to Learn Expression Evaluation in CS I and Its Effectiveness, The Journal of Computing in Small Colleges, Vol 16, No. 4, (May 2001), 34-43.

[16] Kumar, A.N., A Tutor for Using Dynamic Memory in C++, Proceedings of 2002 Frontiers in Education Conference (FIE 2002), Boston, MA, 11/6-9/2002, Session T4G.

[17] Kumar A. Learning the Interaction between Pointers and Scope in C++, Proceedings of The Sixth Annual Conference on Innovation and Technology in Computer Science Education (ITiCSE 2001), Canterbury, UK, (June 2001), 45-48.

[18] Kumar A.N.: Dynamically Generating Problems on Static Scope, Proceedings of The Fifth Annual Conference on Innovation and Technology in Computer Science Education (ITiCSE 2000), Helsinki, Finland, (July 2000), 9-12.

[19] Naps, T.L., Eagan, J.R. and Norton L.L. (2000) JHAVE – an environment to actively engage students in Web-based algorithm visualizations. Proceedings of 31st SIGCSE Technical Symposium on Computer Science Education, March 2000, 32(1), 109-113.

[20] Odekirk-Hash, E. and Zachary, J.L. Automated Feedback on Programs Means Students Need Less Help from Teachers. Proceedings of 32nd SIGCSE Technical Symposium on Computer Science Education, February 2001, 55-59

[21] Rodger, S., and Gramond, E., JFLAP: An Aid to Study Theorems in Automata Theory, Proceedings of ITiCSE 98, Dublin, Ireland, August 1998, 302.

[22] Shah, H. and Kumar, A.N., A Tutoring System for Parameter Passing in Programming Languages, Proceedings of The Seventh Annual Conference on Innovation and Technology in Computer Science Education (ITiCSE 2002), Aarhus, Denmark, June 2002, 170-174

[23] Wood, David and Wood, Heather, Vygotsky, Tutoring and Learning, Oxford review of Education 22(1): 5-16, 1996

[24] Yoo, J.P., Seo, S.J. and Yoo, S.K. Designing an Adaptive Tutor for CS-I Laboratory. Proceedings of the 5th International Conference on Internet Computing, Las Vegas, NV, 2004.

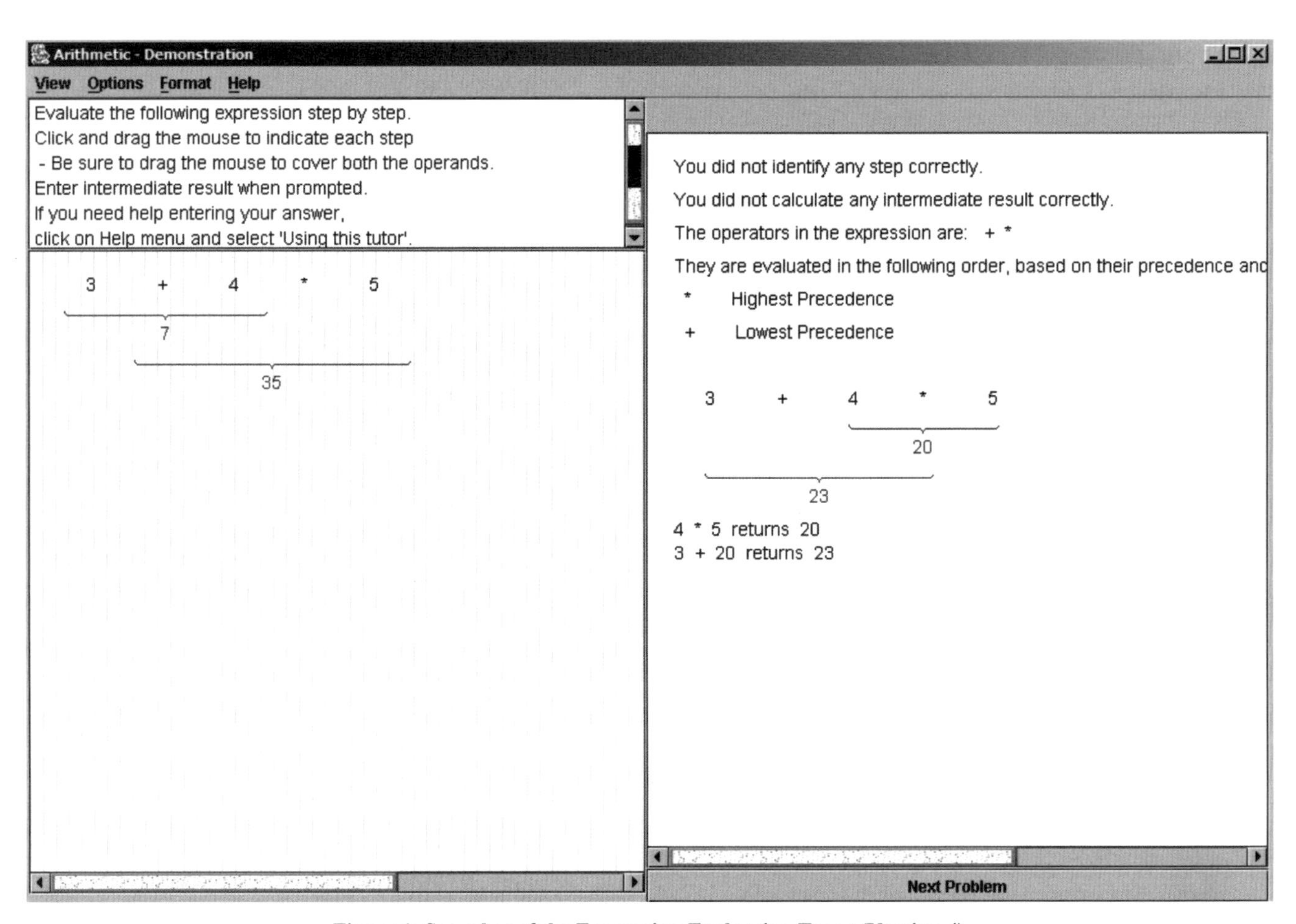

Figure 1: Snapshot of the Expression Evaluation Tutor (Version 4)

PL-Detective: Experiences and Results *

Amer Diwan
Michele H. Jackson
William M. Waite
Jacob Dickerson
University of Colorado
Boulder, CO 80309
{Amer.Diwan,Michele.Jackson,William.Waite,Jacob.Dickerson}@Colorado.edu

ABSTRACT

Last year we described the PL-Detective, a system for building exercises and demonstrations in a programming languages course. One of the main goals of the PL-Detective was to provide an experimental environment with which students could interact in order to discover the information that they needed to complete the exercise. In this paper we evaluate the PL-Detective with respect to this goal. We present data from a class of 29 groups of two or three students that used the PL-Detective for 11 exercises. Our data shows that students are both effective and efficient at getting information from the PL-Detective.

Categories and Subject Descriptors

D.3.m [**Programming Languages**]: Miscellaneous

General Terms

Human Factors, Languages

Keywords

Concepts of programming languages, Education

1. INTRODUCTION

Last year [2] we presented a system, the PL-Detective, for building assignments in a "Principles of Programming Languages" course. The PL-Detective is an extensible compiler for a language called MYSTERY. MYSTERY has a fixed syntax but its semantics are a mystery: different semantics can be selected using command-line options. The current version of the PL-Detective, which is available in open-source form, allows the user to vary the semantics of MYSTERY along 10 dimensions, yielding a total of 9216 combinations. Many educators have expressed an interest in the PL-Detective (the PL-Detective is available for open-source download). Thus, given the growing user base, it is particularly important for us to understand the strengths and weaknesses of the PL-Detective. This paper presents and analyzes data that show that the PL-Detective is effective in meeting its design goals.

We designed the PL-Detective with the goal of helping students to move away from the stage of received knowledge [5, 1]. In other words, we want students to realize that they they can create knowledge (rather than always counting on "receiving" it from an authority figure, such as an instructor). We identified two subgoals that would help us attain our main goal:

1. The PL-Detective should encourage students to collaborate with each other in solving complex tasks. In this way the PL-Detective deemphasizes the instructor as the sole source of information. In our paper last year, we reported that the PL-Detective was indeed successful in this subgoal.
2. The PL-Detective should provide an experimental environment with which the students interact in order to discover the information that they need. In this way, the students learn to generate knowledge as a result of their interactions with the PL-Detective.

In this paper we present data from *language analysis* exercises that demonstrate that the PL-Detective meets the second subgoal. In a language analysis exercise, the instructor fixes the semantics for MYSTERY without revealing them to the students. Students use the PL-Detective to get clues that allow them to determine the semantics of MYSTERY. During these exercises, student interaction with the PL-Detective is similar to that with a compiler or interpreter: students submit programs and the PL-Detective compiles (and optionally runs) the programs. However, the difference in using the PL-Detective is that although students submit programs to a compiler in order to get a working program, they submit programs to the PL-Detective *to get information* so that they can predict the semantics of MYSTERY. Indeed, a program that does not run but produces a certain error message may provide as much valuable information to the student as a program that runs to completion. Essentially, the PL-Detective acts as an oracle, giving useful information to the students provided they ask good questions.

To conduct the exploration reported here, we collected, coded, and analyzed data from eleven exercises using the

*This work was supported by the National Science Foundation under grant EIA 0086255. Any opinions, findings and conclusions or recommendations expressed in this material are the authors' and do not necessarily reflect those of the sponsors.

SIGCSE'05, February 23–27, 2005, St. Louis, Missouri, USA.

```
VAR x: INTEGER;

PROCEDURE f() =
VAR x: INTEGER;
BEGIN
  x := 20;  g();
END;

PROCEDURE g() = BEGIN PRINT x; END;

BEGIN
  x := 10;  f();
END;
```

Figure 1: Distinguishing between static and dynamic scoping (attempt 1)

```
PROCEDURE f() =
VAR x: INTEGER;
BEGIN
  x := 20;
  g();
END;

PROCEDURE g() =
BEGIN PRINT x; END;

BEGIN
  f();
END;
```

Figure 2: Distinguishing between static and dynamic scoping (attempt 2)

PL-Detective over the course of 6 weeks. The study involved 29 groups of two or three students. We used social scientific techniques to conduct our analysis. Our results demonstrate that students use the PL-Detective to effectively and efficiently provide them with the information they need for their assignments.

This paper is organized as follows. Section 2 describes how students use the PL-Detective via an example. Section 3 presents our measurement methodology and environment. Section 4 presents our results. Section 5 discusses some of the lessons we have learned on how to make effective assignments using the PL-Detective. Section 6 concludes the paper.

2. EXAMPLE

We now demonstrate an example exercise that uses the PL-Detective. The goal of this exercise is to determine whether MYSTERY is configured to use static or dynamic scoping. A student may write the program in Figure 1 and submit it to the PL-Detective. If this program produces the output 10, the student can conclude that MYSTERY is configured to use static scoping; if the output is 20, the student can conclude that MYSTERY is configured to use dynamic scoping.

Figure 2 presents an alternate strategy of doing the above. In this strategy, if the submission produces an error message ("x not found"), then it indicates static scoping. If the program prints 20, then it indicates dynamic scoping.

From the above two strategies we see that outputs (or lack of outputs) and error messages (or lack of error messages) can all serve as useful information to the student.

3. METHODOLOGY

In this section we describe our procedures for data collection and analysis.

3.1 What data did we collect?

We collected submissions from a total of 11 PL-Detective exercises that were spread out over 6 assignments, with one assignment per week. These exercises began the third week into a 15 week semester.[1] Students had one week to complete each assignment. In addition, the exercises specified a limit of either the number of programs that students could submit or the number of PRINTs that they could execute (each PRINT outputs a single integer) without having their grade penalized. (Syntax errors did not count against the limit.) Such limits were intended to discourage a trial-and-error approach. Table 1 describes the exercises briefly and also indicates their limits. If the input program to the PL-Detective fails (either at compile or run time) the PL-Detective reports only the first error message to the student. This fixes the amount of information students can derive from a single submission.

We derived the limits based on the nature of the exercise, the instructor's solution to the exercise, and the exercise's level of difficulty. Typically, we set the limit to be twice the number of attempts it took us to answer the exercise. For harder exercises we set higher limits, up to three times the number of attempts it took us to answer the exercise. In general, one can use the limit as an indication of the complexity of the exercise.

3.2 Data Collection

At the end of the Spring 2004 semester, we collected all submissions to the PL-Detective for the exercises described in Table 1. Students worked on all assignments in groups of 2-3 members. There were 29 groups and group membership remained constant throughout the semester. All assignments in the course were submitted in groups, and all members of a group received the same grade. Our previous results (using a survey and focus groups) strongly indicated that most of the groups collaborated throughout each assignment rather than splitting up the labor amongst group members [2].

The PL-Detective records the sequence of submitted programs for each exercise and group. To determine if PL-Detective was successful in meeting its goals we needed to know the characteristics of the PL-Detective as a source of information. Thus, we developed a coding scheme (available from the authors) that coded the explicit information given in the form of error statements and program output. We coded each submitted program based on whether or not error statements or program outputs were useful for answering the exercise. Our coding was conservative in that it considered information to be "useful" if the program outputs or errors provided useful information. With this coding it is possible that someone could extract some useful information from a "not useful" submission. For example, consider a submission that runs to completion, producing some output. If the output was not useful in answering the exercise, we labeled the submission as "not useful" even though the

[1]A PL-Detective exercise appeared in Assignment 2 also, but we did not include it because it was designed just to get students familiar with the syntax of MYSTERY.

#	Description	Assign.	Limit
1	What is the storage binding of local variables (e.g., stack dynamic).	3	3 prints
2	When are two types are equal	3	8 programs
3	Do type declarations create a new type	3	2 programs
4	Does MYSTERY use static or dynamic scoping	4	3 programs
5	What are the semantics of array assignments	5	6 prints
6	What is the evaluation order in a procedure call	5	4 prints
7	Does MYSTERY use short-circuit evaluation	6	3 prints
8	When is one procedure type a subtype of another	6	6 programs
9	What is the parameter passing mechanism	7	10 prints
10	What is the parameter passing mechanism (used a different configuration)	7	10 prints
11	Does MYSTERY use deep or shallow binding	8	4 prints

Table 1: Description of assignments

	Had output	Had error
Useful information	301	81
No useful information	186	223

Table 2: How students use the PL-Detective

	Fully correct	Not fully correct
Useful information	196	60
No useful information	8	32

Table 3: Getting useful information versus getting exercise right

fact that the program ran to completion may reveal some information relevant to the exercise at hand.

Two raters (two of the authors) were trained in the coding scheme and independently coded the same randomly selected subset of the data (approximately 10% of all submissions). Inter-rater reliability was very high, with Cohen's Kappas ranging from .95-1.00. Given this high reliability, one rater then coded the remaining submissions. This methodology is commonly used in the social sciences [4, 3].

In addition to the above ratings we also used the feedback that the class TA gave to the students to determine whether a group was successful or unsuccessful in completing an assignment correctly.

4. RESULTS

While working on the 11 PL-Detective exercises (Section 3), groups submitted a total of 755 programs. Groups completed between 4 and 11 exercises (*mean* = 10.3) and submitted between 8 and 52 total programs (*mean* = 26). On average, students submitted 2.52 programs per exercise.

Table 2 presents data on the 755 programs that students submitted to the PL-Detective. "Had output" means that a program produced some output. "Had error" means that a program did not compile or did not run to completion. Note that these two categories are not mutually exclusive: a program may produce output even if it does not run to completion. "Useful information" means that the program revealed information that was useful for doing the assignment. "No useful information" means that the program did not reveal information (according to our coding) that was useful for doing the assignment.

From this table we see that for programs that produced an output, 62% of them yielded useful information and for programs that produced an error only 27% yielded useful information. In other words, students were more effective at getting useful information from outputs than from errors. Overall, we found that 50% of the submissions produced useful information.[2]

Our past experience indicates that students often follow a trial-and-error approach to coding. One goal for the PL-Detective was to steer students away from such an approach towards a more principled experimental approach. Since such a large fraction of submissions yielded useful information, our results indicate that the PL-Detective accomplishes this design goal.

4.1 Did the students effectively use the PL-Detective as an information source?

Just because half the submissions to the PL-Detective yielded useful information does not mean that students were actually able to use the information to get to a correct answer for the exercise.

We looked at the extent to which receiving useful information was related to whether or not a group answered a exercise correctly. We present the results in Table 3. We used the label "Fully correct" to indicate that a group's answer to an exercise was completely correct. "Not fully correct" means that either the answer was wrong or only partially correct. We use the label "Useful information" to indicate that at least one of the group's submissions for an exercise yielded useful information. "No useful information" means that none of the group's submissions for an exercise yielded useful information.

From this table we see that 196 out of 256 times (77%) when a group came up with a program that would yield useful information for an exercise the group was able to answer the exercise correctly. In other words, students are often able to effectively use the information obtained through the PL-Detective. It is worth remembering that just because a group had a submission that yielded useful information, it does not mean that they had *sufficient* information to fully answer the exercise.

Yet 60 out of 256 times (23%) students had useful information but were not able to capitalize on it to get a correct answer. We had expected that as students use the PL-

[2]Recall that we are conservative with marking submissions as useful: it may be that in reality more than 50% of the submission are useful.

Detective for more assignments they would improve their ability to capitalize on the information received from the PL-Detective. However, we did not find any evidence of this: the exercise that accounts for 15 of these 60 cases occurred late in the semester (Exercise 8 in Assignment 6). Exercise 8 requires students to distinguish between three choices. One of the cases was subtle and students frequently came to the wrong conclusion about it (even though they had useful information about the other two cases).

To generalize the observations for Exercise 8 above, we found that when the exercise asked students to distinguish between just two possibilities (Exercises 3, 4, 5, 7, 11 in Table 1), students were likely to get the exercise right even if they had just one useful submission. When there were more possibilities, students generally needed more than one piece of useful information to get it right.

Surprisingly, we found that 8 times a group had no useful information on an exercise but still came up with the right answer. We examined these cases and found the reasons to be one of the following: (i) Our coding was conservative (focusing only on outputs and errors) so some submissions were marked as "not useful" even though other elements of the submissions could be useful (5 times); (ii) Students used the web link of one PL-Detective exercise to answer a different exercise, thus we did not code some submissions for an exercise as being part of that exercise (1 time); (iii) Students were able to get information from previous exercises (1 time). For example, when doing Exercise 2 (Table 1) groups could gather enough information to also answer Exercise 3;[3] (iv) Grader error (1 time). Reason (i) often indicates particular cleverness and creativity on the part of students and thus it is exciting to see!

Finally there were 32 exercise-group pairs where groups failed to get any useful information from their PL-Detective submissions and also got the exercise wrong. Nearly half of these happened in the first assignment (Exercises 1, 2, and 3) but the others were spread out over later assignments. Thus, we did not discern any obvious pattern.

4.2 Did the students efficiently use the PL-Detective as an information source?

We now consider the exercise of whether or not students were efficient at using the PL-Detective as an information source.

For exercises limited by number of programs, Figure 3 gives the fraction of allowed programs that each group used. A point (x, y) with label e on this graph says that group x used a fraction y of the allowed program submissions for Exercise e. Points that are of the form $(x, 0)$ with label e indicate that group x did not submit any programs for exercise e. For exercises limited by number of prints, Figure 4 gives the fraction of prints that each group used. A point (x, y) with label e on this graph says that group x used a fraction y of the allowed prints for Exercise e. The points of the form $(x, 0)$ with label e mean one of two things: (i) Group x did not submit any programs for Exercise e (6 instances); or (ii) Group x submitted programs for Exercise e but the programs did not produce any output (5 instances). The second case includes one situation where the student

[3]We believe that Exercises 2 and 3 really deserve to be treated as a single exercise but to simplify them we had split them up into two. Some groups actually recognized this and took advantage of this!

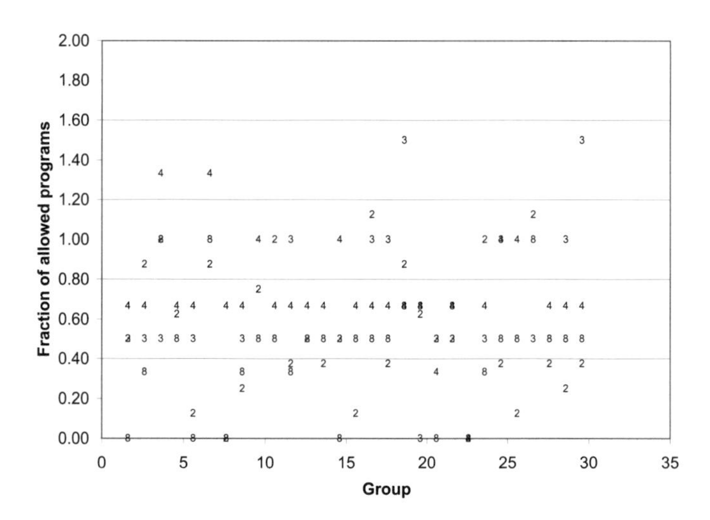

Figure 3: Fraction of allowed programs used by groups.

group was able to get useful information without using any PRINTs. As an example of how the student did this, consider a situation where the value of a variable yields useful information and that the variable's value can be either 10 or 20. Rather than simply printing out the variable (and thus using up a PRINT attempt) one can use an IF statement to print only when the value was 10; in this way when the value was 20, they did not use any PRINT yet they got all the information that they needed! In other words, the fact that the program completed successfully without any output provided the student with useful information.

We clipped the y-axis of both Figures 3 and Figure 4 at 2 to make them easier to read. Between the two graphs there were only four points above 2.

We see that on average students used a little over 50% of the limited attempts. Given that the limits were generally 2-3 times the attempts it took the instructor to do the assignment, students were only a little less efficient than the instructor. We also see that groups rarely exceeded the limit for an assignment (i.e., there are few points above the horizontal 1 line).

We found small but statistically significant correlations between the number of prints or submissions a group used on an assignment and whether the group completed the assignment correctly. First, there is a negative correlation between the percentage of allowed programs that a group used, and whether the group answered the exercise correctly ($p = 0.05$, $r =- .218$); i.e., groups submitting less programs were somewhat more likely to get a correct answer. Second, there is a positive correlation between the percentage of allowed prints that a group used, and whether the group got the exercise right ($p = 0.05$, $r = .155$); i.e., groups submitting more prints were somewhat more likely to get a correct answer.

To summarize, we found that the students were very efficient at using the information gained through the PL-Detective: on average they used about half as many attempts as they were allowed. In fact, we found cases where the student groups were extremely clever about gaining information without using up attempts.

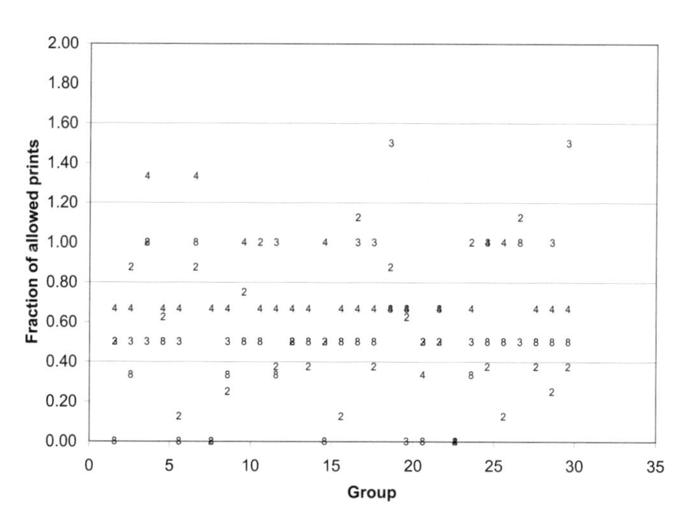

Figure 4: Fraction of allowed PRINTs used by groups.

5. LESSONS LEARNED

We now draw upon our experience using the PL-Detective and the data in Section 4 to highlight the strengths and weaknesses of the PL-Detective.

5.1 PL-Detective as an information source

The PL-Detective enabled us to ask harder exercises than we would normally be able to ask. For example, rather than asking "what will this program print with static scoping and dynamic scoping" we were able to ask "write a program that distinguishes between static scoping and dynamic scoping", which is a much more challenging prospect. However, in order for students to be successful in answering these harder exercises, the PL-Detective has to be a good source of information: students should be able to extract the information they need effectively and efficiently. Our results indicate that this was indeed the case:

- Students were able to get completely correct answers on the exercises approximately 70% of the time.
- Students used up (on average) half of their limited attempts to get to an answer. Given that the limit for the students was 2-3 times the attempts it took the instructor, we see that students were on average only a little less efficient than the instructor in coming up with a correct answer.

We were surprised to find that our data did not indicate a learning curve: in other words, students did not get any more effective or efficient over time. Given that students performed well overall (got completely correct answers on 70% of the time)[4] we hypothesize that the PL-Detective appealed to student intuition: they were able to use the PL-Detective well from the start.

5.2 How difficult was it to design exercises?

To design an exercise, the instructor needs to fix a semantics and set a limit of allowed submissions. Fixing the semantics was straightforward, and usually followed directly from the topics being covered in class. However, determining the limit was difficult. This is reflected in the fact that for some exercises we limited the PRINTs while for others we limited the submissions. Neither of them was satisfactory. For example, if we limit PRINTs, students can easily circumvent the limit by using fewer prints but more submissions; just the fact that a program runs to completion or produces an error can provide useful information (Section 2). As discussed in Section 4 we did encounter a few such situations. We do not yet have a good answer for how to determine and enforce the limits.

5.3 Did the PL-Detective meet its pedagogical goals?

One of the main pedagogical goals of the PL-Detective was to involve students in experimentation: students submit programs and, based on their output, submit more programs. We observed this behavior for the exercises where students had to distinguish between 3+ possibilities (e.g., Exercise 9, Table 1). But there were several exercises (e.g., Exercise 3 in Table 1) where students had to distinguish between only two possibilities and thus did not engage in experimentation. It may be worth either extending the PL-Detective so that it gives more possibilities in the cases where there are only two or combining two exercises with two possibilities each into a larger exercises with more possibilities.

6. CONCLUSIONS

Last year we presented the PL-Detective, a system for teaching programming language concepts. PL-Detective had two design goals: (i) to encourage students to collaborate; and (ii) to provide an experimental environment that students could probe to obtain information necessary to do an exercise. We had already demonstrated that the PL-Detective satisfied the first goal. In this paper we show that the PL-Detective also satisfies the second goal. Our results also provide useful insight into how to use the PL-Detective and how to improve the PL-Detective. We expect these results and insights will be invaluable to others designing similar tools or using the PL-Detective (which is available in open-source form under the GPL).

7. REFERENCES

[1] Mary Field Belenky, Blythe McVicker Clinchy, Nancy Rule Goldberger, and Jill Mattuck Tarule. *Women's way of knowing.* Basic Books, 1997.

[2] Amer Diwan, William M. Waite, and Michele H. Jackson. PL-detective: A system for teaching programming language concepts. In *35rd ACM Technical Symposium on Computer Science Education (SIGCSE)*, Norfolk, VA, March 2004.

[3] J. P. Folger, D. E. Hewes, and M. S. Poole. Coding social interaction. *Progress in communication sciences*, 4:115–161, 1984.

[4] J. P. Folger and M. S. Poole. Relational coding schemes: The question of validity. *Communication yearbook 5*, pages 235–247, 1981.

[5] W. G. Perry. *Forms of intellectual and ethical development in the college years.* Holt, Rinehart and Winston, 1970.

[4]Recall that the 70% figure only reflects situations where a group got an answer *completely* correct. There were many instances where a group got an answer partially correct.

On Understanding the Statics and Dynamics of Object-Oriented Programs

Noa Ragonis and Mordechai Ben-Ari
Department of Science Teaching
Weizmann Institute of Science
Rehovot 76000 Israel
noa.ragonis@weizmann.ac.il, moti.ben-ari@weizmann.ac.il

ABSTRACT

This paper describes research into the influence of using static (class and object) visualization on understanding program flow in object-oriented programming. We found that the advantages of using the static visualization in the first stages of learning could become disadvantages in the advanced stages. The teacher must be aware of these pitfalls and plan the learning sequence accordingly. We think that the BlueJ learning environment that we used should be augmented with dynamic visualization so that students can coordinate the static and dynamic aspects of object-oriented programs.

Categories and Subject Descriptors

K.3.2 [**Computer and Information Science Education**] Computer science education.

General Terms

Human Factors, Languages.

Keywords

Object-oriented programming, program flow, visualization, BlueJ.

1. INTRODUCTION

Many educators believe that there is need to support the learning of abstract programming concepts by using visual tools, although there is a lack of consensus as to the best way of doing so [10]. The BlueJ environment [9] for learning object-oriented programming (OOP) is one of the most popular of such environments. A main feature of BlueJ is the static visualization of the classes and objects, and the ability to interact directly with these icons, thus facilitating understanding of basic concepts of OOP [1, 9, 14]. But in addition, students must understand the program flow, which in OOP is quite complex. While teaching a course in OOP using BlueJ, we became aware of serious learning difficulties on program dynamics, which BlueJ apparently exacerbated.

SIGCSE '05, February 23-27, 2005, St. Louis, Missouri, USA.

In procedural programs, program flow is rather simple: you start with the main program and continue from there, invoking subprograms with parameters as necessary. In the OOP paradigm, there are many classes rather than a single program, and program flow must consider aspects such as: objects are allocated and constructed; their references are assigned to variables in objects of other classes; methods are invoked on objects including an implicit "this" parameter. A novice programmer could ask questions like: Who is in charge of this complicated process? What happens, when and why?

Our research on the dynamic aspects of OOP arose coincidently during the development and evaluation of a high-school course in OOP. Our objective was to investigate if it is possible to teach an objects-first approach to young novices. As such, our concern was with the basic concepts of OOP like class, object and method. We chose to use BlueJ because of its excellent support for learning the basic concepts, in particular, the interactive instantiation of objects from classes and the interactive invocation of methods on objects. This support enabled us to demonstrate and exercise the basic concepts without complications, such as declaring a main method and assigning instances to variables. It was only when we made the transition from individual objects to full programs that it became apparent that there was a problem.

2. RELATED WORK

Researchers have found that there are difficulties in understanding dynamic aspects of program execution in the procedural paradigm just by looking at the static representation of the program [4, 11]. Others claim that the absence of appropriate mental models is one of the main reasons for students' difficulties in understanding program execution [5, 13]. In order to avoid those difficulties, visual environments for teaching elementary OOP have been developed [2, 6, 8]. The ability to reason about program behavior is considered to be an advanced ability that learners of OOP should develop [7, 12, 15].

3. THE RESEARCH

This paper is based on results obtained from a research project on the learning of OOP by high school novices. The students studied OOP in the tenth grade using Java and BlueJ. We taught a two-hour per week course to 18 students during the academic year 2000-1, and to 29 students during 2001-2. During each meeting, one hour was devoted to frontal teaching and the other was used for practical exercises in the computer lab. Extensive data collection was carried out through the entire period: observations and field notes, audio and video recordings, and collection of artifacts. The latter—homework assignments, class work, examinations, final projects—proved to be particularly fruitful in that they showed precisely what concepts were understood and what concepts were problematical. It is important to emphasize that the object of the study was to investigate the process of learning and the ways that students understood the material, rather than to evaluate the specific course or the level of their achievements.

The students continued to take the course in algorithms and programming using Pascal, so as not to interfere with the course of studies required for their diplomas. This affected the research to some degree, but we believe that it does not significantly affect the conclusions that we present here.

4. TEACHING GUIDELINES

At a conceptual level, we wanted the students to achieve understanding of modularity, encapsulation, and information hiding. Operationally, we wanted them to be able to approach a problem by dividing it into classes and implementing the classes in Java. We chose the objects-first approach, in which objects, methods, attributes, classes, object creation, and constructors are presented initially and in an integrated fashion.

In this study, the term "simple class" relates to a class whose attributes are of Java's primitive types or String, while "composed class" refers to a class whose attributes are of a (different) user type. We made two central decisions: (1) we decided, in the interests of better fidelity to the paradigm, to teach composed classes relatively early, and (2) we deferred teaching main methods, believing that they are too procedural, and thus would interfere in understanding the OOP paradigm. We were encouraged in these decisions by the support given by the BlueJ environment for working visually with composed classes without a need to develop a "main program" class. Eventually we came to realize that a main method should not be postponed indefinitely, because that interferes with understanding dynamic aspects of object-oriented programs.

5. CONCEPTIONS OF PROGRAM FLOW

In this section, we present the difficulties that were manifest during the learning process. Each difficulty will be presented by a short description, together with representative evidence. A difficulty was not considered significant unless it occurred frequently. The evidence will be presented by an authentic episode; each episode is described according to the following structure: (a) a short description of the situation in which it occurred, (b) a quotation from a student or an extract from an artifact, (c) an indication of the difficulty that had occurred, (d) an explanation of the probable source of the problem.

• Difficulty 1 – Object state

Novice students have difficulties in understanding the influence of invoking a method on the object state.

a	One of the class exercises referred to a robot game, in which robots in different colors moved on a board that is marked with numbered squares. The simple version included two classes, a simple *Robot* class, in which the attributes were color and the number of square on which the robot stands, and a composed *RobotGame* class, in which the attributes were three robots. We discussed the method that moves a robot one square to the right: *void stepRight( )* *{ numSquare = numSquare + 1; }* Then we asked the students to write the method *stepLeft()* to move a robot one square to the left.
b	One of the answers that we got was: *void stepLeft ( )* *{ numSquare = numSquare + 1 - 1; }* When we asked the student to explain why he wrote +1–1, we got the answer: "Because it [pointed to the *stepRight()* method] had already been done."
c	The student didn't understand that if the method *stepRight()* had been invoked on a robot object, the object state has already been updated, so that the value of the *numSquare* attribute is already increased by one and we need to write only –1.
d	In BlueJ, you can invoke a method from a popup menu on the object icon. We concluded that this interferes with an understanding of the outcome of a method invocation. Even thought there is an option to use the "inspect" feature (which displays the values of the attributes of an object) before and after invoking the method, it seems that student did not understand the concept of the state changing during execution. They looked at it only in a local manner.

• Difficulty 2 – Method invocation

Once students understood the result of invoking individual methods, they still found it hard to understand how a sequence of method invocations relates to solving the problem. They did not immediately understand that each method could be invoked at any time and as often as needed.

a	In class we discussed mutator and accessor methods. We used a simple class *Candle* in which the attributes were the candle color and if it is lighted or not. The following methods were written on the blackboard: *void setColor (String newColor)* *{ color = newColor; }* *String getColor ( )* *{ return color; }* They were written separately, not next to each other.
b	One of the students asked: "If we have a mutator method which determines the new value of the attribute, we already know the new value, so why there is a need to write a method that returns it?"
c	The student didn't understand that each method could be

	executed more than once and not under his manual control. He didn't understand that the source of the value that is used to determine a new value for the attribute is not "us," and that the value could come from many different sources.
d	When invoking a method that has parameters, BlueJ displays a frame in which the user can give values to the parameters. We concluded that this option is the source of the student's problem. They first invoked the mutator method and enter the new value, so it was hard for them to understand the need to invoke (or even to write) the accessor method. It seemed obvious to them that they already knew the current value of the attribute.

- **Difficulty 3 – Parameters**

Novice students have difficulties in understanding where the values of parameters come from.

a	We used an example that included a simple class *Song* in which the attributes were the name, the performer and the length in seconds. (The associated composed class was *Disc*.) Class *Song* included the following method whose goal was to calculate the time it will take to play the song *n* times. *int computeTimesSongLength (int n)* *{ return time * n; }*
b	One of the students asked: "Where did the parameter *n* come from? Where does it appear in the program?" Another question was: "Is a parameter something that is determined later? Where is it determined?"
c	Those students felt uncomfortable with parameters. It was hard for them to get the picture of the data flow of parameters.
d	Difficulties concerning parameters are known from other paradigms but the problem was reinforced by BlueJ. In a very similar manner to what we described in the previous difficulty, we concluded that the difficulty was caused by the extensive use of the feature of the environment that enables the user to insert parameter values directly. If students see frequent scenarios in which parameters get their values from the environment, they miss out on the scenario of executing a sequence of method calls with their parameters.

- **Difficulty 4 – Return values**

Novice students do not understand where the return value of a method goes to!

a	This difficulty arose when we introduced methods that return values.
b	Students asked the following questions: "To where is the return value returned?", "What is done with the value?", "What is the meaning of 'return'; does it [the computer] write the value?" When students were asked in a questionnaire to explain what a return instruction (like *return height*) does, we got the answer: "write the value of the height attribute."
c	Once more we see that students had difficulty understanding data flow, because they hadn't been exposed yet to a complete solution for a problem. They didn't have the opportunity to see what is done with the returned value.
d	In a similar manner to difficulty 3, the use of the static visualization may cause confusion. Invoking a method that returns value from a popup menu causes a frame to appear which shows the returned value. This option disrupted the understanding of data flow when executing a sequence of instructions. Students understood in a local manner the definition that "the method returns a value" but they didn't understand the use of it. Furthermore, the display of the return value in the frame was interpreted as being analogous to an output statement.

- **Difficulty 5 – Input instructions**

Novice students have difficulties in understanding the need for the input instructions.

a	We introduced a class that implemented input of a variety of types.
b	Some students asked: "Why do I need a special instruction for input? We already have the opportunity to get values?"
c	These students didn't see the need for an input instruction and were satisfied with the tool they already have. This also follows because they weren't exposed early enough to a complete solution for a problem.
d	One of the advantages of is that it enabled us to postpone teaching I/O, which is not easy for novices in any language and especially not in Java. Eventually, when input is introduced, they do not see the need for it.

- **Difficulty 6 – Constructors**

Novice students have difficulties in understanding the connections between the constructor declaration, the constructor invocation and the constructor execution.

a	These difficulties arose when we started to introduce a statement that includes the declaration of an attribute, the invocation of the constructor method and the assignment of the returned object to the attribute. For example: *Song song1 = new Song (name, performer, length);* Up until this point, the students were quite experienced with creating objects in the BlueJ environment using the popup menu from the class icon.
b	Students asked: "Where do you write it [the statement]?"
c	While the students had used composed classes, they had yet to see such statements in the code.
d	When executing a constructor method to create a composed object in which the parameters are simple objects, BlueJ enables the interactive assignment of existing objects to attributes by clicking on the object icons. Thus, students were used to see "half" of the above statement, when they used the environment to create an object. Now, they became confused between the "manual" creation and the "real" creation.

- **Difficulty 7 – The overall picture of execution**

The difficulties mentioned so far indicate that novice students have difficulty in capturing the overall picture of program execution. This is succinctly conveyed by the question that came up again and again: What is happening and when?

When students were required to use separate pieces of knowledge, they did very well. They could explain the different concepts, easily operate the BlueJ environment, change given classes and even develop new classes, both simple and composed. But still they didn't have a clear picture about the execution. Nor did they clearly understand the relationships among the Java code, the BlueJ environment and the program flow. Typical expressions of these problems include: "I'm mixed up. When do I need to define each of the things? What is done before what?" One very interesting question was asked when we taught the main program: "Why is it needed? We can do all these things within BlueJ."

The next episode shows one of the situations that points to a lack of understanding of the overall picture of execution.

a	We used as an example a *PhoneCall* class that describes a phone call with the attributes: the calling *Phone*, the receiving *Phone*, the start hour and the end hour. Students were asked to develop a method that calculates the duration of the phone call.
b	Some of the students invoked the method that sets the end time of the phone call as the first instruction in the *phoneCallDuration()* method body. The students justified their solution and told us that they did it to be sure that the end time will be fixed before the phone call duration calculation takes place.
c	Those students thought that they needed to be aware of all the things that matter to the goal of the new method, showing a lack of understanding of the sequence of methods used to solve a problem. (In this case, one method needs to be invoked to fix the end time—a method that the students had already written—and then the new method which computes the phone call duration.)
d	While the BlueJ environment facilitated understanding OOP concepts, it did not help understanding global program flow.

6. Eventually Things Worked Out OK

In spite of the difficulties that arose, students *did* understand the main concepts of OOP as shown in a final questionnaire and project. The questionnaire was based on a program with three classes: *Student*–a simple class with name and grades as attributes, *ClassA*–a composed class with students as attributes, and a *MainProgram* class that created a *ClassA* object, invoked a method on the object (which in turn invoked methods on each student) and displayed the result. Students were asked to: (1) write an explanation of the process that occurred after invoking the main method, (2) draw a sketch of this process, and (3) add instructions to the main method referring to a new object of *ClassA*. In general, the students' answers showed that they had achieved a good understanding of the complex process that takes place when executing the main method. Some of them even used a tree to describe the invocations of all the methods that are involved.

When the students developed their own projects and reached the moment when they executed the main method without using BlueJ, they finally "got it" and were very excited: "Now I understand it all….", "wow… it is working alone…."

7. DISCUSSION

We have shown many misconceptions that novice students have concerning program flow in OOP. We attributed these to the static visualization and interactive features of the BlueJ environment in combination with the way we used it (and even depended upon it) in our teaching process.

The emphasis on teaching the principles of encapsulation and modularization in OOP had caused us to downgrade the teaching of program flow that would have been a central concept in the teaching of procedural programming. The BlueJ environment, which seemed to be a panacea for exercising OOP concepts, reinforced our neglect of program flow. While the results were obtained in a very specific learning environment, we believe that other educators will encounter similar problems, and that they are not necessarily specific to the BlueJ environment.

The topic of program flow needs to be explicitly treated even in an objects-first presentation. A main program class must be presented relatively early so that the students will see: the execution of a sequence of instructions, where objects are created and constructed, what happens to return values, where parameters get their values, why we need input instructions, and so on. The concept of the state of an object must also be explicitly taught and made the subject of exercises. Only then, should instruction move on to compose classes.

We still believe that the BlueJ environment is an excellent teaching tool for novices. However, the distinction between the environment and the execution of a program must be clarified.

Developers of visualizations should combine both static and dynamic aspects; see [3] for our suggestions on this topic. The latest version of Jeliot [2] (http://cs.joensuu.fi/jeliot/) can be used as a plugin to BlueJ and it will be interesting to see if the combination of the two tools can improve the joint learning of the two aspects.

8. CONCLUSION

The conclusion to be drawn from this research is that there are no silver bullets. It is futile to expect that a teaching approach (like objects-first) or a pedagogical tool (like BlueJ) will be able to solve all problems that students have when learning a subject. This emphasizes the importance of evaluation of new ideas in teaching CS: a new pedagogical approach or tool may "crush" one set of misconceptions, but then another set may popup, even one that we thought we had "crushed" before. The results of an evaluation can clarify what aspects must be explicitly taught and how to achieve a good balance between the various aspects of teaching a topic.

9. ACKNOWLEDGEMENTS

We wish to express our gratitude to the school that enabled us to carry out this extensive research project, and in particular to the students who cooperated with our ever-changing ideas on how to teach OOP.

10. REFERENCES

[1] Bailie, F., Blank, G., Murray, K., & Rajaravivarma, R. Java visualization using BlueJ. *Journal of Computing in Small Colleges*, 18(3), 2003, 175-176.

[2] Ben-Ari, M., Myller, N., Sutinen, E., & Tarhio, J. Perspectives on program animation with Jeliot. *Proceedings of the Software Visualization International Seminar*, Dagstuhl Castle, Germany, LNCS 2269, 2002, 31-45.

[3] Ben-Ari, M., Ragonis, N., & Ben-Basat Levy, R. A vision of visualization in teaching object-oriented programming. *Proceedings of the 2nd Program Visualization Workshop*, (HornstrupCentret, Denmark), 2002, 83-89.

[4] Byrne, M. D., Catrambone, R. C., & Stasko J. T. Do algorithm animations aid learning? *Technical Report GIT-GVU-96-19*, Graphics, Visualization, and Usability Center, Georgia Institute of Technology, Atlanta, 1996.

[5] Du Boulay, B. Some difficulties of learning to program. *Journal of Educational Computing Research*, 2(1), 1986, 57-73.

[6] Goldman, K. J. A concepts-first introduction to computer science. *Proceedings of the 35th SIGCSE Technical Symposium on Computer Science Education* (Norfolk, Virginia), 2004, 432-436.

[7] Hadjerrouit, S. A constructivist approach to object-oriented design and programming. *ACM SIGCSE Bulletin*, 31(3), 1999, 171-174.

[8] Hendrix, T. D., Cross, J. H., & Barowski, L. A. An extensible framework for providing dynamic data structure visualizations in a lightweight IDE. *Proceedings of SIGCSE Technical Symposium on Computer Science Education* (Norfolk, Virginia), 2004, 387-391.

[9] Kölling, M., Bruce, Q., Andrew, P., & Rosenberg, J.The BlueJ system and its pedagogy. *Journal of Computer Science Education*, 13(4), 2003, 249-268.

[10] Murray, K. A., Heines, J. M., Kölling, M., Moore, T., Wagner, P. J., Schaller, N. C. & Trono, J. A. Experiences with IDEs and Java teaching: What works and what doesn't. *ACM SIGCSE Bulletin*, 35(3), 2003, 215-216.

[11] Naps, T. L., & Brassler, E. A multi-windowed environment for simultaneous visualization of related algorithms on the World Wide Web. *ACM SIGCSE Bulletin*, 30(1), 1998, 277-281.

[12] Parlante, N. Teaching with object-orientation libraries. *ACM SIGCSE Bulletin*, 29(1), 1997, 140-144.

[13] Perkins, D. N., & Martin, F. Fragile knowledge and neglected strategies in novice programmers. In: E., Soloway, Y., Iyengar (eds.), *Empirical Studies of Programmers*, 1986, 213-229. Norwood, New Jersey: Albex Publishing Corporation.

[14] Thramboulidis, K. C. Sequence of assignments to teach object-oriented programming: A constructivism design-first approach. *Informatics in Education*, 2(1), 2003, 103-122.

[15] Woodman, M., Davies, G., & Holland, S. The joy of software - starting with objects. *ACM SIGCSE Bulletin*, 28(1), 1996, 88-92.

"The Babel Experiment": An Advanced Pantomime-based Training in OOA&OOD with UML

Vladimir L Pavlov, Intel[1]
30 Turgeneva str., Nizhniy Novgorod,
603950, Russia
VLPavlov@ieee.org

Anton Yatsenko, UNN
IT Lab, 23 Gagarin avenue,
Nizhniy Novgorod, 603950, Russia
Yatsenko@wl.unn.ru

ABSTRACT

In this paper we present the original method of intensive hands-on training in Object-oriented Analysis and Design (OOA/OOD) with the Unified Modeling Language (UML). The method has been successfully used by the authors for three years.

During the training, the students:

- go through the communication problems that are typical for large software development projects;
- obtain the successful experience of applying UML to overcome these problems.

The essence of the method is that a team of students is supposed to design a software system. They have several hours to complete the task. During this timeframe verbal and written communication is forbidden, and the UML is the only allowed language. This training is a kind of experiment for students – they are to discover whether UML is "a real language" that is suitable and beneficial for a project team.

The training was successfully delivered more than ten times in both academic and corporate environments and generated positive feedback from students and customers.

Categories and Subject Descriptors

D.2.2 [**Software Engineering**]: Design Tools and Techniques – *Object-oriented design methods;* K.3.2 [**Computers and Education**]: Computer and Information Science Education – *Computer science education.*

General Terms

Documentation, Design, Experimentation, Human Factors, Languages.

Keywords

Unified Modeling Language, UML, IT-education, Object-oriented Analysis, Object-oriented Design, OOA, OOD, OOP, Software Development , Hands-on Training, Pantomime

1. INTRODUCTION

One of the major achievements in the industry at the present time is unification of various notations used in different object-oriented modeling methods. Today all major modeling languages have merged into one – the Unified Modeling Language [1], [8]. UML is de-facto and de jure industry standard for object-oriented analysis and design [8]. This situation also resulted in incorporating UML into standard IEEE/ACM curricula on computer science [3] and software engineering [4].

Although there are a lot of UML courses, many of them have the same drawbacks. Quite often courses are criticized for giving just the syntax of UML with some simple isolated examples of possible UML applications [5]. The authors' experience has shown that the main problem faced by the students, is the gap between knowledge of concepts and ability to effectively apply that knowledge [10]. The authors believe that the best way to improve in any area is practice. Practice makes perfect. As it was shown in Dirk Frosch-Wilke's research [5], after participation in a practical project, students realize the expediency of using UML (see Figures 1 and 2).

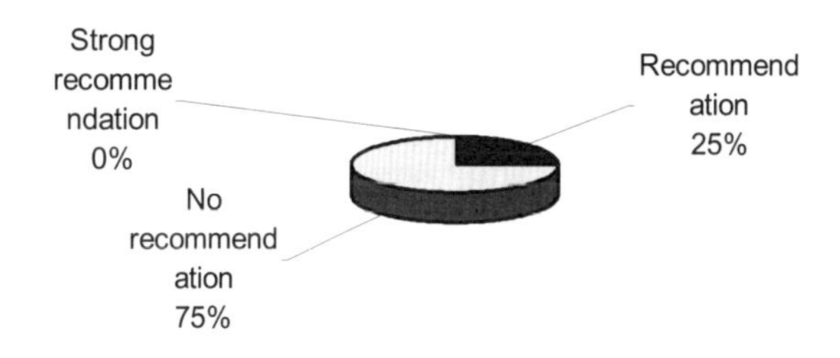

Figure 1 Recommendation of using the UML for software requirement analysis given by students before project work

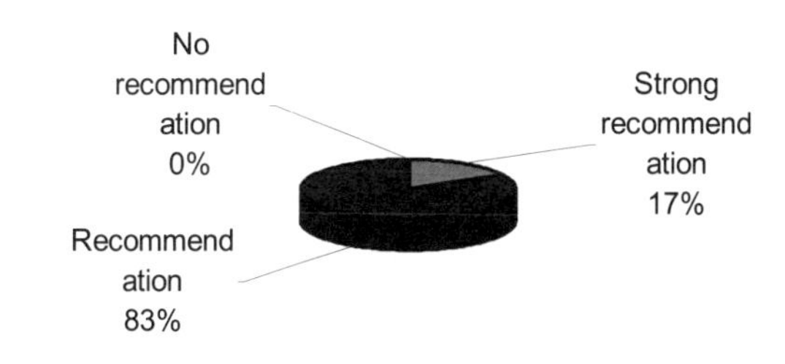

Figure 2 Recommendation of using the UML for software requirement analysis given by students after project work

This leads to another problem of teaching UML in universities: UML is used in large software development projects, and it's quite hard to incorporate such project into university curricula. On the other hand small projects (which could be

[1] This paper discusses the original teaching method that the author had developed prior to he joined Intel.

incorporated into educational process) do not allow students to taste the advantages of UML at full.

To address these challenges, in 2001 Vladimir L. Pavlov developed a training program called "The Babel Experiment". Since then it was successfully delivered a number of times in both software companies and universities. In June 2004 Vladimir L Pavlov and Anton Yatsenko joined their efforts to develop a TTT (Train The Trainer) course for the Babel Experiment.

2. THE TRAINING DESCRIPTION

2.1 Students' background

The method presented in this article was originally conceived as the final stage of traditional academic "OOD with UML" course. Later it was adapted for software development companies whose engineers needed the intensive advanced hands-on training in OOD/UML.

It is supposed that course attendees have some prior knowledge of OOD and UML. Obviously it is impossible to teach the practical aspects of UML if students are not familiar with the syntax of UML. Knowledge of the UML syntax does not guarantee the ability of using UML rationally but it is definitely necessary – if one wants to write meaningful sentences one has to know the letters.

From our point of view students' familiarity with some advanced areas such as design patterns, OCL and UML metamodel is an important landmark on their way to master object-oriented analysis and design [7]. So we usually asked participants of the training to learn these topics prior to attending the Babel Experiment.

Also we always wanted student to have some experience with the Charades game and acquaintance with the parable about "The Tower of Babel" – of course, most students meet these requirements without making any additional efforts.

2.2 The Pantomime Game

There is a well-known student's game called The Charades [2]. This game was one of the prototypes for author's method. This game is known under different names in different places: sometimes it is called "The Crocodile", sometimes – "The Charades" and some people simply name it "The Pantomime Game". In this article we will call it The Charades.

As well as its name, rules of this game vary from one place to another. Here are some exemplary rules.

There are two teams (each from 3 to 10 members). Members of the first team agree on a word and then tell this word to one person from the second team. The chosen person has to pantomime the proposed word to members of his team. At that he can not use speech or writing. Once the word is guessed correctly or the second team gives up, teams exchange their roles. Team, which has guessed the word, proposes new word and the other tries to guess, and so on. To make the game interesting it is preferable to choose really difficult words such as for example: melioration, placebo, expansion, encapsulation and the like.

Students who are going to take part in the Babel Experiment are supposed to practice this game.

2.3 The Tower of Babel

There is a well-known Bible's parable about The Tower of Babel:

"Now the whole earth had one language and few words. And as men migrated from the east, they found a plain in the land of Shinar and settled there. And they said to one another, "Come, let us make bricks, and burn them thoroughly." And they had brick for stone, and bitumen for mortar. Then they said, "Come, let us build ourselves a city, and a tower with its top in the heavens, and let us make a name for ourselves, lest we be scattered abroad upon the face of the whole Earth."

And the Lord came down to see the city and the tower, which the sons of men had built. And the Lord said, "Behold, they are one people, and they have all one language; and this is only the beginning of what they will do; and nothing that they propose to do will now be impossible for them. Come, let us go down, and there confuse their language, that they may not understand one another's speech."

So the Lord scattered them abroad from there over the face of the Earth, and they left off building the city. Therefore its name was called Babel, because there the Lord confused the language of all the Earth; and from there the Lord scattered them abroad over the face of the Earth." Genesis 11.

This legend shows that without having the common language human beings are incapable to achieve the common goal.

2.4 The Experiment description

A group of students who had prior learned OOD&UML is supposed to design some software system. At that verbal and written speech is not allowed and the only languages they may use are UML and pantomime.

Will they be able to design a system under such extreme conditions?

This experiment could be perceived as something quite uncommon for the regular teaching practice in universities. However, our experience shows that such approach is very effective and beneficial to achieve the following goals:

First, this experiment is a test, which can demonstrate to students whether UML is a "real" language or not.

Second, this experiment is aimed to raise students' interest in UML and to be a challenge for further improvement.

Third, experiment gives students an opportunity to obtain experience of team-working on a software design. It also gives them the opportunity to take part in collective research. Of course, the project environment is rather simulated. However, unusual conditions of this experiment allow students to get the teamwork experience similar to what they could learn from a "real" project that would last several weeks. While announcing the experiment to students we usually describe it as "joint eating of salt in the compressed time/space".

It is important to make sure that all experiment participants have committed to do their best during the experiment, that they have "if you pledge, don't hedge" mindset. One of the possible mechanisms to achieve this is to organize the presentation of the experiment results right after the experiment's completion and invite a significant number of spectators (guests). In fact, we did it for all of our Babel Experiments, and it has always been a highly motivating factor.

2.4.1 Approximate schedule of training preparation

The experiment was implemented according to the scheme shown in the Table 1.

Table 1

Days	Activity
1	The event is announced to students;
1-16	Students prepare for the contest (exam); Intensive Charades training
8-16	Spectators receive invitations
17	The contest (exam)
18	The Babel experiment

2.4.2 *Participants selection*

To simplify the communication within a team it is desirable that participants would be of close age – in this case they feel more uninhibited and behave more spontaneously. To ensure emotional balance between participants we've always tried to have both men and women in a team.

It is obvious that everything depends on students' understanding of UML, their imagination and the ability to apply their knowledge in extreme conditions. For the goals of experiment it is useful to organize a competitive selection of experiment participants from the student group. Usually a team of participants consists of 6-10 members who are selected from the group of 20-30 students. This competition between students in a group is made for the purpose of involving into the experiment the most prepared and interested students. It challenges students and encourages them to improve their skills.

Selection is organized as a verbal exam that includes questions both on the UML and on the modeling techniques. Instead of conventional multi-choice questions we prefer open questions. They give an opportunity to look upon the way of thinking of examinee. These questions usually lead to a deeper discussion; they are not supposed to have one simple answer. Most of them are exacted in further discussion by questions: "Why do you think so?", "Where, in which cases, it can be used?" and the similar. Here are some examples of such questions: "What is the difference between the *aggregation* and the *composition*?", "Draw the UML-diagrams, which will retell the fairytale about the Gingerbread Man", "Build the class diagram and statechart diagram for electric chandelier", "You are talking with alien, who understands only the UML language. Explain to alien what the traffic lights are, how it works and how it should be used".

As an alternative to viva voce examination we have always suggested students to earn industry recognized certifications on UML. For example, to be exempt from viva voce exam students can pass the IBM 486 Object-oriented Analysis and Design with UML exam [6] or one of the OMG Certified UML Professional exams [9]. However, students usually prefer not to utilize this option – probably, because of the additional cost associated with certification exams.

2.4.3 *Roles*

In the discussed training we usually had the following roles: participants, trainer, trainer assistant and spectators. In this section we will explain these roles in detail.

Participants are students who wanted to take part in the Babel Experiment and have successfully passed through the selection stage. Their functions in the experiment are:

- designing the system model without using speech;
- presenting the experiment results to spectators.

Trainer is the teacher and the experiment organizer. His role includes preparing the experiment task for participants and controlling conformation to the rules. He is not involved into designing a system, but looks after the process and later gives the feedback to participants.

Trainer assistant supports logistics, organizes lunch and connection with "the outside world". He meets and manages the spectators; he is also responsible for insuring that all Experiment participants strictly follow the rules.

And, as it was stated above, there are spectators (guests), who attend the presentation and whose feedback is important to make the final decision whether the experiment was successful or not (whether it "proves" UML to be a "real language").

2.4.4 *Strike the four matches*

The experiment consists of four phases, and the trainer strikes matches to mark transition from one phase to another. The sequence of the "Strike of four matches" milestones is shown in the Table 2.

Table 2

Milestone/strike	Phase description
The event starts	Instruction of the participants
Switch to speechless mode	Team opens an envelope with the task Team works on the task Light lunch Team moves to the presentation room
Presentation starts	Presentation and discussion of results
The event ends	The end

2.4.5 *Approximate timing*

Approximate schedule of the training is presented in the Table 3. We need a lot of guests on the presentation, so for the purpose of attracting the larger audience the Babel Experiment should be conducted in a non-working day. Usually authors organized it on Sunday because it is desirable to give the participants some time (Saturday) to rest after the working week as well as to get finally prepared for the Experiment.

Table 3

10:00-10:30 – the strike of the first match, the event starts
10:30-14:00 – the strike of the second match, switch to the speechless mode
14:00-15:00 – easy lunch, speech is not allowed
15:00-15:30 – the strike of the third match, switch to aloud mode, presentation starts
15:30-17:00 – presentation ends, the discussion with the spectators starts
17:00-18:00 – spectators leave the auditorium, postmortem with participants starts
18:00 – the strike of the forth match, the event ends

2.4.6 *Experiment task*

Each experiment task consists of two parts. One part is common for all Experiments. The other part is special for every Experiment.

The special Experiment task part is created in secret, so that students could learn it only when the experiment starts, right after the strike of the second match. Special task-part is composed in a way that allows quite different solutions of the task. It should contain some ambiguity for the purpose to test students' ability to understand each other and to uncover and clearly specify all assumptions.

2.4.7 *Special task part sample*

Here is the example of real problem which was posed for the experiment participants in 2002.

"There is a company called BE (the Babel Electronics). The BE is going to launch home TV-systems of new generation. The feature of this product is that remote controls of new systems are something more than just traditional TV remotes.

The new remote control has no buttons; instead of them control has the sensitive screen on the whole control's surface. The control screen may display arbitrary images. The control screen can identify an exact location where a user pushes it by fingers or thick things.

Remote control is at the same time a mobile phone that complies with the GSM standard. This "smart" remote control is able to connect by Internet to the servers containing TV-schedules. Furthermore BE has made an arrangement with BT&T (Babylonian Telephone & Telegraph) company. According to it all WAP-connections of BT&T users with BE's server (where TV-schedules are allocated) will be free of charge during the 5 years from the moment of the new home TV-systems release.

The new TV-systems and their remote controls are supplied with BE-processors. They are capable to run complex software written in modern object-oriented programming languages, such as C++, Java, etc."

Note, that there are two possible usage scenarios for such systems: the user menu may be present either on the control screen or on the TV screen. None of these scenarios is explicitly mentioned to the training participants. This ambiguity was left intentionally in order to provoke students to make unspecified assumptions.

2.4.8 *Common task part*

Here is the common experiment task part which was included with some (not essential) variations in every Babel experiment since the year 2001.

"It's necessary to create and describe with UML the high-level design of the software. This software will be used in above-stated systems. At that using of English (or any other language) on the diagrams is allowed only for naming the diagram elements – use-cases, packages, stereotypes, classes, messages, attributes and so on. Notes, as the UML standard element, are banned.

In the process of designing only using of gestures or UML diagrams (according to above-stated constraints) is allowed.

Above-stated constraints are extended on the period from the moment of designing start (strike of the second match at 10:30) to the moment of results presentation (strike of the third match approximately at 15:00). So that person(s), who will present experiment results to guests, is (are) chosen by the pantomime.

If a participant breaks a rule he'll get a warning. If participant gets three warnings, he loses right of further participating in the experiment. Both the trainer and his assistant may issue warnings."

2.4.9 *Presentation of the Experiment results*

While the Experiment participants finish their assignment in the work-room, the spectators of the Experiment gather in the presentation-room. The spectators are met and hosted by the trainer assistant. When the presentation time comes, the participants move from the work-room to the presentation-room. The trainer strikes the third match and participants are allowed to speak. The presentation is made by person(s), who was (were) previously chosen by the pantomime.

2.4.10 *Discussion*

Discussion is one of the main experiment's stages. It follows the Experiment results presentation, which is made by the Experiment participants. The purpose of this stage is to make the decision about the Experiment results according to the spectators' feedback. During the discussion guests provide their opinions on the presented model (does it contain all important elements, is it produced in logical and consistent manner?). They debate whether it may serve as an input for further detailed modeling and consequent implementation. Discussion is concluded with the final consensual judgment on whether the team has managed to create a sound model.

2.4.11 *Postmortem*

After the spectators leave the auditorium participants and trainer may discuss the Experiment, talk over how they understood each other by the pantomime and UML. They debate the feedback from spectators, highs and lows of the model they have developed as well as the presentation they have delivered. It is a good time to thank each other; it is also an appropriate time to provide feedback to trainer about the Experiment organization – this helps improve future trainings of this kind. Finally the trainer strikes the last match and the event is over.

3. TRAINING RESULTS

The Babel Experiment was conducted more than ten times since it had been invented. It is important to notice that experiment had never failed. During every Babel Experiment students found the common language and generated the common ideas by UML communication, which led them to successful development of the proposed system model. The Experiment has always clearly showed to students that UML is a "complete" language.

It is interesting to mention that once we had two teams[2] working on the same task. One team was limited to using only the UML language and the pantomime in their communication. The other was allowed to use the speech in addition to the UML. The first team (which was not allowed to use speech) coped with a task more successfully than other team. Their diagrams were more detailed, more elaborated and elegant.

Discussing this fact we have come to the following explanation. When a task is discussed by team using the speech, everyone understands each other, so it seems to participants that there is no need to map "obvious" things in the UML diagrams. The problem is that in reality these "obvious" assumptions are quite different for different people. When the team uses only the UML and pantomime, in order to understand each other, participants have to map in the diagram everything very precisely

---

[2] They were participants of the educational project "Virtuoso" that was organized by University of Nizniy Novgorod (Russia) and supported by Intel, Microsoft, IBM, Borland and Kaspersky Lab.

and detailed, much more formal than in normal verbal discussion. This leads to making all assumptions explicitly captured in diagrams hence increases common understanding within a team and helps make final model more clear and coherent.

One of the great training results is stimulation of students' efforts for learning OOA/OOD and UML. In order to pass the UML exam and to win a contest students have to study a lot of materials on the subject. It is necessary to notice that prior to the Experiment we always organize not only the UML exam, but a number of exam rehearsals where everybody has a chance to practice in modeling and get detailed feedback from experts. So, Experiment should be apprehended not as thing-in-itself, but as the culmination of a long-period preparation. The process of intensive students' preparation for the Experiment is overwhelmingly important.

Students always provide very positive responses after they participate in this training. Here are some typical students' comments:

- *"this experience of practical UML-using forced me to change my attitude with regard to UML – now I do understand how it could help me in real-life projects";*
- *"participating in the Experiment helped me to realize that UML is not a kind of abstract "Glass Bead Game", but rather a very practical tool";*
- *"thanks to the Experiment I was able to understand that usage of different UML diagrams (class diagram, sequence diagram, use-case diagram, etc.) really makes sense when they all are used together, representing different points of view for the modeled system".*

Several times we have conducted The Babel Experiment as a kind of capstone project that culminated "traditional" university course in OOD with UML. Students who attended this modified course have shown higher motivation and they have finally received better grades on the final exam in comparison to other students.

So our experience of implementing The Babel Experiments shows that the speechless approach to practice UML is an effective and productive method that helps students fully experience the might of UML.

4. CONCLUSION

In this paper we have presented a pantomime-based method of hands-on training in OOA/OOD and UML. This method has proven itself to be an effective approach to simulate teamwork on complex software projects. It gives students an opportunity to feel the expressive power of UML that significantly simplifies communication within a team.

The training is delivered to students in the form of an experiment with the declared goal to check "Whether UML is a real language". The results of such experiments were always positive – in all cases training participants managed to develop quite elaborated design models without using speech. Once we had two teams working concurrently on the same design task – one team was allowed to use speech while the other was not; the result presented by the speechless team was more elegant and thoroughly developed.

The experimental nature of this method inspires students for deep studying OOA/OOD and UML; the practical nature of this method helps them to recognize OOA/OOD with UML as a practical tool rather then a theoretical method. As a result, after attending the experiment students report that they are eager to apply UML in their real-life projects.

The method was successfully implemented in both academic and corporate environments.

5. ACKNOWLEDGEMENTS

We would like to thank all people who reviewed different versions of this article (either in form of article or presentation) and whose comments helped us to polish our paper:

- Alex Zverintsev (Nokia, Poland);
- Andrey Terekhov (Microsoft, Russia);
- Anna Akousheva (Intel, Russia);
- Dmitry Malenko (Dnepropetrovsk National University, Ukraine);
- Michael Wrinn (Intel, US);
- Nikita Boyko (Dnepropetrovsk National University, Ukraine);
- Nikolay Mitushin (Intel, Russia);
- Stanislav Busygin (University of Florida, US);
- Yury Bushenko (University of Westminster, UK).

6. REFERENCES

[1] Booch G., Rumbaugh J, Jacobson I. *The Unified Modeling Language User Guide*. Addison-Wessley 1999

[2] Charades: http://www.cs.umd.edu/~nau/misc/charades.html

[3] *Computer Curricula 2001: Computer Science* (December 15, 2001) http://www.computer.org/education/CC2001/cc2001.pdf

[4] *Computer Curriculum: Software Engineering* http://sites.computer.org/ccse/volume/FinalReport-5-21-04.pdf

[5] Dirk Frosch-Wilke. Using UML in software requirements analysis – Experiences from practical student project work. *Informing Science + IT Education Conference Proceedings,* Informing Science Institute, Santa Rosa, CA, June 2003, 175-183.

[6] IBM 486 Object-oriented analysis and design with UML. http://www.ibm.com/certify/tests/sam486.shtml

[7] Lew Della, David Clark. Teaching Object-oriented development with Emphasis on Pattern Application. *Proceedings of the Australasian conference on Computing education*, ACM Press, New York, NY, 2000, 56 – 63.

[8] OMG , Unified Modeling Language Specification http://www.uml.org

[9] OMG, UML Certification Program. http://www.omg.org/uml-certification/exam_info.htm

[10] Philip J. Burton, Russel E. Brunn. Using UML to Facilitate the Teaching of Object-oriented Systems Analysis and Design. *Journal of Computing Sciences in Colleges,* vol. 19, issue 3, January 2004, 278-290.

Using Testing and JUnit Across The Curriculum

Michael Wick, Daniel Stevenson and Paul Wagner
Department of Computer Science
University of Wisconsin-Eau Claire
Eau Claire, WI 54701
{wickmr, stevende, wagnerpj}@uwec.edu

ABSTRACT

While the usage of unit-testing frameworks such as JUnit has greatly increased over the last several years, it is not immediately apparent to students and instructors how to best use tools like JUnit and how to integrate testing across a computer science curriculum. We have worked over the last four semesters to infuse testing and JUnit across our curriculum, building from having students use JUnit to having them write their own test cases to building larger integration and use case testing systems to studying JUnit as an example of good application of design patterns. We have found that, based on this increased presentation and structuring of the usage of JUnit and testing, students have an increased understanding and appreciation of the overall value of testing in software development.

Categories and Subject Descriptions

K.3 [**Computers & Education**]: Computer & Information Science Education - *Computer Science Education*.

General Terms

Measurement, Design, Reliability, Verification.

Keywords

JUnit, Testing, Unit Testing, Unit Testing Frameworks.

1 INTRODUCTION

Unit testing has achieved significant prominence in the computer science curriculum over the past several years. This has been driven by several factors: the "test first" mentality of the agile programming community, the available of good unit testing frameworks such as JUnit [6] in the Java software development world, increased interest in knowledge of and experience with testing by industry, and computer science faculty's interest in integrating this into the curriculum.

JUnit has a number of fundamental concepts. A *test case* is a Java class that tests some particular usage of the class in question. A test case consists of one or more *test methods*, which in turn test some component of the class. Multiple test cases can be combined into a *test suite*. Common test data can be organized into a *fixture*, which then can be used with setUp and tearDown methods to isolate activity done across multiple test methods within a test case.

Students quickly see the benefits of a unit testing framework, and indeed they enthusiastically run the tests we provide in our first programming class in Java. However, we originally did not see a reasonable path in our curriculum to help students progress from using unit tests to writing unit tests to developing and understanding more sophisticated testing systems for tasks such as integration testing and use case testing. As we see software development moving increasingly in a test-driven direction, we have worked to structure our presentation of testing with JUnit and infuse testing and JUnit into a variety of courses at various levels in our curriculum.

We have begun using JUnit across our curriculum over the past two years. We start in our first programming course by providing JUnit test cases and suites for our students and trying to instill good testing discipline within them. In our second programming course we move onto asking students to write their own test cases and suites, once they are familiar with concepts such as inheritance and interfaces and they have had more experience with JUnit. In the first software engineering course they use design patterns to build larger testing frameworks that cover integration testing as well as unit testing. Finally, in a senior level/capstone design course, the students study how JUnit makes use of a variety of design patterns. This leads our students to better understand and appreciate the value of testing as part of software development.

2 BACKGROUND

JUnit was created by Erich Gamma and Kent Beck in the mid- to late-1990s in order to provide an easy-to-use framework that encouraged unit testing. JUnit has since become very popular, and can now be considered the flagship of a much larger xUnit family of testing frameworks. There are a number of books [7, 8, 11] that discuss the use of JUnit, both the technical details of using it and to some extent good practice issues. Similarly, there are a variety of articles on the world-wide web (e.g. [3, 4, 5]) that address various aspects of JUnit. Discussion of JUnit has begun to increase in the computer science education literature as well (e.g. [9, 10]).

While many of these books and articles cover technical details associated with using JUnit, relatively few focus on best practices (though see [4,11]) especially as they relate to instruction. This has led us to focus our attention on developing a more methodical approach to the use of JUnit and the teaching of testing from our first course through our capstone courses, so that we can help our students become more skilled in this increasingly significant and important area.

3 UNIT TESTING AND JUNIT IN A FIRST PROGRAMMING COURSE

In our first programming course we try to impress upon the students the value of testing generally and unit testing specifically. We now view this as developing a testing foundation that they will carry through the curriculum, building on this by writing their own unit tests, moving on to integration and other testing, and seeing how testing frameworks can be an example of good software design. As such, we have become more careful to make sure that we provide good test cases and suites for the students.

We start out by providing the students with a lab exercise on JUnit early in the first programming course, and provide JUnit tests for the programming assignments that we assign. As we don't introduce inheritance and interfaces until later in the semester, our focus regarding testing in this course is on having the students directly experience the value of unit testing their code as they develop.

At this level we introduce test suites as well as test cases. While many of the references above focus on test cases and test methods, we are finding that the use of test suites allow us to encourage modular development early, as well as providing a tool by which to evaluate various subsets of functionality or even to evaluate assignments to different levels of quality. For example, we can now give an assignment where we develop an "A" test suite, a "B" test suite, etc., so that students can see that increased levels of unit testing provide additional quality to their work.

We teach the students to place their unit tests in a separate source tree within the same package. For example, under Eclipse, we can have a project JUnitExample that contains a Java folder with the package edu.university.cs.popmachine that contains the domain classes for a Pop Machine system (e.g.PopMachine.java, PopMachineException.java, etc.), and this project also includes a JUnit folder with the same package edu.university.cs.popmachine with the test classes (e.g. TestPopMachineDropPop.java, etc.). We find that this separate source tree organization allows package access for the test classes but doesn't clutter the source tree. It also supports a more modular view of the development of a software system.

We follow a simplified subset of the test case design rules in this first course that we later ask them to use in designing and writing their own test cases in the second programming course (see Section 4). Providing good and consistent examples early encourages the students to follow our model as they move on to designing their own test cases.

4 UNIT TESTING AND JUNIT IN A SECOND PROGRAMMING COURSE

Building on the testing experiences students have in their first programming course, our second programming course explicitly teaches students how to design JUnit test cases for themselves. Obviously, this isn't the focus of the entire course (we focus on algorithms, data structures and their applications), however it does provide a nice opportunity to help students refresh on the concepts from the previous course while learning more about the proper design of JUnit test cases. From their earlier experience, students appreciate the important role of unit testing in software development and have a firm understanding of the appropriate file organization in which to store JUnit test cases. What they lack is the ability to effectively write their own test cases. We have developed a set of JUnit design rules that help students develop a structured and relatively impressive set of testing code. The following section presents our JUnit design rules and illustrates their meaning by applying them to the testing of the following simple source code.

```
public class PopMachine {
    protected List cans;
    protected int costPerPop;
    protected int deposit;

  public PopMachine(int cost) {
    costPerPop = cost;
    deposit = 0;
    scans = new LinkedList();
  }
  public void add(Pop p) {
    supply.add(p);
  }
  ...
  public int dropPop() throws
                       PopMachineException {
    int result = 0;
    try {
      cans.removeFirst();
      if (deposit >= costPerPop ){
        result.change = deposit -
                         costPerPop;
        deposit = 0;
      }
      else {
        throw new NSFException();
      }
    }
    catch (NonexistentElementException e){
      throw new SoldOutException();
    }
    return result;
  }
}
```

This class is meant to simulate the operation of a simple pop machine. Obviously this is a simple example, but the class does illustrate several features intrinsic in more interesting code.

4.1 JUnit Design Rules For A Second Course

Derive one TestClass class from junit.TestCase for each target class. To modularize the test cases, we teach our students to implement an abstract class which extends junit.TestCase for each class they wish to test. The name of each such class should be Test*Class* where *Class* is the name of the given target class (see the example combined with the next design rule).

Define one nested class inside the TestClass for each collaborator of the target class. This nested class is an example of a *mock class* [8]. The idea is that we want to make sure that our test cases test only the target class and not any of the related collaborator classes. By using mock classes we can replace the collaborators with special purpose objects that have hard-coded behavior consistent with our needs. The name of the nested mock class should be Mock*Class* where *Class* is the name of the actual collaborator class. The following code segment illustrates the TestPopMachine class and includes the definition of a mock class to replace the Pop collaborator of our PopMachine class.

```
public class TestPopMachine
                extends TestCase {
  public class MockPop extends Pop { ... }
  public void setUp(){...}
  public void tearDown(){...}
}
```

Derive one TestClassMethod class from TestClass for each method of each target class. Again, to help control complexity and to create modularity within the test cases, we teach our students to define a test case (subclass of TestClass) for each method of each target class. The name of each such class should be Test*ClassMethod*() where *Class* is the name of the target class and *Method* is the name of the specific target method within that class. For example, the following code segment illustrates the TestPopMachineDropPop class that would be responsible for testing the dropPop() method of the PopMachine class.

```
public class TestPopMachineDropPop
                extends TestPopMachine {
  public void testExactChange(){}
  public void testUnderDeposit(){}
  public void testOverDeposit(){}
}
```

Implement one testScenario() method in the TestClassMethod class for each possible scenario of the target method. Typically, there are several paths through a method that must be tested. For example, the method should be tested when it should produce an exception, the method should be tested when it shouldn't produce an exception, and so on. Such tests should be modularized and defined in a common location and thus we group these tests in the TestClassMethod class. Notice how this organizational structure isolates to one class all tests that validate the behavior of a single method. One of the key advantages to this design is that students are forced to explicitly think about the various scenarios for each method. For example, the following code segment illustrates the implementation of the testExactChange scenario for the dropPop() method of the PopMachine class.

```
public void testExactChange(){
  popMachine.deposit = COST;
  assertTrue( popMachine.cans.size()
                        ==originalPopCount);
  try { changeReturned = popMachine.dropPop();}
  catch (NSFException unexpected){
    fail("..."); }
  assertTrue(popMachine.deposit==0);
  assertTrue(popMachine.cans.size()==
                     originalPopCount - 1);
  assertTrue(changeReturned == 0);
}
```

The variable `originalPopCount` used in the above code is initialized by the `setUp()` method of the `TestPopMachine` class to be equal to the size of the list `cans` prior to the actual test code (code not show due to space considerations).

The next code segment illustrates the use of the MockPop mock class in our testing design. In particular, the code segment illustrates the implication of the testAddNotFull() method of the TestPopMachineAdd test case class.

```
public void testAddNotFull(){
  assertTrue( popMachine.cans.size()
                        ==originalPopCount);
  popMachine.add( new MockPop() );
  assertTrue( popMachine.cans.size()==
                      originalPopCount + 1);
  }
```

Notice that by using the hard-coded MockPop class, we can avoid inter-mixing the tests of the PopMachine class and the Pop class. If instead we had actually used the Pop class and an error was encountered, we would not know whether the error was caused by the add( ) method of PopMachine or by some behavior of the actual instance of the Pop class that was given to the add( ) method. Using a hard-coded mock class greatly reduces the chance that the parameter of the add( ) method will be responsible for any errors in the testing of the add( ) method.

Derive one TestClassSuite class from junit.TestSuite for each target class. This class will serve as the focal point for all tests associated with the target class. The constructor for this class should use the static addTest(...) method of the junit.TestSuite class to add an instance of each individual TestClassMethod class to the TestClassSuite.

```
public class TestPopMachineSuite
                extends TestSuite {
  public TestPopMachineSuite(){
    suite.add(new TestPopMachineDropPop());
    suite.add(new TestPopMachineDeposit());
    ...
  }
}
```

4.2 Advantages and Disadvantages

The main advantage to our JUnit design rules is that they create a modularized library of test cases for each class under construction. Further, the organization of this library directly reflects the separation of concerns found in the testing problem – all tests associated with a given method are stored together, all collections of tests associated with a given class are defined under a common ancestor are stored together in a given test suite.

The main disadvantage to our JUnit design rules is that they tend to lead to a massive number of test classes. While this is true, we believe that current development environments combined with the hierarchical nature of the test classes in our result provides a sufficiently powerful abstraction that the volume and numbers of test cases is not a significant burden for the developer.

5 TESTING AND JUNIT IN A SOFTWARE ENGINEERING COURSE

The design rules presented in the previous section not only encourage a coherent set of unit test cases, but also lay the foundation on which we can build other types of test cases including integration tests and use case tests.

5.1 Integration Testing

In our software engineering course, we introduce students to the concept of integration testing. Here the focus is not on the behavior of each isolated class, but rather on the behavior of progressively larger and larger collections of classes working together.

Given the design rules discussed in section 4, the students are in a wonderful position to learn an effective technique for performing integration testing. By using a factory method design pattern [2] to create the instances of all mock classes in our test cases, we can get a fairly effective means of integration testing by simply deriving new test cases from our existing test cases. In these new test cases the factory method of the original test case (which produces instances of the mock object) is replaced with a new factory method that returns the actual object with which we wish to test integration. Consider the example shown in the following code segment.

```
protected Pop createPop() {
  return new MockPop();
}
public void testAddNotFull(){
  assertTrue( popMachine.cans.size()
                         ==originalPopCount);
  popMachine.add( createPop() );
  assertTrue( popMachine.cans.size()==
                        originalPopCount + 1);
}
```

```
public class TestPopMachineAddWithPop
             extends TestPopMachineAdd {
  protected Pop createPop(){
    return new Pop();
  }
}
```

For first section of code illustrates the use of a factory method within the original TestPopMachineAdd class. Notice that the construction of a concrete "Pop" instance is isolated to the `createPop()` method.

The second section of code illustrates how the definition of `createPop()` can be overridden in the new test case so that it integrates with the actual Pop class (not the mock class).

5.1.1 Advantages and Disadvantages

Notice how we essentially get the integration test between PopMachine's add(...) method and the Pop class for free. All we need to do is derive a new test case that simply overrides the factory method so that all the inherited methods of the TestPopMachineAdd class are now performed using an instance of the actual Pop class.

One obvious disadvantage to this approach is that it is difficult to test all possible combinations of a target class with its collaborators. For example, if a class A collaborates with both classes B and C, then to test the integration of A with B would simply derive new test cases that replace the factory of each of our test cases with a factory that creates instances of B. Now to test A, B, and C together, we just derive new classes from our new test cases. These new test cases replace the factory method that produces mock C instances with methods that produce actual C instances. However, if you also want to test the integration of class A with class C alone (not including the actual class B), this requires that we derive new tests directly from the tests for A, replacing the factory of mock Cs but leaving the factory of mock Bs alone. This can lead to a combinational explosion on the number of possible tests cases. We are currently researching ways of removing this combinatorial problem. However, for our current purposes, we simply encourage students to develop tests for A with B, then A+B with C, and so on.

5.2 Use Case Testing

We also teach students how to develop use case tests. Unlike the unit and integration tests, use case tests are not motivated by the implementation classes, but rather by the functional requirements of the system (i.e., the use cases). However, our basic approach to testing still applies. The following use case testing design rules are analogous to the design rules presented in section 4 but they apply to use cases rather than individual classes.

Derive one TestUseCasePackage class from junit.TestCase for each use case package in the system.

Derive one TestUseCase class from TestUseCasePackages for each use case of each target use case package.

Implement one testScenario() method in the TestUseCase class for each possible scenario of the target use case.

Derive one TestUseCasePackageSuite class from TestSuite for each target use case package.

This set of design rules teaches our students to derive a new class from junit.TestSuite for each target use case package (collection of related use cases). Next, students derive new classes from that class, one for each specific use case in the package. Then, each specific scenario (normal flow, alternative flows, exception flows) of each use case is tested in its own method of this class. Finally, test suites are used to create a hierarchical representation of the use case tests.

We have found the symmetry of this approach to use case testing to that of unit testing to be comfortable and familiar to the students

6 DESIGN PATTERNS AND JUNIT IN A SENIOR-LEVEL DESIGN COURSE

In their senior year our students take a course which focuses on design through the use of architectural and design patterns. We have found that a straight catalog approach to this course tends to bore the students. Thus, we spend a lot of time focusing on how to apply patterns to given projects. Some of this work is done through the use of refactoring an existing design to use patterns and some is based on finding patterns from the start. We have found that the JUnit framework is a great example of a system where the types of problems encountered in its design provide nice matches to particular design patterns. In addition, since they have been using JUnit throughout the curriculum they are comfortable with using the framework which provides extra motivation to learn how it is designed.

Instead of tacking the entire design of JUnit at one time and trying cull out the design patterns used, we instead follow the work in

[3]. We start with a blank slate and build up the framework incrementally by applying one pattern at a time, each one solving a particular problem. A short summary of the process and patterns involved follows. Those who are interested in more details should refer to [3].

The first thing we need to do is capture the idea of a test as an object. Developers have different styles of tests in mind and we do not want our framework to be concerned with the types of tests being run – just that there are tests that need to be executed. This is an example of the Command pattern. Thus we make a class called TestCase that captures the test operation as an object. This class will have a run() (acting as the execute() method in "Gang of Four" pattern terminology [2]) to hold the actual test.

Now that we have tests can be manipulated as objects, we can take a look at the development of the tests themselves (i.e. the run() methods). When a developer needs to write a specific test case they will subclass TestCase and override the run() method to implement the concrete behavior of their test. However, all tests contain the same basic steps performed in the same order. Those steps are setup a fixture, run the test using the fixture, then tear down the fixture. This is a classic example of the Template Method pattern where run() becomes the Template Method and setUp(), runTest(), and tearDown() become the Hooks.

Another issue to be solved with tests is that we must collect the results somewhere. We really only care about collecting information on the failures of our tests, thus an efficient way to do this is with the Collection Parameter idiom. This basically states that we want to create a collecting object and pass it to each test where the failure results can be registered with it.

In order to invoke a particular TestCase, we need our invoker to call the generic run() method because of how TestCases were setup as Commands. This in turn calls the runTest() hook method because run() was setup as a Template Method. The issue that this creates is that when the test writer is creating concrete TestCases they need to create a new subclass for each test and put all the testing code in a method called runTest(). This produces a proliferation of classes. One would much rather allow them to create several related testing methods in a single class, as we described earlier in this paper. An Adapter pattern (class version) can be used to solve this problem. It adapts the interface that the test writer wants to use (e.g. testExactChange()) to the interface that the framework needs for polymorphism to work correctly (i.e. runTest()). The best way of providing these adapters in Java is to use anonymous inner classes to subclass the concrete TestCase. Of course this still means all the required anonymous inner classes, one for each testX method the user writes, need to be coded. Here is where reflection comes to the rescue. JUnit provides a default implementation of runTest() that looks for all testX() methods. It creates an adapter specific to each of these methods by creating an instance of a dynamically tailored adapting anonymous inner class.

Lastly we want to be able to abstractly run a single test or a suite of tests. That is, we do not want the invoker of the tests to care if it is running one test or many. This is an example of the Composite pattern where TestCase becomes the Leaf node and TestSuites become the Composite nodes.

We have now built up the guts of the JUnit framework using Command, Template Method, Adapter and Composite patterns, along with the Collection Parameter idiom and reflection. This not only makes a powerful example of how to design with patterns, but it shows the students the inner workings of the testing framework they have been using for years. And for some of the better students it encourages them to dive into the framework and start extending it in an attempt to create a more personalized testing environment.

7 CONCLUSION

We feel that the integration of testing into the curriculum is one of the most important trends in CS today. It enables students to produce cleaner code faster than ever before by catching bugs early in the development cycle. It also facilitates group projects by giving all group members the confidence that each other's code is correct.

Early coverage of unit testing allows students be taught how to write good test cases. Just because your tests pass does not mean your code is correct. The tests are only as good as the test cases themselves. Thus we have developed our methodology for writing good test cases and when to present this information to the students. We have a gradual progression from providing test cases to the students, to students writing their own simple test cases, to the inclusion of mock object and design patterns, to the development of more complex integration testing and use case testing systems. Finally we use the JUnit framework as an example of good design and give students the necessary understand of it allow for possible extension.

8 REFERENCES

[1] Bertolino, A. and Gnesi, S., "Use Case-based Testing of Product Lines," ," *Poster Session from the Proceedings of the 9th European software engineering conference held jointly with 10th ACM SIGSOFT international symposium on Foundations of software engineering*, Helsinki, Finland, 2003, pp. 355-358.

[2] Gamma, Erich, Helm, Richard, Johnson, Ralph, Vlissides, John, "Design Patterns: Elements of Reusable Object-Oriented Software", Addison-Wesley, 1995.

[3] JUnit: A Cook's Tour, http://junit.sourceforge.net/doc/cookstour/cookstour.htm

[4] JUnit Best Practices, http://www.javaworld.com/javaworld/jw-12-2000/jw-1221-ju it.html

[5] JUnit Cookbook, http://junit.sourceforge.net/doc/cookbook/cookbook.htm

[6] JUnit Home Page, http://junit.sourceforge.net

[7] Link, Johannes; "Unit Testing in Java: How Tests Drive the Code", Morgan Kaufman, 2003.

[8] Massol, Vincent, with Husted, Ted; "JUnit in Action", Manning Press, 2004.

[9] Olan, Michael, "Unit Testing: Test Early, Test Often", *Journal of Computing in Small Colleges*, v. 19, n. 2, Dec 2003, pp. 319-328.

[10] Patterson, Andrew, Kolling, Michael, Roseberg, John, "Introducing Unit Testing with BlueJ"; *SIGCSE Bulletin: Proc. 8th Annual SIGCSE Conference on Innovation and Technology in Computer Science Education*, v.35, n.3, September 2003, pp. 11-15.

[11] Rainsberger, J.B., Sterling, Scott; "JUnit Recipes: Practical Methods for Programmer Testing", Manning Press, 2004.

On Integrating Web Services From the Ground Up Into CS1/CS2

Billy B. L. Lim
Illinois State University
School of Information Technology
Normal, IL 61790-5150, USA
309-438-7589
bllim@ilstu.edu

Chu Jong
Illinois State University
School of Information Technology
Normal, IL 61790-5150, USA
309-438-5212
cjong@ilstu.edu

Pruthikrai Mahatanankoon
Illinois State University
School of Information Technology
Normal, IL 61790-5150, USA
309-438-3315
pmahata@ilstu.edu

ABSTRACT
Web services technology is a burgeoning technology that has received tremendous amount of attention in the software industry in recent years under the broader umbrella of service-oriented architecture (SOA). While Web services have been incorporated in many industries in the market place in the last few years, they are only beginning to appear in the academia, primarily in upper division and graduate CS curricula. In this paper, we share our belief that the Web services technology can and should be introduced early in a CS curriculum. We describe a number of scenarios that Web services can be integrated into CS1/CS2 to make them more interesting and more importantly, make the students better prepared for upper division classes and for the industry upon graduation. These scenarios can be incorporated without compromising the core materials presently covered in many CS1/CS2 sequence.

Categories and Subject Descriptors
K.3 [**Computers& Education**]: Computer & Information Science Education – Computer Science Education

General Terms
Design, Experimentation, Languages

Keywords
Web services, service-oriented architecture, Teaching CS1/CS2

1. INTRODUCTION
The introductory programming sequence in computer science has seen its share of changes, in terms of evolution, over the last few decades. From a primarily mainframe based delivery of the courses, through the use of PCs and its accompanying graphical user interfaces (GUIs), to the use of the Web in recent years, the introductory sequence has evolved to meet the needs of the information technology (IT) industry.

During the above period of change, the paradigm shift from procedural to object-oriented (OO) approach to problem solving can also be observed. This is again attributed to the moving forces of IT market where the industry essentially led the movement toward the use of OO technology for software development. This is evidenced from the adoption of OO programming languages such as Smalltalk, C++, Java, and C# in the industry and then in CS1 and CS2 over the years.

Now, similar observation can be made about how the software industry is embracing another wave of change in software development technologies. This time it involves service-oriented architecture (SOA), particularly the use of Web services to speed up application development and reduce costs to access data on disparate systems.

For many years, software reuse and systems interoperability have been primary goals of many IT organizations as means to curb software cost. These organizations have software applications that use the Internet/Web to transfer data, interoperate, and conduct business transactions. OO technology has been utilized to accomplish these goals with relative success over the years. Nevertheless, OO technology itself could not overcome many of the hurdles.

One of them is due to lack of standards. A software component developed in one vendor's technology cannot easily communicate with another vendor's. This is evidenced from the failure of major distributed OO technologies such as CORBA, DCOM, and RMI from becoming mainstream software development technologies. Another difficulty is due to the fact that the majority of software applications reside behind firewalls – security barriers that restrict communication between networks. Here, even if two systems use the same protocol to communicate, the security of firewall prevents the communications from taking place.

Web service [1,3,4,10,11] is the latest buzzword in the industry to address the problems identified above. Web service model is one that utilizes loosely-coupled, platform and language neutral framework for designing the next generation distributed systems. It is based on technologies by the W3C, the international standard body that oversees various Web related technologies. It also has strong support from major industry players such as Microsoft, IBM, Sun, HP, and Oracle. As such, it is projected to be a strong

SIGCSE'05, February 23–27, 2005, St. Louis, Missouri, USA.

technology that many IT organizations will investigate and adopt if proven viable. In fact, Gartner Research compared Web services with previous attempts and stated that this time things may be different because "With Web services, all the major vendors are on board with their support."

Recent studies on Web services have also shown the growth and acceptance of the technology. According to ZapThink, a market research firm, the market for Web services platforms, application development suites, and management tools is projected to expand from a $380 million (US) market in 2001 to over $15.5 billion (US) in 2005. Also, recent survey by market research firm TechMatrix (of 450 IT professionals and consultants) finds that 65% of small and midsize companies and 35% of large companies have adopted Web services to automate business processes between trading partners and for internal application integration. Another important observation is that the use of Web services is now widespread in many industries including retail, financial services, homeland security, transportation, etc.

With the above stunning growth, it is inevitable that Web services will be integrated into CS curricula eventually, if history is of any indication. It is thus a natural evolution for CS1/CS2 to begin exposing the beginning students with this burgeoning technology early on given the current trend of software development. This will not only fascinate the students with its interesting collection of activities (see Section 3), but also inspire and prepare them for real-world software development scenarios when they graduate. First-year undergraduates rarely get the exposure to these technologies because of the need to get to the fundamentals of computing first. This paper describes strategies that can be employed without compromising these fundamentals.

Given today's economic climate and the offshore outsourcing trend to countries such as India and China, which arguably has led to higher programmer unemployment, the adoption of more exciting technologies at the beginning level may help to attract and retain more students. Web services hold great promise in this respect and they are expected to be integrated into the CS curricula pervasively in the years to come.

In fact, it should be noted that efforts are beginning to surface in some CS curricula in the form of upper-division/graduate, seminar type class (e.g., [7,16]). However, it is our belief that ideally one should start to lay the foundation of SOA in the form of Web services in introductory programming courses. Eyeing on the popularity and importance of Web services, their economic argument [2], the need to keep CS curricula as up-to-date as possible, and the importance of laying the right foundation early on, it is thus the goal of this paper to describe scenarios that are viable for integrating Web services into CS1/CS2.

The remainder of the paper is organized as follows. Section 2 gives a brief overview of the underlying technologies behind Web services. The aforementioned scenarios for integration are detailed in Section 3. Section 4 provides a discussion of the implementation of the scenarios, and finally the summary and conclusions are given in Section 5.

2. WEB SERVICES

In a nutshell, Web services can simply be thought of as self-describing services that are HTTP-addressable, i.e., Web-callable. This means that one can shop for a software service much like one can shop for goods on the Web, using exactly the same protocol. Web services relies on SOAP (Simple Object Access Protocol), WSDL (Web Service Description Language), and UDDI (Universal Description, Discovery, and Integration) as the underlying technologies for involved parties to communicate and produce/consume a Web service, as shown in Figure 1. Here, a scenario that shows a brokerage house registering its stock quote service with a registry and a financial software finding and consuming the service is depicted.

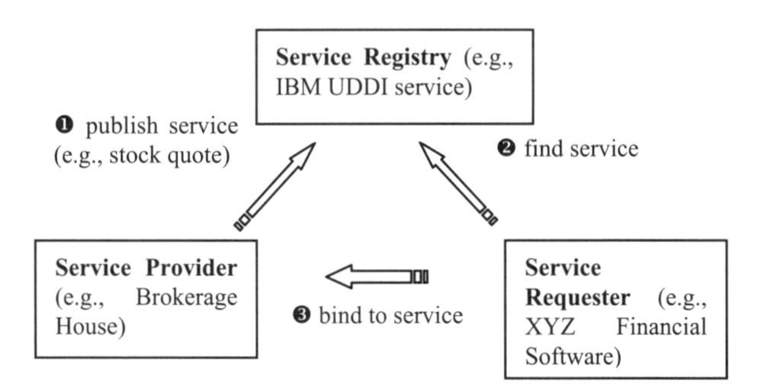

Figure 1: Life Cycle of a Web Service Execution (Registry, Lookup, and Consumption)

Behind the scene, SOAP uses HTTP as the protocol to transmit its message, which is in XML format. This powerful combination of HTTP and XML, both standards of W3C, provides a fully extensible mode of communication between loosely-coupled software systems. The interoperability and scalability of Web services means that developers can rapidly create larger applications and Web services from smaller ones. This adds another dimension to the Web; instead of just person-to-person or person-to-system, it also handles system-to-system.

Given that HTTP is a firewall friendly protocol and XML is becoming more and more popular as a standard for data exchange, it is not surprising that Web services has received so much attention in the industry, including new journals such as International Journal of Web Services Research and Web Services Journal for the coverage of the topic [9,17]. It is the buzz that all major IT corporations are talking about and it is also the centerpiece of the .NET campaign of Microsoft [5], a technology that Microsoft is staking its future in, with $4 billion initial investment.

This new way of application development is mimicking how hardware vendors have been producing hardware components for years. Now, the software vendors even have the Web, one of the most important revolutions in the computer industry, on their side. As stated by Bill Gates [5], Chairman of Microsoft, "The power of the XML Web Services model is amazing. A company offering an online electronic-payment service can expose its service to partners, so that they can deliver it as part of their own offering – regardless of what platform they are using. An airline can link its online reservation system to that of a car-rental partner, so travelers can book a car at the same time they book a flight. … XML Web services help your business break free of its boundaries."

3. WEB SERVICES SCENARIOS FOR CS1/ CS2

This section provides numerous scenarios on how various topics that are typically covered in CS1 or CS2 may be easily enhanced so that students can be exposed to a burgeoning state-of-the-technology – Web services. The scenarios are presented by listing a topic in question, its typical delivery mechanism, its Web services delivery alternative, and finally an example depicting an instance of the scenario. Miscellaneous comments may also be provided under the "Other" subsection.

3.1 Method Invocation

Typical Delivery: This topic is typically covered for methods that are local to the caller's address space or library routines that are external but still from within the same system space.

Web Services Based Delivery: Instead of merely calling methods that are on the same address space, introduce the notion that some methods may have been written by others and that these methods (i.e., Web services) are scattered all over the world but they are callable from the Web.

Example: The Web service method sayHello() may be coded to return "hello" if called from a local machine but return hello in the respective foreign language if the called method is housed in a foreign country (e.g., "你好 (ni hao)" from China, "hola" in Mexico, "konnichiwa" in Japan). This "hello world" of Web services allows the students to be exposed to the new world of SOA with minimal complexity.

Other: The introduction of Web services in this scenario opens up many opportunities to discuss various other subject areas as well. In addition to Web services (SOA in general), one can discuss distributed computing and network communication in general. Also, because of the use of foreign characters, one can talk about character encoding schemes. Lastly, the concept to polymorphism can also be tied to the above when one considers how the objects from different countries are reacting in their own ways (of saying hello) to the same message.

3.2 Sequence, Iterative, and Decision Structures

Typical Delivery: These topics are typically covered by traditional discussion of scenarios that (1) necessitate a certain ordering be imposed in order to solve a problem (e.g., read the input values before processing them), (2) require a loop be used (e.g., processing a collection of numbers to find the average), and (3) need an if-else structure be employed (e.g., find the largest and smallest numbers from a collection of numbers).

Web Services Based Delivery: Instead of merely processing a collection of numbers that may be meaningless (and boring to the students), one could present a scenario where the goal is to solve a problem by using the three fundamental structures and some existing Web services that can be composed to form a solution for the problem.

Example: A plausible scenario here is to discuss a problem where one wishes to find out the warmest temperature in all the U.S. by zip codes at a particular moment in time. Further, the warmest area of the country needs to be plotted on a map.

This scenario, which is much more interesting for today's freshmen, may seem intractable in the traditional CS1/CS2 environment. But there exist various publicly available Web services that can be composed together to solve this problem rather effortlessly. There exists one that retrieves all the US zip codes (GetZipCodes) [14], another one that finds the temperature given a zip code [18], and yet another one that plots a particular area on a map given a zip code (MapPoint Web service) [12]. Thus, one can cover the sequence, iterative, and decision structures all in one shot in the above example.

Other: Variations of the above can easily be done if one wishes to get "closer to home" to find temperatures that are in one's neighborhood. There are Web services that retrieve all the zip codes within a given radius mile of another (e.g., GetNearbyZipCodes [15]) and ones that calculate the distance between two given zip codes (e.g., [8]). With these Web services, one can, for example, create exercises that require two different computations of all the areas that are within, say, 50 miles radius of a city like Chicago given the zip codes.

3.3 Sorting and/or Searching

Typical Delivery: This topic is typically covered by discussions on various sorting and searching methods and their respective Big-O complexities. This is typically followed by examples of applying the algorithms on records of interest such as ranking the top 10 NCAA teams and searching for a team given some criteria.

Web Services Based Delivery: Web services call can be made to return the result of a sort or search, whether this is via publicly available or internally developed Web services.

Example: Web services that implement linear search, binary search, bubble sort, and quick sort may be provided for the students to experiment with and gather the performance of the algorithms. Here, a discussion of the different Big-O notations for the implemented algorithms may be reinforced. Also, students may be asked to observe any network latency as part of the experiments and discuss how the delays compare to the overall performance timings of the algorithms.

3.4 Miscellaneous Data structures

Typical Delivery: This topic is typically covered by discussing scenarios that require the use of compound data structures (e.g., stacks, queues, trees) to effectively produce results for certain problems. For example, one may discuss a simulation of supermarket queues (express lane or otherwise) after the queue and related data structures are presented. The typical scenarios generally do not involve the use of the Web.

Web Services Based Delivery: To make the discussions and potential exercises more interesting, students can be required to consume Web services that directly produce the data structures of interest. Alternatively, they may be asked to create such data structures from the results of Web services themselves to handle the application requirements.

Example: A plausible scenario is to expose the students to the Google Web services API [6] where instead of going to google.com to do searching, a customized version (e.g., better user interface or "create a novel UI for searching" as Google puts it) can be built to serve their own interests. Here, we are still relying on Google's powerful search engine to scour the Web, but we can add the bells and whistles (e.g., add spell check) to make the search experience more fruitful. A discussion of how Google or other search engines typically organizes its data can then follow. For example, Google Directory reuses the data provided by the Open Directory Project and constructs a hierarchical list of Web sites [13]. Instead of generating a compound data structure and constructing a traversal algorithm, the service traverses up and down the already constructed directory tree to get the information to the caller.

Another possibly is to manipulate the search results from a service (one needs to examine the Terms and Conditions carefully here) and create the appropriate data structures that are best suited for the application requirements.

Other: With the above scenarios, one can discuss the concept of Web portals and how Web services are at the core of designing and implementing the portals.

3.5 Use of Different OS

Typical Delivery: For some CS curricula, including one from the authors' institution, part of the introductory sequence needs to expose students to an environment that is other than the "main" one. For example, Windows environment that runs Java may be the main environment that supports the main course activities while an alternate one may be Java on Linux or OS390. Here, the rationale is to expose the students to multiple operating systems and students are typically given a small program to do in the alternative environment.

Web Services Based Delivery: Instead of developing just another program that runs on an alternative environment, students may be shown how to develop a Web service and be challenged to create a useful Web service in a motivating context. Then, one possibility is to require the students to consume the Web service that they have just built. This allows for a discussion on across platforms interoperability when the consumer interoperates with the producer of a Web service.

Example: A Web service on the aforementioned GetZipCodes may be developed and the same service consumer discussed earlier may then be used to consume the newly created Web service. This service may, for example, read from a file that contains all the zip codes and return them to the caller.

4. DISCUSSION

First and foremost, it should be noted that the scenarios and activities discussed in Section 3 are merely intended to be ones that can be used to integrate Web services into CS1 or CS2 and expose students to an increasingly important topic without compromising the core of the courses. They are not intended to replace any of the core topics and their use should be considered an experiment at this point in time.

This experiment is currently being investigated at the authors' institution. (The website http://www.itk.ilstu.edu/lim/ws/ will be used to share Web services materials for integration into CS1 and CS2.) It is anticipated that the overhead of introducing Web services would be minimal given that in many of the scenarios, "black-box" approach would be used. The underlying details are not expected to be fully disclosed until an upper division course that hopefully has a segment that reveals the components of Web services.

Also, with today's technologies, consuming an existing Web service or developing a new one is a relatively easy proposition. For example, to consuming a Web service in Microsoft Visual Studio.NET environment, one needs to simply provide the URI (Uniform Resource Identifier) of the Web service and include it as a *Web reference* in the Solution of the project being built, all of which can be accomplished via point-and-click. Then, to invoke a service, one simply instantiates an object from the associated proxy class (included in the Web reference) and makes a method call.

Similarly, to develop a Web service, one needs to simply create a Web Service project in VS.NET and tag the method that is to be exposed using the [WebMethod] attribute, i.e., just insert this attribute before the method! When done, the method is now exposed and is callable as a Web service.

Both the consumption and the development of Web services can also be achieved easily using technology from the other camp, i.e., Java. Many Java IDEs (e.g., Oracle JDeveloper, Borland JBuilder, IBM Websphere, Sun Java Studio, etc.) provide functionality that is comparable to Microsoft VS.NET and allow for simple integration of Web services technology.

As for the coverage of the general topic of Web services (this is a true overhead as this topic is not known to be covered in any CS1 or CS2 course), this can conceivably be introduced when the general introduction to software engineering is given. An estimate is that no more than 1-week of coverage should be dedicated to this introduction with Web services being a major component here. SOA is changing the landscape of software engineering and Web services technology is at the heart of this evolution and thus deserves the spotlight and time coverage.

5. SUMMARY AND CONCLUSIONS

As industry leaders collaborate to standardize Web services, we can speculate that next generation distributed systems will adopt various Web services-related technologies. Many businesses are currently in the process of implementing the technology to automate their business activities. By exposing our CS students to this concept early on, they will be equipped with the state-of-art software development skill and the knowledge to actively participate in this new industry trend.

Some educators may suggest that Web services should be taught to upper-division undergraduate students, until most students are fully exposed to various concepts in the field, e.g., distributed computing, operating systems, databases, etc. However, we suggest that integrating Web services to the first-year CS curriculum may not only help to attract and retain more students, but will also provide us with newer, advance teaching plans for our upper-division students. Although our examples offer general guidelines of what could be done in the CS1/CS2 level courses, we are equally eager to incorporate Web services vertically as well as horizontally into other curricula, i.e., telecommunication and information systems majors. We anticipated that the overhead of introducing Web services would be minimal given that several of the basic courses requirements of these majors were similar. If "the power of the XML Web Services model is amazing"[5], then this could be the time to introduce such technological foundation to our future IT professionals.

6. REFERENCES

[1] Benfield , S., "Web Services: XML's Killer App," *Java Developers' Journal*, Vol. 6, No. 4., 2001.

[2] Booch, G., "Web Services: The Economic Argument," *Software Development*, Vol. 9, No. 11, November, 2001.

[3] Curbera, F., et al., "Unraveling the Web Services Web," *IEEE Internet Computing*, march/April, 2002.

[4] Dyck, T., "Web Services Wave" (the Cover Story: Web Services Wake-Up Call), *eWeek*, Vol. 18, No. 35, September, 2001.

[5] Gates, W., Microsoft .NET Today, an open letter to the Developers & IT Professionals, June 14, 2001.

[6] Google Web services API, http://www.google.com/apis/

[7] Humphrey, Marty, "Web Services as the Foundation for Learning Complex Software System Development," *35th SIGCSE Technical Symposium on Computer Science Education*, Norfolk, Virginia USA March 3 - 7, 2004

[8] Imacination, http://webservices.imacination.com/distance/

[9] International Journal of Web Services Research, http://www.idea-group.com/journals/details.asp?id=4138

[10] Kiely, D., "WSDL for Defining Web Services," Cover Story, *XML Magazine*, Vol. 2, No. 4, August/September, 2001.

[11] Lim, Billy B. L., Wen, H. J. "Web Services: An Analysis of the Technology, its Benefits, and Implementation Difficulties," *Information Systems Management*, Vol. 20, No.1, Spring 2003, pp. 49-57.

[12] Mappoint, http://www.microsoft.com/mappoint/default.mspx

[13] Ntoulas, A., Cho, J., and Olston C., "What's New on the Web? The Evolution of the Web from a Search Engine Perspective," *WWW2004*, May 17-24, New York, NY, USA.

[14] Remotemethods, http://www.remotemethods.com/home/valueman/validati/zipcodes

[15] Teachatechie, http://teachatechie.com/GJTTWebServices/ZipCode.asmx

[16] Weaver, A., Peden, J., "Integrating Web Services into the Undergraduate Computer Science Curriculum," National Science Foundation, CISE Education Research and Curriculum Development Program, January 12, 2004.

[17] Web Services Journal, http://www.sys-con.com/webservices/

[18] Xmethods, http://www.xmethods.net/sd/2001/TemperatureService.wsdl

Why Structural Recursion Should Be Taught Before Arrays in CS 1[*]

Kim B. Bruce[†], Andrea Danyluk, and Thomas Murtagh
Department of Computer Science
Williams College
Williamstown, MA 01267
{kim,andrea,tom}@cs.williams.edu

ABSTRACT

The approach to teaching recursion in introductory programming courses has changed little during the transition from procedural to object-oriented languages. It is still common to present recursion late in the course and to focus on traditional, procedural examples such as calculating factorials or solving the Towers of Hanoi puzzle. In this paper, we propose that the shift to object-oriented programming techniques calls for a significant shift in our approach to teaching recursion. First, we argue that in the context of object-oriented programming students should be introduced to examples of simple recursive structures such as linked lists and methods that process them, before being introduced to traditional procedural examples. Second, we believe that this material should be presented before students are introduced to structures such as arrays. In our experience, the early presentation of recursive structures provides the opportunity to reinforce the fundamentals of defining and using classes and better prepares students to appreciate the reasons to use classes to encapsulate access to other data structures when they are presented.

Categories and Subject Descriptors

K.3.2 [**Computer and Information Science Education**]: Computer Science Education

General Terms

Algorithms, Design

Keywords

CS1, recursion

*Research partially supported by NSF CCLI grant DUE-0088895.
†currently on leave at UC Santa Cruz.

SIGCSE'05, February 23–27, 2005, St. Louis, Missouri, USA.

1. INTRODUCTION

In the fall of 1999, we implemented a major update of the Williams College CS 1 course. The course is now taught using Java. With the support of the specially designed `objectdraw` library, this course takes an objects-first approach, uses truly object-oriented graphics, incorporates event-driven programming techniques from the beginning, and includes concurrency quite early in the course. As argued in our earlier papers [2, 1], the combination of object-oriented graphics, event-driven programming, and concurrency provides for a very interesting and pedagogically sound introduction to programming.

After the first few offerings of this course, we began to see a troubling pattern: in the second half of the course students were drifting away from thinking about object-oriented design issues. When we introduced arrays, students resisted encapsulating them in classes, instead simply making the arrays available globally as instance variables or passing them around as parameters.

For example, our first array lab involved presenting the Simon game, in which the computer generates longer and longer sequences of notes that the player must repeat. We emphasized to students that there should be a `Song` class in which the array of notes should be an instance variable, and which should support methods like `play`, `endOfSong`, etc. However, many students resisted creating this separate class to encapsulate the array. These students instead declared the array as an instance variable of the class that handled user interactions, and manipulated the array directly within the methods of that class.

Similar things happened with programs involving multi-dimensional arrays, strings, and files. We were concerned that we were teaching the first half of the course in an object-oriented style and the second half in a more procedural style.

Eventually, we devised a reordering of course topics that allows us to more firmly ingrain the object-oriented style of programming in ways that carry over into our introduction of arrays, etc. The key was to move the teaching of recursion from after arrays and strings to before these topics. Moreover, we changed from a focus on method-based recursion over the integers to a concentration on structural recursion. In the rest of this paper we discuss how we approach recursion and the associated benefits to having students design data structures in a more object-oriented style. While our own work took place in the context of using the `objectdraw` library, we believe that the same ideas can be used to improve any objects-early CS 1 course.

2. THE FIRST HALF OF THE COURSE

We begin our introductory course with the use of event-driven programming and truly object-oriented graphics. This use of graphics provides concrete examples of flexible and useful objects from predefined classes. The event-driven programming style allows students to create quite interesting programs using only very basic language constructs. The resulting methods tend to be relatively simple, while the implicit flow of control (e.g., from executing a method handling a mouse press to executing a method handling mouse drags to executing one handling a mouse release) allows students to focus on the manipulation of the objects without worrying about control structures.

After the introduction of conditional statements, students begin the design of multi-class programs. For example, students write programs that allows the user to create and drag around graphical objects generated by a class that they design. Objects on the screen can interact to produce interesting behavior. One such program we have assigned places pictures of two magnets in a window. When one magnet is dragged too close to the other, they either attract or repel, depending on which poles are close enough to interact.

We next introduce `while` loops. Threads (as extensions of our library's `ActiveObject` class) are introduced to provide a context in which simple `while` loops produce interesting behavior. In particular, `while` loops and threads can be used to produce animations as part of a program. As a first example, students write a program in which a click above a line results in the creation of a ball that then falls slowly down the screen. Points are scored if the ball falls entirely within a basket that is placed at a random position at the bottom of the window.

Later, our students write a Frogger game where mouse clicks are used to guide a frog across a four-line highway that includes cars moving in all of the lanes. In this example, there is a class for the frog, a class extending `ActiveObject` representing lanes of the highway, and another class extending `ActiveObject` representing the vehicles on the highway. From these examples, students get a great deal of experience building programs that involve several objects from different classes.

We then introduce Java `interfaces`. We emphasize that if a variable's type is an interface, then the variable can hold objects generated by different classes that implement the interface. This flows into a relatively quick introduction to GUI interfaces using the Swing library.

At this point, we are 5 to 6 weeks into our 12 week semester. Topics to be covered in the second half of the term include one-dimensional and multi-dimensional arrays, strings, exceptions, files, recursion, and simple sorting and searching. Many of these topics are taught in ways fairly similar to those used in procedural languages, though of course the arrays generally hold objects from classes rather than just numbers.

Students learn best when fundamental ideas are reinforced by repetition and are used in different contexts. Because the object-oriented ideas no longer play as important a role in this portion of the course, student understanding of the rationale for object-oriented design seemed to slip, even in situations where the design of classes would provide substantial benefits. In the next section, we discuss how the introduction of recursion before arrays helped us keep the focus on the object-oriented approach.

3. TEACHING STRUCTURAL RECURSION BEFORE ARRAYS

Both arrays and recursive structures can be used to hold collections of objects. In typical introductory texts using procedural or object-oriented languages, arrays are introduced first, and only later are recursively defined structures like recursive lists introduced.[1] In fact many texts reserve their presentation of recursion for one of the final chapters, encouraging instructors to put this material off for discussion in a CS 2 course. We argue here that recursively defined structures are more object-oriented in flavor, and their relatively early introduction can help reinforce important ideas like dynamic method dispatch and the use of interfaces.

In addition, using structural recursion and presenting it before arrays makes it much easier to maintain student interest in the topic. Instructors who teach arrays before recursion have a difficult time convincing students of the value of using recursion. Most of the examples traditionally presented using recursion can easily be handled with loops or arrays or involve problems that appear to have little practical value to the students. On the other hand, at the point we now introduce recursion, students have not yet seen arrays or any other Java constructs that will allow them to represent collections of objects. Learning about recursive structures greatly expands the range of programming problems our students can solve by allowing them to write programs that manipulate such collections.

In this section we present a very simple example to illustrate our ideas. While we will use the `objectdraw` library to create a recursive graphic image, the underlying data structure is simply a specialized recursive list. Instructors can select other examples that fit in the context of their courses, yet illustrate the same fundamental ideas.

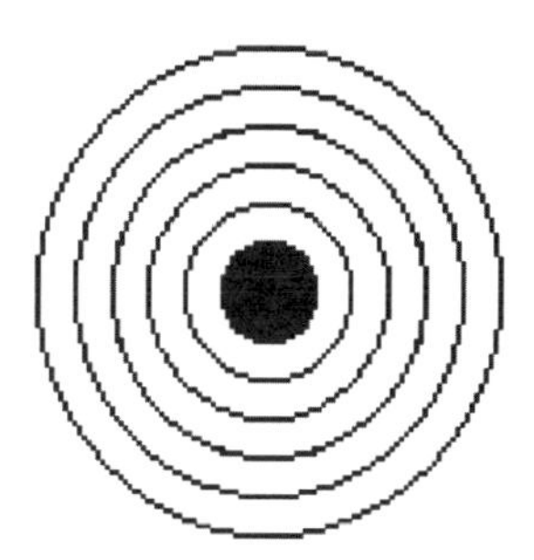

Figure 1: Picture corresponding to an object of a `RingedTarget` class.

For our example we will design a class that represents a target like that shown in Figure 1. A target consists of a small filled oval (the bullseye) and a series of concentric rings. A recursive description of a target is as follows. If the radius of the target is 15 pixels or smaller, the target simply consists of a bullseye. Otherwise the target consists of a framed oval with the given radius and then a smaller

[1]Introductory courses using functional languages, on the other hand, typically cover built-in recursively defined lists early.

target with the same center, but a radius 8 units smaller than before.

We can define classes representing targets that will have exactly this structure. The base class, `BullsEye`, will create the bullseye only, while the recursive class, `RingedTarget`, will represent targets with one or more circles around the bullseye.

We wish to define targets that support a `move` method and a `contains` method. Thus we define an interface with those methods:

```
public interface TargetInterface {
   // move the target by dx in x direction and
   // dy in y direction
   void move(double dx, double dy);

   // return whether the target contains pt
   boolean contains(Location pt);
}
```

Both classes to be defined will implement this interface. We use Java and emphasize interfaces over inheritance, but in courses that use other languages or emphasize inheritance over interfaces, a fully abstract class could be used instead.

Defining a `BullsEye` class implementing this interface is easy:

```
public class BullsEye implements TargetInterface {

   private FilledOval centerCircle; // bullseye

   // bullseye centered at pt with radius
   public BullsEye(Location pt,
                   double radius,
                   DrawingCanvas canvas) {
      centerCircle = new FilledOval(
                 pt.getX() - radius,
                 pt.getY() - radius, 2 * radius,
                 2 * radius, canvas);
   }

   // move the target by dx in x direction and
   // dy in y direction
   public void move(double dx, double dy) {
      centerCircle.move(dx,dy);
   }

   // return whether the target contains pt
   public boolean contains(Location pt) {
      return centerCircle.contains(pt);
   }
}
```

The class above uses the `objectdraw` graphics library, but the intent should be clear enough. The constructor draws a filled oval, while the `move` method moves the oval and the `contains` method determines whether the oval contains the point. As usual the base case of a recursive structure is very straightforward, and neither the constructor nor either method uses recursion.

The recursive class representing targets with one or more rings is more interesting.

```
public class RingedTarget
                   implements TargetInterface {
   // outer ring of target
   private FramedOval outer;
   // rest of target
   private TargetInterface rest;

   // Create target centered at pt with radius
   public RingedTarget(Location pt, double radius,
                       DrawingCanvas canvas) {
      // Create and center outer ring
      outer = new FramedOval(pt.getX() - radius,
                 pt.getY() - radius, 2 * radius,
                 2 * radius, canvas);
      radius = radius - 8;
      if (radius > 15) {
         rest = new RingedTarget(pt, radius,
                                 canvas);
      } else {
         rest = new BullsEye(pt, radius, canvas);
      }
   }

   // move the target by dx in x direction
   // and dy in y direction
   public void move(double dx, double dy) {
      outer.move(dx,dy);
      rest.move(dx,dy);
   }

   // return whether the target contains pt
   public boolean contains(Location pt) {
      return outer.contains(pt);
   }
}
```

The constructor creates an outer ring and then, depending on the size, sets `rest` to be either a new smaller `RingedTarget` inside the outer ring or a new `BullsEye`. The `move` method moves the outer ring and then moves the `rest`. The `contains` method, on the other hand, is not recursive and simply determines if the outer ring contains the location passed in.

While this example introduces the general use of recursion, it also reinforces other important concepts. Interfaces are being used in an essential way, as the value of `rest` can either be a `BullsEye` object or a `RingedTarget` object.

Even more important is how this code illustrates the importance of dynamic method dispatch. In the `move` method, the message send of `move` to `rest` is an excellent example. If the value of `rest` is a `BullsEye` object, then the `move` method of that class moves the `centerCircle`. If the value of `rest` is a `RingedTarget` object, then the `move` method will move its outer ring and then send the `move` message to its `rest` instance variable (which is of course different from the `rest` instance variable of the original receiver).

As noted earlier, the example above is a thinly veiled example of a recursively defined list. We provide students with several other examples of recursive structures that all fit the same pattern (e.g., lists of URLs, scribbles as lists of line segments) as well as one or more examples of somewhat different structures (e.g., fractal drawings of snowflakes or broccoli), each time keeping a focus on the general recursive structure.

4. WHY STRUCTURAL RECURSION?

Most textbooks and instructors introduce recursion via methods in which the recursion is based on integers. For example, one can define recursive algorithms for exponentiation, binary search, or quicksort, where the recursion is based on the number of elements in the slice of the array left to be processed.

Whilc this is finc as an approach to recursion (and examples like binary search and quicksort can be important examples of the use of recursion), we argue that this sort of example is less intuitive to students and does not highlight the important object-oriented features that are brought out by the use of structural recursion. Let's address each of these individually.

Students find it hard to conceptualize recursive functions and procedures. Recursion works by starting one computation, and then interrupting that computation to perform one or more computations using the exact same set of instructions and instances of the same variables, eventually returning to complete the original computation. Instructors know that different copies of parameters and local variables are kept with the stack of activation records corresponding to the various recursive calls. The notion of an activation record, however, is new to the students and difficult for them to grasp because they are allocated implicitly and never explicitly manipulated by the program. While instructors may try to make the underlying execution model more concrete using exercises in which one student begins executing the original computation and calls on others to perform the recursive calls, the notion of procedural recursion resulting in new invocations of procedures is difficult for many students to grasp.

On the other hand, structural recursion is quite concrete. In a course like ours that stresses object-oriented programming, students will have already become familiar with the idea that it is possible to create multiple objects of a single class. Unlike activation records, the creation of these objects is done explicitly in their code. Moreover, they understand that each of these objects has its own copies of the instance variables declared by the class. This knowledge is developed through their programming experience before the subject of recursion is introduced. For example, in the assignment described above in which our students implement a program that lets them drag two magnets around the screen, they know that each magnet must have its own copies of the instance variables that keep track of its position. This is reinforced concretely by the fact that when they invoke the move method of one magnet the other does not move.

This knowledge can be easily exploited when explaining recursion. When they see that the `move` message is sent to a particular object from class `RingedTarget`, one can draw a picture to illustrate the instance variables of the original target and the objects to which they refer. When the recursive call is made to `rest`, the slightly smaller target, another picture can be drawn illustrating the separate instance variables of that object. This can continue all the way down to the base case. These objects are familiar to the students and more concrete than are activations of functions.

We remarked earlier on the fact that using data structures defined by structural recursion highlights and reinforces important concepts in object-oriented programming such as the use of interfaces (subtyping) and dynamic method dispatch. Unfortunately, methods defined based on recursion on the integers illustrate none of these principles. No interfaces are relevant, and the decision as to which code is to be executed is based on a conditional statement rather than on dynamic method dispatch. A binary search or quicksort in an object-oriented language looks extremely similar to one in a procedural language. In fact, many texts illustrate these with static methods, emphasizing their independence from object-oriented concepts.

Another advantage of using structural recursion is that students see these data structures representing collections of objects where the details are hidden inside classes. When we later teach students arrays as an alternative way to hold collections, they are much more likely to see the reasons for hiding the arrays as instance variables in classes that export the more natural methods associated with the data structure. We often show one data structure implemented by structural recursion and another version using arrays. The public methods with their signatures in each are the same, with the differences in implementation hidden inside of the objects. At that point we can discuss how both produce the same results, but with slightly different performance characteristics.

5. EVALUATION

There have been noticeable differences in student programs written in the second half of our course after we moved up the presentation of recursion and emphasized structural recursion over recursion on integers. For example, very few students now resist encapsulating arrays inside classes. Because of their experience with recursive data structures, they now see this as the normal way of handling data structures.

Recall our earlier example of the Simon game, and a class `Song` representing the sequence of notes generated so far. After the introduction to structural recursion, students are much more likely to create a class with an array as an instance variable and where the methods are not tightly associated with array operations. Instead they include methods like `addNote()`, `atEnd()`, `makeNewSong()`, `play()`, etc. As a result of this superior organization, they find this program easier to write and debug.

In checking to find quantifiable evidence of the impact of this change in student perceptions of our course, we examined student course evaluations, in particular the summary scores for course difficulty. Of course there are many variables that can contribute to student perceptions of course difficulty. To adjust for some of these, we compared two offerings of the course that were taught by the same lead instructor in a similar semester. (We see somewhat different student populations between the fall and spring semesters.)

In the spring of 2000, a semester in which arrays were taught well before recursion, students reported an average level of difficulty for the course of 4.0 out of 5, where 1 is the lowest difficulty and 5 is the highest. In the spring of 2002, where recursion was taught before arrays, students reported an average level of difficulty of 3.0 out of 5. The first score was in the highest quintile range for courses in the college, while the latter falls into the second lowest quintile range. We note that most of the lab assignments were essentially the same between these two course offerings.

While there are always minor differences between offerings of the course and indeed the population of students, the changes in student reported level of difficulty suggests that students perceived the course to be easier when recursion was moved earlier. The earlier version of the course introduced integer-based recursion before structural recursion, though the associated lab assignment, both before and after the earlier introduction of recursion, involved designing a recursive class representing a fractal-like picture. Later versions of the course have also included a second recursion lab involving writing a program to handle lists of scribbles.

6. RELATED WORK

There have been many papers on teaching recursion (for example, Wu et al [8]), but only a few have focused on structural recursion. Structural recursion is very common in functional programming languages. An example is the Felleisen et al text [4], which uses Scheme and emphasizes strongly the design of programs based on the structure of the data. Another example is the paper by Henderson and Romero [6], which discusses teaching structural induction with ML.

The text [5] by Felleisen and Friedman breaks from the more usual approaches to Java by developing immutable recursive lists (representing pizzas) from the very beginning. The style used in the book is very similar to that used in functional languages. We do not advocate going as far as those authors, as we believe it is important for students to understand mutable variables and loops, but we do believe that introducing recursion before arrays can have great benefits.

Aside from that text, there has not been as much emphasis on structural recursion early in procedural or object-oriented languages. Our examination of several recent Java-based CS 1 books has shown that most text books either introduce recursion as an optional section in one or more chapters or relegate it to a very late chapter where it is unlikely to be covered. Moreover, virtually all of the examples of recursion presented in these texts involve procedural recursion on integers rather than the structural recursion we are advocating here.

One of the few examples of papers discussing structural recursion we were able to find is Nguyen and Wong's paper [7], which discusses using the visitor pattern on recursively defined data structures, a more advanced topic than we have discussed here.

7. CONCLUSIONS

In this paper, we have argued that the introduction of structural recursion before the presentation of arrays helps solidify students' understanding of object-oriented concepts. It also increases students' understanding of why other data structures, such as arrays, also need to be encapsulated in classes that provide operations more naturally associated with the objects represented by the classes. Moreover, we argued that it is pedagogically easier to explain – and for students to understand – structural recursion than recursion based on integer values. Finally, presenting structural recursion as described here reinforces the use and understanding of interfaces and dynamic method dispatch.

We have been writing a text [3] based on our approach to teaching programming in a CS 1 course. Instructors who are interested in seeing more of the details of our approach to presenting recursion will find them in the draft chapters of the text that are available at:

`http://eventfuljava.cs.williams.edu/`

The text is now scheduled to be published by Prentice Hall in early 2005.

8. REFERENCES

[1] K. B. Bruce, A. Danyluk, and T. Murtagh. Event-driven programming can be simple enough for CS 1. In *Proceedings of the 2001 ACM ITiCSE Conference*, pages 1–4, 2001.

[2] K. B. Bruce, A. Danyluk, and T. Murtagh. A library to support a graphics-based object-first approach to CS 1. In *Proceedings of the Thirty-Second ACM SIGCSE Symposium*, pages 6–10, 2001.

[3] K. B. Bruce, A. Danyluk, and T. Murtagh. *Java: An eventful approach*. Prentice Hall, 2004.

[4] M. Felleisen, R. B. Findler, M. Flatt, and S. Krishnamurthi. *How to Design Programs*. MIT Press, 2001.

[5] M. Felleisen and D. P. Friedman. *A little Java, a few patterns*. MIT Press, 1997.

[6] P. B. Henderson and F. J. Romero. Teaching recursion as a problem-solving tool using standard ML. In *Proceedings of The Twentieth SIGCSE Technical Symposium on Computer Science Education*, pages 27–31. ACM Press, 1989.

[7] D. Nguyen and S. B. Wong. Patterns for decoupling data structures and algorithms. In *Proceedings of the Thirtieth SIGCSE Technical Symposium on Computer Science Education*, pages 87–91. ACM Press, 1999.

[8] C.-C. Wu, N. Dale, and L. J. Bethel. Conceptual models and cognitive learning styles in teaching recursion. In *Proceedings of the Twenty-Ninth SIGCSE Technical Symposium on Computer Science Education*, pages 292–296. ACM Press, 1998.

Use and Assessment of a Rigorous Approach to CS1

John P. Dougherty
Department of Computer Science
Haverford College
Haverford, Pennsylvania 19041 USA
jd@cs.haverford.edu

David G. Wonnacott
Department of Computer Science
Haverford College
Haverford, Pennsylvania 19041 USA
davew@cs.haverford.edu

ABSTRACT

We have developed and implemented a "rigor-first" approach to CS1 instruction, in which we introduce rigorous techniques for understanding algorithms alongside associated programming skills. This core material is developed through a number of engaging problems from more advanced courses in computer science and other natural sciences. These principles are continued in CS2, and the two courses form our "3-2-1" first-year sequence: three programming paradigms and two models of program execution are explored on a single platform. This article discusses the design of our CS1 course, its role in the computer science curriculum, and our experiences with it. Preliminary assessment suggests this approach has merit in our curriculum.

Categories and Subject Descriptors

K.3.2 [**Computers and Education**]: Computer and Information Science Education—*Computer Science Education*

General Terms

Design, Human Factors

Keywords

CS1, gender, multi-paradigm, pedagogy, recursion, rigor, verification

1. OVERVIEW

Haverford College is a small liberal arts institution with programs in the humanities, the social sciences, and the natural sciences. The curriculum in computer science concentrates on the fundamental concepts of the discipline. Most computer science majors continue immediately after graduation onto graduate study.

The Department of Computer Science offers three courses with no prerequisites, of which two are designed for non-majors (CS0). The remaining course is CS205, Introduction to Computer Science, our CS1. This course is populated primarily by computer science majors, computer science minors, and computer science concentrators from mathematics and physics. Discrete Mathematics (CS/Math231) is also required for this population, and is typically studied with CS205 concurrently. CS205 is the initial part of a year long sequence with CS2 (CS206). CS205, CS206, and CS/Math231 together provide the foundation for core and elective courses. Further information about the computer science curriculum can be found at `www.cs.haverford.edu`.

CS205 has always been conducted with an overt emphasis on rigor in terms of mathematical reasoning, invariants and (to some degree) proofs as important tools utilized by the computer scientist. This report documents the goals, motivation, content and presentation of CS1 at Haverford, with special emphasis on the manner in which formal reasoning is incorporated into the course. After a brief discussion of related work in CS1 pedagogy, the conceptual framework of the course is outlined. A description of the topics covered, lecture examples and laboratory assignments is then given. Next we present results from a study to measure the impact of emphasizing rigor early in the process of completing one of the course lab assignments. We also discuss some of the support efforts to aid students throughout the course, and finally review the points of success achieved to date, as well as places where further work is needed.

2. RELATED WORK

There has been a substantial amount of curricular research involving the content of, and approaches for, the introductory course in computer science. The importance of computing as a discipline, and CS1 as the gateway into this discipline, provides motivation for such investigation. A number of plans for pedagogy have been proposed, implemented and deemed successful to some degree. These plans include programming-first [8, 14], objects-first [6], breadth-first (i.e. "top-down") [20], and hardware-first (i.e. "bottom-up") [19]. There has also been work to incorporate such topics as event-driven programming [5], graphics [21, 22] and concurrent programming [10] into this first course. The debate associated with the introductory approaches to the computer science curriculum is summarized in chapter seven of [18].

There are numerous sources that cite the importance of a rigorous treatment of computer science [4, 12, 13, 25]. Some of the motivations for providing a rigorous approach include:

- Rigor is part of the framework for discovery in computer science.

SIGCSE'05, February 23-27, 2005, St. Louis, Missouri, USA.

- Rigor helps students navigate the complementary roles of theory, experimentation, reasoning, and modeling as found in computer science.
- Rigor clearly, and early, distinguishes the science of computing from the programming of computers.
- Rigor helps "level the playing field" of student experiences with introductory computer science.
- Rigor in computer science provides the tools for students to be life-long learners.
- Computer science is a rigorous discipline [23].

A quick review of computer science departments finds many that mention the term rigor. The consensus appears to be that rigor in CS1 should be a goal to some degree (although there are those who disagree [3]). In some cases it appears that courses are designed to balance rigor and accessibility to the material, and each program may need to adjust to the local academic environment.

For example, one computer science program begins with an emphasis on design, theory and empirical analysis [2], where rigor is incorporated throughout, but especially as part of theory. A three-tiered approach has been used where theoretical rigor is separated from lower-level details [27]. A number of computer science programs follow the "MIT/SICP" functional approach to CS1 [1] to facilitate reasoning about programs. An initiative exists to promote the role of math in computer science education, including a working group to integrate mathematical reasoning into computer science curricula (see `www.math-in-cs.org`).

Programming labs are needed to provide skills with current technologies that demonstrate competence with conceptual material [18, 26]. Capabilities such as modular design, clear coding, debugging, and working around failure are also associated with programming experiences.

3. CONCEPTUAL FRAMEWORK

Our approach to teaching CS1 grew out of a need for a single course to both lay a foundation for a liberal arts computer science major and minor, and to provide capabilities suitable for science majors and students seeking programming jobs. This requirement juxtaposed our interest in teaching a "rigor-first" curriculum, which would perhaps be best expressed in Scheme [1] or a functional language, with the objective to use a language such as C++ or Java.

We have reconciled these conflicting goals with an approach to CS1 (and CS2) that we call the "3-2-1" approach, in which we present three programming paradigms (functional and imperative in CS1, and object-oriented in CS2) and two conceptual models of program execution with a single programming language. We currently employ C++ throughout CS1 and CS2, though we believe our approach could be adapted to many languages and are currently exploring the use of Java.

We start with a functional style expressed in a subset of C++ that includes function definitions and calls, variable declaration and initialization (but *not* assignment), and **return** and **if-else** statements. This allows us to spend the first half of the semester discussing, implementing, and analyzing a wide variety of algorithms, with minimal time and effort spent on language features.

While working within the functional programming style, we give the students two cognitive models of program execution. Execution can be viewed as a process of substitution of equals for equals, as in mathematics or most work on pure functional programming, or as a process of working step-by-step through a set of instructions (with call trees serving to connect steps in different function calls). The step-by-step model is typically associated with the imperative paradigm, but it is relevant to functional programming in that it is involved in the actual execution of the program by hardware. This connection to the implementation of the functional program helps students who learn best when they see how something works, and is important to all students when they use the debugger or reason about execution time (which can be affected dramatically by multiple executions of repeated subexpressions).

We move on to study imperative programming in the second half of CS1. Additional language features such as assignment, **else**-less **if**'s, and loops are introduced hand-in-hand with related analysis tools such as static single assignment [17] form, gated single assignment [11], and loop invariants [9]. We discuss the use of the imperative paradigm for program design as well as coding, and mention the possibility of working from a loop postcondition to an invariant before writing any code (this subject is revisited in CS2). Execution of imperative programs is discussed in terms of both of our cognitive models, and we note that execution of a C++ program is, in reality, a process of substitution (in the compiler) and then step-by-step following of instructions.

Of the classifications presented in [18], our CS1 course comes closest to the "algorithms-first", though we use the term "rigor-first" to reflect our agreement with Tucker's emphasis on curricular rigor [24]. We see programming as an important lab skill to express and experience the material we present, much as various lab skills are important in introducing other sciences.

The motivations for this approach include:

- A liberal arts education emphasizes principles, and our intention is to present computer science as a science from the start [4, 25].
- An introductory science course must introduce the proper fundamentals of the discipline, including concepts, vocabulary, reasoning tools, and laboratory experience for present and future investigation.

We spend about a week on each of the following topics:

Introduction: problem instances and general problems; answering problem instances with specific values or general problems with algorithms; overview of algorithm development; correctness and complexity analysis. This week includes a simple computational geometry problem involving the overlap of two rectangular regions and a simple algorithm for exponentiation, and discusses the use of exponentiation in the Phong illumination model in computer graphics [7].

Models of Execution: expression of initial week's algorithms in C++; introduction to our two cognitive models of execution; use of compiler and debugger.

Algorithm Design: design techniques, including derivation of algorithms from specifications, top-down design, enumerate-and-test algorithms, reduction to a known problem. This week also covers `String` manipulation in C++ to allow the use of strings to represent node and edge sets (via a string of one-letter node names, and a string of space-separated pairs); this representation permits the presentation of an example algorithm for finding cliques and for graph coloring.

Correctness: testing, verification, and the strengths of each; preconditions, postconditions, and correctness of non-recursive functions; "making progress" and correctness of recursive algorithms (e.g. exponentiation).

Complexity: asymptotic growth and why it is used to measure computational complexity; exponentiation algorithms that are linear or logarithmic in the exponent. This week also introduces the slow recursive form of Fibonacci sequence generation.

Abstraction and Specification: review of specifications and algorithms; the role of specifications as communication in multi-programmer projects.

Mutable Variables: assignment operators, including =, +=, ++, etc; SSA and GSA as reasoning tools.

Loops: tail recursion using Fibonacci number example; loops as "syntactic sugar" for this form of recursion; thinking in terms of loops rather than recursion; loop invariants and correctness of loops.

Global Variables and References: reference parameters in function calls; global variables and "memoization" for our Fibonacci number function; scoping and dealing with name conflicts during substitution.

Sorting: bubblesort and mergesort applied to strings to test for anagrams; correctness and complexity of each.

Scientific Computing: floating-point representations, limits of precision; arrays and multi-dimensional arrays; discrete simulation. This week focuses on the simulation of heat flow, and includes a lab titled "You can't heat a frying pan with a soldering iron".

Advanced Topics: varies by semester. For example, dynamic programming and gene sequence alignment [16], or an introduction to **class** definitions.

Course Review: recap of major course themes, including techniques for algorithm development, using the relationship between graph coloring and register allocation as an example of reduction to a known problem (coloring appeared in an earlier lab).

This approach lets us discuss recursion early, starting with simple examples such as exponentiation, and adding complexity as students become comfortable. By introducing simple forms of recursion first, we give students familiarity with this idiom before they see its full power.

Our approach also lets us present both the functional and imperative programming paradigms in CS1, without changing languages. We introduce the object-oriented paradigm in CS2, focusing on data abstraction and simple uses of inheritance. Further detail on object-oriented paradigm is presented in our programming languages course (CO3).

4. ROLE OF LAB ASSIGNMENTS

Students are scheduled 1.5 hours per week in closed labs with at least one professor and often a teaching assistant. Assignments are tightly coupled with lecture material, so that students use the intellectual tools demonstrated in the lecture to solve problems related to those they have seen. For example, we use simple problems from computational geometry in the early lectures and labs – the lectures include an algorithm for testing for overlap of rectangular "windows" on a computer screen, and students are asked to develop and implement algorithms for testing for overlap of two circular areas and for overlap of a circular and a rectangular area. An optional exercise testing for line segment intersection helps students with significant prior programming experience understand the difference between programming and algorithm design. Later lectures on algorithm design and analysis use an enumerate-and-test approach to finding subcliques of a graph. The students are then asked for an enumerate-and-test algorithm for finding legal graph colorings (the former involves enumerating subsets; the latter to finding all strings for a given length and alphabet).

Assignments consist of written and programming exercises that together build both reasoning and programming skills.

4.1 Written Exercises

A number of the intellectual tools covered in our CS1 course are best demonstrated by writing *about* programs rather than by writing programs. After we introduce our cognitive models of program execution, we ask students to draw call trees and show how a series of substitutions can be used to deduce the result of a function call (variations on the exponentiation algorithm work well here).

We also ask students to state pre- or post-conditions for functions. This helps to emphasize the distinction between problems and algorithms; a lecture about the difference between the problem of calculating a square root and specifying one is complemented by a lab about the pre- and post-conditions for a function based on the quadratic formula. Function specifications also help to bring out issues of large-scale programming; the multi-part enumerate-and-test lab project gives students the opportunity to write an enumeration function that violates a precondition of the testing function they wrote in an earlier week.

After we discuss imperative programming, we ask the students to develop invariants for numerous loops in subsequent labs. Over the years, we have varied the number and difficulty of proofs assigned to the students. In our experience, requiring a large number of proofs reduces student enjoyment of the course. However, if students do not produce at least one proof of their own, they have trouble understanding what constitutes a good loop invariant. We have currently settled on having the students give correctness proofs for one recursive function and one iterative function. Both functions are given in lecture, and they both embody the algorithm for computing the nth element of the Fibonacci sequence with $n-2$ additions; the similarities between these proofs also helps to drive home the connection between tail recursion and loops. Both proofs are straightforward direct proofs that rely on proof rules for recursive or iterative functions that are stated in lecture and the references [9].

4.2 Programming Exercises

The specific programming exercises are closely tied to lectures, as discussed above. A complete list of our laboratory assignments can be found at `www.cs.haverford.edu`.

We use variants of the C++ `assert` macro to let the students define preconditions and invariants that will be checked at run-time. We ask students to express postconditions in the same manner when feasible; often this is not the case, so comments are used.

5. EXPERIENCES

We have developed our "rigor-first" approach in several stages over the past eight years, and continue to refine it to improve student outcomes.

From the start, we found that our approach had great benefits for computer science majors and other students continuing through the upper-level theory courses. Faculty teaching these courses described an increase in the percentage of students who were comfortable with the use of mathematical rigor to reason about algorithms. Furthermore, we found that our approach has attracted math, physics, economics and music majors into the upper level curriculum.

However, enrollment by students who are not planning to continue in computer science, and enrollment by women, declined dramatically from 1999 to 2002. The work of Margolis and Fisher [15] suggests that a lack of support (or even a perceived lack of support), rather than curricular rigor, could be responsible for the decline in enrollment by women. This explanation is consistent with our belief that students felt that they had less support in our class when we stopped assigning a course textbook. From the late 1990's to 2001, word spread among the students that the text we were using was not very helpful. In 2002 we stopped assigning a course text altogether, as we could not identify any textbook that fully supported our approach. This year was our lowest enrollment ever for CS205.

We have recently improved support for our students:

- We are distributing course notes to provide a written reference that is consistent with our approach.
- We are providing additional faculty-led open lab sessions (beyond the usual required closed lab session scheduled by the registrar).
- We are emphasizing our efforts to support students, letting students know that we will be there to support them during the challenging labs.
- We are expanding the role of student teaching assistants to provide more help with labs, and to present information about the tools used in lab (e.g., subtleties of the IDE or debugger).

These efforts appear to be paying off. Our enrollments for fall 2003 were up overall, and women comprised about 40% of our CS1 enrollment, up from 8% the previous year. For fall 2004, we have seen another increase in student enrollments. Enrollment by women has fallen somewhat from the 2003 level, to 25%, but is still well above the 8% of 2002.

6. ASSESSMENT

We invited students, during the fall of 2003, to participate in a study to gauge the impact of rigor as an aid in completing one of the course labs. The eighth lab of the course was selected for study because it involved nested loops for Selection Sort, providing a vehicle to practice developing preconditions, postconditions and loop invariants.

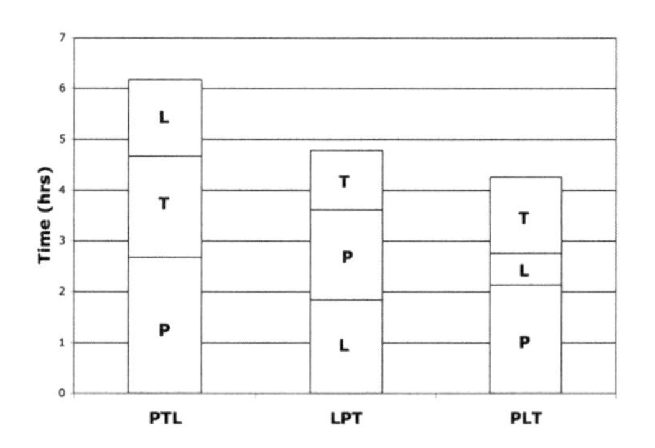

Figure 1: Lab Completion Time, by Group

Students who agreed to participate in this study were partitioned into three groups; namely, PTL, LPT, and PLT. Those in group PTL (Program-Test-Logic) were asked to implement the complete program first, test this code, and then develop logical assertions. Those in group LPT (Logic-Program-Test) were asked to develop the logical assertions before programming, concluding with testing. Those in group PLT (Program-Logic-Test) were asked to write the program, then develop the appropriate logical assertions, and finally test their code. Students in each group were asked to record the amount of (wall-clock) time spent on each phase of the assignment.

There were nine students who participated in this study, with three students in each of the three groups. Mean lab scores (out of 100) for the groups were 95.67 for PTL, 99 for LPT, and 94.33 for PLT.

Of these nine students, only seven submitted complete timing data; two in PTL, three in LPT, and two in PLT. Figure 1 displays the mean time needed to complete each phase of the assignment per group. The bottom segment of each column corresponds to the initial phase of that group, and proceeds simultaneously up the column and across the group name. For example, the mean time for developing logical assertions of the PTL group is depicted by the top segment of the leftmost column of Figure 1.

Programming time and testing time were each least for LPT, the only group that was asked to develop logical assertions prior to coding. The best mean score was achieved by this group as well.

The best reported completion time was realized by PLT, primarily determined by a very small amount of time for developing logical assertions. It could be the the process of programming made the associated logic obvious, or that these students were not interested in the quality of this logic since the programs were already written, and they wanted to proceed quickly to testing. This latter explanation conflicts with the relatively large amount of time developing assertions for the PTL group, where coding had also been completed early. Observations like this one, in conjunction with the small sample size, make it clear that further study is warranted. We hope to perform a similar study in this year's CS2 course (we believe this will provide a better learning experience for the students and reduce the variation in familiarity with loop invariants, which fear may be a as a source of "noise" in our study).

We also requested more informal, qualitative feedback

from study participants. There were observations that developing the assertions after coding seemed unnecessary; hopefully, these students would consider using assertions prior to coding. One student did report a sense of accomplishment in using assertions properly, stating, "Yay! I understand invariants! I never thought this day would come."

7. CONCLUSIONS

This paper reports on the various issues encountered in our pursuit of a rigorous introduction to computer science. Our goal is to give students both a set of intellectual tools to reason about algorithms and strong programming skills. We have structured the course to support these goals by emphasizing fundamentals such as function specifications and loop invariants instead of covering a wide variety of programming language features.

Early usage of intellectual tools sets the stage for future study in core and advanced courses, as well as senior theses. Our students view computer science as a serious, rigorous area of study, like the other science disciplines. Furthermore, our alumni report they are better prepared for the theoretical components of graduate computer science programs than many of their peers, and well prepared for the programming expectations in both graduate school and industry.

Preliminary assessment of this approach in our liberal arts setting has been positive and encouraging. We look to refine this approach, as well as identify other settings where a rigorous treatment of computing topics would prove effective.

8. REFERENCES

[1] H. Abelson, G.J. Sussman, and J. Sussman. *Structure and Interpretation of Computer Programs.* MIT Press, 1996.

[2] D. Baldwin, G. Scragg, and H. Koomen. A three-fold introduction to computer science. In *Proceedings of the 25th SIGCSE Symposium on Computer Science Education*, pages 290–294. ACM Press, 1994.

[3] J.W. Berry. Thoughts on the first year of computer science instruction. unpublished, available at `http://www.cs.duke.edu/csed/fyi/berry.pdf`, 2000.

[4] K.B. Bruce, R.L.S. Drysdale, C.F. Kelemen, and A.B. Tucker. Why math? *CACM*, 46(9):40–44, 2003.

[5] H.B. Christensen and M.E. Caspersen. Frameworks in CS1: a different way of introducing event-driven programming. In *Proceedings of the 7th Conference on Innovation and Technology in Computer Science Education*, pages 75–79. ACM Press, 2002.

[6] S. Cooper, W. Dann, and R. Pausch. Teaching objects-first in introductory computer science. In *Proceedings of the 34th SIGCSE Technical Symposium on Computer Science Education*, pages 191–195. ACM Press, 2003.

[7] J.D. Foley, A. van Dam, S.K. Feiner, J.F. Hughes, and R. Phillips. *Introduction to Computer Graphics.* Addison-Wesley, 1994.

[8] C.G. Gray and M.D. Frazier. Introducing computer science after programming. *The Journal of Computing in Small Colleges*, 18(1):65–76, 2002.

[9] D. Gries. *The Science of Programming.* Springer-Verlag, 1981.

[10] M. Hailperin, D. Arnow, J. Bishop, C. Lund, and L. A. Stein. Concurrency the first year (panel session): experience reports. In *Proceedings of the 31st SIGCSE Technical Symposium on Computer Science Education*, pages 407–408. ACM Press, 2000.

[11] P. Havlak. Construction of thinned gated single-assignment form. In *1993 Workshop on Languages and Compilers for Parallel Computing.* Springer Verlag, 1993.

[12] P.B. Henderson. Mathematical reasoning in software engineering education. *CACM*, 46(9):45–50, 2003.

[13] P.B. Henderson, D. Baldwin, V. Dasigi, M. Dupras, J. Fritz, D. Ginat, D. Goelman, J. Hamer, L. Hitchner, W. Lloyd, B. Marion, Jr., C. Riedesel, and H. Walker. Striving for mathematical thinking. In *Working Group Reports of the 6th Conference on Innovation and Technology in Computer Science Education*, pages 114–124. ACM Press, 2001.

[14] K. Howell. First computer languages. *The Journal of Computing in Small Colleges*, 18(4):317–331, 2003.

[15] J. Margolis and A. Fisher. *Unlocking the Clubhouse: Women in Computing.* MIT Press, 2003.

[16] D. Mount. *Bioinformatics.* Cold Spring Harbor, 2001.

[17] S.S. Muchnick. *Advanced Compiler Design and Implementation.* Morgan Kaufmann, 1997.

[18] The Joint Task Force on Computing Curricula. Computing curricula 2001. *Journal on Educational Resources in Computing (JERIC)*, 1(3es):1, 2001.

[19] Y.N. Patt and S.J. Patel. *Introduction to Computing Systems: From Bits and Gates to C and Beyond, second edition.* McGraw-Hill, 2004.

[20] A.T. Phillips, D.E. Stevenson, and M.R. Wick. Implementing cc2001: a breadth-first introductory course for a just-in-time curriculum design. In *Proceedings of the 24th SIGCSE Technical Symposium on Computer Science Education*, pages 238–242. ACM Press, 2003.

[21] E.S. Roberts. A C-based graphics library for CS1. In *Proceedings of the 26th SIGCSE Technical Symposium on Computer Science Education*, pages 163–167. ACM Press, 1995.

[22] S. Schaub. Teaching Java with graphics in CS1. *ACM SIGCSE Bulletin*, 32(2):71–73, 2000.

[23] A.B. Tucker. From rigor to rigor mortis: Avoiding the slippery slope. In *Proceedings of the 32nd SIGCSE Technical Symposium on Computer Science Education*, 2001. Keynote address, slides available at `www.bowdoin.edu/~allen/sigcse2001/rigormortis.pdf`.

[24] A.B. Tucker. Ensuring a rigorous curriculum: practices and goals. *The Journal of Computing in Small Colleges*, 17(6):.16–.16, 2002.

[25] A.B. Tucker, C.F. Kelemen, and K.B. Bruce. Our curriculum has become math-phobic! In *Proceedings of the 32nd SIGCSE Technical Symposium on Computer Science Education*, pages 243–247. ACM Press, 2001.

[26] H.M. Walker and G.M. Schneider. A revised model curriculum for a liberal arts degree in computer science. *CACM*, 39(12):85–95, 1996.

[27] U. Wolz and E. Conjura. Integrating mathematics and programming into a three tiered model for computer science education. In *Proceedings of the 25th SIGCSE Technical Symposium on Computer Science Education*, pages 223–227. ACM Press, 1994.

Computer Games and CS Education: Why and How

Marianne deLaet
Harvey Mudd College
1250 N. Dartmouth Ave.
Claremont, CA 91711
1.909.607.8312
marianne_delaet@hmc.edu

James Kuffner
The Robotics Institute, Carnegie Mellon University
5000 Forbes Ave.
Pittsburgh, PA 15213
1.412.268.8818
kuffner@cs.cmu.edu

Michael C. Slattery
Marquette University
P.O. Box 1881
Milwaukee, WI 53201-1881
1.414.288.6595
mikes@mscs.mu.du

Elizabeth Sweedyk (moderator)
Harvey Mudd College
1250 N. Dartmouth Ave.
Claremont, CA 91711
1.909.607.8360
z@cs.hmc.edu

SUMMARY
Computer and video games have grown to be a major industry but, until recently, have largely been ignored by academia. The last couple of years, however, have seen the emergence of new academic programs, conferences, and journals dedicated to games studies. This panel discusses a variety of ways, and whys, for introducing games into computer science curricula. Panelists discuss their experiences in designing a broad range of courses including a games course for women, a software development course that uses games as projects, an introductory games programming course in Java, and an advanced graphics course that focuses on games.

Categories and Subject Descriptors
K.3.2 [**Computer and Education**]: Computer and Information Science Education – *computer science education, curriculum.*

General Terms
Design.

Keywords
Computer games, video games, games studies.

Marianne deLaet and Elizabeth Sweedyk
We offer an interdisciplinary course that teaches women to build computer games for women. The course is cross-listed in the Computer Science and Humanities and Social Sciences Departments at Harvey Mudd College and in the Art Department at Scripps College. The only prerequisites are an introductory course in computer science, art, or cultural studies.

SIGCSE'05, February 23–27, 2005, St. Louis, Missouri, USA.
ACM 1-58113-997-7/05/0002.

This pioneering course is part of an effort to increase the number of women in Computer Science at Harvey Mudd College and to improve computer literacy among women at all of the Claremont Colleges.

The course teaches students to analyze the cultural and social content of existing computer games and to design and develop new games that appeal to a female audience. The technical complexity of student projects varies depending on the expertise of team members. At one extreme are simple 2D Flash games and at the other are 3D games built off of a commercial game engine, Torque, with modeling and animation done in Maya.

The students who participate in the course have diverse interests and capabilities, and we capitalize on their abilities to teach each other in project collaborations. All students are required to participate in all phases of game production so artists do some programming and programmers develop some art.

The course is not restricted to women but half of the course spots are designated for women, student teams are typically homogenous with respect to gender, and course projects must target women players.

James Kuffner
Two years ago, I introduced a new graphics course into the Computer Science curriculum at Carnegie Mellon University. The primary goal of the course is to equip upper-level undergraduate and graduate students with practical knowledge and experience programming interactive games and virtual reality simulations. Each year, forty students spend the semester exploring tools and techniques for interactive graphics. All programming is done in C/C++ using open-source, cross-platform libraries such as OpenGL and GLUT. Students work in teams of two designing and programming their own games or virtual reality simulations. There are also several smaller

programming labs designed to provide students with experience implementing common components of game engines. The course topics included event loops and execution threads, rendering and animation in 3D, terrain/background representation, polygonal models, texturing, collision detection and physically based modeling, game AI, and multi-user games and networking. Students in the class are expected to have already completed an undergraduate computer graphics course.

The focus is not on teaching the details of game programming under specific platforms, but rather on providing both a high-level understanding and practical implementation experience of reusable algorithms and coding techniques that can apply to a broad class of large software development efforts. I believe that game programming is a great way to teach valuable software engineering skills to students because so much of a computer science curriculum applies to game development: designing efficient data structures, effective memory management, intuitive user interfaces and rendering displays, networking and concurrency, accessing large data sets and managing system resources, as well as autonomous game entities and artificial intelligence. All of these elements need to function correctly and work together in real-time, so students can see practical motivations for seriously learning computer science fundamentals. In addition, students are highly motivated to study and implement class material due to the fact that they are having fun developing an entertaining and creative product. Students also gain experience programming in teams and using version control software, which are valuable skills for any future professional software developer.

Michael C. Slattery

I have taught an undergraduate Computer Science course entitled "Programming Computer Games" six times since the Spring of 2000. The students are mostly undergrads with a few graduate students each semester. In a typical semester there may be 20-25 students in the class. The course is taught in Java and I assume they have a beginning knowledge of Java programming (perhaps equivalent to CS2). In the past students developed Java applets but this year I'm using a new textbook, which focuses on Java applications. The course does not require a background in computer graphics.

In this course, we study a broad range of computer and video games ranging from 2D games such as Pacman, Tetris, and Mario Brothers to 3D games like Doom and Occarina of Time. Students build games that incorporate 2D and 3D graphics, event handling, music and sound effects, and multi-threading. They also are also exposed to issues in real-time programming and networking.

I've found that programming computer games provides strong motivation for students to learn a variety of techniques and topics in computer science. It prepares them for any job requiring design and implementation of real-time interactive graphics displays, especially game programming, which is a rapidly growing entertainment industry.

Elizabeth Sweedyk

For the past two years, I've used computer games as projects in our software development course CS121. This course is required for CS majors and is typically taken during the sophomore or junior year. The course prerequisite is a data structures course, which introduces students to C++.

CS121 covers the standard fare of most software engineering courses including principles, practices, and patterns in software design and development. In the past, students worked with outside clients on a semester long project. Two years ago I remodeled the course to use games as projects.

Students, in teams of three, build three games across the semester. The first game is a 2D arcade game built off a software framework. This project is primarily an exercise in requirements analysis and feasibility with relatively minor development effort.

The second game is a single-hole miniature golf game in 3D. Students build this game from scratch including the physics engine. This project is primarily an exercise in design and testing. Students learn the necessary graphics through a short OpenGL/GLUT tutorial.

The final game is left to the students to define. This project gives student another opportunity to go through a design/develop cycle, which reinforces the concepts learned earlier in the class. Though not required, students typically use the physics engine they developed in the second project, which helps them understand issues of code reuse. In addition, they often incorporate ideas from other CS courses such as AI, networking, and graphics in their final project.

There were several motivations for the move to games as projects in CS121. First and foremost, using games capitalizes on students' interests; most CS students play games on a regular basis. Students are motivated to work on games, but perhaps more importantly, they are domain experts. They understand games and are their own best critics. Beyond this, however, games are excellent projects in that they incorporate a wide range of techniques from computer science and mathematics. Game projects allow students to exercise their creativity in ways not typically challenged in the computer science curriculum. And finally, students produce projects that can be understood and appreciated by friends, family, and, of course, prospective employers.

IT Offshore Outsourcing: Impact on CS/IS Curriculum

Ernest Ferguson
Dept. of Comp Science / Info Systems
Northwest Missouri State University
Maryville, MO 64468-6001
ferg@mail.nwmissouri.edu

Wing Huen (Moderator)
Dept of Comp Science
University of Wisconsin Oshkosh
Oshkosh, WI 54901-8643
huen@uwosh.edu

Peter B. Henderson
Dept. of Computer Science and Software Engineering
Butler University
Indianapolis, IN
phenders@butler.edu

Clifton Kussmaul
Mathematical Sciences Dept
Muhlenberg College
Allentown, PA 18104-5586
kussmaul@muhlenberg.edu

Categories and Subject Descriptors
K.3.2 [**Computers and Education**]: Computer and Information Science Education – *computer science education, information systems education.* K.4.2 [**Computer and Society**]: Social Issues – *employment.*

General Terms
Management, Measurement, Economics.

Keywords
Curriculum, employment, enrollment, offshore outsourcing, offshoring.

1. SUMMARY
Almost all major news and professional publications e.g. [1,2] document IT Offshoring & Outsourcing (O&O), which has caused job losses in the US and drops in CS/IS enrollment. Public opinion and understanding of O&O are colored by several misperceptions:

- *All software development is going offshore.* Actually, O&O has the biggest impact on lower skilled jobs. Wired Magazine Feb 2004 reported the offshored jobs as custom software development, software maintenance, IT documentation, telephone support, remote networking monitoring, software reengineering, systems management, and IT admin & operations. Reference [5] indicates that an "undergraduate computer science degree is neither common nor appropriate training" for many of these jobs.
- *There will not be onshore jobs in the CS/IT industry.* In fact, the Bureau of Labor Statistics projects that such jobs are among the fastest growing in 2002-2012, with 40-55% increases [3]. 2004 starting IS salaries exceed $34k and CS salaries approach $50k. There are still plenty of available jobs in the US depending on skill set, location, and career goals of the job seekers [6].
- *O&O only affects IT fields.* Actually, it will increasingly affect other areas, such as accounting and legal research.
- *O&O is only about cost savings.* Although cost is the most commonly cited advantage of offshoring, over 70% of CIOs feel the cost factor is overrated; typical savings are 15-25% the first year, and up to 40% later on. Other commonly cited reasons for outsourcing include accessing specialized skills or facilities, being able to increase or decrease developer head count as needed, and increasing development speed [7].
- *All jobs outsourced go to low-wage countries.* In fact, large US outsourcing service companies keep requirements, project management and integration staff onshore.
- *Many IT-producing companies have established significant presence overseas, so they must have transferred software development overseas.* Actually, these companies globalize to enhance their business and in turn help the US economy. Using in-country staff for local content and customization is a common market entry approach.

This panel follows up on the 2004 panel [2] by considering:

1. Which jobs and skills are most affected by O&O?
2. How does this impact CS/IS education?
3. How do we, as computing educators, respond?

SIGCSE'05, February 23–27, 2005, St. Louis, Missouri, USA.
ACM 1-58113-997-7/05/0002.

2. WING HUEN
I have been involved in overseas technology transfers to joint ventures or subsidiaries for 10 years to China and consulting in other countries. As educators we should:

- Produce graduates with skills needed in jobs categorized as conceptualizers and developers[5], including entrepreneur, product designer, research engineer, system analyst, computer science researcher, requirements analyst, system architect, system designer, and others.
- Produce graduates with industry-specific knowledge who can apply computing to make companies/industries more effective. These professionals will be valued as businesses focus more on core competencies. For example, there are innovative IT opportunities in areas like IT Health services (5% of GDP), education (2% of GDP), security, many small

or medium-size enterprises, and the fusion of IT, biotechnology and nanotechnology[8][9].

3. CLIFTON KUSSMAUL

For most of the last 4 years, I have been involved in offshore outsourcing projects in southern India. I expect O&O to increase, but not to overwhelm onshore activity. Thus, businesses will seek employees with:

- broad technical expertise
- communication, teamwork, and project management skills
- familiarity with business issues & application contexts
- multicultural & international experience
- ability to learn and adapt to changing conditions
- leadership potential

There is good evidence for 10X productivity variations across developers and organizations, so very productive groups can overcome differences in hourly rates. To help our students prepare to compete in this environment, we should:,

- Help students understand the IT work life and career. Engineering programs are increasingly using initial "cornerstone" courses as well as later "capstone" courses.
- Emphasize problem solving, analysis, and design.
- Emphasize collaboration and teamwork.
- Provide opportunities to work on distributed teams.
- If necessary, decrease emphasis on technical skills and theories that may be less relevant or obsolete in a few years.

Other ways to increase CS/IS enrollments include:

- Work with math & science colleagues to improve outreach to high school faculty & students.
- Educate students, parents, & administrators (especially admissions officers & deans) about realities of IT job market.
- Seek ways to increase student retention without decreasing standards, through more effective pedagogy and better student support.

4. ERNEST FERGUSON

How has O&O impacted the background sought by companies in filling entry-level positions in applications development? To answer this question the CIO's at companies on *ComputerWorld's* Top 100 Places to Work in IT [4] were surveyed, with 3 pilot in-person or telephone interviews.

This survey asked respondents to complete a survey of skill/background, based on ACM and AITP model curriculum, for each job classification of entry-level positions such as programmer, technical support, network, database systems and so forth. For each category of skills, respondents were asked to rate its importance, and to indicate if the importance of this category had increased, stayed the same, or decreased during the past three years. Even with a return rate of less than 10% due primarily to sensitivity to the O&O backlash, the survey results appear to reflect the impact of an outflow of programming jobs to less costly foreigners and

- An increased importance in the soft skills, i.e. communication, project management, and teamwork.
- High importance of technical backgrounds such as Data Structures, Algorithms and Complexity, and Programming Fundamentals even though there was no perceived increase in importance over the past three years. The technical areas still rank the highest in importance.
- The only category decreasing in perceived importance was Programming Fundamentals.

These preliminary results are congruent with corporate shifts towards using lower cost labor for programming jobs. The jobs remaining place emphasis on the technical skills combined with an increasing emphasis on communication skills, team work skills, project management, and interaction with end users.

5. PETER HENDERSON

High student demand and rapidly changing technology have impeded change. Many computing education programs are behind the curve preparing software practitioners. This is an opportunity to significantly improve the quality of computing education.

Future graduates need to be more general problem solvers and thinkers, develop holistic or "big picture" views, learn to work and communicate with people (colleagues, customers, etc.) and adapt rapidly to changing economy, technology and customer needs. They should be ethical professionals with strong technical skills and an understanding of both corporate and world cultures. I will present several suggested curricula reforms, many of which have been used successfully at Butler and other educational institutions. These include self-directed service learning project experiences, involving the corporate world in the education of students through internships, mentoring, course projects, lunch guests, class and seminar presenters, and a software engineering orientation.

6. REFERENCES

[1] McManes, Chris. "H-1B And L-1 Visas Accelerate Offshore Outsourcing," July 7, 2003 http://www.ieeeusa.org/newspubs/features/070703.htm

[2] Ferguson, E., Kussmaul, C., McCracken, D., Robbert, M. A., "Offshore Outsourcing: Current Conditions & Diagnosis" *Proceedings of the Thirty-Fifth SIGCSE Technical Symposium on Computer Science Education*, March 3-7, 2004.

[3] US Bureau of Labor Statistics, "Occupational Outlook Handbook, 2004-2005 Edition". http://www.bls.gov/oco/home.htm

[4] *ComputerWorld*, June 9, 2003, pp. 28-31. "Cream of the Crop: Computerworld 100 Best Places to Work in IT 2003"

[5] Computing Research Association, Intersociety Study Group on Information Technology Workers, April 1999.

[6] National Association of Colleges and Employers (NACE) Summer 2004 Salary Survey. http://www.naceweb.org/press/display.asp?year=&prid=194

[7] CIO Insight. Research: Outsourcing: How Well Are You Managing Your Partners? 1(33):75-85 November, 2003).

[8] IEEE Spectrum, November 2004, "The View From The Top"

[9] "What is Ahead" section of 75th anniversary issue of BusinessWeek, October 11, 2004.

Outcomes-Based Computer Science Education

Stephen Cooper
(Moderator)
Saint Joseph's University
Philadelphia, Pennsylvania
scooper@sju.edu

Lillian Cassel
Villanova University
Villanova, Pennsylvania
cassel@acm.org

Barbara Moskal
Colorado School of Mines
Golden, Colorado
moskal@mines.edu

Steve Cunningham
Oregon State University and
The National Science
Foundation
Arlington, Virginia
scunning@nsf.gov

SUMMARY

As computer science educators, we are being pushed to define (by accreditation agencies, within our institutions, etc.) our courses and programs in terms of measurable outcomes. The Computing Accreditation Commission (CAC) is responsible for reviewing and accrediting computer sciences departments across the United States. As part of this review process, computer science departments must specify and measure student learning objectives and outcomes (see criteria at http://www.abet.org/cac1.html). The same is true for institution-wide accreditation (for example, by the Middle States Commission on Higher Education). Also, faculty who are composing proposals for NSF or other funding agencies are expected to provide descriptions of objectives and outcomes and how these are to be measured.

Categories and Subject Descriptors

K.3.2 [**Computer and Information Science Education**]: Computer science education, Curriculum, Self-assessment

General Terms

experimentation

Keywords

Computer Science Education, Outcomes, Assessment, Accreditation

1. INTRODUCTION

The mention of the phrase "outcomes-based education" generates a furrowed brow on many a computer science educator's forehead. We have few models to choose from and little experience with using them. The purpose of the proposed panel is to discuss outcomes-based education at both the course level and the curricular level, possible methods for evaluating student outcomes, and its relevance to the accreditation process. This panel will consist of experienced leaders in the following areas: establishing course objectives, assessing outcomes, undergraduate CS curriculum and accreditation. This session is likely to be of interest to computer science faculty members whose departments are seeking CAC accreditation or institutional accreditation/re-accreditation in the near future and to faculty who are composing proposals to NSF and other funding agencies.

Defining objectives and assessing outcomes is a challenge because most computer science faculty are not trained in techniques for setting up objectives and measuring outcomes. Furthermore, most computer science departments do not have access to assessment experts within their own faculty to assist them in establishing an assessment plan. In this panel, we will discuss using outcomes to define our courses in the most general ways, rather than defining them the way we historically have. This focus on outcomes provides a way to develop widely-used assessment tools to measure student success. Having a defined set of outcomes would enable us to be creative in how we design course details as long as we provide the same outcomes. Finally, this lets us use the assessment tools to document our courses for accreditation and to measure student learning for funded projects.

2. POSITION STATEMENTS

2.1 Lillian Cassel

Accreditation has moved from checksheets of detailed criteria to requirements that departments give detailed specification of their goals and demonstrate that they are making good progress in accomplishing those goals. This allows individual programs to have characteristics appropriate for their environment and their students without having to squeeze their own needs into requirements specified by outsiders. At the same time, it makes the process of evaluation more difficult. No longer simple checking off items from a list, today's accreditation assessment requires a clear demonstration that the department has well founded objectives for the program and a working assessment procedure that documents both successes and needs for improvement.

Objectives for a program relate to the institution mission statement and objectives for the department. Once the objectives are determined, effective methods for track-

SIGCSE'05, February 23–27, 2005, St. Louis, Missouri, USA.

ing progress are essential. A good evaluation plan leads to continuous improvement and benefits the program and the students. The new approach opens opportunities for innovation and evolution of programs. Curriculum recommendations from ACM and other relevant organizations provide a starting point from which interesting variations can develop.

Accreditation processes are evolving, moving away from the rigid structures of the past toward more individualized reviews. Examples of changing approaches will be presented and participant feedback will be encouraged.

2.2 Stephen Cooper

When creating a new course, it is important to consider the goals of the course and the expected student outcomes. This is true whether trying to convince the department of the value of the course (where the outcomes can be mapped into the overall objectives of the program), or whether trying to convince a funding agency to support development of the course (where the outcomes can be used to select/develop appropriate assessment instruments to measure the success of the course).

Computing Curricula 2001 (CC2001) [2] serves as a good starting point for determining a set of objectives and outcomes for a course. However, the outcomes mentioned in Appendix A of CC2001 are topic-specific rather than course-specific. In other words, in creating a course, it is necessary to determine which collection of skills (core topics) is appropriate for the course. And taking the union of the outcomes for each of the specific topics may not lead to a coherent set of outcomes for the course. It is also important to note that, for several courses (such as a pre-CS1 course), CC2001 provides little direct guidance. As such, it is necessary to refine the objectives taken from CC2001 into a coherent set of objectives and outcomes for the course, which can then be assessed.

Dr. Cooper has experience with several NSF-funded projects involving the design and development of course-specific objectives and outcomes. He will respond to questions and concerns in the design and development of such objectives.

2.3 Steve Cunningham

For some years we have been working on defining the beginning course in computer graphics, and have found it difficult to deal with the many individual variations in the course. At a workshop last June we took an outcomes-based approach to the course, focusing on the knowledge, skill, and viewpoint that a student should have after the course, and we were finally able to see the real value of the course to the overall computer science curriculum.

This experience shows me that if we look at outcomes at a high enough level to avoid minutiae, we can get a view of a course, a sequence, or a curriculum that is very difficult to achieve any other way. I am eager to see this product-oriented approach applied widely and believe that it can help us cut through much of the process-oriented problems we see in course development. It can also help us see how we might develop alternatives to the usual way of doing a course so we may meet specific local conditions or reach new audiences.

2.4 Barbara Moskal

Assessment has come to the forefront of discussions in many technical fields. Much of this attention can be attributed to the requirements that are set forth by accrediting agencies. Most computer science faculty have not been trained in assessment, leaving computer science departments ill equipped to develop and implement appropriate departmental assessment plans.

One manner to assist departments in the creation of successful assessment plans is to provide examples of such plans. The Department of Mathematical and Computer Sciences (MCS) at the Colorado School of Mines has developed and implemented a departmental assessment plan. This plan was initially implemented in the 1998-1999 academic year and revised and re-implemented in the spring of 2002. The revised plan continues to be used by the department today.

One unique facet of the MCS assessment plan is the existence not only of student goals and objectives but also of faculty goals and objectives. Goals are broad statements of expected student outcomes. Objectives are descriptions of how the attainment of a given goal will be displayed by students. A complete statement that includes both goals and objectives for MCS can be found at:
http://www.mines.edu/Academic/assess/Goals.html.

After establishing goals and objectives, MCS began to plan for the collection, analysis and use of assessment information, using the Olds and Miller Assessment Matrix [1]. In general, the student or faculty goals are recorded above the matrix and the respective objectives are displayed in the first column of the matrix. The second column, the "Performance Criteria", states the observable student performance by which it can be determined whether a given objective has been reached. The third column, "Implementation Strategy", contains a description of the student learning activities supporting the attainment of given criteria. The fourth column, "Evaluation Methods", specifies the measurement instruments to be used to collect the evidence as to whether the performance criteria have been reached. The fifth column, the "Timeline", indicates when each evaluation method was implemented. The sixth column, "Feedback", indicates how the acquired information will be disseminated and used. The complete matrix can be found at
http://www.mines.edu/Academic/assess/Plan.html.

Assessment in MCS does not end with the collection of data. The information acquired through assessment is documented and used for instructional improvement. Examples of the types of changes that have been made in MCS in response to assessment information can be found at:
http://www.mines.edu/Academic/assess/Feedback.html.

Dr. Moskal, has an Ed.D. in Mathematics Education with a doctoral minor in Quantitative Research Methodology. She has acted as a professional evaluator for numerous computer science, engineering and mathematics education projects, and will respond to questions and concerns in the development and implementation of departmental assessment programs.

3. REFERENCES

[1] B. Olds and R. Miller. An assessment matrix for evaluating engineering programs. *Journal of Engineering Education*, 87(2):173–178, 1998.

[2] The Joint Task Force on Computing Curricula. Computing curricula 2001. *J. Educ. Resour. Comput.*, 1(3):1–240, 2001.

Supporting Workflow in a Course Management System

Chavdar Botev, Hubert Chao, Theodore Chao, Yim Cheng
Raymond Doyle, Sergey Grankin, Jon Guarino, Saikat Guha
Pei-Chen Lee, Dan Perry, Christopher Re, Ilya Rifkin
Tingyan Yuan, Dora Abdullah, Kathy Carpenter, David Gries
Dexter Kozen, Andrew Myers, David Schwartz, Jayavel Shanmugasundaram

Department of Computer Science
Cornell University
Ithaca, NY 14853
cms@cs.cornell.edu

ABSTRACT

CMS is a secure and scalable web-based course management system developed by the Cornell University Computer Science Department. The system was designed to simplify, streamline, and automate many aspects of the workflow associated with running a large course, such as course creation, importing students, management of student workgroups, online submission of assignments, assignment of graders, grading, handling regrade requests, and preparation of final grades. In contrast, other course management systems of which we are aware provide only specialized solutions for specific components, such as grading. CMS is increasingly widely used for course management at Cornell University. In this paper we articulate the principles we followed in designing the system and describe the features that users found most useful.

Categories and Subject Descriptors

D.m [**Software**]: Miscellaneous

General Terms

Education, courseware

Keywords

Courseware

1. INTRODUCTION

Managing a large course is a complex task. Many factors may contribute to this complexity: large enrollments; a course staff including several roles such as instructors, teaching assistants, staff assistants, lab consultants, and graders; both individual and group assignments; formation and disbanding of student workgroups during the course; large, multipart assignments whose grading may be partitioned across problems; online student submissions comprising many files; requests for regrading; administration of sensitive information such as scores, statistics, and final grades at an appropriate level of security; and the need to track the progress of these various steps and notify students where appropriate.

CMS is a course management system developed in the Computer Science Department at Cornell University that was designed to meet these needs. It has been developed and used over the past two years with considerable success. In this paper we describe the design of the system and how it solved many of these tasks in a robust and scalable way.

Although existing course management systems support some of these tasks, we are not aware of any system that supports the workflow associated with running a course to the degree that CMS does. For instance, the widely used Blackboard system [1] supports online file submissions and grades, but does not support assigning grading responsibilities, tracking regrade requests, or group assignments. While these other systems do ease the burden of course management, they also introduce new sources of complexity, because users must manually tie together information maintained by the system, such as grades, with information maintained outside the system, such as workgroups and regrade requests.

The main technical challenge we faced in designing a workflow-oriented course management system was scalability. Our objective was to make the system work effectively for a large number of courses, each with possibly a large enrollment and course staff and diverse requirements. Our solution to this challenge involved several ideas. One key principle was decentralization, so that course staff involvement in common course-related tasks was reduced as much as possible. For example, to make the creation of student project groups scalable, we devised an invitation-based group creation model in which students are able to create their own groups without course staff involvement (although staff can also directly manage groups if desired). Similarly, to make regrading scalable, the system directly routes regrade requests to the appropriate grader without requiring any action by other course staff.

Besides scalability, we had the following design goals:

- **Portability:** CMS is web-based and can be run on any operating system platform using a web browser.
- **Security:** CMS users (students and course staff) are authenticated using Kerberos authentication. CMS also supports a fine-grained access control model, with several levels of access for course staff. Decentralized workflow management makes fine-grained access control particularly important.
- **History:** CMS records all update events so users can view the history of changes. Information is never deleted.

- **Selective overriding:** Some policies and rules implemented by CMS can be overridden on a case-by-case basis. For example, a course administrator can override the deadline for submission of an assignment for a particular student.
- **Consistent, powerful GUI:** It is important that the system be easy to learn but also that it provide the power to get work done efficiently. This is accomplished by providing relatively few distinct views of course information but making these views consistent with one another, information-rich, and hyperlinked to allow convenient switching between views.
- **Integration with other software:** CMS integrates seamlessly with other university software for performing authentication and obtaining information about courses and students. Class lists can be imported and final grades exported using a simple ASCII format compatible with Excel.

We should note that the CMS system was not designed to support web-based courses, but rather traditional lecture-based or recitation-based courses. For web-based courses, many design decisions would have been different. For example, some features that other tools support, such as discussion forums, online quizzes, and repositories for lecture notes are not supported by CMS.

CMS is implemented in PHP and runs in a standard 3-tier architecture with multiple application servers connected to a high-performance database server. In Fall 2004, CMS is being used by more than 1900 students in 40 courses in computer science, engineering, physics, and economics. Some of these courses are large, with more than 400 students. Although CMS was originally designed with large courses in mind, many small courses have also chosen to use CMS because of its comprehensive workflow management. A demonstration version of CMS is available for public use at `http://www3.csuglab.cornell.edu/cmsdemo`. Secure authentication is disabled in this demonstration installation.

The rest of this paper is organized as follows. Sections 2, 3, and 4 describe how workflow is supported for the CMS administrator, course staff, and students, respectively. Section 5 discusses related work, and Section 6 presents our conclusions.

2. CMS ADMINISTRATOR WORKFLOW

The CMS administrator is responsible for adding courses to the system and for reporting course grades at the end of each semester. The associated workflow is simple. To add a new course, the CMS administrator enters the IDs of the course and the course instructor; CMS automatically contacts the university systems to import information about the course, such as the course name, registration code, and instructor. Further details about a course, such as information about the course staff and students, are delegated to course staff. Thus, it is easy for the CMS administrator to set up a large number of courses. Similarly, at the end of the semester, the CMS administrator simply activates the reporting feature for active courses and CMS automatically exports the final grades in a format appropriate for the university grade management system. The course is archived in its final state, and students are no longer allowed access after a certain point.

3. COURSE STAFF WORKFLOW

The major portion of course administration falls on teaching assistants and administrative staff. Ordinarily these tasks can be time-consuming and error-prone, but CMS helps simplify and automate these processes.

Managing Course Staff. Large courses usually have a large course staff with several different roles: for example, a principal instructor, assistant instructors, a staff assistant, graduate teaching assistants, undergraduate lab consultants, and graders. To permit decentralized management, it is important that staff members receive only rights appropriate to their staff role, following the principle of least privilege [4]. CMS supports this fine-grained control of privilege with four levels of access: (1) the ability to create assignments and edit their information, (2) the ability to manage student groups, (3) the ability to grade, and (4) complete administrative access including control of staff membership and privilege levels. Any of these privileges can be granted to any staff member. Staff can be added simply by giving their university ID; an LDAP lookup then retrieves all necessary information from the university system, and access rights are assigned with a few mouse clicks.

Managing students. Students can be added to a course either by a bulk upload, perhaps from the university's file for the course, or individually. In both cases, only the university ID of the student is given, and all other information is retrieved from university system using an LDAP lookup. A student may decide to drop a course — in that case, the student can be removed. However, no information about the student is lost, and if the student decides to re-enroll, a click of the mouse button in CMS will do the trick.

Managing assignments. To create a new assignment, a web form is used to enter the relevant information, including (1) the assignment description and associated files, (2) the deadline for submission, (3) a short grace period during which submissions will not be considered late, (4) whether late submissions are allowed, (5) the size of a group and who forms the groups (staff or students), (6) the assignment and source files, (7) the maximum score and the weight for the assignment, (8) whether assignment statistics should be shown, (9) the names of the files that the student should submit, and (10) whether regrades are allowed, whether they are tracked by CMS, and the deadline for a regrade. This information can be changed at any time.

To track the workflow involved in managing an assignment, assignments can be in one of four states: hidden from students (used during assignment creation), shown to students and available for submission, closed to submission but with grades hidden (used during grading), and closed to submission with grades shown to students. Even though an assignment is closed to submission, a staff member can override this setting to allow an individual student or group of students to submit, and can even submit files on their behalf. This flexibility helps when a student has a good reason to submit their assignment after the deadline or has submitted the assignment outside CMS.

Exams. Exams are a special case of assignments for which students usually do not submit files online. The bulk upload feature for grades is particularly useful for exams: a text file of student IDs and grades, compatible with Microsoft Excel, can be uploaded into an assignment or exam. CMS performs consistency checks before allowing bulk uploads: for example, validating student IDs.

Grading and regrading. For each assignment, a course staff member assigns a set of students (or a set of groups, in case of group assignments) to each grader. Figure 1 shows a snapshot of the CMS page that supports this functionality. Student or student groups are selected using check boxes and assigned to a grader selected using a pull-down menu. This page also provides an overview of the files submitted by each group and flags late submissions.

Each grader downloads the files for the students/groups assigned to that grader, grades the assignments, produces a feedback file for each one, and finally uploads the assignment grades and the feedback files (individually or all together). Online grading seems to promote more extensive, detailed feedback. Although a grader is assigned to each student/group, any staff person with the proper

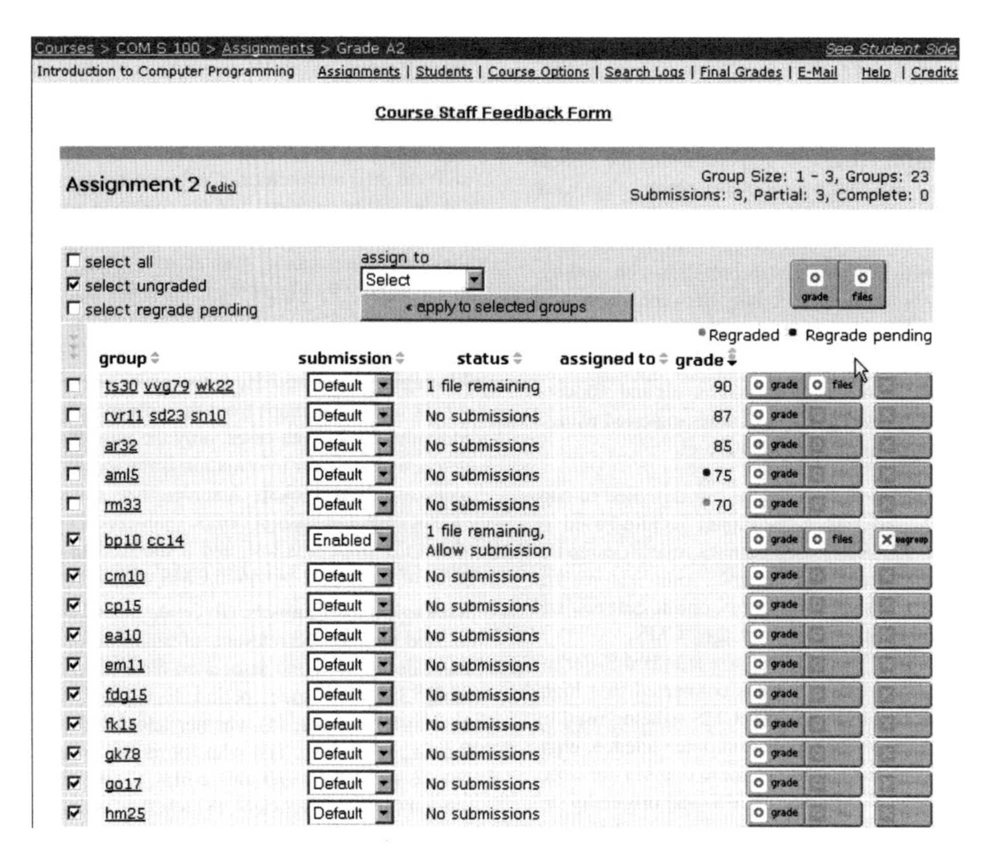

Figure 1: Assigning a Set of Students to a Grader

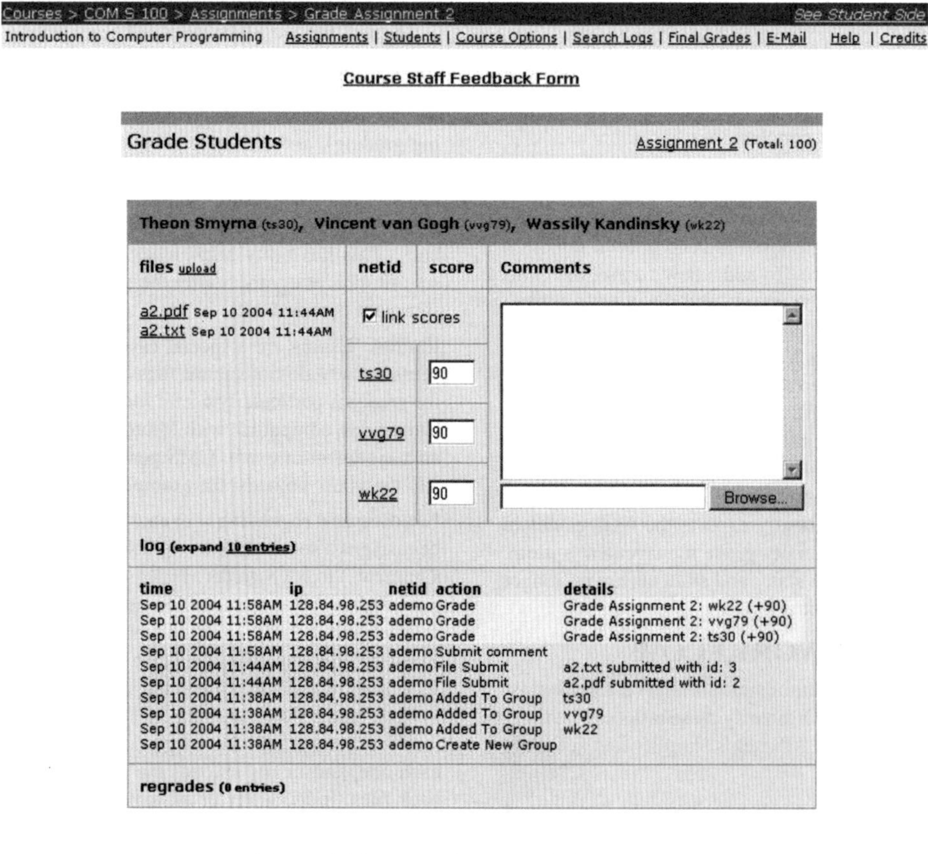

Figure 2: Entering Grades and Comments

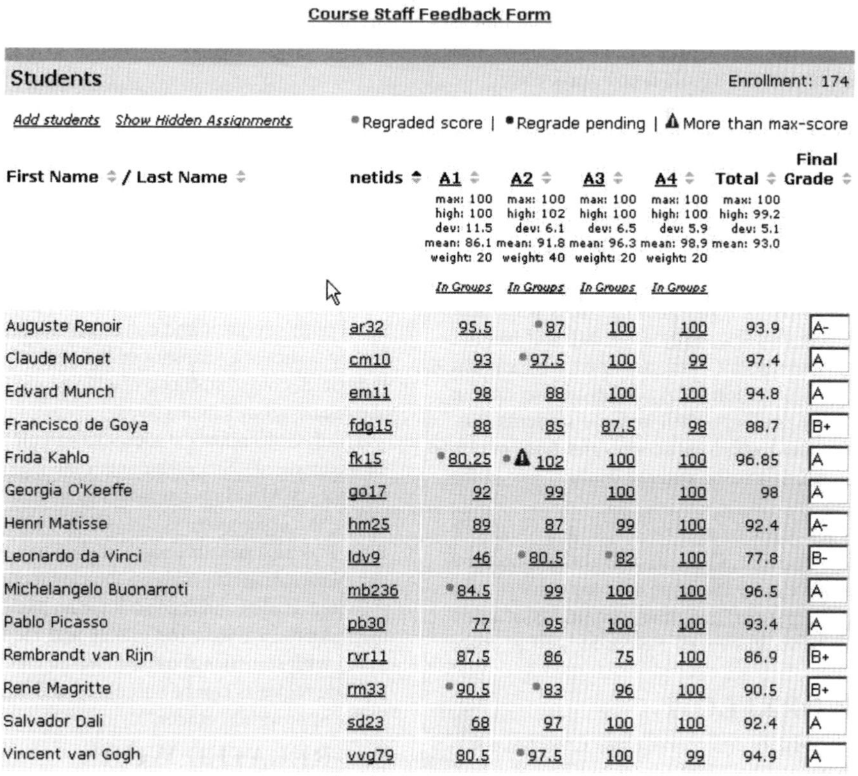

Course Staff Feedback Form

Students — Enrollment: 174

Add students *Show Hidden Assignments*

• Regraded score | • Regrade pending | ⚠ More than max-score

First Name / Last Name	netids	A1	A2	A3	A4	Total	Final Grade
		max: 100 high: 100 dev: 11.5 mean: 86.1 weight: 20	max: 100 high: 102 dev: 6.1 mean: 91.8 weight: 40	max: 100 high: 100 dev: 6.5 mean: 96.3 weight: 20	max: 100 high: 100 dev: 5.9 mean: 98.9 weight: 20	max: 100 high: 99.2 dev: 5.1 mean: 93.0	
		In Groups	*In Groups*	*In Groups*	*In Groups*		
Auguste Renoir	ar32	95.5	• 87	100	100	93.9	A-
Claude Monet	cm10	93	• 97.5	100	99	97.4	A
Edvard Munch	em11	98	88	100	100	94.8	A
Francisco de Goya	fdg15	88	85	87.5	98	88.7	B+
Frida Kahlo	fk15	• 80.25	• ⚠ 102	100	100	96.85	A
Georgia O'Keeffe	go17	92	99	100	100	98	A
Henri Matisse	hm25	89	87	99	100	92.4	A-
Leonardo da Vinci	ldv9	46	• 80.5	• 82	100	77.8	B-
Michelangelo Buonarroti	mb236	• 84.5	99	100	100	96.5	A
Pablo Picasso	pb30	77	95	100	100	93.4	A
Rembrandt van Rijn	rvr11	87.5	86	75	100	86.9	B+
Rene Magritte	rm33	• 90.5	• 83	96	100	90.5	B+
Salvador Dali	sd23	68	97	100	100	92.4	A
Vincent van Gogh	vvg79	80.5	• 97.5	100	99	94.9	A

Figure 3: Administrative View of Students

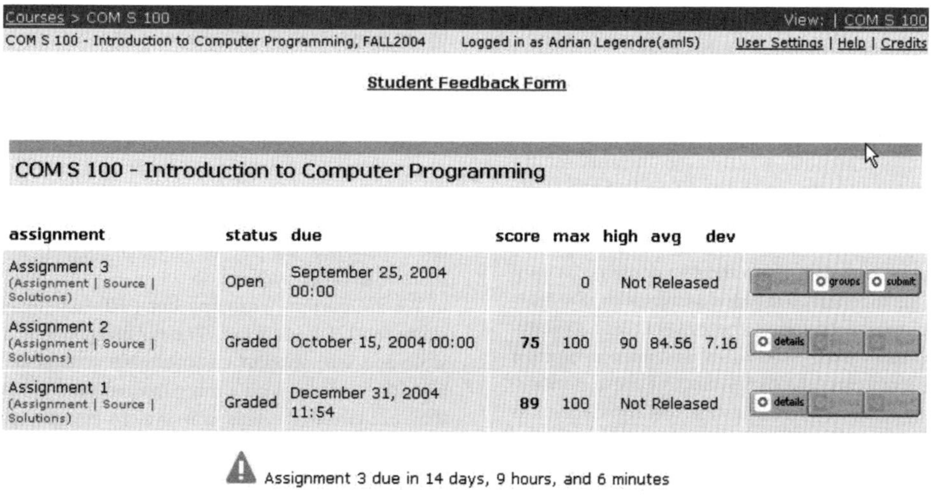

Courses > COM S 100 — View: | COM S 100

COM S 100 - Introduction to Computer Programming, FALL2004 — Logged in as Adrian Legendre(aml5) — User Settings | Help | Credits

Student Feedback Form

COM S 100 - Introduction to Computer Programming

assignment	status	due	score	max	high	avg	dev	
Assignment 3 (Assignment | Source | Solutions)	Open	September 25, 2004 00:00		0	Not Released			groups submit
Assignment 2 (Assignment | Source | Solutions)	Graded	October 15, 2004 00:00	75	100	90	84.56	7.16	details
Assignment 1 (Assignment | Source | Solutions)	Graded	December 31, 2004 11:54	89	100	Not Released			details

⚠ Assignment 3 due in 14 days, 9 hours, and 6 minutes

Figure 4: Course Overview for Students

access level can grade the submission; this is useful for exceptional cases. The CMS page to enter the grades and comments for a single group is shown in Figure 2.

CMS provides direct support for regrading. A student wanting a regrade can submit a regrade request explaining their position; the appropriate grader is alerted and can handle it appropriately.

A log is maintained of all events associated with an assignment, including submission of files, uploading of grades and feedback files, regrade requests, and answers to regrade requests. This log supports complex queries. This capability is useful for grading disputes, for identifying staff errors, and for other special cases.

Administrative views of the students. It is often necessary to maintain several assignments and exams concurrently in various stages of development, submission, and grading. It is important that the course staff be able to track easily what has and has not been done. Figure 3 shows a snapshot of the administrative student view, which provides this information. The administrative student view shows a list of all the students, their names, students IDs, grades on all assignments and tests, total scores, and final grades (if available). Final grades can also be entered in this view at the end of the semester.

Unanswered requests for regrades are marked with a small red dot; answered ones with a gray dot. One can also change the view to see only students who have an outstanding regrade request, who are missing a particular assignment, and other conditions of interest. Thus, course staff receive an overall picture as well as more detailed information.

4. STUDENT WORKFLOW

A student enrolled in more than one course using CMS has a single portal—a single web page—that gives access to all the courses. Students can even access courses that they have taken in previous semesters, if the department allows it.

Managing course information. For each student, CMS provides an overview page for each course in which the student is enrolled. This page shows the student's grades and statistics for each assignment and exam. If a total weighted score is produced, the student can see the weights assigned to each assignment and exam, as well as their total score so far and the statistics for the total score. Finally, when final course grades have been assigned, the students can see them. Figure 4 shows a snapshot of this page.

Different instructors have different opinions on what information should be accessible to students, and should have some control over this. In CMS, the staff can control when the grades on an assignment or exam become viewable, whether the students see the statistics for an assignment or exam, and when (if ever) the students can see their weighted total score or final grade.

CMS also has many ways to notify students about important events. For example, the overview page shows upcoming assignments, due dates, and the time left on the next assignment. Students also receive automatic email notification about events such as availability of grades, feedback on an assignment, and actions on their regrade requests. Students can selectively turn off these notifications if they wish. Thus, CMS is a management tool for students as well as staff.

Managing assignments. CMS provides various ways for a student to manage course assignments. First, CMS provides the ability for students to obtain assignment writeups and other needed files such as source code from the course overview page.

Second, for a group assignment, students can form their own workgroups (and later disband them if necessary). This frees the course staff from a time-consuming chore. Students form groups using an invitation-based model; a student wishing to form a group

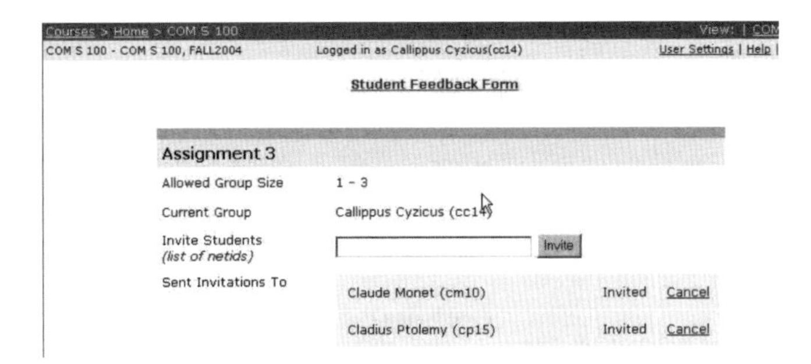

Figure 5: Student Group Formation

invites other students to join the group. The other students are notified of this request and can either accept or decline the invitation. Figure 5 shows a snapshot of the student group management page. If desired, course staff can disable group formation by students and can create groups themselves.

Third, CMS allows students to submit files as part of completing an assignment. Since students may make mistakes when submitting files, CMS allows students to submit files any number of times before the assignment is due. CMS keeps a history of all submitted files. It is also possible for a student to verify that the last recorded submission matches files on their own computer.

When grades and feedback for an assignment become available, the student can view the grades and feedback for the assignment, along with statistics about the overall class performance. If desired, regrade requests can be submitted and will be automatically routed to the appropriate grader.

5. RELATED WORK

Many course management systems have been developed; for a good overview and comparison of these systems, see the Edutools website [2]. However, none of these systems support the entire workflow associated with managing a course. For example, the widely used Blackboard system [1] supports online file submissions and grades, but does not support assigning grading responsibilities, tracking regrade requests, or group assignments.

The ongoing SakaiProject [3] aims to capture course workflow by integrating several existing pieces of software that support different functionality. In contrast, CMS is an operational system designed from the ground up to support a fully integrated workflow.

6. CONCLUSIONS AND FUTURE WORK

CMS is a versatile system designed to support the management of workflow associated with large courses. CMS has been in production use for two years, during which time it has undergone considerable refinement in response to faculty and student feedback. In our experience, the resulting system simplifies course management more than other systems do.

We are currently moving our PHP-based CMS system to Java, using the J2EE platform. The resulting system will be more extensible and will support customizable content delivery. It will also provide students with a more unified view of the courses in which they are enrolled. This new system is expected to be operational in Spring 2005, and we plan to make it publicly available as open-source software.

7. REFERENCES

[1] Blackboard - http://www.blackboard.com.
[2] Edutools - http://www.edutools.info/course.
[3] Sakaiproject - http://www.sakaiproject.org.
[4] J. H. Saltzer. Protection and the control of information sharing in Multics. *Comm. ACM*, 17(7):388–402, July 1974.

Automated Use of a Wiki for Collaborative Lecture Notes

Melissa E. O'Neill
Harvey Mudd College
Claremont, CA, U.S.A.
oneill@acm.org

ABSTRACT

This paper gives a first look at slides2wiki, a new scheme for easily providing collaborative lecture notes. Unlike previous web-based courseware schemes, the slides2wiki approach integrates with existing techniques that computer-science course instructors already use to prepare their classes. This tool is used to create a site where students may collaborate to create their own notes, using the lecture slides as a starting point. Adopting a surprisingly low-tech approach that uses familiar tools and paradigms, slides2wiki avoids many of the stumbling blocks of previous approaches to web-based course support.

Categories and Subject Descriptors

H.5.3 [**Information Interfaces and Presentation**]: Web-based interaction & Collaborative computing; K.3.1 [**Computers and Education**]: Computer Uses in Education & Computer-assisted instruction (CAI)

General Terms

Documentation, Design, Human Factors

Keywords

Wiki, Presentation, LaTeX, XML, Powerpoint, Keynote, Lecture Notes, Collaboration, slides2wiki

1. INTRODUCTION

Teachers who choose to use prepared supporting materials in their classroom face a dilemma not faced by teachers whose materials are generated extemporaneously: what to do when students ask for copies of the materials. When an instructor writes from memory onto a blackboard, students are normally resigned to take notes, but when that same instructor prepares slides, some students will invariably ask for copies of those slides. This dilemma can be "solved" in a number of ways:

1. Refuse to provide the slides and insist on note taking
2. Provide the slides after class
3. Provide the slides before class

SIGCSE'05, February 23–27, 2005, St. Louis, Missouri, USA.

In my personal experience, none of these approaches satisfy enough students. The first approach can cause resentment, as students do not see why they should copy down information that could be provided to them more easily. The second approach also draws criticism as students will often wish that they had had the material beforehand, so that their own notes could be integrated with the text of the slide. The last approach is also problematic, as it removes suspense—students can skip ahead and then feel bored as they wait for you to catch up.

For teachers who mix extemporaneous material and previously prepared overheads, the dilemma is worse. Providing a copy of the prepared material gives it undue emphasis. Students may only keep copies of the lecture slides and forget the material covered in class exercises, discussions, and developed on the board.

Over the last year, I developed a system that addresses many of these issues by using a Wiki site to support collaborative note taking. Unlike existing web-based courseware systems [1, 7, 4, 2], I have taken a lightweight approach that integrates with existing lecture-creation workflow. Instructors have little additional work to do, and students have strong incentives to participate.

1.1 Wikis

A *Wiki* is a website that promotes the collaborative creation of information content. Wiki web pages can be edited by any reader to add or revise content. Information can be easily reorganized—new pages created, existing pages renamed. All changes to the pages are tracked, so it is easy to know who wrote what, promoting a culture of respect in which people generally don't make deleterious changes to a site. There are many Wiki sites on the Internet: the first Wiki was c2.org, created by Ward Cunningham for the discussion of *Design Patterns* [6]; one of the most famous is wikipedia.org, an on-line encyclopedia whose content now rivals that of commercial encyclopedias.

Wiki sites also engender a culture of simplicity. Wiki users can perform all their editing inside a web browser, without needing any advanced browser features such as JAVA or plug-ins. To facilitate easy editing, Wiki sites use a simplified markup language designed for written text.

1.2 Computer-Based Presentation

A number of tools are available to present course materials using a computer. On the commercial front, Microsoft's *Powerpoint* has become the ubiquitous, and often mocked [8], mechanism for presenting lecture slides with a computer, so much so that "powerpoint slides" has almost become a generic term for computer-created slides. There are, however, other options.

On the "easy-to-use application" front, there are several alternatives to Powerpoint. Apple's *Keynote*, for example, operates similarly to Powerpoint (and can read and write Powerpoint files), but uses an XML-based, open file format. Similar functionality is found in OpenOffice.org's *Impress*, Corel's *Presentations*, and KDE's *Kpresenter*.

Adobe's *Acrobat Reader* and Apple's *Preview* can both display an appropriately formatted PDF file as a presentation. This facility allows a number of other tools to be used to create slides, including the LaTeX typesetting system, using packages such as *Prosper* [3] or *foiltex* [5].

Regardless of the tool, I have found that my lecture slides and those of my colleagues follow a similar pattern. For the most part, lecture slides consist of bullet points that provide a skeleton for a part of the lecture—the skeleton is fleshed out both orally and, if necessary, on the board. Some slides also contain graphics, tables, mathematical formulas, or code samples. But, overall, the structural complexity of lecture slides is not high.

1.3 Wiki-Based Lecture Notes

The core idea we will examine in this paper is that of placing skeletal lecture notes onto a Wiki site, and then allowing students to flesh them out with the material they have learned in class. There are several potential benefits to this approach:

- Students gain a valuable collaborative study aid
- The instructor gets to see what students actually understood from the lecture
- The final result should reflect the entirety of the lecture, rather than merely what appeared on the lecture slides

For many instructors, myself included, a scheme such as this one is only likely to be used if it is *easy*. The process of creating a Wiki version of the lecture for collaborative editing should require essentially no work.

2. DUAL-PURPOSE LECTURE MARKUP

In this section, we will examine two schemes for creating dual-purpose markup. The first is based around dual-purpose LaTeX source, and the second is based on creating dual-purpose *Keynote* presentations.

2.1 LaTeX Markup

The LaTeX approach involves a simple slide markup language using the typical commands and environments commonly used in LaTeX documents, augmented with a few convenience commands for slide markup. Figure 1 shows a small example of the markup involved. The usual LaTeX `enumerate`, `itemize`, and `verbatim` environments are available, as is the `\emph` macro, along with counterparts `\strong` and `\code` for boldface and "typewriter" font, respectively.

In addition, code examples can be read from a file by the `codeex` macro, which actually reads in a version of the source that has been reformatted for TeX, with keywords in bold, proper indentation, and so forth. The `\diagram` macro allows a diagram, in the form of a PDF, JPEG, or PNG image to be included in the slides (optional arguments to the diagram command control scaling and positioning).

```
\lectureweek{3}
\lecturenumber{2}
\lectureauthor{Melissa O'Neill}
\lecturecourse{CS 7: Computing with Plants}
\lecturetitle{Calculating with Vegetables}
\lecturefrontpage

\slide{The Value of Vegetables}
Many varieties available...
\begin{itemize}
    \item Carrots, with \emph{emphasis}
    \item Celery, with \strong{boldface}
    \item Leaks, with \code{f(x)}
    \item Potatoes, with a lambda, $\lambda$
\end{itemize}

\subslide{Potatoes, In Depth}
Origins...
\begin{itemize}
    \item Underground
    \item Many varieties
    \begin{itemize}
        \item Russets
        \item Reds
        \item Etc.
    \end{itemize}
\end{itemize}

Growth algorithm...
\codeex{potato.cpp}

\contslide
Potato power in action...
\diagram[0.75]{Potato}
```

Figure 1: Example LaTeX slide markup.

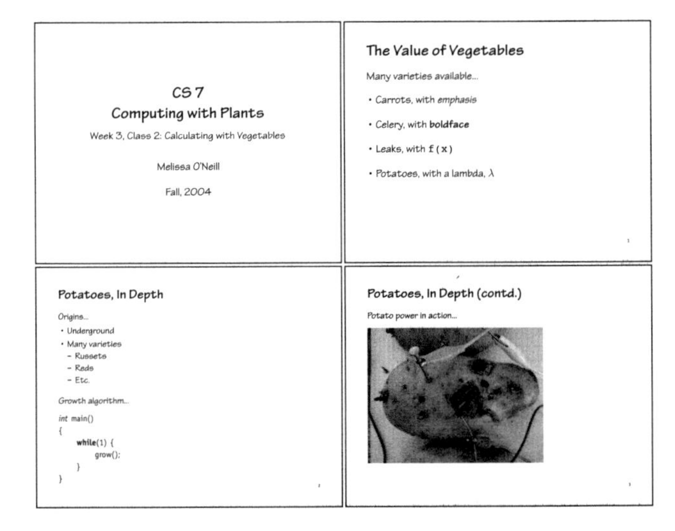

Figure 2: Slides produced by LaTeX.

The result of typesetting the markup from Figure 1 with an appropriate macro package is shown in Figure 2. (The plainness of the slides mostly reflects my own personal leaning towards reduction, rather than any deficiency in the markup.)

A key design goal in the markup language is that it should be both simple enough to be easily processed programatically to create Wiki markup, and expressive enough to meet the needs of that other destination. The result of running slides2wiki on this markup is shown in Figure 3, and the web page rendered from this Wiki markup is shown in Figure 4.

```
---+ The Value of Vegetables

Many varieties available...
   * Carrots, with _emphasis_
   * Celery, with *boldface*
   * Leaks, with =f(x)=
   * Potatoes, with a lambda, &lambda;

---++ Potatoes, In Depth

Origins...
   * Underground
   * Many varieties
      * Russets
      * Reds
      * Etc.

Growth algorithm...
<verbatim>
int main()
{
    while(1) {
        grow();
    }
}
</verbatim>

Potato power in action...

<img src="%ATTACHURLPATH%/Potato.jpg" />
```

Figure 3: Example Wiki markup.

One notable feature of this markup is the idea of a continuation slide. When translated to Wiki markup, the boundary between the two slides is erased to create a continuous section. Another feature of the markup language is that slide topics can be rated as to whether they are a main topic, a subtopic, and so forth, resulting in equivalent sections, subsections, and so forth in the Wiki output version.

Overall, the translation process is fairly mechanical. A few subtleties exist, such as converting PDF or EPS figures to bitmaps for easy web viewing, but these details are easy enough to take care of.

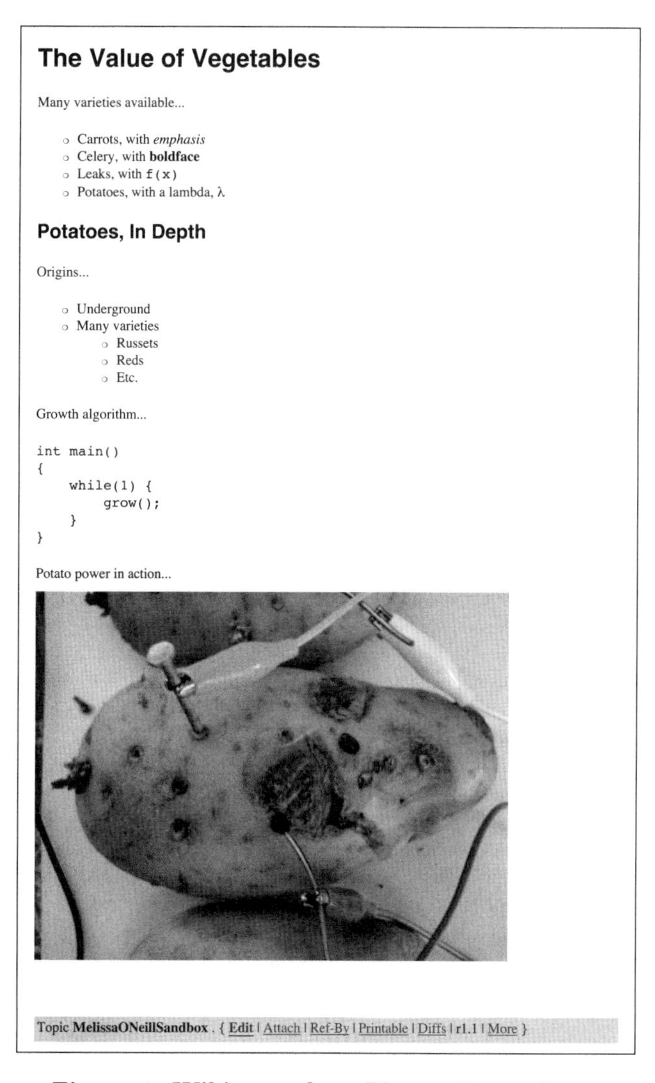

Figure 4: Wiki page from Figure 3's markup.

3. USING PRESENTATION APPLICATIONS

Presentation applications, such as Microsoft *Powerpoint*, Apple's *Keynote*, KDE's *Kpresenter* and OpenOffice.org's *Impress*, provide an easy way to create lecture slides that avoids LaTeX's "arcane" markup syntax. All four tools also provide facilities for making "web-ready" versions of a presentation, but although they can output the lecture content, that content is not intended for collaborative additions from students. What we desire then, as with our previous example, is a tool that can transform a presentation into Wiki markup. For applications with an open file format, such as Keynote, Kpresenter and Impress, writing such a tool is fairly straightforward. We will examine how slides2wiki translates Keynote presentations—similar techniques could be used for Kpresenter and Impress. (Unfortunately, Microsoft Powerpoint does not have an open file format, making the creation of a translation tool more of a challenge—one we do not address in this paper.)[1]

Keynote, Kpresenter and Impress all use XML for their file format, with publicly available DTDs[2] and descriptions. slides2wiki uses off-the-shelf XML-processing tools process presentation XML files. In the case of Keynote, a presentation consists of a description of "master slides", which are used as formatting templates, and a description of the slides themselves, which mostly consist of bullet lists, conceptually similar to those in the LaTeX markup we discussed earlier. Translating these bullet lists is, essentially, a mechanical process. Translating formatting changes is comparable.

There are two issues that complicate the creation of good Wiki markup from presentation applications. The first is recognizing section levels so that the Wiki markup will be structured properly, and the second is dealing with additional material that can be added to a slide, such as an additional text column, diagrams, and so forth.

3.1 Recognizing Slide Types

The LaTeX-based solution from Section 2 understood the concept of a slide hierarchy, which could be ignored when creating presentation slides, but used to create a meaningful

[1]Apple's Keynote will read Microsoft Powerpoint presentations quite successfully, so one option is to convert existing Powerpoint presentations to Keynote ones as a first step.

[2]Document Type Definitions.

section hierarchy when creating the Wiki version. A similar effect can be achieved when translating from Keynote by using different master slides for slides at different levels in the hierarchy. These slides can even have a slightly different look (e.g., slightly smaller text for the title). The translator recognizes when a slide uses one of the "subslide" master slides and creates an appropriate-level section header in the Wiki markup.

The LaTeX-based solution also understood the concept of continuation slides, but using a different master slide to signify a continuation slide is overkill. Instead, the translator considers a slide that has the same title as the previous slide, with the added text "(contd.)" as a continuation slide and elides the slide boundary from the Wiki markup.

3.2 Additions Beyond the Text

Presentation applications typically allow very rich-looking slides, by allowing text and graphics to be placed anywhere, color gradients, progressive builds, and so forth. Much of this additional material can be ignored. For example, in the case of a progressive build, the Wiki markup should just include the final version and so the information describing the build can be ignored. Similarly, background graphics and gradients are usually placed on master slides, which are mostly ignored in the translation process, only being used to differentiate different slide types.

Other text and graphic objects that are added to the page (in addition to the primary bullet list) do present some problems—they can be placed anywhere on the slide, and may not occur in the XML file in the same order as they would be read from the slides. The x- and y-coordinates of the bounding rectangle of these objects are available in the file format, but translating these coordinates is a slight challenge. The algorithm the translator currently uses is

```
while there is more than one object
    find the two closest objects
    combine the two objects into one
        (putting the upper/leftward first)
```

This algorithm only provides a heuristic for the reading order of items on the slide, but it appears to work reasonably well in practice.

4. EARLY EXPERIENCES

So far in this paper, we have focused on the technology issues that arise in developing a system that makes it easy to transition from lecture slides to Wiki markup that supports collaborative note taking. But we also need to address the question of whether all this effort has been worthwhile—do Wiki-based lecture notes work? Although we are not presenting a quantitative study of the impact of the notes here, we can present some anecdotal evidence that indicates that the effort is worthwhile.

These techniques have been used in several classes at our institution; including a C++ and data structures course, an operating systems course, and a programming languages course. Early reaction from students appears to be positive, and reflects the goals we discussed in Section 1.3.

4.1 Real-World Examples

Figure 5 shows a slide from a randomly chosen lecture in our operating systems course. Figure 6 shows the final Wiki version of that same slide (the original Wiki page looked much the same as the slide version, prior to student additions). This example shows how the diagram of a disk was used in class to motivate a discussion of disk and memory terms, and yet that discussion is not apparent from the slide alone. This aspect of the class *is* preserved in the Wiki version. It also shows how students occasionally misunderstand part of a discussion. In this particular example, I made the corrections, but in other cases other students in the class have acted in this role.

Figure 5: A single slide from our operating systems course.

For more examples, the interested reader can examine the actual Wiki sites for some of these classes, at

http://www.cs.hmc.edu/courses/2004/spring/cs182/wiki

and

http://www.cs.hmc.edu/courses/2004/fall/cs131/wiki.

4.2 Caveats

When organizing Wiki-based collaborative lecture notes, one needs to take care to give students clear responsibility for their role. My own experience using this scheme shows that if we make an entire class responsible for the notes to a single lecture, the responsibility is so diffuse that "everyone expects someone else to do it". Instead, I adopted an approach of selecting two students per class as "designated scribes" who would ensure that the Wiki site was a good reflection of what was actually discussed. Other students also had a duty to review their work and make additions or corrections. Including Wiki participation as a small component in the grading of the course also helps to ensure that notes are of appropriate quality.

One additional issue is that when using LaTeX-based slide markup, there is always the temptation to go beyond the subset of LaTeX markup that the translator understands; for example, to perform complex mathematical typesetting. "Cheating" in this way is problematic, because complex equations are difficult to render well in HTML, and even when they can be rendered, the markup itself ceases to be human readable. slides2wiki does not adopt the convention of converting complex equations into graphics because doing so is antithetical to the Wiki approach. Instead, the

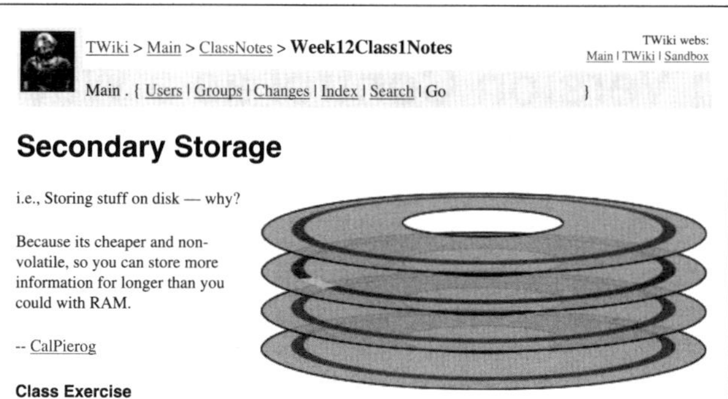

Figure 6: A Wiki excerpt showing the Wiki version of the slide from Figure 5.

preferred solution is to define LaTeX macros for semantic markup—separate macros can be loaded when generating the Wiki page as compared to generating slides.[3]

4.3 Wider Adoption

The Wiki-based lecture notes scheme is already being used across several computer science courses at Harvey Mudd College. The slides2wiki software for automating the Wiki markup process is available under a free software license from http://www.cs.hmc.edu/~oneill/freesoftware/slides2wiki, so that the same approach can be easily tried elsewhere.

[3]Yes, slides2wiki's LaTeX translation actually *does* understand the `\newcommand` and `\newenvironment` commands for defining macros.

5. CONCLUSION

This paper has shown that putting a lecture skeleton onto a Wiki website and encouraging students to flesh out that skeleton can create high-quality lecture notes and provide an instructor with valuable feedback on what students have understood. We have also shown that such a website can be created from existing materials with very little additional effort. The resulting notes are a win/win for course instructors and their students.

The slides2wiki tool works well in practice. It is able to translate from both LaTeX-based slide markup and Apple's Keynote, but it could be extended in various ways to handle more complex slides, and to cover other file formats, such as Kpresenter and Impress.

Other schemes for computer-based collaboration in computer science education may offer more powerful tools for collaboration, and go beyond what occurs in lectures—the advantage of slides2wiki is that it's *easy*.

6. REFERENCES

[1] T. Convery, B. Nuttall, and B. Bodenheimer. Web-based courseware application usability. In *ACMSE'03—ACM Southeast Conference*, Mar 2003.

[2] I. P.-W. Fung. A hybrid approach to represent and deliver curriculum contents. In *Proceedings of International Workshop on Advanced Learning Technologies (IWALT2000)*, pages 209–212, 2000.

[3] F. Goualard and P. M. Neergaard. Making slides in LaTeX with `Prosper`. Feb 2003. `http://www.ctan.org/tex-archive/macros/latex/contrib/prosper/doc/prosper-doc.pdf`.

[4] M. Guzdial. Use of collaborative multimedia in computer science classes. In *The 6th Annual Conference on Innovation and Technology in Computer Science Education*, pages 17–20, June 2001.

[5] J. Hafner. README and INSTALLATION instructions for FoilTeX version 2.1.4a. Oct 2002. `http://www.ctan.org/tex-archive/macros/latex/contrib/foiltex/readme.flt`.

[6] B. Leuf and W. Cunningham. *The Wiki Way: Collaboration and Sharing on the Internet.* Addison-Wesley, 2001.

[7] C. Qu, J. Gamper, and W. Nejdl. A collaborative courseware generating system based on webdav, XML, and JSP. In *ICALT*, pages 197–198, 2001.

[8] E. R. Tufte. *The Cognitive Style of Power Point.* Graphics Press, 2003.

Learning by Doing: Introducing Version Control as a Way to Manage Student Assignments

Karen L. Reid
Dept. of Computer Science
University of Toronto
Toronto, Ontario
reid@cs.utoronto.ca

Gregory V. Wilson
Dept. of Computer Science
University of Toronto
Toronto, Ontario
gvwilson@cs.utoronto.ca

ABSTRACT

Professional software developers use version control systems to coordinate their work, and to provide an unwindable history of their project's evolution. In contrast, students in most programming courses use a homegrown electronic submission program to submit their work, and email to coordinate with partners when doing team projects. In May 2003, we began using CVS, a popular open source version control system, as an assignment submission system. Students receive starter code by checking out the assignment, use the version control system to manage their work, and submit their assignment by committing it to CVS. Teaching assistants grade assignments by checking out each student's repository, and committing the marks. Our experience to date shows that this is both a simpler and a more flexible way to manage student assignments, and also an excellent way to teach them how to use a fundamental software development tool.

Categories and Subject Descriptors

K.3 [**Computing Milieux**]: Computers and Education; D.2.6 [**Software**]: Software Engineering, Programming Environments

General Terms

Education, Management

Keywords

Education, Version control, Software tools, Software Engineering

1. INTRODUCTION

Version control repositories lie at the heart of most modern commercial and open source software projects, as they allow multiple developers to share files in a safe, controlled way, while automatically creating a history of the project's evolution. As several authors have observed [5, 7, 10], one way to predict whether a software project will succeed or not is to ask, "Are developers using a version control system to coordinate their work?"

Prior to May 2003, undergraduates in Computer Science at the University of Toronto were not introduced to version control until their final-year software engineering course. As a result, most students completed their degree with only a hazy understanding of version control's importance and how best to use it. When we introduced a new core second-year course, "CSC207: Software Design", we decided to structure it so that students would acquire such understanding and skills early in their academic career.

Coming into CSC207, students had completed a traditional first-year course using Java. In that course, they used a command-line or web interface to submit their assignments, which copied their files to a course submission directory. If a student ran the submission process a second time, the original submission was overwritten.

Like most open source projects, we chose to use CVS (the Concurrent Versions System) [1]. Its main advantages are that it is free, well-documented, and available on Microsoft Windows, all major flavors of Unix, and Mac OS. Students had no difficulty installing and running it on their personal machines.

In order to ensure that students mastered CVS, we required them to use it to submit their assignments, rather than a traditional electronic submission system. As well as introducing students to a core professional tool, we believed this would:

- make it easier for students to work in pairs or larger groups (an essential skill that is too often shortchanged in undergraduate programs because of the administrative overhead of setting up groups);
- make it easier for students to work on both personal machines and university lab machines;
- make it easier for instructors and teaching assistants (TAs) to assist students during office hours, since they could get an up-to-date copy of students' work at any time; and
- provide a history of student work, which could both help us identify patterns in the way they programmed, and give us additional information in cases of plagiarism.

Below, we describe why we felt it important to introduce students to version control this early, how we actually implemented CVS-based assignments, what our experiences were, and how well we met our goals.

2. PEDAGOGIC VALUE

First and foremost, introducing students to CVS early in their careers helps them see that software development is a process that can be learned and improved, rather than a "black art" which magically yields running programs. It also gives instructors an opportunity to show that good tools and working practices can be used with any language, on any operating system, for any kind of work.

Second, students (like everyone else) are often reluctant to invest time today that will only pay off in the long run. Requiring them to use CVS forces them to get over the initial learning curve. Once they do, and see how much more productive this tool makes them, they are more willing to to learn other tools and practices. This is particularly true when they recognize the advantage of integrated tools in a system such as Eclipse [2]. It also helps that our insistence on CVS forces us to lead by example. Students are more likely to believe that these tools are important when they see their instructors using them on a daily basis.

CSC207 is many students' first encounter with the differences between "toy" programs and larger software projects. While their earlier assignments consist of a handful of Java source files, using CVS allows us to introduce students to the practice of recording how their work has changed over time. Similarly, while they are taught to write meaningful comments describing the state of their code at a particular instant, writing CVS log messages teaches them to describe how that code is evolving. Their practical work therefore helps to introduce them to the concepts associated with "programming in the large".

Finally, giving students a chance to use CVS on their own for several assignments before they use it with a team ensures that they only have to deal with one set of issues at a time rather than trying master a new tool and learning to work with other students simultaneously. Separating these two issues means that when students encounter their first team assignment they will use version control properly rather than using it primarily as a means of submitting their final assignment.

3. IMPLEMENTATION

At the beginning of the term, the instructor creates a repository for each student, with a directory or module for each assignment. The instructor adds starter code or other material to each student's repository using normal CVS commands. We have written a number of simple shell scripts to automate creating repositories and adding files to them. This kind of automation is important because of the course's size: we are currently running 4 sections across 3 campuses with 3 instructors, and a total of 400 students.

It is important that students understand the underlying model, so we spend class or tutorial time explaining how to use CVS. In CSC207, we also spend class time explaining the general principles of version control, and describe how it can be used effectively by professional programmers. Students are given a web page tutorial that has specific instructions about getting started with CVS using our lab machines. One hour of lecture and one hour of tutorial seems to be sufficient to get the students started. Students run "cvs checkout" or "cvs update" to obtain starter code or other files provided by the instructor. To submit an assignment, students simply run "cvs commit" before the due date.

To grade the assignments, the teaching assistants (TAs) check out a copy of each student's repository and compile and test the programs. In the first two terms of using CVS, the TAs added and committed a marks file to each repository containing feedback and evaluation. This led to some confusion since it was not clear to students when the marking had been completed, and it was possible that students saw partial marking results. At present, the TAs edit the marks files in a separate repository; when all grading has been completed, we add the marks files to the students repository in a single batch. This ensures that all students receive their grades at the same time, and that the instructor has a copy of the marks files that the students cannot modify. We also frequently add testing data and code to the students' repositories after the assignments have been graded.

Initially, we decided to use CVS to deliver all course materials including lecture notes, example programs, web pages, and JAR files. Although this made it easy for students to obtain all of the course material, the disk space requirements were prohibitive for a large class. We now use CVS primarily for student assignment work. Lecture notes and other course materials are available through a web page, allowing students to be selective about which materials they download.

One possibility that we have not yet explored is to allow markers to add comments directly to students' programs, and commit the modified files. This would allow markers to comment more specifically and directly on flaws in the students' work, and give students higher quality feedback. However, it requires more care and effort on the part of the marker. To benefit from the marker's comments the students would be best served by understanding how to use the "diff" command. The students would also need to learn to revert to a previous version of their assignment to get back the version they submitted.

3.1 CVS Feature Use

We used a relatively small set of CVS features in our second-year courses. Checkout, add, update and commit accounted for nearly all of the operations performed by students. They occasionally used diff and log to examine their repositories. Students rarely reverted to previous versions and never created branches. A few of the more adventurous experimented with tags, and we are now using tags to manage submissions in upper-year courses.

3.2 Issues

CVS was not designed with educational needs in mind. Three specific issues we encountered were

- the need to prevent naive users from damaging their repository,
- the need to prevent students from seeing one another's repositories, and
- the need to prevent students from rewriting their CVS logs to give the impression that they had completed work earlier than they actually did.

3.2.1 Damaging Repositories

In the first two terms, there were several instances of students directly editing files in their repositories, or creating source files in the repository directory, rather than in a checked-out copy of that directory. In these cases, instructors had to do some repair work on the repository in order to get the student back on track, and students lost some or all of the work they had done. These mistakes were due to students not understanding the distinction between master copies stored in repositories, and working copies storied elsewhere. As we became more experienced in explaining CVS to students, this type of problem almost vanished.

3.2.2 Security

Preventing students from viewing one another's work, while allowing instructors and TAs to see it, was more difficult than anticipated due to limitations in Unix's permissions model. We created two types of repositories:

- An individual repository owned by a single student, but with group permissions set to the group that included instructors and TAs (but not the student).
- Team repositories, for assignments done in pairs (or larger groups). The obvious way to implement this would be to create one group for each programming team, and put the students in the team, the TAs, and the instructors in that group. The problem is that on a standard Red Hat Linux installation, a user can only be in 32 groups at a time. (Users can be added to any number of groups, but only the first 32 actually take effect.) This makes it impossible for instructors and TAs to be in the Unix group for all group repositories at one time. The number is configurable, but requires rebuilding the kernel. Our system administrators solved this problem by creating a setuid script that allowed an instructor to edit the group lists, and to change groups. This worked, but was awkward to set up and maintain.

3.2.3 Potential Cheating

The third problem—students editing their version histories in order to fake early submissions—was never fully addressed. We checked out an instance of the repository shortly after the due time to guard against this problem, but TAs still often checked out their own copy to grade, and the snapshot was treated more as a sanity check if needed. We believe that few students are sophisticated enough to find or exploit this security hole, but recognize that once one does, the technique could quickly spread. We are presently investigating strategies such as secure logging of submission times via CVS triggers as a way to close this loophole. A client-server version control system such as Subversion [3] would also solve this problem.

3.3 Use in Subsequent Courses

Since the introduction of CVS in CSC207, we have begun to use it in follow-on courses. In particular, we have used it in "CSC209: Software Tools and Systems Programming". Students learn C programming in this course and all of their assignments are done as individuals, so we did not take advantage of CVS to manage group work. Because we are in the middle of a shift to the new curriculum, only half of the students in CSC209 had previously used CVS in CSC207. Students in CSC209 did not receive as much tutorial information about how to use CVS, but still mastered it quickly, perhaps because their peers were able to help them when they ran into difficulty.

We are also now using CVS in "CSC369: Operating Systems", a traditional operating systems course. We used the OS/161 simulator developed at Harvard [4] and relied heavily on CVS to manage changes to the simulator over several assignments.

Although the OS course at Harvard also uses CVS, students initialize and maintain their own CVS repositories, and use "cvs diff" and "tar" to collect their work and submit it using a traditional submission system. Based on our experience using CVS, we decided to use the same approach to using CVS as in previous courses with a few changes. Students were asked to tag their repository to indicate the version that they expected to be marked. Unfortunately, students frequently forgot to tag their assignments, particularly in the first half of the term, which meant that the TAs needed to do more work to determine what to grade.

The CSC369 students each had their own repository for the first two assignments. They worked in pairs for the remainder of the course, and team repositories were created for each pair. We used branches in the repository to give students access to solution code and to add starter code for subsequent assignments. Given the size of the code base, the changes made to the code over time by the instructor, and the teamwork, it was essential to use a version control system.

By identifying similarities between the process of releasing and maintaining software products and the process of assignment development and submission we were able to use features of CVS such as tags and branches.

4. EVALUATION

CVS can best be evaluated in comparison with the more traditional submission system it replaced.

4.1 Traditional Submission System

The traditional submission system had the following strengths and weaknesses:

Advantages:

- It is possible to prevent students from making submissions after the posted due time. This makes it completely clear to the students that their work was late.
- A web interface allows students to easily submit files from home.
- It is possible to restrict file names, so that the system can enforce some basic submission rules.
- The submission interface is very simple to use.

Disadvantages:

- Students could see a list of files that they submitted, but could not retrieve their submission. This made it difficult for them to be sure that they had submitted the correct files.
- Students could submit their assignments as many times as they wanted, but each subsequent submission overwrote the previous one, so all history was lost.

4.2 CVS

By comparison, CVS had its own strengths and weaknesses:

Advantages

- Students could check out exactly the material they submitted, so that they could verify that their assignment was complete and that everything had been submitted.
- It was possible to deliver starter code in a more immediately useful form than by posting it on the web in plain files or archived format.
- Intermediate commits were available to the instructor, so if something went wrong, or if a student was unable to complete an assignment for non-academic reasons, instructors and TAs had at least partial information to work with.
- When assessing team projects, there was more evidence of which team members did which parts of the work.
- Use of CVS allowed instructors and TAs to commit marks back to the student repositories, which turned out to be an effective way to manage marking of online submissions.
- Managing student assignments through CVS led us to manage TA interaction through CVS as well, giving us more information about the progress TAs were making and a history of their work.
- Using CVS made it significantly easier for instructors to manage a course of four sections spread across three campuses. It was much easier to keep information up to date and instructors were able to consolidate marking in a way that mailing tar files back and forth did not allow.
- Giving instructors control over repositories made it possible to handle difficult situations gracefully, such as team members switching groups because of personal conflicts, or removing permissions from students who dropped the course.
- Finally, there are obvious advantages to having a record of what students did when in cases of suspected plagiarism, or when students and TAs have different opinions about what was completed when. Making students aware of this gives them one more reason to check in early and check in often.

Disadvantages

- Because students no longer need an explicit action to submit their assignments, it was sometimes difficult to determine which version of the assignment was the final version. In particular, we lacked a good mechanism to handle a late policy, which allowed students to submit the assignment late with some penalty. One approach to solving this problem was to require students to notify the instructor if they chose to submit the assignment late. Requiring a separate mechanism is undesirable.
- The first two terms the course was taught, a significant minority of students used CVS inefficiently because they did not understand the underlying model. For example, we found many students repeatedly used checkout rather than checking out once and using update to refresh their local copy. As we gain more experience with the kinds of mistakes students make, we are able to prevent the most common ones.
- Some TAs had trouble determining which version of the assignment they should mark, and often made mistakes (particularly on early assignments). This was due almost entirely to TAs not understanding how to use CVS. We expect these problems to diminish as TAs become more familiar with the tools.
- Although having the instructor set up and manage the CVS repositories for the teams simplifies the work that students need to do, there is more administrative overhead for the instructor when students drop the course or move between teams. We hope that further work on our shell scripts will automate the administrative work involved.

4.3 Anecdotes

A few anecdotes may help give the flavor of what CVS was like in action:

- More than one student was able to recover files that had accidentally been deleted. This reinforced the tool's value, and made it easier for students to complete their work.
- Students appreciated the way CVS helped them synchronize the work they did at home with the work they did on the lab machines. being able to work on their assignments at home. Later in the term, some students even began using CVS to manage assignments in other courses.
- Some students were alarmed by the fact that times in CVS logs are stored in Greenwich Mean Time (UTC). Since Toronto is on Eastern Standard Time, this led them to believe that their assignments would be considered late.
- There were a couple of cases where students asked for help backing out of recent changes they had made. In one case, the student had discovered that he really wanted to change his strategy and wanted to start over again. In another case, a student realized too late that he was not able to complete a new feature and wanted a previous version of his assignment graded. In addition, we had several cases of students asking us to grade a particular version of their assignment because they were not happy with changes they made later. This was a clear benefit to students who were careful about committing intermediate versions of their code, and reinforced the habits we were trying to teach.
- Students frequently came to office hours asking for help debugging their programs. We insisted that they commit the most recent version of their work before seeking help, so that we could check out their work, compile it and run it without needing to log into the student's account. We had complete freedom to modify their code

until we got it to work, and delete our changes without affecting the student's own work. Students then went back to their own workstation to reproduce what they had just seen us do, which ensured that they really understood what had just happened.

- In one case, we realized that only one quarter of the class had checked out the starter code one week into a three week assignment. We were able to present hard evidence to the class that only a small number of students were working on the assignment, and encourage them to get started. This is a trivial example of how the ability to track student progress on an assignment can help instructors catch problems early.

5. USAGE PATTERNS

Since we now had a wealth of data on how students used CVS and could glean some information on how students worked on their assignments, we conducted a study with Keir Mierle and Sam Roweis to use machine learning techniques to analyze the CVS data [8]. We hoped to be able to tell students that we had discovered that students who made effective use of CVS received higher grades on their assignments. In other words, we hoped that we could find evidence that students with good work habits and good time management get higher grades.

Unfortunately, we were unable to discover any features in the CVS data that strongly correlated with high or low grades. We were, however, able to gather some qualitative information from their repositories. For example this is how we discovered that students were using checkout repeatedly rather than using update. To our surprise, there was no statistical correlation between how early students started on assignments, or how evenly they paced their work, and their final grades. We hope that as we (or instructors at other institutions) collect more data, patterns may begin to emerge. We also intend to see whether there are patterns when we look at student usage of CVS in upper-year courses, as the lack of pattern in the second-year course data may reflect nothing more than the fact that students climb the learning curve at different rates.

6. RELATED WORK

The most closely related work on using CVS for assignment submission is part of Penumbra, an Eclipse plug-in intended to provide a simpler interface to Eclipse for novices [9]. Penumbra also simplifies the interface to the CVS plug-in, allowing instructors to use it for assignment delivery and submission. Penumbra hides the complexity of CVS use from the students under an interface that appears as a more traditional submission system, but students can access the full functionality of CVS by switching to the CVS perspective in Eclipse. This makes it possible to use CVS in a first-year course.

The original version of Penumbra used a single repository for the course and each assignment contained a directory for every student. They used Unix permissions to prevent students from accessing each other's work. We believe it is an advantage to our second-year and upper-year students to have their own repositories. It simplifies management of individual students, and gives the student a more realistic view of how they might use CVS in another context. We now have an undergraduate student working to adapt Penumbra to work with CVS repositories that follow our structure.

Using a version control system as a regular part of assignment management leads to interesting possibilities to evaluate and mentor students. The JRefleX project [6] collects and analyzes CVS history data to produce diagrams that can be used to monitor individual and team progress. This "dashboard" allows instructors to identify problems with assignments early enough to help students recover.

7. CONCLUSIONS

A year and a half after we first used CVS for student assignment submission, we believe that it both can and should be introduced in second year. It forces students to adopt good working practice early enough in their careers for those practices to stick; it make it feasible for us to assign team projects much earlier (and to much larger classes) than was previously possible; and it gives the instructors a powerful tool to manage interactions with students, TAs, and each other. The effort required to set it up is relatively small, and with each passing term we have found ways to avoid those problems that do arise.

Other instructors are already adopting CVS for their courses, and we are convinced the end result will be students who are better prepared to develop software to high professional standards.

8. ACKNOWLEDGMENTS

We wish to thank Michelle Craig, Michael Szamosi, and David Daley, our co-instructors for CSC207.

9. REFERENCES

[1] `http://www.cvshome.org`.

[2] `http://www.eclipse.org`.

[3] Version control with subversion. `http://svnbook.red-bean.com/`.

[4] D. A. Holland, A. T. Lim, and M. I. Seltzer. A new instructional operating system. In *Proceedings of the 33rd SIGCSE technical symposium on Computer science education*, pages 111–115. ACM Press, 2002.

[5] A. Hunt and D. Thomas. *The Pragmatic Programmer*. Addison-Wesley, 1999.

[6] Y. Liu, E. Stroulia, K. Wong, and D. German. Using CVS historical information to understand how students software. In *MSR 2004: International Workshop on Mining Software Repositories*, 2004.

[7] S. McConnell. *Code Complete*. Microsoft Press, 2 edition, 2004.

[8] K. B. Mierle, S. T. Roweis, and G. V. Wilson. CVS data extraction and analysis: A case study. Technical Report UTML TR 2004-002, University of Toronto, Augu 2004.

[9] F. Mueller and A. L. Hosking. Penumbra: an Eclipse plugin for introductory programming. In *Proceedings of the 2003 OOPSLA workshop on eclipse tec eXchange*, pages 65–68. ACM Press, 2003.

[10] J. Spolsky. *Joel on Software*. APress, 2004.

Steganography and Cartography: Interesting Assignments that Reinforce Machine Representation, Bit Manipulation, and Discrete Structures Concepts

Daniel E. Stevenson, Michael R. Wick, and Steven J. Ratering
Computer Science Department
University of Wisconsin – Eau Claire
Eau Claire, WI 54701
715-836-2804
{stevende, wickmr, raterisj}@uwec.edu

ABSTRACT

Today's generation of students crave assignments that are relevant to their world, both in terms of graphical interfaces and, more importantly, the application area. To be fully engaged they must find the application of importance. However, we have found that many assignments in computer science attempt to engage the students by moving further and further away from the underlying machine representations. This causes a disconnect between the applications our students write and the material we present on machine representations and architecture. We present examples of assignments based from the fields of Steganography and Cartography that we have found to be valuable in helping to reinforce the importance of machine representations with today's students. We found that the students were excited and intrigued to see how their discipline could play a vital role in the war on terrorism and how what they were learning in their CS 1 course was directly relevant to what they heard on the nightly news and experience on a daily basis via the Internet.

Categories and Subject Descriptors

K.3 [Computers & Education]: Computer & Information Science Education – *Computer Science Education.*

General Terms

Algorithms, Design, Security

Keywords

Steganography, Cartography, CS 1, Pedagogy, Assignments.

1. RELATING TO TODAY'S STUDENTS

Who are the students sitting in your classes today? They are the students that have grown up watching MTV, playing video games, chatting on AOL, and surfing the Internet. They are the students for which computer technology is not an end but a means. Gone are the students that eagerly studied computer science from the ground up as an exciting new discipline filled with the promise of great applications. Students are not impressed by the technological advances represented by modern computer applications, but rather view them as a natural and essential part of their daily existence.

So, how do we modernize our assignments to deal with this new generation of students? Several people have developed approaches that are interesting and locally successful (for example, [1], [2], [3]). Most of these approaches are centered on the idea of making the programs that students write "look and feel" more similar to the programs that students use. There are two basic approaches to achieving this goal – (1) early use of graphics and graphical user interfaces in the curriculum (for example, [2]) and (2) using specialized multi-media programming languages to allow early computer science students to build sophisticated applications like MPEG movie editors [3]. Both approaches have been shown to still expose students to fundamental programming concepts but tend to create a significant disconnect between the applications the students develop and the machine representation, architecture, and number systems material presented in other courses. And while there may be instructors that believe there is no need for this type of low-level information today, we are not convinced. It is possible to find interesting high-level assignments that actively engage students' interests while still illustrating the real need for and instilling a true appreciation for the knowledge of low-level memory storage issues.

While a modern "look and feel" is a necessary part of assignments for today's students, it is not the most important part. Mark Guzdial and Elliot Soloway said it best in their paper on teaching – "...engaging the students is critical to deep learning..." [3, p.18]. The critical element is what the programs do or allow the students to do. Obviously, programs that involve glitzy interfaces are easier to mesh with the students' past experiences and certainly encourage the use of graphics and graphical user interfaces. However, many applications exist that have this

SIGCSE'05, February 23–27, 2005, St. Louis, Missouri, USA.

feature of the glitzy interface but that also have the look-and-feel of more traditional computer science applications that require and emphasize a knowledge of the underlying machine. In particular, in the remainder of this paper we present five applications from Steganography and Cartography that we have found to be successful in engaging entry-level computer science students and helping to motivate and reinforce fundamental low-level issues currently not in vogue with the students.

2. STEGANOGRAPHY IN BRIEF

Steganography is the science of hiding information in such a way as to make it difficult to discern the presence or contents of the hidden information. Generally the hidden information is a text message or image data. This data is then hidden in a "cover" image (BMP, PNG, JPEG, etc) or other media (MP3, MPEG, etc) in such a way as to minimize the changes in the physical appearance of the cover image, resulting in a "stego" image. The example in Figure 1 shows 32K of image data (the plans for the death star) hidden in a Van Gough cover image.

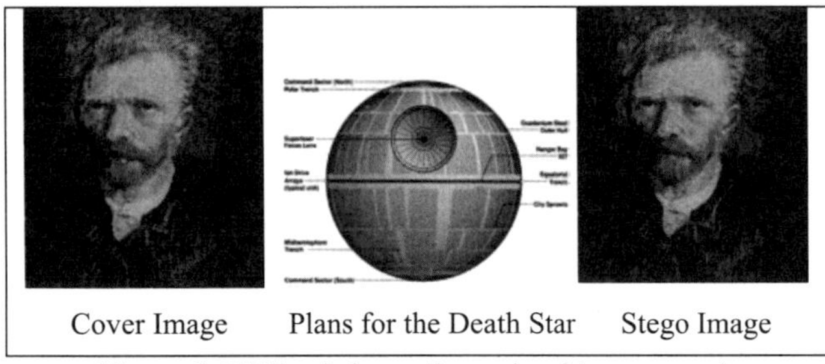

Cover Image   Plans for the Death Star   Stego Image

Figure 1: Hiding information using Steganography

In order to effectively hide data, one has to understand the details of the cover image format. Bitmaps (BMPs), which are used in several of the following assignments, store their pixels directly as 8 bit intensity values (1 intensity value per pixel for grayscale). The standard way to embed data into an image is by least significant bit (LSB) encoding. This encoding modifies the least significant bit of the first N intensity values to match the N bits of the hidden message. This type of embedding not only has the ability to hide a large amount of information, but changing the least significant bits of the intensity values only modifies the perceptual color slightly. However, as with most of the basic steganographic encoding schemes, LSB encoded hidden data can often be discovered by analyzing image statistics (called steganoanalysis) even through the hidden data is not detectable visually. Thus, most hidden data is first encrypted before it is encoded so that if it is detected it still cannot be understood.

Steganographic techniques have made the national news several times over the past two years due to the increased awareness in ways to combat terrorism. In particular, the some people in the U.S. are worried that terrorists are communicating via messages hidden in images on innocent looking web pages. This connects directly with the students' world perception and they immediately find the study of steganographic techniques to be of interest.

3. FOUR ASSIGNMENTS RELATED TO STEGANOGRAPHY

In this section we describe a sequence of four programming assignments taken from the general field of steganography. We present these assignments both to encourage their use at other institutions (the source code is available from the authors) and to serve as demonstrations of the more important topic of choosing programming assignments that connect with today's students while reinforcing lower-level machine representation issues. While the steganography assignments are presented as a sequence (that is how we use them), they can be given independent of one another should an instructor not wish to develop a unifying theme to the assignments in a course.

We are well aware that we are not the first authors to present steganography as an interesting area for computer science assignments (for example, see [8]), however, we have attempted to focus on the lower-level aspect of these systems rather than on the image processing or graphics aspects. Further, while many authors might object to the low-level feel of our code segments (as opposed to a higher-order object-oriented design), we have intentionally targeted imperative-looking code segments to help illustrate the low-level manipulation required by these high-level systems.

3.1 Encryption

The first assignment is a rather simple assignment in which we ask our students to implement an encryption algorithm. Recall that encrypting the data to be hidden is a first step in most steganographic implementations. Every student in the class has heard of encryption and its importance in many areas of "real life" including national security. As such, students seem to grab onto the idea of learning more about this important topic.

We use RSA encryption [4] for this assignment. There are several important issues with RSA. First is that the encryption process involves the computation of an ASCII value to the Eth power, where E is a prime, followed by a mod of that result by PQ, where PQ is the product of two primes. This quickly brings up representation issues as the exponentiation can easily blow out the range of ints and even longs. Certainly BigIntegers solve this problem; however we would like to highlight the machine representation issues so we instead use a modular exponentiation method to solve the problem (see Figure 2).

```
public String encrypt(String plainText) {
  String cipherText = "";
  for (int i = 0; i < plainText.length(); i++) {
    int asciiValue = (int)plainText.charAt(i);

    // Compute (asciiValue ^ E) mod (PQ)
    int tempE = e;
    int cipherValue = 1;
    while (tempE > 0) {
      if ( (tempE % 2) == 1 ) { // If tempE is odd
        cipherValue=(cipherValue * asciiValue)%pq;
      }
      tempE /= 2;  // Integer division
      asciiValue = (asciiValue * asciiValue) % pq;
    }

    cipherText += (char)cipherValue;
  }
  return cipherText;
}
```

Figure 2: Encryption Part of RSA Algorithm

The second issue is that in order to fit the resulting cipher back into a String (to simplify the assignment) we cannot have the cipher values be bigger than 15 bits. Because these values are computed by last moding with PQ, this means that for this simplified assignment PQ cannot be larger than 15 bits. Thus, doing some math tells us that the original primes, P and Q, cannot be larger than 7 bits each. Note that this creates a weak version of RSA that can be easily cracked because the original primes are not large enough. However, this makes a fun class demonstration of how even RSA can be cracked if the keys are not picked well.

The encryption assignment deals with an application area that most student find relevant and exciting. Further, the programming itself serves as a nice illustration of the role of machine representation and simple discrete mathematics.

3.2 Hidden Image Processing

Building on work by Burger [5], we developed an image processing assignment with a special slant toward steganography. Using the Java Image I/O API we asked the students to implement several standard image-processing operations (filtering, intensity modification, and rotating) for simple grayscale raster images. Not surprisingly, students loved the assignment. To illustrate to students the "real world" application of the concepts, during lecture we used the image processing operations they implemented to isolate and highlight edges in an aerial image of a battle scene.

To help lead to the next assignment, we added a slight twist. Using steganographical techniques, we encoded a secret message in the specific image against which the students were required to demonstrate their programs. Figure 3 shows the example test image before and after the image processing. To encoding the secret image we first set the least significant bit of every raster value in the image to zero. Then, for each pixel we wanted white in the decoded secret message, we set the least significant bit to one. The required image processing operations to decode it are:

```
image.mask(1);
image.changeIntensity(255.0);
```

Figure 3: A Secret Image Revealed

To separate the message from the image, the first step masks (bitwise "and"s) each raster value in the image with the value 1. To allow the distinction to be visible to the human eye, the second operation increases the intensity of each raster value by 255%. Talk about engaging students' interest– they were dying to know how we hid the message in the image!

The hidden image processing assignment was both popular and effective. Students enjoyed the assignment and saw the relevance of mathematics to computer science as the image processing algorithms are all based on linear algebra and trigonometry.

3.3 Bitmap Steganography

The next project was the implementation of an actual steganography system. In this assignment, students developed a complete steganography system capable of encoding the contents of an ASCII text file into a bitmap image. To encode the secret message, the user specifies three files – the original text message, the bitmap cover image, and destination for the stego image. The system reads the original text image into a string, and then encrypts it using the simplified RSA algorithm (from the first assignment). The cipher string is then converted (using I/O buffering techniques) into a serialized bit stream. A single bit is inserted at the end of the bit stream and will serve as a sentinel value when the embedded message is extracted. Since RSA is a public key encryption system it is assumed that the receiver of the message already has the private key necessary to decode the message. Byte by byte, the cover image is read into the system. Following the standard bitmap format, the first 54 bytes of header/info in the file are copied directly to the stego bitmap file. For the remaining bytes in the cover bitmap, the least significant bit is truncated and reset based on the next bit in the bit stream and then written to the stego file. The Java code for the heart of this process is shown (in part) in Figure 4.

```
private void stegCopyImage() throws
                 SteganographicalException {
  // Note : textSerializer is the bit sequence
  //        for the encrypted text message
  int b;
  try {
    // Copy the header/info sections - 54 bytes
    for(int i=0; i<54; i++) {
      stego.write(original.read());
    }

    // Embed the message in the image
    for(long i = 0;
            i < textSerializer.countBits(); i++){
      b = truncateLSB( original.read() );
      b += textSerializer.nextBit();
      stego.write(b);
    }

    // Copy the remaining parts of the image.
    while ( (b = original.read()) != -1 ){
      stego.write(b);
    }
  }
  catch (IOException e ){
    ...
  }
  catch (SteganographicalException e){
    ...
  }
}
```

Figure 4: The Heart of the Steganographical Process

As described earlier, the information held in the least significant bits is not perceptible to the human eye. Figure 5 illustrates the end results by showing the before and after bitmap images. While they appear to be identical, the second image contains the entire contents of the Gettysburg Address encoded in its least significant bits.

The steganography system also includes a separate program capable of decoding a secret message held in a bitmap image. In this program, the user specifies the location of the stego bitmap. The system reads the file byte-by-byte skipping the first 54 bytes of header/info. It then reads the remaining bytes from the file, extracting and caching the least significant bit from each one until eight bits have been collected. These eight bits are then grouped as a byte and decrypted using the RSA program together with the correct private key. The resulting byte is then converted to an

ASCII character and appended to the text of the extracted secret message. This continues until the sentinel is reached.

Cover Image Stego Image w/ Gettys Addr

Figure 5: A Secret Message Encoded

The steganography program was incredibly popular with the students even though the program they developed didn't include a single graphical user interface (the bitmap files were displayed using readily available products like Microsoft Photo Editor). While the project obviously involves a visual element, the students were sufficiently fascinated by the techniques involved in the implementation and the social ramifications of the application itself that they were completely engaged in the largely text-based, bit-manipulation project. A few students even took the initiative to research steganography outside of class and learn more about how more complex image formats (such as JPEG) can be used.

From an instructional point of view, the program was also a huge success. The relevance of discrete mathematics on number representations was again reinforced. Students were also able to experience the reuse of their own code they had written earlier (the encryption code). Further, students learned some powerful implementation techniques such a caching, buffering, header values, and sentinel values that are emphasized in courses later in the curriculum. The assignment also included the added benefit that the students gained experience with reading and understanding technical documents (they were required to read and understand the bitmap file format specifications).

3.4 Paint Steganography

In the last program of the semester we finally introduce graphical user interfaces. In particular, we have the students develop a "paint" program through which they can embed an image within another image. Recall the images shown in Figure 3. The first image contains the second black-and-white image embedded in the least significant bits of the file. For the final program the students develop a program that allows the user to hand draw a black-and-white image over a bitmap image. Figure 6 illustrates the simple graphical user interface for the program.

Figure 6: A Simple StegPaint Program

The system initially displays an image read from a .PNG file. We use the .PNG file format because the java.imageio library, used to easily allow the students to display the images, does not support the bitmap file format. The .PNG file format is similar enough to the bitmap format used earlier that the students don't need to relearn another format specification. As the user drags the mouse, the system paints the corresponding pixels white. When the user clicks the Save button, the drawn pixels are embedded into the image using the familiar technique of truncating the least significant bit of all image bytes and then setting the least significant bit of the pixels covered by the painted strokes to one. The code for implementing this portion of the assignment is shown in Figure 7.

```
protected void saveImage(String fileName){
  int[][] raster = image.getRaster();
  int width = image.getWidth();
  int height = image.getHeight();

  // Truncate the least significant bits
  for(int x = 0; i < width; x++){
    for(int y = 0; j < height; y++) {
       raster[x][y] = raster[x][y] & 254;
    }
  }
  // Turn on the bits from the hidden pixels.
  ListIterator pixels = hidden.listIterator();
  while ( pixels.hasNext() ){
    Point pt = (Point)pixels.next();
    raster[pt.x][pt.y] = raster[pt.x][pt.y] | 1;
  }
  image.setRaster(raster);

  try {
    image.write(fileName);
  }
  catch (Exception ex){
    ...
  }
}
```

Figure 7: Saving the StegPaint Hidden Image

In the resulting image the hidden painted image data is undetectable to the human eye until the same "mask then change intensity" operations described earlier are applied.

As expected, the StegPaint program is quite popular with the students as it is their first chance to develop their own graphical user interfaces. Students appear to get a real sense of growth when they look back on the earlier assignment (Hidden Image Processing) and now fully understand the implementation of what then appeared to be magic.

From the instructor's point of view, this assignment is important as it serves to give students hands-on experience with event-driven programming, Java listeners, and the component painting process while still having an explicit tie back to the underlying concepts of machine representation and discrete mathematics.

4. CARTOGRAPHY IN BRIEF

Another application area that requires knowledge of machine representation and is relevant to students' lives is cartography. Cartography is the science of making maps. Most of our students have used online map-drawing programs to find the route from city A to city B and they are curious how the data are represented. The maps used by most map-drawing websites are stored in the shapefile format [7].

Three files in different formats are used to store each shapefile map -- the main file, the index file, and the dBASE file. The main data file is composed of a header record followed by a sequence of data records. The header record gives the length of the file in 16-bit words, but not the number of records. The header record also gives the shape type and the limits of the bounding box. Some integers in this record are stored in big endian order and others are stored in little endian order. The data records are composed of a fixed length record header followed by a variable length record body.

The index file has a header followed by fixed length records, one for each data record in the main file. Each record has the offset and length for its corresponding data record. The dBASE file has any desired feature attributes for the shapes in the main file. Features include areas, perimeters, and place names for regions and lengths for roads.

5. AN ASSIGNMENT RELATED TO CARTOGRAPHY

The assignment we use is to draw a map of the United States. We gave our students some data files in the shapefile format, downloaded from http://nationalatlas.gov/atlasftp.html, and a pointer to some format documentation (www.esri.com/library/whitepapers/pdfs/shapefile.pdf) and said, "Have at it". Well, wc said a little more, but a significant part of the assignment was reading and comprehending the documentation for shapefiles. Another significant part was the software engineering task of determining the details of the problem specification.

The shape type for the provided US map is polygon, though they are not polygons in the usual sense. Each record in the main file stores one polygon which is composed of one or more parts. Each part contains a list of points which are latitude, longitude pairs. The points for all the parts in the polygon are stored in consecutive bytes. The start of each part is determined by a list of indices, effectively a list of pointers.

The file length of the main data file is given in the header record starting at byte 24. This length is stored as a 4-byte integer in big endian order. The shape type is another 4-byte integer given in the header record. It starts at byte 32 and is in little endian order. After reading and perhaps swapping bytes, the 4 bytes need to be converted to an int. The code for implementing this part of the assignment is shown in Figure 8.

```
char headerBuffer[HEADER_SIZE];
char fileLengthBuffer[4];
char shapeTypeBuffer[4];
int fileLength;
int shapeType;
const int LENGTH_SPOT = 24;
const int SHAPE_SPOT = 32;

usMapFile.read( headerBuffer, HEADER_SIZE );

for (int i = 0; i < 4; i++){
  fileLengthBuffer[3-i] = headerBuffer[LENGTH_SPOT+i];
  // 3-i because the file length comes big endian
}
for (int i = 0; i < 4; i++){
  shapeTypeBuffer[i] = headerBuffer[SHAPE_SPOT+i];
}
fileLength = *((int*)fileLengthBuffer);
shapeType = *((int*)shapeTypeBuffer);
```

Figure 8: Reading Big Endian and Little Endian Integers

Our students appreciated the low-level details of reading integers and doubles from a binary file and dealing with big endian and little endian representations and arrays of pointers because the final result is a great looking map of the United States. A nice follow-on assignment would be to give a shapefile containing city, highway, and street data and then find the route from address A in city A to address B in city B.

6. CONCLUSION

We have argued that it is possible to develop interesting CS 1 programming assignments that both include enough glitz to engage students and enough low-level manipulation to reinforce data representation, architecture, and discrete mathematics concepts. In particular, we have found the areas of steganography and cartography to be particularly rich domains from which to develop such programming assignments and have presented several concrete examples. In our experience, the students have found the assignments exciting and engaging while explicitly providing an integrated connection to other aspects of our computer science curriculum.

7. REFERENCES

[1] Naps, T.L. *et al.* Exploring the Role of Visualization and Engagement in Computer Science Education. ACM SIGCSE Bulletin, 35(2), 2003, 131-152.

[2] Astrachan, O. and Rodger, S. Animation, Visualization, and Interaction in CS 1 Assignments, ACM SIGCSE Bulletin, 31(1), 1998, 317-321.

[3] Guzdial, M. and Soloway, E. Teaching the Nintendo Generation to Program. Comm. of the ACM, 45(4), 2002, 17-21.

[4] Rivest, R., Shamir, A., and Adleman, L. A Method for Obtaining Digital Signatures and Public-Key Cryptosystems. Comm. of the ACM, 21(2), 1978, 120-126.

[5] Burger, K. Teaching Two-Dimensional Array Concepts in Java With Image Processing Examples. Proc. of the 34th Technical Symposium on Computer Science Education, ACM Press, 2003, 205-209.

[6] C. LeBlanc and E. Stiller, *Teaching Computer Security at a Small College*, Proceedings of the Thirty-Fifth Technical Symposium on Computer Science Education (SIGCSE), pp. 407- 411, 2004.

[7] Environmental Systems Research Institute, Inc., *ESRI Shapefile Technical Description*, ESRI White Paper, July 1998. http://www.esri.com/library/whitepapers/pdfs/shapefile.pdf.

[8] C. LeBlanc and E. Stiller, Teaching Computer Security at a Small College, Proc. of the 35th Technical Symposium on Computer Science Education, ACM Press, 2004, 407-411.

A Java Framework for Experimentation with Steganography

Dr. Kenny Hunt
The University of Wisconsin - La Crosse
1725 State Street, La Crosse, WI 54601
(608) 785-6822
hunt@mail.uwlax.edu

ABSTRACT

This article describes a Java framework for experimentation with fundamental steganographic techniques. The framework is built on top of Java's image processing libraries and provides extensible handles for customization and experimentation. The framework is designed and presented with a view towards incorporation into an undergraduate computer science curriculum.

Categories and Subject Descriptors

I.4.0 [**Computing Methodologies**]: Image Processing and Computer Vision - *General.*

General Terms

Security, Design

Keywords

steganography, information hiding, computer security, image processing

1. INTRODUCTION

Steganography is a flourishing area of study within computer science and covers a broad range of specialties. In addition, the increasing use of digital images and image processing techniques makes the study of digital image processing an important sub-discipline of computer science. These two fields are brought together in a specialized application of steganography whereby secret messages are imperceptibly embedded in digital images. Steganography can be defined as *"the art of concealing the existence of information within seemingly innocuous carriers. Steganography, in an essence, 'camouflages' a message to hide its existence and make it seem 'invisible' thus concealing the fact that a message is being sent altogether. An encrypted message may draw suspicion while an invisible message will not."* [4]

The study of steganography has become increasingly important since the events of September 11. Shortly after the attacks on the World Trade Center towers it was reported that Osama Bin Laden and his allies had communicated, in part, through the use of secret messages embedded in publicly distributed pornographic images [6]. Researchers quickly sought to develop methods of detecting whether images contained hidden messages and how to decode them if they were present. While this provided the impetus for a sensationalist involvement in the study of steganography, more legitimate and profitable uses of steganographic techniques involve watermarks and digital copyright management.

Digital watermarking is a technique for embedding information transparently into digital media [7]. The embedded information is often a digital signature that uniquely identifies a copyright owner. Identifying information must be difficult to detect without possession of some key data; uniquely identify the legitimate copyright owner, and be difficult to erase or alter even if detected.

2. BACKGROUND

This section provides the technical background necessary for understanding basic steganographic techniques. The technique described here is the well known least significant bit (LSB) approach [5]. More sophisticated methods involve spread-spectrum encodings where a message is embedded across a frequency-based representation of a digital image. While spread-spectrum techniques are beyond the scope of most undergraduate curricula, the LSB approach is easily accessible to undergraduate programming students and directly addresses fundamental issues of data representation and processing.

2.1 Digital Images

A digital image at the most abstract level is a two-dimensional array of colored pixels or dots. When these pixels are displayed on a high-resolution monitor and viewed at an appropriate distance, they appear to be a continuously colored image. Each pixel is a certain color which is typically defined, using the red-green-blue (RGB) color model, as a combination of varying amounts of red, green, and blue light. A color image is therefore said to contain three bands, each of which represents the amount of red, green, or blue light in the image. Whereas a color image contains color and intensity information, a grayscale image is composed of pixels that vary only in intensity, not color. Grayscale images therefore have only a single band. Without loss of generality, the remaining discussion will focus on grayscale images. The discussion is easily extended to cover color images by noting that a color image is the composition of three individual grayscale images representing the red, green and blue bands.

The typical grayscale image has an 8-bit depth which is sufficient to represent 256 unique intensity values ranging from black to white. Most students learn about the binary representation of numeric data early in the CS curriculum but are rarely confronted

SIGCSE '05, February 23–27, 2005, St. Louis, Missouri, USA.

with any low-level issues arising from such a representation. It is this author's experience that many students have never experienced a need for using bit-wise operators nor given much thought to such low-level details. Steganography provides an excellent domain in which to expose students to such issues.

A brief review of binary representation will be instructive when interpreting bit-level pixel data in the context of a digital image. An 8-bit binary numeral has the general form

$$A_7 \cdot 2^7 + A_6 \cdot 2^6 + \ldots + A_1 \cdot 2^1 + A_0 \cdot 2^0$$

where A_n represents a single binary digit. In a digital image it is clear that A_7 is the most significant bit and indicates whether the pixel value is greater than 127. A common means of converting a grayscale image to a binary (i.e. black-and-white) image is to extract the A_7 bit from each pixel. By contrast, A_0 embodies relatively little information and, in the context of a digital image, can generally be understood as a *noise* channel. This is illustrated in Figure 1 where the most significant and least significant bit planes are extracted from an 8-bit image. It is obvious that the more significant bits of each pixel embody greater structural information than the least significant bits.

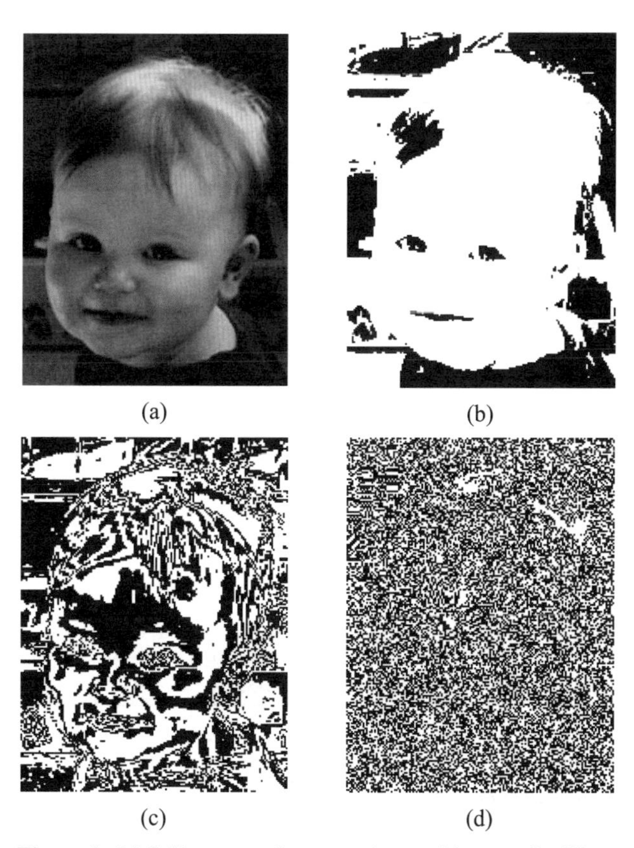

Figure 1: (a) 8-bit grayscale source image (b) most significant bit plane A_7 of the source where white indicates an ON bit and black an OFF bit (c) bit plane A_4 and (d) least significant bit plane A_0 of the source image

2.2 Steganography

The human eye has a resolution far below 8-bits and is typically able to simultaneously discern only one or two dozen intensity levels [1]. This implies that much of the information contained in a digital image is imperceptible to a human observer and that small modifications to a source image will not be perceived. Steganography, in the simplest case, capitalizes on this overabundance of information by replacing the noise channels (i.e. the least significant bit channels) with an arbitrary secret message. Figure 2 gives an overview of a steganographic process flow. A source image, hereafter referred to as a *cover*, is viewed as 8 information carrying channels. A secret message is spread over the least significant channels (in this case the three least significant channels) with the modified channels re-combined to obtain an output, hereafter referred to as the *stego image*, that visually resembles the cover image and contains the injected message.

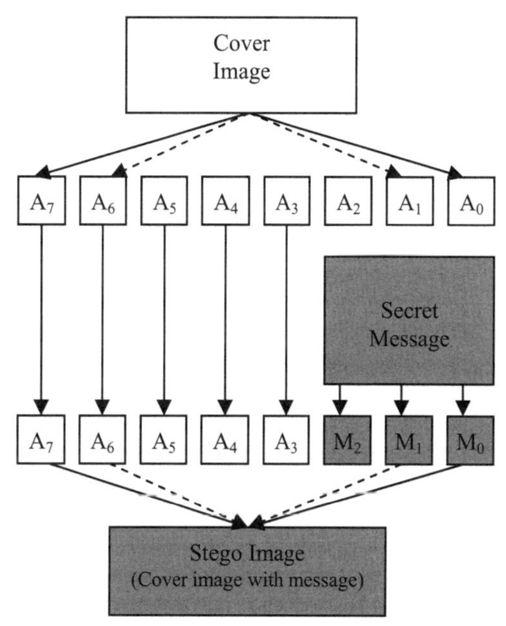

Figure 2: Embedding of a secret message into the three least significant channels of a cover image

The degree to which the resulting stego image visually resembles the cover is dependent upon the number of channels that are used to encode the secret message. In practice, the fidelity of the stego image quickly degrades if more than three channels are used as secret message carriers. While beyond the scope of this article it is worth noting that adaptive techniques exist that allocate carrier channels on a per-pixel basis through evaluation of image texture or morphological structure.

2.2.1 Example

Consider a 2 row by 8 column image with pixel values as shown in Table 1 below. The image can be visualized as generally light-gray towards the left descending towards dark-gray towards the right of the image. Table 2 represents the same information as Table 1 but uses binary notation.

Table 1. A 2 row by 8 column grayscale cover image

209	200	188	192	155	138	100	99
198	155	140	187	154	130	122	99

Table 2. The grayscale cover image from Table 1 represented using binary notation

1101 0001	1100 1000	1011 1100	1100 0000	1000 1010	1000 0011	0110 0011	0011 0010
1100 0110	1001 1011	1000 1100	1011 1011	1001 1010	1000 0010	0111 1010	0110 0100

The secret message "HI" is then embedded into this image. The message, when represented in ASCII text corresponds to the sequence of numerical values {72, 73} or, represented in binary notation, {01001000, 01001001}. The secret message is then viewed as a sequence of 16 individual bits which need to be injected into the original cover image. Since the cover image contains 16 pixels the single least significant bit of each pixel is designated as a carrier of the secret message. In other words, the cover image dedicates a single channel towards carrying the secret message.

Table 3 gives the result of the embedding where the secret message has been distributed over the least significant bits as indicated by underscoring. Note that many of the cover pixel values have not been altered at all in the process. Only the highlighted entries of the table contain pixels that have been modified by the embedding process where the cover pixel has been altered by a single, imperceptible grayscale value.

Table 3. Stego image with embedded ASCII "HI"

1101 0000	1100 1001	1011 1100	1100 0000	1000 1011	1000 0010	0110 0010	0011 0010
1100 0110	1001 1011	1000 1100	1011 1010	1001 1011	1000 0010	0111 1010	0110 0101

While in this case the secret message was textual in nature, any serializable data can be embedded into a digital image using this technique. A practical steganographic tool would include header information prior to the secret message itself all of which has been encrypted and compressed in a preprocessing phase.

3. JAVA IMPLEMENTATION

The standard Java distribution, J2SE [6], includes full support for reading and writing digital images to file, viewing digital images as part of a graphical interface, and manipulating digital images at either low or high levels of abstraction. The presentation in this paper uses the Java 2 Platform, Standard Edition version 1.4 throughout. J2SE supports both immediate and asynchronous mode image processing operations. The asynchronous mode operations are useful for developing applications like web browsers where images can be displayed when the data is available while not blocking operation of the entire browser as the data is loaded. Immediate mode operations block until image data is loaded and, since threads are not utilized, are more suitable for use in an undergraduate curricula.

In J2SE the most generic properties of digital images are captured in a high-level abstract Image class but the most useful class for image processing is a subclass known as BufferedImage. A BufferedImage contains a Raster, representing a two-dimensional array of pixels, and a ColorModel, which specifies how to interpret the Raster data. A Raster contains a DataBuffer, representing the actual low-level pixel data and a SampleModel, which specifies how to interpret this pixel data. Image processing methods will typically take a BufferedImage object as a parameter and manipulate the image through its Raster.

Thorough knowledge of each of these classes is required to perform even the most basic image processing operations. While this is not a substantial overhead for experienced programmers, it is prohibitive to most undergraduates. Even in upper-division courses, it is not tenable to introduce students to the built-in image-processing package solely as a way to introduce steganography or to provide a domain-specific example of the use of bit manipulation. An EasyBufferedImage class has therefore been developed which hides this complexity and provides convenient methods for creating and manipulating digital images. This class is described in greater detail in [2]. Figure 3 shows a UML class diagram of the EasyBufferedImage class highlighting commonly used methods. This class extends the built-in BufferedImage and contains factory methods for creating such images from PNG files as well as from two-dimensional array data.

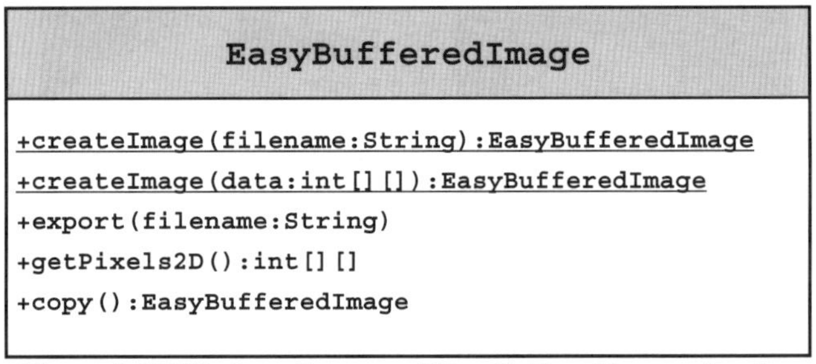

```
EasyBufferedImage
+createImage(filename:String):EasyBufferedImage
+createImage(data:int[][]):EasyBufferedImage
+export(filename:String)
+getPixels2D():int[][]
+copy():EasyBufferedImage
```

Figure 3: UML class diagram of EasyBufferedImage showing only the most relevant methods

A steganographic encoder can be developed which is responsible for both embedding a secret message within an EasyBufferedImage cover and extracting a secret message from an EasyBufferedImage stego. The Steganographer interface shown in Figure 4 captures these responsibilities in the embed and extract methods.

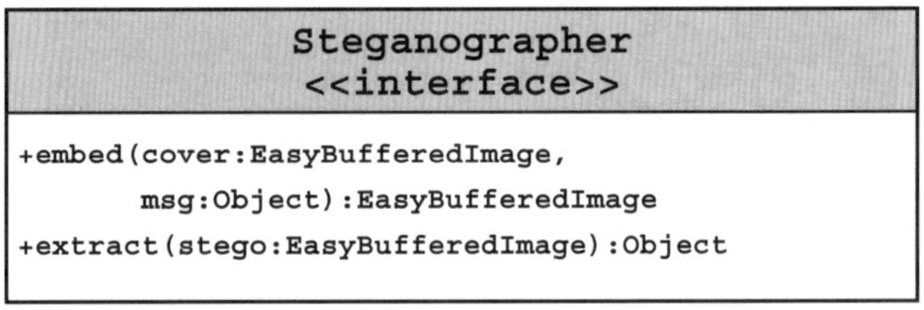

```
Steganographer
<<interface>>
+embed(cover:EasyBufferedImage,
       msg:Object):EasyBufferedImage
+extract(stego:EasyBufferedImage):Object
```

Figure 4: UML class diagram of the Steganographer interface

The embed method accepts an EasyBufferedImage which serves as the cover and an Object serving as the secret message. The method then creates a stego image, embedding the secret message into the cover and returning the result as an EasyBufferedImage. Note that this method does not alter the cover image. The extract method serves as an inverse to the embed method, returning an

Object that has been extracted from a stego EasyBufferedImage. This interface serves as a generic and extensible solution since there is no functional dependency upon the way in which the embedding takes place. These methods simply serve as hooks for customized steganographic algorithms which are provided by implementations of the interface.

For this exercise the Steganographer is implemented as an LSBSteganographer. This implementation performs embedding in the manner previously described by spreading the secret message across the least significant bits of the cover. The LSBSteganographer class is depicted in Figure 5.

```
LSBSteganographer
-----------------
+embed(cover:EasyBufferedImage,
       message:Object):EasyBufferedImage
+extract(stego:EasyBufferedImage):Object
+getChannelCapacity():int
+setChannelCapacity(channels:int)
```

Figure 5: UML class diagram of the LSBSteganographer class

In order to simplify implementation a restriction not defined at the Steganographer level is imposed by the embed method. In particular, the message must be an EasyBufferedImage rather than, in the most general sense, a serializable[1] object. The embed method is allowed to throw an exception if the type of message specified is incompatible with this requirement. A technique for loosening this restriction is presented at the conclusion of this section.

Implementation of the LSBSteganographer can be difficult in light of the low-level bitwise nature of the operations. The work is greatly simplified, however, by the design and creation of an appropriate set of supporting classes. Towards this end ImageInputStream, ImageOutputStream classes are construed to isolate the low-level complexities and to supply a convenient interface to the necessary bitwise operations.

The ImageInputStream class essentially transforms an EasyBufferedImage into a stream of bits, drawn from the least significant channels, which can be sequentially accessed on demand. Convenient auxiliary methods are provided to read an entire sequence of bits and package them into an integer primitive. The ImageOutputStream class supplies the inverse operations, sequentially packaging a stream of bits into the least significant channels of an EasyBufferedImage. The ImageInputStream is best implemented as a subclass of the InputStream class where the abstract read method (equivalent to the getNextByte method) must be implemented. As subclasses of standard input/output classes, the image streams are easily integrated with standard Java stream handling functions. Figure 6 gives a UML overview of the ImageInputStream class.

[1] Serializable is used here in the technical sense of any object that conforms to the Serializable interface

The getNextBit serves as the fundamental method on which the other get methods are constructed. The getNextBit method returns an integer having a value of 0 if the next bit in the sequence is OFF and a value of 1 if the next bit is ON; throwing an IOException if there are no more bits available. The other get methods are easily written by repeatedly executing the getNextBit method and packaging the resulting bit sequence into an int.

Implementation of the getNextBit method is achieved by maintaining indices into the row, column and channel of the current bit and advancing these indices as bits are accessed. The ImageOutputStream class is not specified here but provides functionality inversely analogous to that of the ImageInputStream class.

```
ImageInputStream
----------------
+ImageInputStream(source:EasyBufferedImage,
                  numChannels:int)
+hasMoreBits():boolean
+getNextBit():int
+getNextByte():int
+getNextInt():int
+read():int
```

Figure 6: UML class diagram of the ImageInputStream class

The embed method of the LSBSteganographer is trivial to write in terms of image streams and is given in the pseudocode listing of Figure 7. This implementation will throw an IOException if the carrying capacity of the cover is not sufficient for embedding of the secret message.

The implementation must also generate header information required for later decoding of the secret message. While not described in detail, a typical header will include a magic number along with the height, width, and number of bands in the secret image.

```
public Image embed(cover, message) {
  Image result = cover.copy();
  int k = getChannelCapacity();
  ImageOutputStream rOut =
     new ImageOutputStream(result, k);

  writeHeaderInformation(rOut, message);

  for every pixel P in message
     rOut.writeByte(P)

  return result;
}
```

Figure 7: Pseudocode implementation of the LSBSteganographer embed method

The extract method is also easily implemented in terms of image streams. Since the number of channels used to embed a secret message is not known in advance, the extract method will make attempts to identify the magic number in the header by drawing bits from a single channel. If the magic number is not recognized, the process will be repeated by drawing bits from increasingly more channels until all channels have been exhausted. Once the magic number has been identified, decoding proceeds in a straightforward fashion.

As previously mentioned, the embed method of Figure 7 presumes that the message is an image. This restriction can be eliminated to support the embedding of any serializable data into a cover image. Since the ImageOutputStream is a subclass of the standard OutputStream, an ObjectOutputStream can be used to perform the embedding as shown in the pseudocode of Figure 8. This implementation will throw an exception if the message is not serializable or if the capacity of the cover is insufficient.

```
public Image embed(cover, message) {
  Image result = cover.copy();
  ObjectOutputStream fout =
      new ObjectOutputStream(
         new ImageOutputStream(result,
                               channels));
  fout.writeObject(message);
  return result;
}
```

Figure 8: Pseudocode implementation of a generic LSBSteganographer embed method

Unfortunately, neither the BufferedImage nor EasyBufferedImage classes are serializable and hence are not supported by this method. An embed method can, however, be implemented that determines whether the message is serializable, in which case the technique of Figure 8 is dispatched, otherwise the technique of Figure 7 is utilized if the message is an image.

4. DISCUSSION

The classes presented here form the basic architecture for experimentation with steganographic techniques and provide flexible opportunities for classroom use. Student interest in this topic is naturally high due to media visibility and the intrinsic motivation of developing software to manipulate visual data.

In a pedagogical sense, the value of this exercise lies primarily in two distinct software engineering activities which can be easily adapted to accommodate curricular needs. Perhaps the greatest challenge lies in solving the complex design issues required to compose a reasonable class framework. It is likely that without the development of image stream classes, any attempt to implement a Steganographer will result in a monolithic jumble of non-reusable static methods. Another significant challenge lies in the development of a correct implementation of the design. The design task may be emphasized by providing full implementations of the ImageStream classes while asking students to design and implement a Steganographer. Alternatively, a complete design, specified in terms of interfaces and class stubs, may be provided with implementation left completely to the student. The student, in this case, is given the design but forced to confront the low-level bit manipulation and array processing details.

Also, while the LSBSteganographer class presented in this article embeds information in a left-to-right top-to-bottom fashion, other LSB methods have been utilized in an undergraduate setting [8] and can be implemented by authoring alternate image input and output streams.

A typical application built on top of this framework will involve the loading of a PNG image from a file or URL to serve as the cover. The secret message itself is also loaded into the application, embedded into the cover and then saved to disk or displayed onscreen. Observant readers will note that since the secret message is itself an image, the data hiding process described is recursive in nature. That is to say, the secret message may itself contain a secret message which may contain a secret message and so forth.

Complete implementation of the presented classes and a full-featured lab application are freely available for academic use on request to hunt@mail.uwlax.edu.

5. REFERENCES

[1] Gonzalez, R., and Woods, R. *Digital Image Processing*, Addison-Wesley Longman Publishing Co., Inc, Boston, Ma, 1992

[2] Hunt, K., *Using Image Processing to Teach CS1 and CS2,* ACM SIGCSE Bulletin, Volume 35, Issue 4:86-89

[3] *Java2 Platform Standard Edition 1.4 Release 2002.* Sun Microsystems. http://java.sun.com/j2se

[4] Johnson, N. F., *Steganography*, web article found at http://www.jjtc.com/stegdoc/steg1995.html

[5] Johnson, N., and Sushil, J., *Steganography: Seeing the Unseen*, IEEE Computer, February 1998: 26-34

[6] Kelley, J., *Terror groups hid behind Web encryption*, USA Today, February 5, 2001; available from http://www.usatoday.com/tech/news/2001-02-05-binladen.htm

[7] Steinebach, Martin, Zmudzinski, S., and Chen, F., *The Digital Watermarking Container: Secure and Efficient Embedding,* Proceedings of the 2004 Multimedia and Security Workshop on Multimedia and Security, 2004:199-205

[8] Sutherland, K., *Image Processing Programming Projects in an Upper Division Algorithms Course,* Proceedings of the Midwest Instructional Computing Symposium, 2004

Using Image Processing Projects to Teach CS1 Topics

Richard Wicentowski and Tia Newhall
Computer Science Department
Swarthmore College
Swarthmore, PA 10981
{richardw, newhall}@cs.swarthmore.edu

ABSTRACT

As Computer Science educators, we know that students learn more from projects that are fun and challenging, that seem "real" to them, and that allow them to be creative in designing their solutions. When we have students beating down our office doors wanting to show us what they've done, we know we have designed a project that truly meets its pedagogical goals. In CS1 courses, it is often difficult to come up with large, real-world programming projects that are at an appropriate level and that really excite students. This is particularly true in the first half of the course when students are learning basic programming and problem solving skills. We found that assignments based on image processing are an effective way to teach many CS1 topics. Because students enjoy working on the projects, they come away with a solid understanding of the topics reinforced by the projects. In this paper, we discuss many ways in which image processing could be used to teach CS1 topics. As an example, we present two image processing projects that we use in our CS1 course. These large, real-world programs are designed so that students can successfully master them early in their first semester of programming. Even though our CS1 course is taught using the C programming language, these projects could easily be used by a CS1 course in C, C++, or Java. We provide starting point code for Java and C versions of the projects, and provide sample assignment write-ups on our project webpage [12].

Categories and Subject Descriptors

K.3.2 [**Computing Milieux**]: COMPUTERS AND EDUCATION—*Computer and Information Science Education*

General Terms

Algorithms

Keywords

Computer Science Education, CS1, Image Processing Projects

SIGCSE'05, February 23–27, 2005, St. Louis, Missouri, USA.

1. INTRODUCTION

At Swarthmore College, the computer science curriculum offers a broad exposure to the discipline through three introductory courses, which could be termed CS1, CS1.5, and CS2. CS1 takes an imperative approach using C, often with Roberts' text [10]; CS1.5 takes a functional approach using Scheme with Abelson and Sussman's text [1]; while CS2 takes an object-oriented approach using Java, often with Goodrich and Tamassia's text [6].

Our version of CS1 is called *The Imperative Paradigm: Unix and C*. It is an introduction to programming in the C programming language, and we include an introduction to Computer Science, Unix, and some data structures and algorithms. Typically, we introduce a new feature of the C language each week and give students one or more programming assignments to reinforce this feature. We like to give students several larger programming assignments during the semester so they can experience the benefits of using good modular design, using makefiles, and incremental implementation and testing.

We have found that projects based on image processing are a good way to introduce larger, real-world projects early in a CS1 course. We present as examples two image processing projects that are used in our CS1 course. One version manipulates greyscale images and can be used after teaching arrays early in the semester. Typically, we provide much of the shell of the program and students implement functions to manipulate the image in different ways. The other version manipulates color images and can be used after covering compound data types, such as structs or classes, later in the semester. For this version, students are required to design more of the program themselves.

Most of our CS1 students list the image processing project as their favorite from our course. As a result, we think it is a good vehicle for demonstrating how data structures and algorithms are used in practice, as well as for developing communication, programming, and problem solving skills in students. Based on our own observations, in semesters when we use these assignments, our CS1 students have a better understanding of arrays, and of the semantics of passing arrays to functions, then they do in semesters when we have not used these assignments.

An additional benefit of using these assignments is that students feel a real sense of accomplishment in completing them. The projects initially seem very large and difficult. Students come to realize, however, that their solution to one image manipulation feature can be used as a starting point for adding other features. Thus, what students first see as a daunting assignment turns out to be manageable. Nearly all students implement the required parts. In addition, many students add some impressive extra-credit features.

Our success with these projects made us realize other ways in which image processing could be used to teach introductory CS topics. We are not proposing that one use only image processing projects in CS1, but that there are numerous points when image processing could be used to teach CS1 topics.

There has been prior work on using image processing projects in CS1 and CS2 courses [3, 2, 5, 7]. However, previous work presents either specific image processing projects or image processing libraries. Our work focuses on how image processing projects can be used more generally to meet specific pedagogical goals. Additionally, we present survey results measuring the effectiveness of the application of some of our ideas. In Section 2 we discuss several of our ideas for how to use image processing to teach CS1 topics. In Section 3 we present our two image processing projects, we discuss how they are used, and we present student reaction to the projects, and we conclude in Section 4.

2. USING IMAGE PROCESSING IN CS1

Image processing can be used as an effective way to teach a number of CS1 topics, including both one-dimensional and multi-dimensional arrays, iteration, recursion, pointers, dynamic memory allocation, compound data types, sorting, file I/O, functions, and function call semantics. In Java, projects centered around image processing also can serve as an introduction to teaching event-driven programming, threaded programs, and GUI programming, as well as exploring issues associated with designing user interfaces. For a CS1 course using an object-oriented language such as C++ or Java, a color and greyscale image processing project can be used as a real-world example of inheritance; from Image and Pixel base classes, specialized greyscale and color classes can be derived.

For a CS1 class, an instructor would likely provide students with a library or class containing the I/O routines necessary for translating an image file to a 2-D array of pixel values. In advanced classes, reading the raw image file may itself be a challenging class project. Most modern image formats are quite complex and require that students create supporting data structures to translate the image file into a 2-D array of pixels. For example, the GIF [4] file specification requires that an 8-bit color table be included with the image, and the image data is compressed using LZW compression, a modification of the Lemper-Ziv compression algorithm. For students to extract a GIF image, they would need to create a data structure to hold the color table, then uncompress the image, mapping each pixel to its appropriate color in the color table. This task is beyond the scope of our CS1 course, but could be incorporated into a CS2 project.

Once the image has been stored into a two dimensional array of pixels, there are numerous ways in which the image array of pixels can be manipulated to produce different effects on the image. Some effects give students real-life examples of the importance of finding a generalized solution to a problem. For example, image tiling and splitting effects can be coded in a few lines if students find the general recursive or iterative pattern for how the image is split at each step. On the other hand, if students try to hard code the solution for tiling or splitting an image, they could end up writing hundreds of lines of code to implement the effect (see the infinite splitting effect in Figure 2 as an example).

Image processing projects that require dynamic memory allocation for the image array can be used to reinforce students' understanding of pointers, function call semantics, type, and scope. Effects such as doubling the size of image or rotating the image by an arbitrary angle require dynamic memory allocation. When students are required to write functions to perform such tasks, they need to have a good understanding of pointers, including the ability to return a dynamically allocated 2-dimensional array, and getting the function prototype correct.

Image processing can be used as part of a larger problem that focuses on problem solving. For example, an eight-squares puzzle game with an image manipulation component could be used as a complete assignment, or as an extension of an earlier image processing project. Here students have to solve a more difficult problem where they need to keep state about the game board, modify the image after each step to reflect the move made by the user, detect and disallow invalid moves, and detect when the puzzle has been solved. For the Java version of this assignment, it is straightforward to add mouse click event handler methods for playing the game; for the C version, a text interface may be used to read in the user's next move.

For CS1 courses in Java, there are many image processing effects that can implemented because the Java Swing library is part of the Java language and it is fairly easy to use. Students can easily implement image processing effects in response to mousing events on a displayed image. For example, zooming into an arbitrary part of the image can be triggered by a mouse click, or arbitrarily rotating an image can be triggered by a mouse press-move-release sequence. Also, many drawing effects can be implemented in response to mouse events. In fact, most parts of a simple painting program, such as Microsoft's Paint [8], could be implemented as modifications to a displayed image; in response to mouse events, an eye dropper effect to select a color, a paint brush effect with different brush widths and brush types, a copy and paste effect, and an image cropping effect can be implemented.

3. OUR IMAGE PROCESSING PROJECTS

The primary goal of our CS1 project is to reinforce arrays and compound data types through the use of a real world application. We also accomplish a number of secondary goals: to illustrate the importance of good modular design; to illustrate the importance of implementing and testing code incrementally; to show the importance of efficiency and generalization in designing algorithms; to give students practice implementing sorting algorithms; to give students practice using makefiles; and to provide an opportunity for students to work in teams.

Our image processing project takes an image file as input, and then provides a menu or GUI interface to the user to select different image manipulation features such as blurring the image or rotating the image. Students implement each image modification as a separate function. Each image manipulation function takes the two dimensional image array as input. To solve the assignment, students must know how arrays are passed to functions, how to access array elements, and how to develop algorithms for processing the pixel array to get the desired effect.

Extra credit parts are used to challenge some of the more ambitious students. Some of the image manipulation features we suggest as extensions are quite difficult (like rotating the image to an arbitrary angle). We also encourage students to come up with their own features. This is a nice way to allow for some creativity and flexibility in a course where the assignments are often completely defined.

3.1 Greyscale Image Processing Project

The greyscale image processing project is given to students during the sixth week of class after introducing arrays and simple sorting algorithms. At that point in the semester, students have written functions, they know about local variables and scope, they have done some simple I/O, and they may have learned about C libraries. They have not, however, written large programs, nor do they know pointers or dynamic memory allocation, nor have they had to explicitly link in library code to build an executable file.

As a starting point, we give students a compiled image extraction and display library (such as a .so or .class file). The library contains functions to convert between an image file and a two-dimensional array of pixel values, and functions to display the modified image. We use the Java Swing Library [11] for Java, and libtiff and Tcl/Tk [9] for C. In the C version, image manipulations are stored to a temporary file that is then displayed by the GUI image viewer written in Tcl/Tk. The Tcl/Tk parts of our code could easily be replaced by code that uses an external image viewing program, like xv or a web browser, to view the modified image file after the user selects an effect.

We additionally give students a starting point source file containing a partially complete main function that calls some initialization functions in the image display library, a main loop function that prints a menu and reads in the user's menu option, and function prototypes for some of the image processing features they will implement. In the Java version, instead of a menu, the starting point code creates GUI buttons with associated action methods that will call the student-implemented image manipulation methods. We also provide a complete makefile for students to use to compile their program.

We provide function prototypes in this assignment's starting point because function writing is still quite new to the students, and because the syntax required for passing two dimensional arrays as parameters can be tricky. We also provide them with prototypes because we want them to see how a good, modularly designed solution is structured. Our survey results (see Section 3.3) show that the majority of our students feel that providing them with function prototypes was important to their successful completion of this project.

Students are required to implement a number of different image manipulation features, and are encouraged to implement extra features. For example, in the past we have required 15 features including making a negative of the image, flipping the image vertically and horizontally, switching the top left and bottom right corners, darkening, lightening, polarizing, scrolling both horizontally and vertically, zooming in (to the center or any of the four corners), blurring, rotating 90 degrees, sorting the rows by pixel value, and reverting

Figure 1: Example Image Processing Features. *Top Row, from left: revert to original, make negative, scroll vertically by some number of pixels (200 in this example). Middle Row: Rotate 90 degrees, Zoom (center zoom chosen), Sort Rows by pixel value. Bottom Row: Flip Vertically, Darken Image, Blur Image. (Grace Hopper image from* `www.arlingtoncemetery.net/ghopper.htm`*)*

to the original image (the other effects are cumulative). An example of some of these is shown in Figure 1. Some extra features we propose are edge detection, an eight-squares puzzle effect, displaying a histogram of pixel values, splitting the image, tiling effects, and rotating the image by an arbitrary degree amount. We provide students some pointers to on-line documentation about some of these effects. An example of some of the effects is shown in Figure 2.

Initially, fifteen required image features sounds daunting. However, students quickly see that by starting with some of the easier effects, like producing the negative image, they have a starting point for solving some of the more difficult effects. Some effects, such as blurring the image, cannot be done in-place on the image and require students to discover that they need to make a temporary copy of the image to correctly implement the effect. Students also need to be careful about stepping beyond the row or column bounds in their solutions. Often a strange looking result will help to reinforce this.

A few of the effects are a bit odd, and are included mainly for pedagogical reasons. For example, sorting the rows by pixel value may not be a useful, real-world image effect, but it is a nice way to have students implement a simple sorting algorithm as part of a larger assignment. Another example is the histogram effect where students must create a temporary array for the histogram, step through every pixel in the 2-D array to find the histogram values, and then figure out how to modify the image so that it displays the histogram. One

Figure 2: Example Extra Credit Image Processing Features. ***Top Row, from left: Eight Squares Puzzle, Edge Detect, Histogram of Pixel Values. Bottom Row: Split Image Right, A Tiling Effect, "Infinite Split"***

tricky part to this effect is that the histogram may need to be scaled. If, for example, a single pixel value occurs in the image more than the number of pixels in the height of the image, then the histogram bucket values need to be scaled so that they can be represented by a bar that fits within the height of the resulting image.

3.2 Color Image Processing Project

The color version of the project is introduced in the tenth week of classes after we cover structs. A color image is manipulated as a two dimensional array of RGB pixel structures. The pixels can be implemented as a struct in C, a class in C++ or Java, or as a three element array. Since the color version of the assignment comes later in the semester, we do not give as much starting point code as we do for the greyscale version. We still give students a complete makefile and part of a main function containing calls to our image processing library to create the initial 2-D array from an input image file. However, students are responsible for designing more of the program, including most of the function prototypes, themselves. We also require that students implement a solution that works for a color image of any size. This is a good way to reinforce pointers and dynamic memory allocation.

Many of the greyscale image processing features can be used in the color image assignment. In addition, students implement color "polarizing" features, where they shift all red values (for example) to extremes based on a threshold value. We have also taken pictures in front of a blue screen to create images that students can use for implementing background replacing features. Students can replace the blue background with different colors, different patterns, or with another image.

Some of the greyscale effects cannot be easily implemented in the full color version. For example, sorting rows by pixel value and the histogram effects may not make a lot of sense for color images. Of course, both effects could be done on a single R, G, or B pixel value, or on a function of each pixel's RGB values, but the resulting image will be strange and students can not easily tell if they have correctly implemented the effect.

3.3 Student Response to the Project

One of the most satisfying results of using these projects, aside from meeting pedagogical goals, is that students really enjoy them. It is so much easier for students to learn the material if they are excited and motivated to do the work.

To better quantify how well our projects meet our pedagogical goals, we surveyed 42 students in our introductory course about their experiences with the greyscale version of our project. Overall the students enjoyed the project and felt that it helped them to understand arrays. In Table 1 we show the percentage of students answering either "very helpful" or "helpful" to questions about how well the project help to reinforce their understanding of two-dimensional arrays.

Of the surveyed students, over 80% said that they "really enjoyed" or "enjoyed" the project, and only one student didn't like the project. Almost all students felt that it was at about the right level of difficulty, and most stated that it would have been difficult to complete without being given the function prototypes for some effects. Although a few students felt that the starting point code made the assignment "slightly easy", no student thought that it made the assignment "too easy". Given that students enter our introductory course with a wide range of previous programming experience, it is not surprising that a few students would find this assignment easy. Our survey results reinforced our feeling that giving students the function prototypes is appropriate for this assignment.

This is the first project where we strongly encourage students to work in pairs, and we wanted to gauge student reaction to this experience. Most students (36 out of 42) worked with a partner on this project. Almost all found it helpful to work with a partner; most mentioning that it was nice to split up the work, and that working with a partner was particularly useful for problem solving and debugging. One student stated "I liked working with a partner because we never got stuck for extended periods of time–whenever one of us was stumped the other usually came up with the solution." Another student mentioned that working with a partner "allowed us to brainstorm together and after discussing an idea we could come up with something that we probably wouldn't have thought up on our own." The only negative comments about working with a partner had to do with managing scheduling difficulties.

On both the survey and on course evaluations from previous semesters we asked students what they liked or disliked about the project and why. When we asked in course eval-

Project Helpful in Reinforcing Understanding of:	
arrays in general	86%
semantics of passing arrays	83%
array data access/manipulation	90%
searching and sorting algorithms	67%

Table 1: Survey results showing percentage of students who answered either "very helpful" or "helpful" to questions about how well the assignment helped reinforce their understanding of arrays.

uations which assignment was the favorite and why, nearly all students picked the image processing project. Most mentioned that it was fun and challenging. For example, one student said "The image lab was the highlight of the course." Several students also liked that it was a real-world problem: "I thought the picture lab was a lot of fun...[it] is nice to see how programming can be used in real applications" and "the graphics programs were awesome and very practical." Another student stated that she "thought it was a really cool assignment–it gave us the opportunity to manipulate images and actually feel like we were doing real programming." Another student stated that "I really enjoyed this assignment and felt that it allowed me a chance to see the effects of my program and develop some understanding of how my programs work."

Many students mentioned that they were surprised that they could complete what seemed like a very large assignment: "I liked this assignment because it gave us a chance to put the skills we had learned to use and create a program that produced visually impressive results. It seemed really intimidating at first, but it went pretty quickly and it was satisfying successfully implementing the effects." Some students also liked the open-ended aspect of the assignment: "Pictures were cool because [it was] open-ended." The only negative comments we heard about the assignment was that one student didn't like that we gave them function prototypes: "We were fiddling around with functions that were already given." Another student felt that the image manipulation features were a bit too repetitive and would have liked fewer features.

The survey results support what we had suspected about these projects based on our interactions with students: our students enjoy the projects, they like designing and implementing extensions, they like that the projects are real-world applications, and they feel a real sense of accomplishment in completing the projects. The results also fit our observations that in semesters when we have used these projects, students seem to have a better understanding of arrays and of the semantics of passing arrays to functions.

4. CONCLUSIONS

Image processing projects are an effective pedagogical tool for teaching a wide range of CS1 topics, including multidimensional arrays, function call semantics, and modular design. Although these are large programming projects, they can be structured in such a way that CS1 students can successfully complete them. Student reaction to these fun, real-world applications of CS1 material has been overwhelmingly positive, resulting in students who are more engaged in learning. Students feel a real sense of accomplishment in completing these projects and become more confident and capable programmers.

5. REFERENCES

[1] Abelson, H., and Sussman, G. J. *Structure and Interpretation of Computer Programs, Second Edition.* McGraw Hill, 2001.

[2] Astrachan, O., and Rodger, S. H. Animation, visualization, and interaction in CS1 assignments. *Proceedings of the twenty-ninth SIGCSE technical symposium on Computer science education* (February 1998).

[3] Burger, K. R. Teaching two-dimensional array concepts in java with image processing examples. *Proceedings of the Thirty-Forth SIGCSE Technical Symposium on Computer Science Education* (February 2003).

[4] Compuserve Information Service. Graphic Image Format.

[5] Fell, H. J., and Proulx, V. K. Exploring Martian planetary images: C++ exercises for CS1. *Technical Symposium on Computer Science Education Proceedings of the twenty-eighth SIGCSE technical symposium on Computer science education* (February 1997).

[6] Goodrich, M. T., and Tamassia, R. *Data Structures and Algorithms in Java, Second Edition.* John Wiley and Sons, Inc., 2001.

[7] Hunt, K. Using image processing to teach CS1 and CS2. *SIGCSE Bulletin 35*, 4 (December 2003), 86–89.

[8] Microsoft Corporation. Microsoft Paint. http://www.microsoft.com/.

[9] Ousterhout, J. K. An X11 toolkit based on the Tcl language. *Proceedings of USENIX Winter Conference* (1991).

[10] Roberts, E. *The Art and Science of C.* Addison Wesley, 1995.

[11] Sun MicroSystems. Java Swing Library, part of the Java 2 Platform. http://java.sun.com/j2se/.

[12] Wicentowski, R., and Newhall, T. Two image processing projects for a CS1 course. www.cs.swarthmore.edu/ ~newhall/imagemanip/.

The Impact of Virtual Classroom Laboratories in CSE

Matt Bower
Postgraduate Professional Development Program
Macquarie University
NSW, 2109, Australia
+61 2 98509104
mbower@ics.mq.edu.au

Debbie Richards
Computing Department
Macquarie University
NSW, 2109, Australia
+61 2 98509567
richards@ics.mq.edu.au

ABSTRACT

In order to gauge the pedagogical implications of conducting Computer Science practical sessions remotely, the Division of ICS at Macquarie University conducted a formal experiment using a virtual classroom environment called Macromedia Breeze Live. Research results indicated that students who completed their practical in the virtual classroom: i) felt they performed significantly more collaboration, ii) expressed a preference for this mode of practical session over regular laboratory sessions, iii) felt that they learnt significantly more from their classmates and iv) felt that they learnt significantly more from the practical supervisor than students in the standard classroom. Reasons for these results are proposed in the pedagogical context of offering Computer Science practical sessions online.

Categories and Subject Descriptors

K.3.2 [**Computers and Education**]: Computer and Information Science Education - *Computer Science Education*

General Terms

Measurement, Performance, Design, Experimentation.

Keywords

Virtual Classroom, Survey, Online Learning, Pedagogy.

1. INTRODUCTION

There has been much debate in educational circles regarding whether the media of delivery affects learning outcomes [2, 3]. Coinciding with this debate the need for a more scientific approach to research in Computer Science education has been identified [10]. In order to ascertain the educational efficacy of conducting Computer Science practical (or "laboratory") sessions using a virtual classroom environment, Macquarie University conducted a formal experiment involving eight lab classes.

2. BACKGROUND

There has been reported success in using online collaboration tools in a wide range of educational settings [5, 6, 9]. However these accounts consistently advise of the need to carefully consider the learning context and domain in order to provide an effective educational experience.

Computer Science education is unique because it requires the learner to simultaneously develop a logical understanding of the learning domain and the procedural capacity to implement it on a machine. Expert modeling has been proposed as an outstanding means to purvey proficiency in areas involving complex cognitive schema [4]. However to offer students such a "cognitive apprenticeship" in Computer Science means that students need to be able to hear the thoughts of their instructor at the same time as they see programming being performed. There is less research into whether or not virtual classrooms can effectively deliver this style of instruction to facilitate the learning of programming.

On a separate but related front the efficacy of collaborative approaches to learning has been supported by several Computer Science educators [8, 11, 12]. However there are potential obstacles, for instance a defensive classroom climate, that can stand in the way of effective implementation of collaborative approaches [1]. Given the increasing prevalence of online learning it is important to ascertain the degree to which collaborative processes can be successfully executed in virtual classroom environments and whether or not practical impediments to implementation can be overcome.

The purpose of this experiment was to formally determine the extent to which a virtual classroom environment could be used to offer students a valid learning experience in computer science and to measure the student utility of this approach compared to their standard laboratory sessions.

In the next section we briefly describe the experimental design used to conduct the research. This is followed by a section summarizing student feedback collected using a ten-point survey instrument. Finally a discussion of the findings and their resulting implications for Computer Science education is provided.

3. METHOD

The Division of ICS Breeze Trial was conducted during week 10 practical sessions for the second year Computer Science subject "Object Oriented Programming Practices" in Semester 1, 2004. Four out of 8 practical classes completed their week 10 practical in the "Breeze" virtual classroom environment and 4 in the "Standard" practical laboratory environment. Both groups covered content from the same practical exercises, which related to installation and use of the CVS version control system.

SIGCSE'05, February 23–27, 2005, St Louis, Missouri, USA.

The Macromedia "Breeze Live" [7] platform allows students to collaborate in a virtual classroom environment, either from home or from the on-campus computing laboratories. The environment provides text chat capabilities between all students and the practical supervisor as well as VoIP and webcam broadcast features (the later two facilities were only used by the practical supervisor). The software also provides desktop broadcasting capabilities (that were used extensively by the practical supervisor) and desktop sharing (which was used on occasion by the lecturer to take control of a student's desktop and show the class how to correctly execute a set of instructions).

After completing their week 10 practical students from both the "Breeze" and "Standard" groups were asked to complete the same questionnaire regarding how they felt the mode of delivery for the practical affected their learning. A summary of the responses to the survey is provided below.

4. RESULTS

Fifty-five responses to the feedback survey were received. The questions and results are presented here in sequential order.

Question 1: "For this practical I (H) attended a virtual classroom practical from home, (L) attended a virtual classroom practical in the labs, (N) attended a regular classroom practical in the labs"

Table 1: Distribution of participants

	H	L	N	Grand Total
Breeze	8	24	3	35
Standard	0	2	18	20
Grand Total	8	26	21	55

Note that two students were allocated to the Standard practical group but completed the virtual classroom practical from the labs. Also note that three students were allocated to the Breeze practical but attended the normal classroom practical from the labs. Because these five students self selected their treatment they have been excluded from data analysis for all further questions. This leaves a total of 32 students in the Breeze treatment group and 18 students in the Standard treatment group.

Question 2: "How much collaboration did you perform in this practical (with either your peers or the prac supervisor)?"

Table 2. Amount of collaboration performed

	None (0)	Very Little (1)	Some (2)	A lot (3)	Entirely w\others (4)	Total	Average	Standard Deviation
Breeze	1	4	15	9	3	32	2.28	0.924
Standard	7	5	4	2	0	18	1.06	1.056
Total	8	9	19	11	3	50	1.84	0.973

Highly significant difference ***between mean rating for Virtual Classroom versus Standard groups*** *(5 point Likert scale,* $t = 4.27$, $df = 48$, $p < 0.001$*)*

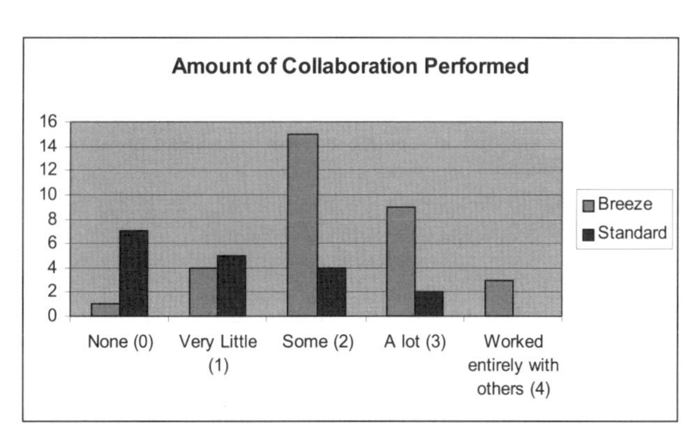

Figure 1: Collaboration - Virtual Classroom vs Standard Lab

Question 3a: "Would you have preferred to (C) collaborate with others during this practical, or (A) just work alone?

Table 3: Collaboration preferences

	Alone	Collaborate	Total	p-value*
Breeze	12	18	30	0.362
Standard	9	9	18	1
Total	21	27	48	0.471

**P-values based upon two-tailed binomial test for difference between proportion favoring collaboration versus working alone. No significant difference between preference for collaborating versus working alone for any groups.*

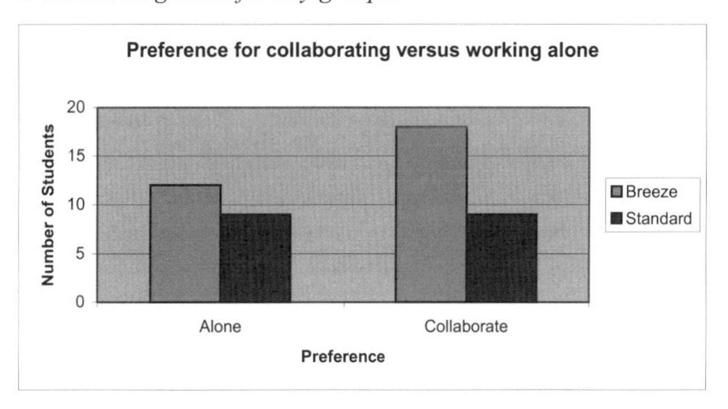

Figure 2. Preference for Collaboration/Working Alone

Question 3b - "How come?"

The open-ended responses to this question were classified by reasons for their learning preference. There were no outstanding differences between the types of reasons provided by students in the Breeze group as compared to the Standard group. The most common reasons for choosing to work alone were "less distractions" (8), "quicker" (4) and "flexibility" (2). The most common reasons for wanting to collaborate were "get help if stuck" (7), "value interacting with others" (4) and "learn more" (3). A broad spectrum of responses was recorded, with some representative comments provided below, for illustrative purposes.

"Don't tend to get distracted when solving a problem. Don't tend to lose track of thought." (Standard)

"Prac work generally progressed at the speed of the slowest student." (Breeze)

"Less distracted, however, it is good to do a little bit of collaboration in case you get stuck on something." (Standard)

"Collaboration after having a go alone. Good to be able to ask questions and get immediate answer and see the supervisor screen" (Breeze)

"it is easier to work with a group, it prevents you being trapped on a subject that you can't know." (Standard)

Question 4a: "Would you have preferred to collaborate in a (R) regular classroom environment or a (V) virtual/online classroom environment?"

Table 4 - Preferred Collaboration Mode

	Regular	Virtual	Total	p-value*
Breeze	7	25	32	0.002
Standard	8	9	17	1
Total	15	34	49	0.009

2-tailed p-value for difference between proportion favoring collaboration versus working alone based on a binomial distribution. Highly significant difference between number of students preferring a Regular classroom environment versus a Virtual classroom environment within the Breeze group and for the two groups combined

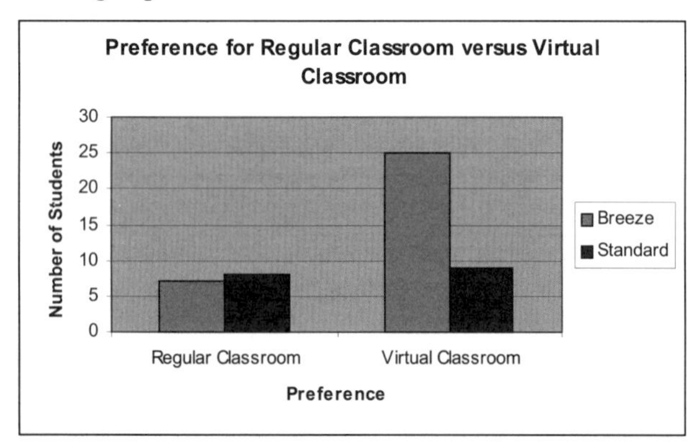

Figure 3: Preferred mode of delivery

Question 4b - "How come?"

When responses to this open ended question were classified into response type the main two reasons that people gave for preferring the Regular Classroom were that it was "clearer" (3) and was "less restrictive" (3) in terms of the pace and material covered. There was no outstanding difference between responses provided by students in the Breeze group as compared to the Standard group. Three representative comments from this group were:

"have to do the prac very quick in the virtual classroom I can take my time to do the prac in regular classroom" (Standard)

"Whilst I thought the online classroom was novel, and could be used well for external teachings, I felt it a bit restrictive in that I felt I had to stay at the same level the class was up to... even if I fell behind." (Breeze)

"I think it's harder to understand online than in the regular classroom, the audio was always breaking up or delayed" (Breeze)

However there was a noticeable difference between reasons provided by the Breeze and Standard groups for students preferring the Virtual Classroom over a Regular classroom. Those who were in the Standard group cited "flexibility" (4) more than all other reasons combined as the rationale for preferring a Virtual Classroom. On the other hand those in the Breeze group cited "more interesting/fun" (7), "clearer demonstrations" (3) and "more interactive" (3) as the main reasons for preferring a Virtual classroom. Some comments from students in the Breeze group expressing a preference for Virtual classroom collaboration include:

"I would prefer both, if I'm late or miss a class. I can go to the virtual classroom and relearn the material. This will obviously give varying advantages. But I like the ability to work from home and really focus on the work." (Breeze)

"I can be more of a participant in the discussion and the virtual (online) classrooom is more exciting and interesting..." (Breeze)

"The interaction between peers appears to be quicker than holding your hand up and waiting for a practical supervisor to come over and help." (Breeze)

Question 5 - "How difficult did you find this practical to follow?"

Table 5. Difficulty following the practical

Group	Very Difficult(0)	A bit difficult(1)	Average(2)	A bit easy(3)	Very easy (4)	Total	Average	Standard Deviation
B	0	9	14	4	4	31	2.10	0.978
S	2	4	9	2	1	18	1.78	1.003
T	2	13	23	6	5	49	1.98	0.989

No significant difference ***between mean rating for Breeze and Standard groups (t = 1.09, df = 47, p = 0.281)***

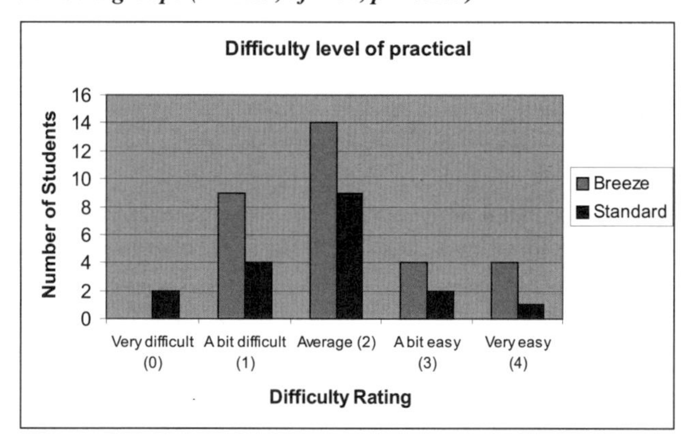

Figure 4: Difficulty of practical – Breeze versus Standard Lab

Question 6 - How much do you feel that you learnt from other students in this practical?

Table 6: Amount Learnt from other students

	Nothing(0)	A little bit(1)	Some(2)	Quite a bit (3)	A great deal(4)	Total	Average	Standard Deviation
Breeze	7	8	8	6	0	29	1.45	1.008
Standard	11	3	2	2	0	18	1.09	1.074
Total	18	11	10	8	0	47	1.17	1.029

Sig. diff. *between groups ($t = 2.23$, $df = 47$, $p = 0.030$)*

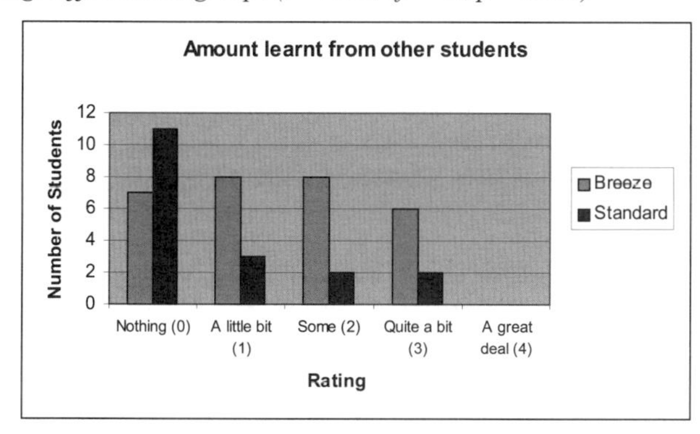

Figure 5: Amount learnt from other students

Question 7-"How much do you feel that you learnt from the practical supervisor in this practical?"

Table 7. Amount Learnt from Supervisor

	Nothing (0)	A little bit (1)	Some (2)	Quite a bit (3)	great deal (4)	Total	Average	Standard Deviation
B	1	7	9	11	3	31	2.26	1.032
S	8	4	6	0	0	18	0.89	0.900
T	9	11	15	11	3	49	1.76	1.182

Highly Significant difference between mean rating for Breeze and Standard groups ($t = 4.68$, $df = 47$, $p < 0.001$)

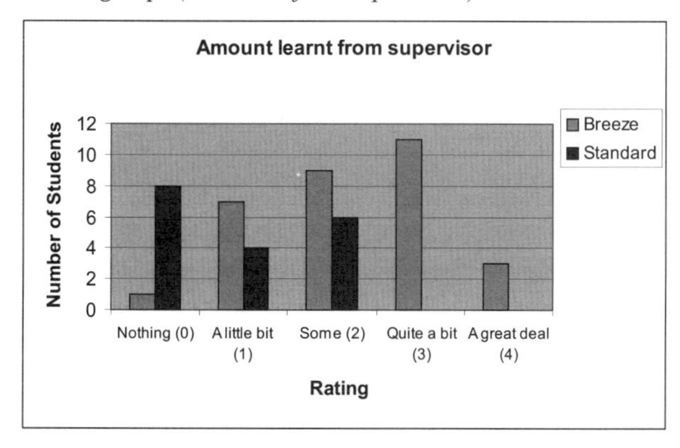

Figure 6: Amount learnt from supervisor

Question 8 -"What were the advantages of the practical you just completed?"

Students from the Standard group cited "learning new concepts" (5) as the main advantage of the practical. There were no other response classifications that occurred more than twice. In contrast students from the Breeze group cited "clearer demonstrations" (10), "interactivity/motivating" (5) and "flexibility" (3) as the main advantages of the practical session. Some comments include:

> "Being able to work thru the prac with vocal help. Even though it was choppy, watching the stepthru of the prac steps were a LOT clearer than the steps themselves" (Breeze)
>
> "we can contact with the presenter at the same time, so that we can ask and get the help at the same time..." (Breeze)
>
> "Have a base knowledge understanding of how to use CVS" (Standard)

Question 9 - "What were the disadvantages of the practical you just completed?"

The main disadvantages suggested by the Standard group were "inability to ask questions/interact" (4) and "difficult to understand" (2). On the other hand the Breeze group identified "bandwidth/audio quality" (7), "slow progress through the material" (6) and "working with the virtual classroom interface" (3) as the main drawbacks of the practical. Four comments include:

> "Very hard to follow what's going on without supervised help" (Standard)
>
> "little interaction with other class members" (Standard)
>
> "our text responses slows things down, plus the audio cuts off and on" (Breeze)
>
> "Hard to multi-task- the breeze window needs to be full screen, and so does the word doc I'm working in." (Breeze)

Question 10-"Please provide any other comments."

The responses to this open-ended question were roughly equally divided between positive and negative comments for both the Breeze and Standard group. The most notable aspect of this section is that 5 of the 7 negative responses relating to the Breeze practical were related to bandwidth/audio quality, particularly from students completing the work from home. A range of responses to this effect are provided below.

> "I'm connected to the system from college within uni, but it cost money!! It's still okay to me, but when I got suck at step 9, the class still solving the problem of step 4. " (Breeze from Home)
>
> "Breeze was excellent! I have broadband and a few words dropped out here and there, but this was not a problem. Quality of speech was excellent, quality of video was good but not required. Mostly was perhaps difficult for [the supervisor] answering different questions about different parts of the prac. Would be better perhaps if students were encouraged to go through the prac at their own pace and ask questions." (Breeze from Home)
>
> "didn't finish the prac. coz the 56k internet connection is too slow for this... if only by typing important messages... I prefer icq or msn. well, still it's good" (Breeze from Home)

5. DISCUSSION

There were several statistically significant results uncovered by this experiment, each with implications for Computer Science education. Firstly, students in the virtual classroom environment on average felt that they performed more collaboration than their peers who completed the standard practical session (ref. Question 2). Reasons for this could include that these students were able to review the text chat from other students in the class and even see their screen on occasions. This speaks well for the potential of virtual classrooms to implement collaborative learning.

The second significant result from this trial was that students who completed the Breeze practical expressed a preference for virtual classroom collaboration over regular classroom collaboration (ref. Question 4a). Obviously students from the Breeze group were as a whole making a much more informed decision about what collaboration in a virtual environment would entail because of the treatment to which they were exposed. It is difficult to ascertain how much of the preference was due to a novelty effect; a popular reason provided for preferring the platform was that it was "more interesting/fun". Also, the possibility of an effect caused by different practical supervisors needs to be considered.

Thirdly, the Breeze group had a significantly higher average rating of "amount learnt from other students" (ref. Question 6) than the Standard group. Assumedly this is a directly related to the fact that students in this group on average (felt like they) collaborated more than students in the Standard group (ref. Question 2). This provides formal evidence that students feel a virtual classroom environment can improve learning outcomes.

Finally, there was a significantly higher average rating of "amount learnt from the practical supervisor" in the virtual classroom group as opposed to the standard classroom group (ref. Question 7). Note that this again may be due to an effect caused by the practical supervisor rather than the Breeze environment. On the other hand it is encouraging that virtual classrooms can be used to provide a learning experience that students feel is substantially better than the practical classes they normally attend.

There are other notable findings from the data collected in this experiment. Firstly, the majority of students surveyed indicated that they preferred a collaborative approach to learning (ref. Question 3), which is encouraging in the context of the number of Computer Science educators who are shifting to this paradigm. Secondly, students who attended the virtual classroom session did not find the laboratory any more difficult than the face-to-face group (ref. Question 5).

On a practical level, Questions 9 and 10 revealed limited bandwidth was the main drawback of the virtual classroom environment trialed. This impacted upon audio and video quality, which are obviously core requirements for effective educational instruction. However it should be noted that a US server was used for this experiment. Subsequent trials with an on campus installation of the Breeze server lead to greatly improved performance both on the internal network and for students accessing the system from home on baseline broadband internet.

Some students commented that they had difficulty working with the virtual classroom interface. However, the fact that they were able to effectively participate in the laboratory session (and reported an improved learning experience across several indicators) without any prior training with the Breeze platform speaks well for the system's usability. Also, as users gain more experience with the platform it would be expected that they would be able to adjust some of the media settings within the Breeze application to further reduce any audio and video latency.

Throughout all open-ended responses words like 'fun', 'exciting' and 'motivating' were used in reference to the virtual classroom environment nine times but not at all for the Standard web module. On the one hand this could be discounted as merely a novelty effect. On the other it is reassuring to know that there is scope to improve levels of student engagement and satisfaction in Computer Science Education through the online medium.

6. REFERENCES

[1] Barker, L. J., Garvin-Doxas, K., and Jackson, M. Defensive climate in the computer science classroom. In *Proceedings of the 33rd SIGCSE technical symposium on Computer science education* ACM Press 2002, 43-47.

[2] Clark, R. E., Media will never influence learning. *Educational Technology Research and Development, 42*, 3 (1994), 21-29.

[3] Cobb, T., Cognitive Efficiency: Toward a Revised Theory of Media. *Educational Technology Research and Development, 45*, 4 (1997), 21-35.

[4] Collins, A., Brown, J., and Holum, A., Cognitive apprenticeship: Making thinking visible. *American Educator, 6*, 11 (1991), 38-46.

[5] English Language Systems (1997) Virtual Classroom Project Report. Last accessed 25th Nov 2004 [Available at: http://people.myplace.net.au/~els/report.htm]

[6] Haghirian, P., and Simon, B. Designing the Virtual Classroom: Towards an Effectiveness Model in International Marketing Teaching. In *Proceedings of the AMA Summer Marketing Educators*. (San Diego). 2002.

[7] Macromedia (2004) Breeze Live Overview. Last accessed Nov 25th 2004 [Available at: http://www.macromedia.com/software/breeze/overview/live/]

[8] Nagappan, N., Williams, L., Ferzli, M., Wiebe, E., Yang, K., Miller, C., and Balik, S., *Improving the CS1 experience with pair programming*, in *Proceedings of the 34th SIGCSE technical symposium on Computer science education*. 2003, ACM Press. p. 359-362.

[9] Prasolova-Forland, E., and Divitini, M. Collaborative virtual environments for supporting learning communities: an experience of use. In *Proceedings of the 2003 international ACM SIGGROUP conference on Supporting group work*. (Sanibel Island, Florida, USA). ACM Press 2003, 58-67.

[10] Valentine, D. W. CS educational research: a meta-analysis of SIGCSE technical symposium proceedings. In *Proceedings of the 35th SIGCSE technical symposium on Computer science education*. (Norfolk, Virginia, USA). ACM Press 2004, 255-259.

[11] Waite, W. M., Jackson, M. H., and Diwan, A., *The conversational classroom*, in *Proceedings of the 34th SIGCSE technical symposium on Computer science education*. 2003, ACM Press. p. 127-131.

[12] Williams, L., and Upchurch, R. L., *In support of student pair-programming*, in *Proceedings of the thirty-second SIGCSE technical symposium on Computer Science Education*. 2001, ACM Press. p. 327-331.

Closed Laboratories with Embedded Instructional Research Design for CS1

Leen-Kiat Soh, Ashok Samal, Suzette Person
Department of Computer Science and Engineering
University of Nebraska
256 Avery Hall, Lincoln, NE 68588-0115 USA
E-mail: {lksoh, samal, sperson}@cse.unl.edu

Gwen Nugent, Jeff Lang
National Center of Information Technology in Education (NCITE)
University of Nebraska
269 Mabel Lee Hall, Lincoln, NE 68588-0230 USA
E-mail: gnugent1@unl.edu, jefflang@unlserve.edu

ABSTRACT

Closed laboratories are becoming an increasingly popular approach to teaching introductory computer science courses. However, as observed in [1], "Considering the prevalence of closed labs and the fact that they have been in place in CS curricula for more than a decade, there is little published evidence assessing their effectiveness." In this paper we report on an integrated approach to designing and implementing laboratories with embedded instructional research design. The activities reported here are part of our department-wide effort to not only improve student learning in Computer Science and Computer Engineering, but also to improve the agility of our Computer Science and Engineering Department in adapting our curriculum to changing technologies, incorporate research, and validate the instructional strategies used. This paper presents the design and implementation of the labs and the results and analysis of student performance. Also described in this paper is how we have employed cooperative learning in our labs and how it impacts student learning.

Categories and Subject Descriptors

Course Related, CS Ed Research, CS1/2, Curriculum Issues

General Terms: Design, Experimentation

Keywords

Closed Laboratories, Cooperative Learning, Instructional Design

1 INTRODUCTION

Rapid and continuous changes in the areas of software development and information technology pose significant pressure on educational institutions in terms of educating and training the next generation of professionals. In particular, maintaining the curriculum in a computer science degree program is a challenge that requires constant attention. The Association for Computing Machinery (ACM) and IEEE Computer Society, the two leading professional bodies in the field of computer science, have recently released guidelines outlining core topics for a computer science degree program [2]. Subsequently, the Department of Computer Science and Engineering at the University of Nebraska-Lincoln reviewed its own undergraduate program in Computer Science with the long-term goal of redesigning and reorganizing the CS curriculum to improve the quality of instruction and student learning. Following this review, the Department approved an innovative curriculum that has the potential to significantly improve the quality of undergraduate CS education. One of the key innovations is the application of a traditional, science-based (e.g., Physics, Chemistry, Biology, etc.) approach to CS laboratories, *supported* by research in educational psychology and instructional design. The scope of this project includes our introductory CS courses (CS0, CS1, and CS2).

Closed laboratories are becoming an increasingly popular approach to teaching introductory CS courses [1], per the recommendations of Denning *et al.* [3] and ACM's Computing Curricula 1991 [4]. Closed labs have several advantages. Students learn at the beginning of their majors to be active learners through goal-oriented problem solving in a laboratory setting [5]. Doran and Langan [6] demonstrated that labs promote students' cognitive activities in comprehension and application, in terms of Bloom's taxonomy [7]. One study in fact, reported that even though their closed labs did not help improve retention or project completion rates in the CS1 course, there was a qualitative improvement in student learning in the closed lab sections [8]. Thweatt reported a statistical design with an experimental group (closed lab) and a control group (open labs) for a CS1 course and found that students in closed labs consistently performed significantly better on comprehensive CS1 exams than those in open labs [9]. Furthermore, exploration opportunities help first-time programmers overcome common hurdles, such as misconceptions about the nature of computers and programs [10]. Parker *et al.* found that closed laboratories demonstrate the scientific method of inquiry and teach skills in data collection and analysis [11]. The laboratory environment also facilitates cooperative learning among students e.g. [12]. Finally, laboratories tend to provide a more flexible environment that can cater to students of different backgrounds and learning styles. However, as observed in [1], "Considering the prevalence of closed labs and the fact that they have been in place in CS curricula for more than a decade, there is little published evidence assessing their effectiveness."

In this paper, we present a systematic approach to design, implement, assess, and evaluate closed labs. To demonstrate the effectiveness of the approach, we focus on measuring the impact of

SIGCSE'05, February 23–27, 2005, St. Louis, Missouri, USA.

cooperative learning in laboratory settings and analyzing the results pedagogically.

2 COOPERATIVE LEARNING

Our approach to incorporating labs in introductory CS courses, as reported in this paper, is based on embedding instructional research design and assessment components into each laboratory. This guides and motivates the design and development process for each laboratory in the way we developed the pre- and post-tests and the activities. In this paper, we report on the incorporation of *cooperative learning* into our labs and studies.

While direct instruction has been shown to be effective in certain domains, studies have shown *cooperative learning* to be an effective pedagogy for CS, producing significant gains in student achievement [13-15]. Other advantages of cooperative learning are the development of communication and problem solving skills [16]. Most of our students intend to join private industry where collaboration and teamwork are the norm, so collaborative learning in college settings better prepares students for what they will most likely encounter after graduation [17]. Direct instruction at the college level tends to emphasize individual skills, and is often removed from environments encountered in industry [18]. Cooperative learning can help students "become aware of the significance of small group dynamics as a tool for task achievement and success in a team environment" [17]. We relied primarily on the work of Johnson and Johnson [19] to model the implementation of cooperative learning in our CS1 laboratories.

For cooperative learning to be superior to individualistic, competitive approaches, five elements are necessary: *positive interdependence*, *face-to-face promotive interaction*, *individual and personal accountability*, *interpersonal skills*, and *group processing* [19]. Positive interdependence requires that group members "encourage and assist each other to do well" [20]. The students should feel that they will succeed or fail together. Face-to-face promotive interaction can be defined as individuals encouraging and facilitating each others' efforts to achieve, complete tasks, and produce in order to reach the group's goals [20]. Individual accountability and personal accountability involve each group member providing their "fair share" of work and feedback. Interpersonal and small group skills address the group members' ability to positively interact and support one another. All five essential "elements" are included in our laboratory design.

3 DESIGN & IMPLEMENTATION

The process of redesigning the CS curriculum was preceded by extensive interactions between researchers from four academic departments: Computer Science and Engineering, Educational Psychology, Curriculum & Instruction, and Instructional Design. Much of the design was formalized through a joint seminar course organized in Spring 2003. The emphasis was not only on the development of novel approaches to deliver and assess course materials that promote "deep" learning, but also on developing a framework in which we can conduct systematic evaluation of the approaches and their short- and long-term effectiveness. Therefore it was important that cognitive and experimental psychologists and instructional designers be an integral part of this effort from the beginning. Due to the vast scope of this project, we decided to first focus on our CS1 course. In addition to lectures, students in our CS1 course attend a programming laboratory that meets for two hours each week. Approximately 25-30 students attend each lab section. The labs provide students with structured, hands-on activities intended to reinforce and supplement the material covered in the course lectures. Although brief instruction may be provided, the majority of the lab period is allocated to student activities.

3.1 Laboratory Design

The first step in developing the labs was to create a base document for each lab that included: the lab's objectives, prerequisite knowledge, tools required, instruction topics, activities and exercises, supplemental resources, follow-on assignments, relevance to course goals, Curriculum 2001 core topics addressed, and ideas for pre- and post-test questions.

After a review of the base documents individually and collectively by CS faculty, each lab was developed by creating a series of five documents in parallel, including (1) a student handout, (2) a laboratory worksheet, (3) an instructional script, (4) a pre-test, and (5) a post-test.

The student handout serves several purposes. It is both the preparation guide and the laboratory script. Each handout includes the lab objectives, a description of the activities that will be performed during the lab (including the source code where appropriate), a list of references to supplemental materials that should be studied prior to the lab and a list supplemental references that can be reviewed after the student has completed the lab. The student handout also provides optional activities that can be completed during or following the lab to give students an opportunity for extra practice.

During each lab, students are expected to answer a series of questions for each activity and record their answers on a worksheet (paper). Worksheets contain questions specifically related to the lab activities and are intended to provide the students with an opportunity to find the answers through programming-based exploration. These worksheets also serve as an assessment tool to gauge the student's comprehension of topics learned and practiced in the lab.

In addition to the student handout, the lab instructor is provided with an instructional script that provides supplemental material that may not be covered during lecture, special instructions for the lab activities, hints, resource links, and useful insights. Additional space is provided at the end of the instructions for each activity to allow the instructor to record his or her comments regarding the activity and suggestions for improving the lab.

The lab pre-tests are on-line and students are required to pass them prior to coming to lab, however, students may take each pre-test as many times as necessary to achieve a passing score (80%). The pre-test is open-book and open-note, and includes multiple-choice, short answer and true/false questions. The goals of the lab pre-test are to encourage students to prepare for the lab and to allow them to test their understanding of the lab objectives and concepts prior to attending the lab. Questions for the pre-test are taken from a variety of sources including the course textbook, other textbooks, and questions found on the web. Questions are categorized according to Bloom's Taxonomy [7].

During the last ten minutes of each lab, students take an on-line post-test as another measure of their comprehension of lab topics. Like the pre-test, questions are taken from a variety of sources and are also categorized according to Bloom's Taxonomy [7]. It should be noted that the goal of the post-test is designed to assess how well they learned the concepts after they have performed the activities specifically designed to reinforce the concepts.

Table 1 shows the list of CS1 laboratories and their corresponding objectives. We incorporated two event-driven programming labs; the first lab introduces students to the differences between event-driven programming and traditional sequential programming; the second lab addresses the capabilities and features of event-driven programming. We designed three testing and debugging labs. The first lab introduces the idea of debugging to students and teaches them how to debug using simple print statements and built-in features of the IDE, and how to identify the different bugs. The second lab describes a more systematic, holistic approach to debugging, with different strategies such as a debug flag. The third lab introduces testing components from the viewpoint of software engineering, such as test cases and drivers. Overall, the three labs progress from simple, reactive debugging to more goal-directed debugging, to standardized testing.

Table 1. Laboratory Topics of Our CS1 Course.

No.	Labs
1	Introduction to IDE & the Computing Environment
2	Simple Class
3	Documentation
4	Testing and Debugging 1
5	File I/O
6	Applets and Applications
7	Event Driven Programming 1
8	Exceptions
9	GUI/Swing
10	Event Driven Programming 2
11	Testing and Debugging 2
12	Inheritance
13	Testing and Debugging 3
14	Recursion

3.2 Instructional Research Design

As mentioned in the previous sections, our approach to implementing CS1 laboratories includes embedded instructional research design to systematically study the effect of our design on student learning. We have modeled our design based on the work of Johnson and Johnson [19] to include the five essential elements discussed in Section 2. Here, we focus on an investigation of cooperative learning in our labs.

3.2.1. Study 1: Effective Pedagogy for CS1 Labs (Part I)

The purpose of Study 1 was to determine the most effective pedagogy for CS1 laboratory achievement. According to the social constructivist view, the cooperative groups should perform higher than the direct instruction group.

Participants: The participants were 68 traditional undergraduate students from the University of Nebraska-Lincoln. Of the 68 students, 5 were female. The study was conducted during the Fall semester of 2003.

Procedures: The three laboratory structures used were: *cooperative group with structure*, *cooperative group without structure*, and *direct instruction*. The difference between the two cooperative groups was the structure of the group: formal versus informal. The cooperative structured group (formal) had defined roles that alternated each week. The laboratory instructor was responsible for monitoring which student "drives" and which students review. The goal of this format was to develop interdependence among the group members based on the environment (a shared computer) and breaking the tasks into smaller parts with each member responsible for a part. By doing so, the group only functioned if each individual contributed his or her part for the whole group to complete their goal.

The cooperative unstructured group was similar to the cooperative structured group in that we wanted to create interdependence among the group members. The difference was that for this group format, we did not control the roles of the group members. The members were responsible for assigning roles and completing tasks. In both groups, the lab instructor served as a facilitator giving both groups the freedom to solve problems themselves.

The last group format used in our study was direct instruction. This is the classical format in which students work individually and competitively against other class members. This group served as the control group. The role of the instructor was to answer individual questions and discourage cooperation while students completed laboratory exercises.

We randomly assigned the pedagogy of each laboratory section (cooperative structured, cooperative unstructured or direct instruction). For the students enrolled in a section employing the cooperative approach, we used stratified random assignment to assign students to their cooperative groups. This was accomplished by ranking the placement test scores used for this course. The scores were grouped into three categories: high, middle, and low. , Students were selected from each group at random and placed in the cooperative group where they would remain for the entire semester. This was to ensure heterogeneous grouping, which has been shown to be the most effective approach [19].

Dependent Measures: We used total laboratory grades and a pre-post-test measuring self-efficacy and motivation as our outcome measures. The combined outcome measures provide evidence of the effectiveness of laboratory pedagogy and achievement. Total laboratory grades were measured by combining post-test grades and worksheet scores for each lab. Although some students worked in cooperative groups, all students were required to individually complete the post-test in the laboratory.

The second outcome measured students' self-efficacy and motivation during the first and last week of the semester. The tool used to measure these constructs adapted eight questions taken from the Motivated Strategies for Learning Questionnaire (MSLQ) developed by Pintrich and De Groot [21]. Students were instructed to respond to a five-point Likert scale (1=strongly disagree to 5=strongly agree) providing their estimated self-efficacy and motivation for CS. Our questionnaire returned a reliability measure (Cronbach Alpha) of .90 with a mean of 3.45 and standard deviation of .09; a Cronbach Alpha value of at least 0.8 is considered sufficient for statistical validity.

Results: The first research question examined was student achievement in the laboratory. Analysis of variance (ANOVA) was used to determine significant differences between the sample means of cooperative groups with structure, cooperative groups without structure, and direct instruction. An ANOVA takes the variance (differences) between the three sample means and normalizes them using the variance (differences) within the groups accounting for sampling error. A significant result, less than .05, indicates that the differences between the group means was something other than chance. Both cooperative learning groups performed significantly higher than the direct instruction group ($F(2,66)=6.325$, $p<.05$) as measured by the final lab grade, as shown in Table 2.

Table 2. ANOVA statistics comparing laboratory grades for each laboratory group. F-statistic is $F(2,66)=6.325$, and significance level is $p=0.003$.

	Sum of Squares	Deg. of Freedom	Mean Sq. Values
Between Groups	100825.8	2	50412.915
Within Groups	526034.4	66	7970.218

The second research question examined differences in students' self-efficacy and motivation before and after CS1 using paired samples t-test. Six of the 8 questions showed statistically significant changes in student perceived self-efficacy and motivation. Troubling was that 7 of 8 questions actually *decreased* from the first application to the second. Table 3 shows the survey questions and the scores before and after the course. The table also shows the t-test scores; a t-score of 2 or greater is considered significant.

Table 3. Self-efficacy measure before and after the CS1 course

Self-efficacy/Motivation Survey Questions	Pre CS1	Post CS1	t values (dof=71)
1. I am confident in my CS knowledge and abilities.	3.47	3.57	-0.54
2. I am motivated to learn more about CS/technology.	4.22	3.5	4.1*
3. I did an excellent job on the problems and tasks assigned for this class.	3.86	3.39	3.14*
4. I valued the opportunity to apply what was taught in lecture in a lab setting.	4.01	3.44	4.25*
5. I valued the opportunities to interact and collaborate with other students in the class.	3.82	3.29	2.64*
6. I was academically prepared to take this course.	3.89	3.53	2.06*
7. Compared to other students in the class, I did well.	3.69	3.44	1.69
8. I think I will receive a good grade in this class.	3.88	3.46	2.6*

** Statistical significance at p<.05*

Discussion: The first question of interest was achievement in the laboratories. Research has shown the importance of laboratories in CS and our study built on this premise. By manipulating the pedagogy used, we determined that cooperative learning is the most effective learning approach. We were surprised that there proved to be no significant difference between the structured and unstructured cooperative groups. We did not control how the unstructured groups chose to define roles (driver vs. reviewer), which may have led to the similar results between the cooperative groups. The significant differences between the cooperative groups and direct instruction support our cognitive-developmental theory that it is better to work in groups than in isolation. The results provide us with enough evidence and reason to continue cooperative grouping in the CS1 laboratories.

The second research question of students' self-efficacy and motivation returned some unexpected results. Students seemed to actually decrease in motivation and self-efficacy from the beginning of the semester to the end. We believe this may be due to inflated self-efficacy coming into the course or even poorly worded items on the self-efficacy/motivation tool. For example, we did not split out the students based on their chosen majors. Therefore, the question asking if the student intended to pursue CS would return a negative value regardless of their experience in the CS1 course since there are a significant number of non-majors in this course due to requirements of many departments to take this course. All the same, students left our class feeling more confident in their CS skills but less motivated to continue in the field of computer science and engineering. The result of our self-efficacy/motivation tool requires further investigation.

3.2.2. Study 2: Effective Pedagogy for CS1 Labs (Part II)

In Study 2, we repeated Study 1 with revisions to the motivation/self-efficacy tool and the addition of qualitative feedback from the students. The participants were 66 traditional undergraduate students from the University of Nebraska-Lincoln. Of the 66 students, 7 were female. The study was conducted during the Spring semester of 2004. The procedures and dependent measures used were the same as in Study 1. Due to the limits on space and the similarity of results with those in Study 1, only a summary of the results are included in this paper.

Results: The first research question examined was student achievement in the laboratory. Both cooperative learning groups performed higher than the direct instruction group ($F(2,64)=2.408$, $p<.05$) as measured by the final lab grade.

The second research question measured students' self-efficacy and motivation before and after CS1 using paired samples *t* test. 6 of the 9 questions showed statistically significant changes in student perceived self-efficacy and motivation. As with Study 1, several measures decreased from the first application to the second.

Discussion: Again, the first question of interest was achievement in the laboratories. The results were different from Study 1 in that statistical significance was not achieved. There was, however, a definite trend towards the cooperative groups achieving higher scores than the direct instruction group. Again, there proved to be no significant difference between the structured and unstructured cooperative groups.

The last research question of students' self-efficacy and motivation returned similar results to Study 1. We continue to feel that students bring with them inflated self-efficacy related to CS knowledge and become less motivated to pursue CS as a major after getting a true feel for the field.

3.2.3. Cooperative Learning: General Discussion

The studies showed that a majority of students preferred working in groups. The reasons provided ranged from the shared problem solving to the social interaction. Not all students assigned to cooperative groups preferred group work. A few stated that they simply preferred to work alone while some students in the direct instruction group complained of the "unfairness" of not being allowed to work with others. The lab instructor corroborated this conclusion and added that a sense of community was developed via grouping.

Implications: Our Reinventing CS Curriculum Project includes a research component focused on discovering the most effective laboratory design. Although laboratories have been used in CS courses in the past, their effectiveness has not generally been measured. The findings of this study have implications for CS laboratory pedagogy. The most significant is the result that shows cooperative groups attain higher achievement than the individual, direct instruction approach. Our results show that the ACM2001 curriculum paired with the cooperative learning pedagogy not only produces higher achievement but also is consistent with the environment students will find in private industry.

4 CONCLUSIONS

We have described an integrated approach using embedded instructional research design to design and implement closed labs for CS1, the first course in a typical CS curriculum. We now have in place a process that guides our lab design and implementation, collects data for our studies based on both quantitative measurements and qualitative surveys, and allows for refinement of the labs as a result of the analysis. We have shown in this paper how we embed cooperative learning and instructional technology into our laboratory design with positive results. We have also shown how qualitative surveys are used to support the validation of our design and guide subsequent lab revisions.

Based on the above results, we have made changes to our labs for CS1. We have also designed and implemented a set of labs for CS2 using the same approach. Both sets of labs were used in the Spring 2004 semester, and will be used in Fall 2004. We have added new labs to include software testing using an on-line tool and complemented the simple class and recursion labs with multimedia flash-based learning objects. For Fall 2004, we will introduce on-line agent-based learning materials for five CS1 labs. We will continue to conduct studies to improve the validity and confidence of the results of our project. We intend to pursue the cooperative learning pedagogy in our CS1 laboratories based on the findings from our studies.

ACKNOWLEDGEMENT

The Reinventing CS Curriculum Project is supported in part by NCITE and CSE at the University of Nebraska. We would like to thank A. Zygielbaum, C. Riedesel, C. Chen, S. Kasinadhuni, J. Bernadt, A. Kosenander, T. Fink, K. Halsted, X. Liu, J. Mallik, and S. Das for their help in implementing this project.

REFERENCES

[1] R. McCauley, W. Parrs, G. Pothering, and C. Starr (2003). A Proposal to Evaluate the Effectiveness of Closed Laboratories in the Computer Science Curriculum, *J. Computing Sciences in Colleges*, **19**(3):191-198.

[2] ACM/IEEE Joint Task Force on Computing Curricula Staff, Computing Curricula 2001: Computer Science, IEEE Press, 2002.

[3] P.J. Denning, D. E. Comer, D. Gries, M. C. Mulder, A. Tucker, A. J. Turner, and P. R. Young (1989). Computing as a Discipline, *CACM*, **32**(1):9-23.

[4] A. Tucker, A., *et al., (*1991). Computing Curricula 1991: Report of the ACM/IEEE-CS Joint Curriculum Task Force", ACM Press.

[5] B.C. Parker, and J. D. McGregor (1995). A Goal-Oriented Approach to Laboratory Development and Implementation, *SIGSCE'95*, Nashville, TN, pp. 92-96.

[6] M.V. Doran and D. D. Langan (1995) A Cognitive-Based Approach to Introductory Computer Science Courses: Lessons Learned", *SIGCSE'95*, Nashville, TN, pp. 218-222.

[7] B.S. Bloom, B. B. Mesia, and D. R. Krathwohl (1964). *Taxonomy of Educational Objectives (two vols: The Affective Domain & The Cognitive Domain)*, David McKay, New York.

[8] A.N. Kumar (2003). The Effects of Closed Labs in Computer Science I: An Assessment, *J. Computing Sciences in Colleges*, **18**(5):40-48.

[9] M. Thweatt (1994). CS1 Closed Lab vs. Open Lab Experiment, *SIGCSE'94*, Phoenix, AZ, pp. 80-82.

[10] R. Lischner (2001). Explorations: Structured labs for First-Time Programmers", *SIGCSE'2001*, Charlotte, NC, pp. 154-158.

[11] J. Parker, R. Cupper, C. Kelemen, D. Molnar, and G. Scragg (1990). Laboratories in the Computer Science Curriculum, *Computer Science Education*, **1**(3):205-221.

[12] S. R. Oliver, and J. Dalbey (1994). A Software Development Process Laboratory for CS1 and CS2, *SIGCSE'94*, Phoenix, AZ, pp. 169-173.

[13] A. Joseph and M. Payne (2003). Group Dynamics and Collaborative Group Performance", *SIGCSE'2003*, Reno, NV, pp. 368-371.

[14] T. Gatfield (1999). Examining Student Satisfaction with Group Projects and Peer Assessment, *Assessment and Evolution in Higher Education*, **24**(4):365-377.

[15] M. Malinger (1998). Collaborative Learning Across Borders: Dealing with Student Resistance, *J. Excellence in College Teaching*, **9**(1):53-68.

[16] Z. Qin, D. Johnson, and R. Johnson (1995). Cooperative versus Competitive Efforts and Problem Solving, *Review of Educational Research*, **65**(2):129-143.

[17] K. A. Yerion and J. A. Rinehart (1995). Guidelines for Collaborative Learning in Computer Science, *SIGCSE Bulletin*, **27**(4):29-34.

[18] J. C. Prey (1995). Cooperative Learning in an Undergraduate Computer Science Curriculum, *FIE'95 Conference.*

[19] D. W. Johnson and R. T. Johnson (1991). *Learning Together and Alone: Cooperative, Competitive, and Individualistic Learning* (3rd ed.), Prentice Hall, Upper Saddle River, NJ.

[20] M. Jensen, D. W. Johnson and R. T. Johnson (2002). Impact of Positive Interdependence during Electronic Quizzes on Discourse and Achievement, *J. Educational Research,* **95**:161-166, 2002.

[21] P. R. Pintrich and E. V. DeGroot (1990). Motivational and Self-Regulated Learning Components of Classroom Academic Performance, *J. of Educational Psychology*, **82**(1):33-40.

An Introductory Software Engineering Course that Facilitates Active Learning

Stephanie Ludi
Rochester Institute of Technology
134 Lomb Memorial Drive
Rochester, NY 14613
(585) 475-7407
salvse@rit.edu

Swaminathan Natarajan
Rochester Institute of Technology
134 Lomb Memorial Drive
Rochester, NY 14613
(585) 475-4663
sxnvcs@rit.edu

Thomas Reichlmayr
Rochester Institute of Technology
134 Lomb Memorial Drive
Rochester, NY 14613
(585) 475-2852
tjrese@rit.edu

ABSTRACT
At the Rochester Institute of Technology, the undergraduate introductory software engineering course has been redesigned from a lecture-lab format to a project-centric studio format. The new format blends the lecture material with the project work. As a result, students drive their own learning experience based on scaffolding created by the course design. The challenges faced and the techniques and strategies utilized in the planning and delivery of the course will be discussed, including the utilization of online learning support infrastructure. This paper presents instructor experiences, analysis of student feedback, lessons learned and recommendations for other educators considering an active learning approach for their courses.

Categories and Subject Descriptors
D.2.9 [**Software Engineering**]: Management- *programming teams.*
K.3.1 [**Computers and Education**]: Computer Uses in Education–*collaborative learning.*
K.3.2 [**Computers and Education**]: Computer and Information Science Education: *curriculum.*

General Terms
Management

Keywords
Software Engineering, Active Learning, Cooperative Learning, Student Teams, Student Centered Instruction

INTRODUCTION
The learning paradigm for computing courses has remained almost intact for the last 25 plus years. Under this paradigm, students in a course meet weekly for lecture and then for a lab, but experience has shown that students often have trouble "connecting" what is taught in class with what is required from them in lab. While research eloquently shows the many advantages of the studio format, implementing an active, studio-centric learning environment presents many challenges. A balanced collaboration between students and instructor is required to achieve the full potential of this approach, with the instructor's role shifting from knowledge disseminator to learning facilitator. Students must accept more responsibility for their own learning and adapt to a classroom style that is different from that experienced in previous courses.

The introductory software engineering (SE) course at RIT (SE361) is a sophomore-level required course for software engineering, computer science and computer engineering majors. RIT operates on a quarter system, consisting of 10 weeks of classes followed by an "exam week" at the end of each quarter. Fifteen to twenty sections of the course with up to 20 students each are taught during each academic year, by 8-10 different instructors. Because of this, the structure and delivery of this course are heavily streamlined. Until the Fall of 2003, this course had been delivered in the classic lecture-lab format with three hours of lecture per week and a two hour lab session.

The primary objectives of our introductory SE course are twofold: First, to give students the opportunity to experience teamwork while working on a term-long project that spans a full development lifecycle, applying effective SE practices, and following a process discipline. And second, to expose students to fundamental concepts of software design and process such as lifecycle models, design patterns, testing and estimation.

Among the problems we experienced with the classic format was that students perceived lecture and lab as two disparate experiences. While the lab allowed them to participate in software engineering activities, the lecture "only taught them a few basic SE principles". Although lectures took significant time per week, students did not see them as adding value to their projects. Lectures became monologues where instructors spoke about subjects the students perceived as tangential to their lab project. Students tended to learn the material for the sake of exams, rather than relating it to their project work and as being fundamental to understanding software engineering.

The even more serious impact of the perceived disconnect between lecture and lab was its influence on perhaps the most important

SIGSCE'05, February 23-27, 2005, St. Louis, Missouri, USA

desired course outcome: understanding the need for process discipline and sound SE practices. It was the lecture that discussed the underlying rationale, but this was viewed as "theory". The labs were graded on a defined set of deliverables, which were viewed as outputs to be produced, without much thinking as to why they were needed.

Over the past two years, we have focused on strategies for the improved delivery of this important foundational course in our curriculum. Our first step was to move the student team project component from a heavy-weight, waterfall development model to an iterative one using a lighter-weight, more agile approach to process [1]. This model allowed students to develop their projects in increments and provided the opportunity to experience a more realistic environment where changes are introduced during the course of a product's development life-cycle. It also provided the instructor with more opportunities for feedback that could be incorporated into future development iterations.

Although the move to an agile project component helped generate enthusiasm among the students, a disconnect between lecture and lab still lingered. To address this issue, we designed our course in a manner that would move students from passive lecture spectators to engaged, active learners, and more effectively integrate the course's project component. The redesigned course structure and its implementation results are the focus of the remainder of this report.

1. TOWARDS A MORE ACTIVE SE361

The Software Engineering Department at RIT has committed itself to engaging students and creating an active classroom environment through systemic change in the courses that make up its curriculum. During the summers of 2002 and 2003 department faculty attended Project Catalyst workshops at Bucknell University [2,3] designed to introduce active learning techniques and aid in course re-design that adopts student centered instruction. Student-centered instruction shifts the responsibility of learning from one that is entirely the instructor's to a shared responsibility between student and instructor [4]. Student-centered instruction requires students not only to passively listen and take notes, but to engage in such higher-order thinking tasks such as analysis, synthesis, and evaluation [7]. This approach transfers the responsibility to students. Students bear the responsibility for constructing their own knowledge and participating in activities that require social interaction between other students and the instructor.

Our goal in redesigning the course was to focus on shifting the traditional lecture portion of the course more towards student-centered interaction as shown in the active learning spectrum in Figure 1. The solid arrows represent the previous SE361 lecture and lab, and the dashed arrows represent goals for the re-designed course.

The active learning spectrum is defined by the following four phases [2]:

- *Active Learning* – students actively participate in learning using individual activities with the opportunity to interact with other students.
- *Collaborative Learning* – more interaction with other students, informal group activities.
- *Cooperative Learning* – formal, structured team activities.
- *Problem Based Learning* – problem situations drive learning activities on a need to know basis.

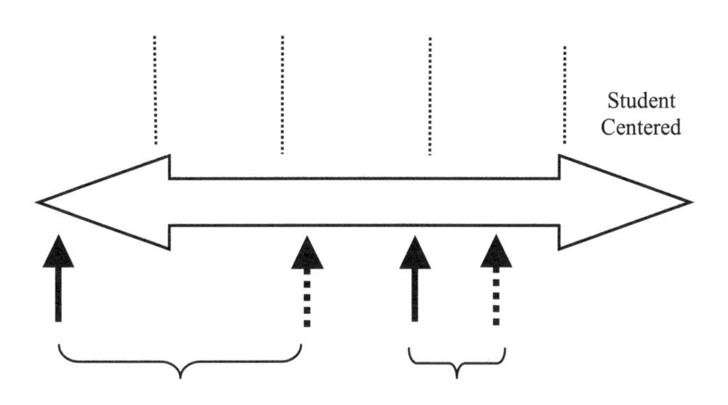

Figure 1. Active Learning Spectrum

Having just gone through a major re-design of the course's project component in the previous year, we decided to leave the format of the project intact. Minor tweaks were made to make the project's problem statement more open ended and provide for creative approaches by the student teams [6].

In addressing the lecture component of the new course we had the benefit of tapping into the experiences of another course in our program that had recently undergone a similar redesign [5]. While that course transformation traversed the active learning spectrum all the way to problem based learning, the experiences gained making lectures more student centered at the active and cooperative learning levels were very helpful here.

2.1 The Redesigned Course

The first step in our redesign was to align the lecture material with the project's flow to achieve their integration. Because so much of the lecture material is needed so early in the course, this proved to be a significant challenge. As mentioned earlier, the project had recently been modified to use an agile, iterative development approach.

The first project iteration, R1, was due at the end of the 5th week, and required basic implementations of the major functionality. The second iteration, R2, due at the end of week 8, added a graphical user interface and included nearly all of the product features. The final iteration, R3, was basically a perfecting release that included thorough testing and bug-fixing, and cosmetic improvements such as help facilities.

This schedule meant that R1 would itself involve a complete software engineering lifecycle, including requirements definition, planning and process choices, architecture and design, integration and testing, and proper configuration management. Therefore we had to provide the student teams the theoretical foundations in all of these areas within the first five weeks of lecture. In addition, students were also being exposed to a new development environment and configuration management tool [8]. Achieving this fast-paced approach to learning while moving away from instructor-centric lectures was particularly challenging.

To accomplish this, we adopted a three-pronged strategy. Firstly, a two-pass strategy was adopted in the coverage of theory material. On the major topics such as design, testing and processes, the first pass focused on the basic concepts and understanding needed for the successful execution of project activities. The second pass covered more advanced topics such as design patterns, dynamic modeling, interface design and evaluation, alternative integration strategies etc., which would be needed for the second and third parts of the project.

The second part of the strategy was to design in-class activities on each topic that would enable students to apply the concepts and familiarize themselves with the practices during class. Some of these activities were related to the project, while others were standalone activities. These activities served as a bridge between theory and practice, and ensured that they gained the competences needed for the project.

The third part of the strategy was to change the role of lectures from covering material to helping students integrate the material and provide perspective. The students were expected to prepare for class by reading relevant sections from the textbook and other sources, and the lectures and in-class activities completed and consolidated this learning process, rather than relying on lectures as the primary source of knowledge.

2.2 Course Structure

The resulting course structure consisted of three components: lectures, in-class activities and project work. We defined weekly milestones for the project, and matched weekly lecture topics to the milestones. The course was scheduled so that there were two two-hour sessions each week. We conceptually divided each session approximately into four half-hour blocks, and allocated these blocks as either lecture, activity or project blocks, with a goal of having roughly equal numbers of each of the three over the course. Most sessions had at least two types of blocks. The idea of this was to facilitate multiple modes of instruction and learning. The resulting course plan is shown in Table I.

The lecture component is relatively high during weeks 2-4 (typically two lecture blocks per session), and tapers off significantly towards the end of the course, with the focus shifting mostly to the project.

The project concept we have been using during the initial offering of the course is to create a game that helps first and second graders to learn math. The target audience is deliberately chosen to be different from the students, to encourage reflection on user characteristics. Each team can design and implement their own game, as long as it serves the customer's need of helping children to learn match. Students manage all aspects of teamwork themselves, and cooperation between teams is encouraged, as also reusing software from outside sources (with acknowledgements).

In-class activities

The in-class activities span a wide range:

- Hands-on tutorials on tools usage, for Eclipse [8] (the development environment), configuration management, and JUnit [9] for unit testing. The JUnit tutorial also shows them how to use a test-driven development strategy if they so desire.
- In-class exercises on writing requirements statements, drawing state diagrams.
- For architecture and design patterns, the instructor and students work through a design example together as a class.
- Role-play in conducting an in-class inspection meeting, where students review sample code to find defects and improvement opportunities.
- Project-related team activities, including creating paper prototypes of interfaces, and later teams evaluating each other's interface based on the prototypes.
- Class discussions on integration strategies that were actually used and those that should have been used in the team projects.
- Case studies of realistic software engineering situations as a course wrap-up. Students work on these first individually and then in teams, followed by an in-depth class discussion.
- Team reviews of the course material before final exams, where each team creates questions and answers on each of the topic areas covered.

Table 1. SE361 Course Plan

Wk	Project Work	Activities	Lecture Topics
1	Set up teams, learn tools	Tool tutorials	Course intro, lifecycle, need for discipline
2	Project concept, requirements	Improve req statements, paper prototype	Requirements, prototyping
3	Test design, planning, process choices	Junit tutorial	Testing techniques, planning
4	Design	Architecting example	Design theory
5	Implement, R1 presentations, reflection	Prototype interface evaluation	Interface design
6	Req change: update plans	Design pattern example, state diagramming	Design patterns, dynamic modeling
7	Development, inspections	In-class inspection mtg	Inspections
8	Release packaging, R2 presentations	Review project integration practices	Testing, integration strategies
9	Cross-team testing	SE case studies	Advanced SE topics preview
10	Final release presentations, postmortem	Create exam questions	-

Course infrastructure

The third part of our strategy involves students being able to drive their own learning processes, rather than relying exclusively on lectures. To facilitate this, we create extensive online materials to help students structure their learning.

"Topic Outlines" were created for each area, that:

- Identify the learning objectives for the area.
- List the various subtopics to be covered, and provides sources for learning each of them. This includes the specific pages in the textbook to read, as well as website URLs that they can go to for additional information if desired.
- Provides a set of "Guiding Questions" that help them to evaluate their learning, and to prepare for exams.

The idea is for the Topic Outlines to serve as a complete self-study guide. For the project, we create a week-by-week list of deliverables, with detailed instructions for each deliverable and project activity. These instructions are written in such a way as to avoid being specific to the project content, so that they can be reused with different projects. Thus each project team knows in advance exactly what was expected of them throughout the project.

Predefined document templates are provided for most project deliverables. Each document is carefully engineered to minimize the work needed to complete it, while simultaneously ensuring that there is due attention paid to all the key content and process discipline aspects. This includes an activity tracker spreadsheet that contains the various project activities and deliverables, where they enter completion status, planned effort, task allocation and later actual effort information on a weekly basis. A "process grid" is created that provides a range of practices of different levels of formality for each process area, and teams can select the level of process they considered appropriate. The objective of this is to shift their mindset from "writing reports and documentation for the instructor" to "creating artifacts to track project progress and decisions", where hopefully they will see more clearly the value that each document is adding to their work.

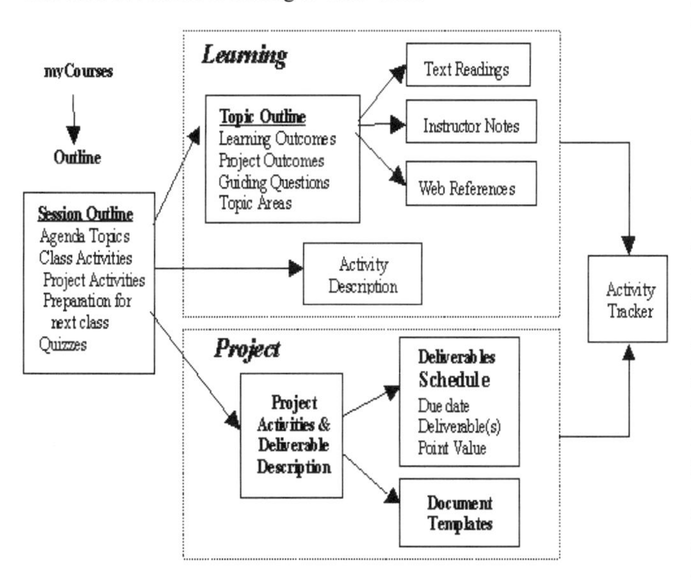

Figure 2. SE361 Course Map

At RIT, online learning support software called "myCourses" is available to make course materials available to students, and organize it by session. We populate each session with information on the lecture topics for the day, in-class activities, project deliverables due, and preparation needed for the next class. This includes hyperlinks to Topic Outlines and other relevant documents. This enables students to see the plan for each day at a glance, and also navigate to the documents that provided more detailed information. A "course map" diagram has been created to help them navigate the course structure, as shown in Figure 2.

The goal in the course materials and their structure is to move away from an instructor-centric concept where the students are constantly dependent on the instructor to lead their learning, tell them what to do and when to do it.

While redesigning the course was a challenge, our work was facilitated by our department's superb facilities. Each class meets in a studio classroom that provides each student with a computer that the instructor can control from an instruction workstation. In addition, to enable student teams to conduct team activities, the departments operates 11 team "breakout rooms" each equipped with a computer hooked to a ceiling-mounted projector, Ethernet connections, and comfortable seating for six.

3. OUTCOMES

In order to assess the new course format, the students were surveyed at both the course midpoint and at the end of the quarter. The survey was administered online to students enrolled in the course during the Fall, Winter, and Spring quarters. The survey administration was piloted during the Fall quarter, while the Winter quarter offered the most representative sample of students from 11 sections of the course.

During Winter quarter, 126 students completed the survey. The survey asked the students to supply demographic information, but concentrated on gauging the effectiveness of the course structure, project, course elements and student preparation. The students also had the opportunity to comment on aspects of the course that they valued and aspects of the course that should be revised.

Since the structure of the course has been designed to rely less on lecture and more on the project, we were interested in gathering feedback as to the pace of the course and the proportion of lecture to project time. While the course is fast-paced, 69% of the students responded that the pace of the course was just right. By comparison 20% of students rated the pace as "Too fast" and 10% of students rated the pace as "Too slow." During the course many students commented informally that the project was very important to them and that they wanted more course time devoted to the project. The statistics supported these comments. In terms of lecture, 47% of students were content with the amount of lecture in the course while at the same time 47% of students wanted less lecture. In terms of the effectiveness of lecture, 31.7% viewed lecture as being either Helpful or Extremely Helpful while 34.1% found lecture to be Moderately Helpful.

The students spoke strongly in terms of the extent of working on the project in class. While 28.6% of students felt that the amount of class time devoted to the project was adequate, a 65.1% of students wanted more class time spent on the project. The students responded to the technical and procedural aspects of the project. In terms of the overall project experience, 79.4% of students found the project itself to be either Helpful or Extremely Helpful. Regarding the deliverables that represented the application of the various Software Engineering concepts covered in the course, 77.8% of students found the various project deliverables to be either Helpful or Extremely Helpful. Such results reinforce the positive impact that the significant course-long project provides in terms of technical and Software Engineering interest.

In terms of the project, a sample of student comments includes:

"The best aspects of the course are being able to go through an entire project's development process, from requirements to final release. Taking a position in the team and being responsibility for those roles throughout the entire quarter helps my understanding of the software development process. I learned a lot from this course."

"I enjoyed working on the project most of all because it gave us a view of real world software development"

"Project provides a way to get practical experience and feel like you are producing a real project rather than a useless piece of code for some trivial application."

"The project was hard but it was a lot of fun"

Since considerable effort was devoted to designing the course infrastructure, we wanted to assess its effectiveness. The results showed that much of the course infrastructure was not perceived as helpful to the students. Only 48.4% of students found the course topic objectives to be either Helpful or Extremely Helpful. Besides the objectives, each major course topic's outline presented a structured view of topic concepts (including references to course readings). Only 50.8% of students felt that the topic outlines were either Helpful or Extremely Helpful. Only 27.8% of students viewed the required readings as either Helpful or Extremely Helpful. This result reflected the perception that students relied on slides for studying rather than reading the text either before class or before a quiz/exam. 62% of students stated that they were prepared for class (in terms of reading) either Rarely or Never. However when the preparation corresponded to a project deliverable, the 97.6% of students were prepared either Usually or Always. When the students see direct value for the preparation (when directly applicable to the project), then the level of preparation is significantly higher. The students want to see clear value in what they are asked to read and do.

The survey contained areas for open-ended comments about the course in any aspects that the student wished to comment. Some student comments regarding the merit of the course include:

"All the group presentations helped us get different perspectives on everything."

"I liked the project and found it very helpful in helping me understand the class as a whole. I liked having set times when things were due so I could plan ahead and be ready for them."

"I like the way this course is structured as compared to the previous CS (Computer Science) courses. Since my professional electives are going to be primarily SE instead of CE (Computer Engineering), this course provided me with a solid foundation in my opinion."

Other comments offer constructive feedback in terms of where to focus efforts in further offerings:

'Lecture didn't always help with project activities, more in class activities would be helpful."

"Need more project time; possibly make the class worth more like 5 or 6 credits and add an hour or two to class time."

The course instructors discussed the survey results, and the feedback was generally consistent with what was observed by instructors in the classroom and with student comments in class. Nearly all of the current course instructors had taught the course in previous renditions. The general perspective was that the new course design had fewer student complaints than previous course offerings. Fewer project failures were also observed.

4. CONCLUSION

The new approach of integrating the lecture and project work has been very successful in reducing the perceived disconnect between the theory and the practice. In-class activities are proving to be both popular and effective in consolidating learning. The attempt to move towards self-guided learning has been markedly less successful, and students are still relying almost entirely on the lecture to learn the concepts. Future efforts will work towards identifying the issues and strategies needed to more effectively address the reliance on lecture.

The new format has certainly succeeded in its goal of more active learning. Only about 30% of class time is spent in classic lecture mode. The strong linkages to the project have increased the effectiveness of the project as a learning vehicle, and made the course more clearly project-centric.

5. REFERENCES

[1] Reichlmayr, T., "An Agile Approach to an Undergraduate Software Engineering Course Project", 33rd *ASEE/IEEE Frontiers in Education Conference*, Boulder, CO, Nov 5-8, 2003

[2] Project Catalyst, "How to Engineer Engineering Education," Bucknell University, 2002-2003, http://www.departments.bucknell.edu/projectcatalyst/

[3] Hoyt, B., Hanyak, M., Vigeant, M., Snyder W., Aburdene, M., et al., "Project Catalyst: Promoting Systemic Change in Engineering Education", 31st *ASEE/IEEE Frontiers in Education Conference*, Reno, NV, Oct 10-13, 2001

[4] Felder, R.M., Brent, R., "Navigating the Bumpy Road to Student-Centered Instruction", *College Teaching*, Vol. 44, pp. 43-47, 1996

[5] Vallino, J., "Design Patterns: Evolving from Passive to Active Learning ", 33rd *ASEE/IEEE Frontiers in Education Conference*, Boulder, CO, Nov 5-8, 2003

[6] Prince, M., Hanyak, M., Hoyt, B., Hyde, D., Mastascusa, E., et al., "A Conceptual Framework for Progressively Developing Students' Team and Problem Solving Skills Across the Curriculum", *Proceedings of the 2002 American Society for Engineering Education Annual Conference & Exposition*, June 16-19, 2002.

[7] Bonwell, C. & Eison, J.. "Active Learning: Creating Excitement in the Classroom". ASHE- ERIC Higher Education Report No. 1, 1991.

[8] The Eclipse Project, http://www.eclipse.org

[9] JUnit, http://www.junit.org

Teaching Entering Students to Think Like Computer Scientists

Elise H. Turner   Roy M. Turner
Computer Science Department
University of Maine
5752 Neville Hall
Orono, ME USA 04469-5257
{eht,rmt}@umcs.maine.edu

ABSTRACT

This paper describes a new course developed at the University of Maine to help students better understand the discipline of computer science and to aid us in recruiting and retaining majors. The course provides an overview of computer science, but also, through focusing on particular topics at an advanced level, begins to teach students how computer scientists think about problems. The course has been taught in Fall 2002, 2003 and 2004. This paper describes the course and discusses our results from the first two years.

Categories and Subject Descriptors

K.3.2 [**Computer and Information Science Education**]: Computer science education

General Terms

Education

Keywords

Introductory Computer Science, Gender Issues

1. INTRODUCTION

At the University of Maine, we are faced with many of the same problems in our introductory courses that face other computer science departments nationwide. In particular, we were concerned about the following problems:

• **Potential majors did not find out what the major was really about until their junior or senior year** [1]. Those students who wanted only to program felt deceived when they were forced to focus on more abstract concepts in upper-level courses. Others, particularly women, left early because they believed the major would lead to a career as a programmer.

• **Non-majors carried into the world the belief that computer science was only computer programming.** Undecided majors, often women, who were talented in mathematics and science and interested in abstract problem solving might not try computer science because they were not particularly interested in programming [2].

• **The details of programming often distracted students from more conceptual information presented in CS-I and II** (see also [3]). Success with this strategy in early courses caused some students in upper-level courses to spend their time on programming assignments to the exclusion of studying the theoretical material presented in the course.

• **Introductory computer science courses did not introduce students to how computer scientists address important problems in their field.** After a year, many students were quite competent programmers but did not know how to think like computer scientists.

To address these problems, Techniques in Computer Science (TCS) was developed to be a rigorous, theoretical, non-programming introduction to computer science. We began teaching the course in Fall 2002 and have taught it each fall since that time. Results from the first two years suggest that the course is successful, and we expect it to be required for all of our students as part of our current curriculum revision.

In this paper, we give an overview of TCS and evaluate the course's success. In Sections 2 and 3, we give a general overview of the course, including the structure of the course and the topics covered. To give an idea of the rigor and depth of coverage of the topics, Section 3 also describes how a single topic, Hamming codes, is presented in the course. Section 4 presents results and Section 5 discusses features of the course that we believe helped retain students.

2. TECHNIQUES IN COMPUTER SCIENCE

Techniques in Computer Science (TCS) was developed to introduce students to the field of computer science in a way that would focus on problem solving, instead of programming, in computer science. Students cover five areas in the course: digital logic, computer organization and architecture, programming languages, operating systems and computer networks. Each area has several topics associated with it. The topics are shown in Figure 1.

By structuring the course in this way, we have intentionally given up some breadth to allow examination of problems in more depth. For each topic, students are presented with

SIGCSE'05, February 23–27, 2005, St. Louis, Missouri, USA.

Digital Logic	Architecture	Programming Languages	Operating Systems	Networks
Boolean Algebra	Daisy Chaining	Variables and PrimitiveTypes	Semaphores	ALOHA Protocols
Circuits from Functions	RAID	Conditionals, Control Structures, and Subroutines	Translation Lookaside Buffers	Hamming Codes
Karnaugh Maps	Booth's Algorithm	Backus-Naur Form	Bankers' Algorithm	Privacy on the Internet
Adders	CPU Organization and Assembly Language			
Registers				

Figure 1: Areas covered, with their topics.

a specific, real problem in computer science and learn the details of a solution to this problem, as well as the reasoning which led to that solution. Students are expected to learn the material at the level of an introductory course in that area. So, often students are exposed to specific topics at the junior or senior level. To determine if students are learning the material at this level, homework problems and exam questions are often taken from upper-level classes. We will discuss the topics in more detail in the next section.

In selecting topics for the areas, the following criteria were used, in order of importance [4]:

1. Does the topic present a challenging technique that will be interesting to the students?
2. Is the topic teachable in an introductory course within a fifty-minute lecture?
3. Does the topic allow us to introduce a way of thinking that is prevalent in computer science?
4. Does the topic cover an aspect of the area that is not covered by other topics?
5. Is the topic central to the area?

No course with a goal of teaching students to think like computer scientists would be complete without teaching the students about abstraction. To do this, we point out abstraction throughout the course. For example, in the introduction to the course, we point out that the areas take us from working close to the machine level to higher and higher abstractions. In the introduction to digital logic, we describe how gates are abstractions of actual circuits. We discuss programming language design in terms of providing an abstraction that allows users to think about their problem at the appropriate level.

Because we are focusing on several specific techniques within each area, we could not cover all areas of computer science. To add more breadth to the course, guest lecturers from our faculty are brought in to talk about their research areas if they have not already been covered. A half-lecture each is devoted to a quick overview of software engineering, artificial intelligence, theoretical computer science and graphics. These introductions simply make students aware of the kinds of problems that are solved in these areas and give them an opportunity to meet our faculty. We expect students to be introduced to techniques from software engineering and algorithm design and analysis in their introductory programming class. In the future, we plan to add artificial intelligence and computer ethics as areas in TCS.[1]

The course is structured to support students trying to master the difficult material covered in this class and to help them develop study habits that will serve them well throughout their college careers. In addition to class meetings there is also a recitation with a teaching assistant each week, and students are encouraged to meet with the instructor in his or her office.

In addition, every effort is made to make each lecture as self-contained as possible. Because there are no prerequisites, and because the material covered is so different from most students' previous experiences with computers, we assume that students are seeing everything for the first time. Although we are able to focus on specific techniques or narrow concepts and examine them in depth, the lectures necessarily devote some time to giving a context for the problem. This context may be background information needed to understand the problem or its solution. For example, to prepare students to learn about adders, we also teach them about representing numbers in a computer and about binary addition. We also have an opportunity to introduce broader issues. For example, to set the stage for a discussion of daisy chaining, we must first tell students that buses allow components to communicate and explain why that communication must be arbitrated.

Homework assignments are given at the end of each topic lecture and cover a single topic. A small number of homework problems drill students on specific skills (e.g., binary arithmetic). Most homework problems and exam questions, however, are similar to or taken directly from assignments in junior and senior level introductions to the area. There are 4–6 questions, usually multi-part, in each homework assignment. Special care is taken to ensure that at least one or two homework problems in each assignment challenge the students to go beyond work in the classroom. Students are explicitly told that the homework is to help them understand the material, and they are encouraged to form study groups and work together on homework problems.

3. COVERING TOPICS IN TCS

In this section we illustrate how most topics were presented, using Hamming codes as an example. But, first it is important to briefly discuss the two areas which have topics that do not obviously fit that pattern: digital logic and programming languages.

The topics covered in digital logic, when possible, adhere to our intention of introducing students to a particular technique for solving a problem in depth. This is clearly the case with Karnaugh maps (How can we minimize circuits?) and registers (How do we store data in a computer?). Although the lecture on algebraic equivalence gives students the background and homework experience to find equivalent circuits and prove their equivalence by algebraic substitution, this topic is less narrow than most others in the class. However, we felt that this was a natural way to give students an opportunity to use proofs and to think about formal reasoning. The topic of moving from functions to circuits is introduc-

[1]We will find space for these areas by replacing in-class review sessions at the end of each area with recitations.

tory material that must be covered if the rest of the area is to be understood. Since gates and an overview of Boolean operations is covered in the introductory lecture, we do not have time to cover creating circuits there. The lecture on adders may seem to be too narrow. However, we use adders to make the point that circuits can be better constructed if we understand the problem and use our insights to inform the solution. We also must introduce number representation and computer addition in the adders lecture, so, although adders can be covered in a few minutes in an upper-level architecture course, we require a complete lecture to present them in TCS.

It may not be clear how the area of programming languages can be presented in a non-programming introduction. Frankly, this was the area that we were most concerned about when developing the course. We wanted this section to introduce students to the constructs of programming languages and to issues in programming language design. The introduction to the area quickly covers the idea of needing to translate a programming language that is helpful to the user to code that can be executed by the computer. The bulk of the introduction is spent on discussing what kinds of tasks people need to perform using programming languages and how we might think about those tasks, using one particular task as an example. This allows us to talk about the basic constructs that are needed to support problem solving. Topics that cover the constructs allow us to talk about exactly what those constructs contribute, the design decisions that are made when the construct is included in a programming language, and how those design decisions are limited by the computer. In the lecture on variables, for example, students first see how variables are used to store values in a program. Next, students learn about the general concept of identifiers and discuss such design issues as the length of variable names and case-sensitive identifiers. Although this course, and particularly this area, were never intended as preparation for the programming course, many students who took TCS reported that they felt their understanding of programming languages from TCS gave them a framework for understanding programming language constructs which made learning about programming easier.

3.1 Teaching Hamming Codes

Hamming codes are presented as a topic in the networks area. As with all topics, we begin with a discussion on why we study Hamming codes. For Hamming codes, we tell students that these are error-correcting codes and that they are used in computer networks and internal memory.

The students have already heard of Hamming codes from studying RAID in the organization and architecture area. There, the RAID level which uses Hamming codes must be glossed over, and we remind students of this connection here. They were also introduced to parity bits when studying RAID. So, we can begin the technical portion of the lecture with a brief review of what parity bits can and cannot do. We also remind them that in RAID architectures we can correct errors because we know the location of the bit that contains the error.

Next, we set up a straw man using the idea of having a parity bit for each bit of data and then a parity bit for the parity bits. We show how the scheme would work and point out that it would more than double the size of memory. Students now see that they need to find the location of the offending bit, but should do it using as little memory as possible.

For the rest of the lecture, we present Hamming codes in the same way that we would present this topic to juniors and seniors. We summarize the goal of identifying the errors using as few bits as possible and give an overview of the basic idea of Hamming codes.

Next, we show how parity bits can be associated with data bits, using a Venn diagram for four bits of data. We then give examples of how to correct the data using the Venn diagram.

Now that the students understand the overall concept, we explain how Hamming codes work in streams of data. By this point in the course, students are comfortable enough with binary arithmetic[2] to understand how checkbits can be added to the data, and to think about the appropriate size for segments of data.

We now go further into detail, explaining how to create a Hamming code for eight bits of data. Finally, we give examples of how the Hamming code can be used to detect and correct data.

The Hamming code homework has the following questions:

1. Assume that the following bits have been sent across the network. Hamming code has been used to encode 8 data bits. Give the *correct* data. Show your work.
   (a) 101110010010
   (b) 111010011111
   (c) 100101100010
   (d) 001001001001
   (e) 111111111111
2. Show how Hamming code can be used for 6 bits of data. Give the location of the data bits within the encoded representation. Give the location of the check bits, and tell which bits they will check.
3. If only a single parity bit is used, what happens when there are two errors? If Hamming code is used, what happens when there are two errors?
4. We said in class that the number of extra bits (in excess of data bits) required for Hamming code is on the order of log_n, where n is the number of data bits. The number of bits required is actually $log_n + x$, where x is the same for any number of data bits. What is x? Make a convincing argument for the value of x you have given.

4. EVALUATION OF THE COURSE

We began teaching TCS in Fall 2002 to test the concept of the course and to see if it should be included in the computer science major. Because it was not required of our majors, first-year students were only encouraged to take the course if they had been placed in remedial programming because they showed little aptitude in math and science. The first

[2]From performing calculations in the digital logic and architecture areas and getting used to logarithms and the amount of data that can be stored in a given number of bits from the operating systems area.

class also included an undeclared major, an upperclassman from a different major, and a woman in our major who was considering leaving the major because she was more interested in problem solving than programming. In Fall 2003, the course was taught for a second time. This time more students were encouraged to take the class. In addition to students who were placed in remedial programming, we also encouraged students who were drawn to computer science because of their interest in programming. This was meant to allow these students to find out if the major was right for them. Because of our success in retaining women the previous Fall [5], we also encouraged all first-year women to enroll in the course. We are currently teaching TCS for the third time. TCS was successful enough in the first two years that this year our curriculum committee recommended it for all first-year majors. The committee also expects to include it as a required course as we complete our curriculum revision this Fall. In this section, we discuss how the course has been evaluated and what we have found.

4.1 Results of Student Surveys

Each year students filled out surveys at the end of the first and last class. At the beginning of the semester in the first two years, most students had little or no programming experience. Although they felt that computer scientists should be good at solving problems, many felt that the most interesting thing they would learn in the class would be some skill used by programmers or computer operators. They also thought that the most important thing they would learn was whether or not the major was a good match for them.

By the end of the semester, students were more sophisticated about computer science. When asked what was the most interesting thing they had learned, most cited an individual topic. When asked what was the most important thing that they had learned, one of two sorts of answers appeared in most responses. Most students who responded in terms of computer science said that they thought everything in the course was important. Other students said that the most important thing they learned from the class was to be a good student.

Although the course was rated as very hard on regular student evaluations and some students mentioned this in their responses to questions on the survey, most students who were computer science majors felt the course was worth their time and effort.

4.2 Retention of Students

One goal of TCS is to retain students who are a good match with computer science. We feel the course achieves this goal.

In the first semester, fifteen students completed surveys on the first day and only nine completed the course. In the second semester eleven students completed surveys on the first day and ten completed the course. We believe there are several reasons for the difference in these numbers. The first time the course was taught, the class consisted mostly of students who would be expected to drop out of computer science in their first semester. Yet, our drop-out rate was slightly less than that of the introductory programming courses (either the remedial courses or CS I). It is also clear from student surveys that most of the students who dropped the course did so for reasons that would make them unhappy with a computer science major. Beginning of the semester surveys indicate that four of these students had previous experience using very specific skills (e.g., installing operating systems, troubleshooting without programming, Web design, certifications, very limited programming skills) and expected a B.S. in computer science to be more of the same, plus programming.[3] Students like these are often frustrated by the major in their junior and senior years. The second year that the course was taught, the New Media major was offered on campus for the first time. This major seems to attract students who are interested in becoming Web designers or computer operators. The student who dropped the course in the second year seems to have taken the course because he believed it was required for another major and dropped TCS when he realized he was in the wrong course.

Although the course was not specifically designed to retain women in the major, all women who took the course in the first two semesters decided to become computer science majors or to enter a closely-related major. In the first year, the women who took the course included a first-year student who was an undeclared major and did not expect to major in computer science and a sophomore computer science major who was planning on leaving the major. At the end of the course, these two women planned to remain in the major. Another woman changed majors from computer science to electrical engineering technology because TCS helped her to recognize that she was more interested in working at the hardware level. These women's perspectives on the course and how it influenced their interest in remaining in the major is the subject of a technical report [5]. In the second year, three women responded to surveys on the first day. All expected to be computer science majors, all completed the class, and all expected to remain computer science majors at the end of TCS.

4.3 Preparation for Further Work in Computer Science

Students who took TCS in Fall 2002 are currently beginning juniors. Consequently, it is difficult to evaluate whether or not TCS will help students to think like computer scientists in their upper-level courses.

Because TCS was never meant to help prepare students for programming, we were surprised by the number of students who told us in casual conversation that their understanding of TCS helped them to better understand programming. As more students complete TCS and we collect more data, we hope to determine if these students feel more comfortable because they are more mature, because they have been exposed to programming language constructs and are better able to focus on programming concepts instead of the syntax of a language, or because they have a feel for the way to think about computer science and do not ignore topics like algorithm design and software design to focus on learning a language in CS-I.

[3]One student withdrew from the University for the semester for reasons unrelated to any courses, and another dropped the course because he thought it was too much work.

5. FEATURES OF THE COURSE THAT HELPED RETAIN STUDENTS

There are several features of TCS that we believe helped us to retain students in the major. Some of these are particularly important to women, but we believe they are helpful to all students.

• **The course was rigorous.** Students were engaged in the types of challenging problem solving that our best majors, and particularly women [6], often find a very attractive aspect of the computer science. It also built students' confidence that they could handle difficult material.

• **Students knew that they were in a "real" computer science course, so they could expect success in CS-T to predict success later in the major.** Students knew that the content of the course and the rigor required were similar to that of other computer science courses. Students were repeatedly reminded in class, especially when homework assignments and tests were returned, that they were doing work usually expected of juniors and seniors in the major. Women and men, majors and non-majors were in the class together, demonstrating to women that they could successfully compete with men in the major (see [7]).

• **The experience that most high school students have with computers was not relevant in TCS.** Consequently, students who entered college with little or no computer experience, as is often the case in our state, were not disadvantaged. In addition, aggressive students who may intimidate others by flaunting their knowledge in introductory programming courses [8, 9] have few opportunities to discuss this knowledge in TCS.

• **The structure of the course supported the students' learning of difficult material, which, in turn, built their confidence** [10]. Although the students reported in surveys and casual conversation that they worked hard, they also believed that the material was not particularly difficult.

• **Students fully appreciated that computer science was not equal to computer programming.** On end of the semester surveys, four students in the first year the course was taught cited this as the most important thing that they learned in the class. For students, often women [2], who are more interested in problem solving than programming, this knowledge can make the difference between staying in the computer science major and leaving it.

• **The course covered a range of areas and a wide variety of topics.** This allowed students to get an accurate sense of the field and helped to satisfy a diversity of interests.

6. CONCLUSION

This paper presents preliminary results from teaching a rigorous, non-programming introduction to computer science. Results from two years of experience with the course suggest that students are interested in learning about important techniques in computer science, even when learning about them requires considerable work. Our preliminary results also suggest that by teaching tham about interesting problems in computer science, students, including women, want to continue in the major.

7. ACKNOWLEDGMENTS

The authors wish to thank Thomas Wheeler and Judith Richardson for helping to create the philosophy of the course and for many helpful discussions about the content of the course. We also would like to thank the students who participated in the course and gave us feedback through student surveys, course evaluations, and casual conversation. We would especially like to thank Cathy Emerton, Christina Logan, and Rebecca Ray, the women in the Fall 2002 class who participated in writing the technical report about their experiences. Parts of two technical reports about TCS [4, 5] have been used in this paper.

8. REFERENCES

[1] T. P. Murtagh. Teaching breadth-first depth-first. *SIGSCE Bulletin*, 33(3):37–40, 2001.

[2] J. Prey and K. Treu. What do you say? Open letters to women considering a computer science major. *Inroads (The SIGCSE Bulletin)*, 34(2):18–20, 2002.

[3] A. B. Tucker, C. F. Kelemen, and K. B. Bruce. Our curriculum has become math-phobic. In *The Proceedings of the Thirty-Second SIGSCE Technical Symposium on Computer Science Education*, pages 243–247, New York, NY, 2001. Association for Computing Machinery, Inc.

[4] E. Turner, R. Turner, and T. Wheeler. A rigorous introduction to computer science without programming. Technical Report UMCS–TR–2004–1, Department of Computer Science, University of Maine, 5752 Neville Hall, Orono, ME 04469, 2004.

[5] E. H. Turner, C. Emerton, R. Ray, and C. Logan. A rigorous introduction to computer science without programming: Three women's perspectives. Technical Report UMCS TR 2004 2, Department of Computer Science, University of Maine, 5752 Neville Hall, Orono, ME 04469, 2004.

[6] M. Barg, A. Fekete, T. Greening, O. Hollands, J. Kay, and J. H. Kingston. Problem-based learning for foundation computer science courses. *Computer Science Education*, 10(2):109–128, 2000.

[7] A. Pearl, M. E. Pollack, E. Riskin, B. Thomas, E. Wolf, and A. Wu. Becoming a computer scientist. *Communications of the ACM*, 33(11):47–57, 1990.

[8] L. J. Barker, K. Garvin-Doxas, and M. Jaskson. Defensive climate in the computer science classroom. In *The Proceedings of the Thirty-Third SIGSCE Technical Symposium on Computer Science Education*, pages 43–47, New York, NY, 2002. Association for Computing Machinery, Inc.

[9] B. C. Wilson. A study of factors promoting success in computer science including gender differences. *Computer Science Education*, 12(1–2):141–164, 2002.

[10] K. Treu and A. Skinner. Ten suggestions for a gender-equitable CS classroom. *The Journal of Computing in Small Colleges*, 12(2):244–248, 1996.

The New Science Students in *Too Much, Too Soon*

An Abbreviated, Accelerated, Constructivist, Collaborative, Introductory Experience in CS

Samuel A. Rebelsky
Grinnell College
Department of Mathematics and Computer Science
Grinnell, Iowa, USA

rebelsky@grinnell.edu

ABSTRACT

Although faculty are most accustomed to teaching semester-long traditional courses, they are encountering an increasing number of situations in which they must teach "courses" of only a few hours that are intended to give others a "flavor" of the discipline. Such situations include alumni events, orientation activities for incoming or potential students, and community outreach programs. In many disciplines, faculty can rely on participants' academic or basic skills (e.g., how to dissect an argument; basic laboratory skills). In computer science, faculty must accept not only a lack of basic skill in the discipline, but also a potential gap in knowledge of what the study of computer science entails.

This paper explores the design of one such introductory experience, which is held in two two-hour sections for selected incoming science students at Grinnell College. The course emphasizes hands-on discovery, algorithm design and algorithm analysis grounded in the problem of sorting. Different faculty members in the department have taught the course three times to general success.

Categories and Subject Descriptors

K.3.2 [**Computers and Education**]: Computer and Information Science Education, *Computer Science Education.*

General Terms

Algorithms, Design

Keywords

Introduction to CS, Short course, Non-majors, Sorting

1. INTRODUCTION

In Fall 2002, Grinnell College asked the Computer Science department to offer a short class for a selected group of incoming students as part of the Grinnell Science Project (GSP). Students interested in science would participate in two "laboratory" sessions of two hours each, which would serve as their introduction to science at Grinnell and to the discipline of computer science. (Further details of GSP follow in section 2.) The faculty of the department found this an interesting design problem: How do you give students with an unknown background in computer science (and, likely, no background in computer science), a realistic laboratory experience in the discipline?

Upon reflection, we came to the conclusion that the design of such a "course" would be useful for many situations. It would certainly serve GSP and even as a recruiting tool to computer science for some of the students in GSP. However, it could also be used for the annual "Alumni College" and for outreach events the college regularly holds for local high-school students. In particularly optimistic moments, we even toyed with the thought of offering it to colleagues in other disciplines who seem not to know much about what we do.

Our initial design goals are reflected in the title of this paper. The course was necessarily *abbreviated*, as we had only four hours to introduce these students to the study of computer science. However, the course was also necessarily *accelerated* in that we hoped and expected to cover material beyond that from the typical introductory course. Because of the GSP requirement that the course be "laboratory-based" and because of our pedagogical preferences, we hoped for a *constructivist* approach that would focus on student-centered activities that would help them develop their knowledge and understanding. Our experience suggests that such activities are best conducted *collaboratively*, in both small and large groups. Finally, the course was to be *introductory*: no prior knowledge of computer science was assumed. These were certainly lofty goals. We will leave it to the reader to judge whether or not we were successful.

Section 2 of this paper grounds the course in the context of the Grinnell Science Project. Although we designed the course particularly for GSP, we do expect that others will be able to use the course in other situations in which such abbreviated courses are necessary, such as those mentioned above. Section 3 summarizes a number of rejected designs, primarily designs suggestions from those outside the discipline. Our reasons for rejecting many of these designs also suggested further goals that helped lead us to the final design. Section 4 provides the core of the paper, the design of the course with comments on the purpose of various components. Because the course described in Section 4 includes somewhat more than can realistically be covered in four hours, Section 5 describes some aspects our actual experiences fitting all of that material

SIGCSE'05, February 23-27, 2005, St. Louis, MO, USA.

in to the time allotted and modifying the "syllabus" for student interest. Finally, Section 6 suggests some future directions for the course and some additional advice to others designing similar courses.

2. CONTEXT: THE GRINNELL SCIENCE PROJECT

In the early 1990's, Grinnell, like many institutions, looked for ways to counter a troublesome trend: Students in traditionally underrepresented groups in the sciences (e.g., students of color, women in the physical sciences, and first generation college students) who had expressed an initial interest in the sciences were more likely than students in other groups to choose majors outside the sciences. Structured student interviews revealed many issues and approaches. In response, Grinnell created the Grinnell Science Project (GSP)[1]. GSP has evolved over the years, and now emphasizes three central components: (1) workshop-style courses in the introductory curriculum; (2) increased opportunities for student-faculty collaboration; and (3) a pre-orientation for incoming students who fit into our target groups. The third component is most relevant for the subject at hand, as the abbreviated course is designed to be part of that pre-orientation.

The pre-orientation addresses a number of important issues. First, it helps the students connect with science faculty through a number of experiences (including joint meals, laboratory projects, other small-group activities). Research suggests that many students who leave the sciences do so because they fail to "connect" with faculty [2]. The early interviews suggested that students in target groups were less likely to approach faculty for help. Surveys with GSP students suggest that we are forming successfully better connections. Second, the pre-orientation helps form a support group for students. The friendships formed during GSP pre-orientation last throughout and beyond students' careers at Grinnell. Third, the pre-orientation helps introduce students to academic culture, particularly Grinnell's culture of science. That culture includes emphases on real problems, on presenting one's work, and on "doing science".

The GSP laboratory sessions help meet two of these goals: They connect a small group of students (typically four or five) with a single faculty member and they give these students an early experience in "real" science that better prepares them for the structure and stresses of their science courses. The laboratory sessions also spark interest in the subject, or so we hope.

For many years, the focus of GSP and of the laboratories was the natural sciences (biology, chemistry, and physics) and mathematics, although GSP did include faculty members from other science disciplines in some activities. In recent years, the program has increasingly tried to incorporate computer science and psychology. As Section 1 suggests, the addition of a laboratory experience in computer science led to the design problem and solution described in this paper.

[1] The project was originally named the "New Science Project" (or NSP), but has been recently renamed.

3. REJECTED DESIGNS

The design of an abbreviated introductory computer science experience is somewhat more difficult than the design of an introductory experience in the other sciences because most work in computer science carries expectations of language skills (while a particular programming language may not be necessary to do computer science, one does need experience in writing and reading algorithms) and of mathematics skills. In many cases, new computer scientists know that their designs (most typically of algorithms) are correct or useful because they implement them and see them working. This situation is significantly different from that of the other sciences, in which the primary abilities one needs are to observe, record data, and analyze data. (GSP includes general data analysis exercises in the days before the laboratory sessions so that students are prepared for such analysis.)

Our first strategy for finding a focus for the laboratory session was to discuss the problem with one of the GSP co-leaders who, although not a computer scientist, had taken our introductory sequence. The co-leader suggested that "How to Build a Web Site" would work. The idea had some merits: Students would likely enjoy learning the topic and would have the experience of learning a new language (and even being able to verify syntax of that language). However, building a Web site is most typically an exercise in computer *skills*, not in computer *science*, and we quickly rejected that idea.

We then looked to what our colleagues did. Many of the other sciences used a variation of a laboratory experience from the introductory sequence. However, our introductory course builds carefully from topic to topic (and requires programming knowledge after the first week), so a topic from the middle of the course would not work. And, while the first laboratory experiences of the course are useful, they focus on language learning and basic programming rather than the vast richness of the study of computer science.

We considered some of the techniques sometimes employed in introductory courses for non-majors, such as those described by Lewandoski and Moorehead [1]. While we adopted some of those techniques, we also worried that using these techniques exclusively would not give students a "typical" laboratory experience, which involves more analysis and more hands-on computer work.

4. OUR SOLUTION AND ITS STRUCTURE

Before moving forward in the design of an introductory experience, we retreated into a more basic question: If this was to be a laboratory experience in computer *science* and not computer *skills* nor computer *programming*, what aspects of computer science is it most important for us to emphasize? We decided that we would emphasize a variety of issues pertaining to algorithms: their design, their specification, their implementation, their asymptotic analysis, and their experimental analysis. Although there are a host of interesting algorithmic problems appropriate for students with little or no prior CS background, we chose sorting as the appropriate algorithmic domain, in part because we introduce sorting in the introductory sequence, in part because students have experience sorting items, in part because there are so many standard "good" solutions.

We then separated the experience into short segments as follows:

Day One [2 hours]
Introduction [10 minutes]
The PBJ Problem [30 minutes]
Designing Sorting Algorithms [30 minutes]
Starting Scheme [40 minutes]
Reflection [10 minutes]

Homework [30 minutes]
Read descriptions of key sorting algorithms

Day Two [2 hours]
Review [10 minutes]
Comparative Analysis [10 minutes]
Experimental Analysis [30 minutes]
Formalizing Requirements [20 minutes]
Comparative Experimental Analysis [40 minutes]
Reflection [10 minutes]

4.1 Introduction

We begin with a ten-minute discussion/lecture designed to help students understand the nature of computer science. Experience shows that even students interested in computer science have difficulty defining the discipline. The ten minutes gives students some chance to find that their notions of computing and their notions of "science" do not cohere. In particular, most can be led to the conclusion that the scientific method focuses on observation, hypothesis generation, experiment design, data gathering, and data analysis. Most then realize that making hypotheses about artificial creations is awkward. Hence, we suggest that the "science" in computer science relies on more than that method. We end by emphasizing the algorithmic nature of CS and the three key ways that computer scientists approach algorithms (as engineers, as mathematicians, and as scientists).

4.2 The PBJ Problem

After convincing students that computer science emphasizes the study of algorithms, we have them participate in a traditional first exercise in algorithm design: The problem of designing an algorithm for assembling a peanut butter and jelly sandwich for someone with little common sense [1]. The exercise helps "break the ice" with a new group of students ("Please, when you tell me to pick up the knife, make sure you specify that I pick it up by the handle; I've used too many band-aids already." "I've been twisting the lid [of this pop-top jelly jar] for over a minute. I don't think it's going to open.") It also helps prepare students for the "the computer is not doing what I tell it to" problems we are likely to encounter in the rest of the laboratory. The problem also gives us a chance to suggest why working together helps (students quickly identify problems in each others' algorithms). We conclude the exercise with a reflection on the key parts of an imperative algorithm (conditionals, built-in operations, loops, subroutines, named variables) and an accompanying handout.

4.3 Designing Sorting Algorithms

Students are now ready to approach the core problem for the course: They are given a stack of CDs and asked to put them "in order". After their experience with the PBJ problem, the students first want to know what basic operations and assumptions they can use, and we give them fairly free reign, as the goal here is to sketch the general scope of a sorting algorithm.

Once the students have ordered their stacks of CDs, we ask them to describe the process by which they put them in order and to attempt to transcribe that process in such a way that others might apply it. Again, there are some interesting problems (and jokes) that occur when one group of students attempts to apply the algorithm another group suggests.

An expected outcome of this stage is that students see that there is more than one algorithm for sorting a group of objects. (If the students do not develop separate algorithms, and they usually do, we explicitly ask them to come up with another way for putting the CDs in order.) We use the difference between algorithms to motivate the analysis in day two's activities.

In practice, a particularly positive aspect of this exercise is that students learn to ask, "what basic operations can I use?"

4.4 Starting Scheme

At this point, more than half of our first two-hour laboratory has passed, and the students are clearly ready to use the computers that surround them (we hold the session in one of our teaching laboratories). We decided that the experience would feel more "real" to them if they saw the algorithms within a programming environment, and not just as a stand-alone simulation that they could run. Hence, the laboratory needs a short introduction to using a programming language. Because it typically runs in an interpretive environment, and because it has a relatively transparent syntax, Scheme seemed like an ideal language (although Squeak might also have been reasonable). In a little more than half an hour, students can learn to use the Scheme environment (DrScheme in our case), write simple Scheme expressions, and understand their output.

4.5 Reflection

Ten minutes at the end of the class are available for students to discuss questions they may have encountered, reflect on what they have learned, and look ahead to the second day.

4.6 Homework

GSP students have many activities that fill their days. Most are preparing a short research report to present to the group at large. They also participate in group-building activities in the evening. Hence, although we are permitted to give the students a homework assignment, we keep it fairly short. We ask the students to read a short (two page) English and pseudocode description of four algorithms: Insertion Sort, Selection Sort, Merge Sort, and Permutation Sort.[2] Insertion and Selection Sort closely resemble the sorting routines students are most likely to present. Merge Sort provides a comparatively easy to understand more efficient algorithm. Permutation Sort ("make all permutations of the original list and then determine which one is sorted") is easy to understand and easy to predict as inefficient.

4.7 Review

We begin the second day with a review of what we learned the first day (the components of algorithms, the reasons

---

[2] Henry Walker suggested the inclusion of Permutation Sort.

computers seem to misunderstand us, the problem of sorting, the basics of Scheme, and some standard sorting algorithms). This short time allows students to ask questions and reminds them of what they are expected to think about and work on for the rest of the day.

4.8 Comparative Analysis

We have told students that "algorithm analysis" is core to the study of computer science. To help them understand the kinds of analysis computer scientists normally do, we first ask them to compare the various sorting algorithms they have just developed or learned about. Students suggest a wide variety of interesting and potentially useful ways to compare algorithms. Most frequently, students include speed, readability, and length of code. With some prompting, they also come to see that correctness is a key attribute of algorithms, if not necessarily a comparative value.

4.9 Experimental Analysis

Students now use the Scheme that they have learned to experimentally analyze one sorting algorithm, selection sort. They see that each portion (identify smallest, remove item) works correctly and that they work correctly in conjunction. They think about what test cases will help them verify whether or not the various portions work correctly.

Once they are confident that the sorting algorithm works correctly, they gather data for the next step in experimental analysis.

For the final step in this stage of experimental analysis, they graph the data points and attempt to find the formula of a "natural" curve through the points. We encourage students to try various functions and see which fits best. Students graph both points and linc in Maplc, which is uscd in thc introductory Calculus courses at Grinnell.

4.10 Formalizing Requirements

In Grinnell's introductory Computer Science sequence, we regularly ask students to write preconditions and postconditions for most of the procedures they write. To give students in this laboratory experience a sense of what it means to specify the meaning of a procedure, we use this portion of the laboratory to ask them to write requirements for the "remove item" portion of list-based selection sort. For this exercise, we adopt an adversarial perspective: We present algorithms that meet their postconditions but fail to do what they expect the algorithm to do (e.g., removing everything from the list often meets students' initial postconditions) and specify initial situations in which may be difficult to reach the postconditions.

4.11 Comparative Experimental Analysis

The formal requirements stage serves also as a pause before the final step of the laboratory experience: a comparative experimental analysis of four sorting algorithms. As in their previous analysis, the students record a variety of time data, graph the data, and use the results to make predictions about the relative speed of different sorting algorithms.

4.12 Final Reflection

In the last ten minutes of the session, we ask students to summarize the key ideas that they have learned over two days. Most report that they have learned that computer science is very different than they had expected.

5. EXPERIENCE

Although this seems like a reasonably large amount of material, we are able to cover most of it in the four hours. The piece that most easily "slips" is the formal requirements specification, primarily because students are getting tired at that point and because they seem to prefer to continue with computer-based exercises.

The introduction to Scheme is certainly one of the more problematic parts of the laboratory. While some students understand that they need to learn the "experimental apparatus", as it were, others are frustrated by trying to quickly learn a programming language and have trouble understanding why they are spending their time on such "basic" (but difficult) activities. Making it clear that the activity is preparatory for other activities helps, but still leaves some students frustrated.

We do not have sufficient data to analyze the effectiveness of this experience as a recruitment or retention tool. Only a few students participate each year, and we have only offered this laboratory experience for the past three years.

The anecdotal outcomes of the laboratory experience have generally been positive. The first time we held the experience, one student noted at the end "All my friends at home told me how awful Scheme is, but it's really cool!" (This student decided to major in Physics, but has taken a number of courses in Computer Science.) Students regularly report that the experience has given them a more positive attitude about computer science ("I hadn't planned to take CS, but maybe now I will"). Few, if any, of the students who have taken these experiences have declared computer science majors, but even fewer had indicated that CS was their primary science interest. (Most students end up in GSP because of their interest in Biology or Psychology; those who end up in our lab are often placed in our lab because their first-choice labs are filled. The problem of incoming student interest in CS is one we must address separately.)

6. CONCLUDING REMARKS

Because our experiences with the laboratory experience have generally been positive, we recommend it to others as a starting point in the design of their own "abbreviated introductions". All materials are available at <http://www.cs.grinnell.edu/~rebelsky/Glimmer/Sorting/>. Even if others do not adopt this particular approach, we hope that it inspires others to design and offer other "abbreviated" introductions to the discipline.

We have yet to teach this laboratory experience outside of the Grinnell Science Program. However, we are beginning to consider whether we can use the laboratory experience as a way of recruiting more students to the introductory sequence (e.g., by offering a few sessions before or at the beginning of each semester).[3] We hope to offer concrete data on the success or failure of such an endeavor at a future SIGCSE.

[3] We would also be willing to help others implement a similar introduction at their institution.

7. ACKNOWLEDGMENTS

The faculty, students, and staff of the Grinnell Science Program very much appreciate the Grinnell College for funding the Grinnell Science Program. I appreciate the advice of my colleague, Henry Walker, during the initial planning of these exercises. Henry also suggested the inclusion of permutation sort in the sorting algorithms students encounter.

8. REFERENCES

[1] Lewandoski, G. and Moorehead, A. Computer Science Through the Eyes of Dead Monkeys: Learning Styles and Interaction in CS I. In *Proceedings of the SIGCSE98 Symposium on Computer Science Education*. New York, NY, 1998, 312-216.

[2] Seymour, E., and Hewitt, N. M. *Talking About Leaving: Why Undergraduates Leave the Sciences*. Westview Press, 2000.

Experiences with a CS0 Course Targeted for CS1 Success

Charles Dierbach, Blair Taylor, Harry Zhou, Iliana Zimand
Department of Computer and Information Sciences
Towson University
Towson, Maryland 21252
410-704-3552
{cdierbach, btaylor, hzhou, izimand}@towson.edu

ABSTRACT

In this paper, we report on an approach taken addressing the issue of the preparedness of students entering CS1. Specifically, we discuss the adoption of a first-day assessment test in lieu of completed course prerequisites for determining students' preparedness, and the development of a corresponding CS0 "fallback" course intended to provide the appropriate background for those students lacking the necessary programming reasoning skills, as indicated by assessment test results. We report here on the adequacy of the assessment test designed, the effectiveness of the CS0 course as targeted for CS1 success, and the perceptions of students as to the impact that the CS0 course has had on their ultimate success in CS1.

Categories and Subject Descriptors

K.3.2 [Computers and Education]: Computer and Information Science Education.

General Terms

Languages, Measurement.

Keywords

Computer Science Education, CS0, CS1, Student Assessment, Curriculum Design.

1. INTRODUCTION

At the authors' institution, the prerequisite for students entering CS1 (a C++-based course) had been "satisfactory completion of a programming course in a high-level programming language" (in addition to fundamental mathematics background). However, the appropriateness of such a prerequisite came into question given that (a) prior satisfactory completion of a programming course does not necessarily guarantee sufficient preparation for the expectations of CS1, and (b) those students who are self-taught or with particular aptitude for the subject would be excluded (until the prerequisite was satisfied).

SIGCSE'05, February 23–27, 2005, St. Louis, Missouri, USA.

Five years ago, the idea emerged that rather than *presuming* whether or not students had the necessary background or aptitude to enter CS1 based on satisfied prerequisites, to actually *test* students during the very first day of class. The questions then became "What kind of test to administer?" "What options to offer students with identified deficiencies?" and "Whether or not to enforce assessment test results?"

It was decided that such an assessment test should be designed not to measure specific programming knowledge, but to measure whether students had the minimal degree of programming reasoning ability expected for success in CS1. With this intension, an assessment test was designed (by the third author) containing a set of ten simple programming questions. In addition, the questions were written in a pseudocode style comprehensible to anyone with sufficient aptitude or experience, regardless of particular prior programming language exposure.

Along with the assessment test, a new "fallback" CS0 course was developed (by the first and second authors) designed to best prepare students for CS1. Thus, the view of this course was not one of providing a particularly broad view of computing for non-majors (as is typical of most CS0 courses), but with the goal of providing *majors* with the appropriate mental models and conceptualization of programming for future success in CS1 [5,7].

Finally, the question as to whether or not to enforce assessment test results, that is, to deny immediate entry into CS1 to those students not achieving adequate scores and requiring them to take CS0 first, was considered and decided against. The reasons for this were both philosophical and practical. If students who performed poorly on the assessment test were so notified, and still decided to remain in CS1, it was felt that they should be allowed to do so. Secondly, making students who have had previous programming courses from area institutions (and who still performed inadequately on the assessment test) take the CS0 course prior to taking CS1 would appear to show lack of confidence in other institutions.

In what follows, we discuss in more detail the approach taken and both the measurable and anecdotal degree of success this approach has had over the past five years of its implementation.

2. CS1 ASSESSMENT TEST DESIGN

The assessment test developed and currently being utilized was designed to be sufficiently simple that if a student performed poorly on it, there was little doubt about the student's lack of preparedness for CS1. The test contains ten simple programming problems presented in pseudocode form, shown in figure 1.

1. Indicate logically incorrect statements in the following, if any:

(a) x = 5 (c) z = x + y (e) x + y = y
(b) y = 10 (d) read (a + b) (f) write (y)

2. Given the input 4 and 6, what is the output in the following?

```
read x
read y
x = x + 3
y = x + 4
write (x, y)
```

3. What is the output in the following?

```
x = 100
if (x < 100) then
  write "Small number"
else
  write "Large number"
```

4. What is the output in the following?

```
x = 3
y = 4
if (x > y) then
  x = 2 * x
  write (x)
else
  y = x + y
  write (y)
```

5. Given the input 1, 3, 5, 7, 11, 15, what is the output in the following?

```
x = 1
while (x < 5)
  read (y)
  write (y)
  x = x + 1
```

6. Assume that x = 2. Execute the following loop 5 times. What is output?

```
loop
  x = x + 2
  write (x)
```

7. Given an array of integers data[10], what is the value of x?

```
a = 1
b = a + 1
data[1] = 9
data[2] = 10
data[3] = 8
x = data[b]
```

8. Assume Sum(x, y) returns the sum of its parameters. What is output?

```
a = 3
b = 5
write (Sum(a + 1, b + 3))
```

9. Write a few statements to swap the values of two variables x and y. (Hint: You may use another variable, if needed.)

10. Which of the following statements are considered either conditional or looping structures in a program?

(a) read
(b) if / else
(c) write
(d) x = 5
(e) while

Figure 1. Assessment test for CS1.

The assessment test is graded out of ten points. Those receiving a score of 0-2 are considered clearly in need of preparation before entry into CS1, and are strongly encouraged to drop the course and register for a section of CS0. Those receiving a score of 3-5 are considered also able to benefit from taking CS0, and are also recommended to so do, although not as strongly. Finally, those receiving a score of 6-10 are considered adequately prepared, and recommended to stay in CS1. (The CS0 courses are scheduled in a way that facilitates students dropping CS1 and adding CS0.)

Given the decision of not to enforce the recommendations made to students, the following procedures were adopted. Each instructor of CS1 administers the exam on the first day of class, grading it before the next class meeting. A form letter is filled out and given to each student containing their final assessment test score and an explanation of how to interpret it. The letter is signed by the chairperson of the department, and indicates that a copy will be kept in their files. (This is done so as to provide sufficient formality to the notification, and to let students know that if they choose not to follow the recommendation, they will have to bear responsibility.)

3. CS0 COURSE DESIGN

Prior to the changes in the introductory curriculum discussed here, the only course within the department satisfying the old CS1 prerequisite of "satisfactory completion of a programming course in a high-level programming language" was an introductory Visual Basic course (referred to as VB0 here). While Visual Basic can be taught in a way that focuses on fundamental programming concepts rather than visual programming-specific features, in practice, this is hard to achieve (given the coverage of Visual Basic textbooks, and the temptations to allow students to "have fun" with GUI development). Thus, the decision was made to develop an alternative fundamentals course to the VB0 course.

The main goal of the CS0 course created was to develop students' ability for algorithmic problem solving and program design, as opposed to knowledge of a particular programming language. In addition, the model of programming introduced was aimed at being simpler than in the CS1 (C++ based) course, given the evidence of the way that novice programmers acquire and utilize mental models of programming [3,4,9] and problems incurred with complex IDEs [1,8]. For these reasons, the course was designed to make use of pseudocode notation for program development (and minimal use of actual program code in order to demonstrate certain concepts, such as compilation). The topics covered in this course (titled "General Computer Science") are given in figure 2.

- Computer Science Overview
- Problem Solving and Computer Algorithms
- Data Representation and Manipulation
- Fundamental Programming Constructs
- Program Modularity (Functions and Procedures)
- Data Structures / Abstract Data Types
- Stacks, Queues, and Lists
- Introduction to Object-Oriented Design

Figure 2. Topics covered in CS0 course.

The course, while presenting some overview of computer science (e.g., introduction to hardware/software) is mainly focused on the understanding of general constructs of programming and proper program design. Thus, while the course is non-programming language specific, the concepts of function and procedures, modular program design, abstract data types, and even gentle introduction to object-oriented design are covered, given the ability to avoid language-specific issues that can clutter and obscure the main points to be made.

4. ANALYSIS OF IMPACT

4.1 Data Collected

The data collected was for those students ultimately taking CS1 with the fourth author. The reasons for not including CS1 students of other instructors in the study was that this author provided detailed records beyond that of other instructors, and for added consistency of final grades, given that this was used as the key measure of success.

Twelve class sections of data were collected over the period from Fall 2001 to Spring 2004. For each student, the following information was attempted to be constructed: the score received on the assessment test taken during the first day of CS1, any prior programming courses taken (i.e., the CS0 or VB0 course within the department, or "other"), and the final grade received in CS1. Of all students over the twelve class sections, complete information on 136 was constructed and used as the data set for the study.

4.2 Assessment Test Adequacy and Predictability

4.2.1 Assessment Test Adequacy

The assessment test was deemed to be adequate by a couple of measures. First, the range of scores realized over all semesters indicates the ability of the exam to consistently distinguish various levels of programming reasoning ability, as shown in figure 3 below.

Semester	Mean	Median
Fall 2001	5.36	6.00
Spring 2002	4.78	4.75
	4.79	4.50
Fall 2002	6.46	6.50
	6.15	6.00
Spring 2003	5.40	6.00
	6.07	6.25
	5.22	5.50
Fall 2003	5.98	6.00
	5.79	5.75
Spring 2004	6.30	6.50
	5.17	5.50

Figure 3. Assessment test means and medians.

The mean values obtained are within the range of 4.78-6.46, a variance of 1.68, with a midpoint value of 5.62. The median correlates well with each mean value for each administration of the assessment test.

4.2.2 Assessment Test Predictability

In order to determine the predictability of assessment test scores to actual performance in CS1, the assessment test scores for all 136 students in the data set were analyzed. Final assigned grades were A, B, C, D, or F (i.e., plus/minus grading was not used). Students were grouped by final grade and the mean of the assessment score at the start of the semester for each group calculated. The result is given in figure 4.

Final Grade	Assessment Score
A	7.44
B	6.17
C	5.43
D	4.46
F	4.75

Figure 4. Correlation of assessment scores / CS1 performance.

Ultimate performance in CS1 correlates well with assessment scores. An exception is shown in the D-F range, where the assessment had indicated overall better expected performance for those ultimately failing the course over those ultimately receiving a D. This can be explained by the fact that only 14 students were in the failing group, and 13 in the group receiving a D (as compared with a total of 109 students receiving a grade of C or better) and thus less statistically significant. However, for the purposes of the assessment test, the ability to predict those most prepared to continue in CS1 versus those that would benefit from further preparation seems to be validated.

4.3 CS0 Effectiveness as Preparation for CS1

4.3.1 Measurement of Ultimate Performance in CS1

Besides determining the effectiveness of the assessment test administered at the start of CS1, the effectiveness of the CS0 "fallback" course as preparation for CS1 was evaluated.

For this evaluation, five (overlapping) groups of students from the original data set were gathered: those that had no programming background at all and remaining in the CS1 course, those that had any previous programming background (including the department's Visual Basic course, VB0), those that had only the VB0 course, those that had prior C++ programming experience, and those that had only the CS0 course. The average performance in CS1 for each of these groups was determined (based on final grade), given in figure 5.

No previous background	2.00
Any (including VB0)	2.53
VB0 Only	2.59
C++ Only	2.50
CS0 Only	2.84

Figure 5. CS1 performance vs. previous background.
(scale of 0-4, where A = 4.0)

There were only five students with no previous background at all who decided to remain in the CS1 course. While a small statistical sample, these students performed poorly (on average), as expected, with an average final grade of 2.0 (C). There were fifty-seven students who had some previous programming background (including the department's VB0 course) other than the CS0 course offered. In addition, those students that had only the department's VB0 course (27) was analyzed. These two groups had essentially the same average performance in CS1, 2.53 and 2.59. In addition, there were eight students having had C++ programming before taking the CS1 course, achieving only an average of 2.50. The group having had only the department's CS0 course (63), however, had the best overall performance in CS1, 2.84. This results shows, therefore, that the non-specific programming language approach of the CS0 course has the potential to better prepare students than courses utilizing specific programming languages, even C++ itself.

4.3.2 Anecdotal Evidence of the Effectiveness of the CS0 Course

In addition to the objective measures of the effectiveness of the instituted CS0 course, subjective measures were obtained by means of a survey given out at the end of CS1. The question given to students was if they felt adequately prepared for the course and if they felt that prior programming experience should be required for entry into CS1. The comments from those students having had the CS0 course before CS1 were overwhelmingly positive. Overall, the comments indicated that students felt both technically prepared and more confident when entering CS1. The comfort level generally provided by the CS0 course (in addition to the technical preparation provided) is seen as additionally relevant to future success in CS1, particularly for women and minorities, as evidenced in the literature [2,6,10]. This is yet to be analyzed.

5. CONCLUSIONS

Based on the initial results presented here, the change from explicit prerequisites for entry into CS1 and a *presumption* of preparedness (based on previous programming courses taken) to a *demonstrated* degree of preparedness (based on assessment test results) appears to have been a move in the right direction. The curriculum change instituted, however, has relied on two critical elements: (a) the design of an appropriate assessment test for determining which students should be recommended to continue in CS1, and which should not, and (b) the design of an appropriate "fallback" CS0 course capable of best preparing students for ultimate success in CS1.

The results obtained thus far have shown the assessment test to be both adequate (for distinguishing the programming reasoning ability of students), and predictive (for determining which students will most benefit from further preparation before taking CS1). The assessment test scores over the past five years have been well distributed, and correlate well with ultimate CS1 performance.

Students opting to take the CS0 course before entry into CS1 have been shown to ultimately perform at a higher level than students with any other particular programming background, on average. Thus, the design of the CS0 course targeted for CS1 success has been shown to be effective. In addition, the comfort and confidence levels of these students appear to have also been positively affected, possibly further contributing to their future success in CS1.

6. REFERENCES

[1] Eric Allen, Robert Cartwright, and Brian Stoler. DrJava: A Lightweight Pedagogic Environment for Java. In *Proceedings of the 33rd SIGCSE Technical Symposium*, Covington, Kentucky, pp. 137-141, 2002.

[2] Sylvia Beyer, Kristina Rynes, Julie Perrault, Kelly Hay, and Susan Haller. Gender Differences in Computer Science Education. In *Proceedings of the 34th SIGCSE Technical Symposium*, Reno Nevada, pp. 49-53, 2003.

[3] Peter J DePasquale III. Implications on the Learning of Programming Through the Implementation of Subsets in Program Development Environments, Ph.D. Dissertation, Virginia Polytech, 2003.

[4] Peter DePasquale, J.A.N. Lee, and Manuel A. Perez-Quinones. Evaluation of Subsetting Programming Language Elements in a Novice's Programming Environment. In *Proceeding of the 35th SIGCSE Technical Symposium*, Norfolk, Virginia, pp. 260-264, 2004.

[5] B. duBoulay, T. O'Shea, and J. Monk. The Black Box Inside the Glass Box: Presenting Computing Concepts to Novices, in *Studying the Novice Programmer*, E. Soloway and J.C. Spoher (eds.), Lawrence Erlbaum, Hillsdale, N.J., pp. 431-446, 1989.

[6] Lilly Irani. Understanding Gender and Confidence in CS Course Culture. In *Proceeding of the 35th SIGCSE Technical Symposium*, Norfolk, Virginia pp. 195-199, 2004.

[7] P. N. Johnson-Laird. *Mental Models*, Cambridge University Press, 1983.

[8] Charles Reis and Robert Cartwright. Taming a Professional IDE for the Classroom. In *Proceeding of the 35th SIGCSE Technical Symposium*, Norfolk, Virginia, pp. 156-160, 2004.

[9] Anthony Robins, Janet Rountree, and Nathan Rountree. Learning and Teaching Programming: A Review and Discussion. *Computer Science Education*, Vol. 13, No. 2, pp. 137-172, 2003.

[10] Brenda Cantwell Wilson. A Study of Factors Promoting Success in Computer Science Including Gender Differences. In *Computer Science Education*, Vol. 12, No. 1-2, pp. 141-164, 2002.

Panel: Using Peer Review in Teaching Computing

Edward F. Gehringer
North Carolina State University
Depts. of Computer Science & ECE
Raleigh, NC 27695-7256
+1 919-515-2066
efg@ncsu.edu

Donald D. Chinn
Univ. of Washington at Tacoma
Dept. of Computing and Software Systems
Tacoma, WA 98402
+1 253 692-4660
dchinn@u.washington.edu

Mark A. Ardis
Rose-Hulman Institute of Technology
Dept. of Computer Science & Software Engineering
Terre Haute, IN 47803
+1 812 877-8226
mark.a.ardis@rose-hulman.edu

Manuel A. Pérez-Quiñones
Department of Computer Science
Virginia Tech
Blacksburg, VA 24061
+1 540 231-2646
perez@cs.vt..edu

SUMMARY

For generations, the academic community has relied on peer review as a way of encouraging scholarship and enhancing the knowledge base. Peer review has been widely used in the classroom since at least the 1970s, with hundreds of papers on its use in diverse academic fields appearing in the literature (for a comprehensive survey, see [1]). Its use appears to be on the upswing, given the current interest in active learning and teamwork. In computer science, peer review seems to have very broad application. It can be used to evaluate the contributions of various members to a project team; it can be used for design documents and code reviews, in writing assignments, and in capstone project courses. The experience of the panelists is illustrative of the wide range of peer-review practices. This panel will serve to introduce the audience to some of these applications. Since many computer-science instructors have experimented with peer review, we are anxious to have them share their experiences during the open discussion period.

Categories and Subject Descriptors

K.3.2 [**Computers and Education**]: Computer and information science education, Curriculum. K.3.1 [**Computer Uses in Education**]: Collaborative learning.

General Terms

Measurement, Documentation.

Keywords

Peer review, collaborative learning, assessment, UML.

1. DONALD CHINN

Learning environments that include student peer review have the potential to provide students with experiences they cannot get otherwise. Peer review is an advanced activity for students. It is a form of assessment at the highest level of Bloom's taxonomy [2] (the Evaluation level). It can also influence student attitudes in a way that advances them in Perry's scheme of intellectual development [3]. For example, students might see other students (and themselves) as legitimate sources of knowledge if the proper evidence is provided, and they might recognize a multiplicity of correct solutions to problems and degrees of quality of those solutions, rather than seeing every problem as having a right or wrong answer, with the right answer possessed by the instructor.

I will discuss issues related to creating learning environments that include peer review, such as how much class time to devote to the activity, the level of difficulty of the problems used in the peer review, and grading schemes. I will also discuss some observations and data from my use of peer review in an algorithms course.

2. MARK ARDIS

In our introductory sequence of courses we use peer reviews of designs and code to teach good style and technique. Since some students enter the sequence with more experience than others, this helps to level the classes.

Peer reviews of protocol proposals are sometimes used to select one protocol for all projects that term. The competitive aspect encourages students to produce better proposals, and the reviewers find bugs that would be difficult to debug. This teaches an important lesson about quality assurance—that review methods may be more effective than testing.

We use peer review for several purposes in our software engineering courses at Rose-Hulman. One purpose is to achieve vertical integration: interaction of students at different levels of education. This has been particularly effective in preparing students for their capstone senior project experience.

Students in junior-level courses review artifacts of senior projects. Juniors get to see some useful examples of artifacts that they are learning to develop, and it shows them what will be expected of them in the next year. Seniors get useful feedback about their work. They are often motivated to produce higher quality work in this environment.

SIGCSE'05, February 23–27, 2005, St. Louis, Missouri, USA.
ACM 1-58113-997-7/05/0002.

Juniors also review presentations by seniors at various stages of their projects. In addition to reviewing the technical content of the presentations they review performance characteristics such as materials, oral skills and attitude. We found that we needed to develop a comprehensive rubric for these presentation reviews, as students need a lot of direction when learning this skill.

3. MANUEL PÉREZ-QUIÑONES

Object-oriented design is difficult to teach early in the curriculum. There seems to be a consensus that with experience, students can do better OO design. We believe that peer review [4] can provide a way to give students more experience with OOD issues without overburdening them with lots of design work. We have built an application to build UML designs that is particularly targeted to first-year students, and designed to support peer-review activities. It supports a very minimal subset of UML, and has numerous usability enhancements, like support for full undo and very flexible printing and exporting capabilities. For peer review, the tool supports writing free-form drawings and electronic sticky notes, and uploading the design plus comments to a remote server.

Before we deployed the tool in our CS2 course, we realized that we did not know what to expect in terms of the levels of feedback that students would provide. But in particular, we did not know if the commenting features would be used more by students who have Tablet-PCs than by the ones who had desktop computers. Thus, we are studying what impact the choice of platform has on the type of peer-feedback provided.

I will report on the design of the tool and an initial study [5] of how paper and pencil, desktop, and Tablet-PC differ when students used them to provide peer-review comments to UML designs. In general, we found that the most natural medium for providing comments was the paper/pencil. The Tablet-PC comments were more similar to the paper/pencil, with the exception that the paper/pencil afforded more fine control in the comments (e.g. crossing out parts of class names). However, that level of comments might not be necessarily appropriate for the task at hand. The Desktop format was the most restrictive of all. Arrows in free form were used only to represent missing UML associations and never as a deictic reference. Furthermore, the comments were always provided in "stickies" but never as free-form annotations.

4. ED GEHRINGER

For several years, I have used a Web-based system called PG [4] for peer review of student work. Students prepare their work, and submit it in the form of a Web page, or a set of Web pages. They are then presented with a set of their classmates' submissions to review, based on a rubric for that particular assignment. Authors can respond to their reviewers on a shared Web page. They can resubmit their work, and have it reviewed again by the same reviewers. After the review period is over, students then assign grades to *reviews* done by other students. This serves to insure careful reviewing, as students who are careless in reviewing their peers will see their own scores suffer.

The power of the peer-review process lies in the fact that it can be used to produce educational resources for subsequent generations of students. Suppose that students choose one of a set of assignments to do—write a paper analyzing a particular topic, make up questions over a particular lecture, or find a set of educational resources that can be hyperlinked to the lecture notes for a particular lecture. Then, from among the submissions for each topic, peer review can be used to identify the best one. The best submissions can be assembled together into a set of resources for the course. This is the core of our Expertiza platform: Students select topics, peer-review each other's work, and then the best work is put into a database of reusable course modules, which can be used in later semesters, or by other instructors. This methodology has been used to produce an award-winning Ethics in Computing Web site [6], annotated lecture notes for several courses, and about sixty problems in parallel computer architecture, which are now available to instructors with accounts on our Conoscenza computer architecture course database [7]. Recently, this methodology has attracted the attention of a major educational publisher, who is interested in it as a means of producing exercises and problems for textbooks.

5. REFERENCES

[1] Topping, Keith, "Peer assessment between students in colleges and universities, "*Review of Educational Research* 68:3, Fall 1998, pp. 249-276.

[2] Bloom, Benjamin S. (editor), *Taxonomy of Educational Objectives: Handbook 1: Cognitive Domain*. New York, Longman, 1956.

[3] Perry, William G., *Forms of Ethical and Intellectual Development in the College Years*. San Francisco, CA, Jossey-Bass, 1999.

[4] Gehringer, Edward F., "Peer review and peer grading in computer-science courses," *Proceedings of SIGCSE 2001: Thirty-Second Technical Symposium on Computer Science Education*, Charlotte, Feb. 22–25, 2001, pp. 139-143.

[5] Pérez-Quiñones, Manuel and Turner, Scott, "Using a tablet PC to provide peer review comments," Technical report TR-04-17, Dept. of Computer Science, Virginia Tech, June 8, 2004.

[6] Gehringer, Edward F., "Building an Ethics in Computing Website using peer review," *American Society for Engineering Education 2001 Annual Conference and Exposition*, Session 1461.

[7] Gehringer, Edward F. and Louca, Tony M., "Web-based databases of course material: Improving the viability," *Frontiers in Education 2000*, Kansas City, MO, October 18–21, 2000, Session S2B in proceedings.

The Year in Review...
Changes and Lessons Learned in the Design and Implementation of the AP CS Exam in Java
Special Session Description

Scot Drysdale
Dartmouth College
scot@cs.dartmouth.edu

Judith Hromcik
Arlington High School
jhromcik@comcast.net

David Reed
Creighton University
davereed@creighton.edu

Reg Hahne, Moderator
Atholton High School
rhahne@hcpss.org

Summary
The 2004 school year marked significant changes in the Advanced Placement (AP) Computer Science curriculum. Most visibly, Java replaced C++ as the exam-testable programming language. More fundamentally, however, the AP CS curriculum now places a greater emphasis on object-oriented design than in previous years. Students are expected to be able to implement interfaces, design and implement class hierarchies using inheritance, analyze the tradeoffs between alternative designs and their associated efficiencies, and make use of Java Collection classes where appropriate. This special session is intended to inform both high school and college teachers as to the extent of these changes and how they affected the development and grading of the 2004 AP CS exams. In addition, it will provide practical insights as to how the new curriculum can be taught in high schools, and how teachers can better prepare their students for the exams.

The AP CS Development Committee's charge is not only to provide a comprehensive testing mechanism, but also to recommend a direction that high school teachers should take in preparing a foundation for more advanced student studies during college. This special session will bring together two college and two high school members of the AP CS Development Committee to share some of their insights into the AP program.

AP teachers will learn valuable information to continue to support their shift to Java in the classroom and about the exam for which they are preparing their students. College teachers will learn more about the AP CS curriculum and test development process, which may aid them in similar course redesigns and in the placement of students with AP credit.

Time will be provided to discuss participant's questions.

SIGCSE'05, February 23-27, 2005, St. Louis, Missouri, USA.
ACM 1-58113-997-7/05/0002.

Categories and Subject Descriptors
D.1.5 [**Programming Techniques**]: Object-oriented Programming

D.3.2 [**Programming Languages**]: Language Classifications - *Object-oriented languages*

D.3.3 [**Programming Languages**]: Language Constructs and Features - Abstract data types, *Classes and objects, Control structures, Data types and structures, Inheritance*

General Terms
Algorithms, Design, Languages

Keywords
AP, AP CS, AP CS Development Committee, Advanced Placement Computer Science, high school teachers, Java, Java Exam, Collection classes, Marine Biology Simulation Case Study, object-oriented design, interfaces, inheritance

1 Free Response and the Collection Classes
Scot Drysdale is Professor of Computer Science at Dartmouth College and has served on the AP CS Development Committee since 2000. Currently he is serving as Chair of the committee. Professor Drysdale's research interests include computational geometry and its applications, and computer science education.

While the core of the AP CS curriculum remains the same (algorithmic thinking, programming fundamentals, and computer literacy), the move to Java in 2004 has introduced and coincided with some significant changes. To take advantage of Java's features and to better match college curricula, the AP CS curriculum was updated to emphasize object-oriented design, the use of interfaces and inheritance, and the application of Collection classes where appropriate. Professor Drysdale will discuss these and other changes in the AP CS curriculum, and how these changes have affected the development of AP CS exams. For example, the more object-oriented Marine Biology Simulation Case Study has allowed for the integration of many object-oriented concepts into the classroom, and serves as a testing framework for these concepts on the exams. Similarly, the use of the Collection classes has given the opportunity to develop free response questions that require knowledge about the implementation of data structures and their appropriate time constraints.

2 Exam Stats and Development

David Reed is Associate Professor of Computer Science at Creighton University in Omaha, Nebraska. His research interests include automated deduction and computer science education, where he has published on topics such as apprentice-based learning, Web-based programming, and innovative instructional methods in introductory computer science. Dr. Reed has been involved with the AP program since 1994, and is the Chief Reader for the AP Computer Science exam since 2004.

With significant changes to the AP CS curriculum and a new programming language tested on the 2004 exam, there were many questions concerning the grading process. Would students (and teachers) be well prepared for the language switch? How would students react to the new areas of emphasis (object-orientation, design, and collections)? Would students stray outside of the Java subset described in the AP CS curriculum? And finally, how would overall student performance compare with previous years?

Dr. Reed will attempt to answer these questions, providing statistics and commentary on the grading process for the 2004 exams. Analysis of student performance in 2004 will provide insights into what concepts the students did and did not master, and may guide AP teachers in better preparing their students for the exams.

3 Tips for Teaching in the Classroom

Judy Hromcik has taught mathematics and computer science at the high school level since 1987. Since 1989 she has taught Advanced Placement Computer Science at Arlington High School, Texas. She developed the AP CS curriculum for the Arlington school system and, in addition to the AP courses, teaches an advanced Computer Science course using Java. Ms. Hromcik has been a College Board consultant since 1995, a reader for the AP CS exam for five years and is a member of the AP CS Development Committee.

The change of programming language, as well as the emphasis on object-oriented methods, has necessitated wholesale changes at the instructional level. While AP- and JETT-sponsored workshops have helped prepare high school teachers over the last few years, the language switch has still placed a burden on teachers to learn a new language, master the Java case study, and develop new teaching materials. Ms. Hromcik will discuss how the language change to Java has affected teaching AP CS I and AP CS II. She will share insights gained from teaching Java for three years, will highlight techniques for teaching objects early in the school year, and will discuss how high school teachers might better prepare their students for the exams.

4 Moderator

Reg Hahne is the Technology Instructional Team Leader and Information Technology Academy Manager at Atholton High School, Columbia, Maryland. He has 15 years experience with the AP CS program. Mr. Hahne has been an AP Computer Science reader for the past eight years, a College Board Consultant for the last 6 years, and is a member of the AP CS Test Development Committee.

Teaching Hands-on Computer and Information Systems Security Despite Limited Resources

Bhagyavati (Moderator)
Columbus State University
4225 University Avenue
Columbus, GA 31907
1-706-565-3519
bhagyavati@colstate.edu

Stephen O. Agyei-Mensah
Clarion University of Pennsylvania
130 Becker Hall
Clarion, PA 16214
1-814-393-2733
smensah@clarion.edu

Rose Shumba
Computer Science Department
Indiana University of Pennsylvania
Indiana, PA 17501
1-724-357-3166
shumba@iup.edu

Iretta B.C. Kearse
Spelman College
350 Spelman Lane, SW, Box 1257
Atlanta, GA 30314
1-404-270-5878
ikearse@spelman.edu

Categories and Subject Descriptors
K.3.2 [**Computer and Information Science Education**]: Computer Science Education, Curriculum.

General Terms
Security, Management, Economics.

Keywords
Computer and Information Systems Security, Hands-on Exercises, Limited Resources, Shoestring Budget.

SUMMARY
Computer and information systems security is an important topic in the computer science curriculum. Teaching courses that raise awareness of the various components of information assurance is a daunting challenge without hands-on exercises to stimulate the understanding of the students. Each panelist has had experience in teaching security courses on shoestring budgets with constrained resources. We will share our experiences in teaching such courses despite limited resources of time, money, equipment and support. We will also illustrate effective hands-on exercises that can be implemented on limited budgets and restricted resources.

Several handouts will be distributed to the audience; these handouts will describe specific hands-on exercises that have been successfully used by the panelists in teaching information security classes. A resources page with annotated URL's will also be made available to interested colleagues and peers. Suggestions from the audience on improving our lab assignments and creatively using existing resources will be welcomed. We anticipate using more than half the allocated time in this manner.

SIGCSE'05, February 23–27, 2005, St. Louis, Missouri, USA.
ACM 1-58113-997-7/05/0002

POSITION STATEMENTS

Bhagyavati

In the Computer Science department where I teach, an optional track of the graduate program deals with information assurance (IA) courses, which can be taken online. The online delivery mode poses particular challenges in developing and administering laboratory exercises to our students. For our undergraduates, we offer computer networking and network security courses, both of which are supplemented by online components; we thus face the challenges of incorporating sufficient hands-on exercises so that students can grasp the applications of security tools.

A small university like ours, with a total enrollment of 7,000 students, cannot afford to purchase equipment and resources as needed for security courses. Remote login equipment is also needed because of the online graduate program. Faculty collaborate freely on sharing effective practices, and pool equipment and course components. For example, old computers were salvaged from IT staff for teaching networking and were reused in the operating systems class to teach Linux concepts. In the following semester, another faculty member used the same machines to demonstrate wireless security attacks and solutions.

Our goal is to develop a set of robust and interactive laboratory exercises for each of the information systems security courses we teach: networking, network security, wireless concepts, computer forensics, advanced system security, risk assessment and software testing and measurement. As each faculty goes to security conferences and information assurance workshops, they bring back a wealth of sharable knowledge about hands-on exercises and best practices in teaching information systems security.

Rose Shumba

The Cybersecurity Basics course is an interdisciplinary course for the Criminology, Management Information Systems and Computer Science students at our university. The course provides an introduction to the theory and concepts of computer security in host systems. In 2002, a project to augment the teaching of a Cybersecurity Basics course was started. Nine laboratory exercises were developed. The project involved:

- evaluation of the effectiveness of Linux host security tools
- developing hands-on lab exercises for teaching the course
- integrating the developed (lab) exercises, and the host theories and principles.

The tools used in the development of the lab exercises were free downloads from two main sites: www.cert.org and www.insecure.org. Examples of representative "best of breed" tools and their chosen categories (from the CERT coordination center at http://www.cert.org) are as follows:

1. Intrusion detection: Ethereal, Tripwire
2. Vulnerability assessment: Nmap and Nessus
3. Audit and monitoring: logsentry, logwatch
4. Encryption: GnuPG
5. User account security: Nutcracker, John the Ripper, Crack

The advantages of using Linux as an approach to improving the teaching of a security course are that: 1) Linux is free, we are using Red Hat 9.1, 2) there is an abundance of freely downloadable Linux security tools, 3) tutorials and documentation are available with most of the tools, which can be tailored to one's teaching environment.

The challenges we face are: 1) keeping up with the tool updates, 2) identifying the ideal tools for teaching such a course with students from diverse backgrounds, 3) dealing with extensive documentation available with some of the tools we require students to install, 4) the installation process for the tools . The main libraries used by most of these tools are libdnet, libpcap and libnids; however, we observed during tool installation that some tools required a certain library version, while others required another version or maybe even an older version of the library. This lengthened the installation process. In addition, installation of some of the tools required advanced Unix/Linux knowledge, and, 5) output from some of the tools is sometimes not very easy to understand. Output from some of the tools requires students to understand network concepts.

Examples laboratory exercise will be shown to the audience.

Stephen O. Agyei-Mensah

Despite a shoestring budget, I have been successful in teaching security to Computer Information Systems students through exercises on wireless networks, which are traditionally less secure than their wired counterparts. The hands-on lab exercises in most college textbooks for wireless security configuration require devices like the Cisco Aironet access point or 3Com AirConnect access point and Cisco Catalyst 1900 switches. The setup and instructions for the lab exercises have been written with these devices in mind. In 2002, these pieces of equipment ranged in cost from $1,000.00 to $2,500.00. They now range between $500.00 and $1,000.00. In a department with an annual budget of $200.00 per faculty member for professional development, resources were scarce and equipment was non-existent when I first taught a security course.

However, a little ingenuity can overcome these obstacles and my experiences with teaching security on scarce resources have been well received by students. Sometimes, students feel more comfortable with reconfiguration of older equipment because of familiarity and the lack of IT staff oversight. There are many inexpensive domestic networking devices on the market whose configuration can offer students the same experience as the expensive Cisco and 3Com devices. For example, Linksys 8-port switches cost about $60.00, Linksys 802.11g wireless access point is under $80.00, a SMC managed switch with VLAN capabilities is under $200.00, and D-Link 802.11b wireless NICs cost about $20.00. The prices for these devices are still falling just like the prices of Cisco and 3Com devices; on the whole, domestic devices are significantly cheaper than that of Cisco and 3Com.

The only drawback in using the domestic devices instead of commercial devices is that professors may have to be a little creative in adapting the instructions in the textbooks for the domestic devices. However, the advantages of such an approach are that students welcome hands-on exercises on familiar devices, scarce departmental and university resources are not stretched, and security loopholes and countermeasures are easily demonstrated by adapting instruction accordingly.

Iretta B.C. Kearse

Spelman College is an outstanding historically black undergraduate private college for women. Spelman promotes academic excellence in the liberal arts, and develops the intellectual, ethical, and leadership potential of its students. As a private undergraduate single-gender college with a total enrollment of 2300, there are limited faculty and financial resources. The Computer and Information Science (CIS) department has a faculty of six full-time instructors, and a yearly network equipment budget of $10,000. The liberal arts CIS curriculum only requires majors to complete three upper-level electives. Many times, an elective is open to both junior and senior undergraduates, and is only offered every other academic year, thus creating the requirement that elective courses be accessible to students with varied levels of computing knowledge.

When teaching the Computer Networks and Security course, what is needed is a set of laboratory assignments that will first establish a base level of student knowledge of networking and then introduce security-related topics. Many network textbooks do not have laboratory assignments related to the lecture topics; or, the assignments are network operating systems specific and require expensive professional grade software and equipment. For these reasons, we have had to create our own labs adapted for use with less expensive devices deigned for the small/home office, and seek out and utilize academic alliance programs, freeware, open source applications, and equipment grant programs that provide resources at little or no cost.

Taming Java for the Classroom*

James I. Hsia jhsia@alumni.rice.edu
Elspeth Simpson elspeth@rice.edu
Daniel Smith dlsmith@rice.edu
Robert Cartwright cork@rice.edu
Rice University
6100 S. Main St.
Houston TX 77005

ABSTRACT

Java is the canonical language for teaching introductory programming, but its complex syntax and abundance of constructs are difficult for beginners to learn. This paper shows how object-oriented programming in Java can be made more accessible to beginners through the use of "language levels", a hierarchy of progressively richer subsets of Java. This hierarchy is implemented as an extension of the DrJava pedagogic programming environment.

Categories and Subject Descriptors: D.2.6 [Software Engineering]:Programming Environments

General Terms: Design, Human Factors, Languages

Keywords: DrJava, language levels, object-oriented programming

1. INTRODUCTION

Programming technology is in the midst of a paradigm shift. Object-oriented programming (OOP) in safe, *object-oriented* (OO) languages like Java and C# is gradually supplanting *object-based* programming in C++ for mainstream applications. Many colleges have recently revised their introductory programming sequence (CS1/CS2) to use Java instead of Pascal or C++. High school courses in AP Computer Science made the transition from C++ to Java last year. In the wake of this paradigm shift, computing educators face a dilemma about what concepts to teach in introductory courses using Java. Should they continue to teach the object-based perspective that has dominated programming curricula for the past decade? Or should they embrace a truly OO approach to program design for which there is little precedent? There is a growing consensus that OOP concepts should be taught in Java as early as possible [9].

Despite the growing consensus in favor of an "objects-first" curriculum, the implementation of this pedagogy has proven to be a challenge. The ACM Education Board recently formed a Java Task Force "to develop a stable collection of pedagogical resources that will make it easier to teach Java to first-year computing students without having those students *overwhelmed by its complexity* [emphasis added]" [1]. Java's complex syntax and plethora of language features are a serious obstacle to learning OOP and interfere with an early focus on OO concepts. Even the traditional first program, "Hello World", seems daunting to a beginner. To run "Hello World" from the command line, the student must write a main method whose declaration looks like this:

```
public static void main(String[] args)
```

In this one declaration, the student is confronted with visibility modifiers, static methods, return types, and arrays—none of which are central to OOP. The instructor faces a choice between taking the time to explain what these complex, unrelated pieces of the language mean or telling the students to blindly cut and paste the code. Neither of these choices is very attractive.

To make Java more accessible to beginners, educators have developed pedagogic programming environments such as BlueJ [8] and DrJava [2] that support simpler, more intuitive programming interfaces. BlueJ provides a graphically based workbench where students can create objects and apply methods to them, while DrJava provides users with an Interactions Pane that transforms Java from a batch-oriented language to an interactive one with a read-eval-print-loop. Both of these interfaces completely eliminate the need to define a `main` method.

While these pedagogic environments are a major step forward over conventional Java environments, they do not fully shield students from the complexities of Java syntax or necessarily encourage OO design. Nearly all Java texts, including those that presume the support of a pedagogic environment like BlueJ or DrJava, cover the major syntactic elements of procedural programming—namely assignment, conditionals, and looping constructs—plus Java language features like `static`, `final` and visibility modifiers, before discussing the essence of OOP: polymorphism (dynamic dispatch). The detour through the mechanics of procedural programming is time-consuming and distracting, making it difficult to teach an OO perspective on program design.

What is needed is a hierarchy of Java *language levels*—progressively richer subsets of the Java language that facilitate a focus on OO design rather than the mechanics of the Java language. The idea of partitioning a language into a hierarchy of language levels dates back to at least the 1970's when Richard Holt *et al* developed the SP/k framework for teaching structured programming in PL/I [7] at the University of Toronto. More recently, the DrScheme environment developed by Matthias Felleisen and his students at Rice

*This research has been partially supported by the Texas Advanced Technology Program and the National Science Foundation.

SIGCSE'05, February 23–27, 2005, St. Louis, Missouri, USA.

University pioneered the idea of partitioning a language into a *semantic* hierarchy of language levels. In DrScheme, the language level hierarchy supports a corresponding hierarchy of computational models, each with a richer data model and more complex semantics than its predecessor. As a result, the progression of language levels in DrScheme directly corresponds to a progression of programming abstractions suitable for teaching. The pedagogy underlying this progression is explained in the textbook *How to Design Programs* (HTDP)[4].

Although HTDP focuses on "mostly" functional programming in Scheme, the underlying pedagogy is largely language independent. In fact, the same programming concepts and principles can be articulated in the context of OOP in Java. In HTDP, program design is *data-directed*, primarily using inductively-defined *algebraic* types like lists and trees.[1] Given the inductive definition for a data domain, there is a corresponding, mechanically generated template for writing a function to process that form of data. In addition, the program development process is *test-driven*; test cases are written for each program function before it is coded.

In an OO context, the design concepts in HTDP correspond to progressively more sophisticated uses of polymorphism that have been codified as *design patterns* in the well-known "Gang of Four" tome [5] on the subject. It is remarkable that two largely disjoint programming cultures have distilled essentially the same principles of program design. The programming methodology from HTDP looks equally familiar when it is translated to an OO context: it is simply Extreme Programming (XP) [10] in-the-small: test-driven development using JUnit.

In this paper, we describe a language levels framework that we have developed for the DrJava programming environment. This framework supports our translation of the programming pedagogy from HTDP into an OO context. With this framework, OO programming in Java is easily accessible to beginners, as demonstrated by the simplicity of the OO program written at the Elementary level in Figure 1.

2. AN OVERVIEW OF DRJAVA

DrJava [2] is a free, open-source, lightweight IDE developed at Rice University by undergraduate and graduate students under the direction of Prof. Robert Cartwright. The user interface is designed to be simple and highly interactive. There are only three panes: a Navigator Pane lists all open documents, a Definitions Pane displays the selected document (typically a file defining a Java class), and an Interactions Pane allows the user to evaluate arbitrary Java program text. The Definitions Pane supports the "intelligent" editing of Java program text through syntax highlighting, brace matching, and uniform indenting to help beginners adjust to Java syntax. The Interactions Pane encourages students to experiment with both their code and Java libraries by accepting an arbitrary series of program statements and expressions and evaluating them cumulatively "on-the-fly". The value of each top-level expression is printed using the `toString()` representation of that value.

A small collection of menus on the title bar provides commands for basic actions, including:

- creating, opening, saving, and closing documents;

[1]A data type is *algebraic* if it can be defined by a *tree grammar* [3]. In OOP, algebraic types are defined by the *composite* pattern [5].

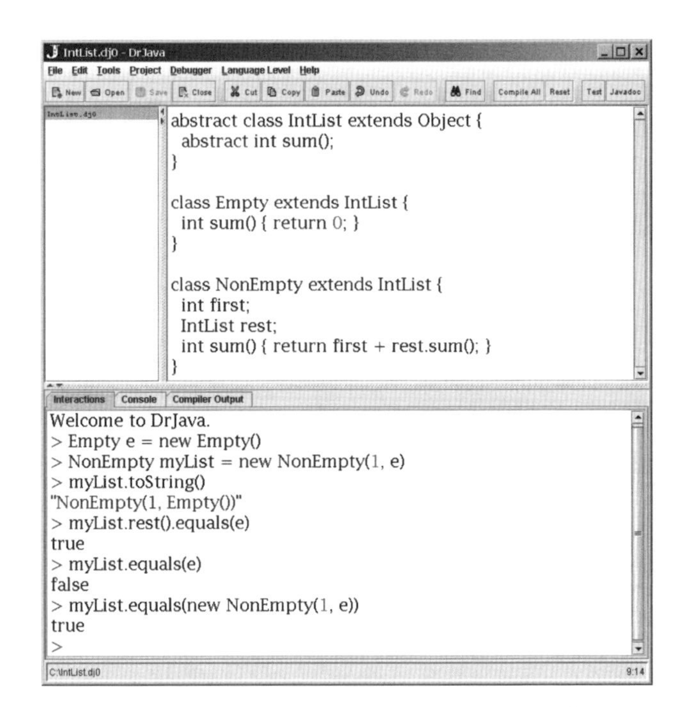

Figure 1: DrJava at Elementary Level

- compiling and unit testing open document(s);
- enabling a source level debugger integrated with the Interactions Pane;
- running `javadoc` on all of the source files to generate HTML output;
- changing the configuration options for DrJava; and
- selecting a language level.

The most common commands are bound to buttons on a tool bar just below the title bar.

Although DrJava is targeted primarily at supporting beginning and intermediate programming courses taught in Java, it is also particularly well-suited to small production programming projects that use test-driven development. In fact, for the past two years, DrJava has been developed using DrJava. The combination of a general read-eval-print-loop (the Interactions pane) with tightly integrated support for unit testing and source level debugging provides an unusually responsive and productive environment for software development. To our knowledge, DrJava is the only IDE, commercial or open-source, that supports a full read-eval-print loop capable of evaluating arbitrary program text in the context of a debugger breakpoint environment.

The most recent release of DrJava fully supports Java 1.5 including generic types and the "Tiger" (JSR-201) language extensions (*autoboxing* and *auto-unboxing*, *foreach*, *enum* types, and *varargs*). It also includes a lightweight project facility capable of building projects like DrJava itself. CVS (the most widely used open source version control package) support has not yet been integrated in DrJava, but will soon be forthcoming. The primary features offered by professional IDE's (like Eclipse and JBuilder) that are missing in DrJava are code completion and refactoring transformations.

3. PEDAGOGY AND LANGUAGE LEVELS

Before describing the design of our language levels framework for DrJava, we must explain an important aspect of our pedagogy that has shaped its design.

In our introductory programming curriculum, we follow the progression of programming concepts in HTDP, adapted to the context of OOP. As a result, we initially focus on programming with *immutable* data objects—objects where all fields are `final`. We impose this restriction for two reasons. First, programming with immutable data is easy for beginners because it is a natural extension of concepts from arithmetic and algebra learned in grammar school. Familiar laws such as the "substitution of equals for equals" hold in the context of immutable data, but break when mutation is added. Second, many computations depend on maintaining the immutability of data as an invariant. Mutating a data object is dangerous because it changes the state of every object that refers directly or indirectly to the mutated object. The integrity of some commonly used classes in the standard Java libraries depends on using immutable data. For example, only immutable objects can safely be used as keys in the `HashMap` and `HashTable` classes in `java.util`. The `String` class in `java.lang` is immutable for this reason.

In our experience as software developers, programming with immutable data confers so many advantages that we teach our students to scrupulously avoid mutation unless there is a specific justification for doing so. Two good reasons for using mutation are:

- **Faithful modeling**. When the entity modeled by a data object can change state, its data representation should be *mutable*. For example, the document objects that are edited in DrJava are mutable.
- **Application efficiency**. If data values are immutable, new values can only be created by explicitly constructing them. In contrast, mutation allows existing values to be updated to form new values. In some applications, the efficiency of the application critically depends on modifying existing values rather than allocating new ones. Consider a compiler that makes multiple passes over the AST representation for a source program. Each pass adds new attributes to the nodes of the AST. Building a new immutable AST on each pass is conceptually elegant, but is often not worth the overhead incurred.

In our framework, the first two language language levels enforce the immutability of data. This restriction guarantees that data structures do not contain cycles, enabling the language levels framework to automatically generate descriptive `toString()` methods for program classes.

4. LANGUAGE LEVELS DESIGN

Designing a language levels framework for Java is a more challenging problem than simply identifying an appropriate hierarchy of language subsets. Full Java requires programmers to write boilerplate methods such as constructors, selectors, and the `equals(...)` and `toString()` methods for simple algebraic data types like the `Empty` and `NonEmpty` list classes in Figure 1. To make programming with algebraic types accessible to beginners, two of our language levels automatically generate these boilerplate methods. Note that immutability plays a critical role in making this process tractable.

Our framework consists of three levels: Elementary, Intermediate, and Advanced, plus the full Java language (which DrJava already supports). Each successive level embodies a richer, more complex collection of abstractions for defining data and performing computation over that data. Nearly all of these abstractions are embodied as design patterns.

The following subsections briefly describe each language level and the associated programming concepts.

4.1 Elementary Level

The Elementary level focuses on computation over immutable algebraic data types such as booleans, integers, lists, and trees. As a result, executing programs is analogous to performing algebraic simplification. In an OO context, the natural representation of algebraic data follows the *Composite* design pattern where each clause of the inductive definition is represented as a concrete class extending an abstract class at the root of the composite hierarchy. Several other basic design patterns can also be taught at this level, including the *Union*[2], *Interpreter*, and *Factory Method* patterns.

Even though many important design concepts can be taught here, only a small subset of the Java language is allowed. Most importantly, data mutation is prohibited, discouraging the use of flags instead of dynamic dispatch. Loops and arrays are also prohibited since their normal usage requires mutation.

To reduce the number of keywords beginners must learn, the only keywords allowed other than the essential four (`class`, `if`, `else`, and `return`) are `this`, `abstract`, and `extends`. The explicit use of `this` naturally arises in some of our early uses of polymorphism, so we include it here. Since `abstract` methods, `abstract` classes, and the `extends` keyword are essential for polymorphism, the `abstract` and `extends` keywords must be supported. However, since beginning students often have difficulty understanding the distinctions between interfaces and abstract classes, we ban interfaces and the `implements` keyword at this level.[3] Many constructs that are not relevant to basic OOP are also prohibited, as shown in the table in Figure 3. Since `import` statements and fully-qualified class names are excluded, no libraries are accessible other than `java.lang` or those placed in the default package.

Significant code augmentation is done at the Elementary level. All fields and variables are made `private` and `final` to enforce the immutability of data, and all methods and classes are made `public`. For the sake of JUnit testing, if a class extends "TestCase", the necessary JUnit framework is automatically imported. Finally, all of the boilerplate methods supporting an algebraic view of data are automatically generated. This code includes accessor methods for all fields; method overridings for `toString()`, `equals(...)`, and `hashCode()` that produce results consistent with an algebraic view of data;[4] and a default constructor that takes in a value for each field of the class. This code augmentation significantly reduces the clerical burden on beginning students. Note the difference between code written at the Elementary level and the corresponding augmented code in Figure 2.

---

[2]We use the term *Union* to refer to a degenerate version of the *Composite* pattern in which there is no recursion in the definition.

[3]We arguably could use interfaces *instead of* abstract classes, but this precludes teaching method hoisting at this level since interfaces cannot include concrete methods.

[4]The `toString()` method returns a string giving the class name of `this` followed by the `toString()` representations of the fields enclosed in parentheses and separated by commas. The `equals(...)` method returns `true` if the argument is an instance of the same class as `this` and all respective fields are `equals(...)`; it returns `false` otherwise (assuming termination). The `hashCode()` method is overridden to be

```
Elementary Code:
    class NonEmpty extends IntList {
        int first;
        IntList rest;
        int sum() {return first + rest.sum();}
    }

Resulting Augmentation:
    class NonEmpty extends IntList {
        private final int first;
        private final IntList rest;
        public int sum() {return first + rest.sum();}

        public NonEmpty(int first, IntList rest) {
            this.first = first;  this.rest = rest;
        }
        public int first() {return first;}
        public IntList rest() {return rest;}
        public String toString() {
            return "NonEmpty("+ first + ", " + rest + ")";}
        public boolean equals(Object o) {
            if ((o==null) || getClass() != o.getClass())
                return false;
            NonEmpty cast = (NonEmpty) o;
            return first == cast.first && rest.equals(cast.rest);
        }
        public int hashCode() {return first ^ rest.hashCode();}
    }
```

Figure 2: Augmentation at Elementary Level

4.2 Intermediate Level

The primary language additions at the Intermediate Level are interfaces, `static` fields, visibility modifiers, `package` declarations, exceptions including `try-catch`, `throw` statements and `throws` clauses, anonymous classes, and explicit casts. Of these features, anonymous classes are the most important because they enable methods to pass "functions" (behavior) as data. In Java, anonymous classes play the same role as `lambda` expressions in functional languages.

The Intermediate level is designed to support the *Command*, *Strategy*, *Visitor*, and *Singleton* patterns, as well as the use of exceptions to signal program errors. Since multiple interface inheritance simplifies the coding of many common uses of some of these patterns, we include interfaces at this level. Since casts are often required to narrow the the output types of Visitor and Strategy classes, explicit casts are also allowed. We permit `static` fields because they are required for the Singleton pattern.

The inclusion of `package` and `import` statements gives students access to all the Java libraries, so the `null` constant (which can be returned by library methods) is allowed. Because students can place classes in named packages, this level requires explicit visibility modifiers for methods and classes so students can learn to distinguish between `private`, `package` and `public` constructs.

Since all program data is still immutable at this level, code augmentation is identical to that done at the Elementary Level, with three exceptions: static fields are automatically made public and final; default visibility modifiers are not generated for methods and classes; and the user must explicitly import `junit.framework.TestCase` to reference the JUnit `TestCase` class.

4.3 Advanced Level

Data mutation (re-assignment) is finally introduced at the Advanced Level. At this level, we teach students how to use procedural programming constructs such as loops, switch statements, and arrays. In addition, named inner classes and interfaces are allowed at this level.

consistent with `equals(...)`. See Figure 2 for an example.

The Advanced Level consists of full Java with the exception of synchronization, bitwise operators, and a few other constructs. Nearly all design patterns can be taught here, including the *State*, *Decorator*, and *Model View Controller* patterns. No code augmentation is done at this level.

4.4 Summary

Figures 3 and 4 summarize the language features and code augmentation for each level.

Language Construct	L1	L2	L3	Full
Classes	X	X	X	X
Non-void methods	X	X	X	X
fields, local variables	X	X	X	X
`abstract` modifier	X	X	X	X
`int`, `double`, `char`, `boolean` types	X	X	X	X
Core operators	X	X	X	X
`if` statement	X	X	X	X
Explicit constructors		X	X	X
`package` and `import` statements		X	X	X
`static` fields		X	X	X
Anonymous inner classes		X	X	X
Casts		X	X	X
Visibility modifiers for classes and methods		X	X	X
`null` value		X	X	X
Exceptions and try-catch statements		X	X	X
Interfaces		X	X	X
Visibility modifiers for fields			X	X
Assignment to fields, variables			X	X
Explicit use of `final` modifier			X	X
Nested classes, interfaces			X	X
`while`, `for`, and `do` loops			X	X
`switch` statement			X	X
`void` methods			X	X
Arrays			X	X
`break` and `continue` statements			X	X
instanceof operator			X	X
All other primitive types				X
Initialization blocks				X
`native` methods				X
`synchronized`, `volatile`, `Thread` classes				X
Bitwise operators				X
Labeled statements				X
Conditional operator				X

Figure 3: Features allowed at each level

Augmentation	L1	L2	L3
Methods, classes automatically `public`	X		
Static fields automatically `public`		X	
Instance fields automatically `private`	X	X	
Fields, variables automatically `final`	X	X	
Constructor generation	X	X	
`toString()`, `equals(...)`, `hashCode()`	X	X	
Accessors	X	X	
Concrete methods automatically `final`	X	X	

Figure 4: Code augmentation at each level

5. IMPLEMENTATION

DrJava translates language level source files based on the file extensions attached to file names. The Elementary, Intermediate, and Advanced levels are identified by the extensions `.dj0`, `.dj1`, and `.dj2`, respectively. This convention enables students to continue using code written at earlier language levels.

Implementation Architecture The translator for each language level maps a language level file to a compilable `.java` file in four stages. If the translator discovers serious errors at any point in this process, it aborts execution of the remaining stages and generates error diagnostics which are displayed for the user. We have placed an emphasis on generating understandable and relevant error messages.

In the first stage, which is identical for all language levels, the translator parses the student's source file into an *Abstract Syntax Tree* (AST), containing nodes for the core language constructs including class definitions, method invocations, variable declarations, and expressions. This parsing pass performs a coarse syntax check, looking for fundamental syntactic errors common to all language levels such as mismatched braces. If it encounters any fundamental errors, it reports them an aborts further translation. However, if the translator discovers an error embedded within an expression, (such as an omitted operator or operand), it encodes the error in the AST rather than immediately reporting it so that a *language-level-specific error message* can be given in the next pass. If no fundamental errors are found, the translator proceeds to the remaining three stages of the translation, which are performed by distinct visitors over the AST. Each "visitor" is implemented using the OO *Visitor* design pattern.

The second stage performs a language-level-specific `syntax check` and constructs a symbol table with information for all classes that are referenced directly or indirectly by the AST. This stage is implemented by a visitor that walks the AST, looking for illegal AST nodes (for example, the `public` keyword at the Elementary level or an inner class at the Intermediate level) and building a symbol table of referenced classes. If any errors are found, the visitor continues its pass over the AST to produce as many user diagnostics as possible. When it has finished, it gives a clear diagnostic for each error (if any) that was discovered.

The third stage performs type-checking. The type-checking visitor insures that all expressions are typed correctly and also performs some syntax checks that cannot be done until program expressions are typed. If any errors are found, the visitor finishes traversing the AST before displaying all error messages to the user.

The final stage performs code augmentation. Source code is copied in pieces from the student's language level file to a new `.java` file of the same name. The augmentation visitor traverses the AST as it copies source code, using the AST to determine where code augmentation is needed. The augmentations include the added modifiers, fields, and methods discussed in Section 4. The resulting `.java` file can now be passed directly to the `javac` compiler where it will compile successfully. More advanced students can also view the `.java` file to see their code's spacing and comments perfectly preserved, supplemented by the necessary augmentation.

Ensuring Reliability Writing and maintaining reliable software is difficult, because bugs can creep into programs of any size. Bugs are particularly pernicious in environments designed for beginners for two reasons. First, beginners have difficulty distinguishing aberrant behavior by the environment from mistakes in their own code or misuse of the environment. Thus, bugs in the environment may lead beginners to believe that they are incapable of writing programs. Second, beginners are much more likely to use unorthodox command sequences and strange coding conventions, stressing an environment in ways that the developers failed to anticipate and exposing hidden bugs.

Our strategy for achieving a high level of program reliability is to follow the tenets of Extreme Programming (XP) [10] with an emphasis on rigorous unit testing. Students and faculty in our introductory programming courses have admirably served as our *on-site customers*.

6. RELATED WORK

We know of only one other effort to support language levels for Java. Kathy Gray and Matthew Flatt at the University of Utah have developed ProfessorJ [6], a plugin for the DrScheme programming environment supporting a hierarchy of three Java language levels. ProfessorJ supports a more conventional Java pedagogy than we do. Mutation is allowed at all levels and no code augmentation is performed. Anonymous and local classes are not supported at any language level which makes it impossible to teach the *Visitor*, *Command*, and *Strategy* patterns in much generality.[5]

From the perspective of most educators using Java, the biggest problem with ProfessorJ is that it is implemented on top of DrScheme rather than a Java Virtual Machine. As a result, it is incompatible with Java binaries (class files) and does not support any of the standard Java libraries (including most of `java.lang`). For example, even the standard wrapper classes `Integer`, `Boolean`, *etc.* are not supported.

7. DIRECTIONS FOR FUTURE WORK

Our immediate goal is to determine which language extensions from Java 1.5 beyond auto-boxing/unboxing (which are already supported at all language levels) should be supported in the language levels framework. Later, we plan to develop a configuration facility for language levels, which will empower instructors to design language levels based on their own pedagogy rather than ours. One of the main issues that we will have to confront is whether we can support code augmentation in the presence of mutation because it breaks invariants on which our current code augmentation depends. At a minimum, we should be able to support configuration options that do not affect the status of mutation.

8. REFERENCES

[1] *ACM Java Task Force web site*, September 2004. `http://www.sigcse.org/topics/javataskforce`

[2] E. Allen, R. Cartwright, B. Stoler. *DrJava: A Lightweight Pedagogic Environment for Java. SIGCSE 2002*, March 2002. `http://drjava.org`

[3] H. Comon *et al. Tree Automata Techniques and Applications.* `http://www.grappa.univ-lille3.fr/tata`

[4] M. Felleisen, R.B. Findler, M. Flatt, S. Krishnamurthi. *How to Design Programs.* MIT Press, 2001.

[5] E. Gamma, R. Helm, R. Johnson, J. Vlissides. *Design Patterns: Elements of Reusable Object-Oriented Software*, Addison-Wesley, 1995.

[6] K. Gray, M. Flatt. *ProfessorJ; A Gradual Introduction to Java Through Language Levels. OOPSLA Educators Symposium 2003*, October 2003.

[7] R. Holt *et al. SP/k: a system for teaching computer programming. CACM* **20(5)**, 1977.

[8] M. Kölling *et al. The BlueJ system and its pedagogy, Journal of Computer Science Education* **13(4)**, 2003.

[9] B. Meyer. *Teaching Object Technology. TOOLS 11*, 1993.

[10] *XProgramming.com web site.* `http://xprogramming.com`

[5] Because all three patterns require forming *closures* in many cases, which are only supported in Java by local and anonymous inner classes.

A Model for Improving Secondary CS Education

Barbara Ericson
Georgia Institute of Technology
801 Atlantic Drive
Atlanta, GA, 30332
678 662-6367
ericson@cc.gatech.edu

Mark Guzdial
Georgia Institute of Technology
801 Atlantic Drive
Atlanta, GA, 30332
404 894-5618
guzdial@cc.gatech.edu

Maureen Biggers
Georgia Institute of Technology
801 Atlantic Drive
Atlanta, GA, 30332
404 894-3181
maureen@cc.gatech.edu

ABSTRACT
This paper describes how the Institute for Computing Education (ICE) at Georgia Tech is trying to improve the state of computer science education in secondary schools in Georgia. ICE is a partnership between the Georgia Department of Education and the College of Computing at Georgia Tech. The goals for this partnership are to increase the number and quality of computer science teachers and increase the number, quality, and diversity of computer science students. One specific goal is to increase the number of students taking the CS-AP course. We believe that this partnership can serve as a model for other states.

Categories and Subject Descriptors
K.3.2 [**Computers and Education**]: Computer and Information Science Education – *computer science education, information systems education, curriculum*

General Terms
Experimentation, Design.

Keywords
Computer Science Education, Teacher Training, Advanced Placement (AP), State and University Partnerships

1. INTRODUCTION
The U.S. Department of Labor predicts that despite the recent decline in the IT industry, computer software engineers and computer systems designers will be among the fastest growing occupations in 2002-2012 [4]. However, the number of computer science students has been dropping across the country [2]. Also worrisome is the lack of women and minorities in computer science [1].

In Georgia there are less than 50 Computer Science Advanced Placement (CS-AP) teachers for over 370 pubic high schools. The Georgia Department of Education would like to offer more computer science classes in high school but doesn't have enough qualified teachers. It is difficult to hire teachers with computer science degrees because they can usually make more money in the private sector. In addition, most people with computer science degrees have not had any teacher training. One way to solve this problem is to train the teachers that schools currently have to teach computer science. In Georgia, the introductory computer science classes are offered in the Technology and Career Education Department. The teachers in this department are business teachers who have little or no computer science experience, other than using computer applications.

Another goal is to increase the number, quality, and diversity of students who take computer science classes in high school. In many of the schools there are very few students taking computer science classes, especially the AP class. Most of the students who *do* take computer science classes in high school are white males. Few of the students who *do* take the AP class actually take the exam and the pass rate among those is low.

These problems are not unique to Georgia. Many states face a shortage of qualified computer science teachers. Most of the students taking the CS-AP course across the country are white males. ICE has been created to address these problems in Georgia, and can serve as a model for other states.

2. WORKSHOP DEVELOPMENT
In the spring of 2004 the Institute for Computing Education (ICE) was created. ICE offered its first teacher workshops in the summer of 2004. ICE is also offering year-round teacher support by the appointment of Barbara Ericson as Director of Computer Science Outreach at Georgia Tech.

2.1 History
In November 2003, the first annual meeting of Georgia Tech's Diversity Advisory Board in the College of Computing took place. Invited members were nationally recognized professionals from academia and business who shared a vested interest in increasing diversity in the field of computing. The Director of Technology and Career Education for the Department of Education in the State of Georgia was one of the participants. As a result of the issues raised that day, Georgia Tech and the Department of Education agreed to work together to address these problems. This partnership was formally announced at a press conference in June of 2004 by the Dean of the College of Computing and the State School Superintendent.

The Institute for Computing Education (ICE) at Georgia Tech was created and its first activity was the creation of two summer workshops: one aimed at teachers of the CS-AP, and one aimed at preparing teachers to teach an introductory computer science course called Programming and Systems Management.

SIGCSE'05, February 23–27, 2005, St. Louis, Missouri, USA.

The goal was to increase the number of qualified AP teachers by both training the current teachers and by starting to train teachers with little or no previous computer science experience. The plan is to get teachers started by having them teach the Programming and Systems Management course. After a year or two of teaching that course, they would take a summer AP workshop and start teaching the AP course.

2.2 CS-AP Workshop Development

The CS-AP exam switched from being in C++ to Java in 2004. The exam also changed to place more emphasis on object-oriented principles. Even experienced AP teachers need some help in making the transition from C++ to Java, and help in understanding object-oriented principles. One teacher on the AP mailing list has complained that his students have gone from doing well on the exam when it was in C++ to failing the Java version.

The College Board does work with institutions to offer summer workshops for AP teachers. However, an institution must start the planning for a College Board Endorsed Summer Institute in the fall of the previous year. By the time the Department of Education and Georgia Tech agreed to hold a summer workshop for CS-AP teachers it was too late to be endorsed for the summer of 2004. Georgia Tech is working with the College Board in order to be an endorsed site for the summer of 2005.

To develop the 30 hour CS-AP workshop for the summer of 2004 we used input from current AP teachers. The teachers reported that they most needed help with how to teach object-oriented principles, the Marine Biology Case Study, and data structures.

Barbara created slides and exercises for the workshop based on her experience teaching undergraduate and continuing education courses. Each lecture was 30 minutes or less and was followed by a hands-on activity that could be used to teach the concepts. Activities included role-playing, object-oriented analysis using UML diagrams and CRC cards, and programming.

2.3 Programming and Systems Management Workshop Development

The goal for this workshop was to begin to prepare teachers with little or no computer science experience to teach the Programming and Systems Management course. This course is an introductory computer science course with a heavy emphasis on learning to program. We also wanted to educate the teachers as to what computing means in the 21st century.

2.3.1 Gathering Information from Teachers

To develop this workshop Barbara visited teachers who were currently teaching the Programming and Systems Management course. The teachers reported that they initially felt unprepared to teach computer science, which wasn't surprising since they usually didn't have *any* training. Some teachers took classes at local colleges, but reported feeling intimidated because of having to take the classes with computer science majors.

Since the teachers didn't have much experience in the field, they tended to teach directly out of the book. In one of the classes Barbara observed, the teacher went step-by-step through the activity in the book while most of the students played computer games. A few students tried to follow along but gave up when they encountered any problems. Several of the teachers reported that students find the exercises in the books to be boring and irrelevant. Some of the students even drop the class when they realize that, contrary to their expectations, they won't be writing computer games.

2.3.2 Workshop Approach

In order to make the workshop interesting for the teachers and the students we adapted an introductory computer science course at Georgia Tech. The course was developed specifically for non-majors and to encourage diversity [3]. This course teaches computer science concepts in the context of manipulating and creating media: pictures, sound, movies, and text. Students at Georgia Tech have found these exercises motivating and creative. One student reported turning in her homework and then, “my roommate and I continued work on it just to see what else we could do.”

This course has been successful at Georgia Tech as seen by an increase in the success rate (defined as getting an A, B, or C in the course versus withdrawing, or getting a D or F). The average success rate for the CS1 course designed for majors was 72.2% for the years from 2000-2002. The average success rate for the course designed for non-majors over the last 3 semesters was 88.83%. The non-majors course is over half female and the females were also more successful in this course. In the fall of 2003 the success rate for women in the course for non-majors was 88.36% which was higher than the success rate for men: 84.71%. In contrast, the success rate for women in the course for CS majors was 77.86%, while it was 82.18% for men.

2.3.3 Language Choice

One of the issues during the development of the Programming and Systems Management workshop was what language should it be taught in? The state was recommending that it be taught in Java but not requiring it. Many of the teachers who were currently teaching introductory computer science courses were using C++ or Visual Basic. The course that we were basing it on at Georgia Tech was using Python.

We chose to teach it in Java because we wanted the Programming and Systems Management course to become a feeder for the AP course. Students should benefit from more experience in Java if they continue on to take the CS-AP. Another hope was that the teachers would develop their Java skills and eventually be able to teach the CS-AP course.

2.3.4 Content

We used image manipulation exercises to give the teachers experience with declaring variables, writing class and object methods, working with one and two dimensional arrays, iteration, and conditionals. Example exercises were negating an image, mirroring an image, doing chroma-key to replace a background, drawing on an image, and creating a simple animation. Each exercise was preceded by no more 30 minutes of lecture and example. After the first week the teachers were asked to create an image collage with the same image appearing at least 4 times in the collage with at least 3 different image manipulations done to it and then the whole thing had to be mirrored horizontally. The collages can be viewed on the teacher pages accessible from http://coweb.cc.gatech.edu/ice-gt/95. Several of the teachers created more than one collage. By the end of the second week we had teachers doing simple animation.

3. WORKSHOP DETAILS

Eighteen teachers registered for the AP workshop and 41 registered for the Programming and Systems Management workshop. However, only 17 teachers actually attended the AP workshop and 30 teachers actually attended the Programming and Systems Management Workshop. Some teachers cancelled and some just didn't show up for the workshops.

The 30 hour AP workshop was held from Tuesday to Friday and teachers earned 3 hours of continuing education credit. The 60 hour Programming and Systems Management workshop was held from Monday to Thursday over two weeks and the teachers earned 6 hours of continuing education credit.

The workshops were held at the Georgia Tech Hotel and Conference Center in Atlanta Georgia. The teachers were required to stay at the hotel. We scheduled lecture and exercises during the day and some additional evening exercises and demonstrations of research at Tech for the evenings.

We offered the teachers more than just computer science instruction. Each workshop had a presentation on how to encourage diversity in the classroom. The Programming and Systems Management workshop had a panel discussion by current Georgia Tech students. And, the teachers got to see current research projects in computer science.

Each teacher received a new laptop to use during the workshop, with all the materials loaded that were needed for the workshops. Most teachers were able to take their laptops home with them at the end of the workshop. We hoped that the laptops would enable the teachers to continue learning on their own at home. All teachers were given a CD with the materials from the workshops as well. We had digital cameras and scanners available so that teachers could use their own pictures in the exercises.

We had a group of undergraduate students who assisted during the workshops as well as three graduate students. This was esential in making sure that all the teachers got help quickly when they were doing exercises.

4. RESULTS

The teachers were asked to fill out a survey at the end of both of the workshops. Participation was voluntary. We got 17 out of 17 responses from the AP workshop and 27 out of 30 responses from the Programming and Systems Management workshop.

The surveys were comprised of a series of five questions to gather information about the teacher (gender, ethnicity, experience), 30 questions with 5 categories of responses (strongly agree, agree, neutral, disagree, and strongly disagree) about the workshop. It also included open ended questions on what areas didn't get addressed in the workshop, how to improve the workshop, and what were their needs throughout the year.

4.1 Overall Results

A combination of the results from the two workshops shows that 79.5% of the teachers reported that they felt more capable in programming after the workshop. 93.18% of the teachers reported getting ideas of *what to teach* from the workshops, and 90.91% of the teachers reported getting ideas on *how to teach* from the workshops.

However, only 56.82% reported feeling ready to teach computer science in the fall. And 45.45% of the teachers wished that the workshops had given them more ideas on what to do in their teaching.

Most of the teachers liked the residential requirement and found it valuable (80%). "Yes, it eliminated personal distractions and allowed me to focus on learning the materials. Also gave me time to collaborate with other teachers after class." "The residential part was phenomenal. It kept us here, allowed for wonderful interaction, and reduced the stress of commuting, home distractions, and meals. The food + service allowed us to relax and took the "school" feeling away (since we are on summer vacation after all)."

The residential requirement was difficult for some, especially if they had small children. "I would have preferred to go home mostly because I have a small child but I did enjoy the demonstrations & the chance to work with the others on assignments / projects."

Most teachers enjoyed the demonstrations of research being done at Georgia Tech. "The demos were awesome. I wish I had thought ahead & had a video camera to record demos." "Awesome! They let us see what type of research is being done using computers - Leave them all & just add to them if possible." Many also enjoyed the panel of students. "The grad students gave excellent info & I think a tape of them talking to us would be a great tool for showing students what computer science can do."

4.2 AP Workshop Results

A majority of the teachers taking the AP workshop were male (see Table 1). Most teachers had previously taught a computer science class and had programmed (see Table 2). By the end of the workshop 94.12% of the teachers felt that they were more capable in programming. 88.24% of the teachers reported getting ideas on *what to teach*, and 94.12% got ideas on *how to teach*. 76.47% of the teachers felt ready to teach computer science in the fall.

Table 1. AP Gender Breakdown

Male	Female
64.71%	35.29%

Table 2. AP Experience Breakdown

Never Taught CS	Never Programmed
11.76%	5.88%

We had interesting results on the question of what needs weren't addressed by the workshop. Nearly a third (29.41%) of the teachers said that they had problems that weren't addressed by the workshop. Most wanted additional information such as lesson plans or sample test questions. One teacher reported that one of the problems was not enough computers.

4.3 Prog. and Sys. Workshop Results

A large majority of the teachers taking the Programming and Systems Management workshop were female (see Table 3). Over 40% of the teachers had never taught a computer science class and over a third of the teachers had never programmed (see Table 4). By the end of the workshop 70.37% of the teachers felt that they were more capable in programming. 96.30% of the teachers reported getting ideas on *what to teach*, and 88.89% got ideas on *how to teach*. But, only 44.44% of the teachers felt ready to teach computer science in the fall.

Table 3. Prog and Sys Gender Breakdown

Male	Female
18.52%	81.48%

Table 4. Prog and Sys Experience Breakdown

Never Taught CS	Never Programmed
44.44%	37.04%

Over a third (37.04%) of the teachers said that they had problems that weren't addressed by the workshop. Of these, four teachers noted their students were, "low-level thinkers that had difficultly grasping abstract ideas." Three teachers requested help with recruitment of students into their classes. One teacher indicated a need for better equipment.

5. ALTERNATIVE SOLUTIONS

The College Board does offer workshops for training high school teachers to teach AP courses. There are summer institutes which usually offer a one week workshop. These are taught by College Board endorsed consultants using College Board materials. There is usually a fee to attend these workshops. It takes 9 months or more of planning to become a site for a College Board endorsed summer workshop and we didn't have that time the first year. We are planning to host a College Board endorsed summer institute this summer (2005) for CS-AP teachers.

Another teacher training approach is the Java Engagement for Teacher Training (JETT) workshops. The JETT Program is a partnership between the Association for Computing Machinery's (ACM) K-12 Task Force and the College Board. JETT's short-term goal is to help teachers make the switch to Java. JETT workshops are offered at universities and also involve a College Board endorsed consultant. These are one to two day workshops. However, the universities are expected to find funding to cover the cost of the workshops. The number of JETT workshops being offered is rising but there still aren't any in Georgia.

Both the College Board summer workshops and the JETT workshops are aimed at teachers with programming experience. While it is important to train the current AP teachers, our goals go beyond that. The Georgia Department of Education would like to increase the number of CS-AP teachers in Georgia. However, there are just not enough teachers with programming experience. Our approach is to train teachers will little or no programming experience to teach an introductory programming course in Java. Our hope is that, with experience teaching the introductory course and additional training, these teachers will go on to become AP teachers. We already have several teachers who took the Programming and Systems management workshop who want to take the AP workshop this summer.

The ICE partnership between the Department of Education in Georgia and the College of Computing at Georgia Tech goes beyond offering workshops. Barbara Ericson has been visiting schools to observe classes and to assist teachers with problems. This has given her a better understanding of the problems that high school teachers face. Teachers value having someone to call or e-mail that is available to come help them or develop materials for them. We are also developing materials to help market computer science, especially to women and minorities. Teachers are bringing classes to Georgia Tech to see demonstrations of research. We plan to have summer camps for high school students. We are also involved in revising the technology curriculum for both middle and high schools in Georgia.

6. CONCLUSIONS

The teachers did say that they learned quite a bit from the workshops. One teacher reported, "This was the best (non-college credit) workshop I have ever taken." The Programming and Systems Management teachers did find the media manipulation approach to be interesting and fun and thought that their students would enjoy it as well. The teachers particularly enjoyed the demonstrations of research projects at Tech and the panel of students. However, many teachers still felt that they weren't completely ready to teach computer science.

Overall the AP workshop teachers felt more prepared than the Programming and Systems Management teachers, probably because they had more experience to begin with. You can't expect teachers without any experience to feel ready to teach computer science after only a two-week workshop. But, with additional support and follow-up workshops we hope that they will be able to teach computer science.

One teacher told us that she hadn't wanted to come to the workshop because she wasn't comfortable with computers and thought it would be boring and too math-based. She was surprised to find that she was having fun. The hope is that some of the Programming and Systems Management teachers will gain confidence over time and eventually become AP teachers.

The features that we feel are the most critical for applying this model to other states are:

- A partnership between the Department of Education and a top technical university.
- Gathering information from teachers about what they are currently doing and what they need.
- Creating short lectures with hands-on activities that are interesting and motivating.
- Covering more than just the computer science concepts. The teachers found both the demonstrations of research projects and the panel of students valuable.
- Year-round support and follow-up.

7. FUTURE PLANS

ICE will be holding one and two-day workshops throughout the year. We have created mailing lists for the teachers. ICE also has a web site (http://coweb.cc.gatech.edu/ice-gt/) where teachers can ask questions and look for resources. Barbara is available to Georgia teachers to answer questions, visit classes, and create materials. Several of the teachers plan to bring their students to Georgia Tech on field trips to see demonstrations of research projects. Several teachers have asked that Georgia Tech students come and talk to their students.

ICE plans to offer the two summer workshops again and hopes to offer additional workshops. One of the survey results was that many teachers (29%) wanted a slower pace, so we would like to have a Programming and Systems Management workshop just for teachers with no programming experience. Another useful workshop would be aimed at teachers who have never taught the AP class.

ICE offered two pilot summer camps in the summer of 2004 with over 60 high school students, primarily women and minorities, attending. We hope to build on that experience and increase the number of students in the future. We would eventually like to offer summer camps to middle school students as well.

Mark Guzdial and Barbara Ericson are working on a book that could be used to teach the Programming and Systems Management course (or as a CS1 text). It should be available by the fall of 2005. Many of the teachers expressed an interest in this book and all teachers were given a working draft of the first chapters.

8. ACKNOWLEDGMENTS

The Institute for Computing Education would not have occurred without the efforts of Jimmy Hogg, Cynthia Greene, and John Barge from the Georgia Department of Education and Paul Ohme the director of CEISMC (Center for Integrating Science, Mathematics, and Computing) at Georgia Tech. As Dean of the College of Computing, Richard DeMillo's vision and support was essential. Kristine Nagel reviewed the workshop slides, taught during the workshops, and was invaluable in running the workshops. Jeremy Goecks and Viswanath Nagarajan created programming exercises and helped with evening exercises. Our thanks to Rachel Knickmeyer who compiled the survey information. Our thanks also to the undergraduate students who helped guide the teachers through the exercises.

9. REFERENCES

[1] AAUW *Tech-Savvy: Educating Girls in the New Computer Age*. American Association of University Women Education Foundation, New York, 2000.

[2] Chabrow, E. Declining computer-science enrollments should worry anyone interested in the future of the US IT industry. *Information Week*, Issue 1002, 2004.

[3] Rich, L., Perry, H., Guzdial, M. A CS1 course designed to address interests of women In *Proceedings of the ACM SIGCSE Conference* (SIGCSE 2004) (Norfolk, VA, USA, March 3-7, 2004). ACM Press, New York, NY, 2004, 190-194.

[4] US Department of Labor, Bureau of Labor Statistics, 2004.

A "Secondary" Look at Digital Image Processing

Alasdair McAndrew
Alasdair.McAndrew@vu.edu.au

Anne Venables
Anne.Venables@vu.edu.au

School of Computer Science and Mathematics
Victoria University of Technology
PO Box 14428, Melbourne 8001, Victoria, Australia

ABSTRACT

For the past few years, we have run a highly successful activity teaching some elementary digital image processing to students at years 9 and 10 of secondary school. The activity involves working with a digital camera, taking, capturing and saving images, and exploring pixel values and their relationship to image brightness and colour. We also perform some elementary processing tasks: thresholding, changing spatial resolution and quantization. Students then have a brief introduction to spatial filtering, followed by some examples: image blurring and edge detection. The activity finishes with some binary morphology. Given that digital image processing is usually offered only at the upper undergraduate or postgraduate level, we have demonstrated that it is quite possible to introduce some image processing concepts in a friendly and supportive environment to students in the middle years of their secondary schooling.

Categories and Subject Descriptors

I.4.0 [**Image Processing And Computer Vision**]: General—*Image processing software*; K.3.2 [**Computers And Education**]: Computer and Information Science Education—*Computer science education, Literacy*

General Terms

Education

Keywords

digital image processing, secondary education, elementary computer science, enquiry-based learning

1. INTRODUCTION

Digital image processing courses are typically offered at the upper undergraduate and postgraduate levels of electrical engineering programs, due, in part, to the mathematical requirements of such courses. These requirements can be considerable: multivariate calculus, linear algebra, Fourier transforms, logic and set theory, to name but a few. Dougherty [3] provides a very large list of different mathematical topics which have relevance to modern image processing. Other authors [13] have stressed the need for mathematics in the study of image processing. However, for explaining the fundamentals much of this mathematics is both unnecessary and obstructive. Since these fundamentals can be explained using minimal, junior high school mathematics [9], is it possible and/or desirable to introduce image processing to secondary students?

Any introduction to image processing should be stimulating and instructive, whilst being appropriate to the skill level of the learners. An inspection of the current prescribed government curriculum for Information Technology at upper secondary school level, the CSF II (Curriculum Standards and Framework) [19] lists amongst its examples of suitable studies in the subject: simulations, robotics, data handling and presentation, multimedia and web authoring. It can be seen that although the study, for example, of computer programming or mathematically oriented computer science is not prohibited by the CSF, it is not actually encouraged. Thus a student may study Information Technology and not have any exposure to these areas, let alone digital image processing.

There are good arguments [18] for image processing to be introduced to students, much earlier in their academic careers than when they eventually arrive at university. As many students have difficulty seeing the relevance of mathematics and science to everyday life, they can lose interest in these areas long before selection of their university course is made. Using image processing as the vehicle, we agree with Raphael and Greenberg [14], that it is possible to create a positive learning experience for secondary students. Our activity would be specifically designed as an introduction to computer science. This idea has already been proposed by Tanimoto et al [18], but as far as we know, has not been implemented. Such an activity would need to be instructive and stimulating, and hopefully it would spark a genuine interest in the sciences amongst the participants, long before the fateful day of university course selection.

On the premise that science should be fun and also inspired by the experiences of the Mathematics Experiences Through Image Processing (METIP) project at the University of Washington [18] and others [8, 14], the first author set about creating a set of introductory image processing exercises targeted at mid secondary school level. These exercises needed to be pedagogically sound and gender neutral.

SIGCSE'05, February 23–27, 2005, St Louis, Missouri, USA

As well the exercises needed to be fun to do since students learn only if they are motivated and ready to learn [7]. Using a set of discovery activities, the exercises would lead students through the seemingly difficult concepts of gray scaling, quantization, resolution, thresholding and convolution. A final consideration in the design of these activities was that, given the appropriate software and hardware, they could be run anywhere and at anytime.

For a number of years, these introductory digital image processing exercises have been presented as the "Fun with Faces" activity for secondary schools by the School of Computer Science and Mathematics at Victoria University. Student and school feedback has been very positive and encouraging. As a result, the "Fun with Faces" activity has become the school's flagship public relations exercise. The next section of the paper describes "Fun with Faces" activity in some detail. Section 3 covers some pedagogical considerations whilst section 4 provides some student feedback. Conclusions and further work are found in section 5.

2. THE ACTIVITY

"Fun With Faces" requires that each student have access to a computer with the freely available software "Scion Image"[1] having been installed. Scion Image, originally written at the National Institutes of Health, is a freely available "powerful and complete image acquisition environment" [17] that supports color and grayscale images. It can be used "to capture, display, analyze, enhance, measure, annotate, and output images".

Additionally, students need access to a digital camera or more conveniently a webcam, commonly available in information technology classrooms, with which to photograph themselves. The activity also assumes that students are familiar with the basic operations of a Microsoft Windows based computer system: that they can open and save files, navigate through different directories, and juggle two or more open applications.

Upon commencement, each student is supplied with a worksheet of instructions punctuated by boxes for students to write down their comments and answer the questions posed throughout the activity. Students are encouraged to work in pairs or even small groups.

2.1 Image capture

Despite the acceptance of digital cameras as commonplace in everyday life, the activity's first step of capturing a suitable image always generates much excitement amongst the students. This image needs to be suitable for further processing: it must be recognizable (not too blurred), and must have a good contrast. This step particularly lends itself to teamwork and joint efforts and the step is usually recorded as a "team photo" of a "group hug". One of the great benefits of using a digital camera is that there is no wastage: there is no film to be consumed or paid for, and students can snap at each other for as long as they like, or for as long as the activity facilitator will let them. Finally, the image they decide to use must then be saved. Scion Image only allows images of type BMP (Microsoft Bitmap) or TIFF (Tagged Image File Format); see [11] for a good account of each. After saving the image, students may either quit or minimize the image capture software/webcam application as the rest of the activity is done using Scion Image only.

[1]This is available from `http://www.scioncorp.com`

2.2 Grayscale and Pixel values

The next step in the activity, is to open the saved image using Scion Image. This image is usually in colour and so one of the first tasks is the conversion of the image from colour to grayscale.

The students are then asked to explore the image by running the cursor over it, and to track the resultant values in the Scion Image window: see figure 1. (For illustrative purposes an image of a bunch keys has been used throughout this paper; however in a "Fun with Faces" activity this would be typically a student's self image.) The reported values are that of the pixel under the student's cursor. For the purposes of this activity, a "pixel" is just one of the coloured dots of which a digital image is made—see [4] for a more precise definition. Students are able to discover that 0 corresponds to black, 255 to white, and that the value of the pixel is a function of its intensity. Scion Image allows two scales of pixel values: 0 for black to 255 for white (this is a standard scale), and 0 for white to 255 for black. In figure 1, the Value for the pixel at the cursor is given as 116.00(139). The first figure of 116 represents the intensity with the standard scale; the second figure of 139 Scion Image's alternative scale. The facilitator then sets the challenge for students to

Figure 1: Scion Image "Info" window

find the lowest value both X and Y. Quickly, students realise that lower values for both X and Y are achieved by placing the mouse cursor in the top left corner of the screen, and the highest values are in the bottom right. A comparison is usually made to the Cartesian co-ordinates X and Y with which students usually have experience.

2.3 Quantization and resolution

These are terms are not generally introduced to the students; however they are important concepts in image processing and display. Fundamentally, resolution refers to the amount of pixels used to display the image; the more pixels, the "smoother" the image will appear; the fewer pixels the "blockier" the image will appear. This blockiness is sometimes called "pixelization". Quantization refers to the number of available gray values. Again, the more values, the better the image will appear; the fewer values will result in a less natural looking image.

Students are then shown how to experiment setting various gray levels used to display an image, creating images similar to those shown on the left in figure 2. By using less and less grayscales for their image display, students see the effects on the appearance of the image, and in particular the appearance of "false contours" in the output.

Quantization: 8 and 4 levels

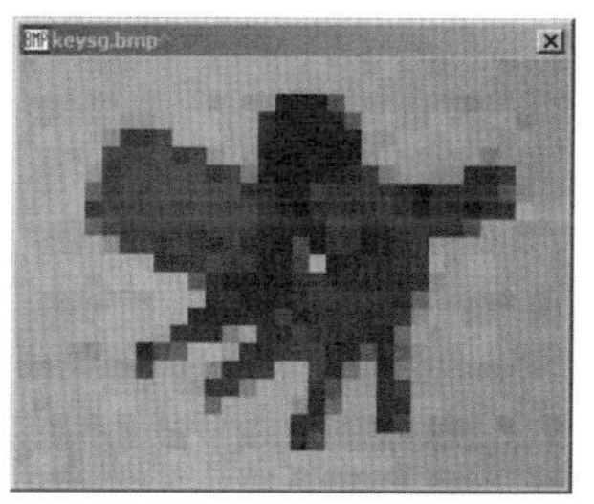

Changing resolution

Figure 2: Quantization and resolution

Allied to quantization is thresholding, where an image is turned into black and white by the application of a simple rule: choose a particular gray value n, and for all pixels in the image, those with values less than n become black, and those with values greater than or equal to n become white. Thresholding is very useful in practice, but it can be difficult to find an appropriate threshold value which will display most of the required information. In Scion Image, thresholding is simply done by adjusting a slider bar, so that visual inspection can find the best threshold value. An example is shown in figure 3. Adjusting the image resolution can be

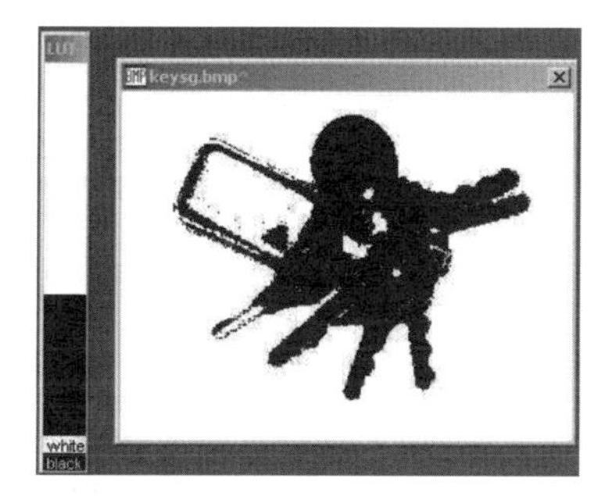

Figure 3: Thresholding

done simply by resizing the image twice: first reducing it in size, and then increasing the result. When adjusting an image size, Scion Image allows the option of using repeating pixels, which leads to the blocky effect alluded to above. Results are shown on the right in figure 2.

2.4 Convolution and spatial filtering

Although formally defined to have different meanings, convolution and spatial filtering are terms that are used interchangeably; the principle involved is one of the most powerful in image processing. Therefore, it is imperative that these concepts are introduced in an easy to understand manner in the "Fun with Faces" activity. For the reader, we may consider a grayscale image as being a very large matrix whose elements are the gray values of the pixels. To perform a spatial filter, we first create a new small matrix M, of size say 3×3 or 5×5. The matrix M is called the *filter*. For every element in the image matrix, place the centre element of M over this image element. Pairing of elements of M with elements of the image, multiply all pairs of elements together and add up these products. For the following filter matrix and image neighbourhood:

$$\begin{matrix} -1 & -1 & -1 \\ -1 & 8 & -1 \\ -1 & -1 & -1 \end{matrix} \qquad \begin{matrix} 10 & 10 & 20 \\ 10 & 20 & 20 \\ 10 & 20 & 30 \end{matrix}$$

the central value in this image neighbourhood, 20, is the current pixel value. The computed output for this position when applying the filter is

$$\begin{aligned} & (10 \times -1) + (10 \times -1) + (20 \times -1) \\ + \quad & (10 \times -1) + (20 \times 8) + (20 \times -1) \\ + \quad & (10 \times -1) + (20 \times -1) + (30 \times -1) = 30. \end{aligned}$$

In the "Fun with Faces" session, the facilitator can introduce the idea that the students' images are in need of a "facial"! This mask or "facial" treatment, will blur their images, and smooth away the wrinkles, or acne as the case maybe. To do the "facial", a mask or filter will need to be applied. Students are asked to open NotePad, or any other small text editor and simply type in the elements of a filter and by using the appropriate commands/mouse clicks in Scion Image, this mask or filter can be applied to the image. Examples of applications of blurring filters are shown in figure 4. By experimentation, students discover that the

Figure 4: Blurring

larger the filter, the greater the blurring.

Students are introduced to filters which have the effect of isolating the edges of the image, or of sharpening the image by enhancing the edges, including the Sobel filters, which are designed to concentrate on edges in one direction only. Examples of the application of these filters are shown in figure 5.

2.5 Morphology

"Morphology" refers to a branch of image processing algorithms which take as their starting point the size and shape of objects in an image. For this activity, students experiment with two basic operations: dilation, which enlarges or

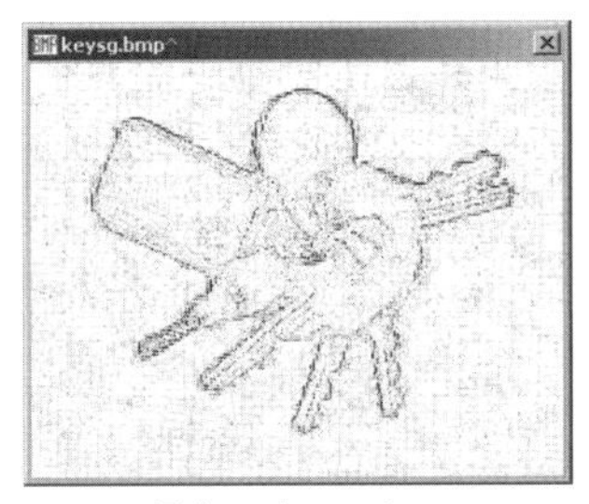

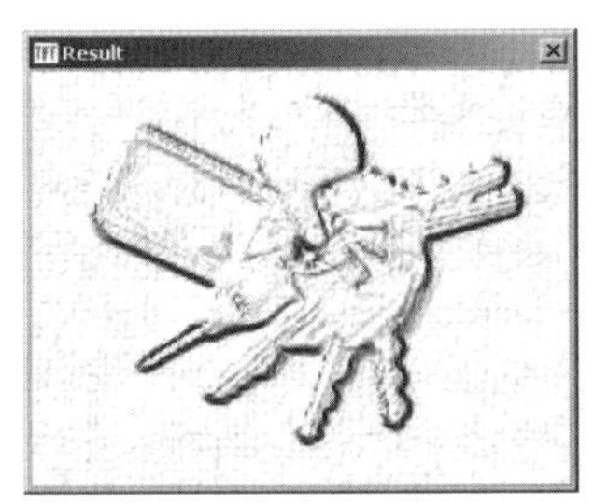

Edge detection | Edge enhancement | Edges using Sobel filters

Figure 5: Edge detection and edge enhancement

thickens objects in an image, and erosion, which shrinks or thins them. The image on the far left in figure 6 shows a binary object formed in Scion Image by taking a grayscale image and thresholding the result.

The results of dilation and erosion are shown in figure 6.

Without going into any of the theory, students can see that dilation really does thicken objects and erosion thins them: the objects from the left image in figure 6 have been thickened by dilation and thinned by erosion.

These two images can now be subtracted to produce an edge map of the original image, as shown on the far right in figure 6.

2.6 Noise

Noise, errors in an image, can be implemented by using the spray can tool (this is available on a floating menu), over a grayscale image. The removal of this "salt & pepper" noise can be done with a *median filter*. This is a filter whose output is the median of the pixels in the image neighbourhood. The affect is dramatic and figure 7 shows an example of noise and its removal by this means.

Figure 7: Noise and its removal

Students see that the median filter does indeed do a very good job of removing the noise. Students can experiment using a larger neighbourhood (5×5 for example), or applying the median filter more than once, to see how this affects the noise removal. They can also experiment with adding different amounts of noise: giving their image "a really good spray", to investigate how the outcome of the median filter is affected by the amount of noise.

3. PEDAGOGICAL CONSIDERATIONS

While digital image processing is typically a graduate study, the literature documents the use of digital image processing as a valuable learning aide in diverse cases such as in medical image processing training [5] and for the teaching of two dimensional arrays in undergraduate computer science classes [2]. In these instances, the inclusion of digital image processing was valued because it engaged students in active experimentation and concrete real world examples. Such inquiry-based activities encouraged students to ask "what happens when I try this?". As Neo and Neo [12] point out active and contextual learning is the hallmark characteristic of the constructivist model in education. In this model, students learn by looking for patterns and significance in their experiences and try to construct their own knowledge by adding to what they already know [16].

Much educational research supports the notion that students do learn according to the constructivist model [6] and the use of inquiry based activities to encourage active learning as been advocated by many authors [6, 10]. Additionally, computer-based technologies have been seen by others [1, 15] as an important vehicle to achieve active engagement amongst students whilst encouraging group participation and exploration of real world scenarios. When image processing activities were introduced in a Cincinnati Public School at 7th grade, Lewis reports [8] that the students found the exercise fun and stimulating and also suggests that the activity fostered a positive learning environment for a broad variety of learners, including gifted students, minorities and females. Similar experiences were also reported by Raphael and Greenberg [14]. These views are supportive of those advocating inquiry-based activities for improved science and mathematics learning throughout the junior high school curriculum [6] and also of our belief that an inquiry based image processing exercise like "Fun with Faces" is both appropriate and desirable for students at this level.

4. STUDENT FEEDBACK

We have deliberately avoided any pre-testing and post-testing of participants, as we wanted the activity to be spontaneous. However, after each "Fun with Faces" session students are invited to comment on this activity by filling out an evaluation form. Without exception, all students agreed that: the activity was worthwhile and enjoyable, the instructions were clear, there were plenty of opportunities to ask questions. When asked: "What did you enjoy about today and why?", many students commented on this activity, which was only one of several offered during the day, with enthusiasm:

"The computer & image thingy was fabulous. I loved it."
"Web camera work!"
"The session with the computers."
"Last session—computers."
"I enjoyed the computer science."
"The computer stuff."

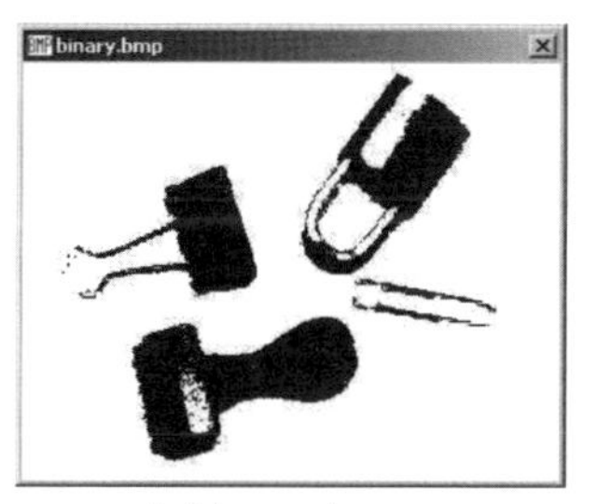

A binary image

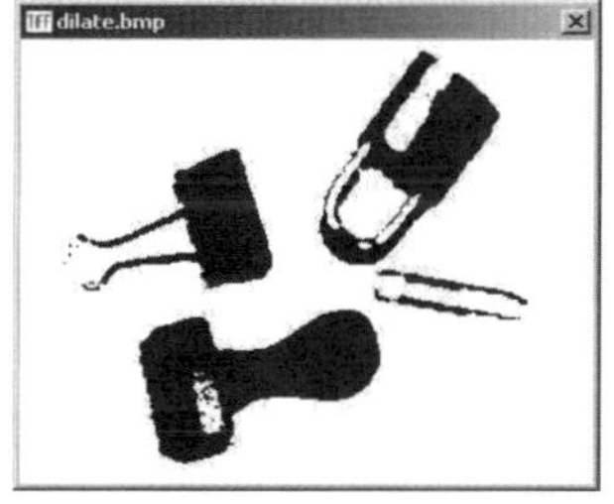

Dilation

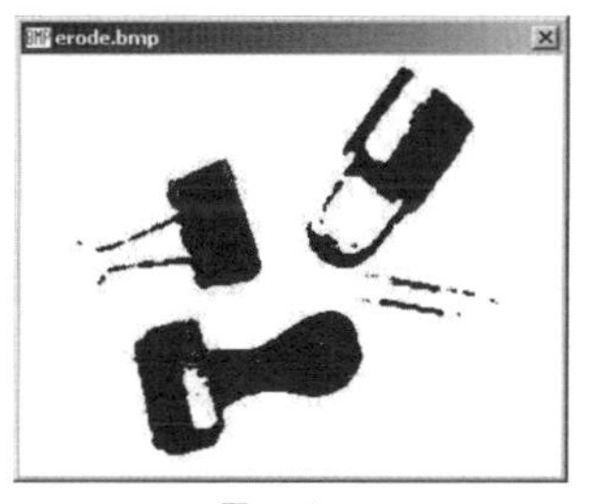

Erosion

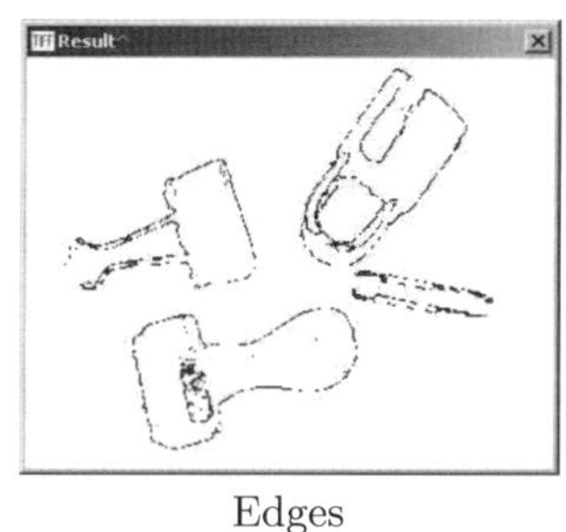

Edges

Figure 6: Morphology

"Fun with photos [sic]!!"

The enthusiasm of the students in the laboratory was also indicative of the fun they were having; this seems to be a very successful activity, illustrating both computer science and mathematics in a positive manner.

5. CONCLUSIONS

We have shown that although image processing—as an area of academic study —is usually reserved for the upper undergraduate years, it is perfectly reasonable to introduce it in a simplified form much earlier. In the course of two hours, students experiment with quantization and spatial resolution, filtering with applications, noise and its removal, and binary morphology. And they leave with a great sense of mastery and satisfaction.

In comparison with previous studies, our activity is designed as a single standalone session aimed at encouraging students to broaden their views of the content and practice of computer science, long before they select undergraduate courses.

There is probably no reason why this activity—perhaps in a further simplified form—could not be offered to high-achieving upper primary level students. However, so far we have restricted our attentions to students at secondary level.

6. ACKNOWLEDGEMENTS

The authors gratefully acknowledge the detailed comments of the referees, who made many valuable suggestions for improving the original draft of this paper.

7. REFERENCES

[1] M. Ally. Foundations of educational theory for online learning. *Theory and Practice of Online Learning*, 2004.

[2] J. Chastine and J. Preston. Teaching 2d arrays using real-time video filters. `http://cims.clayton.edu/jchastine/papers/Teaching2DArraysUsingRealTimeF%ilters.pdf`.

[3] E. R. Dougherty. Editorial. *Journal of Electronic Imaging*, 5(1), 1196.

[4] R. C. Gonzalez and R. E. Woods. *Digital Image Processing*. Prentice-Hall, 2002.

[5] A. Horsch, C. Natscher, M. Tobamn, T. Balbach, M. Danninger, S. Schulz, and D. Stapf. Interactive image processing as learning by doing component of a WBT application. In G. Surján, R. Engelbrecht, and P. McNair, editors, *Health Data in the Information Society. Proceedings of MIE2002*, pages 3–7.

[6] D. Jarrett. Inquiry strategies for science and mathematics learning. it's just good teaching. Northwest Regional Educational Laboratory (NWREL), 1997.

[7] M. Knowles, E. Holton, and R. Swanson. *The Adult Learner: The Definitive Classic in Adult Education and Human Resource Development.* Butterworth-Heinemann, Woburn MA, 2001.

[8] K. O. Lewis. Image processing for teaching (IPT) in science classrooms. *Meridian, A Middle School Computer Technologies Journal*, 5(2). `http://www.ncsu.edu/meridian/sum2002/`.

[9] A. McAndrew. Teaching image processing using minimal mathematics. In T. Greening and R. Lister, editors, *Fifth Australasian Computing Education Conference (ACE2003)*, 2003.

[10] I. Miliszewska and A. Venables. Effective delivery of computer science - a case study. In *Proc. ICCE '99 International Conference on Computers in Education*, page 3, 1999.

[11] J. D. Murray and W. Ryper. *Encyclopedia of Graphics File Formats.* O'Reilly and Associates, 1996.

[12] K. T. K. Neo and M. Neo. A constructivist learning experience: Reconstructing a web site using web based multimedia authoring tools. *Australian Journal of Educational Technology*, 17(3):330–350, 2001.

[13] M. Petrou and P. Bosdogianni. *Image Processing: The Fundamentals.* John Wiley & Sons, 1999.

[14] J. Raphael and R. Greenberg Image Processing: A State-of-the-Art way to learn Science. *Educational Leadership*, 34–37, 1995

[15] J. M. Roschelle, R. D. Pea, C. M. Hoadley, D. N. Gordin, and B. M. Means. Changing how and what children learn in school with computer-based technologies. *The Future of Children. CHILDREN AND COMPUTER TECHNOLOGY*, 10(2):76–101, 2000.

[16] G. Scheuerman. From behaviorist to constructivist teaching. *Social Education*, 62(1), 1998.

[17] Scion Corporation. Scion image beta 4.02 `http://www.scioncorp.com/frames/fr_scion_products.htm`.

[18] S. Tanimoto. Mathematics experiences through image processing (METIP). `http://cs.washington.edu/research/metip/metip.html`, 2004.

[19] Victorian Curriculum and Assessment Authority. Information technology. `http://www.vcaa.vic.edu.au/vce/studies/infotech/infotechindex.html`.

Teaching and Learning Ethics in Computer Science: Walking the Walk

Richard J Botting
California State University, San Bernardino
5500, State University
San Bernardino, CA 92407
(01) 909-880-5327
rbotting@csusb.edu

ABSTRACT

The author shares techniques used in a successful "Ethics and Professionalism" class at California State University, San Bernardino. Ethical issues played a part in designing the class. The author describes active learning and holistic grading. Ethics demanded a novel way to post grades on the web without exposing personal data. This was evaluated by students. The author points out some improvements he has made, or will make.

Categories and Subject Descriptors

K.3.2 Computer and Information Science Education, K.4.1 Ethics, K.6.5 Security and Protection

General Terms

LEGAL ASPECTS

Keywords

pedagogy, ethics, information security, privacy, grading, active learning

1. INTRODUCTION

What ethical considerations apply when you teach ethics? Let me express one of them in the form of the essay questions I use in our "Ethics and Professionalism" course: *Suppose you are a faculty member in a college in California and keep your grades and rosters in an unencrypted spread sheet on a workstation running an MS Windows operating system. Describe two(2) distinct scenarios that expose personal student information(1 paragraph each). What should you do about such a security breach?(1 paragraph)What should you do to stop them occurring?(1 paragraph)*

SIGCSE'05, February 23-27, 2005, St. Louis, Missouri, USA.

This paper includes some ideas that would appear in a good answer to the above question. It describes a recent ethics course[1] that was the most successful course I have ever taught. The student evaluations were so much better than my norm that it is worth noting what I did. The course used active learning[2] and holistic scoring[7]. A new technique for posting grades made identity theft impossible.

In the Fall of 2003, I taught our "Ethics and Professionalism" class for the second time in 6 years. By nearly every criterion the course was a good one. (1) I have clear evidence that all the students achieved my objectives. (2) The student evaluations were the best I have ever had. (3) Anonymous surveys showed that nearly all students liked the innovative way of posting grades. (4) The same surveys in another class indirectly showed that the Ethics course had improved the students understanding of privacy. (5) The course taught me that ethical considerations are vital input into software design. (6) The course was too successful: most students got an *A* or an *A-*.

This paper reviews what I did, how the students responded, and what improvements I plan to make. In section 2 I describe the course and my approach to teaching it. In section 3 I focus on essay questions and how to grade the answers. Section 4 describes the development of a small piece of software to allow students to see their grades without exposing them to identity theft. Section 5 summarizes my conclusions and section 6 acknowledges support. Section 7 contains the references cited in the paper.

2. BACKGROUND

2.1 The Course

The class is a 2 quarter unit course (CSCI488) entitled "Ethics and Professionalism." The catalog description is *Professionalism, ethics, legal issues and social impact and role of computer technology.* It is required for all Computer Science majors in their senior year. It is scheduled each Fall with ten 2-hour classes plus a 2-hour final. Different teachers teach it. The class size is 40 students. We have a diverse student population with a range of cultures, ages, and genders. I had students from every continent in the world. The text was Spinello's *CyberEthics: Morality and Law in Cyberspace* [6]. This is topical and is good on ethical theory and legal issues. I encourage students to read articles and papers in newspapers, magazine, professional journals, and on the Internet. The course web site has copies of the syllabus, a web log, and course related links and resources[1]. I use my own software to generate these web sites from an ASCII- based notation.

2.2 Objectives

In the syllabus the goals are stated as: *To help improve your long term survival in computing by increasing your knowledge, awareness, and thinking about nonmechanical problems facing a computing professional. To help you to act better when faced with difficult choices.* I refined this to requiring evidence of students thinking through ethical problems using material from the book. This was assessed by asking students to write 30 minute structured closed-book essays on realistic topics or problems. All classes ended with the presentation of a scenario, subject, or question and the request for the students to write an essay on the topic. This was handed in, graded and returned at the start of the next class. All but the first and last essay counted and contributed 40% toward the total grade for the class. Similar essays made up the final examination and contributed another 40% of the final grade. Nominal assigned work and participation contributed 20%.

It is essential that grades are assigned to the person who did the work[5]. So, in this class, assigned work contributed only 14.4% to the grade. The rest (85.6%) is supervised. I do not require electronically submitted work because most current technology (1)is slower to use than paper and (2) fails to provide adequate assurance that the work is done by the student.

2.3 Design for a Class Meeting

All students are required to read and study a piece of the text to prepare for each class. As evidence they hand in their rough notes at the start of class. I set them a preliminary discussion question on the topic in the reading, ideally taken from current events. Students are told to think individually and silently about the question and write down their thoughts. They are then told to form a pair and compare their thoughts. Each pair then joins with another pair to generate a common answer that is then shared with the whole class. This is the well known "Think-Pair-Square-Share" pedagogical pattern [2]. While the students did this, I graded the notes (100% if OK, else 0%) and collated them with previously graded work. I returned the work by calling out people's names, while the students continue to work in "squares." This lets me take the attendance roster without wasting time. Each "square" then reports to the class.

The class then goes on to a series of shorter "Think-pair-square-share" exercises. One variation is to ask the students to think about the assigned reading and select a question they want answered. Each group of four asks a question. I and other groups provide answers. Again, whenever possible I call on people by name (initially I use the roster). This is a motivator and places names in my long term memory.

At the end of the class, I set a 30-minute (closed book) written essay. This is graded and returned at the start of the next class.

2.4 Make up work

I allowed one form of make-up work: a student can make a presentation to the class of a relevant topic or situation. This lead to some good sessions when worried students brought up problems and the class provided advice and comfort.

2.5 Evaluation of the Class Process

There is little chalk-and-talk and no bulleted visuals because the selected readings needed little explaining in class. The students are *working* the whole time. The work involves individual thinking and comparing different views. The teacher has the responsibility to control the flow ("*How do we apply Kant's Categorical imperative here? <pause> What do you think, Jo?*"). The teacher also lists answers on the board, compares, contrasts, and summarizes them, digs out missing ideas, and corrects errors ("*Do that and you could go to jail!*").

3. ESSAYS

3.1 Example Questions

I select topics and questions that are relevant and often topical. Here are three questions

1. You see your teacher view some child pornography and save it to a Zip Disk. ***a.*** *Show how* ***two different*** *theories of ethics apply(4 paragraphs).* ***b.*** *How does applying ethical theories help you plan your actions?(1 paragraph)*

2. Spam! ***a.*** *Give an example of how (1) code, (2) the market, (3) norms, and (4) law could control it(4 paragraphs).* ***b.*** *What do you judge will be most effective? Why? (1 paragraph)*

3. ***a.*** *Name and describe four(4) types of intellectual property(4 paragraphs).* ***b.*** *Why do laws protect intellectual property? -- give several reasons(1 paragraph)*

3.2 Grading Essays

It is important to have a simple, rapid, predefined, and published procedure for grading. I think it unethical to change this after the last day that a student can drop. For essays, I make it clear that I am more interested in well reasoned argument than agreement with my opinions. The first essay in the course models the grading but the score is not recorded. I use modified Holistic Scoring [7]. This avoids traits and check lists. The original procedure[7] was to read the item rapidly and assign a score to it based on published criteria and samples. I attach a letter grade to each paragraph as I finish it. I meanwhile mark any mistakes, padding, or omissions. The letters map to scores: A=10, B=9, C=8, D=7, E=6, and F=0. These are averaged, scaled, and rounded to give the score for the essay (0 to 25 in classes, 0 to 50 in the final). These in turn are totaled across the course.

The syllabus defines what each letter grade means. For example an *A* paragraph was described as: *Easy to read, structured, no gross speeling mistooks or grammatical goofs. Content is accurate when factual, well reasoned when debatable, or well expressed when personal and subjective. Sources are given for all non-original work. The original work seems to be something special that you wanted to say. Good use of mathematical ideas and formula. Any humor is an intelligent and polite way to make a relevant point.*

A *D* paragraph was described as *Work that makes your boss wonder about your next pay rise. Many errors of structure, spelling, grammar, fact, and logic. No references. Many ambiguities. Hard to figure out. Content that is inappropriate. It suggests that you don't know what you want. Mathematics is badly wrong or isn't fitted to the situation. Bad jokes.* *B* and *C* paragraphs lie between *A* and *D*. *E* is being worse than a *D*. The *F* is reserved for: *This is identical to something else and you did not say so. F is also used when you omit a required section or topic. Padded, plagiarized, or missing paragraphs.*

An important ethical point: *work must be graded anonymously.* Expectation overrides observation via the halo effect, favoritism, and prejudice. So, I ask students to put their name (and number) *at the end of the work.* I tell them why.

3.3 Student Evaluations of Teaching Effectiveness

I asked for a SETE (Student Evaluation of Teaching Effectiveness) in the class. This is the standard instrument used at California State University, San Bernardino (CSUSB) and uses a 4-point scale (Excellent=4, Good=3, Fair=2, Poor=1) on 10 different items such as the instructor's knowledge, preparation, organization, . . . etc. It is carried out in the ninth week of the quarter. The course is taught by different faculty each year and their student evaluations are not available to me. I usually score close to the averages for a teacher in the College of Natural Sciences (CNS). This time, my median and mode in every question were 4. The averages of all but one rating are close to *one standard deviation higher* than the CNS average. The best score vs. the CNS average was for explaining the objectives and requirements of the course. This score was more than one standard deviation higher. The weakest (0.5 SD > CNS) was for providing clear feedback in grading.

3.4 A Critique of Essay Grading

Students understood the process, but, holistic grades are not good diagnostic tools[7, p 92]. However, with holistic scoring I can grade 40 essays in two or three hours. I plan to research fast ways to give more feedback.

Just about every student wrote essays that met my stated criterion for an A. So, in the future, I will raise the bar. What was an *A* paragraph(see above) will be given a *B*. An *A* will be described as something like this: *The paragraph is a pleasure to read. It is clear, structured, accurate, well reasoned, and has no spelling or grammatical errors. Sources are given for all non-original ideas. New ideas are relevant and either humorous or well reasoned.*

4. POSTING GRADES

4.1 Why Post grades?

Letting students know how they are doing motivates them. It also motivates the teacher to keep up. It lets students spot and correct grading errors before the course is over. So, students should be able see their grades on the Web. It helps if they can also get an idea of the class's overall performance.

4.2 Information Security and Privacy

A fundamental ethical responsibility is to make sure that a student's personal data does not become known to other people. A teacher at CSUSB is required not to expose students' identities and grades. In the USA, Social Security Numbers have been protected at the Federal level for decades. These days, identity theft is common. In California, if personal data is exposed by a security breach, the people at risk must be informed within 48 hours to avoid a fine (The Security Breach Information Act (SB1386) July 2003). This is discussed in the course. So, the students should be more aware of the need to design computerized systems that protect personal data. So, the teacher of this class, must show due diligence in protecting the student's identity and grades.

All networked computers are under attack these days. At the end of the summer quarter in 2003 several MS Windows computers at CSUSB were invaded by viruses and Trojan Horses. The Computer Science faculty web server (Linux) was hacked into via a badly programmed Common Gateway Interface(CGI). Events like these are clearly security breaches. All the data on a cracked computer is open to abuse. The SQL Slammer virus infected 75,000 servers in its first 31 minutes in January 2004 [4]. So, security patches, personal fire-walls, and virus checkers all lag behind the attackers. In Spring 2004, one machine on campus machine was left un-updated for two days and became a zombie file server. No popular system has been proved secure.

My campus was using Social Security Numbers(SSNs) as student identity numbers(SIds) at the start of this class. Clearly *storing unencrypted SIds on any networked machine was not ethical.* I decided to use a spreadsheet that can encrypt my grade sheets using a password as key. Extracting and posting data from this spreadsheet is easy. But what data to publish?

4.3 Analysis

The requirements were: (1) Students can see their own grades. (2) Nobody can figure out other people's grades. (3) Unencrypted names and SSNs must not be placed on any computer connected to the Internet. I looked at creating a traditional id+password system for the class. Such a system must include the ability for users to change passwords and ways to supply alternatives if the password is forgotten. Passwords must not be stored without encryption in case the system is broken into. All this would take time. It would also require students to memorize another id+password. Meanwhile, our systems administrator reacted to the CGI attack by disabling all CGIs. No alternative was set up. As a result I could not use passwords and encryption on the server. I was forced to look for an alternative. I thought a short term secret Id would be secure enough

Asking students to supply a key or identifier can lead to collisions and might lead the unwary to expose personal information. I decided to give each student a temporary secret identity as a database key. There are several candidates: the SId was eliminated by privacy needs. Names are not secure or unique. Hashing names and SIds can generate collisions and needs careful design. The sequence number in the roster is unique but does not preserve confidentially. Allocating a random four digit number (10^4 combinations) as identifier would preserve privacy but would be difficult to memorize. Three letters give 26^3 =17,576 > 10^4 combinations. Memorizing words is easier than numbers. Visualizing a ridiculous image linking a named object and the teacher will do the trick. I developed a list of 100 suitable words (hen, pea, boy, zoo, . . .).

4.4 First Iteration

I used a mail-merge function in a word processor to print out one hundred special forms. Each had a different key. The top of the form was designed to be torn off and kept by the student. It showed their key plus instructions for using it. The bottom half the form was a contract that included the key. Students filled in their name and their SId. It stated the rules for the class such as "no cheating" and "bad work gives a bad grade." The bottom half was signed and returned to me.

I then recorded the key in my encrypted spread sheet. Each week,

I extracted the grades and the keys, sorted by the key, and posted tab-delimited ".TXT" tables to the web.

4.5 A Survey of Student Opinions

A wise or ethical software developer checks with his or her clients and users to see what they think about it. In the tenth week, students did an anonymous and optional survey to see if they used, understood, and liked the scheme.

I got 34 responses. Here are the questions and frequencies of the answers in the survey.

1. I checked my CSCI488 grades
   Every day(0), Every week(14), Some weeks(11), Once or twice(6), Never(3)
2. In other classes I check my grades
   Less often(16) -About the same(16) - More often(2)
3. I found the use of a random word as an identifier in posted grades easy to understand.
4. I found the use of a random word as an identifier insecure.
5. I found it hard to use the random word as an identifier.
6. I prefer this method to using part of my Student IDentifying number.
7. I would like to see this scheme used in my other classes.

Table 1. Responses to question 3 to 7

#	Strongly agree	Agree	Disagree	Strongly disagree
3	19	13	2	0
4	4	8	15	8
5	1	3	15	15
6	12	19	2	1
7	12	18	4	0

The first question showed that most students checked their grades at least once a week. The second question showed that 16 checked their grades more often in CS488 than in other classes and 16 checked their grades the same amount in other classes. Questions 3 through 7 used a four-point ordinal scale. Two students found the random key hard to understand (question 3), four found it hard to use, and three would prefer that I had used their SID. Thirty (out of 34) would like to see the same scheme in their other classes. Twelve thought it insecure. Answers were correlated. For example, the two students who felt that the scheme was hard to understand, also felt that using it was hard, and also did not want it used in other classes. This gave large values for χ^2 tests of association. But (1) the cells had low values and (2) the tests were chosen after noting the correlation. This makes lowers their statitical significance. Such a pattern was, in hindsight, to be expected.

The last question was open ended and asked for comments. Six students noted that when all the grades are visible you can figure out who was who in the class. Another noted it would be better to only display your own grades. One person thought it was too much hassle, and another suggested making the link to the grading more visible on the CSCI488 page. The remaining ten comments were positive.

4.6 Second Iteration

By the end of the quarter, the department web server had PHP [3] running and I was replacing my CGIs with PHP scripts. I developed a script to extract and format the grading data and linked it to the web site. It asks for the student's secret key and does a simple search in the tab delimited data. It selects lines that match the key plus those with a capital letter in the first column. The selected lines are marked up (by the script) as rows in a HTML table (one table per file). The code is less than 40 lines long[1].

4.7 Posting Grades in Other Classes

I used the second iteration for posting grades in later classes. In one (CSci320 Programming Languages, Winter 2004) I repeated the survey. The 28 responses were similar. There was one significant difference. Using a 2><2 contingency table with Yates's correction, gave $\chi^2 = 5.1$ with 1 degree of freedom, P < 5%. So students in the programming language class tended to disagree with the statement "I prefer this method to using part of my Student ID" more often than the "Ethics" students. This shows that the "Ethics" students were more aware of the risks of exposing personal information.

4.8 Evaluation of Grade Posting

Most students liked my technique for posting their grades. It cannot expose a person to identity theft. Still, the use of a secret temporary key to access grades can be cracked by waiting until the quarter is complete and then repeatedly hacking codes and looking for patterns.

Kant's Categorical imperative [6] states that one should adopt maxims that are not invalidated if everybody followed them. If a special identity was used in every class, a student would be overwhelmed by keeping track of them. So, using existing secure identifiers would be better.

5. CONCLUSIONS

It is impossible to say what made this class "excellent" for so many students. Most faculty enjoy teaching the class. To compare responses would require a joint project. This is left to future work.

The next time I teach this class, I want to explore the use of *public key encryption* for grades in the "Ethics" course because it is a topic in the course. In other courses, I could use one of two existing id+password systems. Computer Science students have a Unix account. All CSUSB students have a campus email account and authentication is provided by a special "LDAP" server. By Fall 2004, after a 12 month project, the campus uncoupled student identifiers from social security numbers. Using part of the new SId as a key is now less risky. The PHP code[1] was easily modified.

I think any of the techniques could be used by others with success. But, there are many intangibles, such as teacher enthusiasm, that drive student response. I use active learning techniques and holistic scoring in other classes and get close to average student evaluations. I hope that the students reacted to the effort I put into being ethical.

It will be interesting to see what happens when I toughen the grading and provide more feedback.

I now encrypt all grade sheets and rosters on my computers. I avoid even parts of SSNs and names on servers. I use a script so that students only see their own data. The PHP scripts are as simple as possible to avoid being cracked. Finally, I will continue to be visibly ethical when I teach ethics. Now is the time to glance back to the essay question at the start of this paper and see if you would change your answer.

6. ACKNOWLEDGMENTS

The support of the National Science Foundation under award 9810708 and the Teaching Ethics workshop at the University of Southern Florida [2] is gratefully acknowledged. I thank the anonymous reviewers for their helpful comments. The errors that remain are mine.

7. REFERENCES

[1] Botting, R. J., Archived course materials, data, and PHP scripts, http://www.csci.csusb.edu/dick/cs488/2003

[2] Bower K, *Ethics and Computing*, NSF Workshop (Aug 1998) http://www.cse.nd.edu/~kwb/nsf-ufe/

[3] Doernhoefer, M., Surfing the Net for Software Engineering Notes: Free Software, *ACM SIGSOFT Software Engineering Notes 26* 6(Nov 2001)pp23-24

[4] Jungk, P.; Shim S., S., Y., Issues in High-Speed Internet Security , *IEEE Computer Magazine 37* 7(Jul 2004)pp36-42

[5] Sanders, S. L., Computer Science homework and grading practices: an alternative to the popular model, *ACM SIGCSE Bulletin 20*, 2(June 1988)pp26-29

[6] Spinello, R. A., , *CyberEthics: Morality and Law in Cyberspace* (2nd Edn.), Jones and Bartlett, Sudbury MA, 2003 ISBN 0-7637-0064-9

[7] White, E., "Holistic Scoring: Past Triumphs, Future Challenges" pp79-106 of in Michael Williamson and Brian Huot (eds), *Validating Holistic Scoring for Writing Assessment*, Hampton, Cresskill NJ 1993

Effective Incorporation of Ethics into Courses that Focus on Programming

Mary Elaine Califf
Illinois State University
School of Information Technology
Normal, IL 61790-5150
309-438-5203
mecaliff@ilstu.edu

Mary Goodwin
Illinois State University
School of Information Technology
Normal, IL 61790-5150
309-438-7953
mmgoodw@ilstu.edu

ABSTRACT

This paper discusses some of the issues involved in incorporating ethics material into programming courses. Incorporating ethics into such courses raises particular challenges because of the time-intensive nature of the courses and because of the difficulty of finding material that is both relevant to the course and comprehensible to the students. The paper presents four case studies that we have used successfully when incorporating ethics material into our own programming courses.

Categories and Subject Descriptors

K.4.1 [**Computers and Society**]: Public policy issues – *ethics.*

General Terms

Legal Aspects

Keywords

Teaching ethics, CS1, CS2.

1. INTRODUCTION

Since the appearance of Computing Curriculum '91[3], computer science educators have been increasingly aware of the importance of including some coverage of the ethics of computing in our curricula. The importance of ethics is also emphasized in the accreditation criteria for computer science[6]. Two major approaches can be taken when incorporating ethics into the curriculum. Some institutions take the "ethics course" approach where all students are required to take a course on computer ethics. Other institutions take an approach that spreads ethics coverage throughout the curriculum, expecting instructors to teach small ethics modules in most, if not all, of the courses in the computer science program.

There are clearly advantages to each of these approaches. Consolidating ethics into a single course ensures that students get similar experiences and leaves the teaching of this material to a few instructors, presumably those most qualified to handle it (or at least those most comfortable with the topic). However, this approach may leave students with a picture of ethics as a side issue, disconnected from the main business of computer science. In order to be done well, the ethics course should be taught near the end of the students' academic careers so that ethics relating to the advanced topics can be covered. Typically, the ethics course is taken early on, when students do not have the understanding of the field needed to fully understand the ethical issues. Also, in a field that has many required courses, adding an ethics course requirement might necessitate removing another required course. Integrating ethics into a variety of courses throughout the curriculum encourages students to see ethics as an integral issue in the discipline and allows for ethics issues germane to the specific course to be covered. On the downside, instructors pressed for time might omit the ethics unit. Without careful coordination, students might well cover the same case repeatedly as they progress through the major. Students at universities where multiple sections of CS1 and CS2 are taught necessitating a number of instructors might well be exposed to entirely different ethics cases because the instructor picks the cases. This approach drops the burden of teaching ethics material into the lap of every instructor in the program, many of whom may be quite uncomfortable with these non-technical topics and may have had no training in this area. These are the instructors that we seek to give guidance to in this paper.

The authors teach in a computer science program that asks all instructors to incorporate ethics modules into their courses. Among the courses we teach are several that we consider to be "programming-intensive" courses, such as CS1, CS2 and Algorithms and Data Structures. In incorporating ethics modules into these courses, we had several goals: 1) to engage the students, 2) to leave the overall content and integrity of the course intact, 3) to keep the ethics content relevant to the content of the course, and 4) to meet the ethics requirements of the accreditation board.

In this paper, we first review some of the literature on teaching ethics of computing. Then we discuss some of our "philosophy", what we believe are characteristics of effective (and ineffective) case studies for ethics discussion in programming-intensive courses. We then discuss some available material that we have used in our courses and characteristics of that material that makes it effective for those situations. Finally, we present four original cases, three based on real-life situations and one that is purely fictional, and discuss characteristics of these cases and why they are particularly effective in the courses for which they were developed.

SIGCSE'05, February 23-27, 2005, St. Louis, Missouri, USA.

2. LITERATURE REVIEW

In the past decade, there has been a definite interest in how to "do ethics" in computing curricula. The ImpactCS initiative at Georgetown University defined a set of knowledge units for ethics coverage in computing and provided some online resources[10; 13]. Several papers were written to help faculty face the challenge of adding ethics coverage to their curricula [4; 11; 17; 18; 19]. Working groups were formed to face the challenges of integrating ethics and social issues into a highly technical discipline[9]. However, the majority of the resources were directed primarily at teaching ethics and social issues in a separate course rather than integrating ethical issues into technical courses.

Among those who have looked at providing resources for helping faculty integrate ethics into their existing technically-oriented courses, most have not paid close attention to courses focused primarily on teaching programming issues. The 1997 ITiCSE working group report provides a number of interesting ethics exercises for a variety of computing courses, but none for the introductory programming, data structures, or algorithms courses[9]. Bowyer also has some very nice suggestions for assignments, but none that are clearly geared toward those programming courses[4].

Schulze and Grodzinsky did focus specifically on incorporating ethics material into CS1 and CS2[15]. However, it is worth noting that their suggestions for CS1 have nothing to do with the programming aspects of the course. They suggest looking primarily at "computer user" issues such as appropriate use of email and internet access, because this would be most students' first experience as computer users, particularly their first opportunity to use email and the internet. Their CS2 suggestion for an assignment is very related to programming. They suggest giving a programming assignment that meets pedagogical needs, but is not a "good" solution from the point of view of all those who would be affected by the software. Then students would be asked to read the CACM "How Good is Good Enough?" article[5] and discuss the assignment in light of issues raised by the article. Townsend also suggests incorporating ethics into programming courses by giving a programming assignment that raises ethical issues[17].

3. PROGRAMMING COURSES AND ETHICS: THE CHALLENGES

Why is there a relative dearth of material on teaching ethics in courses that focus on programming? We can easily find ethics exercises for operating systems courses, where issues of security and related ethical and social issues are generally considered absolutely essential to the course, or for artificial intelligence, where ethical and social implications have been the subject of numerous movies and novels. It seems likely that people haven't written a lot about incorporating ethics material into the programming-intensive courses because it's hard to do.

We have come up with some possible reasons for the difficulty of incorporating ethics into courses that focus primarily on programming. First, the courses are highly technical in nature; students expect the focus to be on learning how to **do** things. Ethics are fuzzy material that faculty might view as disconnected from the hardcore content of the course. Second, CS1 and CS2 are generally the first and second, or maybe the second and third courses in the major. Students don't have a lot of background in the field, so instructors have difficulty finding scenarios or activities that students can easily fully understand. Finally, programming courses are usually very time-consuming courses for many students. Students may have to spend many hours outside of class trying to get programs working correctly. Class time is often also at a premium. Thus, ethics activities can easily become a burden on both students and instructors.

This brings us back to programming and a desire for ethics activities and materials that relate specifically to programming and that students can understand and relate to. A quick review of either the ACM Code of Ethics[1] or the Software Engineering Code of Ethic and Professional Practice[2] reveals a number of relevant issues including software safety, software quality, quality of documentation, software correctness, and ownership of code.

In searching for activities or scenarios for use in programming courses, we believe that it's important to address the issues raised earlier. Students often don't see ethics as an integral part of the discipline they're learning. Therefore, we need to select activities that are clearly relevant to the technical course content and inherently interesting, not to us, but to our students. We need to recognize the limitations of student background and time, and avoid using activities that require students to wade through too many complex details, or learn material that really belongs in later courses, just to allow them to understand the scenario they're trying to analyze. For example, the Therac-25 accidents[12] or the Case of the Killer Robot[8] are interesting and valuable cases to analyze, but probably don't belong in programming courses where time is at a premium. We need to make our goal the selection or creation of fairly straightforward ethical scenarios and activities that are not too extensive and resonate with the course material.

4. ASSIGNMENTS THAT WORK

So then the question occurs, "Is there anything out there that works?" And the answer is a definite yes. In addition to possibilities described in papers referenced above, there are a number of ethical case studies or scenarios available that can be effective in programming courses. The key is to look for relatively short cases that can be easily understood by the students and have some relevance to the course material. We've used several existing cases successfully.

"It's Never Right to Copy Software" is a fictional case about a math teacher whose new computers will not be useful without software, but whose principal has limited funding and sees no need to purchase more than one copy of the necessary software[16]. This is probably relevant to students in any course, since it brings up issues of software ownership. It also provides the chance to discuss pirated software that the students might have on their own computers. Students can be asked to view the issue from the perspective of the programmer who wrote the software, and reminded that in a few short years they might be that programmer. The Patriot missile case addresses issues of changing software specifications and software maintenance as well as testing[14]. This can lead to questions of how much testing is enough, whether the amount of testing needed varies based on the use of the software, whether programs should be written to just meet the specifications given, and what documentation should be included with software.

Despite the existence of potentially useful exercises and case studies, it can be most helpful to create a case study more specifically targeted at a particular course or student population. In the following sections, we present four case studies that we have developed and used successfully in our programming courses.

5. IT COULD BE YOU: CASE STUDIES FOR CS2

These case studies are based on recent real life experiences of an acquaintance of the authors. The names of the company and the people involved are changed to protect both the innocent and the guilty.[1]

Case 1: The Firing

The company

Widget Products, a well-established company, decided to begin selling its products online. They hoped to have the online site up and running by January 1, 2003.

The individual

Deborah graduated from college and landed a job as a software engineer at Widget Products in the summer of 2001. A year later, she was established as one of the most capable engineers on staff. Consequently, she was assigned to be in charge of (responsible for) more and more code.

The consultant

David was a software engineer hired as a consultant by Widget Products. He was extremely knowledgeable about making the pieces of the program communicate with each other. He was hired for four months ending December 31, 2002, when the online sales site would be operational. He was a friendly, gregarious 45-year-old, recently married. Despite his knowledge and ability, he had two problems. He was careless when coding, frequently committing code that caused errors. As the release date neared, this became more and more problematic, as the firm's engineers worked 14 hour days to eliminate all bugs. David also spent quite a bit of his time talking with others. This interfered with his productivity and that of the people he was talking to.

The problem

Two weeks before the online sales would begin, management decided to fire David. Someone in the company would have to be responsible for David's code, maintaining it and correcting any bugs found in it, and, therefore, had to know the code. Deborah's manager called her in at around noon and informed her that David would be fired later that afternoon and why. She was then told that she would be responsible for all of his code. Therefore, Deborah's manager told her to spend the afternoon visiting with David and ask him all about his code. She was to learn everything she could from David without letting him know why she was doing this.

Deborah objected. She felt that he was a nice person and his job would end in two weeks anyway, so he should not be fired early. He was newly married, and she thought it would be bad for him to have to go home and tell his wife he'd been fired. Deborah felt like she would be doing something dishonest by pretending just to be interested when getting all the info she could from him before he was fired. She stated that she did not think this was right and would prefer not to do it. Her boss said that David deserved to be fired because his work was causing problems. Furthermore, the company owned the code David had written and had a right to understand it and learn all about the code. He argued that if David were told why he was being asked all about his code, he might refuse to help. He insisted that Deborah do as he asked.

Deborah did spend the afternoon talking with David and learned a lot. When she finished, she headed for the bathroom down the end of the hallway. As she came back, David was already at the elevator with his box of belongings, having been fired. Deborah was quite upset about the events of the day!

This case has been used in a CS2 course very effectively. We generally present the case in pieces, asking students to consider what people should do along the way and then continue telling them what really happened until the next "decision point".

We believe that this case exemplifies several characteristics of effective ethics activities for programming courses. First, the case is engaging. It's an interesting case with a lot of gray. There are a number of points of view and three different people whose actions can be analyzed. David is clearly in the wrong, but his behavior patterns are some that students should recognize in themselves, so looking at his actions is valuable for that reason. Deborah is easier for students to relate to than many figures students see in these ethics scenarios, because she is just a year out of college (we do make a point of informing students that the case is based on real life).

This case is also very relevant to the course and very comprehensible to the students. The case raises real-life issues relating to programming that are often under-emphasized in programming courses, including the importance of maintenance and bug fixes, the importance of care in coding and ownership of code. Despite raising issues that students may be less focused on, the case doesn't really get murky in terms of understanding what the issues are and what's going on—though it may be a bit murky when it comes to the question of what everyone should do.

Case 2: The Hiring

The company

Widget Products, a well established company, decided to begin selling its products online. They hoped to have the online site up and running on January 1, 2003. Widget Products had two engineering divisions, front end and back end. Front end engineers took data provided and prepared the displays to be seen on the web. The back end engineers wrote code that interacted directly with the data base and did the underlying coding for the ordering program.

The individual

Deborah graduated from college with a major in Computer Science. She was well versed in C, C++, and Java. Upon completing her interview with Widget Products, she was offered a job with the front end engineering group. Noticing her hesitancy, the head of engineering told her he

[1] The four case studies presented in this paper are available at http://www.itk.ilstu.edu/faculty/mecalif/Ethics/CaseStudies.htm

did not want to hire her if she were not excited about the job. She explained that her training was for back end work and that she knew almost nothing about the front end work, which would be coded in JavaScript, HTML, XSL, C#, and several other languages unknown to Deborah. The engineering manager explained that the firm was happy to invest the time needed for her to learn the front end material. Deborah then gladly accepted the job offer.

The problem

Deborah's first assignment was to write the code connecting the various sources of data together and incorporating them in graphical displays. No one in the firm knew how to do this. She was told to find online help and purchase any books necessary to do the job. At the end of three weeks, she was no closer to accomplishing the task than when she began. She was frustrated and had no one to get help from. Her immediate boss, the engineer in charge of the front end, called her in for a conference.

Discussion

At this point the students are asked what they think will happen during the conference. They are asked to consult the *ACM code of ethics and professional conduct*. They are asked what the code has to say regarding management of employees and assignment of duties.

The conference

During the conference, Deborah's boss apologized for assigning her a task that she could not do. He said his job was to assign tasks that she could succeed at. He then assigned her to a different task, and explained that the company was going to hire outside consultants to do the task previously assigned to her.

Case 3: The Demo

The company

MMM Software is a start up company in Silicon Valley that began in early 2002. Their product is a software application whose initial release was January 2003. During the following twelve months, the US economy was poor, and consequently sales were slow.

The individual

Sarah graduated from college and landed a job as a software engineer at MMM Software in the summer of 2002. Sarah believed that the product was well done, and that sales would pick up once the economy rebounded.

The problem

A major software development company (we'll call them BigCo) became very interested in using MMM Software's product. They invited MMM Software and one competitor to make presentations. After the initial presentation, BigCo dismissed the competitor and told MMM Software they were impressed and most interested. They gave MMM Software a 100 page document containing their wish list of tasks that they wanted MMM Software's product to perform. MMM Software was invited to give a presentation to the CEO of BigCo in two weeks.

There were many tasks on the wish list that MMM Software could easily incorporate in their product, but that currently were not in the product. The decision was made to hard code the presentation to look like what would happen if the item in fact was operational. Sarah was asked to do some of the hard coding. She was assured that BigCo would be informed regarding which demo items were not currently functional. Sarah was concerned about the ethics of the situation. She would not be present at the presentation.

Discussion

Should Sarah comply with her assignment? What is her obligation to ensure that BigCo is correctly informed of the status of various tasks? What if Sarah's employer had always been honest with her in the past? What if she suspected a fudging of the truth in prior communications from the management? Clearly not all employees could attend the presentation in order to verify that BigCo was correctly informed. Are there alternative solutions to the problem?

All of these cases tend to provoke good class discussion. They raise issues that students have not considered, but that they can understand and do see as relevant. They relate well to Sarah and Deborah, because they easily picture themselves as recent graduates on their first jobs. The issues are comprehensible but not black and white. We find that such cases help students to consider the ethical realities of their intended profession in context.

6. WHAT'S THE ISSUE?: A CASE STUDY FOR AN ALGORITHMS AND DATA STRUCTURES COURSE

The last case study is an example of a completely fictional scenario created very specifically for use in a course. This assignment is used in our algorithms and data structures course, which is the first course in the students' program that seriously examines the analysis of algorithms at all. One of the primary foci of the course is on learning not only the various algorithms and data structures, but also how to select the "right" algorithm or data structure for a specific task. Therefore, we wanted students to have that focus reinforced in an ethics assignment. So we created a writing assignment in which students read the following very short scenario and do a one-page write-up analyzing the case.

Case 4: Search Time

> Dan Johnson is a software developer working for Pflugerville Data Management Services (PDMS). The primary source of revenue for this company comes from clients storing data on servers provided by PDMS and then doing searches on this data. Clients pay a monthly fee based on the storage used for their data, and they pay for searches based on CPU time. Dan's friend Nancy Greene works for one of PDMS's biggest clients, the Pflugerville Pflag. She has made the comment to him that the storage charges seem reasonable, but that the amount of CPU time used for searches seems excessive. Dan has investigated and determined that all of the data is being stored in arrays and searched using simple linear search.

We ask them a set of fairly standard questions about stakeholders, ethical issues, sections out of the code of ethics that apply, possible courses of action, and so forth. Then we also ask them to explain why this case is relevant to the course they're completing.

Students generally have no problem recognizing that linear search is, in fact, a very poor choice of algorithm, and then go on to address the issues of how Dan can bring up the problems and how the company might ensure its continued survival if it loses revenue from having more efficient searches and so on. One of the gratifying aspects of this fairly simple assignment is that students respond very well to it. Almost all of them recognize that there is a major issue here, but one they would never have recognized before taking the course. They also appreciate being given a problem to grapple with that they find straightforward and believable.

7. CONCLUSION

We have presented some thoughts about how ethics can be effectively incorporated into programming courses along with four original case studies that we have used effectively in such courses. We believe that the keys to success in this area are to keep cases short and comprehensible and to make sure that they are relevant to both the students and the course.

8. ACKNOWLEDGMENTS

An early draft of this paper was developed at a writing workshop held by the Center for the Advancement of Teaching at Illinois State University. Thanks to Dr. Kathleen McKinney and Dr. Doug Hesse who organized the workshop as well as to other attendees for their comments.

9. REFERENCES

[1] Association for Computing Machinery. (1997). *ACM code of ethics and professional conduct.*

[2] Association for Computing Machinery, & Institute for Electrical and Electronics Engineers. (1999). *Software engineering code of ethics and professional practice.*

[3] Association for Computing Machinery and Institute of Electrical and Electronics Engineers - Computer Science Joint Curriculum Task Force. (1990). *Computing curriculum '91.*

[4] Bowyer, K. (2000). *Video resources for use in teaching ethics and computing.* In *Proceedings of the Thirty-first SIGCSE Technical Symposium on Computer Science Education*, Austin, TX. pp. 217-221.

[5] Collins, W. R., Miller, K. W., Spielman, B. J., & Wherry, P. (1994). How good is good enough?: An ethical analysis of software construction and use. *Communications of the ACM, 37*(1), 81-91.

[6] Computing Accreditation Commission, Accreditation Board for Engineering and Technology. (2002). *Criteria for accrediting computing programs, 2003-2004.*

[7] DeGuere Jr., P. (Writer), & R. Hardy (Director) (2003). Standards of conduct. In D. P. Bellisario (Producer), *JAG*: Belisarius Productions.

[8] Epstein, R. G. (1997). *The case of the killer robot: Stories about the professional, ethical, and societal dimensions of computing.* New York: Wiley.

[9] Granger, M. J., Adams, E. S., Björkman, C., Gotterbarn, D., Juettner, D. D., Martin, C. D., et al. (1997). Using information technology to integrate social and ethical issues into the computer science and information systems curriculum: Report of the iticse '97 working group on social and ethical issues in computing curricula. *Outlook, 25*(4), 38-47.

[10] Huff, C., & Martin, C. D. (1995). Computing consequences: A framework for teaching ethical computing. *Communications of the ACM, 38*(12), 75-84.

[11] Lelewer, D. A. (1994). *A seminar course in computer ethics.* In *Proceedings of the Twenty-fifth SIGCSE Technical Symposium on Computer Science Education*, Phoenix, AK. pp. 253-257.

[12] Leveson, N., & Turner, C. S. (1993). An investigation of the Therac-25 accidents. *IEEE Computer, 26*(7), 18-41.

[13] Martin, C. D., & Weltz, E. Y. (1999). From awareness to action: Integrating ethics and social responsibility into the computer science curriculum. *Computers and Society, 29*(2), 6-14.

[14] Morgan, T., & Roberts, J. (2002). *An analysis of the patriot missile system*, from http://seeri.etsu.edu/SECodeCases/ethicsC/PatriotMissile.htm

[15] Schulze, K. G., & Grodzinsky, F. S. (1997). *Teaching ethical and social issues in cs1 and cs2.* In *Proceedings of the Twenty-Eighth SIGCSE Technical Symposium on Computer Science Education*, San Jose, CA. pp. 6-9.

[16] Spinello, R. A. (2003). "It's never right to copy software". In *Case studies in information technology ethics* (pp. 59-62). Upper Saddle River, NJ: Prentice Hall.

[17] Townsend, G. (1999). *TheTenthStrand == 3 * EthicalDebates + Solution.* In *Proceedings of the Thirtieth SIGCSE Technical Symposium on Computer Science Education*, New Orleans, LA. pp. 17-21.

[18] Wahl, N. J. (1999). *Yaatce--yet another approach to teaching computer ethics.* In *Proceedings of the Thirtieth SIGCSE Technical Symposium on Computer Science Education*, New Orleans, LA. pp. 22-26.

[19] Werth, L. H. (1997). *Getting started with computer ethics.* In *Proceedings of the Twenty-eighth SIGCSE Technical Symposium on Computer Science Education*, San Jose, CA. pp. 1-5.Bowman, B., Debray, S. K., and Peterson, L. L. Reasoning about naming systems. *ACM Trans. Program. Lang. Syst., 15,* 5 (Nov. 1993), 795-825.

A Discussion Format for Computer Ethics

Alton F. Sanders
Miami University
Department of Computer Science and
Systems Analysis
Oxford, OH 45056
01-513-529-5935
SanderAF@MUOhio.edu

ABSTRACT

This paper, describes a format and grading scheme for a discussion course in Computing Ethics. The teaching of ethics, particularly in a discussion format, can be somewhat problematic in a computer science department where courses tend to be technical and faculty tend to be more comfortable with material presented in a lecture and/or workshop format. Grading of discussion and papers can also be perceived as more difficult or, at least, less grounded in objective criteria. The following describes an approach that attempts to address those particular concerns. The course described was offered in the spring of 2003 when two sections were taught.

Categories and Subject Descriptors

K.3.2 [**Computer and Information Science Education**]: Computer science education, Curriculum, Information systems education

K.7.4 [**Professional Ethics**]: Ethical Dilemmas

K.4.2 [**Social Issues**]: Abuse and crime involving computers

General Terms

Measurement, Design, Reliability, Experimentation, Security, Human Factors, Legal Aspects

Keywords

Computer ethics, social implications, assessment

1. INTRODUCTION

There are three major problems that computer scientists often encounter when faced with the task of teaching a course in computer ethics: the nature of the material being addressed, the desirability of class discussion as an integral part of the course, and the grading of generally non-technical material. It is my purpose here to suggest some concrete ways to address each of these three difficulties. In the next section I shall discuss why we, as professionals, should be the teachers of professional ethics. I shall then make some suggestions on how to conduct a discussion class using methods developed by others and then I shall present the method that I have employed to provide a concrete rationale for the grading of class participation and papers relating to ethical arguments.

SIGCSE'05, February 23-27, 2005, St. Louis, Missouri, USA.

2. PROFESSIONAL ETHICS SHOULD BE TAUGHT BY PROFESSIONALS

Professional ethics and the social implications of computing are subjects that are often viewed as marginal by faculty in computer science departments (or at least the courses that address such subjects are viewed as marginal.) Many professional computer scientists have no problem at all with judging a design document, a technical paper, or a dissertation, but tend to doubt their own ability to judge ethical argument, whether expressed orally or in writing. It is not uncommon for computer scientists to express reluctance at teaching a 'soft subject' as opposed to a course with a strong technical orientation. However, the budding computing profession must attend to the needs of professional practice if we are to "Cross the Chasm" as defined by Denning [3]. Although Denning did not explicitly identify professional ethics as a key issue in defining a profession, his emphasis on professional practice [2,4] is certainly consistent with the assertion that ethics is central to a true profession. Hence, we must view the material as central to our profession.

Currently, although ethics is considered 'officially' part of the core curriculum, it is certainly not being taught by a cross section of computer science faculty. Commonly, the subject is relegated to a single course that is likely to be taught by an adjunct who may be a philosopher rather than a computer scientist. Now philosophers generally know a lot about ethics and the teaching of ethics. Furthermore they are also frequently good teachers who are practiced in teaching ethics. Nevertheless, philosophers are not the best choice to teach a required computer science course in professional ethics. As Michael Davis as argued, "What, for example, can a student think of a course in her profession's ethics if it must be taught by a 'lay instructor'?" [1, p. 231]

Ethics should not be viewed as an ancillary part of our profession. The practice of our profession is just not conducted that way. If we are asked to ship a product that is defective, there will be no philosopher-in-residence who will discuss our ethical obligations. We must be prepared to deal with such matters in the context of our professional environments. We must train our students to do so as well. Davis [1] presents very strong arguments that the *foremost* attribute of a profession, as opposed to a vocation, is the adherence to a code of professional conduct. It is part of our professional obligation to our students to teach them the rules of professional conduct. If we are uncomfortable with the subject, we should undertake steps to reduce that discomfort to the point where we can be effective despite our discomfort. I hope that the following will constitute a positive contribution to such an effort.

3. DISCUSSION FORMAT

The predominant format for computer science courses is a lecture format or a lab/workshop. We have largely been educated via that method ourselves and tend to prefer that approach. Indeed, although the lecture format has gotten somewhat out of fashion in many environments, it may be the best format for certain subjects. Certainly the hands-on aspect of a lab/workshop class can be very valuable in those courses that involve programming or practice with proofs, analysis, or designs.

Although a course on ethics can certainly be taught in a lecture format (indeed, class size may dictate a lecture format in some instances), it is generally considered desirable to use a discussion format. Discussions allow students to more directly and immediately confront multiple perspectives that reveal hidden complexities, unstated assumptions, and varying contexts. Discussions also present some problems to many of us accustomed to lecturing:

(1) Discussions are much more difficult (at least for most of the computer scientists I know) to grade with confidence.

(2) Discussion classes can be much more difficult to control. One must make sure that all students participate, that the discussion remains collegial, and that the discussion remains on point. This is not something that most of us are accustom to doing.

(3) Special steps may be needed to entice students to adequately prepare for class. I heard one student remark about a discussion class he had in another subject, "If you have a gift for gab, then all you have to do is show up and talk in order to get a good grade." Surely none of us would want to teach a course that had that property.

I undertook the design of the course described here as one of those computer scientist with a definite discomfort with the idea of teaching a discussion course on professional ethics. Naturally, I researched the topic in search of assistance in the design of the course and found that there is, indeed, a good deal of literature and available resources. Two significant resources are The Research Center on Computers and Society [6] and The Online Ethics Center for Engineering and Science [5]. I found that most of the literature dealt, quite understandably, with the content of the ethics courses and desired outcomes. While that was certainly useful, indeed essential, it did not address explicit issues of classroom procedures, format and grading that were the main source of my discomfort. Those are the matters I wish to address here.

3.1 Leading the Discussion

Following the analysis of Waite, *et al* [7], the goal of a 'conversational classroom' is to create an environment that resembles the experience of an engaged, intellectual conversation similar to what might take place in a graduate seminar. They cite two principle resources: (1) techniques for creating interaction and (2) techniques for creating a sense of presence (where 'presence' refers to committed involvement in the discussion with obvious interest in the both the outcome and the process.) They provide a number of concrete techniques that an instructor may apply in both cases. I have a couple of simple additional suggestions.

I keep a deck of 3 by 5 cards, each with the name of a student. At any point in the discussion, if I have too many or too few students who volunteer to speak to the topic at hand, I suffle the cards and draw a name. I try to keep the atmosphere light so that the process does not become a frightening ordeal for anyone. Also, if a student is simply unprepared and unable to address the topic, I do not persist, but move on. If one is unable to establish a light atmosphere with a particular class, this policy would probably be a bad one. Instilling fear into the classroom is not consistent with the idea of a conversational classroom.

In order for a student to demonstrate a sense of presence, he or she must be present. Hence, I have declared that any latecomers to class are automatically volunteers. Again, if the atmosphere is kept light and jocular, there is no great trauma associated with such a policy. On the other hand, my feedback from students suggests that it is a significant incentive to coming to class on time. Of course, we instructors must hold our end. I always try to be on time for class and in each class period I ask for a volunteer to be timekeeper (I always get one.) When the timekeeper announces that time is up, I immediately end class. We never run over.

Finally, I believe that certain grading practices can provide incentives that significantly enhance both the creation of interaction and the sense of presence in the classroom. I shall discuss those below.

3.2 Grading Class Participation

I very much agree with Waite *et al* [7] on the importance of listening and absorbing the views of others as expressed in the discussion. I have attempted to emphasize the importance of listening to one's colleagues during class discussion in three ways:

1. Position papers must explicitly cite points raised in class discussion. The citation should be a direct quote.
2. The final exam will be <u>entirely</u> related to class discussions.
3. A small but significant portion of the final grade (10% at last offering) is based on the number of citations that quote a given student (subject to certain qualifications as discussed below.) That portion of the grade will be assigned by using the standard curve on the number of citations for each student.

The rationale here is that we will spend a lot of our time discussing issues. What a student says and how well he or she knows what others have said are both relevant and significant. Both need to be taken seriously.

In order for a student to receive credit for a citation, the quoted remark must be on point, of significance, and reasonable. For example, one paper said "as John Doe said, 'you get what you pay for,' and I agree." Obviously, simply stating a cliché is not worthy of any additional credit. John Doe did not get a citation for that particular remark.

Final student assessment revealed that students, while not fond of having to cite their peers, were tolerant of the practice. Almost all of the students who had any objections to the requirement (a minority of the class) did not object to the requirement as such, but to the number of citations required.

4. ASSIGNING AND GRADING PAPERS

The course described had only the assigned papers and an essay final as graded work. The papers were of two kinds: positional papers that consisted of 3-5 pages and research papers that were very short (three page maximum), but with an extensive annotated bibliography. The format for the research is unusual and was used by another professor at my university. I do not know who used it, but a student once told me of the format and commented on how much he learned from doing those papers. Naturally, that got my attention.

Papers are graded on a "7-Cs" scale, which is a scale that I have been using for years based on seven parameters, all beginning with the letter C. The basic idea is that the attributes of a good paper should be:

The Truth

- Correctness
  - Proper syntax as well as technical correctness
  - Whether the conditions of the assignment have been met
- Cogency
  - Logical validity and relevance of the arguments and examples presented

The Whole Truth

- Completeness
  - Whether everything relevant that could be said has been said.

Nothing But the Truth

- Conciseness
  - Whether there is useless prose, irrelevant material presented, or redundancies of material.
  - Whether any programs presented are developed without extraneous computational overhead.

Told Well

- Clarity
  - Whether the presentation is clear and understandable without a need for additional explanation
- Concreteness
  - Whether abstract concepts are grounded in concrete specific examples
- Creativity
  - Imagination and innovation in both the presentation and in the substance of the paper.

Table 1 shows the current version of the grading rubric that I use to grade student papers. Each row of the table represents a continuous scale. The headings on the columns merely show a rough correspondence between point value and quality assessments. Note that the scales are neither symmetric nor necessarily of equal weight. For example, any paper's presentation is supposed to contain correct statements and sound arguments. Hence, there are few points added for correctness or cogency. On the other hand, in both cases, substantial penalties are assessed for incorrect statements or faulty arguments. Similarly, little is lost by not being creative, but much can be gained by being so. The particular values in the table vary according to the course I am teaching. In some cases, the values are very stable since I have been adjusting them for about 15 years. The values for the course described here are less stable because I am relatively new to teaching the course. In particular, I believe that the maximum value for cogency and, perhaps, correctness should be higher.

Each student gets a copy of the chart with his or her score for each of the seven categories along with comments for each category. Student assessments indicate that students are quite comfortable with the rubric.

Table 1. Grading Rubric

	MIN	*Poor*	*OK*	*VG*	*MAX*
Correct	-100	-20	0	2	5
Complete	-20	-10	0	20	40
Concise	-20	-10	0	5	10
Cogent	-20	-10	0	2	5
Concrete	-20	-10	0	5	10
Creative	-5	-2	0	20	40
Clear	-20	-10	0	5	10

5. MISTAKES

In my initial try at using this format, I made two significant mistakes that I shall attempt to correct the next time I teach the course:

1. I failed to establish an explicit attendance policy.
2. I did not include sufficient assessment of the students' preparation. In particular, often there were some students who had not carefully read the entire reading assignment.

The incentives associated with citations and 'volunteering' were sufficient to motivate most students to come to class prepared most of the time. However, some students nevertheless sometimes came unprepared and a few were absent more than occasionally. There was one infamous occasion when no student had read the entire assignment sufficiently well to present it to the rest of the class. It would therefore seem prudent to establish an explicit attendance policy and additional reading assessments to be conducted frequently.

6. CONCLUSIONS

The discussion format described here worked well the first time it was attempted. Student assessments indicated that students were very pleased with the course and there was a marked difference in the quality of the first student papers compared to the final two or three papers.

I fully intend to use the same format (with corrections as noted in the previous section) when I teach the course again in the spring of 2003. It is, however, my fond hope that in the future that a cross section of faculty in my department will teach the ethics course whether or not they use this format.

7. ACKNOWLEDGMENTS

My thanks to Michael Davis, Robert Ladenson, and Rick Momeyer for stimulating workshops on Teaching Ethics. I also thank Miami University for sponsoring the special faculty seminars known as 'Learning Communities' : (1) *Ethics Across the Curriculum* organized and directed by Rick Momeyer and (2) *Student Assessment* organized and directed by Jerry Stonewater.

8. REFERENCES

[1] Davis, M. *Profession, Code and Ethics* Ashgate Publishing Company, Burlington, VT, 2002.

[2] Denning, Peter J., Computing the Profession, Educom Review, 33,6 (November 1998), 26-30, 46-59.

[3] Denning, Peter J., Crossing the Chasm, Communications of the ACM, 44,4 (April 2001), 21-25.

[4] Denning, Peter J. Great Principles in Computing Curricula, *Proceedings of the Thirty-fifth SIGCSE Technical Symposium on Computer Science Education* (SIGCSE '04) (Norfolk, Virginia, March 3-7, 2004) ACM Press, New York, NY, 2004, 336-341.

[5] The Online Ethics Center for Engineering and Science, http://onlineethics.org

[6] The Research Center on Computing and Society, http://www.southernct.edu/organizations/rccs/index.html

[7] Waite, William M., Michele H. Jackson and Amer Diwan, The Conversational Classroom, *Proceedings of the Thirty-fourth SIGCSE Technical Symposium on Computer Science Education*, (SIGCSE '03), (Reno, Nevada, February 19-23, 2003), ACM Press, New York, NY, 2003, 526-531.

Computer Literacy: What Students Know and From Whom They Learned It

Mark E. Hoffman and David R. Vance
Quinnipiac University
275 Mount Carmel Avenue
Hamden, CT 06518
203-582-8200
Mark.Hoffman@Quinnipiac.edu, David.Vance@Quinnipiac.edu

ABSTRACT

Do new college students already know much of what has previously been taught in our computer literacy courses (assuming a functional definition of knowledge according to which students are proficient with personal computer and Internet applications)? We conducted a survey of incoming first-year students at Quinnipiac University to learn not only their skill level with a representative range of technology tasks, but also from whom they learned these tasks. Results provide a profile of students who report learning many technology tasks primarily on their own. We propose a taxonomy according to which native technology tasks are learned with family support, social and educational technology task categories are supported by friends and teachers, respectively, and optional technology tasks are learned with little support. Our results will help in the design of appropriate computer literacy courses.

Categories and Subject Descriptors

K.3.2 [**Computer and Education**]: Computer and Information Science Education – *literacy.*

General Terms

Management, Experimentation, Verification

Keywords

Computer Literacy, First-Year Students, Technology Tasks, Skill Level, From Whom Learned, Taxonomy

1. INTRODUCTION

"When students entering computer literacy courses already know what was new learning to students of prior years, what then shall we teach them?" This is a reasonable question about incoming first-year college students (referred to as students for the remainder of the paper) given that the background experience of technology use for these students is greater than that of students of prior years. After all, access to personal computers and the Internet among pre-college students has increased dramatically in recent years—particularly Internet access [9]. High speed connections are more widely available in the home [4], and schools have high speed connections that are likely being used to increasingly good effect.

To answer this first question, we need to consider two more specific questions. First, "What is the essential purpose of a computer literacy course?" This question has become more acute with changes in the type as well as the availability of computing technology [3]. "Computer literacy" once referred to familiarity with the basics of operating systems, hardware configurations, and desktop applications, but as computer technology becomes more reliable and personal computers approach the status of household appliances, students are now more involved with the communications and information flow that this technology makes possible.

"Computer literacy," therefore, should now also refer to the literacy necessary to use these means of communication and information with critical understanding. Because the Internet is now a major source of information, computer literacy must increasingly incorporate *information literacy*, especially the ability to evaluate information found online, as well as *critical computer literacy*, the ability to incorporate computing technology in support of critical thinking. Generally speaking, because computing technology is becoming integrated with everyday tasks, the idea of computer literacy is merging with other forms of literacy [10].

Most students would use not a critical but a functional definition of computer literacy, i.e., proficiency with personal computer and Internet applications [2]. Assuming for the moment this functional definition, the second question we need to ask is: "What do students know?" That is, what tasks do they perform proficiently? There is little information in the literature to answer this question. Surveys are available for institutional assessment [2,6], and for student self-assessment [1,7,8]. In some cases, survey results are available [2,5]. Although some of the results are up to date, many are not. Given the recent, rapid rate of change in computing technology, older results are of little value.

We conducted a survey of incoming first-year students at Quinnipiac University. We wanted to learn not only what they knew, their functional computer literacy, but also from whom they learned it. Unlike other surveys in the literature, our survey inquired about a representative, rather than comprehensive, set of technology tasks. The technology tasks we chose ranged from those we were confident many students knew well to those we were confident few students knew well. Understanding from whom students learned each representative technology task provided a new and, as of yet, unexplored dimension.

SIGCSE'05, February 23–27, 2005, St. Louis, Missouri, USA.

Our decision to use this approach was prompted by the question: "How are students learning the functional skills essential to a computer literacy course?" The answer to this question might help us shape content and pedagogy to take advantage of what students are doing before they reach us. For example, just-in-time or on-demand learning through Internet-based organizations such as ElementK[1] allows students to learn specific application features on their own, but we do not well know at this point how a teaching strategy that uses resources such as ElementK integrates with students' prior skills.

Table 1. Technology Tasks and Abbreviations.

Technology Tasks	Abbreviation
Send and receive e-mail messages	E-mail
Send and receive e-mail attachments	Attachments
Create e-mail groups (Personal Distribution Lists)	Groups
Connect to the World Wide Web from Home	Connect from home
Connect to the World Wide Web from your High School	Connect from high school
Participate in chat groups such as instant messaging	IM
Participate in threaded discussions or message boards	Threaded discussion
Search the World Wide Web using a search engine	Search
Create and edit Web pages	Create Web pages
Maintain a Web site	Maintain a Web site
Work with file and folders on my computer	Folders on my computer
Work with files and folders on a networked computer	Folders on networked computer
Create a word processing document such as a Word file	Word processing
Create a presentation such as a PowerPoint file	Create presentations

The decision was also prompted by more general concerns. What are the cultural effects of a generation of students whose native language is punctuated by hyperlinks, whose familiar linguistic spaces are via software applications as much as conversational settings, and whose means of communication and information are chosen from an array of electronic alternatives with personalized settings? If "the limits of my language mean the limits of my world,"[2] then what is the effect on a student's world of a native language so effectively extended by computer technology? These effects are not readily measurable, but should likely change and enlarge our conception of computer literacy.

2. METHODOLOGY

The survey included 4 demographic questions (gender, class in school, school or college in the University, and connection type) and two questions for each of 14 technology tasks. (See Table 1.) For each technology task, students were asked to rate their skill level on a 5-level scale from "poor" to "expert". Students were also asked "From whom did you learn it?" where they selected one of the following persons: Myself, Family, Friend, Teacher, Coworker, Other, or None. Space was included at the end of the survey for any comments students volunteered.

The survey was administered online. Each student required a user ID and password to access the survey. Students were allowed to take the survey only once. Only survey data was supplied to the researchers, therefore, to the researchers, each response was anonymous. For students to submit the completed survey, all questions had to be answered.

The survey was administered during a technology training session over three, weekend-long, orientation sessions for incoming students during June 2004. During the first session only 2 students responded because the survey was omitted from the orientation script. During the remaining two sessions 800 students responded. The entire incoming class consists of approximately 1340 students for a response rate of approximately 60%.

3. RESULTS

In this section we present survey results for connection type, and skill level and from whom learned for each technology task. We also present results comparing connection type with skill level for each technology task, and connection type with from whom learned for each technology task. We do not include results for gender, or school. Since only three students selected "transfer" for class in school, we do not include results for this question.

3.1 Connection Type

Table 2 shows the percent of responses for each connection type. The selection "none" was not offered, however, it is reasonable to assume that a very small number of students do not have one of the three connection types offered.

Table 2. Connection Type Percent

Cable Modem	48.5%
Dial-Up Modem	30.8%
DSL	20.7%

We see that almost half of the students have a cable modem connection, and that almost 70% have a high speed connection (cable modem or DSL). This is our first survey, and although we have only informal past survey results and anecdotal evidence, we think this shows a dramatic increase in high speed connection type among our students over the past two years. We are supported by recent trends in high speed connection installations [4].

3.2 Skill Levels

The average skill level across all 14 technology tasks is 3.68 (where "none" is 1, "poor" is 2, "fair" is 3, "good" is 4, and "expert" is 5). By itself this number is not meaningful, however, it is a number we will be tracking as the survey is administered to students in coming years.

The 14 technology tasks cluster into three groupings by student-reported skill level as shown in Table 3. Looking at the high skill level cluster we see technology tasks that students *want to know*, such as participate in IM, connect from home, and search. In the middle skill level cluster we see technology tasks that students *need to know*, such as folders on my computer and create presentations. In the low skill level cluster we see technology tasks that most students consider *optional*, such as threaded discussions, groups, and create Web pages. Technology tasks in

[1] http://www.elementk.com

[2] Ludwig Wittgenstein, *Tractatus Logico-Philosophicus*, 5.6.

the optional skill level cluster do not necessarily mean that students are not interested. For example, many students have not had the opportunity to learn how to create Web pages; when they learn they often find it the most interesting part of the course.

Table 3. Skill Level Clusters

Technology Task	Average Skill Level
High Skill Level Cluster	
IM	4.56
Connect from Home	4.50
Search	4.34
Connect from HS	4.34
E-mail	4.29
Word	4.27
Middle Skill Level Cluster	
Attachment	3.90
Folder on my computer	3.81
Create presentations	3.63
Low Skill Level Cluster	
Folders on networked computer	3.14
Threaded discussion	3.08
Groups	3.00
Create Web pages	2.43
Maintain a Web site	2.16

3.3 From Whom Learned

Table 4 shows primary and secondary persons from whom students learned each technology task. (Although not specifically stated in the survey, we assume that "myself" includes any aid the student used to learn on their own including trial and error, manuals, training CDs and videos, and online help.) We see that students report learning 10 of 14 technology tasks primarily on their own. For the high skill level cluster, the percent response for "myself" ranged from 68.0% for IM to 61.8% for e-mail. The only high skill level cluster technology task not to rank "myself" first (connect from high school) ranked it second with an percent response of 42.3%. Two technology tasks ranked "teacher" first, and two ranked "none" first. The two that ranked "none" first also have the two lowest average skill levels. The two tasks where "teacher" is ranked first are tasks that are associated with learning at school.

Rank two sources offer an interesting contrast. For the four technology skills that did not rank "myself" one, it was ranked two. "Myself" is either the first or second ranked source for all technology tasks. "Family" is ranked two for 5 technology skills. These technology tasks, such as e-mail, using word processing, and connect from home, form a set of tasks that one would expect of students who have been using computers in the home for a number of years. IM, a relatively new technology task, and one used by high school students to socialize ranks "friend" second. This is the only task where "friend" appears either first or second. "Teacher" is ranked either one or two for tasks considered educational, such as create presentations or connect from high school. Although search is a technology task that virtually all students can do at a high skill level, informal and anecdotal evidence indicates that secondary, and possibly primary, schools are beginning to teach skills beyond keyword search, such as using Boolean operators, and how to evaluate Web pages. That "teacher" is ranked as the second source supports this observation.

We found it surprising that no student reported at any skill level "teacher" as a person from whom they learned word processing. We speculate that students who are 18 years old, born in 1986, have been using word processing over much of their school careers. They may not have had a teacher formally teach them how to do word processing, it may have been informally learned in the home, or they may have simply forgotten. Word processing is one of the early popular personal computer applications; it is likely that sufficient support is available in the home. Since "family" is the second ranking source of learning, this interpretation seems reasonable.

Table 4. Rank one and two responses for the "From whom did you learn it?" question for each technology task. Percent of overall responses across all skill levels is in parentheses.

Technology Task	Rank One	Rank Two
Send and receive e-mail messages	Myself (61.8%)	Family (20.1%)
Send and receive e-mail attachments	Myself (52.9%)	Family (20.2%)
Create e-mail groups (Personal Distribution Lists)	Myself (43.6%)	None (28.4%)
Connect to the World Wide Web from Home	Myself (63.0%)	Family (24.6%)
Connect to the World Wide Web from your High School	Teacher (45.9%)	Myself (42.3%)
Participate in chat groups such as instant messaging	Myself (68.0%)	Friend (22.3%)
Participate in threaded discussions or message boards	Myself (46.6%)	None (30.4%)
Search the World Wide Web using a search engine	Myself (63.2%)	Teacher (19.1%)
Create and edit Web pages	None (39.3%)	Myself (25.3%)
Maintain a Web site	None (48.0%)	Myself (24.3%)
Work with file and folders on my computer	Myself (54.2%)	Family (20.7%)
Work with files and folders on a networked computer	Myself (36.8%)	Teacher (21.9%)
Create a word processing document such as a Word file	Myself (65.7%)	Family (18.2%)
Create a presentation such as a PowerPoint file	Teacher (45.6%)	Myself (31.3%)

By way of contrast, creating presentations is not as well-supported in the home, and is only recently becoming more widely used in secondary and primary schools. "Teacher" as the first ranking person learned from, followed by "myself" supporting this interpretation.

Tables 5 shows skill level versus from whom learned at and above the average skill level of 4.27 for word processing. The table shows "myself" and "family" (the second ranked person from whom the task was learned). Results show that students reporting skill levels above the average learn more frequently on their own, rather than with the support of others. Similar patterns exist for all technology tasks. These results indicate that students at the average skill level learn from a variety of persons. As students' skill level increases above the average, they increasingly learn on their own.

Table 5. Word processing: skill level versus from whom learned.

Skill Level	Myself	Family
5	33.5%	7.2%
4	28.4%	8.7%

3.4 Connection Type versus Skill Level

We analyzed the most frequently reported skill level within each connection type for all technology tasks. For example, for e-mail the most frequently reported skill level for those reporting a cable modem connection type is skill level 4 with 53.7% of the responses. For dial-up and DSL, the skill level is also 4 with 53.4% and 51.8%, respectively. For this task, there is no relationship between skill level and connection type. This lack of relationship was also true of IM, folders on my computer, create presentations, attachments. For six technology task (groups, connect from home, connect from high school, folders on networked computer, word processing, and search), the most frequent skill level is higher for high speed connection types (cable modem and DSL) than for dial-up. This result indicates that for technology tasks that perform better with high speed access, dial-up skill level is lower, whereas, for "light-weight" Internet tasks, such as e-mail and IM, and personal computer specific tasks, such as create presentations, all connection types are equal.

Table 6. Most frequently reported connection type over from whom learned categories.

Connection Type	From Whom Learned				
	Myself	Family	Friend	Teacher*	None**
Cable	13	3	3	3	1
Dial-Up	1	0	7	7	11
DSL	0	11	4	3	3

* No word processing for teacher.

** Cable modem and dial-up modem tied for create presentations.

3.5 Connection Type versus From Whom Learned

We analyzed the most frequently reported connection type within each from whom learned. Results in Table 6 show that cable modem is the most frequently reported connection type for those who report learning by themselves. Dial-up is the most frequently reported connection type for those who report learning from a friend, a teacher, or none. DSL is the most frequently reported connection type for those who report learning from family. Learning in the home, either on one's own, or from the family is related to the presence of a high speed connection (cable modem or DSL), whereas learning from someone outside the home, or not at all, is related to the presence of a dial-up connection.

4. DISCUSSION

The results of this survey show that the typical first-year student at Quinnipiac University has a high speed connection at home; the connection type is most likely to be a cable modem. This student assesses her average skill level over a range of technology tasks closer to "good" than "fair". She considers herself to be highly skilled connecting from home and at school, communicating using e-mail and IM, searching the WWW, and word processing. It is more likely than not that she uses attachments, works with files and folders on her computer as well as networked computers, and uses threaded discussions. It is increasingly likely that the typical student has learned how to create presentations in high school. Students who are highly skilled have learned on their own more often, but the more typical student who is near the mean skill level is likely to have learned with the support of others. The typical student learns traditional applications such as word processing and e-mail with family support and relies on friends for support with IM. She is likely to have had some formal education in searching and in creating presentations in high school.

Students learn what they want to know, and they generally learn what they want to know informally[3]. Aside from connecting from high school, all technology tasks in the high skill level cluster are learned by students on their own. Even creating Web pages, familiar to the fewest number of students, is primarily learned by students on their own. Creating presentations, primarily learned from a teacher, supports this claim since it is unlikely that students want to know how to create presentations, but rather learn it as needed for high school assignments. Instant Messaging, a technology task students want to do, has the highest average skill level and is overwhelmingly learned by students on their own.

Table 7. Taxonomy of technology tasks.

Native	Educational	Social	Optional
E-mail Attachments Connect from home Folders on my computer Word processing	Connect from high school Search Folders on networked computer Create presentations	IM	Threaded discussion Create Web pages Maintain a Web site Groups

The taxonomy of technology tasks shown in Table 7 emerges from the survey results about the other sources of learning. Native tasks are learned informally similar to the way a native language is learned with the support of other native speakers; family is the second ranked person learned from. Native users may not know the formal or "best" way to use a particular feature of an application such as word processing, but they function effectively at some basic level. Educational tasks are learned formally at school with little support at home where teacher is first or second ranked person learned from. Social tasks are learned with the support of friends, where friend is the second ranked person learned from. Optional tasks are learned with little support from any other person, where none is first or second ranked person learned from. This taxonomy gives us a way to understand how students learn technology tasks and their motivation. It also gives a way to predict and track kinds of tasks

[3] We consider informal learning to be self-initiated or learning from a family member or friend.

as they change categories over time. Create Web pages, for example, ranks teacher as the third ranked person learned from. This may indicate that secondary, and possible primary, schools are teaching this task. If this is the case, as is indicated by informal and anecdotal evidence, then this task will become educational. If creating web pages becomes a widely performed task, and it is well-supported in the home, then it may eventually become native.

It may seem that connection type determines students' skill levels for technology tasks, but because high speed connections have only recently become affordable; they may not have been available long enough to have a significant effect on skill levels. Rather, it seems better supported by the results that skill level determines connection type. For 9 of 14 tasks, cable/myself is the most frequent pair reported when connection type was compared with "from whom learned." This may mean that the families of students who are highly skilled invest in high speed connections. Notably, DSL is the most frequently reported connection type for students who reported learning from "family." This could mean that highly skilled students whose families purchased high speed connections early chose cable because of availability and cost at the time. DSL has only recently become widely available, aggressively marketed and priced. Families where students are not as highly skilled, but desire to support their children, may now be selecting DSL in greater numbers.

Students replying to this survey assessed their own skill levels for each technology task. To verify these results, we would need formally to assess their skill levels with task specific assessments. For example, to assess a student's skill level with word processing we would need to identify a set of skills and a performance scale. This remains future work.

After reviewing the results of this survey, we are considering two changes for future use. First, to better understand the effect of connection type on skill level and from whom tasks are learned, it would be helpful to know how long students have had access to the connection in their homes. We speculate that high speed connections are too new in most homes to have had a significant impact yet, but we cannot be sure. Second, we assumed that all students have an Internet connection in their homes. Given the type of student who attends Quinnipiac University, we think this is a reasonable assumption, though we cannot be certain. Adding "none" as an option to future surveys will remove doubt.

5. CONCLUSION

Our survey results are specific for Quinnipiac University, but the taxonomy is generally applicable. For example, if word processing is learned in school more frequently than at home, then native familiarity is lacking and the task is educational. This result changes what can be assumed about students' facility with word processing and how instruction is delivered. Native language speakers who encounter an unfamiliar word or want to know how to use a particular grammatical construction refer to dictionaries or writing guides; they extend the familiarity they already possess in a supportive environment. Non-native speakers must learn the language more deliberately, either socially or formally with reference to explicit grammatical rules. If family members do not speak the language, then acquired familiarity with the language will reflect the peculiarities of the social settings in which the new language is learned. Native users may use appropriate just-in-time tools to expand their knowledge, while non-native users must first learn the basic task. More work needs to be done to validate the taxonomy and to understand its consequences for computer literacy education, but if the border between computer literacy and a larger conception of literacy is blurred in the experience of today's students, then the metaphor of native language used to characterize familiarity with computer applications is more than mere metaphor.

From a cultural perspective, we think that native tasks indicate common ground over generations and therefore are less likely disruptive of a common world-view. If, however, tasks are educational, social, or optional, they are not shared with family or parents and therefore may be more disruptive. We suspect that this, in turn, could exacerbate the digital divide. If technology tasks are taught only in school without considering the students home environment, then they will not become native users, and, thus, be at a disadvantage. These conjectures required further research.

Returning to the beginning: What should we teach in computer literacy courses? Assuming that the number of native tasks is growing, we should begin creating courses that teach functionally computer literate students critical computer literacy skills with regard to these tasks. As we continue this study in coming years, we will test the assumption. At the same time, computer literacy courses should take account of, and develop critical perspectives for, the largely non-native uses of technology, especially socially supported uses, which represent potentially the most disruptive forms of new linguistic space.

6. REFERENCES

[1] Alternative Learning Division. Computer Literacy Self-Assessment. Technology Literacy, (June 26, 2003), Accessed August 16, 2004. <http://matcmadison.edu/ald/lab/tech/selftest.htm>

[2] Computer and Information Literacy. Teaching, Learning, & Technology Round Table, Ursuline College, May 10, 2004 , Accessed August 16, 2004. <http://www.ursuline.edu/tltr/complit.htm>

[3] Hoffman, M. and Blake, J. Computer Literacy: Today and Tomorrow. *JCSC 18,5* (May 2003), 221-233.

[4] Horrigan, J.B. Pew Internet Project Data Memo: 55% of Adult Internet Users Have Broadband at Home or Work. Pew Internet & American Life Project (April 2004).

[5] How Computer Literate are UC Davis Students? *I.T. Times 4,3* (Nov. 1995), Accessed August 16, 2004. <http://ittimes.ucdavis.edu/v4n3nov95/complit.html>

[6] Information Literacy Survey. Accessed August 16, 2004. <http://www2.carthage.edu/ais/survey.htm>

[7] Oxford University Learning Technologies Group IT literacy at Oxford University. Oxford University Computing Services, Accessed August 16, 2004. <http://www.oucs.ox.ac.uk/ltg/literacy/>

[8] Self-Survey of NC Computer Literacy Competencies. Accessed August 16, 2004. <http://www.ceap.wcu.edu/ROFM_CGIv4.1/NCcompetencies.html>

[9] USDoC, *A Nation Online: How Americans are Expanding Their Use of the Internet.* 2002.

[10] Williams, K. *Literacy and Computer Literacy: Analyzing the NRC's 'Being Fluent with Information Technology'.* University of Michigan, 2002. <http://www.literacyandtechnology.org/v3n1/williams.htm>

Design Process for a Non-majors Computing Course

Mark Guzdial
College of Computing/GVU
Georgia Institute of Technology
801 Atlantic Drive
Atlanta, Georgia
guzdial@cc.gatech.edu

Andrea Forte
College of Computing/GVU
Georgia Institute of Technology
801 Atlantic Drive
Atlanta, Georgia
aforte@cc.gatech.edu

ABSTRACT

There is growing interest in computing courses for non-CS majors. We have recently built such a course that has met with positive response. We describe our design process, which includes involvement of stakeholders and identifying a context that facilitates learning. We present evaluation results on success rates (approximately 90% of the students earn an A, B, or C) and impact of the course on students over time (80% report that the class has influenced them more than a semester later).

Categories and Subject Descriptors

K.3.2 [**Computers and Education**]: Computer and Information Sciences Education
; H.5.1 [**Information Interfaces and Presentation**]: Multimedia Information Systems

General Terms

Experimentation,Design

Keywords

Multimedia, CS1, CS2, programming, non-majors

1. DESIGNING COMPUTER SCIENCE FOR THE NON-MAJORS

There is growing interest in the creation of computer science for non-CS majors. One reason for this increase is the recognition that computing now influences every aspect of our society, and it is a competitive advantage for students in other majors to know more about computing. A reason for the interest from CS departments is declining enrollment in the CS major, which inspires CS faculty to look elsewhere for customers [6].

At Georgia Institute of Technology (*Georgia Tech*), the faculty require that every incoming student must take a course in computing, including a requirement to learn and use programming. When that decision was made, the only class available was our majors-focused CS1 based on the TeachScheme approach[7], which did not adequately meet the needs of our liberal arts, architecture, and management students. The course saw low success rates, and the students and faculty were vocal in their dissatisfaction. We saw this dissatisfaction as an opportunity to create a new course and build toward Alan Perlis' vision of programming for *all* students—as a component of a general, liberal education [8].

The course that we developed, *Introduction to Media Computation*, is an introduction to computing contextualized around the theme of manipulating and creating media. Students really do program—creating Photoshop-like filters (such as generating negative and greyscale images), reversing and splicing sounds, gathering information (like temperature and news headlines) from Web pages, and creating animations. Details on the structure and content of the course are available elsewhere [20, 11].

The purpose of this paper is to use our course as an instance, and abstract from it a design process for a non-majors introductory computing course and a set of benchmark evaluation results. Our definition of success is:

- Non-CS majors students should have a higher success rate than in a traditional introductory computing course. If we are designing the course explicitly for that audience, we should be able to satisfy their needs and meet their interests better than we can in a course designed for our own majors.
- The course should have impact beyond the single term. If the course doesn't influence how non-major students think about computing, and they will only take a single computing course (probably), then we will have lost our opportunity to influence these students.

In this paper, we describe how we designed the Media Computation course as an example process for designing a non-majors computing course. A sketch of our process follows, and is detailed in the second section of the paper.

- *Setting objectives*: We set objectives for the course based on campus requirements for a computing course, on ACM recommendations, and on the existing computer science education research literature about what students find difficult about computer science.
- *Choosing a context*: We selected a context that allowed us to meet our curricular objectives and that we

SIGCSE'05, February 23–27, 2005, St. Louis, Missouri, USA.

believed would be motivating to non-major students. Having an explicit context helped them understand *why* they should care about computing, which is significant issue in introductory computing [13].

- *Set up feedback process*: We sought feedback from faculty in the majors that we planned to serve, as well as from students through multiple forums.
- *Define infrastructure*: An early challenge was to choose the language and programming environment, which are critical (and sometimes religious) issues. We found that the process of choosing a language for a non-majors course is as much about culture and politics as it is about pedagogy.
- *Define the course*: Finally, we defined lectures, assignments, and all the details of what makes up a course. Here our decisions were informed by research in the learning sciences [4].

2. DESIGN PROCESS

We detail below each stage of the development process for the Media Computation class. We believe that a similar process could be used to create other introductory computing courses targeting non-CS majors.

2.1 Setting Objectives

The Georgia Tech computing course requirements states that the introductory course curriculum has to focus on algorithmic thinking and on making choices between different data structures and encodings. There is an explicit requirement that students learn to *program* algorithms being studied. We also wanted to build upon the recommendations in *Computing Curricula 2001* [2] as a standard for what should be in a computing introduction, with a "CS1"-level course as our target.

We explicitly decided not to prepare these students to be *software developers*, but instead, we focused on preparing them to be *tool modifiers*. We do not envision these students as professionals ever sitting down to program at a blank screen. Instead, we imagine them modifying others' programs, and combining existing programs to create new functionality. Based on our discussions with faculty in these majors, we realized that these students, as professionals, will very rarely create a program exceeding 100 lines. The implications of these assumptions and findings are that much of the design content and code documentation procedures that appear in many introductory computing curricula are less relevant for these students than for majors.

We also explicitly chose to use this class to attract students currently not being retained within computer science, especially women. Since our audience was non-majors, they clearly fit into the model of students not choosing computer science as a major. We used the 2000 AAUW report [1] and *Unlocking the Clubhouse* [13] as our main sources. We set three objectives based on these studies: Making the content relevant, creating opportunities for creativity, and making the experience social

Relevance: A frequently cited complaint about introductory computing courses is that they are too abstract and not anchored in a relevant context–students do not understand how introductory course content is useful or relevant to their goals or needs. We set an objective to make sure that all the assignments and lectures were relevant to the students' professional goals within that context.

One implication is that we decided to discuss issues of functional decomposition, how computers work, and even issues of algorithmic complexity and theoretical limits of computation (e.g., Travelling Salesman and Halting problems), but at the *end* of the course. During the first ten weeks of the course, the students write programs to manipulate media (which they do see as relevant), and they begin to have questions that relate to these more abstract topics. "Why are my programs slower than Photoshop?" and "Isn't there a faster/better way to write programs like this?" do arise from the students naturally. At the start of the course, the abstract content is irrelevant (from the students' perception), but at the end of the course, it is quite relevant.

Opportunities for Creativity: Comments made by female computer science graduates at a recent SIGCSE session on women in computing suggested they were surprised to find that computer science offered opportunities for creativity—it wasn't obvious in the first few courses, but was obvious later [19]. Providing more opportunities for seeing computing as a creative activity in early classes may help improve retention [1].

Making the Experience Social: We wanted students to see computer science as a social activity, not as the asocial lifestyle stereotypically associated with hackers—a stereotype which has negatively influenced retention [13].

2.2 Choosing a Context

Most introductory computing curricula aim to teach generalized content and problem-solving skills that can be used in any programming application. Research in the learning sciences suggests that, indeed, teaching programming tied to a particular domain can lead to students understanding programming only in terms of that domain. This is the problem of *transfer* [4, 5]. That's why it's important to choose a domain that is relevant to the students. This is not a problem only with students, though—most software experts only can program well within domains with which they are familiar [3]. However, there is strong evidence that without teaching abstract concepts like programming within a concrete domain, students may not learn it at all [12]. Contextualization may offer an important key to improved learning. By teaching for depth instead of breadth, we can teach more transferable knowledge [4].

The argument has been made that teaching programming, especially to non-majors, improves general problem-solving skills. Empirical studies of this claim have shown that we can't reasonably expect an increase in general problem-solving skills after just a single course (about all that we might expect non-majors to take), but transfer of *specific* problem-solving skills can happen [17]. Therefore, teaching programming in a context where students might actually use programming is the best way of teaching students something in a single course that they might use after the course has ended.

Within this context, we were able to address our learning objectives. Issues of data structuring and encoding arise naturally in media computation, e.g., sounds are typically arrays of samples, while pictures are matrices of pixel objects, each pixel containing red, green, and blue values. We were able to address the specifics of a CS1 course in the details of the course construction.

Media computation is relevant for these students because, for students not majoring in science or engineering, the computer is used more for communication than calculation. These students will spend their professional lives creating and modifying media. Since all media are becoming digital, and digital media are manipulated with software, programming is a communications skill for these students. To learn to program is to learn how the students' tools work and even (potentially) how to build their own tools. Our interviews with students suggest that they accept this argument, and that makes the class context relevant for them.

To create opportunities for creativity in assignments, we wanted students to have choices in selecting media to use in their homework whenever possible. For example, one assignment requires the creation of a collage where one image appears multiple times, modified each time. Students get to pick the required image, the modifications to use, and can include as many other images as they would like.

The media computation context also provided something to share which helped to encourage a social class setting. We encouraged students to post their media creations in a shared Web space, our *CoWeb* tool that we had used successfully in previous computer science courses [10]. Such sharing transforms the programming activity. Instead of completing the program for the TA to grade, students are completing the program in order to generate the artifact that can be shared with others. We use the same CoWeb every term of the class[1], so that the "*Galleries*" build up over time. A healthy sense of competition develops–one student told us that her collage "can't be beat by the others" from past terms.

We explicitly encouraged a social context in the traditional parts of the class, as well. We allowed for collaboration on most assignments, only designating two as "take-home exams" on which no collaboration was allowed. We also used in-class quizzes and exams for assessment, but encouraged collaborative studying including collaborative exam review pages.

2.3 Set Up Feedback Process

We frequently involved students in our course design process. When we first started planning this class, we created on-line surveys and asked teachers of freshman campus-wide classes (such as introductory English composition, Calculus, and Biology) to invite their students to visit the pages and address the survey questions. Later, as our questions became more specific, we had follow-up surveys just inviting non-CS majors in our introductory computing courses. These were important mechanisms for gathering impressions and attitudes, and then for bouncing ideas off of students. As the class was taking shape, we invited non-CS majors in our introductory computing courses to attend pizza lunches where we presented the class and got feedback on the course. The lunch forums helped create an interest in the course, and that spurred more discussion and feedback in the on-line surveys.

We also set up an advisory board of eight faculty from around campus who reviewed materials and give us advice on what they wanted for their majors. The advisory board was very helpful in several ways. In several cases, the advisory board told us specific content issues that they wanted to see in the course, e.g., one faculty advisor told us about the kinds of graphing that she wanted to see, and another from Architecture suggested a particular topic that is relevant to architects (the difference between vector and bit-mapped representations) that he hoped we could include. The board was also helpful in creating local expertise in the course when it came time for the various academic units to vote whether or not to accept the new course for their majors. The advisory board members were advertised as the local experts who knew the course better than just what was in the course proposal, which helped to sell the course to the rest of the faculty.

2.4 Define Infrastructure

Our first choice for programming language for the course was Scheme, since it was what we were already using [7]. Scheme was resoundingly rejected by both students and non-CS faculty. Students saw it as "more of the same"—just like our existing introductory computing course. The faculty rejected it for more surprising reasons: *Because* Scheme is perceived as more serious CS. One English faculty member said that she found Scheme unacceptable for her students simply because it was the first language taught at MIT.

We explored several other languages after that, including Java and Squeak [9], since the media manipulation was simple and cross-platform in those languages. Java was unacceptable to the non-CS faculty because we used it in our upper-level courses. That branded it as too complex for non-majors. Squeak was simply unknown–it could not be vetted in the same way that other languages could.

In the end, we settled on Python—in particular, the Jython dialect, implemented in Java, in which we could access cross-platform multimedia easily [18]. Python was acceptable for two reasons:

- First, we could list a number of companies using Python that non-CS faculty recognized, such as Industrial Light & Magic and Google. Having such a list was quite important to them. Non-CS faculty want some measure of quality of materials and content provided for their students, but the non-CS faculty may not have much background in computer science themselves. How can they then vet a programming language for their students? By looking at who else uses it, we discovered.

- Second, unlike a more obscure language like Squeak, there are references to Python everywhere on the Internet, always associated with terms that the faculty members found consoling: Easy-to-use, Internet-ready, and simple for beginners.

While the choice of language was limited by external factors, we were happy with the choice of Python because of the opportunities it gave us to apply lessons from computer science education research–in particular, for teaching iteration and conditionals. We know that learning iteration is hard for students [21], but we also know that if that iteration is expressed as a set operation, novices find it easier to understand [14, 15]. Because of how Python defines a `for` loop, we were able to introduce pixel manipulations as a set operation, e.g., `for p in getPixels(picture):`. Later, we introduced a more traditional `for` loop where an index variable varies across a range of integers, but only after students were successfully programming and dealing with iteration at an easier stage.

[1] `http://coweb.cc.gatech.edu/cs1315`

Once we had chosen our language, we needed to provide tools for this language. We decided to build two sets of tools. The first would be a development environment for the students, JES (Jython Environment for Students) because no such simple development environment existed for Jython. Second, we developed a set of media tools (called MediaTools, implemented in Squeak) to enable students to look at sounds at the sample level, record new sounds, playback movies, and look at individual pixels in pictures. We viewed the MediaTools as important debugging tools for the students.

We have found weaknesses in our original plans. Observations of students programming revealed that the MediaTools were never used as debugging aids. Sitting in a separate application, the MediaTools were simply ignored while students worked on their programs. We have since implemented some of the media exploration functionality in JES, which do get used by the students to help them understand what their programs are generating. The lesson we draw from this is that the context selected for a non-majors course places demands upon the programming environment. A programming environment that works for majors may not be adequate for non-majors, especially if a relevant context is chosen as we advocate. The programming environment must support both context and computing learning objectives.

2.5 Building the Course

We developed the course lectures and assignments to achieve the objectives within the given context and infrastructure. The syllabus[2] for the course walks through each media type, with some repetition of concepts so that conditionals and loops can be re-visited through exploration of different media types.

We only briefly address the issue of inefficiency—it's mostly a distraction in a first course [1, 13]. We do, however, address encoding issues, such as the number of bits per red, green, and blue channel in the pixel, and the theoretical number of colors that such an encoding provides. We consider this a *relevant* technical detail since representations of color are part of the communications focus of the course, and it allowed us to address the Institute requirements of discussing encoding and data structuring. We similarly discuss the number of bits in a sound sample and sampling rate, and relate that to the limitations of sound recording (e.g., the Nyquist theorem).

Student programming assignments built upon the media in relevant communications tasks. As mentioned earlier, one open-ended programming assignment required creation of a collage. A later assignment on text manipulation and HTML was to write a function to generate an HTML index page for all sound and picture files in a given directory. The students' final programming assignment was to write a program to fetch the index page of a news website, find the top three headlines from the page, then generate a ticker-tape movie of those headlines. The programs reached a level of computing and domain complexity that the students seemed to find satisfying.

3. EVALUATION: SUCCESS AND IMPACT

We identified at the start of the paper that our measures for success were (a) improved success rates (percentage of students earning an A, B, or C) and (b) impact of the course over time, after the class was completed. We found that the course has had remarkable success rates and is showing signs of having an impact on students after they leave the course.

[2]The syllabus for the course is summarized in [11].

Course	Success rate
Average for CS1 (2000-2002)	71.2%
Media Computation Spring 2003	90.0%
Media Computation Fall 2003	86.5%
Media Computation Spring 2004	89.9%

Table 1: Success rates of the original CS course compared with three offerings of Media Computation course

Table 1 lists the success rates (defined as the proportion of students who earn an A, B, or C in the course–the additive inverse of those who withdraw or earn a D or F) for our introductory computing course from 2000 to 2002, when all students at Georgia Tech took the course; then the three offerings of the Media Computation course. Around 90% of the Media Computation students succeeded, compared with 72% of the students across all of campus (including CS, science, and engineering majors). Our best-practice comparison is with non-CS majors in a pair-programming offering of CS1 which had a 66.4% success rate[16]. It should also be noted that over half of the students in the Media Computation class have been women [20].

In Spring 2004, we conducted an online survey all the 423 students who took the course in Spring 2003 ($n = 120$) and Fall 2003 ($n = 303$) semester. We sent an email invitation to participate in the survey, which was available as a web form. Sixteen of those students had since graduated, leaving us 407 potential subjects. We had 59 respondents, for a response rate of 14%–not tremendous, but not unreasonable considering we were asking for feedback from non-majors on what was a service course.

The results suggested that students were still engaged with computer science since the course ended. We asked students to report on how much they had talked about computer science with their friends or relatives before and after the course. 64% of the respondents indicated that they engaged in computer science discussions more often since taking the course. Eleven of the 59 respondents (19%) indicated that they had written programs in Python since completing the course–a particularly strong result given our non-CS majors audience. We asked students whether they had edited pictures, sounds, or videos before taking the course, and since. 27% of the respondents indicated that they had edited media since taking the course but hadn't previous to the course. Only one of the students had taken another CS course.

We asked for open ended responses to the question, "How would you say that CS1315 has changed the way you interact with technology, if at all?" 47 of the 59 students (80%) did indicate that CS1315 had an impact on the students' relationship with computing technology.

- That result implies that 20% did *not* indicate that CS1315 had an impact on them. A typical response is, *"No, I think CS was completely irrelevant to my college career. Python is a language I will never remember because it is likely I will never use it again."*
- Others, however, offered a detailed explanation on how

the course had impacted them, such as *"It made me understand more how computers work so I can use them better. Helped me use the normal programs like email and internet better. And I know how picture editing works, which is cool."* and *"I have learned more about the big picture behind computer science and programming. This has helped me to figure out how to use programs that I've never used before, troubleshoot problems on my own computer, use programs that I was already familiar with in a more sophisticated way, and given me more confidence to try to problem solve, explore, and fix my computer."*

We realized that we phrased our last question incorrectly. For many students, what changed after the Media Computation class was not how the students *interacted* with technology, but how they *thought* about technology–in a sense, it served as a "computing appreciation" course. Some example student statements include " *I am uninterested in this field. However, I now have a MUCH better understanding of the people who are interested in this field, how they view things, and how to interact with them more easily.*" and "*Definitely makes me think of what is going on behind the scenes of such programs like Photoshop and Illustrator.*"

4. CONCLUSIONS

The process that we describe in this paper is not specific to designing a Media Computation course for non-CS majors. Rather, we feel that this process is appropriate to follow whenever creating a CS course for non-majors.

The media computation course has been a success at Georgia Tech. There are now non-CS majors asking for *more* CS courses! We are creating a follow-on course, that introduces data structures in a media context. We have also now defined a CS minor option, so that students interested in computing can go into more depth without leaving their own majors.

5. ACKNOWLEDGMENTS

This research is supported in part by grants from the National Science Foundation (CISE EI program and DUE CCLI program), from the Al West Fund at Georgia Tech, and by the College of Computing and GVU Center. We wish to thank all the students who helped create JES and the Media Computation class, and all the students in the class who volunteered to participate in our studies. Our thanks to Adam Wilson who has shepherded development of JES for the last few terms, and to Bob Amar who designed and implemented the follow-up survey.

6. REFERENCES

[1] AAUW. *Tech-Savvy: Educating Girls in the New Computer Age.* American Association of University Women Education Foundation, New York, 2000.

[2] ACM/IEEE. Computing Curriculum 2001. `http://www.acm.org/sigcse/cc2001`, 2001.

[3] B. Adelson and E. Soloway. The role of domain experience in software design. *IEEE Transactions on Software Engineering*, SE-11(11):1351–1360, 1985.

[4] J. D. Bransford, A. L. Brown, and R. R. Cocking, editors. *How People Learn: Brain, Mind, Experience, and School.* National Academy Press, Washington, D.C., 2000.

[5] J. T. Bruer. *Schools for Thought: A Science of Learning in the Classroom.* MIT Press, Cambridge, MA, 1993.

[6] E. Chabrow. Declining computer-science enrollments should worry anyone interested in the future of the U.S. IT industry. *InformationWeek*, 2004.

[7] M. Felleisen, R. B. Findler, M. Flatt, and S. Krishnamurthi. *How to Design Programs: An Introduction to Programming and Computing.* MIT Press, Cambridge, MA, 2001.

[8] M. Greenberger. *Computers and the World of the Future.* Transcribed recordings of lectures held at the Sloan School of Business Administration, April, 1961. MIT Press, Cambridge, MA, 1962.

[9] M. Guzdial. *Squeak: Object-oriented design with Multimedia Applications.* Prentice-Hall, Englewood, NJ, 2001.

[10] M. Guzdial. Use of collaborative multimedia in computer science classes. In *Proceedings of the 2001 Integrating Technology into Computer Science Education Conference.* ACM, Canterbury, UK, 2001.

[11] M. Guzdial. A media computation course for non-majors. In *Proceedings of the Innovation and Technology in Computer Science Education (ITiCSE) 2003 Conference*, New York, 2003. ACM.

[12] J. Kolodner. *Case Based Reasoning.* Morgan Kaufmann Publishers, San Mateo, CA, 1993.

[13] J. Margolis and A. Fisher. *Unlocking the Clubhouse: Women in Computing.* MIT Press, Cambridge, MA, 2002.

[14] L. A. Miller. Programming by non-programmers. *International Journal of Man-Machine Studies*, 6:237–260, 1974.

[15] L. A. Miller. Natural language programming: Styles, strategies, and contrasts. *IBM Systems Journal*, 20(2):184–215, 1981.

[16] N. Nagappan, L. Williams, M. Ferzil, E. Wiebe, K. Yang, C. Miller, and S. Balik. Improving the CS1 experience with pair programming. In D. Joyce and D. Knox, editors, *Twenty-fourth SIGCSE Technical Symposium on Computer Science Education*, pages 359–362, New York, NY, 2003. ACM.

[17] D. B. Palumbo. Programming language/problem-solving research: A review of relevant issues. *Review of Educational Research*, 60(1):65–89, 1990.

[18] S. Pedroni and N. Rappin. *Jython Essentials.* O'Reilly and Associates, 2002.

[19] S. L. Pfleeger, P. Teller, S. E. Castaneda, M. Wilson, and R. Lindley. Increasing the enrollment of women in computer science. In R. McCauley and J. Gersting, editors, *The Proceedings of the Thirty-second SIGCSE Technical Symposium on Computer Science Education*, pages 386–387. ACM Press, New York, 2001.

[20] L. Rich, H. Perry, and M. Guzdial. A CS1 course designed to address interests of women. In *Proceedings of the ACM SIGCSE Conference*, pages 190–194, Norfolk, VA, 2004.

[21] E. Soloway, J. Bonar, and K. Ehrlich. Cognitive strategies and looping constructs: An empirical study. *Communications of the ACM*, 26(11):853–860, 1983.

Just-in-Time Teaching for CS0

Tammy Bailey
Department of Computer Science
Duke University, Durham, NC 27708-0129
tammy@cs.duke.edu

Jeffrey Forbes
Department of Computer Science
Duke University, Durham, NC 27708-0129
forbes@cs.duke.edu

ABSTRACT

Just-in-Time Teaching (JiTT) is a teaching and learning strategy based on the interaction between web-based study assignments and an active learner classroom. The essence of JiTT is the *feedback loop* formed by the students' preparation outside the classroom that shapes their in-class experience. The goal of JiTT is to use feedback to guide teaching and to empower and motivate learners. This paper describes a successful implementation of the JiTT strategy for an introductory computer science course.

Categories and Subject Descriptors

K.3.2 [**Computers & Education**]: Computer & Information Science Education—*Computer Science Education*

General Terms

Human Factors, Design

Keywords

Active learning, CS0, JiTT, non-majors, pedagogy

1. INTRODUCTION

Students in an introductory computer science course are often not aspiring computer scientists. They may be motivated by curricular requirements or curiosity. Instructors must develop a curriculum of sufficient breadth, depth, and rigor along with innovative and creative teaching methods to engage a population of students with diverse knowledge and learning styles. Maintaining student interest while simultaneously providing understanding and appreciation of the course material is an ongoing challenge. Students unfamiliar with the concept of computing as a science often find the combination of theoretical and technical concepts difficult, uninteresting, or of little personal benefit. As such, non-majors tend to lack the motivation required for acquiring the knowledge and skills fundamental to the course material.

Many studies have posited that students are more likely to retain knowledge acquired via active learning strategies such as discussion and practice rather than passive learning strategies such as reading and lecture [5, 7, 11]. Just-in-Time Teaching (JiTT) is a teaching and learning strategy based on the interaction between web-based study assignments and an active learner classroom [10]. Students complete web-based assignments that are submitted online prior to the upcoming lecture. The instructor reviews the assignments "just-in-time" to structure the lecture in accordance with the level of understanding conveyed by the student responses. The subsequent web assignment is then motivated by the in-class discussion. The students' preparation outside the classroom, their experience inside the classroom and the feedback between the two form the *feedback loop* that is the essence of the JiTT strategy.

JiTT was developed in response to the observation that students are not learning as well as they could. In many cases, students focus on their final grade in the course rather than the acquisition of knowledge or skills. In our experience, such cases arise frequently when teaching at the introductory level. JiTT has been shown to be of benefit to courses that students consider to be of secondary importance to their lives or education [10]. The JiTT strategy was first implemented in introductory Physics courses and is now used with success in courses in Mathematics, Biology, Chemistry, and Engineering [8, 9]. JiTT is not widely used in computer science courses and is fairly uncommon at the introductory level, despite the fact that many courses in the area make extensive use of the Internet as a teaching, learning, or communication tool. The use of JiTT in non-introductory undergraduate computer science courses is discussed in [2, 6].

In this paper we present an implementation of the JiTT strategy as described in [9, 10] for introductory computer science courses. This strategy was developed over a number of semesters and implemented when teaching CS0 in Summer 2004. We provide several examples of web assignments and classroom activities for a variety of subject areas.

2. MOTIVATION

At Duke University, Principles of Computer Science (ACM CS0) is designated as a course fulfilling a curriculum requirement and is generally populated with students majoring or intending to major in non-scientific fields. The course curriculum is a result of an ongoing effort at Duke to teach computer science to a diverse audience, addressing a broad selection of topics while maintaining depth and rigor [4], in-

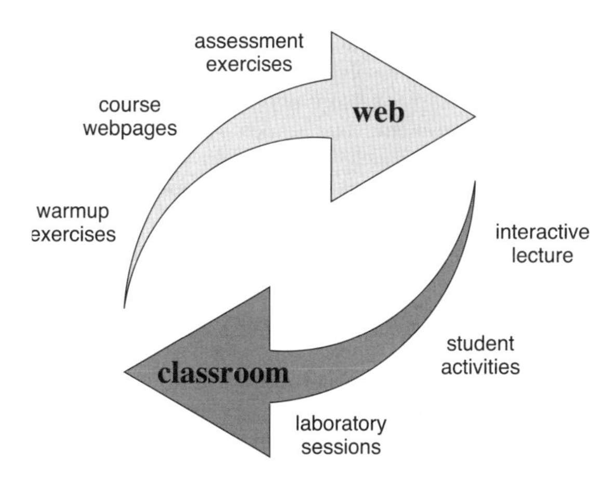

Figure 1: The JiTT feedback loop in CS0.

corporating active learning strategies in laboratory sessions to master technical and theoretical concepts [12], and integrating a series of classroom and web-based activities in which the students take an active role in researching and learning the societal impact of the current technical subject studied in class [3]. While our recent efforts [3, 12] were rewarded with increased student interest, participation, and satisfaction, our main goal as educators is making sure the students learn. Evaluation of students' written examinations show there are still many students who lack understanding of basic concepts or the ability to apply these concepts to unfamiliar problems.

3. METHODOLOGY

The essential element of the JiTT strategy is the feedback between the out of class course work – the *web component* – and the material presented in the classroom, the *classroom component*. In our course, the web component consists of warmup exercises (preparatory and prelab assignments), course web pages (informative, enrichment, communication), and assessment exercises (homework and laboratory assignments). The classroom component consists of lectures, laboratory sessions, and in-class student activities. Figure 1 illustrates the JiTT feedback loop in CS0.

3.1 Web component

Outside the classroom, the students' portal to the class is the web, providing round-the-clock access to course-related materials and a communication channel between the course participants.

3.1.1 Warmup exercises

Warmup exercises are characterized by a clear set of learning objectives, an explanation of unfamiliar terminology, and questions designed to make students confront their previously held notions, stimulate thought and interest, and to create a bridge to concepts introduced later in the course. The exercises ensure that students are familiar with the material prior to class and are aware of the important concepts. Warmup exercises are graded on effort, not necessarily correctness. Students are given credit for correct solutions, incorrect solutions based on correct reasoning, and for providing a clear explanation of where they reached an impasse. Collaboration is encouraged on these assignments.

Preparatory assignments are short, web-based assignments due a set amount of time before lecture. Links are provided to optional supplemental readings that either discuss the subject in greater detail (for students having difficulty with the assignment) or explore the topic in greater depth and context (for students who would like to learn more). The nature of the assignments varies. The assignment can be questions on the reading, solving a simple instance of a problem, or discussing their experimentation with an applet illustrating a particular concept. Whenever possible students are asked to discuss the relation of the preparatory assignment material to material previously learned in class and how they could use what they had already learned when solving the new problem. Students may also provide feedback on the difficulty or appropriateness of the assignment. Questions or comments on the assignment that would be of benefit to the class as a whole are posted on the discussion forums.

Prelab assignments are completed in preparation for the weekly laboratory sessions, and are due prior to the lab. As the laboratory sessions mainly concentrate on computer programming, these assignments generally ask students to formulate pseudocode algorithms for problems that have already been studied conceptually in lecture.

3.1.2 Course web pages

Three types of pages are accessible from the course web page and fit one of three categories. *Enrichment pages* are web sites and links, typically illustrating relevance of course material to everyday life or on topics related to the course material. The enrichment pages are updated throughout the semester and help students answer the questions: what is computer science good for and what is new and interesting in the field? *Information pages* are general course and instructor information, lecture notes, assignments, required reading, and syllabus. These pages also include useful links to resources, such as campus computer labs, instructions for software installation and accessing university network, academic calendars, codes of conduct, and acceptable use policies. *Communication pages* provide discussion forums for student-student and student-instructor conversations and anonymous feedback.

3.1.3 Assessment exercises

Homework assignments are available online and are either graded automatically or require written solutions that are turned in at class time. Homework assignments are strictly graded on correctness, and are thus only assigned after the material has been presented and discussed in class. Students are again encouraged to collaborate, but are told they must write and submit their solutions independently. These assignments contain 2-4 questions that are similar to what a student may expect to see on an exam. *Laboratory assignments*, assigned at each laboratory session, are discussed in Section 3.2.3.

3.2 Classroom component

Our course is split into three fifty minute lecture sessions and one seventy-five minute laboratory session per week. The lab session is designed to be a smaller hands-on experience and has an enrollment cap of thirty students. In both lecture and lab, active learning and peer instruction techniques are employed.

3.2.1 *Lectures with PRS*

The warmup exercises motivate and structure the classroom experience. By reviewing the warmups, the instructor can uncover misconceptions and determine what concepts need reinforcement. The key ingredient of an active classroom is preparation, both for the students and the instructors. After completing the warmups, students can better complete in-class exercises. The instructor is better able to assign appropriate work after reviewing those exercises.

An effective JiTT tool for the classroom is peer instruction. We use Personal Response System (PRS) quizzes along with mini-conferences to assess student mastery and participation. At various points in lecture, the instructor will pose a question along with possible answers. An example question on expression evaluation in Java is below.

Consider the following expression:

```
double C = (F-40.0)*(5/9);
```

If the value of `F` is -40.0, then what is the value of `C`?

a. -40.0
b. 0
c. 40.0
d. error
e. none of the above

The students answer the question by pressing the corresponding numbered button on their PRS transmitter. The student can also indicate his or her confidence (high, normal, low) in their response. We find that using PRS is a far more reliable measurement of overall class comprehension than asking students to raise their hands or volunteer answers. The PRS software records student responses and then graphs the distribution of answers immediately. If the vast majority of students selected the correct response, the instructor can demonstrate the expression evaluation in a program and simply ask the class for an explanation.

PRS is particularly useful when there is some question about the correct response. In that case, students are given time to confer with each other and justify their reasoning to their peers. In discussing the answer to the above question, students bring forth their knowledge of operator precedence, data types, automatic type conversion, and Java syntax. When students are asked to give their answers again, the answers usually converge towards one answer. Of course, that answer is not always the right one which can make for an even more enlightening discussion. In this case, we can demonstrate the expression evaluation in a program.

3.2.2 *Student activities*

Other forms of active classroom engagement also fit within the framework of the JiTT approach. Formal in-class debates also provide a forum for active participation and peer instruction [3]. Debates provide a context for the social aspects of computing discussed in the class. Contests, such as the Othello-playing agent tournament, provide an opportunity for students to demonstrate and describe their work to their peers.

3.2.3 *Laboratory sessions*

The laboratory sessions provide an opportunity for students to experiment with algorithms learned in class. Students either write short programs or participate in hands-on labs as described in [12]. Hands-on labs sometimes do not involve computers at all but rather involve physically manipulating objects while solving problems or simulating algorithms. One example is using posts and disks to solve the Towers of Hanoi problem. The students are guided primarily by undergraduate teaching assistants who are familiar with the misconceptions and difficulties novices face.

4. EXAMPLES

In this section, we provide examples of exercises and activities for a variety of topics discussed during the course.

4.1 Week one

To introduce students to the JiTT structure, a preparatory assignment is given at the first lecture. The students complete the assignment at the beginning of class. The instructor takes a short break to review the responses, and the remainder of lecture is spent discussing the responses.

1. Write down all interactions you have had with a computer today.
2. Would your life change drastically if all computers stopped working? Explain briefly.
3. Complete the following sentence: Computer science is the study of ______________.
4. To the best of your knowledge, what do computer scientists do?

These questions serve as a good way to encourage class participation from the start, illustrate the importance of computing and the effect is has on their everyday lives and address misconceptions about computer science. Invariably, half of the students will respond to the third and fourth questions with *"computers"* or *"programming"*. The instructor should not only clarify these misconceptions but use them to lead the class to a discussion of problem solving and algorithms, which will be the focus of the upcoming lectures.

In the next preparatory assignment, students are asked to read excerpts from George Polya's book on the concept of problem solving [13] and are given an assortment of classic puzzles such as this one:

Tom has three boxes of fruit in his barn: one box with apples, one box with oranges, and one box with both apples and oranges. The boxes have labels that describe the contents, but none of these labels is on the right box. How can Tom, by taking only one piece of fruit from one box, determine what each of the boxes contains?

In lecture, the instructor presents solutions to the puzzles, emphasizing problem solving strategies and addressing common mistakes. This introduces and motivates the upcoming lectures on algorithm design.

4.2 Encryption

A simple example of a substitution cipher is the *Caesar cipher*, which is named after Julius Caesar – not because he invented it, but because he is believed to have used it to communicate with his army. Caesar secured his messages by shifting each letter in his message three letters to the right. After informing his generals of the shift value, he was able to send them secured messages. The Caesar cipher is a a type of substitution cipher called a *shift cipher*, since the ciphertext alphabet is derived from the plaintext alphabet by shifting each letter a certain number of positions, called the *key*. Caesar's cipher uses the key 3. In general, shift cipher keys may be any positive or negative integer value.

> The following message is encrypted using a shift cipher with key 15:
> `CTKTG IGJHI P SDV LXIW DGPCVT TNTQGDLH`
> Decrypt the message.

> Suppose you received the following message:
> `XII VLRO YXPB XOB YBILKD QL RP`
> You were told the message is encrypted using a shift cipher but you forgot the key. Decrypt the message. What is the encryption key?

Most students will be able to successfully decrypt both messages. These preparatory exercises illustrate that if the encryption algorithm is known, then simple encryption algorithms are easy to break. As a class activity (or contest), students are given a message encrypted using a substitution cipher based on a random permutation of the alphabet. Students work together in groups to decrypt the message without knowing the substitution pattern. The objective is to realize that even though there are 26! possible substitution patterns, the cipher is still relatively easy to break using characteristics of the language such as letter and word frequencies and context to reduce the solution space.

The historical example of the Caesar cipher leads to a discussion of modern encryption techniques with particular emphasis on RSA cryptography. The warmup question posed to students is as follows.

> The ability to communicate securely with people all over the world has numerous applications. Is public key encryption the most important invention of the latter half of the twentieth century? Your response should discuss the effect of secure communication on society. In particular, you should consider how RSA along with the Internet has affected different aspects of civilization such as commerce, science, government, and education.

A more technical question used in a homework assignment illustrates the importance of choosing large primes.

> If we encrypt a message using the public key $(5, 299)$ and know that the RSA algorithm was used in generating the keys, what private key can be used for decryption?

4.3 Artificial Intelligence

Consider a scenario where a human judge engages in a natural language conversation with two other parties, one a human and the other a machine. If the judge cannot reliably tell which is which, then the machine is said to have passed the Turing test. A group of programs were developed in an attempt to "pass" Turing's test. The most famous such program, Eliza [14], was one of the first programs that attempted to communicate in a natural language by engaging humans in conversation with a simulated Rogerian psychotherapist.

An applet implementing the Eliza program is available to the students, who then answer the following questions.

> Take some time to chat with Eliza. Would you believe that you are conversing with a human rather than a machine? How long would it take you to be reasonably confident that you were not conversing with a human? Explain your answer.

This warmup can be used as both a preparatory and prelab assignment. In lecture, the student responses illustrate conversational patterns that "break" Eliza, providing an introduction to grammars, parsing, and natural language processing. In lab the students build upon the Eliza grammar, which is simply a file parsed by the Eliza applet.

Eliza was written in 1966 and is relatively simple, using a small database of words and phrases and applying a series of pattern matching rules to the human's statements when forming its replies. Since then, many more complex programs have been developed to simulate conversation. These programs are called *chatterbots*, and their goal is to make a human believe they are engaging in conversation with another human, at least temporarily. One such chatterbot is Alice [1].

> Take some time to chat with Alice. She will tell you she is a robot. How long would it take you to be reasonably confident that you were not conversing with a human pretending to be a robot when you chatted with Alice? Explain your answer.

The chatterbot Alice introduces the reverse Turing Test, that is, one in which the subjects attempt to appear to be a computer rather than a human. In addition, the assignment leads to a classroom discussion of modern artificial intelligence and applications to programs commonly in use including speech recognition, spam filtering, robots, software agents, and game playing.

5. ASSESSMENT

Our first efforts implementing JiTT have been at a small scale in a summer session course with no formal assessment. Our qualitative assessment is given below.

Positive

Students tended to best retain concepts related to assignments and activities that they preferred. The most popular assignments were related to artificial intelligence and game playing, and students performed well on exam questions related to parsing, the Turing test, search trees, and the minimax algorithm. The Towers of Hanoi activity was also noted as being very helpful in demonstrating the concept of recursion, and many students found that while programming the algorithm was difficult, once they discovered the correct solution it made formulating recursive problems much easier throughout the semester. Students generally had more success with concepts that could be illustrated with interactive applets, such as Towers of Hanoi, mazes, fractals, and sorting algorithms. Many students found the supplemental readings on ethical and controversial topics (such as file sharing, cracking and cyberstalking) interesting and read them on their own time, even though they were not required or discussed in class. Students were much in favor of receiving credit for effort on the warmup exercises. Students were also appreciative that failing to understand a particular warmup exercise despite a genuine effort to do so translated to an emphasis of the material in lecture rather than a poor grade on the assignment. Such students were more apt to ask for clarification during lecture and leave class with a better understanding of the material. In general, students felt the problem solving and logical reasoning skills they acquired were of significant benefit and would be useful in their future endeavors. The students were asked about the effectiveness of the course and a representative response is below:

"The web assignments were effective in making me read through the text beforehand so that I would better understand what would be taught in class the next day."

"They gave us a good idea of what to expect during class and of the concepts we were meant to grasp. Often, if I found a web assignment confusing, it let me know what I still needed to understand."

"I like the fact that working with others is encouraged, I believe that it helps a lot when you work with others. I like that we have web assignments and other assignments other than just the tests."

"This is an entirely new subject to me, and one I've never had much interest in, but I see now that it's definitely a creative and interesting field of study."

Negative

The main complaints were the amount of out-of-class work and the pace of the course, although this was noted by some students to be partly because this was a summer course. Providing too many links to supplemental and advanced readings was problematic for a small number of students who felt obligated to read them all on a regular basis. Allowing student collaboration fostered plagiarism in some cases. This abuse mainly occurred on problem solving questions rather than those that were conceptual in nature, although students said they benefited most from the former and least from the latter. As the majority of class assignments were only available on the web, there were recurring issues with Internet access, in particular for students living off-campus. Students also did not always see the connection between the web assignments and the course material, so care must be taken in writing the questions.

6. FUTURE WORK

While student response has been positive, a thorough assessment of the efficacy of JiTT in introductory computer science courses is still required. There are a variety of questions that need to be asked, including:

- Which parts of the model add the most value?
- Does this model encourage students to take future computer science courses?
- Do students from a course like this one actually exhibit better problem solving ability?

JiTT can be instructor and student labor intensive. The students have to regularly turn in assignments and the teaching staff has to review and grade them. Teaching a JiTT course requires a significant library of examples and problems. The web assignments and PRS quizzes have to be crafted very carefully to be effective. Also, the enrichment pages in the web component require continual attention. JiTT can be very time consuming for the instructor compared to a traditional lecture based class, but we hope that after a few iterations, we will have a reasonable array of materials for the web and classroom components. Our goal is to create a resource for other instructors, so that they can apply JiTT in their classes.

There are a number of logistical issues with JiTT that require attention. One issue is how well this system will scale to larger classes and different kinds of institutions with less technical and teaching staff support. Methods for allowing collaboration while minimizing the opportunity for plagiarism are discussed in [10]. In the warmup exercises, credit for effort must be well-defined. Some students tended to abuse this grading system. One idea is to provide several examples of "correct" wrong answers as opposed to "incorrect" ones.

7. CONCLUSIONS

Motivating and engaging students in introductory computer science courses is crucial, particularly in non-major survey courses. Just-in-Time Teaching provides a sensible framework for an active learning environment by blending out-of-class work with lectures and in-class activities. JiTT has been hailed in many of the sciences and is suited for computer science education as well.

8. REFERENCES

[1] The A.L.I.C.E. Artificial Intelligence Foundation. http://www.alicebot.org.

[2] O. L. Astrachan. Non-competitive programming contest problems as the basis for just-in-time teaching. In *Proceedings of the 34th Annual Frontiers in Education Conference*, 2004.

[3] T. Bailey and J. Forbes. Computers and society in CS0: An interactive approach. In *Proceedings of the 34th Annual Frontiers in Education Conference*, 2004.

[4] A. W. Biermann. Computer science for the many. *Computer*, 27(2):62–73, 1994.

[5] C. C. Bonwell and J. A. Eison. *Active Learning: Creating Excitement in the Classroom.* ASHE-ERIC Report Series. Jossey-Bass, 2000.

[6] R. Fleisher. Just-in-time: Better teaching in Hong Kong. In *Proceedings of the Second Teaching and Learning Symposium*, 2004.

[7] R. R. Hake. Interactive-engagement vs. traditional methods: A six-thousand-student survey of mechanics test data for introductory physics courses. *American Journal of Physics*, 66(1):64–74, 1998.

[8] J. Handelsman, D. Ebert-May, R. Beichner, P. Bruns, A. Chang, R. DeHaan, J. Gentile, S. Lauffer, J. Stewart, S. M. Tilghman, and W. B. Wood. Scientific teaching. *Science*, 304(5670):521–522, 2004.

[9] Just-in-Time-Teaching. http://www.jitt.org.

[10] G. M. Novak, A. D. Gavrin, W. Christian, and E. T. Patterson. *Just-in-Time Teaching: Blending Active Learning with Web Technology.* Prentice Hall, 1999.

[11] J. G. Penner. *Why many college teachers cannot lecture.* Charles C Thomas Publisher Ltd, 1984.

[12] S. Pollard and J. Forbes. Hands-on labs without computers. In *Proceedings of the 34th SIGCSE Technical Symposium on Computer Science Education*, 2003.

[13] G. Polya. *How to Solve It?: A New Aspect of Mathematical Method.* Princeton University Press, 1957.

[14] J. Weizenbaum. ELIZA–A computer program for the study of natural language communication between man and machine. *Communications of the ACM*, 9(1):35–36, 1966.

Nifty Assignment

Nick Parlante (moderator)
Stanford University
nick.parlante@cs.stanford.edu

David Levine, Steven Andrianoff
St. Bonaventure University
dlevine@cs.sbu.edu, andrianoff@sbu.edu

Aaron J. Gordon
Fort Lewis College
gordon_a@fortlewis.edu

Alyce Brady, Pamela Cutter
Kalamazoo College
{abrady, pcutter}@kzoo.edu

Paul Kube, Jefferson Ng
University of California, San Diego
{kube, jwng}@cs.ucsd.edu

Richard E. Pattis
Carnegie Mellon University
pattis@cs.cmu.edu

Categories and Subject Descriptors
D.1.5 [**Programming Techniques**]: Object Oriented Programming. K.3.0 [**Computers and Education**]: General.

General Terms
Algorithms, Design, Languages.

Keywords
Education, assignments, homeworks, examples, repository, library, nifty, object oriented programming, pedagogy.

Introduction
I can worry about the strategy of my syllabus, and I can fret over my lectures. Nonetheless, I am always struck that what my students really learn and enjoy in the course depends very much on the assignments. Great assignments are hard to dream up and time-consuming to develop. With that in mind, the Nifty Assignments session is all about promoting and sharing the ideas and concrete materials of successful assignments

Each presenter will introduce their assignment, give a quick demo, and describe its niche in the curriculum and its strengths and weaknesses. The presentations (and the descriptions below) merely introduce each assignment. A key part of Nifty Assignments is the mundane but vital role of distributing the materials – handouts, data files, starter code – that make each assignment ready to adopt. The Nifty Assignments home page, **http://nifty.stanford.edu**, gathers all the assignments and makes them and their support materials freely available.

If you have an assignment that works well and would be of interest to the CSE community, please consider applying to present at Nifty Assignments. See the nifty.stanford.edu home page for more information.

TestMe – David Levine (CS1)
TestMe is a set of programs designed to support the teaching of black-box testing. In each case, the student is provided with the specifications for a complete program and then given executable code. The code is usually, but not always, flawed. It is up to the student to design the testing procedure that will certify the program as correct, or detect the flaws.

A number of different problems are presented. Each problem includes a specification and several executable versions, most with bugs. The programs are all provided in applet form and are thus trivial to install and trivial for the students to use. Depending upon the pedagogical needs, the students may be allowed to "play freely" or be required to design a test suite in advance. The student may be required to submit a description of the bugs and/or the test suite, possibly along with a rationale for why the test suite is complete.

TestMe can be used to help train students how to test abstract specifications before a more formal testing tool such as JUnit is introduced. The key idea can also be applied to more sophisticated assignments where the instructor may provide a flawed solution to a program that the students will later run.

GridPlotter – Alyce Brady and Pam Cutter (CS1)
GridPlotter is a program that emphasizes loops and 2D data structure navigation for CS1. In the GridPlotter assignment, students create patterns by placing color blocks in the cells of a grid. The assignment gives them practice developing loops and nested loops for working with a two-dimensional data structure in a framework that provides immediate visual feedback. The assignment uses a Grid class (provided to the students) with rows and columns, which is a cleaner, simpler data structure to work with than Java 2D arrays. (E.g., Grids are strictly rectangular and provide numRows and numCols methods.)

Students implement methods to navigate the grid in various ways, including traversals, moving down the diagonals, filling in the area beneath a diagonal, etc. All student solutions must scale for different size grids. We provide one method, a row-major traversal, to get them started. The methods are carefully sequenced to become progressively more sophisticated, while the graphical output provides immediate feedback on what the algorithms are doing. Students with previous programming challenging methods. The final exercise requires students to develop three methods of their own that can be combined to form a picture. The assignment is flexible enough to allow both strong

SIGCSE'05, February 23-27, 2005, St. Louis, Missouri, USA.
ACM 1-58113-997-7/05/0002.

and weak students to challenge themselves and succeed, both technically and creatively.background often choose to implement additional, more

Complementary Currency – Paul Kube (CS1)

A common assignment in an object oriented CS1 course has students implement an Account class, composed of a Person object and some other things. (Then later you can derive CheckingAccount and SavingsAccount classes.) But that is a non-nifty assignment. It teaches some useful nuts and bolts of applied computation, but it doesn't do much to inspire your students' imagination about the space of possible computer applications.

We niftified the Account assignment by plugging it into a componentized client-server infrastructure supporting a "complementary currency" in the sense of Bernard Lietaer ("The Future of Money", 2001). A complementary currency is one that exists alongside ordinary currencies; not having the support of a state, complementary currencies depend on, and tend to reinforce, networks of trust in a community. In this assignment, the community is the students in the course, and the currency is exchanged in network transactions with a server process. Now, doing the assignment and implementing the Account class enables a student actually to use the currency and participate in the community. It works, and it's fun: TA's in the lab can sell homemade cookies, students can offer break-dancing or chess lessons or artistic pencil portraits. Students get to know each other a bit, in a noncompetitive, collaborative context; and it widens their horizons about what technology can enable.

Photomosaics – Richard E. Pattis (CS1-CS2)

A Photomosaic™ is a large picture rendered from smaller pictures. When a photomosaic is viewed up close, we can identify each small picture; viewed from afar, these pictures lose their details and we see only their integration into the much larger picture. Often, the pictures form a sort of visual pun: a campus icon constructed from pictures around campus; a student's face constructed from pictures of their classmates.

Fundamentally, this program manipulates arrays: a 1-d array (or collection class) for storing the database of small pictures, repeatedly searching them to find the closest match with a region in the large picture; 2-d (pixel) arrays for representing the images of the small and large pictures, scanning the images when computing the closeness of a match. The concept of closeness can be hardwired, or abstracted to an interface, allowing students to plug-in different metrics.

This program can be written stand-alone, or as the model in an MVC pattern. Other constraints can be added: limiting how often a picture can appear or how closely repeated pictures can appear. What makes this assignment compelling is that students use a large number of interesting objects to produce art (algorithmic aesthetics). At SIGCSE I will briefly discuss patent implications.

ImageLab – Aaron Gordon (CS1-CS2)

Everyone thinks they are a photographer, especially with the pervasiveness of digital cameras. Since digital images, like film-based images, can vary widely in quality, we can use software filters to enhance digital images. In addition, we have the opportunity to use digital filters to artistically modify digital images.

It turns out that many students are not motivated by computing for computing's sake (who knew?). They are more motivated by meaningful programming assignments. ImageLab, written in Java, is a platform for students to write classes for image-filtering and manipulation.

The ImageLab platform provides a GUI with menu items to open and save image files as well as classes and methods to input images, display images, make images available to other classes, and accept images from other classes. It also has a menu of the available filters that can be applied to images. The GUI creates the filter menu dynamically to reflect the available image filter objects. Students can create their own filter objects, have them listed in the filter menu, and apply them to an image.

This unit is intended for CS1 students who are learning about two-dimensional arrays, or CS2 students as an introductory assignment.

BattleShips Project Set – Stefan Brandle and Jonathan Geisler (CS1-CS2)

Niklaus Wirth wrote "... programming courses should teach methods of design and construction, and the selected examples should be such that a gradual *development* can be nicely demonstrated." [CACM, Vol. 14, No. 4, April 1971, pp. 221-227] We decided to improve our projects by developing a set of five increasingly sophisticated versions of the traditional battleships board game which walk students through an incremental development process. These projects also support teaching typical CS1-2 content such as problem decomposition, abstraction, data representation, OOP concepts, and recursion. Adopters control difficulty by choosing which versions to use and how much to provide their students.

Project versions start with a simple one-class program where users just shoot at fixed targets. The final version is fairly sophisticated: it randomly places ships, taunts the user, has an AI that shoots back, uses registered event handlers within a callback system, provides a runtime interface choice (text or GUI), and introduces advanced language features (e.g. dynamically loading objects from the string name, synchronization in an asynchronous environment), and more. Students enjoy the projects. They *really* like writing the AI and then watching the AIs battle it out in our contest manager. Our project kits are in Java and C++, but are portable to a number of languages.

NameSurfer – Nick Parlante (CS1-CS2)

The US Social Security Administration has data for the last 100 years of the 1000 most popular US baby-name choices each decade. The NameSurfer assignment takes that basic data and allows the user to search through it and graph historical trends. The data itself is interesting but unwieldy, so building a GUI application that brings the data to life works very nicely.

Astrachan's law says that an assignment should solve something large and difficult enough that it cannot be done with pencil and paper. NameSurfer makes good use of that idea, since although the data is not that complex, there is a huge volume of it. Building up the program so it can rip through all that data (bless you, oh ArrayList) makes the program more compelling for the students.

We use NameSurfer as one of the last, fairly difficult projects in CS1, or it could be used early in CS2. Our students use standard Java JButtons and JComponent to build the GUI, but any drawing system would work – it's just lines and strings. It is one of the favorite assignments of the quarter, which is pretty shocking for something that is not a game! Students like the assignment because it feels very "real" – reading in a processing a mass of data in an obviously useful way, and because the data itself is interesting to play with and show to friends once the program is working.

Intention-Based Scoring: An Approach to Measuring Success at Solving the Composition Problem

H. Chad Lane
Institute for Creative Technologies
University of Southern California
13274 Fiji Way
Marina del Rey, CA 90292
lane@ict.usc.edu

Kurt VanLehn
Department of Computer Science
Learning Research and Development Center
University of Pittsburgh
Pittsburgh, PA 15260
vanlehn@cs.pitt.edu

ABSTRACT

Traditional methods of evaluating student programs are not always appropriate for assessment of different instructional interventions. They tend to focus on the final product rather than on the *process* that led to it. This paper presents intention-based scoring (IBS), an approach to measuring programming ability that requires inspection of intermediate programs produced over the course of an implementation rather than just the one at the end. The intent is to assess a student's ability to produce algorithmically correct code on the first attempt at achieving each program goal. In other words, the goal is to answer question "How close was the student to being initially correct?" rather than the the ability to ultimately produce a working program. To produce an IBS, it is necessary to inspect a student's online protocol, which is defined as the collection of all programs submitted to a compiler. IBS involves a three-phase process of (1) identification of the subset of all programs in a protocol that represent the initial attempts at achieving programming goals, (2) analysis of the bugs in those programs, and (3) rubric-based scoring of the resulting tagged programs. We conclude with an example application of IBS in the evaluation of a tutoring system for beginning programmers and also show how an IBS can be broken down by the underlying bug categories to reveal more subtle differences.

Categories and Subject Descriptors

K.3 [**Computers & Education**]: Computer and Information Science Education—*Computer Science Education*

General Terms

Measurement

Keywords

intention-based scoring, online protocols, novice programming, intelligent tutoring systems, structured programming

1. INTRODUCTION

Traditional methods of evaluating student programs tend to involve scoring of the final program produced by a student for a given project. Although such a score is certainly appropriate for classroom assessment, it reveals very little about the *process* that went into creating the program. The final program is also prone to influence from a variety of outside sources, such as a tutor or helpful friends. For researchers interested in isolating how different experimental manipulations affect programming skill in a finer-grained way, a metric that targets students *during* the act of programming would be more appropriate. In this paper, we propose such a metric called *intention-based scoring* (IBS) and describe an application of it in the evaluation of an intelligent tutoring system for novice programmers.

Assessing process is a particularly challenging problem. To do so for programming, one approach is to use a *charette*, which requires that a student solve a programming problem in a lab environment and under a time limit [1, 8]. Because no assistance is available (it is typically given as a test), there is no chance for outside influence. Secondly, since most students are not able to complete the full task within the time limit, the resulting score of the "final" version of the program is a actually a measure of success of the student at some point in the middle of their implementation.

Another approach is to collect a student's *online protocol*, which is defined as all files submitted to a compiler during an implementation [12, 13]. This provides a chain of "snapshots" representing a path through the space of development of a program. Lying between each pair of these intermediate programs are compile attempts, which can be explained by a variety of underlying cognitive activities that programmers engage in during programming [2, 4]. In this paper, our goal is not to provide a cognitively plausible account for these activities, but rather to provide a method for scoring such protocols. We seek to quantitatively answer the question "How close was the student to being initially correct?"

2. PROGRAMMING KNOWLEDGE

The knowledge that underlies programming is tacit: a completed program is a poor representation of the knowledge and skills needed to produce it. Studies that focus on the content and structure of this knowledge generally identify structured "chunks" that achieve a variety of goals, sometimes called *schemata* [9] or *plans* [10]. In terms of such theories, two key problems have been suggested as a way of understanding what programmers must do to produce a program [3]:

- **Decomposition problem:** identifying the goals and corresponding plans needed to solve the problem.
- **Composition problem:** implementing and assembling these plans such that the problem is solved correctly.

Although both problems are known to be a challenge for novices, the composition problem is particularly difficult because of subtle interactions and complications that can arise when multiple plans are to be merged [12]. For example, when two goals each imply the need for a loop, the programmer must determine if one loop in the proposed solution can be used to satisfy both plans. Complications such as this are common for novice programmers, and since inspecting only the final version of a program will rarely reveal them, a more targeted evaluation approach is necessary.

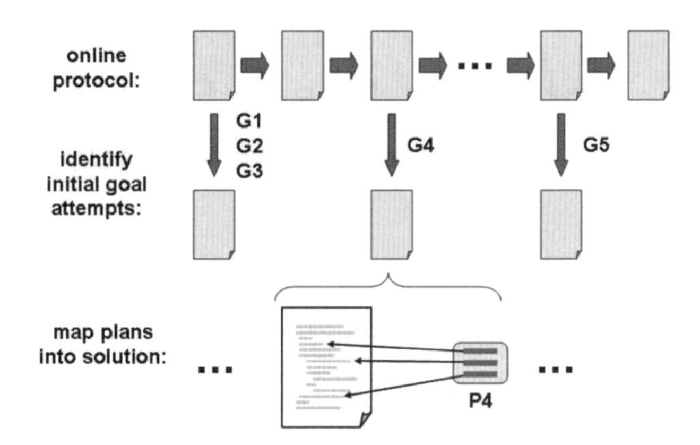

Figure 1: First two stages of producing an IBS.

3. INTENTION-BASED SCORING

IBS derives elements from previous work on identifying bugs in online protocols. Research from this stream has focused on remediation, such as that provided automatically by PROUST [5], as well as on establishing cognitively plausible accounts for how novice bugs are produced [13]. In this section, we present the three phases that are required to produce an IBS.

3.1 Inspecting an online protocol

The first step in producing an IBS is to identify the subset of programs from an online protocol to analyze for bugs. This subset of programs should be the student's *initial attempts* at achieving each goal. A judge begins with the first program submitted and works through the protocol chronologically, checking off goals along the way. This phase is complete when attempts at all goals have been identified or the protocol ends (leaving some goals un-attempted). The process of protocol subset identification is depicted in the top half of figure 1.

The identification process is not always straightforward, however. The first program in a protocol is not always a legitimate goal attempt, for example. Some novices prefer to compile very simple programs to begin, including only things like variable declarations or simple print statements. In cases like this, we ignore such programs and continue searching sequentially for the first substantive attempt at achieving a goal. A related issue is the sometimes fuzzy question of whether or not a program represents an attempt at achieving a goal or not. It is not quite as simple as saying "if any plan component is present, then count it as a goal attempt." For example, some students prefer to declare and initialize all variables at once. This certainly does not imply the student is attempting to implement all plans in which these steps participate.

To handle problems like this, the criteria for selecting programs from a protocol must be agreed upon between multiple judges. In the example we present below, the consensus with the variable declaration issue, for example, was to conclude that by itself, a declaration would not be counted as an attempt at its plan. In other words, more plan components would need to be present than just a declaration or initialization step to count as an outright attempt at that goal. Such issues arise frequently in the subjective tagging of data, which is why it is recommended to tag some subset of the data together under open discussion.

3.2 Bug identification

A critical component of IBS involves the identification and classification of bugs present in a student's protocol. We follow the same two stage process described in [5, 13]. First, the plans being implemented by the student must be identified, and next, compared to the known correct plans of an implementation. Bugs then fall out as differences between these two structures. For IBS, of course, only the plans corresponding to the new goals being implemented at each stage should be considered.

Although there are certainly many ways to characterize the bugs (i.e., plan differences), we adopt here a simplification of the approach taken in [13]. Most generally, an IBS scheme could be constructed from any similar bug classification strategy. Because our goal is not to provide an account of cognitive plausibility, we limit ourselves to categories that relate to solving the composition problem. The top-level categories of bugs in our coding scheme are:

- **omission**: A plan component is missing.
- **malformation**: A component is incorrectly implemented.
- **arrangement error**: A component was placed in the wrong location.

In addition, when inspecting a program, it is also necessary to identify those bugs that are a result of *merging* of plans (e.g., the multiple loop issue mentioned above). We refer to bugs that are *not* a result of confusion between multiple plans as *isolated.* Of course, some bugs can fall under multiple categories. For example, a step can be malformed, out of place, and be a result of confusion between two plans. Because this is a subjective tagging process, it is recommended that multiple judges be used and agreement be checked.

An example of bug identification is shown in figure 2. In this example, the student is attempting to implement a counter plan (shown in the shaded box), but has made three mistakes. First, the incorrect value is used for the initialization step (it should be 0). Second, the increment step is not

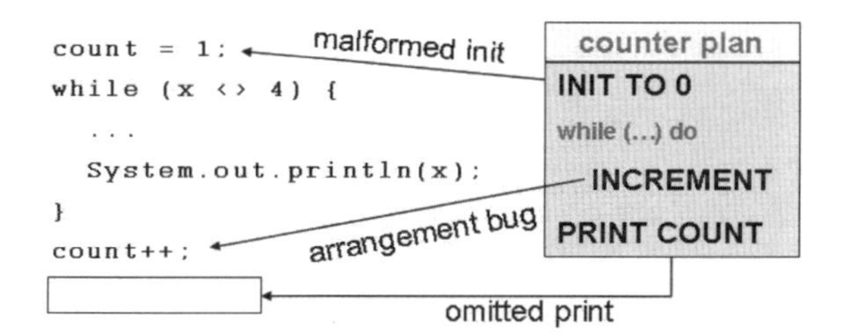

Figure 2: Identifying bugs by plan differences.

placed inside the loop body (an arrangement bug). Finally, there is no print statement (a bug of omission). In this case, the arrangement bug is also considered a plan-merging error since the counter is being integrated into the looping code, which was already in place in this program from a separate plan.

3.3 Scoring

With a bug-tagged protocol, the final step in computing an IBS is to apply a scoring rubric. Although simple bug frequencies could be used, it is less fair since focal steps in plans (i.e., those that are "more" central, such as the increment step of a counter plan) would count the same as less critical components (such as an output statement). To create a rubric, points need to be assigned to the various plan components. Focal steps are weighted more heavily, like updates and conditions, than are supporting steps, like initializations and output statements. This allows us to discount slips (like forgetting to print a value) and highlight errors in critical plan steps. Finally, points for each bug identified during the analysis are taken away from an overall possible score, thereby producing a final intention-based score. In sum, this score represents the accuracy of students' first attempts at achieving programming goals. By looking at points lost from each of the sub-categories (like merge errors or omissions), one can get a better feel for the kinds of errors novices produce.

As an example, for the counter plan in figure 2, one possible assignment could be 3 points for the initialization step, 5 for the increment step, and 2 for the print step. As mentioned, it is best to perform this stage with expert instructors who have experience creating rubrics. In the example, the student might lose 1 point for the incorrect initial value, 3 for the improper location of the increment step, and 2 for forgetting the print step. These partial values need to be agreed upon in the rubric. In sum, this student would receive 4 out of 10 possible points for this attempt at implementing a counter plan.

3.4 Discussion

One difference of IBS with previous work using online protocols is that *all* attempts in a protocol are made available for inspection. Most previous work considered only syntactically correct compile attempts. The reasoning behind "opening" up the protocols in this way comes from the observation that for some students in our protocols, the algorithm intended by the first compile attempt was often different than that in the first syntactically correct attempt. This means that students' algorithms seemed to change, possibly inadvertently, while fixing syntax errors. The very first attempt at assembling an algorithm, in our view, is a more accurate representation of a student's initial impression at how to solve the composition problem. Also, we note that the process is dubbed "intention-based" for two reasons: first, programs are inspected by inferring what goals the student is trying to achieve. Second, when a program statement is not syntactically correct, it is necessary to infer what plan component is being attempted. The line `count + 1;`, for example, is likely an attempt to increment a counter variable. Thus, such a statement is considered equally as correct as a syntactic one.

There are several problems with the IBS method of evaluating programs. First, it is extremely tedious. In no way is IBS intended for regular classroom evaluations – it is only reasonable for use in targeted evaluations that require a fine-grained understanding of student success. Second, the creation of the rubric is subject to the bias of the researcher. In other words, the weighting of the various plan components may indirectly impact the outcome of the study. Finally, in the form presented here, IBS is dependent on a plan-based theory of programming knowledge. The difficulties with this theory, then, are naturally inherited.

4. AN APPLICATION OF IBS

We now turn to an example application of IBS in the evaluation of ProPl ("pro-PELL"), a dialogue-based intelligent tutoring system for beginning programmers [6, 7].

4.1 Experiment

ProPl is intended to help novices do pre-planning of their programs. After the tutoring, students perform their usual, independent implementation. Subjects in the study agreed to allow collection of online protocols. In the sections below, we present the IBS results for the ProPl group when compared to a baseline group of students whoe received no tutoring whatsoever and a control group, who just read the material in a similar environment. The hypothesis being tested was that the program planning skills could be more effectively taught if the interaction occurred as natural language dialogue as opposed to reading alone. In addition to results for two tutored programs (called *Hailstone* and *Rock-Paper-Scissors*), results are also shown for a timed, post-test charette which was not tutored (called *Count/Hold*). The n's were 9, 8, and 9 for the baseline, control, and ProPl groups respectively.

4.2 Training and agreement

After solving the three problems in terms of goals and plans, 15% of all programs were used to train together with two expert judges. After this, another 20% were tagged independently, and then, to confirm agreement, a kappa statistic of .865 was computed on the tags.[1] With consistency of the bug identification procedure confirmed, the remaining protocols were tagged independently.

4.3 Composite intention-based scores

Intention-based scores are shown in table 1 for the three programming projects involved in the study. Some significant and marginally significant differences exist between the

[1]This measure is superior to percent agreement because it factors out agreement by chance. Generally, a kappa value above 0.80 is considered reliable.

problem	baseline	ctrl	ProPL
Hailstone	69.3 (16.4)	79.8 (15.4)	86.1 (9.46)
RPS	67.7 (22.5)	59.5 (18.7)	77.5 (16.4)
CH	n/a	49.1 (26.3)	64.1 (29.8)

Table 1: Composite IBSs, out of 100.

groups. We first consider how the baseline group compared with each of the other groups. For Hailstone, the ProPL students outscored baseline students to a statistically significant level ($t(16) = 2.12$, $p = .0017$) with a very large effect size ($es = 1.03$).[2] The control group also outperformed the baseline group on Hailstone, but not significantly. On the RPS problem, the baseline group outperformed the control group, but the difference is not significant. ProPL students did outperform the baseline students, but again, not to a significant level.

We now turn our attention to the ProPL and control groups. All students in these groups took the same pretest, and so ANCOVAs were used for statistical tests in order to factor out pretest performance. Although ProPL students outperformed the control students on each project, the only significant difference is on RPS. ProPL students were significantly better than control subjects ($F(1, 15) = 7.88$, $p = 0.015$, $es = .96$). On Count/Hold (the untutored posttest charette), ProPL students outperformed those in the control group to a marginally significant level ($F(1, 22) = 3.59$, $p = .072$, $es = .57$).

4.4 Decomposed intention-based scores

The results shown in table 1 are composite scores; that is, the bug categories are lumped together to produce the overall score. To reveal how these points were distributed across the various bug categories, we now proceed to break down the points lost using two sub-categories of bugs.

4.4.1 Merging related errors

In this section, we present the number of points lost related to merging related problems *per opportunity to make an error*. It would be misleading to use the raw points missed. For example, a student who attempts two goals out of a possible five would have far fewer opportunities to produce merging errors than someone who attempts to solve all five. The resulting merge error score would be deceptively low. Similar arguments can be made for plan component omissions and isolated errors. We therefore normalize, and use *total number of goals attempted* throughout the protocol as a denominator. For merge errors, we use the total number of attempted goals, **minus one** because at least two plans are required for a merge error to be possible.

Figure 3 shows the points lost from merging related errors over the three programming problems. For the Hailstone problem, the control group ($M = .38$, $SD = .65$) produced significantly fewer merging related errors than the baseline group ($M = 2.31$, $SD = 1.9$), $t(15) = 2.76$, $p = 0.015$. The ProPL group ($M = .36$, $SD = .45$) performed similarly well when compared to the baseline group ($t(16) = 3.02$,

[2]Effect size was computed using Glass' delta, that is, $\frac{M_{exp} - M_{ctrl}}{SD_{ctrl}}$

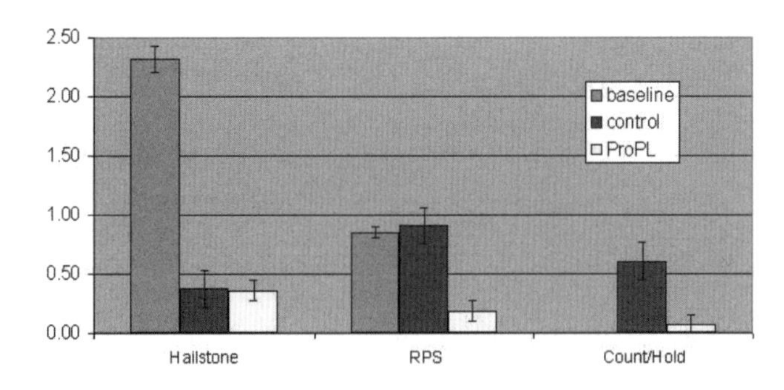

Figure 3: Points lost per plan-merging opportunity. Standard error bars are shown.

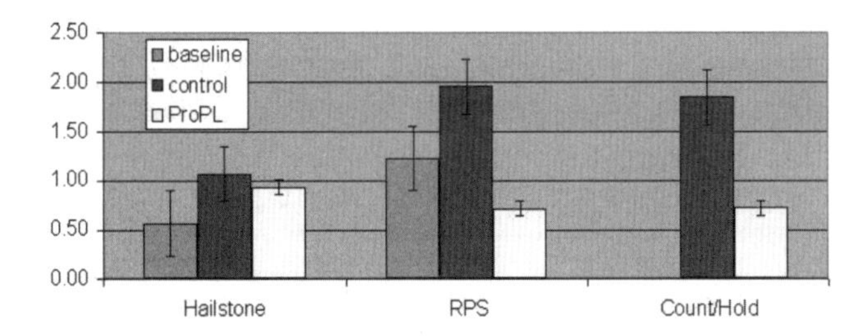

Figure 4: Plan part omission points lost per plan implementation attempt.

$p = .008$). On RPS, the ProPL group ($M = .19$, $SD = .21$) outperformed both the baseline group ($M = .85$, $SD = 1.0$) to a marginally significant level ($t(17) = 1.98$, $p = .075$, $es = .66$) and the control group ($M = .91$, $SD = 1.1$), $F(1, 15) = 3.71$, $p = .076$, $es = .65$. Finally, on the Count/Hold project, the ProPL group ($M = .07$, $SD = .24$) again surpassed the control group ($M = .61$, $SD = .74$) but this time to a highly significant level ($F(1, 15) = 5.77$, $p = .026$) and with an extremely large effect size ($es = 2.3$).

4.4.2 Component omission errors

Moving now to omission errors (figure 4), several differences were found to be significant. Interestingly, the baseline group lost *fewer* points in Hailstone for missing plan parts ($M = .57$, $SD = .59$) than the control group ($M = 1.1$, $SD = .53$) to a marginally significant level ($t(16) = -1.85$, $p = .085$, $es = 1.0$). This suggests the baseline group had a greater opportunity for merging errors because they had more plan components to deal with. When compared to the ProPL group, the difference is not significant. This happened again on RPS with the baseline group ($M = 1.22$, $SD = .62$) outperforming the control group ($M = 1.95$, $SD = .67$), but to a significant level ($t(16) = -2.20$, $p = .046$, $es = 1.2$). The control group, in general, seemed to be more forgetful than the other two groups. The ProPL group ($M = .71$, $SD = .63$) also was significantly better than the baseline group on RPS ($F(1, 15) = 15.6$, $p = .0017$, $es = 1.9$). A similar difference appeared on Count/Hold with the ProPL group ($M = .72$, $SD = .62$) losing significantly fewer points than the control group ($M = 1.84$, $SD = 1.13$), $F(1, 15) = 9.22$, $p = .0065$, $es = .99$.

5. DISCUSSION

Several of the detected differences are suggestive of the impact PROPL had on students in the study. First, the higher composite IBSs of PROPL students suggests that they benefited in general from the tutoring by having initial attempts that were closer to correct than students in the other conditions. Looking at the decomposed scores, both groups receiving intervention did equally well over the baseline group on the first program.

The longer term effect, however, seems to favor the PROPL group. In the following two problems (and most importantly, the third, untutored program), PROPL students lost significantly fewer points from errors related to the interactions between plans. That is, dialogue-based tutoring seems to help novices establish a stronger understanding of the issues involved with achieving multiple goals in one program. Given that this is known to be a major difficulty for novices [12], this result bodes well for the efficacy of natural language tutoring to help novice programmers.

The plan part omission results are not as compelling given the relationship between the baseline and control groups. It is surprising that the baseline group *produced more complete plans* than the control group – the control group received some of this information beforehand. Given the very high level of merging-related problems shown in figure 3, there was a price for being more complete. On the positive side, the PROPL group again demonstrates a trend in the correct direction of getting better with respect to plan completeness. Taking these differences to the most general conclusion, this may suggest that they were able to adopt a more abstract view of programming by thinking at the level of plans rather than the line-by-line view normally adopted by novices.

6. SUMMARY AND FUTURE WORK

In this paper we presented intention-based scoring, an approach to assessing online protocols produced by novice programmers. This metric focuses on the *process* of programming by providing a score of a student's ability to solve the composition problem. An IBS is computed by inspecting the first attempt at solving each programming goal over the course of an entire implementation followed by the application of a traditional rubric to those programs. We then demonstrated how to use IBS to evaluate a tutoring system for novices and were able to break the scores down based on the bug categories to evaluate the system in a finer-grained way.

IBS is limited in its application, however. It is bound to a plan-based theory of programming knowledge and is tedious to compute. These problems suggest two lines of future work. The first is to explore other methods of judging the quality of intermediate programs, perhaps in other programming paradigms. The second, and perhaps more interesting, is to use the large amount of tagged data to build automatic classifiers for bug identification.

7. ACKNOWLEDGMENTS

This research was supported by NSF grant 9720359 to CIRCLE, the Center for Interdisciplinary Research on Constructive Learning Environments at the University of Pittsburgh and Carnegie-Mellon University. We also would like to thank Mark Fenner for his help in tagging the protocols, Bob Hausmann's assistance with the experimental setup and statistical analyses, and the anonymous reviewers who provided insightful and useful feedback.

8. REFERENCES

[1] C. Daly and J. Waldron. Assessing the assessment of programming ability. In *Proceedings of the 35th Technical Symposium on Computer Science Education (SIGCSE)*, pages 210–213, Norfolk, VA, 2004. ACM Press.

[2] W. D. Gray and J. R. Anderson. Change-episodes in coding: When and how do programmers change their code? In G. M. Olson, S. Sheppard, and E. Soloway, editors, *Empirical Studies of Programmers: Second Workshop*, pages 185–197. Ablex, Norwood, NJ, 1987.

[3] M. Guzdial, L. Hohmann, M. Konneman, C. Walton, and E. Soloway. Supporting programming and learning-to-program with an integrated cad and scaffolding workbench. *Interactive Learning Environments*, 6(1&2):143–179, 1998.

[4] M. C. Jadud. A first look at novice compilation behavior using bluej. In *16th Annual Workshop of the Psychology of Programming Interest Group (PPIG 2004)*, Institute of Technology, Carlow, Ireland, April 2004.

[5] W. L. Johnson. Understanding and debugging novice programs. *Artificial Intelligence*, 42:51–97, 1990.

[6] H. C. Lane and K. VanLehn. A dialogue-based tutoring system for beginning programming. In *Proceedings of the Seventeenth International Florida Artificial Intelligence Research Society Conference (FLAIRS)*, pages 449–454, Miami Beach, FL, 2004. AAAI Press.

[7] H. C. Lane and K. VanLehn. Teaching program planning skills to novices with natural language tutoring. In S. Fitzgerald and M. Guzdial, editors, *Computer Science Education*. Swets and Zeitlinger, September 2005. Special issue on doctoral research in CS Education.

[8] M. McCracken, V. Almstrum, D. Diaz, M. Guzdial, D. Hagan, Y. B.-D. Kolikant, C. Laxer, L. Thomas, I. Utting, and T. Wilusz. A multi-national, multi-institutional study of assessment of programming skills of first-year cs students. *ACM SIGCSE Bulliten*, 33(4):125–140, 2001. Report by the ITiCSE 2001 Working Group on Assessment of Programming Skills of First-year CS.

[9] R. S. Rist. Program Structure and Design. *Cognitive Science*, 19:507–562, 1995.

[10] E. Soloway and K. Ehrlich. Empirical studies of programming knowledge. *IEEE Transactions on Software and Engineering*, SE-10(5):595–609, September 1984.

[11] E. Soloway and J. C. Spohrer, editors. *Studying the Novice Programmer*. Ablex Corp., Norwood, New Jersey, 1989.

[12] J. C. Spohrer and E. Soloway. Putting it all together is hard for novice programmers. In *Proceedings of the IEEE International Conference on Systems, Man, and Cybernetics*, Tucson, Arizona, November 12-15 1985.

[13] J. C. Spohrer, E. Soloway, and E. Pope. A goal/plan analysis of buggy pascal programs. In Soloway and Spohrer [11], pages 355–399.

In-Person Grading: An Evaluative Experiment

J. Philip East
Computer Science Department
University of Northern Iowa
Cedar Falls, IA 50614-0507
319-273-2939
east@cs.uni.edu

J. Ben Schafer
Computer Science Department
University of Northern Iowa
Cedar Falls, IA 50614-0507
319-273-2187
schafer@cs.uni.edu

ABSTRACT
In this paper, we discuss in-person or face-to-face grading: what it is, a rationale for its use, our use of it, and an experiment we conducted to evaluate its use. While no statistically significant differences in instructional outcome effects were found, several interesting affective results were seen. Additionally, a number of research methodological suggestions arose from the study.

Categories and Subject Descriptors
K.3.2 [**Computer and Information Science Education**]: Computer science education

Keywords
CS Ed research, classroom management, face-to-face grading, in-person grading, pedagogy, providing programming feedback

1. INTRODUCTION
1.1 Background
Conscientious computer science educators reflect on their practice and seek to improve student learning. Teaching consists of many activities including course planning; lesson planning, delivery, and assessment; assignment planning, assistance, and grading; exam preparation, administration, and grading; and management of various resources. Thus, there are many possibilities for improving instruction and learning. When students make errors or have difficulty, providing feedback is key to enhancing learning. In computer science education, a variety of activities for generating data for such feedback and approaches to communicating the feedback to students have been discussed in the literature ([7], [8]). However, we have found no prior research that actually examined the instructional effectiveness of alternatives for providing feedback to students on their programming assignments.

Ruehr and Orr [8] identify five approaches to providing feedback on students' programming assignments—instructor notes on submitted programs, automated grading, peer review, public presentation, and interactive program demonstration. Cooper [2] and others [1, 5] refer to the latter as face-to-face grading and we have referred to it as in-person grading ([3], [4]). The technique uses personal and private meetings between instructor and student to discuss the student's work and the instructor's evaluation of it. Such meetings may last 20 to 30 minutes and, due to time constraints, may not occur for all assignments for all students.

The first author's introduction to in-person grading occurred via the SIGCSE discussion list in the summer of 2000. The discussion was quite positive and referenced Cooper who said "[face-to-face grading] is probably the single most important improvement that can be made in course management." ([2], p.130) Since then, our study of in-person grading has been a multi-stage research process and is culminating with the work reported here. The first step examined the practice's face-validity (see Kerlinger's discussion of construct validity [6] for general information and [3] and [4] for particular discussions). After concluding that the practice was reasonable theoretically (had face-validity) and was amenable to personal instructional style, the next step checked to see if in-person grading could be implemented by the particular instructor in specific courses [3]. That successful trial led to continued use of the practice, its introduction to the second author, and an eventual informal examination of how students viewed its use [4].

Combined positive results from theoretical, instructor, and student perspectives suggested more formal study was worthwhile. A literature search for prior research was essentially fruitless. The ACM Digital Library contained only two entries under "face-to-face grading" ([1] and [5]), both of which merely mentioned that the practice was not being used. A search for "in-person grading" yielded five entries, none of which actually addressed the subject practice. A search of the Web for the same terms produced about 115 possibilities, most of which were notices or instructions to students concerning someone's use of in-person grading. No actual research on the practice was found. The only actual research we found that related to grading practice was Olson's comparison of analytics and holistic grading of computer programs ([7]).

A more relaxed search of the Digital Library did produce a few results. A brief description of the practice can be found in [2] and more in-depth description and analysis of trade-offs is available in [8].

1.2 Rationale for the Study
Our early use of in-person grading had provided anecdotal evidence of the technique's usefulness. A theoretical analysis led to a similar conclusion with respect to both cognitive and affective outcomes. Several hypotheses were formulated.

Our personal teaching theories are constructivist—we believe student understanding is individually constructed from their experience (that their brains relate and integrate new knowledge and experience with prior knowledge and experience). Thus, they do not necessarily "learn" precisely what we "teach". To better determine student learning then we must attempt to determine the accuracy of their understanding. This cannot be done well by merely examining program assignments and exam items. In-person grading sessions provide an opportunity to interact with students and question their understanding in order to identify and correct misunderstandings. If we are able to do that in a more frequent or more effective manner than with traditional feedback mechanisms, student learning should be improved.

In-person grading provides additional one-on-one interaction to any instructor's teaching and feedback practices. Several facets of instruction and learning should be enhanced by the increased personal attention afforded to students.

First, a more individual discussion of student work should have two positive effects even if instructors provide the same feedback in in-person grading that is given with other techniques. First, students are more likely to perceive and attend to comments from an instructor in the room with them than to written comments on a printout. Additionally, under in-person grading, students will have a much better opportunity to explore the meaning and implication of the feedback. In essence, the feedback should be more effective.

Second, one student activity believed to help learning is questioning. When students do not understand, instructors want them to ask questions. It is believed that the additional one-on-one and relatively informal time that students and instructor spend together under in-person grading will lead students to be more willing to ask questions. The increased questioning should occur both in the in-person grading sessions and during class time and should enhance student understanding and learning.

Finally, for many college instructors, the instructor-student relationship is relatively impersonal. The one-on-one time required for in-person grading is expected to personalize the instructor-student relationship and should lead to students having a better attitude toward the instructor and the class.

Specific hypotheses developed for the study were:

- student learning would be better under in-person grading than with other approaches to providing student feedback
- students being taught using in-person grading would ask more questions during class and, in general, participate in class at a higher rate than students under other feedback conditions
- students would prefer in-person grading over other feedback approaches

2. METHODOLOGY

This study was conducted in a relatively large comprehensive university (13,000 students) in the Midwest. The computer science department has eight faculty and approximately 200 undergraduate majors. In the fall of the 2003-2004 academic year three sections of CS I were taught by two instructors to 84 students.

Anticipated instructor effort (time) was planned and duties allocated in an attempt to divide the work appropriately according to the number of sections assigned each instructor and to control as many of the instructional variables as possible. The instructor assigned one section would do grading for all students except those participating in in-person grading and lead one of the weekly group feedback sessions. The instructor assigned two sections would "teach" (prepare and deliver lessons and prepare assignments), perform the in-person grading for about 10 students per assignment, and lead a second weekly group feedback session.

Class time was on Monday, Wednesday, and Friday. Programming assignments were usually made weekly and were due on Friday. Students were required to submit a report for each assignment that discussed difficulties encountered, learning that occurred, questions on the assignment, and the time spent completing the assignment.

Three treatments (techniques for supplying feedback on programming assignments) were used—in-person grading, instructor-led discussion, and student-initiated discussion. Feedback was presented via personal in-person grading session or through group sessions held at a common evening time during the week. Students were randomly assigned to one of the three groups independent of lecture section.

Students in the student-initiated discussion group attended a Wednesday evening discussion session where the previous programming assignment was returned. Comments identifying problems, point deductions, and positive aspects were written on the program printouts. Students examined their assignments and were encouraged to ask questions regarding them. When no further questions were asked, the students were dismissed. Sessions generally lasted 30 minutes.

For instructor-led discussions, students also attended a Wednesday evening discussion and received their graded assignments. The program printouts had codes indicating problems seen and deductions made. The instructor made a presentation that explained the codes, discussed common problems, identified positive aspects of some student work, and provided alternative approaches to some parts of the assignment. (Codes were determined while grading programs for the student-initiated group and used in an attempt to reduce grading time.) Students were encouraged to ask questions at any time. When the presentation was over and no further questions were asked, the students were dismissed. Sessions lasted approximately one hour.

Students receiving in-person grading would sign up for a 20-minute session with the instructor to be held on Tuesdays. The instructor would examine each student's work and report prior to the appointment and prepare comments and questions for the student. Students were encouraged to ask questions. Only one-third of the in-person group received in-person grading on each assignment. In-person grading students were also randomly assigned to one of the other two groups and would attend the assigned discussion session when not undergoing in-person grading.

There were 10 assignments during the semester with the first being an introduction to the computer system, programming environment, and electronic submission system. Grading for it was not included in the experiment. Thus, each in-person grading student had three one-on-one sessions with the primary instructor and six group sessions.

A variety of data were collected during the semester. All student assignments and reports were kept, thus, the self-reports of time spent on each assignment were available for analysis. Student grades on assignments and exams were noted, as were course grades. Student attendance and participation in class and in the grading discussion sessions had been recorded. At the end of the semester a questionnaire was administered in an effort to determine student reaction and attitude about the experience. Elements of these data appropriate to our hypotheses were subjected to statistical tests of significance.

3. RESULTS

Based on feedback during our Human Subjects Review, students completing the course were asked for permission to include their course data and survey results in this study. The vast majority agreed to participate (only three students chose to withhold permission) with final numbers in each treatment appearing in Table 1.

Table 1 : Study Participants

Treatement	Number of Participants
Student Initiated (SID)	19
Instructor Led (ILD)	20
In Person Grading (IPG)	23
All Treatements	62

All results presented in this section are based on ANOVA tests including both the Tukey HSD and Bonferroni post hoc tests for statistical significance based on an $\alpha = 0.05$.

3.1 Course Results

From a pedagogical point of view we were interested in overall student performance in the course. Since students in the in-person treatment are required to interact with the professor in a one-on-one setting, we were interested to see if students in this treatment were more likely to participate in discussions either lecture or during group lab sections. Furthermore, we were interested in their performance in lab activities, the final exam, and the course overall. Table 2 contains the mean grades earned for students in each treatment for each of these five categories. While an initial examination of Table 2 may suggest that students in the student-initiated treatment performed best on each of these activities, the deviation in these grades is large enough to prevent any statistical significance in these results.

Table 2 : Mean course grade earned on various course activities. No statistical significance exists between mean grades earned for any of these activities.

[* SID=student-initaited discussion, ILD=instructor-led discussion, IPG=in-person grading]

Grade	SID*	ILD*	IPG*
Lab Participation	9.03	7.84	8.85
In-class Participation	5.82	5.39	5.2
Lab Scores	24.19	21.55	22.60
Final Exam	71.21	65.55	63.06
Overall Grade	73.22	66.48	68.50

3.2 Survey Results

While we were interested in the course-level outcomes resulting from using in-person grading, we were also quite interested in the affect on student attitudes toward the course. In order to consider such affects, we administered an end-of-course survey to all students concerning their comfort level, how closely they studied lab feedback, whether feedback was helpful, and their assessment of instructor efforts to improve feedback. Students were presented with a series of statements that they rated on a Likert scale from 1 (disagree strongly) to 5 (agree strongly) with 3 being a neutral score. The content of these statements and the mean score from members of each treatment are contained in Table 3.

Table 3 : Mean Likert score responses to end of course survey statements. Scores marked with an asterisk are different with statistical significance.

Num	Statement	SID	ILD	IPG
1	I feel more comfortable asking questions in this class than in many of my other classes.	3.68*	2.75*	3.48
2	I feel more comfortable going to office hours in this class than in many of my other classes.	3.94	3.35	3.87
3	I carefully examined feedback I received on assignments.	4.42	4.00	4.30
4	The feedback I received on programming assignments was useful.	3.32	3.25	4.04
5	Feedback on programming assignments affected the way I completed later programs.	4.37	4.10	4.57
6	The instructors were interested in my learning.	4.05	3.6	4.09
7	I approve of my instructors' attempts to improve instruction.	4.11	3.75	4.23
8	I would have preferred being in one of the other groups	3.20*	4.48*	1.72*
9	THIS TYPE OF feedback provided better feedback than typically encountered (in CS and non-CS classes).	3.37	3.05*	4.70*
10	THIS TYPE OF feedback improved my learning.	3.63	3.20*	4.22*
11	The instructors should continue using, and improving, THIS TYPE OF feedback.	3.74	2.90*	4.43*

As was the case with course performance, the differences in mean score were statistically insignificant for approximately half of the statements in the survey. However, several significant results were recorded.

Statement one asked students to indicate their level of agreement with the statement "I feel more comfortable asking questions in this class than in many of my other classes." It was our belief that students in the in-person treatment would have more interaction with the professor than students in the other treatments and would thus be more comfortable interacting with the professor. As can be seen in Table 3, the score for students in the in-person treatment is not statistically separable from that of students in the other treatments. However, students in the student-initiated treatment indicate a significantly higher comfort level than students in the instructor-led treatment. In hindsight, this is perhaps explained by the fact that students in this treatment were somewhat forced to ask questions of the instructor. All discussion around performance on previous labs was based on the comments and questions from the students. They very quickly learned that they were expected to ask questions, and as such they would not be denigrated for such questions (likely a common fear among students). Furthermore, students in the instructor-led treatment were meeting with an instructor who was their instructor only for the lab discussion period. As such, they had limited interaction with the instructor over the course of the semester, and it is not surprising that they might never become sufficiently comfortable to freely ask questions.

Items nine, ten, and eleven all ask students to provide their evaluation on the feedback treatment they received. These consist of the statements, "THIS TYPE OF feedback provided better feedback than typically encountered (in CS and non-CS classes)," "THIS TYPE OF feedback improved my learning," and "The instructors should continue using, and improving, THIS TYPE OF feedback." Students receiving in-person feedback provided a much higher agreement ranking than their counterparts in the instructor-led sections. While it is likely that at least part of this difference can be explained by the "different instructors" factor mentioned previously, we suspect that this is largely due to the fact that students found in-person grading to be an effective and helpful method for providing feedback.

We make this previous conclusion based, in large part, on the results of scores received for statement eight. Reading, "I would have preferred being in one of the other groups" this statement was the only statement to produce mean scores that were statistically different for all pair-wise combinations. As can be seen in Table 3, students receiving in-person grading were very likely to disagree with this statement. In fact, with a mean score of 1.72, only three of the twenty-three student receiving in-person grading indicated they would prefer to receive some other form of feedback. This compares to average scores of 3.2 and 4.48 for students receiving student-initiated discussion and instructor-led discussion respectively. While the majority of students receiving in-person grading wanted to stay where they were, the majority of students receiving instructor-led discussion wished to change to a different group.

This data is confirmed by the results to a second part to statement eight. Students were given the option to indicate which treatment they would have preferred receiving. The results of this question are contained in Table 4. Again, it is clear that students receiving in-person grading were very happy where they were, students receiving instructor-led discussion were very unhappy where they were, and students receiving student-initiated discussion were somewhat equally split on their opinions.

Table 4 : Treatment students would have preferred receiving

Wished to be in...	Was in ...		
	SID	**ILD**	**IPG**
SID	10	3	0
ILD	1	3	3
IPG	8	14	20

4. DISCUSSION

While we feel that in-person grading is a promising and effective feedback technique, we were disappointed that results did not more strongly support that belief. We have identified several factors we feel may have influenced the outcomes of this study.

First of all, we must acknowledge the overall weakness of the in-person grading "treatment". Students in this group met only three times over the course of the semester with their instructor. In a perfect setting in-person grading would occur for every lab assignment for every student. If, as we proposed, in-person grading is going to provide additional opportunities for students to ask questions, and instructors to evaluate student learning in a one-on-one setting, it must occur more frequently. In order for this to happen, however, student numbers must be kept reasonable and faculty must be dedicated to the concept of in-person grading. In-person grading for a class of 25 students requires a minimum of 8 hours of meeting times for each lab graded in this manner. We suspect that the majority of instructors are unable/unwilling to dedicate this amount of time to the process.

It is worth repeating, however, that even though student performance was not affected by this limited application of in-person grading, student attitudes were affected. As reported in the previous section, students in this treatment were far more satisfied with their feedback method than members of other groups, and were far less likely to indicate they wanted to switch to another group. Students appeared to recognize the usefulness of this one-on-one time even in its limited form. The following comment is similar to several comments received in the end of semester evaluations.

> "In person grading was an effective way to go through code, line by line and critique each aspect of my programming. It seemed to offer a far better evaluation than the [other groups]."

We also feel that, despite our best efforts to control variables, the results of this study were skewed due to differing instructor styles and the way we divided up the work between the two instructors. Members of the student-initiated discussion group interacted with a single instructor for both lecture and lab discussion portions of the course. Members of the instructor-led discussion group interacted with one instructor for the lecture portion of the course and a second instructor for the lab discussion portion of the course whose primary interaction with them was as grader or fault-finder. Based on student feedback on end of semester evaluations, this was clearly an issue that frustrated them. As one member of the ILD group wrote,

> "The only thing that I truly felt made a difference was having the [lab discussion] taught by a different professor than the classroom instruction. For me as a CS I student just learning to program, any differences in style or otherwise that the two instructors had, can be quite confusing. I think in a more experienced programming class that could be useful when developing your own style so that you could see two ways of doing it. But for CS I when basically fundamentals are the main concern for the course, it should have the same instructor for both lab and instruction."

While this may seem like it goes against what is standard practice at many universities—the use of professors for lecture instruction and the use of TAs for lab instruction—we think there is a significant difference between this "standard" practice and what was experienced in our study. TAs are normally prepared for their role by the lecture professor and taught how to grade and what to recommend. When all else fails, most TAs defer to the lecture instructor. In this study however, we had two well-trained professors who differed in their approach to things and failed to communicate adequately the statements made in one context to maintain continuity with the other context. Additionally, early assignments were relatively easy and much grading focused on style elements not previously agreed upon by the instructors. This clearly was frustrating to students.

Needless to say, our future studies will strive to avoid the multiple-professor problem and to ensure sufficiently strong interventions. We are, however, pleased with this study. It has a solid and explicit theoretical foundation. It was well-designed with random assignment of students to treatments. We hope others can learn from our successes and failures.

5. CONCLUSIONS

Despite results that indicate there may be no effect on the final performance in the course for students participating in in-person grading, we feel strongly that this is a practice that we wish to continue to use, when appropriate, in our own instruction. The majority of students are very comfortable with this feedback technique and seem to feel it helps them learn how to be better programmers.

Furthermore, we feel this is a meaningful first step toward the design and implementation of courses that are nearly entirely laboratory based or "studio" courses. These would provide even more time for one-on-one interaction with students in an environment where students can immediately try the modifications that arise in discussions with the instructor and instructors can better evaluate the student comprehension of these discussions by evaluating the follow-up code written by students. Additionally, instructors would have a much better opportunity to get inside student heads to assess their actual understanding.

Regardless, we feel that in-person grading is a powerful evaluation and feedback tool that more instructors should consider incorporating into their own courses.

6. ACKNOWLEDGMENTS

The authors would like to thank the members of their department for assistance with this study. In particular, Dr. Eugene Wallingford who served as a third party administrator for participation agreements, course evaluations, and study surveys.

7. REFERENCES

[1] Astrachan, O., Smith, R, and Wilkes, J. Application-based modules using apprentice learning for CS 2. In *Proceedings of the Twenty-eighth SIGCSE Technical Symposium on Computer Science Education (SIGCSE '97)* (San Jose, California, February 27-March 1). ACM Press, New York, NY, 1997, 233-237.

[2] Cooper, D. Teaching Introductory Programming (with Oh! Pascal!). W.W. Norton & Company, New York, 1995.

[3] East, J.P. Experience with in-person grading. In Proceedings of the 34th Midwest Instruction and Computing Symposium (on CD-ROM). 2001. [Available on-line via http://MICSymposium.org]

[4] East, J.P. Experimenting with In-person Grading. Proceedings of the 37th Midwest Instruction and Computing Symposium (on CD-ROM). 2004 [Available on-line via http://MICSymposium.org]

[5] Kay, D.G. Large introductory computer science classes: Strategies for effective course management. In *Proceedings of the Twenty-ninth SIGCSE Technical Symposium on Computer Science Education (SIGCSE '98)* (Atlanta, Georgia, February 25-March 1). ACM Press, New York, NY, 1998, 131-134.

[6] Kerlinger, F.N. Foundations of Behaviorial Research (2nd Ed.). Hole, Rinehart and Winston, Inc., New York, NY, 1975.

[7] Olson, D.M. The reliability of analytic and holistic methods in rating students' computer programs. In *Proceedings of the Nineteenth SIGCSE Technical Symposium on Computer Science Education (SIGCSE '88)* (Atlanta, Georgia, February 25-26). ACM Press, New York, NY, 1988, 293-298.

[8] Ruehr, F. and Orr, G. Interactive program demonstration as a form of student program assessment. *Journal of Computing Sciences in Colleges, 18*, 2 (December, 2002), 65-78.

Patterns of Plagiarism

Charlie Daly
School of Computer Applications
Dublin City University
Dublin 9, Ireland
353 1 7005572
cdaly@computing.dcu.ie

Jane Horgan
School of Computer Applications
Dublin City University
Dublin 9, Ireland
353 1 7005260
jhorgan@computing.dcu.ie

ABSTRACT

We used a new technique to analyse how students plagiarise programs in an introductory programming course. This involved placing a watermark on a student's program and monitoring programs for the watermark during assignment submission. We obtained and analysed extensive and objective data on student plagiarising behaviour. In contrast to the standard plagiarism detection approaches based on pair comparison, the watermark based approach allows us to distinguish between the supplier and the recipient of the code. This gives us additional insight into student behaviour. We found that the dishonest students did not perform significantly worse than the honest students in the exams. However, when dishonest students are further classified into supplier and recipient, it emerged that the recipient students performed significantly worse than the suppliers.

Categories and Subject Descriptors

K.3.2 [**Computer and Information Science Education**]: Computer Science Education

General Terms: Management, Measurement.

Keywords

Introductory Computer Programming, Automatic Evaluation, Plagiarism, Watermarks.

1. INTRODUCTION

Academic papers on plagiarism in computer science frequently start by saying that plagiarism is chronic [10] and/or widespread [15, 9] and/or increasing [14], or at least that there is a perception that this is the case [17]. Reliable evidence is hard to come by; some universities do not wish to talk about it [5] and many universities do not check student submissions for plagiarism [5]. When they do check, they are frequently surprised by the scale of the problem, for example, in a well publicised case at MIT, 30% of the students on an introductory programming course were disciplined for plagiarism [16].

This paper concentrates on the problem of plagiarism in an introductory programming course. While we realise that there are many ways to cheat and many definitions of plagiarism, for this paper 'plagiarism' will refer to the case where a student takes code from another student and submits it, possibly with some modification, as their own.

SIGCSE'05, February 23–27, 2005, St. Louis, Missouri, USA.

2. BACKGROUND

We used an automated learning environment, called RoboProf [8, 6], to help teach introductory computer programming to a class of nearly 300 students. The class was taught in the first semester of a four year honours computer science degree at Dublin City University. RoboProf presents programming exercises to the students and marks them automatically, providing immediate feedback to the student. The exercises are viewed using a standard web browser and students can complete them in their own time. There were forty six short programming exercises which were presented in sequential order to the students and which had to be completed before the end of the semester.

Figure 1 shows how the students completed the exercises, with all students completing the first two exercises and approximately half of the students completing the final exercise. Students could pass the coursework element without completing all the exercises.

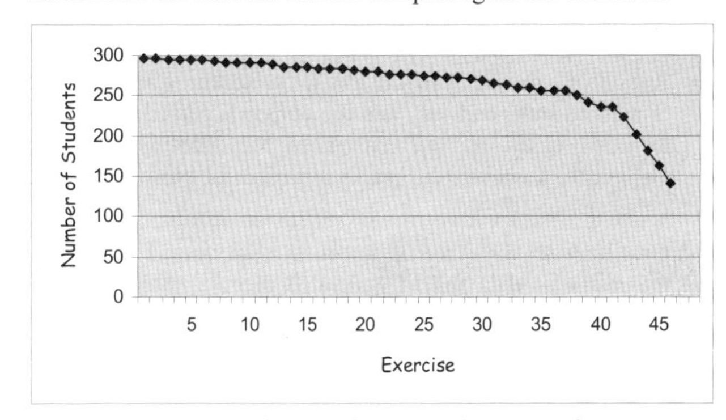

Figure 1. Completion rate of the exercises

Most of the exercises require the student to write or modify a short program and submit it to RoboProf. RoboProf compiles and runs the program and then displays the program's output and the expected output to the student. If the output matches, the student receives full marks, if not, the student can correct the error and resubmit the program without penalty. This process of correcting logic errors is analogous to the method of using compiler error messages to correct syntax errors. On average, each program was submitted 2.5 times before students were satisfied with their mark.

The system was used throughout the semester; Figure 2 shows the number of correct program submissions per day over a period of

11 weeks. As can be seen, there were not many submissions during weekends, and the peaks correspond to the assigned labs which took place on Tuesdays and Thursdays.

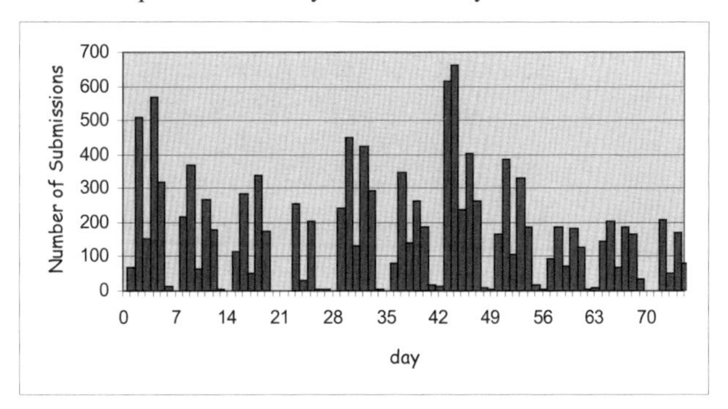

Figure 2. Correct submissions per day

On average, there were over 160 correct submissions per day. Students completed the exercises at a rate of four a week, although the best students averaged seven exercises a week.

There was an end of semester exam which comprised five programming exercises presented by RoboProf. This three hour exam took place in a computer lab under normal examination conditions. Students had to do the exercises unaided. Those who did the course work properly would be expected to do well in the exam.

A few more points are required to complete the context:

- The programming language used on the course was Java.
- Fewer than 10% of the students had programmed before (according to questionnaire responses).
- Dublin City University, in common with other universities in Ireland, requires students to achieve a rather low 40% to pass a course.
- RoboProf can give partial marks for programs. Each test case is marked independently and the output is parsed and marks awarded based on the criteria of the problem designer. Generally, however, the marks awarded for a program were either 0% or 100%.

RoboProf includes a method of detecting plagiarism. This method and the resultant data that it generated are the subject of this paper. We did warn students that we were using software to detect plagiarism. However, for logistical and research reasons, we did not act on any of the cases that we discovered.

3. ROBOPROF DETECTION METHOD

The plagiarism detection system works by adding a watermark to a student's program at submission time. If another student gets an electronic copy of this program (complete with the watermark), and then submits it, RoboProf will recognise it as a copy.

The submission process is controlled by a Java applet which runs the program on the student's machine (it needs local file access permissions to do this). The program and its output are then sent to the server where it is marked. Meanwhile, on the student's computer, the applet writes a watermark onto the program (or overwrites in the case that one already existed). The watermark is a binary number formed by concatenating the year, exercise id, student id and a checksum. Extra white space at the end of a line is invisible, so we represent the number using the tab and space characters as binary digits and write the number at the end of the main method signature. The watermark will not show up in standard editors and is unlikely to be changed by normal editing of the file. An article by Plauger [11], where he was providing evidence in a copyright infringement case, inspired the idea.

Previous automated plagiarism detection systems, e.g. [1, 12] compare pairs of programs with each other and indicate any pairs which are suspiciously similar. Our system has a number of advantages over these pair-wise comparison techniques:

- It can detect plagiarism in very short programs that are typical of introductory programming exercises. With short programs, it is likely that students may come up with similar solutions by chance. Pair-wise detection systems cannot distinguish these chance similarities from cases of plagiarism.
- It distinguishes between the supplier of the code and the recipient of the code.
- It requires no manual intervention. Note that pair-wise comparison techniques merely highlight suspicious cases. Each case needs to be examined to determine whether plagiarism is likely to have occurred. This is naturally subjective and any data generated by pair-wise comparison techniques is thus less useful for research purposes.
- Plagiarism is detected as soon as it occurs. There is no need to gather all the submissions and process them. This feature is especially useful in a self-paced environment where exercise solutions may be submitted at any time.

There are two other minor advantages: it is programming language independent and it works even if a student gets an assignment from a previous year (provided that the system was used the previous year).

There are also some disadvantages:

- It will only detect plagiarism if the copying student gets an electronic copy after the original program has been submitted.
- A student may disturb the watermark inadvertently. However, since the main method signature is not usually changed in Java programs, it is unlikely that a student would try to change it.
- It is easy to bypass the system if the students discover how it works. There is no evidence that students knew about the system; in fact, the number of detected cases of plagiarism increased as the semester went on.

There is another way in which a watermark could be disturbed. Many students keep the editor open as they submit their programs. It is quite possible that, after submitting their program and thus acquiring the watermark, the unmodified version, still in the editor, is saved. This would overwrite the watermark and defeat the detection system.

Some interesting false positives occurred with this system. In some cases, students did not develop programs from scratch, but instead edited a previous program from a previous exercise. If the previous program had been copied and acquired a watermark, then the current program would keep the watermark and it would appear as if it, too, was copied. This error is easy to detect because the exercise id is encoded in the watermark.

There was anecdotal evidence of another false positive. A student claimed that he had developed a program and submitted it. The program received zero marks and the student could not see any difference between the program's output and the expected output. Assuming that there was an error in the system, the student borrowed a program from another student to check the submission process. RoboProf registered this as a case of plagiarism.

3.1 Detection Performance

We decided to measure RoboProf's detection abilities by testing it against a pair-wise comparison system. As already noted, pair-wise comparison systems do not generally work well with short programming assignments, so we chose an exercise which required a longer solution. We collected the students' submissions for this exercise and submitted them to the Moss online plagiarism detector [1]. Moss presents its results as a set of suspicious cases which are then manually checked. The requirement for subjective manual intervention means that this comparison can not be very rigorous.

For the chosen exercise, RoboProf had detected 37 students involved in plagiarism (23 copiers and 14 suppliers). Moss also detected 37 students, but not the same 37 that RoboProf identified. Moss failed to highlight seven similar programs which were the result of plagiarism, but it did identify seven students, in two groups of three and four, which RoboProf had missed. In each group, the students had submitted programs that manual inspection indicated had probably been based on a single program. Of these seven students, six were detected by RoboProf on a subsequent exercise which would indicate that they did not know how to bypass the detection system.

4. RESULTS AND DISCUSSION

We performed a straightforward analysis on the RoboProf plagiarism data. Figure 3 shows that the plagiarism rate per exercise ranges from 0% to 10% with an average of 2.6%.

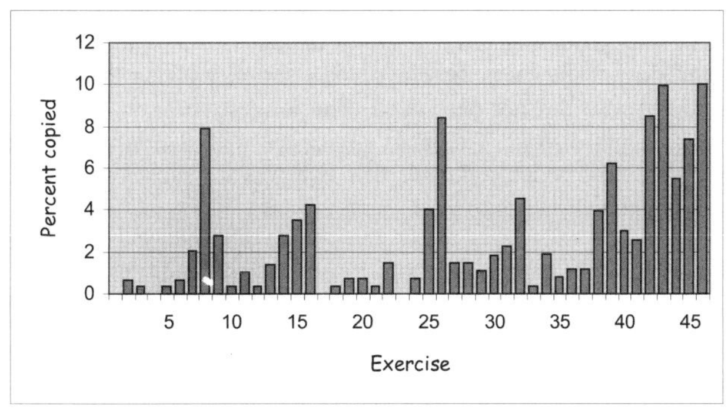

Figure 3. Percentage plagiarism detected for each exercise

Note that this only includes the copiers, not the original authors of the programs. As we move through the exercises, plagiarism tends to increase. There are two outliers, exercise 8 (23 cases or 8%) and exercise 26 (also about 8%). Analysis of the average time taken and the number of attempts would indicate that these exercises were of above average difficulty. It may be that students only copied when they felt that they had no other option. Figure 1 shows that there was a marked drop in the number of students completing the last 10 exercises. This would indicate that the students found these exercises more difficult and this could explain the increased level of copying of these exercises.

It is interesting to compare our detection rate with detection rates on courses at other institutions. According to Alex Aiken, the developer of Moss, large classes will have a plagiarism rate of roughly 10% per assignment, though plagiarism can be reduced through the continued use of plagiarism detection software [2]. At Stanford, Eric Roberts reports a copying rate of between three and five percent [14].

Figure 4 shows the number of times that individual students copied.

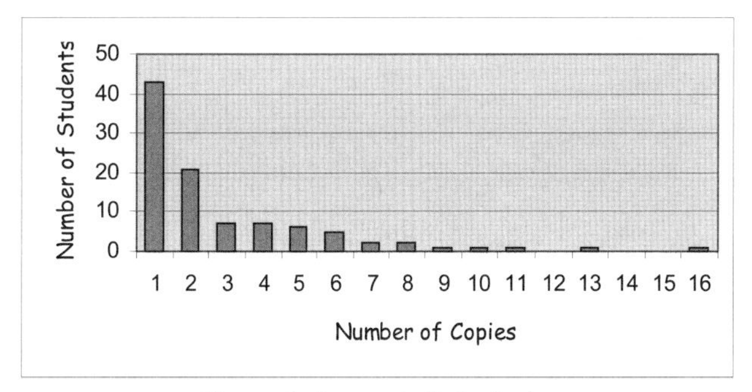

Figure 4. Amount of plagiarism

There is an apparent contradiction between the large number of students who copy and the small percentage of copies per exercise. However, although one student copied 16 programs, most of the copiers (two thirds) copied only one or two programs. These students may have copied to overcome some temporary difficulty that they were having with the course.

4.1 Plagiarism Categories

In Table 1 students are classified as honest or dishonest depending on whether or not they engaged in plagiarism.

Table 1. Honest and dishonest students

Group	N	%
Honest	149	50
Dishonest	147	50
Total	296	100

During the semester, 29 students dropped out, 23 of whom were 'honest'. Some of the students who dropped out early did not attempt many exercises and therefore had fewer opportunities to become dishonest.

Table 2 shows the exam marks of the remaining students:

Table 2. Exam marks of honest and dishonest students

		Mark in the exam	
Group	N	Average	Std Dev
Honest	126	52.6	31.5
Dishonest	141	45.9	30.0
Total	267	49.0	30.6

Although on average, honest students have higher marks than dishonest students, the difference is not significant ($p > .05$).

The watermark detection method enables us to further categorise the dishonest students. Some students had not copied any programs; they were in the dishonest category solely because they had supplied a program or programs to someone else. We called these students suppliers and the remainder we called copiers. It turned out that about a third of the dishonest students were suppliers with two thirds being copiers.

Table 3 shows the exam marks of these new categories.

Table 3. Exam marks of suppliers and copiers

		Mark in the exam	
Group	N	Average	Std Dev
Honest	126	52.6	31.5
Dishonest			
- Suppliers	48	61.8	27.7
- Copiers	93	37.9	28.5
Total	267	49	30.6

A clear difference emerges between the suppliers and the copiers, with means of 61.8% and 37.9% respectively. Duncan's multiple comparison test [13] was performed on the three groups and it was found that the mean of the suppliers, though higher than the mean of the honest students, was not significantly so ($p > .05$), while the mean of the copiers was significantly lower than the means of the other two groups. Most observers would expect this, as these copiers miss the learning value of the exercise. However, it could be argued that they copied because they were not as gifted as the non-copiers and this would explain why they did worse in the exam.

4.2 Staying the Course

We next returned to the coursework data. Figure 1 showed the completion rate for the coursework exercises. We examined the completion rate for each of the three categories: copier, supplier and honest. Figure 5 shows the percentage of students who completed the exercises in each category.

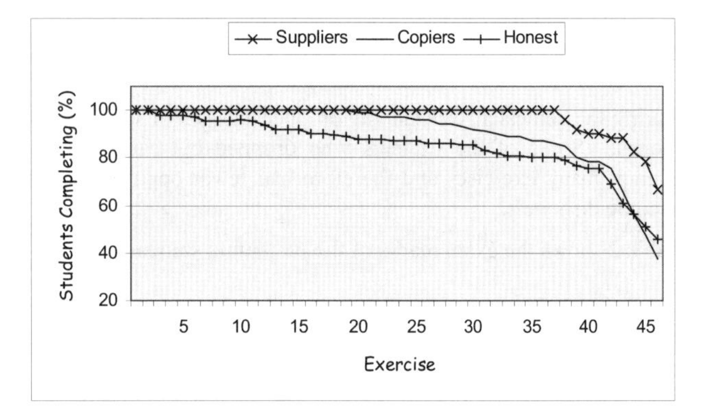

Figure 5. Exercise completion rate by plagiarism category

It can be seen that the suppliers are the best completers, followed by the copiers and then the honest students.

This may be clearer when presented in tabular form (results are shown for four representative exercises):

Table 4. Completion rate of exercises

Category	Percentage Completion Rate by Exercise Number			
	1	20	37	46
Supplier	100	100	100	66
Copier	100	99	86	38
Honest	100	88	80	46

In fact, although all the suppliers had completed exercise 37, 14% of the copiers and 20% of the honest students had failed to complete it. Note also that the fall off of the copiers near the end of Figure 5 follows the fall off in the suppliers. The copiers are running out of source material.

There seems to be a natural explanation for the results of the copiers and of the honest students. If a copier gets stuck at an exercise, they can simply procure a copy from a supplier. An honest student does not have that recourse. Indeed, that could explain why so many honest students dropped out of the course.

It is interesting to consider why the suppliers work so hard at completing the exercises. It may be that the suppliers are encouraged by the possibility of giving their code to their less able colleagues. This would enhance their self esteem and provide the motivation needed to complete the next exercise. If this is the case, plagiarism is bad for the copiers but good for the suppliers.

4.3 Chains of Plagiarism

A chain of plagiarism is where a program moves around a group of students. We hypothesised that a student, who received a copy from someone else, would feel less ownership of it and would therefore be more likely to pass it on resulting in a 'chain of plagiarism'. The evidence does not support this hypothesis. We examined the exercise with most incidents of plagiarism (exercise 8). Thirty seven students were involved, comprising ten simple pairs, two groups of three, a group of four and another group of five. Most of the cases, ten, involved a supplier giving the code to a copier who did not pass it on. The longest chain we observed had a length of four. This is in agreement with the data from the MIT incident which indicates that two was the most typical size of a collaborating group [16].

5. RELATED WORK

Watermarks have long been used in digital documents e.g. [3]. Normally, however, they are used with the knowledge of the author (or the author's agent) to protect copyright. As far as we know, this is the first time that watermarks have been deliberately added to a document without the author's knowledge.

Our work has attempted to deduce motivations based on student behaviour. Previous work into student thoughts on plagiarism used detailed interviews [4] or questionnaires [15]. We see our approach as being complementary; interviews and questionnaires can obviously provide more detail, but the resulting data may not be as objective.

6. CONCLUSIONS

We introduced a new plagiarism detection system and presented results of its use on an introductory programming course. We have compared it with a standard pair-wise comparison system and shown that it is as good at detecting plagiarism, while requiring no manual processing of its results. In addition, our approach reveals more information about the habits of student plagiarism than do standard pair-wise detection systems. We were able to detect a difference between honest and copying students, because the watermark technique allowed us to remove the suppliers from consideration.

We next examined the differences when it came to completing the coursework exercises. Copiers are more likely to complete the exercises than the honest students. These copiers seem to sail along without recognising that there is a problem. The attitude seems to be "can't do the exercise, just get a copy". Unfortunately, when the exam comes around, these students do not do well. If these students were prevented from plagiarising, it is possible that they might engage with the material and improve their programming ability. On the other hand, they might drop out as a number of honest students did when they got stuck. This may suggest a need to improve our support services for weaker students.

It should be noted that there are some significant differences between the exercises presented here and the assignments on a more typical introductory programming course. These exercises require less work than normal assignments and there are no traditional deadlines, the work is self-paced. Assignment difficulty and deadlines are both factors that can affect the amount of plagiarism that occurs in a class [16]. However, we believe that our results do give insights into student behaviour which are more generally applicable.

For those who want to implement this watermark idea, there is another approach. Some assignments require that the student use supporting code. The student downloads the code, does the assignment and submits it. A watermark could be injected at the point where the student downloads the code. In addition to being less ethically dubious, it should be easier to implement and is not subject to the failure mode where a student saves a program over the watermark.

7. REFERENCES

[1] Aiken A. Moss: A system for detecting software plagiarism. Berkeley Computer Science Department. http://www.cs.berkeley.edu/~aiken/moss.html

[2] Aiken A. Personal communication (2004).

[3] Brassil, J. et al. Electronic Marking and Identification. IEEE Journal on Selected Areas in Communications V13 no 8 (1995), 1495-1504.

[4] Carter J. Collaboration or Plagiarism: What happens when students work together? Proceedings of ITiCSE (June 1999), 52-55.

[5] Culwin, F. MacLeod, A. and Lancaster, T. Source Code Plagiarism in UK HE Computing Schools, Issues, Attitudes and Tools, South Bank University Technical Report SBU-CISM-01-02. (2001).

[6] Daly, C. RoboProf and an introductory programming course Proceedings of ITiCSE (June 1999), 155-158.

[7] Daly, C., Horgan, J. Automatic Plagiarism Detection. Proceedings of the International Conference in Applied Informatics (February 2001), 255-259. http://www.computing.dcu.ie/~cdaly/publications/2001/automaticPlagiarismDetection.pdf

[8] Daly C., Horgan J. M. An automated learning system for Java programming. IEEE Transactions on Education, (February 2004), 10-17.

[9] Harris, J. Plagiarism in Computer Science Courses. Proceedings of the Conference on Ethics in the Computer Science Age. (November 1994), 133-135.

[10] Lancaster T., Culwin F. Towards an Error Free Plagiarism Detection System. Proceedings of ITiCSE. (June 2001), 57-60.

[11] Plauger, P. J. Fingerprints, Embedded Systems Programming. (June 1994), 84-87.

[12] Prechelt, L., Malpohl, G., Philippsen M., JPlag: Finding Plagiarisms among a Set of Programs, Technical Report 2000-1, Fakultät für Informatik, Universität Karlsruhe, (2000).

[13] Reilly, J. Understanding statistics and its application in business, science and engineering. Folens, 1997.

[14] Roberts, E. Strategies for Promoting Academic Integrity in CS Courses. 32nd ASEE/IEEE Frontiers in Education (November 2002) http://fie.engrng.pitt.edu/fie2002/papers/1125.pdf

[15] Sheard J. et al. Cheating and Plagiarism: Perceptions and Practices of First Year IT Students. Proceedings of ITiCSE (June 2002), 183-187.

[16] Wagner, N. Plagiarism by Student Programmers, http://www.cs.utsa.edu/~wagner/pubs/plagiarism0.html

[17] Zobel J. "Uni cheats racket": a case study in plagiarism investigation. Proceedings of the sixth conference on Australian Computing Education. (2004), 357-365.

Developing Resources to Support a National Computer Science Curriculum for K-12

Anita Verno
Bergen Community College
400 Paramus Road
Paramus, NJ 07652
201-447-7909
averno@bergen.edu

Debbie Carter
Lancaster County Day School
725 Hamilton Road
Lancaster, PA 17603
717-392-2916
carterd@e-lcds.org

Robb Cutler
The Harker School
500 Saratoga Avenue
San Jose, CA 95129
robbc@harker.org

Michelle Hutton
The Girls' Middle School
423 Dell Avenue
Mountain View, CA 94043
mailto:mfh@pobox.com

Lenny Pitt
University of Illinois at Urbana-Champaign
201 North Goodwin Ave
Urbana, IL 61801
217-244-6027
mailto:pitt@uiuc.edu

ABSTRACT

This session will continue efforts by the ACM and Computer Science Teachers Association (CSTA) to create a comprehensive body of resources to support the implementation of a national K-12 computer science curriculum. The ACM K-12 Computer Science Curriculum Committee, with input from the Computer Science educational community, published a Model Curriculum [1] in 2003. The Model suggests a 4-level curriculum. Level-1 topics, primarily for the K-8 years, closely follow the well-defined ISTE Standards. Level-2 topics are suggested for all students in grades 9 or 10 and are comprised of introductory computer science content. Level-3 topics focus on analysis and design with emphasis on the scientific and engineering aspects of computer science. AP Computer Science and special topics courses comprise Level-4. This special session will focus on the learning objectives and activities for Level 2 of the K-12 Computer Science Model curriculum. Attendees will be invited to provide critical feedback that will help move the curriculum project forward.

Categories and Subject Descriptors

K-3 [Computers & Education]: Computer & Information Science Education – Curriculum.

General Terms

Design, Standardization.

Keywords

K-12, Model Curricula, Pedagogy, Algorithmic Thinking, Computing Workforce, Teacher Preparation, .Teacher Resources, Learning Objectives.

SIGCSE'05, February 23-27, 2005, St. Louis, Missouri, USA.
ACM 1-58113-997-7/05/0002.

1. INTRODUCTION

The ACM K-12 Computer Science Model Curriculum [1] was developed in 2003 to provide a broad outline from which a K-12 computer science curriculum can be developed. The Model Curriculum was a response to the view that computer science education is not clearly defined or well-established at the K-12 level. With an ultimate goal of standardizing computer science content at the K-12 level and providing support for the computer science educational community, the ACM established the Computer Science Teachers Association (CSTA). "The Computer Science Teachers Association is a membership organization that supports and promotes the teaching of computer science and other computing disciplines by providing opportunities for K-12 teachers and students to better understand the computing disciplines and to more successfully prepare themselves to teach and to learn." [2]

The ongoing effort of the CSTA to solidify the computer science teaching and learning experience for American students is critically important. A national computer science curriculum which stabilizes the objectives and content of high school CS has implications beyond K-12 education. It will assist students with further study in computer science / information technology / information systems / engineering and will help with the larger national effort to build America's position as a global leader in technological knowledge and expertise.

This session will continue efforts by the ACM and CSTA to create a comprehensive body of resources to support the implementation of a national K-12 computer science curriculum. The Model curriculum provides an overview of computer science content broken into 4 levels – Level 1 recommended for students in grades K-8, Level 2 recommended for students in grades 9 or 10, Level 3 and 4 recommended for students in upper grades. The Level 1 curriculum closely follows ISTE standards and is therefore a fairly well-developed set of learning objectives with available resource materials. The Level 2 curriculum, suggested for all students, was broadly described in the Model and as such must be detailed to ensure uniform learning across the US.

After a summary presentation of learning objectives, assessment measures, and educational activities, we will engage the attendees in a discussion of the viability of the suggested content and call for resources. The discussion will help inform future initiatives that will keep the ball rolling in the direction of national standards for computer science education in the K-12 community.

2. SESSION OUTLINE

Joint presentation by session participants:

A. Overview of the K-12 curriculum model

Challenge in providing curriculum detail

B. Level 2 Draft Curriculum

General objectives

For each general objective:

- Specific learning goals
- Method of assessing each goal
- Detailed outline of topics including examples of learning activities

Resources required for implementation

C. Discussion:

Value of the topics listed

Ability to implement the curriculum

3. EXPECTATIONS

This session is intended for K-12 and college Computer Science / Information Technology / Information Systems educators and administrators interested in a comprehensive Computer Science educational sequence from Kindergarten through introductory college courses. Continued development of a Level 2 computer science curriculum that can be widely implemented is anticipated as a result of this session.

This special session is important because SIGCSE 2005 will have many K-12 educators in attendance who are interested in the development of computer science curriculum, and who will wish to express their voice to help shape its content. Face-to-face dialogue on objectives, assessment, activities, and resources is essential to ensuring that such a curriculum can be effectively implemented throughout schools. A SIGCSE special session provides the opportunity for input critical to the viability of a national CS curriculum and will help sustain the efforts that are required to achieve this.

The session will describe the K-12 Model Curriculum but will focus on the Level 2 standards. We will distribute a summary of the Level 2 objectives to the participants for use as a reference during the discussion of content, assessment, and learning activities.

Attendees will be asked to provide input regarding the value of the topics listed and the ability to implement the curriculum at their school. Their comments will be recorded and used to update the Level 2 curriculum to help ensure it can be widely implemented. The audience will learn about ways they can participate in the ongoing effort to further detail the various Model curriculum levels.

The session will be moderated by Anita Verno. The participants will present different parts of the outline.

4. REFERENCES

[1] Tucker, Allen, (editor), Deek, F., Jones, J., McCowan, D., Stephenson, C., and Verno, A. *A Model Curriculum for K-12 Computer Science: Final Report of the ACM K-12 Task Force Curriculum Committee.* Association for Computing Machinery (ACM), New York, New York, October, 2003. http://www.acm.org/education/k12/k12final1022.pdf

[2] Computer Science Teachers Association, Mission Statement, 2005. http://csta.acm.org/

Objects-Early Tools – A Demonstration

Joe Bergin
Computer Science
Pace University
berginf@pace.edu

Kim Bruce
Computer Science
Williams College
kim@cs.williams.edu

Michael Kölling
Mærsk McKinney Møller Institute
University of Southern Denmark
mik@mip.sdu.dk

SUMMARY

Various software tools have been proposed or developed for use in introductory programming courses. Usually, presentation of a new tool at the SIGCSE symposium occurs when a tool is first developed, leaving it to interested observers to identify success or failure of tools over their lifetime.

For teachers, it can be difficult to compare available tools and judge potential application in their courses.

In this session, three tools with an established track record of successful classroom use are presented: Karel J Robot [1], objectdraw [2], and BlueJ [2]. In addition to considering each tool individually, opportunities for combinations of these tools are also discussed.

The focus of this session will be on concrete, hands-on advice that teachers can immediately apply in their classrooms.

Categories and Subject Descriptors

K.3.2 [**Computers & Education**]: Computer & Information Science Education - *Computer Science Education*

General Terms: Human Factors.

Keywords

CS1, object-orientation, objects early, pedagogy, software tools.

1. INTRODUCTION AND OBJECTIVES

The idea of teaching a programming course in an 'objects-early' mode has been proposed and discussed repeatedly in the past. A common observation, however, is that many teachers still find it very difficult to find a good entry point into teaching such a course.

Over the last few years, a considerable number of software tools have been developed and presented at the SIGCSE symposium to help with this task. Reports from users consistently show that use of some tools can greatly ease the task of dealing with some of the overhead that teaching of object orientation imposes on teachers and students, and significantly increase understanding of important concepts by students.

New teachers, however, do not have an easy task in finding and evaluating existing tools, identifying those that are still being maintained, and keeping up with recent changes and developments. Frequent questions appearing on various teaching-related mailing lists or being sent to the authors directly bear witness of these difficulties.

SIGCSE'05, February 23–27, 2005, St. Louis, Missouri, USA.
ACM 1-58113-997-7/05/0002.

In this session, three tools that have a proven track record of successful classroom use are being presented by their authors. These presentations aim at achieving three things:

- to give teachers who know little or nothing about the tool a quick and general introduction into capabilities and application areas of the tool;
- to give teachers who already know the tool an update on important recent changes in the tool; and
- to provide concrete, immediately useful ideas about improving programming courses through the use of software tools, that teachers can directly benefit from.

The three projects presented are well known instances of three different types of object-oriented software tools: a micro world (Karel J Robot), a development environment (BlueJ) and a class library (objectdraw).

All three have in common that they have been developed specifically for the teaching of object-oriented concepts in introductory programming courses. All three are also well beyond experimental stages, having been widely used for several years.

Presenting the tools together in a single session provides the unique opportunity to not only discuss each of the software tools individually, but to investigate how these software tools may be combined or complemented to increase their impact.

2. KAREL J ROBOT

Karel J Robot is the current version of a microworld that has evolved since about 1980 into an effective means of teaching programming to novices. It has always focused on correct use of the then dominant programming paradigm. Today that is object-oriented programming. Karel thus introduces dynamic polymorphism as early as reasonable in a course (about the third week of CS1). The Karel world is visual, programming is in Java, and the system is provably a Turing Machine, permitting very complex programs to be written with a very reduced Java subset. Problem solving is stressed over language syntax, and instructors are dissuaded from introducing new language features to solve new problems.

The Karel J Robot (KJR) system is distributed as a Java jar file that has the visual system and a set of classes for primitive robots that the student programmer extends to do interesting things in a simple world. In addition to the "obvious" things (described in the manuscript), KJR provides an agile testing framework (JUnit based) so that test first development can be done in KJR. There is also an acceptance testing framework (KarelFixture) permitting the instructor to present exercises as executable specifications interleaved with text descriptions of the exercise requirements.

KJR also has a remote controller interface permitting students to exercise robots manually. This is built with Java reflection, permitting the student's own code to be so exercised easily. Finally an event driven programming API has recently been added to KJR so that something like programming physical robots via feedback can be simulated.

Web site: `http://csis.pace.edu/~bergin/KarelJava2ed/Karel++JavaEdition.html`

3. BLUEJ

BlueJ is an integrated Java development environment specifically designed for introductory teaching that presents a unique front-end to offer an interaction style that is different to other environment available today.

BlueJ was carefully designed with three fundamental goals in mind: *visualization*, *interaction,* and *simplicity*.

The visualization concept aims at making the main abstractions of object orientation visible on screen: objects and classes. This makes it much easier for students to understand and reason about these fundamental concepts, and easier for teachers to talk about them.

Classes are visualized in a UML-like diagram, which gives an immediate overview over students projects and also shows dependencies. Objects are shown when they are instantiated.

The interaction part enables users to directly interact with the conceptual entities in the environment. Classes can be interactively instantiated, and public method can be invoked on objects. This encourages an exploratory approach to understanding object orientation that involves the student much more than traditional environments.

Simplicity is a key goal in BlueJ's interface design. The environment itself should not become an obstacle in the learning of programming principles. Unfortunately, environments designed for professional developers are of a complexity that poses its own challenges, distracting from the learning of programming itself. BlueJ avoids this by presenting tools custom-designed for student use.

Apart from the general object interaction mechanism, BlueJ offers integrated support for a variety of education-related tools, most importantly an easy-to-use debugger, a *javadoc* generation facility and integrated support for JUnit.

BlueJ was first released in 1998, and is now widely used in many institutions all over the world.

Web site: `www.bluej.org`

4. OBJECTDRAW

The objectdraw library was developed by Kim Bruce, Andrea Danyluk, and Tom Murtagh to support teaching Java to novice programmers. It is designed to support an "objects from the beginning" approach to CS 1. It supports truly object-oriented graphics, makes it possible to incorporate event-driven programming techniques from the beginning, and provides support for introducing concurrency quite early in a course.

Graphical objects both serve as excellent examples of objects and provide visual feedback that makes it easier for students to determine the effects of their code and to detect errors in their programs. The graphical objects provided in the objectdraw library also have the advantage that results of the creation and modification of objects appear immediately on the screen without the need to invoke a paint or repaint method.

The programs that students use most are event-driven. Clicking on a link, selecting an item from a menu, or dragging an icon results in program actions. Students are more highly motivated by writing event-driven programs than using traditional text-based I/O. Moreover, because different events can happen at any time, students learn early that event-driven methods can be invoked in many different orders, just as the methods of other objects can be invoked in different orders. Thus students learn from the beginning not to expect a single monolithic ordering of program statements during execution. The objectdraw library contains a class `WindowController` that extends `Japplet` by inserting a drawing canvas in the center of a window and that serves as a listener for mouse actions on the canvas. The syntactic simplifications that result make it easy for students to program in an event-driven style. In many cases, event-driven programming is easier than more traditional styles.

Web site: `cortland.cs.williams.edu/~cs134/eof`

5. PRESENTERS

Joe Bergin is Professor of Computer Science at Pace University. He has been teaching for 32 years and OO programming since 1986. He is the creator of Karel++ and Karel J Robot, based on earlier work of Pattis, Stehlik, and Roberts. He has written widely on OO programming and especially the central role of polymorphic thinking.

Kim Bruce is the Frederick Latimer Wells Professor of Computer Science at Williams College, and is currently a Visiting Professor of Computer Science at the University of California at Santa Cruz. He is the author of *Foundations of Object-Oriented Languages: Types and Semantics*, MIT Press, and is a co-author of the forthcoming CS 1 text, *Java: An eventful approach*, Prentice-Hall.

Michael Kölling is an Associate Professor of Software Engineering at the University of Southern Denmark. He is one of the developers of the BlueJ environment and has published numerous papers on object-oriented and computing education topics and is co-author of a successful Java textbook.

6. REFERENCES

[1] Bergin, J., Stehlik, M., Roberts, J., Pattis, R., Karel J Robot: A Gentle Introduction to the Art of Object-Oriented Programming in Java, Unpublished manuscript. Available on the web at: http://csis.pace.edu/~bergin/KarelJava2ed/Karel++JavaEdition.html

[2] Bruce, K. B., Danyluk, A., and Murtagh, T. A library to support a graphics-based object-first approach to CS 1. In Proceedings of the 2001 ACM SIGCSE Symposium (2001), pp. 6–10..

[3] Kölling, M., Quig, B., Patterson, A. and Rosenberg, J., The BlueJ system and its pedagogy, Journal of Computer Science Education, Special issue on Learning and Teaching Object Technology, Vol 13, No 4, 249-268, Dec 2003.

Changes in CS Students' Attitudes Towards CS over Time: An Examination of Gender Differences

Sylvia Beyer, Michelle DeKeuster, Kathleen Walter, Michelle Colar, Christina Holcomb
University of Wisconsin-Parkside
900 Wood Road
Kenosha, WI 53141
262 595-2353
beyer@uwp.edu

ABSTRACT

Few women major in Computer Science (CS), which creates a serious bottleneck of women qualified to enter into the CS workforce. To address this bottleneck, this study examines gender issues in CS education. We assessed whether gender differences in CS students' stereotypes of CS and attitudes towards CS classes and the CS program remain stable from one semester to the next. We found that gender differences in CS students are not temporally stable and conclude that one-time assessments of gender differences may lead to erroneous conclusions. We also found that concerns about future work-family conflicts and gender issues in the CS program (e.g., female CS students feeling that they are not being taken as seriously as male CS students) emerged as important concerns for female CS students. The implications of these findings for increasing the representation of women in CS are discussed.

Categories and Subject Descriptors

K. 3 [Computers & Education]: Computer & Information Science Education – Computer Science Education.

General Terms

Measurement, Experimentation, Theory.

Keywords

Gender and CS, Gender Differences, Stereotyping, Attitudes towards CS.

1. INTRODUCTION

This paper examines issues surrounding the question of why there are so few women in Computer Science (CS). We take the position that although structural barriers exist that keep women from advancement in CS careers, the dearth of women in the CS workforce is foremost a pipeline issue (cf. [5]). The most recent available statistics indicate that only 27.7% of Bachelor's degrees in CS are conferred on women [12]. This severely restricts the number of women qualified to enter into the CS workforce. The pipeline of women majoring in CS needs to widen in order to increase the number of women working in CS-related fields. An increased presence of women in CS is imperative if the field wants to benefit from women's special skills and perspectives. We cannot afford to underutilize such a valuable and significant part of our workforce.

SIGCSE'05, February 23–27, 2005, St. Louis, Missouri, USA.

Why do so few women choose to major in CS? We have addressed three reasons for the small number of women majoring in CS in previous publications [1][3][4]. They include low computer confidence, lack of programming and hands-on computer experience, and negative stereotypes regarding the field. We have found similar results for another computer-related field, Management Information Systems (MIS) [1].

In this paper we will examine the stability of gender differences in CS students' attitudes towards CS over time. That is, we will compare CS students' attitudes towards CS in one semester to their attitudes in the following semester. We are especially interested in elucidating whether gender differences in attitudes towards CS remain stable over this time course. Rather than assuming that gender differences assessed at one point in time are set in stone, we propose that they might be fairly fluid: Gender differences in attitudes towards CS that are present when students take their first CS class might be augmented, reduced, or even disappear as students take more advanced CS courses. On the other hand, some differences in attitudes between men and women might not even emerge until students are more advanced in their major. We are not aware of research on CS that has empirically addressed this question. In our research on students in MIS we did find evidence that gender differences in attitudes towards MIS do not remain stable from one semester to the next [2].

We believe that an examination of the temporal stability of gender differences is long overdue. If students' attitudes towards CS change as they progress in the major, and especially if gender differences in attitudes change over time, one-time assessments of students' attitudes might lead to erroneous conclusions. This could lead to premature recommendations for intervention. For example, an assessment of attitudes towards CS in the first required CS course might reveal large gender differences (e.g., male students having much more positive attitudes towards computers). This could prompt calls for intervention to increase the representation of women in CS. However, if gender differences in attitudes towards CS decrease over time, such interventions may not be necessary. On the other hand, if gender differences in attitudes remain stable or are augmented with time, this would indicate that intervention might be advisable to increase women's representation in CS. Thus, our results might have important policy implications.

2. METHOD

This research was conducted at the University of Wisconsin-Parkside, a small public university. In an initial assessment, 234 (81 females, 153 males) students enrolled in CS courses in 2001, 2002, or Spring 2003 returned our initial surveys. In a subsequent semester 94 (39 females, 55 males) of these students also responded to a follow-up survey. Thus, 48.1% of women who participated in our initial assessment completed the follow-up compared to 35.9% of men. (It has been our experience that women's response rates are higher than men's.) In this paper, we are reporting on only the 94 students who provided information at both the initial assessment and the follow-up. Thus, the comparison of initial responses to follow-up responses is based on the same students.

We surveyed two types of CS students: CS majors enrolled in CS1 and students enrolled in computer literacy courses not intended for CS majors. For simplicity we refer to students in these two CS course types as CS "majors" and "non-majors", respectively.

Students received $2 to fill out questionnaires assessing (among other variables not discussed here) their experience with and attitudes towards computers; stereotypes of CS; and attitudes towards CS courses and the program. We used a combination of existing instruments and items created specifically for our research. Following is a description of those items on which we report in the Results section.

We constructed our own "Stereotypes of CS" scale by having students rate the personality characteristics of students majoring in CS. We used individual items from the Role Conflict Scale [7] to assess students' opinions of the compatibility of work and family for women in CS. We asked questions measuring students' general attitudes towards CS courses and the program (e.g., "the choice of CS courses here is too limited", "Female CS students are not taken seriously by male faculty").

3. RESULTS AND DISCUSSION

To understand gender differences in CS students over time, we performed 2 (student gender: female versus male) x 2 (major status: CS major versus non-major) x 2 (assessment time: initial assessment versus follow-up assessment one semester later) repeated measures analyses. Student gender and major status were between-subjects variables, whereas assessment time was within-subjects.

Table 1 gives the means for the analyses. Because the issue of interest for this paper is gender, we will not report on significant main effects of major status. Significant interactions between gender and major status will of course be noted. Differences in N are either due to missing values or the addition or deletion of questions in surveys sent out in different semesters. Please note that when we refer to "CS students", we mean both CS majors and non-majors. If the results apply only to either CS majors or non-majors, we explicitly state that.

3.1 Demographic Variables

The sample consisted of 80.9% Caucasian, 5.3% Asian, 3.2% African American, and 3.2% Hispanic students, with 7.4% choosing not to identify their race. Fifty-six students were CS majors and 38 students were taking a computer literacy course not intended for CS majors (referred to as non-majors).

3.2 Experience with, and Attitudes towards, Computers

Female students were somewhat older than male students when they first became interested in CS, $F(1, 55) = 3.60$, $p = .06$. They were much less likely than male students to have installed RAM into a computer, $F(1, 91) = 23.15$, $p = .0001$.

Males had significantly more confidence in their ability to teach someone to use a computer software package than women at both assessment times, $F(1, 91) = 9.06$, $p = .003$.

We found a significant interaction between time, major, and gender in students' belief that computers are fun, $F(1, 85) = 5.87$, $p = .02$. Female non-majors and male majors increasingly felt that computers are fun, while female majors and male non-majors felt computers were less fun at the follow-up than at the initial assessment.

These results suggest that female students have less computer experience, develop an interest in computers later, and have less confidence in their ability to teach computer skills to others. For these variables no effects of time were found. Gender differences remained stable from one semester to the next. For example, the experience gap in installing RAM did not narrow over time. However, female majors' and male non-majors' attitude towards computers as fun became more negative with time.

3.3 Stereotypes of CS

3.3.1 Work-Family Issues

Over time students became more convinced that female computer scientists who take time off to have children will never catch up again, $F(1, 91) = 9.80$, $p = .002$, and that it is difficult for a woman to combine a career as a computer scientist with family life, $F(1, 91) = 8.55$, $p = .004$.

Female students estimated higher starting salaries than did male students at both times, $F(1, 91) = 4.48$, $p = .04$. However, they also estimated longer work hours than did male students at both times, $F(1, 91) = 16.73$, $p = .0001$.

SELECTED VARIABLES	Initial assessment				Follow-up			
	Non-CS Majors		CS Majors		Non-CS Majors		CS Majors	
	Women	Men	Women	Men	Women	Men	Women	Men
Age when I first became interested in CS	18.3	14.0	20.4	17.3	17.8	14.0	21.2	16.1
Percentage of participants who had opened a computer to install RAM	38	79	27	80	63	86	47	88
I am confident that I can teach someone to use a computer software package****	4.2	5.8	5.5	6.1	5.0	6.0	5.9	6.2
Computers are fun****	6.0	6.1	6.4	6.3	6.2	5.7	6.2	6.4
If female computer scientist takes time off for children, she will never catch up again****	2.2	2.6	2.3	2.2	3.0	3.0	3.1	2.3
It is difficult for women to combine family and career in CS****	2.9	2.2	2.8	3.3	4.0	3.4	3.6	3.2
Estimated starting salaries of computer scientists	44083	42929	49467	44329	46750	44286	49200	42576
Average number of hours worked per week by a computer scientist	49.7	42.2	49.5	45.7	49.7	44.1	48.3	45.2
Having a career is more important than having a family****	2.9	2.5	1.9	2.7	2.3	2.9	2.3	2.5
Students majoring in CS are popular****	3.5	4.3	4.2	4.1	3.9	3.8	4.3	4.2
CS students are "nerdy"****	4.9	5.0	4.2	4.9	4.8	5.4	4.4	4.9
Computer scientists are more interested in numbers than people****	3.5	3.6	2.5	3.5	3.5	3.9	2.2	3.1
Computer scientists enjoy being around people	3.6	4.6	4.3	3.8	3.7	3.8	4.0	4.8
Choice of CS courses here is too limited for my career goal****	3.4	2.6	3.2	3.2	3.0	4.0	2.8	3.3
CS major requires too many credits for completion****	3.2	3.6	3.1	3.0	3.0	4.4	2.9	3.3
The rewards in a computer-related field are worth the sacrifices****	4.7	5.2	4.8	5.7	5.0	3.9	5.3	5.5
I feel tense about my CS assignments****	4.6	3.9	5.2	4.1	4.3	3.8	4.5	4.1
The atmosphere in the CS program is impersonal****	3.2	3.5	3.5	3.2	3.8	3.9	3.3	3.5
There is gender discrimination in the CS program****	2.2	1.6	1.9	1.7	2.3	2.1	1.3	1.5
Female CS students are not taken seriously by male CS faculty****	2.6	1.9	1.9	1.4	3.0	2.4	1.6	1.6
The ability of female CS students is underrated by others****	4.1	3.1	3.4	2.7	3.3	2.7	1.8	1.8
Faculty question the commitment of female students	2.4	1.8	2.3	1.9	2.9	2.6	1.8	1.7

Notes: Higher scores signify stronger endorsement of item.

* 1-4 scale, ** 1-5 scale, ***1-6 scale, ****1-7 scale

When we asked students if they thought that having a career is more important than having a family, we found a significant time x gender x major interaction, $F(1, 90) = 5.77$, $p = .02$. Female non-majors had the strongest career orientation of all the students in the initial assessment. By the follow-up one semester later, their scores had dropped sharply, making them the group that valued career over family the least. Female majors and male non-majors, on the other hand, became more career-oriented over time. Male majors' career orientation decreased slightly over time.

3.3.2 Stereotypes about CS Students and Computer Scientists

The interaction between time, major, and gender for the stereotype that students majoring in CS are unpopular was significant, $F(1, 90) = 3.88$, $p = .05$. While male and female majors' stereotype about the popularity of CS students remained steady around the neutral point, male non-majors' stereotype about how popular CS majors are became more negative while female non-majors' stereotypes became more positive from the initial to the follow-up assessment one semester later.

At both assessment times male students were more likely than female students to believe that CS majors are "nerdy," $F(1, 91) = 6.63$, $p = .01$, and were more likely to subscribe to the stereotype that computer scientists are more interested in numbers than people, $F(1, 91) = 5.26$, $p = .02$.

There was a significant interaction between time, major, and gender regarding the perception that people who choose careers in CS enjoy being around people, $F(1, 90) = 6.24$, $p = .01$. Over time male non-majors' and female majors' stereotype that computer scientists enjoy being around others became more negative. Female non-majors' stereotype remained stable over time. Male majors' stereotype that CS students enjoy being around people became more positive over time.

To summarize, some stereotypes showed a complex pattern of interaction between gender, major status, and time. This indicates that gender differences did not remain stable from one semester to the next. Female students espoused less negative stereotypes than male students. For example, female students were less likely than male students to believe that CS majors are "nerdy". Still, there is reason for concern. Unfortunately, male and female students' perceptions of women's ability to combine family and career became more pessimistic over time. Furthermore, female students estimated longer work hours than did male students. Because women are still considered the primary caretakers of children, female CS students might anticipate greater work-family conflict. Furthermore, over time female CS majors became less convinced that computer scientists enjoy being around others which runs counter to women's greater interpersonal orientation [6][11].

3.4 Attitudes towards CS Courses and the CS Program

3.4.1 General Attitudes toward the CS Program

In analyzing students' reactions to the statement "the choice of CS courses here is too limited for my career goal", we found a significant time x gender x major interaction, $F(1, 90) = 3.81$, $p = .05$. Male non-majors showed a dramatic increase over time in their belief that the course choices were too limited. In contrast, male majors' belief stayed relatively stable. Female majors and non-majors were less likely to believe that their choice of CS classes was limited at the follow-up compared to the initial assessment.

There was a significant interaction between time and gender regarding attitudes that the CS major requires too many credits for completion, $F(1, 91) = 5.53$, $p = .02$. Male majors and non-majors alike became more negative over time, while female majors and non-majors became less negative over time in their perception that the CS major requires too many credits.

There was a significant interaction between time and gender for students' belief that the rewards in a computer-related field are worth the sacrifices, $F(1, 90) = 6.27$, $p = .01$. While both female majors' and non-majors' perceptions became more positive with time, by the follow-up male majors and non-majors alike felt more strongly that the sacrifices in pursuing a CS major were great.

Female students were somewhat more tense about their CS assignments than were male students, $F(1, 75) = 3.28$, $p = .07$.

Students' felt that the atmosphere in the CS program is impersonal more strongly in the follow-up assessment than in the initial assessment, $F(1, 91) = 3.69$, $p = .06$.

3.4.2 Gender Issues in the CS Program

There was a time x major interaction for the belief that there is gender discrimination in the CS program, $F(1, 89) = 6.38$, $p = .01$. Female and male non-majors showed increasing perceptions of gender discrimination over time, whereas female and male majors alike felt that there was less gender discrimination at the follow-up than at the initial assessment in the previous semester.

Female students believed more strongly than did male students that female CS students are not taken seriously by male CS faculty, $F(1, 89) = 3.55$, $p = .06$.

At the initial assessment compared to the follow-up, students felt more strongly that the ability of female CS students is underrated by others, $F(1, 91) = 18.22$, $p = .0001$. At both times women felt more strongly than did men that female CS students' abilities are underrated, $F(1, 91) = 4.04$, $p = .05$.

There was a significant time by major interaction in students' belief that faculty question female Computer Science students' commitment to their studies, $F(1, 88) = 9.53$, $p = .003$. Female and male non-majors became more likely to believe that faculty question women's commitment, while female and male majors over time became less likely to believe that.

To summarize, unfortunately female students felt more strongly than did male students that women are not taken seriously by male CS faculty and that instructors underestimate women's abilities. These perceptions may have a chilling effect on both female CS majors and non-majors. They might increase the attrition rate for female majors and dissuade female non-majors from considering CS as a potential major. Two more troubling findings were that female students were tense about their assignments and both male and female students felt that the atmosphere had become more impersonal at the follow-up compared to the semester before. This should affect female students more negatively than male students because social support and faculty encouragement are even more important to women's than men's decision to enroll in or leave CS [7][10].

An encouraging finding was that over time CS majors were less likely to feel that there is gender discrimination in the department, to feel that female students are underrated by others, and to feel that female CS students' commitment is questioned by faculty. Thus, more exposure to CS faculty had a beneficial effect for majors. Female CS majors also had fewer complaints about the CS program (e.g., choice of courses, credits required) at the follow-up than did male majors.

4. CONCLUSIONS

The purpose of the present study was to investigate whether gender differences in CS students' attitudes towards CS remain stable from one semester to the next. We found that gender differences are less temporally stable than might be expected. In our study of MIS students we also found that gender differences did not remain stable from one semester to the next [2][1].

We conclude from our results that one-time assessments might lead to erroneous conclusions. In the future, researchers should be careful not to jump to conclusions without examining the changing attitudes of both genders over time. It is possible that some gender differences in attitudes towards CS are reduced over time because those who are more involved and more advanced in their CS studies begin to feel assimilated i.e., they see themselves simply as CS students, instead of seeing themselves as male or female CS students. Of course, as with all longitudinal research, an alternative explanation is that other intervening factors (e.g., maturity) are responsible for changes across time.

One limitation of our research is that students were re-contacted in the semester following their initial assessment. Follow-ups over longer periods of time would provide more in-depth information about the stability of gender differences over time. We are presently conducting additional follow-ups to address the stability of gender differences over a two-year period. Especially interesting would be a follow-up study of students entering the workforce. What happens to gender differences as individuals transition into the CS workforce?

A further limitation is that most participants were Caucasian preventing us from conducting analyses by race. More research on minorities in CS is needed. Currently efforts are underway to study CS students at historically Black colleges [9]

We believe that this research has yielded intriguing results. The findings suggest avenues for recruiting and retaining female CS majors, thereby increasing the number of qualified women entering into CS careers. Concerns about possible future work-family conflict and gender issues in the program (e.g., gender discrimination and not being taken as seriously as male students) seem to present problems.

While students' (legitimate?) concerns about future work-family conflict may be intractable for CS departments, the finding that in our CS department greater exposure to CS faculty decreased perceptions of gender discrimination and other gender-related issues is very encouraging. It suggests that faculty and/or departments can greatly affect female students' comfort level. The CS faculty at our institution is 43% female which might explain this result. Mentors and role models play an important role in the success of female students in male-dominated majors [1]. Thus, individual departments that address the issues we highlighted viz., work-family conflict and especially issues surrounding gender discrimination may have increased success in retention and recruitment of CS students.

6. ACKNOWLEDGMENTS

This research was supported by a grant from the National Science Foundation (EIA-0089957) to the first author.

7. REFERENCES

[1] Beyer, S. and DeKeuster, M. Women majoring in Computer Science or Management Information Systems: A comparative analysis. Manuscript under review (2004).

[2] Beyer, S., DeKeuster, M., Rynes, K., and DeHeer, J.. The Temporal Stability of Gender Differences in MIS Students. Proceedings of the Annual Meeting of the AMCIS Conference, New York, NY. i2004).

[3] Beyer, S., Rynes, K., and Haller, S. Deterrents to Women Taking Computer Science Courses. IEEE Society and Technology, 23 (2004), 21-28.

[4] Beyer, S., Rynes, K., Perrault, J., Hay, K., and Haller, S. Gender Differences in Computer Science Students. in Proceedings of the Thirty-fourth SIGCSE Technical Symposium on Computer Science Education (2003), 49-53.

[5] Camp, T. The Incredible Shrinking Pipeline. Communications of the ACM, 40 (1997), 103-110.

[6] Cross, S. E. and Madson, L. Elaboration of Models of the Self: Reply to Baumeister and Sommer and Martin and Ruble. Psychological Bulletin, 122 (1997), 51-55.

[7] Cuny, J., Aspray, W., Cohoon, J., and Jesse, J. Factors Concerning Recruitment and Retention of Women Graduate Students in Computer Science and Engineering. Proceedings of the National Science Foundation's ITWF & ITR/EWF Principal Investigator Conference (pp. 86-90), Albuquerque, NM. (2003).

[8] Lips, H. M. Gender- and Science-Related Attitudes as Predictors of College Students' Academic Choices. Journal of Vocational Behavior, 40 (1992), 62-81.

[9] Lopez, A. M., Jr. and Schulte, L. J. African American Women in the Computing Sciences: A Group to be Studied in Proceedings of the 33rd SIGCSE Technical Symposium on Computer Science Education (2002), 87-90.

[10] Margolis, J., & Fisher, A. Unlocking the clubhouse. Cambridge, MA: MIT Press (2001).

[11] Markus, H. R. and Kitayama, S. Culture and the Self: Implications for Cognition, Emotion, and Motivation. Psychological Review, 98 (1991), 224-253.

[12] U.S. Department of Education, National Center for Education Statistics. Digest of Education Statistics, 2000-2001. (2002).

Diversifying the Images of Computer Science: Undergraduate Women Take on the Challenge!

Carol Frieze
School of Computer Science
Carnegie Mellon University
412-268-9071
cfrieze@cs.cmu.edu

ABSTRACT
This paper tells the story of a student initiative, driven by a desire to diversify the images that surround the field of computer science and those who work in it.

Categories and Subject Descriptors
General Topics: Gender and Diversity issues
K.0 Computing Milieux

General Terms
Documentation, Experimentation, Human Factors,

Keywords
Outreach, Gender Issues, Representation, Diversity, Images

1. INTRODUCTION
This paper tells the story of a student initiative, driven by a desire to diversify the images that surround the field of computer science and those who work in it. We believe it may hold some helpful pointers for those interested in showing that computer science is so much more than "coding". We also offer a useful model for those interested in launching an outreach program for encouraging more girls and women (and boys and men) into the study of computer science.

2. BACKGROUND
Over the past few years we have become well aware of the declining numbers of girls and women entering the computer science major. The problem has been well researched and documented, and disseminated in such well known articles as Tracy Camp's "The Incredible Shrinking Pipeline" [1] and "The Incredible Shrinking Pipeline Unlikely to Reverse" [2].

More recently the issue of declining numbers of students has been felt across the board, as fewer men, as well as women, make the decision to enter the computer science major. Peter Lee, Professor and Associate Dean for computer science undergraduate education at Carnegie Mellon, points out "According to the 2002-2003 CRA Taulbee Survey,[1] enrollment in undergraduate computer science programs has dropped by more than a quarter since 2001. This is stimulating a growing amount of discussion in computer science departments nationwide."[2] [3] Indeed, what was a cause for concern for women's enrollment is now an overall concern.

The issue of declining numbers may actually be a much needed wake-up call for those of us in the field to re-evaluate, re-think and re-shape what computer science really means and how it is perceived in the public consciousness. We may expect greater attention to the issues and a diversity of recommendations and approaches to tackle the challenges. We may find that some of those aspects of the field that have been deterring women from entering are actually deterring all students, and strategies for change may well result in increasing enrollment overall and a more gender balanced environment. But numbers may not be the only issue here, and certainly the field in general should benefit from the resulting re-examination and strategies for action.

The *images* surrounding computer science represent just one among many issues that cloud our understanding of the field. Dominant images still suggest that the field is populated by geeky[3] guys, while at the same time the image of the field itself is seen as little more than coding. *The image of computer science as a broad and exciting field with the potential for diverse participants is, for the most part, missing from the big picture.*

Changing the big picture will be no easy task. Nevertheless, council members from our student organization, Women@SCS, at Carnegie Mellon University, decided to take on the challenge at the local level.

2. WOMEN@SCS ADVISORY COUNCIL
The Women@SCS advisory council is made up of graduate and undergraduate students, and faculty, in the School of Computer Science. The council represents a thriving and significant body of women students[4] and works to create, encourage, and support

SIGCSE'05, February 23–27, 2005, St. Louis, Missouri, USA.

[1] 2002-2003 CRA Taulbee Survey: http://www.cra.org/statistics/

[2] For more on Professor Peter Lee's thoughts see the "Shrinking Pipeline" http://pl.ug.cs.cmu.edu/csd/pmwiki.php?pagename=Main.ShrinkingPipeline

[3] The word "geek" seems to have entered the vernacular in the 1990s as a label for computer obsessed individuals. For an interesting discussion of the term see: http://dictionary.reference.com/search?q=geek

[4] For the full story of how Carnegie Mellon reversed the trend with regards to numbers of women at the undergraduate level see: Blum,

women's academic, social and professional opportunities in computer science and computing-related areas and to promote the breadth of the field and its diverse community.

Lenore Blum, Distinguished Career Professor of Computer Science and faculty advisor to Women@SCS has noted "there is no dearth of ideas generated by the Council and, indeed, the level of energy expended is extraordinary". [4] The council organizes numerous networking, social and professional events on-campus and a busy program of outreach activities.[5] Blum also points out that, "in terms of their increased professional experiences, contacts and growth, their self-esteem, and their academic and leadership successes and awards" council members are deserving beneficiaries of their desires and efforts to reach out to others. [4]

So with the goals of promoting the breadth of the field and its diverse community in mind, council members took on the challenge of developing an outreach program based on their vision of how the field should be represented. And since many strategies that work well for women have been found to work well for all, we may find their contribution, though minor in the larger scale of things, can reach out beyond their initial goals and expectations.

3. THE ROADSHOW STORY

A little under three years ago a small group of our undergraduate women went to the Richard Tapia Celebration of Diversity in Computing Conference[6] and came back to school full of post-conference enthusiasm and energy. This was their first conference experience and it made a huge impact on their view of the field, an impact that would have been hard to replicate even at Carnegie Mellon, where although we have made huge steps forward in improving our gender balance, we still struggle to diversify our computer science undergraduate student body in terms of race and ethnicity.

Following the return of our Tapia contingent the group gave a report to the Women@SCS advisory council at their weekly meeting. They summed up their experiences by unanimously declaring (and I paraphrase): "We must do more Outreach! ....especially to middle school girls! We have to let them know there are women and minorities in the field and that it's not just about coding!" And I said "Okay let's do it!"

The following weekend a group of students worked together and made a powerpoint slideshow which tackled two image topics head-on: "Who can be computer scientists?" and "What can you do with computer science?" At subsequent meetings we talked more about our goals (see 6. below), and the logistics (see 7. below) of putting their plans into action; we improved and revised the content and added new slides and finally began giving presentations of what soon became known as the Outreach Roadshow, a title suggested by our faculty advisor, and soon claimed.

L. Women in Computer Science: The Carnegie Mellon Experience. http://www.cs.cmu.edu/~women/

[5] For more information about the Women@SCS advisory council and their program of activities please browse their web site: http://women.cs.cmu.edu/

[6] The Richard Tapia Celebration of Diversity in Computing: http://www.ncsa.uiuc.edu/Conferences/Tapia2003/index.html#PROGRAM

Since then the Roadshow has become a very popular and valuable program within our organization. It has captured the imagination of our undergraduate students and graduates alike. We have presented on campus, and at middle schools. We have "upgraded" the slideshow to be appropriate for high school students and have presented for middle and high school teachers. More recently we have developed a "research focused" version that is presented by our graduate women to undergraduates. We have provided an online downloadable version[7] and have welcomed requests from students and teachers to use it as their model. We have continually improved the Roadshow as we've collected, and responded to, feedback from students and teachers. When Bill Gates, Chairman and Chief Software Architect of the Microsoft Corporation, came to campus our group was called upon to give a demonstration of the "show".

Over the past year we have produced a more sophisticated version of the Roadshow in which our graduate women present at other campuses to undergraduate students. They discuss the variety of programs in computing related fields available at the graduate level. They talk about the need for more women in the field in academia and how to pay for graduate school. The students tell their personal stories, give overviews of their departments and give short talks on their individual research. At the last graduate Roadshow the students represented such diverse areas as Robotics, Language Technologies, Computational Neuroscience and Computer Science.[8]

Perhaps the most meaningful and exciting moment for us was going back to the Richard Tapia conference in 2003 and actually presenting our Roadshow at the site of its inspiration!

4. WHAT IS THE ROADSHOW?

The Roadshow is a presentation by a group of women undergraduates and graduates from the School of Computer Science at Carnegie Mellon who talk about their thoughts on the field, why and how they began studying the area, their early and current experiences, what computer science means to them now, and their future hopes and expectations. The presentation includes a slide show to illustrate the breadth of the field of computer science and computing related areas, question and answer interaction, a guessing game and (for younger audiences) a simple robot demonstration.

There are currently three versions of the Roadshow targeted at middle school, high school and undergraduate students. They all share the goals of a) bringing women's personal experiences of computer science and computing related fields to the audiences and b) getting students excited about the field and what it offers. In this way the Roadshow challenges stereotypes and promotes new images of computer science and computing related disciplines.

A description of the Roadshow fails to do it justice. It is the students themselves who give the presentation the potential to be effective. Their energy, visibility, technical know-how and interaction with the audiences combine with the slideshow images to challenge stereotypes and offer new images of the field and the people in it.

[7] http://women.cs.cmu.edu/What/Outreach/

[8] At Carnegie Mellon we have the advantage of having the School of Computer Science which is comprised of 6 departments representing a diverse range of areas. Our students are exposed, directly and indirectly, to a wealth of research areas and world-class faculty.

With that in mind, below is a description of what the Roadshow looks like and includes:

- images of the students to illustrate their personal stories as they introduce themselves (these include their baby pictures or photos from outside of the work situation.)
- an interactive guessing game (diverse images of computer scientists and of non-computer scientists)
- an interactive discussion on what is computer science and what you can do with it? (children are asked about their use of the internet, instant messenger, etc.)
- a step by step math puzzle and introduction of the term algorithm (answers and more puzzles are provided)
- the breadth of the field is illustrated with a "talking heads" demo, simple robotics videos, the CAPTCHA project (which serves to identify humans from robots as they log in to such things as Yahoo), video graphics, speech recognition, computer science and biology, and more
- depending on the age of the audience the students will add information about the classes they take, job opportunities, the companies they can work for, and graduate school options
- depending on the age of the audience we use simple robot demos such as a "lego robot bug" and a Sony Aibo Robot dog
- the students conclude with a question and answer session (they encourage questions throughout) and then leave contact addresses and the web site address in case members of the audience want more information or have further questions

5. AUDIENCES

The content of the Roadshow changes to suit audiences such that the presentation for younger students is fast paced and fun with a guessing game and puzzles, while the undergraduate audience gets a taste of real research areas and advice on funding and applying to graduate school. While targeting girls and women, we nevertheless are inclusive of boys and men, because one of our primary goals is to show women in leadership and teaching roles to all audiences.

We feel the Roadshow is appropriate for the following audiences:

- middle school girls and boys
- high school students
- parents and teachers
- undergraduates from computer science and other fields
- representatives from industry
- all who are interested in gender equity and computer science

Our presentation for undergraduates has been given to small audiences at three universities thus far and we are currently preparing to present at the University of Pennsylvania and at Columbia University. We will also be presenting the graduate level Roadshow at the Grace Hopper conference[9] in Chicago this October.

[9] The Grace Hopper Celebration of Women in Computing 2004 http://www.gracehopper.org/

6. GOALS

The Roadshow serves a variety of goals, in fact we deliberately want to make the most of all such presentations.

- to increase the visibility of young women in computer science
- to challenge traditional stereotypes
- to show the breadth of fields that computer science and related areas can encompass
- to spark interest in the science
- to provide an interesting and enjoyable learning experience
- role modeling
- to provide leadership/mentoring opportunities for our young women computer science students
- to challenge current images of the field and those in it
- to diversify current images of the field and those in it
- to expose undergraduates to the possibilities of research
- to provide opportunities for our graduate women to network with faculty and students from other schools

7. LOGISTICS

My current motto is "Be prepared for anything!" Although our Roadshows are carefully arranged we never quite know the make-up of the audience and the setting until we arrive on the scene. The range has been surprisingly wide. We have presented in private schools to the entire student body in splendid auditoriums, and to public school classes in the main cafeteria having struggled in with our own screen, laptop and projector. In all cases, however, we have found the audiences to be wonderfully responsive! Perhaps the most meticulously and diligently arranged Roadshow, with numerous emails going back and forth, turned out to be the most disappointing because the session was set for a time when, unfortunately, undergraduate students were busy with classes and unable to attend. The rest of the day, however, was carefully thought out, with productive meetings, and our graduate women were able to network with faculty and other graduates so that overall it became a very worthwhile experience!

8. FEEDBACK

We are currently reviewing how best to evaluate the effects of the Roadshow program. Getting enough feedback is perhaps one of the most difficult aspects of the Roadshow. Ideally we would like to know if the presentation has had any impact and if there has been any follow-up or other initiatives as a result. We have a teacher questionnaire that has proved to be very helpful and we have listened closely to their comments and incorporated them where possible.

When we work with high school and middle school teachers we hear again and again how much they need, and appreciate, the examples and materials we use to demonstrate the breadth of computer science. There seems to be a desperate need for teaching resources that situate programming in the wider context of the field. Teachers seem to share our desire to try to break down the stereotypes that surround the field but rarely have the resources to do so.

Teachers also repeatedly affirm that the personal stories of our students, "their energy and enthusiasm" are what make the Roadshow so effective and unique. Something as simple as young women explaining how and why they decided to major in computer science can be very valuable and effective parts of such presentations.

Quotes:

"Some day I hope to be a computer scientist just like you" (7th grade girl)

"I think what you do is really awesome" (6th grade girl)

"The show is unique, you should keep it this way." (high school teacher)

"I liked that you showed a mixture of races" (high school teacher)

At one presentation a computer science professor pointed out that the "show" glossed over the grunt work of computer science in favor of the exciting parts. I had to admit this was absolutely true and somewhat deliberate since our focus was always on trying to get the students excited about the science. I was rescued by a young African American woman in the audience who argued that while our culture was so intent on getting kids excited about football and sports, we paid so little attention and energy to getting them excited about science!

My favorite feedback comment, though frivolous, came from a young child at an on-campus presentation. The children were asked by their summer camp organizer what they had leaned about computer science. One little boy put his hand up and said very seriously "I've learned that computer scientists are very pretty"!

9. BENEFITS FOR OUR STUDENTS

Our undergraduates and graduates are in very intensive academic programs. I am always amazed that they manage to volunteer so much of their time, energy and expertise to outreach work. The Roadshow is a clear example of the activism of the Women@SCS council members and their strong drive to give back to the community. I also hear again and again from our students that doing the Roadshow is such fun. When pressed they often explain that they wished they had been given similar presentations in their own schools.

Quotes from Student Presenters:

- "I really enjoy sharing my experience and enthusiasm with others while gaining valuable presentation experience."
- "I participated in the Roadshow because it is one way I can help students understand the boundless opportunities an education in computer science can bring."
- "What I got out of the Roadshow was a chance to improve my presentation skills and even learn some applications of computer science that I didn't even know of."
- "I see the Roadshow as a way to hopefully generate an interest in technology and its applications so that students will consider pursuing the field in the future."

Both the undergraduate and the graduate Roadshows provide our students with leadership and public speaking opportunities. By having graduates and undergraduates team up together to develop and implement the presentations, numerous opportunities for mentoring and learning from each other arise. The Roadshows help our students with confidence building and provide them with opportunities to illustrate their knowledge in a fun environment.

10. CONCLUSION

We live in a culture which specializes in manipulating our thoughts and attitudes through images. Image so easily becomes reality. But culture is constantly changing and we can challenge current images and try to change them as much as be affected by them. Indeed, as I listen to students' perspectives (men and women) as they discuss computer science stereotypes I hear them constantly redefining and reshaping the images that surround them.

The students who initiated the Roadshow did so with the aim of challenging and diversifying current images. As women they did not see themselves fitting naturally into the traditional image dominated by "geeky guys" but, *perhaps more importantly, as students of computer science, they did not see images of the field that matched their learning and exposure to an exciting field of study with the potential to impact many lives.*

Professor Lee suggests that to address the current state of computer science "demands a concerted effort by top scientists" [4]. In the meantime some of our women students are making one small contribution to meet his "call to action".

While it remains to be seen if the Roadshow has any real local impact, for the students involved it is clearly a very worthwhile experience, as one students commented: "Knowing that even one kid changed their views of computer science after all the presentations we did is enough for me to feel like I've made a difference!"

ACKNOWLEDGMENTS

Our thanks to the wonderful students who have created and presented the Roadshow and have given their time and energy to try to impact the images surrounding computer science. And our thanks to all the children, teachers and students who have participated as Roadshow audiences and organizers.

REFERENCES

[1] Camp T. *The Incredible Shrinking Pipeline*. Communications of the ACM, 40 (10): 103-110, 1997. http://www.mines.edu/fs_home/tcamp/cacm/paper.html

[2] Camp, T. *The Incredible Shrinking Pipeline Unlikely to Reverse,* ACM-W, January, 2000. http://www.mines.edu/fs_home/tcamp/new-study/new-study.html

[3] Lee, Peter. *Shrinking Pipeline* http://pl.ug.cs.cmu.edu/csd/pmwiki.php?pagename=Main.ShrinkingPipeline

[4] Frieze, Carol, and Blum, Lenore. *Building an Effective Computer Science Student Organization: The Carnegie Mellon Women@SCS Action Plan* Inroads SIGCSE Bulletin Women in Computing; vol.34.no.2, 2002, June, p. 74-78

[5] Blum, L. *Women in Computer Science: The Carnegie Mellon Experience.* In Resnick D.P.and Scott , D., eds., The University of the Future: The Future of the University. 2001.

Climbing Onto the Shoulders of Giants

Antonio M. Lopez, Jr.
Xavier University of Louisiana
Computer Sciences and
Computer Engineering Department
504.520.5248
tlopez@xula.edu

Lisa J. Schulte
Xavier University of Louisiana
Department of Psychology
504.520.5421
lschulte@xula.edu

Marguerite S. Giguette
Xavier University of Louisiana
Computer Sciences and
Computer Engineering Department
504.520.7458
mgiguett@xula.edu

ABSTRACT

The "incredible shrinking pipeline" problem has become the euphemism for the dilemma of declining numbers of women seeking bachelor's degrees in a computing discipline. The problem is well recognized, and many have suggested reasons for it. Unfortunately, much of what has been written is based on anecdotal evidence or inferences made from statistical results from small samples of very specific groups in the computing disciplines. There have been few multi-disciplinary approaches to analyze the problem with even fewer attempts to create a model that might explain it. This paper is the end of a beginning. Having received a National Science Foundation grant to study gender-based differences and ethnic and cultural models in the computing disciplines, the principle investigators document the work that has led to launching a nationwide study of the problem to commence in Fall 2004.

Categories and Subject Descriptors

K.3.2 [**Computer and Information Science Education**]: Computer Science Education

General Terms

Experimentation, Human Factors, Verification.

Keywords

Gender, Ethnicity, Culture, Social Cognitive Career Theory

1. INTRODUCTION

Investigating with scientific rigor the decline in the number of women seeking bachelor's degrees in a computing discipline is a daunting task. Data are spread throughout the various computing disciplines and findings are typically published in journals specific to a discipline. Statistics on populations within a computing discipline, such as African American women in Computer Engineering, have been sparse. Descriptive statistics of a computing discipline's population are offered more often than statistical support of a theory that represents the phenomenon and can predict those population characteristics that result in successful recruitment and retention of women and minorities in the computing disciplines. The theories recognized in the behavioral sciences regarding career choices have not been incorporated, for the most part, into the published works of the computing disciplines.

In this paper, the term "computing discipline" means an academic program that leads to a bachelor's degree in: Computer Engineering (CE), Software Engineering (SE), Computer Science (CS), Computer Information Systems (CIS), Information Systems (IS), Management Information Systems (MIS), Information Technology (IT), or the like. Each of the computing disciplines has elements of commonality with the others as well as elements that distinguish one from the others. Thus the term computing discipline will be applied when commonality is the focus. That stated, much has been written about the under-representation of women in the computing disciplines [5, 6, 7, 9, 18 to reference but a few]. Research seeking to understand the cause of the decline of women in the computing disciplines have ranged from a small group analysis at one institution of higher education to larger statewide studies, and from developing statistics that describe what currently exists to presenting anecdotal evidence that is used to support a program of change within an institution.

Researchers must be cautious in reviewing previous studies. Very often data regarding computing disciplines are embedded in studies done on student populations from the STEM (Science, Technology, Engineering, and Mathematics) disciplines. Under such circumstances the statistical confounding of variables can easily occur. The confounding of variables can also occur when studies make no distinction between computing disciplines. Dryburgh's [11] critical review of the research conducted in the 1990s regarding the under-representation of girls and women in CS highlights additional reasons to be cautious, one being that "findings are sometimes generalized to females of all ages or educational levels, when empirical studies on gender and computing tend to test hypotheses on one age group or on students at a specific level of education."

In September 2003, Xavier University of Louisiana was awarded a National Science Foundation (NSF) grant to conduct a study of gender-based differences as well as ethnic and cultural models in the computing disciplines. The proposed research is a mixed design, primarily a three-year longitudinal study (beginning in Fall 2004) with a new sample of first-year undergraduates being introduced in the second and third year. The project will involve a total of 50 institutions of higher education from across the nation. Twenty-five of these institutions will be Historically

SIGCSE'05, February 23–27, 2005, St. Louis, Missouri, USA.

Black Colleges or Universities (HBCUs) and 25 will be Predominantly White Institutions (PWIs). Every year of the study each institution will have approximately 70 of their computing discipline undergraduates (both male and female) surveyed; these subjects will range from first-year students to seniors. As a control/baseline each year, 30 first-year undergraduates from non-computing disciplines at each institution will also be surveyed.

This paper presents the journey to the point where the principle investigators (PIs) now find themselves, ready to launch their survey. This journey included forming an Advisory Board, finding Corporate Partners, and recruiting Research Partners as well as Higher Education Partners. This paper provides the rationale of the study. It reports some findings from the pilot study conducted in Spring 2004. Analysis of the pilot data brought forth the survey that will be used in Fall 2004.

2. GIANTS

The award of a planning grant in October 2001 allowed the PIs to assemble an Advisory Board of leaders. A number of them have published in the area of gender differences in CS. Others have directed funds or urged faculty to investigate key questions not only about gender but also about ethnicity and culture. The academic members of the Advisory Board are:

Sylvia Beyer, Associate Professor of Psychology, University of Wisconsin-Parkside. Her research focuses on gender differences in self-perceptions in male-dominated domains. She is currently the PI on an NSF funded project entitled "Predictors of Women's Interest and Retention in Undergraduate IT Majors."

Doris Carver, Professor of CS and Associate Vice Chancellor of Research and Graduate Studies, Louisiana State University. She is an IEEE Fellow and Editor-in-Chief of *Computer*. She was the PI for the NSF funded virtual workshop entitled "Research Foundation for Improving the Representation of Women in the IT Workforce."

Joanne McGrath Cohoon, Research Assistant Professor in the Curry School of Education, University of Virginia. She is a sociologist who studies technology, gender, education, and their interaction. One of her current investigations is a national study of gendered attrition from undergraduate computing majors.

Andrea Lawrence, Associate Professor and Chairperson of CS, Spelman College. She is the President of the Association of Departments of Computer and Information Sciences and Engineering at Minority Institutions.

Jane Margolis, Research Educationist, University of California Los Angeles in the Graduate School of Education and Information Studies. She has recently worked on an NSF funded three-year study titled "Out of the Loop: Why So Few Underrepresented Minority and Women Students are Studying Computer Science?" – an investigation of African American and Latino/a male and female high school students' decisions to study (or not study) CS in three public Los Angeles high schools.

Although matching funds were not required with the proposal, the PIs thought it was important to invite Corporate Partners with demonstrated cash commitments for two reasons. First, the progress of women and minorities in the computing disciplines does not end when they graduate. Corporations, large and small, national and local, need to be involved and committed to scientific studies. They need to take what is learned and incorporate it into their training programs and corporate cultures [10]. Second, the request for proposal sets limits on the amounts that NSF can award. These amounts do not cover all the costs of a study. The PIs want to do a pilot study in Spring 2004, annually have a face-to-face meeting of the Advisory Board and the research team, and in Spring 2007 be able to finalize the study. Requesting money for these activities would put the project's budget over the NSF limits. Microsoft, Inc. and Apogen Technologies, Inc. stepped forward in support of the work. A representative from each is on the Advisory Board.

Another element of support for this study comes from the Research Partners. Early in the planning, the PIs obtained commitments for assistance with the design of the survey instruments and analysis of the collected data from three established and recognized researchers in the behavioral sciences. The Research Partners have experience with gender and ethnicity issues as well as cultural models. They are:

Madonna G. Constantine, Professor and Chair of the Psychology Department, Columbia University. She is a Fellow of the American Psychological Association (APA), consulting editor for the *Journal of Cultural Diversity and Ethnic Minority Psychology* and an associate editor for the *Journal of Black Psychology*.

Robert W. Lent, Professor and the Director of Counseling Psychology for the Department of Counseling and Personnel Services, University of Maryland, College Park. He is a Fellow of the APA and a co-developer of the Social Cognitive Career Theory (SCCT). SCCT attempts to explain how people develop their academic and career interests, how they translate those interests into career choices, and what additional influences, such as cultural and environmental factors, contribute to their choices and achievements at school and work.

Frederick G. Lopez, Professor and the Director of Training in Counseling Psychology for the Department of Educational Psychology, University of Houston. He is an APA Fellow, a former Fulbright Senior Scholar (Portugal), and a member of the editorial board of the *Journal of Counseling Psychology*.

The following subsections briefly highlight some of the contributions and findings of these colleagues.

2.1 Lent

Bandura [1] introduced self-efficacy theory into the psychological literature 27 years ago. Self-efficacy focuses on the cognitive means people use to guide their own behavior. Shortly after its introduction, Hackett and Betz [12] noted the potential of the self-efficacy construct to help explain certain aspects of women's career development, such as the tendency of many women to underutilize their career talents and to avoid male-dominated career paths. One of the major streams of research on academic and career-related self-efficacy has involved STEM disciplines. Because adequate preparation in math serves as a "critical filter" affecting entry into a wide range of scientific and technical careers [4], researchers have studied the utility of math self-efficacy in explaining students' interest in, choice (or avoidance) of, and performance in, science and math-intensive academic courses and disciplines. Findings have shown that math self-efficacy beliefs are predictive of science and math-related interests [15]. While research on math self-efficacy has been beneficial, researchers in career selection [16] have also studied additional variables that along with math self-efficacy form the core of Bandura's social cognitive theory [2]. Outcome expectations and personal goals are two such variables. Outcome expectations refer to beliefs about the outcomes of various courses of action (e.g., "a degree in *X* will allow me to receive things I value"), while goals involve one's determination or intention to pursue a particular course of action (e.g., "I am fully committed to getting my degree in *X*").

To incorporate a wider range of social cognitive mechanisms and processes in the study of academic and career behavior, Lent, Brown, and Hackett [13] developed the SCCT. SCCT consists of three overlapping models aimed at explaining the processes through which people (a) develop basic academic and career interests, (b) make and revise their educational and vocational plans, and (c) achieve performances of varying quality in their chosen academic and career pursuits. Self-efficacy, coping-efficacy, outcome expectations, interests, and goals play key roles within each of these three models, operating in concert with a variety of additional personal, contextual, and learning variables (e.g., gender, race/ethnicity, social support, external barriers) to help shape people's career trajectories. Recent findings [14] indicate that SCCT variables were strongly predictive of engineering students' persistence goals across gender and university type (i.e., HBCUs versus PWIs). SCCT provided the primary theoretical and empirical approach for the pilot study.

2.2 Margolis

The foundation for the analysis found in [18] is more than 230 interviews over a four-year period with CS students at Carnegie Mellon University. Thirty non-CS undergraduates were also interviewed. The gender distribution among the CS students was 51 females and 46 males. Among the females there were 24 European Americans, 16 International students, 8 Asian Americans, and 3 African Americans. Among the males there were 28 European Americans, 7 International students, 6 African Americans, and 5 Hispanics. Margolis and Fisher did not disaggregate the students beyond the issue of gender, except when international students were considered.

Almost every woman in this study came to CS by being a "math and science" student in high school, enjoying problem solving, doing puzzles, and the like. Beyer [5] replicated these findings in a smaller population at another single institution; her work is discussed later. Margolis and Fisher also confirmed how influential home environments (i.e., family) are for students' developing an interest in CS. This reflects positively on Lent's work. Interest is an element of the SCCT, and family support or lack of it is part of the social supports or barriers of the model.

Although Margolis and Fisher had numerous findings, two resonated with the PIs and warranted further investigation. The first was the concept of "computing with a purpose." Women find the study of CS more persuasive and meaningful when connected to other fields in human and social contexts. The second was the notion of Stereotype Threat. Steele [21] defined Stereotype Threat as the danger of being viewed through the lens of a negative stereotype, or the fear of doing something that would inadvertently confirm that stereotype. In subsequent work Steele [22] suggested that stereotype vulnerability might explain the decline of interest especially among women in male dominated fields and among African Americans in academic settings in general. The PIs wanted to include in the pilot study survey components that would test the affinity of women to programming in context and the impact of Stereotype Threat.

2.3 Cohoon

In 1999, Cohoon [8] suggested that gender characteristics such as early sex role socialization, mathematical achievement, computer interests, etc. were not sufficient to explain the disproportionate loss of women from CS. Her unit of study was the CS department as opposed to individual CS students. The original work looked at all 22 Virginia colleges and universities that granted CS degrees and tracked the retention of declared CS majors (sophomores, juniors, and seniors) from Fall 1992 through Spring 1996, with no new cohorts being added each year. To avoid confounds, only those students who switched to a different major at the same institution were considered part of the departmental attrition rate; those who dropped out of the institution or transferred to another institution were excluded from consideration. The observed result was that female attrition rates varied by CS department more than male attrition rates. Although the analysis may not be generalized to the entire U. S., it does suggest that departmental characteristics might overcome or exaggerate gender differences.

A follow-on study expanded the population to 23 CS departments at Virginia institutions from 1992 to 1997 and added 23 biology/life sciences departments at the same institutions [9]. In addition to the analysis of departmental attrition data, there was qualitative analysis of interview data (chair, faculty, and students at 5 CS departments) and discipline comparisons (CS versus biology/life sciences) of quantitative survey data. The findings were that faculty practices, the availability of same-sex peer support, and institutional and community environment influenced CS gendered attrition. Faculty practices included mentoring, teaching enjoyment, and believing that faculty share responsibility for success with their students. Departments with higher female proportions of enrollment were more likely to retain women at comparable rates to men. Institutional environment included such things as the department having at least one woman faculty member and above average support from the institution.

The PIs wanted to include in the pilot study elements that would investigate Cohoon's findings by way of a sampling of a national population of students. Where CS and biology had been compared, the PIs wanted to compare different computing disciplines. They also wanted to compare first-year students in computing and non-computing disciplines. Furthermore, there was the question of what might be revealed when ethnicity was factored into the study. Typically in CS departments at HBCUs, there are an equal number or more of women than men. Analysis of NSF data from 1989 to 1997 revealed that HBCUs awarded African American women CS degrees in greater numbers than their male counterparts, and the exact opposite was true for African American women and men attending PWIs [17]. A concept of "culture" seems to present itself when students view their institutional environment and faculty practices. Meeden et al. [19] found it difficult to write the cultural survey questions that were administered in Spring 2002 to 133 students in every CS class at two institutions (39 at Bryn Mawr and 94 at Swarthmore). But they found that male and female students often hold different views of the culture within the same CS department. Analyzing

U. S. National Center for Education data (994 institutions granting 41,240 CS/IS degrees in 2001), Barker and Garvin-Doxas [3] found that the overall nature of the institution, along with its culture and teaching, has predictive power for women persisting in CS/IS. Is culture driven more by institution, department, discipline, ethnicity, or gender?

2.4 Beyer

Beyer et al. [5] also did a multivariate investigation, both gender differences and discipline differences – CS versus non-CS, but the unit of study was students. Fifty-six students were involved in this study, all from the University of Wisconsin – Parkside, and the data were collected in Fall 2001. The students were each paid $8. Twenty-four students were female and 32 were male. Twenty-eight of the 56 students were CS majors and 28 were not (14 were Business majors, 6 were in other majors, and 8 did not indicate their course of study). All the CS majors were in an Introduction to CS course and the non-CS majors were enrolled in a Computer Productivity class. The ethnic distribution of the students was one African American (2%), four Asians (7%), five Hispanics (9%), and 46 Caucasians (82%). Some of the variables studied were educational goals and interests, stereotypes and knowledge of CS, support and encouragement, and attitudes toward CS courses and instructors. There were more than 35 findings from this study. Listed below are some findings that will be referred to later in this paper:

1. There was no gender difference in the number of hours spent on schoolwork per week.
2. CS students spent significantly more time on their schoolwork than did non-CS students.
3. More men than women had, outside of class assignments / requirements, installed hardware (e.g., RAM, hard drive, etc.) in a computer.
4. There was no gender or CS versus non-CS differences at first computer use age.
5. There was no gender or CS versus non-CS differences for the estimated percentage of women computer scientists.
6. There was no gender or CS versus non-CS differences in support and encouragement from others.
7. There was no gender or CS versus non-CS differences in perceptions of the CS faculty, the social atmosphere in the CS department, and programmatic issues.

This study had elements that are found in the SCCT, but provided additional elements targeted at the student population in the computing disciplines. Overlapping elements included educational goals and interests as well as support and encouragement. The study had strong elements of computer self-efficacy and attempted to capture the "culture" of CS in courses and faculty. The PIs gained insights from this work and used many of the survey questions in the pilot instrument.

3. PILOT STUDY

At many institutions in the U. S., a "major" cannot be declared until the sophomore year. For this reason, the PIs avoided the word using instead the word "discipline." Survey questions were posed as, "In your discipline, ..." and use of the subject's demographic information provided the means for response distillation. This also facilitated distinguishing responses from subjects in any of the computing disciplines as well as the non-computing disciplines while focusing the subjects on their discipline. The former is important because a recent study of a state higher education system reported that there were significant differences in the population of women in CS, IS, and IT [20]. The latter is important in determining if there is any variation in how first-year students see the difficulty of their discipline.

Psychometric properties of survey scales are not typically a topic of discussion among computing discipline faculty. However, such properties play an important role in the reliability and validity of the instrument used in obtaining inferential results. With all the variables seemingly impacting gender differences in the computing disciplines as well as adding concerns about ethnicity and culture, there are a plethora of scales from which to select, all of which have established psychometric properties. The problem in the pilot study was one of selection. The scales of Lent and Beyer were easy to include. However, even though the SCCT has a self-efficacy component, other researchers suggest the importance of math self-efficacy, and should not computer self-efficacy be included as well? Scales to test for Stereotype Threat are not abundant, but scales to test for the concept of "computing with a purpose" do not appear to exist. The survey items for Stereotype Threat came from Steele whereas items to determine "computing with a purpose" were developed by the PIs. There was also the question of "culture." Not knowing with certainty which scales might be more appropriate than others, the pilot incorporated too many of them and took an hour or more to complete.

Thanks to a very dedicated group of higher education partners and their students the pilot study helped the PIs find their way. The pilot study took place in Spring 2004 and analysis of the data was accomplished during the summer. Students were paid $10 to take the survey. One hundred ten students took the survey (36 from two HBCUs, 73 from two PWIs, and 1 did not specify); of these 44 were female and 66 males. Seventy-one students were in a computing discipline and 39 were in a variety of non-computing disciplines (Anthropology, Business, Communications, etc.). In both groups, the majority of the students were not in their first year. The ethnic distribution of the students was 40 African Americans (36%), three Asians (2%), two Hispanics (2%), 57 Caucasians (52%), one Multiracial (1%), six indicated Other (5%), and one who did not respond (1%).

4. SOME FINDINGS

The intent of a pilot study is analogous to a rehearsal. A myriad of flaws and failings are typically revealed and these are addressed prior to the launch of the study. The PIs' pilot study served that purpose. The scales used in the pilot were reviewed in light of the data; some scales were discarded, others modified, and yet others left as is. The pilot had almost 600 questions, but the study will have fewer than 200 and take less than 30 minutes to complete.

Even though pilot studies are not typically used to render results, sometimes when the evidence is strong comments can be made. Since Beyer's work was involved in the pilot, and the pilot had a larger and more diverse sampling giving greater ethnic and discipline distributions, the PIs believe it appropriate to highlight some findings. Substituting computing discipline for CS, evidence from the pilot supported findings 1, 3, 4, 6, and 7. The pilot found evidence supporting a variant of 6: There was no gender or computing discipline versus non-computing discipline differences in support and encouragement from family. The pilot found no significant difference with regard to finding 2; this is probably due to a variation in responses, which affects the statistical tests.

In the pilot the CS question that had resulted in finding 5 was replicated to ask about women in CIS and CE as well as African American women in all three disciplines. The pilot found that there was no significant computing discipline versus non-computing discipline differences in responses. However, females compared to males estimated significantly more women and African American women with CE degrees. African American females compared to Caucasian females estimated significantly more African American women in all three disciplines. These ethnicity findings need further investigation.

5. END OF BEGINNING

The purpose of this paper is to document some of the intricacies of the "incredible shrinking pipeline" problem and some of the many efforts in various disciplines to develop a model for it. With the completion of a pilot study, the PIs climbed onto the shoulders of giants, developing a survey instrument that will investigate: Collective self-esteem, Computer self-efficacy, Coping self-efficacy, Gender role, Goal, Interest, Math self-efficacy, Outcomes expectation, Self-efficacy, Social support and/or barriers, Stereotype threat, and computing with a purpose.

6. ACKNOWLEDGMENTS

This material is based upon work supported in part by the National Science Foundation under Grant No. HRD-0332780, Microsoft Inc., and Apogen Technologies Inc. Any opinions, findings, and conclusions or recommendations expressed herein are those of the authors and do not necessarily reflect the views of the National Science Foundation, Microsoft, or Apogen Technologies.

Special thanks to the Higher Education Partners involved in the pilot study: Appalachian State University (Cindy Norris and Dianne Dula), George Washington University (Rachelle Heller), Winston-Salem University (Elva Jones), and Xavier University of Louisiana (Lynda Louis).

7. REFERENCES

[1] Bandura, A. Self-efficacy: Toward a Unifying Theory of Behavioral Change. *Psychological Review, 84* (1977), 191-215.

[2] Bandura, A. *Social Foundations of Thoughts and Actions: A Social Cognitive Theory.* Prentice-Hall, Englewood Cliffs, NJ, 1986.

[3] Barker, L. and Garvin-Doxas, K. Poster: The Effects of Institutional Characteristics on Participation of Women in Computer Science Bachelors Degree Programs. *ITiCSE'03,* June 30 – July 2, 2003, Thessaloniki, Greece, 242.

[4] Betz, N. and Hackett, G. The Relationship of Mathematics Self-efficacy Expectations to Selection of Science-based College Majors. *Journal of Vocational Behavior, 23* (1983) 329-345.

[5] Beyer, S., Rynes, K., Perrault, J., Hay, K. and Haller, S. Gender Differences in Computer Science Students. *ACM SIGCSE Bulletin – inroads, 35,* 1 (2003), 49-53.

[6] Borg, A. What Draws Women to and Keeps Women in Computing? *The Annals of the New York Academy of Sciences, 869* (1999), 102-109

[7] Camp, T. The Incredible Shrinking Pipeline. *CACM, 40,* 10 (1997), 103-110.

[8] Cohoon, J. Departmental Differences Can Point the Way to Improving Female Retention in Computer Science. *ACM SIGCSE, 31,* 1 (1999) 198-202.

[9] Cohoon, J. Toward Improving Female Retention in the Computer Science Major. *CACM, 44,* 5 (2001), 108-114.

[10] Czetli, S. Business Scene: Why aren't more women in tech fields? The Interactive Edition of the Pittsburgh Post-Gazette, www.post-gazette.com/pg/pp/03093/171152.stm.

[11] Dryburgh, H. Underrepresentation of Girls and Women in Computer Science: Classification of 1990s Research. *Journal of Educational Computing Research, 23,* 2 (2000), 181-200.

[12] Hackett, G. and Betz, N. A Self-efficacy Approach to the Career Development of Women. *Journal of Vocational Behavior, 18* (1981) 326-336.

[13] Lent, R., Brown, S. and Hackett, G. Toward a Unified Social Cognitive Theory of Career/Academic Interest, Choice and Performance. *Journal of Vocational Behavior*, 45 (1994) 79-122.

[14] Lent, R., Brown, S., Schmidt, J., Brenner, B., Lyons, H. and Treistman, D. Social Cognitive Predictors of Engineering Students' Academic Goals: Do Sex or University Type Moderate Predictor-criterion Relations? *Proceedings of the 111th Annual Convention of the American Psychological Association,* Toronto, Canada, 2003.

[15] Lent, R., Lopez, F., and Bieschke, K. Mathematics Self-efficacy: Sources and Relation to Science-based Career Choice. *Journal of Counseling Psychology, 38* (1991) 424-430.

[16] Lent, R., Lopez, F., and Bieschke, K. Predicting Mathematics-related Choice and Success Behaviors. *Journal of Vocational Behavior, 42* (1993) 223-236.

[17] Lopez, A. and Schulte, L. African American Women in the Computing Sciences: A group to be studied. *SIGCSE'02,* February 27-March 3, 2002, Covington, KY, 87-90.

[18] Margolis, J. and Fisher, A. *Unlocking the Clubhouse: Women in Computing.* The MIT Press, Cambridge, MA, 2002.

[19] Meeden, L., Newhall, T., Blank, D. and Kumar, D. Using Departmental Surveys to Assess Computing Culture: Quantifying Gender Differences in the Classroom. *ITiCSE'03,* June 30 – July 2, 2003, Thessaloniki, Greece, 188-192.

[20] Randall, C., Price, B., and Reichgelt, H. Women in Computing Programs: Does the Incredible Shrinking Pipeline Apply to All Computing Programs? *ACM SIGCSE Bulleting – inroads, 35,* 4 (2003) 55-59

[21] Steele, C. Race and the Schooling of Black Americans. *The Atlantic Monthly, 4* (1992) 68-78.

[22] Steele, C. A Threat in the Air: How Stereotypes Shape Intellectual Identity and Performance. *American Psychologist 52,* 6 (1997) 613-629.

Factors Influencing the Shrinking Pipeline in High Schools: A Sector-Based Analysis of the Israeli High School System

Larisa Eidelman and Orit Hazzan
Department of Education in Technology & Science
Technion - Israel Institute of Technology
Haifa, Israel 32000
<elarisa , oritha @ techunix.technion.ac.il>

ABSTRACT

The study described in this article continues research on gender-related issues in Computer Science education by focusing on the differences between two sectors in the Israeli high school system – the Jewish sector (majority) and the Arab sector (minority). As it turns out, the under-representation of female high school students in CS studies is significantly more salient in the majority sector. This study explores this situation and attempts to explain it. We also explain how the findings of this research can be applied to other countries and societies.

Categories and Subject Descriptors

K.3.2 [**Computers and Education**]: Computers and Information Science Education – *CS education.*

General Terms

Human Factors.

Keywords

Computer science education, high school, gender, culture, Israel.

1. INTRODUCTION

Worldwide surveys indicate that the number of women studying undergraduate-level Computer Science (CS) is constantly decreasing [3]. According to Galpin [5], the low participation of women in the computing studies is recognized worldwide. As it turns out, the situation is similar among high school students as well. However, while many studies are carried out at the university level and programs are implemented in order to change the situation, high school students do not attract such attention. In Israel too, as far as we know, no research has ever been performed that focused on female high school students studying CS. This article presents such a study. Specifically, it focuses on high school students studying advanced-level CS.

Based on data collected in Israel, significant differences were found in the percentages of female high school students studying advanced-level CS among different sectors. More specifically, while the percentage of female high school students studying advanced-level CS is about 50% for the Arab *minority* sector, the percentage of female students studying CS at the same level among the Jewish *majority* sector is only about 25%.

SIGCSE'05, February 23-27, 2005, St. Louis, Missouri, USA.

Different studies around the world identified various factors that discourage women from studying CS and from persisting in the field. By focusing on the Israeli high school female students studying CS at the highest level, we suggest that the research presented in this article may partially explain the above-mentioned phenomenon.

2. RESEARCH BACKGROUND

Margolis and Fisher [7] suggest that the under-representation of women in computing fields is important on two levels: On the personal level and on the societal-cultural level. Therefore, they suggest that the significant differences between the representation of women and men in the CS fields in general, and in high school CS classes in particular, should not be ignored. This under-representation has a special significance in Israel, a small country in which the efficient utilization of its human resources is of great importance.

2.1 Under-Representation of Women in the Computing Fields – A Worldwide Perspective

As mentioned in the introduction, the under-representation of women in the computing fields is recognized worldwide [5]. However, recent in-depth analysis of this phenomenon reveals that the problem is not universal, but rather is restricted to specific countries and cultures [1, 5, 6]. More specifically, in certain countries and cultures, such as Greece, Turkey, Mauritius, and Romanic countries (e.g. France and Italy), the representation of women in CS is relatively high and constant, in contrast to the US, Anglo-Saxon countries, Scandinavian and German-speaking countries, in which the representation of women in CS is relatively low and decreasing. Accordingly, it is reasonable to assume that cultural factors play an important role in encouraging or discouraging women from studying CS.

2.2 Under-Representation of Women in the Computing Fields – An Israeli Perspective

The Israeli high school CS syllabus includes the core of the discipline and is considered to be relatively advanced in comparison to the CS syllabi of other countries. The syllabus is modular and thus enables the study of CS on different levels, ranging from the basic level to a more advanced one. Most of the advanced-level students take the CS matriculation exams at the end of 12th grade, after having taken (and successfully passed) the lower-level exam at the end of 11th or 10th grade. In most cases, advanced-level CS students are required by the school to study advanced-level mathematics in parallel to their CS studies.

Most Jewish and Arab students attend separate educational systems with similar curricula in most subjects. The CS syllabus is identical in both systems and the only differences are in the teaching language and the language of the matriculation exam.

High school is a critical point in the CS pipeline, at which many female students are lost, mainly in the Jewish sector. As mentioned previously, a significant difference exists in the percentages of female high school students studying advanced-level CS between the Arab and Jewish sectors. Specifically, while 50% of those studying high school CS in the Arab *minority* sector are female students, only 25% of those studying the same level of high school CS in the Jewish *majority* sector are female students. This situation prompted us to initiate this research, which examines the factors that influence the enrollment and persistence of Israeli high school students in advanced-level CS studies. In addition to gender difference research, the co-existence of two populations (Arab and Jewish) in Israel provides an opportunity to examine cultural differences as well.

There is, in fact, another advantage of conducting such research in Israel. One solution that has been suggested for countries in which women are under-represented in CS (and which would like to change this situation) is to visit countries in which this problem does not exist, and to identify the cultural differences, as well as actions taken to encourage women to study CS, which may explain why women in such countries find CS an attractive field. From this point of view, Israel is a perfect place for such research. Specifically, in order to understand the low participation of Jewish female high school students in CS, there is no need to visit another country. It is sufficient to investigate the differences that exist between the two populations that live in the same country and study according to the same curriculum, one of which (the majority) suffers from this under-representation, while the other population (the minority) does not.

The research described in this paper takes advantage of this situation. The specific research questions were:

- What considerations are involved in the decision of Jewish and Arab high school female students to study advanced-level CS?
- What considerations influence the persistence in such studies in each sector?

3. RESEARCH METHOD

The research examined both gender and cultural differences among Israeli high school students studying advanced-level CS. Three comparisons were conducted, as follows: Jewish female students vs. Jewish male students, Arab female students vs. Arab male students and Jewish female students vs. Arab female students. This paper focuses on the differences between Jewish and Arab female students.

3.1 Research Population

The research population consisted of 12th grade CS students from 9 typical high schools, from both sectors (5 schools from the Jewish sector, 4 schools from Arab sector). The schools were selected based on the agreement and permission given by their principals and the willingness of the CS teachers in those schools to let their classes participate in the research.

146 students participated in the research. Table 1 describes the distribution of the students according to gender and sector.

Table 1. Distribution of research population

	Total	Male	Female
Number of students from the Jewish sector	90	(72%) 65	(28%) 25
Number of students from the Arab sector	56	(39%) 22	(61%) 34
Total	**146**		

The CS teachers and school counselors were included in the research population as well.

3.2 Research Tools

The research applied both quantitative and qualitative approaches. Data were gathered using the following research tools: comprehensive questionnaires completed by all students, ethnographic interviews with female students, and classroom observations during CS lessons. In addition, interviews were conducted with CS teachers and school counselors.

Questionnaires: The comprehensive questionnaire included mostly closed questions in addition to several open questions. The questionnaire addressed the following topics: personal and demographic information; ICT usage; areas of interest in higher education; attitudes towards CS studies; perceptions of CS; stereotypes related to CS; support and encouragement resources; factors that may influence the decision to study CS; attitudes towards the under-representation of women; and considerations in choosing a high school major. The questionnaire was administered to all students in the selected CS classes.

The data collected in the questionnaires were coded and analyzed using the statistical application SPSS. Closed questions were analyzed using statistical tests such as the Kruskal-Wallis test, Mann-Whitney test and logistic regression; open questions were analyzed using content analysis techniques.

Interviews: Ethnographic interviews with 18 Jewish and Arab female students were semi-structured interviews lasting between 45 to 90 minutes. All interviews were transcribed and analyzed using content analysis techniques.

Observations: Observations were made during CS lessons in different schools and classrooms, both during lab lessons and traditional classroom lessons. The manuscripts of the observations were also transcribed and analyzed.

4. PRELIMINARY RESULTS

This section presents data from the questionnaires and the interviews related to three topics: support and encouragement, future and success orientation, and the perception of CS. These data will be discussed in Section 5.

4.1 Support and Encouragement

Several questions in the questionnaire addressed the issue of the support and encouragement to study CS that students receive from different sources. One of the direct questions was: "Who encouraged you to choose CS studies?" Figure 1 presents the distribution of answers to this question.

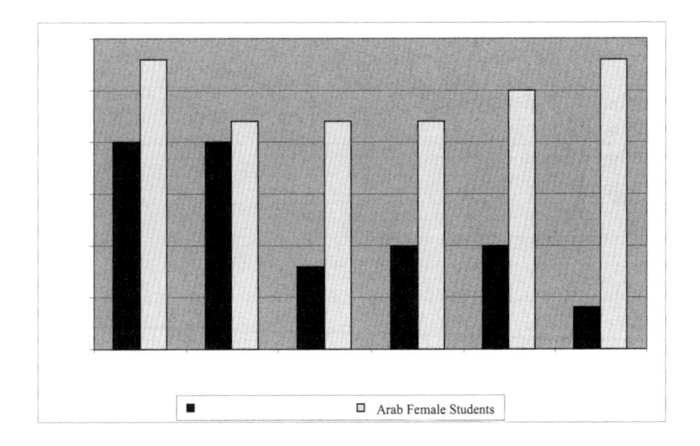

Figure 1. Percentages of females' encouragement by others

Figure 1 reflects an unequivocal conclusion: Arab female high school students (*n=34*) receive much more encouragement to choose CS than do their Jewish counterparts (*n=25*). Specifically, Arab female high school students are encouraged more by their mothers (56% vs. 40%), fathers (44% vs. 40%), siblings (44% vs. 16%), friends (44% vs. 20%), acquaintances who had studied CS (50% vs. 20%) and – with the greatest difference – by their teachers (56% vs. 8%).

In another part of the questionnaire, the students were asked to rate their agreement with the following statement: "*Our school encourages its students to study advanced-level CS*". The difference between the two populations was significant (p=0.000): 91% of the Arab female high school students agreed with the statement compared to only 28% of the Jewish female high school students.

Additional evidence can be found in students' answers to the question in which students were asked to rate the influence of different factors on their choice to study advanced-level CS. Significant differences were found in the influence of the following 4 factors:

a. "*Supporting and helpful CS teachers*": On a 1-3 scale, the Arab female high school students gave an average rank of 2.4, while the average rank given by Jewish female high school students was 1.2 (p=0.000).

b. "*School recommendation (teacher, counselor, principal)*". Arab female students gave an average rank of 2.0 vs. 1.2 by Jewish female students (p=0.000).

c. "*Family recommendation (parents, siblings, uncles/aunts)*": Arab female students gave an average rank of 2.3 vs. 1.9 by Jewish female students (p=0.024).

d. "*Friends' recommendation*": Arab female students gave an average rank of 2.3 vs. an average ranking of 1.4 by the Jewish female students (p=0.000).

In their answer to one of the questionnaire's open questions, Jewish students explained: "*Parents don't encourage the girls enough to begin studying CS and since the female students are influenced by their female friends' attitudes towards computing, they don't turn to CS studies (and not because of a lack of required capabilities, since they do have them)*" or "*There is not enough encouragement for girls! They are afraid CS is a difficult and complicated subject!!! Similar to advanced-level mathematics, where we are a lot of girls, the same can be true for CS as well!!!!!*".

The difference in the participation of female high school students in CS studies between the two sectors is reflected not only in the number of female students attracted to study this subject, but also in the number of female students that persist in their CS studies. As it turns out, Jewish female students are more likely, compared to their Arab counterparts, to abandon their CS studies during the high school years (especially at the beginning of 12th grade, when the material becomes more complicated).

In the interviews, the female students were asked about their own and their friends' persistence in CS studies. Here is an example of an Arab female student's attitude to this issue, which highlights the importance of the support the female Arab students receive from their environment: "*It depends if someone encourages them at all. Look, there are many girls who think that they ought to be satisfied by little, by staying at home and helping out. There are girls who want to be the ideal woman, to study and to do things and get the equality we need, so they fight... Girls need more encouragement than boys, because we (the Arab girls) have a lot of burden and responsibility, more than the boys have.*" When encouraged by the interviewer to elaborate, "*In what sense?*" she explained: "*In all aspects, at home and in the society, since we are criticized more. And if ... she doesn't have the strength to struggle with the criticism and the studies, it is difficult for her, so she needs someone to encourage her more.*"

4.2 Future and Success Orientation

Another question that appeared in the questionnaire asked the students to grade the influence of future- and success-oriented factors on their decision to study advanced-level CS. Significant differences (p=0.036) were found in respect to several statements: The average rating (on a 1-3 scale) by Arab female students of the statement "A *matriculation certificate with CS will help me find a job*", was 2.3 compared to 1.8 among their Jewish counterparts. The average rating by Arab female students of the statement "*CS is an essential subject for academic studies*" was 2.5 vs. an average grade of 1.9 given by Jewish female students (p=0.001).

In the questionnaire, the female students were asked about the field they plan to major in, in their academic studies. 45.5% of the Jewish female students were still undecided as to what they would like to major in at the university, as opposed to 9.1% of the Arab female students. 31.8% of the Jewish female students intended to major in a CS related subject, as opposed to 21.2% of Arab female students. 22.7% of the Jewish female students indicated subjects that are unrelated to CS vs. 69.7% of the Arab female students. Figure 2 illustrates these findings.

When asked about gender-related considerations involved in the choice of majors, some of the female Arab students stressed their duties as wives and mothers: "*The boys consider how to earn a living, but the girls consider both how to earn a living and be at home*"; "*A girl, when she decides what subject to study, thinks first about all the time she will need in order to take care of the children she will have in the future, and only then does she think about what subject to study. The boys first think directly about themselves*".

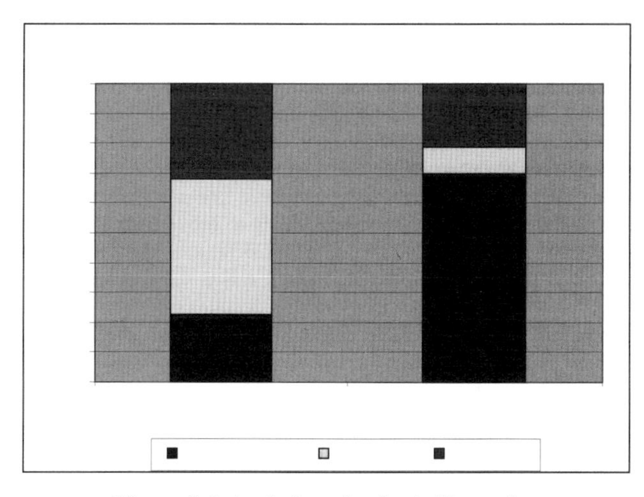

Figure 2. Intended academic studies major

At the same time, however, at the high school level, female Arab students conceive of CS as a way to increase their self-esteem. During her interview, one Arab female student was asked: "*Is it possible that Arab female students find studying CS to be a way to increase the chances of finding a job and achieving economic independence?*" The answer was: "*Yes, sure. CS is like I have a job. People will regard me as...if I have a higher status. They will see a girl with intellect, not just a simple girl. There is a different perspective on a girl who is studying CS. There is more appreciation...When my parents tell their friends that I'm studying CS it gives them more pride and appreciation.*"

4.3. Attitudes towards CS Studies

A difference in the female students' perspectives was observed also with respect to their conception of the field of CS. As can be seen in Table 2, the female students from the two sectors view CS in a significantly different way. Only 32% of the Jewish female students who are already studying CS think that CS is important. A higher percentage of Arab female students think that CS is difficult and frightening, but yet a much higher percentage of Arab female students like and enjoy CS.

Table 2. Attitudes towards CS among Jewish and Arab female students

Attitude toward CS	Jewish female students	Arab female students	Difference
Interesting	68%	85%	**
Difficult	16%	35%	**
Essential	56%	38%	**
Boring	16%	9%	*
Enjoyable	28%	53%	**
Frightening	8%	21%	**
Important	32%	77%	**
Liked	8%	50%	**
Surprising	0%	47%	**

$^{**}p<0.01$, $^{*}p<0.05$

In addition, one of the questions in the questionnaire asked students to rate factors that relate to attitudes towards CS studies, according to their influence on their decision to study advanced-level CS. Significant differences were found in the average rankings (on a 1-3 scale) by Arab female students and Jewish female students with respect to the following statements: "*CS is a prestigious subject*" – 2.4 by Arab female students vs. 2.0 by Jewish female students (p=0.049), "*I conceive of CS studies as a challenge for success*" – 2.4 by Arab female students vs. 1.9 by Jewish female students (p=0.035) and "*I enjoy studying CS*" - 2.4 by Arab female students vs. 2.1 by Jewish female students (p=0.032). When asked about their agreement with the statement "*Studying advanced-level CS is a challenge*", 82% of Arab female students agreed with this statement as opposed to only 36% of the Jewish female students.

5. DISCUSSION

In the discussion we will explain and discuss the findings presented in the previous sections.

5.1 Subject Diversity: Is it Good or Bad?

Currently, the Jewish and Arab sectors in Israel study in separate educational systems. As mentioned previously, both educational systems have a similar structure in terms of the basic curriculum. In what follows, we explain the above findings through some of the structural differences that do, nevertheless, exist between the two educational systems.

High school students can choose to specialize (advanced-level studies) in specific subjects taken from two groups: Group A includes the traditional scientific fields: mathematics, physics, chemistry and biology; and Group B includes CS, economy, communication, psychology, sociology, languages, law, art, drama, music, tourism and theater. As it turns out, the most prominent difference between the two educational systems is in the diversity of the subjects offered at an advanced level. Both systems offer the same variety of Group A subjects; however, while most Jewish schools offer a variety of Group B subjects, most Arab schools offer very few subjects from Group B. As a result, when 10th grade students are required to choose specialization subjects for their high school years, Jewish students have many options to choose from in Group B compared to Arab students who have less choice. Specifically, Jewish female students have the option of choosing traditional "feminine" subjects (like psychology) while Arab female students are, in most cases, restricted to a choice of more "masculine" subjects (such as CS). Moreover, most of the other Group B subjects are considered by students to be easier and to require less effort compared to CS. Thus, for Jewish female students the alternatives seem much more attractive.

This situation is reflected clearly in the interviews, in which the female students were asked: "*Which subjects did you have doubts about when you had to choice your majors?*" A typical answer given by a Jewish female student was: "*I didn't choose physics, because I didn't really see myself there ... I didn't feel the connection in any way. And versus chemistry I had drama, so I preferred drama, because I felt a connection. Later I changed drama to social sciences and instead of physics I took CS*". Such answers clarify the idea that because of the alternatives that exist in the Jewish schools, the choice of CS is not trivial or obvious. A typical answer of an Arab female student was: "*There were biology, physics, chemistry and CS. I had doubts between CS and physics*". Arab female students were then asked what their choice would have been had their school offered more Group B subjects, such as art. Following is an answer given by one of the Arab female student: "*Yes. First of all it's easier and it explains why there are more boys then girls (in the Jewish sector), because boys won't take drama, theater or art though they will take CS. It suits them more. But the girls think it's easier, so why not. It suits the girl's personality*".

Ultimately, we see that the limited option in the Arab sector actually benefits Arab female students and exposes them to prestigious areas, such as CS. At the same time, the existing diversity offered in Jewish high schools, while aiming to enable all students to study subjects according to their capabilities and areas of interest, draws female students away from CS. *Well, subject diversity - is it good or bad?*

5.2 High School Female Students As a Minority or Majority: What Can Be Gained?

In this section, we analyze the situation described in this article by examining the unique characteristics of the Arab–Israeli society that are likely to influence Arab female students to choose and persist in CS studies. Furthermore, we ask what can be learned and adopted from such findings, by the Jewish-Israeli society in particular, and by other countries dealing with a similar high school female student minority in CS in general.

As shown in Section 4.1, noticeable differences exist in the extent of encouragement Arab female students receive from various agents, especially from teachers, in comparison to Jewish female students. Even in light of the renowned, greater appreciation and respect given to teachers in the Arab sector, the differences, we suggest, are still enormous. One possible explanation for such an extent of encouragement is based on findings of other studies that explored cultural and familial differences between Arab and Jewish adolescents. According to these studies, since Arab students are part of an Eastern, collective culture, as well as a minority group, it is likely that they are "pushed" by their parents to higher scholastic achievement in order to improve their social status [8].

In addition, Arab students perceive their family environment as more authoritarian than do their Jewish counterparts. The hierarchical structure of the Arab family is based on age, and traditionally requires the young to obey the old and adhere to their expectations [8]. Furthermore, it was found that peer influence in the Arab sector is much more positive than it is in the Jewish sector, possibly because of the relative independence from family and friends that exists in the Jewish sector [2]. This might explain the lower influence of parents and peers in the Jewish sector.

Despite the fact that Arab female students are about half in CS classrooms in high schools, according to their future orientations (Section 4.2), this will probably not help to expand the "shrinking pipeline" in Arab sector. Most of the female students have already decided on their future professions and only a small percent of female Arab students are considering majoring in CS. Thus, the better starting point might not carry over to higher education and industry.

The picture painted by the results of our study is that Arab female students perceive CS studies as a way to provide themselves with increased professional opportunities and especially social status (Section 4.3). This assumption is reinforced by results of general research focusing on the future orientation of Arab adolescents, which concluded that Israeli-Arabs perceive high school education as a crucial element in the opening up of employment opportunities and in achieving a higher economic status [2]. In order not to be inferior in the eyes of their family in particular and society in general, it seems that Arab female students are highly motivated to study CS since they consider these studies as a way in which to prove their skills and capabilities. They also hold relatively positive attitudes toward CS compared to Jewish female students (Section 4.3). Since it was found that positive attitudes of the female students towards computing influenced their continued enrollment in computer courses [4], the attraction and retaining levels of CS studying among the Arab female students is clear.

Different social and cultural characteristics stimulate the extensive encouragement the Arab female students receive. Naturally, we can conclude that encouragement may be one solution for attracting female students to study CS and keep them there. By creating an atmosphere that supports the development of positive attitudes towards CS, we can probably attract more female students to study advanced levels of CS.

6. ACKNOWLEDGMENTS

We would like to thank the Samuel Neaman Institute for Advanced Studies in Science and Technology and the Technion MANLAM Fund for their generous support of this research.

7. REFERENCES

[1] Adams, J., Bauer, V. & Baichoo, S. (2003). An Expanding Pipeline: Gender in Mauritius, *Inroads-SIGCSE Bulletin* **35**(1), pp. 59-63.

[2] Azaiza, F. & Ben-Ari, A.T. (1997). Minority Adolescents' Future orientation: The Case of Arabs Living in Israel, *International Journal of Group Tensions* **27**(1), pp. 43-57.

[3] Camp, T. (2002). Message from the Guest Editor, *Inroads-SIGCSE Bulletin, Special Issue – Women and Computing*, pp. 6-8.

[4] Charlton, J.P. & Birkett, P.E. (1999). An Integrative Model of Factors Related to Computing Course Performance, *Journal of Educational Computing Research* **20**(3), pp. 237-257.

[5] Galpin, V. (2002). Women in Computing Around the World, *Inroads-SIGCSE Bulletin, Special Issue – Women and Computing*, pp. 94-100.

[6] Lopez, A. & Schulte, L. (2002). African American Women in the Computing Sciences: A group to be studied, *Inroads-SIGCSE Bulletin* **34**(1), pp. 87-90.

[7] Margolis, J. & Fisher, A. (2002). *Unlocking the Clubhouse-Women in Computing*, MIT press.

[8] Peleg-Popko, O., Klingman, A. & Abu-Hanna Nahhas, I.(2003). Cross-Cultural and Familial Differences between Arab and Jewish Adolescents in Test Anxiety, *International Journal of Intercultural Relations* **27**, pp. 525-541.

Programming: Factors that Influence Success

Susan Bergin
Department of Computer Science,
National University of Ireland Maynooth,
Maynooth, Co. Kildare.
sbergin@cs.may.ie

Ronan Reilly
Department of Computer Science,
National University of Ireland Maynooth,
Maynooth, Co. Kildare.
ronan@cs.may.ie

ABSTRACT

This paper documents a study, carried out in the academic year 2003-2004, on fifteen factors that may influence performance on a first year object-oriented programming module. The factors included prior academic experience, prior computer experience, self-perception of programming performance and comfort level on the module and specific cognitive skills. The study found that a student's perception of their understanding of the module had the strongest correlation with programming performance, $r = 0.76, p < 0.01$. In addition, Leaving Certificate (LC) mathematics and science scores were shown to have a strong correlation with performance. A regression module, based upon a student's perception of their understanding of the module, gender, LC mathematics score and comfort level was able to account for 79% of the variance in programming performance results.

Categories and Subject Descriptors

K.3.2 [**Computer and Information Science Education**]: Computer science education

General Terms

Human Factors, Measurement, Performance

Keywords

CS1, Programming, Predictors

1. INTRODUCTION

Student retention on third-level (post high school or equivalent) Computer Science (CS) and Information Technology (IT) courses is a significant problem. Students find computer programming difficult and struggle to master the core concepts. A multi-national, multi-institutional study on the programming skills of first year CS students found that students struggled to achieve an average above 30% on assessments administered as part of their study [14]. Furthermore, introductory programming modules tend to have a very high student to lecturer ratio (100:1 or greater) and often lecturers do not know how well students are doing until after the first assessment. In general the first assessment does not take place until six or eight weeks after the module has commenced and given the typically high number of students, marking the assessments can take a considerable length of time. At this stage, it may be too late to intervene to prevent struggling students from failing. Even if intervention is possible, a lecturer is unlikely to know a student well enough or be able to identify individual student problems and therefore recognize the most suitable interventions to make.

The research documented in this paper is part of a longitudinal study on early identifiable factors that influence performance on an introductory programming module. If such factors can be identified then it may be possible to develop a tool to provide an early diagnosis of a student's likely performance on a programming module. Interested parties could use the tool to make more informed decisions on appropriate courses of action and to decide upon personalized interventions that foster a student's intellectual strengths.

2. RELATED RESEARCH

While a considerable amount of research has been carried out on factors that affect programming performance our interest is on factors that affect programming performance on an introductory third-level object-oriented programming module where such factors can be determined early in the academic year. These factors can be categorized as: (1) previous academic and computer experience, (2) cognitive skills, (3) personal information and (4) experience on the module. A brief review of some research studies in each of these categories is presented next.

Previous academic experience and programming experience have often been cited as predictors of programming success. Several studies have found that mathematical ability and exposure to maths courses are important predictors of performance on introductory computer science modules [2, 3, 4, 6, 13, 19]. Similarly, although less studied, performance in and experience of science subjects has also been shown to be important [2, 19]. Studies have also found prior programming experience and non-programming computer experience (for example, experience of computer applications, emailing, game playing and surfing the web) to be related to programming performance [9, 10, 6, 4, 18].

The role of cognitive factors in programming has also received research attention. Certain cognitive factors, including problem-solving, abstract reasoning, problem translation

SIGCSE'05 February 23–27, 2005 St. Louis, Missouri, USA.

skills, logical ability and cognitive style have been identified as possible predictors [7, 12, 11, 15].

Numerous studies have been carried out on demographic and self-reported personal information. Some studies have examined specific attributes related to study, for example preference for working alone or in a group to solve a programming problem and encouragement or support from others to study computers [4, 2, 8].

In recent times researchers have examined the relationship between students' expectations of and experiences on an introductory computing module. A positive relationship between a student's mental models of programming and self-efficacy for programming and performance has recently been identified [18]. The grade a student expected to achieve in an introductory module was found to be the most important indicator of performance in another recent study[17]. A recent longitudinal study found that the most important predictor of students' performance on an introductory computer science course was comfort level, determined by the degree of anxiety a student felt about the course [4].

Although a considerable number of research studies have examined factors that influence programming performance, comparisons between the various studies and application of the results are difficult because the studies are carried out using different parameters. These parameters include:

- the type of students (novice to experienced programmers, academic students to employees),
- the content of the course (some courses are solely programming courses while others are introductory computing courses),
- the programming language being taught (older studies tend to be based on procedural languages),
- the educational setting (many of the research studies are based on the US educational system) and
- the reference criterion (for example continuous assessment, end-of-year exam, job performance).

In the rest of this paper we describe our study, which builds upon existing research, in particular the work of [2, 4], to identify early factors that influence performance of first year students, on an introductory object-oriented programming module, using the Java programming language. The course is based on the Irish educational system and the reference criterion is the overall result achieved on the module.

3. RESEARCH DESIGN

The introductory programming module at our university is composed of a one and a half hour Problem-Based Learning (PBL) workshop, a one and a half hour laboratory session and three one-hour lectures per week over two semesters. Students in Ireland do not study programming in secondary school and the majority of students taking this module have recently completed second level education.

Selection of factors for this study was restricted for a number of reasons, including availability of participants, length of completion time needed for each instrument and stage in year. With this in mind we attempted to examine the relationship between and the predictability of fifteen factors and performance on our introductory module. The factors fall into four broad categories:

1. previous academic and computer experience: as measured by performance in the Irish Leaving Certificate (LC) examinations in mathematics and science subjects and self-reported computer experience,
2. specific cognitive skills: as measured by an in-house cognitive test,
3. personal information: gender, age, work-style preference, encouragement from others and the number of hours per week working at a part-time job and
4. experience on the module: students own perception of how well they are doing and how comfortable they feel with the module material.

Performance on this module is based on continuous assessment (30% of the overall mark) and a final examination (70% of the overall mark). The measure of performance reported upon in this paper is the overall module mark. Continuous assessment and final examination marks render similar results and are reported in [1].

3.1 Participants

The study was carried out in the academic year 2003-2004. Students enrolled in the first year 'Introduction to Programming' module in our department voluntarily participated in this study. Ninety-six students completed the module in the academic year 2003-2004.

3.2 Instruments

Two instruments were used to collect data: a questionnaire and a custom-made cognitive test. The questionnaire collected data on the following items: (1) LC mathematics grade, (2) LC physics grade, (3) LC biology grade, (4) LC chemistry grade, (5) highest LC science grade, (6) comfort level on the module, (7) perceived understanding of the module material, (8) prior programming experience, (9) prior non-programming computer experience, (10) work-style preference (preference to work-alone or as part of a group), (11) encouragement from others to study computer science, (12) number of hours per week working at a (part-time) job. The cognitive test was developed in-house[1] and comprised items involving numerical and letter sequencing, arithmetic reasoning, problem translation skills and logical ability. In addition, information on gender, age and overall module results was available for all students taking the module.

In total 80 students (49 male, 31 female) completed the cognitive test and 30 (19 male, 11 female) students completed the survey. Both instruments were completed in the second semester of the module and data collection for both was paper-based.

4. RESULTS

An a priori analysis was carried out to verify no significant difference existed between the mean overall module scores of the class and the sample. Test assumptions on normality (Kolmogorov-Smirnov test) and the equality of variance (Levine test) were performed and a t-test on the overall results, ($t(124) = 0.795, p = 0.428$), found no significant differences between the mean scores of the class and

[1] Developed by Jacqueline McQuillan, Department of Computer Science, NUI Maynooth.

Table 1: **Pearson correlations for previous academic results and performance**

	LC Maths	LC Phys	LC Chem	LC Bio	High Sci
r	0.46**	0.59*	0.4	0.75*	0.48**
n	30	18	11	10	28
Female only					
r	0.72*	0.89**	0.88	0.93**	0.84**
n	11	7	4	7	11
Male only					
r	0.16	0.27	-0.04	0.9	0.16
n	19	11	7	3	17

** Correlation is significant at the 0.01 level (2-tailed).
* Correlation is significant at the 0.05 level (2-tailed).

the sample. In the remainder of this section the findings on the relationship between each of the factors studied and programming performance is presented, followed by an analysis of the combination of factors that best predicts performance.

4.1 Previous academic and computer experience

To establish the relationship between previous academic experience in mathematics and science, the achievable grades for each subject were ranked, with the highest rank given to the highest possible grade and the lowest rank given to the lowest possible grade. Table 1. provides the Pearson correlations for each of these measures and notable relationships are identified. LC mathematics was found to have a statistically significant relationship with performance, $r = 0.46, p < 0.01$. LC physics was found to be moderately strong and significant, $r = 0.59, p < 0.05$ as was LC biology, $r = 0.75, p < 0.05$ for the final examination. Highest science result, which includes other less commonly studied science subjects, was also found to be statistically significant, $r = 0.48, p < 0.01$. No relationship was found between LC chemistry and performance. Secondary analysis, based on gender revealed that none of the measures were significant for male students and resulted in notably higher correlations for the female students, as shown in Table 1. A recent study on gender differences in LC examinations found that (1) more female students are taking higher level LC examinations than male students and (2) female students are outperforming male students on LC maths and physics examinations (no other science subjects were reviewed in the study) [5]. This may relate to our findings and further research is necessary.

The findings on the relationship between experience in mathematics and science subjects, and programming performance is in line with previous research findings. The strength of the correlations between LC physics scores and particularly LC biology scores and programming performance is interesting and would suggest that science in general has a significant influence on performance. However, the lack of correlation with LC chemistry appears contradictory and further research is required.

Table 2: **Dichotomous values for personal factors**

	Values
Gender	Male, Female
Age	Under 23, 23+
Work style preference	Individual, Group
Encouragement	Yes, No
Part-time employment	No, Yes

Table 3: **Pearson correlations for comfort level and perceived understanding with performance**

	Comfort level	Understanding
r	0.55**	0.76**
n	30	30
Female only		
r	0.62*	0.82**
n	11	11
Male only		
r	0.79**	0.84**
n	19	19

** Correlation is significant at the 0.01 level (2-tailed).
* Correlation is significant at the 0.05 level (2-tailed).

Previous computer experience was measured by prior programming experience and previous non-programming computer experience. In both cases student responses were separated into those with previous experience and those without previous experience. Descriptive statistics for each group are given in Table 4. T-tests for independent samples were used to examine the differences between the overall module results of each group. Before each t-test was carried out assumptions of normality and equality of variance were confirmed. No significant differences were found between students with or without previous programming experience or between students with or without non-programming computer experience and performance module. Although previous research has found previous programming experience and non-programming computing experience to be indicators of success our results may be partially accounted for by the fact that students cannot study programming or application software at examination level in secondary schools in Ireland.

4.2 Specific cognitive skills

A correlation of $r = 0.31, p < 0.01$ was found between performance on the cognitive test and performance on the module. Although this result is weak, subsequent analysis found that a number of items in the test were highly correlated with programming performance. We anticipate that a redesign of the test could result in more significant findings in the future.

4.3 Personal information

Gender, age, work-style preference, encouragement by others and part-time employment were treated as dichotomous

Table 4: **Comparison of the mean and standard deviation for overall results (as a percentage) grouped by: gender, age, work-style preference, encouragement by others, prior programming (Prog. exp.) and non-programming computer experience (Non-prog. comp. exp.)**

		n	Mean (%)	S.D. (%)
Gender	Female	36	51	24
	Male	60	49	22
Age	Under 23	92	50	23
	23+	4	56	28
Work-style preference	Individual	12	50	22
	Group	18	43	23
Encouragement	No	21	44	21
	Yes	9	50	25
Part-time job	No	18	47	24
	Yes	12	45	20
Prog. exp.	None	25	46	23
	Some	5	44	18
Non-prog. comp. exp.	None	4	49	21
	Some	26	45	23

variables for analysis purposes. The possible values of each factor are given in Table 2. Students were grouped according to the responses they provided for each of the factors. Descriptive statistics for each group are given in Table 4. T-tests for independent samples were used to examine the differences between the overall module results for each of the factor values, for example the mean overall module result for male students was compared to the mean overall module result for female students. Before each t-test was carried out assumptions of normality and equality of variance were confirmed. In each instance, the t-tests revealed no significant differences between any of the factors and the overall results on the module. We intend to further examine the relationship between work-style preference and performance, as since the introduction of PBL workshops into the module mean scores have increased, at the top, middle and bottom levels of the class. We feel this is a result of the PBL workshops and students repeating the module appear to concur with us [16].

4.4 Experience on the module

Comfort level was measured as the cumulative response to questions on a student's understanding of programming concepts, difficulty designing programs without help and difficulty for completing lab assignments. Each question had a number of ranked answers and the cumulative rank was used to analyze comfort level. The Pearson correlations are given in table 3. Comfort level was found to be a statistically significant indicator of performance with $r = 0.516, p < .01$.

Understanding was measured by ranked responses to a single question 'How do you rate your level of understanding of the programming module?' A strong significant relationship between understanding and performance was found, $r = 0.76, p < 0.01$.

Given the earlier findings on gender differences between previous academic experience and programming performance, gender based analysis was carried out on comfort level and understanding. Comfort level was found to have a higher correlation with performance for male students.

Like the Cantwell Wilson and Shrock [4] study comfort level was found to be highly correlated with programming performance. The most significant finding, however, is the very strong correlation between a students' perception of their understanding of the programming module. As this study was carried out in the second semester we intend to conduct a further study to identify the point in time perception of module understanding becomes such a reliable indicator. If a similarly high correlation can be found early on in the module then it would be very powerful in diagnosing and subsequently mediating struggling students.

4.5 Regression Analysis

To investigate whether the various factors studied were predictive of performance on the module a number of regression analyzes were conducted. Each analysis was motivated by the literature review, the authors' experience working with first year students and the strength of the correlation coefficients generated in this study. Although, both LC biology and LC physics rendered high correlation coefficients for programming performance, neither variables were directly included in the regression models as the sample size for each was deemed too small (n=10, n=18 respectively). Instead the highest LC science result was included (n=28).

The first model was designed to determine the earliest indicators of programming performance. Consideration was given to gender, previous academic experience, cognitive test score, previous programming and non-programming computer performance, encouragement from others, work-style preference and hours working at a part-time job. Using a stepwise regression method a significant model emerged with $F(2, 27) = 7.113, p < 0.01$ with an adjusted R square =30%. Significant values were found for: LC maths ($\beta = 0.390, p = 0.021$) and gender ($\beta = -0.368, p = 0.028$).

The second model considered all of the predictors used in the first model but also included the results of the first class test. Class tests are typically the first test given to first year students and although they do not test a student's ability to design and code up a solution to a programming problem they do test a students' understanding of basic programming concepts. A stepwise regression method found a significant model of $F(2, 27) = 14.882, p < 0.001$ and adjusted R square =49%. Significant values were found for the class test ($\beta = 0.563, p = 0.000$) and LC maths ($\beta = 0.375, p = 0.01$).

The third model included the predictors from the second model but also considers the results of the first lab test. The lab test is similar to the final examination in that students are required to design and code up a solution to a programming problem. Although the lab test may be a better predictor of the overall result, a trade off takes place in that this information is not available until near the end of the first Semester and at this stage struggling students may have dropped out or given-up hope of succeeding. A stepwise regression method resulted in a significant model of $F(2, 25) = 26.38, p < 0.001$ and an adjusted R square = 65%. Significant factors were found for the first lab test ($\beta = 0.700, p = 0.000$) and highest science result ($\beta = 0.700, p = 0.000$).

The fourth model includes the predictors from the second model but takes into account a students' comfort level with the module and perceived understanding of how they are doing. Using a stepwise regression method a significant model emerged with $F(4,23) = 26.03, p < 0.001$, adjusted R square = 79%. Significant values were found for: understanding ($\beta = 0.505, p = 0.000$), gender ($\beta = -0.494, p = 0.000$), comfort level ($\beta = 0.301, p = 0.022$), and LC maths ($\beta = 0.197, p = 0.047$). If the results of the first lab test is also considered 84% of the variance in performance can be accounted for with $F(4,23) = 36.92, p < 0.001$.

The factors known at the start of the academic year result in a poor prediction of programming performance. The results of the first class test (model 2) and subsequently the first lab exam (model 3) results in an improved prediction ability. However, when a students' perception of their understanding of the module is considered a very strong prediction model occurs. As with the strength of the Pearson correlation coefficient for this variable a further study to determine the stage at which a student's self-perception becomes so accurate would be valuable.

5. CONCLUSIONS

This study examined the relationship and predictive ability between fifteen factors and performance on a programming module. Comfort level on the module, LC maths and LC science scores were shown to have a strong correlation with performance, with notable gender differences identified. A predictive combination of factors was found to be a student's perception of their understanding of the module, comfort level on the module, LC maths score and gender, accounting for 79% of the variance in programming performance.

The study found that the strongest relationship existed between a student's perception of their understanding of the module and programming performance. The need to understand the role of self-perception in the process and to investigate how early it becomes a reliable predictor warrants further research.

6. REFERENCES

[1] S. Bergin and R. Reilly. Discovering the likely performance of novice programmers on an introductory programming module. In *Technical Report NUIM-CS-TR-2004, Department of Computer Science, National University of Ireland, Maynooth*, 2004.

[2] P. Byrne and G. Lyons. The effect of student attributes on success in programming. In *Proceedings of the 6th annual conference on Innovation and technology in Computer Science Education*, pages 49–52, 2001.

[3] P. F. Campbell and G. P. McCabe. Predicting the success of freshmen in a computer science major. *Commun. ACM*, 27(11):1108–1113, 1984.

[4] B. Cantwell-Wilson and S. Shrock. Contributing to success in an introductory computer science course: a study of twelve factors. In *Proceedings of the thirty-second SIGCSE technical symposium on Computer Science Education*, pages 184–188, 2001.

[5] J. Elwood and K. Carlisle. *Examining Gender. Gender and achievement in the Junior and Leaving Certifcate Examinations 2000/2001.* National Council for Curriculum and Assessment, 2003.

[6] G. E. Evans and M. G. Simkin. What best predicts computer proficiency? *Commun. ACM*, 32(11):1322–1327, 1989.

[7] D. C. Gibbs. The effect of a constructivist learning environment for field-dependent/independent students on achievement in introductory computer programming. In *Proceedings of the thirty-first SIGCSE technical symposium on Computer science education*, pages 207–211, 2000.

[8] A. Goold and R. Rimmer. Factors affecting performance in first-year computing. *SIGCSE Bull.*, 32(2):39–43, 2000.

[9] D. Hagan and S. Markham. Does it help to have some programming experience before beginning a computing degree program? In *Proceedings of the 5th annual SIGCSE/SIGCUE ITiCSEconference on Innovation and technology in computer science education*, pages 25–28, 2000.

[10] E. Holden and E. Weeden. The impact of prior experience in an information technology programming course sequence. In *Proceeding of the 4th conference on Information technology curriculum*, pages 41–46, 2003.

[11] T. R. Hostetler. Predicting student success in an introductory programming course. *SIGCSE Bull.*, 15(3):40–43, 1983.

[12] B. L. Kurtz. Investigating the relationship between the development of abstract reasoning and performance in an introductory programming class. In *Proceedings of the eleventh SIGCSE technical symposium on Computer science education*, pages 110–117, 1980.

[13] R. R. Leeper and J. L. Silver. Predicting success in a first programming course. In *Proceedings of the thirteenth SIGCSE technical symposium on Computer science education*, pages 147–150, 1982.

[14] M. McCracken, V. Almstrum, D. Diaz, M. Guzdial, D. Hagan, Y. B.-D. Kolikant, C. Laxer, L. Thomas, I. Utting, and T. Wilusz. A multi-national, multi-institutional study of assessment of programming skills of first-year cs students. *SIGCSE Bull.*, 33(4):125–180, 2001.

[15] R. Nowaczyk. Cognitive skills needed in computer programming. In *Annual Meeting of the Southeastern Psychological Association*, 1983.

[16] J. O'Kelly, A. Mooney, J. Ghent, P. Gaughran, S. Dunne, and S. Bergin. An overview of the integration of problem based learning into an existing computer science programming module. In *Pleasure By Learning, (PBL 2004)*, 2004.

[17] N. Rountree, J. Rountree, and A. Robins. Predictors of success and failure in a cs1 course. *SIGCSE Bull.*, 34(4):121–124, 2002.

[18] D. L. S. Wiedenbeck and V. Kain. Factors affecting course outcomes in introductory programming. In *Proceedings of the 16th Workshop on Psychology of Programming, PPIG'04*, pages 97–109, 2004.

[19] L. H. Werth. Predicting student performance in a beginning computer science class. In *Proceedings of the seventeenth SIGCSE technical symposium on Computer science education*, pages 138–143, 1986.

Tracking an Innovation in Introductory CS Education from a Research University to a Two-Year College

Allison Elliott Tew
College of Computing, Georgia Tech
801 Atlantic Drive
Atlanta, GA 30332-0280
404-385-1105
allison@cc.gatech.edu

Charles Fowler
Gainesville College
PO Box 1358
Gainesville, GA 30503
770-718-3803
cfowler@gc.peachnet.edu

Mark Guzdial
College of Computing, Georgia Tech
801 Atlantic Drive
Atlanta, GA 30332-0280
404-894-5618
guzdial@cc.gatech.edu

ABSTRACT

Innovations in teaching and learning computer science education can easily be overly-specific to a given institution, or type of institution. For example, an innovation may require special hardware, or may make assumptions about the background of the students. This paper tracks one such innovation, a multimedia-focused introductory computing course, as it moved from a research-focused university to a public two-year college. At both institutions, the new course resulted in dramatically improved retention. Students at the two-year college were even more motivated and more positive about computing after the course than students at the research university. The results suggest ways of approaching innovation that is easily adaptable to other institutions.

Categories and Subject Descriptors

K.4 [**Computers and Education**]: Computer and Information Sciences Education; H.5.1 [**Information Interfaces and Presentation**]: Multimedia Information Systems

General Terms

Design.

Keywords

Adoption/adaptation, multimedia, CS1, programming.

1. INTRODUCTION

While we hope that our teaching and learning innovations are usable in any computer science classroom, the reality doesn't always match our expectations. An innovation may require hardware that isn't available at all institutions. For example, a particular approach may be too slow on older processors to maintain student motivation at institutions that can't afford new, faster processors. Or an innovation may not be successful if students don't have adequate mathematics background.

SIGCSE'05, February 23–27, 2005, St. Louis, Missouri, USA.

Therefore, we cannot assume that an innovation that is successful at a research-focused university would be as successful at a smaller institution, such as a public two-year college. This paper describes an exploration of exactly that kind of a transition. We hope that our experience might inform others developing teaching and learning innovations that are portable between institutions. We describe in this paper the innovation that we developed and the result of its use at Georgia Institute of Technology (Georgia Tech). We then describe the use of the same innovation at Gainesville College. Based on demographic data, grade distributions, and surveys used at both institutions, we describe how the innovations worked similarly and differently at each institution. We end with our explanation of what happened and why.

1.1 Media Computation as an Introductory CS Course

In Spring 2003, Georgia Tech first offered a new introductory computing course whose goal was to motivate non-Engineering and non-CS majors [5,7]. Georgia Tech has had a requirement for all students to take a course in computing, but only had one version of CS1 until Spring 2003. The new course had an explicit focus on *media computation*. Students were introduced to programming and computing concepts by creating Photoshop-like filters, splicing and reversing sounds, writing programs to mine Web pages, and generating animations.

Table 1. Success rates at Georgia Tech before and with Media Computation class.

	Enrollment	Success Rate
Georgia Tech's CS1		
Average 2000 – 2002	930	71.2%
Media Computation		
Spring 2003	120	90.0%
Fall 2003	303	86.5%
Spring 2004	395	89.9%

The new course met with improved success rates (the percent of the course earning an A, B, or C in the course—that percentage of the course that did not withdraw or earn a D or F) over the general course (Table 1). Students enrolled in the media computation class were generally more motivated to study computer science—they told us that they understood better why computing was relevant to them and their careers [7].

The Media Computation course approach was explicitly designed to attract students who were not succeeding at a traditional computer science class [1,6]. The students in the Media Computation class were not majoring in technical fields and were mostly women. We explicitly designed the course to address the issues that research had found were barriers to students' success in computer science. In particular, we aimed at:

- *Relevance*: We explicitly made the argument that understanding media computation was useful and important to students in Management, Architecture, and Liberal Arts, with examples drawn from those domains.
- *Creative*: We created opportunities to explore computing as a creative medium. Where possible, assignments were open-ended. For example, one assignment required the creation of a collage where the same image had to appear four times, three with modifications. Students could choose their images and their manipulations, and add whatever other images they wanted.
- *Social*: We encouraged collaboration at several points in the class, and made on-line forums so that the results of students' programs could be shared in a gallery of student created images, sounds, and animations.

2. ADAPTING THE COURSE

The Media Computation class was used at Gainesville College in the CSCI 1100 – Introduction to Computing and Computer Programming course. This was the course taken by students who did not feel that they had adequate background in computing to take the traditional CS1 course (CSCI 1301). The Gainesville College version of the course used the same text [4], lecture slides, assignments, and overall structure.

The adaptation of the course occurred to allow for additional topics usually found in a computer literacy course and to allow generous amounts of time for students to complete programming assignments. The Gainesville course covered slightly more than half of the material in the textbook. Pair programming was encouraged but not required. Some class time was reserved for students to work on programming assignments or in-class exercises. The instructor was available in the classroom to help students who were stuck and/or frustrated. Some assignments, such as the picture collage, became great fun for some of the students.

Table 2. Success rates at Gainesville College before and with Media Computation class.

	Enrollment	Success Rate
Gainesville's CSCI 1100		
Average 2000 – 2003	28	70.2%
Media Computation		
Summer 2003	9	77.8%
Fall 2003	39	84.6%
Spring 2004	22	77.3%
Summer 2004	11	90.9%

In the three year period before CSCI 1100 became a media computation class, the average success rate was 70.2%. Gainesville College has enjoyed similar increases in success rate as previously demonstrated at Georgia Tech (Table 2)[1]. These results at a very different institution indicate that this innovation is adaptable to new environments.

3. COMPARING THE STUDENTS

The most relevant comparison for these courses at these institutions is probably the students. We would expect that the students who choose Gainesville College and those who choose Georgia Tech would differ in terms of their interests, their academic goals, and perhaps their demographics.

3.1 Coming in to the class

The majority of the students surveyed at both institutions were female (averaging 53.8% female at Georgia Tech and 69.2% female at Gainesville College) and Caucasian, although Georgia Tech did have students representing a more diverse set of ethnic backgrounds.

Table 3. Gender of Survey Participants

	Georgia Tech		Gainesville	
	Male	Female	Male	Female
Sp03	32.9%	67.1%	--	--
Su03	--	--	20.0%	80.0%
Fall03	51.1%	48.9%	37.5%	62.5%

Table 4. Ethnicity of Survey Participants

	Georgia Tech	Gainesville
African-American	6.4%	0.0%
Asian	7.0%	0.0%
Caucasian	80.8%	96.2%
Hispanic	0.3%	0.0%
Other	5.4%	3.8%

During Spring 2003 and Summer 2003 semesters at Georgia Tech and Gainesville respectively, students were surveyed at the beginning of the course to gather information about their academic background and experience with and attitudes about Computer Science. All students at both institutions intended to complete a traditional 4-year bachelor's degree and were majoring in areas such as Business, Liberal Arts, Nursing & Architecture (Table 5). While not enrolled in traditionally math or science focused programs, these students did not consider themselves to be technophobes. Only 32.9% and 31.2% of the students at Georgia Tech and Gainesville agreed

[1] We considered using statistical comparative techniques on the entire data set, but the dramatic variation in sample size across institutions precluded meaningful statistical analysis.

with the statement "I do *not* think of myself as being good with technology."

Table 5. Survey Participation by Degree Program

	Georgia Tech	Gainesville
Architecture	12.8%	--
Business	45.3%	22.2%
Liberal Arts	38.4%	33.3%
Nursing	--	11.1%
Sciences	3.5%	11.1%
Undecided	--	22.2%

Gainesville and Georgia Tech students did have different priorities or goals for the class. The top 5 goals of at each institution listed in Table 6. Gainesville students were much more focused on learning how to programming (60.0% of the students listed this as one of their goals for the course) and gaining general computing knowledge and skills (30.0%). Georgia Tech students included both of those goals, (22.1% & 27.9% respectively) but also listed getting a good/passing grade (24.4%) and learning skills that would be practical/relevant for their major (22.1%) equally as frequently.

Table 6. Student Goals for Media Computation class.

	Georgia Tech	Gainesville
1	General Computer Knowledge	Programming Knowledge & Skills
2	Good or Passing Grade	General Computer Knowledge
3	Programming Knowledge & Skills	Good or Passing Grade
4	Practical/Relevant Skills for Major	Fulfill CS Requirement
5	Media Skills	Computer Science Knowledge & Skills

3.2 During the Class

In addition to the initial surveys during Spring & Summer 2003 semesters, a mid-term survey was also collected asking for students' opinions about the course in progress.

From the initial survey, we found that a majority of students at both institutions had been looking forward to the class (Figure 1), while many more students at Gainesville reported they were satisfied with the course while enrolled. After the course, 68.8% of students at both institutions reported they had enjoyed the class.

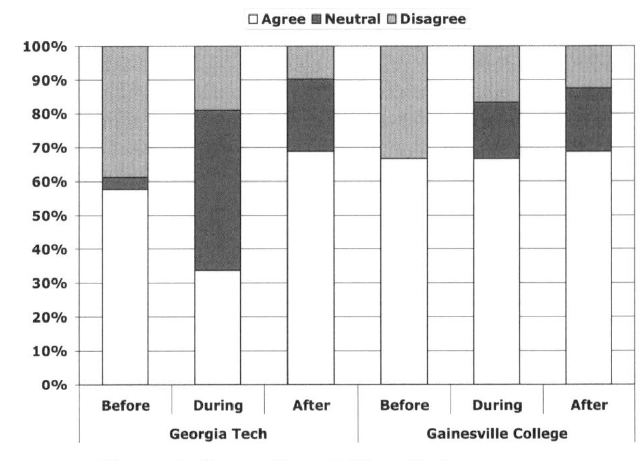

Figure 1. Perception of Class Enjoyment

Students at both institutions responded very favorably to the instructor and social atmosphere of the class. 96.8% of the students at Georgia Tech found the instructor to be enthusiastic about the material while 93.8% of Gainesville students did so.

Since one of our goals in the course was to make the study of computing a more social endeavor, we asked students about some of the social aspects of the classroom. Students at both institutions found the class atmosphere to be conducive to asking questions (Table 7), with more students at Georgia Tech feeling positive (strongly agree or agree) about that aspect.

Table 7. Class Atmosphere was Conducive to Questions

	Georgia Tech	Gainesville
Strongly Agree	26.6%	6.2%
Agree	53.2%	56.2%
Neutral	14.0%	37.5%
Disagree	4.0%	0.0%
Strongly Disagree	2.2%	0.0%

And students at both institutions were very supportive of allowing students to collaborate on homework assignments (Table 8), again with Georgia Tech students being more positive about this opportunity.

Table 8. Liked Collaboration on Assignments

	Georgia Tech	Gainesville
Strongly Agree	50.4%	37.5%
Agree	35.3%	31.2%
Neutral	12.0%	25.0%
Disagree	1.8%	6.2%
Strongly Disagree	0.5%	0.0%

In addition to their positive attitudes regarding course operations, an overwhelming majority of students at both institutions reported at midterm that they believed they were learning to program, 96.6% at Georgia Tech and 83.3% at Gainesville.

3.3 Upon leaving the class

During Fall 2003, students at both institutions were given surveys at the end of the term asking them to reflect on their experiences during the semester. They reported on their programming ability, their experience in the class, and their attitudes about computing.

Almost all students reported that they had improved their programming skills during the term: 91.6% at Georgia Tech and 87.5% at Gainesville College. Georgia Tech students had slightly higher levels of confidence in their programming abilities 75.8% strong or very strong vs. 68.8% at Gainesville (Table 9).

Table 9. Programming Skills – Fall 2003

	Georgia Tech		Gainesville	
	Before	After	Before	After
Very Strong	1.4%	5.5%	0.0%	0.0%
Strong	8.1%	70.3%	12.5%	68.8%
Not Much	16.6%	17.8%	25.0%	25.0%
Very Little	18.4%	6.4%	6.2%	6.2%
No Skills	55.6%	0.0%	56.2%	0.0%

While one of the goals of the course design was to increase relevance of the computing materials for our students, our findings on that aspect are decidedly mixed (Table 10). Only 39.2% of Georgia Tech students found the homework assignments to be personally relevant and even fewer (31.2%) of Gainesville College students did so.

Table 10. Homework Assignments were Relevant to Me

	Georgia Tech	Gainesville
Strongly Agree	6.2%	6.2%
Agree	33.0%	25.0%
Neutral	31.7%	50.0%
Disagree	25.0%	18.8%
Strongly Disagree	4.0%	0.0%

However, when students were asked about the relevance of the skills they learned in the class, their responses were much more positive (Table 11). 59.9% of Georgia Tech students agreed that the skills learned from this class will be useful in other areas of their life. 56.2% of Gainesville students agreed. Georgia Tech students reported greater relevance to their professional career, with 45.5% students agreeing; 37.5% of the students agreed at Gainesville College.

Table 11. Skills from this Class will be Useful in

	Georgia Tech		Gainesville	
	Life	Career	Life	Career
Strongly Agree	12.6%	6.8%	6.2%	0.0%
Agree	47.3%	38.7%	50.0%	37.5%
Neutral	23.9%	31.5%	12.5%	25.0%
Disagree	13.1%	16.2%	25.0%	37.5%
Strongly Disagree	3.2%	6.8%	6.2%	0.0%

Another goal of the course was to grow students' appreciation for and understanding of computing. After completing the course, a majority of students at both institutions did recognize that programming can have a creative component. 61.5% of survey respondents at Georgia Tech agreed with the statement "Programming can be a creative outlet," while 56.2% of Gainesville students agreed with the statement. And an overwhelming majority of both students (89.0% at Georgia Tech and 87.5% at Gainesville) reported they felt more knowledgeable about computers as a result of this class.

As society's definition of literacy grows to include digital technologies the use of computers as a communication tool, particularly for non-science and engineering majors, becomes a vital professional skill [2]. We asked our students not only whether they recognized the need to use the computer as a communication tool, but whether they could actually use it at as such. The results are shown in Table 12. A majority of students at both institutions reported that they did know how to use this new communication tool and even more so reported that the skills learned in this class will enable them to be able to better communicate with programmers in the future.

Table 12. Know How to Use Programming to Communicate

	Georgia Tech		Gainesville	
	with Others	with Programmers	with Others	with Programmers
Strongly Agree	8.0%	10.8%	0.0%	6.2%
Agree	50.9%	49.3%	56.2%	50.0%
Neutral	23.7%	24.2%	31.25%	31.2%
Disagree	14.3%	14.8%	12.5%	12.5%
Strongly Disagree	3.1%	0.9%	0.0%	0.0%

After completing the course a significant population of students at both institutions would like to take additional courses in Media Computation: 50.0% of the students at Gainesville College indicated such an interest; 42.6% of Georgia Tech students indicated so (Table 13). However, students were much less inclined to take additional CS courses, with only 31.2% of Gainesville students and 23.4% of Georgia Tech expressing interest. While these results do not indicate a majority of students with either of these opinions, at Georgia Tech this is a significant improvement over the only

3.5% who reported planning on taking additional CS courses in the pre-course survey.

Table 13. Would Like to Take More Courses in

	Georgia Tech		Gainesville	
	CS	Media Comp	CS	Media Comp
Strongly Agree	4.1%	16.1%	6.2%	12.5%
Agree	19.3%	26.5%	25.0%	37.5%
Neutral	23.8%	23.3%	43.8%	18.8%
Disagree	37.7%	22.9%	25.0%	25.0%
Strongly Disagree	15.2%	11.2%	0.0%	6.2%

These results demonstrate that students at both institutions, even after completing the course, perceive media computation and CS quite differently. When asked "Media Computation teaches a different set of skills than other intro CS courses", 66.2% of the Georgia Tech students and 56.2% of the Gainesville College students agreed with this statement. We believe these finding are consistent with our goal of reaching out to students who currently are under-served by traditional introductory CS courses.

4. EXPLAINING THE RESULTS

In general, we found that we had similar improvements in success rates at both Georgia Tech and at Gainesville College. We hesitate to use the word *significant*, since it's difficult to imagine applying a statistical model to these results, but it's clearly a *notable* and even *dramatic* improvement. What's perhaps more striking is that the Gainesville College students were even *more* enthusiastic about the class than the Georgia Tech students: They were more positive about the class upon coming in, and were even more positive about being interested in future computing courses than the Georgia Tech students.

There are several possible explanations for this difference. The Gainesville College classes were much smaller than the Georgia Tech classes at the same time, by more than an order of magnitude. A smaller class may lead to better teaching and better opportunities to learn. The Gainesville College students also had hands-on experience in the classroom and the class proceeded at a slower pace, covering approximately half of the material in the textbook. The Gainesville College students may have been enthusiastic about trying a new course developed at Georgia Tech.

An explanation that we find compelling is that the course was explicitly designed to attract students most at-risk at failing computer science, based on research results [1, 6]. The course was successful in meeting those students' needs at Georgia Tech. It's not surprising, then, that the course was even more successful at Gainesville College where *more* of the students look like at-risk students according to the research, e.g., there were more female students, and the students in the Gainesville College class were the ones self-selecting as having inadequate background for CS1. In a real sense, the goals for the course made it an even better fit for Gainesville students than Georgia Tech students.

The lesson for developers of learning and teaching innovations might be to know one's (student) audience and to build on existing research. The Media Computation class worked [2,5] because we carefully followed recommendations of research studies. The students who were most likely to succeed when following these recommendations were the kinds of students whom we invited into the class at both Georgia Tech and Gainesville College. The innovation was portable because those kinds of students were at both institutions. We could imagine innovations with a particular focus (e.g., drawing upon work in high performance computing or computational science) that might attract a student audience that is not common in all institutions. Because we aimed at a common group of students that were available at both institutions, the innovation was adaptable, and we might imagine that it would be adaptable at other institutions with similar audiences.

The results presented here do not include any qualitative data analysis. Such analyses have been done on the Media Computation course at Georgia Tech [3,6], but we have not yet been able to conduct similar studies at Gainesville College. In the future, we hope to be able to do so to gain further insight into the adaptation of this innovation at other institutions.

5. ACKNOWLEDGMENTS

Our thanks to the National Science Foundation (DUE and CCLI Educational Innovations programs) for their support of this work, as well as the NSF ADVANCE project at Georgia Tech (SBE-0123532), and Dr. Mary Jean Harrold specifically. We also thank Andrea Forte who designed the surveys that we used at Georgia Tech and Gainesville.

6. REFERENCES

[1] AAUW. *Tech-Savvy: Educating Girls in the New Computer Age*. American Association of University Women Education Foundation, New York, 2000.

[2] A. Forte and M. Guzdial. Computers for Communication, Not Calculation: Media as a Motivation and Context for Learning. In *Proceedings of 37th Hawaiian International Conference of Systems Sciences*. Big Island, Hawaii, 2004.

[3] M. Guzdial and A. Forte. Design Process for a Non-Majors Computing Course. *Proceedings of the ACM SIGCSE 2005 Conference*, pages In-Press, St. Louis, MO, 2005.

[4] M. Guzdial. *Introduction to Media Computation: A Multimedia Cookbook in Python*. Prentice-Hall, 2004.

[5] M. Guzdial. A media computation course for non-majors. In *Proceedings of the Innovation and Technology in Computer Science Education (ITiCSE) 2003 Conference*, 104-108, New York, 2003. ACM, ACM.

[6] J. Margolis and A. Fisher. *Unlocking the Clubhouse: Women in Computing*. MIT Press, Cambridge, MA, 2002.

[7] L. Rich, H. Perry, and M. Guzdial. A CS1 course designed to address interests of women. In *Proceedings of the ACM SIGCSE Conference*, pages 190–194, Norfolk, VA, 2004.

What Can Computer Science Learn from a Fine Arts Approach to Teaching?

Lecia J. Barker Kathy Garvin-Doxas
University of Colorado
Boulder, CO 80309
303-735-6004
{barkerl, garvindo}@Colorado.edu

Eric Roberts
Stanford University
Palo Alto, CA 94305
650-723-3642
eroberts@cs.stanford.edu

ABSTRACT
Two pedagogical techniques of IT programs are compared, a traditionally taught computer science (CS) major and an IT certificate program using a fine arts approach to pedagogy. The latter graduates a higher percentage of women than of males. Although the two programs are quite different in the nature of the material and what students are expected to learn, CS instructors can borrow from the certificate program in ways that could increase attraction to and retention of women in CS, especially by allowing students to hear each other articulate what they are learning; mentioning practical applications of theoretical principles; and requiring that students display their knowledge and solutions to their peers.

Categories and Subject Descriptors
K.3.2 [**Computers and Education**] Computer and Information Science Education

General Terms: Human Factors

Keywords: Gender issues; CS education research; Classroom management; Pedagogy

1 INTRODUCTION
The attrition of women in computer science (CS) in the U.S. is much higher than that of men [3, 4]. Several explanations are offered in the literature. Many women lose confidence in their ability to complete the tasks required for earning acceptable grades, despite evidence that they perform equally to men when lack of experience is factored out [5, 6]. This is partly because the individualized classroom climate of introductory courses makes it difficult for students to accurately gauge their abilities in comparison to their peers [1]. Margolis and Fisher reported that a loss in confidence often precipitated a student's decision to leave the CS major [11]. Other explanations include the low number of female faculty role models in computer science, poor student-mentor relationships caused by impersonal and non-collaborative computer science classes, classroom environments characterized by unchecked one-up-man-ship, and a "chilly" climate where woman experience difficulty entering peer study groups and face "pervasive stereotypes" that women cannot be technical or must use their feminine wiles to get good grades [1, 2, 4, 15]. Many women experience the double bind described by Seymour, in which being feminine or attractive is interpreted as being incompetent, while playing down one's femininity is interpreted as unnatural or unattractive [16]. A particularly large, multi-university study showed that leaving a major was related to teaching practices [17].

There is a relationship between attracting students to and retaining them in an established program. When students are considering a program of study, they ask other students, professors, family, and friends about their experiences or what they have heard. For example, when asked what computer science was about or why they had not entered a CS major, ITC students interviewed as part of this study perceived CS as narrow; CS students as focused on learning programming; the major as not permitting them to apply their skills to other fields; as antisocial; and as a major where they could not exercise creativity. This extreme view has some elements of truth, according to our observations and CS majors; thus when CS majors tell other students about their experiences, these are less likely to enter the CS major.

Many interventions have been proposed to increase retention of women in computer science. These include offering introductory or immigration courses with a broader view of the IT industry or which accommodate different abilities at the early stages of the program; increasing student collaboration (e.g., through pair programming); and including projects which are more meaningful to women [7, 12, 14, 15, 18]. Ensuring that visible role models are presented to students, making available faculty and student role models, and improving student-faculty and student-student relationships through mentoring programs are also recommended [2, 7, 10, 12]. A combination of strategies is advised [3].

In this paper, we offer a method of increasing retention by creating a classroom culture in which learning is a social or community process, not private and individualized. We conducted more than 600 hours of classroom observation in a multi-disciplinary information technology certificate program and a traditional computer science major. The certificate program's project courses use a fine arts approach where public critique and collaboration are routine and required; this program, though based in technology, both attracts and retains women at higher rates than does computer science. Below we present the background of the study, including a brief description of each curricular program and our research methods. We then describe two differences across these two classroom settings: knowledge sharing and assessment techniques. We conclude with some ideas on how CS instructors might adapt some of the pedagogical techniques of the certificate program to, in combination with other strategies, improve recruitment and retention of women.

This material is based upon work supported by the National Science Foundation under Grants 0090026 and 0082915.

SIGCSE'05, February 23-27, 2005, St. Louis, Missouri, USA.
Copyright 2005 ACM 1-58113-997-7/05/0002...$5.00.

2 BACKGROUND

2.1 University, Students, and Programs

The two programs observed were a traditional computer science (CS) major and a six-course, multimedia-oriented IT certificate program (ITC). We are not suggesting that these two programs of study are comparable; we suggest only that pedagogical techniques from the ITC's fine arts approach could be introduced into CS to improve learning and retention for all students, and in particular, women. Both curricular programs were observed in the same university, a public, doctoral-extensive university enrolling 24,000 undergraduates in 2003.

2.1.1 CS Major

The CS department, housed in a school of engineering, had ~700 majors in 2000 when the study was begun, but like most CS departments across the country, these numbers have decreased over the past few years. The CS major is consistent with Computing Curricula 2001's description of a "programming first" approach [9], in which early instruction concentrates on programming. Instruction tends to occur in a large lecture, with students independently learning skills in labs [1].

This CS program typically graduates fewer female undergraduate majors than the U.S. national average, at about 17 percent. Between 1994-2000, its attrition rate for women was 11.4%, higher than men at 10.5%; this was not a statistically significant difference. (Note, however, that this may be due to very low power, given the very small population of women on which to base the analysis.) The attrition rate for CS women at this institution is not as high as the national average (cf. [4]), but entry is lower. As Cohoon has demonstrated in her research, the problems of attrition and entry are not experienced uniformly across programs [4]; the cause of low graduation rates of women in CS can be low entry, high attrition, or a combination of these.

CS students interviewed as part of this study[1] reported many instances in which males and females are treated differently in class. As has been reported in other studies (e.g., [11]), women believed they were held to higher standards than were men, such that if they were called upon, they could not afford to answer incorrectly for fear it would reinforce a belief that women did not belong. Not surprisingly, about 2/3 of the men interviewed never felt discomfort asking questions in class, while only 1/3 of the women claimed they experienced no discomfort. Some women reported feeling isolated, but at the same time conspicuousness in class, and felt that they had to hide their femininity. One student said, "heaven forbid I talk about nail polish when I'm in that programming class."

2.1.2 ITC Program

In the ITC program, students acquire in-depth skill with high-end, software packages (e.g., Photoshop, Flash) as well as some HTML programming, with the goal of designing multimedia materials and interactive programs. Programming courses (e.g., C++ or Java) are optional. The certificate program, open to all undergraduates, requires that students take six courses; three are taught exclusively by ITC core faculty. The introductory course teaches basic HTML with course content centering on societal aspects of communication technologies; three are project courses with both individual and group assignments; and the remaining two courses focus on social or theoretical implications of technology from the viewpoint of any of several disciplines.

In ITC, student enrollment is slightly more than half women (52%), and 62% of those who have completed the certificate are women. Both ITC males and females complete the certificate at 92%. ITC students interviewed described a supportive and collaborative learning environment. Students interviewed did not perceive that women were treated differently from men in their ITC classes.

2.2 Research Method

Our data collection and analytical methods fall within ethnographic inquiry, the goal of which is to systematically document and understand interactions and their meanings within a particular social context, such as a classroom or curricular program. Using this approach, social scientists hope to articulate what is often implicit and unarticulated in social settings: both typical behavior and the shared norms and beliefs prescribing what is appropriate. Ethnographic research leads to in-depth knowledge of particular situations and should not be generalized, but used by analogy. When the reader believes their situation is similar in essential features, then ethnographic research can help to shine a light on the interactional details of their classroom.

During two sequential academic years, we observed seven CS courses, eight ITC courses, and six courses cross-listed between the two programs, totaling more than 600 hours of classroom observation (see Table 1). The results we present here are not isolated in particular classrooms, but typical features of learning and assessment in the two programs.

For each class, we systematically recorded: number of students attending, sex, and appearance; physical layout of classrooms and seating arrangements; and descriptions of teaching and interaction (student-student, student-instructor) and interactants (male/ female; major if known). Observation notes were typed and the resulting text bound into 21 "books."

Table 1 Observation Details

Term	Program	Courses	Hours
Fall 2000	CS	2	46
	IT	3	50
Spring 2001	CS	2	70
	CS/IT*	2	38
Fall 2001	CS	2	103
	CS/IT*	2	48
	IT	3	95
Spring 2002	CS	1	21
	CS/IT*	2	60
	IT	2	73
Total		21	604

*Cross-listed in CS and ITC.

3 KEY DIFFERENCES OBSERVED

3.1 Knowledge Sharing

3.1.1 Knowledge Sharing in CS

In all the computer science courses we observed (except for the cross-listed courses), lecture and lab were separate. In lecture, students tended to sit and listen, looking forward at their professor. When a teacher stands at the front of the room, attention is focused on one person, object, or action, implying that

[1] 141 (89 women, 52 men) students were interviewed in another part of this study, including 41 ITC students, 85 CS students, and 15 students who switched out of the CS major. The report is not yet published; acknowledgment to Liane Pedersen-Gallegos and Elaine Seymour will be made in the final version of the paper.

the learning or knowledge will be imparted by that person and the contributions of others is of lesser value. Teachers have the right to move around the class, while students have no such right without permission from the teacher [13]. Further, the lectern is a signal to students that one-way transmission of information will predominate. Spatial arrangements have additional meaning for participants in a classroom; for example, "in a non-circular configuration . . . in which there is one member at the apex of a triangle, . . . the member at the apex typically has the right (and obligation) of sustained speech" [19, p. 184].

The subject matter of lectures was often taught with general principles preceding reasons why a person might need to know the theory or method. In one class, when a student asked why they needed to know a particular algorithm, the professor replied that he was proving its efficiency. Thinking he had not been clear about his question, the student asked again. After probing the student to better understand the question, the professor apologized for not understanding the question and moved forward with the lecture. From the perspective of an outsider (the observer), it felt like an embarrassing moment, where people simply don't understand each other's perspectives. The professor's focus was theoretical (algorithmic efficiency); the student's focus was on specific application contexts where the algorithm might be used.

The professor was thinking (and teaching) in terms of general principles that could be applied to specific contexts, while the student was hoping to understand a specific context in which the general might apply in order to learn. Deductive instruction was similarly observed across many classes, where abstract principles and reasoning were described prior to mention of any practical application of that knowledge. Because students may be trying to understand computer science in quite different ways from how professors teach, it can be very helpful for students to hear other students articulate what they are learning.

CS professors occasionally experimented in lecture, demonstrating the trial and error process of computing. Once, for example, a professor worked through a program to produce a graphic image, using trial and error and eliciting the knowledge of students. Though it was the end of the class period, when students in most classes are noisily zipping their notebooks into their backpacks as a signal to professors, on this occasion they were too engaged to behave like typical students. More often, professors came to class with working programs and complete lectures, giving the illusion to their less experienced students that they always had the right answer and that programming ran smoothly for them. Thus CS professors were perceived as experts and students as novices. If professors were to teach in a lab or work through problems in class (e.g., ask students for problems that the professor could then try to program on the spot), students would have more opportunities to learn from each other and experience the process of programming through the eyes of their professors.

In lab, students faced their computers working independently on their assignments. Most talk among students was subdued and brief. Cheating in computer science is a significant and possibly increasing phenomenon.[2] Like most CS departments, this takes seriously its responsibility to reduce cheating. When a student is detected using another student's code, both are punished. We learned from students that the reason they avoided talking to other students in labs and blocked their screens was fear that someone else would see their code. As documented elsewhere, when we began this research, collaboration was equated with cheating in non-subtle ways on course syllabi in an effort to reduce cheating [1]. The byproduct was that students were not clear about the difference between cheating and collaborating, erring on the side of caution by not talking to each other.

Although the tone of anti-collaboration statements has softened, syllabi typically continue to include statements like this:

> "Some of the homework that you do in this class may be done with other students. However, other work must be done on your own, with no help except from the instructors. For your assignments, you will be asked to accept the student honor pledge: *'On my honor, I have neither given nor received unauthorized assistance on this work.'* In your submission you should clearly indicate which students helped you in the assignment and on what questions. Breaking this rule for homework or exams will result in an F for the entire course (not just for the assignment)."

It is clear that students had trouble determining the difference between authorized and unauthorized assistance. In interviews conducted by one of our graduate students studying an experimental, group-based introductory course, CS students said that in this course, they could do things that their friends had told them was considered cheating in their traditionally taught courses (e.g., discussing how to write an algorithm as a group). These kinds of messages are the beginning of students' socialization into their chosen discipline, as shown by a comment from CS senior, who said, "you shouldn't have to collaborate to get a job done."

The combination of the instructor-centered learning environment where the instructor is the principle source of knowledge, subject matter abstracted from the world of human experience, and fear that talking to another student might be construed as cheating resulted in very little observable knowledge sharing among students. A substantial tradition of research shows that students benefit from cooperative learning and hearing each other articulate what they are learning and that women prefer collaborative learning environments. Thus it is no surprise that ITC students interviewed describe their classroom environments as one of the most attractive features of the program.

3.1.2 Knowledge Sharing in ITC

The introductory ITC course is, like the CS courses, taught using lecture and lab, but with the additional requirement that students discuss what they are learning. In addition to the professor, this course includes a series of guest speakers who speak about their experience (e.g., e-commerce or other domains). We observed faculty calling on students frequently and encouraging them to ask questions during lecture. They also were required to analyze what they had heard orally by means of a conceptual framework, defined early in the term and threaded through the semester. The nature of the material was meaningful in and of itself, since students can look around and see the subject matter, the increasing prominence of technology, as part of their everyday lives.

The project-based courses were taught using a fine arts or studio approach. Faculty used both lecture and hands-on activities, but lecture occurred in the lab and directly preceded the hands-on experience. For example, the professor would teach a concept, show a concrete example, and then students would put their hands directly on their keyboards and practice it. The professor was always in the lab with the students, walking around, helping them

[2] That is, the rise in cheating incidents could be a function of cheat-detecting software or the easy availability of others' code is available on the Internet. Most likely, it is a combination of these.

learn. When he was satisfied that most in the class had learned, he would ask them to look away from their monitors to hear more lecture. In addition, the professor was not always the only person conveying knowledge about design principles, software, or subject matter. As a multi-disciplinary program, it should be expected that students bring a variety of skills and perspectives with them. So, for example, we observed some environmental design students whose skill with certain software, such as Form Z, far exceeded the instructor's. In such a case, we sometimes heard students explaining certain concepts to the professor and to other students; in this way students could come to count on each other to help them learn.

In project courses, initial assignments were personalized. Students were asked to perform general tasks or produce web sites, but to do so by means of their own interests or experiences. The learning objective was for students to understand how to manipulate features and capabilities of the software they are using. To do in-class and after-class assignments, students were told early that there was no reason for them to re-invent the wheel; that is, professors explicitly told students that they should search for and find source code before creating it themselves. Instructors demonstrated web sites with HTML tips, samples of JavaScript and java code, etc., much like computer science professors refer to libraries. This created an expectation that students would either teach themselves a large part of what they were supposed to learn (a sometimes unwelcome expectation, according to interviews) or to seek out the knowledge of their peers.

Student interaction was not forbidden in any way: assignments were personalized, so there was no real way to "cheat." It was not uncommon in labs for a student to call out the professor's name to ask for help; indeed, labs were noisy with student talk. When the professor was busy, which was often the case, students came to expect help or information from anyone, calling out, for example, "does anyone know what the image needs to be saved as to open in Flash? A jpeg?" Anyone who already knew how to do something would guide the student to help, often standing up and looking over the less-experienced student's shoulder to look at the monitor and give very specific instructions. Page after page of observation notes taken from the ITC project courses is filled with students helping each other in a variety of ways.

Students become socialized in ITC to expect learning with each other and professors in the lab, which became evident from student reactions to the way CS professors taught cross-listed courses. In one of these, an ITC student said, "I'd rather do the database assignment on a server, having you there to guide us. We can do the reading outside of class, instead of you lecturing about it." Another student added, "We could have class up in the lab, and maybe do half lecture and half lab." The professor replied that she was already giving them too much time to work collaboratively during lecture time, referring to it as "foreign" in engineering. She then reported to students that when she said told other engineering faculty about the students' requests, they had exclaimed, "they want what?"

Knowledge sharing was multi-directional and occurred at any time in ITC courses. Students showed their professors how to do things; professors asked students how to do things; and it was not uncommon for professors to say "well, I'll have to figure that out later" or "I don't know how to do that." These kinds of comments did not undermine the professors' authority; instead, they suggested the reality of using technology: weird things happen that can't be solved immediately and it is okay to not know it all. The expert/novice divide we observed in CS did not hold in the ITC classes, revealing as myth the alignment of expert/non-expert roles corresponding with professor/student roles.

3.2 Assessment Techniques

3.2.1 Assessment in CS

Assessment of all programming assignments in the CS courses we observed used a computer program. This program, in addition to assessing whether a student's program worked, could tell if a student's program was too much like another program and therefore identify cheaters. Undergraduate teaching assistants briefly reviewed comments to ensure that students had completed the assignment's requirements. Though the grading program had a name and was talked about as if it were a person, it did not take the place of human interaction, as a professor or a tutor or teacher might. Further, while professors frequently talked about the importance of the process of programming as well as of planning and design, in most cases grades depended almost exclusively on whether or not the program generated appropriate output, etc. Even if a student's mistake was in syntax, they got little credit if their program didn't work. This assessment policy reinforces the message that computer science is about programming and, in spite of what we heard CS professors tell students in class about elegant programs, reinforces the notion that it doesn't matter how you get there, the only thing that counts is getting it to work.

Although Computing Curricula 2001 mandates that students learn to critique programs, we did not observe students critiquing their own or others' programs in lecture or in lab. In contrast, ITC used assessment methods that one would typically find in a fine arts or performance arts setting.

3.2.2 Assessment in ITC

In ITC, students would produce something, then be required to demonstrate what they had produced in front of the entire class before submitting it to the professor for individualized assessment. In addition, rather than simply observe and clap their hands, other students were required to make comments aloud about what they liked or didn't like. For example, one student presented an animation showing a woman getting ready to go out, drinking by herself, and partying with friends. After discussing the meaning of the animation, a male student evaluated its aesthetic aspects, saying one part was too long and another too short. The professor suggested that the student do more with music. A female student suggested that the animation be broken up into two different animations. Even the most skilled students were publicly evaluated by their professors and peers.

Clearly, this was a difficult situation for students, who had to become accustomed to public judgment. It is even more difficult for students who avoid public situations. It was not uncommon to observe a student turning red from the neck up to his forehead as more experienced students, either technically, in terms of design, or in terms of particular subject matter, evaluated his work. Yet all students were required to articulate the choices they made in front of each other and all students listened to others making comments on their work. The effect was the leveling of the playing field, since everyone had to suffer the same fate. Most importantly, students gained in two significant ways: 1) they heard each other talk about doing the work rather than hearing only the more theoretical, didactic, and discipline-specific words of a professor; and 2) hearing what other students knew permitted them to make more accurate assessments about their own skills and levels of understanding, decreasing the likelihood that they will lose confidence without good cause and leave the program.

The language students and professors used often suggested that the works displayed were works in progress and that therefore, students were in the process of learning. In other words, the presentations were not finished pieces, but were a way of practicing new skills and then reflecting publicly on them. Student criticism of each other's work was taken seriously not only by students, but also by professors, implying that student feedback was valuable. Students became accustomed to asking each other for help and critique and were exposed to more examples of similar work.

4 SUMMARY AND IDEAS

In CS, students had few opportunities to share knowledge with each other, either when they were learning (i.e., in lecture or lab) or when they were assessed. In contrast, the fine arts approach to teaching of the ITC puts the burden on students to elicit knowledge from each other and their professors and to put their own knowledge on public display. As a result, students became accustomed to hearing one another talk about their work – in students', rather than only in professors', terms and through different ways of learning by example as well as principle.

One must consider the differences in pedagogy that are mandated by differences in the underlying notions of mastery and the nature of the material. Computer science is an entire curricular program and cannot possibly be taught using a fine arts approach for every class, especially considering the theoretical nature of much of the subject matter. However, the underlying principles of students sharing knowledge with each other and putting their own knowledge on public display can be integrated into every course. In particular, we believe that CS professors can:

- Ensure opportunities for students to hear each other articulate what they are learning; this does not have to be on graded assignments, but could be practice in constructing algorithms, for example, in groups or pairs in labs. Students could then present their solutions to the rest of the class.
- Begin lectures by telling students a practical application of what they will later describe at the theoretical level. For example, at the beginning of a lecture on finite state machines, a professor might mention that vending machines would fall into the category. That is, what human contexts are made better, more efficient or secure, etc., by using a program or algorithm?
- Require that students display their solutions to the class and require that their classmates give them feedback. In this way, students can learn by example, learn in more than one mode, and hear each other articulate what they are learning. For example, a professor might select a certain number of students to present the design principles of their assignment to the rest of the class.

These techniques allow students to more accurately gauge their progress, overcoming female attrition due to loss of confidence when their performance is equal to that of their peers. Women will be less likely to see themselves as performing below the men around them. In addition, integrating knowledge sharing into lectures and labs can go a long way toward addressing the different ways in which students and faculty work to understand computer science. Also, the interaction among students builds in an environment characterized by sharing and camaraderie that is preferable to most students, but especially to women. Creating a departmental culture in which students work hard to learn together can be a mechanism for both attracting and retaining female computer science majors.

5 REFERENCES

[1] Barker, L. J. & Garvin-Doxas, K. (2004). Making visible the behaviors that influence learning environment: A qualitative exploration of computer science classrooms. *Computer Science Education, 14*(2).

[2] Borg, A. (1998). What draws women to and keeps women in computing? In C. C. Selby (Ed.) *Women in science and engineering: Choices for success.* New York: New York Academy of Sciences.

[3] Cohoon, J. M. (2001). Toward improving female retention in the computer science major. *Communications of the ACM, 44*(5), 108-114.

[4] Cohoon, J. M. & Chen, L. (2003). Migrating out of computer science. *Computing Research News, 15*(2), 2-3.

[5] Farenga, S. J., & Joyce, B. A. (1998). Science-Related Attitudes and Science Course Selection: A Study of High-Ability Boys and Girls. Roeper Review, 20(4), 247-251.

[6] Fisher, A. J., Margolis, J., & Miller, F. (1997).Undergraduate women in computer science: experience, motivation and culture. *Proceedings of the 28th SIGCSE Technical Symposium on Computer Science Education*, San Jose, CA.

[7] Gürer, D. (1999). Testimony to the Committee on Workforce Needs in Information Technology. ACM Committee on Women in Computing. URL: www.acm.org/women/work_shortage.shtml

[8] Haller, S. M., & Fossum, T. V. (1998). Retaining women in CS with accessible role models. *Proceedings of the ACM SIGSCE Conference.*

[9] IEEE and ACM Joint Task Force. (2001). *Computing Curricula 2001.* URL: www.computer.org/education/cc2001/final/index.htm

[10] Information Technology Association of America (1999). Building the 21st century information technology work force: Underrepresented groups in the information technology workforce. Arlington, VA. URL: www.techworkforce.org/recruiting.htm

[11] Margolis, J. & Fisher, A. (2002). *Unlocking the clubhouse: Women in computing,* MIT Press.

[12] Margolis, J., Fisher, A. J., & Miller, F. (1998). Living among the "programming gods": The nexus of confidence and interest for undergraduate women in computer science. URL: www-2.cs.cmu.edu/~gendergap/confidence.html

[13] McHoul, A.W. (1978). The organization of turns at formal talk in the classroom. *Language in Society, 7,* 183-213.

[14] McDowell, C., Werner, L., Bullock, H., & Fernald, J. (2002). The effects of pair-programming on performance in an introductory programming class, *Proceedings of the 33rd SIGCSE* Technical Symposium on Computer Science Education, Northern Kentucky, KY.

[15] O'Leary, D. P. (1999, Version 1: June 1999). *Accessibility of computer science: A reflection for faculty members.* Dianne P. O'Leary. URL: www.cs.umd.edu/users/oleary/faculty/whole.html

[16] Seymour, E. (1995). The loss of women from science, mathematics, and engineering undergraduate majors: An explanatory account. *Science Education, 79*(4), 437-473.

[17] Seymour, E. & Hewitt, N. (1997). *Talking about leaving.* Westview Press, Boulder, CO.

[18] Williams, L. A. (2000). Strengthening the case for pair programming. *IEEE Software, 17*(4), 17-25,

[19] Wilson, B.G. (1995). Metaphors for instruction: Why we talk about learning environments. *Educational Technology, 35*(5), 25-30.

The Effects of Individual Differences on CS2 Course Performance Across Universities

Tracy L. Lewis
Radford University
Department of Information Technology
Radford, VA 24142
+1 (540) 831-5358
tlewis32@radford.edu

J. D. Chase
Radford University
Department of Information Technology
Radford, VA 24142
+1 (540)831-5997
jchase@radford.edu

Manuel Pérez-Quiñones
Virginia Tech
Department of Computer Science
Blacksburg, VA 24061
+1(540) 231-2646
perez@cs.vt.edu

Mary Beth Rosson
Pennsylvania State University
School of Information Sciences and Technology
State College, PA
+1 (814) 863-2478
mrosson@psu.edu

ABSTRACT

Research is presented that examined the effects of various measures of prior computer science experience and cognitive abilities on overall performance in a CS2 course. Participants selected from the CS2 course at two southeastern state universities were used within this study, resulting in a sample size of 161 (School A, n = 76; School B, n = 85). School A is a mid-sized comprehensive university and School B is a large research-intensive university.

Self-reported data were collected on measures of experience in object-oriented processing, UNIX programming, web design, computing platforms, and various CS experience. Further, cognitive abilities measures of spatial orientation, visualization, logical reasoning, and flexibility were administered.

The results show that the schools significantly differed on all measures of cognitive ability and most measures of prior computer science experience. The schools also differed on the extent to which these measures were related to overall course performance. The results suggest that, for school A, the cognitive ability visualization and the prior computer science experience measure of OO processing were significantly related to course performance. However, when examining school B, no measures were found significant.

Categories and Subject Descriptors

K.3.2 [**Computers and Education**]: Computer and Information science education – *self assessment, cognitive abilities, and individual differences.*

General Terms

Measurement, Performance, Experimentation.

Keywords

Individual differences, cognitive abilities, course performance, prior computer science experience, object-oriented design

SIGCSE'05, February 23-27, 2005, St. Louis, Missouri, USA.

1. INTRODUCTION

Enormous bodies of theoretical and empirical studies are readily available on the topic of predictors of course performance and achievement. In reviewing historical studies, there appears to be a growing list of explanatory variables. For example, studies before 1977 focused on demographic variables and high school achievement to account for enhanced computer science performance [2, 5, 15]. Unfortunately, the models developed from the aforementioned studies demonstrated only limited predictive power [9]. Between 1977 and 1981, investigators broadened their research models to include the use of IBM's Programming Aptitude Test (PAT) [11, 17]. However, the use of linear regression or factor analysis models in these studies failed to account for half of the total variation in course performance. Due to programming paradigm shifts, IBM's PAT soon became obsolete and researchers began to look for other possible predictors of success.

Since 1985, scholars have explored the relationships between computer science ability and general cognitive processes [3, 9, 10, 11, 19, 20]. Although not every study reported significance in the use of cognitive measures, many of the surveys produced a wealth of valuable information on supporting the use of demographics and prior academic performance as possible indicators of computer science course success.

A sizeable number of the studies mentioned found correlations between their selection of independent variables and course performance. However, when several of these studies were replicated at other institutions, the results were inconclusive [3,10]. Based on these findings, the current research sought to investigate measures of individual differences across universities. More specifically, this research answered the following research questions:

1. To what extent, if any, do the students differ (prior computer science experience and cognitive abilities) across universities?
2. To what extent do the differences in individual differences across schools affect performance on an specially constructed design task and the final grade in a CS2 course?

2. BACKGROUND

The following subsections present a brief summary of literature on prior computer science experience and cognitive abilities as predictors of performance. For this research, four measures of course performance were used. However, because of page constraints, only data related to the final course grade is presented.

2.1 Prior Computer Science Experience

Prior computer science experience has been loosely defined as any experience/exposure to computing languages, equipment, and/or applications prior to the student's enrollment in the current course [20]. Fayad and Jakiela (1989) noted that prior computing experience was a significant predictor of course grade in an introductory engineering design course. When investigating programming language prediction, it was shown that prior BASIC knowledge was a positive predictor of performance on the second exam in the course [9].

Studies involving introductory computer science courses have uniformly described that prior computer science experience was a significant predictor of course performance [12, 14]. In fact, Morrison and Newman not only showed that prior programming course experience was positively linked to introductory computer science course performance, but also demonstrated that it was particularly significant when that prior programming course was offered at the university level. Using a sample of 65 students, Katz et al. reported that the significance of prior computer science experience was only indirectly affected by gender since males generally had more prior computer science experience.

Two recent studies have reported findings contrary to the widely accepted belief that prior computer science experience is a reliable predictor of course performance [18, 16]. Rountree et al. noted that only 18% of the students who claimed to already *know* a programming language had an appreciably higher success rate. They further noted that 12 of the 84 students who indicated prior experience actually failed the course. They concluded that knowing a programming language was no guarantee of course performance in an introductory computer science course. Ventura reported similar findings wherein a student's belief about his or her ability to program was not correlated with any measure of course performance. It was further noted that students without prior Java programming experience in fact did better than those who had programmed in Java prior to the objects-first course.

2.2 Cognitive Abilities

According to [22]. cognitive abilities are the characteristic, self-consistent, modes of functioning that individuals show in their perceptual and intellectual activities.

2.2.1 Spatial Orientation

Ekstrom et al. (1979) defined spatial orientation as the ability to perceive spatial patterns or to maintain orientation with respect to objects in a space. Spatial orientation tests require participants to distinguish between the faces of an object. Each problem in the test features drawings of pairs of cubes or blocks. The second cube may be a rotated version of the first cube, and the subject has to determine if the two cubes are the same or different.

2.2.2 Visualization

Visualization is the ability to manipulate or transform the image of spatial patterns into other arrangements. The visualization and spatial orientation factors are similar but visualization requires that the figure be mentally restructured into components for manipulation, while the whole figure is manipulated in spatial orientation. Carroll (1974) concluded that both visualization and spatial orientation require the mental rotation of a spatial configuration in short-term visual memory; however, visualization requires the additional component of performing serial operations. Some subjects may employ an analytic strategy in visualization tests and search for symmetry and planes of reflection as clues to the solution.

2.2.3 Logical Reasoning

Logical reasoning reflects the ability to evaluate the logical correctness of possible conclusions for a given set of information. Ekstrom et al. (1979) defined logical reasoning as the ability to reason from premise to conclusion, or to evaluate the correctness of a conclusion. The complexity of this factor has been pointed out by Carroll (1974), who describes it as involving both the retrieval of meanings and of algorithms from long-term memory and then performing serial operations on the materials retrieved. Carroll suggested that individual differences on this factor could be related not only to the content and temporal aspects of these operations, but also to the attention that the subject gives to details of the stimulus materials.

2.2.4 Flexibility

Flexibility of use is the mental mindset necessary to think of different uses for objects. Flexibility tests typically ask the subject to practice "practical resourcefulness" in naming two objects that can be used together to make something or do something that is required (to solve a particular task).

2.2.5 Perceptual Style

The final cognitive ability of interest within this research is perceptual style. Perceptual style is the manner in which a person cognitively approaches a learning situation. In terms of perceptual style, an individual can be classified as field-independent or field-dependent. Field-dependence/independence (FD/I) is the most extensively researched cognitive control. Initiated over 40 years ago, FD/I remains among the most prescriptive of learning and instructional outcomes [17]. Stevens, Wileman, and Konvalina (1981) and Werth (1986) are particularly renowned for using measures of FD/I as reliable predictors of success in computer science courses.

Individuals who prefer a field-dependent (FD) perceptual style tend to perceive globally, i.e., perception is dominated by the overall organization of the surrounding field, and parts of the field are experienced as "fused" [19]. Individuals who prefer a field-independent (FI) perceptual style tend to view concepts more analytically, finding it easier to solve problems.

3. METHOD

3.1 Sample

Students enrolled in CS2 courses at two southeastern state institutions were asked to participate in this study. Grades were obtained from the course instructors. The duration of the data collection was one semester (January through May, 2004).

Based on student population categories as reported in *U.S. News and World Report* (2004), School A was selected from what was considered to be a medium-sized university (~16,500 students). School B was selected from the list of larger state universities (~25,000 students). All participants were enrolled in a CS2 course during the spring semester of 2004. Both universities follow the IEEE/ACM Joint Task force on Computing Curriculum (CC2001) syllabus for object-first pedagogy. Specifically, CC2001 stated that a CS2 course should cover topics related to the introduction of object-oriented programming and design.

While the university admission requirements differ, the specific course of interest is hypothesized to be fairly consistent across universities. According to syllabi, obtained from the course websites, the universities covered the same topics and used the same textbook.

3.2 Measures

This research administered measures of prior computer science experience and cognitive abilities (spatial orientation, visualization, logical reasoning, flexibility of use, and perceptual style).

Each variable was assessed using formats to be described in subsequent sections. Responses to the respective variable statements were tallied to generate a total score based on correct/incorrect responses to specific items.

CS2 course performance was determined by the participant's performance on a specially constructed pre/post instruction design task as well as the final grade in the course.

3.2.1 Prior Computer Science Experience Scale

The prior computer science experience scale was novel to this research. Participants responded based on their self-assessed proficiency in various areas of computer science. Five subscales were identified (UNIX Programming, Object-Oriented Processes, Web Designing, Computing Platforms, and Various CS), each of which was named according to the majority of the items represented by the subscale.

Participants responded to the prior computer science experience scale using a 5-point Likert-type scale, 1 (None), 2 (Novice), 3 (Intermediate), 4 (Proficient), and 5 (Expert). The use of a 5-point scale is supported through existing research suggesting that coefficient alpha reliabilities tend to increase up to the use of 5-points and level off thereafter. Each subscale within the prior computer science experience was determined by calculating the average of the sum of the proficiency levels for each item.

3.2.2 Cognitive Abilities

A detailed description of the measures used within this study is omitted. For further details please contact the author at tlewis32@radford.edu.

Spatial Orientation was assessed using the Cube Comparison Test – S-2, available through the Kit of Factor-Referenced Cognitive Tests [8].

Visualization was assessed using the Surface Development Test – VZ -3, available through the Kit of Factor-Referenced Cognitive Tests [8].

Logical reasoning was assessed using the Inference Test - RL-3, available through the Kit of Factor-Referenced Cognitive Tests [8].

Flexibility of use was assessed using the Combining Objects Test – XU-1, available through the Kit of Factor-Referenced Cognitive Tests [8].

Perceptual style was measured by the Group Embedded Figures Test – GEFT [22].

3.2.3 Pre/Post Instruction Design Task

The pre/post training design task asked participants to create a multi-player "survival of the fittest" terrarium game. The participants were asked to identify the essential classes and interactions between those classes. Each participant was instructed that s/he was not required to *code* any of the specifications of the game, however, they were required to *design* the game in such a way that a coder could advance from their design directly into coding of the system.

The design tasks were evaluated using an adapted version of the Student Individualized Performance (SIP) rubric developed by Custer, Valsey, and Burke (2001). The SIP consists of six categorical anchors: cohesion, clarity, completeness, clarity, consistency, and correctness. Each category was evaluated using a 5-point Likert-type scale, 1(Novice) to 5(Expert). The category points were totaled to suggest an overall score on the design task. Criteria for each category and evaluation point varied across the SIP.

Three evaluators—two external evaluators and the primary investigator of this research—were trained to assess the design tasks using the SIP. For this study, inter-rater reliabilities ranged from .81 to .83.

4. RESULTS

To explore the relationship among prior computer science, cognitive abilities, and CS2 course performance, this research utilized *path analysis* because of its predictive power in exploratory studies. Path analysis was used in combination with other multivariate methods (multiple regression, correlation, and factor analysis).

4.1 Demographic Analysis – School A

This sample was 87% male, with a mean age of 19.5 (SD = 1.36). The mean high school grade point average was 2.93 (SD = .38), and the mean college grade point average was 2.83 (SD = .38). 95% of the participants were enrolled as full-time students and 91% reported English as their native language. Thirty-eight percent were classified as freshmen, 25% as sophomore, 22% as junior, and 15% as senior. Thirty-seven percent reported being computer science majors, and 23% reported being information systems majors. The remainder of the group was evenly distributed among the database, software engineering, and networks majors. More than half of this group (61%) reported taking one or more computer science courses in high school, 23% took one or more advanced placement computer science courses in high school, and 10% took the advanced placement computer science examination.

4.2 Demographic Analysis – School B

This sample was 98% male, with a mean age of 18 (SD = .68). The mean high school grade point average was 3.56 (SD = .39), and the mean college grade point average was 2.95 (SD = .35). 98% were enrolled as full-time students and 96% reported English as their native language. Eighty-six percent of the students were classified as freshman, 11% as sophomore, and 2% as junior. Ninety-six percent reported being computer science majors. A majority (81%) reported taking one or more computer science courses in high school, 39% took one or more advanced placement computer science courses in high school, and 29% took the advanced placement computer science examination.

4.3 Demographic – School Comparison

Chi-squares and Independent-sample *t* tests were conducted to evaluate the differences between the schools using demographic variables previously reported (age, high school grade point average, college grade point average, enrollment status, native language, classification, major). School A (men – 87%; women 13%) had significantly more women than did School B (men – 98%; women – 2%); $X^2(1) = 6.79$; $p < .01$. It was found that the two schools significantly differed in the means of age ($t(159) = 6.63$, $p = .00$), high school grade point average ($t(159) = -9.72$, $p = .00$), classification ($t(159) = 7.68$, $p = .01$), and advanced placement courses taken ($t(159) = -2.40$, $p = .02$). It is noted that the schools did *not* significantly differ in college grade point average.

4.4 Reliability and Factor Analysis

The Cronbach's alpha for the previously validated measures of cognitive ability—spatial orientation ($\alpha = .92$), visualization ($\alpha = .94$), flexibility ($\alpha = .85$), logical reasoning test ($\alpha = .69$), and perceptual style ($\alpha = .84$) — were within acceptable ranges established in previous studies of college students [8, 22]. Factor analysis was conducted on the prior computer science experience scale. Factors were analyzed using principal components analysis and Kaiser's normalized varimax orthogonal rotation. Employment of Kaiser's criterion of factor acceptability (associated eigenvalue greater than one) yielded six factors. Solutions of lower dimensionality and scree plots were examined and a five-factor solution was determined to be most meaningful.

4.5 Means Analysis

Independent-sample *t* tests were conducted on measures of cognitive abilities and prior computer science experience.

4.5.1 Cognitive Abilities

Mean comparisons were conducted to determine if the schools significantly differed on measures of cognitive abilities (spatial orientation, visualization, logical reasoning, flexibility, and perceptual style).

It was found that the schools significantly differed on all measures of cognitive abilities. Participants from School A ($M = 13.34$, $SD = 8.52$) scored significantly lower on the spatial orientation test than those from School B ($M = 20.80$, $SD = 8.43$), $t(159) = 5.58$, $p = .00$. Further, participants from School A ($M = 26.14$, $SD = 18.68$) scored significantly lower on the visualization test than those from School B ($M = 40.35$, $SD = 16.22$), $t(159) = 5.12$, $p = .00$. In addition, participants from School A ($M = 8.11$, $SD = 5.68$), scored significantly lower on the logical reasoning test than those from School B ($M = 11.25$, $SD = 5.41$), $t(159) = 3.68$, $p = .00$. Also, participants from School A ($M = 18.87$, $SD = 5.33$) scored lower on the flexibility test than those from School B ($M = 22.79$, $SD = 5.88$), $t(159) = 4.41$, $p = .00$. Finally, participants from School A ($M = 10.13$, $SD = 4.76$) scored significantly lower on the perceptual style test than those from School B ($M = 13.16$, $SD = 4.27$), $t(159) = 4.27$, $p = .00$.

4.5.2 Prior Computer Science Experience

Means comparisons were conducted for each subscale of prior computer science experience (UNIX programming, object-oriented processes, web designing, computing platforms, and various CS).

It was found that the schools significantly differed on all subscales of prior computer science experience. Participants from School A ($M = 1.33$, $SD = .46$) had significantly more UNIX programming experience than those from School B ($M = 1.17$, $SD = .30$), $t(159) = 2.76$, $p = .01$. Further, participants from School A ($M = 2.29$, $SD = .60$) had significantly less experience in object-oriented processing than those from School B ($M = 2.75$, $SD = .72$), $t(159) = 4.37$, $p = .00$. Also, participants from School A ($M = 2.85$, $SD = .66$) had significantly less experience in computing platforms than those from School B ($M = 3.1$, $SD = .61$), $t(159) = 2.74$, $p = .01$. Finally, participants from School A ($M = 2.69$, $SD = 1.34$) had significantly less experience in various CS tasks than those from School B ($M = 2.26$, $SD = .55$), $t(159) = 2.76$, $p = .01$.

4.5.3 Pre/Post Training Design Task

Means comparison was conducted to evaluate whether the two schools significantly differed on results of the pre-training, post-training, and design task change scores. It was found that the participants from School A ($M = 11.90$, $SD = 3.27$) scored significantly lower on the pre-training design task than did participants from School B ($M = 14.00$, $SD = 3.69$). However, the schools did not significantly differ on the scores of the post-training design task. Further analysis of the data found that the change from pre-training to post-training design task was significantly greater for School A ($M = 2.11$, $SD = 3.18$) than for School B ($M = -.88$, $SD = 4.36$).

4.5.4 Final Course Grade

Means comparison was conducted to evaluate whether the participants from the two schools significantly differed on the final grades issued in the course. It was determined that the schools did not significantly differ on the final grade, with both schools final grades averaging in the mid-80s.

5. DISCUSSION

In summary, it was determined that School A (the comprehensive university) consistently scored lower on measures of cognitive ability, prior computer science experience, and pre-training design task than did School B (the research-intensive university). However, at the end of the semester when the post-training design task was administered, it was found that student performance across schools did *not* significantly differ. Further, the final grades in the courses were not significantly different.

The promising finding in this research is that associated with the performance on the design task. While students clearly showed a difference in backgrounds, cognitive ability, and design knowledge at the beginning of the semester, by the end of the semester the knowledge gap had narrowed to the point of being insignificant. The result of this study essentially shows that students of differing backgrounds attending different universities eventually reach a similar level of design skill by the time the time the CS2 class is completed. Further research is needed to justify the statement that *maybe* CS2 is the OOD leveling course across universities.

One could speculate that course depth/breadth and differing levels of student expectations would account for the steep improvement curve seen in School A. This may hold as a plausible explanation for overall course grade, however this has no significant bearing on the unbiased post-training design task.

While teaching methodology may play a role in overall learning and performance in the course, the results of this research sparked interest in other measures of individual differences that may explain performance on the post-training design task. For example, maturity, motivation to learn, course satisfaction, self-efficacy, and measure of performance anxiety provide plausible explanations for these results. Future research will examine measures of these factors to assess their role in task and course performance; along with specific assessments of teaching methodologies.

The ultimate goal of this research is to equip educators with the tools necessary to assess knowledge, engage students, and facilitate learning.

6. REFERENCES

[1] ACM Computing Curricula. (2001). *Computing curricula 2001 final report*. Joint Task Force on Computing Curricula – IEEE and ACM.

[2] Alspaugh, C.A. (1972) Identification of some components of computer programming aptitude. *Journal of Research in Mathematics Education, 3*, 89-98.

[3] Bishop-Clark, C. (1998). An undergraduate course in Object-Oriented Software Design. *Proceedings from Frontiers in Education Conference '98*. Tempe, AZ.

[4] Carroll, J.B. (1974). *Psychometric tests as cognitive tasks: A new structure of intellect* (p. 74-16). Princeton, NJ: Educational Testing Service.

[5] Denelsky, G.Y. & McKee, M.G. (1974). Prediction of computer programmer training and job performance using the AABP test. *Personal Psychology*, 129-137.

[6] Mazlack, L J. (1980). Identifying potential to acquire programming skill, *Communications of the ACM, 23*(1), 14-17.

[7] Deckro, R.F. & Woundenberg, H.W. (1977). MBA admission criteria and academic success, *Decision Sciences*, 765-799.

[8] Ekstrom, R. B., French, J. W., & Harman, H. H. (1979). Cognitive factors: Their identification and replication. *Multivariate Behavioral Research Monographs, 79*(2).

[9] Evans, G E. & Simkins, M G. (1989). What best predicts computer proficiency?, *Communications of the ACM, 32*(11), 1322-1327.

[10] Goold, A., & Rimmer, R. (2000). Factors affecting performance in first-year computing, *ACM SIGCSE Bulletin, 32*(2), 39-43.

[11] Glorfeld, L. W., & Fowler, G. C. (1982). Validation of a model for predicting aptitude for introductory computing. Association for Computing Machinery Special Interest Group *Computer Science Education Bulletin, 14*(1), 140-143.

[12] Katz, S., Aronis, J.D., Allbritton, C. Wilson, C & Soffa, M.L., (2003). An experiment to identify predictors of achievement in an introductory computer science course. *ACM Conference on Computer Personnel Research.*

[13] Jakiela, M., & Fayad, L. (1989). Identification of factors that contribute to engineering design skill. Transactions of the IEEE.

[14] Morrison, M. & Newman, T. S. (2001). A study of the impact of student background and preparedness on outcomes in CS I, *Proceedings from SIGCSE 2001*, Charlotte, NC,179-183.

[15] Petersen, C.C., & Howe, T.G. (1979). *Predicting academic success in introduction to computers*. Association of Educational Data Systems Journal, 182-191.

[16] Rountree, N., Rountree, J. & Robins, A.V. (2002). Predictors of success and failure in a CS1 course. *Special Interest Group on Computer Science Education Bulletin,* 34(4):121-124.

[17] Stevens, L.J., Wileman, S., & Konvalina, J. (1981). *Group differences in computer aptitude*. Association of Educational Data Systems Journal, 84-95.

[18] Ventura, P. (2004). Unpublished Dissertation: *On the origins of programmers: Identifying predictors of success for an objects-first CS1*. Computer Science, University at Buffalo, SUNY.

[19] Werth, L. (1989). *Predicting student performance in a beginning computer science class,* Proceedings of the 17th SIGCSE Technical Symposium on Computer Science Education, Cincinnati, Ohio.

[20] Wilson, B. (2000). *Contributing factors to success in computer science: A study of gender differences*. Unpublished dissertation from the Department of Curriculum and Instruction, Southern Illinois University at Carbondale.

[21] Witkin, H., Moore, C., Goodenough, D., & Cox, P. (1977). Field-dependent and field-independent cognitive styles and their educational implications. *Review of Educational Research, 47*, 1-64.

[22] Witkin, H., Oltman, P., Raskin, E., & Karp, S. (1971). *A manual for the embedded figures test.* Palo Alto, CA: Consulting Psychologists Press.

Towards Concrete Concurrency: occam-pi on the LEGO Mindstorms

Christian L. Jacobsen
Computing Laboratory
University of Kent
Canterbury, Kent, CT2 7NF
clj3@kent.ac.uk

Matthew C. Jadud
Computing Laboratory
University of Kent
Canterbury, Kent, CT2 7NF
matthew.c@jadud.com

ABSTRACT

In a world of ad-hoc networks, highly interconnected mobile devices and increasingly large supercomputer clusters, students need models of computation that help them think about dynamic and concurrent systems. Many of the tools currently available for introducing students to concurrency are difficult to use and are not intrinsically motivating. To provide an authentic, hands-on, and enjoyable introduction to concurrency, we have ported occam-π, a language whose expressive powers are especially compelling for describing communicating dynamic reactive processes, to the LEGO Mindstorms.

Categories and Subject Descriptors

D.1.3 [**Programming Techniques**]: Concurrent Programming

General Terms

Human Factors, Languages

Keywords

LEGO, occam-π, concurrency, parallelism, CSP, fun

1. INTRODUCTION

This paper is about a philosophy of instruction and the tools we have developed for teaching concurrency in the context of this philosophy.

Our philosophy regarding instruction is that students should have fun engaging in authentic, hands-on learning, and they should look forward to those learning experiences. When we say fun, we mean our students should find learning to be enjoyable, challenging and enriching in obvious ways. "Hands-on" means that the learning process is not passive from the learner's perspective (like a typical lecture), but active, requiring students to participate mentally and physically in the learning process. We define authentic learning experiences as those that are true unto themselves; they are not contrived. And when a student walks into our classroom, we want them to look forward to the lesson—even if they don't know what it is going to be.

Our goal is to remain true to our philosophy, and at the same time develop a platform upon which we can explore concurrency and parallelism with our students. We believe the LEGO® Mindstorms™ provides an ideal starting point in this regard. Little robots have to deal with big problems, and the problems students face programming these robots are *real*: navigating around a room, while reading from multiple sensors and communicating with other little robots is an obvious goal, but a difficult task nevertheless. In bringing occam-π[5] to the Mindstorms, we believe we can explore concurrency more deeply, more tangibly and more enjoyably than with the technologies otherwise available to us.

We begin our paper with a brief introduction to occam-π and the run-time environment that we have developed for use in our own classrooms. We then examine a number of other tools and methods for teaching concurrency in section three; in particular, we consider these tools through the lens of our own philosophy of instruction. Lastly, we provide a worked example demonstrating occam-π's expressiveness on the LEGO Mindstorms, and close with a brief discussion of future directions of our work.

2. BACKGROUND

occam-π is a new, explicitly concurrent language, which combines the best features of the Communicating Sequential Process (CSP) algebra, first introduced by Professor Sir Tony Hoare in 1985[15], and the π-calculus, developed by Robin Milner[22]. occam-π has a small number of syntactic constructs (like Scheme) and uses indentation to denote logical blocks of code (like Python). Modeled closely on the CSP algebra, occam-π compilers provide guarantees about the run-time behavior of programs. For example, it is not possible for data race-hazards to take place at run-time. Additionally, one of the defining features of the language is the ability to express non-deterministic choice over communications channels. For example, it is possible to easily respond to any one of many sensors on a little robot. This process of alternating over communications channels (as expressed by the `ALT` construct) is demonstrated in our worked example in section four.

SIGCSE'05, February 23–27, 2005, St. Louis, Missouri, USA.

The CSP model of concurrency provides a clear and simple framework for expressing parallel programs. This is accomplished through the use of unidirectional, point-to-point, blocking *channels* through which data is passed from one process to another while executing in parallel. Unidirectional, point-to-point channels are part of what make occam-π a safer language for programming concurrently. Additionally, because all communications block, each communication becomes an explicit synchronization point in our program. This makes it unnecessary to use spin locks, semaphores, and other error-prone constructs commonly employed when writing parallel programs in other languages.

The CSP model of communicating processes is widely used today: Erlang[2] and Handel-C[3], for example, both build on concepts that originated in CSP. Additionally, occam-π is continually evolving in the form of KRoC –the Kent Retargetable occam-π Compiler[4, 32]. Our efforts extend this work: we have built the *Transterpreter*, a virtual machine interpreting a byte-code that includes instructions directly supporting CSP primitives for concurrency[16]. The byte-codes generated are an integral step of the KRoC compiler, thereby providing the Transterpreter with an existing and proven tool-chain.

Written in strict ANSI C, the Transterpreter runs on all major operating systems and architectures. Because of the Transterpreter's small memory footprint (roughly 5Kb), it is well suited to embedded applications. In addition to being able to execute occam-π programs on Macintosh OS X, Linux, Solaris and Windows, we planned from the beginning for our software to run on small devices like the LEGO Mindstorms.

Because of the extremely portable nature of the Transterpreter, we can execute the exact same occam-π program on the LEGO Mindstorms as we would in our simulator or on larger robotics platforms. The Transterpreter also offers an excellent run-time environment for exploring concurrency; in this regard, occam-π is a language that allows students to develop their skills in concurrency over examples that range from real-time systems to high performance clusters and grid-like architectures.

3. TEACHING CONCURRENCY

Motivation matters. We believe students should have fun exploring authentic tasks in constructive ways[17]. In this section, we examine some pedagogic approaches to introducing concurrency, from the perspective of our beliefs that learning should be fun, authentic and constructive.

3.1 Learning should be fun

In their paper "Using robotics to motivate back door learning," Marion Petre and Blaine Price studied children using the LEGO Mindstorms in robotics competitions[25]. Their research echoes what Fred Martin[21] and others[7] have observed in their own work: little robots can provide a focus for learning and collaboration. It is this engaging, motivational element that we feel is missing from languages like SR[1] and Oz[29] that have been developed for introducing concurrency to students.

Micro-worlds have often filled this motivational void in the past. StarLogo, developed by Mitchel Resnick and others at the MIT Media Labs, is a massively parallel micro-world designed to help children explore and play with decentralized systems[27]. occam-π, like LOGO, is a small and simple language, designed originally for use in embedded systems. We believe the use of the Transterpreter on the Mindstorms will provide us with an environment and metaphor for exploring concurrency in the real world.

3.2 Learning should be authentic

Many students studying operating systems encounter the *dining philosophers problem*[15]. Invented by Dijkstra, this problem may involve (for example) five philosophers who share five chopsticks and one plate of spaghetti. They sit, they think, and they eat, repeating this process indefinitely. Problems arise when one philosopher is infinitely refused the use of a chopstick, by another greedy philosopher, who always pick up their chopstick immediately after putting it down. This will lead to starvation of the first philosopher. Another bad condition, known as deadlock, can occur when everyone picks up one chopstick and no one can pick up the second needed to eat the spaghetti; this leads the philosophers to wait indefinitely for the second chopstick to become available. A number of pedagogic environments have been developed to allow students to explore this problem, visually or otherwise[20, 28].

The dining philosophers problem is authentic in that it accurately captures the problem of sharing resources (like memory and disk) by two or more simultaneous processes in a computing system. However, the problem lacks real-world authenticity: it is an analogy. When programming a LEGO Mindstorms equipped with multiple sensors, process starvation, deadlock, livelock and race-hazards are *real* problems. Failing to read from one of two light sensors may prevent a robot from following a line, or cause it to wander off a student's work surface (sometimes much to their delight). We think using a language like occam-π on the LEGO Mindstorms introduces students to the challenges and delights of concurrent real-time system design; and it provides a powerful tool for executing those designs.

3.3 Learning should be constructive

We agree with Einstein when he said: "Things should be made as simple as possible—but no simpler." Relevant here is that there is no reason why learning to program in the concurrent paradigm should be any more difficult than learning any other paradigm. Too many approaches to teaching concurrency are too complex, introduced too late and their value is therefore obscured.

Many examples exist where industry-standard libraries like PVM[13] or OpenMP[31] have been employed in the classroom[10, 18, 24]. However, all of these industrial-strength packages suffer from the same problem: while their primitives may be few and simple, correct and safe application of them can be surprisingly hard. They are designed for professional software engineers, not first-year undergraduates; the usability issues that can result from this mismatch may have a significant impact on what students can accomplish[9].

In an attempt to deal with this dissonance, pedagogic libraries like ThreadMentor[8] have been developed—but all of these (industrial and pedagogic alike) suffer from a larger problem. Libraries provide students with primitives for implementing concurrency in their programs, but they do not help students to *design* solutions with concurrency in mind. These libraries represent the imposing of one computational paradigm (concurrency) in a fundamentally serial paradigm.

occam-π, on the other hand, has concurrency built into the heart of its language, by design, that makes it natural to express ideas about processes, networks, communication, time-outs, non-deterministic choice etc. Furthermore, we only ever need to think about one component process at a time, so that there is true compositionally and, hence, scalability.

Our goal is to make students fluent in concurrent design and implementation, not to teach them how to use one set of primitives for concurrency before they fundamentally understand the paradigm. We encourage students by giving them programming tasks that are fundamentally concurrent in nature: programming little robots, for example. In this respect, we appreciate Lynn Andrea Stein's work in "Rethinking CS101," which involves motivating students to think about agent—and event—based computing sooner, rather than later, in the curriculum[30].

3.4 Learning on the LEGO

Our implementation of occam-π for the Mindstorms opens new possibilities for the teaching and learning of concurrent programming using this small robotics platform. Languages like Not Quite C (NQC)[6] and ROBOLAB[26] provide basic multitasking facilities that students can use, although interprocess communication is difficult and awkward at best. The implementation of Ada for the Mindstorms, developed by Fagin et al., translates Ada programs to NQC, and therefore shares many of NQC's limitations[11]. Despite the existence of concurrency primitives in Ada, Ada/Mindstorms does not currently take advantage of these. Tasking is however a future goal for the Ada/Mindstorms environment[12].

Unlike many languages available for the Mindstorms, our implementation of occam-π will be complete. At the time of writing, all core concurrency mechanisms have been implemented. Capabilities for dynamic memory, mobile processes and channels (allowing the creation of dynamically evolving process networks) are currently work in progress. Other complete languages do exist for the Mindstorms. pbForth is a complete Forth implementation for the Mindstorms by Ralph Hempel[14]. There also exists a complete environment for programming the Mindstorms in C, BrickOS, written by Markus Noga[23]. BrickOS requires GCC to build C programs for the Mindstorms, which is a non-trivial environment to set up and maintain. We would hesitate to use it in the classroom. However, we have made extensive use of BrickOS in our own work, as we host the Transterpreter within it.

We believe Klassner's work on Mnet, a LISP environment for the LEGO Mindstorms, is motivated by concerns regarding authenticity similar to our own[19]. In teaching the fundamentals of classic AI (search, planning, etc.), it is much more interesting to do the work on real robots as opposed to working in a virtual microworld. Further comparison, however, is unfair to both projects: Frank Klassner is interested in motivating students studying AI, while we are looking for an authentic environment for studying concurrency in real-time systems.

4. OCCAM-PI ON THE MINDSTORMS

We have discussed occam-π and the Transterpreter, and how our pedagogic goals relate to other approaches to teaching concurrency. We have also discussed how the Transterpreter relates to other languages and environments available for the Mindstorms, and will now provide a worked example to further ground this discussion in the technologies we are making available to the larger computer science education community.

In all the languages and environments available for the Mindstorms, a robot that can bump-and-wander its way around a room is a simple task. A more difficult challenge is to build a robot which allows the bump-and-wander robot to be interrupted, if it reverses into an obstacle, during its timed reversal sequence. The robot this example is using has two bump sensors, one in front and one at the back. When the robot bumps into an obstacle at the front, it starts a reverse turn. The reverse turn can be interrupted either by a time-out, or at any time the robot reverses into an obstacle, which would be detected by the triggering of the back bump sensor. Due to the use of two separate conditions for termination of the robot's reversal, implementing this program can be a difficult task in many other languages.

occam-π is a language of communicating processes. The primary mechanism for these communications are *channels*, which are unidirectional, synchronizing, unbuffered pipes through which data (or references to data) can be safely passed. These channels can carry everything from single booleans to complex structured data, and serve as explicit synchronization points in occam-π programs, and guarantee the complete absence of data race-hazards, a property enforced by the compiler.

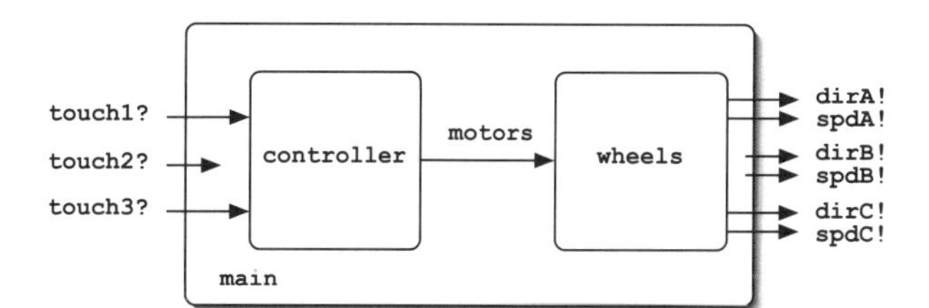

Figure 1: A simple process diagram

```
 1 #INCLUDE "legolib.inc"
 2 PROTOCOL Motors IS BYTE; BYTE; BYTE; BYTE:
 3 VAL INT backupTime IS 1000:
 4
 5 PROC main ()
 6   CHAN Motors motors:
 7   PAR
 8     controller (touch1?, touch3?, motors!)
 9     wheels (motors?, dirA!, spdA!,
10                      dirC!, spdC!)
11 :
```

Figure 2: `main` gets things started

Figure 1 is a simple process diagram that we might develop with our students to represent a collection of processes on a Mindstorms—just two in this example.

There is a `controller` process, containing the control logic, and a `wheels` process, used to mediate communication with the motors. There are also three external input channels, one for each touch sensor, and six external output channels, that directly drive actuators on the wheel motors. These external channels are provided by our *legolib*—see figure 2 (line 1). There is also one internal channel, `motors`, carrying information between the two processes.

Figure 2 lists the top-down presentation of this system. We start by specifying the `main` process that declares the internal channel, and creates and starts the two concurrent sub-processes. Of interest is the declaration of the `Motors` protocol (line 2), which declares that all communications over a channel of type `Motors` will involve sending four bytes: left motor direction, right motor direction, left motor speed, right motor speed; the channel variable `motors` is locally declared in the procedure `main` on line 6.On line 7, we spawn two processes in parallel using the `PAR` construct: the controlling process, and the process that drives the wheels.

In creating the `controller` and `wheels` processes, we see that each have been passed a different end of the `motors` channel. The end of the channel passed to each process is signified by a '?' suffix (for reading) or '!' suffix (for writing). We will use this `motors` channel to set the direction and speed of the two motors attached to the LEGO Mindstorms. Messages passed set the direction and speed of the two motors connected, as programmed by the `wheels PROC` (figure 3).

```
1 PROC wheels (CHAN Motors moto?,
2      CHAN BYTE dirA!, spdA!, dirC!, spdC!)
3   WHILE TRUE
4     BYTE dLeft, sLeft, dRight, sRight:
5     SEQ
6       moto ? dLeft; sLeft; dRight; sRight
7       PAR
8         dirA ! dLeft
9         spdA ! sLeft
10        dirC ! dRight
11        spdC ! sRight
12 :
```

Figure 3: `wheels` handles motor control

A common idiom in occam-π programs is for each process to contain an infinite loop (line 3); in a language that is inherently concurrent, this is not a problem. We see on line 1 the parameter `moto?`, which is our motor control channel; the other end of this channel is connected to the `controller` process (this fact is not relevant to the design and implementation of this process however). In `SEQ`uence (line 5), we read in four bytes from the `moto` channel (line 6), and then in `PAR`allel we set the direction and speed of motors attached to ports A and C on the Mindstorms by the relevant channel communications.

```
1 PROC controller (CHAN BOOL touchFront?,
2      touchBack?, CHAN Motors moto!)
3   WHILE TRUE
4     BOOL touched:
5     TIMER clock:
6     INT curTime:
7     SEQ
8       moto ! FWD; FULL; FWD; FULL
9       touchFront ? touched
10      moto ! BWD; HALF; BWD; FULL
11      clock ? curTime
12      ALT
13        touchBack ? touched
14          SKIP
15        clock ? AFTER curTime PLUS backupTime
16          SKIP
17 :
```

Figure 4: `controller` is the interesting bit

In figure 4 we see the `controller` process; this `PROC`ess does all of the "work" in our example. On lines 1-2, are the parameters—in this case, two input channel ends from the touch sensors and the output end of the `motors` channel. On line 3 is the idiomatic infinite loop, followed by three local variable declarations. The `clock` defined on line 5 has a special type, a `TIMER`. This is treated as a read-only channel from which the current system time (in milliseconds for this platform) is always available.

We begin by moving forward (line 8); we accomplish this by sending library-defined constants for direction and speed down the channel `motors`, which given its `PROTOCOL` must take four bytes of information. Sending data down a channel is accomplished via the syntax

$$< channel > \; ! \; < valexp >$$

where the result of the value expression on the right-hand side is sent down the channel (as long as the compile-time type check passes).

In the next line, we take advantage of the fact that occam-π channels are synchronized; the `controller` process will block on line 9 until the `touchFront` channel becomes ready with a value—meaning the touch sensor has been pressed. Here, we see the occam-π syntax for reading from a channel,

$$< channel > \; ? \; < variable >$$

where a value is read from the channel into the variable provided.

Once the `touchFront` channel is triggered, line 10 tells the motors to run in reverse (at different speeds, so we pivot), and the interesting part of the program begins.

The `ALT` construct (line 12) provides for passive waiting for one of two or more events to become ready; it allows the expression of the non-deterministic behavior of a process. In this case, we are waiting for either the back touch sensor (`touchBack`, line 13) or the `clock` (line 15). In particular, we are watching to see if a number of milliseconds equal to the variable `backupTime` (line 3, figure 2) have elapsed since the time this process first read the clock on line 11.

If either the touch sensor or the time-out on the clock becomes ready for communication, we do the same thing in both cases: we drop out of the `ALT` with the `SKIP` instruction (a no-op). This takes us up to the top of the loop, where we once again set the motors moving in a forward direction, and begin the process all over again.

For information, the source-code for the above occam-π program, is 42 lines long. A Java solution, programmed by an expert colleague, using a standard OO event-driven paradigm, occupies 165 lines.

5. CONCLUSIONS AND FUTURE WORK

The Mindstorms is an excellent introductory platform for introducing students to the issues involved in developing concurrent and parallel programs. It is an authentic application of these ideas, as even small robots have big problems dealing with the immediacy and concurrency of the real world.

Our plans for future work are driven by technological, pedagogic and research concerns. The Transterpreter will continue to grow until it supports the full extent of occam-π. Additionally, we look forward to experimenting with the Transterpreter as a platform for exploring grid computing in the context of dynamic clusters—another natural application of occam-π. We have begun collecting resources for teaching and programming with occam-π at `www.transterpreter.org`, intended for use by instructors and students interested in our work. Lastly, more research of this nature regarding the use of robotics for motivation and concurrency in the curriculum is absolutely necessary.

6. ACKNOWLEDGMENTS

We would like to thank David Barnes for his comments and feedback on an early draft of this paper. In addition, thanks to Peter Welch at Kent and Mark Smith of Colby College for their insights during the revision process.

7. REFERENCES

[1] G. Andrews and R. Olsson. *The SR Programming Language: Concurrency in Practice.* Benjamin/Cummings Publishing Company, Inc., 1993.

[2] J. Armstrong, R. Virding, C. Wikström, and M. Williams. *Concurrent Programming in Erlang.* Prentice-Hall, second edition, 1996.

[3] M. Aubury, I. Page, G. Randall, J. Saul, and R. Watts. *Handel-C Language Reference Guide.* Oxford University Computing Laboratory, August 1996.

[4] F. R. Barnes. *Dynamics and Pragmatics for High Performance Concurrency.* PhD thesis, University of Kent, June 2003.

[5] F. R. M. Barnes and P. H. Welch. Communicating Mobile Processes. In *Communicating Process Architectures 2004*, pages 201–218, 2004.

[6] D. Baum and R. Zurcher. *Dave Baum's Definitive Guide to Lego Mindstorms.* APress L. P., 1999.

[7] R. D. Beer, H. J. Chiel, and R. F. Drushel. Using autonomous robotics to teach science and engineering. *Commun. ACM*, 42(6):85–92, 1999.

[8] S. Carr, J. Mayo, and C.-K. Shene. Threadmentor: a pedagogical tool for multithreaded programming. *J. Educ. Resour. Comput.*, 3(1):1–30, 2003.

[9] S. Clarke. Measuring API usability. *Dr. Dobbs Journal*, May 2004.

[10] J. C. Cunha and J. Lourenco. An integrated course on parallel and distributed processing. In *Proceedings of the twenty-ninth SIGCSE technical symposium on Computer science education*, pages 217–221. ACM Press, 1998.

[11] B. Fagin. An Ada interface to LEGO Mindstorms. *Ada Lett.*, XX(3):20–40, 2000.

[12] B. Fagin. Ada/mindstorms 3.0: A computational environment for introductory robotics and programming. *IEEE Robotics and Automation Magazine*, 10(2):19– 24, June 2003.

[13] A. Geist, A. Beguelin, J. Dongarra, W. Jiang, R. Manchek, and V. Sunderam. *PVM 3 Users Guide and Reference manual.* Oak Ridge National Laboratory, Oak Ridge, Tennessee 37831, May 1994.

[14] R. Hempel. The pbForth Home Page, 2004. `http://www.hempeldesigngroup.com/lego/pbForth`.

[15] C. Hoare. *Communicating Sequential Processes.* Prentice-Hall, Inc., 1985.

[16] C. L. Jacobsen and M. C. Jadud. The Transterpreter: A Transputer Interpreter. In *Communicating Process Architectures 2004*, pages 99–107, 2004.

[17] M. C. Jadud. Teamstorms as a theory of instruction. In *Systems, Man, and Cybernetics, 2000 IEEE International Conference*, volume 1, 2000.

[18] L. Jin and L. Yang. A laboratory for teaching parallel computing on parallel structures. In *Proceedings of the twenty-sixth SIGCSE technical symposium on Computer science education*, pages 71–75. ACM Press, 1995.

[19] F. Klassner. Enhancing lisp instruction with RCXLisp and robotics. In *Proceedings of the 35th SIGCSE technical symposium on Computer science education*, pages 214–218. ACM Press, 2004.

[20] B. L. Kurtz, H. Cai, C. Plock, and X. Chen. A concurrency simulator designed for sophomore-level instruction. In *Proceedings of the twenty-ninth SIGCSE technical symposium on Computer science education*, pages 237–241. ACM Press, 1998.

[21] F. G. Martin. *Circuits to Control: Learning Engineering by Designing LEGO Robots.* PhD thesis, Massachusetts Institute of Technology, 1994.

[22] R. Milner. *Communicating and mobile systems: the π-calculus.* Cambridge University Press, 1999.

[23] M. Noga. BrickOS for the LEGO Mindstorms. `http://freshmeat.net/projects/brickos/`.

[24] Y. Pan. An innovative course in parallel computing. *Journal of STEM Education*, 4(0), 2003.

[25] P. B. Petre M. Using robotics to motivate 'back door' learning. *Education and Information Technologies*, 9(2):147–158, 2004.

[26] Pitsco LEGO Dacta. The ROBOLAB system, 2000. `http://www.pitsco-legodacta.com/Products/robolab.htm`.

[27] M. Resnick. *Turtles, Termites, and Traffic Jams: Explorations in Massively Parallel Micorworlds.* MIT Press, 1994.

[28] S. Robbins. Starving philosophers: experimentation with monitor synchronization. In *Proceedings of the thirty-second SIGCSE technical symposium on Computer Science Education*, pages 317–321. ACM Press, 2001.

[29] P. V. Roy and S. Haridi. *Concepts, Techniques, and Models of Computer Programming.* MIT Press, 2004.

[30] L. Stein. Challenging the computational metaphor: Implications for how we think, 1999.

[31] The OpenMP Architecture Review Board. OpenMP Specifications version 2.0. `http://www.openmp.org/drupal/mp-documents/cspec20.pdf`.

[32] D. Wood and P. Welch. The Kent Retargetable occam Compiler. In B. O'Neill, editor, *Parallel Processing Developments, Proceedings of WoTUG 19*, volume 47 of *Concurrent Systems Engineering*, pages 143–166. IOS Press, Netherlands, 1996. ISBN: 90-5199-261-0.

Efficient Use of Robots in the Undergraduate Curriculum

Judith Challinger
California State University, Chico
400 West First Street
Chico, CA 95929
(530) 898-6347
judyc@ecst.csuchico.edu

ABSTRACT

In this paper we describe how a single Khepera II robot was used for an assignment in a senior level course on graphical user interface implementation. The assignment required each student to implement a graphical user interface for remotely controlling a Khepera II robot. From the author's point of view, the focus of the project was how to efficiently and effectively allow the 35 students enrolled in the course to have access to the robot for the purposes of testing and debugging. Furthermore, two of the students were enrolled through the distance education program and were remotely located. The intent was to see if an assignment making use of the robot would stimulate student interest, and whether it could be done with a minimal investment in hardware, lab, and instructor resources. The students were surveyed at the conclusion of the assignment in order to assess the effectiveness of the assignment. The results of this survey are presented, along with plans for future work.

Categories and Subject Descriptors

K.3.2 [Computers and Education]: Computer and Information Science Education ---Computer Science Education

General Terms

Algorithms, Design, Human Factors, Languages.

Keywords

Java, Swing, GUI, Graphical User Interface, Robotics, Khepera.

1. INTRODUCTION

Using the enticing qualities of a robot to attract and retain student interest in computer programming is nothing new [1]. Pedagogy based on the use of robots to engage students has become fairly common. It is especially prevalent in CS1/CS2, as well as in courses that specifically address the topics of robotics and artificial intelligence. [2] The most interesting robots are still quite expensive, however. The result is that this equipment is typically reserved for the use of a select few graduate students or advanced undergraduate students, working directly under a faculty member. When our institution recently received a grant to acquire the equipment necessary to establish an Intelligent Systems Laboratory [3], the goals of the principle investigators included encouraging the use of the equipment in supporting undergraduate education, and promoting interdisciplinary and faculty collaboration. With their encouragement, the author decided to attempt to utilize one of the more interesting robots, the Khepera II, for an assignment in a senior level course on graphical user interface implementation.

In this course the students learn to implement graphical user interfaces using the Java Swing API. The assignment that was selected required each student to implement a graphical user interface (GUI) for remotely controlling a Khepera II robot. From the author's point of view, the focus of this investigation was how to efficiently and effectively allow the 35 students enrolled in the course to have access to the single robot for the purposes of testing and debugging. Furthermore, two of the students were enrolled through the distance education program and were remotely located. The intent was to see if an assignment making use of the robot would stimulate student interest, and whether it could be done with a minimal investment in hardware, lab, and instructor resources. The students were surveyed at the conclusion of the assignment in order to assess the effectiveness of the assignment. Information on the assignment, the methods used to give students access to the robot, and the results of the student survey are presented here, along with plans for future work.

SIGCSE'05, February 23–27, 2005, St. Louis, Missouri, USA.

2. THE KHEPERA II

The Khepera II (see Figure 1) is a moderately expensive robot. It is small, only 70mm in diameter, and is round. The robot has 8

Figure 1. The Khepera II Robot.

infrared proximity detectors - three to the front and left, three to the front and right, and two at the back. They can be seen around the outside circumference of the robot. It has wheels that can be controlled in a variety of ways, and it also has position counters on each wheel. The Khepera II has a variety of running modes. For this assignment the robot was connected to a host computer via a serial cable and configured to process a simple command protocol [4].

3. STUDENT ASSIGNMENT

The assignment requires each student to implement a graphical user interface (GUI) for remotely controlling the Khepera II robot. The result of the student's work will be a client program that can connect to a robot server, can query the state of the Khepera II, and can send motion commands to the Khepera II. The GUI consists of graphical components to display the state information, buttons and menu elements to control the robot, and a map representing the robot's environment as discovered during navigation (see Figure 2). The student is provided with a Java archive (jar) of classes that implement a model for the robot and all the necessary client communication software. Their task is to implement the GUI precisely as described in the assignment[1], using the classes provided in the jar file. As the purpose of the course is to learn how to use the Swing API, from the perspective of the student this assignment has the following goals in terms of the GUI implementation:

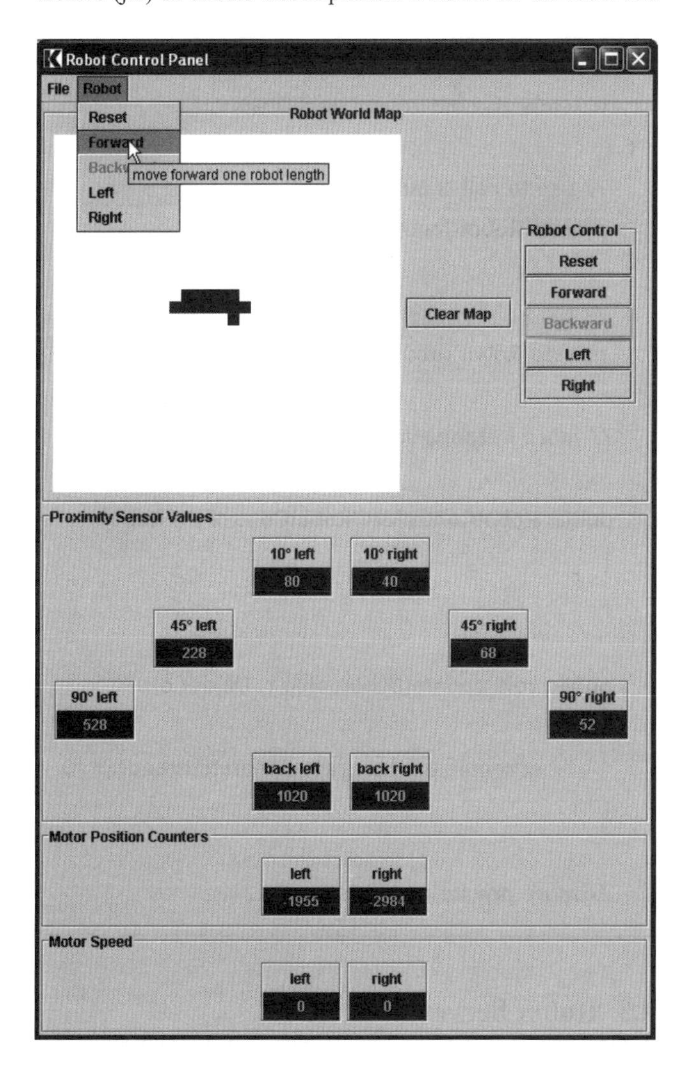

Figure 2. The student will implement this Robot Control GUI.

- Implement a fairly complex GUI with several different panels and files.
- Customize a JPanel by extending and then overriding paintComponent( ).
- Use Action objects to create both buttons and menu items.
- Use TitledBorders to group and organize components.

An additional, very important, aspect of the assignment is the continuing exposure of the student to design patterns. In fact, a main theme of the course is design patterns [5]. One in particular that is studied is Model – View – Controller. Swing provides a particularly rich demonstration of the MVC design pattern in action. The application of this design pattern is further emphasized in the separation of the Model for the robot (a class provided to the student) from the View – Controller (implemented in the classes the student will develop).

4. ROBOT CLIENT AND SERVER

Several problems needed to be considered in order to make this assignment feasible:

- How to minimize the effort needed to communicate with the Khepera II so that the student could focus on the GUI implementation.
- How to provide a connection to the Khepera II to students as they design, implement, test, and debug, their GUI.
- How to ensure fairness among the students in terms of connect time to the robot.
- How to ensure that only one student GUI is controlling the Khepera II at any given time.
- How to ensure the safety of the Khepera II.
- How to allow the student to see what the Khepera II is actually doing.

The robot physically resided in the author's office. A special table was constructed with walls around the edges to prevent the robot from leaving the table. Rounded corners helped to minimize situations where the robot would become stuck. An apparatus was placed above the table to hold both a web cam and the cable providing the connection between the Khepera II and the host computer. Students could view images from the web cam

[1] The complete assignment using the Khepera II may be seen at www.ecst.csuchico.edu/~judyc/0304S-csci233/program03.html

remotely, providing them with visual information about what the robot was doing. Communication between the Khepera II and the host computer was accomplished over a serial link. A software package was developed by the author, which supplies the classes necessary to build both a client application and the robot server application. Some of these classes are discussed in the sections that follow.

4.1 Robot Class

A class was developed to provide a model for the robot. This class is used both by the robot server, and by the robot client (for which the student is implementing the GUI), to instantiate an object that will represent the state of the robot. The Robot class is both Observable and Serializable. The student does not instantiate the Robot object directly. Communication between the client and the server is part of the functionality that is provided to the student in the jar file. When the client establishes communications with the robot server, the Robot object on the server is serialized and sent in its entirety to the client and instantiated.

The Robot class provides the following functionality in its public interface:

- A method is provided for each type of low-level command that can be sent to the robot. This is similar to the approach taken by Harlan, et al [6]. The students do not know about these methods, and are instructed to use the high-level commands discussed next. An example is:

```
public void  sendWheelSpeed(int left, int right)
```

- Several methods are provided that implement high-level commands. These can be used by the student to make the robot perform certain actions (turn right 90 degrees, for example) without having to worry about calculating the parameters needed for the low-level commands to accomplish this. Examples of high-level commands include:

```
// move forward one robot length
public void moveForwardOne()
// turn right 90 degrees
public void turnRightNinety()
```

- An entire set of synchronized methods to access the state of the robot (as maintained in the Robot object). This includes such things as the current proximity readings, wheel motor position and speed, and so on. For example:

- The Robot class also provides a method that will parse a command from the robot and update the instance variables accordingly. This method is also synchronized. Again, this is a method the students are not told about. The client communications will pass any commands received from the robot (via the robot server) to the Robot class to parse. Since the Robot class is Observable, the students can arrange to receive events for Robot state changes just by registering their GUI object(s) as an Observer of the Robot.

4.2 Robot Client Communications

Included in the jar file provided to the student is the RobotControl class. This class contains the main method for the client application. The main method instantiates the RobotControl object and then immediately calls a method on the object that will loop forever, reading from the server. During initialization, the RobotControl object will establish a connection with the server, receive the initial state of the Robot object and instantiate it, and instantiate an object of type RobotControGUI, passing it a reference to the Robot object and to the RobotControl object. The student is given an empty class to fill in as the basis for their GUI:

```
// RobotControlGUI.java

package robot.control;
import robot.shared.*;
// more import statements

public class RobotControlGUI
   extends JFrame implements Observer
{
   // use to call shutdown( )
   private RobotControl robotControl;

   // the Robot model
   private Robot robot;

  // more instance variables as needed

  public RobotControlGUI(RobotControl rc, Robot r)
  {
  }

  public void update(Observable r, Object o)
  {
     // schedule on the event dispatch thread!
  }

  // more private methods are OK
```

4.3 Robot Server

A robot server application was developed. This application runs on the host machine to which the Khepera II is connected via a serial communications link. The server establishes communications with the robot, and then waits for connections by client applications. The server provides the following services:

- In the running mode that was selected, the Khepera II does not have any way to generate events to the host computer. Therefore, it must be polled. The server polls the robot several times per second and updates the state maintained in the Robot object (the server uses the same class as the client for this purpose).

- The server will accept multiple client connections. Each client that establishes a connection is sent the current robot state in the form of the serialized Robot object. All messages coming in to the server from the robot (in response to polling, for example) are parsed and used to update the Robot object, and are also passed along to each client connection.

- Only one of the clients is allowed to send commands to the robot at any given time. Messages coming in from a client are passed to the Khepera II robot, assuming that client is currently selected to be controlling the actions of the robot. These messages are passed directly through the server to the robot. The Khepera II will generate a message in response to a command that changes its state. It is this confirmation message from the robot that is parsed, used to update the state of the Robot object, and passed along to all client connections. This approach ensures that the state of the Robot object will accurately represent the state of the real robot.

- One of the first problems encountered was the need for a timeout on client connections. The problem arose when the client application written by a student would have an exception, but the student would not kill all the threads. This could cause the connection to the server to exist for quite some time without the student even realizing it. Not only did this take up a connection, but also if that client was the one selected to control the robot then other clients were prevented from doing so. A timeout of 10 minutes was settled on and seemed to satisfy most people.

- Another problem was encountered in which some students' client applications would put the Khepera II into a state where it was spinning madly, or running continuously even though it was up against a wall. It is again possible that the student inadvertently left a thread running that was sending commands to the robot. The intent of the assignment was for the user to be able to control the robot remotely to explore an environment by moving forward or backward one robot length at a time, or turning left or right. Using the high-level command methods of the Robot class, this should have proceeded at a fairly sedate pace. However, things don't always get used as intended! The solution that was effective was to have the server refuse to forward a "move" command to the robot unless the current wheel speed was zero.

- The server logs the date, time, and IP address for each client connected or when a connection is closed. Any time a command is refused, this is logged as well. All error conditions are logged. The logging functionality was essential for solving problems with the server.

5. RESULTS

All students were able to complete the assignment. Most of them enjoyed the challenge, although it certainly wasn't without some level of frustration at times. The Khepera II robot survived the experience without any damage. The author was generally able to keep one step ahead of the students in solving problems such as the need for a timeout on client connections.

Students were asked to complete an anonymous survey in order to give feedback on the quality of the assignment. Ten questions for which the student could answer either Excellent, Good, OK, Not Good, or Terrible, were as follows:

1. How clear were the learning goals for the robot control assignment?
2. How clearly did the robot control assignment specify what you were to implement?
3. How helpful was the robot control assignment in giving you direction as to how to get started?
4. How appropriate was the level of difficulty of the assignment?
5. How relevant was the robot control assignment to the course objectives and to your academic goals?
6. How stimulating was the robot control assignment in terms of inspiring you to want to work on the project?
7. How stimulating was the robot control assignment with respect to the level of interest it generated in you for further investigations into graphical user interfaces, robotics, or some other aspect of the assignment?
8. How effective was the robot control assignment in helping you learn more about the implementation of graphical user interfaces?
9. What did you think of the robot control assignment overall?
10. How effective was the robot control assignment at minimizing technical difficulties that might hamper your learning?

In addition, there were two free response questions:

- Please share what you liked and/or didn't like about the robot control assignment. Be as specific as possible about why you liked or disliked any aspect of it.

- Do you think this assignment, or one similar to it, should be used in this course in the future? Please share any suggestions you have for improving the robot control assignment, or make any other comments you would care to.

There were 23 students that chose to complete the survey. A summary of the responses is given in Table 1. The results show that the majority of the students found the assignment clear, stimulating, and relevant to their learning goals. The survey also shows that technical difficulties encountered by the students were a large source of frustration. It is impressive that most students rated the assignment as well as they did in spite of the problems. The free response answers give a lot of insight into what the problems were. Most had to do with access. Students did not like

Table 1. Results of Student Survey.

Question Number	Excellent	Good	OK	Not Good	Terrible
1	13%	83%	0	4%	0
2	35%	52%	9%	4%	0
3	13%	43%	40%	4%	0
4	26%	40%	26%	9%	0
5	22%	57%	13%	9%	0
6	48%	26%	4%	9%	13%
7	17%	48%	17%	9%	9%
8	17%	48%	22%	9%	4%
9	9%	61%	9%	4%	17%
10	0	17%	26%	52%	4%

having to conform to a schedule. Many like to work late at night, and the server and robot were turned off in the evening. With the current configuration of the client software, students could not test and debug when the server was not running. On the other hand, many of the students found the assignment very stimulating. Some of their comments are illuminating:

- "I really enjoyed the assignment. It was just really cool controlling a robot over the internet with a program I wrote."
- "I liked the fact that this assignment utilized some real world technology. Too often programming assignments are trivial in their purpose. This one was fun and accomplished its purpose."
- "I liked the robot assignment because it was different than the usual assignments."
- "I liked writing a program that was used to control hardware."

6. FUTURE WORK

There are many possible directions that can be explored, and a few development tasks that will improve future assignments of this type. The most important improvement to the software that has been developed would be to include a simple simulator in the client software that is provided to the student. This would not be difficult to do, and would mean that the students could do their initial testing and debugging offline. Quite a few students suggested this in their free responses to the last survey question. It is interesting that this agrees with the findings of Fagin and Merkle [7], even though they were examining the use of robots at the introductory level.

The Khepera II is a stackable architecture. There are several different types of turrets available – circuit boards with additional capabilities that can be inserted into the connectors on the top of the Khepera II. For example, there is a turret with a video camera, one with a gripper, and one that performs radio communications so the robot does not need to be tethered to the host. It is easy to envision projects similar to this one in a variety of different courses.

One advantage to utilizing a resource such as the Khepera II in a classroom situation is that it makes the students aware of the availability of the lab and the research equipment in it. It is not quite so intimidating once they have used it in such a controlled manner. They feel more confident in proposing a senior project, master's project, or independent study, which uses the lab and its resources. This assignment has already spun off several interesting student projects, and it is not uncommon to have students stopping by to ask if the "robot project" will be offered again.

7. ACKNOWLEDGMENTS

This classroom project was made possible through funding from a CSU Internal Grant for Faculty Development, and support from the College of Engineering, Computer Science, and Technology. An initial version of the client/server software was developed under an industry contract with Pacific Media Technologies, who graciously permitted this adaptation of their software. The use of the Khepera II robot was made possible by a National Science Foundation (NSF) Major Research Instrumentation (MRI)/Research in Undergraduate Institutions (RUI) grant EIA-0321385 for 2003-2006. Special thanks go to the Spring 2004 students of CSCI 233 Graphical User Interface Implementation for making this investigation so much fun.

8. REFERENCES

[1] R. Pattis, *Karel the Robot: A Gentle Introduction to the Art of Programming*, John Wiley & Sons, Inc., 1981.

[2] M. Goldweber, C. Congdon, B. Fagin, D. Hwang, and F. Klassner, The use of robots in the undergraduate curriculum: experience reports. In *Proceedings of the thirty-second SIGCSE technical symposium on Computer Science Education*, p. 404-405, ACM Press, 2001.

[3] http://isl.ecst.csuchico.edu/index.htm

[4] http://k-team.com/robots/khepera/index.html

[5] O. Astrachan , G. Mitchener , G. Berry , L. Cox, Design patterns: an essential component of CS curricula. In *Proceedings of the twenty-ninth SIGCSE technical symposium on Computer Science Education*, p.153-160, ACM Press, 1998.

[6] R. Harlan and D. Levine and S. McClarigan, The Khepera robot and the kRobot class: a platform for introducing robotics in the undergraduate curriculum. In *Proceedings of the thirty-second SIGCSE technical symposium on Computer Science Education*, p. 105-109, ACM Press, 2001

[7] B. Fagin and L. Merkle, Quantitative analysis of the effects of robots on introductory Computer Science education. Journal on Educational Resources in Computing (JERIC), Vol. 2, No. 4, 2002.

Creating Emergent Behaviors: Two Robotics Labs That Combine Reactive Behaviors[i]

Robert M. Harlan
Computer Science Department
St. Bonaventure University
Shelley McClarigan
Dresser-Rand Company
{rharlan,smcclar}@cs.sbu.edu

ABSTRACT

Most undergraduate robotics courses introduce reactive behaviors, behaviors that are not mediated by world knowledge or a world model. What is missing from these courses, however, is the experience of combining reactive behaviors to create emergent behavior, behavior that is not anticipated by the robotocist but generated by the interaction of behaviors and the environment. We discuss two laboratory exercises that introduce reactive behaviors and combine them to produce emergent behaviors.

Categories and Subject Descriptors
I.2.9 [**Computing Methodologies**]: Artificial Intelligence – *robotics.*

General Terms
Algorithms, Experimentation

Keywords
Behavior-based robotics, emergent behavior, robotics laboratory assignments.

INTRODUCTION

The late 1980's and early 1990's witnessed the development of a new approach to building behavior control algorithms for autonomous robots. In contrast to the traditional or hierarchical approach, in which the robot's model of the world was used to interpret sensor readings and plan appropriate actions, researchers such as Arkin [1] and Brooks [2] introduced a reactive or behavior-based approach in which motor actions of the robot were tightly coupled with sensor readings, eliminating the need for world knowledge or an internal model of the world to produce appropriate behavior.

A wide variety of laboratory exercises for undergraduate robotics courses using low-cost, Lego-based robots have been developed to illustrate this approach [e.g., 9]. Most exercises illustrate individual reactive behaviors such as following a line, seeking a light source or avoiding obstacles. Some [3] show how the reactive behaviors can be sequenced to carry out a task such as vacuuming.

An important aspect of the reactive paradigm, however, is not covered in most lab exercises. Proponents such as Brooks argued that simple behaviors – by this we mean a tightly coupled sensor reading and corresponding motor action – can be combined to produce emergent behavior, viz., behavior that is elicited by the environment by the interaction of the simple behaviors but that is not programmed in advance by the robotocist.

The fact that emergent behavior is not controlled directly by the programmer is an important reason to add this experience to the undergraduate curriculum. It is difficult to understand the causes of unexpected emergent behavior and to predict the effect changes in the properties of one of the underlying simple behaviors will have when it interacts with the environment. A premium is placed on careful observation and building robust traces to reveal the robot's dynamic changes of state.

We have developed two laboratory assignments that implement and combine simple reactive behaviors, obstacle avoidance and light seeking, into an emergent behavior. The labs are motivated by Murphy [8]. The first lab uses subsumption to combine the two, where the light-seeking behavior subsumes or overrides the avoidance behavior. The second lab uses potential fields: obstacles provide a repulsive force and the light an attractive force which can then be combined to produce the emergent behavior.

The labs were developed using the Khepera miniature robot. However, the methodology can easily be extended to other platforms.

SIGCSE '05, February 23-27, 2005, St. Louis, Missouri, USA.

Figure 1: Lab set-up includes a host computer, a Khepera robot and a 110 x 80 "world" for each team of two students.

THE ROBOTICS COURSE

Our robotics course is designed to present an overview of the development of behavior control algorithms for autonomous robots. Following the taxonomy of the discipline presented in the text used in the course, Murphy's [8] *Introduction to AI Robotics,* the lecture component introduces three distinct paradigms: the traditional, top down approach to robotics that emerged from early work in artificial intelligence; the behavior-based or reactive approach that developed in response to the failures of the traditional approach; and more recent hybrid approaches that combine the two. The text is supplemented by various readings, especially articles presenting different hybrid approaches.

The course is a four credit, one semester course that consists of two one-hour lectures and two two-hour labs per week. The number of students taking the course has ranged from six to twelve. Students work in teams of two using the paired-programming model.

The laboratory component of the course introduces the traditional approach and the reactive approach to designing behavior control algorithms [4]. The lab utilizes the Khepera robot from K-Team, [7] a miniature mobile robot (5.5 cm diameter) which permits micro-world experimentation with control algorithms in a reasonably compact space (Figure 1). It has eight infrared sensors that can sense both ambient light levels and proximity to nearby objects. It also has two DC motors that are capable of independent variable-speed motion, allowing the robot to move forwards, backwards, and to complete a variety of turns at different speeds (Figure 2).

We use a previously developed object-oriented interface for the Khepera that provides methods for controlling effectors and accessing sensor data by abstracting from low-level communication between the controlling program and the robot [5]. The interface enables students to write behavior control programs in the first lab and to focus on the design, implementation and testing of their programs.

Our laboratory sequence differs from many undergraduate lab courses in that the traditional approach is introduced before the reactive or behavior-based approaches. We have two reasons for this divergence: one practical, the other philosophical.

The practical reason is that the Murphy text uses a historical approach that begins with the traditional, AI inspired approach. The search-based planning techniques developed in AI were used to guide autonomous robots.

The second reason is philosophical. It is one thing to argue that the reactive or behavior-based approached arose because of the failure of the traditional approach to build robots that were capable of functioning in the real world. It is another to have students experience this failure themselves!

For example, the A* algorithm enables a robot to plan an optimal route between two points and then carry out the plan only under two assumptions, neither of which are applicable to the real world. First, the robot must have perfect knowledge of the world: the location of all obstacles must be known in advance, because a change in position of one obstacle disrupts the plan and makes it impossible to carry it out. Second, the algorithm requires a perfect robot to carry out the plan: wheel drift and slippage soon make it necessary for what our students call "the hand of God" to intervene and place the robot back on course.

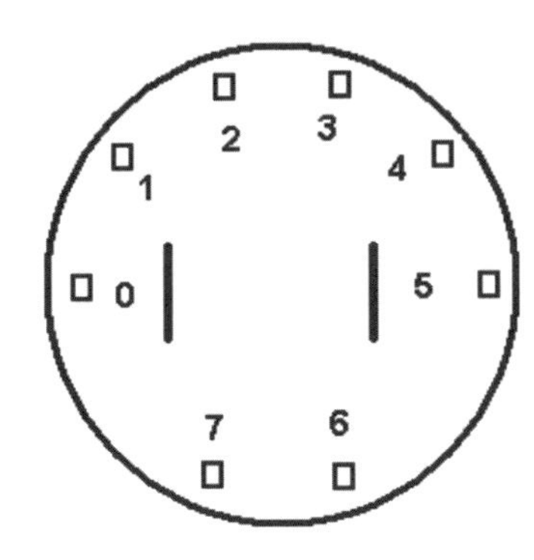

Figure 2: Schematic showing the Khepera's eight IR sensors and two effectors.

This experience motivates the transition to the reactive approach.

THE BEHAVIOR-BASED APPROACH TO ROBOTICS

The behavior-based approach to designing robot control algorithms addressed weaknesses in the traditional, representation-based approach. The traditional approach fails when the control program designer fails to anticipate situations in which the robot might find itself. The behavior-based approach holds that behavior should be motivated (stimulated) by the perceived environment without the intermediary of either a world model, through which the perceived environment is interpreted, or memory, which enables previous internal states to influence the current internal state of the robot. Perception is ``direct,'' and percepts of specific types give rise to corresponding behaviors without any intermediation.

Murphy distinguishes two distinct architectures for implementing reactive behaviors. The first, subsumption, was developed by Brooks in the 1980s. Each behavior is a sensory input – motor response pair. These pairs, modeled on stimulus-response pairs found in animals, are designed at the lowest level to ensure the survival of the entity. In robotics, an example would be obstacle avoidance, where the sensing of an obstacle results in a motor response on the part of the robot.

Brooks proposed that a robot, like an animal, can have multiple behaviors operating simultaneously, and that some combinations of behavior form a hierarchy that enable higher-level goals to be achieved. For example, a robot may be designed to explore an environment. In order to explore safely, it must still avoid obstacles, but do so in a way that still enables it to move about in the world in a directed way.

In Brooks' terms, the higher level goal of exploring must subsume the lower level goal of not running into obstacles. The resulting behavior is "emergent" in that it is the particular environment that elicits the behavior from the robot rather than a specific programmed routine that anticipated a specific set of inputs and generated the behavior.

COMBINING BEHAVIORS USING SUBSUMPTION

Our first attempt to create observable emergent behavior followed the discussion above: a "wander" behavior subsumed the lower-level obstacle avoidance behavior.

The wander behavior simply made the robot move forward. For the avoid behavior, the six side- and forward-facing sensors (sensors 0 through 5) generated an obstacle percept of one of six values: NONE, LEFT, LEFTFRONT, FRONT, RIGHTFRONT, and RIGHT. The FRONT percept triggered the collide reaction: the robot stopped and turned around 180°. The directional percepts other than FRONT triggered the runaway reaction, causing the robot to move in a direction 180° opposite of the direction in which the obstacle is seen. The NONE percept did not affect the robot's behavior.

We used a Boolean switch to determine when the wander behavior would subsume or suppress the avoidance behavior. An obstacle in front of the robot would always force the robot to stop and turn around. Obstacles on either side of the robot would force the robot to go in the opposite direction when the wander goal was not in effect, and to combine the wander direction and the avoid direction when it was.

However, the behavior change caused by the interaction of the wander and avoid behaviors was very difficult to observe. Our solution was to use the Khepera's light-sensitivity sensors to produce a light-following behavior that would subsume the avoidance behavior.[ii] All eight sensors were used to identify a light source: one sensor with a reading significantly below the average of the other sensors generates a goal percept indicating the location of the light. We modified the wander behavior to move forward if the robot doesn't sense a light source, or move in the direction of the goal percept if it does. The runaway behavior is also modified by the goal percept. If the robot does not perceive a light source, it still turns 180° away from the obstacle. However, if the robot does sense its goal, it turns only a fraction of that, resulting in a direction shaped by the environment encountered by the robot. (Figure 3)

The result is visually quite striking and makes the emergent behavior caused by the interaction readily apparent. The robot wanders around avoiding obstacles until a light source is seen. A light source to the left or right of an obstacle will cause the robot to move toward the light while avoiding the obstacle. At present the robot moves around an obstacle in a stair-case fashion: for example, a light source to the right of an obstacle causes the robot to move away from the obstacle, then towards the light, then away from the obstacle, enabling it to "step" around the obstacle towards the light.

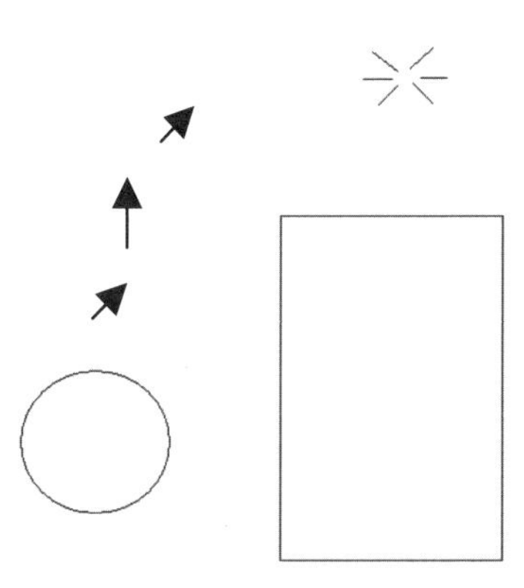

Figure 3: Path Generated by the Interaction of Avoid and Light-Following Behaviors

Achieving this solution required a significant amount of trial and error and illustrates the point made above regarding the difficulty of reasoning about emergent behavior. Specific obstacle positions would trigger iterative behavior that made no progress towards the light source. Attempts to "smooth out" the stair-case behavior resulted in the robot hitting obstacles.

COMBINING BEHAVIORS USING POTENTIAL FIELDS

A second method for combining reactive behaviors presupposes that each behavior is treated as if the environment were exerting a force on the robot. A force has both a direction and a magnitude. Two distinct forces, eliciting different behaviors, can be summed, producing a single force with its own direction and magnitude.

The second lab guides students in reengineering the obstacle avoidance and light-following behaviors using the potential field approach.

Obstacle avoidance is implemented by associating a potential field object with each forward or side facing sensor. The object includes the threshold of the sensor as well as the orientation of the sensor on the robot. We use a 360° circle to assign sensor orientation and force direction (Figure 4).

The proximity sensors are updated and the force operating on each sensor is calculated on each cycle. If the threshold of a sensor is met, a repulsive force with a direction opposite to that of sensor is generated. The forces acting on all sensors are summed, resulting in a direction for the robot. A function then orients the robot in that direction. Magnitude is not considered at present: any force acting on a sensor has a magnitude of 1, no force a magnitude of 0.

No change was required for the light-following behavior: an activated light sensor generated an attractive force in the direction of the sensor. This direction is passed to the function setting the direction of the robot.

Combining the behaviors resulted in an example of just how difficult it is to understand emergent behavior. We simply averaged the direction of the obstacle-avoiding and light-following forces by adding them together and dividing, which had worked for the simple avoidance behavior. While the resulting behavior was correct in most cases, periodically the robot would turn the wrong way and hit an obstacle.

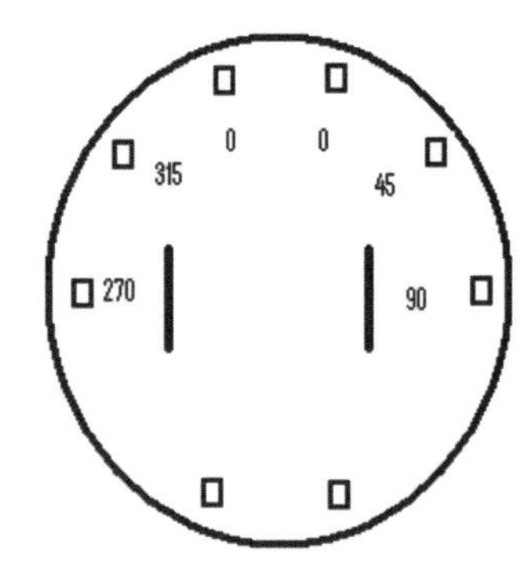

Figure 4: Orientation of the 8 Light-Sensing Sensors

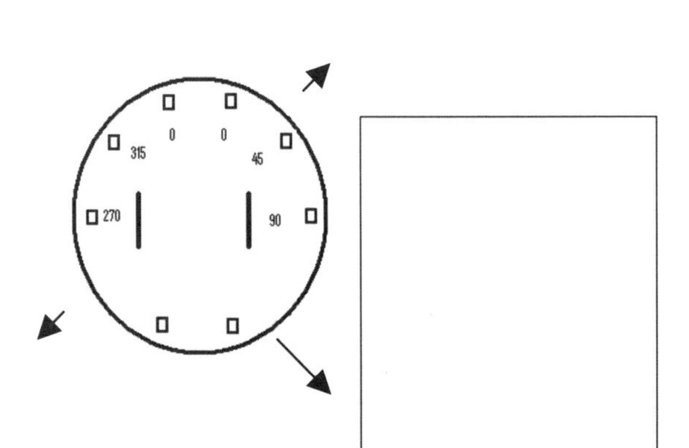

Figure 5: Error Generated by Naive Addition of Force Directions. Robot turns into the Obstacle.

The cause of this problematic (but certainly emergent!) behavior is shown in Figure 5. An obstacle seen on, e.g., the right side of the robot would generate a repulsive force with a direction of 235°. A light source seen to the right center of the robot would generate an attractive force with a direction of 45°. The resulting direction of 140° would cause the robot to turn into the obstacle!

Once recognized the problem was solved by changing the representation of the direction and using the math library to sum the force directions.[iii]

As was the case in preceding lab, the resulting emergent behavior is both robust and easily observed.

CONCLUSIONS

The two labs discussed above contribute the undergraduate robotics lab experience by guiding the students in generating emergent behavior that is easily observed.

There are two important reasons to adapt at least one of these labs for any undergraduate robotics course. First, the labs do provide hands on experience in both implementing and combining reactive behaviors. When emergent behavior occurs students have the experience of creating a truly autonomous agent.

Second, we found that it was more difficult to reason about combined or emergent behaviors than it was either to reason about traditional behavior control algorithms or even individual, reactive behaviors. Small changes to thresholds, for example, resulted in unexpected (and often untoward) emergent behavior. The difficulty of isolating causes of and fixes for problematic emergent behavior enables students to experience first hand the empirical nature of computer science in general and robotics in particular. As noted above, a premium is placed on close observation of the interaction between the robot and the environment as well as developing traces that permit the examination of dynamic changes in the robot's internal states.

The Khepera robot proved to be an ideal platform for creating emergent behavior. However, the labs should be adaptable to any platform that supports multiple sensors.[iv]

REFERENCES

[1] Arkin, R., *Behavior-Based Robotics*. MIT Press, Cambridge, MA, 1998.

[2] Brooks, R., *Cambrian Intelligence: The Early History of the New AI*. MIT Press, Cambridge, MA, 1999.

[3] Burhams, D. and Kandefer, M. Dustbot: Bringing Vacuum-Cleaner Agent to Life. In *Accessible Hands-on Artificial Intelligence and Robotics Education* (Stanford University, March 22 – 24, 2004). AAAI Press, Menlo Park, CA 2004, 82 – 84.

[4] Harlan, R. AI and Robotics Labs at the Undergraduate obotics Laboratory, St. Bonaventure University. In *Accessible Hands-on Artificial Intelligence and Robotics Education* (Stanford University, March 22 – 24, 2004). AAAI Press, Menlo Park, CA 2004, pp 85 – 87

[5] Harlan, R., Levine, D. and McClarigan, S. 2001. The Khepera Robot and the kRobot Class: A Platform for Introducing Robotics in the Undergraduate Curriculum. In *Proceedings of the 32nd SIGCSE Technical Symposium on Computer Science Education* SIGCSE Bulletin vol. 33(1) ACM Press, New York, NY, pp. 105 – 109.

[6] Kumar, D., and Meeden, L. A Robot Laboratory for Teaching Artificial Intelligence. In *Proceedings of the 29th SIGCSE Technical Symposium on Computer Science Education* SIGCSE Bulletin vol. 30(1), ACM Press, New York, NY, 1998), pp. 341 – 344.

[7] Mondada, F., Franzi, E., and Ienne, P. Mobile robot miniaturization: A tool for investigation in control algorithms. In *Experimental Robotics III, Proceedings of the Third International Symposium on Experimental Robotics,* Springer Verlag, 1994, pp. 501-513.

[8] Murphy, R., *Introduction to AI Robotics*. MIT Press, 2000.

[9] Walker, E Lego Mndstorms Robotics in a Small Liberal Arts College. In In *Accessible Hands-on Artificial Intelligence and Robotics Education* (Stanford University, March 22 – 24, 2004). AAAI Press, Menlo Park, CA 2004,s pp 115 – 117.

---

[i] The laboratory equipment discussed in this paper was funded in part by National Science Foundation CCLI-AI grant 9980999.

We wish to thank our colleagues, David Levine and Steven Andrianoff, for their help in preparing this paper and to the robotics students who assisted in the development and testing of the labs.

[ii] Like many of our good ideas this one arose from a discussion of just this problem and was suggested by a student, Steve Gewand.

[iii] If your students are like ours and balk at trigonometry, the function can be provided as a black box. The function is passed force directions in degrees and returns a direction in degrees which in turn can be used to orient the robot. The naive summation of directions worked for the avoidance behavior because obstacles generated forces that never crossed the 360º barrier.

[iv] The lab assignments and solutions are available at http://web.sbu.edu/cs/roboticsLab/. The Khepera interface is distributed under the GNU General Public License and is avai able through SourceForge at https://sourceforge.net/projects/krobotif/

Multidisciplinary Teamwork in a Robotics Course

Jerry B. Weinberg, William W. White, Cem Karacal, George Engel, Ai-Ping Hu
School of Engineering
Southern Illinois University
Edwardsville, IL 62026
(618)650-2541
(jweinbe, wwhite, skaraca, gengel, ahu) @siue.edu

ABSTRACT

Real-world systems are comprised of interdependent components creating integrated systems. These systems are developed by multidisciplinary teams. The goal of this project is the development of a comprehensive undergraduate course in robotics that encompasses various fields that are integral to robotic systems: Computer Science, Electrical and Computer Engineering, and Mechanical Engineering. A main pedagogical goal of the course is to teach group dynamics and the skills necessary for interaction with people in different disciplines in multidisciplinary teams. Descriptions of the course and the hands-on lab assignments are presented along with course assessment.

Categories and Subject Descriptors

K.3.2 **[Computers and Education]**: Computer and Information Science Education--*Accreditation, Computer science education*; I.2.9 [**Artificial Intelligence**]: Robotics--*Autonomous vehicles, Kinematics and dynamics, Manipulators, Sensors*

General Terms

Design.

Keywords

Robotics, sensors, manipulators, kinematics, feedback control, localization, navigation, multidisciplinary, cross-functional, teamwork.

1. INTRODUCTION

Real-world complex systems are comprised of an assortment of integrated components from multiple disciplines. The development of such systems has shifted from designing individual components in isolation to working in cross-functional teams that encompass the variety of expertise needed to devise such systems [8,14]. This means that students must learn the team building and communication skills to work with others outside of their own discipline. The Accreditation Board for Engineering Technology has acknowledged the importance of these abilities in its *Criteria for Accrediting Engineering Programs* [5]. The study of robotics provides an excellent instrument for teaching and learning about working in multidisciplinary teams.

Robots are complex integrated systems comprised of interdependent electrical, mechanical, and computational components. Because of the variety of concepts that robots engender, they have become a valuable tool for teaching the practical, hands-on application of concepts in various engineering and science topics [1,4,9]. The multidisciplinary character of robots makes them a natural focus of study for teaching and experiencing teamwork that includes members from cross-functional vocations.

The overall goal of this project is the development of a comprehensive undergraduate course in robotics that emphasizes multidisciplinary teamwork by encompassing many of the diverse fields of engineering which are integral to robotic systems: Computer Science (CS), Electrical and Computer Engineering (ECE), and Mechanical Engineering (ME). This is a two-year project supported by a grant from the National Science Foundation's Division of Undergraduate Education under the Course, Curriculum, and Lab Initiative – Adaptation & Implementation Program. The course adapts material from [4,6,7,10,14,16].

The course is cross-listed for credit to students in each of the areas. It incorporates team-based robotics projects in which the teams are composed of one student from each area. The pedagogical goals of the course include:

- To gain hands-on experience in practical robotics
- To learn about integrated system design
- To learn to interact with people in different disciplines in a cross-functional team
- To learn about group dynamics and teamwork

This paper presents the outcome of the first offering of the course, which was taught by a team of faculty members from all of the represented areas. An eventual goal of the project is to adapt the materials so that the course can be taught at undergraduate institutions that do not offer a degree in robotics, an active robotics research center, or even have the full range of engineering expertise that is represented in such a comprehensive course. Informed by the assessment of the first year the material will be further developed to allow the course to be taught by a single faculty member.

SIGCSE'05, February 23-27, 2005, St. Louis, Missouri, USA.

2. COURSE ORGANIZATION

The course, entitled "Robotics: Integrated System Design", was offered for the first time in Spring 2004 as a senior-level elective in the three majors: CS, ECE, and ME. Enrollment limits were used to achieve a balanced enrollment between the majors for the purpose of team formation. Following the guidelines put forth in [4], nine teams were formed using the criteria of major, availability, and grade point average. To ensure that teams were multidisciplinary, each team was assigned at least one student from CS, ME, and ECE. On the first day of class, students completed a survey that included a request for the times during which they were available for team meetings. The amount of face-to-face meeting time is important for successful teamwork [13,14,15], so availability was the second criterion used to formulate teams. To ensure that all teams would have an equitable distribution of skill levels, grade point average was used as the final criterion.

The schedule of class topics is presented in Table 1. The general topics covered were control theory (i.e., kinematics, feedback control), sensors (i.e., circuits and signal processing, computer vision), and artificial intelligence (i.e., localization, planning).

Table 1: Week-by-Week Schedule of Class Topics

Day 1	Day 2
Introduction to Robotics	Teamwork/Group Dynamics
Robot Technical Fundamentals	Forward/Inverse Kinematics
Forward/Inverse Kinematics	Introduction to Handy Board
Feedback Control	Feedback Control
Electronics Primer/Sensor Fundamentals	Circuits
Sensor Operating Principles	Advanced Sensors
ME & ECE Quiz	AI and Reactive Control
Computer Vision/Image Processing	Localization/Navigation
Localization & Navigation	Planning
Problem Analysis/System Design	Final Project Assignment
Multi-Robot Coordination	Multi-Robot Coordination
Time & Space Complexity	Robot Competitions
CS & IME Quiz	Project Troubleshooting
Final Project Presentations	Final Project Presentations
Final Project Demonstrations	Final Project Demonstrations

The topics were ordered using a layered abstraction approach [3], beginning at the lowest level of information, where relative position is used to determine movement (kinematics), proceeding to the attribute layer, where sensor input is processed to determine situations (behavior-based robotics), and finishing at the model layer, where abstractions of the world are used to make planning decisions.

Coverage of each topic area included some basic concepts of the respective discipline in order to provide students outside of that discipline with a sufficient framework for understanding the more advanced concepts. To mitigate the potential for disinterest caused by presenting basic concepts to students within their respective discipline, concepts were covered from the perspective of their application to robotics.

The grading policy was set to emphasize the hands-on, team-based aspects of the course. However, a significant amount of the grade was set aside for quizzes and the final exam to ensure that students made a sincere effort to learn concepts from disciplines that were complementary to their own: Team Assignments 25%, Team Project 30%, Quizzes 25%, and Final Exam 20%

To enhance the multidisciplinary teamwork aspects of the course, students were encouraged to utilize their lab project teams to form study groups for the quizzes and the final exam. Although this aspect of the course was not specifically formalized (as suggested in [4]), both single teams and multiple teams were observed studying together prior to the quizzes and the final exam.

On the day that the teams were announced, lecture material and in-class exercises were presented to emphasize how teams work and how team members may interact within their group [2,4,16]. The specific topics included:

- What defines a team?
- Team process: team roles, decision making, conflict resolution
- How to run an effective team meeting
- Characteristics of good and bad team members
- The difference between constructive and destructive criticism
- Individual personality types and their impact on how individuals work and interact
- Brainstorming methods

During the in-class exercises, the teams were instructed to practice the same team process they were expected to use during their team meetings. This included assigning team roles, setting a meeting agenda, and recording results. The identified team roles were Chief Technology Officer (CTO), Scribe, and Rat Hole Watcher. The CTO is the identified leader of the project, and this role was expected to rotate between team members based on the emphasis of the particular assignment. The Scribe is responsible for recording the results of each team meeting. Team minutes were required to be submitted as part of the grade for each assignment. Finally, the Rat Hole Watcher is empowered to stop a line of conversation that is off topic in order to keep the discussion focused.

The choice of robotics platforms for the team assignments and projects included LEGO mechanical pieces and the Handy Board Controller [11]. This platform was chosen for its mechanical flexibility, its ability to easily interface with custom-built sensors, the availability of a C development environment, and the availability of a low-cost color camera, the CMUcam. Robot kits developed by the KISS Institute for Practical Robotics were purchased (www.kipr.org). Each kit cost $1245 and included a vast amount of LEGO pieces, geared and servo motors, a variety of pre-built sensors, a CMUcam, and a Handy Board. In addition, electronic parts were purchased for labs that required the development of custom sensors as discussed in Section 3.

3. HANDS-ON LAB ASSIGNMENTS

The overall philosophy of the lab assignments is to provide a hands-on, multidisciplinary design experience that complements the lecture material. This approach to teaching creates an active learning environment in which students can explore a significant design area, make hypotheses about how things work, and conduct experiments to validate their assumptions [12]. In this way, it creates a type of "directed constructionism" learning experience in which students are asked to explore related topics in a specific order [14].

3.1 Assignment 1: Rube Goldberg Machine

The first assignment involved the design and implementation of a Rube Goldberg Machine (www.rgmc.com) that would capture a mouse without harming it. In addition to familiarizing the students with the building materials in the kit, this assignment was designed to place the students in a frame of mind for designing and building. The main intention behind this lab was to provide students with an opportunity to participate in a fun activity while moving through the early stages of team formation.

3.2 Assignment 2: Mobile Bug Behavior

The second assignment was designed to help students learn about the electronics components of their kits and give them experience with the programming environment. The assignment involved simulating bug behavior. Using the Handy Board, various sensors and motors, and a team-designed 1-DoF joint mechanism, each team would gain experience on an integrated system that included mechanics, electronics, and computation.

The objective was to build a mobile bug that would "wake up" when exposed to a light. Using a sonar sensor on a turret mechanism, the bug was to scan the area in front of it for the closest object, which it would interpret as a food source. Once the bug identified the object, it was expected to move in the direction of the object. Using touch sensors as "antennae", the bug would find the food and stop to "feed". If the food source was removed, the bug was to search for a new food source.

3.3 Assignment 3: Homing Light Sensor

The third assignment required the design and fabrication of a custom light sensor that could "home in" on a light source. The goal area was defined as the set of all points in the working plane within six inches of the light source. The robot's initial position and orientation with respect to the source would be unknown, but was about 24 inches away, and the initial heading would diverge by no more than approximately 45 degrees from the optimal path to the source. The robot was required to remain "quiet" until the light source was activated, whereupon the robot was expected to "home in" on the source as quickly as possible.

3.4 Assignment 4: Robotic Arm

The fourth assignment involved the design of a two-link manipulator robotic arm that would accurately track a one-inch-radius circular closed path with its tip. The manipulator parameters would lead to two inverse kinematics solutions to the given task. The implementation of a Proportional Derivative (PD) closed-loop control was required to achieve the desired accuracy. In addition, two rotational potentiometers were required to be used to sense the joint angles.

3.5 Project: Autonomous Search & Rescue

The objective of the culminating project was to design and implement an autonomous urban search and rescue robot for an earthquake-damaged building, as detailed in Figure 1.

The project assignment was designed to have each team explore localization methods (including the design and implementation of a sensor for sound localization), and develop an algorithm for navigation.

> ***An earthquake registering 7.5 on the Richter scale along the New Madrid Fault has caused extensive damage across Missouri, Southern Illinois, and Tennessee. An emergency response team was sent out to search for potential victims in a warehouse near I-255, which has suffered severe damage in part of its storage facility.***
>
> ***In the midst of their heroic efforts to find and save factory workers, an aftershock measuring a 5.3 on the Richter scale hits and 7 emergency workers, scattered throughout the factory, are too badly injured to escape. Rescue workers have asked that your Robotic Rescue Team dispatch a robot to help identify where the workers are trapped so that critical resources can be focused on the rescue of the emergency workers.***
>
> ***The local rescue workers have provided you information about the warehouse that you might find useful for your robot. They have provided a blueprint of the area needed to be searched as well as photos of the facility prior to the earthquake. Your team has been given 25 minutes to search the facility for the rescue workers.***

Figure 1: The Urban Search & Rescue Back Story

The search area was a 10'x10' area with various obstacles, divided into five rooms with a sixth room located in an upper level that was only accessible by means of a ramp. The robot's mission was to locate all victims wearing uniforms of a specific color and one victim that was "screaming for help". The screaming victim was a sound source generating a 2 kHz tone. When a victim was detected, the robot was to approach the victim, set off a series of beeps, and record the location of the victim in a two-dimensional array. The array representing a floor map was downloaded after the robot's run to check for accuracy.

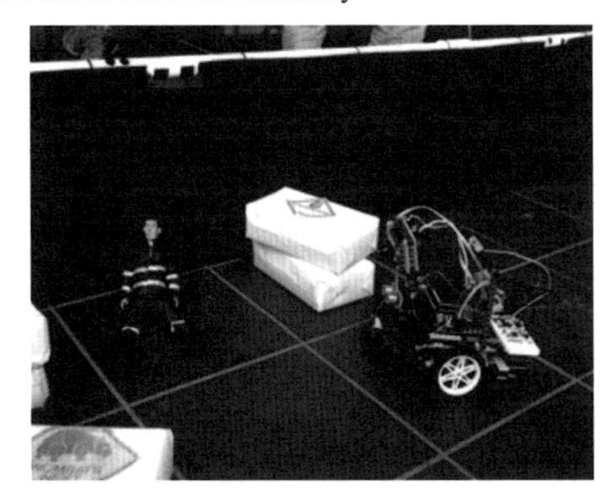

Figure 2: A Robot Finding a Victim

The evaluation of the project was based upon the extent to which a robot visited rooms and discovered victims. Teams could do well even if they did not accomplish a search of every room and the location of every victim. In a challenging project such as this, with so many real-world variables to overcome and control, if a robot found three to four out of seven victims, it would be considered successful. In addition, to help promote progress being made in each discipline, extra credit was given if the teams demonstrated certain aspects in isolation:

- The implementation of feedback control to improve the robot's accuracy for going in a straight line.
- The implementation of feedback control to improve the robot's accuracy and reliability for making a 90-degree turn.
- The implementation of the sound localization sensor.

4. ASSESSMENT AND EVALUATION

A number of assessment tools were designed to gauge the effectiveness of various aspects of the course. While the other members of the research team were instructors for the course, one member was designated the course assessor, who was responsible for implementing the assessment tools.

4.1 Multidisciplinary Teamwork Assessment

Peer reviews and team interviews were specifically designed to facilitate the assessment of the extent to which the course successfully provided students with effective experiences within multidisciplinary teams.

On the peer reviews, students were asked to evaluate their teammates with respect to four desired attributes: commitment, cooperation, motivation, and participation. As expected, personalities and different work ethics frequently affected mutual perceptions in the peer evaluations. Common complaints included apathy, procrastination, closed-mindedness, and chronic unavailability. Such comments were far outnumbered by complimentary remarks, however, emphasizing helpfulness, creativity, organization, experience, and pragmatism.

Each project team met with the course assessor within a few days of demonstrating its search-and-rescue final project, to discuss the course's emphasis upon teamwork, and to suggest improvements that might be made to the projects in future versions of the course. In the presence of the entire team, individual team members tended to downplay personality conflicts and praise each other's efforts on the projects. However, there was a certain consensus that the distribution of labor across the disciplines was not equitable. Many teams voiced the opinion that each project should be easily divisible into equal CS, ECE, and ME components, or, alternatively, that preliminary projects should take turns in focusing on particular disciplines, with the final project composed of three comparable, distinguishable parts.

Most of the other comments from students during these team interviews concentrated upon the relative lack of time allocated to some assigned projects, particularly the final search-and-rescue project. A specific recommendation of several teams was to enhance the quality of the final project by designing the earlier lab assignments to serve as components of the final project.

4.2 Cross-Functional Learning Assessment

Assessment mechanisms designed to gauge the course's success in imparting cross-functional learning included a mid-point questionnaire, discipline-specific discussions, term quizzes, a pre-course survey, and the final exam

Conducted halfway through the course, the mid-point questionnaire queried the students regarding their background in their own and their teammates' disciplines, as well as the extent to which they and their teammates were contributing to team understanding of the course projects. While students from each discipline expressed confidence in their preparation in their own discipline, CS students felt very unprepared for ME material, while ECE students felt somewhat weak in ME and ME students felt rather weak in CS. These perceived shortcomings were rather effectively addressed, however, with ME students evaluated as contributing significantly to their CS and ECE teammates' understanding of the ME discipline's role in the assignments, and CS students evaluated as contributing tremendously to their ME teammates' understanding of the CS discipline's role in the assignments.

The course assessor conducted open discussion sessions with the students from each of the three disciplines about two-thirds of the way through the course, concentrating on any cross-disciplinary problems that had been perceived by the students. While all three groups expressed favorable impressions of the course as a whole, a common theme in these discussions was the perception that CS students were rather overburdened in the projects, while ME students often had little to contribute. Most students from each discipline advocated a more equitable distribution of the assignment workload across the disciplines.

Term quizzes were administered in each of the course disciplines, and each quiz contained some questions that were designed to help assess the success of cross-functional instruction in the course. Each discipline's instructor designed questions for which students from that discipline (who had completed discipline-specific course prerequisites) were expected to know the associated course material before taking the robotics course, while students from other disciplines were not. While students unsurprisingly tended to perform better on quiz questions from their own disciplines, it is notable that the gap between the mean performance of students from a particular discipline and the mean score of all of the students in the course was usually quite narrow.

A primary mechanism for measuring the cross-functional learning that occurred in this course was the administration of an ungraded pre-course survey on the first day of the course and a graded final exam on the last day of the course, containing equivalent questions from the disciplines of CS, ECE, and ME. The pre-course survey was ostensibly administered to assess student background and to help formulate project teams. The students were not informed that the survey's technical questions would also appear on the final exam, and the surveys were not returned to the students.

As expected, students performed reasonably well on questions from their own discipline on the pre-course survey, and somewhat better on those questions on the final exam. Cross-functional improvement was much more pronounced, with substantial improvements in ECE and ME scores by non-majors, and vast improvements in CS scores by ECE and ME students. An analysis of the academic backgrounds of the students in this course provides a satisfactory explanation for this disparity. CS and ECE students frequently take calculus and physics courses, in which certain introductory ME topics are introduced. Similarly, CS and ME students usually take beginning circuits courses. However, the programming courses to which most ECE and ME students are exposed usually do not cover the more advanced CS topics that were included on the pre-course survey and final exam.

5. FUTURE WORK

The multidisciplinary robotics design course will be taught again in Spring 2005. The assignments and course material shall be altered to reflect the student feedback and instructor perceptions of what did and did not succeed in the pilot version of the course.

5.1 Lab Assignment Restructuring

A common complaint from students in the pilot version of the course was the perception that preliminary assignments failed to adequately prepare the teams for the culminating project. Many teams reported having difficulty adjusting to the volume of new skills needed on this final project, including camera operation, sound localization, and navigational mapping. A strong consensus was reached among both students and instructors that a more progressive, modular approach to the lab assignments would be more appropriate in the next version of the course, rather than the discipline-centered assignment approach taken in this first version.

In addition to this anticipated restructuring of the lab assignments, students have expressed a desire for more competitive contests between teams in the course. Demonstrations of the search-and-rescue culminating projects in the pilot version of the course were conducted in a public arena, with dozens of student spectators and extensive local media coverage. This fact proved quite motivating for students, and many indicated that such good-natured competition, even without any impact on grades, provided teams with additional an incentive to excel on the assignments. As a result, the inclusion of head-to-head demos, perhaps with web-posted results, is being considered for the next version of the course.

5.2 Improved Team Management

Perhaps the most counterproductive characteristic of many team efforts in the pilot version of the course was the tendency to "pipeline" the lab assignments, i.e., awaiting the full implementation of prerequisite components of the assignment before proceeding with the design and implementation of later components. This problem usually took the form of CS students failing to construct the software framework for an assigned robotics application until their ECE and ME counterparts completed the implementation of their respective parts of the assignment. This practice often resulted in the last-minute discovery of fundamental design flaws and, consequently, the rushed implementation of only partial functionality.

To encourage teams to better manage their lab assignments, the revised version of this course will require each team to submit an initial design document early in the development process for each assignment (e.g., within the first week of each three- or five-week cycle). These documents will be quickly evaluated, assessing the practicality of the design, the equity of the workload distribution among team members, and the appropriateness of the test plan. With at least half of the allocated time for each assignment still available, it is expected that this practice will alleviate the pipelining problem and improve the overall quality of each team's submitted assignments.

5.3 Reduction in Number of Instructors

While the pilot version of this course had four actively participating instructors, the Spring 2005 version will only have two and, with the refinement of course materials, the expectation is that future incarnations of the course may be taught by a single well-prepared instructor from any of the four disciplines, with the possibility of an occasional guest lecture by an expert from one of the other areas.

6. ACKNOWLEDGMENTS

This project was funded in part by the NSF, Grant Award # DUE-0311434. We would also like to thank Howie Choset for allowing us to adopt materials from his General Robotics Course at CMU.

7. REFERENCES

[1] Beer, R., Hillel, C., and Drushel, R. Using Autonomous Robotics to Teach Science and Engineering. *Communications of the ACM 42*, 6, June 1999, 85-92.

[2] Beyer, H. and Holtzblatt, K. *Contextual Design: Defining Customer-Centered Systems*. Morgan Kaufmann, Inc., 1998.

[3] Crabbe, F. Unifying Undergraduate Artificial Intelligence Robotics: Layers of Abstraction Over Two Channels. *2004 AAAI Spring Symposium Technical Report SS-04-01*, AAAI Press, 2-7.

[4] Csernica, J., Hanyak, M., Hyde, D., Shooter, S., Toole, M., and Vigeant, M. *Practical Guide to Teamwork*. June 2002. http://www.departments.bucknell.edu/projectcatalyst/EngEdWksp2003CD/

[5] Engineering Accreditation Commission (Accreditation Board for Engineering and Technology, Inc.). *2001-2002 Criteria for Accrediting Engineering Programs*. December 2000. http://www.abet.org/images/ eac_criteria_b.pdf/.

[6] Greenwald, L. Tools for Effective Low-Cost Robotics. In *Working Papers of the Spring 2001 American Association of Artificial Intelligence Spring Symposium*; Session on Robotics & Education, March 2001.

[7] Greenwald, L, and Kopena, J. Mobile Robot Labs. *IEEE Robotics and Automation 10*, 2, June 2003, 25-32.

[8] Hartfield, B. The Designer's Stance. In *Bringing Design to Software*. T. Winograd, ed., Addison-Wesley, 1996.

[9] Klassner, F. A Case Study of LEGO Mindstorms Suitability for Artificial Intelligence and Robotics Courses at the College Level. In *Proceeding of the 33rd SIGCSE Technical Symposium on Computer Science Education* (Northern Kentucky), February 2002, 8-12.

[10] Kumar, D. and Meeden, L. A Robot Laboratory for Teaching Artificial Intelligence. In *Proceedings of the Twenty-Ninth SIGCSE Technical Symposium on Computer Science Education* (Atlanta), 1998, 341-344.

[11] Martin, F. *Robotic Exploration: A Hands-On Introduction to Engineering*. Prentice-Hall, Inc., 2001.

[12] Miller, G., Church, R., and Trexler, M. Teaching Diverse Learners Using Robotics. In *Robots for Kids: Exploring New Technologies for Learning*. A. Druin and J. Hendler, eds., Morgan Kaufmann, 2000, 165-192.

[13] Pinto, M.B., and Pinto, J.K. Project Team Communication and Cross-Functional Cooperation in New Program Development. *Journal of Product Innovation Management 7*, 1990, 200-212.

[14] Rosenblatt, M. and Choset, H. Designing and Implementing Hands-on Robotics Labs. *IEEE Intelligent Systems 15*, 6, November/December 2000, 32-39.

[15] Song, X.M., Montoya-Weiss, M.M., and Schmidt, J.B. Antecedents and Consequences of Cross-Functional Cooperation: A Comparison of R&D, Manufacturing, and Marketing Perspectives. *Journal of Product Innovation Management 14*, 1997, 35-47.

[16] Weinberg, J. B. and Stephen, M. A Laboratory Experience for Teaching Participatory Design in a Human-Computer Interaction Course. In *Proceedings of the 2002 ASEE Annual Conference & Exposition* (Montreal), June 2002.

Resolved: Objects Early Has Failed

Owen Astrachan (Moderator)
Duke University
Durham, NC 27708
ola@cs.duke.edu

Kim Bruce
Williams College
Williamstown, MA 01267
kim@cs.williams.edu

Elliot Koffman
Temple University
Philadelphia, PA 19122
koffman@temple.edu

Michael Kölling
Computing Laboratory
University of Kent
m.kolling@kent.ac.uk

Stuart Reges
University of Washington
Seattle, WA 98195
reges@cs.washington.edu

SUMMARY

The participants will use a debate format with a provocative thesis to explore the pedagogical approach known as "objects early" or "objects first." By arguing in the affirmative, Elliot Koffman and Stuart Reges will point out concerns that have been raised about the approach. By arguing in the negative, Kim Bruce and Michael Kölling will describe schools that are succeeding with the approach and ways to address significant concerns. Owen Astrachan as moderator will ensure that the debate remains civil and will provide some humorous and possibly even insightful commentary on the evidence presented by both sides.

Categories and Subject Descriptors

K3.2 [**Computers and Education**]: Computer and Information Science Education – *computer science education, curriculum.*

General Terms: design

Keywords: CS1, object oriented programming, objects first.

1. INTRODUCTION

As table 1 makes clear, the volume of email traffic on the SIGCSE mailing list spiked during the fourth week of March, 2004. The normally tame list suddenly had five times the usual number of messages and together those messages constituted seven times the usual number of lines of text. And then just as suddenly as it had begun, the list went back to the usual flow.

The spike started during the third week of March when Eric Roberts posted a message about the new ACM Java Resource Task Force [4]. Several people expressed concern about the implications of an ACM-endorsed set of tools for teaching Java.

SIGCSE'05, February 23-27, 2005, St. Louis, Missouri, USA.
ACM 1-58113-997-7/05/0002.

The volume exploded when the discussion turned to the question of whether the push to teach objects early has been worth the effort. Clearly many people have strong opinions on this subject.

Table 1. Email traffic on SIGCSE list (2004)

Week	Messages	Total Lines of text
1st week of March	16	1,794
2nd week of March	18	1,002
3rd week of March	24	1,659
4th week of March	95	9,207
1st week of April	13	1,823
2nd week of April	7	481
3rd week of April	24	1,262
4th week of April	19	1,263

The volume was so high, however, that many people couldn't keep up with it. This is evidenced by the fact that the discussion so quickly faded away (a sign that people were worn out) and the fact that Kim Bruce was asked to write a summary of the discussion for *Inroads Magazine* [1].

We have proposed this debate as an attempt to chip away at the complexity of this difficult question. By limiting the number of people who can speak and forcing them to adopt a debate format, we hope to clearly articulate the issues on both sides. We also chose the debate format to underscore the fact that this issue will not be settled in 75 minutes. As with any controversial subject, both sides of the argument have merit. So we see this more as the beginning of a discussion rather than as an attempt to settle the question.

2. A TRADITION OF FRIENDLY COMBAT

In choosing this format we are emulating a tradition long established at the annual OOPSLA conference of exploring complex questions by taking things to an extreme and interjecting humor. At their 1999 conference they featured "The Show Trial of the Gang of Four for Crimes Against Computer Science" in which they explored the question of how useful design patterns have turned out to be [2]. In 2002 they had a debate "Resolved: Objects Have Failed" in which they explored the question of whether object-oriented programming has lived up to its promised potential [3].

We are also taking a page from William F. Buckley and the many debates sponsored by the television show Firing Line on controversial subjects like affirmative action, abortion rights and political correctness. In particular, we liked the way that Michael Kinsley as moderator of the debates was able to use humor to keep tempers from flaring. He reminded the participants and the audience that, even though we may disagree bitterly, that we still respect each other and want to be friends at the end of the day. We invited Owen Astrachan to play this role for our debate. The combination of Owen's well-known equanimity and his sangfroid under fire makes him the perfect choice to judiciously stir this caldron of controversy.

3. THE PARTICIPANTS

It is fitting that the four who will debate this issue all participated significantly in the March debate on the SIGCSE mailing list. The most difficult choice was whom *not* to include. Particularly among those arguing for the objects early approach, we simply couldn't include all of the passionate and articulate advocates. Their absence from the debate should not in any way be construed as a reflection on the merits of their arguments. We simply couldn't include everyone.

Oddly enough, the difficulty was in finding people willing to argue against objects early. Elliot Koffman opined on the mailing list that there is a "silent majority" that is not comfortable expressing their concerns, which could explain why few were eager to argue the affirmative side of this debate.

Below is a brief biography of each debate participant and some of their professional experience that is relevant to the debate.

Arguing in the affirmative that objects early has failed are:

Elliot Koffman: Elliot is a Professor of Computer Science at Temple University. He is the author of several popular CS1 and CS2 textbooks, is a past chair of SIGCSE and has been involved in computer science curriculum issues for many years, including serving as the chair of the committee that rewrote the course descriptions for CS1 and CS2 in 1984.

Stuart Reges: Stuart is a Senior Lecturer in Computer Science and Engineering at the University of Washington. He served as the second chief reader for the AP/CS exam and was heavily involved in the design of intro courses and undergraduate curricula first at Stanford University and then at the University of Arizona.

Arguing in the negative that objects early has not failed are:

Kim Bruce: Kim is the Frederick Latimer Wells Professor of Computer Science at Williams College. He has been a long-time contributor to SIGCSE discussing such issues as the inclusion of mathematics in the computer science curriculum. Recently he has co-developed a library to support the early use of event-driven programming and graphics in CS1. This library is used in a forthcoming objects-early CS 1 text book. Kim is spending the 2004-2005 academic year as a visiting professor at the University of California at Santa Cruz.

Michael Kölling: Michael is a Senior Lecturer at the Computing Laboratory at the University of Kent at Canterbury.. He has been a frequent contributor to SIGCSE and is one of the creators of the popular BlueJ integrated Java development environment designed for novices. He is also the coauthor of an objects early CS1 textbook.

Moderating the debate is:

Owen Astrachan: Owen is a Professor of the Practice of Computer Science at Duke University where he serves as Director of Undergraduate Studies. Owen has been heavily involved with the AP/Computer Science program, serving as a committee member, the third chief reader and as chair of the task force that recommended the recent switch to Java. Owen has also been a frequent contributor to SIGCSE and provided a memorable talk at the 2003 conference when the keynote speaker was unable to attend.

4. REFERENCES

[1] Bruce, K. Controversy on How to Teach CS1: A discussion on the SIGCSE-members mailing list. *Inroads Magazine (in production).*

[2] Cunningham, W. The Show Trial of the Gang of Four for Crimes Against Computer Science. Described at http://c2.com/cgi/wiki?ShowTrialOfTheGangOfFour.

[3] Gabriel, R., and Steele, G. Resolved: Objects Have Failed. Opening arguments available at http://dreamsongs.com/Essays.html.

[4] Roberts, E.. Resources to support the use of Java in introductory computer science. *Proceedings of the 35th SIGCSE technical symposium on Computer science education.*

Emerging Areas in Computer Science Education

Amruth N Kumar
Ramapo College of NJ
Mahwah, NJ
amruth AT ramapo.edu (Moderator)

Bina Ramamurthy
University at Buffalo
Buffalo, NY
bina AT cse.buffalo.edu

Rose K. Shumba
Indiana University of Pennsylvania
Indiana, Pennsylvania
shumba AT iup.edu

Lawrence D'Antonio
Ramapo College of NJ
Mahwah, NJ
ldant AT ramapo.edu

SUMMARY

Computer Science is an evolving discipline. It continues to reinvent itself every 5-7 years. In order to keep up, Computer Science educators have had to continually modify the curriculum, either changing existing courses or introducing new ones. It is next to impossible for educators to keep abreast of all the developments in the discipline - learning a new area can place substantial demands on their time and effort.

Therefore, this panel is intended as a quick introduction to some of the emerging areas and practices in Computer Science that deserve inclusion in the undergraduate curriculum. The panelists will present four new emerging areas - Grid Computing, Cybersecurity, Bioinformatics, and Robotics in the traditional Artificial Intelligence course. Each panelist will present a typical syllabus, list sample resources, and recount his/her experience developing the course. It is hoped that this panel will help interested faculty adopt successful practices.

Categories and Subject Descriptors

K.3.2 [**Computers and Education**]: Computer and Information Science Education

General Terms

Algorithms, Design, Security.

Keywords

Grid Computing, Wireless Networking. Bioinformatics, Cybersecurity, Robotics, Artificial Intelligence.

1. BINA RAMAMURTHY – GRID COMPUTING

I will present a comprehensive package that will guide small school educators to setup, teach and use grid technology in their curriculum. Grid technology is being hailed as a major innovation that will revolutionize business models and scientific research methods. A grid is a network of computational units cooperating to share compute cycles, data and other resources using an open and standardized service-based framework. Prominent industries are promoting it under different names such as utility computing and on-demand computing. Scientists as well as practitioners believe that the grid developed for scientific computing is on the brink of making computing freely available as yet another "utility," similar in ease of accessibility to the power grid that supplies electricity and the telephone grid that enables voice communication. It (grid) will potentially impact all levels of the society similar to how the Internet did when it matured into a mainstream technology. It is important that our students and workforce are prepared for the new roles and opportunities grid infrastructure may create.

Though vast amount of information from many different sources are available about the grid technology, it is not in a form that is readily usable for educators. This situation is further complicated by various versions of different implementations of the grid infrastructure and software. Anyone wanting to learn about grid has to wade through a number of publications in a wide range of topics from certification authorization for security to service deployment. To address theses issues, we have initiated a project called GridForce (**Grid For Collaboration and Education**) that will serve as a single point of dissemination for materials needed for grid technology education. I will provide sample curricula for grid technology courses, laboratory exercises, instructions to set up a grid laboratory environment, and application and user models for interaction with national grid facilities.

SIGCSE'05, February 23-27, 2005, St. Louis, Missouri, USA.
ACM 1-58113-997-7/05/0002.

2. ROSE SHUMBA - CYBERSECURITY

IUP offers an information assurance track. Two of the courses in the track are the Cybersecurity Basics course and the Network security course. The Cybersecurity basics course is an interdisciplinary course for the Criminology, Management Information Systems and Computer Science students. This is a host security course. Upon completion of the Cybersecurity course, students then take the Network security course. IUP has started work towards developing outcome based standards for teaching the two courses. The main idea is that we need to move towards standards-based programs that are not vendor dependent but contain a solid body of theory and principles based on "best practices" taught consistently in all programs. We have surveyed existing programs, textbooks and the two non vendor specific certification programs GIAG and ISC2 in an effort to establish the core content that should be covered in the two courses. We are recommending outcome based assessment of students and educational programs based on this core content. Setting such a standard with measurable outcomes could be an important step to achieving uniformity in professional preparation programs and could quickly raise the bar for entry level professionals. The work done so far emphasizes "best practices" using the "best of the breed" tools, and how to collect and observe evidence. I will present the work done so far towards developing standards for teaching the two courses.

3. LAWRENCE D'ANTONIO - BIOINFORMATICS

Computational methods are playing an increasingly important role in answering questions in biology. Bioinformatics is the interdisciplinary field that deals with these methods. It brings together a complex mix of biology, chemistry, algorithms, computing power, heuristics, and statistics to analyze enormous amounts of data, such as DNA or protein sequence data.

There are various ways that bioinformatics can be incorporated in the computer science curriculum (for example, using DNA sequence alignment as an example of dynamic programming in an algorithms course). Another approach, which I will outline, is to develop an upper level course in bioinformatics for computer science majors. Students need only a background in data structures. The molecular biology needed for the course can be easily taught.

The primary focus of such a course is studying sequence alignment algorithms which allow for comparison of nucleic acid sequences. Both optimal and heuristic versions of these algorithms are analyzed, with applications using public sequence databases. Hidden Markov models are introduced to perform profile alignment. Another major topic is DNA fragment assembly (including the shortest common superstring problem). In addition, problems may be discussed in constructing phylogenetic trees to determine evolutionary relationships. Such a course is a natural extension to the computer science curriculum, and will give students exposure to a major area of scientific research.

4. AMRUTH KUMAR – ROBOTICS IN AI

Both Artificial Intelligence and Robotics are seasoned courses in the Computer Science curriculum. However, using robots in the traditional undergraduate Artificial Intelligence course is an emerging practice, fueled by the availability of inexpensive, yet fairly powerful robots. Educators have used robots in this course in various ways, and for different purposes. My approach has been to: 1) Use robots to emphasize high-level knowledge-based AI algorithms, not robotics. Therefore, introduction of the robots does not disrupt or add to the normal coverage of topics in the course. Instead, the robots serve as the platform for the assignment of traditional projects. 2) Use plug-and-play robots such as the LEGO MindStorms robot. Plug-and-play robots need less skill and are hence, less stressful to build, but entail the same thrill of robotics as any other robot. 3) Use robots for open, rather than closed-laboratory projects. Therefore, there is no need to set aside expensive new laboratory facilities for the course. 4) Instruct students to purchase their own robot individually or in groups. Therefore, there is no need for the institution to commit additional funds to the course, or for the instructor to engage in book-keeping.

I have been using LEGO robots in my Artificial Intelligence course since fall 2000. My experience has been that students find the robot projects more challenging, yet more enjoyable than symbolic projects in AI; and the projects are effective at helping students learn AI concepts. I will present the logistics of using robots in the AI course – the design of the projects, robot hardware, demonstration props, and robot software; share experiences and point out pitfalls in the design and execution of robot projects; and provide pointers to resources useful for potential adopters. Time permitting, I will discuss alternatives to LEGO robots and knowledge-based projects.

5. THE PANELISTS

Amruth Kumar is Professor of Computer Science at Ramapo College of New Jersey. His research interests include Computer Science education and Intelligent Tutoring Systems. He is on the eastern and northeastern boards of the Consortium for Computing Sciences in Colleges. Partial support for his work was provided by the National Science Foundation's Course, Curriculum and Laboratory Improvement Program under grant DUE-0311549.

Bina Ramamurthy is a Research Assistant Professor in the Department of Computer Science and Engineering at University at Buffalo (SUNY). Her current NSF-supported project GridForce aims to spread grid awareness among educators and to improve technical preparedness of our workforce for the grid technology.

Rose K. Shumba is a Professor of Computer Science at Indiana University of Pennsylvania, which is one of the Centers for Information Assurance. She has taught the Cybersecurity course for the last two years. She has also been involved in other security projects at IUP.

Lawrence D'Antonio is Associate Professor of Mathematics and Computer Science at Ramapo College of New Jersey. He is currently involved in a research project that is trying to identify DNA sequences that may play a major role in gene expression.

A Design for Team Peer Code Review

Deborah A. Trytten
University of Oklahoma
200 Felgar; Room 108
Norman, Oklahoma 73019
405-325-4299
dtrytten@ou.edu

ABSTRACT

The software industry needs our graduates to have significant and meaningful experiences with teamwork. A new design has been developed for a teamwork exercise based on peer code review. This design uses the three Ss of building assignments for cooperative learning: Same problem, Specific choices, and Simultaneous report. Students perform peer code review individually, and within and between stable small groups. The code can be sanitized student work or may be altered by the instructor to meet specific course learning objectives. The review is done in three phases. First, individuals answer yes or no to questions that evaluate the quality of the design and code. Then each group answers the same set of questions. When the groups have completed their evaluation, the class joins together to reveal and discuss the answers. This design was successfully implemented during the 2003-2004 academic year in an introductory programming class. This design is applicable to more advanced classes with significant programming assignments. Future work includes extending this structure to give students experience with other software engineering artifacts early in their academic careers.

Categories and Subject Descriptors

D.2.5 [**Software Engineering**]: Code Inspections and Walk-Throughs.

General Terms

Management, Documentation, Design.

Keywords

Software Engineering, Education, Peer Code Review, Cooperative Learning, Team Work.

1. INTRODUCTION

The size and complexity of today's software programs dictates that software engineers work in teams during their entire professional life. Industry needs graduates with teamwork skills.

SIGCSE'05, February 23–27, 2005, St. Louis, Missouri, USA.

Unfortunately, taking a collection of people and giving them a project to work on creates a group, not a team. A team is cohesive, interdependent, and shares resources, goals, and rewards [5]. A collection of people without these attributes is a group. The University of Oklahoma Sooners Football program is a team. The House of Representatives is a group.

Developing teamwork exercises for college classes is an important teaching challenge. It is tempting to think that any experience that students have working with others is beneficial to their professional development; and this point of view has merit. But sometimes working together creates more frustration than benefit. Group members can be bossy, lazy, rude, show up late for meetings (if they show up at all), be unprepared, and fail to meet deadlines. While these behaviors are not unknown among groups in industry, frustrating group experiences in college will probably not result in an appreciation for the importance and value of teamwork that is essential to students who are entering the software engineering profession.

The design of exercises given to collections of students is one factor that determines whether they will experience group work or teamwork. Three critical attributes of successful designs have been identified in the cooperative learning literature, and these will be reviewed in Section 2. Section 3 will discuss peer code review. The design the peer code review exercises using cooperative learning principles will be developed in Section 4. Section 5 contains a description of the implementation of this design. The final section will identify opportunities for future work.

2. COOPERATIVE LEARNING

The distinction between groups and teams comes from the literature on cooperative learning [5]. Two factors that interfere with teamwork are social loafing and transaction costs. Social loafing occurs when people work less diligently when grouped together. When a group of students produces a report that some members have neither contributed to, nor sometimes even read, social loafing has occurred. Anyone who has served on a University-wide committee is probably familiar with social loafing. Transaction costs are the amount of time and effort that it takes to compare group member schedules, find a time when everyone can meet and negotiate conflicts, find a location for a meeting, and communicate this information to group members. Anyone who has tried to get ten faculty members together for a meeting on short notice, is probably familiar with transaction costs.

Any exercise design that is intended to achieve cooperative learning must have a strategy for managing both social loafing and transaction costs. One way to defeat social loafing is to implement peer evaluation, where a percentage of the student's grade is dictated by the other group member's evaluation of the quality and quantity of work performed by the individual. Allowing teams to work during class time can eliminate transaction costs.

Although these strategies will improve group work, they are not the only factors that determine whether teamwork will be achieved. The structure of the exercise has been found to be a significant factor [6]. For example, long writing assignments have been identified as one of the worst possible group assignments [6] as have computer programming projects [9,10].

Michaelsen has identified three factors that lead to successful teamwork experiences [6]:

- Same problem
- Specific choices
- Simultaneous report

The structure that Michaelson pioneered for teamwork experiences is to give a multiple-choice test repeatedly. These tests are typically open book and open note, necessitating multiple-choice questions at the high levels of Bloom's taxonomy be generated [2]. First the test is given to individuals. This promotes individual accountability and helps to alleviate social loafing. Next, the exact same multiple-choice test is then given to the team as a whole. Since the individuals have had time to form their own opinions, the group discussion is both educated and intense.

After the groups have submitted their work for grading, each team is required to simultaneously and publicly vote on the correct answer for each multiple-choice exercise (Simultaneous report). The discussion in which teams defend and critique each other's reasoning as they try to reach consensus on the correct answer can only result if the teams are working on the Same problem, and making Specific choices. Competition among cooperating teams is an ideal environment for learning. Since the entire exercise takes place during class time, transaction costs are eliminated.

The biggest challenge in using this framework is writing the multiple-choice tests that evaluate student attainment of high level learning objectives. Simple factual tests are obviously inappropriate, since they do not represent high levels in the Bloom taxonomy and are not reflective of the learning objectives in most worthwhile courses. If the problems are not truly challenging, all of the teams may be able to find the correct answer. While this is a desirable result in one sense, it does not generate the deep, hotly contested and intellectually rich class discussion that is the most desirable end product.

3. PEER CODE REVIEW IN INTRODUCTORY PROGRAMMING CLASSES

3.1 Motivation

Peer code review is a staple of the software industry. It is one way that practicing professionals continually increase their technical skill. If it is done thoughtfully and properly, it also can drastically improve the quality of code that is generated. Cohen describes code review, explains it virtues, and gives practical advice [3]. A web based system for anonymous peer code review has been developed for introductory programming courses [8].

Using peer code review in classes outside of software engineering, particularly in the introductory programming classes that are my primary area of interest, has additional objectives. First it allows students to see that software engineers talk to each other. In classes where copying a single line of code from another student can result in academic misconduct charges, students may get the impression that programming is a solitary activity. Nothing could be further from the truth. If peer code review helps solitary students see that they must learn to connect with others, and lets social students see that there is a place in our discipline for them, it is worth the effort.

Another objective of peer code review is to encourage students to learn to read code. Writing code and reading code are very different activities, and both have value in the professional context.

Another advantage to peer code review is that students can examine alternate methods to solve a problem that they have already solved. Good engineering within any discipline demands the examination and evaluation of alternative designs. Unfortunately, beginning programming students are usually so happy to think of one way to get a program to run that they forget to look for alternate solutions. By encouraging students to see other options, we can help them become reflective practitioners of their craft.

3.2 Mechanics

If the value of peer code review for introductory programming classes is accepted, the design of these exercises needs to be determined. Peer code review in industry is typically unstructured. The code is often projected on a screen, and individuals meticulously read it one line at a time, asking questions and making improvements until they agree that the revised code is correct.

This is not an appropriate structure for the freshman students that typically populate beginning programming classes. Poorly defined assignments are both futile and unfair with this population. Properly done code review is an evaluation activity. Evaluation is the highest level of the Bloom taxonomy. To expect students who are new to collegiate expectations to independently jump to the highest level of learning objectives in the Bloom taxonomy is unrealistic.

An alternative structure is to give students specific questions to answer. These questions are the same ones that the trained software engineer would ask herself automatically.

- Are the classes properly differentiated? If not, give example(s) of poorly defined classes.
- Are data and methods properly assigned to instances and classes? If not, give example(s) of improper usage of instances and classes.
- Are the access modifiers correct? If not, give example(s) of incorrect access modifiers.
- Is the program well documented? If not, list documentation shortcomings.

Providing students with directed questions accomplishes two goals. First, it shows students the criterion for well written code.

Secondly it gives students experience applying these criterion to programs. Together, the directed questions can lead students to recognize good programs when they see them, and ultimately to build better programs of their own.

As the semester progresses the questions can change. Initially, the questions are shallow. For a beginning programmer, figuring out whether the class names start with capital letters and the instance names with small letters (a common code convention in Java) is a non-trivial task. As the semester progresses, the sophistication of the questions can increase. By the end of the semester, students could be asked if the program is properly documented. To answer this question, they would have to apply the individual criterion used in earlier peer reviews. Questions about the quality of a design will be some of the most challenging to answer.

4. THE EVOLUTION OF THE DESIGN

4.1 The Original Design

In the Fall 2002 semester, a colleague and I began experimenting with peer code review ideas in the first programming class in our computer science degree program. Students were assigned by the instructor to permanent groups of between four and five students during the first week of classes, using previously developed methods [8].

Students were required to bring copies of their own code to share with their group. Groups would review the code by answering a series of 10-30 questions provided by the instructor about the quality of the code. The graders would read the student responses (one from each group) evaluate them individually. Each student was required to have his or her program reviewed at least once during the semester.

While the idea of using peer code review was appealing, the results were poor. The selection mechanism for group membership had been developed for upper division classes with a less diverse student population. Critical questions about prior programming experience were not included in the screening questionnaire used to organize the groups. This left some groups with two or three people that had programmed before, and others without that precious resource.

Many logistic problems occurred. Students would forget, conveniently or otherwise, to bring their code for review. It was not unusual to have the first thirty minutes of a two-hour lab wasted while a student scurried to a laboratory to print out multiple copies of his or her code. It was also not uncommon for the student whose code was to be reviewed to suddenly disappear from lab for the day, leaving an awkward situation for the remaining group members who would then have to rush to print out their programs for review.

Another problem occurred because the groups had been assigned so early in the semester. There is significant attrition in this class. The failure to distribute people with prior programming experience throughout the groups meant that some groups were left with only one or two students. These groups were at a tremendous disadvantage since they lacked the breadth of resources that a larger group would have.

The last difficulty with this strategy was that having each group review a different program made it hard for graders to evaluate the quality of the peer code reviews efficiently. While this factor alone would not have eliminated this activity if it were otherwise beneficial, it was a burden on top of the other difficulties.

4.2 The Improved Design

In the Spring 2003 semester, major improvements were made to the structure of the exercise. Groups were assigned later in the semester, in an attempt to avoid assigning students who would drop the class to groups. Attrition still produced a few small groups by the end of the semester.

The critical question about prior programming experience was included on the screening questionnaire, making it possible to distribute knowledge more uniformly throughout the groups. This radically improved the quality of the code reviews and also reduced the number of clueless groups.

To address the logistics issues, a program submitted by one student was selected for code review by all groups. Student names or other personal identifiers were removed. Sometimes the program was modified a bit to make the code review more challenging or interesting. Having the instructor control the selection of code to review also meant that all students saw a wide variety of code, from mediocre to the best.

The peer review questions were nearly identical to the earlier design. Since every group was now reviewing the same code, grading was easier and as a result, more consistently and correctly done.

Student reaction to this design, although only indirectly measured, was more favorable. Reliable students weren't mysteriously absent during code reviews. Lab time devoted to code review was being well spent. The quality of the code reviews was also improved, probably due to more consistent and correct feedback. A few students complained that code review was busy work, but the student reaction was otherwise at least neutral if not favorable.

This is a viable structure for a peer review assignment in an introductory programming class. It isn't, however teamwork. These groups weren't cohesive and interdependent. They did share resources and rewards, for example by getting the same grade for the code review. But they didn't have any of the other characteristics of a team. For example, they didn't choose to sit together in class, and no team developed any identity (for example by giving themselves a name that they used). While these are not essential learning objectives of the class, it was an indication that this assignment could be improved.

4.3 The Final Design

In the Fall 2003 and Spring 2004 semester, the insight that the three Ss hadn't been applied to this assignment finally arrived. From the first to the second semester, one S had been inserted. They were now working on the Same problem. But we were still two Ss short of teamwork.

The prospect for writing multiple-choice tests of high level learning objective questions for peer code review was daunting. Since programming projects have to be changed every semester to prevent academic misconduct, these questions would have to be reworked every semester. While this wasn't impossible, it was discouraging. Making a time consuming course harder to teach isn't wise, and perhaps as importantly, won't transfer to the next instructor.

Finally, I realized that true and false questions are multiple-choice questions in binary. Each of the questions had already been posed in this fashion. The only difference was that an explanation had been required afterwards. By removing the explanation, the individuals and teams would be making Specific choices. And if we required the teams to share their choices using flash cards (green for true and red for false) at the end of the lab, then we would have Simultaneous reporting. The grading could be done very simply, both for the individual and group work. The class discussion could focus on why the program was or was not meeting some criterion. The end result is a very easy assignment to implement and evaluate.

A few other modifications were done to improve the logistics.

- Students are assigned to permanent groups after the third programming project is complete. This leaves four projects for code review and circumvents most of the attrition.
- Since teamwork is now sought, we perform a team building exercise before the first peer code review. The structure of this exercise is in the literature [9].

A variation of this structure would omit the individual multiple choice peer code review. This would make the exercise less time consuming, but would diminish individual accountability and might increase social loafing.

5. RESULTS

These ideas were developed for CS 1323 Introduction to Programming. The course uses the Java programming language. The prerequisite for the class is high school algebra. No prior programming experience is assumed. Students taking this class typically major in computer science, computer engineering, electrical engineering, industrial engineering, meteorology, and mathematics. Although the bulk of the students are freshmen computer science and computer engineering majors, the course is taken by students of all levels.

The class initially contained approximately 150 students distributed across two sections for lecture and three sections for lab. Lectures are 50 minutes, three times a week, or 75 minutes, twice a week, and run by the instructor. Labs are 2 hours, once a week. Each lab is taught by team of two teaching assistants, with support from the instructor as needed. There are three teaching assistants for the course.

This class has a long history of high student attrition and a high rate of student failure, as is typical of introductory programming courses. As a result, a number of new strategies are currently being used simultaneously to try to improve student success in this course including a new active learning strategy, continuing development of the use of TuringsCraft software (www.turingscraft.com)[1], and a different approach to homework assignments. Also, the composition of computer science classes has recently changed, due to declining enrollment. While retention appears to be improving, the presence of so many confounding factors has complicated the evaluation of this effort.

Before the peer code review assignment was implemented, the laboratories were used to provide students with help on programming projects and homework. Laboratories were fairly well attended shortly before a project was due, but otherwise sparsely attended. It was clear that laboratory time was not an educationally meaningful experience for most students a significant amount of the time.

The implementation of the final design was accomplished during the Fall 2003 and Spring 2004 semesters. A previous experience with the success of exercises with the three Ss gave cause for optimism [9,10]. This optimism was justified by the student response. Students consistently attended lab during the peer code review and completed the exercise. With fifteen questions, the exercise usually takes about one hour to complete. Performing peer code review during laboratory time results in more students spending lab time on a meaningful educational activity. On this basis alone, this exercise is worthwhile.

Writing the questions for the peer review is relatively easy. A project is selected from the online student project submissions. It is sanitized to remove personally identifiable information (including the name of the person who created the file, visible in Windows systems). I then perform a code review and spot things that were particularly good or bad about the given program. Questions are created to probe student knowledge of the evaluation. If I run out of material, I modify the code. For example, a common error that beginning students make in Java is to construct objects multiple times unnecessarily, as shown below. The numbers in parentheses are line numbers.

```
(77) String[] results = new String[10];
(78) results = reader.readLine().split();
```

Several questions that would probe for this error (in order of increasing difficulty) are:

- The reference results did not need to be constructed in line 77.
- The reference results was constructed twice.
- The reference results was properly constructed.
- There is a reference that was constructed twice unnecessarily.
- All objects were properly constructed.

Question topics were found to be largely reusable between semesters. Even though the details of projects change between semesters, the learning objectives remain essentially the same. By the end of the second semester, the process of building questions took around 30 minutes. Grading is extremely quick and easy.

Unlike building questions, determining the answers for the questions was challenging. Initially, I let the teaching assistants determine the answers on the fly in the laboratory. This resulted in different sections having different answers, usually because of minutia discovered by a student in the lab. This made the teaching assistants look disorganized and feel insecure, and made the answers seem random to students. We had to make improvements.

Holding a meeting with the teaching assistants to determine the correct answers before the laboratory was found to be essential. The three teaching assistants work the exercises independently and we compare answers. We then rewrite the questions or code until we all agree upon one answer. This process typically takes less than thirty minutes.

Using this method we improved the quality of the questions significantly. We usually still have one question out of 15 that we have to discard in a typical quiz (usually because both answers are reasonably well justified). I consider this to be acceptable. In these cases all students receive credit for answering the question correctly.

We found that performing this exercise during the first half of the laboratory was more successful than the second half. By the second half of lab some students are anxious to leave. This was inhibiting the discussion of questions since a small number of students were rolling their eyes, shuffling papers, making audible sounds of impatience, and generally being snarky during the discussion between groups. Moving the peer code review to the first half of lab removed this problem.

We had some difficulties during the first peer code review with the discussion between groups getting hostile. This typically happened when a pair of aggressive students would disagree on an answer and attempt to obtain supremacy at all costs. Having the option of discarding the question if both answers are truly justified, and encouraging the teaching assistants to intervene more quickly and strongly when these situations arise has removed this problem.

It is difficult to measure the success of this plan. Peer code review is a small part of the project grade, and the projects are only a modest part of the overall course grade. With the number of confounding factors, a definitive proof that the value of this structure cannot be done at this time. However, these students have some experience reading code, have seen alternate designs for code they have written, and have learned something about the value communication skills in this discipline.

6. FUTURE WORK

Although it seems unlikely that an exercise that plays a small part in a complex class will improve student retention significantly, or raise student course grades, it is possible that students might experience affective gains (changes in attitude) that could be measured. These type of non-cognitive gains are included in the model presented by Fink [4].

For example, students who have done this type of code review might have a deeper appreciation of the collaborative nature of computer science. They might see software engineers as team players, and develop more confidence in their ability to work with others productively. Making students aware of this important aspect of our discipline at a time when students are making academic choices that will either include or exclude them from computer science is worthwhile. Of course, this is a lot to expect from an exercise that plays a small part in a multi-faceted class.

Taking other software engineering activities and structuring them using this framework is also future work. Activities that focus on code design are a particularly attractive target, particularly for our second programming class CS 2334 Programming Structures and Abstractions.

7. ACKNOWLEDGMENTS

The author gratefully acknowledges the contributions of Scott Swindell, to the development of both peer code review and peer design reviews in computer science classes at the University of Oklahoma. The insight that peer code review should be done by introductory students is his.

The author also gratefully acknowledges the contributions of L. Dee Fink of the Instructional Development Program at the University of Oklahoma, and Larry Michaelson, formerly of the Division of Management in the Michael F. Price College of Business.

8. REFERENCES

[1] Arnow, D., Barshay, O., "WebToTeach: A Web-based Automated Program Checker", Frontiers in Education (FIE99), San Juan, Puerto Rico, November 1999.

[2] Bloom, B. S., Taxonomy of Educational Objectives. Handbook I: Cognitive Domain, David McKay Co., 1956.

[3] Cohen, L., "Code Reviews", Linux Journal, Volume 2001, Issue 81, January 2001, Article 11.

[4] Fink, L. D., Creating Significant Learning Experiences: An Integrated Approach to Designing College Courses, Jossey-Bass, 2003.

[5] Fink, L. D., "Beyond Small Groups: Harnessing the Extraordinary Power of Learning Teams" in Team-Based Learning: A Transformative Use of Small Groups, Praeger, Michaelsen, L.K., Knight, A. B., and Fink, L.D. editors, 2002.

[6] Michaelsen, L. K. and Knight, A. B., "Creating Effective Assignments: A Key Component of Team Based Learning" in Team-Based Learning: A Transformative Use of Small Groups, Praeger, Michaelsen, L.K., Knight, A. B., and Fink, L.D. editors, 2002.

[7] Michaelsen, L. K., "Getting Started with Team Based Learning" in Team-Based Learning: A Transformative Use of Small Groups, Praeger, Michaelsen, L.K., Knight, A. B., and Fink, L.D. editors, 2002.

[8] Trivedi, A., Kar, D. C. Patterson-McNeill, H., "Automatic Assignment Management and Peer Evaluation", The Journal of Computing in Small Colleges, Volume 18, Issue 4, April 2003, pages 30-37.

[9] Trytten, D. A., "Progressing from Small Group Work to Cooperative Learning: A Case Study from Computer Science, Journal of Engineering Education, Volume 90, No. 1, January, 2001, pp 85-92.

[10] Trytten, D. A., "Progressing from Small Group Work to Cooperative Learning: A Case Study from Computer Science", *Proceedings of the 1999 Frontiers in Education Conference*, November 1999.

Enhancing Team Knowledge: Instruction vs. Experience

D. Smarkusky, R. Dempsey, J. Ludka
Information Sciences and Technology
The Pennsylvania State University
120 Ridge View Drive
Dunmore, PA 18512 USA
+1 570 963-2593
{dls102, rfd, j4l}@psu.edu

F. de Quillettes
Information Sciences and Technology
The Pennsylvania State University
P.O. Box PSU, Old Rt. 115
Lehman, PA 18627 USA
+1 570 675-9277
fxd4@psu.edu

ABSTRACT
Information technology projects are growing in complexity and require teams to solve problems and develop solutions. With current undergraduate, computer science and information systems curricula, students graduate with technical skills, but lack team project experiences. We have identified and developed team knowledge modules that are being taught to students in an effort to increase awareness of team process fundamentals and build the foundation of an effective team player. In this paper we present the challenges that we face with team projects and then discuss team knowledge modules that are being taught to incoming freshmen to engage students in a curriculum that requires team projects in each course. We conclude with our assessment results and show comparisons of student team knowledge by instruction and experience.

Categories and Subject Descriptors
K.3.2 [**Computer and Information Science Education**] *Computer science education, Curriculum, Information systems education,* D.2.9 [**Management**] *Programming teams*

General Terms
Management and Experimentation.

Keywords
Software engineering, information technology education, team knowledge, team process, curricular initiatives.

1. INTRODUCTION
The philosophy of the Information Sciences and Technology (IST) Program at Penn State University is a triad of information, technology, and people, which conforms to that proposed in [3], and incorporates a mix of teamwork, computer science knowledge, problem-solving, communication, and organizational processes. We adopted the software engineering principle of working in teams as each course in the curriculum requires students to complete a team project. As the software engineering, computer science, and information technology fields advance, so does the knowledge that students should have when they graduate, but we cannot squeeze additional courses into the curriculum [6]. Instead, we need to provide future graduates/professionals with a strong technical core coalesced with highly developed teamwork skills, and teach them how to understand and apply this knowledge to make a difference in business, government, and education [1].

1.1 Motivation
Faculty and students often refrain from using teams because of the effort involved with individual vs. team assessment, time management, team dynamics, team member roles and functions, and process knowledge and maturity [4]. What knowledge and experience is required to work effectively in teams? Can faculty assume that students know how to effectively work in teams when they enter college, or that students have prior team project experiences? How do faculty address the challenges that students face when working in teams? How do faculty prepare students to work effectively in teams? We believe that team projects provide students with an opportunity to share ideas, learn new concepts, expose different points of view, and experience the satisfaction and challenges of working with others, while remaining in an academic setting.

The team knowledge modules presented in this paper were created based on the challenges we experienced. Most of our students work at part-time jobs and commute to campus, which causes a problem when trying to find non-class time for projects. The time management, meeting process and team communication modules were designed to address some of these issues. We also discovered that there were two types of problem students, "poor drivers" and "free riders". "Poor drivers" were students who had a dominating personality and did not know how to delegate responsibility and wanted to do all of the work on their own. "Free riders" were those types of students who were more than willing to let other students do the work. The team contract, team roles and responsibilities, and the self and peer assessment modules were developed so that students could be held responsible for their tasks, know what their role in the group should be and then be able to properly assess other students based on their roles and responsibilities within the project. Students had difficulty selecting problem solutions or respecting team decisions that did not match their individual answer. Students also had difficulty resolving conflicts that arose within the team. The team building, team dynamics and problem solving modules were developed to increase awareness of team dynamics and provide direction when conflicts arose and problems needed to be solved. We understand that not all students may enjoy working in a team environment, but our goal is to increase student awareness and provide them with team experiences that will allow them to become effective and productive team players in society and the workplace. In the remaining sections of this paper, we summarize the team knowledge modules and present our assessment results.

2. TEAM FUNDAMENTALS

We understand the importance of the Personal Software Process (PSP) and the Team Software Process (TSP) in training students to become disciplined and productive problem solvers and software professionals [3, 4]. Thus, our goal is not to replace these software processes, but to provide a foundation that will enhance the team project experience and provide a solid foundation upon which the TSP and PSP can be constructed.

A committee of faculty and staff from our university, including instructional resource specialists and representatives from Penn State's Royer Center for Learning and Academic Technologies, combined efforts to develop team knowledge modules that introduced freshman students to the world of team project experiences. Each module contains an objective/purpose, activity, assignment, and corresponding rubric for student assessment.

The team knowledge modules were integrated into the introductory course and associated first year seminar course. These courses meet each week for three lecture hours with two lab hours, and one lecture hour, respectively. Both courses are taken concurrently during the fall semester of the freshmen year. For courses in which team fundamentals were taught, class size was limited to 25, the same instructor taught both courses, and there were no teaching assistants assigned to the course. We summarize each of the team fundamental modules in the following sections.

2.1 Time Management

Objective: Upon completion of these exercises the students will recognize priorities and identify constraints and milestones that will impact their ability to successfully complete their personal or project tasks.

At the individual level, students are required to use an academic planner or PDA to complete weekly schedules that include academic, work, and personal tasks. To help students with prioritizing tasks to avoid waiting until the last minute to complete academic tasks, students also maintain a prioritized task list. Students assign a priority of (A, B, C) and keep a status (Completed, Forwarded, Deleted, Assigned to individual, InProcess) of each task.

At the project level, students define and recognize the development phases of a project, the associated constraints with regard to time and resources, and project milestones. A timeline reflecting the business plan of development phases of an assignment project is then constructed. Students analyze their individual schedules and then assign roles and tasks according to the defined milestones. Students incorporate meeting times into their project. Finally, students incorporate project time constraints and milestones established by the academic calendar and faculty member. If time permits, students are introduced to MS Project where they record project tasks and milestones, and assign team members to their associated tasks.

2.2 Team Building

Objective: Students will gain knowledge of other team members and build a common bond within their team.

In this lesson, students will interview each other with the purpose of learning at least one new thing about each person on their team. To better understand each individual and build unity in the team, students need to have knowledge about the goals and values of other team members. This knowledge will provide students with information about how other team members prioritize their academic, personal, and work activities. To build unity within the team, students need to have a common bond. The common bond will be a team poster/logo in which all team members will contribute something that is important to them and will provide motivation to them during the productive and challenging times of the project. An activity example follows:

Mini-Poster and Team Name. You are to create a team mini-poster that includes a team name and something important to and suggested by each member of the team. This mini-poster must be in electronic format (PDF, MS Word, or PPT). Be as creative as you like. Your mini-poster, when printed should fit on 8.5" x 11" paper. One individual on the team may be asked to briefly present the concepts (graphics, text) of your poster to the class. Be prepared to talk about how the poster components relate to the members of your team.

Team building takes time and this exercise is only an introductory step. Effective team dynamics, confidence, and trust between team members play critical roles in strengthening teams [2].

2.3 Team Roles and Responsibilities

Objective: The student will realize the importance of assigning different roles to team members, and how members should act and function within a group.

An in-class team activity would include assigning students to groups (arbitrarily assigned) for about 10 minutes, with an assignment requiring input from everyone, but eventually deciding on a single answer with supporting statements. For example [5]:

- "If you could remove any of the 50 states, which state would it be and why?", or
- "Which way should the key turn in a car door to unlock it?"

After the 10 minutes, have the students individually fill out the questionnaire, shown in Figure 1, concerning the functioning of a group, and individual actions and participation within a group.

Name ____________________
Group ____________________

Questionnaire:
What did you add to the group discussion?
What percent of the discussions were you involved in? 0 – 100%
Were there any "sleepers" in the group (someone making almost no contribution)?
Was there anyone who decided to "run the show" (talked most of the time)?
How were decisions made within the group?
Was everyone encouraged to add to the discussion?
Did you feel free to disagree with someone else's opinion/suggestion?
Were your opinions/suggestions taken seriously?
How well do you think the group performed AS A GROUP?
What suggestions would you make that would make the group function better?

Figure 1. Roles and Responsibilities Questionnaire

Finally, collect and examine the questionnaires. Explain members' roles (leader, recorder, etc.) within a group and how individuals should function and act within a group. Using examples from the questionnaire, point out how much better the team(s) could have performed. If time permits, assign different groups, and try it again (with a different problem to be solved) and/or assign a group project to be done as homework. Have the students fill in another questionnaire stating the roles each student in the group performed, the contributions made by each member, and (maybe) how group decisions were made.

2.4 Team Communications

Objective: The student will realize the importance of sharing information with other team members with respect to project documentation, team discussions, and the sharing of information via e-mail, chat sessions, formal meetings, hallway chats, or written documentation.

During this exercise, students brainstorm ways in which they can share information with other students under various circumstances and then discuss what would happen if this information were not shared with others.

2.5 Team Contracts

Objective: Students will develop a contract that includes team responsibilities, expectations, communication plans, and task responsibilities.

Students are to write a team contract. If there are problems with the teams during the semester, they will be held to this contract. At a minimum, their contract must contain a brief description of:

- Communication plan
- Team member responsibilities/expectations
- How missed meetings will be handled
- Who is responsible for delinquent work and how this work will be completed
- Printed names /signed names
- Date of signing

Firing of fellow team members is allowed, but the conditions for termination must be included in their contract if they plan to exercise this right. A termination statement must be submitted to the instructor one week prior to termination of any team member. This statement must include the reasons for termination, documented attempts to resolve stated issues and results of these attempts. If any teams fire a team member, the remaining team members will be responsible for completing the assignments. Fired team members will also be required to complete the assignments on their own or in conjunction with other fired team members, unless hired by another team, not to exceed four members per team. Teams with less than 4 members will have an opportunity to interview and hire anyone who has been fired. Team members cannot be fired after 50 percent of the work has been completed.

2.6 Team Dynamics

Objectives: At the end of this lesson, students will be able to identify and explain the goals and values that are important to each of their team members. Students should also be aware of the different personalities within their team, how these differences may influence the effectiveness of their team with regard to team interactions, task performance, conflict resolution and problem solving.

Did you every wonder why people react differently to different situations? Why are the values and goals of individuals so important? What things have an effect on them? What makes them "tick" as a person? Often times we make decisions on what is most important to us. Having an understanding of the important goals and values of each of their team members will give students information about how their team members may prioritize their tasks, perform activities and make decisions. An example is described below:

Determining Values and Goals. Using the values and/or goals, listed in Figure 2, select the **five (5)** that are **most important** to you and then rank these five items in order of importance. Once complete, share these with your fellow team members and explain why they are important to you.

Power To have control of others	**Location** To live where I want to live	**Family** To have time with my family
Security To have a secure and stable position	**Prestige** To be seen as being successful, as having stature	**Leadership** To become influential
Loyalty To be loyal to the Company and my boss and to have in return their loyalty	**Challenge and Self-Realization** To do work that is personally challenging, that helps me grow	**Friendship** To work with people I like and to be liked by them
Expertness To become an authority in what I do	**Wealth** To earn a great deal of money	**Enjoyment** To like my work, to have fun in it
Service To contribute to the satisfaction of others	**Achievement** To accomplish important things	**Independence** To have freedom of thought, time and action

Figure 2. Values and Goals

2.7 Meeting Process

Objective: At the completion of this lesson, students will by able to construct a team meeting agenda, explain the need for prepared pre-meeting materials, know how to conduct an effective meeting, record meeting minutes, and perform necessary meeting follow-up.

In this lesson students will identify the key elements of an effective meeting and learn the need for planning in order to effectively accomplish the designated task(s). Some activities include:

- Students list common complaints they have about team meetings and hold a group discussion on how planning and preparation might have averted them.
- Students prepare a list of different meeting purposes and discuss how this could affect the agenda.
- Students prepare a list of meeting elements: agenda, minutes, summary action items, sign-off, and next meeting date.

2.8 Problem Solving

Objective: At the end of the lesson, students will be able to take an unstructured set of facts and circumstances and be able to define a problem as a group, use critical thinking skills to develop alternative solutions, develop a methodology to choose among competing alternatives, make a group decision, and present the problem solution.

An assignment that incorporates problem-based learning follows:
"Ma and Pa Kettle, owners of Plum Awful Scooter Skates (PASS for short) request your assistance in solving what is turning into a significant problem for them. They inherited this company from their parents in the early 40's, shortly after scooters went out of favor as a vehicle for children. They have managed to eek out a living, staying one step ahead of the tax collector, with a record keeping system that was all manual. All customer and vendor records were kept on paper in a rusty old filing cabinet in the shed where the still used to be. They could probably find a record on every transaction over the last 50+ years.

But as of late, a real significant problem has occurred. There has been a resurgence in demand for scooters. Ma and Pa can no longer keep up with the inquiries and orders. To make matters even worse, for some reason these new customers want all sorts of crazy little wheels on their scooters. This has caused Ma and Pa to have to locate a whole new set of vendors to supply parts. Now they are also having a problem keeping track of vendors and processing timely orders for parts.

One new vendor suggested that they could download that company's entire parts list over the web. These words really puzzled Ma and Pa. They hooked up the horse and buggy and went to town to visit their favorite computer consultant, I. KnowItAll, hoping to get a solution to their problem. Mr. KnowItAll, being extremely busy himself, has commissioned your group to help find a solution to the Kettle's data storage problem.

Investigate different storage media that could be used to store needed data for the Kettles. Factors to consider during the investigation should include but are not limited to the amount of data, the data access frequency (how often is data read and written), the time it takes to read and write data from/to the media, and the amount of time the data will be stored (days, months, years). The Kettle's also don't own a computer, so you will also need to investigate different computer systems (hardware and software) that will help the Kettles in solving this problem. Prepare a report that lists the storage media considered, the characteristics of each, which one(s) you would recommend and why you are making this recommendation. Once you have selected the storage media, identify a computer system (hardware and software) to support your recommendation. Ma and Pa Kettle haven't been selling many scooters as of late, and therefore don't have much money in their savings account. Therefore, they have asked Mr. KnowItAll to find a computer system that meets their needs, but does not exceed $3592.79. For this assignment, students should utilize the following problem solving process:

1. Identify the constraints for the problem to be solved.
2. Determine the system requirements that need to be included in the solution.
3. Investigate and identify possible solution alternatives.
4. Based on the problem solution criteria, evaluate and critique the alternatives.
5. As a team, discuss all possible alternatives, keep track of the pros and cons for each and then select the solution that best solves the problem.
6. Be able to defend and describe in detail why this alternative is best."

2.9 Peer evaluation

Objective: The students will understand the importance of providing and receiving feedback in addition to the criteria used for both self and peer evaluations.

Self and Team Evaluation

☐ Check the box if this is a self evaluation. Date: ____________

My Name: ______________________

Name of Person I am evaluating: ______________________

Complete one of these forms for every member of your team, including yourself. **Evaluations will be scored on a scale of one (1) to five (5) with one being the lowest and five being the highest**. Circle the number that MOST closely represents the person's attributes. After completing the evaluation, add up the total points, and then complete the constructive comment and bonus sections on the back of this page. **Your individual grade will be made up of the average of all team member evaluations, including your own.** Take your time in filling out this form and most importantly, be honest!

**** Remember, your instructor will be the only one to see these evaluations.**

(1) *Process:* *1 2 3 4 5*
- Models a caring attribute about goals
- Exhibits leadership skills
- Helps direct the group in setting goals
- Helps direct group in meeting goals
- Exhibits on-task behavior consistently

(2) Communication: 1 2 3 4 5
- Shares many ideas related to the goals
- Encourages all group members to share their ideas
- Listens attentively to others
- Asks questions for clarification
- Builds upon others' comments

(3) *Interpersonal Skills and Social Interaction:* *1 2 3 4 5*
- Involves whole group in problem-solving
- Actively participates helping the group work better together
- Respects the views of others
- Reflects awareness of other's views and opinions in discussions
- Empathetic to other people's feelings and ideas

(4) Contribution: 1 2 3 4 5
- Contributes in a positive way to the group work
- Contributes to decision making
- Encourages group to evaluate how well they are working together

(5) *Shares Responsibility:* *1 2 3 4 5*
- Participates actively
- Thoroughly completes assigned tasks
- Ensures responsibility for task is shared evenly

Total Points: ______________________ (25 points maximum)

Constructive Comments. If completing this evaluation for yourself, then explain your role within the group and provide a list of your responsibilities in the comments section. If you are completing this form for a team member, please make any additional comments about their performance. Please include any constructive comments that you might have that would improve an individual, the workings of the group, and/or the project.

Comments:

Bonus.

You have a $10,000 bonus to split amongst the members of the team. Based on the team members contribution to the total project, list the amount that you would give to the team member you are currently evaluating.

Figure 3. Self and Peer Evaluation Form

A sample self and peer evaluation form is shown in Figure 3. This form is completed by students and reviewed by the instructor. Students complete both self- and peer evaluations. The first section of the form provides students with an opportunity to evaluate the process, communication, interpersonal skills, contribution and responsibilities of team members. The second section of the evaluation is more open-ended. Using the level of detail provided and a comparison of stated task assignments among team members, instructors receive an indication of student involvement in the project. There are times when team members report conflicts and problems with team member performance during project development, but these problems are not reported on the evaluation forms and all team members receive positive evaluations. When dealing with this problem, bonus money seems to make the difference. Each student is instructed to distribute bonus money among all members of the team, based on their contribution to the project. The amount of money distributed should support the contributions stated in previous section of the form. When dealing with effective and productive team members, the money is never equally divided between team members. The bonus amounts may be close in value, but never equal. When a non-productive team member submits an evaluation, the bonus money is almost always divided equally (i.e. $3,333.33, for a 3 person team). This is just an observation, and may not be true for all cases. Once the evaluation forms are reviewed, instructors discuss the project challenges and lessons learned with the entire class.

3. ASSESSMENT AND SUMMARY

The goal of our study was to determine how students learn team knowledge skills. Could this knowledge be learned by instruction or only gained with experience? With this in mind, we completed a study that included 72 baccalaureate degree students, from which the freshmen class of 25 students was selected as the pilot group to receive instruction using the team knowledge modules. The freshmen class completed a team knowledge skills assessment at the start of the Fall 2003 semester to obtain baseline values. This same assessment was given to all freshmen, sophomores, juniors and seniors, at the start of the Spring 2004 semester. This data would provide insight into whether team knowledge skills are learned by instruction or experience. The results of these assessments are presented below.

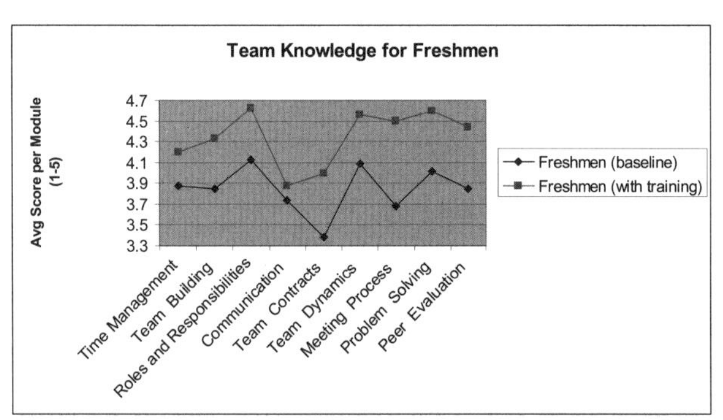

Figure 4. Team Knowledge – Instructional Comparison

The results in Figure 4 show a comparison of the team knowledge areas for freshmen. The bottom line represents the baseline of team knowledge for the freshmen students at the start of the Fall 2003 semester. The top line represents their level of knowledge after completing the team knowledge modules described in this paper. For these students, their average knowledge in each area increased with the greatest increase being in meeting process and the smallest increase in team communications.

The results in Figure 5 show a comparison of knowledge among the Spring 2004 freshmen (including those with training) with that of the sophomores, juniors and seniors who have not received formal training using the team knowledge modules, but who have gained team project experience in each course throughout the curriculum. From this we can see that the students who received the formal team training had higher average scores with the greatest positive differences in the team building, meeting process and problem solving areas.

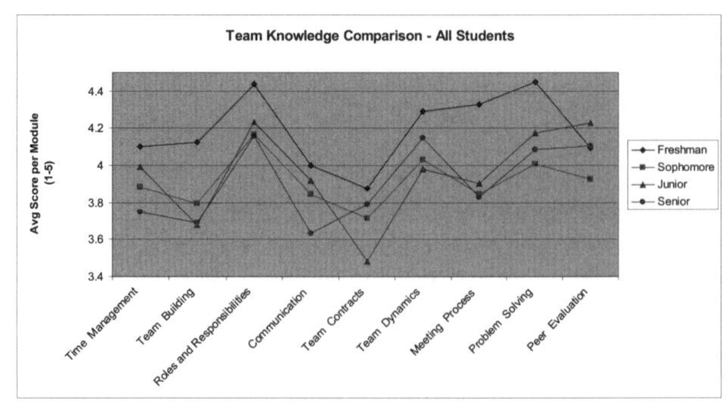

Figure 5. Team Knowledge – Instruction vs. Experience

Based on the results of this study, we would like to continue tracking these students to determine the impact on team-based learning as they continue their academic careers. The team knowledge modules will continue to be evaluated and improved. In addition, we will continue to incorporate the team knowledge areas into the course team projects so that these concepts can be enhanced, reinforced and re-evaluated in all courses with required team-based project deliverables and assessment (team contracts, MS Project deliverables, and individual and peer assessments and feedback). We need to continue to assess the effectiveness of using teams in all courses and the best practices in which to increase student awareness of team knowledge fundamentals. This empirical data can be collected over time to study the various issues related to women, minorities, etc. in the context of team processes.

4. ACKNOWLEDGEMENTS

We would like to thank the students who formally and informally provided feedback on their team experiences. Special thanks to the faculty and instructional resource specialists who participated in the development of the team fundamentals. Their efforts were greatly appreciated by all involved.

5. REFERENCES

[1] Blake, M.Brian, and Cornett, T., "Teaching an Object-Oriented Software Development Lifecycle in Undergraduate Software Engineering Education", *Proc. of the 15th Conference on Software Engineering Education and Training (CSEET'02)*, February 2002, pp.234-240.

[2] Ferguson, C., Little, S., McClelland, M., "Developing Teamwork through Experimental Learning", *The Journal of Computing in Small Colleges*, Volume 16, Issue 2, January 2001, pp. 268-280.

[3] Hilburn, T.B., "Software Engineering Education: A Modest Proposal", IEEE Software, Nov./Dec. 1997, pp. 44-48.

[4] Hilburn, T.B., "Teams Need a Process!", Proceedings of the 5th annual SIGCSE/SIGCUE ITiCSEconference on Innovation and technology in computer science education, Helsinki, Finland, July 2000, pp. 53 – 56.

[5] http://halcyon.usc.edu/~kiran/msqs.html, Microsoft Interview Questions.

[6] Parnas, D.L., "Software Engineering Programs Are Not Computer Science Programs", *IEEE Software*, November 1999, pp. 19-30.

Affective Assessment of Team Skills in Agile CS1 Labs: The Good, the Bad, and the Ugly

Dawn McKinney and Leo F. Denton
School of Computer and Information Sciences, University of South Alabama
Mobile, AL 36688
(251) 460-6390
{dmckinney,ldenton}@usouthal.edu

ABSTRACT

Team experiences can be important learning experiences, and industry highly values team skills in graduates. Low retention rates might also be improved with early team experiences because team experiences have been linked to increases in the sense of belonging, a key retention factor. Team experiences in upper-level courses could also benefit from earlier team experiences. The purpose of this paper is to describe and evaluate an early use of teams in the second semester of our CS1 sequence. The instructional methodology drew heavily upon the professional practices of an agile software development model, Extreme Programming. These professional practices fostered the development of team skills during a semester-long project in a closed lab. The evaluation of our experience revealed aspects of the good, the bad, and the ugly. Areas for improvement and future work are also explained.

Categories and Subject Descriptors

K.3.2 [Computing Milieux] Computer and Information Science Education – *Accreditation, Computer science education, Curriculum, Information systems education, Self-assessment.*

General Terms

Measurement, Experimentation, Human Factors.

Keywords

Active Learning, Adaptability, Affective Assessment, Agile Software Development, Commitment, Communication, Cooperative Learning, Cooperation, CS1 Labs, Extreme Programming, Internalization, Retention, Sense of Belonging, Team Skills, Work Ethic.

1. INTRODUCTION

The use of teams in education is supported by the literature. Studies show that active and cooperative learning experiences are beneficial to students [18], and active and cooperative learning can easily become integral components of team experiences. The National Association of Colleges and Employers (NACE) includes team skills in its top-ten list of characteristics that industry most wants in college graduates: communication skills, honesty/integrity, teamwork skills, interpersonal skills, motivation/initiative, strong work ethic, analytical skills, flexibility/adaptability, computer skills, and organizational skills [2]. Moreover, with enrollments dropping in the computer and information sciences at many institutions, retention has become an important issue. An important factor leading to students leaving colleges is a lack of a sense of belonging [11, 19, 21]. Because the sense of belonging can be fostered by positive team experiences, the use of teams in introductory courses could increase retention. At our university, students are required to take a Small Group Communications course and a Software Engineering course both of which are sophomore level courses. Later team experiences include Senior Project.

This paper describes the experimental use of teams in CS1 to assess the potential benefits of team experiences for students at the introductory level. Students at this level often have limited prior practice or instruction supporting team skills. Studies show that students require instruction on team skills [6, 10]. Nonetheless, an early introduction to teams could help students develop these needed skills. Further reasons supporting this early use of teams include: (1) studies show that women and minorities benefit from quality team experiences [18], (2) our earlier work which has shown that the sense of belonging, along with other affective factors, is correlated with student achievement [3], and (3) team activities provide a context that allows for efficient and effective assessment of affective objectives [4].

This paper focuses on the team aspects of our Spring 2004 experience. Using the NACE list as a springboard, this effort specifically identified, promoted, and assessed five affective team skills: communication, cooperation, work ethic, adaptability, and commitment. We will describe our instructional environment, methodology, use of professional practices, assessment, and improvements planned for Fall 2004. The description of this experience includes elements of the good, the bad, and the ugly.

2. OUR CS1 ENVIRONMENT

CS1 at our School of Computer and Information Sciences is a two-semester sequence for majors focusing on problem-solving and programming concepts. Both semesters have a closed lab which meets for 75 minutes each week. The students are required to bring personal laptops to class and lab. Graduate assistants help students with technical problems during class and lab and support the instructor as needed. Our class sizes are relatively small, usually between 15 and 30 students. The programming language used during both semesters is Java.

SIGCSE '05, February 23–27, 2005, St. Louis, Missouri, USA.

3. METHODOLOGY

During Fall 2003 and Spring 2004, students in the second semester of CS1 were provided instruction about team skills [6] and Extreme Programming practices [9, 20], grouped into teams, and assigned a semester-long project to be completed during the weekly lab sessions. Extreme Programming has become a well known agile approach to software development [7, 8, 15, 16, 22]. This approach was chosen primarily because of its strong emphasis on the development of team skills.

3.1 Forming of teams

We allowed students to form their own teams of between 5 and 9 students each. The team size allowed for diversity, more pairing, and prevented teams from becoming too small due to drops or absences. Friends tended to stay together as did minorities. The more experienced or confident students also tended to form teams as did the less experienced. The "loners" had to be encouraged to join teams. Teams chose team names which seemed to give them a sense of identity and "team spirit." However, we did experience problems with this approach, such as teams with unbalanced skill levels. Some studies suggest that teams be carefully chosen by the instructor [6, 17] which is our plan for Fall 2004.

3.2 Affective objectives for team skills

The affective objectives connected with the agile lab experience related directly to five team skills: communication, cooperation, commitment, work ethic, and adaptability. Table 1 lists these course objectives which emphasize team skills. These affective objectives were not separate from the cognitive framework of the course but rather integrated into it.

Table 1. Affective objectives included on course syllabus.

Communication	Communicate with students and faculty about course concepts and practices.
Cooperation	Cooperate with a team in an effort to solve problems and develop software.
Commitment	Demonstrate a commitment to quality software development with good design and testing practices.
Work Ethic	Demonstrate a strong work ethic by attending class and participating fully.
Adaptability	Demonstrate adaptability in software development practices.

3.3 Semester-long project

The teams in each semester were assigned the same project. Each team was independent and had different ways of approaching the project, but being in the same room, ideas were often shared between teams. In each semester, the project was a "real" program that the instructor of the class was interested in using as a customer. For example, in Spring 2004, the project involved the development of an automated survey builder which was to be used to capture and evaluate data. Even though students at this level were not ready to provide software solutions for real world customers yet, we believed they would benefit from producing something they knew was worthwhile for an actual "customer," even if it was their instructor. This approach also oriented students toward an important industry concern, the development of software that satisfied the customer rather than software that simply fulfilled written requirements. The duration of the semester-long project allowed the students to experience three project iterations and provided a sufficient time frame to allow for affective growth in team skills.

3.4 Agile Practices

The agile practices of Extreme Programming incorporated into the class were: the planning game, small releases, metaphor, simple design, test-driven development, refactoring, pair programming, collective ownership, continuous integration, sustainable pace, on-site customer, coding standards, and stand-up meetings [9]. Details of the Fall 2003 work and its assessment can be found in an earlier paper [13]. Although our main focus was teams, we introduced all of the agile practices because the practices work together [9]. Still we devoted most of the attention to those Extreme Programming practices that had the highest impact on the team-based objectives relating to communication, cooperation, commitment, work ethic, and adaptability. Those practices identified as having high impact were pair-programming, collective code ownership, on-site customer, stand-up meetings, and test-driven development. Each of these is described in subsequent subsections.

3.4.1 Pair-programming

Students were required to write code in pairs only. As part of this process, they were instructed to briefly document their pair programming experiences. The student typing at the computer was the "driver", while the "co-pilot" corrected typos, and suggested code, techniques, and solutions. [8, 16]. Recorded information included driver, co-pilot, date, task, and start/stop times. This routine helped encourage each student to rotate between driver and co-pilot and to pair with other members of the team. Students needed to communicate with one another and cooperate in order to make orderly progress. "Pair pressure" also played an important role in fostering a good work ethic and commitment to the project. Observations indicated that students struggled with and benefited from working with other people with different ideas. This process was particularly apparent when observing a programming pair work together and when observing multiple pairs attempting to coordinate their work. These experiences helped students to develop and practice adaptability skills.

3.4.2 Collective code ownership

The program code for each project was kept on a server available during lab and all team members had access to all the code. There was no physical impediment for any member of the team to change the code at any time. Orderly development of the software project required adaptability, communication, and cooperation.

3.4.3 *On-site customer*

The instructor played the role of customer and the graduate assistants played the role of project managers for each team. Students were required to communicate with the customer frequently during the software development process. The customer made various project changes just as real world customers do. The students, though at times frustrated, learned to accept the normalcy of change and the importance of adapting to and cooperating with the customer.

3.4.4 *Stand-up meetings*

Stand-up meetings are quick meetings, typically lasting from 2 to 5 minutes, where each team member briefly states what he or she has been working on and what progress has been made. During these meeting, all team members must stand. The meetings were fun, and the students seemed to appreciate having an efficient way of communicating and maintaining accountability. The standing component of the meeting also tended to ensure that everyone was alert and attentive (students were not allowed to use their laptops or other resources during the meeting). Stand-up meetings also motivated the students to make meaningful contributions so that they could have something significant to report. These meetings were announced with little warning, on an as needed basis, but typically were held at the beginning and the end of lab sessions. This practice was an important way to encourage the development of commitment, work ethic, and communication.

3.4.5 *Test-driven development*

Test-driven development was attempted with JUnit, an automated test-driven development tool. Though not expected to impact team skills significantly, test-driven development became a central practice in this regard. Because the tool was new to the students, and because the students were inexperienced programmers, and because the students did not have sufficient instruction or guidance in using the tool, there was much frustration associated with this practice. Nonetheless the attempt to follow this practice created opportunities for the development of team skills. While adaptability was certainly required, the other team skills were also needed: communication, cooperation, commitment, and work ethic. Unfortunately, from a technical perspective, the project-wide use of JUnit was largely unsuccessful. We believe an IDE that better integrates the use of JUnit and earlier instruction on test-driven development with more examples could be beneficial.

3.5 Peer Evaluations

We were able to schedule three iterations of the project, each about three calendar weeks, or 225 minutes of lab time. After each of the three iterations, students were required to evaluate each team member using a peer evaluation instrument which consisted of five items: (1) " Specific positive contributions of this team member," (2) "Best qualities this member added to the team effort," (3) "Weaknesses of this member," (4) "Would you want this member on your team again? (yes/no)," and (5) "Overall level of contribution of this team member (Low to High on a 5 point Likert scale)." Table 2 shows sample student responses from the instruments. We have categorized them as the good (positive), the bad (negative), and the ugly (out-of-line). Based on these comments, students received informal feedback from the instructor which was probably an insufficient means for promoting sustained affective growth. In the future, while protecting anonymity, we intend to provide more complete and appropriate feedback to students reflective of observations from peers, instructor, and project managers.

Table 2. Sample peer-review comments representing the team-skills factors showing aspects of the good, the bad, and the ugly.

	The Good	The Bad	The Ugly
Communication	"He is good at explaining things to those who are not grasping a particular concept."	"He sometimes talks over weaker members."	"Maybe you should discuss appropriate behavior toward women with him."
Cooperation	"A good quality is her positive attitude and willingness to participate and help where needed."	"Does not contribute to group discussions/effort noticeably or effectively."	"I think he talks out of turn, his comments are inappropriate, and he is disrespectful toward the customer."
Commitment	"He has probably shown the most improvement and most effort on the team. His attitude as well as his ability to program has changed a lot since the first lab. His willingness to improve I think inspires our team"	"The only thing that worries me about her is her lack of enthusiasm. I don't think college is a real priority in her life right now."	"I don't think he really cares about team work."
Work Ethic	"She is willing to learn and take extra steps to dig for material. I feel she is determined to do well."	"He is normally absent and when present never wants to work on the project."	"Sleeps during class, is absent a lot, doesn't really help during lab, just kind of sits back and watches"
Adaptability	"She has an open mind and wants to hear and learn about what others bring to the table. She is also a good listener."	"He is set on his way of thinking."	"Insists on doing things his own ways, not according to the rules and what the customer wants the team to do."

4. ASSESSEMENT AND RESULTS

Data from the first and second peer evaluation instruments included (1) open-ended questions about the abilities and contributions of each team member with no explicit mention of team skills and (2) a quantitative measure of the overall effectiveness of each team member. The third peer evaluation instrument explicitly asked each student to rate each team member on each of the five team skills: communication, cooperation, commitment, work ethic, and adaptability.

As a measure of the level of internalization of the team-based objectives, the instructor examined the student responses and identified comments which referred to one of the five team skills. A score was then assigned to each student indicating the number of times, per evaluation form, that he or she referred to one of the skills. These *frequency of use* scores were correlated with (1) *adjusted* course grade (team project grade components were removed from the final course grade to lessen the potential interactions with the grade variable), (2) the student's overall peer evaluation scores from the first and second peer evaluations, and (3) the five team skill scores (e.g. communication) from the third peer evaluation. We found significant positive correlations with *adjusted* course grade, the overall peer evaluation scores from the first and second peer evaluations, and with several team skill scores from the third peer evaluation. The significant results are shown in Table 3. These results indicate that a student's unprompted application of team skills terminology correlated with other students' perceptions of how well that student contributed to the project. This correlation suggests that some students not only learned about team skills cognitively but also chose to apply those skills in their in-lab practice.

For the Spring 2004 semester, data on the levels of affective factors was collected using adapted versions of the Intrinsic Motivation Inventory [12] and the Belonging Scale [1]. We used these validated instruments to measure students' sense of value of the course, perceived competence, effort, lack of pressure, and sense of belonging at 5 weeks into the semester and 10 weeks into the semester. Our earlier work has shown significant correlations of these factors with student achievement [3] as well as significant drops in all affective factors except student belonging over the semester in CS1 [14]. Paired samples *t*-tests were performed to measure the increases or decreases in each of these factors. The agile CS1 labs showed significant increases in overall belonging, student belonging, and a lack of pressure from 5 weeks into the semester to 10 weeks into the semester. These results are shown in Table 4. These results support the idea that team experiences contribute to the sense of belonging and a decrease in student pressure.

Additional Pearson correlations were made between *adjusted* course grade and (1) the overall peer evaluation scores from the first and second peer evaluations and (2) the team skill scores from the third peer evaluation. Significant positive correlations were found in the overall scores from the first peer evaluation, work ethic, and communication. These results are shown in Table 5. There was no significant difference between the 1st and 2nd overall peer evaluation scores. We believe that better feedback to the students about their peer evaluations could lead to significant improvements in the 2nd peer evaluations and promote more affective growth.

Table 3. Correlations with Frequency of Use Scores.

	Pearson Correlations with Frequency of Use	N	*p*-value
Course Grade	0.447*	24	0.029
1st Peer Evaluation	0.537**	24	0.007
2nd Peer Evaluation	0.661**	23	<0.0005
Work Ethic	0.690**	23	<0.0005
Communication	0.683**	23	<0.0005
Cooperation	0.615**	23	0.002
Commitment	0.677**	23	<0.0005
**** Significant at the 0.01 level (two-tailed)**			
*** Significant at the 0.05 level (two-tailed)**			

Table 4. Increase in belonging and decrease in pressure.

Early/Late Factors	*t*-value	N	*p*-value)
Pressure	-3.637**	23	0.002
Belonging	2.282*	23	0.035
Student Belonging	2.773*	23	0.013
**** Significant at the 0.01 level (two-tailed)**			
*** Significant at the 0.05 level (two-tailed)**			

Table 5. Correlations with *adjusted* course grade

	Pearson Correlations with Course Grade	*N*	*p*-value
1st Peer Evaluations	0.541**	26	0.004
Work Ethic	0.462*	23	0.026
Communication	0.641**	23	0.001
**** Significant at the 0.01 level (two-tailed)**			
*** Significant at the 0.05 level (two-tailed)**			

5. RECOMMENDATIONS

Our results, experience, and reflections suggest the following recommendations. To tackle the bad, we recommend that: (1) instructors choose teams using a defined process, (2) students receive concrete definitions about team skills and timely feedback about how they are doing as team members, (3) students receive adequate instruction on test-driven development, and (4) test-driven development is implemented using an IDE that incorporates an automated testing tool. To prevent and mitigate the ugly, we recommend that: (1) swift corrective actions be taken to correct situations where students are disrespectful or uncooperative and (2) persistently disrespectful or uncooperative students be required to work alone or among themselves rather than be an undue burden to other students' team experiences. To carry on the good, we recommend that: (1) extreme programming practices be utilized as a means to support the development of team skills, (2) semester-long lab projects be utilized to support the objectives of second semester CS1 courses, (3) peer evaluations be implemented to effectively monitor the progress of teams, and (4) that positive team experiences be used to enhance the students' sense of belonging and lack of pressure.

6. FUTURE PLANS

In Fall 2004, we plan to continue using agile teams and practices for the lab component of our second semester of CS1. The instructor will choose teams using specific team-forming strategies [6]. After each iteration cycle, a peer-manager-instructor evaluation summary will be provided to each student in order to facilitate affective growth in weak areas. Finally, we intend to better prepare the students to accomplish test-driven development by providing an in-depth instruction in the use of JUnit early in the semester and by the adoption of an IDE that facilitates the use of JUnit.

7. ACKNOWLEDGEMENTS

We would like to extend our appreciation to Dean David Feinstein, Computer Science Coordinator Michael Doran, and to our students.

8. REFERENCES

[1] Anderson-Butcher, Dawn, and David E. Conroy. Factorial and Criterion Validity of Scores of a Measure of Belonging in Youth Development Programs. *Educational and Psychological Measurement*, Vol. 62, No. 5, October 2002, p. 857-876.

[2] *ACM/IEEE Computing Curricula 2001, Computer Science Volume, Chapter 10: Professional Practice.* Available at http://www.acm.org/sigcse/cc2001/cs-professional-practice.html

[3] Denton, Leo F., Dawn McKinney, and Michael V. Doran. Promoting Student Achievement With Integrated Affective Objectives, *Proceedings of the 2003 American Society for Engineering Education Annual Conference & Exposition*, Nashville, Tennessee, USA (2003).

[4] Denton, Leo F., Michael V. Doran, and Dawn McKinney. Integrated Use of Bloom and Maslow for Instructional Success in Technical and Scientific Fields, In the *Proceedings of the 2002 American Society for Engineering Education Annual Conference & Exposition,* Montreal, Canada (2002).

[5] Denton, Leo F. and Dawn McKinney. Affective Factors and Student Achievement: A Quantitative and Qualitative Study, *34th ASEE/IEEE Frontiers in Education Conference*, Savannah, GA, October 20 – 23, 2004.

[6] Felder, Richard M., and Rebecca Brent. The ABC's of Engineering Education: ABET, Bloom's Taxonomy, Cooperative Learning, And So On. *Proceedings of the 2004 American Society for Engineering Education Annual Conference & Exposition,* (2004).

[7] Fenwick, James B., Jr. Adapting XP to an Academic Environment by Phasing –In Practices. *Extreme Programming and Agile Methods – XP/Agile Universe 2003, Third XP Agile Universe Conference,* New Orleans, LA.

[8] Hanks, Brian, Charlie McDowell, David Draper, and Milovan Krnjajic. Program Quality with Pair Programming in CS1. *ITiCSE'04*, June 28-30, Leeds, United Kingdom.

[9] Jeffries, Ron, Ann Anderson, and Chet Hendrickson. *Extreme Programming Installed.* Addison – Wesley. 2001.

[10] LeJeune, Noel. Critical Components for Successful Collaborative Learning in CS1. *Consortium for Computing Sciences in Colleges*, 2003, p. 275-285.

[11] Light, Richard. *Making the Most of College.* Harvard University Press, 2001.

[12] McAuley, E., Duncan, T., & Tammen, V.V. "Psychometric properties of the Intrinsic Motivation Inventory in a competitive sport setting: A confirmatory factor analysis." *Research Quarterly for Exercise and Sport*, 60, 48-58, 1987. http://www.psych.rochester.edu/SDT/measures/intrins.html

[13] McKinney, Dawn, Julie Froeseth, Jason Robertson, Leo F. Denton, David Ensminger. Agile CS1 Labs: eXtreme Programming Practices in an Introductory Programming Course, *Proceedings of XP/Agile Universe 2004, Calgary, Canada, August 15-18, 2004. Lecture Notes in Computer Science,* Springer, 2004.

[14] McKinney, Dawn and Leo F. Denton. Houston, we have a problem: there's a leak in the CS1 affective oxygen tank, *Proceedings of the 35th SISCSE Technical Symposium on Computer Science Education*, Norfolk, VA, March 2004.

[15] Melnik, Grigori, and Frank Mauer. Introducing Agile Methods in Learning Environments: Lessons Learned. *Extreme Programming and Agile Methods – XP/Agile Universe 2003, Third XP Agile Universe Conference*, New Orleans, LA.

[16] Nagappan, Nachiappan, Laurie Williams, Miriam Ferzli, Eric Wiebe, Kai Yang, Carol Miller, and Suzanne Balik. Improving the CS1 experience with pair programming. *Proceedings of the 34th SIGCSE technical symposium on Computer science education*, 2003, Reno, NV.

[17] Oakley, Barbara, Rebecca Brent, Richard Felder, and Imad Elhajj. *Turning Student Groups in to Effective Teams. Journal of Student Centered Learning*, Volume 2, No. 1, 2004, p. 9-34.

[18] Ormrod, Jeanne Ellis. *Human Learning*, Third Edition, Merrill, 1999.

[19] Seymour, Elaine, and Nancy M. Hewitt. *Talking About Leaving: Why Undergraduates Leave the Sciences.* Westview Press, 1997.

[20] Steinberg, Daniel H., and Daniel W. Palmer. *Extreme Software Engineering: A Hands-on Approach.* Prentice-Hall, Inc., 2004.

[21] Tinto, Vincent. *Leaving College: Rethinking the Causes and Cures of Student Attrition.* Second Edition, the University of Chicago Press, 1993.

[22] Wainer, Michael. Adaptations for Teaching Software Development with Extreme Programming: An Experience Report. *Extreme Programming and Agile Methods – XP/Agile Universe 2003, Third XP Agile Universe Conference*, New Orleans, LA.

Cooperative Learning Techniques in CS1: Design and Experimental Evaluation

Leland L. Beck
Department of Computer Science
San Diego State University
San Diego, CA 92182-7720
(619)594-6807
beck@cs.sdsu.edu

Alexander W. Chizhik
School of Teacher Education
San Diego State University
San Diego, CA 92182-1153
(619)594-1222
achizhik@mail.sdsu.edu

Amy C. McElroy
Dept. of Mathematics and Statistics
San Diego State University
San Diego, CA 92182-7720
(619)594-2059
amcelroy@sciences.sdsu.edu

ABSTRACT
A set of cooperative learning exercises were designed for use in a Java-based CS1 course. The exercises used specific roles to focus students' attention on key concepts of the Java language, and on key mental processes of programming and problem solving. A controlled experiment was conducted to evaluate the effectiveness of this approach. The results show that the cooperative learning experience had a significant positive effect on student performance, and may have been of special benefit to women and minority students.

Categories and Subject Descriptors
K.3.2 [**Computers & Education**]: Computer & Information Science Education – *computer science education, curriculum.*

General Terms
Human Factors

Keywords
Cooperative learning, Classroom management, Pedagogy, CS1.

1. INTRODUCTION
This paper reports on the development of a set of cooperative learning materials for use with a Java-based CS1 course, and on the evaluation of the effectiveness of these materials using a controlled experimental design. Cooperative learning is not a new idea; however, our approach has some innovative features, which are discussed later in this paper.

Section 2 describes some of the educational techniques that were applied in our exercises, and the reasons for using them. Section 3 places these techniques in the context of previously published work, and identifies the innovative aspects of our approach. Section 4 describes the experimental design that was used in evaluating the effectiveness of the materials, and Sections 5 and 6 present the results of this experiment. Section 7 concludes and offers suggestions for future research.

SIGCSE '05, February 23–27, 2005, St. Louis, Missouri, USA.

2. DESIGN OF THE MATERIALS
Our cooperative learning exercises were designed to help students achieve a fundamental understanding of key concepts. One important technique we used was the assignment of specific roles to students during the group exercises. For example, in an early exercise, one group member (the Variable Manager) was assigned to keep track of names and contents of variables, using pencil and paper. A second group member (the Program Reader) read a simple Java program that contained variable declarations and assignment statements, and issued the appropriate instructions to the Variable Manager. A third member (the Method Executor) was responsible for performing simple I/O operations, following a different set of instructions. A fourth student was assigned the role of Facilitator (helping the whole process stay on track and helping the other group members stay in their assigned roles).

The division of roles in this exercise was intended to reflect the underlying process of sequential program execution and the storage and use of variables, thus helping the students to develop their own mental model of the way programs are executed by a computer. Other exercises used roles to help students gain an understanding of data type conversions (and when these conversions are required), the execution of different types of control structures (including nested structures), and the processes of creating objects and invoking instance methods associated with these objects.

The cooperative learning exercises were also designed to help students learn about key mental processes of programming and problem solving. For example, one exercise began by asking students to read and understand simple 'if' statements, and then to modify these statements in specified ways. This was intended to focus students' attention on the syntax and semantics of the statements.

Later in the same exercise, the students were presented with simple problems involving logical conditions, and with Java statements that were proposed as solutions to these problems. Students were asked to determine whether or not the proposed solutions were correct, and to correct those proposed solutions that contained errors. This was intended to help the students learn to look critically at a piece of code (their own or someone else's), and to find and correct program bugs.

Finally, the exercise asked students to write and test their own solutions to simple problems involving logical conditions. Roles were used during this process as well: some students were assigned the role of Coder (writing the desired Java statements), and others the role of Tester (checking to see whether those statements really solved the problem). If errors were found, the Java statements were returned to the Coders for rewriting (and were then re-examined by the Testers). These roles were intended to focus attention on the process of testing a program (and on the need to do so). Roles were rotated during the exercise, so that students who had the role of Coder on one problem would have the role of Tester on the next.

Other exercises used a similar approach to focus attention on the processes of program design (using pseudocode), coding, and testing. This time, students in one role (Designer) were asked to write a pseudocode description for how to solve a problem. Students in a second role (Coder) were asked to examine the pseudocode to determine whether it really solved the problem and whether it was precise enough to be a basis for coding. (If not, it was returned to the Designers to be rewritten.) When the Coders were satisfied, they wrote Java statements corresponding to the pseudocode and gave them to students in the Tester role (as described above).

In the past, we have often observed that students tend to short-cut the process of program design. ("Write the code first, do the design and documentation later — but only if you have to!") By separating the roles of Designer, Coder, and Tester, exercises like the one just described can help students learn the value of a disciplined approach to programming.

3. RELATIONSHIP TO PREVIOUS WORK

Cooperative learning is not a new idea, and most of the educational techniques used in this project have been used before in other situations. The innovative aspect of our work lies in the combination of these techniques and the application of this combined approach to the teaching of introductory computer programming. This section briefly reviews the existing educational research base related to cooperative learning, and identifies some of the ways in which our approach differs from previously published work.

3.1 Cooperative Learning

Cooperative learning techniques have been applied with a wide variety of subject matter and a broad spectrum of populations. In general, cooperative learning involves students working together as part of a collaborative effort to understand material or complete a task. A strict definition of cooperative learning [7] requires several specific elements: Positive interdependence (students in a group depend on each other to succeed), Individual accountability (each person must contribute and learn), Group processing (reflecting on how the group is working), Social skills (communication, leadership, etc.), and Face-to-face interaction. Some researchers and practitioners have adopted a broader definition, considering group-based learning methods that may lack one or more of these elements.

Good discussions of cooperative learning methods and research can be found in [5, 14, 15, 16]. Accumulated evidence suggests that cooperative learning results in higher student achievement, more positive attitudes toward the subject, improved student retention, and a variety of other benefits [7, 15, 16]. It appears that the cooperative learning approach may be especially beneficial for women and members of under-represented minority groups [12, 16, 25]. One possible explanation for this is that cooperative learning changes the atmosphere of the classroom, making it more supportive and less competitive. For some women and minorities (and, indeed, some members of the male majority in Computer Science), this may be a very positive change.

A number of educators have studied the use of cooperative learning techniques in Computer Science courses. Some of these recent efforts are described in [3, 4, 9, 13, 17, 18, 24]. Anecdotal evidence indicates that these cooperative learning experiences are valuable, and instructors and students seem to be pleased with the results. However, it has often been difficult to perform objective evaluations of the outcomes. Some of these difficulties arise from small course sizes, differences in student and instructor preparation, and possible changes in course content and standards over a period of years. (See, for example, the discussions in [3] and [18].)

Most previous efforts to apply cooperative learning in Computer Science courses have simply divided students into small groups to work on programming problems or laboratory exercises. Typically, these problems or exercises are very similar to those that might be given as individual assignments in a traditional course. It is expected that students will learn from each other as they work cooperatively on an assignment; however, the assignments are not designed specifically to take advantage of the structure of the group. In most cases, any special roles are purely functional (such as having one group member working at the keyboard), rather than being related to the concepts being studied.

In contrast, our cooperative learning exercises assign specific roles to group members. Some of these roles are used to focus attention on the most important concepts being learned. We believe that this approach is more useful in helping students develop an accurate mental model of the concepts and the underlying processes. We also use roles that are related to the overall functioning of the group (such as Facilitator and Reporter). Most theories of cooperative learning hold that this division of group responsibilities into roles significantly improves the effectiveness of the learning process. (See, for example, [6], [15], and [16].)

3.2 Pair Programming

An educational technique that has elements in common with cooperative learning is pair programming. In this form of collaboration, two programmers work side by side at one computer. At any particular time, one member of the team (the "driver") is typing at the computer or writing down a design. The other member (the "navigator") is actively observing the work of the "driver" — watching for defects, thinking of alternatives, asking questions, etc. The "driver" and "navigator" roles are switched periodically between the two team members.

Pair programming was originally popularized as part of the Extreme Programming software development methodology [2]. Research results indicate that pair programmers produce higher quality code in about half the time, as compared with programmers working alone [19, 21]. Pair programming techniques have also been found to be effective for student programmers, leading to improved student learning and satisfaction as well as reduced frustration [8, 10, 20, 22, 23].

Our cooperative learning exercises use methods similar to pair programming to help students learn about the processes of programming and problem solving. However, our exercises lead students through a number of different levels of cooperation. In the early stages, the entire group is asked to brainstorm together in solving a problem. At a later stage, students work in pairs to solve a problem, and then compare their solutions with those developed by another pair in the group. Still later, other exercises give students the opportunity to work on problems on their own, with consultation from the other group members if needed. We also use pairs to separate and highlight the processes of program design, coding, and testing.

We believe that this incremental approach offers even more advantages than strict pair programming. At first, everyone in the group is learning how to approach a programming task. Thus it is useful to have as many different points of view as possible. As students' programming and problem-solving skills develop, they progress to working in pairs. Finally they have the chance to build confidence by solving problems individually (still with support from the group).

Including more than two members in a collaborative group also allows us to assign the type of concept-related and process-related roles discussed previously. These types of roles would be more difficult to implement in a strict pair-programming environment.

4. EXPERIMENTAL DESIGN

Our cooperative learning exercises were evaluated as part of the introductory Computer Science course at SDSU (CS 107). This course follows the imperative-first model described in the ACM/IEEE Computing Curricula 2001 report [1].

Our experiment was conducted with students who were enrolled in one relatively large section of CS 107 during Fall 2003. At the conclusion of the add/drop period (the first three weeks of the semester), we used a random sampling process to divide the students in this class into an experimental group and a control group.

Table 1 shows the distribution of students in the class by gender and ethnicity. (The "other" category includes all ethnicities with fewer than 5 members in the class.) The random sampling was done within the subgroups shown in this table; approximately one-half of the students in each gender/ethnicity grouping were selected for the experimental group. The main exception to this was the subgroup composed of white males, which was twice the size of any other gender/ethnicity grouping in the class. Approximately one-third of the white male students were selected for the experimental group, because of physical limitations on the size of this group.

Table 1. Distribution of students by gender and ethnicity

Ethnicity	Gender	Number
White	Male	30
	Female	15
Filipino	Male	11
	Female	2
Mexican-American and other Hispanic	Male	9
	Female	3
Other	Male	8
	Female	6

All students in the class met together for two lecture hours per week. During the third hour, students in the control group met in a traditional classroom setting to work on additional problems and ask questions related to the current lecture material. Students in the experimental group worked on cooperative learning exercises and problems in teams of 4 or 5 students each. Each of these cooperative learning teams included students from a variety of gender/ethnicity groupings and with a range of prior programming courses and experience. Students remained within the same cooperative learning teams for the duration of the semester.

The experimental (cooperative learning) group was led by the first-named author of this paper. The control group was led by a different instructor with prior experience in teaching this introductory programming class. The primary instructor for the underlying CS 107 section (from which the experimental and control groups were selected) had no direct involvement with either the experimental group or the control group. This was done in order to avoid any appearance of favoritism to students in either group.

There were two in-class midterm exams (given approximately one-third and two-thirds of the way through the semester), and a final exam. Students from both groups (experimental and control) took the same examinations at the same time. Exam papers from the experimental and control groups were mixed together during the grading process, to ensure uniformity of grading.

5. EXPERIMENTAL RESULTS

Table 2 shows the mean score achieved by students from the experimental and control groups on each of the three examinations.

Table 2. Mean exam scores

Group	N	Exam 1	Exam 2	Final
Experimental	36	89.9	79.8	82.7
Control	48	86.5	73.2	73.0

Students from the experimental and control groups performed at approximately the same level on the first midterm exam. The difference in exam scores between groups increased as the course progressed. This strongly suggests that the differences in student performance on the final exam (about 10%) were due to the cooperative learning experience, rather than to any inherent difference between groups. (This aspect of the results is discussed quantitatively in the next section.)

Previous studies have indicated that cooperative learning may be especially beneficial for members of ethnic minority groups. Our results, summarized in Table 3, support this. Students from all gender and ethnicity categories seemed to benefit from the cooperative learning approach. However, non-white males appeared to benefit even more than other students, with a difference in average score between groups of 17.6 points on the final exam. Females also seemed to benefit more than white males; however, this indication is not as strong and will need further study.

It also appears that the cooperative learning approach may have had a beneficial effect on student retention, especially among non-white males. Four of the 16 students in the non-white male control group (25%) stopped attending class and doing course work before the final exam was given. In contrast, only 1 of the 12 students in the non-white male experimental group (8%) stopped attending before the final. These students are not represented in the average final exam scores shown in Tables 2 and 3; thus, the actual benefits from the cooperative learning approach may be even greater than the tables show.

Table 3. Mean exam scores by gender and ethnicity

Gender, ethnicity	Group	N	Exam 1	Exam 2	Final
Female, non-white	Experimental	6	88.7	78.8	71.3
	Control	5	93.2	68.2	68.6
Female, white	Experimental	8	90.6	78.1	87.4
	Control	7	87.1	62.1	73.6
Male, non-white	Experimental	12	91.0	77.5	83.1
	Control	16	81.7	71.2	65.5
Male, white	Experimental	10	88.9	84.4	84.8
	Control	20	88.5	80.0	79.1

There were only two other students who stopped attending class before the final exam. Both were white males (one from the experimental group and one from the control group).

An analysis of different types of exam questions suggests that the cooperative learning approach was especially useful in helping students understand and apply important conceptual skills. Table 4 shows the scores achieved by students on questions of various types from all three exams. Students who did not take all three exams (either because of attrition or because of excused absences) are not represented in this table.

Table 4. Mean total score on questions by type

Group	Applying basic rules	Tracing code execution	Writing programs
Experimental	52.8	59.3	72.6
Control	53.1	51.9	64.8

There was virtually no difference between experimental and control groups on the questions that called for the application of basic syntactic and semantic rules (for example, punctuation of statements and evaluation of simple Boolean expressions). This seems to indicate that there was no inherent difference between the two groups in their initial approach to the course material. However, the other question types required students to apply a deeper level of understanding of language constructs and the programming and problem solving process. Students from the cooperative learning group performed substantially better on these types of questions, which suggests that they had a better understanding of the key concepts involved.

6. STATISTICAL ANALYSIS

Many standard statistical techniques, such as the t-test, rely on the assumption that the data are approximately normally distributed. The exam scores from our experiment do not meet this assumption of normality: they are sharply skewed to the left, with many high scores and a long tail of lower scores. (We believe that this distribution is typical of exam scores in courses like ours.)

Instead of using techniques that rely on the assumption of normality, we began by converting the scores on each of the exams into a letter grade, according to percentile. The top 15% of grades on each exam were assigned a letter grade of A, the next 20%=B, next 30%=C, next 20%=D, and remaining 15%=F. We then performed a statistical analysis using the General Linear Model (GLM) [11], taking into account the experimental design using gender/ethnicity blocks as described in Table 1.

This analysis showed that the overall difference between experimental and control groups on the final exam (Table 2) was statistically significant (p=0.010), with the experimental group scoring on average one-half to one full grade higher on the A-F scale (0.7557).

Table 3 suggests that there may have been differences between gender/ethnicity categories — that is, that students in some of these categories may have benefited more than others from the cooperative learning experience. However, our analysis using the GLM did not find these differences to be statistically significant. We speculate that this lack of significance may be due to the relatively small sample sizes for some of the gender/ethnicity categories. One of our goals for future work is to replicate the study with larger numbers of students in order to investigate this aspect further.

We also performed a repeated measures analysis using the GLM to investigate the change in exam scores over time, where time1 = exam 1, time2 = exam 2 and time3 = final exam. The same conversion of numeric grades to letter grades was applied. As Figure 1 shows, the experimental and control groups performed similarly on the first exam, but the control group decreases on both the midterm and final, whereas the experimental group increases on both subsequent exams. The difference in slopes for the lines indicating the progress of the two groups is highly statistically significant (p=0.0073). This provides further evidence that the differences in performance between the groups were due to the cooperative learning experience, rather than to any inherent difference between the groups.

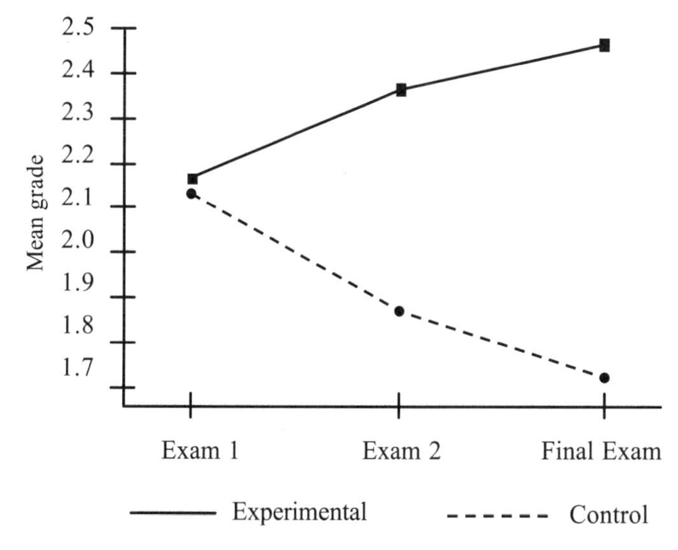

Figure 1. Progress of Experimental and Control Groups

7. CONCLUSIONS AND FUTURE WORK

It seems clear that there were substantial educational benefits for the students who took part in our cooperative learning experiment. Students in the experimental (cooperative learning) group performed substantially better on exams than students in the control group, and these differences increased during the progress of the course. The differences in performance between the groups were statistically significant ($p \leq 0.01$). There are strong (although not quite statistically significant) indications that cooperative learning was especially beneficial for women and non-white students.

However, there is more work to be done. Although we did our best to create a carefully controlled experimental design, we recognize that it is very difficult to conduct a perfect experiment when doing educational research. We are now beginning work on a project that will evaluate the effectiveness of our cooperative learning approach when it is used by different instructors, with different populations of students, and in different educational environments. These further experiments will include larger numbers of women and minority students, in order to further investigate our indications of special benefits to students in these categories.

In the near future, we will be seeking faculty who would like to take part in this follow-up project. If you are interested in participating, please contact the first author of this paper.

8. ACKNOWLEDGMENTS

This work was supported by the National Science Foundation under CCLI grant DUE-0127534.

9. REFERENCES

[1] ACM/IEEE, *Final Report of the Joint ACM/IEEE-CS Task Force on Computing Curricula 2001 for Computer Science,* December 2001.

[2] Beck, K., *Extreme Programming Explained: Embrace Change,* Addison-Wesley, 2000.

[3] Chase, Joe and Okie, Edward, "Combining Cooperative Learning and Peer Instruction in Introductory Computer Science," *Proceedings, 2000 SIGCSE Technical Symposium on Computer Science Education,* pp. 372–376.

[4] Finkel, David and Wills, Craig E., "Computer Supported Peer Learning in an Introductory Computer Science Course," *SIGCSE Bulletin,* Special Issue, 1996, pp. 55–56.

[5] Johnson, D. W. and Johnson, F. P., *Joining Together: Group Theory and Group Skills,* Prentice-Hall, 1975.

[6] Johnson, D. W. and Johnson, R. T., *Learning Together and Alone* (4th edition), Allyn and Bacon, 1994.

[7] Johnson, D. W., Johnson, R. T., and Smith, K. A., *Active Learning: Cooperation in the College Classroom,* Interaction Book Company, 1991.

[8] Katira, N., Williams, L., Wiebe, E., Miller, C., Balik, S. and Gehringer, E., "On Understanding Compatibility of Student Pair Programmers," *Proceedings, 2004 SIGCSE Technical Symposium on Computer Science Education,* pp. 7–11.

[9] Keeler, Carolyn and Anson, Robert, "An Assessment of Cooperative Learning Used for Basic Computer Skills Instruction in the College Classroom," *Journal of Educational Computing Research,* 1995, pp. 379–393.

[10] McDowell, C. and Werner, L., "The Effects of Pair-Programming on Performance in an Introductory Programming Course," *Proceedings, 2002 SIGCSE Technical Symposium on Computer Science Education,* pp. 38–42.

[11] McNeil, K. A., Newman, I. and Kelly, F. J., *Testing Research Hypotheses with the General Linear Model,* Southern Illinois University Press, 1996.

[12] Nelson, C. E., "Student Diversity Requires Different Approaches to College Teaching, Even in Math and Science," *American Behavioral Scientist,* vol. 40, pp. 165–175, 1996.

[13] Priebe, Roger, "The Effects of Cooperative Learning in a Second-Semester University Computer Science Course," Presented at Annual Meeting of the National Association for Research in Science Teaching, March 1997 (available as ERIC document ED406189).

[14] Sharan, Shlomo (ed.), *Cooperative Learning: Theory and Research,* Praeger Publishers, 1990.

[15] Sharan, Shlomo, *Handbook of Cooperative Learning Methods,* Greenwood Press, 1994.

[16] Slavin, Robert E., *Cooperative Learning: Theory, Research, and Practice* (2nd edition), Prentice Hall, 1995.

[17] Troeger, Douglas, "Formal Methods, Design, and Collaborative Learning in the First Computer Science Course," *New Directions for Teaching and Learning,* Spring 1995, pp. 55–66.

[18] Walker, Henry M., "Collaborative Learning: A Case Study for CS1 at Grinnell College and UT–Austin," *Proceedings, 1997 SIGCSE Technical Symposium on Computer Science Education,* pp. 209–213.

[19] Williams, L., *The Collaborative Software Process,* Ph.D. Dissertation, University of Utah, 2000.

[20] Williams, L. and Kessler, R. R., "Experimenting with Industry's 'Pair-Programming' Model in the Computer Science Classroom," *Computer Science Education,* March 2001, pp. 7–20.

[21] Williams, L., Kessler, R., Cunningham, W. and Jeffries, R., "Strengthening the Case for Pair Programming," *IEEE Software,* July/August 2000, pp. 19–25.

[22] Williams, L. and Upchurch, R., "In Support of Student Pair Programming," *Proceedings, 2001 SIGCSE Technical Symposium on Computer Science Education,* pp. 327–331.

[23] Williams, L., Wiebe, E., Yang, K., Ferzli, M. and Miller, C., "In Support of Pair Programming in the Introductory Computer Science Course," *Computer Science Education,* September 2002, pp. 197–212.

[24] Willis, Craig E., Finkel, David, Gennert, Michael A., and Ward, Matthew O., "Peer Learning in an Introductory Computer Science Course," *Proceedings, 1994 SIGCSE Technical Symposium on Computer Science Education,* pp. 309–313.

[25] Yerion, Kathie A. and Rinehart, Jane A., "Guidelines for Collaborative Learning in Computer Science," *SIGCSE Bulletin,* December 1995, pp. 29–34.

SIGCSE Special Projects Showcase

Sally Fincher
Computing Laboratory
University of Kent
Canterbury, Kent
+44 1227 824061

S.A.Fincher@kent.ac.uk

SUMMARY

This session showcases the projects that have received support from a SIGCSE Special Project Award in the previous year.

Categories and Subject Descriptors

K.3.2 [**Computer and Information Science Education**]:.

General Terms

Management

Keywords

SIGCSE Special Project Awards

1. INTRODUCTION

SIGCSE launched Special Project Awards in 2002 to help its members investigate and introduce new ideas in the learning and teaching of computing. SIGCSE members may apply for funds up to $5,000 USD per proposal, which must provide some clear benefit to the wider disciplinary community in the form of new knowledge, developing or sharing of a resource, or good practice in learning, teaching, or assessment.

Since March 2003, SIGCSE has received thirteen proposals and made five Special Project awards, described here, to a total sum of $17,967 USD. The first project described was funded in the previous year, but before the 2003 showcase.

2. CREATING COMPUTER EXERCISES INVOLVING COMPUTER SECURITY

Charles Ashbacher, Mount Mercy College

This project will develop software to demonstrate particular concepts in computer security: code obfuscation and steganography (in this case, the hiding of messages in image files). The final source code and documentation will be released as open source and posted on the SIGCSE web site

SIGCSE'05, February 23-27, 2005, St. Louis, Missouri, USA.
ACM 1-58113-997-7/05/0002.

3. A REMOTE PROGRAM VIEWER

Charles Dierbach, Towson University

The objective of this project is to provide students the ability to remotely interact with instructors and other students on specific problems they may be having on a given program assignment. Currently, a student has two means of such interaction at their disposal. They may either be in the presence of another person, or they may email their program to another individual as an attachment. While emailing programs does provide a means of remote interaction, such interaction is not in real time. Since often times the resolution of one programming problem immediately brings to light another, such delayed interaction is not the optimal scenario for students. The project proposed would provide a viable alterative to the current means of interaction.

4. PROJECTS IN WIRELESS AND AD-HOC NETWORK SIMULATION

Chris McDonald, University of Western Australia, Crawley

This Special Projects Grant application seeks funding to support three objectives:

- to extend the *cnet* simulator to support the exciting new areas of mobile and ad-hoc networking. *cnet* currently supports both either workstations and routers, connected by point-to-point (WAN) or Ethernet (LAN) links. This project will add mobile nodes, whose movement patterns may be programmed, and IEEE802.11 (wireless Ethernet) and Bluetooth communications, whose signal propagation and power consumption may also be programmed.
- to develop a set of core laboratory and project exercises, and sample solutions, on mobile and ad-hoc routing protocols. These will include a number of standard table-driven and on-demand mobile routing protocols, and some newer power-aware protocols in which the objective is to minimize battery consumption.
- to port the simulator and all examples to the new Apple Mac-OSX platform and its new Aqua graphical interface. *cnet* currently runs on many Linux and Unix platforms using the Tcl/Tk windowing toolkit. The Apple platform is experiencing a renaissance in Computer Science Education, and porting *cnet* to Mac-OSX will make *cnet* accessible to an even wider CS Education audience.

5. TOWARDS THE DEVELOPMENT OF "BEST PRACTICES" FOR TEACHING INFORMATION ASSURANCE COURSES

Rose Shumba, Indiana University of Pennsylvania

The output from this project; a list of the "best breed" set of tools, associated tool evaluation reports, and a set of penetration testing exercises will be made available at the SIGSCE Education Resource Centre. This will benefit SIGSCE members and others who are either about to start an information assurance program or want to improve on existing courses. The challenge is that there is an abundance of CERT recommended security tools, faculty are not sure how they work. The result is most information assurance courses have no tool-based hands-on exercises. A cursory survey of a random sample of 50 security courses so far shows that less that 10% of the programs have hands-on experiences with tools [4]. There is no existing documentation that we know of, on evaluation of security tools..

6. A VISUALISATION SYSTEM TO SUPPORT SOFTWARE DEVELOPMENT COMPREHENSION: EVALUATION

Charles Boisvert, Norwich City College, UK

eL-CID supports students' understanding of program development by allowing them to study programs' development history rather than view only their finished form. It is available at `http://www.boisvert.uklinux.net/`.

The system attempts to resolve a simple problem: students understand programs presented to them, yet cannot develop their own. In their own words, "I understand this solution, but I don't understand how to get there".

To do this, it uses an annotated development history of the programs. Students can view, print and execute the program at any stage of its development or follow an animation of the development process. The annotations are shown alongside the animation or can be aggregated to form a developer's description.

This project aims to test eL-CID in the classroom. I will build a set of introductory level programs. A cross-over study will compare the performance of students using eL-CID with that of a control group. This evaluation will be triangulated with questionnaires and analysis of forum transcripts in the near future.

7. DESIGNING AND EVALUATING PROGRAMS IN COMPUTER SCIENCE EDUCATION

Justus Randolph, University of Joensuu, Finland

Although there are a number of evaluation reports on CSE programs, there is a paucity of research done to synthesize these reports and to develop sound guidelines that will benefit CSE designers and evaluators.

The purpose of this project is to increase student achievement in CSE by providing empirically-verified practices for designing and evaluating CSE programs. Beneficiaries of this project include CSE practitioners, researchers, evaluators, designers, and students. Project activities include a critical review of CSE evaluation resources, a systematic review of CSE program evaluation reports, models for CSE evaluation, and case studies regarding the design and evaluation of a number of Finnish CSE programs.

Design Patterns for Parsing

Dung "Zung" Nguyen
Dept. of Computer Science
Rice University
Houston, TX 77005
+1 713-348-3835
dxnguyen@rice.edu

Mathias Ricken
Dept. of Computer Science
Rice University
Houston, TX 77005
+1 713-348-3836
mgricken@rice.edu

Stephen Wong
Dept. of Computer Science
Rice University
Houston, TX 77005
+1 713-348-3814
swong@rice.edu

ABSTRACT
We provide a systematic transformation of an LL(1) grammar to an object model that consists of

- an object structure representing the non-terminal symbols and their corresponding grammar production rules,
- a union of classes representing the terminal symbols (tokens).

We present a variant form of the visitor pattern and apply it to the above union of token classes to model a predictive recursive descent parser on the given grammar. Parsing a non-terminal is represented by a visitor to the tokens. For non-terminals that have more than one production rule, the corresponding visitors are chained together according to the chain of responsibility pattern in order to be processed correctly by a valid token. The abstract factory pattern, where each concrete factory corresponds to a non-terminal symbol, is used to manufacture appropriate parsing visitors.

Our object-oriented formulation for predictive recursive descent parsing eliminates the traditional construction of the predictive parsing table and yields a parser that is declarative and has minimal conditionals. It not only serves to teach standard techniques in parsing but also as a non-trivial exercise of object modeling for objects-first introductory courses.

Categories and Subject Descriptors
D.1.5 [**Programming Techniques**]: Object-oriented Programming.

General Terms
Algorithms, design, languages.

Keywords
Parsing, grammar, CS1/CS2, objects-first, design patterns, pedagogy, modeling.

1 INTRODUCTION
The 2001 ACM Computing Curricula lists the objects-first approach as a legitimate way to teach object-oriented programming (OOP) in introductory computer science courses [1]. OOP educators would concur that in order for such courses to be effective, they must progress normally yet quickly to cover topics that are complex enough to make a compelling case for OOP (see for instance, [2][3]). A wealth of problems in various phases of a compiler can be appropriately modeled as object-oriented systems. However, such problems are rarely discussed at the introductory level in current computer science curricula.

A quick tour of web sites and extant textbooks [4][5][6][7] seems to indicate that context-free grammars (CFG) and their related topics are usually relegated to upper division courses in programming languages and compiler construction. Efforts have been made to introduce object-oriented design patterns such as the composite and visitor patterns into such courses at the semantic analysis phases but not at the syntax analysis phase [5][8]. Perhaps because it is considered well understood, the current treatment of predictive recursive descent parsing (PRDP), typified by the construction of a predictive parsing table and the use of a large stack of conditionals on the token type to select the appropriate production rule, offers no innovation and incorporates no object-oriented concepts. Such a procedural approach does not scale, is rigid and cannot easily adapt to change: a small modification in the grammar such as adding a new production rule for an existing non-terminal symbol will require a complete rewrite of the code.

We present in this paper an object-oriented formulation of PRDP for LL(1) grammars that is flexible and extensible, yet simple enough to be taught in a CS2 objects-first course. At this level, it is pedagogically prudent to start with a simple grammar and gradually expand it to enforce and enhance the student's understanding. Thus, it is crucial that an open-ended number of tokens, non-terminal symbols and production rules can be added to a given grammar with minimal perturbation to the existing code. The key design element is to equip the tokens with the capability to perform an open-ended number of tasks and to shift the responsibility of determining what production rule to parse to the tokens themselves. Such capability is effectuated via a variant of the visitor pattern [9] whose formulation will be described in Section 2.

We also need to model the non-terminal symbols of a grammar and their corresponding production rules, which define the syntax for all sentences generated by the given grammar. Section 3 illustrates via a simple example a systematic transformation of a given LL(1) grammar to an equivalent grammar where each non-terminal symbol translates to a class/interface whose production rules are expressed in terms of "has-a" and "is-a" relationships. The composite pattern [9] is used extensively here, resulting in an object model that represents the meta-structure of the parse tree.

In our parsing framework, the parsing of each non-terminal is modeled as a visitor to a token. To decouple the parsing visitors

```
public abstract class AToken {
   private String _lexeme;
   public abstract Object execute(ITokVisitor algo, Object param);
}
// ---------------------------------------------
public interface ITokVisitor {
   public Object defaultCase(AToken host, Object param);
}
// ---------------------------------------------
public class NumToken extends AToken {

   public static interface INumVisitor extends ITokVisitor {
      public Object numCase(NumToken host, Object param);
   }

   public static abstract class AChainVis implements INumVisitor {
      private ITokVisitor _successor;
      protected AChainVis(ITokVisitor successor) {
         _successor = successor;
      }

      public Object defaultCase(AToken host, Object param) {
         return host.execute(_successor, param);
      }
   }

   public Object execute(ITokVisitor algo, Object param) {
      return (algo instanceof INumVisitor)?
            ((INumVisitor) algo).numCase(this, param):
            algo.defaultCase(this, param);
   }
}
```

Listing 1: Modified visitor pattern for tokens (constructors omitted)

and achieve a much higher level of modularity, we apply the abstract factory pattern [9] and relegate the manufacturing of parsing visitors to appropriate concrete factories instead. Section 4 explains how such a design helps produce a robust object-oriented predictive recursive descent parser that requires only local knowledge of each grammar rule and as a result is flexible and readily extensible.

Section 5 demonstrates the flexibility and extensibility of our parsing approach with an example of how expanding the original grammar with several new tokens, non-terminals and production rules only results in minimal perturbations of the existing code.

2 DESIGN PATTERNS FOR TOKENS

Our object-oriented formulation of LL(1) grammars seeks to delineate and decouple the task of parsing each grammar rule for each non-terminal from the task of selecting the appropriate rule to parse. The parsing algorithm for each non-terminal X knows exactly what the rules are for X and how to proceed with each of the rules but does not know which rule to apply without identifying the current token. On the other hand, the current token intrinsically knows its type and thus can select the appropriate rule but does not know what the rule needs to do at that juncture. The visitor pattern allows these two classes of objects to cooperate to carry out the correct parsing task at the correct time without querying the current input token for its type: the tokens serve as hosts and the parsing algorithms are the visitors.

However, the standard visitor pattern requires that the number of hosts is invariant, which does not meet our design goal of being able to add an arbitrary numbers of tokens, i.e. hosts, to the system. At the core of the visitor pattern is the guarantee that any given host only calls the method of the visitor corresponding to that host. Instead of a single visitor interface that offers a fixed number of methods to a fixed number of hosts, consider a union of interfaces, one per host.

We implement this union as an interface called *ITokVisitor* with a single default case method corresponding to the abstract host, *AToken* (see Listing 1). Thus, every concrete host accepts this visitor. Each concrete host defines its own visitor sub-interface with a method specific to that host. When a concrete host accepts a visitor using *AToken*.execute(...), it checks if that visitor is its own specific visitor and calls the host-specific method of the visitor if this is the case, otherwise it calls the default case method. For instance, in Listing 1, the NumToken host checks if the visitor, algo, is of type INumVisitor. If it is, the host-specific method of the visitor, numCase(...), is called, otherwise the default case method, defaultCase(...), is called.

The visitor pattern is designed for situations where the host's type is unknown at run-time. During parsing, the current token may be one in a set of valid tokens. To enable the current token to select the appropriate visitors, we apply the chain of responsibility design pattern [9] to chain together all the visitors of the valid tokens. The assumption that the grammar is LL(1) guarantees that exactly one visitor in the chain corresponds to the current valid token. This point will be further elucidated in Section 4, where we describe the lazy manufacturing of appropriate visitors using factories.

The tokens so designed do not have any knowledge about any grammar or any action one wants to do with them. This allows the tokens from the same set to be used in different grammars. Moreover, we can add any new token to the system by sub-classing *AToken* and defining a corresponding nested sub-interface for *ITokVisitor* without affecting any of the existing code. Section 5 will further illustrated the flexibility and extensibility of our design.

We now tackle the problem of modeling the non-terminals and their production rules.

3 DESIGN PATTERNS FOR NON-TERMINALS AND PRODUCTION RULES

As a simple example, consider the CFG for infix arithmetic expressions using only addition, numbers and identifiers:

E :: F | F **+** E   F :: **num** | **id**

The above grammar is not LL(1) but can be left-factored to yield the following equivalent LL(1) grammar.

E :: F E'   F :: **num** | **id**
E' :: *empty* | **+** E

This grammar isn't quite ready to be modeled as classes however. This is because there is still a sequence of symbols, "+ E", that is not yet associated with a unique symbol. So, we perform one more grammar transformation where each distinct sequence of two or more symbols on the right-hand side of the production rules is given a unique non-terminal symbol on the left-hand side of the rules ("+ E" is replaced by E1a). Single tokens occurring in a branch also receive their own non-terminal (**num** and **id** are replaced by F1 and F2, respectively). It is clear that this is an equivalent grammar because it simply gives names to existing sequences of symbols or tokens. Below, we have changed the names slightly to remove the primes and create Java-legal symbol names:

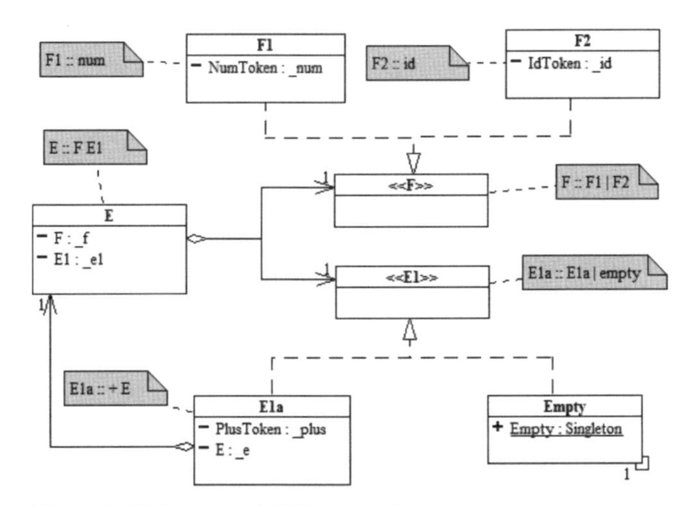

Figure 1: Object model of the example grammar.

E :: F E1	F :: F1 | F2
E1 :: ***empty*** | E1a	F1 :: **num**
E1a :: **+** E	F2 :: **id**

In an object model, there are two fundamental types of relationships, "is-a", represented by inheritance, and "has-a", represented by composition. Thus, in order to create an object model of our grammar, we need to see if these two relations are expressed by the grammar. We find that non-terminals with more than one production rule ("branches") can be represented with an "is-a" inheritance relationship because the union of those production rules says that any term on the right-hand side can be a representation of the left-hand side. F in the grammar above is such a branch: F1 "is-a" valid representation of F, and so is F2. On the other hand, some rules represent a sequence of terms, such as the rules E and E1a above. The left-hand side of these "sequences" can be said to be composed of the right-hand side terms. Thus, the distinct non-terminal sequences can be represented by compositional relationships. E, for example, "has-a" E1 and an F.

We can now simply and directly create our object model of the grammar. In Figure 1 we see that all the non-terminals are represented by classes or interfaces. Branches are represented by interfaces to allow multiple inheritances, and sequences are represented by classes because they require fields. In addition, all the terminal symbols, which are the possible tokens "+", identifiers and numbers, are represented by their own classes. The empty term and the end-of-file token are represented individual classes as well. The recursive nature of the grammar is immediately evident as the composite design pattern in the class structure.

If the above object structure is indeed a good representation of the grammar it models, then it will contain all the relationships, features and other information in that grammar. Therefore, instead of doing a large-scale case analysis over the entire grammar, if we let the object structure drive the processing of a token stream, then all the necessary case information will automatically be present.

4 FACTORIES

The goal here is to maximally decouple the elements of the grammar, which will lead to a parsing system that is robust and extensible. The problem with directly defining and instantiating the parsing visitors is that at any given stage, one must analyze the details of the grammar to the level of knowing all possible tokens at that stage. This analysis may require one to look beyond the immediate relationships a class may have with any other classes. For instance, to find the possible tokens that could be the start of an E term, one must look down to the F term. However, the code to process an E term should only be concerned with the fact that an E term is composed of a F term and an E1 term, and should not be coupled to the internal nature of the F, E1 or any other terms. Likewise, when parsing a branch, such as F, one must create the union of all the visitors that parse the branch's subclasses. Luckily, an LL(1) grammar insures that there are no conflicts between methods of the visitors to the branch's tokens because each token uniquely determines a sequence. However, if a branch consists of further branches, again, this would entail delving into the details of the grammar at deeper levels. In addition, the presence of loops in the grammar further complicates the analysis as it impacts the construction order of the visitors.

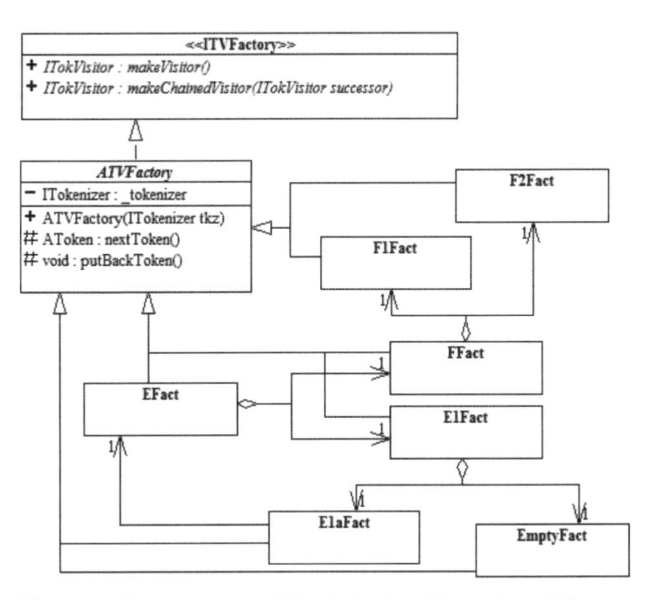

Figure 2: Class diagram of the factories of the token visitors.

To remedy this problem, one must re-think the instantiation process of the visitors. In particular, in order to decouple the construction of the visitor for one term from the details of other terms, one must abstract and encapsulate the construction process. This is done by the abstract factory design pattern. Using factories to instantiate the parsing visitors

- enables each term to be decoupled from any other term by hiding the instantiation details.
- enables the construction of the union of visitors by chaining, which is used to implement branches.
- enables the lazy construction of already installed visitors which is needed to create circular relationships.

Each non-terminal symbol (and its corresponding class) is associated with a factory that constructs its parsing visitor (see Listing 2). All factories adhere to a basic factory interface which provides the methods to instantiate the parsing visitors. For convenience, all the factories are derived from an abstract factory, *ATVFactory*, which provides access to the tokenizer.

The factories for sequence terms (e.g. E and E1a) are initialized with the factories of their composed terms. The actual creation of the visitors is delayed until the first call to makeVisitor() or

```
// E1aFact is an inner class of EFact

// parse "+" followed by an E
private class E1aFact extends ATVFactory {
  private EFact _eFact;
  private ITokVisitor _parseE;

  private IInit _initializer = new IInit() {
    public void init() {
      _initializer = NoOpInit.Singleton; // do it only once
      _parseE = _eFact.makeVisitor(); // make visitor
    }
  };

  public E1aFact(ITokenizer tkz) { super(tkz); _eFact = EFact.this; }

  public ITokVisitor makeVisitor() {
    _initializer.init(); // lazy initialization
    return new PlusToken.ADefaultVis() {
      public Object plusCase(PlusToken host, Object inp) {
        return new E1a(host, (E) nextToken().execute(_parseE, inp));
      }
      public Object defaultCase(AToken host, Object param) {
        throw new IllegalArgumentException("Wrong token");
      }
    };
  }

  public ITokVisitor makeChainedVisitor(final ITokVisitor succ) {
    _initializer.init(); // lazy initialization
    return new PlusToken.AChainVis(succ) {
      public Object plusCase(PlusToken host, Object inp) {
        return new E1a(host, (E) nextToken().execute(_parseE, inp));
      }
    };
  }
}
```

Listing 2: Typical factory for a sequence parsing visitor.

makeChainedVisitor(), since only then is it guaranteed that all factories have been created and circular references can safely be established. The initializer object _initializer, which performs this lazy construction, is instantiated anonymously and replaces itself with a no-operation to ascertain it is executed only once. This is an example of the state design pattern. Listing 2 shows how the use of anonymous inner classes in the makeVisitor() method to instantiate the parsing visitor creates a closure that includes the stored visitor, _parseE.

The factories for branch terms (e.g. F, see Listing 3) are initialized with the factories for all their right-hand side terms. A visitor that parses a branch is the union of all the visitors that parse its subclasses. Since the grammar is LL(1), and each method of a visitor corresponds to a particular token, none of the subclasses' visitors utilize the same method for processing. Thus the union of the subclasses' visitors can be accomplished by using the chain of responsibility design pattern [9]. But since the factory for the branch doesn't know what methods are utilized by the subclasses' visitors, it is forced to delegate the process of creating this chain to one of the factories of the subclasses. Hence, all factories provide a method, makeChainedVisitor(*ITVFactory* succ), to produce a visitor that, in case itself is not the intended receiver (i.e. defaultCase() is called), delegates to another visitor, the successor succ, thereby establishing the chain of responsibility. The E and ***empty*** terms are special cases since they have defined behaviors for all token cases. Thus the visitors for these terms can only be the end of a chain.

```
// FFact is an inner class of EFact

// parse either an F1 or an F2
private class FFact extends ATVFactory {
  private F1Fact _f1Fact;
  private F2Fact _f2Fact;

  public FFact(ITokenizer tkz) {
    super(tkz);
    _f1Fact = new F1Fact(tkz);
    _f2Fact = new F2Fact(tkz);
  }

  public ITokVisitor makeVisitor() {
    return _f1Fact.makeChainedVisitor(_f2Fact.makeVisitor());
  }

  public ITokVisitor makeChainedVisitor(ITokVisitor succ) {
    return _f1Fact.makeChainedVisitor(
        _f2Fact.makeChainedVisitor(succ));
  }

  private class F1Fact extends ATVFactory { ... }
  private class F2Fact extends ATVFactory { ... }
}
```

Listing 3: Typical factory for a branch parsing visitor.

The result is that instead of constructing the parsing visitors directly, one now constructs the parsing visitor factories displayed in Figure 2. Note that the object structure of the factories matches that of the grammar object model in Figure 1, except that all the factory-factory relationships are compositional. Each factory's construction only requires the factories of those terms it is directly related to, either by composition or by subclass. One thus need only know the grammar one level at a time, no global knowledge of the grammar is needed. This decoupling of the grammar terms makes the system very robust with respect to changes in the grammar. To start parsing, we simply ask the top-level factory, EFact, to make its visitor and apply that visitor to the first token. Note that we can avoid using mutating setXXX() methods usually necessary to produce a circular relationship if we create factories as inner classes inside the closures of other factories that use them. In Listing 2, EFact.this can be accessed directly because EFact closes over E1aFact. In Listing 3, instances of F1Fact and F2Fact can be created directly since they are implemented as inner classes of FFact. We have demonstrated this technique in an automated parser generator; unfortunately, this nesting of factory classes tends to generate a single unwieldy source file for a large grammar.

5 EXTENDING THE GRAMMAR

Consider a grammar that adds parenthesized expressions and multiplication to the grammar used above:

E :: S E1	T :: **num** T1
E1 :: ***empty*** | E1a	V :: **id** T1
E1a :: **+** E	T1 :: ***empty*** | T1a
S :: P | T | V	T1a :: ***** S
P :: **(** E **)**	

For this new grammar, we have changed the composition of E, added five more non-terminals, three tokens, and seven production rules, and removed a non-terminal and a rule. To parse this grammar, we have to change only two fields and one constructor parameter in the E class, and replace the F factory, FFact, with the new S factory, SFact, in the factory for E. The remaining classes can be added without modifying any of the

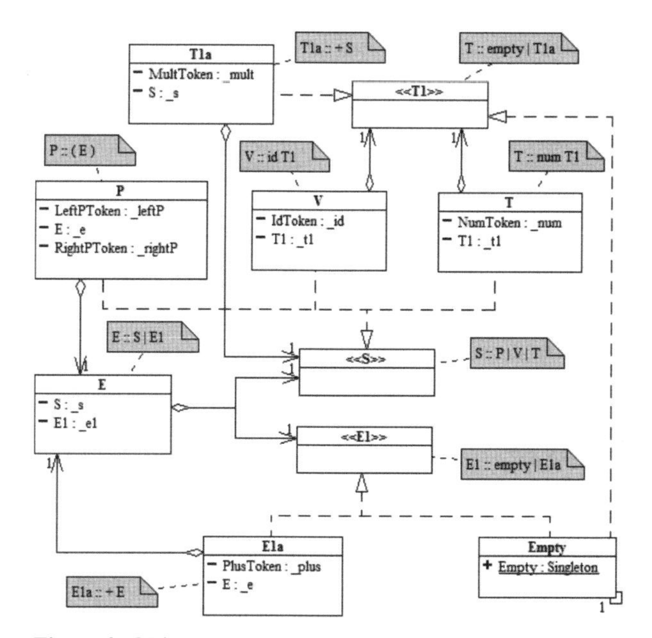
Figure 3: Object model for the extended grammar.

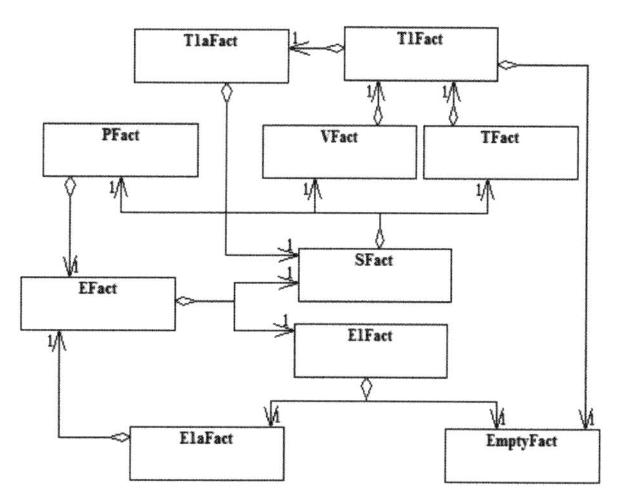
Figure 4: Factories for the extended grammar.

existing code. The UML class diagram for the terminals and non-terminals is depicted in Figure 3, the diagram for the factories can be found in Figure 4. Again, the structure of the factories matches that of the grammar.

In a procedural style it is hard to achieve the same extensibility that our object-oriented formulation exhibits. Traditionally, the addition of the "(" token as legal beginning of an expression would require a pervasive change to the existing parser. Our modified visitor pattern combined with the factory pattern provides the desired decoupling that pinpoints where the changes should be made and prevents a propagation of changes through the system.

6 CONCLUSION

We have created an object-oriented predictive recursive descent parser by starting with an LL(1) context-free grammar and applying a simple transformation. The resulting equivalent grammar was directly modeled by a class structure using inheritance to represent branches and composition to represent sequences. Since the tokens determine whether or not the input corresponds to the grammar, a variant of the visitor design pattern was used to provide direct dispatching to the appropriate parsing code, thus eliminating conditionals, and to allow the open-ended addition of tokens to the grammar with minimal perturbation of the existing code. The code thus became declarative in nature. The abstract factory pattern was used to decouple the individual grammar elements from each other and create a flexible, extensible system. The traditional global case analysis, predictive parsing table and attendant stack of conditionals gave way to a simple local analysis and delegation-based behavior. The chain of responsibility pattern was used to model the union of parsing behaviors needed under branching conditions. While it is beyond the scope of this paper, the object structure of the parse tree can easily be extended with its own visitors to enable semantic analysis of the parsed input.

It is important to recognize that OO PRDP cannot be taught in isolation. It must be carefully integrated into an objects-first curriculum that emphasizes OOP/OOD, design patterns, and abstract decomposition. At our institution, this material is covered near the end of CS2, which is an OO data structures and algorithms course. At this point in the curriculum, the students are already versed in basic OOP/OOD practices, including all the design patterns mentioned here. The PRDP formulation serves not only to expose the students to fundamentals of syntactic analysis, but also as a vehicle for teaching them how to decompose a problem into a flexible and extensible object system.

REFERENCES

[1] Computing Curriculum 2001, Computer Science Volume, Dec. 15, 2001 (http://turing.acm.org/sigs/sigcse/cc2001/)

[2] Madsen, Ole, Keynote speech at OOPSLA 2002, Seattle, WA, Nov. 7, 2002. (oopsla.acm.org/fp/files/spe-concepts.html).

[3] Alphonce, C., Nguyen, D., Ventura, P. and Wong, S., "Killer Examples" for Design Patterns and Objects First Workshop, OOPSLA 2002, Seattle, WA. Nov. 4, 2002. www.cse.buffalo.edu/~alphonce/OOPSLA2002/KillerExamples.

[4] Aho, A., Sethi, R., and Ullman, J., *Compilers: Principles, Techniques and Tools*, Addison-Wesley, 1986.

[5] Appel, A., Palsberg, J., *Modern Compiler Implementation in Java, 2nd ed.*, Cambridge University Press, 2002.

[6] Grune, D., Bal, H., Jacobs, C., and Langendoen, K., *Modern Compiler Design*, Wiley, 2000.

[7] See for instance:
- inst.eecs.berkeley.edu/~cs164/
- penguin.wpi.edu:4546/course/CS544/PLT4.4.html
- www.cs.cornell.edu/courses/cs211/2000fa/materials/Lecture09-Sept-26-Recursive-Descent-Parsing.pdf
- www.cs.nyu.edu/courses/spring02/G22.2130-001/parsing1.ppt
- http://www.cs.rit.edu/~hpb/Lectures/20012/LP/
- http://www.owlnet.rice.edu/~comp412/Lectures/09.pdf

[8] Neff, N., *OO Design in Compiling an OO Language*, SIGCSE Bulletin, 31, 1, March 1999, 326-330.

[9] Gamma, E., Helm, R., Johnson, R., and Vlissides, J. *Design Patterns, Elements of Reusable Object-Oriented Software*, Addison-Wesley, 1995.

Teaching Inter-Object Design Patterns to Freshmen

Prasun Dewan
University of North Carolina
Department of Computer Science
Chapel Hill, NC 27516
919 962 1823
dewan@unc.edu

ABSTRACT
The benefits of object-oriented programming apply only to programs consisting of multiple objects. Inter-object design patterns make it, in theory, possible for beginning programmers to create well-understood forms of such programs. However, their descriptions have been targeted at experienced programmers with knowledge, for instance, of the implementation of compilers. We show that it is possible to explain and motivate several of these patterns including the iterator, model-view-controller, model-interactor, observer, façade, composite, and factory patterns by showing them working "in the small" in simple examples. We have effectively used this approach to teach an undergraduate class including several college freshmen and one high-school junior, who were able to exercise the patterns "in the medium."

Categories and Subject Descriptors
D.1.5 [**Programming Techniques**] – Object-oriented programming. D.3.3. [**Programming Languages**] – Language constructs and features – *Patterns*.

General Terms
Design, Languages.

Keywords
Iterator, observer, factory, façade, MVC, interactor, composite.

1. INTRODUCTION
In courses on object-oriented programming, it is not only important to learn object-oriented constructs such as classes, interfaces, and inheritance, but also exercise these constructs in programs that demonstrate their benefits. This implies that these programs must have multiple objects. As students cannot be expected to write arbitrarily complex multi-object programs, typically one or more examples are given of the kind of programs they must write, with the students expected to see the relationships between the problems solved for them and those they solve on their own. We have found that this approach has drawbacks. The less strong students often have trouble with the unimportant differences between the examples and exercises, becoming confused, for instance, by an example class taking no constructor and an exercise analog requiring a programmer-defined constructor. The stronger students are able to solve the problems but do not quite understand what precisely they have learnt from the exercise. They have difficulty if they are asked to solve the same kind of problem later but not pointed to the relevant solved example as a guide.

This is exactly the problem *design patterns* solve. We will use this term to denote any recurring theme in programming (not captured by a programming language), and unlike some others, not distinguish between patterns, frameworks, and architectures. A design pattern is associated with a problem context in which it is applied, a solution that abstracts away irrelevant details, and a comparison of the solution with alternative solutions. Design patterns can be classified into intra-object design patterns such as [1], which describe abstract algorithms implemented by individual objects, and inter-object design patterns, which describe abstract ways in which multiple objects can work together.

Introducing object-oriented programming using inter-object design patterns is currently mainly a wish. The reason is that the initial and definitive book on them [2] is aimed at experienced software professionals. To motivate them, it uses complex examples such as compilers not known to many undergraduates, especially in early classes. This problem has been realized before and attempts have been made to simplify some of these design patterns [3-9]. This paper contributes to this work by creating the simplest examples we could devise for several seemingly complex patterns. This approach of showing a pattern working "in the small" relies on the ability to see that the problems solved by it would be more severe in bigger projects.

Our simplifications have been successfully presented by the author in Fall '03 to a class including several college freshmen and one high-school junior. The prerequisite for the course was experience with procedures, arrays, conditionals, and loops. The course not only taught the presented design patterns but also the basic object-oriented constructs of interfaces, classes, and inheritance, familiarity with which is assumed here. It was taught in Java – therefore, our examples make use of predefined Java (1.1) classes and interfaces. As equivalent classes can be built in other languages, our contribution is largely language-independent. The public methods of each of the classes mentioned here are defined by an interface. Depending on the example, we omit the full definition of either the class or the interface, as it is implied.

2. ITERATOR
An advantage of Java is that its libraries provide examples of several important design patterns. One of these is the `Enumeration` interface, which is essentially an interface for iterating arbitrary Java objects. An implementation of this

interface is provided by the popular `Vector` class. However, there is no clear reason for using this interface - as the iterated elements are also stored in an indexable collection, students always have the alternative of indexing the collection. Moreover, it is impossible to get a deep understanding of a pattern without seeing an implementation of all the objects participating in it. Therefore, we present below an example that motivates the pattern and requires both the implementation and use of an iterator interface.

Consider two similar programs that process a string argument. One prints the upper case letters in the string in the order they appear in the string, while the other one prints them both in this order and its reverse. Assume that the string can be long, so we do not want to scan it more than one time. Consider first solutions to the two problems without the iterator pattern. Here is a code fragment from a solution to the first problem:

```
for (index = 0; index < args[0].length(); index++) {
    char currentChar = args[0].charAt(index);
    if (Character.isUpperCase(currentChar))
        System.out.print(currentChar);}
```

while the following is a code fragment from a solution to the second problem: :

```
for (index = 0; index < args[0].length(); index++) {
    char currentChar = args[0].charAt(index);
    if (Character.isUpperCase(currentChar)) {
        System.out.print(currentChar);
        storeChar(currentChar, collection); }}
printReverse(collection);
```

In the second fragment, `collection` is an object that can store the scanned characters. The problem here is that the two programs duplicate the code for finding uppercase letters. This duplication may not seem an issue in this simple problem, but imagine a more complex and familiar scanning problem – that of reading lines from standard input. Imagine if every program that processes lines had to also scan the input characters to collect them into lines. Fortunately, Java implements a library that automates the scanning task for us. The library provides a method (`readLine()`) to scan the standard input for the next line so that our program can simply process the line. We need to similarly create a class, `AnUpperCaseScanner`, that scans the input string for the next upper case letter. Unfortunately, Java's input library does not provide a convenient way to tell us when the standard input has been closed, that is, when there are no more lines available. We can fix this problem by having our scanning class export a method that tells us if there are more upper case letters available. Thus, its interface is:

```
public interface CharEnumeration {
    public boolean hasMoreElements();
    public char nextElement();
}
```

All *iterators* implement equivalents of these two methods – they differ only in the type of element they produce. We can now replace the first code fragment above with:

```
CharEnumeration charEnumeration =
    new AnUpperCaseScanner(args[0]);
while (charEnumeration.hasMoreElements())
    System.out.print(charEnumeration.nextElement());
```

and the second code fragment above with:

```
CharEnumeration charEnumeration =
    new AnUpperCaseScanner(args[0]);
while (charEnumeration.hasMoreElements()) {
    char currentChar = charEnumeration.nextElement();
    System.out.print(currentChar);
    storeChar(currentChar, collection);}
printReverse(collection);
```

As we can see, there is no duplication of scanning code this time as the scanning task is carried out by a separate class. If we decide on a new scanning algorithm, we have to change one and not two classes.

3. MVC & OBSERVER

The next example we present motivates several patterns. As before, it involves writing related programs that should share code. The programs allow a user to add a (positive or negative) value to a counter, and view the current counter value. They provide four different user interfaces to the counter semantics, which are shown in Figure 1. In Figure 1(a), the counter is shown as a slider that can be moved to change its value. In Figure 1(b), the program allows the user to enter counter increments in the console window, and after each input value, it shows the current value of the counter in the console window. Figure 1(c) retains the mechanism of Figure 1(b) to change the counter but, instead of printing the result in the console window, it creates a new "message" window on the screen that shows the value. Figure 1(d) shows that it is possible to combine elements of Figure 1(b) and (c). It also retains console-based input, but displays the counter in both the console window and the message window.

Ideally, these four programs should share the implementation of the common counter semantics. This means the implementation of these semantics should have no user-interface code. To separate the user-interface and semantic code, we must create a separate *model* object representing the semantics, which exports two kinds of methods: *read methods* that expose its external state, and *write methods* that change its state. The following class defines such an object for the counter example:

```
public class ACounter implements Counter {
    int counter = 0;
    public void add (int amount) {counter += amount;}
    public int getValue() {return counter;}
}
```

We can now define each user-interface in a separate class:

```
public class AMonolithicConsoleUI {
    static Counter counter = new ACounter();
    static public void main (String args[]) {
    while (true) {
        int nextInput = readInt();
        if (nextInput == 0) return;
        counter.add(nextInput);
        System.out.println("Counter:" + counter.getValue());
}}}
```

The problem with the above implementation of Figure 1(b) is suggested by its name – the input and output code are mixed in one class. This means that when we implement the code for the user-interface of Figure 1(c), we would duplicate the input code above. Similarly, when we implement Figure 1(d), we would have to duplicate both the input and output code above. Thus, input and output processing should be in separate objects, which are called *controllers* and *views*, respectively. This pattern is therefore called the *MVC* (*model-view-controller*) pattern.

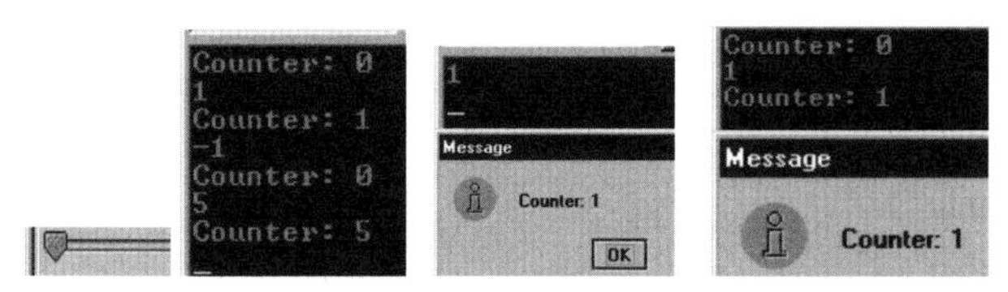

(a) Slider (b) Console UI (c) Message UI (d) Combined UI

Figure 1 Multiple User Interfaces to Same Semantics

A model may be connected to multiple views and controllers. For example, to create the user-interface of Figure 1(d), we would connect our counter to the two views created for Figure 1(b) and 1(c). This raises the following issue: When a controller processes an input command, how do all the views know they should update their displays? For instance, if a counter controller increments a counter, how do all the views know that they should display the new counter value? We can, of course, make the controller notify all the other views after it has invoked a write method in a model. This approach does not allow views to be updated autonomously, that is, without user input. Imagine a counter being updated every second. Fortunately, a simpler, centralized approach can be taken that addresses this problem. Whenever the model is changed, it notifies all of its views. As a view can be dynamically created/destroyed, it registers/unregisters itself with the model so that the model knows who it should notify. A notifying object such as the model is called an *observable* and a notified object such as the view is called an *observer*. Together they implement the *observer pattern*. Even though this pattern appeared first within the context of the larger MVC pattern, it is now recognized as an independent pattern.

To make the counter an observable, we add methods to its interface that allow its observables to be added and removed:

```
public void addObserver(CounterObserver observer);
public void removeObserver(CounterObserver observer);
```

An observer defines a notification method that takes an observable as an argument:

```
public interface CounterObserver {
    public void update(ObservableCounter counter);
}
```

The method is invoked by the observable to announce a change to it. An implementation of this method is illustrated by the console view:

```
public class AConsoleView implements CounterObserver {
    public void update(ObservableCounter counter) {
        System.out.println("Counter: " + counter.getValue());
}}
```

The method calls read methods of the model to retrieve its state and displays it to the user. It is itself called by write methods of the model – in our example, the `add ()` method.

```
public void add (int amount) {
  counter += amount;
  for (int index = 0; index < observers.size(); index++)
    ((CounterObserver)observers.elementAt(index)).update(this);
}
```

Write methods, in turn, are invoked by controllers in response to user input, as shown in the implementation of the console controller below:

```
public class ACounterController implements CounterController{
    public void processInput(Counter counter) {
        while (true) {
            int nextInput = readInt();
            if (nextInput == 0) return;
            counter.add(nextInput);
}}}
```

To summarize, a controller responds to a user command by calling a write method in the model, which updates its state and calls a notification method implemented by all of its observers. View observers implement this method by calling read methods in the model to retrieve its new state and update the display. A model can also have non-view observers, as shown below:

```
public class ARocket implements CounterObserver {
    public void update(ObservableCounter counter) {
        if (counter.getValue() == 0) launchRocket();
}}
```

4. INTERACTOR AND FAÇADE

We have not considered above how models, views, and controllers get instantiated and connected to each other, and who performs this task. We could have the main program do all of these tasks, as illustrated by the following main method for Figure 1(b):

```
public static void main (String args[]) {
    Counter model = new ACounter();
    model.addObserver(new AConsoleView()));
    (new ACounterController()).processInput(model);
}
```

The problem with this approach is that all of this code must be duplicated in the implementation of Figure 1(d), or in an applet-based implementation of Figure 1(b). The solution is to create a separate reusable class for composing a controller and view. A class that instantiates and composes multiple objects allows its users to see a new object that represents the combination of the composed objects. It is called a *façade* because, like the façade of a building, only selected aspects of its units are available to the outside. In our example, the façade, called AConsoleInteractor, gives its users a way to connect the model to the view-controller combination:

```
public class AConsoleInteractor implements ConsoleInteractor {
    public interact(Console model) {
        model.addObserver(new AConsoleView()));
        (new ACounterController()).processInput(model);
}}
```

It does not bother them with the details of connecting the model to the individual view and controller. The following rewrite of the main method above shows the use of this façade:

```
public static void main (String args[]) {
    (new AConsoleInteractor ()).interact (new ACounter());
}
```

We will refer to a class, such as `AConsoleInteractor` above, that represents the functionality of both a controller and a view as an *interactor,* and the division of interactive programs into models and interactors as the *model-interactor* pattern. In this example, the interactor was created as a façade that combines an existing view and controller. It is also possible to create such an object from scratch when input and output processing cannot be easily separated. For example, in Figure 1(a), it is not clear if the slider belongs to a view or a controller as it is both an input and output device. In this case, we may create the combined functionality as an atomic interactor.

5. COMPOSITE

Consider now a program that allows a user to enter the title of a course, and returns the department and course number if it is offered (Figure 2). The programs must search some list of course objects to answer the user queries. Each course object must provide the list object with methods to get the associated title, department, and course number, which are defined by its interface given below:

```
public interface Course {
    public String getTitle();
    public String getDepartment();
    public int getNumber();
}
```

Consider now the list object that stores and searches for courses. There are advantages of making this list a hierarchical tree. Information about courses may come in a hierarchical form from organizations. For example, the programming and other groups submit courses to computer science department, the computer science and other departments submit courses to the school of arts and science, and the various schools submit courses to the university. Moreover, a hierarchical course tree easily allows the answering of hierarchical queries such as "show me all computing science courses" or "show me all programming courses". We will not attempt to support such queries here, pointing them out simply to motivate the tree.

```
Please enter course title:
Intro. Prog.
TITLE            NUMBER
Intro. Prog.     COMP14
Please enter course title:
```

Figure 2 Course Example

Let us assume that the interface of the list object is `CourseList`. What makes it a tree is the ability to offer an `addElement()` method that takes elements of both `Course` and `CourseList` as its argument. Let us assume that the added course is stored in an array, `contents`. We must decide, then, on the exact type, T, of the argument of `addElement()` and the elements of `contents`. We need a type that describes only the legal tree nodes – courses and course lists. This means we need a new interface, `TreeNode`, that is extended by both `Course` and `CourseList`. Thus, we must change the header of the above definition of `Course` (while retaining the body):

```
public interface Course extends TreeNode { ... }
```

We could define `CourseList` as follows:

```
public interface CourseList extends TreeNode {
    public void addElement(TreeNode element);
    public Course matchTitle (String theTitle);
}
```

Let us create class, `ACourseList`, to implement this interface. It could implement `matchTitle()` as follows:

```
public Course matchTitle (String theTitle) {
    for (int index = 0; index < size; index++) {
        TreeNode element = contents[index];
        if (element instanceof Course) {
            if (((Course) element).getTitle().equals(theTitle))
                return (Course) element;
        } else {// instanceof CourseList
            Course course = ((CourseList)
                            element).matchTitle(theTitle);
            if (course != null) return course; }}
    return null;
}
```

There are many problems with this solution. First, the programmer must write tedious code that narrows the type of a `TreeNode`. Second, and more important, if we add a new extension of `TreeNode`, say `FlatCourseList`, that stores a flat list of courses, we must change this code. The key to solving these problems is to move `matchTitle()` from `CourseList` to `TreeNode`:

```
public interface TreeNode {
    public Course matchTitle (String theTitle);
}
```

thus requiring even a `Course` object to implement it. Each tree node must implement this method by checking if the subtree rooted by the node has a leaf node with the specified title. The method's implementation in `Course` is straightforward:

```
public Course matchTitle(String theTitle) {
    if ( title.equals(theTitle)) return this;
    else return null;
}
```

Its new implementation in `ACourseList` is simpler than the previous version and has none of the problems of the latter:

```
public Course matchTitle (String theTitle) {
    for (int index = 0; index < size; index++) {
        Course course = contents[index].matchTitle(theTitle);
        if (course != null) return course;}
    return null;
}
```

We have seen here an example of the *composite pattern* in which leaf and composite nodes of a tree provide different implementations of one or more common interface methods.

6. FACTORY

Now imagine a variation of the example above that allows us to gather statistics about the courses queried by users. In particular, each time a user request for a course matching a title is successful, we want to increment a counter associated with the course, and provide a method to access this counter. We do not want to directly modify the previous course objects, as some might prefer to use the version that does not gather and store statistics, for efficiency and other reasons. For example, they might feel that these statistics give misleading information and do not allow an unpopular course to become popular. Thus, we would like to inherit rather than change the previous code, as shown in the following interface of the new course object:

```
public interface LoggedCourse extends Course {
    public int getNumberOfQueries();
}
```

Some sites can use normal courses while others can use logged courses. It would be nice if it were easy to switch between the two sets. Fortunately, by using interfaces, we have already taken a step towards this goal. For example, if we look at `CourseList`, we see no method that is aware of the exact class of the stored courses. The interface refers only to the `TreeNode` interface, which is implemented by both sets of course classes. The only code that must be aware of the exact classes is one that actually creates the course objects. The following method is an example of such code:

```
static void fillCourses() {
    courses.addElement (new ACourse (
                        "Intro. Prog.", "COMP", 14));
    courses.addElement (new ACourse (
```

```
                    "Found. of Prog.", "COMP", 114));
    ... // add other courses
```

How do we make it easy to change object-creation code when we decide to switch classes – in our example from normal courses to logged courses? The answer is to create special classes, called *factories*, that provide methods to instantiate other classes. In our example, we can create the following factory:

```
public class ACourseFactory {
    public static Course getCourse (String title, String dept,
                                    int num) {
        return new ACourse(title, dept, num);
}}
```

The `fillCourses()` method would now be rewritten to use this factory:

```
static void fillCourses() {
    courses.addElement (ACourseFactory.getCourse (
                    "Intro. Prog.", "COMP", 14));
    courses.addElement (ACourseFactory.getCourse (
                    "Found. of Prog.", "COMP", 114));
    ...// add other courses
```

If we later decide to fill logged courses instead of regular courses, all we have to do is change one line in the course factory:

```
return new ALoggedCourse(title, dept, num);
```

We do not have to change each statement in `fillCourses()`. Thus factories are useful when we have multiple classes with a common interface among which we want to easily switch.

7. CLASSROOM EXPERIENCE

As mentioned above, these examples and explanations were actually used in the classroom. The students practiced the patterns in a project that incrementally created a spreadsheet. They created three pairs of scanners and evaluators for expressions – one for unparenthesized number expressions, another for parenthesized number expressions, and finally, one for parenthesized expressions involving both numbers and spreadsheet variables. A factory was used to create instances of the current scanner and expression-evaluator choice. A façade was used to combine these two objects into a spreadsheet cell. The dependents of a cell were made its observers. The spreadsheet itself was a model manipulated by an interactor. The scanners implemented the iterator pattern and the expression evaluators for the parenthesized expressions implemented the composite pattern. The spreadsheet consisted of about forty classes/interfaces. Thus, while students learned the patterns "in the small," they were able to exercise them "in the medium."

The students did very well and were generally happy with the course, as shown by their exams, grades, and evaluation (posted at the course home page: www.cs.unc.edu/~dewan/comp114). The freshmen did better than the general class, and the high school student received the highest grade on the first midterm. This perhaps shows that enthusiasm and intellect rather than background and college-experience are required to learn this material. 27 students (including 10 college freshmen and the high-school junior) answered three independently-posed questions asking them to indicate for each pattern they were taught, whether they did *not* understand it well, whether they would make it a point to remember it, and whether they would make it a point to forget it. Table 1 shows the survey results. These numbers can be derived from the shown numbers. The table shows that these patterns can be better taught. It also shows the vast majority of students understood the patterns, and significantly more were keen to make a special effort to remember them rather than forget them. The likely reason for the MVC and Observer patterns being relatively less well-understood/appreciated is that, unlike the other patterns, students had not studied them for exams (at the point of time at which the survey was taken)

Table 1 Survey of Students

Pattern	Not well understood	Memorable	Forgettable
Iterator	0	5	1
MVC	6	8	3
Observer	5	7	4
Composite	0	9	0
Factory	3	7	3
Facade	2	9	2

8. CONTRIBUTION

This paper makes several contributions. First, for each of the discussed patterns, it does a "before and after" comparison in which solutions to the same problem with and without the pattern are compared in detail by showing actual code. Second, it presents the smallest detailed and motivated examples we have seen to date for the covered patterns. Finally, it describes classroom experience with the presented material, showing survey results that indicate how effective it was, and more important, point out directions for improvement. To the best of our knowledge, no other work makes these contributions.

9. ACKNOWLEDGMENTS

The main credit for this experiment goes to the students of my Fall '03 Comp 114 class at UNC, who were excited rather than scared by the idea of learning material that had never been taught before. I am indebted to Ralph Johnson for introducing me to MVC long before it became popular. The comments of the referees strengthened the paper. This research was funded in part by NSF grants ANI 0229998, EIA 03-03590, and IIS 0312328.

10. REFERENCES

1. Astrachan, O. and E. Wallingford. *Loop Patterns*. in *PLoP*. '98.
2. Gamma, E., et al., *Design Patterns, Elements of Object-Oriented Software*, Reading, MA.: Addison Wesley, 1995.
3. Clancy, M.J. and M.C. Linn. *Patterns & Pedagogy*. in *SIGCSE*. '99.
4. Gelfand, N., M.T. Goodrich, and R. Tamassia. *Teaching Data Structure Design Patterns*. in *SIGCSE*. '98.
5. Hansen, S. *The Game of Set - An Ideal Example for Introducing Polymorphism & Design Patterns*. in *SIGCSE*. '04.
6. Nevison, C. and B. Wells. *Teaching Objects Early and Design Patterns in Java Using Case Studies*. in *Innovation and technology in computer science education*. '03.
7. Nguyen, D., M. Ricken, and S. Wong. *Design Patterns for Marine Bilology Simulation*. in *SIGCSE*. '04.
8. Nguyen, D. and S.B. Wong. *Patterns for Decoupling Data Structured and Algorithms*. in *SIGCSE*. '99.
9. Preiss, B.R. *Design Patterns for the Data Structures and Algorithms Course*. in *SIGCSE*. '99.

Teaching Design Patterns in CS1: a Closed Laboratory Sequence based on the Game of Life

Michael R. Wick
Computer Science Department
University of Wisconsin-Eau Claire
Eau Claire, WI 54701
wickmr@uwec.edu

ABSTRACT

Design patterns are an important element of today's undergraduate curricula. However, their inherent complexities often make them difficult for entry-level students to even partially grasp. In this paper, we describe the latest in our continuing efforts to build educational materials appropriate for infusing design patterns in entry-level computer science courses.

Categories and Subject Descriptors

K.3 [**Computers & Education**]: Computer & Information Science Education – *Computer Science Education.*

General Terms

Design.

Keywords

Design Patterns, Game of Life, CS1, Laboratory.

1 INTRODUCTION

Design patterns [1] have emerged over the last decade as a necessary component of a software educator's arsenal of design and implementation techniques (for example, [2]). Some authors argue that the use of design patterns can create designs that are far more complicated than necessary for entry-level computer science applications (for example, [3]). The key point is that the use of design patterns can add complexity that is called for. However, we have found that with the proper simplification and customization, many popular design patterns can be presented to entry-level computer science students in such a way that the resulting design is understandable and that the presence of the design pattern has real and significant advantages for the system. While we are the first to admit that the resulting designs are typically more complicated than those that entry-level students would develop on their own, we believe that it isn't the complication that students object to; it is the fruitless complication of using design patterns without significant and real value-added.

SIGCSE'05, February 23–27, 2005, St. Louis, Missouri, USA.

Over the last few years, we have worked on developing a collection of exercises, lectures, and laboratories designed to introduce entry-level students to the power and elegance of design patterns (for example, [4] [5]). This paper presents the outcomes of our latest work in this area - a series of closed laboratory assignments designed to introduce students to the power and elegance of design patterns through their application to the classic Game of Life [6] program.

2 GUIDING PRINCIPLES

Before diving into the details of the Game of Life laboratory sequence, it is worth pausing for a moment to reflect on the guiding principles that steer us in our work to infuse design patterns in the entry-level computer science coursework. These principles fall into two categories for the purpose of this paper – General Principles and Design Pattern Principles.

2.1 General Assignment Selection Principles

Use assignments that involve graphical user interfaces. This doesn't mean that the students need to implement the graphics. Rather, given the ubiquitous presence of "sexy" computer applications in their lives, students will be more engaged in assignments that look and feel like the computer programs with which they are familiar.

Use assignments that include an element of chance, experimentation, or surprise. We have found that students are more engaged in the software development process when the end artifact is something with which the students can "play" and experiment.

Use assignments that have a connection to the student's perception of the "real world". Seemingly more so every year, our students want to see applications even in the first semester that have some kind of connection to the real world. We have found it much easier to keep students engaged if they can see some real-world application for the system they are developing.

2.2 Design Pattern Assignment Selection Principles

Use classic computer science assignments as the basis for the design pattern assignments. According to Webster's Dictionary, "classic" is defined as 1) a work of enduring excellence; 2) historically memorable; 3) a traditional event. Classic computer science examples by their very definition are excellent examples for illustrating key computer science concepts. We should harness the proven value of these classics even when attempting to introduce students to additional concepts beyond the original intent.

Remove all unnecessary complication from the design pattern without removing the essential characteristics. Design patterns, in their full glory, typically involve the use of abstract classes, interfaces, inheritance, polymorphism, and so on. This can be a daunting list of concepts for an entry-level student to consume at one time. However, many specific applications of design patterns do not really call for this generality. Design patterns can be simplified for presentation to entry-level students without losing the essential characteristics that make the design patterns valuable.

Choose only design patterns that have a real value-added to the application. As with almost any software development concept, design patterns can be applied in places where they really don't have anything to add to the design. Doing so tends to leave students with the feeling that all design patterns add to a design is complexity [3]. It is important to carefully choose the design patterns for entry-level students so that the value-added of the design pattern is obvious and real.

Use refactoring as a mechanism for helping students to understand the power and impact of design patterns. Entry-level students are highly unlikely to come up with the designs suggested by typical design patterns. Rather, they tend to take the fastest and easiest solution to the problem (which doesn't mean the best solution). By starting students with a design that they find reasonable and understandable and then refactoring that design to introduce design patterns, students get a better appreciation for value-added by the design pattern.

The Game of Life fits particularly well with most of these guiding principles. The Game of Life is a classic computer science assignment with a proven record of teaching students important programming techniques. The graphical user interface for the Game of Life is simple enough to provide as a pre-cooked software component but sufficiently interesting in appearance so as to keep the students' attention. While the Game of Life is driven by deterministic rules, the behavior of those rules over sufficiently many generations is interesting and surprising. The Game of Life also provides a fertile ground for introducing important design patterns that have a real and significant value-added to the student. The Game of Life, however, does not score very well on the "real-world" metric. Certainly, one can show the types of biological populations that the Game of Life can be used to model, but for most students this is a stretch. However, given the other qualities of the Game of Life assignment, we have still found it to be a popular and engaging exercise for the students.

3 THE LABORATORY SEQUENCE

This section outlines a series of closed laboratory assignments based on the Game of Life that, one by one, introduce entry-level computer science students to the Observer, State, Singleton, Command, and Visitor design patterns [1].

3.1 Pre-Laboratory Design

At the beginning of the first laboratory, students are given a complete implementation of the Game of Life as summarized in the design shown in Figure 1. This design is best described as the "monolithic" design that an entry-level computer science might originally develop. The design centers on a single class that includes both the domain rules of the Game of Life and the user interface. The implementation is straight-forward enough that nearly all students can quickly and easily digest the code. However, it doesn't typically take very long before the students realize that this simplistic design lacks the kind of generality and robustness appropriate for the Game of Life application.

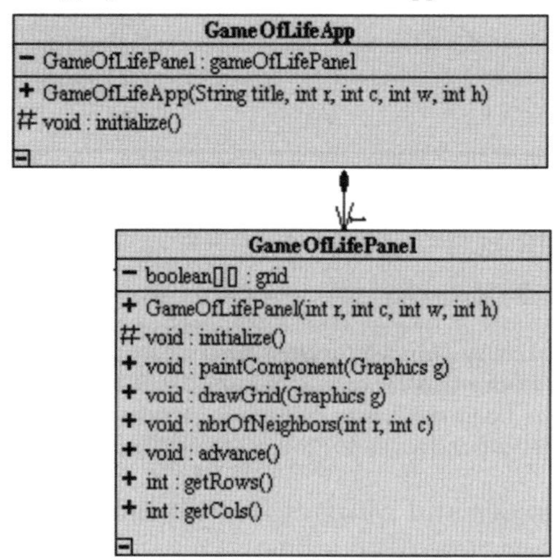

Figure 1: A Starting Design

3.2 The Observer Design Pattern

The first improvement that we introduce to the students is the concept of separating the presentation and domain layers of the system. In particular, we introduce the Observer design pattern [1,p.293]. The Observer design pattern is applicable and appropriate in many situations including when 1) the application has two separate aspects that can be varied independently of one another; or 2) the application involves objects that when changed require changing other objects.

The Game of Life has both of these characteristics. Students see that the visual representation of the Game of Life and the actual structure of "live" and "dead" cells are two separate aspects of the system. Further, the students are quick to point out that when the cells of the game change state (from "live" to "dead" or vice versa) the domain must notify the graphical user interface to allow it to update itself. Likewise, when the user clicks on a cell in the user interface to toggle the cell from "live" to "dead" or "dead" to "alive", the user interface must notify the domain so that it can record the appropriate changes to its model.

The students are then introduced to the refactored design summarized in Figure 2.

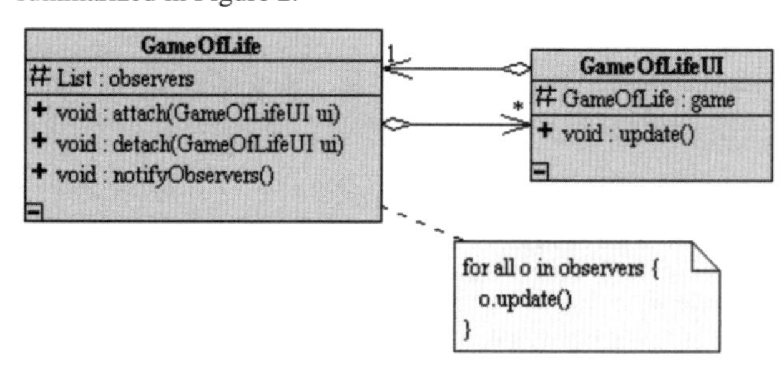

Figure 2: The Observer Pattern in the Game of Life

Students are given the code for this improved design but asked to complete several critical elements that achieve the desired realization of the Observer design pattern:

- o Implement the “attach(GameOfLifeUI)” method of the GameOfLife class that allows additional user interfaces to be attached to the game.
- o Implement the “detach(GameOfLifeUI)” method of the GameOfLife class that removes a user interface from the list of observers for the game.
- o Implement the “notifyObservers()” method of the GameOfLife class which involves the for-loop shown in Figure 2.
- o Modify the “advance()” method of the GameOfLife class so that it correctly causes all observers to be notified of changes to the domain.
- o Modify the “update()” method of the GameOfLifeUI class so that it correctly retrieves the model from the GameOfLife and renders the new state on the screen.

Notice that while the students are given considerable portions of the design already coded, they are asked to gain first-hand experience with implementing the primary aspects of the Observer design pattern.

3.3 The State Design Pattern

The next stage of the laboratory is designed around two primary lessons: 1) software solutions should be designed around the language of the problem not the language of the solution; and 2) polymorphism is a powerful technique for enabling objects to change their behavior over their lifetime. To help instill these lessons into the students, we next introduce the State design pattern [1,p.305] which is appropriate in many situations including when an object’s behavior depends on its state and it must change its behavior at run-time depending on its state.

In the previous implementation, the “state” of a cell (“alive” versus “dead”) is represented as a matrix of Boolean values. This of course leads to conditionals that ask “if cells[i][j] is true then...”. Clearly, the domain of the Game of Life does not involve Boolean values. Rather, the language of the problem talks about cells as either “alive” or “dead”. We illustrate to students that by using a Boolean matrix, we have exposed a design decision.

Further, students also see that a given cell conceptually changes state some times as the program executes. Using the State design pattern we present the students with the refactored design summarized in Figure 3.

In this design, we replace the matrix of Boolean values with a matrix of Cells. Each Cell instance holds an instance of a CellState. The CellState is either an instance of DeadState or AliveState. When an instance of the Cell class receives a message, the Cell instance passes the message onto the CellState instance whose behavior is determined by its actual (dynamic) type. For example, an instance of AliveState, when requested to “toggle()” returns an instance of DeadState. This new instance is saved by the Cell. In the future, the Cell will now behave as if it were actually DeadState.

Again, students are given the code for this design and asked to complete a few critical methods involved in the concrete implementation of the State design pattern:

- o Implement the “live()” method of the Cell class to simply call the “live()” method of the CellState class and save the returned CellState as the new CellState for the Cell object.
- o Implement the “die()” method of the Cell class following the same mechanism as the “live()” method described above.
- o Implement the “live()” method of the DeadState class so that it defines the behavior of a dead cell coming to life.
- o Implement the “die()” method of the AliveState class so that it defines the behavior of an alive cell dieing.
- o Modify the “advance()” method of the GameOfLife class so that it uses a matrix of Cells.

This specific set of exercises gives the students hands-on experience with the implementation of the delegation which lies at the heart of the State design pattern.

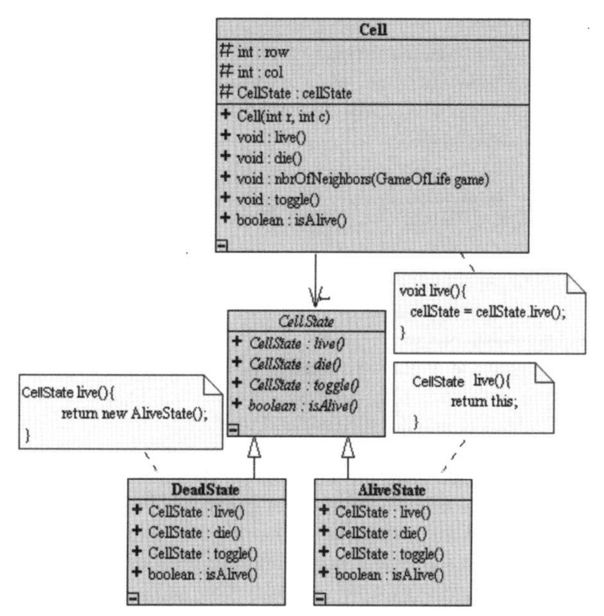

Figure 3: The State Pattern in the Game of Life

3.4 The Singleton Design Pattern

Next, the students are shown that AliveState and DeadState just added to the design have no local state themselves. That is, they have no attributes. It thus seems rather silly and inefficient to keep generating new instances of these two classes as the program proceeds from generation to generation. The Singleton design pattern [1, p.127] is applicable in many situations including when 1) there must be exactly one instance of a class; or 2) a class contains no local state

Figure 4 summarizes the application of the Singleton design pattern to the Game of Life.

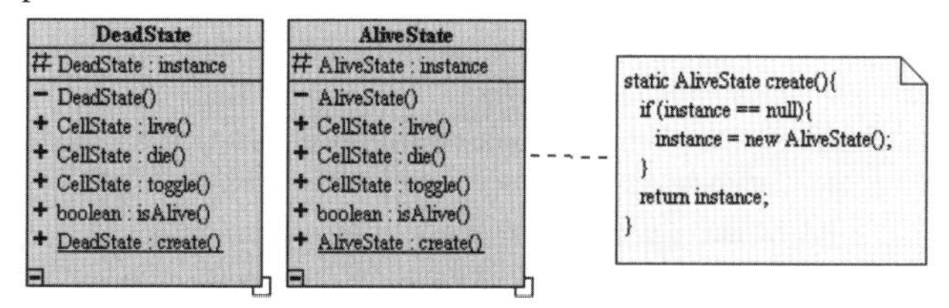

Figure 4: The Singleton Pattern in the Game of Life

Notice that this design involves the use of a private constructor and a public "create()" method to gain access to the single shared instance of each class. Again, the students are given code and asked to complete several key aspects:

- Implement the static "create()" method in the AliveState class as shown in Figure 4.
- Modify the "die()" method of the AliveState class so that it uses the "create()" method to get an instance of the DeadState rather than using the now private constructor.
- Initialize the static variable in the DeadState class that holds access to the one shared instance of the DeadState class.
- Modify the "live()" method of the DeadState class so that it uses the "create()" method.
- Modify the constructor of the Cell class so that it is implemented using the "create()" method of either the DeadState or AliveState class.

This particular set of exercises gives the students hands-on experience with the use of a static variable and a private constructor to control class instantiation – the essence of the Singleton design pattern.

3.5 The Command Design Pattern

Recall that the Game of Life uses the states of the surrounding cells to determine the state of each cell in the next generation. For example, based on the particular rules used, a live cell with a certain number of live neighbors dies (starvation). However, you can't simply use a pair of nested for-loops to walk through the matrix of cells changing them as appropriate. To do so would then change the number of alive and dead cells for the neighbors of the mutated cell and thus would destroy the environment that should have determined the states of the neighboring cells. The typical solution used by entry-level programmers is to create a second copy of the matrix, using the original matrix to decide if cells live or die and then actually mutating them only in the copy of the matrix. After all cells are processed, the original matrix is replaced with the new copy. This seems to strike students as silly and inefficient (because it is). The real problem is that we need to separate the time between when we decide that a live cell must die or a dead cell must live. The Command design pattern [1,p.233] is appropriate when you wish to specify, queue, and execute requests a different times. Figure 5 summarizes the application of the Command design pattern to the Game of Life.

The solution involves the creation of two classes that represent the "live" command given to a dead cell or the "die" command given to a live cell. As the GameOfLife moves through the matrix of cells, it creates instances of the LiveCommand or the DieCommand as appropriate. Notice that both LiveCommand and DieCommand are subclasses of LifeCommand which holds the actual cell involved in the command. When the matrix is completely processed, the "execute()" method of each saved LifeCommand is run which in turns sends the appropriate request (live() or die()) to the appropriate Cell.

The students are given an implementation of the Game of Life using the Command design pattern and are asked to:

- Implement the constructor of the LifeCommand class so that it saves the specific Cell instance for which the message is intended.
- Implement the "execute()" method of the DieCommand class as shown in Figure 5.
- Implement the "execute()" method of the LiveCommand class analogous to the "execute()" method of the DieCommand class.
- Modify the "advance()" method in the GameOfLife class so that it creates a list of LifeCommands as it moves through the Cell matrix. It must also include a loop to move through the resulting list asking each LifeCommand to "execute()".

This specific set of exercises allows the student to gain hands-on experience with the single most important aspect of the Command design pattern; namely the ability to separate the construction of a request from its actual execution.

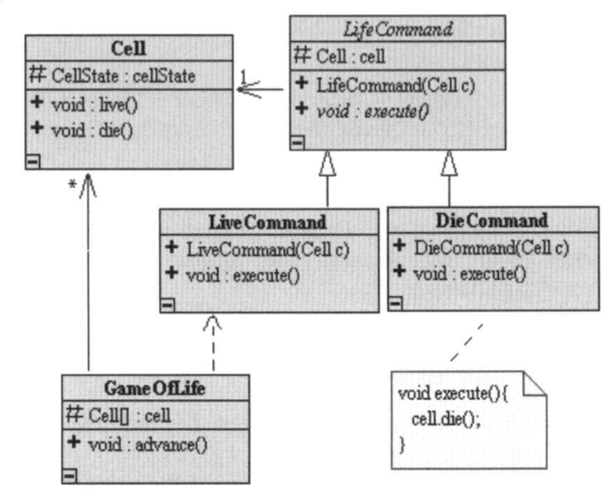

Figure 5: The Command Pattern in the Game of Life

3.6 The Visitor Design Pattern

At this point in the laboratory, the students have created a rather robust design for the Game of Life implementation. One (at least) serious defect still remains, however. Namely, the survival rules of the Game of Life, for which there exist numerous variations, have been coupled to the implementation of the production of new generations. This is where the Visitor design pattern comes in [1,p.331]. The Visitor design pattern can be used in several situations including when 1) many distinct operations need to be performed on objects in an object structure and you want to avoid "polluting" their classes with these operations; or 2) the classes defining the object structure rarely change, but you often want to define new operations over the structure.

For the Game of Life, the object structure is the matrix of cells. The distinct operations are the survival rules that we wish to apply to the matrix of cells to create the list of LifeCommands. Most variations of the Game of Life focus on variations in the survival rules and not on the states of a cell (alive vs. dead) and therefore the object structure doesn't need to change but the operations (survival rules) do need to change. Figure 6 summarizes the application of the Visitor design pattern to the Game of Life.

The basic idea is that each Cell in the matrix is given a method "accept(...)" that allows a particular LifeVisitor (survival rule) to be applied to each Cell. The Cell, as it always does, simply delegates the "accept(...)" request to its CellState instance. The CellState class (which is either an instance of DeadState or AliveState) invokes the appropriate "visit*X*(...)" method from the LifeVisitor (for example, "visitLiveCell(...)". This method applies the particular rules which define how to visit a live cell and either places a new LifeCommand in a list or does not, as appropriate. Notice that in this design, the detail of the survival a rule are decoupled from the operation of the Game of Life and thus can be allowed to vary independently and dynamically as the game operates.

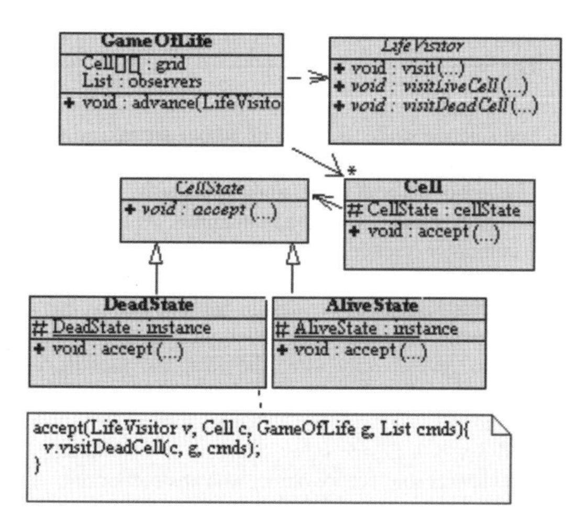

Figure 6: The Visitor Pattern in the Game of Life

Again, the students are given code for this design of the Game of Life and asked to:

- Implement the "accept(...)" method of the Cell class which simply delegates the method call to the current CellState instance.
- Implement the "accept(...)" method in the AliveState class by having it invoke the "visitAliveCell(...)" method of the LifeVisitor.
- Implement the "accept(...)" method of the DeadState class analogous to the same method in the AliveState class.
- Implement the "visit(...)" method of the LifeVisitor class using double dispatching to invoke the appropriate state-specific visit method.
- Modify the "advance()" method in the GameOfLife class to use the explicit LifeVisitor rather than the hard-coded survival rules.
- Implement the "visitDeadCell(...)" method in a LifeVisitor subclass to correctly define the appropriate survival rule for the traditional Game of Life implementation.

This set of exercises is by far the most extensive and challenging for the students. As is shown in the next section, for our specific laboratory sequence, this portion of the laboratory sequence is a single closed laboratory by itself.

3.7 A Sample Division of the Lab Sequence

Our entry-level course includes a 2-hour per week closed laboratory setting. The entire Game of Life sequence involves three of these laboratories periods (of a total of 15 laboratory periods). The laboratory sequenced is introduced in the final third of the semester after the students have already experienced laboratories on rather standard CS1 material. In the first laboratory, the students are introduced to the concept of design patterns, given the monolithic starting design, and asked to update the design to include the Observer design pattern and the State design pattern. In the second laboratory, the students are refreshed on the application and asked to incorporate the Singleton and Command design patterns. The third and most challenging laboratory is the third laboratory which involves the incorporation of the Visitor design pattern. Again, however, this is just a sequence that we have found useful and appropriate.

4 SUMMARY AND CONCLUSION

We have described a series of closed laboratory experiences that help students to learn the fundamentals of the five powerful design patterns within the context of the classic Game of Life computer application. We have developed a specific set of exercises that allow each student to gains hands-on experience with the essential characteristics of these design patterns without becoming overwhelmed by the need to implement the other aspects of the system. Further, by selecting core intertwined functionality for the students to implement, we avoid the kind of "blind coding" that can be a problem with "program-in-progess" assignments in which students add a single line here or there but never understand the bigger picture. The students don't need to understand the details of how the entire system works but rather are focused on understanding just those aspects that are affected by the design pattern under study.

We have also found that from this first-year experience, most students are well prepared to further study and apply these and other design patterns in subsequent courses. More importantly, each student has the case studies of this laboratory sequence in their background as a common example of how object-oriented design and separation of concerns can lead to robust and powerful designs.

REFERENCES

[1] E. Gamma, R. Helm, R. Johnson, J. Vlissides, **Design Patterns: Elements of Reusable Object-Oriented Software**, Addison-Wesley Publishing, (1994).

[2] D. Nguyen, and S. Wong. *Design Patterns for Sorting,* ACM SIGCSE Bulletin 33(1):263-267, Proceedings of the thirty-second SIGCSE technical symposium on Computer Science Education , 2001.

[3] O. Astrachan, *OO overkill: when simple is better than not,* ACM SIGCSE Bulletin 33(1): 302-306, Proceedings of the thirty-second SIGCSE technical symposium on Computer Science Education, 2001.

[4] M. Wick, *An object-oriented refactoring of Huffman encoding using the Java collections framework,* ACM SIGCSE Bulletin 35(1): 283-287, Proceedings of the 34th SIGCSE technical symposium on Computer Science Education, 2003.

[5] M. Wick, *Kaleidoscope: using design patterns in CS1,* ACM SIGCSE Bulletin 33(1): 258-262, Proceedings of the thirty-second SIGCSE technical symposium on Computer Science Education, 2001

[6] M. Gardner, *The fantastic combinations of John Conway's new solitaire game "life",* Scientific American, 223: 120-123, 1970.

Teaching Design Patterns By Stealth

Stephen Weiss
Department of Computer Science
University of North Carolina at Chapel Hill
Chapel Hill, NC 27599-3175
919-962-1888
weiss@cs.unc.edu

ABSTRACT
Learning design patterns is tough, even for seasoned programmers who have seen lots of programs and hence have a sense for constructs that tend to recur. Teaching design patterns to new programmers is even tougher. As Asher Sterkin states, "Teaching design patterns in isolation is similar to studying a foreign language with only a dictionary." [4]. It is far better to try to teach design patterns using killer examples to help motivate and illustrate each pattern. I propose here something a little more radical: to teach by stealth. With a small number of principles of good program design, and using a running case study that grows in complexity through the semester, we can, through class discussions and exercises, "invent" programming solutions that turn out to be some of the important design patterns. The official names and definitions of the pattern [2, 3] are revealed only after the fact, if at all.

Categories and Subject Descriptors
K.3.2 [**Computers and education**]: Computer and information science education – *Computer science education, Curriculum.* D.1.5 [**Programming techniques**]: Object oriented programming. D.3.3 [**Programming languages**]: Language constructs and features – *Patterns.*

General Terms
Languages, Design

Keywords
Programming pedagogy, design patterns

1. INTRODUCTION
Learning design patterns is hard, even for seasoned programmers. But we've seen enough programs to understand their value. It is a far more difficult task to try to motivate and teach design patterns in early programming courses where students have not experienced enough programs to have seen anything repeated significantly. The difficulty is compounded at this university where our CS-1 course is strictly a service course for arts and science students, most of whom are taking their one and only computer science course. And our CS-2 course, while required for our undergrad CS majors, is taken by many students in other sciences, business, or the humanities, who are not going further in computer science.

So I have decided not to cover design patterns per se, but rather to try to motivate the underlying principles using running case studies and to reveal, only after the fact, the identity of the design pattern. I also do not make a big deal of the pattern names so students need not puzzle over, for example, whether what they did was a façade or an adapter, an enumerator or an iterator, or whether the factory object was abstract or not.

In this paper, I outline a series of in-class discussions with companion exercises that introduce students to some of the important design patterns.

The underlying design principles I stress, often with examples from outside programming, are:

- Change happens; expect it; design for it.
- It should be easy to locate the place where a change is needed.
- A change to a single artifact in a program should be able to be made in just one place.
- A change to an artifact should require a minimum of change (or better yet, no change) to the rest of the program.
- If an error is introduced in the change process, it should affect only the thing being changed and not jeopardize other parts of the program.

2. AN ANALOGY
A typical car battery has an expected life far less than the expected life of the car. So (unlike some small cordless electronic devices), a car battery is designed to be replaced. It is easy to unbolt the old battery, install a new one, connect it up, and nothing else needs to be replaced. The only additional changes required are possibly resetting the clock, the radio presets, and the remote entry system. The change is localized and does not require a change to the rest of the system. All but the last of the design principles are illustrated by this analogy. It makes an interesting class discussion to consider how you might protect a car's various electronic components from an error (connecting the battery cables to 110 volts AC, for example), and the horrendous changes that would be required to replace a car's 12 volt battery with a battery of a different voltage.

SIGCSE'05, February 23–27, 2005, St. Louis, Missouri, USA.

3. CASE STUDY

A good case study to use is a simple payroll program.[1] It can start out very simple and then get as complex as you want. I begin with an array of hourly employees, each represented as object of an HourlyEmployee class. Each employee object in the array has a name, number of hours worked this week, and an hourly wage. An employee's weekly salary is hourly wage times hours for the first forty hours with time and a half after forty hours. The students' task is to go through the array and generate "paychecks": a list of each employee, the raw data, and their weekly salary. This is a good first assignment in CS-2 containing everything that they should have learned in CS-1: straight line code, selection, iteration, arrays, classes with multiple objects, and methods. It is also a good refresher exercise for students not coming directly from CS-1. In addition, many of our CS-2 students have waived our CS-1 course based on a high school programming course, making our CS-2 course their first college level computer science course. This exercise is both a refresher for some of these students, and for others who struggle, is a gentle nudge back to CS-1.

Most student programs will have very a simple employee class with only reader and writer methods, with the raw data display and salary calculation done in the main method. This is a trap I allow (even encourage) students to fall into in order to better motivate what's to come.

Once they have the basic payroll program written, I start making changes and additions. First, I change the overtime threshold to 35 hours. I've been temped to make this change an hour before the assignment is due, but I have been afraid that students would view this as cruel and unusual. A properly written program can be changed and retested in less than a minute. But if the program has "magic numbers" embedded in the code, the process could take much longer and be less likely to be correct. The lesson here is to use constants and if the same constant value is to be used in more than one class, then define it once only, and don't repeat its definition.

4. EXPANDING THE CASE STUDY

4.1 More Employees

Next, I expand the variety of employees by adding a salaried employee (whose weekly pay is their annual salary divided by 52), and a commission employee (whose weekly salary is gross sales that week times their commission rate). I also add a couple of new properties (employee's state of residence and number of dependents) anticipating tax calculations later on. We begin in class discussing how to accommodate multiple employee types. The first problem is how to get different object types into a single array. We could use an array of Object and figure out (using the `instanceof` operator) the class of each object and retrieve the appropriate raw data and calculate the salary accordingly. Bad idea! Instead, we could create an Employee class with subclasses HourEmp, SalEmp and CommEmp. Then the array would be of Employee descendant objects. But we would still have to figure out the specific type so that salary could be computed correctly. Better, but still messy. A better idea, and an important lesson, is to move the data retrieval and salary computation to the specific employee classes. Then the main method could call common methods, toString() and getSalary(), to retrieve the needed information. Now the responsibility for calculating salary resides where it belongs: with the specific employee. The main method can now go through the Employee array getting the raw data and salary without having to know the type of employees, exactly what data to retrieve, and how to calculate salary. Lessons here are the virtue of polymorphism, and of putting responsibility in its proper place. Also properties and methods common to the subclasses (e.g. name, state, dependents and their associated readers and writers) can be brought into the parent class so that they appear only once. Lesson: avoid repeating things in multiple places; we've discovered a bit of refactoring.

4.2 Federal Tax

Next I add Federal tax to the paycheck beginning with a simple 20% of gross salary. Where should the tax be calculated? We already know that it should not be in the individual employee classes. That would create multiple instances of the same code. It shouldn't even be in the Employee parent class; tax is not a property of employees. So we can create a separate FederalTaxCalc class with a static method to compute tax given the relevant parameters. But why should the employee have to know which of its properties are relevant to the Federal calculation? A better approach would be for the employee to call the tax calculator sending it a reference to itself (this) giving the tax calculator full access to whatever properties it needs. Again, the lesson here is to give full responsibility to the method calculating the tax rather than splitting the responsibility between the employee (knowing what information to send) and the tax calculator (actually computing the tax). This lesson is driven home by changing the tax calculation to include a deduction for each dependent. Students are amazed by how easy this change is added to the tax calculator without any change in the employee methods. In particular, the call to the tax calculator method is unchanged even though additional information is now being used in the tax calculation.

4.3 State Tax

Next I add state tax. For this exercise I start with only three states, each with its own formula for computing state tax (percent of gross and dependent deduction). One of the states (e.g. Nevada) has no state tax. Students are told to imagine what the program would be like with fifty states, each with its own tax formula. The new tax motivates a discussion of where the state tax calculator should reside and how we should determine which formula to use. We propose (and later reject) the possibility of having a state tax calculator class and a single state tax calculator method (just as was done with the Federal calculator). And just like with the Federal tax, the Employee object would call the state tax calculator sending it a reference to itself. The state calculator would, with a huge case statement, figure out which formula to use and perform the calculation. The problem with this is that to change a single state's tax formula, we must find the relevant code within a large method, and a careless change could jeopardize all state tax calculations, not just the one being changed. We're better off having fifty individual state tax calculator classes, all of which implement a common tax calculator interface. This results in a much larger number of

[1] Because of the vastly different backgrounds of the students in our course, we must choose examples very carefully. This is one that everyone should understand.

classes than before, but each one is very small. If a state tax formula changes, it's easy to locate which class to change, and errors introduced affect only that state. But now, how to determine which class/method to call? Again, we don't want a huge case statement cluttering up the Employee class. Instead, we propose a special class with a method that examines the employee object, creates a reference to a new state tax calculator object of the appropriate type, and returns a reference to that object. The employee can then compute state tax with only two lines of code: one line in the employee constructor that gets a reference to an appropriate state tax calculator and one line to call the method to actually compute the tax. And this code is exactly the same, regardless of the state. We have created a factory! And we quickly discover that since the state tax calculator doesn't store any information specific to the employee, we really need at most one copy of each state calculator: voila, the singleton.

What happens if an employee moves to another state? Easy! Just add a second line to the state writer method to invoke the state tax factory to create (if necessary) and return a reference to the new state tax calculator. This might also be a motivation for an observer that is notified every time the employee object is changed. But this is not a very compelling motivation for the observable/observer pattern.

4.4 Processing the Array

If all the employees got paid on the same schedule, then we could go through the array with a simple **for** loop.

```
for (int i=0;i<empList.length;i++)
    // Process employee i.
```

But what if we wanted some times to process only a subset of employees? For example we might want to pay hourly employees every week, and the salaried and commission employees biweekly. We don't want to change the code every time we run the program in order to choose the desired subset. How can we modify the program so that a program parameter (or value read in from an environment file) specifies the desired subset? We could, for example, specify the desired selection criteria as a set of Boolean flags, one for each employee type. In class discussions we develop the necessary code using either a case statement or a series of if statements. For example,

```
for (int i=0;i<empList.length;i++)
  {  if (employee[i] instanceof SalEmp &&
         salFlag
     ||  employee[i] instanceof CommEmp &&
         commFlag
     ||  employee[i] instanceof HourEmp &&
        hourFlag)
     // Process employee[i]
  }
```

It's messy, but it gets the job done. But if we have to add another employee type, say, one who earns a base salary plus a commission, we not only have to create a new Employee subclass, but also must add a new flag and a new test to the selection. How can we do better?

As an analogy, think about a busy doctor's office. The doctor is occupied healing the sick and doesn't want to be bothered about maintaining the waiting line. An assistant tells the doctor "who's next" and, at the end of the day, "no more." We can do the same in our payroll program.

We delegate the list scanning to a new class that provides the main method with only three operations: reset (start the list anew), next (get the next element that meets the selection criteria), and hasMore (returns a boolean that tells if the list contains any more elements matching the selection criteria.) A true value of hasMore is a precondition of next. Now processing the employee list is simple.

```
while(enum.hasMore())
     // Process enum.next() employee
```

All that needs to be done is to instantiate the desired enumerator object (enum). Again, we have created a bunch of small classes, each dedicated to only a single task. If changes are needed, the place to change is easy to locate and errors introduced are restricted to just that one class. The errors are easy to locate and do not jeopardize other parts of the program.

5. ADDITIONAL COMPLEXITY

I can now go back and add even more complexity. For example, an additional employee type, say, an employee who receives both a base salary and a commission on sales. And I can provide the students with an appropriate class, but one that does not match exactly the employee interface. Students quickly see the value of creating a simple adapter class rather than try to write the new class from scratch. They also see how easy it is to incorporate the new employee type into the existing program.

6. SUMMARY

By the end of this exercise, the students have written about five different versions of the payroll program, each more complex than the previous. More importantly, they have learned a bunch of design patterns. They have learned these patterns not by reading their descriptions, but by developing them as solutions to problems. They may not know the names of the patterns they know, but now when they read the Gang of Four [2], they can recognize some old friends. More important still, they come away with some important programming principles and some experience putting those principles to work.

7. REFERENCES

[1] O. Astrachan, G. Berry, L. Cox, G. Mitchener. *Design Patterns: An Essential Component of CS Curricula.* SIGCSE Bulletin, 30,1 (March 1998), 153-160.

[2] E. Gamma, R. Helm, R. Johnson, and J. Vlissides. *Design Patterns.* Addison Wesley, 1995.

[3] A. Shalloway, and J. Trott. *Design Patterns Explained.* Addison Wesley, 2002.

[4] A. Sterkin. Teaching Design Patterns. http://www.hadassah-col.ac.il/cs/staff/asterkin/advCPlusProg/Teaching%20Design%20Patterns.pdf

[5] S. Stuurman, and G. Florijn. Experiences with Teaching Design Patterns. *Proceedings of the 9th Annual Conference on Innovation and Technology in Computer Science Education* (ITICSE), 2004.

Synthesis and Analysis of Automatic Assessment Methods in CS1

Generating intelligent MCQs

Des Traynor
Dept. Computer Science
National University of Ireland, Maynooth
Co.Kildare, Ireland
dtraynor@cs.may.ie

J. Paul Gibson
Dept. Computer Science
National University of Ireland, Maynooth
Co.Kildare, Ireland
pgibson@cs.may.ie

ABSTRACT

This paper describes the use of random code generation and mutation as a method for synthesising multiple choice questions which can be used in automated assessment. Whilst using multiple choice questions has proved to be a feasible method of testing if students have suitable knowledge or comprehension of a programming concept, creating suitable multiple choice questions that accurately test the students' knowledge is time intensive.

This paper proposes two methods of generating code which can then be used to closely examine the comprehension ability of students. The first method takes as input a suite of template programs, and performs slight mutations on each program and ask students to comprehend the new program. The second method performs traversals on a syntax tree of possible programs, yielding slightly erratic but compilable code, again with behaviour that students can be questioned about. As well as generating code these methods also yield alternative distracting answers to challenge the students. Finally, this paper discusses the gradual introduction of these automatically generated questions as an assessment method and discusses the relative merits of each technique.

Categories and Subject Descriptors

K.3.2 [**Computer and Information Science Education**]: Computer Science Education, Self-assessment

General Terms

Design, Human Factors

Keywords

Assessment, Program Comprehension, First Year Programming

SIGCSE'05, February 23–27, 2005, St. Louis, Missouri, USA.

1. INTRODUCTION

It is difficult to assess the programming ability of students in introductory computer science. This was highlighted in 2001[10] when an international study showed that the majority of students lack the basic programming skills after they have completed a year of computer science studies. If suitable programming assessment was in place, this lacuna in student knowledge would have been far more obvious. Whilst it is convenient to place the blame on students, and it may seem reasonable to place blame on lecturers, it is true to say that if effective programming assessment was enforced then the impact of such a large study would have been greatly reduced. For too long, improper assessment had incorrectly awarded students artificially high grades, thus leaving the discipline in a state of shock when the results from the study arrived. Assessment is the key to learning[16]. Poor assessment presents two problems, it does not highlight the weak students accurately, nor does it challenge the promising students appropriately[1].

Automated assessment methods involving machine analysis of output from programs[3] have proved to be a successful method of analysing students' ability to write code; however this is not the only learning outcome we expect from introductory computer science. It is also important that students can understand and comprehend code. It has also been argued that comprehension should be examined, before asking students to apply their knowledge, in Blooms taxonomy of educational objectives[2] comprehension is one stage before application.

One clear and objective means to estimate students' ability to comprehend programs is to use multiple choice questions (MCQs). It is a common misconception that MCQ tests are easy and the lazy way out for lecturers, it has been noted by Lister and others that *Quality MCQs are not the work of the lazy!*[9]. The MCQs used by Lister typically involves a piece of code, and questions regarding the behaviour of the code when executed. It is the goal of this research to automate the process of creating high quality MCQs through using automatically generated fragments of code and providing a restricted number of 'intelligently chosen' possible answers.

[1]An alternative outcome from poor assessment occurs when the assessment is too challenging. In this case students are demotivated by poor scores and the lecturer again gains little insight from analysis of the results.

Which of the following is the correct declaration for the main function in Java?

a) Begin Program ()

b) public start main()

c) public static void main(String args[])

d) int program;

e) System.out.println("Hello World");

Figure 1: Weak MCQs encourage surface learning

1.1 Overview of the paper

The next section introduces some of the difficulties in automated assessment, and discusses the requirements for reasonable multiple choice questions. The third and fourth section of this paper details the two approaches we have taken to solving the problem, and presents sample output from each attempt. The fifth section compares the output from both methods and discusses their strengths and weaknesses. The final section presents preliminary results from using this technology in Maynooth University and also discusses future work for the project.

2. AUTOMATED ASSESSMENT

The clear advantages of automated assessment are objectivity and convenience. Assessment involves creating questions, carrying out the examination and marking the scripts. It is both difficult and time consuming to mark 100 student scripts in an accurate, unbiased manner. If this procedure can be automated in some way, whilst maintaining the quality of assessment, this will allow the teacher/lecturer more time to concentrate on the preparation and delivery of course material. It is important to state that many projects such as ExamGen[13] offer what they refer to as automatic test generation. Whilst this may seem a similar goal, what distinguishes the work in this paper is that the questions themselves are automatically generated. The majority of the other projects simply provide students with a random subset of a large question bank.

Educationalists have argued that MCQs encourage *surface learning* where the student can pay lip service to a topic by skimming through their notes and achieve a sufficient score in the exam[1]. It has also been said that the only real advantage is that of speed and convenience. As a result of these misconceptions, departments are justifiably cynical about the adoption of MCQs as an assessment method. Often they will cite extremely weak MCQs they have seen as examples of why it is an unsuitable assessment method. For example, the multiple choice question in Figure 1 could be correctly answered by any student with little or no knowledge of programming in Java, simply through skimming throw the first section of notes on most programming courses. This method of learning deserves little reward in any assessment method.

Lister[8] shows a more extreme example of this where all incorrect answers have artificially low feasibility thus rendering the question of no value. Another common criticism from educationalists is that any form of selected response testing is only capable of testing the lower levels of Bloom's taxonomy[2], however in the field of computer science examining students' ability to comprehend a program is of great value. The next section discusses the specifications of the requirements as a set of criteria for evaluating the quality of the MCQs

2.1 Requirements for effective MCQs

To ensure that the MCQs that will be generated by this system will be of a high quality, there are certain requirements that each question must meet[2]. The current requirements are detailed in the following list.

1 **Good quality code.** Any code presented to the students must be of a high quality, and follow all proper guidelines given to students. Obfuscated code and spurious examples within code should not be allowed.

2 **No Tricks.** The question should focus on teaching the normal behaviour of programs, not the badly coded exceptions. There should be no *tricks* in the majority of the questions. (For example in C++ the statement `if(i=size)`will compile, but is bad programming, similarly the expression `x+=x++;` is valid code but not good practice).

3 **Quality Distractors.** The alternative incorrect answers (distractors) must have a suitably high feasibility so as to ensure students are challenged by each question.

These requirements are useful as they serve to both clearly define what can be generated, and also ensure the quality of the output. The approaches to generating both code and questions were influenced by these requirements.

We studied a variety of different approaches for generating code and questions, ranging from grammatical evolution[14] to various different techniques extracted from genetic programming[11]. Two approaches that we deemed achievable were that of template based mutations, and random walks through a predefined syntax tree. These approaches were selected as they lend themselves to formal definition and could be implemented within the allowed time. We decided to pursue both of these approaches with the intent of evaluating their success as a means of assessment.

3. TEMPLATE BASED MUTATION

Template based mutation uses the mutation phase from genetic programming and applies it to a pre-approved population of problems.

In practice this means the lecturer will supply what they consider to be a suitable suite of problems, each one consisting of of a piece of code, and a question regarding its behaviour. This style of question was first proposed by Lister[7] in 2000 and has proved an effective method of probing student knowledge.

The mutations of the code take the form of minor changes that guarantee different behaviour from the program. The result of this is that one input template can result in a multitude of different questions generated. The mutations are performed by randomly selecting a set of substitutions that

[2]It is current research beyond the scope of this paper to refine these requirements and construct models against which we can verify questions

should have an effect on the outcome of the code. These substitutions are usually related to the topic under examination. For example if a lecturer wished to examine students' knowledge of boolean operators, the substitutions could replace $<$ with $\leq$, $=$ with $\neq$ etc. The new program is then compiled and the correct answer is then retrieved through execution. Figure 2 gives a short example of how a piece of code can be automatically mutated to produce several different pieces of code, each with alternative outputs.

4. RANDOM TREE WALKS

The second approach investigated involves using randomization techniques for creating short pieces of code. Each piece of code is generated using a random *walk* through a very rich tree of potential programs. In Java there are certain lines of code that each program must display to compile and execute independently. The first part of the tree involves placing these declarations into the code and then making decisions based on the input parameters about how the program will be developed.

4.1 Input Parameters

The input parameters are used to define the constraints which govern the program being generated. The parameters are

- **The level of difficulty required.** This parameter (currently an integer 1..10), defines how difficult it should be to comprehend the program. It affects variables such as the length of statements, the levels of nesting (of both `if` statements and loops), the simplicity of loops(e.g. a simple loop would run from zero to some arbitrary number in increments of one, whereas a complex loop might have a variety of termination conditions, and non-trivial increments). In practice, code generated at a high level of difficulty can resemble obfuscated code which is not suitable as it does not satisfy the requirements.

- **The length of the program.** Depending on the length of the exam, certain lecturers may wish to have a small number of long programs, or a large number of short programs to test their students' knowledge. Whilst the authors find the latter yields more significant data, it was deemed necessary to include such a parameter to make the system adaptable. The length of a program is represented using an integer ranging from 1..10, where 1 would yield a program of approximately 5 lines, and 10 returns a program with between 40 and 60 lines of code.

- **The assumed knowledge of the students.** This parameter corresponds to a set of concepts that the students already have covered. For example, when writing a question based on arrays, it would aid in question construction to know that students have already covered `for` loops, `if` statements etc. This is implemented as an integer which corresponds to which level of learning the students are at. The lecturer supplies the level of learning and which concepts they represent.

- **The concept(s) being examined** This parameter represents the cynosure of the question. When creating the code the overall behaviour of the system should depend on this concept, thus making it crucial to understand when attempting to answer the question. In early tests of the system this necessity was overlooked and this resulted in poor questions. For example a question which alleged to examine `for` loops, would output code with `for` loops that would never be reached due to preceding `if` statements.

All of the above input parameters serve to influence the decisions made during the random code generation, for example if the difficulty of the question was set to 10 it is very likely that loops will nest inside each other, and that there will be more complicated boolean expressions inside `if` statements etc.

However generating code is not all that is required to generate questions. The third requirement was to generate a set of feasible answers that will distract the students sufficiently. This method for this is discussed in the next subsection.

4.2 Generating Feasible Answers

Automatically generating feasible answers requires a formal and reasonably rigorous definition of the concept of feasibility. This is a very difficult notion to define and represent in a program. Initial research showed that the most effective distractors were those that were based on student misconceptions. When writing feasible answers we believe the authors were intentionally mimicking the incorrect thoughts of their students, e.g students may confuse the AND operator (&&) with the OR operator (||) or confuse an array item's index with its value, so in a question examining knowledge of the operators one or more of the answers should check for this misconception. This is an effective method of generating feasible answers, and one which is also easily automated.

Novice misconceptions have been monitored in computer programming for a long time. Whilst the most significant work in this area covers older languages such as Basic[12] or Pascal [15] the work tends to be abstracted sufficiently to represent potential mistakes and misconceptions in most languages. In particular DuBoulay[4] identified the origins of these misconceptions and provided a list of mistakes common to all languages.

Modern, language specific studies have highlighted the most common programming mistakes in Java[6]. Complimentary to this a study of students' understanding of Java focused on many misconceptions that students use as rules when programming in the language[5]. Combining this recent research with the guidelines offered in the earlier works, it was decided to use misconceptions as a framework for creating alternative incorrect answers. This process is described as follows.

Each generated code segment is compiled initially and the correct answer is extracted by running the program. Then a set of substitutions based on the student misconceptions are performed and the code is recompiled and the alternative answer extracted. This is done once for each answer, until enough answers have been retrieved. If a substitution produces output that is already in the list of answers it is discarded. Table 1 shows an abbreviated list of the substitutions used for generating questions based on `for` loops and arrays; these substitutions can be performed in either direction and will usually alter the output of the program. During development it was found useful to also produce a highly infeasible answer, as this can identify students who are extremely weak in the subject and have resorted to clue-

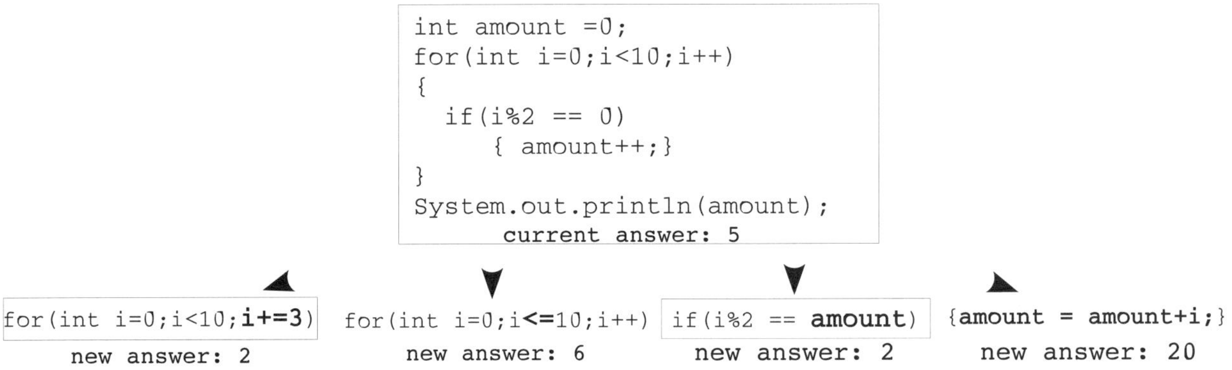

```
int amount =0;
for(int i=0;i<10;i++)
{
  if(i%2 == 0)
     { amount++;}
}
System.out.println(amount);
      current answer: 5
```

for(int i=0;i<10;i+=3)	for(int i=0;i<=10;i++)	if(i%2 == amount)	{amount = amount+i;}
new answer: 2	new answer: 6	new answer: 2	new answer: 20

Figure 2: One short code snippet can examine many concepts when altered slightly.

Misconception	Substitution
Division and Modulo	% with /
Confusing and with or	|| with &&
bounds checking	> with >=
if-else chains	`else if` with `if`

Table 1: Misconceptions and their Substitutions

```
int x = 89/9;
int y = x %5;
        if (x > y || y ==1)
        {
         System.out.println("test" );
        }
        else if (y<=x)
        {
                while(x <= 10)
                {
                 x++;
                 y+=x;
                }
        }
System.out.println("x=" + x + ", y="+ y );
```

Figure 3: The output from a typical run of random tree walking.

less guessing. The final answer list is then shuffled to ensure a random ordering of the answers.

4.3 Example of output

Figure 3 shows a sample output from the random code generation where the topic examined was conditional statements (`if-else`) and while loops. The assumed knowledge in this case was operators, and this sample question had inputs of length=3 and difficulty=5. Applying the substitution technique yielded the list of answers seen in figure 4. The misconception associated with each answer is in square brackets.

a) test x=8,y=1 [correct answer]

b) x=11, y=25 [confusing % with /]

c) test x=11,y=31 [doesn't understand `if-else`]

d) test x=9,y=4 [confusing && with ||]

e) test x=10,y=10 [Highly infeasible, student could only guess.]

Figure 4: Generated answer set for question in figure 3.

5. RESULTS AND EVALUATION

This assessment method was in testing for the academic year 2003-2004, and was presented to students as an optional self-assessment method and proved extremely popular. Students were requested to provide feedback and comments about the system to aid in its development. Whilst the overall feedback was positive, when asked which style of questions (template based, or random) they preferred students provided some enlightening comments on which we can base future work.

The typical responses were that template based questions were good questions that examined given concepts very well. Students felt that if they scored highly in the template based tests, they were happy with their level of knowledge. The question were generated based on ten templates provided by the course lecturer.

The results were less encouraging for the fully random questions. Whilst the input from the lecturer was minimal (no work was required), the feedback was more critical. Students remarked that the questions did achieve a uniform difficulty and that sometimes the topic being examined was not central to the question. These issues were resolved later in the year, when the input parameters were modified to account for this.

In summary, whilst the template questions achieve a sufficiently high quality they require additional work from the lecturer; the randomly generated programs require little or no effort but produce less satisfactory results.

There will be a structured experiment in the following academic year comparing the re-developed system against traditional assessment methods. This will enable a full rigorous evaluation of automated assessment and The system will be deployed as a significant aspect of the students continuous assessment and feedback will again be requested to assist in further development.

6. CONCLUSIONS

The two alternative approaches have both shown that it is possible to achieve reasonable automated assessment. The system has been modified with the students' feedback taken into account and will be used in the following academic year for a series of assessment tests. In particular the output from template based mutations is highly satisfactory, whereas the full random code generation is still in its infancy as a method for question generation.

We acknowledge that automated assessment is by no means yet a suitable replacement for other, more traditional assessment methods. However we feel that this project provides a resource light additional assessment type which can work in unison with the more traditional methods. This complementary integration of traditional and innovative assessment is a more natural and pragmatic progression toward automating assessment techniques.

6.1 Future Work

We have decided to apply the techniques used in template based mutation to a variety of question styles. At present they are only suited to question asking students about how a program will behave (e.g. "What is the output? "), however there are a plethora of MCQ styles to which the techniques can be applied. At present all questions present code that will compile, however this technique could also be used to test if students can understand and apply basic rules of syntax and static semantics for compiling programs (e.g "Does this program compile, if not what is the error? ").

7. ACKNOWLEDGMENTS

The work presented in this paper is part of ongoing research in the National University of Ireland, Maynooth funded by the Irish Research Council for Science Engineering and Technology (IRCSET). A special word of thanks for Professor Benedict du Boulay who helpful words motivated this research.

8. REFERENCES

[1] R. F. Biehler and J. Snowman. *Psychology Applied to Teaching.* Houghton Mifflin Company, 8th edition, 1997.

[2] B. S. Bloom and D. R. Krathowl. *Taxonomy of educational objectives.* McKay & Co, 1956.

[3] C. Daly and J. Waldron. Assessing the assessment of programming ability. In *Proceedings of the 35th SIGCSE technical symposium on Computer science education*, pages 210–213. ACM Press, 2004.

[4] B. duBoulay. Some difficulties of learning to program. In E. Soloway and J. C. Spohrer, editors, *Studying the Novice Programmer*, chapter 15, pages 283–301. Lawrence Erlbaum Associates, 1989.

[5] A. E. Fleury. Programming in Java: student-constructed rules. In *Proceedings of the thirty-first SIGCSE technical symposium on Computer science education*, pages 197–201. ACM Press, 2000.

[6] M. Hristova, A. Misra, M. Rutter, and R. Mercuri. Identifying and correcting Java programming errors for introductory computer science students. In *Proceedings of the 34th SIGCSE technical symposium on Computer science education*, pages 153–156. ACM Press, 2003.

[7] R. Lister. On blooming first year programming, and its blooming assessment. In *Proceedings of the Australasian conference on Computing education*, pages 158–162. ACM Press, 2000.

[8] R. Lister. Objectives and objective assessment in CS1. In *Proceedings of the thirty-second SIGCSE technical symposium on Computer Science Education*, pages 292–296. ACM Press, 2001.

[9] R. Lister and J. Leaney. Introductory programming, criterion-referencing, and Bloom. In *Proceedings of the 34th SIGCSE technical symposium on Computer science education*, pages 143–147. ACM Press, 2003.

[10] M. McCracken, V. Almstrum, D. Diaz, M. Guzdial, D. Hagan, Y. B.-D. Kolikant, C. Laxer, L. Thomas, I. Utting, and T. Wilusz. A multi-national, multi-institutional study of assessment of programming skills of first-year CS students. *SIGCSE Bull.*, 33(4):125–180, 2001.

[11] N. Pillay. Using genetic programming for the induction of novice procedural programming solution algorithms. In *Proceedings of the 2002 ACM symposium on Applied computing*, pages 578–583. ACM Press, 2002.

[12] R. Putnam, D. Sleeman, J. Baxter and, and L. Kuspa. A summary of misconceptions of high school BASIC programmers. *Journal of Educational Computing Research*, 2:459–472, 1986.

[13] A. Rhodes, K. Bower, and P. Bancroft. Managing large class assessment. In *Proceedings of the sixth conference on Australian computing education*, pages 285–289. Australian Computer Society, Inc., 2004.

[14] C. Ryan, J. J. Collins, and M. O'Neill. Grammatical evolution: Evolving programs for an arbitrary language. In *Proceedings of the First European Workshop on Genetic Programming*, pages 83–96. Springer-Verlag, 1998.

[15] J. C. Spohrer and E. Soloway. Novice mistakes: are the folk wisdoms correct? *Commun. ACM*, 29(7):624–632, 1986.

[16] R. C. Sprinthall, N. A. Sprinthall, and S. N. Oja. *Educational Psycholgy.* McGraw-Hill Education, 7th edition, 1998.

Using a Pre-Assessment Exam to Construct an Effective Concept-Based Genetic Program for Predicting Course Success

Gary D. Boetticher
UHCL
2700 Bay Area Blvd.
Houston, Texas 77058
1 281 283 3805
boetticher@cl.uh.edu

Wei Ding
UHCL
2700 Bay Area Blvd.
Houston, Texas 77058
1 281 283 3871
ding@cl.uh.edu

Charles Moen
UHCL
2700 Bay Area Blvd.
Houston, Texas 77058
1 281 283 3848
moench@cl.uh.edu

Kwok-Bun Yue
UHCL
2700 Bay Area Blvd.
Houston, Texas 77058
1 281 283 3864
yue@cl.uh.edu

ABSTRACT

There is a limit on the amount of time a faculty member may devote to each student. As a consequence, a faculty member must quickly determine which student needs more attention than others throughout a semester. One of the most demanding courses in the CS curriculum is a data structures course. This course has a tendency for high drop rates at our university. A pre-assessment exam is developed for the data structures class in order to provide feedback to both faculty and students. This exam helps students determine how well prepared they are for the course. In order to determine a student's chance of success in this course, a Genetic Program-based experiment is constructed based upon the pre-assessment exam. The result is a model that produces an average accuracy of 79 percent.

Categories and Subject Descriptors

K.3.2 [**Computer and Information Science Education**]: *Computer science education, Information systems education, Self-assessment.*

General Terms

Management, Measurement, Performance, Experimentation

Keywords

Pre-assessment Exam, Concept-based, Machine Learner, Genetic Program, Academic Success Prediction, Course Prediction, Classroom Management, Data Structures

1. INTRODUCTION

Anyone who teaches can appreciate the challenge of assessing students early in a semester in order to identify those students who may need additional attention. Poorly qualified students may not be competent enough to know that they are incompetent, thus overestimating their preparedness for the course. The key question is, ***How to effectively identify high-risk students early in a semester?***

This paper addresses this question by using a twofold process. Students entering the data structures course are required to take a pre-assessment examination where questions are classified into concepts according to the ACM curriculum guidelines on Computer Science programs [2]. The results culled from this exam serve as the basis for constructing a Genetic Program (GP) model for predicting students' grades, with emphasis on the pass/failure results.

An efficient and accurate grade predictor provides many benefits:

- Students can better plan for the targeted course. Weaker students typically overestimate their expected grades and underestimate the necessary effort. This is in agreement with the general study on the premise that incompetent persons may not be competent enough to evaluate their own competency [8]. A feedback in the beginning of the course thus assists these students in managing their study time more efficiently and realistically.
- Instructors can quickly realize what concept deficiencies exist in a class and adjust lectures accordingly.
- Administrators obtain timely feedback on important issues, such as student retention and resource management.

There are many existing experiments on academic performance predictions. Many of them utilize readily available information as predictive factors, such as GPA and SAT. Alternatively, this approach uses an automated Web-based pre-assessment examination, which is taken by the students at the start of the semester. Using a concept-based pre-assessment examination provides additional benefits:

- The examination focuses on problem-solving and critical thinking skills. The questions, which are language independent, are built on essential programming facts and skills conforming to ACM Curriculum Guidelines on Programming Fundamentals [2].
- Feedback to instructors and students can be more targeted. For example, weak responses on given concepts can prompt the instructors to devote more time for reviewing the concepts in the class. Similarly, instead of receiving just

SIGCSE'05, February 23–27, 2005, St. Louis, Missouri, USA.

bleak predictions, lagging students can improve their study habits by committing extra time to their academic deficiencies.

- The examination can easily be integrated to support concept-based outcome assessments, which are preferred by many accreditation organizations.
- The examination can easily be modified to serve as a placement examination, in order to take advantage of its predictive nature [10].

This approach uses Genetic Programs (GPs) to predict course outcome. Traditional approaches often need large sample data sets, which may be difficult to attain over one semester. An important advantage of GPs is that they work well with small data sets and require minimal assumptions [3]. The average enrollment in the data structures class over the last 10 semesters is 91.5 students per semester. Thus, the GP approach fits well in this application domain.

This research uses the results from the pre-assessment exam to determine whether a model can be constructed to predict the probability of success. If this is possible, then the approach can be universally applied to other courses at other universities.

Initial results of the GP experiment for predicting a student's chances of success in the data structures class are encouraging. Four sub-experiments produce an average accuracy of 79 percent in predicting student success.

2. RELATED RESEARCH

Academic performance prediction has captured the interest of educators and researchers for a long time and there are a wide variety of results.

Many models predict broad academic performances, such as GPA, degree completion and earned credit hours [4]. Alternatively, other researchers, including this paper, focus on more specific courses or group of courses [9, 11, and 15].

Various factors have been used to build these predictive models. Important categories of predictive factors include:

- General background of the students, such as race, age and gender [4, 15, and 17]
- General academic background, such as SAT, ACT, GPA, etc. [1, 4, 9, and 17]
- Technical academic background, such as Mathematics background, grades in Computer Science courses, etc. [17]
- Behavioral factors: such as personality, attitude, etc. [9, 15, and 17]
- Internal examination results [10]

This paper differs from other authors in the use of a pre-assessment examination at the beginning of a semester for building a predictive model. This is in contrast to Rosbottom's research where a formative assessment is performed close to the final examination [13], whose primary goal is to help students to prepare for their final examination.

Finally, different educators/researchers use different techniques for constructing the predictors. The majority of the experiments use traditional statistical methods of varying degrees of sophistication [1, 9, 11, and 15]. However, there are also works that are based on other techniques, such as artificial neural network [4].

Compared to others, this paper is distinct in the following aspects:

- A pre-assessment examination is used.
- A GP is used as the basis for building a predictor.
- Examination questions are classified by concepts. Instead of using only the overall examination score, every concept score is used as a factor for constructing the predictive model.
- The predictor model is validated by using a four-fold stratified cross-validation.

To the authors' best knowledge, no other researchers have incorporated a similar approach.

3. APPROACH

3.1 The Pre-assessment Exam

The undergraduate Computer Science (CS) program at the University of Houston-Clear Lake (UHCL) is an ABET-accredited program. It is unique in that it does not offer lower level undergraduate courses. As a consequence, undergraduate students transfer into the program after completing their first two years of study at another academic institution. There is no guarantee of the quality of education at their previous institutions. One of the first classes taken by an undergraduate is a data structures course. This is one of the most critical courses within the computing programs. The data structures course serves as a prerequisite for six other undergraduate CS courses. Doing well in this class is absolutely essential to the successful completion of the undergraduate computing programs. Historically, the drop rate for this course ranged between 20 to 40 percent. Similar problems are shared by other academic institutions. For example, Glasgow University experienced a 42.2% failure rate in their introductory computer science course [12].

To address the high drop rate, a pre-assessment exam has been created for the data structures course. The pre-assessment exam is an hour-long quiz that consists of twenty-nine technical questions and three demographic questions in multiple-choice format.

The technical questions test the student's programming knowledge by asking about programming topics that would have been addressed in the first CS course. The questions were designed by ten faculty members, all of whom had taught the data structures course. The questions were designed to be language-independent, and they uncover variables and assignments, mathematical expressions, conditional control structures, iterative control structures, functions and recursion, parameter passing, arrays, records, and syntax and semantics. All these topics coincide with the core fundamental programming constructs from the Programming Fundamentals area of the ACM's Computing Curricula guidelines for Computer Science [2].

The pre-assessment exam was implemented as an online quiz in WebCT [14], a learning management system that facilitates distance learning. Instructors can use it for developing and teaching online courses, and it supports posting lecture notes, creating discussion boards, and giving Web-based quizzes to assess the students' progress. An important feature of WebCT is its capability to grade and track all quizzes automatically. This feature dramatically reduces the amount of time an instructor needs to commit to monitoring and maintaining a quiz.

The pre-assessment exam was administered to all three sections of data structures during the spring 2004 semester, and each of these three sections had a different instructor. While it is acknowledged that the differences between the three instructors may have affected the modeling process, no obvious effect was observed.

Students could access the pre-assessment exam immediately after the first class of the semester. A slight grade incentive, independent of a student's score, was offered to motivate students to complete the exam.

3.2 Genetic Programs

A Genetic Program (GP) learner is chosen for conducting the experiment for the following reasons:

- It is able to produce a human-readable solution in the form of a polynomial equation.
- It requires minimum human intervention with very little previous domain knowledge.
- Relevant attributes receive greater emphasis.
- GPs tend to scale well with problem size.
- GP modeling does not introduce human bias (quantity/quality of rules) in solution formation.
- GPs allow better abstract representation [7].
- GPs can learn on small data samples.

GPs solve problems by evolving solutions. The GP algorithm consists of the following steps [5, and 6]:

```
1. Initialize the Population
2. While a Desired Fitness not reached
    3. Select Parents          ┐
    4. Perform Crossover       ├── For entire Population
    5. Perform Mutation        │
    6. Evaluate Fitness        ┘
7. End While
```

Collectively, a group of *chromosomes* (polynomial equations) make up a *population*. All the data is plugged into a chromosome. The calculated results are compared with actual values in order to determine the chromosome's fitness value. In *crossover*, chromosomes are paired up and a subtree equation is chosen and swapped. In *mutation*, a random node is chosen from the new equation tree and that value is slightly modified. See Whitely [16] for further information regarding GPs.

An in-house, vanilla-based GP is used for the experimentation process. This program is available at the following link: http://nas.cl.uh.edu/boetticher/GDB_GP.ZIP. Figure 1 shows a sample screenshot with the GP from one of the sub-experiments.

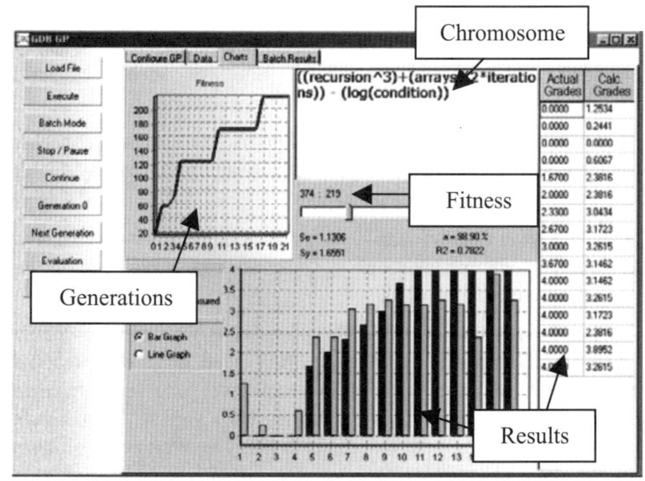

Figure 1: Sample Genetic Program Screenshot

4. EXPERIMENTS

4.1 Experiment Overview

The goal of this experiment is to determine whether a GP can successfully predict whether a student will succeed in a data structures class using the results from a pre-assessment exam.

Sixty-three out of seventy-four data structures students completed the pre-assessment exam. The average score and standard deviation are *21.63* and *4.85* respectively. An *A* is defined as *4.0*, an *A-* is *3.67*, a *B+* is *3.33*, etc. A *WX* grade is assigned a numeric value of *0*. For this course, *Success* is defined is defined as a score of 1.67, which equates to a *C-*, or higher.

A four-fold validation is performed by dividing the initial data set into independent groups. Four separate sub-experiments are performed when each independent group is rotated into the test set. This insures experimental integrity and validates the results.

4.2 Concept-Based GP Experiment

A raw dataset consists of 30 columns. The first 29 columns contain binary values where a "1" means the student answered a question correctly, and a "0" means a student missed the question. The last column is the course grade, which ranged from 0 to 4 as explained earlier.

One difficulty in building models on the raw dataset is that the binary values for the independent variables make it difficult to perform subtle discriminations between questions. Thus, the data was processed by characterizing each of the 29 questions into one of nine concepts which best describes the nature of the question. Table 1 shows the distribution of each question to a corresponding concept.

Mapping questions into concepts offers several advantages. It allows knowledge to be assessed at a higher abstract level, which may be applied to various courses in multiple disciplines. The data now assumes a wider range of values, which makes it easier to differentiate between students.

Table 1. Questions Distributed by Concept

Concept	No. of Questions
Variables and assignment	2
Mathematical expressions	2
Conditional control structures	5
Iterative control structures	5
Functions and recursion	1
Parameter passing	6
Arrays	5
Records	1
Syntax and semantics	2

After identifying a question to concept mapping, the results for each concept are averaged. For example, if 5 questions map to one concept and a student had 4 out of these 5 questions correct, then the student would receive a "0.8" for that concept. Table 2 shows the data layout for this experiment.

Table 2. Data Layout for Concept-Based GP Experiment

	$Concept_1$	..	$Concept_N$	Course Grade
$Student_N$				

The 4-fold stratified cross-validation partitions the data into independent groups of 16, 16, 16, and 15 samples respectively. All 4 sub-experiments use a GP configuration of 1000 chromosomes, 100 generations, and a maximum equation length of 9999 characters.

Figure 2 shows the results from the experiments. For each experiment, the black vertical bar represents the actual grade a student received in the course. The actual grades are sorted from lowest to highest along the *x*-axis. Next to each black bar is a gray (red) bar which shows the predicted grade. The black horizontal line in each graph represents the threshold for success in the data structures class.

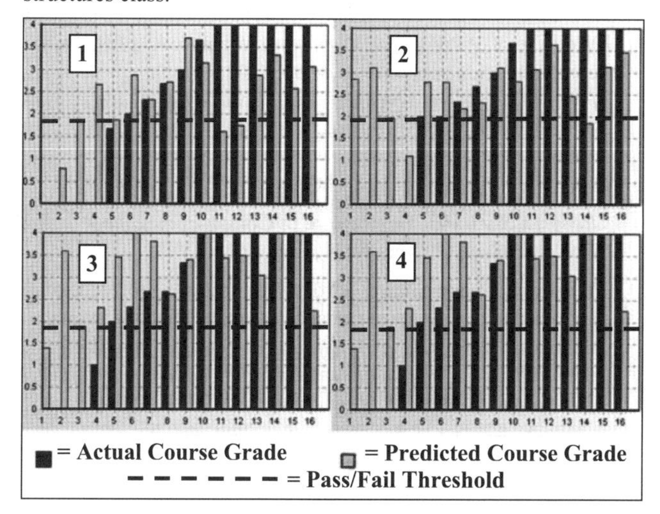

Figure 2: Results from the Concept-Based Experiment

Table 3 shows the results in terms of how well the GP did in predicting whether a student would pass the data structures class. These results show modeling consistency in all experiments.

Table 3. Results from Each Sub-Experiment

	Predicted to Pass		Predicted to Repeat	
Sub. Exp. #	Actually Passed	Had to Repeat	Had to Repeat	Actually Passed
1.	11	2	2	1
2.	12	3	1	0
3.	12	3	1	0
4.	10	3	1	1
Total	**45**	**11**	**5**	**2**

As seen in Table 3, the GP could predict which students would pass the course with 80.3 percent (45/(45+11)) accuracy. This same model could predict which students would need to repeat the course with a 71.4 percent (5/(5+2)) accuracy. Overall, this model is correct for 79 percent (50/63) of the cases.

5. GP VERSUS STATISTICAL MODELS

Various exponential regression models and second order non-linear models are produced using DataFit 8.0. These statistical models use the exact same data configuration (4-fold stratified partition) as the GP. Thus, each model produces 4 sets of results.

The GP and exponential regression models produce results within 1 percent of each other. On average, the GP appears to be superior to the second order non-linear model by 5 percent. However, a t-test assessment between the GP and each of the statistical models does not reveal any superiority of any of the approaches. This is probably due to the limited sample size of 4 experiments per model.

6. DISCUSSION

Considering this experiment was conducted for only one semester and that there are many other contributing factors which influence a student's chances for success, the results are interpreted to be very good. The pre-assessment exam tries to correlate pre-requisite knowledge with the probability that a student will successfully acquire data structures for the remainder of the semester. A major reason for the good results is that the participating faculty brought extensive academic domain knowledge and related teaching experience into the process in terms of what preliminary knowledge is needed to succeed. The exam offers both breadth (nine concept areas) and depth (multiple questions in most areas).

Developing a tool to predict a student's specific grade with 100 percent accuracy is unrealistic and unnecessary. Instead, a major goal of this research is to identify high-risk students. Even when high-risk students are notified, it is their responsibility to determine their course of action. This may require enrolling in one or more foundation courses, improving study habits, or considering another major.

A second major goal seeks to identify concept deficiencies. An automated process aggregates the results by concept then ranks these results by score. This enables an instructor to focus on areas of greatest academic need.

This approach is characterized as bottom-up. It assesses success by course, rather than by program. As a consequence, this approach may be adapted to other courses in other disciplines at other universities.

7. CONCLUSIONS

A process for developing and analyzing a pre-assessment exam is described. Conducting a GP-based experiment predicts success and failure with 80.3 and 71 percent accuracy respectively. These results were comparable and slightly superior to various statistical models. This exam allows students to decide what is necessary to succeed in the course. It also shows an instructor what concept deficiencies exist in a class.

8. FUTURE DIRECTIONS

This whole process is an evolving process. Natural improvements to this research include data, modeling, test, and pedagogical improvements.

- **Data improvements.** Collecting more data samples, especially failure rates (grades of *D+* or lower) would help the GP learn better. It might also be interesting to include more attributes such as SAT score, or High School GPA.
- **Modeling improvements.** Different machine learners could be utilized. Results could be compared/contrasted with the GP results.
- **Test improvements.** A larger test pool may be added which randomly selects questions (by concept). This would allow a student to take the exam multiple times to gauge their progress.
- **Pedagogical improvements.** Adding a corresponding set of tutorials would allow a student to not only identify deficiencies, but to acquire the knowledge or skills that they might be missing.

9. ACKNOWLEDGEMENTS

This work is supported in part by the UHCL Alumni Association Program Endowment, July 2003.

We would also like to thank Dr. Bettayeb, Dr. Davari, Dr. Murphy, Dr. Perez-Davila, Dr. Perkins-Hall, and Dr. Shiau, for their comments and ideas throughout this whole process.

10. REFERENCES

[1] Butcher, D.F., and W. A. Muth, Predicting performance in an introductory computer science course, *Communications of the ACM,* Volume 28, Issue 3, 1985, Pp. 263-268.

[2] CC2001 Joint Task Force. (2001, Dec.). Computing Curricula 2001: Computer Science. ACM/IEEE-CS. [Online].

[3] Chidambaran, N.K., "Genetic Programming with Monte Carlo Simulation for Option Pricing," *Proceedings of the 2003 Winter Simulation Conference,* December 2003.

[4] Cripps, Al, "Using artificial neural nets to predict academic performance," *Proceedings of the 1996 ACM Symposium on Applied Computing*, February 1996, Pp. 33-37.

[5] Goldberg, David, *Genetic Algorithms in Search, Optimization, and Machine Learning.* Addison-Wesley, USA, 1987.

[6] Grefenstette, John J. *Incorporating Problem Specific Knowledge into Genetic Algorithms.* In L. Davis, editor, *Genetic Algorithms and Simulated Annealing,* Chapter 4, Morgan Kaufmann Publishers, Inc., 1987, Pp. 42-60.

[7] Koza, John. (1992) *Genetic Programming: On the Programming of Computers by Means of Natural Selection.* MIT Press, Cambridge, Massachusetts.

[8] Kruger J. and David Dunning, Unskilled and Unaware of It: How Difficulties in Recognizing One's Own Incompetence Lead to Inflated Self-Assessments, *Journal of Personality and Social Psychology*, Dec. 1999 Vol. 77, No. 6, Pp. 1121-1134. (http://www.apa.org/journals/psp/psp7761121.html).

[9] Lending, D. and S. E. Kruck, "IT Education: What predicts student performance in the first college-level IS course?: is it different for men and women?" *Proceedings of the 2002 ACM SIGCPR conference on Computer personnel research*, Kristiansand, Norway, May 2002, Pp. 100-102.

[10] Miller, N.E. and Donna S. Reess, A placement examination for computer science II, *ACM SIGCSE Bulletin*, Volume 33 Issue 2, June 2001.

[11] Newsted, P.R., "Grade and ability predictions in an introductory programming course," *ACM SIGCSE Bulletin*, Volume 7 Issue 2, June 1975.

[12] Roddan, M., The determinants of student failure and attrition in first year computer science.

[13] Rosbottom, John, "Computer managed, open question, open book assessment," *ACM Proceedings of the 2nd conference on Integrating technology into computer science education*, 1997, Pp. 100-102.

[14] WebCT Campus Edition. [Computer software]. Lynnfield, MA: WebCT, Inc.

[15] Werth, L.H., "Predicting student performance in a beginning computer science class," *ACM SIGCSE Bulletin, Proceedings of the seventeenth SIGCSE technical symposium on Computer science education*, Volume 18 Issue 1, Feb. 1986.

[16] Whitley, Darrel, "A Genetic Algorithm Tutorial," *Technical Report CS-93-103*, Department of Computer Science, Colorado State University, November 10, 1993.

[17] Wilson, B.C. and Sharon Shrock, "Contributing to success in an introductory computer science course: a study of twelve factors," *ACM SIGCSE Bulletin, Proceedings of the thirty-second SIGCSE technical symposium on Computer Science Education*, Volume 33 Issue 1, February 2001.

Designing, Implementing, and Analyzing a Placement Test for Introductory CS Courses

Leen-Kiat Soh, Ashok Samal, Suzette Person
Department of Computer Science and Engineering
University of Nebraska
256 Avery Hall, Lincoln, NE 68588-0115 USA
E-mail: {lksoh, samal, sperson}@cse.unl.edu

Gwen Nugent, Jeff Lang
National Center of Information Technology in Education (NCITE)
University of Nebraska
269 Mabel Lee Hall, Lincoln, NE 68588-0230 USA
E-mail: gnugent1@unl.edu, jefflang@unlserve.edu

ABSTRACT
An introductory CS1 course presents problems for educators and students due to students' diverse background in programming knowledge and exposure. Students who enroll in CS1 also have different expectations and motivations. Prompted by the curricular guidelines for undergraduate programs in computer science released in 2001 by the ACM/IEEE, and driven by a departmental project to reinvent the undergraduate computer science and computer engineering curricula at the University of Nebraska-Lincoln, we are currently implementing a series of changes which will improve our introductory courses. One key component of our project is an online placement examination tied to the cognitive domain that assesses student knowledge and intellectual skills. Our placement test is also integrated into a comprehensive educational research design containing a pre- and post-test framework for assessing student learning. In this paper, we focus on the design and implementation of our placement exam and present an analysis of the data collected to date.

Categories and Subject Descriptors
Course Related, CS Ed Research, CS1/2, Curriculum Issues

General Terms: Design, Experimentation

Keywords: Placement Examination, Bloom's Taxonomy

1 INTRODUCTION
Student preparation for the undergraduate study of computer science has been and will likely continue to be extremely varied. Not only is the level of preparation diverse, but also the form and content are inconsistent. High school computer science is generally taught with a mathematics, science, or business emphasis and may or may not be associated with an advanced placement (AP) program. It may cover programming, networking, or web page development, and may utilize functional, object-oriented, or imperative programming paradigms supported by an assortment of programming languages. This observation applies not only to the rural Great Plains states, but also to most other universities that teach computer science. A placement examination that *accurately and reliably* assigns students with diverse backgrounds to the most appropriate first course in computer science will have widespread applicability.

Our research group, a collaboration between faculty from the Department of Computer Science and Engineering (CSE) and the College of Education and Human Sciences (CEHS) at the University of Nebraska-Lincoln (UNL), has taken on the challenge of creating a placement test as one component of a broader "reinvention" of the introductory computing curriculum in CSE. In addition to assigning students to their first course in computer science, the test is designed to serve as a dependent variable in a pre-post research design, validate the instructional impact of CS1, and serve as a knowledge measure in other research designs to determine ways to maximize student learning and retention. This paper documents the processes our research group has followed in planning, creating, implementing, and analyzing a placement test, and describes the group's anticipated future work. We detail the design and implementation of the test itself, including initial work, building the question pool, categorization of questions by topic and level of knowledge, integration with a delivery system, and testing of the entire package. We discuss the results and analyses based on student performance, and we conclude with our plans for future work.

2 BACKGROUND
The primary purpose of the placement exam is to appropriately place students into one of two introductory computer science courses offered by our CSE department. The first option, CSE105 (pre-CS1), is an introductory course intended for students who lack prior exposure to logic constructs and fundamental computer science terminology, and students who are not CSE majors but who want to gain a basic understanding of the field of computer science including programming. Credits earned in CSE105 count towards a degree for most college majors, but not for a computer science or computer engineering degree. The second option, CSE155 (CS1), is intended for students who already have a basic understanding of computing concepts including basic control-flow structures and Boolean logic and who have programming experience in a high-level programming language. These students typically plan to major in an area related to computer science and engineering. The needs of each group of students are different; therefore our placement test is designed to distinguish between the groups and place students into the appropriate course. In the past, students entered the same introductory course regardless of their major field of study or prior computing experience. This left some students feeling overwhelmed while others complained of bore-

SIGCSE'05, February 23–27, 2005, St. Louis, Missouri, USA.

dom. Having two separate introductory CS courses allows our CSE Department to better serve students with diverse backgrounds and different goals.

The placement test is based on the recommendations of the ACM/IEEE Computing Curricula 2001 (ACM/IEEE-CS, 2001) document. The document details the topics leaders in the field of computer science deem to be most critical. The CSE Department at the University of Nebraska-Lincoln has used the ACM2001 guidelines to design their introductory CSE courses and to determine the topics to be covered on the placement exam. Each topic included in the placement exam is also addressed in both introductory courses (pre-CS1 and CS1).

The exam covers each of the major topics recommended by the Computing Curricula 2001 guidelines and tests the students' knowledge of each topic at multiple levels of competency. Testing at multiple levels is accomplished by developing our question pool based on Bloom's Taxonomy [1] such that each question is categorized into one of the cognitive domains, from the simplest to the most complex. The use of Bloom's Taxonomy allows the research team to better assess the level of understanding and knowledge of a student.

3 RELATED WORK

Using a placement exam to assign students to a CSE course is not a novel idea. Some examples are summarized below:

- At the Department of Computer Science at Northwestern University, the CSE placement exam is designed to evaluate students' programming skills. There are three possible outcomes of this exam: 1) students are allowed to enter any course that requires pre-CS1 or C/C++/Java programming experience, 2) students are allowed to enter any course that requires "basic programming experience" but not courses requiring pre-CS1 or C/C++/Java experience, or 3) students must take pre-CS1 or other introductory CSE courses that do not require programming experience.
- At California Institute of Technology the CSE Department has a placement exam for students who want to skip CS1 course (http://www.cs.caltech.edu/placement). Incoming freshmen are the intended audience for the exam. This placement exam also serves as the basis for case-by-case consideration placement into more advanced CSE classes. In the CS1 exam, the students are required to describe the representation (data structures) for a singly linked list of integer-string pairs, write a routine (or routines) to manipulate the linked lists, describe how his or her "sort"procedure is invoked, and perform a complexity analysis on their algorithm. If a student wants to test out of CS2 (skipping both CS1 and CS2), an additional exercise requires the student to write a specification in clear English for a class to represent a graph, provide two different implementations meeting the specification/interface, and write a procedure to find the length of the shortest path between two graph nodes on top of the interface specified.
- At the Department of Computer Science and Engineering at the Washington University at Saint Louis, students with significant computer science background and experience in object-oriented programming are invited to take the CSE placement exam during the orientation week for possible placement in a course beyond CSE101G (CS1). The placement exam is designed assuming a working knowledge of Java that is sufficient to read, modify, and write Java source code.
- The Computer Science and Engineering Department of Arizona State University has an exam to place students into CSE110 (pre-CS1) or CSE200 (CS1). The placement exam has 40 multiple-choice questions on the syntax of Java and Java-based programs. Most of the questions are not specifically tied to problem solving in general computer science, but are about program syntax.

There are other CSE placement exams that focus on placement in CS1. In some CSE departments these exams are mandatory while in others, they are optional or only required under certain circumstances. Most of the placement exams we researched serve one purpose—to place incoming, first-semester CSE students into the appropriate introductory CSE course (generally pre-CS1 or CS1). In contrast with our exam, most of the placement exams do not explicitly consider pedagogical contexts such as Bloom's taxonomy nor are the results used to improve course instruction. We are unable to find any references or publications that evaluate the quality of these examinations—there are no formative or summative analyses available. Furthermore, our placement exam design is also based on problem solving using computers rather than on programming. Our objective is to place students who demonstrate comprehension and application capabilities into CS1 and to advise the other students to take pre-CS1. Overall, in our project, we aim to emphasize pedagogical contexts as well as validation of our work. In the next section, we discuss the detailed design of our placement exam.

We would like to note that The Advanced Placement (AP) exams administered by the College Boards also is designed to test the ability of high school students to perform at a college level in 19 subjects, including Computer Science. The exams consist of both free-response and multiple-choice questions, with the former are graded by college professors and high school teachers, while the latter are automatically graded by computer. The computer science test is designed to test students' ability to design, write, analyze, and document programs and subprograms. To ensure that AP Exams accurately measure college-level knowledge and performance in each discipline, the development process includes college curriculum surveys, pretesting of multiple-choice questions, and college comparability studies. These AP tests have been extensively researched, with numerous reliability and validity studies conducted to ensure appropriate psychometric properties. For example, reliability statistics for the 2003 computer science advanced placement exam range from .91 to .95. Validity studies compare how students with a given AP grade perform in an advanced college course. If students consistently succeed in that course, those AP grade levels provide an indication that they have the prerequisite skills. To check the validity of such decisions, studies are conducted in which the AP Exam is administered to students taking the college courses in question. The college students' grades on the AP Exam are then compared with their grades in the college course. The College Board also conducts numerous item statistics, and may remove items that do not meet certain criteria, such as a low or negative correlation with performance on the entire exam. These statistics and procedures are similar to ones we used and are described in a later section.

4 DESIGN

Designing and validating a good placement test is challenging. Several dimensions must be considered in order to develop an exam that accurately and reliably assigns students to the proper first course in computer science. First, the areas of student knowledge and skills to be assessed must be carefully selected. Secondly, the exam questions must be designed to match the level of understanding expected of the students. Furthermore, the questions must have an appropriate level of difficulty. If the questions are too difficult or too easy, the exam will not effectively distinguish between the knowledge and skill levels of the students. In addition, the test must be reliable and valid. And finally, placement criteria that reliably assign students to the proper course must be established. Each of these aspects is described below.

4.1 Knowledge and Skills

As described earlier, we have designed our placement test to serve two purposes: (a) to determine the readiness of a student for our CS1 course, and (b) to validate student learning in our CS1 course. In order to accomplish these objectives, it is important to accurately identify which topics should be tested as prerequisite skills for the course and which should be tested as post-test measures. We used the ACM/IEEE Computing Curricula 2001 guidelines as the basis for what to expect from the students. Using these guidelines and our CS1 course descriptions we determined five content areas to be tested for prerequisite skills and five content areas to assess student learning in our CS1 course. For each content area, CSE instructors and researchers teaching and developing the curriculum for the lower level CSE courses developed a detailed list of topics and associated levels of competency expected of students in each course. Table 2 (in Section 5.2.1) lists the ten content areas covered on our placement test. The first five content areas (1-5) address prerequisite skills and second five content areas (6-10) represent the topics students are expected to know after completion of CS1.

4.2 Individual Questions

Exam questions were drawn from multiple sources, including textbooks, previous exams and classroom exercises. It was also necessary to generate new questions to ensure that all content areas were adequately covered. Both CSE and education educators and researchers carefully reviewed all questions to verify their appropriateness.

The quality of a question can be measured in different ways. The *degree of difficulty* (mean) of a question is determined by the percentage of test takers who answer the question correctly. If a question is too easy (very high mean) or too difficult (very low mean), it does not provide a meaningful discriminator and should be carefully considered for revision or exclusion. For our test, the target mean for each question was between 0.4 and 0.85.

The *item-total correlation* for a question shows the strength of the relationship between the students' response to a question and their total score. A good question should have a strong positive correlation between the two. Low values for this measure—i.e., a student who scores high overall yet fails to answer the question correctly, and vice versa—indicate that the question may be confusing, ambiguous or even wrong. While a value of 0.3 is generally regarded as a good target, we chose a value of 0.2 as acceptable.

For multiple-choice questions, the frequency of response for the choices also may be used to measure the overall quality of a question. If students choose only two of the five possible choices, then the three unpicked choices are not providing any discrimination and should either be modified or dropped.

At the end of each testing cycle, exam questions in the pool are evaluated for their effectiveness and discrimination power. Questions that are either too easy or too difficult are eliminated or modified and returned to the question pool for validation before being used in the next placement test. Similarly, questions in the pool must be periodically replaced to keep the questions from being repeated too many times.

4.3 Reliability and Validity

In addition to careful delineation of the skills and knowledge to be measured, the test must exhibit reliability and validity. Reliability is the degree of consistency, precision, and repeatability. Scores on reliable measures are not greatly influenced by random error. Although there are several types of reliability, we focused on *internal consistency* reliability, which is a measure of the item-to-item consistency of a subject's responses within a single test. This type of reliability is measured by a reliability coefficient, which ranges from 0 (no reliability) to 1 (perfect reliability). In assessing the reliability of our test, we used *Cronbach's Alpha* statistic. Reliability measures of our test have ranged from .70 to .74, which is acceptable for research purposes. We do not, however, believe that our reliability index is high enough, given that we are making critical, individual decisions about student placement. Our goal is to continually refine the test, with the goal of reaching a reliability coefficient of .80 or higher.

While reliability reflects the consistency of test scores, validity refers to how well the test measures what it purports to measure. Our main concern is with *content* validity and *predictive* validity. Content validity reflects how adequately the test samples and represents the content domain. It is not measured statistically, but instead is judged by expert opinion on the representativeness of the items. The panel of CSE and education researchers carefully reviewed the items to determine content validity. Predictive validity is used for making predictions about the individual, which in our case is the student's readiness to take CS1. Predictive validity for our test was determined by correlating a student's total score on the placement test (all 50 questions) with his/her exam scores in the course. The correlation for Spring 2004 semester was .58, providing evidence of this type of validity. Another statistical test involved correlating students' scores on the first twenty-five questions with their total points in the course. The results show that student's score on the first half of the placement exam was a significant predictor of their total points in the course.

4.4 Placement Criteria

Determining the cutoff score for placement is a critical decision and must be arrived at carefully. Ideally, students who are placed into a CS1 course should succeed in the course. A cutoff score that is too low will result in a higher percentage of students having difficulty in the course. In our placement test, we give one point for each correct answer irrespective of the difficulty of the question. There is no penalty for a wrong answer. During the development of the test, we initially chose 50% to be the cutoff score. Students who receive at least 40% but less than 50% are interviewed individually and are advised to be placed in CS1 or pre-CS1 based on their programming background. As the test is updated and revised to improve measurement statistics, however, the cutoff scores have been adjusted as described below.

5 IMPLEMENTATION

Software developed by the National Center for Information Technology in Education (NCITE), within the College of Education and Human Sciences at UNL, was used for administration of the placement exam (Feese & Zygielbaum, in press). The system allows students to go back and change answers until a final submission of the entire test. It also allows instructors to set up tests using a specially developed teacher interface and to view the results on-line. The individual student information captured is student ID, student response to each question, correct and incorrect statistics for each test item, total correct for first 25 questions, total correct for second 25 questions and a total score.

The duration for the placement exam is one hour, with a total of 50 questions and 10 content areas. There are five questions in each category and each question is classified into one of the Bloom's competence level. Students are not informed about the competence level of each question. The presentation order of the questions is by the competence level within each content area. All the "knowledge" questions are presented first, followed by the "comprehension" questions, and so on. This procedure allows higher level questions to build upon the lower level questions, e.g. to answer a comprehension question, one should understand the requisite knowledge.

6 DISCUSSION OF RESULTS

At the end of the Summer 2003 session, we asked our CSE155 (CS1) students to take the placement exam to fine-tune the logistics of test administration and the questions themselves. Subsequently, the placement exam was refined prior to administration to students enrolling in the regular sessions of CSE155 in Fall 2003 semester.

6.1 Fall 2003 Session

At the beginning of the Fall 2003 semester, students scheduled for CSE105 (pre-CS1), CSE155 (CS1), and CSE156 (CS2) took the revised version of the placement exam. Fifty-five CSE105 students, 78 CSE155 students, 13 CSE155H (honors) students, and 23 CSE156 students took the test. The reliability of our instrument was approximately the same as the test given in Summer 2003 (coefficient alpha = .74); however, the larger number of students who participated during the fall (n=223) resulted in better stability. The following statistics summarize the results.

- In general, CSE156 students performed the best on both sets (first and second 25) of questions (61.6% and 63.2%, respectively). Honor students in CSE155H (61.5% and 58.6%, respectively) also did better than other CSE155 students (53.8% and 52.8%, respectively). Most students performed better on the first set of questions than on the second set; however this was not true for the CSE155H honors students. CSE105 students performed most poorly overall (43.1% and 42.4%, respectively).
- In general, CSE105 students spent the least amount of time on the exam (22.9 min) and CSE155 students spent the most time (46.2 min). However, CSE155H students spent considerably less time on the test (29.3 min), compared to their counterparts in CSE155. We also observed that CSE155H students performed very "efficiently"—scoring a high average with very little time.

Other statistics based on the Fall 2003 placement exam scores are:

- In general, students who performed well did so on both the first set of questions and the second set of questions.
- Students who scored 48% or better on the first 25 questions spent more time on the exam (44.4 minutes) than students in the borderline group (39.7 minutes) and the group of students who scored below 40% on the first 25 questions (36.8 minutes).
- CSE155H students scored well on the first 25 questions (61.5%), much better than their counterparts in CSE155 (53.8%). The majority of CSE105 students scored below 40% on the first 25 questions (38.2%) or were in the borderline group (34.5%). Most of the CSE155 and CSE155H students scored 48% or better on the first 25 questions. Based on these statistics, we think the cutoff score (placement criteria) for the exam was appropriate.
- Pre-post comparisons from Fall 2003 semester showed an increase from pre- to post-testing. A t-test for the significance of difference between these two mean values showed that the difference was highly significant ($t(63) = 11.036$, $p < .001$), providing validation of the instructional effectiveness of the CS1 course. Placement test score also served as a significant predictor of total test scores in CS1, an indication of the test's predictive validity.

6.2 Spring 2004 Session

The placement test again underwent revision based on Fall 2003 measurement statistics and was administered to 84 students scheduled for either CSE105 or CSE155 in Spring 2004 semester.

6.2.1 Bloom's Taxonomy and ACM Content Area

Spring 2004 results were further analyzed to determine any differences between student responses to questions representing the levels of Bloom's taxonomy, as well as the ten content areas identified by the ACM Computing Curricula 2001. Results are presented in Tables 1 and 2, showing that students scored highest on the comprehension questions and lowest on the higher-level analysis questions. This is to be expected, since comprehension knowledge is a precursor to higher-level analytical skills. Using this reasoning, students should have scored best on the knowledge level questions. However, students did worst on "knowledge" questions than "comprehension" questions. Our hypothesis is that students are coming from high schools without the necessary computer science factual knowledge, including terminologies and definitions, but are able to use general mathematical and reasoning abilities to perform well at the comprehension level. In other words, students can logically come up with a solution for the comprehension questions more easily than they can generate a definition for a concept they have not previously encountered.

Table 1. Student Mean Scores on Placement Test by Level of Bloom's Taxonomy

Bloom's	Knowledge	Comp.	Appl.	Analysis
Mean	.54	.64	.48	.44

Table 2 clearly indicates that students tend to score high on machine level representation of data and low on algorithms and problem solving. The high scores on machine level data representation are expected due to the lower-level type of knowledge in this content area. Algorithms and problem solving, on the other hand, requires higher order thinking skills. The relatively high score in object-oriented programming indicates students have a fairly well developed idea of objects, even if they cannot at this stage write programs using objects. The low scores on syntax and semantics of programming constructs indicate that students are coming from high school without sufficient knowledge of programming languages and the relevant syntax and semantics – concepts which students are expected to apply in CS1.

Table 2. Student Mean Scores on by Content Area

Content Area	Mean
1. Functions, relations, sets; basic logic	.58
2. Fundamental data structures	.48
3. Fundamental programming constructs	.64
4. Algorithms and problem-solving	.39
5. Machine level representation of data	.87
6. Fundamental data structures (data types)	.57
7. Fundamental programming constructs (syntax and semantics)	.36
8. Object-oriented programming	.67
9. Fundamental computing algorithms, sorting & searching	.45
10. Event-driven programming; software engineering	.61

Our primary reason for using Bloom's Taxonomy is to gain a greater understanding of the depth of a student's knowledge; however this means we sacrifice internal reliability because questions that are very easy or very hard add little to the test's reliability. Ideally we would set a cutoff point using a predetermined score of student proficiency and present questions near or at the determined proficiency that would increase the reliability of scores. This makes our test different from other tests such as those developed by Educational Testing Service in that our student population is heterogeneous, yet our questions assess different levels of knowledge.

6.2.2 Other Analyses

Earlier in the paper, we reported that there were significant positive correlations between total scores on the placement test for students in CSE155 and their total exams scores, as well as student's scores on the first 25 questions and their total points in the course. Another analysis we performed involved looking at differences in total points scored in the CSE155 course between students scoring less than 48% (the cut percentage for CSE155) and those scoring above 48% on the first twenty-five questions on the placement test. A one-way ANOVA found a significant difference between these two groups on total course points ($F(1, 64) = 4.76$, $p < .05$), indicating that students who scored higher on the placement test accumulated more course points and consequently received a higher grade.

In keeping with the second purpose of the placement exam, to determine gains in student knowledge, we again conducted pre-post analyses. The mean for the pre-test was 27.09, which improved to 33.6 for the post-test. A t-test for the significance of difference between these mean values was highly significant, $t(68) = 11.81$, $p<.001$, providing validation of the instructional effectiveness of the course. Statistical tests were also run by Bloom's level and the results show highly significant results ($p< .001$) for all levels. Students showed greatest improvement on the knowledge questions, $t(68) = 8.27$, $p<.001$, providing further support for our observation that students are coming from high school without the necessary computer science factual knowledge. CS1 provides a venue to obtain the background knowledge needed for success in future computer science courses

7 CONCLUSIONS

Although we have used the placement exam to assign students to pre-CS1 and CS1 for the past two semesters, we plan to make additional changes to the exam and conduct more comprehensive analyses and investigations. A significant change we plan to incorporate for the upcoming semesters is to include questions using specific programming languages instead of pseudo code. Our observation indicates that students are good at problem solving, but without any programming experience perform well in the placement test and hence are placed into CS1. However, they experience considerable difficulty in the programming components (homework, labs) of the course. Since we use Java in our CS1 course, we will replace all pseudo code examples in our questions with Java code examples. We will also add a few Java-specific questions to test students' knowledge and comprehension of the Java language.

We have described a placement exam designed within the overall context of a Reinventing CSE Curriculum Project. As such, we have utilized educational research components in the design of the exam, such as Bloom's taxonomy, and we have adhered to the ACM/IEEE Computing Curricula 2001 guidelines. We have presented the process we followed to develop the exam, discussed preliminary results of administering the exam and highlighted interesting observations. We plan to carry out further investigations in an effort to continually refine the placement exam, provide additional insights to our preliminary findings, and improve our introductory CSE courses and our overall curriculum.

ACKNOWLEDGEMENT

The Reinventing CS Curriculum Project is supported in part by NCITE and CSE at the University of Nebraska. CSE. The authors would like to thank Art Zygielbaum, Chuck Riedesel, Chao Chen, Smitha Kasinadhuni, Joseph Bernadt, Andhy Kosenander and Traci Fink for their invaluable help in implementing this project.

REFERENCES

[1] ACM/IEEE-CS (2001). Computing Curricula 2001. Retrieved May 12, 2004, from http://www.sigcse.org/cc2001/.

[2] Bloom, B. S. (1956). *Taxonomy of Educational Objectives: Book 1, Cognitive Domain,* New York: Longman.

[3] Feese, R. and A. Zygielbaum (in press). Affinity Learning. In L. PytlikZillig, L, Bodvarsson, M., & Bruning, R. (Eds.), *Technology-based Education: Bringing Researchers and Practitioners Together*, Greenwich Connecticut: Information Age Publishing.

A Multi-Institutional Investigation of Computer Science Seniors' Knowledge of Programming Concepts

Laurie Murphy
Pacific Lutheran University
murphylc@plu.edu

Renée McCauley
College of Charleston
mccauley@cs.cofc.edu

Suzanne Westbrook
University of Arizona
sw@cs.arizona.edu

Timothy Fossum, Susan Haller
University of Wisconsin Parkside
{fossum,haller}@cs.uwp.edu

Briana B. Morrison
Southern Polytechnic State Univ.
bmorriso@spsu.edu

Brad Richards
Vassar College
richards@cs.vassar.edu

Kate Sanders
Rhode Island College
KSanders@ric.edu

Carol Zander
University of Washington, Bothell
zander@u.washington.edu

Ruth E. Anderson
University of Virginia
ruth@cs.virginia.edu

ABSTRACT

Research on learning suggests the importance of helping students organize their knowledge around meaningful patterns of information. This paper reports on a multi-institutional study to investigate how senior computer science majors articulate and organize their knowledge of programming concepts using a card-sorting technique adopted from knowledge acquisition. We show that card-sorts are an effective means of eliciting students' knowledge structures and suggest they can also be used to help students organize their knowledge throughout the curriculum.

Categories and Subject Descriptors

K.3.2 [**Computer and Information Science Education**]: Computer Science Education – computer science education research.

General Terms

Experimentation.

Keywords

Content analysis, Card sort, Knowledge, Expertise.

1. INTRODUCTION

Some students are able to effortlessly apply knowledge they acquired in one context to another, for example, when computer science students use their knowledge of programming concepts to solve a problem in an upper-level course. These students' programming knowledge appears to be well organized and integrated into their understanding of computer science as a whole. One might ask "what conceptual structures do computer science students, especially those who are highly successful, have about programming concepts? What pedagogical implications do their knowledge structures have for computer science education?"

There is evidence to indicate that the way subjects organize concepts reflects their mental representation of the way these concepts are related. Adelson gave novice and expert programmers randomly ordered lines of computer code and observed which lines they recalled and in what order [1]. The order in which lines were recalled indicated that subjects were imposing their own structure on the unstructured data. Experts organize or "chunk" information differently from novices: they form abstractions based on deep (semantic) characteristics rather than on surface (syntactic) characteristics (See, e.g., [2,3]). Also, expert subjects tend to be more consistent, and novices more variable in the ways they organize information [1,2 p. 638]. Davies et al. gave subjects code fragments to organize. Given Adelson's evidence, Davies et al. expected experts to base their categorizations on objects and inheritance relationships and novices on syntactic elements [4]. Instead, their results indicated experts mainly based their classifications on functional relationships and novices on object-based categorizations.

Our objectives were to learn how senior computer science students articulate and structure their knowledge about programming concepts and to discover if there are differences among the knowledge structures of students who are about to graduate. In our multi-institutional study, we used a card-sorting technique adopted from knowledge acquisition to elicit computer science seniors' articulable knowledge of programming concepts. Card sorting is designed to elicit information from subjects by observing how they categorize and relate a group of concepts [8]. This study grew out of a study of the conceptual structures of novice programmers conducted in 2001-2003 by Petre et al. [7].

2. STUDY DESIGN

Subjects were given a set of 26 index cards, each containing a "minimalist" one-word prompt for a programming concept. The concepts, which were the same as those used in the study of novice programmers [7], were general in nature and not constrained by any programming task or the syntax of a particular language . (See Figure 1.) Each subject was asked to sort these 26 cards into categories using a single criterion. Subjects provided names for each group (category) and for the overall criterion by which he or she sorted the cards (students were allowed to use

SIGCSE'05, February 23-27, 2005, St. Louis, Missouri, USA.

1 function	8 if-then-else	15 encapsulation	21 expression
2 method	9 boolean	16 parameter	22 tree
3 procedure	10 scope	17 variable	23 thread
4 dependency	11 list	18 constant	24 iteration
5 object	12 recursion	19 type	25 array
6 decomposition	13 choice	20 loop	26 event
7 abstraction	14 state		

Figure 1: Stimuli used in card sort task.

"don't know" and "not applicable" as category names). An example sort from one subject used the criterion "Dependency Groups," and provided categories named "general requirement," "storage," "function calling," "control flow," "data structures," "object-oriented" and "don't know." Subjects were asked to perform sorts repeatedly until they were unable, or unwilling, to carry out additional sorts.

2.1 Subjects

Our subjects were 65 senior students at eight colleges and universities in the United States who were eligible to complete computer science baccalaureate degrees during 2004. At each school, the study was advertised and students volunteered to participate, although some effort was made to recruit female students and students with a range of academic abilities. Fourteen (22%) of the subjects were female, 51 (78%) were male. The mean computer science and overall grade point averages of the subject population were both 3.25 on a 4-point scale. Subjects ranged in age from 18 to 43 years and reported first programming exposure ages from 6 to 39.

2.2 Data Collection

Data were collected during spring 2004 following a standard protocol. All researchers participated in the novice study [7], so they were familiar with the sorting and data collection procedures.

i. *Demographic and background data:* Demographic and background information was collected for each subject including: expected graduation date, age, gender, first spoken language, first and second programming languages, age at first exposure, programming experience, overall GPA, computer science GPA, and grades in computer science courses.

ii. *Card sort data:* Subjects were asked to sort the cards/concepts into categories using a single criterion. Criterion and category names were recorded verbatim. Cards in each category were recorded by number. Sixty-five subjects generated 291 sorts.

2.3 Data Analysis Techniques

Although subjects articulated the category and criterion descriptions in their own words, we noticed their articulations were often based on similar themes or ideas. For example, several subjects performed sorts based on level of difficulty or abstraction.

We also observed that sorts based on the same verbalized idea were often quite different. For example, subjects used different numbers of categories, assigned the same name to different groups of cards, or gave different names to very similar groups of cards. Some students appeared more articulate than others. For example, they used more descriptive category names, or names that were well known computer science terms (e.g., "control structures"), rather than common words or phrases (e.g., "verbs", "things").

To classify the sorts, we used content analysis on the category and criteria names given by the subjects. Content analysis is a systematic, replicable technique for analyzing a body of text and assigning units of that text into categories or named groups [9]. We then examined these groups to identify the common characteristics or unique properties of the sorts within each group.

2.3.1 Content Analysis Groups

In our content analysis we used the criterion and category names for a single sort as the unit of analysis. Initially, two pairs of researchers independently identified and named groups (called "Content Analysis Groups" or "CAGs") using the data from three schools. These same four researchers, working together, then compared the two sets of CAGs and agreed on a set of 16 CAGs to be used to classify all sorts. Two other researchers then independently classified each of the 291 sorts into one of the CAGs. Sorts for which they disagreed were assigned to a CAG by consensus.

The five most popular CAGs (those into which the largest numbers of sorts were classified) are: *Abstract/Concrete* - sorts that refer to levels of abstraction or abstract concepts; *Big Sort* - sorts that appear to encompass a subject's broad understanding of programming[1]; *Language Paradigm / Programming Language Concepts (PLC)* - sorts based on single or multiple paradigms and other PLCs like language translation; *little sort* – sorts that are narrowly focused on one or a few specific aspects of programming; and *Parts of a program* – sorts that assigned only concrete programming concepts into meaningful categories.

2.3.2 Sort Similarity Metric

We wanted to know if sorts within a given CAG had similar structure – that is, when subjects articulated similar criteria did they also use comparable numbers of categories containing similar card groupings. We also wanted to measure whether individual subjects performed unique categorizations – that is, whether a subject's set of sorts represents truly different ways of organizing the concepts, or if they are simply variations on the same theme. To answer these questions, we applied the *Normalized Minimum Spanning Tree (NMST)* metric [5] to the card sort data. NMST, a distance metric based on the minimum spanning tree of the edit-distance between sorts, measures how dissimilar a set of sorts is. If a set of sorts is essentially the same sort over and over structurally (similar number of categories with similar cards in each), then the NMST will be smaller than if the sorts are truly different in structure.

3. RESULTS AND DISCUSSION

3.1 Quantitative results

3.1.1 Performance Quartile Statistics

We assigned each subject to a performance quartile based on his or her computer science GPA. We then calculated the total and average number of sorts performed by students in each quartile as well as the average number of categories per sort (excluding "don't know" and "not applicable" categories). Finally, we

[1] The "Dependency Groups" sort, mentioned in the Study Design section, was classified into the *Big Sort* CAG.

	Performance Quartile				
	top	second	third	bottom	all
CS GPA range	4.00 → 3.62	3.58 → 3.33	3.32 → 3.00	2.96 → 2.31	4.0 → 2.31
total subjects	16	16	16	17	65
total sorts performed	86	61	75	69	291
avg. sorts per subject	5.38	3.81	4.69	4.06	4.48
avg. categories per sort	3.48	3.23	3.64	3.84	3.55
avg. dissimilarity (NMST)	8.33	7.10	6.63	6.16	

Figure 2: Performance Quartile Statistics

computed the mean NMST value for each quartile, where the NMST metric was applied to each subject's set of sorts independently. These results are shown in Figure 2.

Sorts executed by top quartile students were structurally more dissimilar on average (as indicated by higher NMST values) than sorts by students in other quartiles. The Mann-Kendall test for randomness against a monotone trend, the "trend" being an increase in student performance levels relative to the four quartiles, was used to verify this observation. It yielded a z score of 2.97 (p=.0025) suggesting the sorts performed by top quartile students were significantly more diverse than those in the lower quartiles. By contrast, while the average dissimilarity decreases monotonically as we move from the top quartile to the bottom, the other measures (total sorts, avg. sorts, and avg. categories) do not.

3.1.2 CAG distribution

We calculated the number and percentage of subjects who performed at least one sort in a given CAG for the entire population and by performance quartile. The percentage of total subjects executing sorts in the top five CAGs was: *Abstract/Concrete* (40%), *Big Sort* (42%), *Language Paradigm/PLC* (45%), *little sort* (40%) and *Parts of a Program* (32%). The number of subjects from each quartile who executed at least one sort in each of these CAGs is shown in Figure 3. We see that top quartile students performed more sorts associating the programming terms with levels of abstraction. Better students also executed more sorts related to programming language paradigms or concepts. Top performers did more *Big Sorts* which implies a greater ability to see a *big picture* or overall view, while they executed fewer of the more narrowly focused "*little*" and "*parts of a program*" sorts.

3.1.3 Sort Structure within CAGs

We assigned sorts to CAGs based on the words the subjects used to name their categories and criteria. To validate the CAG assignments, we wanted to know if the actual partitioning of the concepts was similar for sorts within a given CAG. To answer this question, we used the NMST metric to evaluate the similarity/dissimilarity of the sorts within each CAG. If a CAG represents a collection of sorts that have conceptual similarity, we expect its sorts to be similar with respect to their categorizations, and therefore the NMST of the CAG should be relatively small.

To quantify "relatively small", for each CAG we compared the NMST of the *n* sorts in the CAG to an NMST obtained by randomly choosing (without replacement) *n* sorts from the 291 sorts in our study. A meaningful CAG should have an NMST

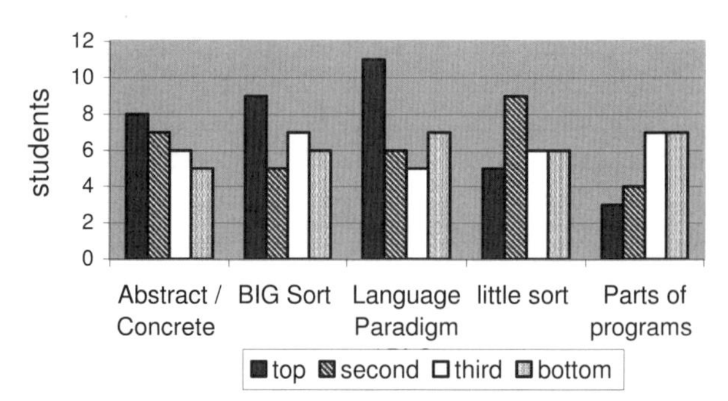

Figure 3: Distribution of the top 5 CAGs by quartile.

value that differs significantly from that of randomly-selected groups of sorts. Four of our five top CAGs had significantly smaller NMST values than were found in random groupings, indicating their contents were more structurally similar than random groups. One of the top five, *Big Sort*, had a significantly larger NMST, indicating its contents were more dissimilar than expected from a random group.[2]

We expected the high similarity among sorts in the *Abstract /Concrete* CAG because of its dichotomous nature. We also expected high similarity among sorts in the *Language Paradigm/PLC* CAG because it focuses primarily on object-orientation. There was also high similarity among sorts in the *little Sort* and *Parts of a Program* CAGs. This may be due to a tendency for subjects to produce large "not applicable" categories in these sorts. The sorts in *Big Sort* were highly dissimilar. This was not entirely unexpected since most subjects seemed inclined to produce at least one sort that categorized all the cards in some meaningful way, resulting in diverse categories for these sorts.

3.2 Qualitative Results

We assessed the qualitative differences among the sorts within each CAG, especially sorts by subjects in the top and bottom quartiles. We focused on these high and low performers because students in the study tended to be better performers overall, thus there is little difference in the GPA ranges of adjacent quartiles. Furthermore, focusing on students at the top and bottom makes our results less susceptible to variations in the curricula and grading norms at the eight participating institutions. Below we discuss our results for the top five CAGs.

3.2.1 Big Sort CAG

"Experts' knowledge is ... organized around core concepts or 'big ideas' that guide their thinking about their domains." [6, p 36] The *Big Sort* CAG contains sorts that appear to encompass a subject's broad understanding of programming including abstract concepts. Twenty-seven of the 65 subjects (42%) performed one or more *Big Sorts*, expressing a broad or "big picture" view of programming. Top quartile students did more *Big Sorts* (12 by 9 students) than the bottom (8 by 6 students) although there is little difference in the average number of categories (top = 5.25, bottom = 5.13) or criteria names, which tend to be very broad across quartiles. However, the category names reveal noticeable differences between these two groups.

---

[2] All results were significant at p<<.005 except for "Parts of a program", which was significant at p<.025.

	abstraction	choice	decomposition	dependency	encapsulation	event	iteration	list	object	recursion	scope	state	tree	type
top	75	63	88	75	88	38	50	25	50	75	75	75	38	13
bottom	80	80	40	80	80	60	40	0	40	80	80	80	20	60

Figure 4: Percentage of top and bottom quartile students categorizing terms as abstract.

While high and low performers are similar in their mentions of some intermediate concepts, such as data structures (top=66%, bottom=63%) and object oriented (25% for both), the top quartile subjects use control ("control flow", "control structures") much more often (50%) than do the bottom quartile subjects, with only one (13%) mention of "program control".

The top quartile also makes associations with fundamental concepts like problem solving ("ways to solve a problem"), transitions/interactions ("transitions", "controls how parts of a program interact or how programs interact"), language constructs ("constructs in a language", "basic programming constructs"), mathematics ("more mathematical or theoretical terms") and the program stack ("advanced function calling and program stack"). They also draw connections to advanced topics like concurrency ("events and concurrency", "method dispatching"), software engineering, design, programming methodologies and algorithms. By contrast, bottom quartile students almost never mention these concepts.

In addition to noticing bottom quartile students were less likely to associate the concepts to advanced topics, we also observed that some were clearly inarticulate. For example, one student labeled a category "unnamed but related". Many more appeared unable to distill a single idea for a group of related cards, instead using general names or simply concatenating ideas such as "two things I can create with general coding" or "abstraction of sequence of statements or events or functions." Such inarticulate names were not generally found among top quartile sorts, although one was unable to give a criterion name for a *Big Sort*.

3.2.2 Abstract/Concrete CAG

The *Abstract/Concrete* CAG categorizes sorts that refer to levels of abstraction or abstract concepts. The term "abstraction" appeared to hold meaning for almost all of the senior students with only eight (12%) failing to place the term into at least one meaningful category for at least one sort. Only four of these students, two each from the second and bottom quartiles, admitted they did not know the term "abstraction".

Overall, 26 subjects performed 28 *Abstract/Concrete* sorts. Synonyms for *abstract* included "high level", "theory" and "conceptualizations". Terms synonymous with *concrete* included "low level" and "things that take physical space". Students from all quartiles performed *Abstract/Concrete* sorts, although slightly more top-performers executed them: top quartile students performed 8 sorts (8 subjects); second quartile did 8 sorts (7 subjects); third did 7 sorts (6 subjects); bottom quartile, 5 sorts (5 subjects). Although the tendency to execute *Abstract/Concrete* sorts increased with performance, we did not notice any obvious qualitative differences in the category and criterion names used by students across quartiles.

We also examined which terms the top and bottom quartiles categorized as *abstract* or *most abstract*. Figure 4 shows general agreement between the two quartiles for many of the terms with only a few notable exceptions. Nearly 90% of top quartile students categorized "decomposition" as abstract, while only 40% of the bottom quartile did. We also see a sharp contrast in these students' views of "type". Only one top quartile student (13%) indicated "type" was abstract, while 60% of the bottom quartile students did. Sixty percent of bottom quartile students also categorized "event" as abstract compared to 38% of the top students. *(Note: terms categorized as abstract by fewer than two students from both quartiles are not shown in Figure 4.)*

During the novice study [7], 11 of the 21 researchers (all experienced educators) were asked to categorize the 26 terms as "abstract" or "concrete". All 11 classified "abstraction", "dependency", "decomposition", and "encapsulation" as abstract and seven of 11 classified "state" and "tree" as abstract. All other terms were deemed abstract by less than half of the researchers. Seniors were more likely than the researchers to view "scope" and "recursion" as abstract and less likely, particularly the bottom quartile, to categorize "tree" as abstract. This is notable, since "tree" is often presented to students as an *abstract data type*. This suggests that top quartile students' views of abstraction are more similar to that of experienced educators.

3.2.3 Language Paradigm/PLC CAG

Almost half, 45%, of all subjects created at least one *Language Paradigm/Programming Language Concepts (PLC)* sort. Most top quartile subjects, 69%, performed one or more. While the researchers named this CAG *Language Paradigm/PLC*, only eight students (two in each quartile), 28%, used the word "paradigm" in their criterion name. Of these eight students, only one used "language paradigm". Most criteria referred to one or more specific paradigms, e.g., "OO vs. non-OO" and "Associated primarily with procedural languages, OO, or both."

As a paradigm, object-oriented was mentioned most often. Figure 5 shows the distribution of the number of paradigms mentioned by quartile. While 50% (8/16) of top quartile students referred to at least two language paradigms, only 19% (3/16), 25% (4/16), and 18% (3/17) of the second, third, and bottom quartiles respectively, performed sorts other than OO vs. non-OO related. The tendency of top quartile students to use more language paradigms in these sorts demonstrates they have a greater ability

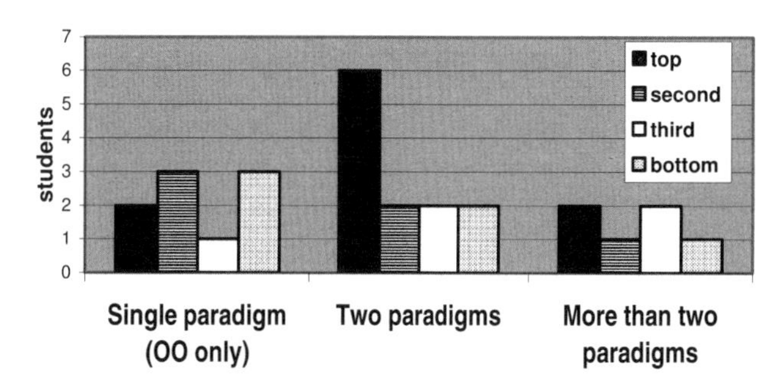

Figure 5: Number of paradigms mentioned in "Language Paradigm/PLC" CAG sorts by quartile

to retrieve and apply their knowledge of language paradigms within the context of the programming terms.

3.2.4 *little Sort and Parts of a Program CAGs*

The *little sort* CAG focuses on sorts with only one or a few specific aspects of programming. They typically have few categories and often have categories consisting of only one or two cards. A large "not applicable" group is also characteristic of *little sorts*. Sixty percent of these sorts were dichotomous (excluding "don't know" / "not applicable"), with 77% of subjects who did *little sorts* performing at least one dichotomous *little sort*.

The *Parts of a Program* CAG is similar to *Big Sort* excluding most abstract ideas. This sort was done by 32% of all subjects. Twice as many students in the third and bottom quartiles performed this sort than did top and second quartile students.

In *little sorts*, frequently occurring criteria themes were control flow, objects, functions, and data. Some *little sorts* expressed the subject's personal perspective of the programming terms such as "things I've learned here in my CS classes". Many *little sorts* were based directly on the card names verbatim. More top students related terms to other computer science concepts such as information hiding and OO design. When executing *little* and *Parts of a Program* sorts, bottom quartile students focused more on surface, syntactic details, while top quartile students based more sorts on deep, semantic characteristics suggesting that better students' knowledge structures are more like those of experts [1].

4. CONCLUSIONS

To summarize, we found evidence that suggests

- Subjects performed sorts that could be grouped into a fairly small number of well-defined categories.
- Top quartile students performed more structurally diverse sorts.
- Top quartile students were more likely to use abstract concepts such as "control structures" or "design methodologies," and as a result, gave more precise names.
- Top quartile students were more likely to perform *Big Sorts*, implying a greater ability to see the big picture.
- Top quartile students were more likely to perform sorts associating programming terms with levels of abstraction and to use multiple paradigms in their *Language Paradigm/PLC* sorts.
- Bottom quartile students were more likely to perform narrowly focused *little sorts* and *Parts of a Program* sorts and to focus on surface details in those sorts.

It is not surprising that top performers are better at card sorting - we expect top students to have a greater understanding of programming concepts. However, when we consider the skills students must employ to perform more complex and diverse sorts, we observe not only basic programming knowledge but also expert behavior such as an ability to see the "big picture", the ability to fluently retrieve relevant knowledge, and the ability to apply knowledge in different contexts. This enables them to "notice features and meaningful patterns of information that are not noticed by novices." [6, p.31]

That card sorts provide an effective means of eliciting expert knowledge structures of top performing seniors, suggests card sorts can also help students organize their knowledge throughout the curriculum. Educational research on expertise "suggests the importance of providing students with learning experiences that specifically enhance their abilities to recognize meaningful patterns of information (e.g., Simon, 1980; Bransford et al., 1989)." [6, p.35] For example, students in an algorithms class could be given cards, each containing a different algorithm, and asked to sort the cards by criteria such as "application", "algorithmic technique" or "runtime complexity", with students providing category names. The same could be done in a programming languages class with languages on the cards and the criteria "paradigm", "domain" or "implementation". Introductory students could perform a constrained (with predefined categories) *Big Sort*, which could help them organize a "big picture" of concepts learned over a term.

The immediate value of such exercises is to identify gaps in knowledge that can be used to guide class discussion or review. Their value can be amplified if students are explicitly made aware of the organizational structures the sorts represent. That is, exercises should be "approached from the perspective of helping students ... become metacognitive about their learning so they can assess their own progress and continually identify and pursue new learning goals" [6, p. 50]. A natural follow-up to this study is to empirically investigate how card-sorting exercises can be used to improve students' ability to articulate and organize their knowledge of computer science.

5. ACKNOWLEDGMENTS

We are grateful to Sally Fincher, Marian Petre, Josh Tenenberg and the other participants of the *Bootstrapping Research in Computer Science Education* project for their support. This material is based in part upon work supported by the National Science Foundation under Grant No. DUE-0122560.

6. REFERENCES

[1] Adelson, B. Problem solving and the development of abstract categories in programming languages. *Memory and Cognition*, 9(4):422–433, 1981.

[2] Allwood, C. M. Novices on the computer: A review of the literature. *International Journal of Man-Machine Studies*, 25:633–658, 1986.

[3] Chi, M. T. et al., ed. *The nature of expertise*. Erlbaum, 1988.

[4] Davies, S. P., Gilmore, D. J., and Green, T. R. G. Are objects that important? The effects of expertise and familiarity on the classification of object-oriented code. *Human-Computer Interaction*, 10(2 & 3):227–248, 1995.

[5] Fossum, T. V., and Haller, S. M. Measuring Card Sort Complexity. CogSci 2004, Chicago IL, URL www.cogsci.northwestern.edu/cogsci2004/papers/paper411.pdf.

[6] National Research Council. *How People Learn: Brain, Mind, Experience, and School*. National Academy Press, 2000.

[7] Petre, M., Fincher, S., Tenenberg, J., et al "My criterion is: Is it a Boolean?": A card sort elicitation of students' knowledge of programming constructs. Technical report 1682, University of Kent, June 2003.

[8] Rugg, G., and McGeorge, P. The sorting techniques: A tutorial paper on card sorts, picture sorts, and item sorts. Expert Systems, 14(2):80-93, 1997.

[9] Stemler, S. An overview of content analysis. Practical Assessment, Research & Evaluation, 7(17), 2001.

An Address Translation Simulator

Steven Robbins
Department of Computer Science
University of Texas at San Antonio
srobbins@cs.utsa.edu

ABSTRACT

Virtual memory is a major topic in undergraduate operating systems courses. One aspect of virtual memory, address translation, is often covered in an abstract way. When examples are given, only a piece of the translation is done, using a small translation lookaside buffer or a small single-level page table. Since most students learn best by doing rather than watching, the topic is best understood by having students do realistic address translations. This is problematic since it involves lookup from several large tables of data which are difficult to fit on a piece of paper. The address translation simulator described here solves this problem by presenting the student with complete page tables in a way that allows simple navigation of these tables. The simulator can be used for both teaching and student evaluation.

Categories and Subject Descriptors

K.3 [**Computers & Education**]: Computer & Information Science Education—*Computer Science Education*

General Terms

Virtual memory, address translation

Keywords

operating systems

1. INTRODUCTION

Virtual memory and address translation are standard topics in an undergraduate operating systems course. Although address translation in modern computers is mostly done by hardware, the topic of address translation is usually taught in the undergraduate operating systems course because that is where virtual memory is typically taught. Operating systems courses that delve into the details of the operating system by having students write (or modify) an operating system are usually good at giving students hands-on experience with the details of operating system issues. Since it is primarily a hardware topic, address translation is an exception to this.

Although students learn best by doing rather than watching, most presentations of address translation are abstract and cover only the simplest of address translation problems, mainly because of the nature of address translation. Translation requires access to a large amount of data: a translation lookaside buffer and at least one page table. Since this information does not easily fit on a sheet of paper, instructors find it difficult to design problems that students can do. Also, hand manipulation of binary address strings up to 64 bits in length is prone to errors. Even a hexadecimal representation of a 64-bit address is daunting, and hexadecimal is often not suitable because the sizes of bit fields are not always multiples of 4.

This paper discusses a simulator that makes it simple (and fun) to manipulate address bit fields and allows students to practice address translation using a translation lookaside buffer (TLB) and single or 2-level page tables. The simulator can also be used for evaluation of student skills by keeping a log file in HTML format that can be displayed with a standard browser or printed. The simulator is written in Java and will run on any computer system having a Java runtime environment. It is available for download or can be run directly from the web without the need for any installation.

The address translation simulator is part of a suite of simulators that have been developed for the undergraduate operating system curriculum [5]. These simulators have a consistent look and feel so that students who have used one can easily master another.

2. ADDRESS TRANSLATION IN MODERN TEXTBOOKS

Topics in address translation that are typically addressed in modern operating systems textbooks [1, 2, 3, 6, 7, 8] include:

- partitions
- single-level page tables
- multiple-level page tables
- segmentation
- segmentation with paging
- inverted page tables

This paper concerns itself with address translation using a TLB with one and two level page tables. Experience has shown that students do not grasp this concept until they have done problems involving concrete examples. It is particularly difficult to produce problems of this type and some

SIGCSE'05 February 23-27, 2005, St. Louis, Missouri, USA

TLB

page	frame
5	9
3	7
2	4
6	3

page table

valid	frame
0	5
1	6
1	4
1	7
0	8
1	9
1	3
...	

Figure 1: A small TLB and the beginning of a page table.

textbooks do not even try. The exercises involving address translation in some books [2, 3, 6] deal only with questions concerning the location or number of bits in various fields of the virtual address or the size of page tables. Some books do not even have exercises on this topic [1] while others [7, 8] have exercises involving a small (6-16 entries) single-level page table. None of the standard operating systems textbooks have any exercises combining TLB lookup with page table lookup or using multilevel page tables.

It is useful to have students actually perform address translation in some simple cases. I have found that about half of the students in my undergraduate operating systems courses cannot do this without practice, indicating that they really do not understand the process. Address translation requires looking up an entry in a TLB and then possibly looking through one or more page tables. Just displaying a typical TLB requires a lot of space. A full page table will not easily fit on a piece of paper. For the past decade, I have been using a toy problem based on the TLB and page table shown in Figure 1. The page size is 256 bytes. I give my students a few addresses such as the ones below and ask them to determine the page number and the physical address or if a page fault occurs. I also combine this with an access time calculation.

a) 01010100010
b) 10001000101
c) 00110110100

While this type of problem is useful, it is still much too small to test understanding. A similar problem with a 2-level page table would be unmanageable on paper, even if only the page tables needed to do the problem are given. Since part of the problem is to determine which second-level page table to use, giving only the needed page tables defeats the purpose of the exercise. The Address Translation Simulator allows students to experiment with more realistic problems in address translation.

3. GOALS OF THE ADDRESS TRANSLATION SIMULATOR

The goals of the address translation simulator are twofold: practice and testing. In practice mode, help is available for each stage of the translation. In testing mode, help can also be available, but each action of the student is recorded. In either mode, the simulator displays a logical address along with the parameters of the system. Sample parameters are shown in Figure 2.

There are several levels of practice mode available depending on the skill level of the user. Help menus are available for

Page Table Levels	2
Page Size	4096
Level 2 Page Table Size	512
Virtual Address Bits	30
Physical Address Bits	23
TLB Entries	16
Page Table Width (bytes)	4

Figure 2: Parameters for the simulator

all objects displayed. At the lowest level of skill, a progress list like the one shown in Figure 3 shows the steps the user must take to complete the address translation. As steps are completed, a colored dot appears at the start of the item, indicating that it has been completed. Clicking on any of these items produces a dynamically generated help menu describing in detail what needs to be done. Two possible menus obtained by clicking on the first unchecked item in Figure 3 are shown in Figure 4. Since the menus are dynamically generated, the information shown depends on the current state of the address translation. The upper menu is used if the TLB has not yet been displayed. Clicking on the **do it!** line displays the TLB and changes the menu accordingly. The lower menu corresponds to the case in which the TLB has been displayed but the user has incorrectly determined the sizes of the page number and frame number fields. As the students become more skilled, the progress list and help menus can be removed, requiring the students to know which steps must be completed.

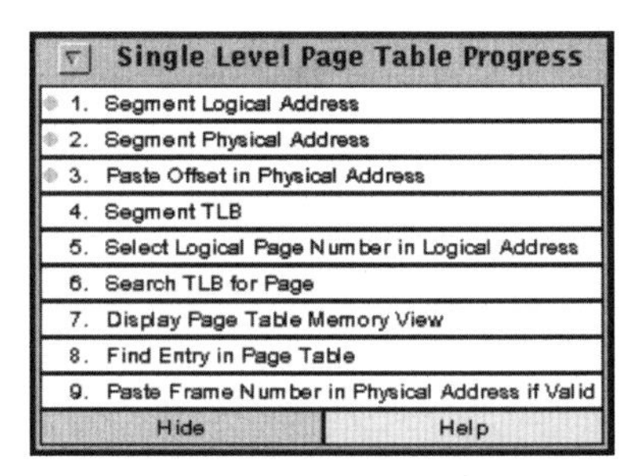

Figure 3: A progress list for a single-level page table.

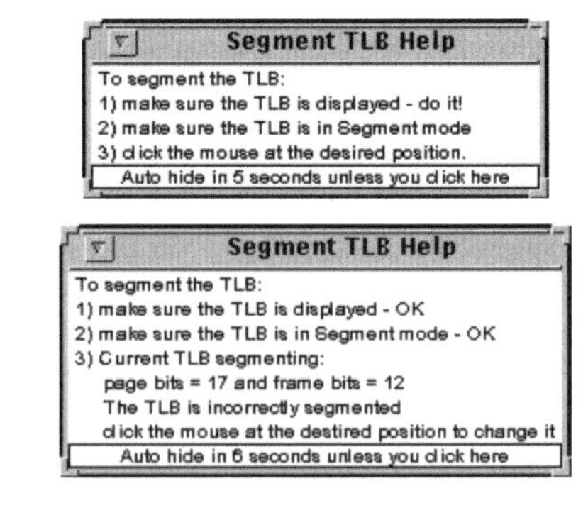

Figure 4: Two possible help menus for the 4th entry of Figure 3.

In testing mode there are several options as to how much help the student can get, starting with complete hints as to what to do next as in practice mode up to no indication as to correct procedure until the physical address is found. Testing mode can be set up with a fixed number of *lifelines* in which the user can ask for help a certain number of times.

In testing mode all actions of the user are logged, and written logs can be produced with varying degrees of detail. At the highest level of detail all actions by the user are reported. At the lowest level only the number of correct and incorrect answers are displayed.

The log can be automatically sent to the instructor (or to another account) by email so that the log cannot be modified by the student. Alternatively, the log can be saved to a file in HTML format so that it can be displayed by a browser or printed.

The simulator can be used to enhance and test the following skills necessary to the understanding of address translation:

Identifying the fields of a logical address
Identifying the fields of a physical address
Determining the sizes of the fields in the TLB
Looking up a page number in a TLB
Calculating the address of a page table entry
Looking up an entry in a page table
Using the valid bit

4. LOOK AND FEEL

The simulator has the same look and feel as other simulators developed for the operating systems curriculum [5]. Three new general purpose widgets have been added: a clipboard, a segmented string and a calculator.

Binary fields are manipulated in the simulator using a familiar copy and paste paradigm. Copying a string representing a binary number moves it into a clipboard. There is only one clipboard, but the contents are displayed in each widget that uses it. A Calculator widget, shown in Figure 5 allows binary numbers to be manipulated in simple ways: add, subtract, multiply, divide and shift. Numbers are manipulated by copying them into the clipboard (the **Select** operation), pasting them (**Paste**) into the **x** or **y** fields of the calculator, performing an operation, and copying the result back into the clipboard (**Select** again).

Calculator
Clipboard 110111100
Select Paste << >> valx: 111110000000000000 x+y x-y
Select Paste << >> valy: 11011110000 x*y x/y
Select Paste << >> valz: 111110001101111000 Base: 2
Hide Size: 30 Help

Figure 5: A calculator widget.

An example of a simple operation using the clipboard is the lookup of a page in the TLB. To do this, the user places the appropriate bit field of the logical address in the clipboard. The same clipboard is shared by the TLB, so pushing the **Lookup** button on the TLB locates the corresponding entry. This is explained in more detail in the next section.

Some operations such as the calculation of the memory address of page table entry require the calculator. The start address of the page table is put in the clipboard. The value will then be shown in the clipboard of the calculator (top line of Figure 5). Pushing the **Paste** button of the **x** value of the calculator (second line of Figure 5) sets the value of **x** in the calculator. Next, select the page number in the logical address and similarly paste it in the **y** field of the calculator. If the page table entries are 4 bytes each, shift the page number left twice by pushing the shift left button (<<) for the **y** value. The add button (**x+y**) puts the sum in the **z** value of the calculator, and the corresponding **Select** button puts the result in the clipboard, making it available to the memory module.

The **Help** button of the calculator displays general information about using the calculator. Depending on the level of help selected, it can display additional information when appropriate, such as *Do not forget to shift the page number to the left.*

5. SINGLE PAGE TABLE

In this section we describe using the address translation simulator in practice mode with a TLB and single-level page table. The user is presented with an address translation problem in a window like the one shown in Figure 6.

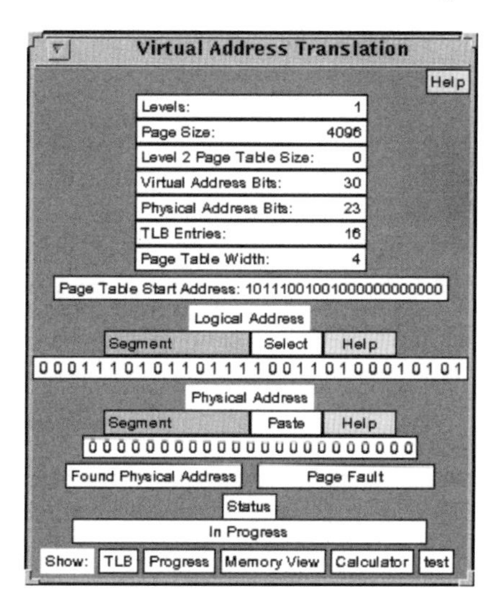

Figure 6: An address translation problem using a single-level page table.

The page size is 4K bytes, the virtual address is 30 bits, and the physical address is 23 bits. Page table entries contain 4 bytes and the TLB has 16 entries. The starting address of the page table is shown along with the logical address of 000111010110111100110100010101. Below the logical address is a place for the user to fill in the corresponding physical address. The buttons below the physical address are for the user to report either having found a physical address or that a page fault will occur. Below this is the status of the physical address determination. When one of the above buttons is pushed, it either reports that the corresponding value was correct or incorrect. At the bottom of the window are some buttons for popping up various windows.

The steps required to solve this problem are shown in Figure 3. Since a single-level page table is being used, the logical and physical addresses each have two parts, an offset and a page or frame number. The first step tested by the simulator is the determination of the boundary between the offset and the rest of the address. Both the Logical Address and Physical Address widgets are shown in Figure 6 and start in **Segment** mode. In this mode an address is segmented by clicking the mouse in the appropriate place on the address. If done correctly, the step is indicated in the progress list. The logical and physical addresses are displayed in a segmented string widget that allows the string shown (in this case a binary number) to be divided into parts. In this case there is only one dividing line, and if students make a mistake, they can just click again in another place.

Once the students have segmented the logical and physical addresses, they can change the logical address widget to **Select** mode and the physical address to **Paste** mode. Now, clicking on one of the fields of the logical address puts that field into the clipboard. Clicking on a field of the physical address pastes a copy of the clipboard into that field. Only two clicks are needed to copy the offset from the logical address to the physical address.

The next step is the lookup in the TLB shown in Figure 7. First the student segments the TLB into fields containing page and frame numbers. The process is similar to the segmenting of the logical or physical address, except that one click segments all of the entries in the TLB. After segmenting the TLB, students click on the **Lookup** button to look up the page number contained in the clipboard. If the simulator finds a corresponding entry, it highlights the frame number and puts the frame number in the clipboard. Alternatively, if students see a matching page number in the TLB, they can just click on the corresponding frame number after setting the TLB to be in **Select** mode. In either case, if the page is found in the TLB, students can put the corresponding frame in the physical address by clicking on the appropriate field in the physical address. This action pastes the frame address into the physical address from the clipboard.

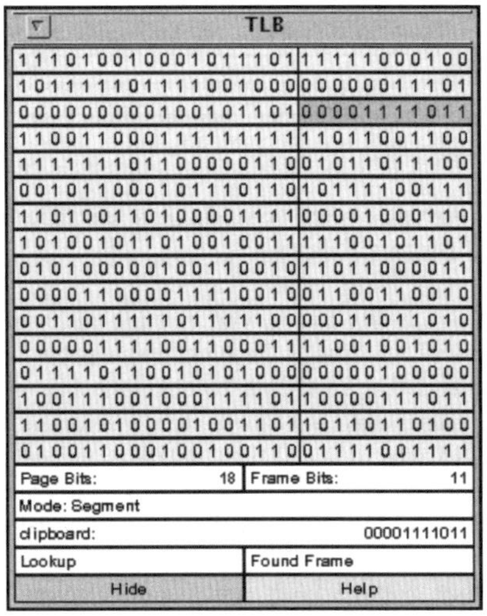

TLB

111010010001011101	11111000100
101111110111001000	00000011101
000000000100101101	00001111011
110011000111111111	11011001100
111111101100000110	01011011100
001011000101110110	10111100111
110100110100001111	00001000110
101001011010010011	11100101101
010100000100110010	11011000011
000011000011110010	01100110010
001101111101111100	00011011010
000001111001100011	11001001010
011110110010101000	00000100000
100111001000111101	10000111011
110010100001001101	10110110100
010011000100100110	01111001111

Page Bits: 18 | Frame Bits: 11
Mode: Segment
clipboard: 00001111011
Lookup | Found Frame
Hide | Help

Figure 7: The TLB after a successful lookup.

If the page is not in the TLB, students must examine the page table. The simulator provides several views of memory. One view is the page table view. For single-level page tables the simulator displays page table entries (with valid bit) for the entire page table as shown in Figure 8. When there is only one page table, students do not have to set the address of the start of the table. Students can either scroll down to the needed entry (tedious if the page table is large) or can put the entry number in the clipboard and click the **Entry** button on the memory display. A lookup is done by putting the page number into clipboard and clicking the **Entry** button.

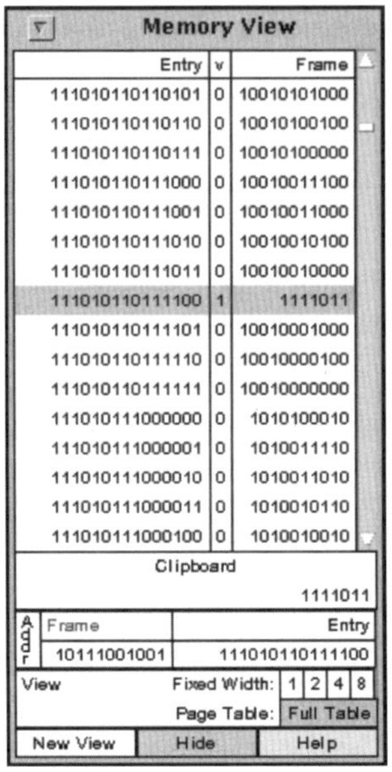

Memory View

Entry	v	Frame
11101011011010 1	0	10010101000
111010110110110	0	10010100100
111010110110111	0	10010100000
111010110111000	0	10010011100
111010110111001	0	10010011000
111010110111010	0	10010010100
111010110111011	0	10010010000
111010110111100	1	1111011
111010110111101	0	10010001000
111010110111110	0	10010000100
111010110111111	0	10010000000
111010111000000	0	1010100010
111010111000001	0	1010011110
111010111000010	0	1010011010
111010111000011	0	1010010110
111010111000100	0	1010010010

Clipboard
1111011

Addr	Frame	Entry
	10111001001	111010110111100

View   Fixed Width: 1 2 4 8
Page Table: Full Table
New View | Hide | Help

Figure 8: The single-level page table view of memory after a successful lookup.

6. TWO-LEVEL PAGE TABLE

There are several ways of implementing 2-level page tables. For this simulator, the top level page table entry contains a valid bit and the frame number of the start of the corresponding second-level page table. The second-level page tables contain valid bits and frame numbers. A page fault can occur at either level. The TLB entries, if used, contain the combined first and second-level page numbers and a frame number. If an entry is present in the TLB, the frame number is directly available and no page table lookups are needed. In this case the procedure is the same as for a single-level page table.

If the combined page number is not in the TLB, students must segment the logical address again so that it is divided into three parts. The high order field is the first-level page number. Students select this to use as an index into the first-level page table. If the corresponding entry is invalid, a page fault occurs. Otherwise a second-level page table lookup is necessary. Figure 9a shows the result of a successful first-level lookup. After the entry is found, the frame number of the start of the second-level page table is in the clipboard. Students now switch to the second-level page table view. In this view students need to indicate the starting frame number of the page table. Since the starting frame number is in the clipboard from the previous step, students should click the **Frame** button. After selecting the second-level page number from the logical address, do an **Entry** lookup in the second-level page table. Figure 9b shows the result of this. The frame number is 1111011.

The address translation simulator assumes that page tables start on frame boundaries, which is almost always the case. When multi-level page tables are used, page tables are often one frame in size. In the first-level page table of Figure 9a, as in the single page table case, the start address is fixed (there is only one such table per process) and each line gives a table entry labeled with the entry number. In the second-level page table shown in Figure 9b, the starting frame number of the page table must be set by the user. Students can do this either by putting the frame number in the clipboard and pushing the **Frame** button or by putting the address of the desired entry in the clipboard and pushing the **Addr** button. In either page table at most 16 entries are displayed on the screen and the students can scroll through the entire page table if they desire.

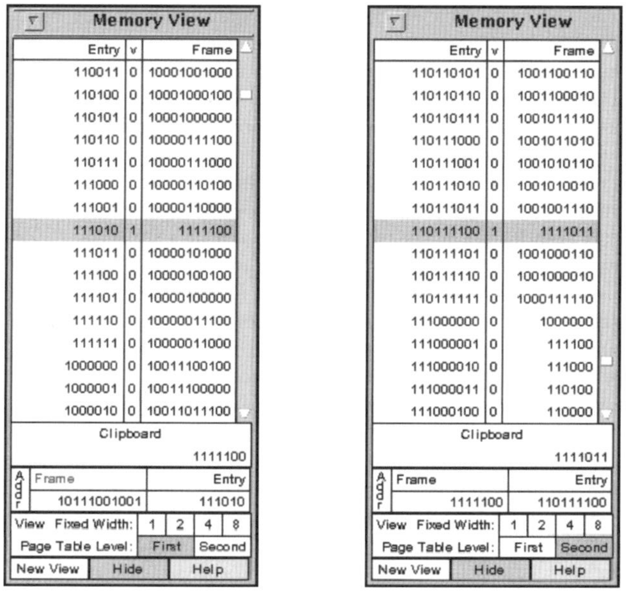

Memory View

Entry	v	Frame
110011	0	10001001000
110100	0	10001000100
110101	0	10001000000
110110	0	10000111100
110111	0	10000111000
111000	0	10000110100
111001	0	10000110000
111010	1	1111100
111011	0	10000101000
111100	0	10000100100
111101	0	10000100000
111110	0	10000011100
111111	0	10000011000
1000000	0	10011100100
1000001	0	10011100000
1000010	0	10011011100

Clipboard
1111100
Addr Frame: 10111001001 Entry: 111010
View Fixed Width: 1 2 4 8
Page Table Level: First Second
New View Hide Help

a)

Memory View

Entry	v	Frame
110110101	0	1001100110
110110110	0	1001100010
110110111	0	1001011110
110111000	0	1001011010
110111001	0	1001010110
110111010	0	1001010010
110111011	0	1001001110
110111100	1	1111011
110111101	0	1001000110
110111110	0	1001000010
110111111	0	1000111110
111000000	0	1000000
111000001	0	111100
111000010	0	111000
111000011	0	110100
111000100	0	110000

Clipboard
1111011
Addr Frame: 1111100 Entry: 110111100
View Fixed Width: 1 2 4 8
Page Table Level: First Second
New View Hide Help

b)

Figure 9: The first-level page table view of memory (left) after a successful lookup and the corresponding second-level page table (right).

Figures 8 and 9 show page table views of memory. In these views, data is arranged in blocks that correspond to the width of the page table and valid bits are shown. Students can also display a frame of physical memory in a more generic way. Figure 10 shows a frame of memory with a data width of 4 bytes. The valid bits are not available from this memory view. A separate valid bit view may be used to determine whether a given page number is valid. This separate view is more appropriate for those machines that store the valid bits in the MMU rather than in the page tables.

7. CONCLUSIONS

The address translation simulator can be used in three ways: for demonstration, for practice and for evaluation. Instructors can perform in-class demonstrations of how address translation is done. After students have seen the demonstration, they can use the simulator to practice performing address translations. The practice problems can be run with varying levels of help, from guiding the students at each step

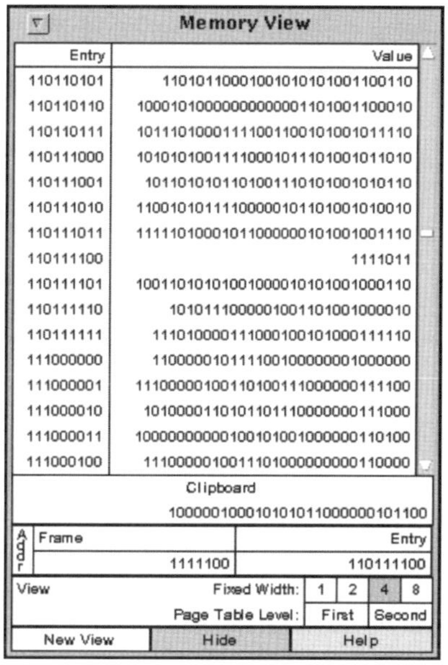

Memory View

Entry	Value
110110101	110101100010010101010100110011 0
110110110	10001010000000000001101001100010
110110111	10111010001111001100101001011110
110111000	10101010011110001011101001011010
110111001	1011010101101001110101001010110
110111010	11001010111100000101101001010010
110111011	11111010001011000000101001001110
110111100	1111011
110111101	10011010101001000010101001000110
110111110	1010111000001001101001000010
110111111	1110100001110001001010001111 10
111000000	110000010111100100000001000000
111000001	11100000100110100111000000111100
111000010	1010000110101101110000000111000
111000011	10000000000100101001000000110100
111000100	1110000010011101000000000110000

Clipboard
10000010001010101100000010110 0
Addr Frame: 1111100 Entry: 110111100
View Fixed Width: 1 2 4 8
Page Table Level: First Second
New View Hide Help

Figure 10: The view of memory arranged in 4-byte words.

to just providing hints if a student gets stuck. A user's manual is available on line.

Lastly, the simulator can be used for testing. The simulator can generate a log for the instructor showing in a settable detail how the student did. Usually, instructors only need to test for completion. That is, instructors should ignore student runs in which errors were made and just check to see that at least one run of each type was computed without error.

The simulator can be run directly from a browser [4] without the need of any installation. If customization is required, the simulator can be downloaded and installed on any host that has a modern Java virtual machine.

8. ACKNOWLEDGMENTS

This work has been supported by an NSF grant: *A Course in Experimental Techniques for Computer Science Majors: Proof of Concept*, DUE-0088769.

9. REFERENCES

[1] W. S. Davis and T. M. Rajkumar, *Operating Systems, A Systematic View,* Addison Wesley, 2005.

[2] H. M. Deitel, P. J. Deitel and D. R. Choffnes, *Operating Systems, Third Edition,* Prentice Hall, 2003.

[3] G. Nutt, *Operating Systems, Third Edition,* Addison-Wesley, 2003.

[4] S. Robbins, The Address Translation Simulator, 2004. Online. Internet. Available WWW: **http://vip.cs.utsa.edu/nsf/address/run/**

[5] S. Robbins, Simulators for teaching operating systems, 2003. Online. Internet. Available WWW: **http://vip.cs.utsa.edu/nsf/simulators**

[6] A. Silberschatz, P. B. Galvin and G. Gagne,, *Operating System Concepts, Sixth Edition,* John Wiley and Sons, Inc, 2002.

[7] W. Stallings, *Operating Systems, Fifth Edition,* Prentice Hall, 2004.

[8] A. Tanenbaum, *Modern Operating Systems, Second Edition,* Prentice Hall, 2001.

Experiences Teaching Operating Systems Using Virtual Platforms and Linux

Jason Nieh
Department of Computer Science
Columbia University
New York, NY 10027
nieh@cs.columbia.edu

Chris Vaill
Department of Computer Science
Columbia University
New York, NY 10027
cvaill@cs.columbia.edu

ABSTRACT

Operating system courses teach students much more when they provide hands-on kernel-level project experience with a real operating system. However, enabling a large class of students to do kernel development can be difficult. To address this problem, we created a virtual kernel development environment in which operating systems can be developed, debugged, and rebooted in a shared computer facility without affecting other users. Using virtual machines and remote display technology, our virtual kernel development laboratory enables even distance learning students at remote locations to participate in kernel development projects with on-campus students. We have successfully deployed and used our virtual kernel development environment together with the open-source Linux kernel to provide kernel-level project experiences for over nine hundred students in the introductory operating system course at Columbia University.

Categories and Subject Descriptors

D.4.0 [**Operating Systems**]: General; K.3.1 [**Computers and Education**]: Computer Uses in Education—*distance learning*; K.3.2 [**Computers and Education**]: Computer and Information Science Education—*computer science education*

General Terms

Design, Experimentation, Human Factors

Keywords

Operating systems, computer science education, virtualization, virtual machines, open-source software

1. INTRODUCTION

Programming projects are an important aspect of learning about operating systems. The hands-on experience is crucial for helping students to understand how the textbook concepts can be applied in practice. However, developing and administering programming projects that teach students about real-world operating system design and implementation is difficult for two important reasons.

First, unlike other application software which runs at user-level, operating system code runs in supervisor mode. To write or modify operating system code that runs in supervisor mode, students must be given root privileges to do many of the things required for kernel development such as installing a new kernel, rebooting, kernel testing and debugging, etc. In addition, the kernel development cycle of plan-implement-reboot-test-debug results in system downtime that necessitates exclusive access to a computer to avoid inconveniencing others. For a large introductory operating systems class, providing each student with a computer on which to run as root to do kernel development would be difficult to administer and prohibitively expensive.

Second, real production operating systems are large, complex pieces of software. The sheer size of these systems makes them difficult to understand and learn about. These operating systems are also not primarily designed as teaching tools, but instead to be used in commercial deployment. For example, such operating systems are already fully functional and do not have major missing subsystems that students can design and implement. These factors make it difficult to design projects for students that enable them to learn about interesting and important aspects of real-world operating system design.

To address these issues, we created a virtual kernel development environment in which operating systems can be developed, debugged, and rebooted in a shared computing lab environment without affecting other application users. Using virtual machines and remote display technology, our virtual kernel development laboratory enables even distance learning students at remote locations to participate in kernel development projects with local on-campus students. We have combined our virtual kernel development laboratory with a set of novel programming projects using the Linux kernel to provide real-world project experiences for students. These projects enable students to modify and replace substantial subsystems of Linux in a manner that provides many of the benefits of building new operating system subsystems from scratch. We leverage the benefits of the Linux open-source software base and widely available development tools to enable students to effectively manage the software complexity associated with a production operating system.

SIGCSE'05, February 23–27, 2005, St. Louis, Missouri, USA.

Both our virtual kernel development environment and programming projects build on production technologies that are widely used. Our virtual kernel development environments builds on virtual machines provided by VMware [9] and remote display mechanisms such as VNC [7]. Our programming projects are based on Linux. Building on production technologies enables us to leverage other large development efforts to support operating system education without the need to to maintain substantial pedagogical infrastructure on our own. We do not need to maintain our own simulators or pedagogical operating systems, which is difficult to do given the rapid pace of industry practice and the limited teaching resources available at most universities. Instead, our approach inherently keeps up and evolves as technology changes without requiring an in-house development effort.

We have deployed, refined, and used our virtual kernel development environment together with Linux kernel programming projects in teaching an introductory operating systems course at Columbia University. We were the first to use this approach for teaching operating systems [6], and have used it successfully over the last five years to teach over nine hundred students. These students range from sophomore undergraduates to doctoral students and include even distance learning students located halfway around the world. Our experiences using our virtual kernel development lab together with Linux demonstrate the utility of this approach for enhancing operating systems education by providing effective kernel-level project experiences for students.

This paper describes how we developed our approach to operating systems education and our experiences with it in the classroom. Section 2 discusses related work. Section 3 describes the development of our virtual kernel development environment. Section 4 describes the design of our Linux kernel programming projects. Section 5 discusses experiences using the virtual kernel development laboratory and the Linux kernel projects. Finally, we present some concluding remarks.

2. RELATED WORK

The two main approaches to providing programming experience in operating system courses can be loosely categorized as *user-level* or *kernel-level*. User-level projects require only developing code designed to run in unprivileged mode. Examples of such projects include writing modules for a user-level simulator such as Nachos [1], user-level threads programming, or systems programming with a production operating system such as Linux, Solaris or Windows XP. Operating systems courses with only user-level student projects are much more common because the projects are typically no more difficult to setup and administer than other user-level applications. While user-level projects do provide students with some hands-on experience with operating systems, they do not provide direct kernel-level development experience. As a result, user-level projects do not effectively address important issues such as bootstrapping, handling interrupts, the kernel-level development and debugging process, or understanding the kernel internals of a full-featured operating system.

Some operating system courses offer kernel-level programming projects. Kernel-level projects require writing or modifying code designed to run in supervisor mode. Kernel-level projects can provide a better pedagogical vehicle for learning about real-world operating system design and implementation. However, because of the complexity of production operating systems, such projects are typically based on a small pedagogical operating system like MINIX [8]. While MINIX can be setup and run on modest PC hardware, this would require providing every student with their own machine on which to do kernel development, which is impractical in most university settings and does not scale to large class sizes or supporting distance learning students effectively. Since pedagogical operating systems are small though, they can often be used with a machine simulator instead, such as Bochs [5]. One may even design a pedagogical operating system to be used only in a simulated environment [4]. At the same time, because pedagogical operating systems are smaller than production operating systems, developing code in one does not expose students to many of the real-world issues that arise in practice. Furthermore, because pedagogical operating systems are not used in practice, keeping them from becoming dated can require substantial effort and they may have more limited lifetimes due to changes in technology and operating system practice [4]. Examples of pedagogical operating systems that have become obsolete include Xinu [2] and TOY, which was originally developed by Brian Kernighan in 1973. In contrast, a production operating system such as UNIX predates both TOY and Xinu yet continues to be widely used today.

3. A VIRTUAL KERNEL DEVELOPMENT LABORATORY

To support kernel-level programming projects for students to learn about operating systems, what we would like to do is provide each student with effectively root access on a dedicated machine which the student can use to test kernel code and crash and reboot at will. However, we would like to do this without the expense and administrative difficulties of providing a dedicated physical machine for each student. Note that the key issue is testing and debugging kernel code, not writing kernel code. Many users can share the same machine to write and compile kernel code since that activity does not result in frequently crashing and rebooting a machine due to student programming errors.

Our solution was to use VMware [6, 9] virtual machine technology to create a virtual development platform that looks like a real machine but in fact is only a virtual one. We used VMware's Workstation product, a virtual machine monitor [3] for the x86 architecture. A virtual machine monitor is an additional layer of software between the hardware and the operating system that virtualizes all of the hardware resources of the machine to provide a virtual hardware execution environment called a *virtual machine* (VM). Multiple VMs can be used at the same time, and each VM provides isolation from the real hardware and other activities of the underlying system. Because it provides the illusion of standard PC hardware within a VM, VMware can be used to run multiple unmodified PC operating systems simultaneously on the same machine by running each operating system in its own VM. An operating system running as a user-level application on top of VMware is called a *guest OS*. The native operating system originally running on the real hardware is called the *host OS*. VMware provides a GUI as the visual interface to the VM which makes it look like a real computer from the moment the VM boots.

VMware is low-level enough to make a guest OS appear to be receiving hardware interrupts, such as timer interrupts, and behave as if it were the only operating system on the machine. At the same time it provides isolation so that a failure in or misbehaving of a guest OS does not affect other guest OSes or the underlying system. For instance, a guest OS crashing will not crash the underlying system. As opposed to a software simulator, much of the code running in a VM executes directly on the hardware without interpretation. Only privileged instructions are trapped and impose additional overhead. A key advantage to using a VM as opposed to a simulator is the performance improvement possible through direct execution of unprivileged instructions.

We designed our virtual kernel development platform to be used in a shared computer lab facility. As is typical at many universities, such a facility is generally not available to be dedicated as an operating systems lab. VMware enabled us to configure a guest OS as a kernel development environment for a group of students working together on a kernel programming project. We could give students root access to guest OSes running in VMs without compromising the security of the lab machines. Since faults that occur in running the guest OS are contained within its respective VM, students could crash and reboot their guest OSes without interfering with the operation of the host. Students debugging their kernel could thus work in a shared computer lab facility and share the same computer as other students without disrupting the work of the other students.

To properly isolate VMs and their guest OSes from the underlying host machine, there are a few important VMware disk and network configuration options that need to be set properly. VMware allows the guest OS to mount raw disk partitions or use virtual disks. A virtual disk in VMware is simply a large file in the host OS file system that is treated by the VM as a disk. We configured the VMs to use virtual disks so that disk problems caused by a misbehaving guest OS that a student installed would not affect the host disk partitions. The use of virtual disks made it much simpler for students to re-install a guest OS in the event of a disk crash in the VM. Since a virtual disk is just a regular file on the host OS file system, we just provided clean versions of the virtual disk so that students could use them to overwrite their own in case of unrecoverable disk crashes in the VM. Restricted access to the virtual disks was achieved using user groups. Each virtual disk was owned by a different user group and permissions were set on the virtual disks so that they could only be accessed by the teaching staff or members of the respective user group. Students were each assigned to one user group.

The VM network configuration options determine the type of networking available to the guest OS. The options are no networking, host-only networking, and bridged networking. The no networking option does not export a network interface to the VM. The host-only networking option exports a network interface to the VM that only allows communication between the VM and the host machine. Under bridged networking, the host OS acts as a bridge between the VM and the LAN, effectively allowing the VM to run as a real networked machine with an IP address. To allow students to access their files on the host machine, we configured the VMs for host-only networking. Using host-only networking, students were able to use ftp to backup their work onto their regular home directories, which alleviated much of the problems of a virtual disk crash while working on an assignment. We did not provide full bridged networking to the VMs because of the security implications of allowing students to have root access on a full networked machine on a LAN.

Because VMs are virtual and there is no need to provide additional hardware in creating additional VMs, we could easily provide multiple VMs for each student. By design, our virtual development platform provides two VMs per student group, one which serves as a primary test VM and the other which serves as a backup test VM. Because students frequently crash their VMs when running their kernel code, it is not uncommon for a student to corrupt the virtual disk associated with the VM. Just like a real machine with a bad disk a corrupted virtual disk prevents a VM from booting. By providing a backup test VM for each student, a student can continue working with the backup test VM while the primary test VM is repaired by copying over a clean virtual disk and thereby restoring the VM to its initial starting configuration. However, any modifications stored on the corrupted virtual disk are lost.

Because of the likelihood that a VM can lose its persistent storage state, VMs are only used for testing and debugging, not actual kernel code development. On each host machine, we allocate a separate disk partition for each student group to use. That partition includes space for the student group's VM virtual disk as well as a development area in which to do kernel builds and write kernel code. All code developed by the students resides on the host machine itself, not within the VM. As a result, VM disk crashes and reinstalls do not cause any loss of kernel development work by the students. This separation of the development environment from the testing and debugging environment is critical for preventing students from losing their work.

Perhaps the most important advantage of using a VMware VM for kernel debugging is that a VM can be powered on and off with the click of a mouse as opposed to a physical machine which requires that its power be physically turned on or off. Machine problems that can only be fixed by power cycling are therefore much more convenient to fix when the machine is a VM. Furthermore, power cycling a VM can be done by a student who is not physically co-located with the respective host machine without the need for any specialized power management hardware.

Since distance learning students are increasingly common and many commuter students often work from off-campus, we augmented our virtual machine platform with remote display functionality to support remote kernel development and debugging. While VMware Workstation runs like a normal X application under Linux that can displayed its GUI on another machine via X, any extended loss network connectivity between machines would cause the X application to terminate, the equivalent of powering off the VM without properly shutting down the guest OS. This could result a corrupted virtual disk. We instead used VNC [7] to provide remote access to a VM because it allows a VM to continue running even when its display on another machine is interrupted due to loss of network connectivity. Using VNC, students did not have to compete for console access to use VMware. VNC could be used by distance learning and off-campus students in industry who could not access VMware using X because of corporate firewalls. VNC also provides screen sharing technology so that users can see and control the exact same screen on multiple machines, which made it much easier for students to collaborate in their project. This remote display functionality enabled us to teach operating systems using the virtual kernel development environment to students at remote locations around the world.

4. LINUX KERNEL PROJECTS

Our virtual kernel development laboratory enabled us to provide kernel-level programming projects with either real production operating system or a pedagogical one. We chose to use Linux, a production operating system, for this purpose for eight important reasons. First, since Linux is used in the real world, it enables students to learn about real-world operating system issues that are difficult to glean from simplified pedagogical tools alone. Second, because Linux is open-source and widely used, there is a wealth of documentation and tools available to learn about the system. For example, there are a number of Linux source code navigators available that make it extremely easy to follow code through the system and search for various functions to understand how the system works. Third, there are many utilities such as kernel debuggers available for use with Linux which are of high quality because many people use them given the popularity of Linux. The same useful tools that are available to real kernel developers are available to students. Fourth, since Linux is immensely popular, students were more interested in doing the projects since they were working with something they felt was practical and relevant. Fifth, by applying operating system concepts to Linux, students gain skills in a real production system that can be immediately applied in the workforce after graduation. Sixth, by using a real production operating system, students gain experience dealing with a large, complex piece of software and understanding of how to read production code to figure out how a system works. Being able to manage software complexity is of tremendous importance in the real world given that operating system and other software developers spend much of their time working with others on large software projects, not developing isolated single-person systems. Seventh, as Linux evolves to keep up with the pace of innovation necessarily in production systems, it also naturally evolves as a pedagogical tool that enables students to learn in the context of modern operating system design trends. Finally, all of this support for Linux is provided without any need for us to maintain the operating system or any of its utilities, allowing us to focus limited teaching resources on teaching rather than a difficult in-house development effort that becomes outdated in less than a decade [4].

Because Linux is a production operating system, it does not naturally provide pedagogical opportunities by leaving out various operating system functionality for students to implement as is commonly done with pedagogical operating systems. However, many interesting aspects of important operating system subsystems can be designed in a variety of ways. Our approach to developing kernel programming projects for students is to create projects that allow them to add or replace existing operating system functionality. This provides two important advantages over the approach of leaving out parts of an operating system for students to fill in. First, the opportunities for projects are not fixed to the set of holes that were created at a given point in time which may not be the right set of projects for students to work on at a later time as technology evolves. Second, by replacing existing operating system functionality, students can learn by example from the design of existing code as written by real-world operating system developers.

Using this approach, we developed a number of kernel programming projects that can be used for an operating systems course to provide hands-on experience for students in understanding key operating system concepts. While discussing these projects in-depth here is not possible due to space constraints, we highlight five representative projects that we have developed corresponding to major operating system topics such as operating system structure, synchronization, scheduling, memory management, and file systems. Each assignment is designed to be done in two weeks or less by small student groups of two to three students.

As a first kernel project, we have students learn basic Linux kernel development and operating system structure. They first learn how to build a kernel and install and boot it. We then teach students how to apply patches and use a kernel debugger by downloading and applying the patch for the KDB kernel debugger for Linux. Students install the kernel with debugger support and walk through some simple debugging instructions. The final part of the assignment allows students to learn about operating system structure by adding a new system call that obtains some basic information about a process from its internal kernel structure. This assignment not only eases students into the sometimes intimidating process of kernel development, but it also illustrates the operation of a system call and its difference from a normal library function call.

As a second kernel project, we have students learn about synchronization through an assignment consisting of two parts. The first part involves a user-level POSIX-like threading implementation, similar to the GNU libc's *linuxthreads* library. Students are given an incomplete version of the library and a test-and-set function, and asked to implement mutexes, semaphores, and reader-writer locks. We start with synchronization in user-level to stress that the concepts are not specific to kernel programming, and in fact are necessary in any threaded programming environment. The second part involves implementing a new kernel synchronization primitive that allows multiple processes to block on an event until some other process signals the event. When the signal occurs, all processes blocking on the respective event are unblocked. This assignment exposes students to synchronization issues for both user-level thread libraries as well as kernel-level synchronization primitives.

As a third kernel project, we have students implement a new kernel CPU scheduler. This scheduler is called User-Weighted Round-Robin (UWRR), and operates by switching, round-robin, between users, giving each user's processes a full share of the CPU when it is that user's turn. This scheduler was chosen both because it is easy to understand and implement, and because students can easily see why such a scheduling policy might be useful. This is the first assignment that requires students to deal with a more substantial kernel subsystem but still only involves modification of a relatively modest number of lines of kernel code. The assignment builds on the previous two kernel programming projects as students need to write new system calls to control the UWRR scheduler and they need to be careful to protect kernel data structures with proper locking mechanisms.

As a fourth kernel project, we have students replace the stock Linux kernel's page replacement algorithm with the classic two-bit clock algorithm taught in operating system textbooks. This assignment requires students to learn in detail how the stock Linux kernel's page replacement mechanisms are implemented and to understand the Linux paging system in reasonable detail. Because the virtual memory subsystem of an operating system is often its most complex part, our focus in this assignment is less on building a new virtual memory subsystem and more on demonstrating working knowledge of the stock kernel's memory subsystem. Once students understand the stock kernel well, implementing the two-bit clock algorithm is fairly straightforward and requires less than thirty lines of new kernel code.

As a fifth Linux kernel project, we have students implement a new access control list mechanism for the commonly used Linux ext2 or ext3 file systems. This assignment requires students to gain practical understanding of how the virtual file system (VFS) infrastructure is designed, which is the key file system abstraction layer that every file system designer needs to understand. In addition to learning about file systems, the project also gives students an opportunity to learn a bit about security issues as well.

5. EXPERIENCES

The experiences of both students and instructors with this approach to teaching operating systems have been very positive. We have taught the course in this manner for five years running, and enrollment has consistently increased. When we started this program, operating systems was not a required course in the computer science undergraduate curriculum at Columbia, yet enrollment increased 50% in just the first year. Since we started this approach to the course, we have had to double the number of sections taught, and the course has gone from a once-per-year offering to a staple course offered every semester to accommodate the large course enrollments. In Fall 2004, the course had the highest enrollments of any Computer Science course at Columbia.

The popularity of the course is attributable to what students see as its relevance to popular and modern real-world operating systems. Although many students find kernel-level programming very difficult at first, they often say the work investment is warranted because they are learning a useful and applicable skill. We have received many comments from alumni who say the course turned out to be very useful to them after graduation. While our intent in teaching an introductory operating systems course is to convey understanding of general principles, and not to teach Linux kernel programming as such, our approach leverages the natural interest many students have in working with such a popular system. This has turned out to be a very powerful incentive—we have had students take the course as early as their sophomore year and perform extremely well. Not surprisingly, students are more willing to put forth extra effort to learn difficult material if they perceive that the material may be useful to them again after the course is over.

The virtual kernel development laboratory itself has also led to positive student experiences with the course. The virtual machine and VNC setup allows students to collaborate more easily without necessarily being physically in the lab. We have had students as far away as Japan take the course in a distance learning capacity. Our approach holds benefits for students that can work locally as well. The virtual machines reboot more quickly and are more easily recovered from kernel-bug catastrophes than physical machines are, leading to fewer frustrations for students.

The virtual kernel development laboratory has also been favorably received by machine administrators in our department's information technologies staff. Virtual hardware is not subject to failure and virtual machines for students mean that administrators do not need to deal with the difficulties attendant upon managing extra machines running potentially buggy kernels. If a student corrupts her virtual root disk, she merely gets a new copy—no administrator must reinstall a base operating system.

Our success with using virtual kernel development platforms and open-source Linux in teaching operating systems has prompted educators at a number of other universities to adopt our approach for their own operating system courses. These universities include both top-tier and smaller schools, demonstrating the viability of our approach for a variety of educational settings.

6. CONCLUSIONS

We have developed a virtual kernel development platform that enables kernel-level projects to be conducted by students in shared computer lab facilities without affecting other application users. We have used this platform together with kernel programming projects in the Linux kernel to teach students about important operating system concepts in conjunction with real-world operating system design issues. We have used this approach to teach a wide range of students, including sophomore undergraduates, doctoral students, and distance learning students located in distance countries around the world. Our experiences in deploying this approach to teach more than nine hundred students have demonstrated the effectiveness of learning about real production operating system kernel development using virtual platforms. We hope our experiences can continue to serve as a basis for improving operating system education at other institutions as well.

7. ACKNOWLEDGMENTS

This work was supported in part by an NSF CAREER Award and NSF ITR grant CNS-0426623.

8. REFERENCES

[1] W. Christopher, S. Proctor, and T. Anderson. The Nachos Instructional Operating System. http://http.cs.berkeley.edu/~tea/nachos/nachos.ps.

[2] D. E. Comer. *Operating Systems Design: The XINU Approach*. Prentice-Hall, 1984.

[3] R. P. Goldberg. Survey of Virtual Machine Research. *IEEE Computer*, 7(6):34–45, June 1974.

[4] D. A. Holland, A. T. Lim, and M. I. Seltzer. A New Instructional Operating System. In *Proceedings of the 33rd SIGCSE Technical Symposium on Computer Science Education*, pages 111–115, Feb. 2002.

[5] K. Lawton. Bochs. http://bochs.sourceforge.net/.

[6] J. Nieh and Özgür Can Leonard. Examining VMware. *Dr. Dobb's Journal*, Aug. 2000.

[7] T. Richardson, Q. Stafford-Fraser, K. R. Wood, and A. Hopper. Virtual Network Computing. *IEEE Internet Computing*, 2(1):33–38, 1998.

[8] A. Tanenbaum. A UNIX Clone with Source Code for Operating Systems Courses. *Operating Systems Review*, 21(1):20–29, Jan. 1987.

[9] VMware. http://www.vmware.com/.

Configuring a Multi-Course Lab for System-Level Projects

Joel C. Adams W. David Laverell
Department of Computer Science
Calvin College
Grand Rapids, MI 49546
1-616-526-8562
{adams, lave}@calvin.edu

ABSTRACT
Having students modify an actual operating system kernel or network protocol stack opens their eyes to what is going on "beneath the hood" of a computer. However student modifications to a system may result in an unstable computer. Because of this, giving students such experience has in the past required a lab and/or computers dedicated to the students in the system-level course, and computer science departments without such dedicated facilities have been unable to provide their students with system-level experience. In this paper, we present two ways of giving students system-level experience in a non-dedicated lab; one using commercial software (VMWare), and another using open-source freeware (User Mode Linux Kernel).

Categories and Subject Descriptors
K.3 [**Computers & Education**]: Computer & Information Science Education – *Computer Science Education.*

General Terms
Management, Design, Reliability, Experimentation,

Keywords
Laboratories, Operating Systems, Networking, User Mode Linux Kernel, VMWare.

1. INTRODUCTION
Most laboratory and programming projects are intended to provide students with a concrete, hands-on experience to help them better understand abstract concept(s). In computer science courses where students are studying system-level concepts, it may be desirable to give students system-level experiences, such as requiring them to modify a real kernel in an *Operating Systems* course [8], the actual protocol-stack in a *Computer Networking* course [9], and so on. Because students must have access to the system's source code, projects using a real kernel or stack are limited to laboratories that use an open-source system, such as Linux, FreeBSD, OpenBSD, etc.

A student-modified system tends to be unstable until the student successfully completes their project. Since it is inconsiderate to subject students from other courses to such instability, system-level projects have in the past required a dedicated computing laboratory, separate from other general-purpose laboratories [2][5]. Because of this, computer science departments with a single laboratory have often used hardware emulators [3] that provide less authentic experiences.

Even at institutions with separate, dedicated laboratories for systems courses, the following issues must be addressed:

1. *The instability of a student-modified system makes that system unusable by anyone else.* Two mechanisms for resolving this problem include: (i) assign each student their own machine and system to modify; or (ii) have multiple students share a specific machine, whose disk contains a separate, bootable partition for each student assigned to it. Both of these solutions require a student to always use the same machine.
2. *If the number of students N exceeds the number of available machines M, then an instructor must allocate the M machines among the N students.* Common ways to resolve this issue include: (i) having multiple students use the same machine, or (ii) having students work in groups of size N/M. (If N » M, then multiple *groups* may have to use the same machine.)
3. *If a laboratory configuration requires each student (or group) to use a specific machine for their project, then students (or groups) may have to contend with one another for that machine.* A common mechanism for resolving this problem is a *reservation system*, in which students (or groups) are required to sign up for a particular time-slot during which they will have sole access to their machine.
4. *If a laboratory configuration requires each student (or group) to use a specific machine for their project, then a student (or group) will be unable to work on their project while their machine is in use by another student (or group), even if other machines are open.* The only obvious means of resolving this problem is to not require each student (or group) to use a particular machine, but doing so creates a conflict with the solutions for issue 1 above.

In a nutshell, the problem is this: to limit the potential instability of student-modified systems (or the abuse of super-user privileges), students doing system-level projects have in the past been required to work on a particular machine. However most departments have insufficient resources to provide each student with their own machine, making machine-sharing a necessity. As a result, students lose flexibility as to *when* they may work. This is especially inefficient if other machines are sitting idle.

In this paper, we present a solution to all of these problems. Our solution can be used in either a general-purpose lab or a dedicated lab, making it applicable at virtually any institution. As such, it makes system-level projects possible at institutions where they were impractical in the past. It also makes such projects easier to manage at other institutions.

2. BACKGROUND

The recent development of software like *VMWare* [10] creates new possibilities for resolving the four issues listed in Section 1. VMWare provides an x86-emulating *virtual machine* that allows a user to run another operating system "on top of" the machine's real operating system, as shown in Figure 1:

"Top" level OS (Windows or Linux)
VMWare (x86 virtual machine)
"Bottom" level OS (Windows or Linux)
Hardware (x86 actual machine)

Figure 1. VMWare

VMWare works by allowing a user to set up one or more *virtual disks*. Each virtual disk can contain its own operating system, that may be the same as or different from the "bottom" level operating system. To run VMWare, one simply specifies a virtual disk; the virtual machine then begins running and loads whatever operating system (or boot loader) it finds on that virtual disk. If for some reason the "top" level system should lock up (e.g., because of a student's modifications), the "bottom" level OS is safely isolated from the problem. Recovery from a disaster as thus as simple as restarting VMWare – the real "bottom" level OS need not be rebooted.

When it starts, VMWare loads the specified virtual disk into a RAM-disk which it treats as its boot disk. When VMWare is shut down, if its RAM-disk has been modified, it asks the user if they want to (i) save the changes, (ii) discard the changes, or (iii) defer the decision. Thanks to this mechanism, any changes one makes to the system remain local to the RAM-disk, until the user saves them to the virtual disk. This allows a user to thoroughly test any modifications they've made to their system before they actually alter their virtual disk.

In [7], Jason Nieh describes a dedicated operating systems laboratory in which each machine was equipped with VMWare. ([6] describes a similar networking laboratory.) While Nieh's laboratory resolved issues 1, 2, and 3, it failed to address issue 4; student-groups had to use particular machines, and if their machine was in use by another group, they were forced to wait even if other machines were vacant.

This paper describes our *Systems Lab*, a laboratory that also uses VMWare to resolve issue 1. However our laboratory uses an alternative approach to resolve issues 2 and 3, that also resolves issue 4. In addition, our approach does not require a dedicated laboratory; it can be used in either a dedicated- or a shared-lab environment.

3. VMWARE + FAST ETHERNET + NFS

To resolve issues 1-4, we designed a shared *Systems Lab* in which we could assign system-level projects in our *Operating Systems* and *Computer Networking* courses. For lab machines, we purchased 25 off-lease 3-year-old PCs. Each PC had a 450-MHz Pentium-II CPU, 128 MB RAM (which we upgraded to 256MB), a 9 GB hard disk, and a 10-100Mbps Ethernet card.

For a network, we connected machines into "workgroups" of 3 via a 5-port 100 Mbps Ethernet switch, each of which was then connected to a central 24-port switch (for future expansion). By configuring a 25th PC as both a firewall and an HTTP proxy server, and using it as the connection between our switch and our campus network, we were able to isolate our lab from the outside world, but still provide each PC with web-access.

Our *Operating Systems* and *Computer Networking* courses both meet during the same semester, and the enrollment in each is greater than the number of machines in our lab. To deal with the resulting congestion, we felt it was imperative to resolve all four of the issues described in Section 1, so that each student or group could work at any open machine.

To resolve issue 1, we installed VMWare on each machine, and used it to run Linux on top of Linux, as shown in Figure 2:

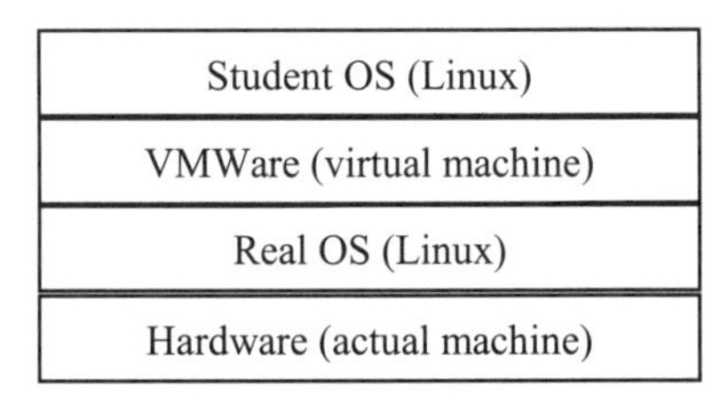

Figure 2. Linux on top of Linux via VMWare

For the "top" level OS, we prepared a 2 GB VMWare virtual disk containing a full Linux installation. This virtual disk was saved in a public directory, with its permissions set to read-only.

To resolve issues 2, 3, and 4, we added a 26th PC as a file server, plus a RAID array containing four 120GB disks. Configured as a RAID-5 device, this array provides 360GB of usable disk space – enough to give 180 students 2 GB of disk space each.

To provide students with home directories, we created a Linux `/home` partition on this RAID array, and created student home directories within `/home`. Each lab PC was configured to mount `/home` via the Network File System (NFS) service, and student accounts were managed via the Network Information Service (NIS) from the file server. The resulting configuration is shown in Figure 3, below.

With home directories in place, students were instructed to copy the read-only virtual disk from its public directory to their home directories, and were given the root password to the OS on the virtual disk. (This password was different from that of the "bottom" level OS). Since every PC in the lab accessed their account information via NIS and mounted `/home` via NFS, students could now login to any PC in the lab, and then boot VMWare using their own virtual disk. From any PC in the lab, they could modify their kernel, recompile its source code, save changes, and so on, without affecting anyone else's virtual disk or the "bottom" level OS.

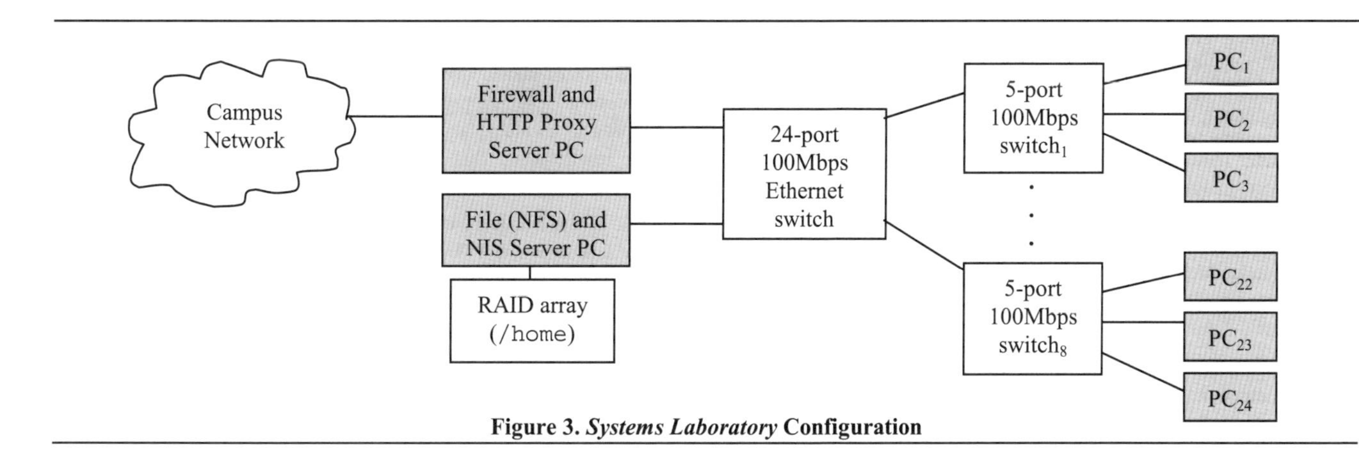

Figure 3. ***Systems Laboratory*** **Configuration**

It required some time and effort to get all of this working properly. However, this approach has let us realize these benefits:

1. It resolves issue 1 by allowing students to work on system-level projects. Students using the lab may be in the same or in different courses. Different virtual disks can be created for different courses, as necessary or appropriate.
2. It resolves issues 2, 3, and 4 in the same way as any other lab – students may work at any open machine.
3. It lets instructors assign group or individual projects as pedagogically appropriate, rather than as a work-around necessitated by limited computing resources.
4. It lets students test the changes they make to their system before they save those changes to their virtual disks (or defer making the decision).
5. If students manage to irreparably mangle their virtual disks, it lets them easily start over by recopying the original read-only virtual disk from the public directory into their home directory.
6. Aside from removing the student accounts, no special action is required to restage the machines, either at the end of the semester, or the next time the course is offered, saving time in the long run.
7. Although we used this approach in a separate Systems Lab, there is nothing that prevents this approach from being used in a general-access lab. This solution can thus be used at departments or institutions that have a single computing laboratory.

Because of these benefits, we believe the time spent to get this arrangement working was time well spent.

4. OBSERVATIONS

After having used the Systems Lab in our curriculum, we have the following observations:

- Students enjoyed being able to "get down and dirty" with the low-level system source code. Many expressed amazement at the ugly *spaghetti code* (i.e., extensive use of C's `goto`) they encountered in the Linux kernel.
- Students appreciated VMWare's permitting them to test out their system modifications before committing them to their virtual disks. Just two *Operating Systems* students (out of roughly 30) mangled their hard disks by neglecting to use this feature. All these students had to do was recopy the original read-only virtual disk from the public directory into their home directory, and they could work again.
- Students rose to the challenge of doing system-level projects that no previous class had been assigned. Having to wrestle through issues with which older students could not help created a certain *esprit de corps* in the course.
- Our 100 Mbps (fast) Ethernet was fast enough to provide adequate performance. VMWare could take a few seconds to start up, as it accessed a virtual disk across the network via NFS. However once it was running, very little speed difference was discernable between it and the local machine.
- If many students started VMWare simultaneously, our PC file server could bog down under the load of downloading so many virtual disks at the same time. To remedy this, we have since replaced our PC file server with a dual 2.4GHz Xeon multiprocessor, which has solved the problem.
- Compiling the 2.2 Linux kernel required about 10 minutes on our 450MHz Pentium-II CPUs. This meant students could no longer use the compiler as a substitute for careful design, coding, and debugging, as some were in the habit of doing. For most students, this was a new experience and a revelation. It was also the biggest source of student complaints. To compile the 2.4 kernel in a similar length of time, we have recently upgraded to 1GHz Pentium-IIIs.
- Students from different system-level courses (*Operating Systems* vs. *Computer Networking*) used the lab simultaneously without interfering with one another. In the second semester, students in two different system-level courses (*Computer Security* vs. *Network Administration*) used the lab without interfering with one another.
- Though the Systems Lab is a dedicated lab, this approach could be used in *any* lab shared by multiple courses. We are presently considering adding it to our general-access labs to provide greater flexibility in where students work.

5. USE IN OTHER COURSES

Our *Operating Systems* course used the Systems Lab for modified (updated) versions of some of the assignments found in [8]. Other courses and activities using the lab include:

- *Computer Networking*, which used the lab for exercises in TCP/IP socket programming, packet sniffing, protocol study, and so on. This course met concurrently with our *Operating Systems* course during the fall semester.
- *Computer Security*, which used the lab for exercises in password breaking, attack methodologies, intrusion detection, and so on. VMWare also allows the creation of a *virtual honeypot* [1] – a honeypot installed on a "top" level OS – that completely hides the "bottom" level OS from an intruder, allowing the "bottom" level OS to surreptitiously monitor the intruder's behavior without being detected.
- *Network Administration*, which used the lab for network administration exercises including configuration of network services, routers, firewalls; network analysis; and so on. This course met concurrently with our *Computer Security* course during the spring semester.

Each course is an upper level elective in our curriculum.

6. BUDGET

Table 1 (below) presents the cost of building our lab:

Table 1. Systems Lab Expenses

Item	Qty.	Unit Cost	Total Cost
3-Year-Old Used PCs	26	$150	$3,900
128MB Memory Upgrades	26	$25	$ 650
VMWare Licenses	25	$113	$2,825
VMWare Support	25	$24	$ 600
5-port Fast Ethernet Switch	8	$40	$ 320
24-port Fast Ethernet Switch	1	$800	$ 800
RAID Array (Promise RM8000)	1	$3415	$3,415
Total			**$12,510**

Our original 3-year-old PCs were 450 MHz Pentium-IIs. As mentioned above, we have since replaced them with (3-year-old) 1 GHz Pentium-III machines, at the cost shown in Table 1.

We could have either purchased a smaller central switch (e.g., 16-port), or purchased a larger central switch (e.g., 32-port) and eliminated the eight 5-port switches. We chose the configuration above for its flexibility and expandability.

Some of these prices have already decreased. However these prices should provide an approximate cost for building a laboratory with capabilities similar to (or better than) ours.

In addition to the items in Table 1, we purchased additional networking hardware specifically for our *Computer Networks, Computer Security,* and *Network Administration* courses, including a hub and router for each "work group", cable tray, patch cables, and so on. Since these are not directly required to give system-level projects, we have omitted their cost here.

7. USER MODE LINUX KERNEL

At the risk of stating the obvious, VMWare is not inexpensive – its licenses and support account for more than 27% of the expenses in Table 1, and push its total cost above $10,000. For many institutions, this extra expense may be prohibitive and prevent a budget officer from approving funds for a lab.

Thankfully, there is a freeware alternative to VMWare called **User Mode Linux Kernel (UMLK)** [4]. UMLK allows a user to run a Linux kernel at the user level. As such, it provides a way to give students a system-level programming experience, and since it is free, it can significantly reduce the cost of doing so (compared to VMWare). We hope to someday read a SIGCSE paper reporting on the use of UMLK in assigning system-level projects.

Where VMWare is an x86 hardware emulator (i.e., a virtual machine) that boots from a virtual disk, UMLK is a kernel with its own file system that runs directly on top of another Linux kernel, as shown in Figure 4:

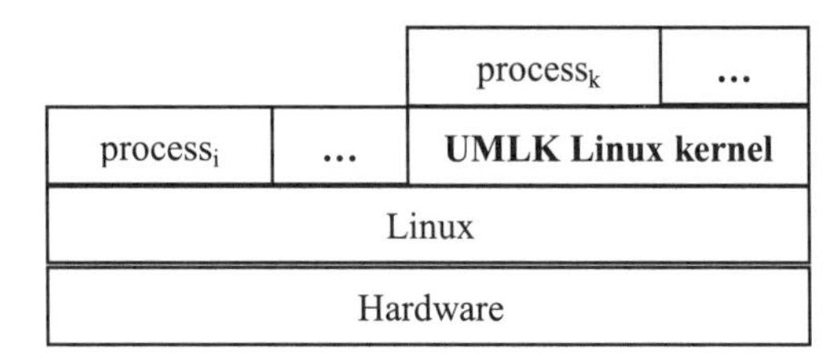

Figure 4. UMLK Structure

Because of these differences, UMLK is not quite as flexible or full-featured as VMWare. At present:

- UMLK runs only Linux on top of Linux – neither the "top" nor the "bottom" level operating system can currently be any other OS. This may limit its applicability at some institutions.
- Where VMWare allows you to install any x86-based OS on your virtual disk, UMLK runs whatever Linux kernel is installed in its file system. Different kernels can be run at different times in UMLK, but changing the kernel requires that the new kernel be (re)installed into the file system. By contrast, switching kernels in VMWare is simply a matter of booting from a different virtual disk on which the new kernel has been installed – one can easily revert to a previous kernel without having to reinstall it.
- Where VMWare allows a user to test system modifications before committing them to their virtual disk, UMLK users must commit such modifications to their UMLK file system before testing. One might argue that if students have never been "spoiled" by using VMWare, they will never know what they are missing. However the absence of this mechanism significantly increases the cost of helping a student recover from a catastrophic mistake, since a new kernel must be reinstalled on their file system to recover from such an error.

UMLK thus provides a viable alternative approach for giving system-level projects in a (shared or dedicated) lab setting. It may be attractive at institutions with existing laboratories running Linux, or who are willing to add a dual-boot option in a laboratory running Windows. Compared to VMWare, it trades off some convenience and flexibility for expense.

8. CONCLUSIONS

The commercial product VMWare provides a robust, flexible, and convenient means of building an environment in which students can work on system-level projects. By isolating the system the student is working on from the operating system running on the actual hardware, VMWare permits a student to safely modify their "top" level system, without danger of the "bottom" level system being compromised and rendered unstable. VMWare also allows students to test changes they've made to their systems before permanently committing those changes. VMWare thus provides a convenient tool by which students can work on authentic system-level projects, either in a dedicated systems lab, or in a general-purpose computer lab.

For institutions seeking a less expensive solution, the non-commercial product User Mode Linux Kernel provides a viable alternate means of providing students with an authentic system-level programming experience, though at the price of some features and flexibility available in VMWare.

For institutions where the general-purpose lab is already heavily utilized, we have demonstrated how to build a separate, dedicated Systems Lab for use in operating systems, networking, security, and other "low level" courses. By having students access their VMWare virtual disks via NFS over a fast network from a centralized file server, a student can work on a system-level project from any open machine, and students in different "low level" courses can share the same laboratory with a minimal level of conflict.

We hope that our experience will provide a useful model for other institutions seeking to build their own facilities.

9. REFERENCES

[1] R. Barnet, Monitoring VMWare Honeypots, http://honeypots.sourceforge.net/monitoring_vmware_honeypots.html

[2] M. Claypool, D. Finkel, C. Wills, An Open Source Laboratory for Operating Systems Projects, *Proceedings of 6th Annual Conference on Innovation and Technology in Computer Science Education (ITiCSE),* June 2001, pp. 145-148.

[3] J. Dickinson, Operating Systems Projects Built on a Simple Hardware Simulator, *Proceedings of the 31st SIGCSE Technical Symposium*, March 2000, pp. 320-324.

[4] J. Dike, The User Mode Linux Kernel Home Page, http://user-mode-linux.sourceforge.net/.

[5] J. Hill, C. Carver, J. Humphries, and U. Pooch, Using an Isolated Network Laboratory to Teach Advanced Networks and Security, *Proceedings of the 32nd SIGCSE Technical Symposium*, February 2001, pp. 36-40.

[6] B. Kneale, and I. Box, A Virtual Learning Environment for Real-World Networking, *Proceedings of the Informing Science + IT Education (InSITE) Conference*, June 2003, pp. 671-683.

[7] J. Nieh and O. Leonard, Examining VMWare, *Dr. Dobb's Journal*, August 2000, pp. 70-76.

[8] G. Nutt, *Kernel Projects for Linux*, Addison Wesley, 2001.

[9] B. Richards, Teaching Network Protocols Through Debugging, *Proceedings of the 31st SIGCSE Technical Symposium*, March 2000, pp. 256-260.

[10] VMWare, http://www.vmware.com/.

We've Been Working on the Railroad: A Laboratory for Real-Time Embedded Systems

John W. McCormick
University of Northern Iowa
Computer Science Department
Cedar Falls, IA 50614-0507
mccormick@cs.uni.edu

ABSTRACT

This paper describes a laboratory used to support a junior level course in real-time embedded software development. Thirteen years of data comparing programming languages for a real-time systems course are presented. Funding provided by the Maytag Corporation and Rockwell-Collins makes it possible to provide other schools with low cost electronics necessary to duplicate this laboratory with a minimum of effort.

Categories and Subject Descriptors

C.3 [**Special-Purpose And Application-Based Systems**] – *real-time and embedded systems, process control systems*

D.2.2 [**Software Engineering**]: Design Tools and Techniques – *state diagrams, object-oriented design methods*

D.3.3 [**Programming Languages**]: Language Contructs and Features – *concurrent programming, classes and objects.*

K.3.2 [**Computers and Education**]: Computer and Information Science Education –*computer science education.*

General Terms

Design, Languages, Reliability, Experimentation, Verification

Keywords

Laboratory, Project, Curriculum, Real-Time, Embedded, Ada, C

1. INTRODUCTION

Over 99% of all microprocessors manufactured today are used in embedded systems. These systems are distinguished by their interaction with unique hardware, concurrent measurement and control of analog environmental variables, predictable response times, reliability, and safety. Unfortunately, very few undergraduate computer science programs address the special issues involved in the specification, design, implementation, testing, or verification of embedded software. Clifton [4] reports that in the previous ten years only four papers have been presented at SIGCSE on this topic. This paper shows how one course and laboratory can fill the embedded systems gap in computer science curriculums. I emphasize the hardware aspects of the laboratory for a software savvy audience.

SIGCSE'05, February 23–27, 2005, St. Louis, Missouri, USA.

An introductory undergraduate course in real-time embedded software development should acquaint students with the fundamental scientific issues of real-time computing [3] and practical skills in embedded software development. While the theoretical issues can be covered without a laboratory, real-time embedded software development skills require the experiences that a laboratory provides. A major problem is finding equipment suitable for teaching these skills.

Simulators are commonly used to give students experience with real-time embedded systems programming [1]. Typically these simulators do not provide many of the frustrating problems associated with physical systems. In most embedded systems projects, hardware and software are developed in parallel. Gathering evidence for the determination of whether a fault is in the hardware or the software is an important skill for the embedded systems programmer. Lack of experience with real systems is a prime reason cited by engineers who would exclude computer science graduates from their development teams.

For the past 21 years I have used a computer controlled model railroad in my real-time embedded systems course. Some of the advantages of using a model railroad in the laboratory are:

- Model railroad equipment is readily available and priced well below typical laboratory equipment.
- Model railroads provide a wealth of problems from both the discrete and continuous real-time domains.
- Undergraduate computer science students easily understand the electronics and physics.
- Students are highly enthusiastic about writing software to control a model train layout.

With the support of the Maytag Corporation and Rockwell-Collins, I have designed and implemented an affordable real-time embedded systems laboratory that other institutions can easily duplicate. The cost of the interface electronics for a small layout is about $1,200. Interface costs for my large layout were $2,900.

2. The Real-Time Embedded Systems Course

The University of Northern Iowa is a mid-size school whose programs are founded on a strong liberal arts curriculum. The Computer Science Department offers traditional degree programs based on CC-2001 [7]. The real-time embedded systems course is one of several project courses in our curriculum. Each project course is centered on a large software project requiring knowledge from core computer science courses. The prerequisites for the real-time embedded systems course are CS1, CS2, CS3, discrete mathematics, computer organization, and software engineering. Over half of the students enrolled in the course have also completed a course in operating systems.

A major goal of the course is the preparation of software engineers capable of working as members of an interdisciplinary development team. Many topics are covered at a survey level. For example, students in the course learn just enough of the basic concepts of control theory to be able to communicate with a control engineer and to implement a simple control algorithm. Graduates of the course have gone on to work in a wide range of domains including avionics, communications, manufacturing, medical instrumentation, and railroads. Feedback from graduates and their employers has been extraordinarily positive.

2.1 Laboratory Assignments

The four credit-hour course has three 50-minute lectures and a two-hour laboratory session each week. The early laboratory sessions are used to review (or learn) and practice with the features of the implementation language that are important for the completion of their project. These features include data types and structures, control structures, modules and packages, input/output, classes and objects, concurrent programming, and exceptions. Later laboratory sessions are devoted to developing code that will be directly applied to their projects, including polling and interrupt-based device drivers and the implementation of simple railroad classes such as diesel horns and turnouts (switches).

2.2 Course Project

Students work in teams of three or four to complete a substantial project. Each team writes all the code necessary (from low level device drivers to high level control logic) to produce a bootable image. Teams are free to formulate their own projects. Minimum project requirements include:

- Running multiple trains.
- At least one train controlled by a human engineer.
- No train collisions.
- Detecting and recovering from hardware failures, such as turnouts, sensors, lost cars, and devious professors.

Over the years, train races, train wars, and dynamic scheduling problems have been the most popular project themes. Many teams also implement additional safety features such as throttle limits and protection for locomotive transmissions.

Deliverables used in grading the project include:

- A one-page system concept document.
- A detailed (10 to 20 pages) user's manual.
- Object modeling documents (based on [10]).
  - Class diagrams.
  - Dynamic model (state) diagrams.
  - Functional model diagrams.
  - Data dictionary.
- Class specifications.
- Unit (class) test plans.
- Implementation code.
- Unit test programs.
- Self and team assessments.

These deliverables are used as milestones throughout the course to help ensure that students keep up with the demanding schedule necessary to complete the project. One of my first tasks is to work with teams on their systems concept document to reduce overly optimistic proposals into ones that can be completed. Students are aware of the high completion rates of past teams (presented later in this paper) so they understand that they can complete the project by the end of the semester.

Students keep an engineering notebook [11] with a detailed record of their individual and team activities. They maintain a separate time log that I review and sign once a week.

Student teams do exhaustive module testing. All test plans are approved and test results certified by a member of the team selected as the team's test manager. Integration testing is based on meeting the requirements of their user's manual.

3. The Laboratory

My first model railroad laboratory was constructed in 1983. Construction of the new railroad layout funded by Maytag and Rockwell-Collins was completed in 2001. The track plan of this model railroad is shown in the Appendix.

3.1 Model Railroad Equipment

The model railroad is HO scale (1:87). While smaller scales would permit more equipment in the laboratory, they are more expensive, more difficult to maintain, and less readily available.

To run multiple trains on their layouts, model railroaders traditionally divide the track into electrically isolated sections called *blocks*. Modelers use many toggle and rotary switches to connect a particular power supply (called a *cab*) to a group of track blocks beneath each train. In my layout, the computer controls the voltage and polarity applied to each of 40 blocks. Today's model railroad enthusiasts often use more modern direct digital control of locomotives to solve the problem of multiple train control. I have rejected this approach as it provides fewer software development problems and less experience with analog electronics.

Turnouts (commonly called switches) are controlled by gear- and screw-driven switch machines. The software can determine and modify the state of each of the 26 turnouts on my layout.

In order to do closed loop control, it is necessary to obtain feedback on the process being controlled. For the model train this feedback consists of the trains' locations as a function of time. On my layout, this information is obtained from 51 Hall effect sensors installed on the track. These sensors are triggered by small magnets attached to the front of every locomotive and to the rear of each caboose.

Engineers drive a train via a hand-held control unit. This is a small box with two buttons, a knob, and two toggle switches that a human engineer can use to control a train. Typical student projects assign knobs for train throttles, buttons for horns and brakes, and toggle switches for train direction (forward or reverse) and for setting the next turnout ahead of the train (left or right).

A final piece of railroad hardware generates sounds from digital recordings of diesel locomotives, air brakes, air horns, and bells.

3.2 Computing Hardware

A number of different hardware configurations have been used over the long history of this project. In the first laboratory, students developed their control software on a Digital Equipment Corporation PDP 11/24. They used a serial link to download executable programs to the PDP 11/23 target computer. In 1989 I replaced the PDP 11/24 with a microVAX II and the PDP 11/23 with an rtVAX (optimized for real-time). The current laboratory has inexpensive PCs for both development and target machines.

3.3 Interface Hardware

The interface hardware connects the control computers to the railroad hardware. Figure 1 is a diagram showing the layers within a model railroad control system.

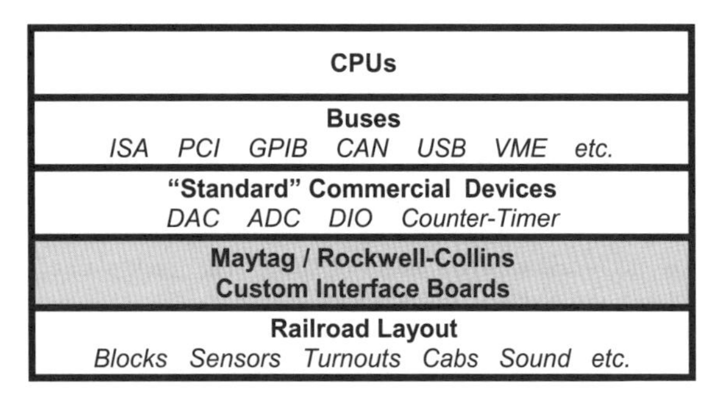

Figure 1. Hardware layers connecting the control computers to the model railroad

One or more CPUs are connected to commercial analog-to-digital converters (ADC), digital-to-analog converters (DAC), TTL level digital I/O (DIO), and counter-timers. The connections may be made through any of a number of different buses. I use custom hardware to connect these devices to the railroad layout. In the past, this interface layer was hand built on wire wrapped and soldered prototyping boards. It took considerable effort to construct all the necessary circuits. With the support of Maytag Corporation and Rockwell-Collins, I have designed and manufactured circuit boards that make this aspect of building the laboratory much easier for those wishing to duplicate my efforts. The interface hardware consists of four major subsystems (block control, turnout control, train sensors, and sound) detailed in the next sections and two minor subsystems (cabs and hand-held controllers).

3.3.1 Block Control

The block control subsystem controls the power applied to each block of track in the railroad layout. Figure 2 shows a single track block circuit. Each Maytag / Rockwell-Collins block circuit board contains 12 such circuits.

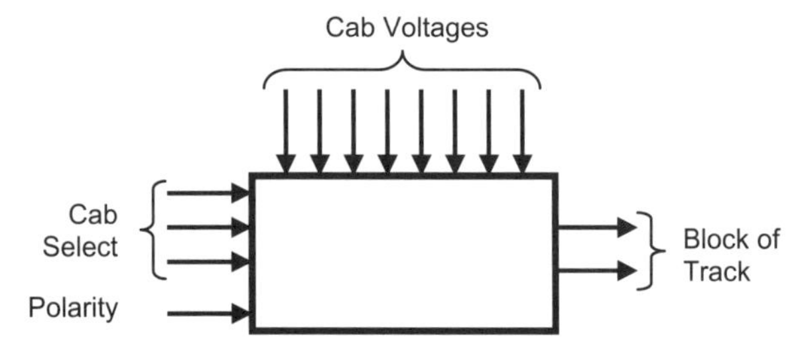

Figure 2. Track Block Control Circuit

The two analog outputs of the block control circuit are connected to the rails of a block of track to supply power to the train on that block. Each circuit has four digital inputs and eight analog inputs. Three of the digital inputs (*cab select* in Figure 2.) are used to select which one of the eight analog inputs will be used to power the track block – an analog version of the multiplexer students study in computer organization. The remaining digital input is used to select the polarity of the voltage applied to the track. The polarity controls the direction the train moves on the block. The analog inputs (*cab voltages* in Figure 2) may be supplied by either digital-to-analog converters or by programmable counter-timers. The latter provide a pulse width modulated signal for controlling the speed of a train. Pulse width modulation gives more precise control of the DC motors in the locomotives than is possible with simple voltage level control.

3.3.2 Turnout Motor Control

The turnout control subsystem is designed to control Tortoise™ brand switch machines. Other brands can be used. Figure 3 shows a single turnout control circuit. Each Maytag / Rockwell-Collins turnout circuit board contains 24 such circuits.

Figure 3. Turnout Motor Control Circuit

The two analog outputs of the turnout motor control circuit are connected to a switch machine motor. A series of contacts on the switch machine provide an analog signal (*sense* in Figure 3.) that indicates whether or not the linkage has reached the end of its travel.

A single digital input (*direction* in Figure 3.) selects the direction to turn the switch machine motor. Because switch machines take two to three seconds to change, a turnout has four possible states: left, right, moving left, and moving right. Rather than use two output lines to determine the state of the turnout, we use the desired direction (the input value) in combination with an output value (*in position* in Figure 3.) that reports whether the switch machine motor has reached the desired direction.

3.3.3 Train Sensors

This subsystem connects the Hall effect sensors on the track to a digital input/output (DIO) board with interrupt capabilities. It may also be used with other TTL level sensors. Each Maytag / Rockwell-Collins sensor circuit board handles 64 sensors. LED's are provided to aid in debugging interrupt handlers.

The Hall effect sensors are located on the boundaries between track blocks. When a locomotive is detected, the software must power up the next block before the wheels bridge the gap between blocks. This is a hard real-time deadline. Failing to power the next block in time will blow the block power supply fuse.

3.3.4 Sound

The optional sound subsystem provides an interface to up to four Dallee LocoMatic™ railroad sound units [5]. Each unit provides diesel engine sounds that vary in proportion to throttle settings, air brake release sounds, air horn sounds, and bell sounds.

4. Software

The final product for a team is the software to monitor and control the railroad as described in their user's manual. The teams write nearly all of the code (12K–15K lines) to create a bootable program that runs on the bare hardware with a minimal executive.

4.1 Requirements and High Level Design

Much of the semester is devoted to analysis and design. Many students remark that this is the first time they have experienced benefits from design. We use a subset of UML [10] as our primary analysis and design technique. Students are familiar with object-oriented programming from previous courses but have little experience with object-oriented design of non-trivial systems. Their first object models are often rich in operations and weak in associations. Modeling a generic railroad layout provides a good exercise in discovering ordinary and qualified associations, aggregations, and generalizations.

Temporal relationships of a real-time system are difficult to understand. The object model shows the static structure at a single moment in time. We use a dynamic model to show changes to objects and their associations over time. State diagrams graphically illustrate the primary dynamic modeling concepts – events and states. The behavior of many railroad objects requires further abstraction through concurrent and nested state diagrams. For example, a turnout's state includes both the position of its switch points (left, right, moving left, or moving right) and, concurrently, its condition (OK or failed).

Students are not kept away from their editors and compilers while working on their high level designs. Because the specifications of the specialized I/O devices used by the railroad are already well defined, students can write the code for the various device drivers early in the semester.

4.2 Low Level Design

Students use their object and dynamic models to design the individual classes making up their system. The model railroad, like most embedded systems, consists of external elements that exist in parallel. A major problem associated with the creation of software for such systems is how to express that parallelism in the structure of the software. While students study alternative approaches such as cyclic executives, they use explicit concurrent processes in the design of their railroad systems.

During the low level design process, students determine which objects are active (generate events spontaneously) and so require their own thread of control. They must also consider communication, synchronization and mutual exclusion needs. Additional objects, such as bounded buffers, needed to support concurrent operations are included in the design at this point. A typical project has over 30 concurrent processes.

4.3 Implementation

During the first six years that the real-time systems course was offered, students developed their railroad control code in C. As shown in Figure 4, no team successfully implemented the minimum project requirements when the C language was used. To ease student and teacher frustrations I made an increasing amount of my solutions available to the teams. Figure 4 shows that even when I provided nearly 60 percent of the project code, no team was successful in implementing the minimum project requirements.

Thinking that the low level of tasking provided through semaphores was the major contributor to the problem of incomplete projects, I selected a language with a much higher level of tasking abstractions – Ada. I expected a disaster the first year with both new equipment and a new language. As in a real-life embedded

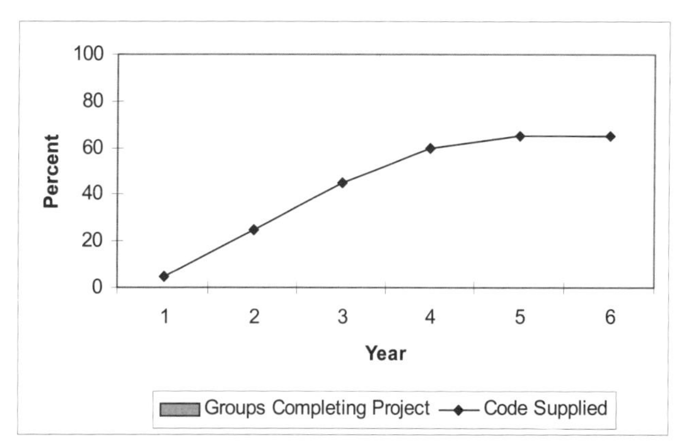

Figure 4. C language project completion rate (zero) and amount of code supplied by instructor

systems project, I was building the hardware while my students were writing the software. I finished the hardware with only four weeks remaining in the semester. But to my amazement, nearly 50 percent of the student teams had their projects working before the end of the semester. I had supplied them with only two sample device drivers. As shown in Figure 5, when I supplied some additional software components, **more than 75 percent of the student teams completed their projects**.

Through an analysis of the students' engineering notebooks, I found my original hypothesis, that the major problem was C's low-level tasking mechanism, to be incorrect. While Ada's high level of abstraction for tasking did reduce development time for the students, it was the accurate modeling of scalar quantities (integers, real numbers, and enumeration values) that contributed the most to Ada's success in this course. Hours spent locating a C function call with two swapped *int* parameters was reduced to a quick fix of a syntax error in the equivalent Ada code. Similarly, the calculation of an out of range track block number that took a team a full day to find in their C program is detected and reported immediately by the Ada run-time system. This conclusion is consistent with studies done on the nature of *wicked bugs* in software [6, 8] where 88 percent of the programming errors in the C/C++ programs studied were a result of problems with scalars; problems that do not exist in Ada. A more recent study [9] shows that such problems also exist in Java.

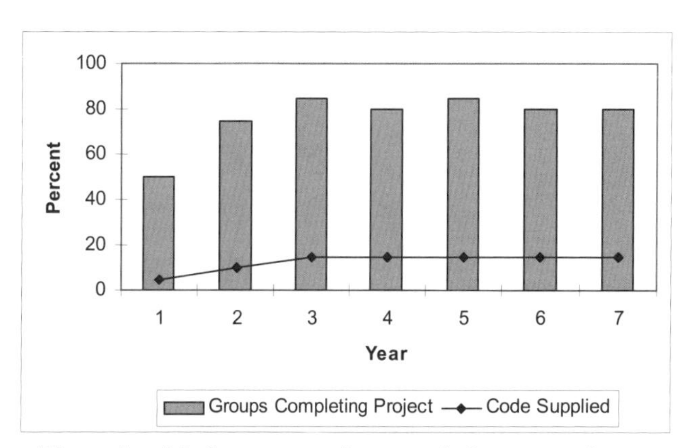

Figure 5. Ada language project completion rate and amount of code supplied by instructor

5. Future Work

The next project in the hardware area is the development of train telemetry to provide more precise location data than provided by the Hall effect sensors. This data will allow students to implement speed limits, cruise controls, closer spacing between trains, and additional safety features. New wireless technologies such as Bluetooth or ZigBee radio may provide both the telemetry capability and new learning experiences.

As society assigns more critical functions to embedded systems it is crucial that the software running them possess high degrees of safety and reliability. To meet these challenges, I plan to bring more formal methods to my course. SPARK [2] (a subset of Ada and a suite of tools - *Examiner*, *Simplifier*, and *Proof Checker*) provide the means for students to use formal analysis on their code. As it requires little more than running a tool, simple use of proof in showing that a program is free from exceptions due to run-time errors is now well within their reach.

6. Conclusions

The model railroad provides an exciting environment for teaching a real-time embedded systems course – a course in which most student teams successfully complete a major software project. I have developed the interface hardware to allow other schools to easily connect a variety of computers to a model railroad at minimal cost. Contact me for more information. In addition to circuit and wiring details, I can supply a spreadsheet that you may use to produce part lists and cost estimates for whatever size railroad you care to build. A sample user's manual, photographs, and a video of the laboratory described in this paper may be found at http://www.cs.uni.edu/~mccormic/RealTime/

7. ACKNOWLEDGMENTS

Thanks to the many "train course" students for keeping meticulous notes on the mistakes they made over the years.

8. REFERENCES

[1] Amirijoo, M., Tešanović, A., and Nadjim-Tehrani, S., Raising Motivation in Real-Time Laboratories: The Soccer Scenario, *SIGCSE 2004 Proceedings*, 265-269, 2004.

[2] Barnes, J., *High Integrity Software, The SPARK Approach to Safety and Security,* Addison-Wesley, 2003.

[3] Burns, A. and Wellings, A., *Real-Time Systems and Programming Languages* (3rd Ed.), Addison Wesley, 2001.

[4] Clifton, J., A CS/SE Approach to a Real-Time Embedded Systems Software Development Course, *SIGCSE 2001 Proceedings*, 278-280, 2001.

[5] Dallee Electronics, Inc. Railroad Sound Systems. http://www.dallee.com/sound_systems.htm

[6] Eisenstadt, M., My Hairiest Bug War Stories, *Communications of the ACM*, vol 40, no 4, 30-37, 1997.

[7] IEEE Computer Society/ACM Joint Task Force on the "Model Curricula for Computing". http://www.computer.org/education/cc2001/final/

[8] McCormick, J., Forum Letter, *Communications of the ACM*, vol 40, no 8, 30, 1997.

[9] Potratz, E., A Practical Comparison Between Java and Ada in Implementing a Real-Time Embedded System, Proceedings of the ACM SIGAda 2003 Conference, *Ada Letters*, vol 25, no 1, 71-83, 2004.

[10] Rumbaugh, J., Blaha, M., Premerlani, W. Eddy, F., and Lorenson, W., *Object-Oriented Modeling and Design*, Prentice Hall, 1990.

[11] Writing Center at the Colorado State University. http://writing.colostate.edu/references/documents/notebook/

9. APPENDIX Track Plan of the Model Railroad

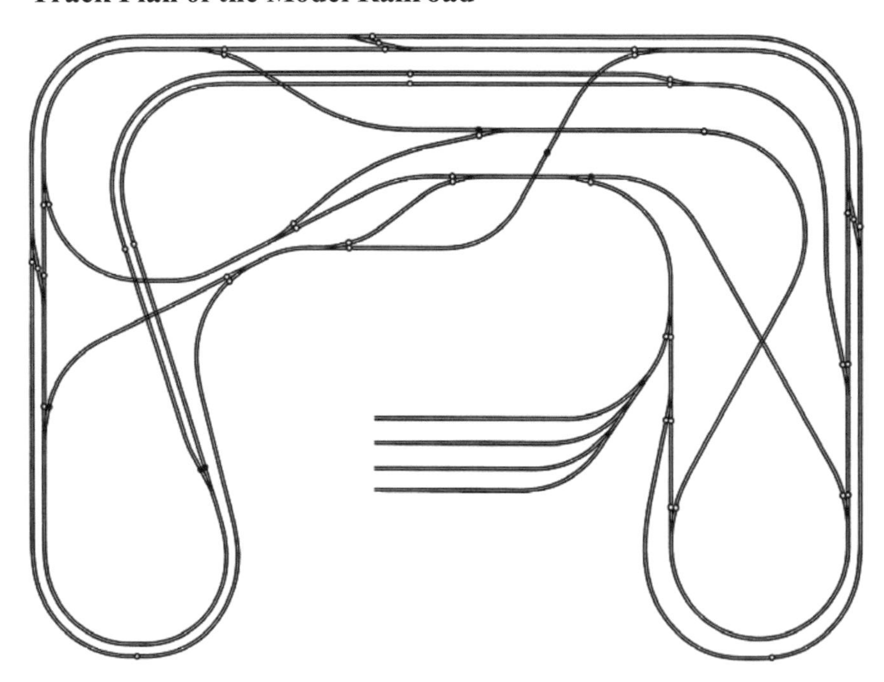

Fostering a Creative Interest in Computer Science

Gary Lewandowski, Elizabeth Johnson, Michael Goldweber
Department of Mathematics and Computer Science
Xavier University
Cincinnati, OH 45207-4441
513-745-2836
{lewandow, ejohnson, mikeyg}@cs.xu.edu

ABSTRACT

In this paper, we describe activities undertaken at our university to revise our computer science program to develop an environment and curriculum which encourages creative, hands-on learning by our students. Our main changes were the development of laboratory space, increased hands-on problem solving activities in the introductory course, open-ended programming projects in the early courses including a requirement of an open-ended project extension for an A grade, and the integration of a seminar into the senior project requirement. Our results suggest that these changes have improved student skill and willingness to deal with new problems and technologies. An additional surprising side-effect appears to be a dramatic increase in retention over the first two years, despite lower overall grade averages in those courses.

Categories and Subject Descriptors

K.3 [**Computer & Information Science Education**]: Computer Science Education

General Terms

Measurement, Performance, Design, Experimentation.

Keywords

Major retention, curriculum, hands-on activities, learning community.

1. INTRODUCTION

The rapid pace at which technology evolves requires computer science graduates, whether they enter industry or academia, to have the ability and desire to use existing technology (e.g., computing platforms, language features) in new ways and to apply their existing knowledge of computer science to new, emerging technologies. The goal of our senior project capstone course had long echoed this requirement; students were asked to create their own project demonstrating their computer science skills, exploring any topic in which they were interested. Unfortunately, the results of the senior project were often disappointing. Our seniors produced senior projects that demonstrated technical programming skills but did not really show deeper computer science skills and rarely veered into completely unknown areas. We eventually concluded that many of the students simply lacked the imagination to consider more interesting projects. But how does one teach students to be creative and willing to explore?

This paper describes our curricular and cultural changes over the past several years as we translated the lofty goal of enhancing creativity and a willingness to explore into concrete curricular changes without revising our overall course sequence. We have noticed a significant increase in student creativity and exploration. An unexpected side-effect appears to be a dramatic increase in retention over the first two years of our program. While the physical space we describe is of course unique to our institution, we believe the curricular and cultural changes described here are exportable to a wide range of institutions.

Section 2 describes our general approach to the problem of developing more adaptive students. Section 3 describes our computer science laboratory. Section 4 describes three main course revisions we implemented. Section 5 outlines the results we noted. Section 6 outlines our conclusions.

2. APPROACH

The problems of student preparation for creative, independent work have been noted at other institutions. In particular, the lack of insight-building activities and an emphasis on topical rather than abstract knowledge in the curriculum have been identified as prime factors in producing students without the skills to work independently on projects [2]. Inattention to the development of advanced information-processing skills that allow students to identify information needed to solve a problem, gather that information from diverse sources, and apply it in new ways is also a major shortcoming of many curricula [3].

We reasoned that successful undergraduate research required the skills we were trying to build. Thus, our search for how to improve our students' creative abilities led us to several schools with reputations for success in undergraduate research. In particular we examined Swarthmore, Bryn Mawr and Hope College. These schools were similar to our university in some respects -- small, with a focus on liberal arts, but many more students from these schools went on to graduate school, thus indicating an interest and aptitude in doing research. We noticed two key differences between Xavier and these schools. Unlike our program, the three model schools had dedicated space for their majors; this allowed the students to work independently and

SIGCSE '05, February 23-27, 2005, St. Louis, MO, USA.

to work for long hours as necessary. These schools also offered electives that required independent student projects.

We did not believe that simply creating more electives would help our students become creative explorers -- this, after all, was essentially the role of the senior project. Thus we decided to adapt the approaches of these schools into a curriculum-wide revision, funded by a National Science Foundation CCLI Adaptation and Implementation grant (DUE-9952548). Our goal was to encourage creative exploration and problem solving at all levels of the curriculum, culminating in creative senior projects.

3. COMPUTER SCIENCE LABORATORY

Before we undertook the course revisions, we purchased equipment and identified space for our first dedicated computer science laboratory. Prior to the establishment of this lab, our majors worked at home, in their residence hall rooms, or scattered among the public computing labs on campus. Their interaction with other computer science majors occurred primarily in class or by happenstance around campus. While there was a reasonable amount of social interaction among classmates, students socialized mainly with other students at their level of the program, and there was little interaction while actually working on computer science activities.

Our goal in establishing the lab was to increase the feeling of community among the computer science majors. We reasoned that the creation of an informal learning community outside of the classroom would increase the opportunities for students to interact in academically meaningful ways outside the classroom and thus promote engagement in the subject. As has been shown in previous work [4], this can also lead to higher retention of majors.

Our initial conception of the lab revolved around three features. The first was a variety of computing platforms; along with PCs and Macintoshes we purchased Sun Workstations. Since the initial purchase we have added handheld machines, laptops (PC and Mac) and even XBoxes. We believed the heterogeneity of platforms would help establish a basic ability to adjust to changes in computing environments, increasing student willingness to explore. The variety of platforms, particularly the Suns also served as a notice to students and the university community that this was a computer science space, not just a computing space, laying a foundation for convincing students that we belong to a culture of exploration.

The second feature of the laboratory was specialized space. The space was divided into three distinct rooms, each targeting a particular need. The main workroom space was used for projects and coursework that did not require a specialized machine configuration. This area included a couch and work table, as well as a large whiteboard. Two smaller rooms connected to the main workroom. One was a server room for fileservers, nameservers and any specialized servers needed for projects or courses. The other room was designed to be dedicated to independent and senior projects.

The third feature of the laboratory was a student advisory board. Students in the second year and later of study were chosen to provide advice on rules and organization of the lab. We believed this would hand ownership of the lab to the students. Indeed, before the lab was opened, the students changed the original layout of the main room, merged the project room with the server room, and established a "quiet" room where students who wanted to work without distraction could spend time.

After two years in the original space, we obtained a Major Research Instrumentation (MRI) grant from the National Science Foundation (EIA-0215836) for parallel and distributed computing equipment, necessitating a move to a larger space. The new laboratory has the same essential features as the first lab but has a much larger main workroom including space for approximately fifteen workstations, several empty tables, a couch, cubbyholes for student books/backpacks and a large whiteboard. Overflow from workstations is handled with laptops. The project room shares space with a quiet area. Since its inception, students have used the lab both as a social and academic gathering place. The lab doors have card-swipe locks allowing access to all students who are taking a computer science course other than the first one. By student demand, the lab is open until 2 am during the school year and all night during the week before finals. As will be discussed in section 5, this common space has become an important part of the culture in Xavier's computer science program.

4. COURSE REVISIONS

The main purpose of the original NSF CCLI grant was to fund curricular revisions in our program. While courses throughout the curriculum were revised to incorporate more creative, hands-on activities, we chose to concentrate our evaluation efforts on three courses that occurred at important milestones in student careers – Computer Science I (CSCI 170), Data Structures and Algorithms (CSCI 220), and the Senior Seminar and Project (CSCI 390). Our approach was to add increasing opportunities for creative activities as the students progressed through the major. So, in Computer Science I, the emphasis was on hands-on activities while in Data Structures and Algorithms, students were given the opportunity to choose one of several creative project enhancements. Finally, in the senior project students were permitted to work on a project of their own choosing, under the guidance of a mentor. This section describes the evolution of each course.

4.1 CSCI 170: Computer Science I

Since a major curriculum revision implemented in 1997, our first course for computer science majors has presented a breadth-first view of computer science rather than teaching the syntax and semantics of a particular programming language. Students looked at algorithms as the central concept in computer science and used pseudocode to write these algorithms. Karel++, a simple object-oriented programming language which allows students to direct a robot through a graphical world, was used at the end of the semester as another embodiment of algorithms.

The main goals of the course redesign were to increase the number of hands-on activities, which we believed would foster an attitude of exploration, and to show the students computer science in society which we believed would broaden their perspective on uses for technology (and possibly plant some seeds for independent projects down the road).

In the fall 2001 semester, students experienced the initial revised version of Computer Science I. We increased hands-on activities in two main ways. First, we used Karel++ rather than pseudocode to teach basic algorithmic structures (sequence, conditional, iterative statements). Using an actual language, we reasoned, would allow more trial and error exploration. The second hands-on revision introduced LEGO robots, programmed by the students using Java classes. The Java classes were developed by a junior computer science student to provide the same interface as is used in the Karel++ language so that students could see the similarities and differences in writing programs for a real environment versus a simulated one without the overhead of learning a new syntax. To introduce uses of computer science in society, articles from the popular media were given to students weekly, along with reflection questions. To introduce a broad sense of computer science, algorithms in application areas such as cryptography, artificial intelligence, and networks were also examined.

The course has continued to evolve. We found that students retained little from the topic-a-week algorithm-application section. We now emphasize the notion of algorithm throughout the course, first in the context of general problem solving (using pseudocode), then in contexts of computer circuits, hardware and LEGO robots. We have increased the hands-on activities, sometimes in non-computational contexts such as algorithms for origami. One of our most popular activities is a day dedicated to having pairs of students build a computer from simple components. Suggested by one of our students, the activity encourages exploration while demonstrating that the von Neumann model they learn is essentially the model still used This activity proved to be very popular, prompting upper-level students to ask if they could also have the opportunity to build a computer. Our final set of hands-on activities explores computational efficiency as students modify Java implementations of sorting and searching algorithms to include counters, then run the algorithms on a variety of inputs.

4.2 CSCI 220: Data Structures and Algorithms

The Data Structures and Algorithms course is taken in the third semester of study. The unrevised course was a fairly typical programming course with 4 to 6 unrelated projects along with periodic homework. The main goal of our revision was to incorporate a sense of exploration into the projects, encouraging the students to think creatively.

The revision consists of two main changes. First, students are introduced to C++ at the beginning of the course after having learned Java in the first programming course (Computer Science II). While many aspects of the two languages are similar, the differences can, of course, cause students some frustration. We want them to understand that the language is simply the tool for implementing the algorithm, echoing the variety of algorithm descriptions encountered in Computer Science I. We insist the first projects be implemented in both languages, then do a few in C++ only, and offer a choice of either language on the final project.

The second revision is the incorporation of open-ended projects. In the first offering we used the web cache and search engine project from Swarthmore [1] over the last half of the course. Since then we have also used unrelated projects, each with its own open-ended possibilities (e.g. a traffic simulation suggested students explore the impact of stoplights, stop signs, lane mergers or lane additions; a file-comparison-via-hashing project suggested students explore using the tool on code trees or modifications to catch a variety of small file modifications that would foil noticing sections of code that are the same). An essential piece of the open-ended project revision is a grading rubric given to the students with each project. The rubric establishes the need for achievement in the open-ended segment in order to get an A. It makes clear that analysis and exploration are important and establishes an expectation that excellence in the course includes a willingness and ability to explore on one's own.

4.3 CSCI 390: Senior Seminar and Project

In the unrevised Senior Projects course, students worked on individual projects, meeting weekly with an advisor. Our main goal in the revision was to emphasize that the skills gained through the curriculum went beyond programming. In particular, we wanted to see students work on projects requiring independent research and creative problem solving.

In the revised course, first offered in 2001, students were required to prepare a research proposal within the first two weeks of class. The proposal would define an exploration area, providing the students an opportunity to demonstrate their ability to find interesting topics to explore. We added a one-hour seminar each week. After the first two weeks, a pair of students was in charge of each session. They chose a reading from 'The Turing Omnibus,' by Dewdney and prepared a list of questions for their classmates to answer prior to class. During the class session the student pair led the discussion on the material. We also required a final presentation on each project at a public forum. This allowed younger students to see what the seniors had accomplished. Thus, the offering of this revised course was important not only for the seniors but also for the expectation it suggested to students in the other years.

The course has continued to evolve. While the Dewdney book covers important topics that the students had not been exposed to previously, the students did not find it to be a very accessible or compelling book. In the 2002 offering, we allowed students to choose readings from any source, after giving them some guidance as to what is appropriate for the course. A timeline was incorporated into the proposal because although projects were of greater consequence than in previous semesters, student effort was not evenly distributed across the semester. In spring 2003, we made the final revision to the course, narrowing the student discussion leader's seminar reading selection choices to material related to their own senior project. Thus students had an opportunity to talk with their classmates about the research they were conducting. We made this change so that students would more closely connect the idea of reading technical material and doing research.

5. RESULTS

Our overall goal was to increase our students' ability to do creative, independent problem solving. As this is a somewhat nebulous concept, assessing our results is non-trivial. We chose to examine student work at the end of the three revised courses described above, to track non-classroom evidence that student activity in open-ended projects had increased., and to follow the retention rate of incoming computer science majors over the first three courses (corresponding to the first two programming courses).

5.1 Assessment Data

In the Computer Science I course, two common questions were used on the final in 2000 (unrevised) and 2001 (revised). The first question involved comparing two search algorithms. The second asked students to write a predicate for a Karel or LEGO robot. On a scale of 0 to 6 for the question about comparing two search algorithms, students in 2000 scored an average of 3 while students in 2001 scored an average of 2.86. On the question about writing a predicate for Karel (2000) or Lego robots (2001), the 2000 average was 3.56 of 4 and the 2001 average was 3.04 of 4.

In the Data Structures and Algorithms course we used a similar open-ended analysis question on finals in 2001 (unrevised), 2002, and 2003. Students were asked a question whose solution involved gathering and updating real-world data. If all the data were given ahead of time, a solution could be suggested that involved static processing, e.g. with a graph search algorithm. Since the data needed to be processed and revised as the information arrived however, a solution involving priority queues or binary search trees along with graph traversals was likely to yield better results. We re-graded the question from the three semesters on a 5-point scale to ensure a uniform rubric. The results are displayed in Figure 1.

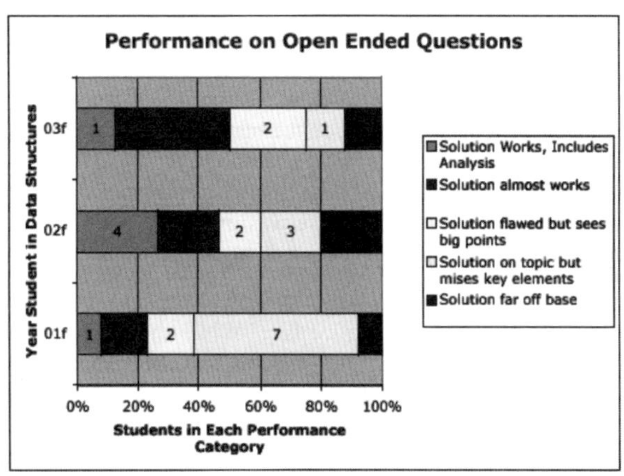

Figure 1: Results from CSCI 220

Senior projects for 2000 (unrevised curriculum) and 2004 (students who had taken several of the revised courses and had access to the lab all four years) were evaluated using a rubric that evaluates students on a four-point scale (0 is low) in terms of three metrics: 1) the choice of a project (how interesting is the project in a computer science sense), 2) the student process on the project (how steady and independent), and 3) result (quality and interest), The rubric was applied in summer 2004, ignoring grades received in the course. Figure 2 shows the scoring in these categories for the seniors in 2000 (bars marked with 0) and 2004 (bars marked with 4). Each bar represents one student.

We tracked the following as non-classroom evidence of interest in or success with open-ended exploration: participation in summer research projects, school-year non-course research projects, interest in graduate school, conference presentations, conference attendance, scholarly articles. Table 1 summarizes the results as a comparison of 1994-2000 with 2001-2004.

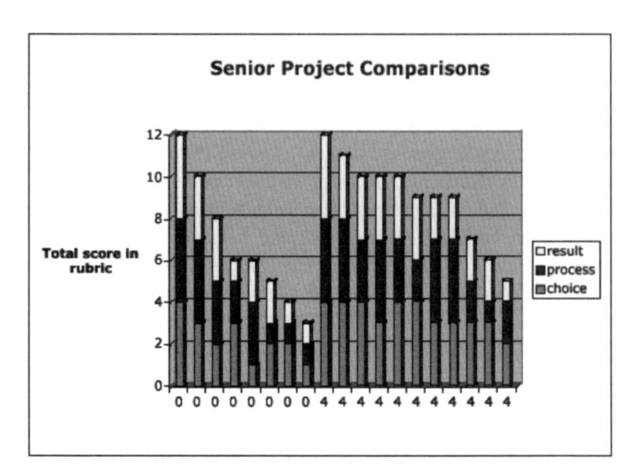

Figure 2: Results from three metrics on senior projects

Non-classroom activity	Number of Students, 1994-2000	Number of Students,2001-2004
Summer Research	3	14 (8 in off-campus REUs or CRA distributed mentor)
School-year Research	0	11 (10 through CRA/CREW)
Interest in Graduate School	4	13 (9 in CS, 1 im Math, 1 in business, 1 in medicine, 1 in non-profit management)
Published papers (with or w/o faculty co-author)	1	5
Conference Presentations	2	7
Conference Attendees	2	12 (Grace Hopper, ITICSE, SIGCSE, Supercomputing, NCUR)
Applied for NSF Fellowship	0	6 (3 honorable mentions)

Table 1: Non-classroom evidence of interest in open-ended exploration

The average retention rate from 1997-2000 (four years) over the first three courses of the curriculum is 57.8% (37/64 students entering CS I as a major entered Data Structures and Algorithms as a major). The average retention rate for 2001-2004 (three years) over the first three courses of the curriculum is 77.4% (24/31).

5.2 Discussion

The impact of open-ended questions is not noticeable in the Computer Science I course. This is not surprising, given that the opportunities for such questions are limited in the first course. The impact, however, appears significant by the completion of the third course, Data Structures and Algorithms. As can be seen from the graph in Figure 1, the percentage of students with working or nearly working solutions (the two leftmost categories) has increased over the course of the three offerings. In particular, less than 30% of the students in the pre-revision course had acceptable solutions; by the third offering, this had increased to 50%.

As we had hoped, we found that integrating open-ended projects into the curriculum helps encourage more interesting, open-ended senior projects. We see a marked improvement between seniors in 2000 and 2004, particularly in the choice of project. The increase in interesting projects is also reflected in the number of students attending and presenting at conferences.

We note that the communal lab became an integral part of encouraging students to succeed at open-ended projects and to explore their interest in research. In particular, we found that in addition to the expected interaction between students within a course or year of study, we also had older students helping younger students in the courses they had already taken. Similar to Montessori classrooms, our lab became a place where advanced students introduce newer students to the culture and expectations of the major.

A second impact of the space has been an increase in ongoing projects by the students. Independent student projects (i.e. not associated with any course) conducted in the lab include

- building a Beowulf cluster,
- development and analysis of a survey on high school students' attitudes towards computer science,
- building a CAVE Automatic Virtual Environment, and
- development of a seminar for other majors that provides hands-on networking experience.

We believe the ongoing projects in the lab, along with the open-ended projects in the early courses are a factor in the increased research interest. These projects intrigue lower-level students who feel encouraged to explore topics they are interested in and resulted in an increase of students working on summer or school year research projects.

Finally, although increasing retention was not the goal of the project, we did find that introducing open-ended projects and rubrics for assessing work in this way appears to have a positive impact on retention. The retention is not related to a particular instructor: all three of the computer science faculty taught the first two courses during the time period covered by our data. Moreover, this retention comes despite a lower average grade-point average (GPA) for those students taking all three courses. This lower GPA does not reflect lesser ability or effort on the part of the students in the courses, but rather resulted from a concerted effort on the part of the faculty to adopt higher grading standards in the computer science courses. One would expect that these lower grades would drive some students from the major, especially in this era of rampant grade inflation. We found instead that students were challenged by the higher expectations and felt a sense of pride in succeeding in a difficult major. The common lab space has also helped in providing both peer encouragement during tough times and a community that even struggling majors are reluctant to leave.

6. CONCLUSIONS

The main contribution of our work is to demonstrate that one can create a cultural change among their students, encouraging exploration and creativity, and, as a by-product, increase retention of majors in the program. We believe the changes most vital to this improvement are a dedicated lab, projects that encourage exploration, and a grading rubric expressing an expectation of creativity and exploration to reach excellence.

7. ACKNOWLEDGMENTS

Richard Pulskamp, Director of Institutional Research at Xavier University, provided statistical consulting on the project. Barbara Walvoord of the Kaneb Center for Teaching and Learning at the University of Notre Dame provided assessment consulting on the project. Mary Kochlefl, Director of Grant Services at Xavier University, provided invaluable assistance over the course of designing and carrying out this curriculum revision. This material is based upon work supported by the National Science Foundation under Grant No. 9952548. Any opinions, findings, and conclusions or recommendations expressed in this material are those of the author(s) and do not necessarily reflect the views of the National Science Foundation.

8. REFERENCES

[1] Tia Newhall , Lisa Meeden, A comprehensive project for CS2: combining key data structures and algorithms into an integrated web browser and search engine, *ACM SIGCSE Bulletin*, v.34 n.1, March 2002.

[2] Greg Scragg, Doug Baldwin, and Hans Koomen. Computer Science Needs an Insight-Based Curriculum. *Proceedings of the 25th SIGCSE Technical Symposium,* March 1994. pp. 150-154.

[3] Martin A. Siegel. From Content-Centered to Problem-Centered Design: The Need for Information Processing and Critical-Thinking Skills. In Barbara B. Seels (Ed.), *Instructional Design Fundamentals: A Reconsideration* (pp. 201-207). Educational Technology Publications, Inc., 1995.

[4] Uri Treisman. Studying students studying calculus: A look at the lives of minority mathematics students in college. *The College Mathematics Journal*, 23(5): 362-372, 1992.

Intra-Curriculum Software Engineering Education

James B. Fenwick Jr. and Barry L. Kurtz

Computer Science Department
Appalachian State University
Boone, North Carolina, USA
1-828-262-2708

jbf@cs.appstate.edu

ABSTRACT

We have been funded by the National Science Foundation to investigate the feasibility of distributing large software engineering projects across the academic curriculum (DUE 0127439). This paper reports on the pedagogical aspects of the intra-curriculum methodology we have developed including motivation, goals, instructor responsibilities, and variations of the approach. The paper also reports on three applications of the methodology including lessons learned.

Categories and Subject Descriptors

K.3.2 [**Computing Milieux**]: Computer and Information Science Education – *computer science education, information systems education.*

General Terms

Human Factors

Keywords

Software engineering education, pedagogy.

1. INTRODUCTION

An important part of education in an academic setting is the practical application of concepts. However, the application of software engineering in the academic world is very different from software engineering in a professional setting. Major differences include:

- students are earning academic credit and not their livelihood,
- students will normally spend only about 10 hours per week (3-4 hours in class and 5-6 hours outside class) on a course compared with 40+ hours per week in industry,
- student team members have difficulty meeting together (except for the limited in-class time) compared with the accessibility of coworkers in industry,
- students are constantly switching focus between a variety of academic activities in the course of a single day compared with the focus on a single project in industry,
- the size and scope of the projects are in no way comparable,
- the availability of expertise in the problem domain is in no way comparable, and
- the availability of expertise in the solution domain is in no way comparable.

Despite these differences it is the job of instructors of software engineering to provide as realistic an experience as possible to prepare students for work in the "real world."

Some schools are introducing software engineering concentrations or degree programs. These approaches use a set of courses to introduce and apply software engineering concepts. Another approach is the addition of one or two courses into a traditional computer science curriculum. Concepts are taught earlier in the curriculum and a capstone project course often provides the practical application of the concepts on a large, long-term project.

At Appalachian State University, a senior-level required course is used to introduce students to software engineering concepts. It is well known that a practical exercise aids in student assimilation of the concepts, thus a "large" project is also attempted. A large project requires a significant amount of programming effort, yet programming skill development is not the goal of this course. Rather, our project goal for this course is more focused on earlier lifecycle activities such as analysis and design and also project management.

In the face of the restricted setting mentioned earlier, we still need a project with sufficient scope to make analysis, design, and management interesting and challenging yet doable in a single semester. We have focused on distributing components of a large software engineering project across several courses and potentially between many universities.

The remainder of this paper describes other approaches and then provides an overview and the goals of our intra-curriculum methodology. Three applications of the approach and discussion of variations are described. Also, some tools developed to support this approach are described briefly. The paper ends with conclusions and future plans.

2. RELATED WORK

Educators have attempted a number of approaches to address the problems facing software engineering education. Some schools offer a degree program in software engineering, which uses an entire curriculum targeting these issues. Other schools have created a software engineering sequence or concentration by adding additional courses, usually with a capstone project course; yet the fundamental problems facing educators in an academic setting remain.

Daigle and Niccolai[1] attempted to create an "inter-class synergy" between a low level software engineering theory course with a senior level project course. Our approach similarly

SIGCSE '05, February 23-27, 2005, St.Louis, Missouri, USA.

attempts a synergy between classes, but involves a more active participation with the lower level courses.

Faulkner and Culwin[4] also noticed the complementary relationship between a software engineering course and advanced elective courses. They argue that human-computer interfaces should be more fully integrated into the software engineering curriculum. However, our approach targets a program offering a computer science degree. Moreover, our approach doesn't change the curriculum (which can sometimes be a difficult proposition).

Villarreal and Butler[7] described a software engineering educational reform effort that "merged" a database course and a software engineering course in order to provide a more real-world project experience. Rather than form a "superclass" giving two course credits, our methodology centers on the software engineering course and uses other courses already existing in the curriculum as resources.

Last and Hause, et.al.[5,6] have conducted research on the effects of software development performance due to the interaction factors of project teams that are not co-located. Their study focuses on collaborating teams separated by wide geographical distances.

Our methodology lies between the work of Last and a traditional, in-class team. Our teams are only marginally distributed. The next sections detail our intra-curriculum methodology.

3. THE INTRA-CURRICULUM APPROACH

Facing the difficulties of software engineering education in the academic setting mentioned in the previous section, we realized that other courses in our curriculum were also requiring project implementations. Thinking of these other courses as potential resources in a collaborative effort spawned the intra-curriculum methodology. The overview of this approach is to simultaneously involve multiple courses in the curriculum in the development of a single software engineering term project. Below are the goals we established for the intra-curriculum methodology.

- *Maintain core software engineering practicum components.* As a practical exercise of concepts, the software engineering project must remain large enough to warrant the typical engineering activities (e.g., modeling, documentation) and the use of larger teams.
- *Decrease the level of programming implementation performed by the software engineering students.* Software engineering should rightly focus on other crucial activities including requirements, design, testing, and management. Individual programming skills development is the responsibility of other courses in the curriculum.
- *Increase student understanding of project management issues.* Practical experience in dealing with items of risk and planning is essential in modern software engineering education.
- *Increase student understanding and appreciation for system design.* An important aspect of development is a flexible design. Students at all levels should get an early and meaningful exposure to design notations (e.g., UML).
- *Increase student dedication to software quality issues.* Quality is a fundamental objective of software engineering, but is too frequently sacrificed by students working on projects that are discarded after the assignment.
- *Minimize interference on collaborating courses.* In order to attract collaborating courses, the approach should not cause large disruptions in how the other courses already function.

4. APPLICATIONS OF THE INTRA-CURRICULUM APPROACH

We have applied the intra-curriculum approach three times. The first time was the fall 2002 term and we only wanted to use two courses. In the spring 2003 semester, we altered the approach to include the software engineering course, and a senior-level human/computer interfaces (HCI) course. In the fall 2003 term, we expanded the approach to partner the software engineering course with a CS2 class and a junior-level database course.

Software Engineering + Low Level Course

In the first application of the intra-curriculum approach we attempted a typical project; that is, we were not concerned with the project having large enough subsystems to hand over to other courses. Rather, the software engineering teams were encouraged to use a Data Structures course as a resource for low-level implementation duties. However, none of the software engineering teams took advantage of this opportunity. In post-mortem analysis, students explained that they felt they could implement the simpler components (the ones suitable for a lower level class) more quickly and with higher quality themselves.

Lesson learned #1: mandate collaboration with lower level students.

Software Engineering + Specialized Course

In the next attempt, an integrated restaurant system project was attempted. Three software engineering teams ranging from 6-8 students each collaborated with HCI teams of 4-5 students each. There was some "cross-pollination" between the two courses as two of the software engineering teams contained one or two students who were simultaneously enrolled in the HCI course.

Software engineering teams were allowed to choose a subsystem of the restaurant system for their project. The restaurant system consists of integrated ordering, inventory, reservation, and financial subsystems. All the HCI teams designed an interface for the ordering subsystem. One software engineering team (with no HCI students) chose the inventory subsystem, and the remaining teams selected the ordering subsystem.

The results of this application of the approach were mixed; we are achieving our goals but not completing the software engineering project fully. Students were generally receptive and saw the value in collaborating with the other course. Some students reported having similar experiences with collections of teams in summer jobs or internships. However, there were instances of false assumptions between cooperating teams. At some times, one team assumed the other team was responsible for certain decisions. For example, the interface team decided they weren't responsible for how to handle special orders. At other times, both teams assumed responsibility; for example, how to select menu items into the order. Yet, this provided a useful educational experience in project communication and management.

Instructor collaboration turned out to be easier than expected. Before the term began, instructors agreed upon a mutually beneficial and appropriate project. Some background work was necessary to ensure the resulting interface could be incorporated into the larger project. We decided on using Visual Tcl [8] and used a Tcl extension to link with C/C++ code. Unfortunately, the final interface was delivered too late to get fully integrated with the software engineering project leaving that project with a rudimentary interface.

Lesson learned #2: prepare for component delivery failure.
Lesson learned #3: manage component progress carefully.

Software Engineering + Low Level Course and Specialized Course

In this application of the intra-curriculum software engineering project we again used the restaurant system, but collaborated with a low level CS2 course and a junior-level database course. There were two software engineering teams of 6-8 students and 6 database teams of 4 persons each; however only two database teams worked on the restaurant ordering persistent storage subsystem. The other database teams worked other projects selected by their instructor.

To insure collaboration with the low level class, the software engineering project contained a "contractual requirement" to include a group from the low level class. This group was considered as "interns from the local University" and thus they possessed fewer skills but still must be accommodated. This required the software engineering students to perform technical management activities relating to an evaluation of their initial system structure in order to identify small components (e.g., a class) that were suitable for the low level students. There was some student angst regarding the quality of the low level student work, but they soon realized that they had a part in this through the development of unit tests. The software engineering teams selected suitable components and then presented their requirements to the CS2 students as part of an extra credit assignment for their CS2 course. Fortunately, we were able to get enough interested students, some of them the better students in the CS2 course.

The software engineering students also acted as "customers" for the database teams. The database teams developed their various work products which were given to the software engineering teams for evaluation. This evaluation was content-specific; the database instructor evaluated the work products for a grade.

The results of this application of the approach were also mixed. There were several changes requested by the database customer (the software engineering teams) as the requirements became better understood. Since the database component was the final project for the database course, it wasn't required to be completed until the end of the term which did not leave adequate time for the software engineering students to fully integrate the final work product into their project. Fortunately, the software engineering teams had designed and built a simple, limited, non-persistent data component to enable testing of interface code. Also, one software engineering team was forced to abandon the component delivered by their lower level partner. While originally frustrated, the software engineering students realized they had poorly designed their unit test verification mechanism.

Lesson learned #4: beware two <u>final</u> projects depending on each other.

Reflections on Application of Approach

Results of applying our intra-curriculum approach to the software engineering project have been encouraging. Using qualitative assessments with students and instructors, we believe we are achieving the goals of the approach. The *amount* of implementation done by the software engineering students does not appear to have decreased, but the abstraction level has changed. These students are coding less at the statement level (e.g., assignments, conditionals, loops, etc.) and are doing more integration of high level components. By working with student groups in other courses, the software engineering students became cognizant of the importance of tracking the progress of these groups. Moreover, by working with other groups, all students have exhibited an increased awareness of quality. It seems the larger and more technically diverse this group, the more sensitive students become to quality. The software engineering students have grown in their understanding of design notations as vehicles of communication to the other groups. They also understand the importance of flexible designs that provide the substitution of backup components. Although this was learned the hard way, it is a valuable lesson in software engineering education nonetheless.

5. COLLABORATION VARIATIONS

This section discusses some of the issues in considering your own (and our further) applications of the intra-curriculum methodology. We examine these issues as collaboration variations in terms of courses, projects, team composition and grading.

5.1 Course Collaboration

The software engineering course is central to the approach we describe. Low level courses are intended to provide implementation resources for the software engineering course project. We have used a CS2 course, but CS1 and Data Structures courses are also viable alternatives. Specialized courses are intended to provide implementation resources for more complex components. An instructor considering this approach could examine her own departmental curriculum to find suitable specialized courses; possibilities include database, interface, and networking courses, and possibly translator or architecture courses. It is also possible to use multiple collaborating courses; for example, to use a CS1 <u>and</u> a CS2 course as low level course partners and a database and interface course as specialized partners.

When appropriate collaborating courses have been identified, the next process to engage is deciding on the nature of realizing the collaboration. Our original vision was being able to leverage the work products that other courses are already creating. For example, the database course was already doing a project, we just would like their project to assist us in our software engineering project. This approach causes less change for the other instructors, which provides more opportunity for collaboration. However, this also causes restrictions. Our collaboration should minimally disrupt the normal flow of the other course project. That is, we don't want to change *how* these courses conduct their project, rather we just want to dovetail the nature of the project.

In some cases, there will need to be some give-and-take regarding timings of work products. Coming to agreement on how to mutually benefit each other requires flexibility and being able to work well with other instructors.

An important aspect in a collaboration as prescribed by the intra-curriculum methodology is the timing of interactions between the courses. Typically, the software engineering project spans an entire term. Collaborating courses can also include term projects or projects with a smaller duration. Working with a course that also uses a term-long project involves timing to communicate requirements to the other course early enough and getting the final component with enough time in the term to accommodate integration. Working with a course with shorter duration projects is easier. However, the software engineering course must be careful to know when the other course will possess the necessary skills, possibly delaying requirements communication.

5.2 Team Collaboration

Typically, a project course contains more students than can reasonably make up a single team; thus, several teams are used. One strategy for organizing multiple teams on a single project is competition. All teams are given the same set of requirements and each team makes local decisions resulting in multiple solutions. Another strategy is collaboration, whereby the multiple teams are given mutually dependent pieces of the project. This strategy results in a single system solution, and can often have a larger scope.

Our intra-curriculum methodology can accommodate both of these strategies in many variations. Several such variations are described below and illustrated in Figure 1. Multiple software engineering teams can compete with each other. They can share single solutions to components from other classes; thus, collaborating with these courses (Figure 1(a)). Alternatively, the competing software engineering teams could work separately with different teams in other courses. Thus, there would be competition combined from multiple courses (Figure 1(b)). A hybrid variation is shown in Figure 1(c), competing software engineering and specialized course teams collaborating with a single CS2 team.

Collaboration between multiple lower level course teams and the software engineering team(s) is somewhat simplified since the component complexity is typically lower. In this case, there are usually enough smaller components to give different components to each lower level team.

Since the software engineering course and the specialized course are likely at the upper division level, it is possible that some students are in both classes in the same term. It is also possible that some of the software engineering students have already had the specialized course or conversely that students in the specialized course have already had software engineering. We refer to these student distributions as "cross pollination." These types of distributions can be leveraged to assist in the communication between the collaborating teams and to increase an understanding of the issues facing the developers of the other team. For instance, consider a software engineering team that contains a member of the database team. If the software engineering team needs to update the database requirements the database team member can communicate the requirements change and its motivation to the database team directly.

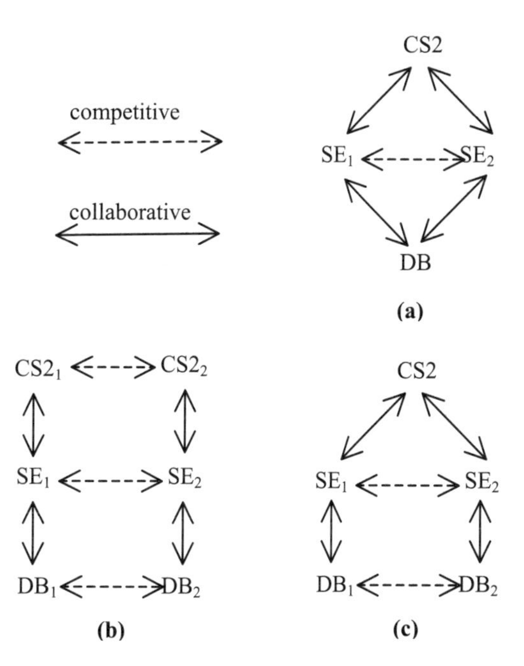

Figure 1 – Variations of Course Collaborations

5.3 Grading Collaborative Work

While students don't "grade" other students work, team assignments typically include an element of student feedback regarding the performance of each team member. In the context of our intra-curriculum project methodology, this includes feedback concerning the collaborating teams from other courses. Can a specialized course team that failed to deliver their component on time cause the software engineering team's grade to suffer? The answer could be yes, if the software engineering team failed in providing a clear specification and managing the progress of the component. The answer could be no, if they can verify that they took appropriate measures; that is, the failure to deliver really is through no fault of theirs. Can a software engineering team negatively affect the grade of a specialized course team project? The answer could be yes, if the component specification was suitable and the team did not indicate to the software engineering team any problems with the specification. The answer could be no, if the software engineering team repeatedly failed to provide an acceptable specification.

Can a lower level course team negatively affect the software engineering team project grade? The answer could be yes, if the software engineering team failed to provide a clear specification failed to provide an acceptable verification mechanism, or failed to manage the progress satisfactorily (this is somewhat difficult since the components are less complex, thus they "turn around" much quicker). The answer could be no, if the lower level class just didn't get it done although they thought all along they could. Similarly to above, the lower level course team could have their grade negatively affected if they failed to deliver or failed to indicate a problem with the specification or verification.

6. SUPPORTING TOOLS

Using an intra-curriculum approach adds new dimensions of communication. Students in different courses must communicate specifications, progress, verification methods with each other. To assist in performing this additional communication, we have developed several tools. These tools have been described in more detail elsewhere [2,3]; however, awareness of the communication support is relevant here and so we provide brief descriptions..

6.1 SECT

The Software Engineering Collaboration Tool (SECT) is a prototype system to help collections of teams communicate and share work products. While these types of communication tools are available individually (e.g., email, IM, ftp, etc.), there remains a need to integrate them into a common tool framework that targets and supports student project development. Many collaboration tools lack features to enable instructor monitoring of student communication and progress. The design of SECT integrates all these capabilities.

6.2 CppAT

We have developed a C++ Acceptance Testing tool that is modeled on the FIT acceptance testing framework for Java [4]. FIT and CppAT allow customers (usually non-technical) to specify acceptance tests (inputs and expected outputs) in HTML tables. The system parses the HTML, creates a test program, executes this test program, and indicates success/failure by color-coding cells in the original HTML tables. We have limited, yet positive, experience with students using this system.

6.3 Quiver

Quiver is a quiz and verification system that is implemented as a self-contained and locally installed web service. It is a robust tool that can run on Windows and Unix-based platforms. Used as a quizzing system, Quiver allows an instructor to specify a programming quiz and release the quiz to students. Students then login and take the quiz in a controlled and monitored environment (e.g., a closed lab). Student code is compiled and executed as part of instructor specified test cases. Feedback of test case results is returned to the student, and the instructor can control the amount of this feedback. We have used Quiver extensively in quizzing mode with students at all levels.

Used in verification mode, Quiver allows the specification of a software component and the verification of the correctness of the component (i.e., test cases). Thus, software engineering students specify a component and provide verification test cases. Collaborating teams refer to the specification and verify the components they build. We are continuing improvements to Quiver aimed at simplifying the building of test cases.

7. CONCLUSIONS

We have presented an innovative pedagogical approach to teaching software engineering. The intra-curriculum approach aims to involve multiple courses simultaneously in the development of a large system. For example, a software engineering course can collaborate with both a database course and a CS2 programming course on a single project. This collaboration frees the software engineering students from some low level implementation allowing them to focus more on the analysis, design, and management engineering aspects. We also provided rich detail of our own applications of the intra-curriculum approach and discussed several alternative collaboration frameworks.

Qualitative assessments are encouraging; we and the students themselves feel that the students are having positive learning experiences. Some have reported frustration with the dependence on others for their project success, but also reporting that they understand this is realistic.

8. FUTURE WORK

We are continuing to use the intra-curriculum software engineering project. This term (fall 2004) we are again collaborating with the database course. At this time, we are unsure what implementation language we will use for the software engineering project which impacts our collaboration with lower level courses.

We have received another NSF grant (DUE 0341506) that is investigating an expansion of the intra-curriculum approach to courses at different universities. This work is just underway and is expected to provide more quantitative assessment.

REFERENCES

[1] Daigle, R. and Niccolai, M. Inter-Class Synergy by Design. In *Proceedings of the SIGCSE conference on Computer Science Education (SIGCSE '97)*. ACM Press, New York, NY, 1997, 92-95.

[2] Ellsworth, C.E., Fenwick, J.B. and Kurtz, B.L. *The Quiver System.* In *Proceedings of the SIGCSE conference on Computer Science Education (SIGCSE '04)*, ACM Press, New York, NY, 2004, 205-209.

[3] Ellsworth, C.E., Holland, J., Krishna C.B., Fenwick, J.B. and Kurtz, B.L. *Software Tools to Support Software Engineering Education.* In *Proceedings of the IASTED Conference on Computers and Advanced Technology in Education (CATE '04)*, August, 2004.

[4] Faulkner, X., Culwin F. Enter the Usability Engineer: Integrating HCI and Software Engineering. *SIGCSE Bulletin, 32,* 3 (Sep. 2000), 61-64.

[5] Hause, M.L., Last, M.Z., Almstrum, V.L. and Woodroffe, M.R., Interaction Factors in Software Development Performance in Distributed Student Teams in Computer Science. In *Proceedings of the Conference Integrating Technology into Computer Science Education.* ACM Press, New York, NY, 2001, 69-72.

[6] Last, M.Z., Hause, M.L., Daniels, M. and Woodroffe, M.R., Learning from Students: Continuous Improvement in International Collaboration. In *Proceedings of the Conference Integrating Technology into Computer Science Education.* ACM Press, New York, NY, 2002, 136-140.

[7] Villareal, E.E. and Butler D. Giving Computer Science Students a Real-World Experience. In *Proceedings of the SIGCSE conference on Computer Science Education (SIGCSE '98)*. ACM Press, New York, NY, 1998, 40-44.

[8] Visual Tcl, http://vtcl.sourceforge.net.

Game Design & Programming Concentration Within the Computer Science Curriculum

Ron Coleman, Mary Krembs, Alan Labouseur, Jim Weir
Marist College
School of Computer Science and Mathematics
Poughkeepsie, New York 12601-1387
1 845-575-3000
{Ron.Coleman, Mary.Krembs, Alan.Labouseur, Jim.Weir}@Marist.edu

ABSTRACT

This paper describes initiatives at Marist College to develop a Game Concentration in the undergraduate Computer Science curriculum. These initiatives contemplate recommendations for existing courses as well as adoption of new courses. We also consider activities of the Association of Computing Machinery (ACM) in this area and opportunities for students beyond the classroom.

Categories and Subject Descriptors

K.3.2 [**Computers and Education**]: Computers and Information Science Education – *Curriculum.*
K.8.0 [**Personal Computing**]: General – *Games.*
D.1.m [**Software**]: Programming Techniques – *Miscellaneous*

General Terms: Algorithms, Design, and Experimentation.

Keywords: Curricular initiative, Game Programming

1. INTRODUCTION

Experience tells us that students are keenly interested in videogames. For many, game systems like the *GameBoy*, *PlayStation*, *Xbox*, etc. represent not only a student's initial experience of computers and computing, in all likelihood these students may well have played videogames before even using the Internet. Indeed, videogames are the initial draw to technology for a number of students in the first place.

Students are also drawn to cutting-edge and emerging technologies. They want to be "where the action is", as it were, and videogames are all about action and interaction. Advances in hardware and software have made game programming accessible to virtually anyone, including teenagers, with even modest programming skills. [6]

Yet videogames embody a considerable amount of computer science, aspects of which are not typically covered by computer science curricula. Consequently, as we explain further below, students have had to look outside traditional academic settings to formally study game development.

The paper focuses on recommendations for existing courses as well as adoption of new ones as we perceive them at Marist. Given the similarity of programs of study across different institutions, we believe these initiatives may potentially have applicability for many other institutions as well. On the other hand, this paper does not consider game development in broad artistic, cognitive, and socio-communicative terms. For instance, while there are some artistic considerations in our analysis, we are mainly concerned with issues related to computer science, physics, and mathematical coursework—the "hard core" of game development, as it were. Thus we have no specific recommendations for coordinating with or influencing the Art, English, or Psychology departments. While an initiative as such may be possible, perhaps even desirable, it is beyond our scope here.

2. MOTIVATION

A review of computing history suggests a curious and distinctive divergence between conventional and videogame applications.

Conventional applications generally emphasize managing and supporting organizational operations and objectives. These include business functions like accounting, sales, inventory tracking, student registrations, etc. These applications are supported by systems programming and employ best practices for optimization, searching and sorting, messaging, and the like, which are fundamental computer science issues usually taught in traditional academic settings.

Videogame applications, on the other hand, generally emphasize entertainment objectives.[†] Once relegated to hulking consoles in dimly lit juke bars and noisy bowling alleys, videogames have truly come into their own on home consoles, on cell phones and personal data assistants (PDAs), on handheld game machines like the *GameBoyAdvance®*, and – thanks to the Internet – online with multiple players scattered around the globe.

While videogames employ fundamental computer science, they also work in real-time and bypass the operating/windowing system, directly accessing hardware devices like video processor

[†] Many videogames emphasize educational and training objectives (e.g., flight simulators) that are also relevant for our purposes.

SIGCSE'05, February 23-27, 2005, St. Louis, Missouri, USA.

units, sound cards, analog, digital, and force feedback controllers—subjects not typically covered by mainstream computer science curricula. Games furthermore incorporate physics simulations, mathematical models, and game-specific principles that distinguish them from conventional applications. For instance, games are *non-linear*, meaning they provide the player with more than one way to be successful or victorious. Games are often written in non-traditional, game-specific languages and scripts supported by a *game engine*—the underlying software that automates game functions from loading and playing animations and sounds to handling collision detection and particle systems. Furthermore, videogames routinely employ artificial intelligence, which broadly speaking is relatively rare in non-entertainment applications.

Thus, we have the status quo: an applications bifurcation. It implies that conventional and videogame software designers rarely talk to one another or compare notes. [1] This situation similarly explains, in our experience anyway, why many game programmers are often self-taught; why they learn the art of game development in their spare time, outside of coursework, as a "labor of love"; why they have little or no formal computer science training, sometimes reinventing solutions to problems long since solved by computer scientists. By the same token, many computer scientists and IT professionals we know are frequently unaware of the challenges and diversity and uniqueness of games, that is, as serious applications. Legendary game designers and pioneers are virtually unknown outside game circles, although their games, e.g. Pong, Pac-Man, Quake, Halo, are widely admired and enjoy, in some cases, cult-like appeal. [4]

Game trade schools have emerged to fill this gap. However, game development is very encompassing and integrative. Indeed, industry experts are now recognizing that students need to be exposed to a broader range of subjects such as history, art, music, creative writing, etc. — the very strengths of liberal arts colleges. [1]

Game trade schools, furthermore, exist for another, perhaps an even more important reason: They satisfy a demand. In other words, game schools, by their existence, suggest that students not only want to be formally trained, but students (and their parents) also consider this training to be worthwhile.

3. OBJECTIVES

We approached the above challenges with the following three objectives (not necessarily in this order):

(1) Coordinate courses consistent with the International Game Developer's Association (IGDA) *Curriculum Framework* with focus on the study of Game Design and Game Programming topics. [5] We give more details below.

(2) Attract, retain, and prepare new Computer Science students for further game studies and/or to pursue careers in the game industry.

(3) Remain competitive as an Institution of higher learning.

We found these objectives could be facilitated within the context of an existing Computer Science curriculum with relatively minor changes. To accomplish this, we take advantage of a few opportunities presented by the policies and the currently recommended schedule.

- Full-time tuition at Marist buys students 16 credits per semester. Most semesters use only 15 of them. This is especially true of the fall semesters. By offering a one-credit GAME seminar in the fall of each year, the Gaming Concentration students get their own "special" course sequence where the faculty can present very game-specific topics, all at no additional expense to the students – more "bang for their buck".
- We are also adding the one-credit Computer Networking Lab in the spring of their junior year in support of massive multiplayer online games (or MMOGs).
- Since game programming requires knowledge of Physics, we specify "General Physics" in the program. This does double duty, also satisfying a core science requirement, so it doesn't reduce the number of electives available to the student.

4. NEW FEATAURES

The Computer Science department has already adopted a yearlong sequence of two courses, Game Design & Programming I and II, which form the core of the proposed concentration. Game Design studies interface design, world design, design of play rules and mechanics, and integration of audio and visual components. Game Programming considers not only "hard core" Computer Science – searching, sorting, path finding, finite state automata – it also incorporates real-time programming for animations, input control, sound playback, collision detection, and applications of physics simulations (e.g., forces, rigid body collisions, particle systems, explosions, etc.) and mathematical methods (vector transformations, random deviates, etc.).

The Concentration has additional features. For instance, we are proposing a Game Seminar as well as recommendations for related courses like Artificial Intelligence, Computer Graphics, and others. We've furthermore included a new math course on computational geometry.

4.1 The Gaming Algorithms Methods & Execution Seminar (GAMES)

This one-credit seminar provides a forum for teaching and exploring issues specific to game design and implementation. It sets apart game concentration students from the outset.

The GAME Seminar meets once a week throughout the fall semester of each year. Various topics are discussed. There are quizzes, tests, and projects. A letter grade is awarded.

Potential topics, in no particular order, may include:

- Game design
- Games and strategy theory
- Business of games in industry
- Game computer architectures
- History of games
- Language processing and adventure games
- Wireless games
- Internet games
- Humor in games
- Non-linearity in games

- AI in games
- Physics in games

Each topic may be covered in a single meeting or span several meetings. We can use this seminar to cover areas that don't require a full course, but are still important to the topic. (Finite State Automata comes to mind. A few classes should suffice.)

4.2 Topics in Applied Geometry

This upper-level Computer Science or Applied Math class covers topics primarily from Computational Geometry and Curve and Surface Design. Subjects to study include plane-sweep algorithms, convex hulls, Voronoi Diagrams, triangulations, parametric equations of curves and surfaces, spline curves and surfaces such as Bezier and NURBS. The course covers the mathematics, algorithms and data structures of these two areas.

These areas of study have applications in Gaming but also Graphics, Computer Aided Design, Molecular Biology, GIS, etc.

Pre-requisites are Calculus II, Linear Algebra, and Computer Science I or equivalent programming expertise. Assignments embody rigorous mathematics as well as programming projects.

5. INFLUENCE ON OTHER COURSES

Since we have neither the faculty time nor classroom space to entirely fill the gaming concentration with brand new courses (we already have three: Game Design and Programming I & II and Topics in Applied Geometry), we recommend small changes and adjustments to some existing courses and a few exchanges in the course requirements. See the appendix for more detail on this subject.

- We recommend that students in the Gaming Concentration substitute our required "Logic Design" course with "Computer Networking and Distributed Systems".
- The language study course uses the language of the Game Design and Programming I and II and gaming concentration capstone course. Currently this is C++.
- Students in the Gaming Concentration take Game Design and Programming I in place of Software Development, which is currently a requirement.
- Advanced Data Structures is required for the Concentration. Currently it is an elective.
- Artificial Intelligence is required for the Concentration. Currently it is an elective. AI would be taught with an eye towards gaming applications in addition to the traditional academic AI topics. As such, we don't need to have two AI courses. Some topics applicable to gaming and AI include chasing and evading, pattern movement, flocking, path finding and navigation, and targeting and threat assessment under uncertainty. [2, 9] Some of these are not typically covered in traditional academic AI study.

6. TRANSFER STUDENTS

As the gaming concentration develops, no doubt new students that didn't start at Marist as freshmen in the Concentration will want to enter the program. At the very least, we need to support transfer students at the Junior year level. (We are thinking, in particular, about transfers from community colleges in the Marist area.) We have considered this as a strong possibility and structured the Concentration accordingly.

Ideally, the transfer students will have already taken Computer Science I and II and Calculus I and II. If not, these courses will need to be taken before matriculation into the Gaming Concentration can be granted. Hopefully, the transfer students will also be ahead on their Core and Liberal Studies courses, so that Topics in Applied Geometry can be worked into their schedule early on.

Since no transfer student will have had the benefit of the GAME seminars we mentioned earlier, a special two credit "transfer version" of the GAME seminar is offered in the spring semester (so as not to add further burden to the Faculty responsible for the fall GAME seminars.)

7. OPPORTUNITIES

A concentration in games presents a number of opportunities for students to further their studies in games or perhaps pursue game careers.

- Every year Marist hosts two large, student-organized gaming events. These events don't have to be all play and no work. We are considering setting up a booth, developing a flyer, and whatnot, to reach out to prospective students and tell them about the Concentration and encourage them to participate in *game programming* competitions rather than just a game playing contests.
- We are considering setting up a forum for game vendor representatives (e.g., NVIDIA, Alienware, and others) and students to discuss game internships, careers, requirements, etc.
- We hope further to engage game vendors to donate hardware to support game design, programming, and student research. For instance, Marist already conducts non-game related joint studies with a major computer vendor. This vendor also makes processors for Nintendo's *GameCube®* and graphic processor units for NVIDIA, and will soon be making the next generation of processor chips for Microsoft's *Xbox®*. Also, *Direct3D®*, which our students use in the Game Concentration, is the software driver for the *Xbox®*. We believe there are opportunities here for the vendor to help prepare the next generation of game developers.
- Indeed, anticipating that students may have expectations for careers in gaming, we plan to work with Career Services to reach out to game vendors to support Marist's Career Fair.

8. THE ACM AND GAMES

The ACM has published no official position on game curricula, as far as our research indicates.

The ACM has, however, approved an agreement to cooperate with International Game Developers Association (IGDA) in 2002. As we mentioned earlier, the IGDA authored *The Curriculum*

Framework, [5] which is the basis for our Game Design and Programming courses.

We note further that key ACM publications have featured game-related papers. For instance, the February 2004 issue of the forward-looking *ACM Queue* was dedicated entirely to game development. [9] In the flagship journal, *Communications of the ACM*, a series of related papers in 2002 were published dedicated to game engines for scientific research. [8] In 2000, the *CACM* published another series of related papers related to physics-based game simulation. [7] Earlier still, Nolan Bushnell (1996), game design pioneer and founder of Atari, also published in the *CACM* a perceptive paper on entertainment computing.

We may conclude from these activities that there is growing interest in and support for game-related development and curricula within the larger computer science community. We believe the ACM will (eventually) need to formalize its position on computer science related game studies if demands from students for formal training grow as it would appear poised to do.

9. OPEN ISSUES

Adding course requirements to an already rigorous field of study is challenging. We don't want to overburden the students with so many required classes that they have no time to explore other intellectual interests through free electives. Marist students have an option use free elective credits for work internships, which is absolutely crucial, as that often enhances opportunities obtaining employment upon graduation.

Our recommendations accommodate free electives in both the major and general areas of study by maximizing any "double duty" opportunities (e.g., the Artificial Intelligence course) and minimizing the number of entirely new courses (e.g., the GAME Seminar is not a new course but replaces the computing studies seminar. The presence of general electives means that there is room for internships and some diversity in course load. However, from the Concentration perspective, the course load structure is still a little too strict. We would do much better shape if we could get two Art courses to count as Core / Liberal Studies courses. That would greatly help to preserve the remaining electives. This needs to be worked on further, and is not accounted for here.

Workload is another issue. After four years, all four levels of the GAME Seminar will be running simultaneously. There may also be a spring "GAME I and II for transfer students". This may present scheduling and/or teaching load challenges.

We furthermore have been asked several times about game design and programming at the graduate level. We have not fully taken these requests into account, although the opportunities would seem considerable since graduate students generally have deeper computer science backgrounds and programming experiences.

Then there is the issue of whether or not we need game-specific hardware. If so (and this is likely), who will control access to it? How do we support it?

10. EXAMPLE COURSE SEQUENCE

Table 1 presents an example course sequence along with notes specific to the Gaming Concentration.

11. ACKNOWLEDGMENTS

Thanks are due to Dr. Roger Norton, Dean of the School of Computer Science and Mathematics at Marist College for his encouragement and support of the initiative. We'd also like to thank the faculty in the School for their comments and feedback on this topic.

12. REFERENCES

[1] Adams, E., *Break into the Game Industry*, Osborne, 2003

[2] Bourg, D.M., Seemann, G., *AI For Game Developers*, O'Reilly, 2004

[3] Bushnell, N. "Relationships between fun and the computer business," *CACM*, vol. 39, no. 8, p. 31-37 (August 1996)

[4] Burnham, V. *Supercade*, MIT Press, 2003

[5] Education Committee, *The Curriculum Framework*, International Game Developer's Association, v2.3, igda.org (February 2003)

[6] Sethi, M., *Game Programming for Teens*, Premier (2003)

[7] Various authors, "Physically Based Computer Animation," CACM, vol. 42, no.2 (February 2000)

[8] Various authors, "Game Engines in Scientific Research," *CACM*, vol. 45, no. 1, (January 2002)

[9] Various authors, *ACM Queue* (2004). vol. 1, no. 10, (February 2004)

Table 1 – Example Course Sequence

	Number	*Name*	*Credits*	*Gaming Concentration Notes*
Freshman	CMSC 110	Computing Studies Seminar	1	
Fall	CMSC 120	Computer Science I	4	
	MATH 241	Calculus I	4	was Introduction to Statistics I
	PHIL 101	Introduction to Philosophy	3	
	ENG 116	College Writing I	3	
	CMSC ?	GAME Seminar I	1	
			16	

Spring	CMSC 121	Computer Science II	3	
	MATH 250	Discrete Mathematics I	3	
	IS 130	Computer Studies Concepts	3	
	ENG 117	College Writing II	3	
	MATH 242	Calculus II	3	was Core / Liberal Studies
			15	
Sophomore	CMSC ?	Lower-level CS elective	3	
Fall	MATH 210	Linear Algebra	3	was Calculus I
	Science	Lab Science I	4	should be PHYS 211 - General Physics
	Core/LS	Core / Liberal Studies	3	
	Core/LS	Core / Liberal Studies	3	
	CMSC ?	GAME Seminar II	1	
			17	
Spring	CMSC 230	Assembly Language Programming	3	
	MATH ?	Topics in Applied Geometry	3	was Calculus II
	Science	Lab Science II	4	
	Core/LS	Core / Liberal Studies	3	
	Core/LS	Core / Liberal Studies	3	
			16	
Junior	CMSC 406	Computer Networks/Distributed Systems	3	was Logic Design
Fall	CMSC 331	Theory of Programming Languages	3	
	CMSC 233	Language Study	3	may be OOP in C++
	CMSC 446	Computer Graphics	3	was Math or Science elective
	Core/LS	Core / Liberal Studies	3	
	CMSC ?	GAME Seminar III	1	
			16	
Spring	CMSC 415	Computer Organization and Architecture	3	
	CMSC 414	Game Design and Programming I	3	was Software Development
	CMSC 335	Advanced Data Structures	3	*Required for Gaming Concentration*
	PHIL 300	Ethics	3	
	Core/LS	Core / Liberal Studies	3	
	IS 407	Data Communications Networking Lab	1	
			16	
Senior	CMSC 422	Operating Systems	3	

Fall	CMSC 404	Artificial Intelligence	3	was Upper-level elective
	CMSC 424	Game Design and Programming II	3	was Upper-level elective
	?	General elective / Internship	3	
	Core/LS	Core / Liberal Studies	3	
	CMSC ?	GAME Seminar IV	1	
			16	
Spring	CMSC ?	Upper-level elective	3	
	CMSC ?	Upper-level elective	3	maybe a Gaming Project, a capstone course
	?	General elective / Internship	3	
	?	General elective / Internship	3	
	Core/LS	Core / Liberal Studies	3	
			15	

Total = 127 credits

Informatics: A Focus on Computer Science in Context

David G. Kay, André van der Hoek, Debra J. Richardson
Department of Informatics
Donald Bren School of Information and Computer Sciences
University of California, Irvine
Irvine, CA 92697-3425 USA
+1 949 824 6326
{kay,andre,djr}@ics.uci.edu

ABSTRACT

Because the field of computer science has broadened so much in recent years, traditional degree programs are becoming crowded with new courses, each introducing its own "essential" topic. However, with more and more such courses, it is no longer possible to cover every topic in a single, coherent, four-year program. Many alternative approaches are available to address this situation. At UC Irvine, we have chosen a solution in which we offer four coordinated degree programs: a B.S. in Computer Science & Engineering, a conventional B.S. in Computer Science, a new B.S. in Informatics, and a broad overview B.S. in Information and Computer Science. Of these, the B.S. in Informatics is the most innovative, focusing on software and information design. Context plays a particularly strong role in our B.S. in Informatics: Placing software development in context is critical to the delivery of successful solutions, and we educate our students accordingly. We present our definition of informatics, detail our curriculum, describe its pedagogical characteristics and objectives, and conclude with some critical observations regarding informatics and its place in computer science education.

Categories and Subject Descriptors

K.3.2 [**Computers and Education**]: Computer and Information Science Education – *computer science education, curriculum*

General Terms: Design

Keywords: Informatics, education, computer science education, software engineering education, contextual learning

1. INTRODUCTION

In recent years, the field of computer science has grown tremendously in both breadth and depth. On the one hand, new subfields have emerged: bioinformatics, security, gaming, and others. On the other hand, existing subfields such as software engineering, computer networking, programming languages, and theory have grown significantly in knowledge and pedagogical approaches.

It is now recognized that undergraduate computer science degree programs can no longer cover all aspects of the field comprehensively [1]. Institutions across the country are employing a variety of approaches to designing their undergraduate computing curricula to counter this problem. Four canonical strategies may be applied: (1) survey the field at a high level, (2) provide a more configurable program, (3) lengthen the degree program, and (4) offer separate, diversified degree programs.

Survey the field at a high level. Under this strategy, students learn about a broad range of topics. A typical program may include, for example, courses in programming, computer architecture, operating systems, networking, programming languages, compilers, databases, graphics, artificial intelligence, software engineering, human-computer interaction, and social and ethical issues. Other courses may be included, usually depending on the interests of the faculty. This kind of degree program is often the result of incremental modification; as new topics emerge, the program changes to incorporate new courses on these topics. A problem with this strategy, though, is that as the number of topics increases that "any undergraduate really should know," the program strains at the seams, reducing opportunities for elective courses and sacrificing depth for breadth.

Provide a more configurable program. Under this strategy, a curriculum is partitioned into core and optional courses. In some degree programs, students may arbitrarily choose optional courses, but a more typical approach is to group optional courses into concentrations and require students to take one or more concentrations to bring some depth to their studies. While increasing flexibility, this kind of strategy also has drawbacks. As the number of optional courses rises, chains of prerequisites restrict which courses can be taken when; since a given course is seldom offered every term, care must be taken in scheduling. Students may become stuck, may simply choose concentrations based on which courses best fit in their schedules, and may not have a good grasp of how the different classes in their program complement each other to form a coherent course of study.

Lengthen the degree program. Although not an option often considered, the five-year bachelors/masters combination common in Europe is one form of lengthening the degree program. Adopting such an approach is possible, for example with a six-year bachelors/masters program. This, however, requires a commitment of time and funding that many students may be reluctant to make as they graduate high school. Moreover, economic downturns and outsourcing notwithstanding, current projections indicate a high demand for technology-skilled workers over the next decade [2]; constricting the pipeline at the front end may not be wise policy.

Offer separate, diversified degree programs. This solution strikes a balance between depth and breadth: By offering multiple degree programs, each with its own particular focus, it is possible to offer a range of options to students and still provide an in-depth education within each option. Especially when the degree programs share some courses in the first year, this option allows sufficient flexibility for students who may wish to change while at the same time providing in-depth treatment of specialized topics in each degree in the later years. (The greater the overlap of early courses across programs, the easier it is for the student to switch programs.) The drawback is, of course, that students must choose a focus early, although this is slowly but surely mitigated by the introduction of computer science in high-schools; prospective students can familiarize themselves with a range of computing topics before they enter college, enabling them to make finer sub-disciplinary distinctions early in their college career.

The Donald Bren School of Information and Computer Sciences at UC Irvine has chosen this latter option: Instead of offering one configurable degree program (as it has done for many years), it now offers four closely coordinated programs. These programs allow students the choice of focusing on the lower layers of computer science (e.g., hardware design, embedded systems, computer networks, sensor networks) with a B.S. in Computer Science & Engineering (offered together with the Henry Samueli School of Engineering), on the middle layers (e.g., databases, computer systems design, theory, programming languages, artificial intelligence) with a B.S. in Computer Science, and on the upper layers (e.g., software engineering, human-computer interaction, computer-supported collaborative work, organizational information systems) with a B.S. in Informatics. In addition, they may still choose the generic, configurable B.S. in Information and Computer Science, should they desire an overview of the field rather than the in-depth exploration provided by the other three degree programs.

Here we describe the Informatics program, which we developed and now offer with support from the U.S. Department of Education's Fund for the Improvement of Post-Secondary Education (FIPSE). We designed it from the ground up to focus on the upper layers of computer science, complementing the school's other degree programs, to serve as an example of innovative curricula and effective pedagogy, and to promote inclusive participation by a broadly representative student body. This program admitted its first students in September 2004.

2. INFORMATICS

The term "informatics" has long been used in Europe to describe the entire field of computer science, from computer engineering to information systems and related fields, but in the U.S., that usage has not caught on. A small but growing number of U.S. universities are now developing new programs in informatics [3, 4, 5, 6], programs not equivalent to general computer science but concentrating instead on the upper layers of the field, moving away from a focus on computers alone to a focus on *computing in context*. Defined as the study of the design, application, use, and impact of information technology, informatics applies information technology to real world problems, designs and develops new uses for information technology, and aims to understand the impact information technology has on people [6].

To position Informatics clearly in the broader area of computing, we augment two diagrams of the Computing Curricula 2004 draft (CC 2004) [1]. Figure 1 presents the first diagram, with Informatics filling the hole that exists between "software" and "organizational needs" with "context". This signifies that Informatics builds a bridge from computer science and software engineering to information technology, a bridge that is formed by making context central to the education. The motto is that software is not developed as an isolated artifact, but is always a solution to a problem, addressing software *and* information, development *and* design, technical *and* social factors, as well as creation *and* study of implemented solutions [7].

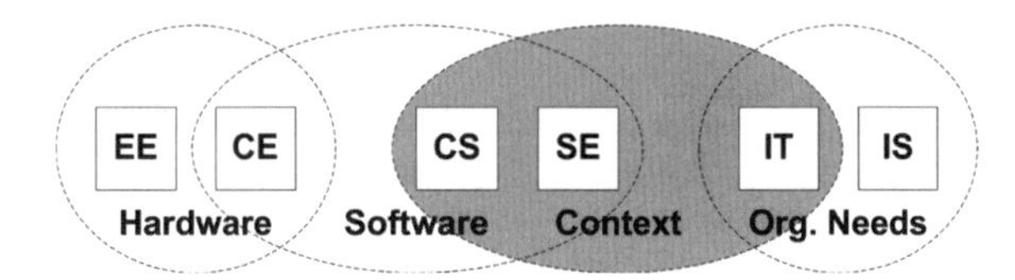

Figure 1. Informatics centers on context.

The second augmented diagram identifies the coverage of different areas of concern for Informatics. In Figure 2, we have drawn a complement to the diagrams in the CC 2004 draft that show the areas of concern for CE, CS, SE, IS, and IT. Informatics sets itself apart by focusing squarely on application domains and software development, from both a theoretical and practical perspective. The superimposed grey oval represents the additional context that Informatics addresses, both in terms of the organization and systems issues to be supported and the system infrastructures available. Of note is that Informatics encompasses most of the areas covered by the SE diagram in the CC 2004 draft. This is by design, since we believe software engineering is at the heart of Informatics. We believe that SE must be augmented to give students an adequate education for addressing real-world problems effectively. An Informatics education includes significant aspects of other disciplines, among them social science, cognitive science, computer-supported collaborative work, human-computer interaction, organizational studies, and particular application areas as well as a considerable portion of the core of computer science.

At present, the field of Informatics is still searching for the best way to educate its students. Different institutions take different approaches. At Indiana University, students take a set of core courses in computer science, followed by one or more application area specializations [6]. At the University of Washington, students focus more on the information aspects of Informatics, with

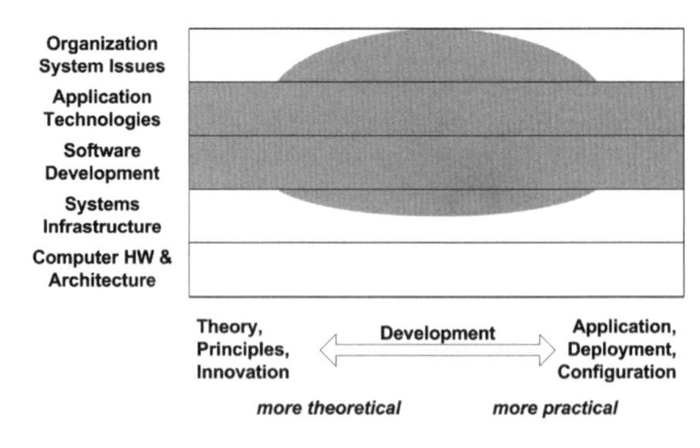

Figure 2. Areas of concern for Informatics.

courses in databases, information management, information system design, determining information needs, searching for and presenting information, etc. [3]. More experience is needed, and we anticipate that many more programs will emerge in the near term. While these may differ in their precise implementations, we predict they will fall in the outlined domain and revolve around issues of design, context, and understanding impact.

Our B.S. in Informatics distinguishes itself from existing degree programs in Informatics in two ways: (1) its solid technical foundation, building upon a very comprehensive software engineering background, and (2) an integrated social and technical approach from the beginning. Starting with the introductory course in the first year and continuing all the way through the capstone senior project course, we train students continually to examine the broader picture, develop an understanding of the problem context, and apply their technical skills to design and develop an appropriate solution. We achieve this with a curriculum that balances course sequences in software engineering, programming languages, human-computer interaction, organizational computing, and databases with a variety of individual courses in project management, computer-supported collaborative work, information retrieval, information visualization, and so on.

3. INFORMATICS CURRICULUM

Our new Informatics curriculum, shown in

Table 1, is designed in accordance with the definition and observations above. Our courses all run on the quarter system. We marked each course as follows: unmarked courses are taught and specified by Department of Informatics faculty; courses marked with (cs) originate in the other degree programs in the school and are typically offered by faculty in its other departments; courses marked with (o) discuss non–computer-science topics; and courses marked with (b) signify electives or courses that satisfy the university's breadth (general education) requirements.

We designed our program from scratch, without being limited by existing courses. We did take advantage of existing courses when they fit our vision, but we were not constrained in any way. The result is a curriculum consisting of fourteen new and thirteen existing courses in computing, as well as three mathematics courses and the required breadth (general education) courses.

The first year provides students with a hands-on introduction to the broad field of Informatics, anchored by the new core course. This three-quarter sequence introduces students to the Informatics philosophy of considering context from their first quarter in the program. We want the students to develop a mindset in which context and design come first, rather than starting off with a focus on programming alone. The course does have a strong emphasis on writing programs in the functional and object-oriented styles (as does the rest of the curriculum; students will practice more programming than is common in most CS programs), but the assignments and class meetings put contextualized problem solving and design first and programming second.

The first year also teaches students formal reasoning (logic) and problem solving skills through a sequence of three courses: abstract reasoning, discrete math, and data structures analysis and implementation. Together with the statistics course in the second year, the materials introduced in these courses lay the mathematical foundation for the rest of the program.

The second year builds up a portfolio of foundational techniques and skills that further establish the discipline of Informatics and provide a "toolbox" that students will use in future years to solve large-scale information and software design problems. Courses discuss the role of various programming languages and conceptual approaches (including how special-purpose languages can help solve certain problems elegantly); introduce user interface design (from the multiple perspectives of theory, established practices, and hands-on development); present software engineering methods, notations, and tools; and establish the roles of requirements elicitation and quality assurance in successfully carrying out a system design and development project.

The third year builds upon the foundational techniques and skills introduced in the second year; it covers information and software design from two different but related perspectives. First, there is a three-course series that describes how information and software design affect the real world, i.e., the social and organizational context in which a solution is ultimately placed. A second three-course sequence (actually starting in the last quarter of the second year) introduces technical approaches to design and large-scale problem solving with software. Combined, the two sequences present a comprehensive overview of design from both a technical and social perspective.

The fourth year is built around a year-long capstone project in which groups of students address a significant project, typically from an outside client. In addressing this project, students must bring together materials from previous years (tools, skills, processes, ethnographic methods, design approaches, and many others) to complete their project successfully. The fourth year also includes more advanced courses on databases, information retrieval, information visualization, project management, and computer-supported cooperative work.

This program, unlike many current computer science and engineering curricula, affords students the flexibility to take elective courses or to undertake undergraduate research projects. Providing these opportunities allows students to pursue interdisciplinary interests and maintains their enthusiasm and motivation.

The program has several distinguishing characteristics:

- *A smaller number of math courses.* Traditional computer science programs often include math courses intended mainly to enhance students' "mathematical maturity" and formal reasoning skills. While we value mathematics as a discipline and accept that math helps students develop reasoning skills, we designed our program to include only those math or other foundational courses that contribute directly to an understanding of software and information design. We believe students can develop critical thinking skills in many ways and we particularly advocate building these skills in the domain in which they will be applied. Hence, many of our courses are structured to require formal or quantitative reasoning, weighing of alternatives, and creative thinking. A good example is the software design series, which emphasizes creative problem solving and designing appropriate solutions to challenging problems.
- *An interdisciplinary approach.* Our Informatics major addresses the broad set of issues surrounding design, including initial requirements gathering, estimating and measuring the

impact of alternative solutions, and implementing those solutions—all from a multi-disciplinary perspective that includes computer science, information science, organizational science, social science, cognitive science, and others. It is not sufficient to teach mechanical design notations and principles; these must be placed in context, examined from multiple perspectives, and honed and practiced to develop the designer's ability to propose solutions that effectively solve the problem at hand. We address these issues throughout, particularly in the third-year sequence on social and organizational impact and the fourth-year senior design project.

- *A focus on design.* As the linchpin of our curriculum, we take a distinctly design-oriented approach to the materials in the Informatics program. Traditionally, design is underrepresented in current computer science curricula; at best, a typical software engineering class introduces notations and lets students practice, at best, a few designs. With the exception of some specific software engineering programs [8, 9], there simply is no room in the curriculum to teach additional material and practice more. Our curriculum turns this notion on its head. We introduce design from the beginning, have multiple course sequences on the topic, examine it from a multi-disciplinary perspective, and promote extensive practice in actually creating high-quality designs. Even compared to existing software engineering degree programs, this is a much broader and more in-depth treatment.

We anticipate that our students will be able to function in a variety of different jobs. They will be familiar with all aspects of the software development process, from initial requirements gathering to the delivery of a solution. They will know that software is merely a part of an overall solution that addresses the information that an organization manages, manipulates, and visualizes. They will design and develop integrated software and information systems. They will be technically solid. They will know that their activities have both a technical and social aspect, and know how to create and also analyze solutions. In sum, they will be prepared to deal with real-world problems in context and approach them from an informed computing perspective.

4. PEDAGOGICAL CHARACTERISTICS

We designed the Informatics major to incorporate a set of best pedagogical practices. To meet the program's goals, we felt it was critical not just to provide the right set of courses but also to address the pedagogy for structuring, sequencing, and delivering those courses. Not surprisingly, then, the curriculum makes wide use of multi-course sequences. These course sequences provide continuity, help place the topics in their broader context, and provide added depth as one topic builds upon another. In our software design sequence, for example, students in the first course ("Design I") are introduced to software design notations and principles, refinement into code, architectural styles, and design patterns. The second course ("Design II") broadens the study to large-scale systems, reuse, product families, real-time systems, and application frameworks. Finally, the third course ("Software Architecture, Distributed Systems, and Interoperability") expands the repertoire to distributed, decentralized design.

Group work is often required in our courses. In the first year, we start with pair programming and build that up in later courses to larger group projects. In the final year, groups of students participate in a year-long senior design project. We support this teamwork by addressing the tools and approaches necessary to manage the work effectively. The second-year "Methods and Tools" course, for instance, introduces tools for such tasks as configuration management, bug tracking, and process management. In the senior year, students take a full course in project management as they start on their senior design project.

We use case studies to provide realistic, practical experiences to our students. This starts with a case study of a web store that we introduce in the first quarter. Students are not expected to build the entire store, of course, but will build individual components that must be integrated with the existing implementation. Having

Table 1. Required Curriculum for the UC Irvine B.S. in Informatics.

	Fall	*Winter*	*Spring*
First	Informatics Core	Informatics Core	Informatics Core
			Informatics Research Topics Seminar
	(o) Critical Reasoning	(o) Discrete Mathematics	(cs) Fundamental Data Structures
	(b) Writing	(b) Writing	(b) Writing
Second	(o) Statistics	Human-Computer Interaction	Project in HCI & User Interfaces
	(cs) Concepts Programming Languages I	Concepts Programming Languages II	Software Design I
	Software Methods and Tools	Requirements Analysis & Engineering	SW Specification & Quality Engineering
	(b) Breadth	(b) Breadth	(b) Breadth
Third	Social Analysis of Computerization	Organizational Information Systems	Project Social/Org. Impacts of Computing
	Software Design II	SW Arch, Dist. Sys., & Interoperability	(cs) File and Database Management
	(b) Breadth	(b) Breadth	(b) Breadth
	(b) Breadth / Elective	(b) Breadth / Elective	(b) Breadth / Elective
Fourth	Senior Design Project	Senior Design Project	Senior Design Project
	(cs) Project in Database Management	(cs) Information Retrieval	Information Visualization
	Project Management	CSCW	(b) Breadth/ Elective
	(b) Breadth / Elective	(b) Breadth / Elective	(b) Breadth / Elective

access to the full working example, however, is critical, as it provides relevancy and forms a context for the concepts that are taught. Moreover, students can freely explore other aspects of the application and interesting problems arise that frame the theory of design and allow practical examples of the theory. These case studies occur throughout the program. The design courses, for instance, study and dissect designs of actual systems. The senior design course is, in some ways, a large, experiential case study with an actual customer, in which the students must manage, design, and implement an entire project from start to finish.

Each year culminates with a project course in which a particular case study wraps up the year. We will have showcase days in which students at all levels in the program present their projects to a public audience that includes representatives from local industry. Such industrial contact further motivates the students.

We use varied teaching approaches throughout the curriculum. Principled use of case studies, as described above, puts us in the domain of problem-based learning. A speaker series in the first year introduces students to the broad topics and research problems in Informatics, further enhancing the context. We dissect, study, and analyze from a design perspective actual software and information systems. Real customers provide the projects for the senior design course. Advanced software engineering simulations let students work through more aspects of the software development process than they could experience in the field. Together, these and other approaches provide the students with an engaging experience that is clearly related to their future endeavors.

Putting all these pieces into place requires a significant commitment from the faculty with a huge potential payoff. Specifically, the above factors—increased program coherence, ties to realistic problems, and practical, creative exercises accompanying theoretical course materials—are among the strongest factors contributing to increased participation of underrepresented populations in CS programs [10].

5. CONCLUSIONS

We created this B.S. in Informatics degree with three goals: (1) build a complementary degree program focused on both software and information design, (2) develop an exemplary program with effective pedagogy and an engaging curriculum emphasizing real-world problems and creative solutions, and (3) promote access to the program, retention, and degree completion for a broadly representative group of students.

This major (and the other new majors in the school) were proposed, approved by the campus, and implemented successfully in a very cooperative climate. Incoming students have chosen among the programs, with an initial first-year class of 31 in Informatics (out of approximately 180 first-year students schoolwide).

The program has the strongest technical component of any current U.S. Informatics program, befitting its home in an information and computer science school with a long tradition of technical excellence. The program meets a particular real-world need for broadly trained system designers with strong implementation skills [2]. It also resists outsourcing, since high-level design requires intensive interaction with clients and an understanding of their organizational, social, and cultural context, all of which is hard to achieve from halfway around the world. It should particularly attract students with more interest in designing solutions to real problems than in designing smaller, faster, and cheaper computers.

With enrollments in computer science programs currently trending downwards, schools must explore ways of attracting more students to the field. The approach taken at UC Irvine is to diversify degree offerings, providing programs tailored to diverse students' goals and interests. Our B.S. degree in Informatics is one part of this strategy, offering a novel combination of concepts and skills that expands the range of computing curricula.

6. MORE INFORMATION

More information about the UC Irvine B.S. in Informatics can be found at: http://www.ics.uci.edu/informatics.

7. ACKNOWLEDGMENTS

The Informatics major at UC Irvine is sponsored in part by the Fund for the Improvement of Postsecondary Education (FIPSE), U.S. Department of Education.

8. REFERENCES

[1] ACM, AIS, and IEEE-CS Joint Task force for Computing Curricula 2004, *Computing Curricula 2004,* http://www.acm.org/education/curricula.html.

[2] U.S. Bureau of Labor Statistics, *2002-2012 Employment Projection*, http://www.bls.gov/news.release/ecopro.nr0.htm.

[3] University of Washington Information School, B.S. of Science in Informatics, http://www.ischool.washington.edu.

[4] York College of Pennsylvania, B.S. of Informatics, http://www.ycp.edu/academics/.

[5] Montclair State University Department of Computer Science, B.S. in Science Informatics, http://cs.montclair.edu/undergraduate.html.

[6] Indiana University School of Informatics, B.S. of Informatics, http://www.informatics.indiana.edu/.

[7] A. van der Hoek, D.G. Kay, and D.J. Richardson, *A B.S. in Informatics: Contextualizing Software Engineering Education* (in submission).

[8] Rochester Institute of Technology Department of Software Engineering, B.S in Software Engineering, http://www.se.rit.edu/degrees.html.

[9] Milwaukee School of Engineering, B.S. in Software Engineering, http://www.msoe.edu/eecs/se/.

[10] Margolis and Fischer, *Unlocking the Clubhouse: Women in Computing.* Cambridge: MIT Press, 2001

Randomness and Probability in the Early CS Courses

David Ginat
(moderator)
Tel-Aviv University
ginat@post.tau.ac.il

Richard Anderson
University of Washington
anderson@cs.washington.edu

Daniel D. Garcia
University of California, Berkeley
ddgarcia@cs.berkeley.edu

Richard Rasala
Northeastern University
rasala@ccs.neu.edu

ABSTRACT

Randomness and probability are essential notions in CS studies. They are invoked and employed in diverse courses at different levels. Although a structured course on these notions does not usually appear early in the curriculum, students and educators may benefit from their encapsulation already in CS0 and CS1. The special session will involve motivation, demonstration, and discussion with the audience of the assets of such an encapsulation. Attending CS educators will enrich their teaching perspectives, pedagogical tools, and assignment repertoires.

Categories & Subject Descriptors

K.3 [**Computers & Education**] Computer & Information Science Education – *Computer Science Education.*

General Terms

Algorithms, Design.

Keywords

Randomness, Probability.

1. OBJECTIVE

The early CS courses – CS0 and CS1 – introduce the students to programming and CS fundamentals. They emphasize task analysis and solution design, which are practiced through a variety of tasks, of diverse characteristics – some are technical exercises; some are numerical calculations, some involve data processing, using basic data structures; and some may be simulations of real world occurrences or other phenomena.

The main objective of the early courses is the fundamentals of design, analysis, and implementation. Yet, a variety of additional topics are embedded in these courses in limited respects. These may include programming environments and HCI, basic architecture considerations, discrete mathematics, problem solving heuristics, and more.

SIGCSE'05, February 23-27, 2005, St. Louis, USA.
ACM 1-58113-997-7/05/0002.

One additional topic that may be nicely embedded at a very basic level is probability and statistics. CS students usually learn this topic in a systematic course later in the curriculum (e.g., [4]). Yet, they may refresh and enhance their initial pre-college familiarity with it already in CS0 and CS1. Such an enhancement, involving basic notions of randomness and probability, may be beneficial in several respects:

- Students will comprehend the meaning of randomness and basic probability rules.
- They will realize the relevance, appearance, and use of randomness and probability in programming tasks. This may involve stimulating invocations of random generation and probabilistic computations.
- The corresponding programming tasks may often be colorful and attractive. In particular, they may involve diverse simulations of real world phenomena (in nature or among people), random events, guessing activities, and games.
- The notions of non-determinism and probabilistic algorithms may be introduced, at a very preliminary level, through guided examples.

The objective of the special session is to motivate and show the benefits and assets of encapsulating randomness and probability in the early CS courses, and offer ways for performing this encapsulation. The session's presentation will include the motivation and rationale as well as appealing illustrations.

We believe that CS educators will benefit from such presentation, as it uncovers a less illuminated, yet very relevant perspective, which may be naturally integrated in the teaching of CS0 and CS1. The various illustrations may serve as valuable didactical tools, and enrich CS tutors' repertoire of examples, tasks, and projects.

2. OUTLINE

The session will be partly a tutorial and partly an interactive seminar. It will include motivation, illustrations, audience participation, and conclusion. The general structure will be as follows.

- **Rationale.** The relevance of encapsulating randomness and probability in CS0 and CS1.
- **Encapsulation illustrations.** Each participant will display a couple of approaches and illustrations of embedding probability and randomness in the early courses.

- **Audience participation.** The audience will be encouraged to comment on the presented illustrations, and contribute additional ones.
- **Suggestions for educators.** Pedagogical lessons of encapsulation approaches will be discussed with the audience and summarized.

The presented ideas will involve various elements, which range from basic statistical and probability notions to their diverse appearances in programming. Below is a list of such elements.

- **Basic utilization of the *random* function.** The *random* function is relevant in numerous applications, for selecting elements. The elements may be drawn from various numerical ranges or from classes of objects. One often needs to define a <u>mapping</u> from the standard range [0,1] of the *random* function to an integer range [0,K], and then needs to further define a mapping from [0,K] to the task's domain of elements. Key questions may arise when one debates different ways of returning random selections through elementary or complex objects.
- **Random set generation.** One may need to randomly generate a set, or a list of elements, and therefore repeatedly invoke *random*. This may occur, for example, upon generating a random permutation. An algorithmic scheme of repeated *random* invocations should be carefully designed, in order to guarantee suitable randomness; e.g., each domain instance (permutation) should be generated with equal probability.
- **Real-world applications.** Randomness is required in diverse forms, in a wide range of applications that emulate real world situations, such as arbitrary arrivals of entities, social events, nature occurrences, and more. Such applications may be the basis for programming assignments, of various scales, in any paradigm, be it functional, procedural, or object-oriented.
- **Particularly colorful applications.** Games, graphical applications, and instructive simulations may be particularly attractive; e.g., one may program Black-Jack, dice games, animations, and simulations such as the Buffon Needle for the estimation of π [2] or the Galton Board for studying the normal distribution [3].
- **Probabilistic evaluation of randomness schemes.** Various algorithmic schemes that involve repeated invocations of the *random* function may be evaluated with respect to probabilistic considerations. Such an evaluation may illuminate the ties between randomness and probability in programming.
- **Basic embedment of probability.** A variety of basic tasks may involve simple probability rules; e.g., a task for computing the chances of team A to beat team B in the World Series, given that the probability of a win for A in a single game against B is *p*. The integration of simple probability rules in a computational scheme may enhance comprehension of these rules and their application in programming. The use of spreadsheets may also be relevant for enhancing comprehension.
- **Simulation means and probabilistic analysis.** The very basic (unconditional) probability rules may be considered simple and intuitive. Yet, the probabilistic analysis of even simple phenomena may sometimes yield counter-intuitive results; e.g., the Monty Hall dilemma [5] and the Birthday problem [1]. As a first step, prior to the analysis one may simulate the phenomena and realize the results. The evidence from repeated simulations may be used for realizing probability rules and being careful with intuition.

The above elements may be embedded in various places during the teaching of CS0 and CS1, mostly through examples in class and homework tasks. A series of such examples and tasks may yield an initial, yet valuable comprehension of the notions of randomness and probability.

3. EXPECTATIONS

The expected audience is computer science educators that are interested in pedagogical aspects of programming, design and analysis. The presented approaches and illustrations of including randomness and probability in CS0 and CS1 offer a novel perspective and pedagogical means, which educators my employ in class. In addition, the audience comments and participation may yield fruitful discussions, and possibly further suggestions and means for class utilization.

REFERENCES

[1] http://mathworld.wolfram.com/BirthdayProblem.html

[2] http://mathworld.wolfram.com/BuffonsNeedleProblem.html

[3] http://mathworld.wolfram.com/GaltonBoard.html

[4] Hogg, R. V. and Tanis, E. A., *Probability and Statistical Inference*, Macmillan (2000).

[5] Von Savant, M., *The Power of Logical Thinking*, St. Martin Press (1996).

The Many Facets of Diversity

Jack Beidler (Moderator)
University of Scranton
Computing Sciences
Scranton, PA 18510
570-941-7774
beidler@scranton.edu

Hilary Holz
California State Univ. Hayward
Dept of Mathematics and Computer Science
Hayward, CA 94542
hholz@csuhayward.edu

Ken Yasuhara
Univ. of Washington
Comp.Sci.&Engr.Ed. Group
Seattle, WA 98195-2350
206-616-7046
yasuhara@cs.washington.edu

Evans J. Adams
Fort Lewis College
Computer Science
1000 Rim Drive
Durango, CO 81310
970-247-7211
adams_e@fortlewis.edu

ABSTRACT

The panelists approach diversity from different points of view and experiences to produce a positive and productive foundation for an open discussion on the many facets of diversity, it potential, and positive impact on our profession.

Categories and Subject Descriptors

K.7.0 [**The Computing Professional**]: Diversity, ethical issues, minority issues, gender issues.

General Terms

Human Factors, Legal Aspects, Management.

Hilary Holz

Diversity in computer science stands in marked contrast to all other major science, technology, engineering and math (STEM) disciplines. The role and representation of women in the STEM disciplines has been studied intensively since the late seventies, resulting in a progressively deeper understanding of myriad aspects of STEM education. Women's representation and experience is by no means equal in many STEM fields, nonetheless, model programs have applied the results of diversity research, resulting in gains for women (and minorities) at all levels. Computer science has seen no such gains.

The lack of progress in computer science education takes on new significance when viewed in the context of the broader methodological gains resulting from the research into women in STEM education. One fundamental lesson of the last two decades is surely that successfully diversifying the pedagogy of a discipline strengthens that discipline for all students. Basic research on the difference between CS and other STEM fields needs to be done, so that practitioners can effectively exploit existing STEM education knowledge.

Our research approaches the problem of diversity in computer science via the lens of the disparity between the experience of CS and other STEM fields. Based on preliminary results, our current project focuses on the acquisition of computer science research methods (CSRM.) We are exploring formal and informal educational interventions. In order for our work to be replicable and generalizable, we are working with students, faculty, administrators and researchers in multiple institutions.

Ken Yasuhara

Diversity is and isn't about gender, race, and ethnicity Effective education strives toward offering all able students the opportunity to excel in their studies. Supporting a diverse enrollment requires teaching practices, courses, curricula, and student support that are designed with an understanding of the ways in which students differ. Particularly with the visibly white, male majority in our field, discussing diversity in terms of women and racial/ethnic minorities is convenient but comes with the threat of furthering negative stereotypes about intrinsic ability (or lack thereof) of these underrepresented students. As effective educators, we should place equal focus on attributes that more directly (and accurately) inform our teaching: our students' academic and social preparation, academic interest and motivation, and learning styles. This by no means justifies removing considerations of gender, race, and ethnicity from the discussion. Indeed psychology, sociology, and education research suggest exactly the opposite, because gender, race, and ethnicity are frequently correlated with the above attributes. In their landmark study of women in CS, Margolis & Fisher emphasize that cultural and curricular obstacles in CS tend to affect women more but also affect some men.

The challenge, then, is to plan our teaching practices, course designs, and curricula to not only accommodate but support the

SIGCSE'05, February 23-27, 2005, St. Louis, Missouri, USA.
ACM 1-58113-997-7/05/0002.

success of students of varying academic and social preparation, academic interest and motivation, and learning styles. At the risk of oversimplification, achieving a more diverse enrollment boils down to something the SIGCSE community has been doing for years: making general (i.e., not ostensibly diversity-motivated) improvements in teaching. SIGCSE's recent emphasis on best practices in collaborative learning; lightweight, formative assessment (e.g., CATs); and learning
styles are all likely to help us more effectively educate a more diverse audience. (Notably, state institutions in Washington and California are required to frame any diversity efforts in gender- and race/ethnicity-neutral terms by anti-affirmative action legislation.)

The real challenge lies in understanding the obstacles that underrepresented students face in CS programs and focusing changes in teaching to directly address these obstacles. This not only helps "level the playing field" for underrepresented students but also results in an improved educational experience for all students. Understanding these obstacles is the work of CS education researchers, in cooperation with educational sociologists and the like. Again looking to Margolis & Fisher for an example, CMU decided to drop prior programming experience from its
admissions criteria when it found that (a) it did not correlate at all with long-term success in the major and (b) it filtered far more female applicants than males. This change contributed substantially to their famous increase in female enrollment.

Evans Adams

For the past 15 years, I have been the Computer Science Coordinator at Fort Lewis College in Durango, Co. Fort Lewis College continues to honor its historic commitment to Native Americans by offering tuition scholarships to all qualified American Indians who meet admission requirements. It is the only college in Colorado to do so, as it has for more than 100 years. We get Native American students from all over the United States, including many from Alaska and a few from Hawaii. By virtue of our geographic location in southwest Colorado, we also attract many Hispanic/Latino students. We have an extremely small number of African American students, but a very rich ethnic diversity nonetheless. Approximately 20% of the student population of 4100 is Native American.

The impact on the entire campus is extremely interesting. We have a very prominent Anthropology program and our Center for Southwest Studies is home to many Native American artifacts. Our Native American Center serves as a meeting place for Native American students. There are also many programs which focus on integrating the Native American students into the broader campus culture, and programs that are educating the non-Native students to the American Indian culture.

The impact on courses and curriculum is significant. A number of the Native American students come from high schools on their reservations and received poor academic preparation. The campus has consistently received federal grants to try to bridge the gap between their high school preparation and our expectations for college freshmen. The retention rate for Native American students is low. They tend to stop out for a number of reasons such as family concerns, poor academic achievement, and the need to work to raise funds for college. Many Native American students eventually return and earn their bachelors degrees.

Students of color face unique challenges and demands when enrolled in institutions where they are underrepresented. Hence, team interaction may be initially difficult for them. I often try to have more than one Native American student, particularly in lower division courses on a team and have had some success with this approach. This semester, I am experimenting with pair programming and its potential benefits to students of color.

John Beidler

I address diversity from the perspective of the **Agile Manifesto** (http://www.agilemanifesto.org/). Recall, the agile manifesto states,

> "We are uncovering better ways of developing software by doing it and helping others do it. Through this work we have come to value:
>
> **Individuals and interactions** over *processes and tools*
>
> **Working software** over *comprehensive documentation*
>
> **Customer collaboration** over *contract negotiation*
>
> **Responding to change** over *following a plan*
>
> That is, while there is value in the items on the right, we value the items on the left more".

Consider the four items on the left. What is the impact of diversity on the four items on the left? My claim is that addressing diversity, by which I mean doing, instead of just talking, directly improves our ability to address three of the items on the left – individuals and interaction, customer collaboration, and responding to change – resulting in a positive impact on working software. My presentation focuses on how addressing diversity enhances the career opportunities of our students.

Computing Accreditation: A New Criteria Structure and New Flexibility

Stu Zweben
The Ohio State University
Computer Science & Engineering
2015 Neil Avenue
Columbus, OH 43210
1-614-292-9526
zweben@cse.ohio-state.edu

Han Reichgelt
Georgia Southern University
Department of IT
P.O. Box 8150
Statesboro, GA 30460
1-912-486-7679
han@georgiasouthern.edu

Gayle Yaverbaum
Penn State University
777 W. Harrisburg Pike
Middletown, PA 17057
1-717-948-6152
gjy1@psu.edu

SUMMARY

The Computing Accreditation Commission (CAC) of ABET has proposed changes in the structure of the criteria used to accredit computer science and information systems programs. The new structure combines, into so-called "general criteria," components of criteria that apply to *any* computing program accredited by CAC. Individual program areas will supply criteria that only apply to that specific program area, to supplement the general criteria. The new criteria format allows CAC to accredit additional program areas, such as information technology. In fact, program criteria for information technology also have been proposed. This session will discuss the new criteria structure, including the proposed general and program criteria, changes to existing criteria, and the timetable for implementation of the new structure.

Categories and Subject Descriptors

K.3.m [**Computers and Education**]: Accreditation.

General Terms

Standardization.

Keywords

Accreditation, ABET, information technology, information systems.

1. OVERALL OBJECTIVE OF THE SESSION

The Computing Accreditation Commission (CAC) of ABET has proposed changes in the structure of the criteria used to accredit computing programs. The new structure combines, into so-called "general criteria," components of criteria that apply to *any* computing program accredited by CAC, including computer science and information systems programs. Draft general criteria have been published by ABET for review and comment [1], and pilot visits using these general criteria are being conducted by CAC during the 2004-05 ABET accreditation cycle.

Individual program areas such as computer science and information systems will supply additional criteria that only apply to that specific program area, to supplement the general criteria. Draft program criteria for computer science and for information systems have been proposed.

This new criteria structure parallels that used by other commissions of ABET, such as the Engineering Accreditation Commission which accredits computer engineering and software engineering programs. It allows CAC to accredit additional program areas, such as information technology. In fact, program criteria for information technology also have been proposed. It also allows computing programs that do not fall into one of the designated program areas to be accredited using only the general criteria. Thus, the general criteria define minimum requirements for a program to be accredited as a computing program.

It is important that the computing community be aware of these new developments and have the opportunity to provide feedback during ABET's review and comment period. Thus, the objective of this special session is to discuss and obtain feedback about the new criteria structure, including the proposed general and program criteria and the timetable for implementation of the new structure.

2. OUTLINE OF THE SESSION

The session will be organized as follows:

a. New criteria format and proposed general criteria (Zweben)

b. Proposed program criteria for CS (Zweben)

c. Proposed program criteria for IS (Yaverbaum)

d. Proposed program criteria for IT (Reichgelt)

e. Proposed timetable for implementation (Zweben)

f. Discussion

SIGCSE'05, February 23–27, 2005, St. Louis, Missouri, USA.
ACM 1-58113-997-7/05/0002.

Presentation of the first four items will take 10 minutes each, and the fifth item will take 5 minutes, allowing 45 minutes for discussion, questions and answers. It is possible that some questions and answers will be allowed after each of the speakers, to help calibrate for the entire audience those aspects of the presentation that appeared to be unclear.

3. EXPECTATIONS

The intended audience for this special session includes faculty from computer science or information systems programs currently accredited by CAC, faculty from computer science or information systems programs that are not currently accredited but are considering or otherwise interested in accreditation, and faculty from computing programs such as in information technology that are considering or otherwise interested in accreditation.

The session is important because the new criteria structure is very different from the current criteria structure. For example, each category in the current criteria includes a statement of "intent" and a set of "standards," each of which must be satisfied for the intent to be met unless a satisfactory alternative implementation of the intent statement is provided. The new structure does not include these "standards" as part of the criteria. Thus, faculty who are familiar with the current structure need to be aware of the changes, as they likely will apply to programs seeking accreditation or re-accreditation in the near future.

The session will explain the new structure and the reasons for it. It will explain the general criteria as published by ABET for review and comment, and the proposed program criteria in the areas of computer science, information systems, and information technology. Changes to existing criteria will be noted. Feedback on both general and program criteria will be sought as part of the discussion in the session. Additional feedback can be provided directly to ABET, and the mechanism for doing this will be explained. Finally, the timetable and transition plan proposed for instituting the new criteria will be explained.

The participants each were involved in the development of the general criteria as members of the CAC Criteria Committee. Each has expertise and training as an evaluator for CAC visits in one of the three areas in which program criteria have been proposed.

4. ACKNOWLEDGMENTS

We thank Doris Lidtke for her encouragement of this session, and for her review and comments on an earlier version of this session description.

5. REFERENCES

[1] ABET Computing Accreditation Commission, *Criteria for Accrediting Computing Programs,* http://www.abet.org/images/Criteria/C001%2004-05%20CAC%20Criteria%2011-18-03.pdf, 19-20.

NOTES

Keynote Talk

Increasing the Number of Women Majoring in Computer Science: What Works?

Maria Klawe
Princeton University
Princeton, NJ, USA
klawe@princeton.edu

Abstract

This talk examines approaches taken at a variety of universities and colleges to increase the number of women majoring in computer science. We also discuss the new National Center for Women in Information Technology and its role as a repository for best practices.

Bio

The speaker is the Dean of Engineering at Princeton University, the Past President of ACM, and Chair of the Board of Trustees of the Anita Borg Institute for Women and Technology. She received her Ph.D. in Mathematics from the University of Alberta in 1977. Prior to moving to Princeton in 2003, she was the Dean of Science at the University of British Columbia where she also held the NSERC-IBM Chair for Women in Science and Engineering from 1997 to 2002. Her previous positions include eight years with IBM Research in California. Klawe's research interests include interactive multimedia, educational technology, and theoretical computer science.

SIGCSE'05, February 23-27, 2005, St. Louis, Missouri, USA.
ACM 1-58113-997-7/05/0002.

SIGCSE 2005 Workshops

The following workshops were available to attendees of the SIGCSE 2005 Symposium for a nominal fee.

Wednesday Workshops, 7:00 p.m. to 10:00 p.m.

1. Microsoft .NET Programming: Building Applications with C#, J#, C++ and VB.NET

Joe Hummel, *Lake Forest College* **Room: Landmark 1**

Microsoft .NET is an exciting new framework for programming not only on Windows platforms, but Linux and FreeBSD as well. This workshop will introduce attendees to .NET programming, in particular with regards to building console-based, GUI, and database-driven applications. Both command-line tools (free) and Visual Studio .NET will be demonstrated. The purpose of this workshop is to introduce .NET, allowing attendees to evaluate its use in a CS or IS curriculum. PowerPoint presentations will be example-based, and suitable for introducing .NET to students; attendees will have access to electronic copies of all materials used in the workshop.

2. Taking the Hard Edge off Technical Education: Strategies for Integrating Soft Skills in the CS Classroom

Elizabeth Howard, *Miami University*
Martha Petrone, *Miami University* **Room: Landmark 2**

In reports from employers, computer science graduates receive stellar marks for their technical knowledge. At the same time, employers express concern about underlying abilities, such as listening, interpersonal effectiveness, intercultural sensitivity, and teamwork in their entry level employees. In this workshop, participants will learn specific pedagogical strategies to help students develop these fundamental soft skills that will better prepare them for success in the computer science field. Using a model for increasing intercultural awareness and a series of activities, participants will experience for themselves the exercises that they can use in their own classrooms.

3. From Nand to Tetris in 12 Steps

Shimon Schocken, *IDC Herzliya*
Nisan Noam, *Hebrew University of Jerusalem* **Room: Landmark 3**

As CS and EE courses become increasingly more specialized, students are increasingly unable to grasp major ideas that cut across traditional course lines. This workshop presents an approach that restores the big picture by covering architecture, compilers, and OS topics in one course, requiring only programming as a pre-requisite. Using a modular series of 12 projects, students are guided through the gradual construction of a complete working computer system. Starting with elementary logic gates, they build a general-purpose hardware platform and a modern software hierarchy, yielding a simple but surprisingly powerful computer system. This is achieved in a one-semester course by virtue of extreme focus and modular design. The course is completely self-contained, requiring no special equipment or software beyond what is given in the course web site, and is accompanied by a new MIT Press textbook. For more details see `www.idc.ac.il/tec`.

4. More Nifty Examples in Discrete Mathematics

William Marion, *Valparaiso University*
Peter Henderson, *Butler University*
Susanna Epp, *DePaul University* **Room: Portland**

Good examples are powerful tools for enhancing student understanding of the important connections between topics in discrete mathematics and fundamental ideas in computer science. This follow up to the SIGCSE 2004 "Nifty Examples in Discrete Mathematics" workshop will illustrate examples for use in the classroom or as assignments covering a broad spectrum of discrete mathematics topics. These include: analyzing and building a geodesic dome, mathematics of the Josephus problem, penny pile problems, reverse binary tree traversal, keys and locks, two color argument, and many more. Some of these were developed by participants in the NSF-funded summer 2004 workshop on discrete mathematics under the auspices of the MAA's Professional Enhancement Program. Participants will work in groups on additional examples. All materials presented will be posted on a workshop web page and will feed into the work of the SIGCSE Committee on the Implementation of a Discrete Mathematics Course.

5. Incorporating User-Centered Design Methods in a Human-Computer Interaction Course

Jerry Weinberg, *Southern Illinois University Edwardsville*
Mary Stephen, *Saint Louis University*
Charlotte Schwendeman, *Perficient, Inc.*
Joe Haschart, *Edward Jones* **Room: Westmoreland**

Creating usable software means taking into consideration who is using the system, what they are using it for, and how it fits within their overall workflow. It is important to educate students in the techniques of user requirements gathering, analysis and design that embrace human activity as an integral component of the process. This workshop will introduce User-Centered Design (UCD) techniques and present course material for teaching these methods in an HCI class. Industry leaders from St. Louis-based companies will discuss how UCD methods are used in their business practices and the skill sets they look for when hiring.

6. How to Run a Programming Contest

Lee Wittenberg, *Kean University* **Room: Benton**

Programming contests, most notably the ACM's International Collegiate Programming Contest, have become quite popular. Unfortunately, there is very little help available for those who wish to run such a contest, and there are many technical obstacles to overcome. Participants will learn how to overcome these obstacles and run a successful programming contest: setting up a server, configuring clients, and using the popular PC^2 software package to manage program submission and evaluation during the contest. Particular attention will be paid to the tools and steps necessary to create bootable CD-ROM's providing a common working environment for contestants.

7. Intellectual Property Law Basics for Computer Science Instructors

David G. Kay, *University of California, Irvine* **Room: Parkview**

An introduction to the basics of intellectual property law (patents, copyrights, trade secrets, trademarks) designed to give computer science instructors a framework for answering student questions, debunking misconceptions, and understanding how the law and computing interact.

8. Constructing QuickTime Movies Programmatically

Jay Martin Anderson, *Franklin and Marshall College* **Room: SLU Shannon Hall**

I will present the "model – view – controller" paradigm for the construction of animations as QuickTime movies, and apply this to some simple examples using Objective-C. The major exercise will be to construct an animation of a simple algorithm or other visualization. The workshop will be illustrated with examples from computer science, computational mathematics, and computational geometry (HANDS-ON, OFF-SITE).

9. Teaching Introductory Computer Science with JPie

Kenneth Goldman, *Washington University in St. Louis* **Room: SLU McDonnell Douglas Hall 1003**

JPie is a tightly integrated visual programming environment that supports live construction and modification of Java applications through direct manipulation of graphical representations of program constructs. JPie enables a concepts-first introduction to computer science by simplifying the programming process and supporting experimentation through modification of running programs. This hands-on workshop will provide experience using JPie in the context of a variety of course projects that have been used in a concepts-first curriculum to introduce object-oriented design and fundamental software concepts to college students without computer science background. Additional information about JPie is available at `http://JPie.cse.wustl.edu` (HANDS-ON, OFF-SITE).

10. Quick Web Application Development using JavaServer Pages and the JSP Standard Tag Library

Ariel Ortiz, *Tecnologico de Monterrey, Campus Estado de Mexico* **Room: SLU McDonnell Douglas Hall 1066**

The JavaServer Pages (JSP) technology allows mixing regular, static HTML with dynamically generated content. The new version 2.0 of JSP allows developers and designers to use this technology without needing to learn how to write Java scriptlets. In this workshop, participants will be introduced to the core elements of JSP 2.0, including its new expression language and the JavaServer Pages Standard Tag Library 1.1 (JSTL). Using the Model-View-Controller design pattern, a modular and extensible simple on-line Web game application will be designed, implemented and deployed. Attendees should be familiar with HTML; prior basic Java knowledge is desirable (HANDS-ON, OFF-SITE).

11. Introducing Embedded Systems in the Digital Logic Laboratory

Robert Pilgrim, *Murray State University* **Room: SLU McDonnell Douglas Hall 2030**

In this hands-on workshop participants learn to integrate microcontrollers into an undergraduate digital logic and computer architecture course. The workshop introduces a laboratory that combines theory, simulation and real hardware using low cost microcontrollers. Through a series of experiments participants begin using preprogrammed microcontrollers to design and test digital logic circuits and then write their own microcontroller programs for embedded systems applications. All laboratory hardware, software and documentation is provided. No previous electronics experience is required. Participants should have knowledge of a high-level programming language (HANDS-ON, OFF-SITE).

12. Experimenting with Formal Languages

Allen Stoughton, *Kansas State University* **Room: SLU McDonnell Douglas Hall 2001**

Many of the results of formal language theory are proved using algorithms. In typical courses on the subject, students apply these algorithms to toy examples by hand, but aren't able to experiment with them on a larger scale. To enable such experimentation, the presenter has developed the Forlan computer toolset, and is writing an introductory textbook based on Forlan. Both the toolset and textbook are open source and are available at `www.cis.ksu.edu/~allen/forlan/`. Participants will learn how to use Forlan in their teaching. We will focus on ways of synthesizing automata using algorithms for combining and transforming automata and regular expressions (HANDS-ON, OFF-SITE).

Friday Workshops, 7:00 p.m. to 10:00 p.m.

13. Using BlueJ to Start an OO Intro Course

Michael Kölling, *University of Southern Denmark* **Room: Landmark 1**

Getting started is one of the hardest parts in an object-oriented introductory programming course. BlueJ is designed to help with these problems. Knowing the technical capabilities of BlueJ, however, does not make it obvious how to use it to achieve good results. In this workshop, we will discuss pedagogical principles and give concrete advice on starting an objects-first style-programming course. Examples are presented that can immediately be used in class. The presenter is one of the principle BlueJ developers, and co-author of a successful textbook: Barnes/Kölling: *Objects First With Java.* In this workshop, the important principles underlying the BlueJ design and the textbook pedagogy are presented.

14. Kinesthetic Learning in the Classroom

Andrew Begel, *University of California, Berkeley*
Daniel Garcia, *University of California, Berkeley*
Steven Wolfman, *University of British Columbia* **Room: Landmark 2**

This workshop will focus on kinesthetic learning activities, i.e., physically engaging classroom exercises. These might, for example, teach recursion by simulating the Towers of Hanoi with students instead of disks, or highlight the difference between pipelined and non-pipelined execution using a human assembly line. The workshop will begin with a brief kinesthetic learning activity to motivate the value of these activities. We will follow with a variety of examples, and discuss how to deploy these in a classroom. Most of the workshop will be devoted to facilitated group work to help the participants design and test their own activities.

15. Active and Cooperative Learning Techniques for Computer Science Education

Jeffrey McConnell, *Canisius College* **Room: Westmoreland**

Active and cooperative learning provides a powerful mechanism to enhance depth of learning and increase material retention. Active and cooperative learning gets students involved with the material rather than passively listening to a lecture. This workshop will use introductory material on active and cooperative learning for a number of activities that will give participants direct experience with and the chance to observe these techniques in action. There will also be opportunities for open discussion of situations that participants may have already encountered.

16. Teaching Ethics Using Structured Controversy

James Bohy, *Simpson College* **Room: Portland**

Instruction related to ethical, social, and moral material in computer science must have as a key component some form of active engagement with the issue at hand. Structured controversy is a cooperative learning technique first proposed in science education in the late 1970s. The activity engages students and instructors in a process of presenting both sides of a given issue and arriving at a consensus solution. This workshop focuses on instructor responsibilities for setting up and running a structured controversy in his/her classroom, culminating in some of the participants actually walking through the activity.

17. Computer Security Essentials, Part 1 — System Footprinting and Vulnerability Assessment

Paul Wagner, *University of Wisconsin - Eau Claire*
Andrew Phillips, *University of Wisconsin - Eau Claire*
Daren Bauer, *University of Wisconsin - Eau Claire*
Tom Paine, *University of Wisconsin - Eau Claire*
Jason Wudi, *University of Wisconsin - Eau Claire* **Room: Landmark 3**

This is the first of two hands-on workshops for CS educators seeking to develop curricula in computer security. We provide guided hands-on instruction on various Windows and Linux based tools commonly used for gathering information about, and assessing the vulnerability of, other systems. Participants will experiment with these tools as the presenters guide them through typical tool use scenarios. The session concludes with an information gathering exercise on an isolated network. Participants will use laptops running both Windows and Linux images preconfigured with common security "holes" so that they may experience first-hand the process of information gathering and vulnerability detection (HANDS-ON).

18. Writing Computer Books

Barry Burd, *Drew University*
Rick Decker, *Hamilton College* **Room: Benton**

This workshop covers the computer book-writing process from start to finish. It covers both textbooks and books for the general public. Workshop topics include choosing a subject, writing a proposal, submitting sample chapters, finding a publisher, contacting an agent, reading a contract, meeting deadlines, working with coauthors, reviewing copy edited material, responding to technical reviews, creating ancillary materials, and marketing your book. The presenters are computer science professors so (naturally) the discussion will be honest, informative, and unbiased.

19. Quick and Easy GUIs for 2D Array Assignments

Alyce Brady, *Kalamazoo College*
Pamela Cutter, *Kalamazoo College*
Kathleen Larson, *Kingston High School* **Room: Parkview**

Many introductory programming assignments such as games, mazes, and various types of simulations, involve objects in a two-dimensional data structure. These projects lend themselves to graphical representations, but the overhead involved in implementing graphical user interfaces, especially interfaces that support user interaction, and is non-trivial. The Grid Package provides a set of simple Java classes for modeling objects in a two-dimensional grid, and provides a library of other classes that make it easy to create interactive, graphical user interfaces to control and display 2D array applications. This workshop will introduce the Grid Package and how to use it in assignments in introductory courses.

20. Learning to Program with Alice.

Stephen Cooper, *Saint Joseph's University* **Room: SLU McDonnell Douglas Hall 2001**

This workshop will offer a hands-on introduction to programming with Alice. Alice is a powerful program visualization tool that enables students to "see" objects and work with object-oriented programming. Participants will learn how to use Alice to build virtual worlds and how to use this approach in introductory-level computing courses (introductory programming for majors, programming for non-majors, computer literacy, etc.). Participants will receive a CD containing the latest version of the software and curricular materials (lectures, closed laboratory assignments, take-home assignments, and sample exams) developed as part of NSF-0126833 and NSF-0339734 (HANDS-ON, OFF-SITE).

21. Teaching Mobile and Ad-hoc Networking using Simulation

Chris McDonald, *The University of Western Australia* **Room: SLU McDonnell Douglas Hall 1032**

This workshop will demonstrate that students' understanding of mobile and ad-hoc wireless networking can best be developed and assessed through quality interactive simulation tools. Classroom-tested material will demonstrate detection and recovery from data corruption and loss, collision detection and avoidance, data-link protocols, table-driven and on-demand routing algorithms, and the security of mobile and ad-hoc wireless networks. The workshop draws on our 13 years' teaching experience with the simulation of wide-area, local-area, and mobile and ad-hoc wireless environments, in undergraduate courses of up to 180 students each year. Faculty will be introduced to exercises and assessments suitable for undergraduate open- and closed-laboratory sessions, and even capstone projects (HANDS-ON, OFF-SITE).

22. Using Software Testing to Improve Programming Assignments and Grading

Stephen Edwards, *Virginia Tech* **Room: SLU McDonnell Douglas Hall 2030**

This workshop provides a practical, hands-on introduction to how one can incorporate software testing activities as a regular part of programming assignments. It presents five different models for how one can incorporate testing into assignments, provides examples of each technique, and discusses the corresponding advantages and disadvantages. Approaches to assessment—using testing to assess student code, assessing tests that students write, and automated grading—are all discussed. Advice for writing "testable" assignments is given. Hands-on examples are used throughout to illustrate the techniques (HANDS-ON, OFF-SITE).

23. Introductory Lego MindStorms for Introductory Computer Science

Frank Klassner, *Villanova University* **Room: SLU McDonnell Douglas Hall 1066**

This workshop will explore how to use LEGO MindStorms as an active-learning platform for teaching topics ranging in the CS 0 - CS 1 - CS 2 portion of the typical computer science curriculum. We will identify common problems first-timers may face in adopting the platform, and describe approaches to overcome them. Participants will work with pre-built robots and learn how to use Java to program and control the robots. C++ support material will be available upon request. This workshop is strictly for instructors who have not previously used MindStorms in their classroom. (HANDS-ON, OFF-SITE).

24. Bioinformatics Basics for Computer Scientists

Debra Burhans, *Canisius College*
Gary Skuse, *Rochester Institute of Technology* **Room: SLU McDonnell Douglas Hall 1003**

This workshop is designed to introduce computer scientists to the emerging field of bioinformatics. The workshop will include an overview of basic biological concepts, including fundamental structures such as cells, genes, chromosomes and proteins along with higher-level concepts such as genomes, proteomes and bibliomes. Some important algorithms for bioinformatics analysis will be introduced, in particular those related to sequence assembly and gene prediction. Hands-on experience with Perl programming for bioinformatics will be incorporated into the workshop. An exploration of bioinformatics resources for educators, including software, databases, course and laboratory materials, exercises, and on-line teaching tools, will conclude the workshop (HANDS-ON, OFF-SITE).

25. Teaching Pre-AP with HTML and Javascript

Richard Kick, *Hinsdale Central High School* **Room: SLU McDonnell Douglas Hall 2101**

The Advanced Placement Computer Science curriculum has evolved from a procedural based curriculum, to the current object oriented curriculum. A significant understanding of object oriented concepts and techniques is essential in order for students to find success in AP CS courses. This workshop will provide teachers with hands-on experiences in using HTML and Javascript to introduce the object concept to pre-AP students. In particular, tools for creating and viewing HTML and Javascipt documents will be presented and discussed. A large number of web documents and Javascript code examples will be presented and electronically distributed to participants (HANDS-ON, OFF-SITE).

Saturday Workshops, 4:00 p.m. to 7:00 p.m.

27. Multimedia Projects for CS1 and CS2

Mark Guzdial, *College of Computing, Georgia Tech*
Barbara Ericson, *College of Computing, Georgia Tech* **Room: Landmark 2**

Constructing and manipulating media is a motivating context for students in CS1 and CS2. Modern computers are capable of interesting media effects in reasonable running time, using simple and obvious algorithms that fit within the constraints of introductory courses' curricula. In this workshop, we will present algorithms (mostly in Python) and working code (in Java) for the creation and manipulation of sound, image, and video data. Example techniques will include sound splicing and reversing, chromakey ("blue screen") image effects, animation, and Photoshop-like image filters.

28. Computer Security Essentials, Part 2 — Intrusion Detection and System Defense

Paul Wagner, *University of Wisconsin - Eau Claire*
Andrew Phillips, *University of Wisconsin - Eau Claire*
Daren Bauer, *University of Wisconsin - Eau Claire*
Tom Paine, *University of Wisconsin - Eau Claire*
Jason Wudi, *University of Wisconsin - Eau Claire* **Room: Landmark 3**

This is the second of two workshops for CS educators developing curricula in computer security. Participation in workshop part one is recommended as a prerequisite. We provide guided hands-on instruction and experimentation on both defensive techniques and the understanding of exploits for the purpose of better defending systems. The session concludes with a hands-on exercise giving the participants an opportunity to participate in a carefully constructed and monitored cyberwar scenario; i.e. the participants will harden their systems, identify potential exploits and threats, and work to understand the mindset of the attacker by identifying weaknesses in all systems on the network (HANDS-ON).

29. Facilitating Student Written Operating Systems in the Undergraduate OS Course

Michael Goldweber, *Xavier University*
Renzo Davoli, *University of Bologna* **Room: Landmark 3**

Ideally, the most meaningful learning experience for students in an undergraduate OS course would be to develop fully functional OS's on their own. This can be accomplished using µMPS, a hardware simulator for a pedagogically undergraduate-appropriate architecture, along with Kaya, a specification for a multi-layer OS supporting multiprocessing, VM, thread synchronization and external devices; disks, terminals, tape and printers. Attendees will not only learn all that is necessary to begin using µMPS/Kaya but will receive all the curricular materials (Student Guide and Instructor's Guide) needed to make immediate (i.e. "out-of-the box") and effective use of this courseware system.

30. Assigning Team Projects: Problems, Pitfalls, and Solutions

Joanna Wolfe, *University of Louisville*
Timothy Hardin, *University of Louisville* **Room: Portland**

This workshop draws on the presenters' experiences observing, videotaping, and interviewing members of over 15 student teams. We will analyze short videotapes illustrating common problems in student teams and discuss practical ways to avoid these problems. Topics will include evaluating team projects, managing student teams, assigning discrete roles to team members, and avoiding gender bias. We will also review examples of successful team assignments, grading guidelines, and software for managing team projects. All participants will receive a CD and handouts containing instructor supplements, including videos that can be used to discuss teamwork. NSF support is gratefully acknowledged.

31. Advanced Lego MindStorms for the Advanced CS Curriculum

Frank Klassner, *Villanova University* **Room: Benton**

This workshop will explore how to use LEGO MindStorms as an active-learning platform for teaching advanced CS topics ranging from Computer Architecture to Operating Systems to Wireless Networking to Artificial Intelligence. In this workshop, COMPUTER SCIENCE is emphasized over robot-building. Participants will receive material on how to use Java, C/C++, and Lisp to control and program MindStorms. This workshop assumes participants have already used MindStorms for at least one semester.

32. Model-Driven Programming Education

Jens Bennedsen, *IT University West*
Michael Caspersen, *University of Aarhus* **Room: Parkview**

Motivated students, efficient learning, and a 90% pass rate are the results of applying a model driven approach to introductory object-oriented programming. We explore a CS1 course based upon a model-driven approach to programming focusing on systematic techniques for program construction. Exercises and assignments take a class model as starting point, and progression in the course is based upon complexity of class models rather than syntactical structures of a programming language. After the workshop attendees knows how to adopt the model-driven approach; a wealth of material supporting the approach is provided. Working knowledge of Java or C++ is required.

33. The Polymorphism Challenge

Joseph Bergin, *Pace University*
Eugene Wallingford, *University of Northern Iowa* **Room: SLU McDonnell Douglas Hall 2101**

Facility with polymorphic programming is a valuable skill for a programmer or an instructor. This hands-on workshop will give you ideas and practice with the techniques required to program with dynamic polymorphism. As a participant you will practice the polymorphism etude with a partner under direction of the workshop leaders. You will re-write simple but complete programs that normally use if statements, to completely remove all selection structures in favor of polymorphism. This will give you important design experience and improve your skill as an object-oriented programmer and as a teacher. The workshop will stress techniques applicable to CS1 (HANDS-ON, OFF-SITE).

34. Fostering Classroom Engagement with DyKnow Vision and Tablet PCs or other Pen-based Computing Devices

Dave Berque, *DePauw University*
Scott M. Thede, *DePauw University* **Room: SLU McDonnell Douglas Hall 2001**

Pen-based computing devices ranging from Tablet PCs to inexpensive graphics tablets (costing less than $100) are being used increasingly in the computer science classroom. Participants will learn how effective pedagogies can be fostered using such devices in conjunction with a software system named DyKnow VISION (`www.dyknow.com`, patent-pending). After a brief introduction to pen-based hardware, participants will learn how to use DyKnow VISION in (freely available) presentation mode. Participants will then experience how the full power of the licensed version of DyKnow VISION can support numerous interactive pedagogies that center on allowing students and teachers to share and annotate classroom materials (HANDS-ON, OFF-SITE).

35. Using Eclipse to Teach Java Programming

Barry Burd, *Drew University* **Room: SLU McDonnell Douglas Hall 2030**

The Eclipse development environment is great for both large and small classroom projects. Eclipse is an industrial strength IDE, but it can be customized and simplified for use by novice programmers. Eclipse's smart Java editor compiles code as you write. It provides hierarchical views of the class/method structure, and comes with optional plug-ins for UML diagramming and visual drag-and-drop programming. Eclipse's refactoring operations encourage good program structure. Over 40% of all professional Java developers use Eclipse. Best of all, Eclipse is being developed by the open source community. It's free to use, and free to modify (HANDS-ON, OFF-SITE).

36. Taming Java in CS1 Using Language Levels

Robert Cartwright, *Rice University*
Zung Nguyen, *Rice University*
Stephen Wong, *Rice University* **Room: SLU McDonnell Douglas Hall 1066**

Java is the canonical language for teaching introductory programming, but its complex syntax and abundance of constructs are difficult for beginners to learn. This workshop will show how Java programming can be made more accessible to beginners through the use of language levels, a hierarchy of progressively richer subsets of Java. This approach to teaching Java minimizes the clerical burden involved in learning to write Java programs and reinforces the specific programming abstractions taught at each language level. The workshop will focus on providing hands-on experience using DrJava, an open source-programming environment supporting language levels (HANDS-ON, OFF-SITE).

37. Advanced Graphics Application Development with OpenGL

Dan Cliburn, *Hanover College* **Room: SLU McDonnell Douglas Hall 1003**

Do you want to make your graphics course a little more entertaining for your students? This workshop is designed to introduce advanced graphics topics that can be incorporated into an undergraduate level graphics course that teaches OpenGL. Specifically, participants will learn how to add lighting, textures, fog, picking, billboards, sound (using DirectX), and joystick input (using GLUT) to their OpenGL applications. Each participant will develop a "dungeon crawl" game during the workshop that illustrates these concepts. Some prior C++ and OpenGL experience is required (HANDS-ON, OFF-SITE).

SIGCSE 2005 Birds-of-a-Feather Sessions

The following Birds-of-a-Feather sessions were organized for attendees of the SIGCSE 2005 symposium.

jGRASP: Improving Usability for Novices

James Cross, Dean Hendrix and David Umphress, *Auburn University*

jGRASP is a freely available integrated development environment, which generates visualizations to improve the comprehensibility of the software. These visualizations include Control Structure Diagrams, UML Class Diagrams, Object Viewers, and a highly visual debugger. As jGRASP enters a new phase of development and refinement, it is important to balance usability with functionality. This session will focus on how the usability of jGRASP can be significantly improved, especially for first-time users, while adding important functionality.

It's a Small World: International High Schools

Jenka Guevara, *American School Foundation, Mexico City*

At this session school teachers from international schools will describe and share their positive and negative experiences. Naturally, non high school and non international people are also welcome.

Professional Certifications in CS Undergraduate Programs

Ariel Ortiz Ramirez, *ITESM Campus Estado de México*

As CS educators we know the importance of education over professional training. Yet we cannot ignore that employers commonly affirm that recently graduated students have a lack of practical skills required in "real world" situations. Important IT companies, such as Sun Microsystems, CISCO and Microsoft, have academic programs that allow students to get certified in their specific technologies before they graduate. This session will discuss the merits and drawbacks of incorporating professional certification training into CS programs.

Curriculum Issues: Coping with Offshore Software Development Outsourcing

Anthony Duben and Ken Surendran, *Southeast Missouri State University*, and John Impagliazzo, *Hofstra University*

Recent studies project a trend of continued loss of entry-level programming jobs - usually taken up by Computer Science graduates - due to offshore software development outsourcing. The purpose of this session is to identify curriculum-related strategies for addressing issues such as coping with reduced enrollments in CS programs, preparing the graduates adequately for higher-level jobs without the usual on-the-job training in entry-level positions, and other academic issues resulting from this trend.

Wall Posters for Computer Science

Ken Vollmar, *Southwest Missouri State University*

There are evidently no widely distributed or currently available wall-mounted posters with Computer Science educational topics! We need ideas on poster themes and presentation styles in anticipation of printing and distribution. Suggestions will probably include themes and topics such as achievements of "well-known" and "unknown" people; artistic/graphic representations of concepts, algorithms, and solutions; and introductory topics for elementary school levels. In exchange for your input, take home* a piece of artwork (*subject to production by the artistic co-"PI").

Incorporating Service Learning into a Capstone Course

Roger Ferguson, *Grand Valley State University* and Mary Last, *University of Mary Hardin-Baylor*

Service learning has become part of the curriculum of many post-secondary institutions. The incorporation of service-learning in capstone courses was advocated by Lazar and Lidtke in Managing IT/Community Partnerships in the 21st Century (2002). This session will focus on how CS/IS educators can incorporate service learning in capstone courses. The intent is for participants to share their experiences with others having a similar interest. Ideas exchanged during the session will be recorded and sent to interested participants.

Both Sides Now: Transition from Graduate Student to Faculty Member

Peter DePasquale, *The College of New Jersey* and Tracy Lewis, *Radford University*

This session seeks to bring together recent Ph.D. graduates who are now in faculty positions and soon-to-be graduates in order to facilitate a discussion of transition "lessons learned" (both professionally and socially) from graduate student to new faculty member. Discussion points will include the following: how other (more established) faculty members perceive and treat you; the politics of academia; great ways of launching research and obtaining funding; social life (within and outside the department); ethical issues; top things to do to get your new career on the right foot; "if only someone had told me this when I started out..."; gender specific barriers (e.g., what to do when you teach all males); age specific barriers (e.g., what happens when your students are older than you); mentor/mentee relationships; academic preparedness to teach; the perfect departmental fit.

Working Effectively with Underprepared Potential Majors

Marcia Schlafmitz, *New Jersey City University* and Lonnie Fairchild, *SUNY – Plattsburgh*

Many institutions enroll potentially talented students who want to major in computer science but are academically unprepared. We will share strategies for identifying these students and helping them "catch up." Possible topics: How are students underprepared: skills in math? abstract thinking? lack of computer experience? Can a CS0 course develop necessary skills? What teaching techniques help: collaborative approaches? reflective journal writing? What else can help: how the CS curriculum is organized? mentoring? how/when math concepts are taught?

Increasing Retention in CS101 and CS102

Deborah Whitfield and Paul Mullins, *Slippery Rock University*

Regardless of the language used in the ACM defined CS101 and CS102, teaching structured programming and problem solving at an introductory level is a challenge. The leaders will describe techniques they have used for increasing student learning in CS101 and CS102 and present preliminary retention data. Participants will be asked to identify themselves, their institutions, the CS101 - CS102 sequence they teach, the type of students that take the courses and techniques they have used.

Deciding on Objectives and Outcomes

Doris Lidtke, *ABET, Inc.* and Gayle Yaverbaum, *Penn State University at Harrisburg*

This session will enhance the computing community's consciousness of assessment by discussing the first step of the process: deciding on objectives and outcomes. Attendees are encouraged to bring their own educational objectives and student outcomes so that the group can discuss their strengths and weaknesses. Additionally, attendees will be given some model materials, which they can modify with their own constituencies to suit their own program environment. As time permits, measurement of outcomes will be discussed.

Recruiting and Retaining Underrepresented Groups in CS Programs

Bridget Baird, *Connecticut College*

Computer science programs generally have low numbers of women and domestic students of color. This session will focus on strategies to address this problem, particularly in the CS1 course. How can we induce more underrepresented students to enroll in the CS1 course, and how can we keep their interest so that they consider majoring in CS? Some of these strategies include introducing a broader range of applications, mentoring, training TA's, offering scholarships and creating a gathering place.

Big Brother or "Oh, Brother": Course Management Systems in Computer Science

Jeffrey Popyack, *Drexel University*

This discussion will focus on the use of course management systems (WebCT, Blackboard, TopClass, et al.) by computer science educators to administer their courses. The typical CMS is usable by a wide audience of educators, not only those with sophisticated computing expertise. However, our experience has been that computer scientists have specialized needs and perspectives on CMS use that differ from those of the typical academic users. Come share success stories, "war stories", workarounds, advice, and the like.

ACM Programming Contests: Building a Team and Attending a Contest
Howard Whitston, *Albion College*

This session will explore ways of building a team that works well together to solve at least one problem and overcoming administrative resistance. It could be the ultimate group project – limited time and resources, unlimited creativity with bragging rights for the next year. Practices, on-line resources, non-ACM sponsored contests, and your suggestions for getting less competitive students involved will also be discussed.

CS1 for the Non-major: Challenges, Opportunities and Best Practices
Jeffrey Stone and Tricia Clark, *Penn State University at Schuylkill*

As introductory computing becomes an increasingly ingrained aspect of many college majors, a larger number of non-CS majors are enrolling in CS1 courses in order to satisfy general education or program requirements. In this session we will discuss the challenges facing those CS1 faculty who teach sections involving a significant number of non-majors. Opportunities for pedagogical innovation will be explored, and "best practices" employed to address the interests of non-major students will be considered.

Teaching the History of Computing
David Hemmendinger, *Union College* and John Impagliazzo, *Hofstra University*

Computer history can be woven into computer science courses or can be the subject of an entire course. One of us teaches an NSF-supported survey course that uses computer history as a vehicle for introducing computing topics; the other teaches a course on the history of computing for CS majors and non-majors. We propose to exchange ideas about the two approaches, the kinds of audience for which they are appropriate and the resources available for them.

Town Meeting: SIGCSE Committee on Expanding the Women-in-Computing Community
Gloria Townsend, *DePauw University*

At SIGCSE 2004 we launched a SIGCSE committee to identify "best practices" for increasing the population of high school girls and college women enrolled in computing classes. The goals of this Birds-of-a-Feather session are to increase membership in our committee – and thereby increase our viewpoints and results; to report and evaluate 2004 committee progress; and to identify new committee goals for 2005. See `http://www.sigcse.org/topics/committees.shtml` to join our listserv.

Laboratories in CIS: Pedagogic (and Practical) Issues
Frank Friedman, *Temple University;* Richard Enbody, *Michigan State University;*
Gayle Yaverbaum, *Penn State University at Harrisburg;* and Michael Feldman, *George Washington University*

We intend to discuss the pros and cons of the laboratory experience in CIS, including staffing, grading, the pedagogic importance of labs, and the differences between labs for non-majors and various levels of upper division majors.

Peer Review of Team Projects and Term Papers
Edward Gehringer, *North Carolina State University*

Peer review is frequently used in a classroom setting to give students greater feedback on their work than the instructor and/or TA's can provide. As collaborative learning and team projects play an increasing role in computing education, peer review within teams and/or among teams offers an effective way to improve learning and assessment. In this session participants will discuss effective strategies for peer review of team projects and term papers. These include the organization of peer-review sessions, when they should occur, and how much they should count, as well as the development of rubric questions for students to evaluate their peers' work.

BlueJ Users' Forum
Ian Utting, *University of Kent;* Michael Kölling, *University of Southern Denmark*

This is a forum for teachers using the BlueJ IDE to share their experiences and to discuss recent and future developments with members of the BlueJ team.

Concepts-Based Teaching of Programming: Lessons for Concurrency
Peter Van Roy, *Université Catholique de Louvain*

We propose to teach computer programming in terms of programming concepts, not programming languages or paradigms. We start with a small set of concepts and add concepts exactly when they are needed. We end up covering most concepts used in programming today. We have taught with this approach since 2001. We'll concentrate on the topic of concurrency in this session.

Mathematical Reasoning in Computer Science

Peter Henderson, *Butler University* and Judith Gersting, *University of Hawaii at Hilo*

Mathematics and mathematical reasoning are central to computer science, and mathematical concepts should become an integral part of the entire CS curriculum. This birds-of-a-feather session will be a forum for educators to discuss the role of mathematics in computer science curricula.

Can One Database Course Fit All? CS and IS in a Single Course

Catherine Ricardo, *Iona College* and Mary Granger, *George Washington University*

Because of small enrollments, many institutions cannot support two different introductory database courses and are forced to put computer science and information science students together. CC2001 and IS2002 both include database courses, but the objectives do not match. Surveys on the database curricula actually taught also showed significant differences between CS and IS departments. This session is an opportunity for those who teach database to discuss the issues they face in trying to meet the needs of both audiences.

SIGCSE 2005 Faculty Poster Sessions

Posters present work-in-progress and other topics for which dialog with Symposium attendees is particularly appropriate.

The Effect of Paired-Programming and Instructional Design on Student Performance and Satisfaction in a Beginning Programming Course
Terence C. Ahern, *California State University at Monterey Bay*

Guild-based Group Learning for Computer Science Courses
Rebecca A. Bates, *Minnesota State University, Mankato*

Instructional Multimedia for Mathematics, Science and Technology Educators
Andrew Beiderman, Donna Tupper, and Sylvia Sorkin, *The Community College of Baltimore County*

Visualising Software Development: eL-CID Evaluation
Charles Boisvert, *Norwich City College*

A Quasi-Experimental Research Methodology to Evaluate a Pedagogical Change in System Administration
Charles Border, *Rochester Institute of Technology*

Fun Yet Rigorous Laboratories for a Java-Based CS2
Mark A. Boshart and Martha J. Kosa, *Tennessee Technological University*

The JVMViewer: An Interactive Interpreter for Java Bytecodes
Carl Bredlau, *Montclair State University*

Introduction to Informatics — A First Course Designed to Introduce the Discipline of Informatics
John P. Buerck, *Saint Louis University*

Activities of the ACM Two-Year College Education Committee
Robert Campbell, *Rock Valley College*
Elizabeth K. Hawthorne, *Union County College*
Karl J. Klee, *Alfred State College*

Fibonacci Numbers in Computer Science
Darrah Chavey, *Beloit College*

Objects and Algorithms using Visual Logic Puzzles
John Cigas, *Rockhurst University*
Wen Hsin, *Park University*

RoundHeads: An Introductory Lab Experience with Objects in CS1
Blase B. Cindric, *Mount Union College*

Undergraduate Science Informatics at Montclair State University
Dorothy Deremer, *Montclair State University*

A Research Robot at Lego Prices: Pushing the Limits of Evolution's ER1
Zachary Dodds, *Harvey Mudd College*

S^2C Student Service in Computing
Roger Ferguson, *Grand Valley State University*
Mary Z. Last, *University of Mary Hardin-Baylor*

Implementing a Video Game as a Final Student Project in Computer Science 1
Gabriel J. Ferrer and W. Dwayne Collins, *Hendrix College*

Linked Lists Animation Using Macromedia Flash
Ahmad Ghafarian, *North Georgia College & State University*

Apprenticeship-based Software Engineering Educational Project
Bruria Haberman, *Holon Institute of Technology and The Weizmann Institute of Science*
Cecile Yehezkel, *The Weizmann Institute of Science*

Computer Science ≠ Computer Programming
Charles R. Hardnett and Iretta C. Kearse, *Spelman College*

Greenfoot — A Development Environment Supporting Object Interaction and Visualization
Poul Henriksen and Michael Kölling, *The Maersk Mc-Kinney Moller Institute for Production Technology*

How is Everyone Doing? Automatic Project Feedback and Monitoring for Programming Courses
David Hovemeyer, Bill Pugh and Jaime Spacco, *University of Maryland*

A Lab Component for an Advanced Databases Course
Orlando Karam and Kai Qian, *Southern Polytechnic State University*

Programming with Python for Non-Majors — Innovative Teaching Approach
Yana Kortsarts and Jeffrey Rufinus, *Widener University*

Significant Findings Regarding Computer Science Major Retention When Pair Programming is Used in Introductory Programming Courses for Both Women and Men
Charlie McDowell and Linda L. Werner, *University of California at Santa Cruz*

Teaching Database Backward: A Mini-Projects Approach
Kirby McMaster, Bilyeu-Dittman and Ashley Blake, *Weber State University*

Discrete Math as a Programming Course
Kirby McMaster, Brian Rague and Trevor McMaster, *Weber State University*

A Model for a Liberal Arts Project-Based Capstone Experience
David R. Musicant and Jeff Ondich, *Carleton College*

Architectural Styles Laboratory for Software Architecture and Design
Kai Qian and Orlando Karam, *Southern Polytechnic State University*
Jigang Liu, *Metropolitan State University*

Simulators for Experimentation in Operating Systems
Steven Robbins, *University of Texas at San Antonio*

Accessibility First: Teaching Web Design "Backwards"
Brian J. Rosmaita, *Hamilton College*

MARS: An IDE for MIPS Assembly Language Programming
Pete Sanderson, *Otterbein College*
Ken Vollmar, *Southwest Missouri State University*

.NET in a Programming Paradigms Course
Christelle Scharff, Dennis Anderson and Viktor Geller, *Pace University*

Problem Solving, Programming, and Process: A CS Course for High School Students
Linda B. Sherrell, Allen Thomas and Larissa Klimple, *The University of Memphis*

Incorporation of a 3D Interactive Graphics Programming Language into an Introductory Engineering Course
Jason S. Snook, Vinod Lohani, Jenny Lo and Hayden Griffin, *Virginia Polytechnic Institute & State University*

Demonstrating the Use of Logic Emulation to Bring Computer Organization and Architecture Concepts to Life
Timothy Daryl Stanley, *Brigham Young University Hawaii*

Teaching Client-Server Software Development by Example
Evelyn Stiller and Cathie LeBlanc, *Plymouth State University*

Centrally Stored and Delivered Virtual Machines in the Networking Lab
Mark Stockman and John Nyland, *University of Cincinnati*

Using a Virtual Laboratory to Teach Online Information Assurance Courses
Wayne C. Summers, *Columbus State University*

International Curriculum Design for Undergraduate Computer Science
Carol Taylor and Slava Popovsky, *University of Idaho*
Barbara Endicott-Popovsky, *Seattle University*

An Undergraduate Level Course on Cryptography
Soe Than, *Virginia Military Institute*

Creating a League of Our Own: Grace Hopper's Scholars Program for Attracting Women to Computer Related Fields
Donna Tupper and Barbara Leitherer, *The Community College of Baltimore County*

Are There Gender Differences in the Way People Program?
Linda Werner, *University of California, Santa Cruz*
Jill Denner, *ETR Associates*

New Beginnings for CS1: The Experience of Introducing a Socially Focussed Pre-term Group Activity for Computing Undergraduates
Su White, *University of Southampton*

Instructional Calculators for Numeric Representations in Computers
James B. Wilkinson, *The College of Charleston*

Unifying the Undergraduate Applied CS Curriculum Around a Simplified Microprocessor Architecture
David Wonnacott, *Haverford College*

Talking about Entering: Why Women and Men Choose/Reject the Computer Science Major
Ken Yasuhara and Richard Anderson, *University of Washington*

SIGCSE 2005 SRC Graduate Student Research Abstracts

Personalized and Adaptive Promotion Delivery System For Wireless Devices

Karthik Harihar, *Columbus State University*

Emergence of m-commerce has been attributed to the significant growth of popularity of mobile devices and wireless technologies. Market studies forecast high demand for mobile applications and services. Mobile devices offer unique characteristics such as portability, mobility and personalization that facilitate new classes of applications offering targeted services based on the needs of the individual users. Several mobile marketing frameworks have been designed to deliver promotional information to the users based on location information. However, these systems often require specialized sensors or tend to spam the users with unwanted information. We present an intelligent framework for mobile marketing that delivers targeted promotions to the consumers based on the context of their location and precise matching to their preferences. Our framework guards its users from any unwanted information (spam), dynamically adapts to the user's changing shopping habits, and does not require any special sensors or GPS equipment. A fully functional prototype for Pocket PCs running Windows CE has been implemented as a proof of concept.

Showing Where Blind Relevance Feedback Fails

Chris Jordan, *Dalhousie University*

In Information Retrieval, relevance feedback has been used to effectively improve retrieval performance. Traditionally users generate feedback for this process. Blind relevance feedback (BRF) automates this process by only considering the top ranked documents as relevant. BRF has been shown to improve retrieval performance though it has no means for dealing with noisy documents that may be in the top rank. Thus it should not work well for low quality queries. By using relative entropy to derive sets of queries of varying quality, I believe that it can be shown precisely when BRF will fail.

Expressway Over Chord in Peer-to-Peer Systems

Hathai Tanta-Ngai, *Dalhousie University*

We introduce the expressway - an auxiliary fast coarse-grained routing layer on top of structured peer-to-peer systems. The expressway is developed and tested over Chord. It provides fast routing on the same identifier space as the underlying system. The expressway consists of peers that can forward requests over a longer distance than peers in the underlying system. These expressway peers forward a request until no expressway peer exists in the last hops to the destination. Then, they defer the request to be routed in the underlying system to its destination. Our expressway is suitable for environment where peers have different amounts of resources. The routing performance is improved as expressway peers contribute more resources to the routing service.

Updating the Partial Singular Value Decomposition

Jane E. Tougas and Henry Stern, *Dalhousie University*

Latent semantic indexing (LSI) is an information retrieval method that uses the partial singular value decomposition (PSVD) of the term-document matrix representation of a dataset. Calculating the PSVD is computationally expensive. When terms or documents are added to an existing dataset, it is beneficial to update the previously calculated PSVD to reflect these changes. Our work has shown how updating can be used in LSI to significantly reduce the computational cost of finding the PSVD, with little loss of accuracy. Moreover, we show how the computational cost can be reduced further, using a combination of updating and folding-in.

Developing Verifying Compiler for LIPS (Language for Implementing Parallel Distributed Systems)

Amala Rajan, *Middlesex University*

A verifying compiler proves that a program is correct before allowing it to run. Developing a verifying compiler is a challenge in the field of Computer Science due to difficulties in mechanical theorem proving, and difficulties in writing assertions. With the advancements in technology and theorem proving, significant progress has been made since 1969. The research aims to develop a verifying compiler for LIPS, a Language for Implementing Parallel Distributed System. The objective of the research is three fold: (a) develop a compiler for LIPS with out verifying capabilities; (b) identify the methods/techniques, which could be used for verification; and (c) incorporate the method to the LIPS compiler to make it a verifying compiler.

ForNet: A Distributed Forensic Network

Kulesh Shanmugasundaram, *Polytechnic University*

This paper introduces ForNet, a distributed forensics network. Unlike the state-of-the-art solutions in network forensics, ForNet uses a novel concept called synopses to reduce raw network traffic to succinct form such that relevant information can be stored for prolonged periods of time. ForNet also introduces the concept of monitoring and privacy policies. Synopses and distributed nature of ForNet allow it to scale well across large networks. We believe the inclusion of policies and informing users of monitoring allow ForNet to be more acceptable form of monitoring than the mechanisms used today.

Ramifications of Gift Exchange in Multiagent Systems

Shah Jamal Alam, *Saarland University*

We explore in this thesis the implications of applying the idea of gift-exchange mechanism inspired from Pierre Bourdieu's sociological theories into a market-based multiagent system. The market in our case comprises of customers and providers agents; the former places call for proposals for tasks in the market, while the latter proceed with the execution of tasks based on their abilities and other circumstances. In our work, the agents are either profit-oriented, or those who prefer exchanging gifts and are in pursuit of other gift giving agents. We scrutinize various hypotheses to investigate the implications of gift exchange in our system.

Unfolding Polylines by "Shaking"

Thomas Young and Shaaz Noormohammad, *University of South Alabama*

We compute polyline unfolding in two-dimensional space using a stochastic algorithm, similar to "shaking out" Our algorithm consists of three major phases for every joint, which is repeated as necessary: moving the joint angle by some small random amount, propagating the movement throughout the polyline, and ensuring that no lines cross both during and after the movement has been completed. We utilized polar form coordinates in our implementation of the algorithm to both simply the procedures and to prevent slight variations in segment length. This research can be used in a classroom setting to introduce polyline unfolding to students.

Query Optimization in the WHAT Tool Using Genetic Algorithms

Emeka Nwaneshiudu and Andrew Murray, *Villanova University*

Web Host Access Tools (WHAT) is a java based metasearch engine that provides users with relevant information by streamlining results from various search engines and ordering them by a predefined user context. In the WHAT, we used genetic algorithms (GA), which allow for complex-programming anomalies to be solved by mechanisms based upon the principles of genetics, to create queries with different order and complexity of keywords for a given search task. Recall and precision standards were applied to our results and we discovered the precision was the highest with two to three query words and that GA improved the recall values over the WHAT ranking algorithm.

SIGCSE 2005 SRC Undergraduate Student Research Abstracts

Digitization of Fingerprint to Obtain Key for One Time Pad Cryptography

Navina, V. Kirthika and T. Eswari Priya, *Anna University*

In this paper we have encoded the fingerprint of sender and generate an intermediate key which is dependent on fingerprint patterns. Next, we use a 128-bit key and using this key and the intermediate key we generate the original key that will be used for encryption. Since our original key is not merely based on fingerprints only, even if anyone is able to obtain the fingerprints being used he will not possibly arrive at the key. In these methods, the intermediate key generated is of quite large length and we diffuse the 128-bit key into it. For the encryption we use one time pad cryptography. This method enables us to use one time cryptography without bothering about how to memorize or remember a large length of key but the 128-bit.

Enhancing a Pen-Based Groupware System Through Image Caching and Gesture Recognition

Mike Oren and Laura Schafer, *DePauw University*

The goal of this project was to improve the user interface for a pen-based collaborative note taking environment. We explored image caching techniques as a way to speed up user navigation through the environment. We also explored the use of gesture recognition in order to provide users with a more natural interface when using the program with pen-enabled hardware. Solving this problem involved investigating various algorithms as well as conducting a user study to measure user preferences for various interaction techniques.

Virtual Fireflies for the Study of Firefly Mating Preferences

Matthew P. Glover, Duane P. Mohney, Brian S. Vysocky Jr., Joshua M. McKinnon, and Michael E. Taft
Fitchburg State College

Our group designed and constructed virtual fireflies to empower biologists to perform experiments that explore aspects of firefly flash communication. Flash shape and timing identify the many firefly species and separate the sexes. Using microcontrollers, LEDs, and photodiodes we built hardware capable of producing flash sequences modeled from actual fireflies. Paired with the right software algorithms our devices recognize valid flash sequences and respond appropriately. They have successfully engaged in conversation with real fireflies. These virtual fireflies are a portable, field-programmable product biologists use and demonstrates how computer science can be paired with other disciplines to enhance scientific research.

User Interface Considerations for Older Users

John Gould and Matthew Schaefer, *George Washington University*

This research addresses the unique processes and human-computer interface considerations needed when designing software for older computer users. The software industry does not appear to be recognizing the technology gap that exits between older users and younger, more-experienced users. SilverMail, an e-mail client simulation, was developed via paper prototyping and usability testing with older adults. SilverMail incorporates special, senior-specific design features such as menu and task-based program flow, file system abstractions, and postal-mail metaphors. This research also highlighted the problems many older adults have with standard GUI widgets and applications, providing an increased understanding of their technology needs.

Web Raveler: A Web Mediation Infrastructure

Sam Martin, Stephane Nyombayire, and Cassie Schmitz, *Grinnell College*

The growth of the World Wide Web has led to the development of a number of services that modify Web pages before they are presented to the user. Such mediations include translators, content filters, annotation systems, and many others. Too often, authors of such services must "reinvent the wheel," and build a framework for sending and receiving Web queries, as no standardized infrastructure exists for providing these services. At the same time, users of such mediators generally cannot combine the services they provide. In this paper, we describe our initial design and preliminary implementation of Web Raveler, an infrastructure for providing Web mediation services. Web Raveler is designed to provide an easily extensible, rich environment for programmers to develop mediators of Web content.

Using Practical Toys, Modified for Technical Learning: A Class Aimed at Increasing Children's Interest Level in Computer Science

Tracey Lynn Weisheit, *Hanover College*

Can educating children inspire technological change? While it is true that many children are "computer literate", their knowledge of topics actually relating to the computing sciences is often limited. With the growing decline in computer science professionals, I decided to test whether introducing younger kids to the computing science helps raise interest in computing. To do so, I designed and taught a Robotics course as part of a larger camp that studied elementary school students. I surveyed the campers and instructors before and after camp to determine if their opinions on computing topics such as Artificial Intelligence and Programming changed.

Dense 3D Mapping with Monocular Vision: Bridging the Gap Between Robotics and Computer Vision

Kamil Wnuk, Harvey *Mudd College*

Currently, the vast majority of autonomous mapping in robotics relies on direct measurements from costly devices such as sonar, infrared, and laser range finders. Adapting established methodologies from the structure-from-motion (SFM) subfield of computer vision to data commonly available in robotics, we have created a unique toolkit, able to render visually dense 3d maps from odometrically annotated monocular vision. Though computationally intensive, monocular vision provides a low-cost, yet highly capable alternative to currently popular mapping sensors. Future research on application of our work for navigational uses hopes to create inexpensive monocular robotic systems capable of autonomous navigation.

Does Programmer-Defined Formatting Improve Code Comprehension?

Melissa Gifford, Leslie Tableman, and Sara Henry, *Hope College*

Programmer-defined formatting is when the writer of a program may emphasize parts of the code by using options such as fonts, color, and bolding in a non-algorithmic way. We designed an experiment to discover if programmer-defined formatting helps programmers understand what code does better than syntax-highlighting. We also investigated how well the new type of formatting was received by those who were tested. The results from a beta-test are generally in favor of the new type of formatting, although the small group of subjects renders those results unreliable. Continuing research with a larger test group is planned for the future.

A Learner and Instructor Centered Collaborative Electronic Textbook

Christopher Johnson, James Boerkoel, and Benjamin Worrel, *Hope College*

Electronic textbooks can significantly enhance the traditional paper textbook, allowing both in and out of class interactions among participants that are not practical using paper texts. Electronic textbooks also allow the reader to take more effective notes and to organize those notes. During the summer of 2004, we used usability and usefulness feedback from previous courses to improve the eTextReader, an electronic textbook application developed by other members of our research group. This poster describes the results of our work and outline why we believe our work will lead to significant improvements in users' perceptions and use of the eTextReader.

Evolving Steerable Bipedal Locomotion in Simulation

Brian Allen, *Iowa State University*

This work uses evolutionary reinforcement learning to discover steerable controllers for bipedal locomotion in simulation. Higher overall fitness and greater complexity of resulting behavior is observed through the gradual introduction of more challenging fitness criteria using a schedule based on observed fitness of the population. Steerable, bipedal walking controllers with cyclical behavior are shown to arise de novo from the evolved recurrent neural networks.

JIT Program Optimization via Compile-time Information

Nathan Kuchta, *Lake Forest College*

Effective program optimization by a compiler requires a significant amount of time, primarily due to the sophisticated program analyses required. A growing proportion of today's software runs on virtual machines, implying that many common optimizations (e.g. register allocation) must be performed at run-time. This places the optimizer under severe time pressure, and ultimately limits the aggressiveness of the optimization. Our approach is to improve optimization while reducing cost by passing analysis information collected during compilation to the VM in the form of annotations (hints in the generated code). We are using Microsoft's Rotor framework for implementation and collecting results.

Design and Implementation of a Web-Based Academic Program Assessment System Using XML and Relational Databases

Rebecca Buhman and Crystal Ward, *Northwest Missouri State University*

Collection of assessment data is widespread and systems are implemented in a number of universities to display the results in various formats. The ultimate purpose of assessment is to improve the curriculum, but only by tying assessment data to detailed curriculum goals can such improvements be made. Our goal is to build a framework that can then be used to analyze the assessment data to improve academic programs. Our system will incorporate a database to store the information, XML to transport the information between applications, and a web interface to allow easy accessibility.

Software Obfuscation

Mikhail Sosonkin, *Polytechnic University*

Software obfuscation is one of the methods for protecting software against reverse engineering and intellectual property theft. In the past many methods were developed to obscure the low-level flows of a program. However, in an object-oriented program, the class hierarchy and relationships reveal a significant portion of the design. We propose three methods to obfuscate the high-level design of a program. These methods were successfully implemented and tested to see the affects on the run time of obfuscated programs.

Accessibility in Introductory Computer Science

Gustavo R. Lima, Alexander V. Fairley, and David Gerry, *University of Massachusetts – Boston*

This project seeks to integrate software accessibility into the CS1 curriculum. Accessibility is an important aspect of modern software systems for both legal and ethical reasons. The acceptance of Java as language for CS1 gives us the opportunity to teach accessibility from the beginning, since Java Accessibility is simple and integrated into Swing components. We present simple guidelines on how to incorporate Accessibility into a Java based CS1, and describe programming projects that incorporate accessibility.

Global Teleconnection Patterns and their Impact on Local Hydrological Processes

Hui Nee Chin, *University of Nebraska-Lincoln*

This study is part of the Intelligent Joint Evolution of Data and Information (IJEDI) project, which has the overall goals of creating a hydrological drought index for drought monitoring and mitigation support. To obtain such an index, better understanding of hydrological data is needed. This study focuses on the relationships between Multivariate ENSO Index (MEI) and hydrological data such as precipitation, streamflow, and underground water level, and on the relationship between MEI and crop yields. The research component of this study is to develop an approach that identifies such relationships systematically and reliably which will include data modeling and analysis.

Using Algorithm Visualization to Improve Students' Understanding of Parameter Passing Methods

Orjola Kajo, *University of Wisconsin Oshkosh*

The learning tool that has been developed in this project creates a random instance of a parameter-passing problem and solves it by using a pair of methods, either by-reference and copy-restore or by-name and macro processing. The solution to the problem is hidden with the purpose of being unveiled by the student through a sequence of snapshots supplemented with interactive questions that force the student to predict what will happen next. The results of the statistical testing of the effectiveness of this tool show that it can significantly improve students' learning of copy-restore and by-name methods. Very significant contributions to this project were made by Jessica Gowey during the academic year 2003-2004 while she was an undergraduate student at University of Wisconsin Oshkosh.

Author Index/Panelist Index

NOTES

NOTES

NOTES